The Artizan, Volume 8

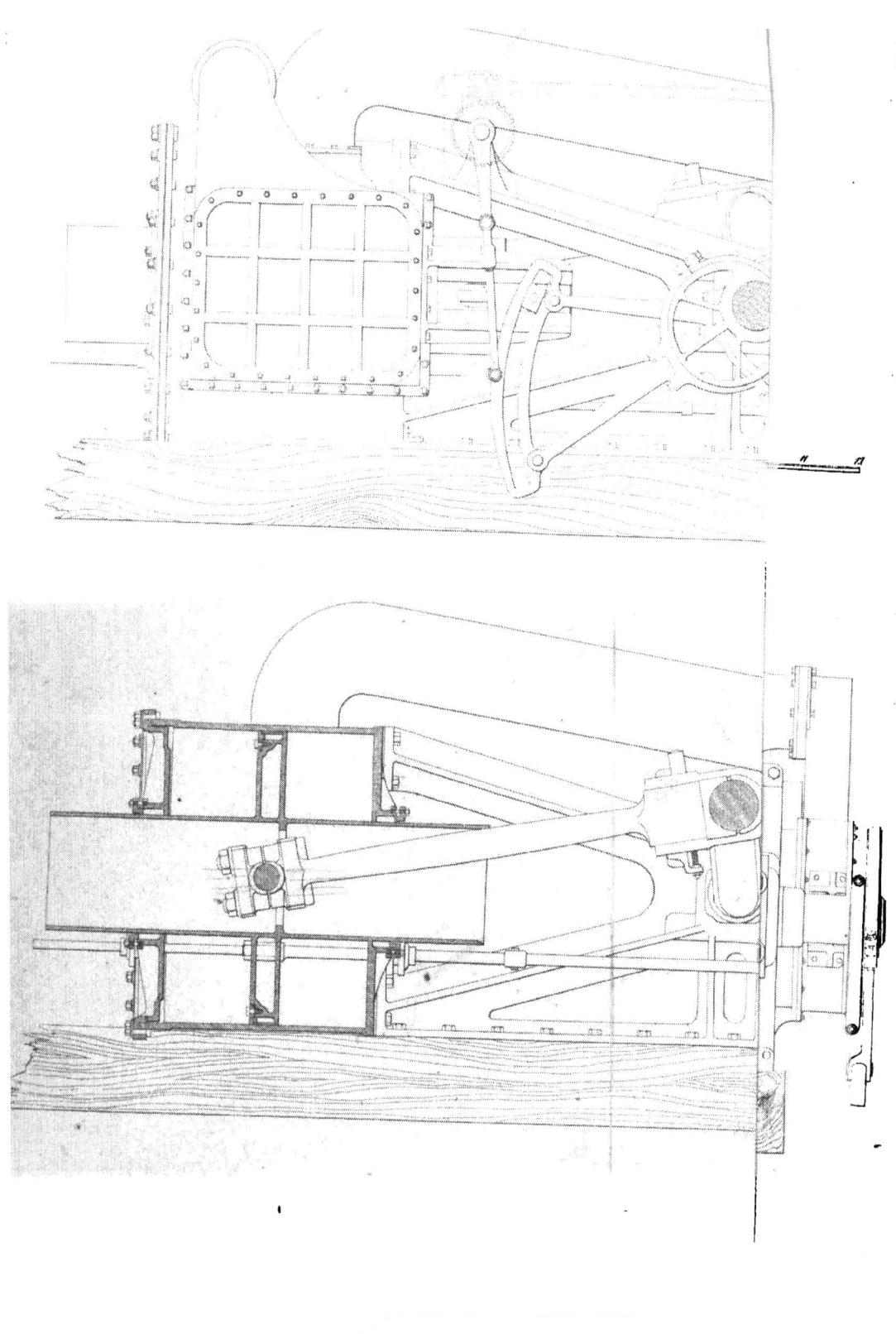

THE ARTIZAN.

A Monthly Journal

OF

THE OPERATIVE ARTS.

VOL. VIII.

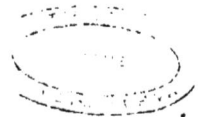

LONDON:

OFFICE OF "THE ARTIZAN" JOURNAL, 69, CORNHILL.

1850.

LONDON.
JOSEPH RICKERBY, PRINTER,
SHERBOURN LANE.

INDEX TO VOL. VIII.

1850.

DIRECTIONS TO THE BINDER.

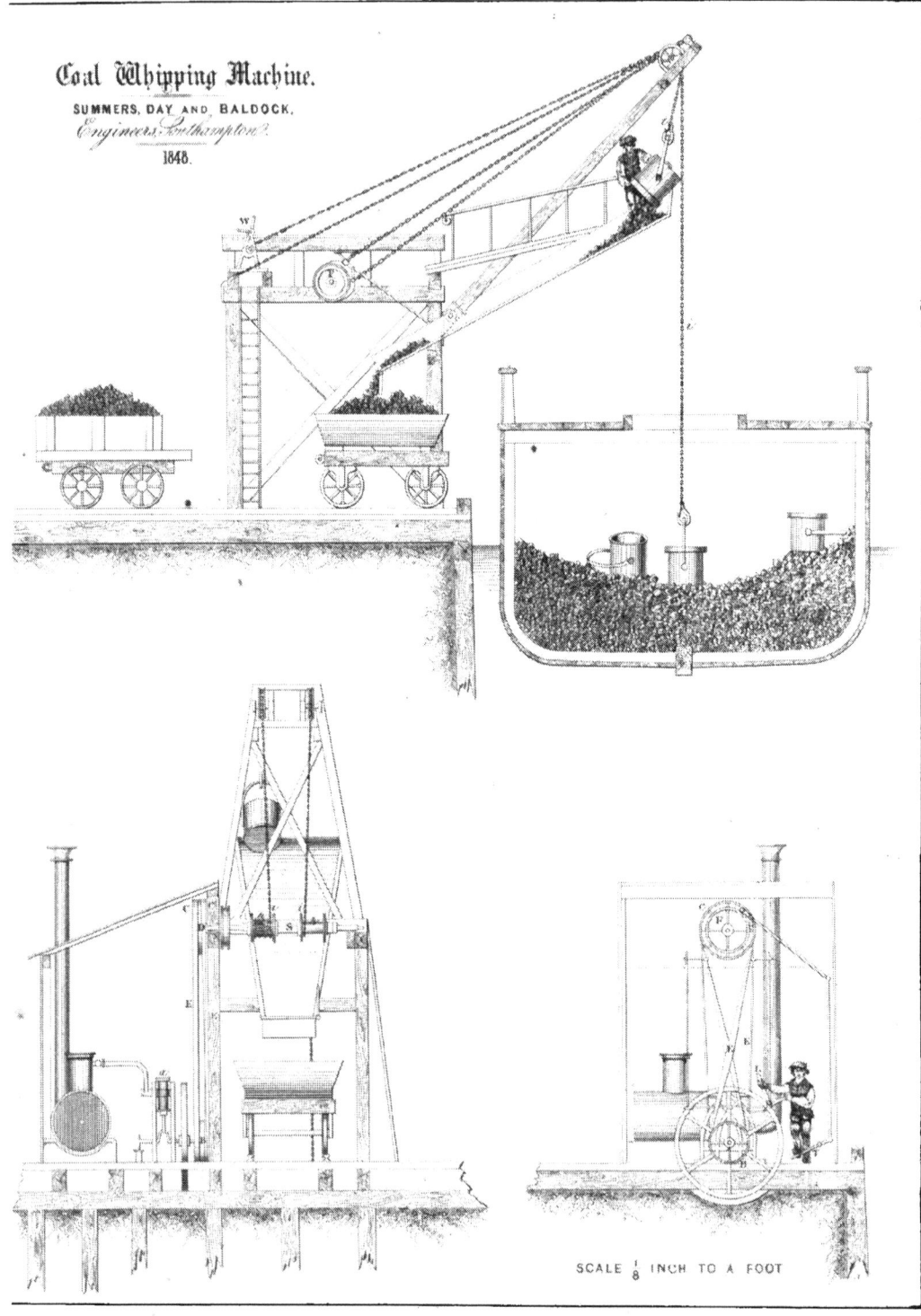

Coal Whipping Machine.

SUMMERS, DAY AND BALDOCK,
Engineers Southampton
1848.

SCALE ⅛ INCH TO A FOOT

THE ARTIZAN

No. I.—Vol. VIII.—JANUARY 1st, 1850.

MECHANICAL ENGINEERING.

STEAM COAL-WHIPPING MACHINERY, AS CONSTRUCTED BY MESSRS. SUMMERS, DAY, AND BALDOCK.

At page 241 of our last volume we gave a drawing and description of the steam machinery in use at Lowestoft Harbour, for the purpose of unloading colliers at the Railway Company's wharf. We have now the pleasure of publishing a plate of another machine for a similar purpose, constructed by Messrs. Summers, Day, and Baldock, engineers, of Southampton, which offers the means of making an interesting comparison between the different methods of solving the problem, "How to raise a loaded bucket, and lower an empty one, with the least expenditure of power and time." It will be observed that the main difference between the two machines consists in the present one being double-acting, having two buckets, passing each other in the middle of their journey—one being raised while the other is being lowered; whilst the Lowestoft machine is single-acting, only one bucket being in motion at a time. Consequently, if the maximum speed at which it would be convenient to move the buckets and their maximum contents be fixed, the double-acting machine would raise twice as much as the single-acting machine, in a given time, although it would take double the power. In machinery of this kind, however, it is convenient to be able to perform a large quantity of work on an emergency, and men generally prefer to work at their maximum strength, when working piecework.

The coal-whipping machine represented in the annexed drawing was erected and set to work in May, 1848, on a wharf belonging to Mr. Moller, of that port, since which time it has been in constant use, chiefly in discharging vessels laden with coal for the coke ovens of the London and South-western Railway Company.

A small oscillating engine of 2-horse power is fixed to the wharf, as at a. b is a pulley keyed fast on to the engine crank shaft. c c are two pulleys which run loose on the barrel shaft, s. d is a pulley keyed fast on to the barrel shaft, s.

e e are the two driving straps, one of which is an open strap, and the other a crossed one, which are alternately moved on to the fixed pulley, d, as the buckets require to be raised or lowered into the vessel's hold. The two levers, l l, which are used for shifting the straps, e e, are fixed in a convenient situation for the engine driver to stand with one of them in each hand, and his foot upon the treadle, t, which communicates with the break wheel, f, with which, when the bucket is at its proper height above the shoot for being tipped, he holds it firm. The instant he perceives, through the glass door of the engine-house, that the bucket is emptied, h

releases with his foot the break lever, and shifts one of the straps on to the fast pulley, d, which lowers the emptied bucket into the vessel's hold, and raises the full one, which has been hooked on below. There are several buckets in the hold, so that no time is lost in filling and hooking them on. The hooks used for this purpose are made very strong, and of the very best iron, and are provided with a keeper and spring, somewhat similar to the common well-hook.

The engine driver does not require to regulate the admission of steam to the engine every time he lifts, because the work is, as nearly as possible, uniform, as there are two buckets used, and the time required to tip the bucket being so very short, the engine does not accelerate its speed, but continues at a nearly uniform velocity the whole time it is at work. It will be observed that the two buckets always move in opposite directions, and, consequently, the weight of each bucket is balanced by the other one; this is effected by passing the winding chains, i i, to which the buckets are attached, round the barrels, h h, in opposite directions, viz., above and below the barrels, so that one is winding up, while the other is unwinding the chain. In order to accommodate the length of the chains to the rise and fall of the tide, the barrels, h h, are attached to the shaft by clutches, by releasing these, the barrels may be easily turned, so as to take up the chain, or let more out, as may be necessary; each chain having three or more turns round the barrel than is ever unwound, for safety.

The shears are raised or lowered to allow a vessel to pass under them, by the crab winch, w, but are always carried by two strong guy chains when at work.

This machine is very simple in its construction, and has been found very economical and satisfactory in its operation; and, although the steam engine is of only 2-horse power, when working at 30 lbs. per square inch on the boiler (the highest pressure used), it has raised 329 tons of coal in 13h. 20m., actual working time, or at the average rate of nearly 25 tons per hour.

These machines may be either fixed on a wharf, as shown by the drawing, or upon the deck of a barge or hull; and, from the ease and rapidity of their operation, will be found very valuable in discharging the cargoes of colliers and other ships, or for warehousing goods from waggons, trucks, &c. &c.

ANALYSIS OF THE STEAM ENGINE.

We have at various times received requests from our correspondents to point out some works from which they might obtain practical instruction in the art of designing steam engines and general machinery, and we have accordingly called their attention to various treatises on the steam engine, which might be supposed to contain the most modern and approved examples of different makers. These works, however, seem not to convey the exact information required by the tyro. "What I want to know," says an "Apprentice," in a letter before us, "is how I am to set about making the drawings for an engine, so that the pattern-makers and smiths can go right on with the work, and bring everything in, to make a good job." We propose to supply this want, and to lead the tyro step by step; first discussing the various details, and then arranging these details into the various forms required under different circumstances.

We shall commence with the details of a low pressure condensing engine; and, in order to prevent any misconception into which our readers might fall, from the (at the present day) vague term, "low pressure," we wish it to be understood to apply to steam, not exceeding ten pounds per square inch. There is no special reason for fixing this particular pressure, but we consider it to be, on the average, the highest which we would willingly apply to an engine after the old type of condensing engines. The most judicious designers make the rubbing parts much larger than is required for strength alone, with a view to save wear and tear; and then the other parts being made a little stronger than the rule, to correspond, we get an engine which can be worked with safety, though not with such economy, at a much higher power than it was designed for.

We must also premise that we shall not, under this head, give all the modifications of which the details of an engine are capable, for this would only confuse the student; but shall confine our remarks to those arrangemenss which we can guarantee from practice, without contending that they are the best under all circumstances. We shall be glad, however, to receive sketches from any of our readers, of any novelties, which it may be in their power to give.

The piston in plate 1 is of 30 inches diameter, drawn quarter size, which is what is commonly called a 30 horse engine. Although rather against our inclination, we shall *call* this engine of thirty horses power. The area of 30 is 706, which divided by thirty horses power, gives 23.5 square inches of piston per horse power; we will not stop now to inquire to what indicated power this engine will work, but take this area as a standard of what is expected by the buyer of the maker.

The diameter of the cylinder being thus ascertained, the length of stroke must be fixed, and this will depend upon the purpose to which the engine is to be applied. If the first cost be not an objection, a long stroke will be preferred, on account of its offering the means of working more expansively, and consequently with a less consumption of fuel. From four to six feet may be taken as a fair proportionate stroke for a land engine, and we will therefore fix upon the average, or say five feet stroke, bearing in mind that the cost of the engine and buildings increases with the length of the stroke, to a considerable extent.

The piston must first be drawn, in order to fix the length of the cylinder, and its depth in the centre is usually made 1-5th of the diameter, or six inches. The diameter of the piston-rod 1-10th the diameter of the cylinder, say 3 inches; it is made, say $3\frac{1}{4}$ inches, where it passes through the piston, in order that the rest of the rod may pass freely, and not for strength, because the rod is turned down smaller where it enters the cross-head, and in both places has the same strain on it. The amount of taper on the rod in the piston—is shown, perhaps smaller than many engineers would make it, for fear of splitting the piston by its wedge-like action. It is 4 inches diameter at bottom, giving a difference of $\frac{3}{4}$inch, which is at the rate of $\frac{1}{8}$ inch taper for an inch in depth, and we have found this enough, when the boss is made of sufficient strength, whilst it must be remembered that the less the taper the more secure will be the junction between the rod and the piston; a junction which ought never to be disturbed, after once being made, if it can be avoided. The rod is keyed up by a steel key, a little taper, as shown, which theoretically would perhaps be better if thinner and deeper, but a thin key, which has to be driven home under a heavy blow, is apt to get upset and damaged. Two opposite ribs of the piston are cast double, to form the key-way, and serve to strengthen the piston at that part. On the driving side more room must be left than on the opposite side, in order to drop in the key, and the space ought to be cast full wide, except just where the key bears, to save chipping. The efficacy of a key depends so much on the nicety with which it is fitted, that this point can hardly be too sharply looked after.

As far as strength is concerned, the piston may be made of less depth at the edges than at the centre, and the proportion shown appears to give sufficient depth of packing ring, more particularly at the present day, when our improved tools enable us to bore with such great accuracy. The taper is all on the top side, and the bottom of the piston is flat; this makes the bottom of the cylinder flat, and allows all the water to run off from it (if the slide valve be suitably designed), and also from the top of the piston, if the engine be left at top stroke.

The top and bottom plates of the piston are $\frac{3}{4}$ thick. The piston flange and cover are shown 1 inch thick; the cover is sometimes made of wrought iron, and may then be lighter than in the present instance. It is held down by six $\frac{7}{8}$ bolts, screwing into gun-metal nuts, made deep to get a good thread, and let into the body of the piston; the nuts are sometimes made of wrought iron, but gun-metal is preferable, to obviate the rusting of the bolts and nuts together. The heads of the bolts are sunk into the piston-cover to give clearance at the top of the cylinder, and the recesses must be made of sufficient diameter to admit the head of the socket-spanner to turn the bolts. The top and bottom plates of the piston are connected together with six ribs, $\frac{7}{8}$ thick, which run from the centre boss to the bosses cast around the recesses for the nuts. These ribs divide the piston into six compartments, and, consequently, holes have to be cast to get out the cores. These holes, shown at *d*, are afterwards bored out with a little taper, and plugs fitted in, and each screwed with two small studs, tapped half into the plug and half into the piston.

The packing ring is a plain eccentric ring, cut on the thin side, and sprung together before it is turned to the right diameter. There are varieties of pistons innumerable, but we cannot say that we should prefer any of them to this form, unless we were to make an exception in the case of very large engines.

A tongue piece, *c*, is tenoned into the junction of the ring, and fixed on one side by tapped pins, as we described for the plug holes. These pins also fasten a stop piece *b*, on the inside of the piston. The wrought iron guard *a*, serves very conveniently to bring the ring together when it is to be taken in or out of the cylinder, in the following manner:—The guard is bolted to the lower side of the ring (as shown in plan), but the bolt hole on the other side is slotted out to allow the guard and ring to slide on each other. Therefore, by driving a key in between the stop piece *b*, and the guard, the ring will be either distended or drawn together, according to the side on which the key is driven.

The tongue piece, we need hardly add, serves to prevent any leakage of steam past the junction of the ring. The piston is shown an inch thick on one side and half an inch on the other.

(To be continued.)

INDICATOR CARDS.

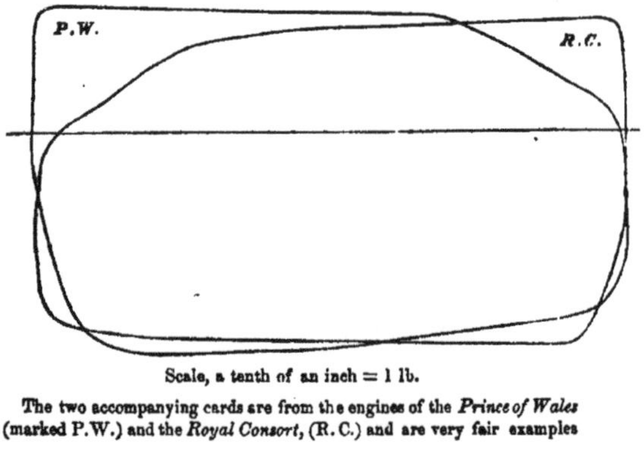

Scale, a tenth of an inch = 1 lb.

The two accompanying cards are from the engines of the *Prince of Wales* (marked P.W.) and the *Royal Consort*, (R.C.) and are very fair examples

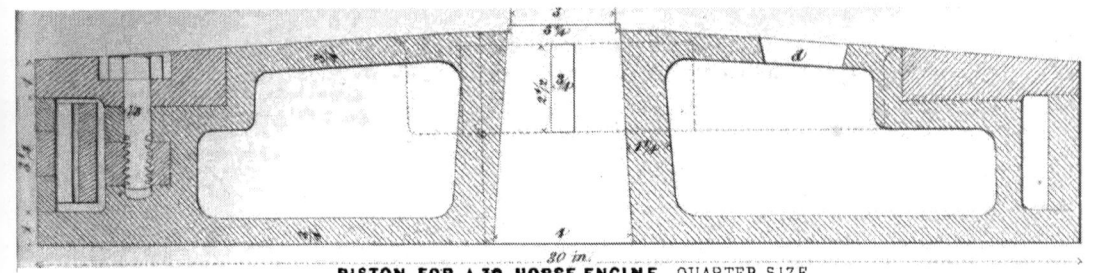

PISTON FOR A 30 HORSE ENGINE . QUARTER SIZE.

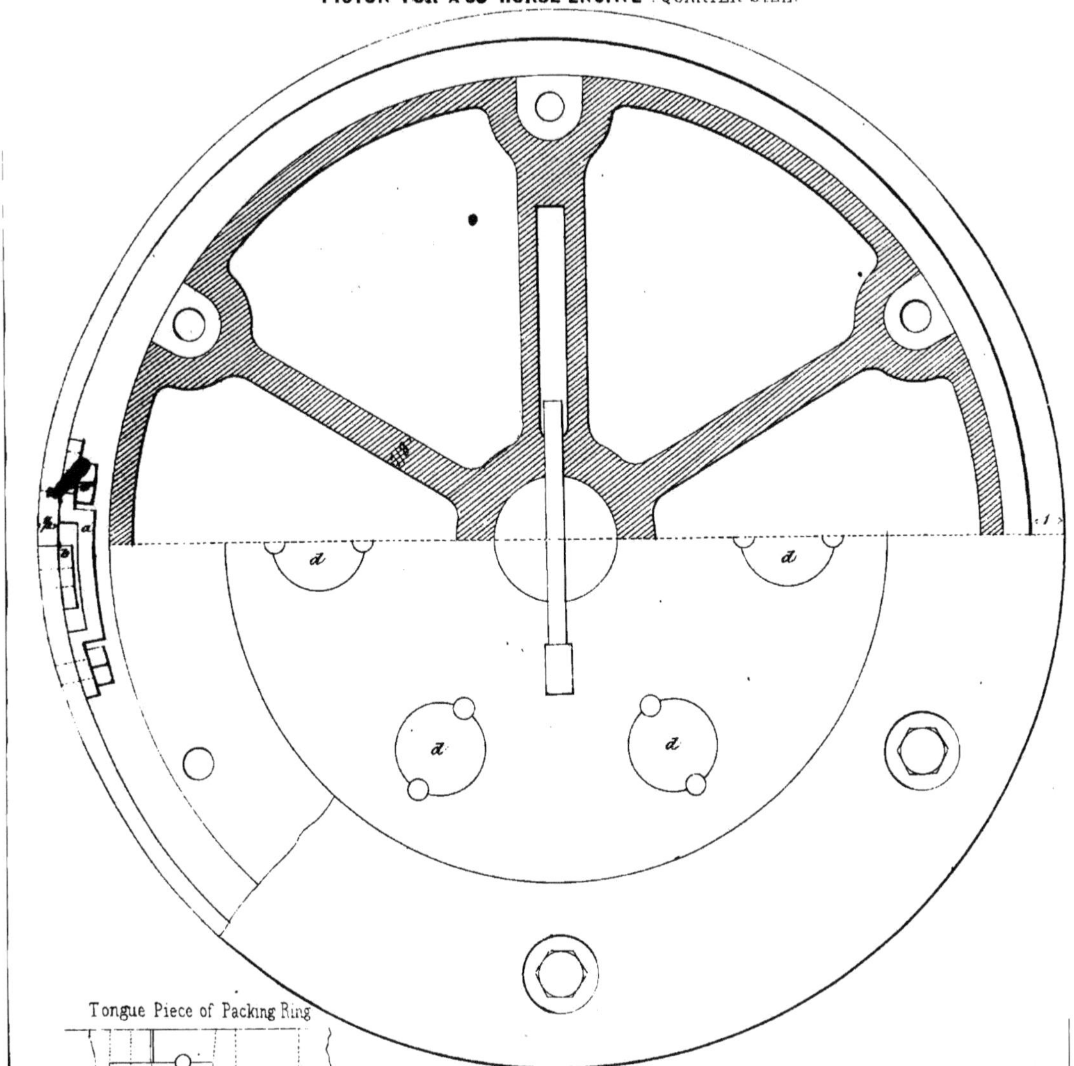

Tongue Piece of Packing Ring

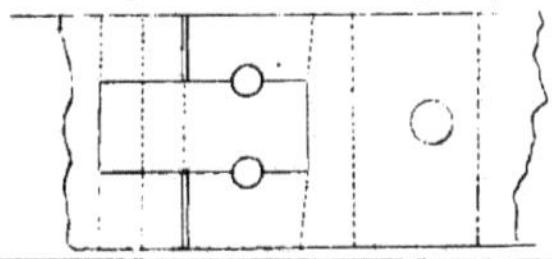

Litho Waterlow & Sons London

ARTIZAN 1850

of seagoing engines, which do not carry so much pressure of steam as the river boats.

The card from the *Prince of Wales* is from the larboard engine, at 19 of revolutions per minute. Particulars of the engines of the *Royal Consort* will be found in our last No.

To some of our readers the way in which these cards are arranged, right and left-handed, may be a novelty. It is a very convenient way in which to take the two cards off the top and bottom of one cylinder, on one piece of paper, the atmospheric line remaining the same in both cases. It is effected by mounting the indicator on a pipe, which can be connected alternately with the top and bottom of the cylinder by means of two cocks, one above, and the other below the indicator socket. As the indicator does not require to be moved during the operation of indicating one engine, it saves the trouble of shifting the string for working it—a trouble which often serves as an excuse for not indicating the engines at all, more particularly in direct-acting engines, which have no parallel motion to connect the string to, and require a special apparatus for the purpose. A large and small pulley are generally used to reduce the stroke of the piston to that of the indicator, and we find it convenient to have the small pulley to ship on the large one, and then, by having a number of small ones of different diameters, any length of stroke can be suited.

DIMENSIONS AND DETAILS OF NEW STEAMERS.

LONDONDERRY AND GLASGOW STEAM NAVIGATION COMPANY'S STEAMER, "LONDONDERRY."

Built by Messrs. Robert Steele and Co., Greenock. Engines by Mr. Robert Napier, Vulcan Foundry, Glasgow. Boilers by Messrs. James and George Thomson, Clyde Bank Foundry, Glasgow.

	Ft.	in.
Builder's measurement.		
Length aloft ...	160	8
Ditto keel and fore rake ...	159	1
Breadth of beam ...	25	3
Ditto over the paddle-boxes ...	43	9
Depth of hold amidships ...	15	11
Length of engine space ...	60	11
Tonnage.	Tons.	
Hull ...	488$\frac{11}{94}$	
Contents of engine space ...	206$\frac{45}{94}$	
Register ...	281$\frac{62}{94}$	
New measurement.	Ft.	
Length on deck ...	157.1	
Breadth on ditto amidships ...	22.9	
Depth of ditto, ditto ...	15.7	
Length of quarter-deck ...	40.4	
Breadth of ditto ...	25.6	
Depth of ditto ...	2.9	
Length of engine space ...	60.9	
Tonnage.	Tons.	
Hull ...	480$\frac{1744}{3500}$	
Quarter-deck ...	32$\frac{1508}{3500}$	
Total ...	512$\frac{3252}{3500}$	
Contents of engine space ...	235$\frac{1348}{3500}$	
Register ...	277$\frac{184}{3500}$	

A pair of side lever engines of 240-horse nominal power. Cylinders, 57½ ins. diameter × 5 feet stroke. Paddle wheels, diameter extreme, 21 feet 5 inches; ditto effective, 20 feet 10 inches. Floats, 7 feet 7 inches × 2 feet 4 inches. Two sets of 18 arms and floats. Revolutions, 23 per minute; speed, 12 miles an hour. Draught of water, 10 feet 6 inches forward, and 11 feet aft. Present boilers, 2 return flue, with 3 furnaces in each; steam pressure, 7 lbs. She had formerly 3 flue boilers, with 9 furnaces, put in in 1841.

The *Londonderry* is at present chartered by the North Lancashire Steam Navigation Company, and plies between Londonderry and Fleetwood, making the passage in 19 to 20 hours.

The crew consists of 24 hands: 11 in the captain's department, 9 in the engine room, and 4 in the cabins.

Description—Full female figure head, false quarter-galleries, standing boltsprit, 3 masts, schooner-rigged, square-sterned and carvil-built vessel of timber. Port of Londonderry. Master, Robert Gentle.

THE NORTH LANCASHIRE STEAM NAVIGATION COMPANY'S IRON VESSELS, "PRINCE OF WALES" AND "PRINCESS ALICE."

Built and fitted by Messrs. Tod and M'Gregor, Glasgow.

	Ft.	in.	Ft.	in.
Builder's measurement.				
Length of keel and fore rake ...	160	7	164	0
Breadth of beam ...	26	4½	24	1
Ditto, including the paddle-boxes ...	42	8	40	8
Depth of hold amidships ...	13	9	14	0
Length of engine space ...	50	0	50	7
Hull ...	525$\frac{24}{94}$		479$\frac{31}{94}$	
Contents of engine space ...	164$\frac{61}{94}$		174$\frac{11}{94}$	
Register ...	350$\frac{57}{94}$		305$\frac{39}{94}$	
New measurement.				
Length on deck ...	159.6		164.7	
Breadth on ditto amidships ...	24.6		23.3	
Depth of hold, ditto ...	13.5		13.9	
Length of break-deck ...	51.4		48.1	
Breadth of ditto ...	24.0		21.7	
Depth of ditto ...	0.9		1.1	
Length of engine space ...	50 0		50.6	
Tonnage.	Tons.		Tons.	
Hull ...	487$\frac{88}{100}$		422$\frac{7}{100}$	
Break-deck ...	12$\frac{8}{100}$		12$\frac{41}{100}$	
Gross ...	499$\frac{96}{100}$		434$\frac{48}{100}$	
Contents of engine space ...	187$\frac{0}{100}$		177$\frac{34}{100}$	
Register ...	312$\frac{96}{100}$		257$\frac{14}{100}$	
A pair of steeple engines in each vessel.				
Nominal power ...	270 h.p.		212 h.p.	
Diameter of cylinders ...	0	61	0	54
Length of stroke ...	5	0	5	0
Diameter of paddle-wheels, extreme ...	25	7	22	9
Ditto, ditto, effective ...	25	0	22	2
Length of floats ...	6	6	6	2
Breadth of ditto ...	1	9	2	3
Number of arms and floats ...	24		21	
Sets of ditto ...	3		3	

Prince of Wales.—Two tubular boilers, 11 feet, 6 inches long × 10 feet, 6 inches broad × 11 feet high. Steam-chests, 3 feet, 6 inches high. Four furnaces in each boiler, 7 feet, 6 inches long × 2 feet, 2 inches broad. The four middle furnaces have been lengthened, making them 9 feet, 6 inches long. The consumption of fuel remains the same, viz., 28 cwt. per hour, but the steam-pressure has been increased from 8½ to 9½ lbs. Number of revolutions per minute, 20; and the passage between Fleetwood and Belfast, 120 miles, is done in 10 hours. The floats have been drawn up, making the effective diameter of the paddle wheels 23 feet, 3 ins.

She had flue boilers when she was launched in 1842, and has been constantly running since that time.

Frame of vessel 3½ × 3½ × $\frac{7}{16}$ inches, and 2 feet apart.

The crew consists of 27 hands:—11 in the captain's department, 10 in the engine-room, and 6 in the cabin.

Description—Bust, male figure head ("Infant Prince") false quarter galleries, three masts, schooner rigged, standing bowsprit, common bow, square sterned, and clinch and carvil built vessel, Port of Fleetwood (Port of Preston) commander, Mr. Archibald M'Neilage.

Princess Alice.—Two tubular boilers, by Messrs. Thomas Vernon & Co., 1848, length 18 feet, breadth 9 feet, 4 inches; 3 furnaces in each boiler, length 7 feet; breadth, 2 feet, 4 inches; depth, 4 feet; 36 tubes each boiler, diameter 6 inches × 13 feet; the bunkers are between the engines and boilers, length fore and aft 5 feet 2 inches, and all the depth and breadth of the vessel, except a tunnel or passage, 4 feet broad, and 5 feet, 10 inches high, at boiler end, and 8 feet at engine end, to help the draught to the furnaces. The ash-pits are fitted with doors, so that the draught can be regulated at pleasure; the guage cocks, instead of being above the tubes, as is common, are below them, having pipes in the inside leading down to them, instead of long rods being attached to the guage cock handles. Consumption of fuel, 20 cwt. per hour; 23 revolutions per minute; steam pressure, 10lbs.; vacuum 28 inches; average draught of water, 9 feet; average speed, 12 knots per hour. This vessel has rather the advantage of the other in speed. Frames $3\frac{1}{2} \times 2\frac{1}{2} \times \frac{3}{8}$ inches, and 2 feet apart.

Description—Bust female figure head, sham quarter galleries, three masts, schooner-rigged, standing boltsprit, clipper bow, square-sterned clinch and carvil-built vessel. Port of Fleetwood (port of Preston). Commander, Mr Leonard Humphries.

THE NORTH LANCASHIRE STEAM NAVIGATION COMPANY'S IRON VESSEL, "FINELLA."

by Messrs. Thomas Vernon and Co., Liverpool. Engines. etc., by Messrs. George Forrester and Co., Vauxhall Foundry, ditto.

Builder's measurement.	Ft.	in.
Length of keel and fore rake	160	0
Breadth of beam	20	4
Ditto of the paddle-boxes	34	7
Depth of hold amidships	11	4
Length of engine space	35	8
Tonnage.	Tons.	
Hull	$327\frac{81}{94}$	
Contents of engine space	$79\frac{34}{94}$	
Register	$248\frac{47}{94}$	
New measurement.	Ft.	
Length on deck	157.8	
Breadth on ditto amidships	19.3	
Depth of hold at ditto	11.1	
Ditto at break-deck	1.9	
Length of engine space	35.7	
Tonnage.	Tons.	
Hull	$252\frac{94}{100}$	
Contents of engine space	$82\frac{76}{100}$	
Register	$170\frac{18}{100}$	

A pair of side lever engines of 110-horse nominal power. Cylinders, 41 inches diameter × 3 feet 6 inches stroke. Overhung paddle-wheels, diameter, extreme, 19 feet 6 inches; ditto effective, 19 feet. Floats, 5 feet 4 inches × 1 foot 6 inches. Two sets of 9 arms and 18 floats. Two tubular boilers—length, 10 feet 9 inches; breadth, 7 feet 4 inches; height, 9 feet. Steam-chests—length, 10 feet 9 inches; breadth, 3 feet 9 inches; depth, 2 feet 6 inches. Two furnaces in each boiler—length, 8 feet 5 inches; breadth, 2 feet 7 inches; depth, 3 feet 4 inches. 180 tubes in each boiler. Diameter, $2\frac{3}{4}$ inches × 6 feet 3 inches. Steam pressure, 10 lbs. Consumption of fuel, 18 cwt. of coals per hour. Revolutions, 28 per minute. Average draught of water, 6 feet. Frames, $3\frac{1}{2} \times 2\frac{3}{8} \times \frac{7}{16}$ inches, and 1 foot 6 inches apart. The *Finella* formerly plied between Douglas (Isle of Man) and Fleetwood, 54 miles, which was generally performed in $4\frac{3}{4}$ to 5 hours.

Description – A full female figure head, no galleries, clipper bow, standing boltsprit, 2 masts, schooner-rigged, square-sterned clinch and carvil-built vessel. Port of Fleetwood (port of Preston).

December 5th, 1849.—This steamer was tried on the Wyre, with 100 tons of pig iron on board (dead weight), the draught of water being 6 feet 10 inches fore and 7 feet aft. Steam pressure, 10 lbs.; the floats being drawn in towards the centres, making the paddle-wheels 17 feet effective diameter, the engines making 25 revolutions per minute. The vessel ran several times round the Screw Pile Light-house, under the command of Mr. J. J. Wheeler, and the speed of the vessel was highly satisfactory, being at the rate of 10 knots per hour. (It is intended to raise her forward, to make the deck on a level with the break-deck.)

"ORION."—(Further Particulars of Boilers, continued from page 270). —Present boilers: length, 10 feet 4 inches; breadth, 7 feet 6 inches; depth, 8 feet 8 inches. Steam-chests: length, 10 feet 4 inches; breadth, 4 feet 6 inches; depth, 4 feet. Four furnaces, 2 in each boiler: length, 4 feet; breadth, 3 feet; depth, 3 feet 6 inches. 360 tubes, 3 inches diameter. Consuming 16 cwt. of coals per hour. Steam, $9\frac{1}{2}$ lbs. 27 revolutions per minute. In August last the present boilers received new tube plates, with 80 tubes, $5\frac{5}{8}$ inches diameter; the furnaces lengthened 2 feet, making them 6 feet long, consuming 8 cwt. of coals per hour. Steam the same; revolutions the same. F. B.

DEATH OF SIR M. I. BRUNEL.

The distinguished engineer. Sir Marc Isambart Brunel, Knt., Chevalier de la Legion d'Honneur, Vice-President of the Royal Society and of the Institution of Civil Engineers, &c., died on Wednesday, the 12th inst., at his house in St. James's-park, in the 81st year of his age.

By birth he was a Frenchman, but his life and genius was almost wholly devoted to the invention and construction of works of great public utility in this country, Sir I. Brunel was born at Hacqueville, in Normandy, now in the Department de l'Eure, in the year 1769, a year since remarkable for having given birth to many eminent men. His family has for many centuries held, and now hold, the estate on which he was born; and the name of Brunel is found constantly mentioned in the ancient archives of the province. He was educated for the church, with the prospect of succeeding to a living, and was accordingly sent at an early age to the seminary of St. Nicain, at Rouen. But he soon evinced so strong a predilection for the physical sciences, and so great a genius for mathematics, that the superiors of the establishment recommended he should be educated for some other profession than that of the church. His father strongly objected to his adopting the profession of an engineer, as one more likely to prove beneficial to others than himself, and he, therefore, determined that he should be educated for the naval service, in which he thought his son's proficiency in mathematics might lay the foundation of his advancement in that profession. At the proper age he entered the royal navy, being indebted for his appointment to the Mareschal de Castries, then the Minister of Marine. On one occasion he surprised his captain by producing a sextant and quadrant of his own construction, and which he used for making observations. He made several voyages to the West Indies, and returned home in 1792. At this time the French Revolution was at its height. As Mr. Brunel entertained royalist opinions, which he was not very careful to suppress, his life was more than once in danger, and he was, like many others at that time, forced to seek safety in flight. He emigrated to the United States, where necessity, fortunately, compelled him to follow the natural bent of his mind, and to adopt the profession of a civil engineer. He was first engaged to survey a large tract of land near Lake Erie. He was employed in building the Bowery Theatre, in New York, which not many years ago was burnt down. He furnished plans for canals, and for various machines connected with a cannon foundry then being established in the state of New York. About the year 1799 he had matured his plans for making ship blocks by machinery. The United States was not then a field for so inventive a genius as Brunel's. He determined upon visiting England, and offering his services and plans for this purpose to the British Government. Lord Spencer, then we believe First Lord of the Admiralty, became his friend and patron. He became a frequent guest at Spencer-house, and never failed to speak warmly of the assistance and encouragement he derived from the friendship of Lord and Lady Spencer. From this time he continued to reside in England, and refused to entertain many propositions made to him to leave England, and settle abroad under the auspices of other Governments.

After much opposition to his plans, for a very powerful interest was arrayed against him, not lessened in that day by his being a Frenchman, he was employed to execute them in Portsmouth Dockyard. To perfect his designs, and to erect the machinery, was the arduous labour of many years. With a true descrimination, he selected Mr. Henry Maudslay to assist in the execution of the work, and thus, possibly, was laid the foundation of one of the most extensive engineering establishments in the kingdom, and in which perhaps, a degree of science and skill has been combined and applied to mechanical invention and improvement, scarcely exceeded by any other in the world. The block machinery was finished in 1806, and has continued ever since in full operation, supplying our fleet with blocks of a very superior description to those previously in use, and at a large annual saving to the public. It was estimated at the time that the saving, in the first year, amounted to 24,000*l*. per annum; and about two-thirds of that sum were awarded to Mr. Brunel. It is needless to describe the originality and beauty of this well-known machinery. Even after the lapse of 40 years, notwith standing the marvellously rapid-strides we have made in the improvement and construction of machines of all kinds, it remains as effective as it was when first erected, and unaltered. It is still an object of admiration to all persons interested in mechanics. A few years afterwards he was employed by Government to erect sawmills, upon a new principle, in the dockyards of Chatham and Woolwich. Several other inventions were the offspring of his singularly fertile mind about this time—the circular saw, for cutting veneers of valuable woods; and the beautiful little machine for winding cotton threads into balls, which greatly extended its consumption. About two years before the termination of tho war, Mr. Brunel, under the countenance of the Duke of York, invented a machine for making shoes for the army by machinery, the value and cheapness of which were fully appreciated, and they were extensively used; but, the peace of 1815 lessening the demand, the machinery was ultimately laid aside. Steam navigation also at that time attracted his attention. He was engaged in the building of one of the first Ramsgate steam-boats, and, we believe, introduced the principle of the double engine for the purpose. He also induced the Admiralty to allow him to build a vessel to try the experiment of towing ships out to sea, the possibility of which was then denied. Many other objects of great public utility occupied his mind, which in this mere outline of a long and active life must be excluded.

The visit of the Emperor Alexander to this country, after the peace, led him to submit to the Emperor a plan for making a tunnel under the Neva, where the accumulation of ice, and the suddenness with which it breaks up on the termination of winter, rendered the erection of a bridge a work of great difficulty. This was the origin of his plan for a tunnel under the Thames, which had been twice before attempted without success. In 1824, however, a company was formed, and supported by the Duke of Wellington, who took from first to last a deep interest in the work. Many men of science also joined it, amongst whom the late Dr. Wollaston was the most prominent, and whose brother long continued one of the most active and able promoters of the scheme. The work was commenced in 1824. It was stopped more than once during its progress by the breaking in of the river, and more effectually at last by the exhausted finances of the company, which never extended beyond the command of 180,000*l*. At length, after the suspension of the work for many years, by a special Act of Parliament, a loan was sanctioned, the Exchequer Loan Commissioners advanced the funds necessary for the completion of the work under the river; and, notwithstanding many weighty professional opinions were advanced against the practicability of the work, from both the loose alluvial nature of the soil through which it had to be constructed, and the superincumbent flood of water, it was finished and opened to the public in 1843. In a scientific point of view this work will always be regarded as displaying the highest professional ability, an amount of energy and perseverance rarely exceeded, and a fertility of invention and resources under what were deemed insurmountable difficulties which will always secure to Sir I. Brunel a high place amongst the engineers of this country. During Lord Melbourne's administration Mr. Brunel received the honour of knighthood, on the recommendation of the late Lord Spencer, then Lord Althorp. Sir I. Brunel was a vice-president of the Royal Society, a corresponding member of the Institute of France, and a vice-president of the Institution of Civil Engineers. He was also a Chevalier of the Legion of Honour. He was unaffected, simple in his habits, and benevolent, and as ready to do a kind act as he was to forget an injury. He died in his 81st year, after a long illness which first visited him soon after the completion of the Tunnel. The care, anxiety, and constant strain of body and mind, brought on a slight attack of paralysis, from which he never thoroughly recovered. He leaves a widow, Lady Brunel, one son, the eminent engineer, and two daughters, the eldest married to Mr. Hawes, the Under-Secretary of State for the Colonies, and the youngest to the Rev. Mr. Harrison, the vicar of New Brentford.—*Times.*

GREAT EXHIBITION OF THE WORKS OF INDUSTRY OF ALL NATIONS.

Since we last penned some remarks on this subject the arrangements have made rapid progress towards completion, so rapid, indeed, as to take us by surprise, as we doubt not, it has done many of our readers It

appears from the papers, at length published, that as long ago as the 7th of November, a contract was entered into between the Society of Arts, and Messrs. George and James Munday, by which the latter gentlemen bound themselves to pay £20,000 for the prize fund to erect the building, and to take all the risk of the exhibition repaying them for their outlay. It would appear, from a semi-official journal, that proposals were *privately* made to some of our large capitalists, and that the only parties who did not decline to entertain them, were the Messrs. Munday. We confess that we can see no reason why the intervention of any capitalist was necessary, in the matter. Could not the Council of the Society of Arts rely on the liberality of an English public, to raise the sum of £70,000 (the maximum estimated cost?) It will be observed that certain concessions are proposed to be made by the contractors, on account of the increased interest with which the question has been taken up; but we should be glad to know, why tenders were invited before the state of the public mind was sufficiently ascertained! When public opinion had once declared itself in favour of the proposed Exhibition, it would be absurd to suppose that any loss could be sustained. We give abstracts of the contract (from the *Athenæum*) which, having received the approbation of His Royal Highness Prince Albert, may, we presume, be considered as decided upon.

"Deed No. 1 recites that His Royal Highness Prince Albert is President of the Society of Arts, that His Royal Highness and the Society were desirous for the promotion of the Arts, Manufactures, and Commerce of the country, to institute a Great Exhibition in 1851, and for this purpose that prizes to the value of £20,000 at the least should be awarded. That (in accordance with a previous understanding) a site would be provided by the Commissioners of Woods and Forests—that it was deemed necessary by His Royal Highness and the Society that the sum of £20,000 for prizes should be lodged to secure the payment of such prizes—that Her Majesty should be petitioned to issue a Royal Commission, of which His Royal Highness should be President—that capacious buildings should be erected, the design for which is contemplated to be obtained by public competition —that prospectuses or other descriptions and announcements of the proposed design, and all other necessary means for promulgating, advancing, and completing, should be circulated and advertised—that it was necessary, in organizing the arrangements, that Members of the Society should visit the principal cities, &c.—that Managers, Secretary and officers in general should be provided—that as the funds of the Society were inapplicable to such payments, and though it was anticipated that a considerable sum would be raised by subscription and other means, still it was doubtful whether the sums so raised would be sufficient, that, therefore, an agreement was entered into between the said contractors and the said Society for carrying out the design; for providing £20,000 for prizes, and for immediately paying £500 towards preliminary expenses, as well as such further sums as should be requisite, and for indemnifying the Society against expenses.

"That the said Society had appointed an Executive Committee, including a nominee on the part of the Contractor, and also Trustees for the £20,000 and other monies allotted for prizes, with Treasurers of Exhibition Funds.

"That it had been agreed that if before the 1st of February, 1850, a Royal Commission should not have been issued, the Contractors might refer further proceedings to arbitration.

"That in performance of such agreement the contractors on their part had paid £500 on the 30th of August, and a further sum of 20,000*l*.; and it had also been agreed that the Exhibition should be carried out in the manner expressed in these presents, and in another indenture of even date—that trusts, &c. of 20,000*l*. and 500*l*. actually paid, and all other monies to be paid, should be declared—that certain payments made, and liabilities incurred, by the Society, should be considered as part of the expenses of the Exhibition. The contract then sets forth that the contractors covenant to pay from time to time, until the 1st November, 1851, all such money as may be required for the Exhibition—that the contractors shall within three months after the Exhibition shall have been carried out, pay such a sum as, together with monies previously paid, shall be adequate to pay all expenses whatsoever, of advertisements, printing, agents, offices, superintendents, clerks, workmen, buildings, insurances, decorations, and all other the costs, charges, and expenses of every kind whatsoever, to which the Society may be liable, and will indemnify the Society from such expenses, except the cost of the preparation of the deeds and premiums for designs for buildings. It is then declared that the said 20,000*l*. shall be invested in the names of the Trustees in Government or other securities, as His Royal Highness may direct—add that the 500*l*. already paid, and all monies to be hereafter paid by the contractors, as also all donations, &c. shall be invested.

"It is provided that if donations and subscriptions shall exceed £30,000, then, and in addition to the 20,000*l*., certain further sums may be set apart for prizes.

" And the Society shall hold in trust the receipts to repay the contractors the 20,000*l.* advanced for prizes, with interest at five per cent. ; also all such sums as they shall have paid in pursuance of their covenants, with interest, as aforesaid, except certain expenses, which are to be exclusively paid by the contractors :—but it is agreed that, if the receipts shall more than cover all such payments, the residue shall be held upon trust, one-third to be held in trust by the Society of Arts, for the establishment of future exhibitions, and the remaining two-thirds to be paid to the contractors, out of which the contractors are to pay all expenses of managers, officers, attendants, salaries, advertisements, printing, and other incidental expenses.

" That if a Royal Commission shall not be issued before the 1st February, 1850, the contractor may refer the further performance of the agreement to arbitration, that if the contractors neglect to fulfil the covenants, the Society shall stand possessed of the said 20,000*l.*, and all other sums paid by the contractors, for the purpose of indemnifying the Society from all expenses and liabilities in relation to the said exhibition, the Society's right to demand the performance of the contract to indemnify, not however to be prejudiced ; that the Society shall be enabled to determine the contract, upon receiving on or before the 1st February, 1850, a request to do so from the Lords Commissioners of Her Majesty's Treasury, and that the Society is not answerable for involuntary losses."

" In the second indenture, of even date with the first, it is recited that the contractors have paid £20,000 for prizes mentioned in deed No. 1, and £500 ; and have covenanted to pay such other sums as shall be required. The indenture witnesseth that it is agreed between the Society and the contractors, that certain specified arrangements relating to the exhibition, are to be under the control of the executive committee, unless a Royal Commission shall be issued. That on or before the 1st of May, 1850, plans, &c , of building, are to be submitted to His Royal Highness—that the plans, &c., approved by His Royal Highness shall be delivered to the contractors on or before the 1st of June, 1850, when the contractors are to be put in possession of site. The contractors within one month, engage to deliver a statement of quantities and a tender ; that if the contractor's tender be considered excessive, the plans, &c., and the tenders, be referred to arbitrators ; that the price reported by the arbitrators shall be the price to be paid to the contractors for the building ; that the contractors shall complete the building on or before the 31st of March, 1851.

" The indenture then provides that the materials shall be the absolute property of the contractors, after the termination of the exhibition on the 1st of October, 1851, and makes other provisions merely technical—the statement of which is not necessary to the public understanding of this matter.

" Thus it will be seen that the Messrs. Munday have taken upon themselves the entire risk of this vast speculation—relying solely on the public zeal, and the liberality which that may beget, for their repayment and their reward. In the administration of the funds by them advanced they are to have no share ; those funds will be distributed by the Society of Arts in the person of its executive Committee, under the authority and supervision of a Royal Commission, having the Prince Consort at its head.—Since the contract was signed, (But why was it signed ?—Ed. *Artisan*) we understand that the spirit exhibited by the public in answer to the appeal made to it in behalf of this vast scheme, having greatly improved the prospects of the speculation, the Messrs. Munday have consented to certain modifications in the terms of the original deed, at the request of Prince Albert—anxious in every way to guard the interests of the public. The time within which the conditional power reserved to Government of terminating the contract is to be exercised, has been extended to two months after the first meeting of the Royal Commission—and the Messrs. Munday have agreed, if the contract is not terminated by the Government, to put a limit on their profits—being " willing that an arbitration shall determine, when the exhibition is closed, the proportion of any surplus, after payment of all expenses whatever, to be allotted to them as remuneration for the capital employed, the risk incurred, and the exertions used."—In all respects, the liberality and public spirit displayed by the Messrs. Munday have alone, as is acknowledged by the Prince Consort, rendered it possible to give to this scheme a form and substance for presentation to the Government :—and we are glad to add, that the Prince has written a letter to them expressive of his sentiments to that effect. This part of the matter, and the care which has been taken of the public interests, will be better understood from a perusal of the following correspondence :—

" TO HIS ROYAL HIGHNESS THE PRINCE ALBERT, PRESIDENT OF THE SOCIETY OF ARTS.

" Guildford, December 7, 1849.

" Sir,—I have had the honour to receive by your Royal Highness's commands the following extract from the Minutes of the Executive Committee of the Exhibition of Industry of all Nations :—

" The Prince inquired whether Mr. Cole was prepared to report on the willingness of the contractors to place a limit on their profits, and was informed that the contractors had stated they were disposed to entertain at all times any wishes of His Royal Highness, and to refer them to arbitration.

" His Royal Highness expressed his great satisfaction at this proof of confidence, and thought it expedient that the contractors should write a letter to accompany the deeds, agreeing that the Council of the Society of Arts should have power to determine the contract by arbitration on the 31st of March, or at any time His Royal Highness might think desirable.

" ' Resolved—That a copy of the Minute entered on Friday last, referring to the contract, be officially sent to Mr Drew, with a request that he obtain an answer to it from the contractors as soon as possible.

" To the two proposals above mentioned, respecting, first, the willingness of the contractors to place a limit on their possible profits, and, secondly, to assent to a further extension of the term for determining the contract, I have to inform your Royal Highness that I am authorised by the contractors, Messrs. Munday, to reply on their behalf as their nominee.

" Before considering the first proposal, I submit it is necessary to dispose of the obvious preliminary question whether the minute implies that the Government or the Society of Arts, or anybody else, in desiring to limit the possible profits, is prepared to limit the possible losses that may be sustained under this contract. As the minute does not allude to this contingency, I have taken it for granted that no one is so prepared. Under this view, I proceed to discuss the proposal, which I am authorised to say the contractors are quite prepared to consider in accordance with your Royal Highness's suggestion, because they fully sympathise in the desire of your Royal Highness to protect to the utmost the public interests in this matter. They admit the full force of the fact, that the undertaking now appears under an aspect very different from that which it wore in July last, when it was first propounded by your Royal Highness. At the same time the contractors submit it should be borne in mind, in considering their position, that, before the proposition for holding the Exhibition, accompanied with the offer to the world of prizes to the amount of £20,000, could be published, it was obviously necessary that there should be some guarantee that the proposal would become a reality. The contractors apprehend there can be no doubt that the Government, the Society of Arts, or some one, must have taken the preliminary risk before any public steps whatever could be taken, and the contractors, for certain considerations, were then willing to undertake that risk. If a contract had to be made now, in the month of December, for the first time, the present information as to the expression of public feeling might, perhaps, cause the terms of that contract to be different.

" The contractors, however, do not wish to take advantage of the state of uncertainty which existed in July last, and are willing that the better knowledge and experience in this matter, which have been obtained at their risk and by the expenditure, should be fairly considered. But in so doing, I submit that the circumstances of the early period when the agreement was made ought not to be forgotten. In July there was no evidence at all to indicate how far the public would respond to the proposal, and there was no pecuniary guarantee whatever to secure its eventual success, as indeed there is none certain even now.

" The contractors were invited to enter into an engagement binding themselves to carry out this great work, involving a certain liability of £75,000 ; to be prepared at once when called upon to deposit £20,000 for a Prize Fund ; to advance all necessary capital for preliminary expenses ; and to make an outlay immediately without any tangible commercial security whatever. If they had viewed this proposal simply as tradesmen, they would probably have declined it, as I knew that others had already done, but they were induced to entertain it principally by my knowledge (obtained from the perusal of minutes of meetings held at Buckingham Palace and Osborne House, and shown to me by Mr. Fuller) of the interest taken by your Royal Highness in the plan, and of the confidence displayed by your Royal Highness in this matter in Messrs. Cole, Fuller, and Russell, from whom (then personally unknown to the contractors) the latter received an assurance of willingness to co-operate with the Executive.

" Upon such moral rather than commercial security, the contractors entered into this arrangement, binding themselves to carry out the proposal, which was not indeed defined in its extent, but was to be carried out to such an extent and in such a way as your Royal Highness, or a Royal Commission if issued, should direct.

" The receipts by which this outlay was to be repaid, either as respects the amount, or the regulations for obtaining them, were to be altogether beyond their control. How and whence they should arise they could not determine ; this point resting with the public themselves and with the Royal Commission. It was agreed, when the receipts were sufficient to repay the £20,000 advanced for the Prize Fund, the expenses of the building and some expenses mentioned in the deed, that the residue of the receipts if any, should be divided in certain proportions between the Society of Arts, as trustees for the public in this matter, and the contractors. Out of their share the contractors undertook, further, to pay the expenses, necessarily very considerable, of all management, salaries, offices, advertising, printing, &c. ; and the Society of Arts, I understood, would hold their proportion in trust for future similar exhibitions ; so that, even after the Prize Fund and the building had been paid for, the contractors still had a risk, whilst the public were sure of a future fund, if the receipts from the undertaking afforded any surplus whatever beyond the outlay for prizes and the cost of the building. During the preparation of the deeds for giving effect to the arrangements already mentioned, a still further protection of the public was asked of them, and they consented to the proposition made by Mr. Cole, that the contract should be altogether cancelled upon arbitration before February 1850, if the Government desired it : thus practically agreeing that, if a better arrangement for the public could be devised, there should at least be an opportunity of making one.

"I have now to state to your Royal Highness that, as the contractors still entertain the same confidence towards the undertaking and its promoters as they did when they came forward in July, and by so doing enabled the proposal to be announced to the world, so they are now willing that an arbitration shall determine, when the Exhibition is closed, the proportion of any surplus, after payment of all expenses whatever, to be allotted to them as remuneration for the capital employed, the risk incurred, and the exertions used.

"With regard to the wish of your Royal Highness that the contractors should agree to a still further extension of the time within which Her Majesty's Government shall be at liberty to determine the contract, and the suggestion made, as I understand, by your Royal Highness, that the period of extension should be the end of two months after the first meeting of the Royal Commission, I have to state that the contractors consent that the contract shall be liable to be determined at any time within the period suggested, upon the desire expressed by the Lords of the Treasury in the manner in all other respects provided in the deed.

"In conclusion, I beg leave to submit to your Royal Highness that, while I have no wish to parade the willingness of the contractors thus to make further concession or to submit to further modification in the terms of the contract for the public benefit, I think it only fair to call to mind the position in which they now place themselves.

"Your Royal Highness has the guarantee that the proposal will be carried out in such a way as a Royal Commission may direct. The Society of Arts have the honour of being the organ for executing the proposal without any risk or loss to themselves. The public not only have no risk of loss, but will have in fact all the profits of the undertaking, because I submit that a fair remuneration for risk and employment of capital cannot be considered as any other than an ordinary charge. In fact, the contractors are the only parties unprotected, and are liable to all the risks whatever.

"I have the honour to be, Sir, with the greatest respect, your Royal "Highness's most obedient and faithful servant,
    (Signed)   "GEORGE DREW."

"Osborne, December 10, 1849.

"Sir,—I am commanded by His Royal Highness, the Prince Albert, to acknowledge the receipt of your letter of the 7th of December, and to express to you His Royal Highness's sense of the public spirit and confiding readiness which were displayed by the contractors in the original acceptance of the contract at a time when the risk of the undertaking could in no way be ascertained or limited.

"His Royal Highness has no hesitation in acknowledging that it was owing to liberality and public spirit, thus displayed, that it became possible for him to bring the scheme of the Exhibition of the Industry of all Nations before the Government and the public in a shape insuring the practicability of its execution.

"His Royal Highness is happy to trace the same feelings in the answer which he has received from you on the part of the contractors, under the present much altered circumstances of the undertaking; and the Prince is induced to hope that the position in which the present contract can be laid before the Government and the public will prove satisfactory to both.

"Firstly, because the present agreement enables the Royal Commission, should it decide that the present contract will not be conducive to the public benefit, to determine that contract, within a limited time, upon equitable terms.

"Secondly, because the contractors have consented to an arrangement by which the share to be assigned to them of any profits that may result from the exhibition, after payment of their expenses, shall be determined by arbitration, under the then existing circumstances of the case, whilst they still remain liable for any possible losses, trusting solely to the liberal support of the public of a scheme which they have already so warmly received.

"It is in appreciation of this fact that His Royal Highness feels it a duty to furnish to them the earliest information with regard to the scheme in which His Royal Highness, as President of the Society of Arts, in conjunction with the British public, stands now morally pledged to the world ; and therefore the Prince is pleased to direct that the contract, with the modifications agreed to in your letter, together with this answer written by His Royal Highness's command, shall be published without delay.—I have the honour to be, sir, your obedient humble servant,
    (Signed)   "C. B. PHIPPS.
"George Drew, Esq."

The Royal Commission for inquiring into the best mode of carrying out the Exhibition will shortly be issued ; and will consist of heads of parties and interests, members of the present and late administration, representa-tives, of agriculture, art, science, mechanics and manufactures. It is proposed, in addition, to nominate any number of local commissioners desirable, represent the interests of various places, both at home and abroad.

SANITARY HINTS.

CLARK'S SELF-ACTING VALVE-TRAP.

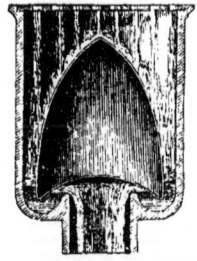

This is an ingenious substitute for the common bell-trap. Its action will be perceived at a glance. The outer case is formed of lead, and the floating-valve of copper. When water runs through the grating the valve rises, and allows a free discharge down the waste-pipe, whilst at the same time it forms a perfect water-seal against the return of any effluvia from the drain, after the flow of the water has ceased. Its great advantages are, its simplicity, cheapness, and non-liability to get out of order.

ANALYSIS OF AMERICAN PATENTS.

Arunah S. Macomber, Bennington, Bennington county, Vermont, for an improvement in a turning-lathe for wheels. January 2.

THE patentee says,—" The nature and principle of my invention consists in placing the box to be turned or rimmed out on a lathe within a revolving chuck, through which passes a fixed spindle with a cutter attached to it, and connecting the said chuck and stock-head to a saddle, which, by a slot or slots therein, and pivots or centres connecting the said saddle to the slide, allows the saddle, poppet-head, and chuck, to be set at any angle with the cutter on the spindle, whereby boxes of any required taper may be cut or rimmed out, as the chuck revolves around the cutter and moves with the slide."

Claim.—" What I claim as my invention is the saddle, constructed with a slot or slots, combined with pivots or screws, or swivels, and with another slot or slots in the flanch below, whereby the said swivels will act as centres or swivels, for the saddle to be moved either transversely or set at any angle with the point of the cutter on the fixed spindle, so that when the box and chuck revolve round the cutter, and with the slide as it moves horizontally on the bed of the lathe, boxes for carriage and other wheels may be turned or rimmed out of any required interior taper."

Benjamin W. Warner, City of New York, for an improvement in making shears. January 9.

THE patentee says,—" The nature of my invention consists in attaching the lower blade of the shear to a bar, and making it work in combination with the upper blade by means of a short arm or lever worked by the upper hand lever, by which arrangement the blades are made to act, in cutting, more nearly parallel to each other than those of the ordinary shears, thus increasing the facility of their use by lessening the spread of their points, and keeping the lower part of the shears constantly in contact with the surface upon which the material is laid to be cut, at the same time that the power of the hand is applied more equally on the whole blade than in any other plan hitherto in use."

Claim.—" What I claim as my invention is the construction of the lower blade separate from the upper lever and jointed to it."

Adrian Bancker and Charles F. Alvord, City of New York, for an improvement in making hats. January 9.

THE patentees say,—" Our invention, discovery, or improvement consists in substituting for the ingredients usually employed, a solution of gutta percha, prepared in any usual manner, for the purpose of stiffening the body of the hat.

Claim.—" What we claim as our invention is the application of a solution of gutta percha for the purpose of stiffening hat bodies, and uniting the plush or other cover to the body, as a substitute for shellac, glue size, and seed lac, or other articles hitherto used for such purposes."

Benjamin H. Green, Princeton, Mercer county, New Jersey, for an improvement in coating telegraph wires. January 9.

CLAIM.—" What I claim as my invention is the construction of an apparatus for aiding in the painting or coating of telegraph wires (or for other purposes), by the combination of rotating and stationary brushes, and suspension pulleys or their equivalents, with a portable receptacle for paint or other coating matter, not intending by this claim to limit myself to the particular form, number, and arrangement of the parts composing the apparatus for aiding in the painting or coating telegraph wires, but to vary the same as I may deem expedient, whilst I attain the same end by means substantially the same."

Bliss Coiser, Mount Morris, Livingston county, New York, *for an improved machine for sawing clapboards.* January 16.

THE patentee says,—" The nature of my invention consists in so constructing the carriage and combining it with other parts of the machine. that when the thick plank, or piece of timber of suitable thickness, is placed upon the carriage, and the machine put in motion. it will automatically operate as follows:—The portion of the carriage upon which the timber rests will have its side most distant from the saw alternately elevated and depressed, so as to incline the front edge of the timber, in combination with the feed movement, in such a manner that the saw will cut from the timber. at each forward movement of the carriage, clapboards, double the thickness at one edge that they are at the other, their thick and thin edges regularly alternating from the top to the bottom of the piece of timber."

H. G. Ty.r and John Helm, New Brunswick, Middlesex county, New Jersey, *for an improvement in the manufacture of India-rubber.* Jan 30.

THE patentees say,—" The nature of our invention consists in forming a compound of caoutchouc, carbonate of zinc, or other preparations of that metal, and sulphur, which is perfectly elastic, impermeable to air or water ; unchangeable in extreme tem eratures, preserving its colour without ' bloom,' and free from the deadly action upon the constitution and health hitherto experienced by the operatives employed in the preparation of metallic vulcanised rubber."

Claim.—" What we claim is the combination of caoutchouc, in its several varieties, with either carbonate of zinc, sulphate of zinc, or the other salts of zinc, with sulphur, in manner, form, and proportion, as hereinbefore set forth."

John Sourbeer, Mount Joy township, Adams county, Pennsylvania, *for an improvement in flood fences.* January 30.

THE patentee says,—" The nature of my invention consists in constructing such a fence that, when the water rises to the first rail, it will raise it out of the mortise in the post at one end, and hold fast by the hook and staple to the post at the other end, and swing round in any course the current may take it, and as the water rises the rails will be raised out one by one, until the water course will have no other obstacle than the posts, and when the water falls the rails are soon put to their place again."

Frederick Harbach, Cleveland, Ohio. *for an improved multiple grate furnace for locomotive boilers.* January 30.

THE patentee says.—" The nature of my improvement consists in an arrangement or combination, with the main tubular flue and water section of the boiler of a locomotive engine, of a series of two or more fire boxes (each including a fire-place, grate, and ash pit), and one or more water chambers or spaces between, or connected with, each two of said fire boxes, the whole being so disposed and made to operate as not only to greatly increase what is usually termed the grate surface. but the water surface also exposed to the action of the flame or heat proceeding from the fuel in combustion. Each of the said . re boxes is to have all the usual appendages for burning coal (whether anthracite or bituminous) separate from the other : oxygen, or atmospheric air containing the same, in addition to the ordinary draught created by the exhaust steam, being supplied by a blower driven by the main sugine or a separate one. as circumstances may require."

Claim.—" What I claim as my invention is the combination and arrangement of two or more fire boxes, and the water chamber or chambers between them, with each other, and the main boiler and flues, when said fire boxes are arranged vertically over each other ; the whole being arranged. constructed, connected. and made to operate. as above si ecified, and for the purpose of using anthracite coal, and increasing the fire and water surface in boilers whose position is such that it is difficult to extend the fire surface horizontally, and thereby improving the capacity of the boiler to generate steam."

Isaac L. Bennett, Westerloo. Albany county, New York, *for a piston-valve inclosed in the steam cylinder.* February 6.

CLAIM.—" What I claim as my invention is the employment of the two sliding ring valves. in combination with the cylinder and reciprocating piston. for admitting the steam to, and discharging it from. the cylinder in reciprocal succession. by the alternate direct action of the piston on the ring valves, and without the intervention of any other agents. whether the valves be connected in the manner described, or in any other way which is substantially the same, and by which analogous results are produced."

William Sewall, jun., Williamsburg, Kings county, New York. *for an apparatus for ascertaining the saltness of water in steam boilers.* Feb 6.

THE patentee says.—" The nature of my invention consists in constructing and arranging an apparatus containing a hydrometer. a d with or without a thermometer, and so connected with a steam boiler as to readily pass a current of water from any part of the boiler through it, for the purpose of ascertaining at all times, by inspection, the exact degree of saltness of the water at such desired part of the boiler."

Warren S. Bartle, Newark, Wayne county, New York, *for a method of regulating the supply of water to steam boilers.* February 6.

THE patentee says,—" The nature of my invention consists in regulating the quantity of water forced into steam boilers, and thus maintaining it at a uniform height therein, by means of a float placed in the boiler, or in a chamber communicating with it, which float, by its rising and falling, directs the points of one or more clicks, moved longitudinally to and fro by the engine, alternately upon, or away from, adverse ratchets attached either to a cock in the pump, so as to turn the cock alternately one way and the other, and admit and shut off the water in its passage to the boiler (the pump all the while moving), or to a lever moving a clutch or other device, which stops and starts the wheel, pulley, or shaft, that drives the pump, and thus starts and stops the pump."

Claim.—" What I claim as my invention is regulating feed in boilers by means of an arrangement of a float, a rocking shaft, kept in constant motion by the engine, vibrating clicks, and circular or straight ratchets, acting upon the cock stem, valve spindle, or pump shaft, so that the float is required to exert no direct force to regulate the supply, the whole machinery constructed and acting as described."

Henry Jenkins, Pottsville, Schuylkill county, Pennsylvania, *for an improvement in wire fences.* February 13.

THE patentee says, —" My invention consists in forming a fence of wrought iron in a cheap and economical manner, by the construction and arrangement of its several parts, by which a light and durable fence, of a highly ornamental character, can be made at as cheap a rate as one formed of cast iron, and in many cases cheaper."

Claim.—" I claim constructing the wrought iron wire fence, by forming the top and bottom rails and posts of the panel, of grooved bars, through which the ends of the wires, of which the meshes are made, are drawn, and the ends turned down into said grooves, and then covered by other similar bars to hold them in place, by which a perfect finish is effected, and the expense and difficulty of riveting is avoided."

Asa Hill and Samuel G. Blackman, Norwalk, Fairfield county, Connecticut, *for an improvement in composition for filling teeth.* February 13.

THE patentees say,—" This article is made by taking the gutta parcha of commerce, freeing it from its impurities and colouring matter by boiling and working it, or by maceration, and combining with it, when sufficiently heated with a dry heat to render it plastic, about two parts quick lime, and two parts each of quartz and feldspar, all reduced to an impalpable powder."

Claim.—" What we claim is the combination of gutta percha as a base, with such other mineral, earthy, and metallic substances as will make such a compound, of such a character, and adapted to such purposes, as we have described—viz., its combination with such of those substances as will shorten it and render it less tenacious, harden it and render it fit for a useful filling, and give it the desired colour, without any noxious quality, and without destroying its plasticity when heated, and the application of the compound substance for that purpose."

Nelson E. Chaffee, Ellington, Tolland county, Connecticut, *for an improvement in drying machines.* February 20.

THE patentee says,—" The nature of my invention consists in providing a wheel composed of two circular sides, united together by an axle passing through the same, so as to leave a space between the said two sides, the which space I divide into four separate chambers by wire wicker work, into which I put the wool or cloth to be dried, and, by giving the wheel a great velocity, the air impinges through the wicker work on the periphery of the wheel on the cloth or wool, and dries the same in an incredibly short period."

Claim.—" What I claim as my invention is a wheel divided into chambers, open to the free circulation of the atmosphere around the periphery, and through the passage around the interior parts of the chamber ; also for the purpose set forth. I do not confine my claim to the chambers formed of iron wires or rods : for some purposes wood would be preferable ; neither do I confine my claim to four chambers in the wheel, but to two or more formed as described."

James Mulbury, Parkesburg, Chester counter, Pennsylvania, *for an improvement in short slide valves for chamfering the corners.* February 20.

THE patentee says,—" My improvement consists in making the sides of the steam ways in the seat of the valve, and the sides of the steam way in the valve or slide, join their respective faces by rounded or flattened corners ; also the joining of the outer sides of the seat, and that of the outer sides of the slide, with their respective faces by rounded corners."

Claim.—" What I claim is the rounding or flattening of the corners joining the sides of the steam ways in, and the outer sides of the seat of the valve with its face. Also the face of the valve or slide being joined to the sides of the steam cavity therein, and in its outer sides, by corners rounded or flattened as set forth."

INSTITUTION OF CIVIL ENGINEERS.
Tuesday, November 27, 1849.
JOSHUA FIELD, Esq., President, in the Chair.

THE paper read was a "Description of the Old Southend Pier-head, and the extension of the pier; with an inquiry into the nature and ravages of the 'Teredo Navalis,' and the means hitherto adopted for preventing its attacks," by Mr. John Paton.

After describing the form of construction of the old pier-head, and showing the adoption of copper sheathing for protecting it from decay, and the important considerations involved in the attempt to preserve marine structures the paper explained the ravages committed by marine worms ("Teredo Navalis," "Lymnoria Terebrans," and others) on the piles, both above and below the copper sheathing. This sheathing extended from the top of the mud to three feet above low water-mark; the worm destroyed the timber from two feet below the surface of the mud, to eight feet above low water spring tides, and, in fact, out of thirty-eight fir timber piles, and various oak piles, not one remained perfect, after being up only three years; indeed, some were entirely eaten through.

A general outline of the extension of the pier, and a minute description of the pier head, were then given, showing the means adopted by the use of iron piles and by scupper-nailing the inner piles, to preserve the structure from decay. The greater portion of the extension of the pier, the length of which was one mile, as well as the whole of the pier head, were constructed of square, hollow, iron piles, and scupper-nailed fender piles; the iron piles being forced to a depth of from eight feet to sixteen feet, by pulling them backwards and forwards with ropes attached to them, and not by driving in the usual manner; they were then filled with gravel and concrete to within five feet of the top, and the fir piles to sustain the superstructure were fitted into them. The pier head was constructed with forty cast iron piles, and twenty fender piles, nailed from five feet below the bed of the sea to eight feet above low water; its greatest height was twenty-five feet above low water spring tides.

The paper then entered into an investigation of the nature and operations of the "Teredo Navalis," and shewed, as a remarkable peculiarity, that no chemical means had hitherto prevented wood from being destroyed by these animals and the "Limnoria Terebrans," whose destructive powers were likewise noticed, and as having penetrated between the copper sheathing and the wood at Southend. The operations of the "Teredo," although most destructive in warm climates, extended themselves to all places, having been found almost in the Polar seas.

The chief peculiarities which distinguished the "Teredo" were stated to have been ascertained by minute microscopical investigation, and that woody fibres of an extremely minute nature had been discovered in the body, thus setting at rest the question as to whether the "Teredo" did actually feed upon the wood. It was stated, that the failure of chemical means to preserve timber from destruction by the marine worm was believed to proceed from two causes, namely, of poisonous compounds having no seriously injurious effect upon them, and the sea-water, and other things decomposing the poisonous ingredients contained in the wood. In corroboration of the first of these views, accounts of experiments made by Mr. Paton were adduced; and Physiological facts, quoted from the *British and Foreign Medical Review*, were brought forward to show, that cold-blooded animals were much more tenacious of life, than those of a higher temperament; and hence it was argued, that, as it required a very large quantity of poison of the most virulent nature, to destroy animals of a much higher order than the "Teredo Navalis" it would take a still greater quantity to affect those animals as they existed in their own element; and it was questioned, under these circumstances, whether wood could ever be so completely and thoroughly saturated, as in any degree to affect them. The corrosive action of the sea-water, its extended influence and constant variableness in different parts of the globe, were then commented on, and some of the various salts held in solution mentioned. It was believed to be impossible to form any general notion of the precise action of sea-water on timber, whether chemically saturated, or not, without a series of most minute experiments, and a large body of facts, carefully collected in different parts of the globe—as that which might be advantageously used in the Thames, might not be of the slightest avail in the Tropics, and 'vice versa;' it was thus questioned, whether any generally applicable principle could be found for the counteracting of that universal solvent of soluble matter. The conclusions arrived at were, that the ravages of the marine worm were not prevented by any chemical application, and that nothing but mechanical means could ever prove completely successful; studding with broad-headed nails was considered to be the most effectual remedy, and various authorities were quoted, proving its success. The paper concluded with a list of places where wood, prepared with various chemical ingredients, had been destroyed from various causes.

At the next meeting, on December 4, the discussion was continued, and extended to such a length as to preclude the reading of any original communication.

Numerous specimens were exhibited, and commented on, of timber thoroughly perforated by worms; whilst beside them, under the same circumstances, the "Jarrow wood," from Australia, was shown to have remained completely free from injury.

The reference to the age of Homer, as an instance of the ancient ravaging habits of the "Teredo" induced a return to Geological questions; and it was shown, that in the London clay, remains had repeatedly been found, of timber perforated by sea worms. The Oolite and Greensand formations also exhibited petrified wood, filled with boring Moluscæ. This led to the consideration of the formation most likely to withstand the attack of the "Pholas;" and it was shown, that the Portland stone was, from the quantity of silica it contained, least liable to be attacked.

The "Pholas," was shown to have been in active operation upon certain rocks from the earliest periods, but never upon Portland stone. Hence it was argued, that kind of stone should be used for breakwaters and other works exposed to the action of the sea.

The early state of the "Teredo" was noticed; when escaping from the egg, in the shape of a free swimmer, it was drifted about with the tide until it met with a log, a pile, or the side of a ship, to which it attached itself, and making an inroad into it, became a non-locomotive animal of different form and habits, never again to leave the habitation it had burrowed for itself in the body of the timber. The question, of whether the boring operation of the marine worms was carried on by chemical, or by mechanical means, was lengthily discussed. The thin shell, covered by its delicate membrane, was instanced as not possessing strength enough to cut away timber; but it was on the other hand shown, that the shape of the two shells, forming the extremity of the animal, admirably adapted them for powerful cutting, or rasping tools, when moved rapidly in a circular direction, as was evidently the case, from the uniformly cylindrical character of the holes.

The shells of the "Pholas" were also shown to be used in that manner, and the opinion appeared generally to lean to a mechanical cause, for the effects observed.

This bearing of the discussion naturally induced remarks upon the ravages of the white ants of India; which, however, appeared to have been little studied, and less understood, as far as attempting to arrest, or to prevent its inroads.

The various materials, such as Kyan's Corrosive Sublimate of Mercury, Sir W. Burnett's Chloride of Zinc, Margary's Salts of Metals, Payne's combination of Muriate of Lime and Sulphate of Iron, forming an insoluble compound, and Bethell's Creosote or Oil of Coal Tar, were discussed. All had their partisans, and were stated to have succeeded and failed under certain circumstances. Specimens of piles from Lowestoft harbour, whose waters were notoriously full of worm, showed that timber in a natural state was in a few months thoroughly perforated by "Teredo" in the centre, and "Limnoria" on the surface; but that piles, which had been properly saturated according to Bethell's system, in exhausted receivers, and subjected to such pressure as insured the absorption of about ten pounds weight of the creosote, or oil of coal tar, by each cubic foot of the timber, were perfectly preserved from attacks of marine animals of any kind.

The discussion was interrupted by the monthly ballot, when the following candidates were elected:—M. Jones and T. C. Gunn, as Members; T. A. Hedley, J. Allan, H. O. Bridgeman, and Captain J. Estridge, as Associates.

Tuesday, December 11, 1849.
JOSHUA FIELD, Esq., President in the Chair.

THE paper read was "On the facilities for a Ship Canal Communication

1

between the Atlantic and Pacific Oceans, through the Isthmus of Panama," by Lieut.-Colonel Lloyd, Assoc. Inst. C. E.

In treating this subject, which, on account of recent events, has become one of great importance to the political and the mercantile world, the author brought to bear all the knowledge and experience acquired during a lengthened residence in South America, when serving in the Colombian Engineers, under General Bolivar, from whom, after much difficulty, he obtained permission to make the first survey of the Isthmus, which he accomplished in the most complete manner, as well as making soundings throughout the principal rivers and in the chief harbours; compiling, at the same time, a mass of minute and valuable information relative to the country, which he transmitted to the Royal Society, in whose archives they were deposited, and a paper on the subject was published in the Philosophical Transactions in 1830. Thus may Great Britain claim not only the projection of one of the greatest works of modern ages, but also for one of her sons the merit of having, for the pure love of science, been the first to demonstrate the facility of the accomplishment of that, which so many have since descanted upon, and to some extent, appropriated without acknowledgment.

The general views of the author incline to the formation of a Ship Canal, in preference to a Railroad; he denies that there are any obstacles to its accomplishment, but, on the contrary, asserts so many local advantages to exist and to be concentrated nearly at one point, that in after ages it will be a matter of wonder why so many generations should have neglected, or refused to render them available, towards the establishment of this long-coveted communication between the two Oceans.

The paper first reviewed the surveys of Garella, of Morel, and others, who had examined the country subsequently to Colonel Lloyd. It then examined the various lines proposed, and gave reasons for preferring that which, starting from the beautiful bay of Limon, would proceed by a short canal, through a flat country, to the River Chagres, thence up the River Trinidad, as far as its depth would suit, and then cutting a canal into the Rio Grande, debouching at Panama. This line, it was contended, in the present state of the science of Engineering, presented no obstacles, except-ing the climate and the expense, to prevent a canal being cut of sufficient depth and dimensions to float, from one river to the other, the largest ship in Her Majesty's Navy.

The climate was stated, from personal experience, to be quite as good as in any tropical country, except in some particular spots, where, from local causes, certain complaints were rife.

The expense could only be accurately estimated by the survey of expe-rienced Engineers; but in a country abounding in fine timber, and the best building materials of all kinds, whilst no great chain of mountains, as had been fancifully depicted on suppositious charts, had any existence, except in the imagination of the designer, it was only fair to allow, that the cost of a canal of such limited length could not be very great, and the supply of water might be presumed to be ample, in a climate where there was copious rain for nine months in each year.

The disadvantages of a Railroad, in such a humid climate were descanted upon at length, and it was shown, that the risk of injury to merchandise from that cause alone, independent of that to be anticipated from breakage and pilfering, during the various trans-shipments, must induce preference for a canal, through which vessels should pass from sea to sea without delay, and continue their voyage to their destination without breaking bulk.

The means of accomplishing the work were then fully considered. The proposition for a certain number of convicts, to be contributed by Great Britain, France, and America, was shown to be untenable; but it was argued that a portion of the convicts from this country might be more advantageously sent there than to our present penal settlements. The means of preventing their escape were shown, and a proposition made for introducing with them a number of convicts from Bengal, and the other Presidencies, whose lan-guage and habits would effectually prevent their mingling with the British convicts, whilst their power of enduring fatigue under a tropical sun, and during rains, and their simple mode of living, would render them valuable pioneers for the more robust Englishmen.

It was stated, also, that a great deal of native labour might be obtained at a cheap rate; sixpence, or ninepence per day, and his rations, consisting of a pint of rice, a pound of dried beef, and a "golpe d'aguardiente," being the ordinary pay of a "Peon."

The chief point, insisted on by the author, was the great field opened in the Isthmus, for emigration, for the surplus population of this country. He contended, that it was far preferable to the Canadas, where the poor but industrious and honest mechanic, or labourer, on arriving, found that the rich lands he had heard of, could only be reached by a weary journey and after such hardships, in a severe climate, as his limited means and broken strength rendered impossible for him to bear.

Australia, with its arid, trackless wastes, held out still fewer temptations to the emigrant; for the ordeal of misery to be encountered by the majority, was such as to deter all but the stoutest hearts from encountering it.

The Isthmus had none of these disadvantages. It was comparatively within an easy distance; the emigrant would be at his destination almost on landing; the resources of the country were great, and the productions varied and cheap, whilst the present population was infinitely disproportioned to the superficial area of the country.

The point was strongly insisted on, and it was argued, that a grant of land might be easily obtained, in liquidation of the debt owing by the Govern-ment of the country, and as the British had once possessed an establishment there in 1675 to 1690, under the charter of the "Scotch Darien Company," so a footing being again obtained, a barrier of the most formidable character would be opposed to the annexation propensities of our transatlantic brethren, who were making rapid strides towards the possession of this valuable tract.

Appended to the paper was a copy of the commission granted to Lieut.-Colonel Lloyd, by General Bolivar, authorising his examination and survey of the Isthmus, and of the rivers, which had previously been most jealously refused to every one. This document was alluded to with some natural pride, as proving that to an English engineer was due the merit of having been the first to examine and propose a work of such vital importance to the whole world, but which had been since claimed, and, in fact, appropriated by other persons without acknowledgment.

The discussion upon this interesting subject was announced to take place at the meeting of January 8th.

Tuesday, December 18, 1849.

JOSHUA FIELD, Esq., President, in the Chair.

THE Annual General Meeting of the Institution was held on Tuesday evening, December 18th, when the following gentlemen were elected to form the Council for the ensuing year:—

William Cubitt, *President*; I. K. Brunel, J. M. Rendel, J. Simpson, and R. Stephenson, M.P., *Vice-Presidents*; J. F. Bateman, G. P. Bidder, J. Cubitt, J. E. Errington, J. Fowler, C. H. Gregory, J. Locke, M.P., I. R. M'Clean, C. May, and J. Miller, *Members*; and J. Baxendale, and L. Cubitt, *Associates of Council.*

The Report of the Council, which was read, alluded to the past season of unexampled depression in the Engineering world, but at the same time held out hopes of improvement, on account of the agitation of the subjects of better supplies of Water and Gas, the Sewerage and Drainage of Towns, the construction of Abattoirs, and other sanitary questions; whilst the im-provement of Canals, in their struggle with the Railways for the heavy traffic, the construction and amelioration of Harbours, the embanking and improving of Rivers, the recovery of marsh-lands from the sea, and nume-rous other works, which had been neglected on account of the more attractive railways, would resume their former importance, and eventually afford ample employment for the majority of the members of the profession.

It was shown, that the careful administration of the funds had been attended to, and that a considerable quantity of publications had been issued.

The alteration of the commencement of the Session was shown to have worked well; and, in general, the report of the progress of the Society was very satisfactory, in spite of the bad times for engineers.

The debt contracted for the improvement of the House of the Institution was stated to have been entirely liquidated, by the liberality of a number of the members.

Telford Medals were presented to Lieut.-Colonel Harry D. Jones, R. E., Mr. R. B. Dockray, and Mr. J. T. Harrison; Council Premiums of Books to Messrs. J. T. Harrison and J. Richardson; and Telford Premiums of Books to Messrs. R. B. Grantham, T. R. Crampton, W. Brown, and C. B. Mansfield—the President addressing a few complimentary expressions to each of these gentlemen on presenting the Premiums.

Memoirs were read of the following deceased members:—Messrs. J.

Green, P. Rothwell, R. Sibley, and D. Wilson, Members; A. Mitchell; Lieut.-Colonel A. W. Robe, R.E.; C. K. Sibley, W. Mitchell, and J. C. Prior, Associates; and J. Woods, Graduate.

The thanks of the Institution were voted unanimously to the President, Vice-President, Members, and Associates of the Council, to the Auditors, Scrutineers, and the Secretary, for their attention to the interests of this Institution.

The President returned thanks very briefly, and on retiring from the chair, after holding it most worthily for the two past years, he recommended to the members his successor, Mr. Cubitt, whose active energy and high position in the profession rendered him every way fit to occupy the chair of such a Society.

The address was very warmly received, and it was proposed to the Council to consider by what means the eminent past Presidents could be enabled to continue their valuable services, in conjunction with the acting Council.

The meeting was adjourned until Tuesday, January 8th, when the following papers were announced to be read:—"An Account of the Black-friars's Landing Pier," by F. Lawrence; and "A Description of a Timber Bridge, erected on the line of the Lynn and Ely Railway," by J. S. Valentine, member of the Institution of Civil Engineers.

INSTITUTION OF MECHANICAL ENGINEERS.

ON RAILWAY AXLES.—BY MR. M'CONNELL.

When the railway system was first introduced into this country, the question of the strength of the materials for constructing the new stock was (it is to be presumed) materially influenced by the amount of experience derived from the vehicles which had previously been in use for the conveyance of traffic.

As the new system became extended and improved in all its arrangements, and the facilities which it possessed for conveying greater loads at higher speeds were gradually developed, the working stock was necessarily changed from time to time in conformity with the greater demands for convenience and stability. Improvements in almost every point have been carried out until we have now in operation the railway stock, generally speaking, in an excellent condition for the purpose to which it is applied.

It is remarkable that, notwithstanding the importance of proportion and quality as first elements in considering the strength of the materials of which railway moving stock is composed, no rule, generally applicable for even the main features of this great system of machinery, has been established.

Without attempting to embrace the whole subject, although one of great importance to proprietors of railways and the public generally, I conceive it is proper in this place to express my strong conviction that the general question of the strength and quality of those materials justly proportioned to the strains to which they are subject, and bearing reference to accidents from collision, faults of road, deterioration from a variety of causes, &c., must eventually be treated with great attention and consideration; and in order to insure safety to life and property for all who use railways, as well as the greatest possible economy for the profit of those who have embarked their capital in their construction, I believe it will be found essential to have some regulations founded upon the joint experience of those parties who have been practically engaged in managing and working the different departments of railways.

It is well known that short-sighted economy has been practised in many instances in giving directions for the purchase and repair of railway stock, and it is only dear-bought experience which can effectually convince those parties who, to make a little saving by purchasing a cheap ill-constructed machine, gain a great and constant loss whilst it is in use.

The advantages of a general and constant interchange of opinion among those parties to whose judgment and management the working expenses of the different railways are entrusted is most important; and if such varied experience could be collected regularly and systematically into one focus, where it might be digested and prepared for practical use, the effect for good to the general system of railways would be very great, and, in a scientific point of view, the results recorded would prove highly interesting.

Having thus briefly stated a portion of my views as bearing upon the introduction of the best means of producing uniformity in the working stock of railways, I will now proceed to consider "Railway Axles," which,

as an important part of the great machinery, are deserving of marked attention.

I have endeavoured to ascertain whether any data were available which might assist me in forming a groundwork of the results of combined experience on this subject; but I regret to say that, although my inquiries have been in all cases promptly and carefully attended to, yet the object which I had in view has not been attained.

As an example of the diversity of opinion, or rather perhaps the want of some certain rule to guide engineers in proportioning the strength of axles to their weights and strains, I would refer to the different forms of axles now in use on one portion of one railway, and in doing so would remark, that a clearer proof could not be afforded of the desirableness of some defined principle to guide us in deciding on the strength for railway axles.

For obvious reasons I wish particularly to guard against expressing, directly or by inference, any opinion on any description of manufacture of axle, or even quality of iron of which axles are composed. I would wish to limit the scope of the present paper simply to the question of the form and dimensions of axles, with the changes and deterioration to which they are subject in process of working, assuming in all cases the material of which the axles are made, and the mode of manufacture, to be of the most approved description.

In order to arrive at a knowledge of the best form and dimensions of axles, we have first to ascertain the load and friction to which they are to be exposed; and, secondly, to estimate as nearly as possible the strains to which they will be subject whilst in motion.

Supposing a waggon or carriage to be constantly in a state of rest, it would of course then only be necessary to consider the axle as a beam or girder, sustaining a load of five tons upon the two journals, the points of support being the wheels resting upon the rails; the middle portion of the axle being of sufficient strength to sustain the wheel or prop in its perpendicular position. We then require to find out the proportionate strength, so that each section of this beam or girder shall only be sufficiently strong to resist the strain or load to which it is then subject.

It is ascertained, by an approximate calculation, that a journal 1.128 inch diameter, is not capable of sustaining a heavier load when in a state of rest than 2½ tons, or 5,600 lbs.; and allowing in practice that the waggon or carriage axle is made ten times the breaking strength, the diameter of the journal would be, adopting the same calculation, 2.43 inches. In these calculations the strength alone is considered, but we have also to take into account the question of friction and likewise the tendency to abrasion.

With our present means of information no accurate data are available for determining the best proportion of journal or bearing according to the weight it has to bear, or the velocity at which it is required to move. A great variety of proportion is in use, but it is fair to note that in engine-axles particularly, the length of bearings depends to a certain extent upon the construction and arrangement of the engine: as a general rule the length of the bearing is not in due proportion, according to our general experience, to the diameter.

It has always been considered that, having first ascertained, from example and experience, the strength of sectional area necessary under every circumstance to sustain the load which the journal has to carry, the length of it was determined by the velocity or amount of friction to which it is liable. Judging from axles at present in use in carriages and waggons, the length of bearing is twice the diameter of the journal; but on this, as well as other points on strength of material, there exists a great variety of opinion. Even the forms of journals are found to differ very much. Without attempting to decide on the merits of any of them, I shall, in the present instance, content myself with stating that all my experience has proved the desirableness of maintaining the rubbing or wearing surfaces of bearings as free as possible from sharp abrupt corners, and sudden alterations in diameter or sectional strength.

Having thus treated the journals as regards the load and the friction upon them, I now proceed to estimate the various strains to which the axle is exposed whilst in motion.

The first strain to which the axle is subject is that arising from the weight of the waggon and load, which, being received or resting on the journal, produces the greatest effect upon the axle at the outer face of the wheel-boss, and to which is to be added the momentum of the load in falling through the spaces caused by inequalities in the joints of the rails.

The injurious consequences upon the axle of inequalities of the road surface, and flat places on the surface of the wheel-tyre, by the jolting or perpendicular motion which they produce, cannot be accurately estimated, and these are very much increased when the bearing springs of the waggon or carriage are not sufficiently elastic, and do not yield to the shock or blow downwards, so as (to use the expression) to cushion its effect. As an instance of the imperfect action of the springs, I would allude to those in use on many waggons, in which the form and construction cause them to be so rigid, that the downward blow is more like a hammer upon an anvil. To obviate this strain as much as possible, it is necessary to proportion the spring so as to sustain the load properly, and yet to be of sufficient elasticity to absorb the effect of the load oscillation.

The strain arising from the oscillation of the waggon on curves from imperfect coupling, is increased by the lateral freedom or space on the bearings or play between the rails and flanges of the wheels; which, when an irregularity occurs on the side of the rail, or any sudden cause disturbs the direct motion of the waggon onwards, is in effect the same as a blow upon the flange of the wheel, the radius of the wheel tending to act as a lever to break the axle at the inner face of the boss of the wheel.

This strain is in the compound ratio of the momentum of the load, the angle at which the wheel strikes the rail, and the distance from the centre of the axle to the point of impact, producing an effective strain upon the axle at the inner face of the wheel-boss, which extends proportionately over the whole axle between the wheels. To lessen in practice as much as possible the deteriorating effect of these descriptions of strains upon the axle, the following conditions are important:—

That the bearings or journals of the axles fit as closely to the brasses as is consistent with freedom, the allowance of flange-guage of wheel being quite sufficient for the carriage to move freely round curves and meet any irregularity in the guage of the rails.

That the waggons or carriages be as equally loaded as possible, and the draw chains be exactly in the centre; and as side chains are dangerous, they should be completely removed, provision being made for a duplicate centre draw chain, should a failure take place. As the damage to the loading of waggons is in proportion to the oscillation, they should all be screwed together by means of screw-couplings, having spring-buffers upon both ends of every waggon.

It is well known that the injury to the waggon, to the load which it conveys, to the axle which carries it, and to the road over which it runs, is very much aggravated if the waggons are allowed to oscillate from side to side, and become like so many battering rams, injuring themselves and all substances in contact with them. A train of waggons or carriages should be jointed together similar to the vertebræ of an animal, by which means any sudden lateral action would be neutralised by the support derived from the neighbouring vehicles.

The road to be kept as accurate as possible to guage and line.

The third class of strains to which axles are liable are the shocks produced by starting and stopping a train, and which are in proportion to the momentum of the wheel and axle at the time of collision when stopping, and to the velocity of the impelling force and the inertia of the wheel and axle when starting; these strains are felt principally on the neck of the journal.

Fourth strain—the torsion or twisting caused by the wheels travelling over curves of the line; the difference in length of surface of the inner and outer rail compels one wheel to grind or slide upon the rail, while the other is free to roll. This strain is proportionate to the load on the wheel, determining the amount of friction upon the rails and the length of axle between the wheels; a slight amount of torsion is also caused by any variation in the diameter of the wheels on the same axle, by any inequality upon each journal, the quality of the brasses, or the amount of lubrication proportionately, and the strain of the break block on one side, because when any of these occur separately or jointly, one-half of the extra strain on one journal is transmitted through the axle to the other, and twisting or weakening the axle is necessarily produced. To lessen the amount of the above strain, it is obvious that the wheels should be kept in the best possible state of repair so far as equal diameters and true circular surfaces are concerned, the

waggons or carriages should be loaded equally on each side, the journals carefully lubricated, and all break blocks adjusted to bear the same pressure on both wheels of the same axle.

Fifth strain—the constant vibration of the whole axle. This is more particularly the case and is accelerated when the axle is fixed in a rigid, unyielding wheel. My experience has proved that the axles fixed in cast iron wheels are very much more liable to deterioration than those in wrought iron wheels, and the jar or vibration tending to deteriorate the quality of the iron, by altering its texture from fibrous to crystalline, is clearly visible in its effects in several fractures which I have seen. It would appear that the cast iron wheel acted more like a hammer on the axle, and as in the cold-swaging process, a gradual breaking up of the fibre at the back of the wheel goes on, which is shown by an annular space, varying from $\frac{3}{8}$ inch to $\frac{3}{4}$ inch in breadth; the strength is completely destroyed of this outer portion, and a sudden shock of the wheel upon some point of the road completes the fracture of the axle.

Among other causes which contribute to the deterioration of axles may be mentioned the practice of throwing cold water on the axle to cool it, when it has become nearly red hot from the want of proper lubrication of the journal.

With regard to the strain to which the portion of the axle between the wheels is subject, there can be no doubt if the form of the axle is so proportioned, that any blow transmitted through the wheel is received equally along the whole body of the axle, and the sectional strength at each point is fairly balanced to resist the effect of the blow, the axle will then be best suited to prevent deterioration at any particular place.

With the view of determining the weakest point of a common waggon axle under different circumstances, I made a few experiments, as follows:—

In the first experiment the power was applied to the flange of the wheel, and the resistance (as in the case of a railway axle when running) at the centre of the opposite wheel; the result was that the axle began to bend from a straight line at $12\frac{1}{2}$ inches distance from the boss of that wheel to which the power was applied, and there is no doubt that if the power had been continued the fracture would have taken place within the $12\frac{1}{2}$ inches.

As a proof of this, in the second experiment, an axle of precisely the same dimensions and form, on being bent alternately backwards and forwards (the power being always applied on the same wheel at opposite points) was broken at the twelfth time of bending, within 6 inches of the back of the wheel.

In the third experiment the power and resistance were exactly in a parallel line to the centre of the axle, and the result, as might be expected, was a curve of a nearly uniform radius, proving that, although the form of this axle was adapted to receive the blows of both wheels at precisely the same instant, and to the same extent (an impossible circumstance in practice), it was not suited to receive alternate strains or shocks, to which all axles are subject in ordinary use.

The sizes of the axles in the above three experiments were precisely alike.

In the fourth experiment another axle of the same dimensions was taken, and reduced at the centre in a lathe to the following dimensions:—The axle was divided into eight equal spaces from the back of the wheel to the centre of the axle. Immediately at the back of the wheel the axle was 4 inches diameter, and the deflection was $9\frac{1}{4}$ inches; at the first space the diameter was $3\frac{4}{5}$ inches, and the deflection was $8\frac{3}{4}$ inches; at the second space the diameter $3\frac{7}{10}$ inches, and deflection 7 inches; at the third space the diameter $3\frac{1}{10}$ inches, and deflection $5\frac{3}{4}$ inches; at the fourth space the diameter $2\frac{1}{10}$ inches, and deflection $4\frac{1}{4}$ inches. Up to this point the axle maintained a straight form from the back of the wheel, and from this point to the centre of the axle, as shown by the deflections, it assumed a fair curve, proving that the axle was weaker towards the centre than it ought to have been, and that the first 12 or 14 inches from the wheel, having maintained the straight form, was stronger in proportion.

In the fifth experiment the axle was reduced to two inches and a half in the centre, and, with the power applied as in the last case, the weakness at the centre was more perceptible.

In the sixth experiment the axle was made of another form, weaker immediately at the back of the wheel and at the centre. We had here two bends or curves, with a straight portion between them.

In the seventh, there was an improvement upon the sixth, but it did not realise a perfect balance of strength at the different points.

In the eighth experiment this was fairly accomplished, the proportion being as follows:—From the back of the wheel to the centre of the axle the sizes were 4$\frac{1}{10}$ diameter, 3$\frac{1}{4}$ diameter, 3 inches diameter, 2$\frac{3}{4}$ diameter, 2$\frac{11}{16}$ diameter, 2$\frac{5}{8}$ diameter, 2$\frac{1}{2}$ diameter, 2$\frac{11}{16}$ diameter, 2$\frac{5}{8}$ diameter; the half-length of the axle being divided as before into eight equal spaces.

It must be evident that this can only be an approximate result, but we found that these proportions enabled us to attain the nearest approach to a regular curve in bending the axle; and it is worthy of notice that when the dimensions of the axle at the journal and in the boss of the wheel are determined, a calculation to ascertain the exact proportion between the wheels seems to confirm the above statement of dimensions in the eighth experiment.

The greatest strain to which this portion of the axle is subject, being received at the bottom flange of the wheel, and transmitted through its radius, the amount of strain which any portion of the axle has to resist is inversely as its angular distance from the point of impact is to the radius of the wheel.

Assuming the blow on the flange of the wheel to exert a breaking force equal to 102,229 lbs., and the diameter of the axle to be be 4.71 inches to resist this blow, then, dividing the axle into four equal spaces to the centre, the proportionate breaking force at each point would be as follows:—At the first, 94,381 lbs., relative diameter, 4.59 inches; at the second, 80,697 lbs., relative diameter, 4.35 inches; at the third, 67,796 lbs., relative diameter, 4.11 inches; at the fourth, 58,899 lbs., relative diameter, 3.92 inches.

With regard to engine axles, these proportions will apply where no circumstances exist of employing the centre of the axle for transmission of power. The crank axles of locomotive engines cannot be treated by any of the rules applicable to straight axles; and our experience would seem to prove that, even with the greatest care in manufacturing, these axles are subject to a rapid deterioration, owing to the vibration and jar, which operates with increased severity, on account of their peculiar form. So certain and regular is the fracture at the corner of the crank from this cause, that we can almost predict in some classes of engines the number of miles that can be run before signs of fracture are visible; a certain amount of injury can be prevented by putting counter-balance weights opposite to each crank, which lessens the vibration very considerably.

It is right to observe in this place, that to some extent the injury to all axles may be increased, if the wheels in which they are fixed are not properly balanced; and I have no doubt that a great portion of the constant vibration to which they are subject may be traced to the knocking action of the wheel upon the rail, owing to a want of balance.

The question of deterioration of axles arising from the various causes, which I have enumerated, is a very important one to all railway companies; that some change in the nature of the iron does take place is a well-established fact, and the investigation of this is most deserving of careful attention.

I believe it will be found that the change from the fibrous to the crystalline character is dependant upon a variety of circumstances. I have collected a few specimens of fractured axles from different points, which clearly establish the view I have stated. It is impossible to embrace in the present paper an exposition of all the facts on this branch of the subject; but so valuable is the clear understanding of the nature of the deterioration of axles, that I am now registering each axle as it goes from the workshops, and will endeavour to have such returns of their performances and appearances at different periods as will enable me to judge respecting their treatment. When it is considered that on the railways of Great Britain there are about 200,000 axles employed, the advantage of having the best proportions, the best qualities, and the best treatment for such an important and vital element of the rolling stock, must be universally acknowledged.

The Chairman observed, that as there were many members present well versed in the qualities of iron, he hoped they should have some observations from them tending to confirm or to call in question the positions taken by Mr. McConnell in his paper.

Mr. Henderson thought the subject was a very important one, and had been well treated in Mr. McConnell's paper; and he hoped the investigation would be carried out by further experiments.

The Chairman said, that Mr. McConnell had expressed a strong opinion, that a change took place from a fibrous structure in iron to a crystalline one during the time of its being in use; and it would be satisfactory if an instance could be pointed out where this change had occurred, owing to vibration or any other treatment, for he had not been able to satisfy himself from many experiments that any such molecular change took place. Hammering a piece of hot iron till it is cold produced a hardness called crystalline; but the question for consideration was, supposing an iron axle were annealed by heating to a dull red heat and being allowed to cool slowly, would the "texture" of that iron undergo any alteration afterwards from the vibration of the railway or any piece of machinery they were in the habit of employing. He had not been able to detect an instance of the kind; and in giving evidence before the Iron Girder Bridge Commission, he mentioned cases of vibration going on from year to year without any sensible change occurring in wrought or cast-iron. For instance, they had the Cornish engine beam with a strain of 50 lbs. per inch, working eight or ten strokes per minute for more than 20 years; and certainly if a molecular change was introduced by vibration, it ought to be by that continual concussion and vibration, but none was perceived. Again, the connecting rod of a locomotive was a piece of iron in a most perplexing situation, for one having more to do and having the strain changed more frequently it was difficult to conceive; and yet he had known the connecting rod of a locomotive engine to vibrate eight times in a second for several years' regular work, making more than 200 million times altogether, but the iron retained its fibrous structure; and he thought axles could not be subject to so much vibration. When, therefore, he found that a connecting rod did not change its molecular texture, he must say there were good grounds for doubting that iron changes its state in axles. Then with regard to the experiments made by Mr. McConnell, with a view to ascertain where axles were most exposed to tension, he could not quite agree with him, for he subjected the wheels and axles to a slow steadily increasing pressure, till he bent the axles in different positions. The results were correct as far as regarded the slow pressure on the flanches of the wheel under the circumstances of the experiments recorded by him, but they were not a faithful representation of what takes place in practice, for it would be found that when the wheels of a carriage jarred, a violent blow was inflicted on the rail, and the strain on the axle was totally distinct from a slow pressure. He would refer to the experiments made some years ago by Mr. John Gray, on the Hull and Selby Railway, and which were published in the Engineers' and Architects' Journal, or the Mechanics' Magazine, to show how important is the element of time in the fracture of an axle. He took a round bar of iron, 3 feet long and 2 inches diameter, and turned it down in the middle, to 1 inch in diameter for 2 inches in length. He then took another bar, 1 inch in diameter uniformly throughout, and he tried the strength of these bars under *concussion* and not mere pressure. Now the severest point of strain would evidently be the middle of the bars where the diameter was the same in both, and consequently, if weights were gradually and quietly laid on, the results would be alike in both bars; but when small weights were let fall on them, the bar 1 inch in diameter throughout its whole length was found to be much stronger than that which was in the main 2 inches, and 1 in the middle. For as time is an element when the resistance of material is concerned, regarding the axle as elastic like a piece of india-rubber, the only particles that could yield to percussion from the falling weight were those between the shoulders in the part of the axle that was turned down, but in the case of the bar an inch in diameter throughout its whole length the whole of the particles would yield; the one being a good spring and the other a very bad one. It therefore appeared to him that the experiments recorded by Mr. McConnell, though correct as regarded the position in which he put them, were not correct as regarded concussion. The axles rarely if ever broke in the middle, but generally at the end close to the boss of the wheel; because of the sudden change in the elasticity of the axle at that point; the portion of the axle fixed within the boss of the wheel being very rigid, whilst the rest remained elastic, which caused the vibrations to be suddenly checked at that point. No doubt the plan of weakening axles in the middle had done good because it made them spring, and in crank axles it relieved the strain in the cranked part.

Mr. H. Smith suggested that in the case of bar-iron, the exterior portion had greater tenacity than the interior or under part; and the strength would be more than proportionately diminished where the exterior portion was cut through. He also referred to some experiments in which he had cold-hammered fibrous iron till it became crystalline, and the effect produced corresponded with the description given by Mr. McConnell of the fractured axles.

Mr. McConnell observed, that he had met with several cases of broken axles in which a distinct annular space was observable all round the surface of fracture, that was quite short-grained and appeared changed into a crystalline texture, whilst the centre of the axle remained fibrous. He admitted that his experiments were only approximate, and that he had not put the strain in the natural way; but it was almost impossible to do so in consequence of the great trouble and expense that would have accompanied it; at the same time the results were proportionate in each case, and the accuracy of the experimental results had been confirmed by calculation. With regard to the axle fitting into the wheel, they now allowed only a very small shoulder, not exceeding a sixteenth of an inch, and this shoulder was not square but tapered, and the boss of the wheel was slightly coned to fit the shoulder.

Mr. Cowper did not believe that any axle which when broken proved to be crystalline had ever been fibrous in its character.

Mr. Ramsbottom considered that a change took place in the axle from the effect of mere mechanical action, and his observations had tended to confirm him in that opinion. Some time ago he selected an axle which had not a very good form of journal, and the end broke off with two blows of a 12 lb. hammer. This axle had for three years been subject to a strain vertically, which was reversed at every revolution, and it came off with a crystalline fracture. He then tried the part that had been within the boss of the wheel, which had not been subject to this great strain, and found the strength was very much greater than that of the journal, for it required 79 blows to break it off, and in that case the fracture was fibrous. A parallel case might be observed with reference to an ash stick, which, if doubled, would break with a fibrous fracture; but if subjected to vibration, however slight, running through it a great number of times, it would break in a different mode. He thought the strain on a locomotive connecting rod was by no means so great for the sectional area as upon an axle journal; and the latter had two reversed strains for every revolution of the small wheels, but the connecting rod had only two for each revolution of the driving wheels.

The Chairman said, he was only desirous to put the members on their guard against being satisfied with less than incontestible evidence as to a molecular change in iron, for the subject was one of serious importance, and the breaking of an axle had on one occasion rendered it questionable whether or not the engineer and superintendent would have had a verdict of manslaughter returned against them. The investigation hence required the greatest caution; and in the present case there was not evidence to show that the axle was fibrous beforehand, but crystalline when it broke. He therefore wished the members of the Institution, connected as they were with the manufacture of iron, to pause before they arrived at the conclusion that iron is a substance liable to crystallize or to a molecular change from vibration. For his own part, he was now induced to look upon wrought iron as literally elastic, like a piece of india-rubber; for in the case of the Britannia Tubular Bridge, where they had two 10-inch square chains or bars, each 100 feet in length, it was found that before the tube was raised the chains or bars stretched nearly 2 inches in length at each time of lifting, but resumed their original length when the strain was withdrawn; the same action being repeated every time the tube was lifted. He could therefore only regard these 10-inch bars of iron as analogous to a piece of india-rubber.

Mr. McConnell said, he had one specimen of an axle which he thought furnished nearly incontestible evidence of the truth of his position, that a change took place in the texture of the iron. One portion of this axle was clearly fibrous iron, but the other end broke off as short as glass. The axle was taken and hammered under a steam hammer, then heated again and allowed to cool, after which they had to cut it nearly half through and to hammer it a long time before they could break it.

The Chairman remarked, that this was a case of converse reasoning; for it was an instance of a piece of crystalline iron being converted into fibrous iron. Iron when it was once heated and allowed to cool gradually, acquired a close and fine grain but, became neither crystalline nor fibrous; if cooled suddenly it acquired a crystalline grain, and if rolled while being cooled it

became fibrous, but he did not think that it underwent any molecular change from mechanical action after it was cold.

Mr. Henry Smith observed, that throwing cold water upon hot journals did great injury by crystallizing both portions of the axle.

Mr. Slate did not think that any change from a fibrous to a crystalline texture was produced in iron unless it were strained beyond the limit of its elasticity. Some of the pump rods in Staffordshire which had been in use for 18 or 20 years, were subject to a strain of 3½ tons per square inch; and a short time ago he had occasion to ascertain their actual performance with reference to this very question, and this not being considered conclusive, he had made a machine in which he put an inch square bar subjected to a constant strain of 5 tons, and an additional varying strain of 2¼ tons, alternately raised and lowered by an eccentric 80 or 90 times per minute, and this motion was continued for so long a time that he considered it equal to the effect of 90 years' railway working, but no change whatever was perceptible; and therefore he was one of those who did not believe in a change from a fibrous to a crystalline structure in iron. He remembered a case where a question havng arisen as to the manufactures of a certain shaft, it was agreed to hammer it until it split as a means of discovering the nature of the manufacture of the shaft; the result was satisfactory; and the iron appeared still fibrous in texture.

Mr. Henry Smith promised to furnish some results of cold-hammering iron, at the next meeting.

The further consideration of the paper was then adjourned, and the Chairman said he wished that more of the Members had been present at the meeting, and hoped they would attend and assist in the further discussion of the subject.

A vote of thanks was passed to Mr. McConnell for his communication.

SOCIETY OF ARTS.

PRESIDENT—H.R.H. PRINCE ALBERT, D.C.L., F.R.S., &c.
Session XCVI.

NOTES OF PROCEEDINGS.

Abstract of the Prize Essay by Mr. J. A. Leon on the Cultivation and Manufacture of Sugar, part of which was read on the 28th November, and concluded at the Meeting on the 5th December.

BENJAMIN ROTCH, Esq., V.P., in the Chair.

The modern agricultural improvements, irrigation and subsoil drainage are little known in most of the British colonies, and very few of the commonest agricultural implements have been introduced there The chief alteration which has been adopted is the planting the canes at a greater distance from each other than formerly. The theory of clearing, planting, moulding and cutting the cane in suitable season is understood, but seldom practised. It is erroneous to suppose that European labourers cannot endure the climate in the sugar-growing colonies, and European emigration ought to be encouraged. The first improvement in the West Indies should be the organisation of a new system better adapted for emancipated negroes. The planter of the present day cannot do better than lease his fields to a set of negroes, on condition of their planting for him three-fourths of the land with sugar-canes; so that the negroes will be dependent for support on the produce and its quality, and will not fail to cultivate the land in a proper manner; the owner of the estate erecting improved steam-machinery, giving up the cultivation of the land, and remaining a sugar manufacturer. The ex-planter, in his new establishment, will then no longer require hired negroes for the people of his manufactory being British emigrants, the colonial sugar will be produced by Creole growers and European manufacturers. Small West India proprietors should join their lands, so as to form a farm of 700 or 800 acres, to be cultivated as before mentioned, and erect thereon a central sugar manufactory capable of working the produce from 500 acres of sugar-canes, which will be on an average, 1000 tons of Muscovado sugar from 10,000 tons of canes. Thus they would farm in a small space, and manufacture with powerful machinery, in which consists the required agricultural improvements, and isolated estates might send their concentrated saccharine matter, or crude sugar, to a parochial central factory.

The cultivation of the sugar-cane requires more labour than other plants, and in that respect a cane-field may be compared to a garden, and, like it, requires constant care and attention.

The woody part of the ripe sugar-canes is generally consumed as fuel in the process of manufacturing sugar ; other portions are used as seed, forage, and manure, the green leaves being given as food to cattle. It is found that 100 lbs. of canes generally yield 50 lbs. of juice ; these 50 lbs. of juice produce by the old process of manufacture 5 lbs. of Muscovado sugar and 5 lbs. of molasses scum ; the remainder, 40 lbs., is the quantity of water to be evaporated by the manufacturing process.

Nothing can surpass the slovenly, unscientific way in which sugar is made on those estates where the common process is in use ; and in the whole British dominions only four sugar plantations have received complete steam machinery. The author recommends steam, not only as a moving power, but also for heating and evaporating purposes, and refers to a Colonial Steam Generator which he has invented, as answering every purpose that can be required ; but this modern apparatus will be only beneficial when worked on a large scale.

In selecting the ground on which a manufactory is to be erected mainly depends its future success.

The essay then describes the various existing mills made use of in the manufacture of sugar, of which the chief defects are—

1. Overspeed in motion.
2. Mismanagement in feeding.
3. Inefficiency of the moving power.

The great price of coal, however, in the West Indies, being £2 16s. per ton. (when used), renders the working of steam power very expensive ; however, the steam may be economised and employed in subsequent processes.

With reference to the proper inclination of the feeding-board, Mr. Leon states that, in the ordinary horizontal three-roller mill, it ought to make an angle of 90 degrees with a line drawn between the centres of the two front rollers, and that no other position answers so well for the regular distribution of the canes.

The essay proceeds to describe the Steam Defecator, and other apparatus employed in the manufacture of sugar, and the advantages peculiar to each.

A great improvement in sugar manipulations, even greater than the concentration *in vacuo,* is the application of animal charcoal for manufacturing and refining sugar. The discovery of revivification allowing the same carbon to be used again enables the refiner to produce the best quality of sugar from the raw material by a single operation ; *and by improving* on the same principle of filtration, the colonial manufacturer will succeed in producing refined sugar direct from the cane, and thereby dispense with the secondary manipulation in Europe.

Concentrated cane-juice, containing more than 50 per cent. of saccharine matter, will be altered if boiled at a high temperature, or re-concentrated at a low one ; but if boiled *in vacuo,* the saccharine liquid may be rapidly concentrated at even a low temperature. The author recommends the use of Clark's Condenser, in which the steam is distributed all at once, in 216 vertical pipes, radiating to a single collecting pipe, communicating with the air-pump, and a double-evaporation apparatus constructed by himself, and operating,

1st. Without altering the saccharine matter, as well with a minimum as a maximum of water.

2d. Without borrowing any water.

3d. Without requiring active superintendence, and saving fuel to a large amount.

In building a sugar manufactory, the main flue of the steam generators should pass close to the curing-house wall before reaching the chimney,—cast-iron tubes lying across the flue, having one end in the curing-house, whilst the other receives the outside air, being heated from the caloric from the furnace, warms the inner air passing from the yard into the curing-house. Thus a hot-air apparatus is formed with great economy. The direct bleaching, *i.e.* the artificial mode for separating the liquid from the solid sugar, is done by sprinkling water on the sugar with a small instrument made for that purpose, and, according to the number of ablutions, this operation will produce crushed lumps, or stamped loaf-sugar.

The modern steam apparatus for manufacturing sugar with profit requires the fulfilment of several conditions.

During crop-time, continuous work night and day,—from whence three advantages arise :

1st. The cane-juice does not become sour, as when left standing during the whole night in the heated apparatus

2d. Fuel is saved, because the fire has not to be re-lit.

3d. Double work being done, the expenses of the machinery are reduced 50 per cent.

A better class of labourers must be procured, and work for the whole year round provided for them.

Mr. Leon is of opinion that nothing but such a total change can restore the British sugar colonies ; and to prepare for this, two things are necessary :

1st. A thorough knowledge of the modern art of building, erecting, and working the improved apparatus.

2nd. Regular theoretical and practical information on sugar manipulation for the instruction of colonial factory managers, to be given in a London laboratory, furnished with the necessary utensils for working on a small scale. The sugar for experiment should be extracted from the beet-root, the juice of which is nearly identical with that of the sugar-cane.

The subject was resumed on the evening of the 12th inst., when Mr. Leon alluded to the defects of the present system of revivification, the charring cylinders being too large in diameter, so that the outside of the charcoal was burnt in endeavouring to reach the interior. A letter was read from Boston, U.S., to Mr. Perkins, describing a steam battery for boiling Muscovado sugar, used in the island of St. Croix, in which no other fuel was used than the Megass. The engine was non-condensing, and the steam, after being admitted to the cylinder at 60lbs. pressure, and cut off at half stroke, was blown through a series of copper pipes, two inches diameter, and so arranged that they could be turned up out of the sugar-boiling pans which they served to heat, and at the bottom of which they were placed. The back pressure was stated to be 3 lbs. per square inch. [This method of using the waste steam, we may observe, is not new by any means. The hottest liquor should be first exposed to the steam to extract a portion of its excess of temperature, and the cold liquor will finally condense it, so that distilled water may be returned into the boiler, and a much less supply of feed water is required. The writer stated that the steam was used directly from the boiler at 60lbs. in a subsequent operation, or it is questionable whether the pressure might not be reduced with advantage. Less expansion would be required to do the same work, but less heat would be lost by radiation. The object would seem to be to lose as little heat in the engine as possible. If steam is to be used for boiling, any advantage taken of its expansibility in its passage from the boiler to the sugar-pans must be regarded as so much clear gain.—Ed. *Artisan.*]

Mr. E. Highton next read a very interesting paper on electricity and its application to the arts and sciences. Mr. Highton first enumerated the various terms applied to electricity to express its different states, the apparent complication of which was sufficient to deter the student from this interesting branch of science. Various specimens of electrotyping were exhibited, and the method described of preserving animals, insects, and plants, by depositing on them a thin coat of gold. The subject was first covered with a solution of phosphorus, and then a solution of nitrate of silver. This caused a deposit of the silver on the subject, and afforded a proper ground on which to electrotype the gold in the ordinary way. It was finally exposed to a high degree of temperature to dessicate the animal matter and prevent its decomposition. Butterflies, spiders, &c., were exhibited, treated in this manner, and it was stated that Captain Ibbetson was engaged in electrotyping a spider's web. Electrotype copies of daguerreotypes were also exhibited, which, it was stated, possessed all the fidelity of the originals.

Mr. Highton then alluded to the application of electricity to the art of war by the ready means it afforded of exploding, at a precise instant of time, cases of gun-powder, placed either under ground for the defence of fortified places, or sunk at the entrance of rivers and harbours, to destroy a vessel as she passed over them. It was also proposed, as a means of testing the state of the air in coal mines, by exploding the gas before the men entered the mine, if it had been allowed to accumulate. Mr. Highton stated that this idea occurred to him while making experiments on the passage of the electric current, and testing the presence of the spark by its igniting the vapour of alcohol. An ingenious machine was described, by which very minute portions of time could be measured; such as the falling of a body for a small distance, and also the method of ascertaining the temperature of the ocean at great depths, by the action of a galvanometer, influenced by thermo-electricity.

The different theories on the formation of hail were likewise treated on; the size of the hailstones was accounted for by the rapidity of their descent through the air, caused by the united forces of gravity and electricity, which promoted evaporation from their surfaces, and cooled them below the freezing point, so that they rapidly accumulated the moisture in the atmosphere, in the form of layers of ice.

The effects of thermo-electricity were explained, and the manner in which cold could be produced, through its agency, by the application of heat. In conclusion, Mr. Highton entered into an interesting disquisition on its property of producing direct circular motion, and therein differing from all other known forces of nature. It thus became a most valuable analytical test for ascertaining whether certain other forces were simple and direct acting in one straight line, or the resultant of a combination of forces acting in various directions. This test was applied to the motions of the heavenly bodies. A vote of thanks was passed to Mr. Highton, and the discussion postponed to the next meeting.

The discussion on the paper was resumed on 19th instant, after some additional remarks by Mr. Highton on the formation of hail, and the application of the electrotype process to chronometer springs. Among the specimens exhibited was some iron tubing covered with a deposit of brass, or rather, a new kind of brass, composed of copper and cadmium, instead of zinc. The interesting fact was mentioned, that the addition of a very small quantity of the sulphuret of carbon to the cyanide of silver in the decomposing cell had the property of precipitating the silver perfectly bright, instead of dead. Mr. Highton stated, on the authority of Messrs. Elkington, that the silver could be deposited so hard as to resist the file, and that the degree of hardness depended on the intensity of the battery power.

Mr. Hunt stated that the deposits of the two different metals on the same object was effected by stopping out the required parts with a varnish of shellac, dissolved in coal tar naptha, which resists the action of the cyanide, and saves the more precious metal. He also mentioned the labours of Dr. Braun, who has been engaged for some time in copying the antique vases in the Vatican, by means of flexible moulds, which are then blackleaded inside and electrotyped. In this manner the most graceful specimens of ancient art are reproduced, with a correctness unapproachable by manual labour, and at a price which will bring them within the reach of all.

The question of the use of electro-magnetism as a motive power having been raised, Mr. Hunt stated that it had been found, in the experiments of Jacobi, undertaken at the expense of the Russian Government, that a reaction of the magnetic current was generated against the motion of the magnets, which was assigned as the cause of the failure of those experiments. Mr. Hunt promised to lay before the Society the particulars of some experiments which he is now carrying on, upon the same subject.

A paper was then read on Messrs. Fox and Barrett's patent method of constructing floors and roofs, so as to render them fireproof, without any increase in the cost.

PATENT LAW REFORM.

(Concluded from p. 282.)

SELECTIONS FROM EVIDENCE.

MR. WILLIAM NEWTON EXAMINED.

1075. But for matters of fact involved in an invention, does he rely upon the information he obtains from patent agents ?—Yes, I think he does; I do not see how he can avoid doing so. Matters of fact are reduced into a very small compass. The Crown is never answerable for the absolute validity of a patent. The thing may be old, and the agent ought to know whether it is or not.

1076. Do you think the practice with respect to caveats is satisfactory ?—I think it is a very desirable practice, and one of the best things about the whole system, and prevents frequently very serious robberies of inventions.

1077. Do you think it would be desirable to give a more general notice than is given under the present system to the public ?—I do not think it would be desirable, because in many cases it would only create opposition from parties who might get hold of the inventor's idea the moment the subject was mentioned. Sometimes an invention is of that character that the mere mention of its object discloses the nature of the invention.

1078. You do not think it desirable that a public notice should be given of an intention to apply for a particular patent ?—No ; I think it highly objectionable. It has always been considered objectionable to allow any person to inspect the caveat-books, to know what caveats there were.

1079. That is, in order that the public may not obtain such a knowledge as would lead them to anticipate a patent, and very likely to pursue another course ?—Yes ; for the publication would have the effect of giving publicity to the applicant's intentions.

1080. Now, supposing the law were so far altered as to make the patent date from the period of the petition ?—Which I think it ought to be.

1081. In that case, should you see any objection to a notice that could not convey any knowledge that would lead to an encroachment ?—I do not know that there would be any advantage in that public notice. The ultimate granting of the patent, though it might take date from the petition, would, in case of an opposition, be dependent upon the hearing before the Attorney or Solicitor General, and if too much publicity were given to the application, it might call forth a successful opposition. That would be very likely to occur, as I, for instance, have often discovered the nature of an invention from the mere wording of its title.

1082. Would it be any inconvenience to the applicant that there should be that knowledge of his invention, he having the start of all competitors ?—I can hardly trace all the effects upon the instant, but I do not see any advantage in its publicity.

1830. Would not the advantage be this, that A. B., applying for a patent for an improvement in the steam-engine, notice is given to the public that A. B. has made that application for a patent for an improvement in the steam-engine ?—Yes, it would call public attention to the application.

1084. Then other persons are enabled to come forward with their caveats, who think that it is likely to be an encroachment upon their inventions ?—It very frequently happens that a man in a large way of business can by any means conceal his invention from his work-people. A discussion at some adjacent public-house has very often drawn the secret out, or enough of it to make an effective opposition to the patent. Now, if a man applies for a patent for what does not strictly belong to him, it is most likely that the real inventor (who is perhaps proceeding with experiments) will have entered a caveat, to prevent his being superseded, and there is the advantage.

1085. Under the existing practice, anybody being engaged in such inventions may ; and people are very much in the habit of entering general caveats, are they not ?—Very few. Some speculative men—such a man as the late Lord Stanhope—would have half a dozen floating caveats, to know what was going on. I do not find that it is all common ; in fact, I hardly know an instance of a caveat having been entered by a person who had not really something in progress which he was endeavouring to perfect and protect. He does it for the protection of himself against his workmen, or those who by some accident might become acquainted with his invention.

1086. You consider that the great majority of general caveats are *bona fide* ?—Yes, I do. The expense is very small for entering them.

1087. Assuming that the Attorney-General's report is favourable, a second opposition may be made at the Patent Bill Office ?—Yes.

1088. A caveat may there also be lodged ?—Yes.

1089. Do you think it important to preserve that second stage of the opposition ?—Yes, I do ; for I have often known that, after an application for a patent has been reported upon favourably, a party, who was previously interested in the invention, has then first become aware of such application, but, from the existence of a second stage of opposition, he has been enabled to stay the further progress of the patent until the intending patentee guaranteed him a suitable interest in the invention.

1090. What time generally elapses between the report and the issue of the bill from the Bill Office?—The report goes to the Queen, who, upon the faith of that report, issues a warrant to the Attorney-General to prepare a bill for her signature. The Queen's warrant is returned within a week from the time the report was received.

1091. Might not that object be accomplished by giving another week to the notice?—Yes; but I think already the delays in passing patents are objectionable; for sometimes the subject leaks out in some way or other (particularly if it is a small matter) while the patent is in progress; somebody makes the article, and sells it, and the invention becomes public property. I should, therefore, like the patent to date from the presentation of the petition, or from the granting of the report.

1092. There are three stages in which oppositions may be made at present —twice before the Attorney-General, and once before the Lord Chancellor? —Yes, there are.

1093. Do you think that three are necessary?—Would not two stages be sufficient?—They are guards which are very inexpensive, and sometimes very effectual. I could name one instance—in fact, a great many—wherein they have been very beneficial. A man came to me, from Birmingham, and said, "I am afraid I am about to be superseded in an invention of great importance to me." He was a chemist, He said, "I have been treating with certain parties (whom he named), and suddenly, yesterday, they broke off the negociation, by telling me that they should have nothing to do with my invention." He said, "I was alarmed at this proceeding, and came up to consult you." On inquiring, I found that the parties named had no patent, nor could I at first find that they had one in progress; but, on looking further, I discovered that they had commenced a patent more than a year before; and, having followed it through the several offices, I learned that it had actually passed the Privy Seal, without our knowledge, it being an old application, and was then going to the Great Seal. I immediately entered a caveat at the Great Seal Office. This brought the parties immediately to an arrangement, and the man, who thus narrowly escaped the loss of his invention, received £1000, to let the patent proceed.

1103. Do you think that the present mode of paying the fees upon patents, and the great variety of the payments, are convenient?—To a certain extent, perhaps, it is, for parties are very anxious to proceed with their patents, but they cannot, perhaps, at first command sufficient money. I am frequently told that parties are uncertain of the result of their inventions, and want to test their value, but they fear to try their invention without some sort of protection. I therefore recommend this course:—that they go to the expense of about 10l., and get the Attorney-General's report, which is, to a certain extent, a security. They very often do that. I have known instances of patents lying by for years before inventors have completed their experiments, and are satisfied that they ought to go on.

1104. Do you think it desirable that there should be a power of keeping an application for a patent in suspense for a whole year?—That depends upon another circumstance. If you give protection, or what is, in fact, the same thing, if you make the patent take date from the application in the first instance, then the public ought to be made acquainted with it as quickly as possible. If you do not do that, the patentee obtains no real protection until the Great Seal is secured. At present the patentee runs the risk of losing his patent by delay.

1105. If the patent were made to date from the application, would it not be necessary to require that the applicant should prosecute the patent to completion within a limited time?—Certainly, most decidedly. And more than that, it would be necessary that he should deposit at once a preliminary specification, showing the elements of his invention. I should look at the patent in this way; first of all to get an intelligible title, that title may be "An improvement in steam-engines;" but there are a thousand different parts in a steam-engine, and who can tell the part to which the improvement refers? When, therefore, an application is made to the Attorney-General, there should always be deposited at the same time a specification, giving a general notion of the invention. As for instance,

that the improvement refers to the valves, or to the packing of the pistons, and that it was intended to effect so-and-so; just a general idea of the advantages which the inventor contemplated obtaining. Now that is done at present in cases where there is opposition; but I have often urged that *I* should be done in all cases. That, in fact, a man may not be able to obtain a "fishing patent," which will serve for the insertion of anything that may fall in his way, before the enrolment of his specification; but that he shall state positively what he has invented before he gets the Attorney-General's report.

1106. Do you think that the present fees upon English patents are excessive?—Yes, I do. I think it would be desirable if they were reduced.

1107. To what extent would you propose to reduce them?—If I remember rightly, my former notion was to grant an English patent for 60l., and the other two patents for 20l. each, thus making the cost 100l., instead of their exceeding 300l., as at present.

MR. BENNETT WOODCROFT EXAMINED.

1158. Supposing a person now wishes to apply for a new patent, what means has he of ascertaining whether there is or not already a patent existing for the same invention?—The only mode he has is one that is so tedious and expensive that only one patentee in a thousand will go to it, and that is by tracing such of the titles of patents that have been granted as are to be found in various publications, and then going to the offices and making searches through each specification. I once was three weeks making searches myself, and on one occasion (the 6th November, 1846,) I paid in fees for searches alone in the Petty Bag Office as much as 2l. 8s. in one day.

1159. Is it the fact that a person who seeks to obtain a patent generally takes no steps to ascertain whether or not a patent is already in existence for the same invention?—I think most inventors are of opinion that it is quite a hopeless task.

1160. And they leave it to chance?—They ask the patent agent whether he knows anything of it, and I have no doubt he speaks very conscientiously when he says that he does not know of any such invention.

1161. If there be a previous patent in existence for the same invention, the second patent is void?—It is, because the contract by the Crown is that after the 14 years' monopoly it becomes public property, and the public are entitled to use the invention.

1162. Does it often happen that a person takes out a patent when there is another patent in existence for the same invention?—Very frequently. There is nothing of more frequent occurrence.

1163. In that case all the money expended on the patent is lost?—Yes, and all the money expended in making experiments and in establishing a business for the supposed invention.

1164. Have any steps ever been taken to procure something like a complete body of information as to existing patents?—No step has been taken to publish those inventions. I think there are 400 patents for propelling. I was at the trouble to make searches. I think the searches in one way or another took me almost 12 months' time. I made a copy of the drawings, and an abstract of the specifications, and I wished to publish the collection thus made, but the publisher asked me 1500l. for the publication of the work. I thought I would publish it to show the monstrous evil of that particular part of the patent law by which information is virtually withheld from the public. If, to-morrow, I thought I had made an original invention and I was desirous of ascertaining the fact, there is another crying evil which I will state. I go first to the Enrolment Office. There are three Enrolment Offices. One at the top of Chancery-lane is called the Enrolment Office, another the Petty Bag Office, and the other the Rolls Chapel Office. If I want to see Thomas Savery's patent of 1696, I go and ask, "Have you Thomas Savery's patent of 1696?" They say, "We will look in the list," and whether they find it or not they make you pay a fee, besides unavoidably detaining you some time, and then perhaps the answer is, "No, we have not got it." "Where can I find it?" "We cannot direct you to either office. Then I go to the Rolls Office and say, "Have you Thomas Savery's patent of 1696?" A search is made, and they say, "No; we have no such patent." But there is the fee to pay. Then there is a third search to make, provided the specification had not been enrolled in the last office

and they say, " No; the patent was granted, but there is no specification."
But there is the fee to pay. It is not the fees alone that I complain of, but
the great time lost by the inventor in going from one office to another; for
if you go for a second search that you wish to make, you have all the same
ground to go over again.

MR. CHARLES BARLOW EXAMINED.

1226. What amount of reduction would you propose?—I would propose that the first skin should have a stamp of 1*l.*, and each following skin
5s.; and in the same way with respect to the enrolment fees. They are
very heavy, in Scotland particularly, being three times heavier than in
England; for what cause I am quite unable to say, but they are so.

1231. Supposing a person is about to apply for a new patent, what
means has he of obtaining information as to existing patents on the same
subject?—His only course is to obtain a list from some agent of the patents
which have been taken out for that purpose, and then to go and read those
specifications at the three offices; a most troublesome, tedious, and expensive business, inasmuch as there are no means of ascertaining whether such
specification is enrolled at one office or the other, but he has to go to all
three, and pay a fee at each, until he has found it. The fee at one office is
1s., the fee at another office is 1s., and the fee at the third is 3s. 6d. It
takes a long time to read many specifications and is also expensive.

1232. Do patentees often go through that process?—They are often
obliged to do so; but I cannot say that they do generally; they rather
avoid it, and run the risk of taking out a patent for what has already been
done before.

1233. Does it often happen that they take out patents for inventions
which are already the subject of patents?—Very frequently indeed, which
would be avoided if they could, as in America, read the specifications and
drawings of every patent at the Government office, free of charge, and find
them with facility.

1234. Do you think it would be desirable to print all the specifications
in extenso for the use of the public?—I think it would be extremely desirable that the specifications should be enrolled in book form by the patentee,
not as at present upon a skin of parchment, and then afterwards copied upon
a roll or skin, which is very tiresome to read, being in old English. They
should be enrolled in legible characters in book form, and kept classified,
and be open for reference upon payment of either 6d. or 1s. We do not
object to a fee, provided it is at one office only.

JOSEPH CLINTON ROBERTSON, ESQ., EXAMINED.

1303. Do you think an enormous multiplicity of patents would be an
advantage?—Decidedly not.

1304. Do you think that the owners of such patents would in the end
be gainers by their monopoly?—Very few indeed; but the manufacturers
get trammelled and embarrassed by the pretensions of people of that description. It is common with all manufacturers to have claims made against
them by parties thinking that they are using their inventions, and a manufacturer rather than go to law with them will compromise the matter, and
pay something by way of hush-money. I think it would be found a hinde-
rance to trade and manufactures.

1305. Would not a multiplicity of patents lead to litigation?—Certainly it would, in proportion to the number of patents. It seems to me
that if patents were excessively cheapened, it would be then requisite to
subject all applications for patents to a much stricter scrutiny than is now
the case; and then possibly the Attorney-General might require to have
some person in the way of an assessor to enable him to go through them
not allowing every one to pass, simply because it happens to be unopposed.

1306. Assuming that it is not desirable to make them extremely cheap,
and that some obstacle ought to be offered to the grant of a monopoly upon
grounds of public policy, do you consider the present amount of fee too
large?—A great deal too large in any point of view.

1307. What would you say should be the proper sum?—I think parties
would not object to something between 25*l.* and 40*l.* I gather that from
inventors themselves, and there are very few that could not muster that.

1308. Would you require an additional fee for the extension of a patent
to Scotland or Ireland?—I think so.

1309. What amount of fees would you suggest?—I should think they
might be put on a par, say half the price of the English patent. The
Scotch patent is the more valuable of the two. But it would hardly be
worth while to make any distinction between the Scotch and the Irish.

1310. You would grant an English patent, setting aside the charges of
agency, for 40*l.*, and you would extend that patent to either Ireland or
Scotland for a fee of 20*l.* for each kingdom?—Yes.

1311. Therefore the patent would be obtained for the three kingdoms
for 80*l.*?—Yes.

1312. Exclusive of the cost of agency?—Yes.

1313. Have you any suggestion to make with regard to the present
mode of preparing the specification?—None; I think it is proper to allow
six months to complete the outline specification; supposing the outline specification lodged at the time of the report in every case, I see no objection
to that.

1314. Do you think there is sufficient check now upon the preparation
of the specification?—I think that parties must be left to prepare them as
they think proper, and that there should be no public interference in that
respect. I should recommend one Enrolment Office. There is great inconvenience in having patents enrolled in three different offices.

1322. Are you acquainted with the French law as to patents? Yes, I am.

1323. Do you think that any part of the French regulations can be
advantageously introduced into this country?—In France every patentee
pays so much per annum, and if that system were adopted here I think it
would produce much more revenue than our own.

1324. Do you think it desirable that a tax should be paid by annual
instalments rather than by a gross sum in the first instance?—Yes. In
France if a patent does not turn out well, the parties drop it altogether.
There is a day appointed for payment of the annuity, and if it is not paid the
patent falls; and that system gives a man an opportunity of dropping it if
he has been mistaken in his views.

1325. Is not the result of that mode of payment this—that the Government only gets the entire sum upon the successful patents?—Yes.

1326. In that manner the Government must lose a great deal of revenue?—Yes, put in that way; but successful inventors here would be
very willing to pay a per centage on their receipts. There is a universal
feeling entertained of this kind. It is repeatedly said that the Government
might get a very large revenue from successful patents.

CORRESPONDENCE.

To the Editor of the Artizan.

SIR,—At page 267, last number, your correspondent, W. W. R., insists
on calling the instrument described at page 205, an Elliptograph, and has
put himself to a great deal of trouble to perfect the fallacious instrument,
drawing the distinction without the difference, the principle and action of
the two instruments being exactly the same.

At the time I noticed that, by J. S., the error appeared so palpable and
self-evident, that I thought the mere allusion to it would be sufficient to
convince any one at all acquainted with the ellipse of its utter incapability
of describing one, and quoted the fact in the common reciprocating steam
engine, which is known generally by every practical engineer, most of whom
know nothing of *the conic section.*

Your Falmouth correspondent need not have travelled so far for his

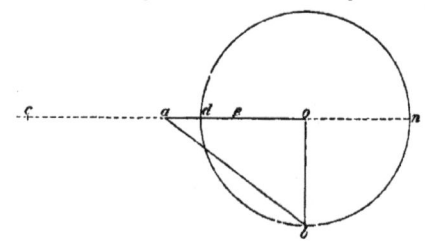

proof, for a slight knowledge of geometry will be sufficient to show the principle contained in the instrument is incorrect.

In the annexed figure let the right-angled triangle, $a\ o\ b$, on the line, $c\ n$, have its sides, $a\ b = 5$, $a\ o = 4$, and $b\ o = 3$; from o as a centre, with radius $o\ b$, describe the circle, $d\ b\ n$, and make $c\ d = a\ b$, then $c\ d + d\ o = e\ o = 8$, and $c\ o - a\ o = c\ a = 4$; $c\ d + 2\ d\ o = c\ n = 11$; make $e\ n = a\ b$, then $c\ n - e\ n = c\ e = 6$, and $c\ e - c\ a = a\ e = 2$.

Now, the principle of the instrument is, that the end a, of $a\ b$ slides on $c\ n$, while the other end b, revolves in the circle $d\ b\ n$, and when $b\ o$ makes a right angle with $c\ n$, every point in $a\ b$ will be at its greatest distance from $c\ n$, and therefore in that position will give the greatest minor axis to the figure described by the instrument. It has been shown that $c\ a = 4$, and $d\ o = 3$, but $c\ a$ has been passed over by the end a, of $a\ b$, in the same time that $d\ o$ has been passed over by the end b, which has still to travel to n, $o\ n$ and $o\ d$ being equal; but the end a, has only to travel to e, $a\ e$ being to $a\ c$ as 2 is to 4. It follows, therefore, that the nearer the pencil is fixed to b, on $a\ b$, the nearer will the figure described approach to an ellipse, but, like hope deferred, when it is at b it describes a circle.

In passing the pencil to the other end of $a\ b$, and fixing it almost at a, there will be an elongated figure described, having its minor axis (if we take the figures as inches) only about two inches from one end, which cannot be an ellipse, and so on for every point in $a\ b$, not one of which would describe an ellipse. In proportion as $a\ b$ is greater than $b\ o$, the less will be the error, but were it infinitely long, so long would it be in accomplishing the end, for then it would describe circles.

I therefore, do not fail to perceive, on reconsidering the matter, the incorrectness of the principle, and that the instrument propounded by W. W. R. will *not* describe a perfect ellipse.

I am, sir, yours truly,

London, December 5, 1849. N. D.

Sir,—In your report of the Cornwall Polytechnic Society there is a Saw Set by J. Harris, of Camborne, for which he received the second bronze medal.

Fig. 1.

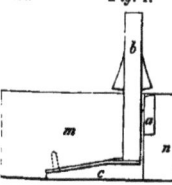

As I believe this is a late report, and that all inventions for which they give medals are understood to be new, you will oblige me very much, and at the same time do an act of justice, in giving a similar invention a place in your pages.

It is now nearly two years since I first saw the instrument, and was so much pleased with its simplicity, that I made a sketch and a note of the same at the time, which I give verbatim.

"I have just seen a very novel Saw-Set, which the Patternmaker, who owns it, made ten years ago. It is very simple, and is of the following construction:—

Fig. 2.

Fig 1 is a section at the punch b. Fig. 2 is a plan; m is a piece of beech about 7 ins. long, $3\frac{1}{4}$ wide, and $2\frac{1}{2}$ thick, with a strip of iron let into one edge; n is a piece of the same length, about an inch wide, screwed fast to m; a is a piece of hardened steel, $1\frac{1}{8}$ inches square, $\frac{5}{16}$ thick, having chamfers of various sizes on the four edges to suit saws of various sizes, and fitted loose into n, so that it can be removed and re-inserted with the most suitable edge uppermost. The punch b, is of steel, $\frac{3}{8} \times \frac{5}{16}$ and $3\frac{1}{4}$ long; it has two projections, shaped to suit both the tenon and hand-saws; c is a small spring in the bottom, which raises the punch after every stroke of the hammer, and allows the saw to be moved along. This spring is a late addition."

You will see from the sketch that there is a great similarity between it and that by J. Harris, and, seeing that this one has now been in existence about 12 years, it bids fair to lay claim to priority, the which I claim for its maker, whose name is Bradley, a working man in London.

I am, sir, yours truly, N. D.

[Our correspondent must remember that the same idea occurs not unfrequently to different persons, with a most marvellous coincidence as to time and manner, and we have no need to suppose that the later inventor was aware of the existence of any previous scheme for the same purpose. We may here remind our readers that they would consult their own interest as well as that of their fellow-workmen, by recording their ideas in the *Artizan*, in order to place their priority beyond a doubt, and to save others from expending their ingenuity in a wrong direction.—Ed. *Artizan.*]

ROYAL STEAM NAVY.

APPOINTMENTS.

Chief Engineer.—James P. Rundle, to the *Terrible*.

Assistant Engineers.—Richard E. Percival, to the *Fire Queen*. R. J. Sargeant, Andrew Douglas, Richard Cattew, John A. Ritchie, Robert Moore, John Oliver, R. H. Alvin, to the *Terrible.* Henry Brown, Robert Moore, George Crichton, and John Bell, to the *Fisgard.* John T. Obree, to the *African.*

DOCK YARD INTELLIGENCE.

Woolwich.—Lieut. Robertson and Mr. Casey, with engineers and stokers of Captain Austin's steam department, have returned to Woolwich after being engaged in trying the steaming qualities of the *Amphion*, 30, steam-frigate, for four successive days, between the Nore and Nob channel. The trials lasted on each day from daylight in the morning until dusk in the evening, anchoring each evening so as to be ready to start at an early hour on the following morning. The result of the trials gave an advantage over those previously made, the speed being, on the average of four runs at the measured distance between the Nore and Mouse lights, very nearly $6\frac{3}{4}$ knots per hour; the engines making about 48 revolutions per minute, with a pressure of steam of about 9 pounds. The draught of water was 17 feet, 10 inches forward, and 18 feet, 9 inches aft., and the diameter of the screw 16 feet, with a pitch of 21 feet. New India rubber valves have been supplied, and they worked well during the trials.

Woolwich.—The *Minx*, screw vessel, fitted with the disc engine, was tried down the river, on the 12th instant, on an experimental trial. The vessel is 130 feet long, 21 feet beam, and 301 tons burden. The engine is of 10 horse nominal power, and occupies a space 5 feet 2 inches $\times$ 3 feet. The speed was ascertained to be 5.148 knots per hour; the mean pressure of the steam being 53.5 lbs. on the square inch, and the number of revolutions 104 per minute. The speed on the last trial was 4.659 knots, and with the former reciprocating engines of 10 horse nominal power, by Messrs. Seaward, it was only 4.515 knots. The consumption of fuel with the disc engine is stated to be 18 per cent. less than with the other engines, though we can see no reason why the disc should use the steam more economically than the reciprocating engine, but rather the reverse.

The plates of the condemned boilers of the steam-frigate, *Retribution*, are to be used up for building some iron barges.

Chatham.—The *Tiger* steam-ship did not go out of dock on the 30th ult., as it was intended, in consequence of there not being sufficient water in the river, to float her out. The ceremony of christening the ship was gone through; it was performed by Mrs. A. Lawrie, the wife of the chief engineer of the yard, breaking a bottle of wine over her bows, and naming the vessel. This war-steamer is built on the plan of Mr. John Edye, Sub-surveyor of the Navy; her outside planking is that of the best seasoned teak. She was floated out of dock on Saturday. The following are her dimensions:—

	Feet.	In.
Length between the perpendiculars	205	0
Length of keel for tonnage	180	$5\frac{7}{8}$
Breadth, extreme	35	$11\frac{7}{8}$
Breadth for tonnage	35	7
" moulded	35	0
Depth in hold	24	6

Burden in tons, 1,220 52·94.

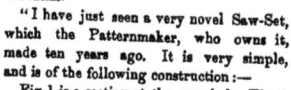

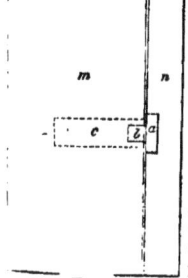

This steam-ship was built by Mr. F. J. Laire, master-shipwright, and she will carry the following armament on her spar-deck, viz., 1 gun 68-pounder, 95 cwt.; 1 16-in., 85 cwt.; and 4 guns, 32-pounders, 56 cwt.; and on her main-deck she is to carry 4 guns, 32-pounders, 56 cwt. each. Her draught of water is 17 feet.

PORTSMOUTH.— *Termagant,* steam-frigate, by White of Cowes, 1,556 620 horse power, by Seaward, went out on Wednesday, the 12th, under Commander Stephens, of the *Blenheim,* navigated by Mr. Robert C. Allen, master of that ship, to the measured mile in Stokes' Bay, to make a further trial of her steaming powers—a better result than heretofore achieved being desired by the Admiralty in return for the immense cost of the ship—about £70,000! Captain Ellice, Controller of Steam Machinery, on behalf of the Admiralty, came down expressly to witness and report upon this result. Two members of Messrs. Seawards' firm also came down to attend the trial. Mr. Murray, chief engineer of the dockyard, also went out in the ship, and numerous other officers. She was trimmed as if in commission, and drew—forward, 16 feet 2 inches; aft, 17 feet 10 inches; making her 20 inches by the stern. She made six runs, at the measured mile, with the following result:—

Runs.				Knots. Reduced mean.
First	...	...	...	10.112
Second			...	6.452—8.282
Third	...	...	...	10.256—8.354—8.318
Fourth			...	6.779—8.517—8.435
Fifth			...	10.112—8.455—8.481
Sixth	...	...	...	6.629—8.370—8.407

Mean of means. - 8.400 knots per hour.

The engines performed all their functions in the most perfect and eminently satisfactory manner, and elicited marked praise and attention from the Admiralty Controller. They made from 31 to 33 revolutions. The thermometer in the stokehole indicated 100°, and in the engine-room 89°. The trial was under favourable auspices; the wind was E., with a strong topgallant breeze and smooth water, in which she made the half-circle in 3½ minutes. With the tide the wind was on the quarter; running against the tide the wind was three points on the bow. The result was considered more favourable than that obtained on her last trial on the 20th ult., which we do not clearly comprehend, as she then made as the mean of six runs, 8.544 knots; whereas on the present trial, she made 8.400 only. She will be docked in a few days, and have divers means tried to improve her, after which she will be tried again with a new screw.

AMERICAN STEAM NAVY.
From the Journal of the Franklin Institute.

Within the last twenty years, the navies of England and France have undergone a great change by the introduction of steamers, and in any naval contest this country, at the onset would suffer from the want of a suitable number of vessels of that class. By the liberal aid which the English Government have extended to private companies, they have in reserve a very large number of first class steamers at a nominal expense. Our own government are now trying, in a measure, to make up for lost time, and contracts have been made with parties, who are to build the following steamers for the routes designated, with the understanding that, in case of war, the Navy Department may take the vessels at a valuation.

4 of 2700 tons, to run from New York to Liverpool.
4 „ 2400 „ „ New York to New Orleans.
3 „ 800 „ „ Panama to Oregon.
3 „ 1800 „ „ New York to Bremen.

Of these vessels, there are 2 of the New Orleans line finished, 3 of the Pacific line, and 2 of the Bremen line; the rest are in a state of forwardness, and will probably be all done in 12 months. In addition to the above, there are 13 sea steamers, from 500 to 1000 tons burthen, employed in private service between New York and New Orleans, at the different ports, making an aggregate of 40,000 tons, which could be at the disposal of the government when required, although several of the vessels have no mail contract.

Having spoken of the private steamers, those that the government may

have, I propose to go on, and speak of those vessels which really belong to the Navy, most of which have been built from the designs furnished by the proper departments, and may, therefore, be considered indicative of the ideas entertained at the Navy Department in relation to war steamers. This, of course, applies to those now building, and not to those already built, of which I shall speak first.

The first of the naval steamers we now have is the *Fulton,* built about 12 years since. It is much to the credit of the Department, that no person had been willing to assume the responsibility of having designed this vessel; like Japhet, she has long been in search of a father, but without any prospect of success. She is now at anchor at the Brooklyn Navy Yard, being of no service, except to be used in the harbour of New York. The Department would do well to remove the machinery, which is very good, and, with some changes, would answer for a ship of 1000 tons; as she now is, she would not be safe out of the harbour, and cannot be considered as of any account when speaking of *sea steamers*.

Our second vessel is the *Mississippi,* a fine steamer. built in 1841, about 220 feet long, 40 feet beam, 23 feet hold, with two English marine side lever engines, of 460 horse power, and four copper boilers for bituminous coal. This vessel has been in commission about 8 years, during much of which time she has been in active service and has always given satisfaction. She has recently made the passage from Norfolk to Gibraltar in 16 days, with an average consumption of 30 tons of coal in 24 hours. The *Missouri,* a sister ship, but with inclined engines, was burnt a few years since at Gibraltar.

Our third vessel is the *Princeton,* a propeller. This ship is about 160 feet long, 30 feet beam, and 20 feet hold; has two semi-cylinder engines, and a propeller of 14 feet diameter; three boilers of iron, and uses a fan to increase the draught, natural draught not being sufficient to supply the required head of steam. This vessel may be considered the best of her class, and has done considerable service. She has just returned from a two years' cruise in the Mediterranean, and her hull has been condemned. She was built in 1843, of white oak, obtained in a hurry, and her rapid decay is, in a great measure, no doubt, owing to the great heat of the boilers.

Our fourth vessel is the *Allegheny,* built of iron at Pittsburg, two years since. She is about 180 feet long, 32 feet beam, and 19 feet hold. She is propelled by two of Hunter's submerged wheels, of 14 feet diameter, and 4 feet face, with engines of 60 inches diameter of cylinders, and 4 feet stroke; usual number of revolutions, 30; two boilers for bituminous coal, with natural draught. The model of this ship is peculiar to this mode of propelling, being cut away under the water line, so as to allow the paddles to project. This vessel has been in service about two years, most of the time at Brazil and the Mediterranean, from whence she recently returned. Her speed at sea is not more than 6 miles per hour, and she is probably the last of her class, as this mode of propelling has nothing to recommend it to favour.

Our next vessels are the *Massachussetts* and *Edith,* propellers, both now in the Pacific. These vessels were bought from private service during the Mexican War, and were transferred to the Navy Department at its close. They are about 500 and 700 tons, with a speed of from 6 to 7 miles per hour, and would most likely be used as transports.

The *Water Witch* comes next, a small iron steamer, with side wheels. She was originally built with Hunter's wheel, but condemned, then lengthened and Loper's propeller put in; she then made the passage from Philadelphia to Norfolk, was then again condemned, and a condensing engine and side wheels put in. She is now considered a fair vessel of about 250 tons.

The last we have is the *Vixen,* a small vessel 118 feet long, 22 feet beam, and 8 feet hold, originally built for the Mexican Government; engine with 36-inch cylinder, 6 feet stroke; speed 8 miles per hour. This and the *Spitfire,* a sister vessel, were constantly employed, during the Mexican War, on the coast of Mexico, where their light draught of water rendered them invaluable.

These are all the vessels at present belonging to the Navy that are finished, and can be brought into use on our seaboard. I will continue the subject, and speak of the steamers now building, in your next.

                             X.

STEAM NAVIGATION.

STEAM COMMUNICATION WITH THE WEST INDIES, MEXICO, AND THE PACIFIC.

We learn from the Southampton Correspondent of the *Times*, that a new and improved scheme for the performance of their mail contract, has been submitted to the Lords of the Admiralty by the Directors of the West India Mail Packet Company, and that there is every probability of the proposed changes being sanctioned by them. The necessity of some alteration has been long apparent, but it is questionable whether it might not have been postponed some years longer had not the American line of steamers started with the usual go-a-head spirit of our transatlantic brethren, entered seriously into competition as regards the most valuable portion of the traffic with our own line of mail packets. The Americans have not been very successful, as yet, with their Atlantic steam ships, which have rarely made a voyage without some accident or delay; but they are not the sort of people to sit down quietly, and let such mischances at the onset interfere in carrying out any of their schemes.

In lieu of the semi-monthly mails, now despatched, it is proposed to substitute a communication once in three weeks to all parts of the West Indies and South America. This curtailment of accommodation is not so serious as might, at first sight, appear. On the present system it frequently happens that the outward steamers reach their destination so short a time before the closing of the homeward mail, that parties in the interior, say of Jamaica, are obliged to postpone their replies to the following packet, so that a fortnight is lost. The service will be performed with more certainty, and the bi-monthly communication can always be reverted to, when the increase of traffic shall demand it. The Gulf of Mexico, Havannah, the Spanish Main, and the Isthmus of Panama, will also be assimilated with the British West Indies, and will have a mail every three weeks, instead of once a month, as at present.

The *détour* to Bermuda, made by the steamers to the Gulf of Mexico, has been a fruitful source of danger to the vessels, as the losses of the Company sufficiently prove. The numerous and ever-varying rocky shoals, and the set of the Gulf Stream across the Atlantic, against which the outward steamers to Bermuda have always to run, are sufficient to justify the abandonment of this station, which is to be given up in favour of the Danish island of St. Thomas, which will be henceforth the head quarters for coaling. and transfer of the mails, passengers, and cargo.

"The main (or trunk) line of communication between England and the Isthmus of Panama, touching only at St. Thomas, is to be accomplished by new steam-ships, which are about to be constructed. They will be of between 2,000 and 3,000 tons burden, with proportionate steampower, and they are intended to attain a regular average speed of at least 12 knots. These ships, it is stipulated, shall be of even* superior qualities to those vessels on the Cunard line of the Niagara and Europa class, which have performed such wonders in Atlantic steaming, but whose speed, taking the duration of the most successful voyage, has barely exceeded 11 knots, and on the average is not more than 10. As these steamers will be receptacles for the whole of the passengers, mails, specie, and cargo collected from the Pacific and the Spanish Main for transmission to Europe, and, by means of the subsidiary lines, from Mexico and the various West India Islands, concentrating at St. Thomas for the homeward voyage, they will doubtless be provided with accommodation for a large number of passengers and for the considerable freights that will have to be conveyed by them. The present steamers will be employed on the intercolonial and branch services, and will be in sufficient number to provide for the due regularity of this portion of the scheme, while spare vessels will always be at hand in the event of any accident or derangement from unavoidable causes.

"The main line steamer starting from Southampton will reach St. Thomas in 12 days; at that island several branch steamers will be waiting her arrival. To one of them will be transferred the mails and passengers

---

* We trust, for the sake of the shareholders, that the Directors w ill do as well as Mr. Cunard has done. The distance is much the same as the run to New York, and we shall be glad to know the terms on which the contractors will guarantee an average of 12 knots in all weathers.

---

for Havannah and the Gulf of Mexico; to another the mails for Porto Rico, Hayti, Jamaica, San Jago de Cuba, and the other ports intended to be accommodated by the Jamaica route; another ship will receive the mails for the Windward and Leeward Islands and Demerara; these vessels having previously effected a mutual interchange of intercolonial mails for the various parts of the West Indies. Such operations completed, the through or Southampton steamer will instantly proceed to the Isthmus of Panama, while the branch steamers will as quickly depart from St. Thomas for their respective destinations.

Homeward the mode of operation will be of a similar character. The Main steamer, from Chagres having reached St. Thomas with the Pacific mails on board, will find waiting for her the several branch steamers which have come up from the Gulf of Mexico, Jamaica, Demerara, &c. These vessels will immediately transfer their mails to the Atlantic steamer, and she will without delay set sail for Southampton, having on board the mails, specie, passengers, and cargo from all parts of the West Indies, Mexico, Spanish Main, and Pacific; the various intercolonial steamers remaining at St. Thomas to coal and prepare for the arrival of the succeeding outward steamer from England. In point of detail and arrangement this plan will have vast advantages over the old and intricate plan of two separate routes outward and two homeward, and the whole scheme will merge into one of increased simplicity with far less probability of derangement.

The routes will be as nearly as possible as follows:

Main or Through line.—Southampton to Chagres, embracing the mails for the Pacific and California, and conveying all the West India and South American mails as far as St. Thomas:—Southampton to St. Thomas, 3,622 miles, in 12 days, one day stoppage; St. Thomas to Chagres, 1,120 miles, in six days; total 4,742 miles from Southampton to Chagres, to be accomplished in 18 or 19 days, against 5,850 miles from Southampton to Chagres, *via* Madeira, Barbadoes, St. Thomas, Porto Rico, Jacmel, Jamaica, Santa Martha, and Carthagena, occupying 35 days as hitherto, and effecting a saving of fully 16 days.

HAVANNAH AND GULF OF MEXICO ROUTE.

	miles.
Southampton to St. Thomas by main line steamer	3,622
St. Thomas to Havannah by branch steamer, taking her course through the old Bahama channel	1,010
Havannah to Vera Cruz	810
Total	5,442

from Southampton to Vera Cruz, against 5,899 miles by way of Bermuda, Nassau, Havannah, and Mobile, as at present. Tampico, 205 miles from Vera Cruz, may be accommodated with a call either outwards or homewards, or both if found necessary. It will be seen by the above that Mobile is to be omitted as a port of call, and that all the traffic of passengers from Mexico, which has hitherto left the West India steamers at Mobile-point to proceed to England *via* the United States, will in future be secured to the through line. The traffic from and to Havannah, which has almost ceased by these vessels, will also be secured. The voyage to Havannah will be performed in 15 days against 34 days as at present; to Tampico, in 20 days against 35 days; and to Vera Cruz in 21 or 22 days, against 33 days, occupied hitherto by the Bermuda steamers.

JAMAICA ROUTE.

	miles.
Southampton to St. Thomas (by main line steamer)	3,622
St. Thomas to San Juan Porto Rico (by branch steam r)	65
Porto Rico to Jacmel (Hayti)	388
Hayti to Kingston (Jamaica)	255
Total	4,330

from Southampton to Jamaica, against 5,025 miles by way of Madeira, Barbadoes, St. Thomas, Porto Rico, and Hayti; and 4,895 miles *via* Bermuda, Nassau, and Havannah; which are the respective routes now taken to Jamaica by the outward steamers. It is needless to say that a great saving of time will be hereby effected. Jamaica will be reached in 16 or 17 days; Jacmel (Hayti) in 14 or 15; Porto Rico in 13; against 30, 28, and 27 days respectively as at present.

From Jamaica the mails will be sent by branch steamers to St. Jago de Cuba, to Grey Town (Mosquito), to Carthagena, and Santa Martha, by such arrangements as will facilitate in a commensurate degree their intercourse with and to England. Jamaica will besides be greatly benefitted by being in constant communication with those ports on the main land between which and herself a large trade will be encouraged to mutual advantage.

"The same may be said of Belize (Honduras), the mails for which colony are to be sent from and received at Jamaica by a branch steamer instead of to and from Havannah as at present.

WINDWARD AND LEEWARD ISLANDS AND DEMERARA ROUTE.

	miles.
Southampton to St. Thomas (main line steamer)	3,622
St. Thomas to Tortola (branch steamer)	23
Tortola to St. Kitts ,,	128

			miles.
St. Kitts to Nevis	,, - - - -		11
Nevis to Montserrat	,, - - - -		33
Montserrat to Antigua	,, - - - -		32
Antigua to Guadaloupe	,, - - - -		70
Guadaloupe to Dominique	,, - - - -		45
Dominique to Martinique	,, - - - -		40
Martinique to St. Lucia	,, - - - -		45
St. Lucia to Barbadoes	,, - - - -		100
Barbadoes to St. Vincent	,, - - - -		90
St. Vincent to Curaçoa	,, - - - -		50
Curaçoa to Grenada	,, - - - -		32
Grenada to Trinidad	,, - - - -		94
Trinidad to Tobago	,, - - - -		85
Tobago to Demerara	,, - - - -		329
	Total- - - -		4,820

from Southampton to Demerara, occupying at present 28 to 30 days, but this will be accomplished in 20 to 22 days, including all stoppages for landing and receiving mails at the islands between St. Thomas and Demerara, such islands also receiving their mails from the St. Thomas steamer proportionately earlier, according to their several positions on the route.

The Venezuelan mails heretofore conveyed from St. Thomas to La Guayra will in all probability be carried in a small steamer either from that island or Barbadoes.

STEAM COMMUNICATION WITH THE BRAZILS.

At page 61 of our last number, we gave an account of the contract entered into between the Lords of the Admiralty, and the directors of the Royal West India Mail Packet Company, for the conveyance of the mails between Southampton or Liverpool, and Pernambuco, Bahia, and Rio de Janeiro. From the latter port the mails were to be conveyed to Montevideo and Buenos Ayres, by branch steamers running in conjunction with the main line. Nearly a year has now elapsed without the Company having taken any active steps in the matter, and as the Southampton correspondent of the *Times* has taken up the matter, we conclude that some gentle pressure is about to be applied.

It is understood that a long time has been occupied in deciding whether paddle-wheel or screw steamers were to be employed, and that the paddle-wheel system has been decided upon. Great stress seems to be laid upon the supposed fact that no screw steamer has yet attained an equal speed to that of a paddle-wheel steamer—that if one of a pair of paddle-wheel engines breaks down, the speed is not seriously diminished, and that repairs to the paddle-wheel can be effected at sea, whereas the screw cannot be repaired without going into port. That these circumstances combined prove " that there is a degree of certainty about the voyages of a steamship worked with paddles, which cannot be obtained by a steam vessel trusting to a screw, which, if broke or deranged, leaves the ship at the mercy of the winds and waves, in the midst of the ocean, and possibly in a dangerous position on a lee shore."

The route proposed to be adopted is, we understand, as follows :—

		miles.
Southampton to Funchal, Madeira	- -	1,306
Madeira to Santa Cruz, Teneriffe	- -	260
Teneriffe to Porto Praya, Cape Verd Island (allowing 20 miles for winding the islands)		945
Cape Verd to Pernambuco	- - -	1,535
Pernambuco to Bahia	- - -	410
Bahia to Rio Janeiro	- - -	680
Total (Southampton to Rio Janeiro)		5,136
Rio Janeiro to Montevideo	- -	1,040
Montevideo to Buenos Ayres (allowing 20 miles for winding the shoals)	- - -	130
		6,306

Supposing the voyage to be performed by steamers running at an average speed of eight miles an hour, and allowing for stoppages, the time occupied to Pernambuco would be about 22 days, to Bahia 24, and to Rio Janeiro 27 days. At a speed of 10 miles the voyage to Pernambuco would occupy 18 days, Bahia 20 days, and Rio Janeiro 24 days. At a speed of 12 miles the distance to Pernambuco would be performed in 15 days,

Bahia in 17 days, and Rio Janeiro in 19 to 20 days. We believe the medium, or 10-knot speed, is the one that will be adopted.

The route thus marked is undoubtedly the best one that can be laid from Southampton to Brazil. The stoppages are at judicious and convenient distances, and afford a regular communication to and from Madeira, the Canaries, and Cape Verde. The distance from Southampton to Pernambuco direct is 3,953 miles, against 4,046 with the proposed stoppages, and from Southampton to Rio Janeiro direct 5,565 miles, against 5,136 as intended, so that a very trifling increase of distance is required to be traversed on account of the detour to the various islands and ports.

Sierre Leone is only 710 miles from Praya (Cape Verde,) one of the ports of call, and therefore, if needful, a branch steam-vessel, or fast-sailing schooner, could bring up the mails thence, and thus a direct line of steam communication be established with the coast of Africa at a small additional expense.

It is suggested, that if these steamers were allowed to call at Lisbon, they would secure a large amount of traffic between Portugal and the Brazils, countries which are bound together by a community of language, customs, and commerce. This line would also supersede a proposed line of steamers between Cadiz, the Canaries, and Cape Verde, organized by a company of Cadiz merchants. It would also give us an additional communication from England to the Tagus ; and would also act as a feeder to the Peninsula and Oriental Company's line. Another peculiar feature in this line is, that from Porto Praya. Cape Verde, nearly half the distance from England to the Cape of Good Hope, the line can at any time be extended to our South African possessions, so that the Cape of Good Hope will be brought within 36 days' steam of England.

Up to this time no vessels have been built by the West India Mail Company for this service, but it is understood that it is intended to detach four vessels from the West India fleet, which are to be razéed and improved, so as to bring their average speed up to ten knots. But, as these steamers cannot be spared, until the new steamers, mentioned in the previous article, are ready for sea, which cannot be done under a year, there is little chance of the commencement of the Brazilian service till the middle of 1851.

We withdraw a portion of this article to insert an important correction on the authority of Mr. J. Laming, the managing director of the General Screw Steam Shipping Company, who states the following to be the facts of the case :

In June, 1848, the attention of the General Screw Steam Shipping Company was requested by the late Lord Auckland, then head of the Admiralty, to steam communication with the Brazils. On the 5th October the basis of a negociation was proposed by the Admiralty, and on the 9th accepted by the Company, who were desired to have the ships ready in April following. The contract was approved by the Post-office, but finally rejected by Sir C. Wood, of the Treasury, who recommended public competition for the service. This was done on 25th January last. Four parties tendered. The tender of the Royal West India Mail Packet Company was twofold—viz., for paddles at a high rate, and for screw vessels. Their tender for the screw vessels, being the lowest of the four parties, was accepted, and that for paddles rejected. The next lowest tender was that of the General Screw Steam Shipping Company, being precisely similar in terms to the arrangement previously made by them with the Admiralty.

As Mr. Laming justly remarks, any comparison he might offer between screw vessels and paddle-wheel vessels, might be considered partial ; he, however, points to the fact, that the screw was accepted by the Admiralty, and that it is on the screw system that the Royal West India Mail Packet Company now hold their contract.

We shall make some further remarks on this subject next month, and in the meantime call attention to the performances of the *Bosphorus* and *Hellespont*, screw vessels by Messrs. Maudslay and Co., belonging to the General Screw Steam Shipping Company, particulars of which have appeared in our pages. The statement from Southampton appears to us a feeler thrown out by the West India Mail Company to ascertain whether they can get their contract altered to suit their own views. For ought the public know, however, things may have been "made pleasant" at the Admiralty already.

THE PROPELLER STEAM SHIP "CAROLINA."
From the Journal of the Franklin Institute.

This fine steamer made a trial trip on Tuesday, the 25th of September, and, I understand, gave general satisfaction to her builders, and met their fullest expectations. I therefore furnish you with the following particulars of her construction:—Length over all, 164 feet; between perpendiculars, 149 feet; length of keel, 139 feet; breadth of beam, 29 feet; and depth of hold, 18 feet 6 inches.

She has two direct action condensing steam engines, with the cylinders placed directly over the shafts. Diameter of cylinders, 44 inches, and 3 feet stroke. One engine is directly abaft the other, and both are attached to the same shaft, at right angles. There are two air pumps, of 30 inches diameter and 20 inches stroke. These pumps are geared from the propeller shaft by spur wheels, so arranged that, while the engines make 60 revolutions, the air pumps each make but 25 strokes. Thd object of this reduction of speed in the air pumps (which is not a new idea) was to avoid the shock produced on metal valves by high velocity. This objection is entirely obviated by the use of valves of vulcanised India rubber. By this great reduction in the speed of the air pumps, the relative capacity between them and the cylinders is very much changed, reducing them to about $\frac{1}{10}$th the capacity of the cylinders, while the usual proportion is $\frac{1}{8}$th. With a moderate pressure of steam, and cutting off at one-half, no difficulty may be found, but I think the air-pumps would be found too small for a full pressure of steam, and working full stroke.

The propeller is Loper's, made of composition, 11 feet 4 inches diameter; angle at the hub, 20°; at the periphery, 48°. There are four blades, and the extreme width of each at the periphery is 7½ feet. The pitch of the screw is such that, working in a solid, the centre of effort would advance 27⅞ feet per revolution. On her trial trip she is reported to have averaged 42 revolutions per minute; the speed of the propeller was then 13$\frac{1}{15}$ miles per hour. The speed of the vessel at the same time was 10 miles per hour. Pressure of steam, 20lbs., cutting off at one-half.

She has two boilers, and burns anthracite coal, with natural draught. Blowers are now being added, which will increase the pressure of steam, but with a corresponding increased consumption of fuel.

As a whole, the *Carolina* is a very creditable job. Messrs. Reanie, Neafie, and Co., who built the engines, and Messrs. Byerly and Son, who built the hull, have certainly done justice to their work; and, although I think it an error of judgment, on the part of those who designed her, to place the centre of weight so far abaft the centre of buoyancy, which renders it necessary to carry a considerable quantity of ballast to bring her on an even keel, still, as it has evidently been intentional, I suppose there are good reasons for it, although not made public.

W.

STOVES AND FIRE-PLACES.
WALKER'S PATENT SELF-FEEDING STOVE.

A press of other matter has prevented our following up this subject, which we commenced in our last volume, with the regularity we could wish. Now, however, that we have turned over a new leaf, we intend to pursue the subject.

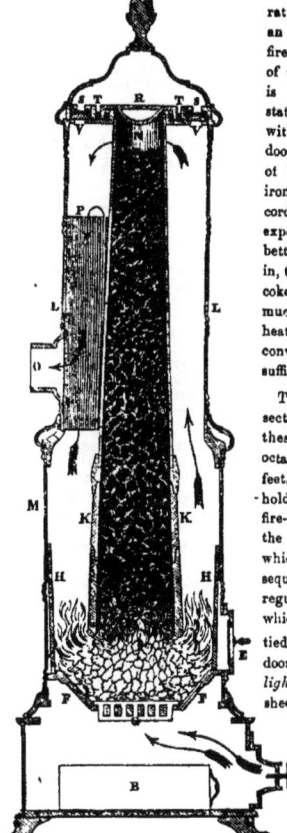

The stove now under consideration, is distinguished as being an entirely closed stove, though fire is visible by means of a plate of talc in the furnace door; this is a convenience, because the state of the fire is ascertained without opening the furnace door. It has also the peculiarity of being constructed entirely of iron; and although we have recorded our opinion, derived from experience, that fire brick is a better material for burning coa in, than iron; yet in a case where coke is used, burning without much fluctuation or intensity of heat, the cast-iron may be more convenient, and its durability sufficient for the purpose.

The engraving represents a sectional elevation of one of these stoves. The base is of an octagon shape standing on four feet. F, is a cast-iron pan, which holds the fire. G, is the set o fire-bars. C, is the regulator in the ash-pit door, by means of which the draught and the consequent intensity of the fire is regulated. B, is the ash-pan, which can be removed and emptied at pleasure. E, is the fire-door, through which the fire is *lighted*, and which contains a sheet of transparent talc, through which the fire can be seen. H is a cast-iron lining, which surrounds the ignited fuel, and prevents the outer case from being over-heated, an accident which, as we have before observed, is dangerous from the risk of fire, and unwholesome, from the burning of the air in the apartment.

On the furnace part of the stove stands "the radiator" L L, which, as it is cooled by the outer air, abstracts the heat from the products of combustion which finally escape down a back flue P, formed of two partitions closed at the bottom, and communicating with the chimney-pipe O.

In the centre of the stove is fixed the fuel-holder K K N, which is filled, from the top, the fuel descending as fast as it is consumed. The top of the fuel-holder is fitted with a ring T T, filled with sand, into which the lid R, drops, in order to make an air-tight joint, which is essential, in order to prevent the fuel in the feeder from igniting.

The stove is lighted in the ordinary way, through the fire door E, and when thoroughly alight, the fuel is put in at the top by means of a funnel. The fire will then burn from 12 to 18 hours without further attention, except regulating the draught to suit the temperature required.

As the inside of the radiator will require sweeping at the end of the season, the ring S S, at the top, is made moveable, and, by means of a small brush introduced through V V, all the dust may be brushed off and will fall into the ash-box.

The patentee claims an advantage for this stove, over many others, in the thinness of the fire, which makes the combustion more perfect, and therefore economizes the fuel.

A stove 15 inches square on the base, and 4 feet 3 inches high, is estimated to warm a room 20 × 20 × 10 feet high, keeping it at a temperature of 66° in frosty weather, with a consumption of two pecks of coke, and to burn 12 hours with once filling the feeder.

It has been applied to several churches, and other large buildings, and the patentees have favoured us with the various testimonials, which, however, we think our readers will not require us to repeat, as their opinion will rather be formed on its apparent merits.

NOVELTIES.

PRACTICAL MODE OF ASCERTAINING THE RATE OF A CLOCK.—All the *stars* are found to be unanimous in giving the same exact duration of 23h., 56m, 4·09m. for the *sidereal* day; this being the case, to ascertain the rate of a clock or watch, "an observer need only station himself to the north of some well-defined vertical object, as the angle of a building, and placing his eye exactly at a certain fixed point (such as a small hole in a plate of metal nailed to some immoveable support), notice the successive disappearances of any star behind the building by a watch—taking care that the part of the edge behind which the star disappears be quite smooth; the verticality of the edge should be secured by the use of a plumb line.—*Herschel's Outlines of Astronomy*.

AMERICAN ENGINE MAKING.—The engine trade is exceedingly busy in New York, chiefly upon marine work. The orders consist of the large ocean steamers. Those for the *Antarctic* are said to cost 250,000 dollars.

The Russian Scientific Academy has announced that, in obedience to the directions of the Emperor, a committee has been appointed to report on the project of the French chemist, M. Archcrot, for lighting St. Petersburgh with electricity, and experiments are to be made on a large scale in several parts of the city.

CORK PACKING FOR STUFFING BOXES.—An interesting experiment is being made on the use of cork shavings instead of gasket in the stuffing boxes of steam engines. The cork is cut by a machine which gives the shaving a curl, and it was originally used in this state to make the patent safety mattrasses for ship use. The same material, however, has now been applied to the piston rod stuffing box and has worked, without grease, for upwards of two months. If this should, on further trial, prove satisfactory, it will effect an important saving both in time and expense.

LIVERPOOL WATER WORKS.—Messrs. D. Y. Stewart and Co. of St. Rollox, are casting the pipes for the Liverpool Corporation Water Works, of which Mr. Hawksley of Nottingham is the engineer. They are 12 feet lengths of 44 inch pipes, weighing 2 tons, 13 cwt. each length. The quantity required is 10½ miles, and they are being turned out at the rate of a quarter of a mile per week.

LIST OF ENGLISH PATENTS,

FROM NOVEMBER 19, 1849, TO DECEMBER 21, 1849, INCLUSIVE.

Thomas Worsdell, of Birmingham, manufacturer, for certain improvements in the manufacture of envelopes and cases, and in the tools and machinery used therein. November 19.

John Webster Hancock, of Melbourne, in the county of Derby, manufacturer, for improvements in the manufacture of hosiery goods, or articles composed of knitted fabrics. November 17.

Charles Edouard Francois Constant Prosper De Changy, of Brussels, now residing in Tavistock-street, Westminster, civil engineer, for improvements in the preparation and manufacture of flax, hemp, and other like fibrous substances. November 20.

Charles Cowper, of Southampton-buildings, Chancery lane, for certain improvements in the manufacture of sugar. November 20.—(Communication.)

Francis Justin Duburguet, of Cahors, in the Republic of France, for certain improvements in hydro-pneumatic engines. November 22.

Joseph Pierre Gillard, gentleman, of Paris, in the Republic of France, for certain improvements in the production of heat and light in general. November 22.

William Garnett Taylor, of Binton House Hall, in the county of Westmoreland, gentleman, for improvements in lint, and in linting machines. November 24.

George Callaway, of Putney, in the county of Surrey, station agent, and Robert Alee Pinkus, of the same place, engineer, for certain improvements in propelling ships and other vessels; also in apparatus for ploughing land. November 24.

Charles Cowper, of Southampton-buildings, Chancery lane, for certain improvements in piling, faggotting, and forging iron for plates, bars, shafts, axles, tyres, cannons, anchors and other similar purposes. November 24.

Joseph Barrans, of St. Paul's, Deptford, in the county of Kent, engineer, for improvements in axles and axle boxes of locomotive engines and other railway carriages. Nov. 24.

Ambroise Ador, of Paris, in the Republic of France, engineer, for improvements in producing light. November 24.

Henry Lamplough, of Snow Hill London, consulting chemist, for a new mode of supplying pure water to cities and towns. November 24.

James George Hewey and James Newman, of Birmingham, for improvements in the manufacture of buttons, studs, and other dress fastenings and ornaments. November 28.

Francis Tongue Rufford, of Prescot House, Worcester, fire-brick manufacturer, Isaac Marson, of Cradley, in the same county, and John Finch, of Pickard street, City-road, Middlesex, manufacturer, for improvements in the manufacture of baths and wash-tubs, or wash-vessels. November 28.

Frank Clarke Hills, of Deptford, in the county of Kent, manufacturing chemist, for an improved mode of compressing peat for making fuel or gas; and of manufacturing gas, and of obtaining certain substances applicable to purifying the same. November 28.

Louis Napoleon Le Gras, of Paris, in the republic of France, civil engineer, for improvements in the separation and disinfection of fecal matters, in the manufacture of manure, and in the apparatus employed therein. November 30.

Charles Barlow, of Chancery-lane, London, esquire, for improvements in the manufacture of a certain pigment. November 29.—(Communication.)

Walter Crum, of Thornliebank, in the county of Renshaw, Scotland, for certain improvements in the finishing of woven fabrics. December 3.

Conrad Montgomery, of the Army and Navy Club, St. James's-square, in the county of Middlesex, esquire, for improvements in brewing, distilling, and rectifying. December 3.

William Eccles, the elder, William Eccles, the younger, and Henry Eccles, of Blackburn, in the county of Lancaster, cotton spinners, for certain improvements in machinery or apparatus for preparing, spinning, and weaving cotton and other fibrous substances. December 3.

Joseph Paradis, of Lyons, in the Republic of France, merchant, for improvements in the manufacture of elastic mattresses, cushions, and paddings, part of which improvements are applicable to other purposes, where sudden or continuous pressure is required, to be sustained or transmitted. December 3.—(Communication.)

George Buchanan, of the city of Edinburgh, civil engineer, for improvements in cocks valves, or stoppers; and in the use of flexible substances for regulating or stopping the passage of fluids; and also in making joints of tubes and pipes or other vessels. Dec. 3.

Baron James Ulric Vaucher de Strubing, of Margaret-street, Cavendish-square, for improvements in the manufacture of axle-tree boxes for carriages, and of the bearings of the axles of railways; and in the making of an alloy of metal suitable for such and like purposes. December 3.

George Edmund Donisthorpe, of Leeds, in the county of York, manufacturer, for improvements in wheels of locomotive carriages. December 3.

Peter Fairbairn, of Leeds, in the county of York, machinist, and John Hetherington, of Manchester, for certain improvements in machinery for preparing and spinning cotton, flax, and other fibrous substances. December 3.

Samuel Fisher, of Birmingham, in the county of Warwick, engineer, for improvements in railway carriages, wheels, axles, buffer and draw-springs, and hinges for railway carriage and other doors. December 5.

Edward Carter, of Merton Abbey in the county of Surrey, machinist, for improvements in printing calico and other fabrics. December 5.

Jonah Davies and George Davies, of the Albion Iron Foundry, Tipton, Staffordshire, engineers and iron founders, for improvements in engines worked by steam, air, water and other fluids, and whether locomotive, marine, or stationary, and also in boilers, the principle of which improvements is likewise applicable to blowing air and pumping water. December 10.

Jean Baptiste Ecarnot, of France, for improvements in the manufacture of sulphurous, acetic, and oxalic acids, and nitrates. December 10.

David Christie, of Saint John's place, Broughton, in the borough of Salford, in the county of Lancaster, merchant, for improvements in machinery for preparing, assorting, straightening, tearing, teasing, doubling, twisting, braiding, and weaving cotton, wool, and other fibrous substances. December 10.

John Houghton Christie, of Craven-street, Strand Esq, for an improved construction of wrought iron wheels and machinery for effecting the same. December 10.

Thomas Grimsley, of the city of Oxford, in the county of Oxford, sculptor, for improvements in the manufacture of bricks and tiles. December 10.

The Baron Louis Lo Presti, of Paris in the Republic of France, for improvements in hydraulic presses, which are, in whole or in part, applicable to pumps and other like machines. December 10.

William Holt, of Preston-place, Bradford, organ builder, for certain improvements in the construction of the pallets or valves of organ sound-boards or wind charts, the same being applicable to seraphines, colophons, harmonicums, harmoniums, and all other musical instruments, in which the tone is produced by the admission of wind, supplied by bellows or other machinery, to pipes, reeds or springs, and played upon by a key board or keyboards, and also to various other purposes connected with all the above named musical instruments. December 10.

John Henry Jenkinson, of Salford, in the county of Lancaster, machine-maker, and Thomas Priestly, of Shuttleworth, in the same county, manager, for certain improvements in machinery or apparatus to be used for preparing, spinning, and doubling cotton, wool, flax, silk, and similar fibrous materials. December 12.

William Birkmyre, of Fulbech Cottage, Hampstead, chemist, for improvements in the manufacture and refining of sugar. December 12.

Alfred Dalton, of West Bromwich, in the country of Stafford, iron founder, for improvements in reverberatory and other furnaces. December 15.

Charles Cowper, of Southampton-buildings, Chancery-lane, for improvements in instruments for measuring, indicating, and regulating the pressure of air, steam, and other fluids, and in instruments for measuring, indicating, and regulating the temperature of the same, and in instruments for obtaining motive power from the same. December 15. (Communication.)

Charles Lizars, of Paris, in the Republic of France, engineer, for improvements in gas meters. December 15.—(Communication.)

Thomas Rock Shute, of Watfort, in the country of Hertford, silk throwster, for improvements in spinning, doubling, and throwing organzine silk. December 16.

Timothy Hackworth, and John Wesley Hackworth, of the Soho Works, Shilden, in the county of Durham, engineers, for improvements in locomotive and other engines. Dec. 15.

Benjamin Fawcett, of Old Jewry, in the city of London, builder, for improvements in pigments, paints, and vehicles for painting. December 15.

Isaac Lewis Pulvermacher, of Vienna, engineer, for improvements in galvanic batteries, in electric telegraphs, and in electro magnetic and magneto-electro machines. Dec. 15.

Robert Harcourt, of Birmingham, manufacturer, for certain improvements in knobs, handles, and fastenings for doors and drawers; and in fastenings to be used in fastening window sashes, curtain and other rods, and for other like purposes. December 15.

James Oldknow, of Lille, in the Republic of France, lace-manufacturer, for improvements in the manufacture of lace and other fabrics. December 15.

Henry Roberts, of Connaught square, Hyde park, in the county of Middlesex, gentleman, for improvements in the manufacture of bricks and tiles. December 15.

George Wythes, of Reigate, in the county of Surrey, contractor for public works, for improvements in apparatus for receiving and retaining the rails on railways. Dec. 3.

Richard Hobson, of Leeds, doctor of medicine, for certain improvements in the manufacture of horse shoes, and in apparatus for taking the measurement of horse-shoes or horse's-hoofs. December 15.

Edward Lyon Berthon of Fareham, in the county of Southampton, clerk, Master of Arts, for certain improvements for ascertaining and indicating the course or way, velocity, trim, and draught of ships, and the rate of currents: also for discharging water from ships; and for taking altitudes and levels on sea and on land. December 19.

James Smith, of Deanston, in the county of Perth, now residing in Glasgow, for certain improvements in treating the fleeces of sheep when on the animals. December 19.

William Ackroyd, of Birkenshaw Mills, near Leeds, in the county of York, for improvements in dressing and cleaning worsted, and worsted mixed with cotton and other fabrics after they have been woven. December 19.—(Communication.)

Warren De la Rue, of Bunhill row, in the county of Middlesex, manufacturer, for improvements in the manufacture of envelopes. December 19.

Frederick Hale Thomson, of Berners-street, Oxford-street, and Edward Varnish, of Kensington, in the same county, for improvements in the manufacture of ink stands, mustard-pots, and other vessels of glass. December 19.

Henry Fox Talbot, of Lacock Abbey, in the county of Wilts, esquire, and Thomas Augustine Malone, of Regent street, in the county of Middlesex, photographer, for improvements in photography. December 19.

Joseph Whitworth, of Manchester, engineer, for certain improvements in machinery or apparatus for cutting metals, and also improvements in machinery or apparatus, applicable to agricultural and sanatory purposes. December 19.

Frederick George Spray, and George Wevell, of Hampstead road, engineers, for an improved steam engine, parts of the arrangements of which may be applied to apparatus for regulating, measuring, and registering the flow of liquids and gases. December 21.

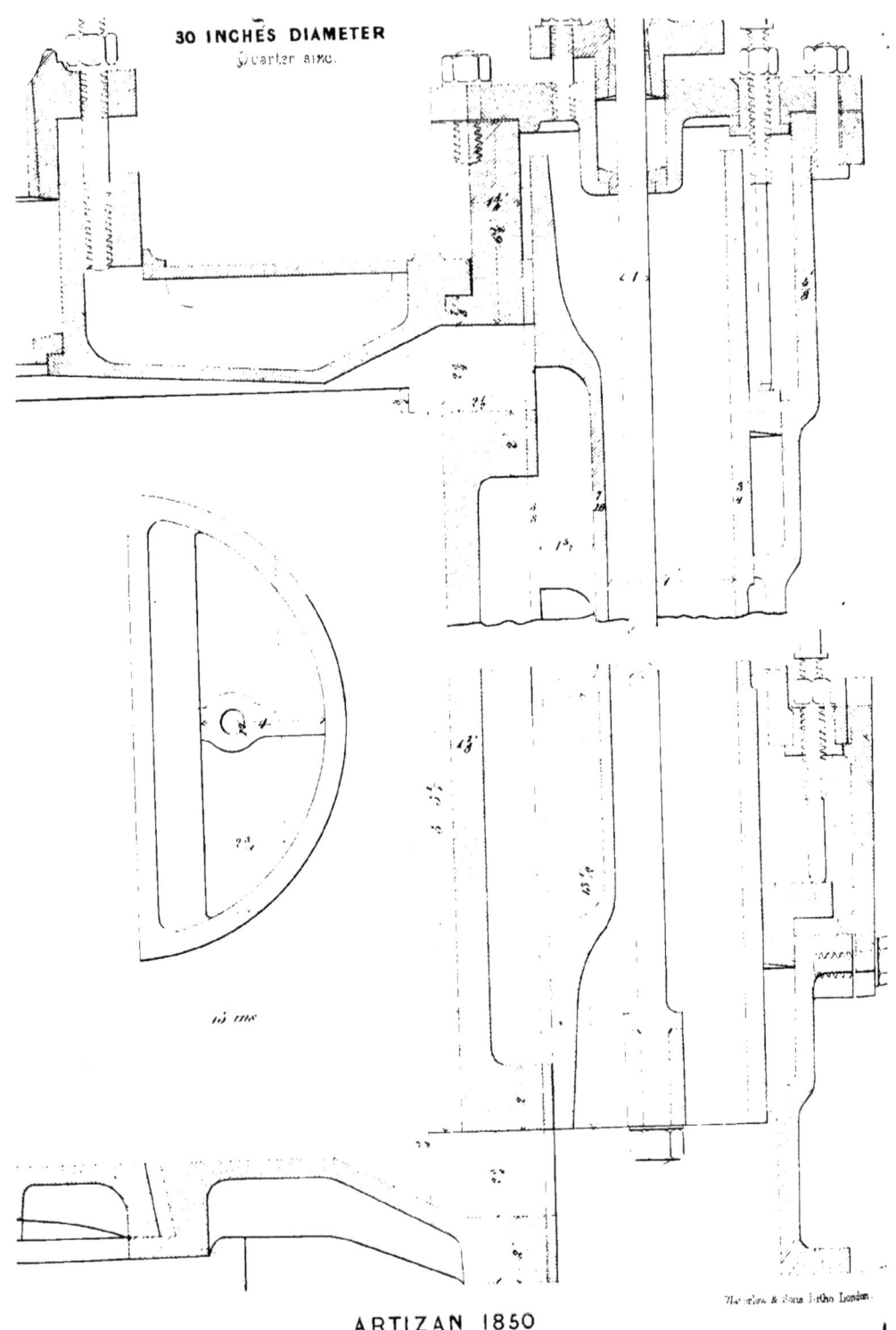

30 INCHES DIAMETER
Quarter size.

ARTIZAN 1850

Waterlow & Sons Litho London.

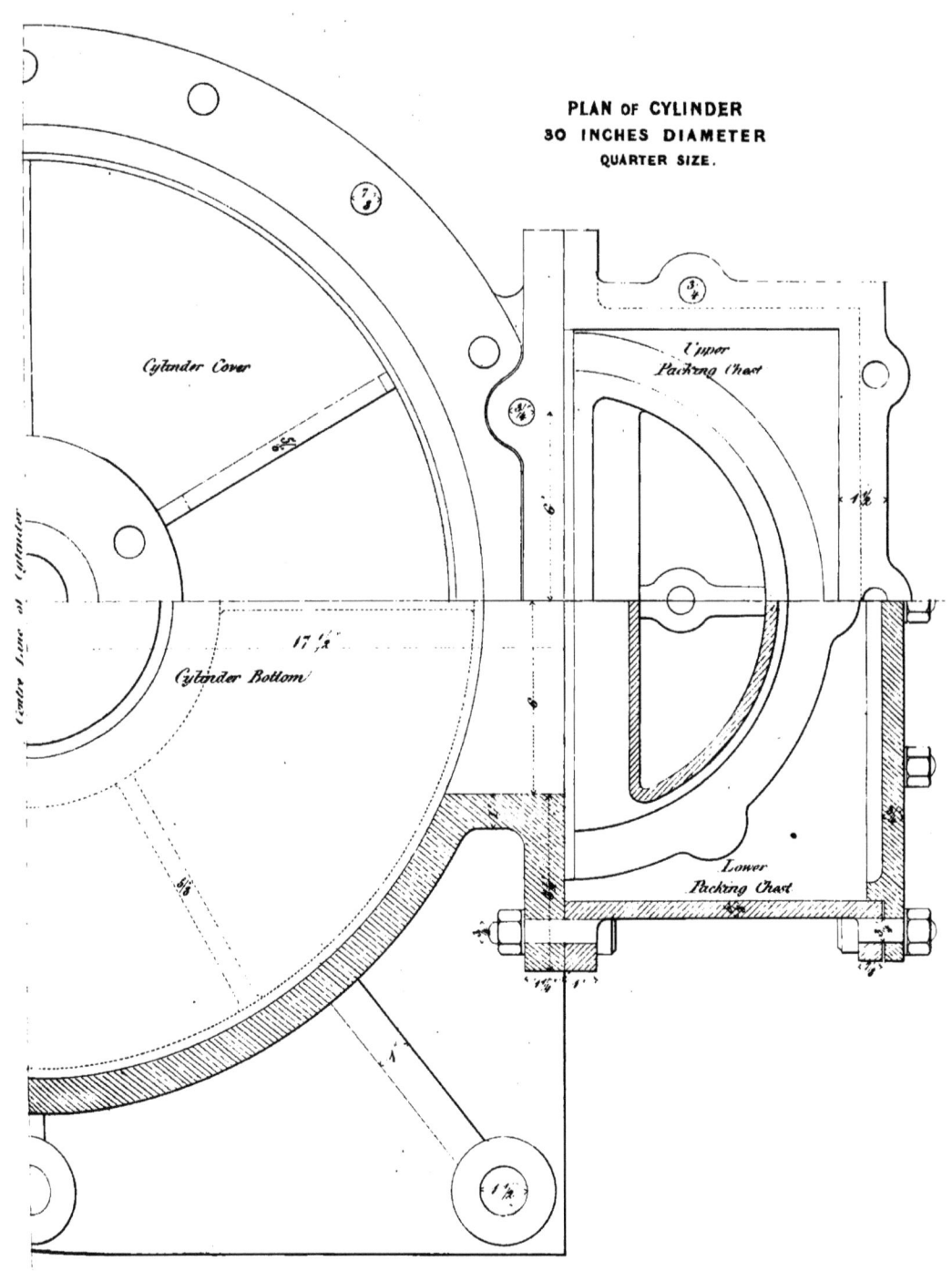

PLAN OF CYLINDER
30 INCHES DIAMETER
QUARTER SIZE.

Cylinder Cover

Upper
Packing Chest

Centre Line of Cylinder

Cylinder Bottom

Lower
Packing Chest

ARTIZAN 1850.

THE ARTIZAN.

No. II.—Vol. VIII.—FEBRUARY 1st, 1850.

MECHANICAL ENGINEERING.

ANALYSIS OF THE STEAM ENGINE.

(*Continued from p. 2.*)

The Cylinder.—Having fixed the diameter and depth of the piston, we can now proceed to set out the cylinder. The size of the ports is the first point to be considered, and it is one for which a great many rules have been made. A square inch per horse power is an old rule for low pressure engines. Much depends upon the speed of the piston, the degree of expansion used, and the amount of lead given to the valve. In locomotives we have arrived at our present maximum speed of piston and size of ports, to which all our present system of engineering tends; this is particularly the case with marine engines, which, in the case of those applied direct to the screw, approximate nearly to the velocity of the locomotive. In the case of paddle-wheel engines, the size of ports has, perhaps, not been increased, the higher pressure of steam and greater expansion compensating for the increased speed of the piston.

In the present engine the ports are made 2¾ inches × 12 inches = 33 inches area, which will admit of the speed of the engine being increased to, say 260 feet per minute, should it ever be necessary. Large ports and slides are objectionable from the increased weight and expense of the parts, and the waste of steam at every stroke; the latter point being felt more strongly when an engine of long stroke is fitted with a short slide, which will take, say 4 per cent. of the *contents of the cylinder* to fill the passages. Supposing then that the steam be cut off at ⅓, the loss would be 12 per cent. on the steam consumed. The convenience of using short slides is, however, sufficient in many cases to counterbalance the loss of steam.

The distance between the ports is made such that the piston will just come to the edges of the ports at top and bottom stroke; this distance, therefore, will be the length of stroke added to the depth of edge of piston—in this case 5 feet 5½ inches. To this must be added the clearance at each end of the cylinder, to ascertain the distance between the bottom of the cylinder and the underside of the cylinder cover. The amount of clearance varies with the opinion of the maker; one aiming at superfluous nicety, and another calculating upon the foundations sinking, the brasses wearing, or the piston rod being made too long or too short, and the various other

> "Perils that do environ
> The man that meddleth with cold iron."

We are also informed, upon good authority, that a small amount of clearance strongly affects the smooth working of the engine, which, as a principle, is doubtless very true. The clearance in this case is given as ⅜ inches at each end, which we consider the least that could with safety be allowed on a 5-feet stroke. Next, the thickness of metal over the upper port, say ⅞ inch, being settled, will give the face of the top flange of the cylinder, and the line of clearance above the port will give the underside of the cylinder cover, which will be made of the same shape as the top side of the piston, in order to give an equal amount of clearance all over. The thickness of metal of the cylinder should not be less than 1 to 1½, and it is better to be on the safe side and have enough to take another cut out of, in case of accident. The top of the cylinder, as far as the lower side of the port, say 3⅜, ought to be bored out about ⅜ inch larger in diameter than the working part, in order to get the piston in easily, and to save giving that part the finishing cut; this and the cylinder flange will be more clearly shown when we give a section of the whole cylinder on a smaller scale.

A brass gland is fitted into the bottom of the cylinder cover stuffing-box, and being kept ½ inch short, gives a clearance for the taper end of the piston rod in the piston. The width allowed for packing is 1 inch all round, and the total depth of the stuffing box is 6½ inches, or rather more than twice the diameter of the rod; for high pressure steam this depth might be increased with advantage. A recess ⅝ inch deep is turned out of the top of the stuffing-box, to form a receptacle for the grease, and serves to prevent waste and keep the cover clean. The Cornish engine makers make this recess an addition to the flange, and much deeper, so that the flange of the gland sinks completely into it: this, however, hardly appears necessary, and there may be a difference of opinion as to its neatness. The flange is made deep enough to meet the loose plate which covers up the feathers on the cylinder cover, and which is supported on its internal and external circumference by the feathers, which are faced, at those parts, in the lathe.

The gland is circular, of cast iron, with a brass bush, fitted in with a slight taper; unless the gland be entirely of brass, the circular shape is to be preferred, as offering greater facility for lathe work. It is held down by three ⅞ bolts, the nuts of which should be made rather deeper than the diameter of the bolt (the standard size), as indeed should all nuts similarly used. An oil cup is turned out of the gland at top, and the surfaces bearing on the packing are bevilled to throw the packing against the rod. The cylinder cover is ⅝ thick, and the ribs the same.

The cylinder bottom is cast in, and is stiffened like the cover by six feathers, of same thickness. A hole is cast in the bottom to get the boring bar through, the size of which will be fixed by that of the bar proposed to be used. It is closed by a plug, as shown, the vacancy between being filled in with iron cement, and the taper preventing its coming loose. The plug is sometimes bolted in, for convenience of removal, a case which seldom occurs, for an engine ought to be superseded before the cylinder requires re-boring.

The face of the cylinder and the slide is the next point.—The distance of the face from the inside of the cylinder will be fixed by the amount of surface for making a tight joint of the cylinder cover over the port, and the thickness of metal in the face. Taking the latter at 1¼ inch, and supposing ¼ inch to be lost in the larger diameter of the cylinder at the mouth and the clearance, 2½ inches total will give 1 inch surface for the cylinder cover at the narrowest point. The cylinder is here shown faced with brass ⅝ thick, the slide being of cast iron. There exists some difference of opinion as to whether the brass face wears better than the cast iron would do. There can be no doubt, however, that the brass offers greater convenience when the faces require scraping and bringing up to a true surface. These faces are fastened on by brass screws tapped into the cast iron, and rivetted their whole depth in the brass.

Erratum.—In the last line but one of our previous article, for "piston" read "packing-ring."

The stroke of the slide varies with different makers, but may be taken at 2¼ times the depth of the port, or rather more—the increased stroke giving a quicker motion to the valve. In this case, with 2¾ inches port, say 8 inches stroke of slide. The total length of the slide is made such as just to close the two ports when at the middle of its stroke, and may, therefore, readily be found, an ⅛ of an inch being generally allowed in addition, say 5 feet 11 inches over all.

In the drawing the slide is shown at the top of its stroke, the upper port being, therefore, opened to the fullest amount allowed by the length of the slide face. If the slide face were cut away so that the steam was admitted the full size of the port, there would be no *lap* on the slide, but in this case lap is added, and the port is never opened more than half way. The steam is, therefore, cut off sooner when the slide descends, and is worked expansively. We shall reserve what we have to say in explanation of this branch of the subject until we come to the setting of the eccentric.

Two inches surface is allowed below the upper port, and above and below the lower one, the amount being such as is considered necessary for keeping steam-tight. Four inches is allowed at top where there is ample room.

As the steam, after being admitted in the most convenient manner into the slide case, can only get into the port through the space left between the brass face on the cylinder and the front of the slide, care must be taken to allow sufficient room between them. If it were intended to work the engine with the ports full open, the distance must not be less than the port, or 2¾ inches; but as in this case the port is only opened 1⅜ inches, that amount would be sufficient. But as it might be requisite at some future time to take the lap off, it is made 1¾ inch, so that the port could be opened to that extent.

The thickness of metal of the slide, where it is not faced, is $\frac{7}{16}$ inch.

The size of the slide from front to back must be ascertained by setting it out in plan, as shown. The port is dotted in, and it will be seen that the slide is struck at such a radius, that the segment, 4 inches, is equal in area to the port after deducting the corners. The back of the slide is packed to take the pressure of the steam off it, and to separate the middle of the slide jacket, which contains steam, from the top and bottom, which communicate with the condenser. The space for packing at the top commences on a level with the port, which is the lowest point to which the top of the slide descends. The depth of packing is 5 inches. The space for its reception is bored out, and the back of the slide is turned, and is made ¾ thick to allow for fresh surfacing. As will be observed in the plan, the slide jacket is just a semi-circle; consequently, if two engines were being made, the two jackets, after their faces had been planed, might be bolted together and bored out simultaneously. If they were smaller segments than a semi-circle, packing pieces would be put between them. The slides would be treated in the same way. It is obvious that the radius of the slide and jacket will be affected by the proportion of the depth to the breadth of the port, and the amount of surface given on each side of the port, in plan.

The turned ends of the slide are made of such a length, 13½ inches, that they will not be drawn through the packing.

The packing is compressed by brass packing rings, and screwed down by three or more screws. Brass nuts for these screws are let into the jacket, having a collar below, and being rivetted over on top. The lower packing ring requires lugs for the screws to bear on; these, with the door, will be shown in plan.

The length of the cylinder face above the upper port is fixed by the clearance necessary for the valve at top stroke. The slide-rod, 1 inch diameter, passes through the boss at bottom of the slide; it is kept as near the face as it can be got. The slide-stuffing box presents no object for remark. Lugs 1½ inch deep are cast on the slide jacket to bolt on the cover, which is ⅞ inch thick. The gland of the stuffing-box is held down by ⅝ bolts.

An exhaust-pipe would be required to be bolted to the bottom of the slide jacket, if the cylinder stood upon the sides of a cistern; but if it stood directly on the sole plate, as in a side lever engine, this would be unnecessary. We have purposely refrained from any details connected with the arrangement of the parts into a beam, or direct-acting species of engine. This point we shall leave, until we have made the tyro thoroughly acquainted with the parts themselves.

(To be continued).

To the Editor of the Artizan.

SIR,—Inclosed I forward you the following table for obtaining the ordinates of semi-elliptic arches, so as to construct the arch with expedition and accuracy,

Let A D (see figure) = semi-span = s
B D = height = h

To find the ordinate x at $\frac{1}{10}$ the semi-span from A towards D.

Then, from conic sections, we shall have

$$\text{As } (s \times s) : h^2 :: \tfrac{1}{10} s \left(s + \tfrac{9}{10} s\right) : x^2$$

Or,
$$s^2 : h^2 :: \left(\tfrac{1}{10} s^2 + \tfrac{9}{100} s^2\right) : x^2$$

Taking the extremes and means,

$$\text{we have } s^2 x^2 = \left(\tfrac{1}{10} s^2 h^2 + \tfrac{9}{100} s^2 h^2\right)$$

Dividing by s^2

$$\text{then } x^2 = \left(\tfrac{1}{10} h^2 + \tfrac{9}{100} h^2\right), \text{ adding these values,}$$

$$\text{we have } x^2 = \left(\tfrac{10}{100} h^2 + \tfrac{9}{100} h^2\right) = \tfrac{19}{100} h^2$$

$$\therefore x = \tfrac{1}{10} h \sqrt{19}$$

$$\text{Taking } h = 1, \text{ then we have } x = \tfrac{1}{10} \sqrt{19}$$

$$= .43589 \text{ the tabular number at } \tfrac{1}{10} \text{ the semi-span.}$$

It is evident, from the above result, that in any semi-elliptic arch, if half the span is divided in the same proportion corresponding with the fractional parts in the table, the only variable quantity will be the height of the arch.

NOTE.—The ordinate at ⅕ the semi-span of any arch, reckoning from A to D, is equal ⅗ the height of the arch; and the ordinate at ⅖ the semi-span is equal ⅘ the height.

Example of the use of the Table.

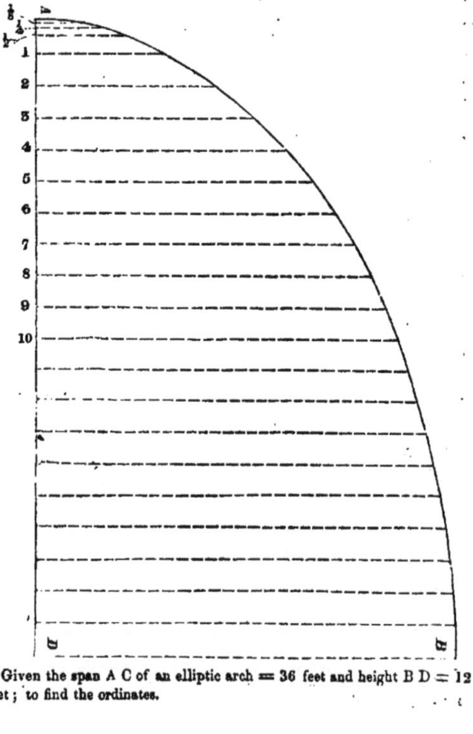

Given the span A C of an elliptic arch = 36 feet and height B D = 12 feet; to find the ordinates.

· Now, suppose we want 20 ordinates to half the span A D, here we make use of column 20

Then $\frac{36}{2}$ = 18 the half span,

And $\frac{18}{20}$ = .9 the length of each division.

Now, referring to column 20, and opposite 1, we have the tabular number .3123, then .3123 × 12 feet the height = 3.7476 the ordinate for the first division.

Again: to find the ordinate for the second division; opposite 2, we have the tabular number .4359 × 12 the height, gives 5.3308 the ordinate to the second division, we proceed in the same manner 1, 2, 3, 4, &c., to the 20th division; then, when we have all the ordinates taken out, we may proceed with the construction. The number of each column represents the denominator and the vertical numbers 1, 2, 3, 4, &c., the numerators of the fractional parts of the semi-span.

The use of the fractional parts at the top of the table is evident from an inspection of the figure. For instance: the first division from A to 1 is divided into $\frac{1}{4}$, $\frac{1}{2}$, $\frac{3}{4}$, &c.; then we look in column 20, and opposite these fractions we have the tabular numbers .2222, .1576, .1116; then, each being multiplied by the height, will give the ordinates at $\frac{1}{4}$, $\frac{1}{2}$, $\frac{3}{4}$, &c., of the first division.

If we should investigate the ordinates to semi-circular arches, we should come to the same conclusion as above ; and it may be here stated that the same remarks are applicable to the semi-circular as well as to the semi-elliptic-arch.

TABLE OF THE ORDINATES OF SEMI-ELLIPTIC AND SEMI-CIRCULAR ARCHES WHEN THE HEIGHT = 1.

Column No. 4.	Column No. 8.	Column No. 5.	Column No. 10.	Column No. 20.	Column No. 40.	Tabular Numbers.
		$\frac{1}{16}$	$\frac{1}{16}$	$\frac{1}{8}$	$\frac{1}{4}$	.1116
		$\frac{1}{16}$	$\frac{1}{8}$	$\frac{1}{4}$	$\frac{1}{2}$	.1576
						.1765
$\frac{1}{16}$	$\frac{1}{8}$	$\frac{1}{8}$	$\frac{1}{4}$	$\frac{1}{2}$	1	.2222
						.248
$\frac{1}{8}$	$\frac{1}{4}$	$\frac{1}{4}$	$\frac{1}{2}$	1	2	.3123
						.348
$\frac{1}{4}$	$\frac{1}{2}$				3	.38
		$\frac{1}{2}$	1	2	4	.4359
					5	.4841
$\frac{1}{2}$	1		$\frac{1}{2}$	3	6	.5268
					7	.5651
		1	2	4	8	.6
					9	.632
1	2		$\frac{1}{2}$	5	10	.6614
					11	.6888
			3	6	12	.7141
					13	.7378
			$\frac{1}{2}$	7	14	.76
3					15	.7806
	2		4	8	16	.8
					17	.8182
				9	18	.8352
					19	.8511
2	4		5	10	20	.866
					21	.88
				11	22	.893
					23	.9052
			3	6	12	24
5						.9165
					13	26
						.9457
			7	14	28	.9539
					29	.9614
3	6			15	30	.9683
					31	.9744
			4	8	16	32
					33	.9846
	7			17	34	.9887
					35	.9922
			9	18	36	.995
					37	.9972
				19	38	.9988
					39	.9997
4	8	5	10	20	40	1.0000

B. C. K.

CLAY'S PATENT ROLLED TAPER IRON.

The very ingenious machinery invented and patented last year by Mr. Clay for the purpose of rolling iron of any section into taper bars, has now been brought extensively into use, and promises to confer an especial advantage on ship-builders, who can now purchase iron rolled ready to bend into ships' knees at a cost considerably under that of forged iron, which has been hitherto used for the purpose. It is also applicable to anchor shanks and stocks, windlass necks, levers, mill shafting, railway switches, &c.

The machinery is very simple, consisting of a pair of hydraulic cylinders, fitted with solid pistons and rods, extending through the usual screw that holds down the upper roller. The cylinders are provided with two valves, one for the entrance and the other for the exit of the water, which are both self-acting. When the cylinders are filled with water, and the pressure of rolling a bar of iron is applied, the upper roller forces the water out of the cylinder by the exit valve, which allows the roller to rise, and the bar being rolled, to become gradually thicker. It is obvious that, by regulating the aperture of the valve for the exit of the water, the taper of the bar will be in a like manner regulated at the discretion of the workman.

Mr. Clay tells us in a note recently received from him—"We are at present making the taper iron at an ordinary large mill, just in the usual manner, at which has already been made taper bars at the rate of rather more than 2 tons an hour, or 25 per shift."

Licences have been granted to the Mersey Steel and Iron Company, on the west coast of Great Britain, and Messrs. Losh, Wilson and Bell, of Newcastle-upon-Tyne, for the east coast.

IMPROVEMENTS IN IRON MANUFACTURE.

Sir F. C. Knowles has recently patented an improved method of making iron direct from the ore, which appears to be based on sound chemical principles. The patentee states that the method was suggested to him by a consideration of the fact, that coal, in the process of coking, whether in coke ovens, or in the blast furnace, as raw coals, loses a large portion of its weight in the form of gaseous matter, composed chiefly of carbon and hydrogen, and by considering the well-known superior de-oxidising and cementing power of these elements in the aeriform state, as compared with their solid and crude condition in coke or bituminous coal. This loss is increased by the action of the blast on the materials in the lower parts of the blast furnace, which has been computed at upwards of eighty per cent. of the entire weight where raw coal is used. In addition to this, only the poor earthy ores have been used, while the nearly pure ores have been neglected; and we import foreign iron for the purpose of conversion into steel.

For the first process—that of making the iron direct from the ore, without any previous smelting—the patentee selects those ores most free from earthy matter, and the nearer they approach to pure oxides the better. For another process—the preparing iron ores by cementation in retorts, to make cast-iron, by smelting afterwards—the ores are taken indifferently, excepting such as contain much sulphur and arsenic. They are first broken into pieces of moderate size, so as, when placed together in a heap, there may be interstices between them capable of admitting a gas, or vapour, through them without obstruction. They are then placed in retorts, rendered gas-tight, and brought up to a red heat, each of which is connected with gas-tubes, having stop-cocks for the purpose of injecting and regulating a current of gas among the ore. For this purpose two sorts of gasses are used by the patentee—common carburetted hydrogen, or coal-gas, and carbonic oxide, prepared by slow combustion of charcoal, or coke. The patentee does not confine himself to coal-gas, but employs any hydro-carbon which can be produced economically. When the retorts are charged, and the gas generated, the *rationale* of the process will be as follows:—The ore being mainly an oxide of iron, the hydrogen of the hydro-carbon unites with the oxygen of the ore to form water, while the carbon unites with another portion of oxygen, forming carbonic oxide or carbonic acid, as the case may be, leaving metallic iron as the result. The ore being so far reduced, the next stage of the process, when malleable iron is the proposed product, is to shut off the gas on both sides of the retorts, and transfer the contents of the retorts to the puddling furnace, where the iron is treated in the common way. It may be cut, piled, re-heated, and rolled as usual, according to the nature of its distinction or quality required. If steel be required, the cementation must be carried farther, until the reduced metal has absorbed about 1 per cent. of carbon. The reduced and cemented ore is then put into crucibles, or melting pots, to be run down into ingots in wind-furnaces, as is now done in the making of cast-steel. If the earthy matter in the ore require it, some proper flux is to be added, according to the usual method of fluxing iron ores. If cast-iron be required, the cementation must be carried on until about 3 or 4 per cent. of carbon is absorbed, after which it is transferred to the blast-furnace, with a proper flux. The patentee further claims, where cast-iron or steel is the product required, the separate cementation of iron ores with charcoal, coke dust, anthracite coal, coke, &c., on the following iron ores:—Pure specular ore, red and brown hematite, black oxide, red and brown ochreous ores, magnetic iron ores, spathose ores, being carbonates of protoxide of iron, and different from the argillaceous iron ores of the carboniferous series of rocks above the mountain limestone. Lastly, the patentee claims the use of spathose iron ores and "soft mine" as a flux, to supersede the use of limestone; the ore is first roasted, to drive out the carbonic acid, and then mixed with other ores in such proportion that the lime contained in the aggregate may bear a due proportion to the silica and alumina in the other iron ores to be smelted.

DIMENSIONS AND DETAILS OF NEW STEAMERS.

THE PORTUGUESE GOVERNMENT WAR STEAMER, "MINDELLO."

Built by Messrs. Green, of Blackwall, from the designs, and under the superintendence, of the contractors, Messrs. J. and A. Blyth, engineers, London.

				Ft.	in.
Length of keel for tonnage	...	...	...	149	5
Breadth for ditto	...	...	...	27	7
Ditto, extreme	...	...	...	27	11
Ditto, moulded	...	...	...	27	0
Tonnage, O.M.	...	...	...	604 tons.	
Depth of hold from underside of deck to underside of keelson				17	6
Length between engine-room bulkheads				38	9

A pair of side lever engines of 220-horse nominal power. Cylinders, 56¼ inches diameter × 5 feet stroke. Air pumps, 31 inches diameter × 2 feet 9¼ inches stroke. Paddle-wheels, diameter, extreme, 23 feet; ditto over the floats, 22 feet 6 inches. Three sets of arms and floats. Floats, 8 feet × 1 feet 10 inches. Revolutions per minute, 21. Average draught, 11 feet 3 inches.

Two tubular boilers—breadth, 19 feet 6 inches; length, 10 feet 7 inches; height, 12 feet 10 inches. Ditto over steam chests, 16 feet 3 inches. Eight furnaces, 8 feet 4 inches long. Fire bars, 7 feet 6 inches long × 1 foot 9 inches wide. 344 iron tubes, 3¼ inches inside diameter × 7 feet 3 inches long. The total weight of the whole machinery, including water in the boilers, and the bunkers is only 15 cwt. per horse-power, showing the lightness to which beam engines can be brought by the more extensive adoption of wrought iron, and attention to the details of construction.

This vessel was built and equipped in 1845, at a time when the affairs of Portugal were at a very critical juncture. Soon after her arrival she was wrested from the possession of the Government by the Junta of Oporto, and, after having suffered great neglect from the Portuguese who were put on board as engineers during nine months' service, was finally recovered by the assistance of the English admiral, and placed in the hands of the legitimate authorities. The boilers, as may be imagined, suffered most, and it was only by the greatest exertions on the part of the English engineers on board that they were kept running so long. Neither did the interior of the engines entirely escape, although, with the exception of these unavoidable drawbacks, their external appearance elicited the highest commendations from several eminent engineers, who visited her on her arrival under the command of Captain Jose de Silva.

We had the opportunity of inspecting her on a trial trip, after receiving a thorough repair to her boilers, and noted down a few remarks on the general arrangements.

The side-levers, and framing, are all of malleable iron, and the arrangement of the latter, from the fewness and simplicity of the parts, struck us as being especially judicious. The entablatures are of cast iron, supported by eight wrought iron columns, which are stayed fore and aft, and transversely with horizontal stays, and there are two diagonal stays to each pair of columns—the lower one connected directly to the column, and the upper to the entablature. These are connected again to the arched frame, sketched below, which binds the cylinder to the condenser. The appearance of the whole is so light, that doubts might be entertained as to its sufficiency, had not four years' hard work been unable to strain a single bolt or stay. This satisfactory result is no doubt attributable to the manner in which the paddle and engine beams are trussed diagonally together, and braced with long through bolts (thus distributing the strain of propulsion) as if the engines had been of the direct acting kind, with no other fixing but the deck beams to depend upon.

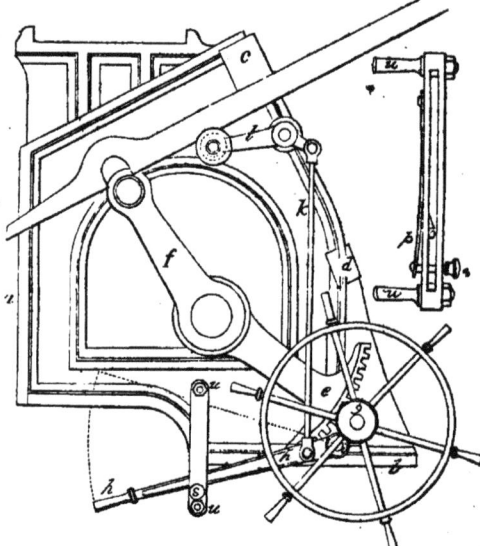

Scale ¼ inch to a foot.

The starting gear appeared to us to possess some points of novelty and convenience, and we accordingly noted it down for the benefit of our readers. *a b* is a cast iron frame, connecting together the cylinder faces, and the top of the condenser; the latter being cast on the sole plate, this frame serves to hold the cylinder very securely at top, without incurring any risk of breaking cement joints, as would be the case were the condenser jointed to the sole plate. The frame also serves to carry the weigh shaft brasses, and the plummer blocks for the motion shaft; the malleable iron stays to the entablature and the columns, are bolted to the lugs *c* and *d*. The toothed segment *e* is keyed on the weigh shaft lever *f*, and is worked in the usual way by the starting wheel and pinion *g*. The throwing out lever *h*, serves to throw the eccentric rod out, and the starting wheel into gear (and *vice versa*), at the same instant, in the following manner. The lever *h* is centred upon the pin *i*, which is fixed in the frame *a b*. The upper end of the lever carries the pin, on which the starting wheel works; and, by the motion of the lever, the pinion may be thrown in or out of gear with the segment; at the same instant the rod *k* raises or depresses the lever *l*, the end of which carries a roller, on which the eccentric rod travels, when out of gear. The lever *h* is retained in its lowest position, as shown, by the catch *o* (drawn to 1½ inch scale in the detached sketch), which is in a piece with the spring *p*. Its bevilled edge allows the lever to pass it, when brought down, whilst its return is prevented until the engineer wishes to throw the eccentric rod in gear, when he has merely to push back the handle *z*, which throws back the catch *o*, and allows the weight of the eccentric rod to throw it into gear, and the starting wheel and pinion out of gear. The studs *u u*, are screwed into the frame and into the condenser, and carry the catch frame.

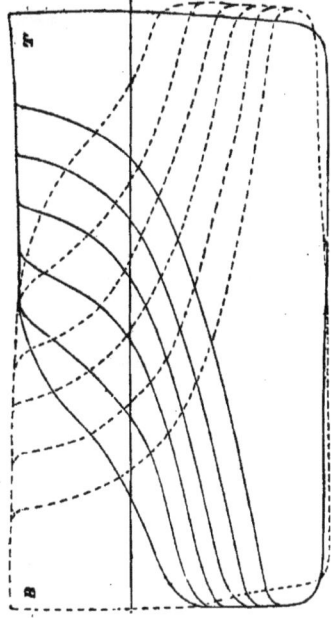

Scale, ½ inch = 1 lb.

The annexed card was taken at sea, off the North Foreland, and shows the work performed at top and bottom of the piston. The number of revolutions varied with the expansion from 12 to 20 per minute. The expansion gear is placed within reach of the engineer, and is so arranged that he can alter the degree of expansion in an instant.

We were gratified to observe that the comfort of the stokers had been fully cared for by a due attention to the ventilation of the engine room—a point which, we are sorry to say, is too often overlooked, as of minor consideration.

The armament consists of four broadside guns, 32-pounders, and two 8-inch pivot guns, fore and aft.

The *Mindello* left the Thames on 30th ult., and, having touched at Vigo, arrived at Lisbon after 5 days 11 hours steaming.   K.

THE CORK STEAM NAVIGATION COMPANY'S IRON VESSEL, "MINERVA."

Built by Messrs. Thomas Vernon and Co., Liverpool. Engines, &c., by Messrs. Bury, Curtis, and Kennedy, Clarence Foundry, ditto.

Builder's measurement.				Ft. in.
Length of keel and fore rake	...	...	...	197 0
Breadth of beam amidships	...	...	...	26 6
Depth of hold, ditto	...	...	...	16 6
Length of engine space	...	...	...	57 0
Tonnage.				Tons.
Hull	...	...	...	652⁴⁴⁄₁₀₀
Contents of engine space	...	...	...	204⁸⁸⁄₁₀₀
Register	...	...	...	447⁷⁴⁄₁₀₀

New measurement.				Ft.
Length on deck	...	...	...	197 0
Breadth on ditto amidships	...	...	...	25.2
Depth of hold ditto	...	...	...	16.3
Length of engine space	...	...	...	57.0
Tonnage.				Tons.
Hull	...	...	...	677⁴⁴⁄₁₀₀
Contents of engine space	...	...	...	253⁷⁸⁄₁₀₀
Register	...	...	...	424⁶⁶⁄₁₀₀

A pair of side lever engines of 384-horse nominal power. Cylinders, 70 inches diameter × 6 feet 2 inches stroke. Paddle-wheels, diameter, extreme, 26 feet 9 inches; ditto, ditto, effective, 26 feet 1½ inches. Floats, 9 feet 10 inches × 2 feet 1 inch; 3 sets of 4 arms and 22 floats. Two tubular boilers, 19 feet long, fired fore and aft, 3 furnaces at each end; total, 12 furnaces. 526 tubes in each boiler, diameter, 3 inches × 7 feet 1 inch long. 17 strakes of plates from keel to gunwale. Average, 19 revolutions per minute.

Description—Bust female figure head, no galleries, elliptical stern, and clinker and carvil-built, standing bowsprit, 2 masts, schooner-rigged (no top masts), one main and break deck. Port of Cork. Commander—Mr. Thomas Hirste.

The following quick run, performed by this vessel, is extracted from the captain's log book, dated Friday, the 16th of March, 1848.

"Clock to Cumbray, 15.6 miles, in 55 minutes."

SHANDON AND GLASGOW STEAM-PACKET COMPANY'S IRON STEAMER, "SUPERB."

Built by Messrs. John Reid and Co., Port Glasgow, 1839. Engines, &c., by Mr. Robert Napier, Vulcan Foundry, ditto.

Builder's measurement.			1839. Ft. ins.	1844. Ft. ins.
Length of keel and fore rake	...	...	119 2	164 4
Breadth of beam	...	...	17 2	17 2
Depth of hold	...	...	9 6	9 6
Length of engine space	...	...	37 6	47 6
Tonnage.				Tons.
Hull	...	...	179⁴⁄₁₀	206⁴⁴⁄₁₀₀
Engine space	...	...	57⁴⁄₁₀	75¹²⁄₁₀₀
Register	...	...	115	124⁶⁴⁄₁₀₀

New measurement.			Ft.	Ft.
Length on deck	...	...	119.2	186.4
Breadth on ditto amidships	...	...	16.5	17.0
Depth of hold	...	...	9.4	9.0
Length of engine space	...	...	35.7	47.7
Tonnage.			Tons.	Tons.
Hull	...	...	151⁷⁷⁄₁₀₀	163⁷⁷⁄₁₀₀
Engine space	...	...	59⁷⁰⁄₁₀₀	79⁷⁰⁄₁₀₀
Register	...	...	91⁷⁷⁄₁₀₀	84⁷⁷⁄₁₀₀

One side lever engine of 74-horse nominal power. Diameter of cylinder, 47⅝ inches. Length of stroke, 3 feet 9 inches. Diameter of paddle-wheels, extreme, 15 feet 2 inches; ditto, ditto, effective, 14 feet 3 inches. Floats, 7 feet 3 inches × 1 foot 3 inches. Three sets of 14 arms and floats.

The first boiler was a common flue boiler, having 4 furnaces 7 feet long, the engine going 28 revolutions per minute, consuming 96 cwt. of coals per day. Steam pressure, 6 lbs.

The second boiler was put in in 1844 (when the vessel was lengthened 17 feet 2 inches), being tubular. Tubes, diameter, 12 inches × 12 feet; and 5 furnaces, 7 feet long.

At the beginning of 1849, the two tubular boilers formerly on board of the *Jenny Lind* were put in. Length, 11 feet 3 inches; breadth, 5 feet 7 inches; height, 6 feet. Length of steam-chests, 8 feet; breadth, 3 feet; height, 2 feet 10 inches. Two furnaces each; but were too small, and the present tubular boiler was put in July last. Length of boiler at centre,

17 feet 9 inches; length at bottom, 16 feet; breadth, 15 feet 8 inches; depth, 7 feet. Five furnaces—length, 6 feet 4 inches; breadth, 2 feet 7 inches; open below. Oval steam-chest—length, 7 feet 6 inches; breadth, 6 feet 3 inches; depth, 6 feet. 48 tubes, diameter, 6 inches × 9 feet long. Steam pressure, 13 lbs. Consumption of fuel per hour, 17 cwt. of coals. Average, 35 revolutions per minute. Frames, 3 × 3 × ½ ins., and 3 feet apart. Ten strakes of plates from keel to gunwale.

This was the first iron steamer built at Port Glasgow, and the first built with the clipper-bow upon the Clyde, and was designed by Mr. John Wood. Since that time, there have been upwards of 95 steamers built upon that principle, showing the superiority of the clipper over the common bow; because, the cutwater and the hull being in one shell, prevents the cutwater from being so liable to be damaged or knocked off. There is still another advantage, that is, reducing the tonnage of the vessel by the new act of 1836.

This steamer was built to ply upon the Forth, between Stirling, Alloa, and Newhaven, with passengers, &c.; but, drawing more water than was intended, she was then put upon the station between Glasgow, Port Glasgow, Greenock, Helensburgh, Row, Roseneath, Shandon, Garelock Head, &c. The steamer *Albert* was built to supply her place in 1840.

Description—One deck (standing bowsprit, bust female figure head, clipper bow, 1839), no bowsprit, or figure head, common bow (1844) sham quarter galleries, square-sterned and clinch-built vessel, 1 mast, sloop-rigged. Port of Glasgow. Captain Stewart.

THE ISLAY AND GLASGOW STEAM-NAVIGATION COMPANY'S IRON VESSEL "ISLAY."

Built and fitted by Messrs. Tod and M'Gregor, Glasgow.

Builder's measurement.	Ft. in.
Length of keel and fore rake	167 0
Breadth of beam	21 6
Ditto, including paddle-cases	39 5
Depth of hold amidships	11 0
Length of engine space	58 1
Tonnage	Tons.
Hull	385 $\frac{21}{94}$
Contents of engine space	155 $\frac{18}{94}$
Register	230 $\frac{3}{94}$
New measurement.	Ft.
Length on deck	167.0
Breadth on ditto amidships	20.8
Depth of hold ditto	10.6
Length of quarter-deck	35.9
Breadth of ditto	20.0
Depth of ditto	2.2
Length of engine space	58.1
Tonnage.	Tons.
Hull	307 $\frac{58}{100}$
Quarter-deck	17 $\frac{6}{100}$
Gross	324 $\frac{64}{100}$
Contents of engine space	138 $\frac{59}{100}$
Register	186 $\frac{5}{100}$

A pair of steeple engines upon Mr. David Napier's four piston-rod principle, of 152 horse nominal power; cylinders, 46 inches diameter × 5 feet stroke; feathering paddle-wheels, diameter, 22 feet; length of paddle-boards, 6 feet × 2 feet 6 inches; fourteen paddle-boards. Two common flue boilers, length, 22 feet 3 inches; breadth, 9 feet 6 inches; depth, 8 feet 6 inches. Steam chests, length at top, 6 feet 9 inches; below, 7 feet; breadth, 3 feet 9 inches; depth, 3 feet 3 inches. Six furnaces, three in each boiler; length, 6 feet 6 inches; breadth of ditto, 2 feet; depth, 3 feet 9 inches; diameter of chimney, 3 feet 6 inches; steam pressure, 9 lbs.; vacuum, 26 inches; average 23 revolutions per minute; consumption of coals, 17 cwt. per hour. The coal bunkers hold 40 tons of coals, and are placed between the engine and boilers, a system coming greatly into use, since the introduction of tubular boilers especially, being superior to the old mode of having the coals on the top of the boilers, which tends to decay the sides of the vessel and the top of the boilers. There is a tunnel in the middle of the bunker, the same length as ditto; breadth, 3 feet; height, 6 feet 8 inches.

Keel, bar iron, 4½ × 2 inches; for 80 feet, 4½ × 2½ inches; scarphs, 10 inches; stem, 3½ × 1½ inches; stern-post, 4 × 2½ inches; 3 feet kneed to form part of keel; frames, 3½ × 2½ × $\frac{5}{16}$ inches, and 1 foot 6 inches apart at midships, and 1 foot 8 inches fore and aft. There are nine strakes of plates from keel to gunwale, tapering in thickness from $\frac{7}{16}$ to ¼ of an inch. Has a hurricane deck between the paddle-boxes, 32 feet 2 inches in length, and 20 feet 9 inches in breadth, and is about 8 feet above the main-deck; the engines at the top are 14 feet above the deck. Height of forecastle deck, 3 feet 6 inches. Sponced 3 feet afore, and 2 feet 6 inches abaft, the paddle-wheel space. Carries three boats, one being a life boat; three anchors, No. 916, weight, 8 cwt. 2 qrs. 22 lbs.; No. 917, weight, 8 cwt. 3 qrs.; Kedge anchor, No. 944, weight, 3 cwt. 7 lbs., made by Messrs. H. Wood and Co. The *Islay* plies between Glasgow, Greenock, Port Ellen (Islay), West Tarbert, and Port Askaig (Islay), &c. Makes the passage between Greenock and Port Ellen, on an average, in eight hours (distance 90 miles). Commenced running October 11, 1849.

Description—A bust female figure head, sham quarter bridges, standing bowsprit, two masts (no topmasts), schooner rigged, square-sterned and clinch-built vessel. Port of Glasgow. Commander—Mr. Luke Skelly.

GREENOCK AND GLASGOW TOWING COMPANY'S STEAMERS, "VENUS" AND "CHIEFTAIN."

"Venus," built at East Jarrow, in the County of Durham, 1845. Engines, boilers, &c., by Mr. J. P. Almond, North Shields.

"Chieftain," built at Stockton, in the County of Durham, 1845. Engines, boilers, &c., by Messrs. Conley and Scott, North Shields.

	"Venus."	"Chieftain."
Builders' measurement.	Ft. ins.	Ft. ins.
Length of keel and fore rake	82 3	80 1½
Breadth of beam	15 0	15 8½
Ditto, including paddle-cases	32 6	33 4½
Depth of hold amidships	9 0	9 0
Length of engine space	36 0	36 3
Tonnage.	Tons.	Tons.
Hull	88 $\frac{44}{94}$	95 $\frac{11}{94}$
Contents of engine space	43 $\frac{22}{94}$	50 $\frac{30}{94}$
Register	45 $\frac{22}{94}$	45 $\frac{11}{94}$
New measurement.	Ft.	Ft.
Length on deck	81.0	78.0
Breadth on ditto amidships	14.2	14.4
Depth of hold ditto...	8.8	8.9
Length of engine space	36.0	36.3
Tonnage.	Tons.	Tons.
Hull	69 $\frac{13}{100}$	76 $\frac{49}{100}$
Contents of engine space	48 $\frac{5}{100}$	50 $\frac{49}{100}$
Register	21 $\frac{8}{100}$	26
One half-lever engine in each vessel.		
Nominal power	40 h.p.	40 h.p.
	Ft. ins.	Ft. ins.
Diameter of cylinder	0 34½	0 34½
Length of stroke	3 7	3 8
Diameter of paddle-wheels, extreme ...	12 4½	12 4½
Ditto, ditto, effective	11 11	11 11
Length of floats	7 3	7 4
Breadth of ditto	1 6½	1 9½
Number of arms and floats	12	12
Sets of ditto	2	2

Venus—Two common flue cylindrical boilers—length, 17 feet; diameter, 7 feet 2 inches. Four furnaces, 2 in each boiler—length, 5 feet 10 inches; breadth, 2 feet 4 inches; depth, 3 feet 3 inches. Funnel—diameter, 2 feet 8 inches; height above deck, 26 feet 7 inches. Safety valve, $4\frac{1}{2}$ inches diameter. Steam pressure, $12\frac{1}{2}$ lbs. Steam pipe, $4\frac{1}{2}$ inches diameter. Consumption of fuel, 7 cwt. of coals per hour, and the bunkers hold 10 tons. Average speed, 31 revolutions per minute, and 8 knots per hour. Engine, No. 37. Master—Mr. John Campbell.

Chieftain—Two common flue cylindrical boilers—length, 19 feet; diameter, 6 feet 2 inches. Four furnaces, 2 in each boiler. Bunkers hold 12 tons of coals—consumes about 6 cwt. per hour. Revolutions, 37 per minute. Steam pressure, 10 lbs. Speed, 8 knots. Engine, No. 12. Master—Mr. Peter Dick.

Description—One flush deck, no figure head nor galleries, short bowsprit, one mast, sloop-rigged, round-sterned and clinker-built vessels of timber. Port of Greenock.

THE GLASGOW CASTLE ROYAL MAIL STEAM NAVIGATION COMPANY'S IRON VESSELS, "PIONEER" AND "PETREL."

Built and fitted by Messrs. Barr and M'Nabb, Abercorn Foundry, Paisley.

	Pioneer.	Petrel.
Builder's measurement.	Ft. in.	Ft. in.
Length of keel and fore rake	160 10	166 7
Breadth of beam	18 $2\frac{1}{2}$	17 10
Ditto, including paddle-cases	34 $2\frac{1}{2}$	34 0
Depth of hold amidships	9 0	7 11
Length of engine space	54 2	56 1
Tonnage.	Tons.	Tons.
Hull	$252\frac{31}{94}$	$248\frac{52}{94}$
Contents of engine space	$82\frac{74}{94}$	$91\frac{47}{94}$
Register	$169\frac{3}{4}$	$157\frac{24}{94}$
New measurement.	Ft.	Ft.
Length on deck	159.8	165.5
Breadth on ditto amidships	17.8	17.4
Depth of hold ditto...	8.8	8.7
Length of quarter-deck	45.0	47.6
Breadth of ditto	14.0	14.1
Depth of ditto	0.6	0.6
Length of engine space	54.2	56.1
Tonnage.	Tons.	Tons.
Hull	$192\frac{47}{100}$	$167\frac{68}{100}$
Quarter-deck	$4\frac{9}{100}$	$4\frac{35}{100}$
Total	$196\frac{58}{100}$	$191\frac{27}{100}$
Contents of engine space	$91\frac{48}{100}$	$91\frac{21}{100}$
Register	$104\frac{68}{100}$	$100\frac{7}{100}$
A steeple engine in each vessel.		
Nominal power	95 h. p.	100 h. p.
	Ft. in.	Ft. in.
Diameter of cylinder	0 $52\frac{3}{8}$	0 54
Length of stroke	4 3	4 3
Diameter of paddle-wheels extreme ...	19 0	19 1
Ditto, ditto, effective	18 6	18 7
Length of floats	6 0	6 3
Breadth of ditto	1 4	1 3

Pioneer—Nine arms and 18 floats; steam ports, 2 feet 1 inch × $3\frac{1}{2}$ inches; centre to centre, 4 feet $3\frac{1}{2}$ inches; piston-rod, diameter, $5\frac{3}{8}$ inches; paddle shaft journals, $8\frac{1}{2}$ × $10\frac{3}{8}$ inches; ditto at outer ends, $6\frac{1}{2}$ × $7\frac{1}{2}$ inches; between centres, 14 feet 2 inches. Two common flue cylindrical boilers; four furnaces, two in each. Bunkers hold 12 tons of coals. Consumption, 10 tons per day of 13 hours on an average. Makes 28 revolutions per minute at 10 lbs. steam pressure, and 30 revolutions at 12 lbs.

Frames, $2\frac{1}{2}$ × $2\frac{1}{2}$ × $\frac{5}{16}$ and 2 feet 3 inches apart; eight strakes of plates from keel to gunwale; draught of water, mean, 5 feet 3 inches. Plies between Glasgow, Greenock, and Ardrishaig, east end of Crinan Canal. The voyage going and returning is usually made in 13 hours—total, 180 miles per day. She has made the passage from Greenock to Rothesay in one hour, at 31 revolutions per minute. Launched, 1844. Captain, Mr. A. Shields.

Petrel—Boilers same principle as the *Pioneer*; the bunkers hold 12 tons of coals; consumption, about 14 cwt. per hour; 28 revolutions per minute at 10 lbs. steam pressure, and 30 revolutions at 12 lbs.; frames, same as *Pioneer*. Plies from Glasgow to Greenock, 21 miles; ditto to Gourock, $3\frac{1}{2}$ miles; ditto to Dunoon, $8\frac{1}{2}$ miles; ditto to Rothesay, 13 miles; total 46 miles going, and 46 returning, making 92 miles. Draught of water, 5 feet. Both vessels were designed by Mr. Alexander Denny. Launched, 1845. Captain, Mr. C. Gillies.

Description—No figure head, galleries, nor bowsprit; two masts, schooner rigged, square-sterned, and clinch-built vessels. Port of Glasgow. F, B.

COFFEY'S PATENT STILL AND CONDENSING APPARATUS.

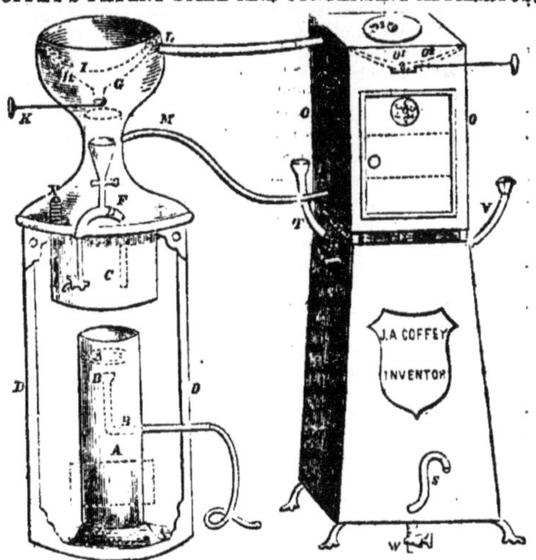

This is a very ingenious apparatus for performing the multifarious laboratory operations of distilling, decocting, and evaporating. The heat is supplied by a gas burner B, which can be regulated to the greatest nicety. C is the boiler or still, containing the liquor to be evaporated, the vapour from which ascends into the still head G, and communicates part of its heat to to the cup H, which contains an evaporating pan I, which may be used for preparations requiring a gentle steam heat. A portion of the vapour will be condensed and running down the still head will pass through the pipe M, to the refrigerator, of which only an outside view is shown, but which from its novelty we shall give a section of, next month. The vapour which is not condensed in the still head passes through the pipe L, to the hot chamber above the refrigerator, and circulates around the oven which it contains, and which may be used in various processes; or the heat may be applied to the evaporating pan O 1; the condensed vapour passing thence into the refrigerator, and being drawn off through the pipe S. T is a funnel pipe by which the refrigerator is filled with cold water, U being the overflowing pipe. The pipe V communicates with the interior of the refrigerator, to act as a safety pipe, and the pipe W is for the purpose of cleaning it out. By shutting the valves K and 2, the pans H and O 3 may be used to heat a retort, the loose pans being removed. X is a steam guage and thermometer. C is a pipe for filling the still, with a glass liquor guage and funnel.

This apparatus combines great compactness and portability with efficiency, and ought to find a place in every chemist's laboratory.

To the Editor of the Artisan.

SIR,—I beg to request the insertion, in your valuable journal, of a statement regarding the public service, which the following paragraph in the *Herald* of 19th instant, has tended to malign:—

"EXPENSIVE SYSTEM OF COALING AT PORTSMOUTH.—The *Terrible* was two days and nights alongside the *Malabar*, coaling, which process has not been much expedited by the mechanism, railways, and tomfooleries, that have cost so much money, and with which this ship has been fitted. The money expended on her would have sufficed to have built a good pier and wharf—with sufficient room for stacking quantities of coal at the entrance of the Clarence Creek, where there is sufficient water for large ships. A wharf at this point has long been talked of, and it is high time it was built. All vessels in a hurry are now obliged to come alongside the yard jetty to coal, and the coal as it is at present stacked about the jetties is a great nuisance to the dockyard. The *Sidon* coaled alongside the yard on Thursday, and took on board as much in 12 hours as she would have done alongside the *Malabar* in three days."

The repeated attacks upon dockyard authorities which have for some time been so fashionable, too often impose upon the credence of the public, from want of any better knowledge of the truth than some self-constituted critic may choose to supply; and the characters as well as the skill of "good men and true," are always considered "fair game" to be held up to ridicule by the unfathomable wisdom of the writer.

The practice of coaling all classes of steam vessels from coal depots is well known, and must owe its continuance to the superior economy and facility of taking both the colliers and steamers alongside such hulks in preference to taking the same vessels alongside a wharf or jetty; and we are, therefore, not surprised that, in Portsmouth Harbour, there have been for several years floating coal depots, alongside which the innumerable Government steamers are constantly being coaled, with perhaps an occasional solitary exception of some steamer like the *Sidon*, in a "very great" hurry, being "obliged" to be taken alongside the wharf for that purpose.

The coaling in all these depots has hitherto consisted in the employment of large gangs of convicts, who are constantly engaged in filling an incredible number of coal sacks, which, being neatly stowed between the decks of the depot, are ready to be thrust on board of a steamer, and shot into her coal-bunkers, on the instant of her being put into commission. This process is carried on at an immense cost of human labour, and expense of sacks, and it is not to be wondered at that, with all the modern improvements of machinery, the government should be advised to endeavour to reduce this immense annual outlay, by the application of steam power to raise the coals in iron buckets, from the interior of the depot, and shoot them at once into the steamer.

That the government should have possessed the alternative of choosing between a steam-worked floating depot, and the acknowledged inconvenience of even a well-arranged wharf, only reflects the more credit on their determination to prosecute the adaptation of steam power to the identical process which had hitherto proved most convenient for the special object in view. For this purpose, the *Malabar* frigate was selected, and was fitted throughout with every convenience to enable the coal buckets to be filled instantaneously, and with the least possible drudgery. A steam engine of large power was erected on board; but, as there was great choice of expedients for raising the bucket from the floor of the depot, after being filled, and, as economy of the public money does, however incredible it may appear to the correspondent of the *Herald*, enter into the mind of the greatest naval board in the world, *only one-fifth of the raising machinery* was permitted to be supplied, in order to have its merits fairly tested. This one-fifth part was set to work in the beginning of last year, and has been, since that time, generally employed in coaling steamers, and it was with this one-fifth part that the *Terrible* coaled on the occasion referred to. I, should also be understood that these negligent and incompetent authorities, having seen good cause in the course of last autumn for so doing, without the consent of the *Herald*, actually order the remaining four-fifths of the machinery to be made; and further that the said four-fifths of the machinery is now fixed on board the *Malabar*, and only requires some connecting gear to put the whole in operation. Now, whether all the machinery above stated, shall be capable of being concentrated upon the bunkers of one steamer, and thereby coaling her in one-fifth of the time alluded to by the *Herald*, matters little; it will soon be tried, and confident expectations are entertained of even a much larger result. But surely enough has been said to show that, in this case, the authorities have acted in accordance with the dictates of the most ordinary human wisdom, with the most ordinary attention to the economy of the public purse, and in that inventive, or rather, improving, course, most likely to lead to a satisfactory issue.

Let any thinking man judge of the ignorance of facts with which the *Herald* sits down to condemn methods and men, and then apply their impressions of the motives that must have actuated this carping "Momus" in the instance before us, to the numerous scurrilous attempts to depreciate the conduct of our navy board in the estimation of the public. Apologising for occupying so much of your valuable space,

I am, sir, your obedient servant,
A LOVER OF FAIR PLAY.

P. S: I inclose you my name and address to show you that I have no interest in the matter beyond promoting the truth.

FEN DRAINAGE.
To the Editor of the Artisan.

SIR,—Having observed that you request communications of all engineering news, I think that you may like to know what we are doing in the fens. We have just started a new 70-horse engine in the Feltwell district. The cylinder is 40 inches diameter × 7 feet stroke. The scoop wheel is 40 feet diameter over the floats, which are 3 feet wide, and 6 feet long, and there are 48 of them, dipping 9 feet into the fen. This is, I think, the grandest wheel in the fens, and is by Messrs. Blyth, of London. The engine is on a regular sole plate, and the beam carried on two columns, 12 inches diameter. There are three large boilers, 24 feet long, and 6 feet diameter; with a fire tube, 3 feet 3 inches diameter, and the furnace is 7 feet long. There is a water tube in the middle of the other, about 18 inches diameter. The first 24 hours after she was started, she worked the water down 30 inches, throwing as is calculated, 12,000 tons an hour. The commissioners have named her the *Gyr Falcon*, being the swiftest bird that flies. Yours truly. T. C.

[We are ashamed to confess that our ignorance of the noble art of Falconry, prevents us from appreciating, so fully as our correspondent appears to do, the felicity of the nomenclature, adopted by the commissioners. If, however, he or any other of our readers can enlighten us on the subject we shall feel deeply indebted to them.]

CORROSION OF BOILERS.
To the Editor of the Artisan.

SIR,—I observe, in your valuable magazine (*ante* 272), a method proposed for preventing the corrosion of marine boilers, by means of coal tar. Now, I do not think the party making the suggestion knows where corrosion actually takes place, and where it is most destructive; it is not where the water acts on the surface of the iron, but where the steam acts, viz., the roof and steam chests; the flues and sides of boilers never do corrode inside, and, if kept free from water on the outside, would last double the time that is generally allowed for boilers. If your correspondent could furnish a receipt to prevent the corrosion that takes place in the roofs, steam-chests, and steam pipes (when made of malleable iron), he would confer a great benefit on steam-ship proprietors.—Yours, &c.,
L.
Aberdeen, Jan. 18, 1850.

[The great importance of the subject induces us to insert our correspondent's letter; though it would seem to have escaped his notice—if we understand him rightly—that if the application of coal tar be really efficacious, there would be no impossibility in applying it over the whole surface, both *inside and outside the boiler*. We confess to be rather incredulous on the point, but we shall be glad to hear of the plan being fairly tried.]

To the Editor of the Artisan.

SIR,
I have to thank your correspondent "N. D." for the trouble he has taken to expose the incorrectness of the "Elliptograph," described in a former number. I quite agree with his remarks on my letter, and only regret I did not give the subject more attention before occupying your pages with an attempt at improving an instrument which is certainly next to useless.

I am, Sir, your obedient servant,
W. W. R.
Falmouth, January 8, 1850.

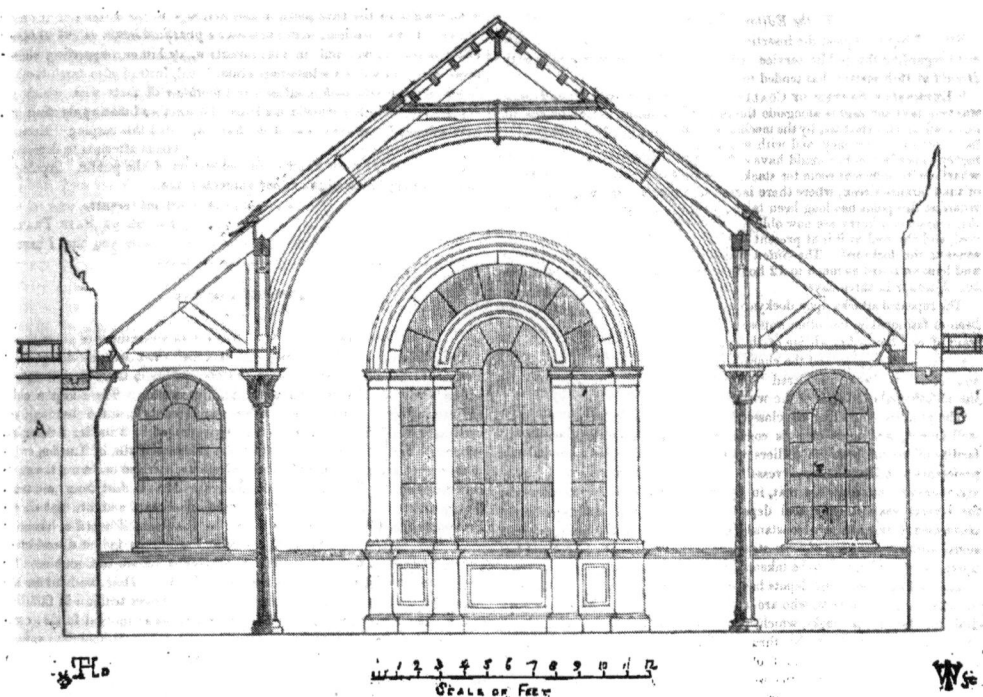

SCALE OF FEET

THE ARTIZANS' HOME, SPITALFIELDS.

The accompanying engraving is a cross section of the coffee-room in the building lately opened for the occupation of mechanics and workmen. This room is of large and lofty proportions, and cannot fail to win the approbation of those for whose enjoyments it has been built, when they compare it with the little pent-up cribs to which of necessity they have been accustomed. We do not think it possible habitually to occupy such a room as this, without feeling a certain expansion of thoughts as well as lungs, both of which are so essentially neccessary to the welfare of man. This room is 45 feet long and 35 feet wide, and is warmed by hot water pipes. It is divided into two side aisles and an open central part by cast iron columns, four on each side, from which spring four laminated semi-circular arches, of 20 ft. 9 in. span and 9 feet rise and in 4 thicknesses. The roof is entirely open, of stained timber, and, by an elegant simplicity of construction, adds considerably to the general appearance of the room ; it is in its entire extent covered with rough plate-glass. The aisles and a third side of the room are divided into comfortable boxes, supplied with substantial tables, and in the fourth side are the windows, the centre one of which, without pretensions but of a large size, has a good effect. Over the door is a bust of Watt, who, without a tithe of the advantages here offered to the working man, effected so much for himself and the world.

We have visited this building with the intention of laying before our readers some *practical* and *professional* observations relating to the details of arrangements and construction, and now propose to submit them to their attention, merely premising that the building has been erected from the designs and under the superintendance of W. Beck, Esq., architect, by Mr. S. Grimsdell, the builder, the amount of contract being £9,560. The engineer is Mr. Reeve.

On entering the hall of the building we pass by the superintendent's office and rooms on the left, and the cook's store-room and chambers on the right. From the hall we pass under the staircase into the coffee-room, above mentioned ; to the left of this is the lecture and reading-room, 60 feet long by 21 feet 9 inches wide ; it is lighted by 6 windows of 3 feet 6 inches opening ; it is warmed by open fire-places, and lighted, as well as the rest of the building, by gas ; at one end of this room is the library. The reading-room is to be supplied with daily papers and periodicals, and decorated, as we hear, by busts and maps.

To the right of the coffee-room is the common kitchen, ranging in length parallel to the coffee-room ; it is 45 feet long and 21 feet 9 inches wide, and contains two of Sherwin's ranges, with large ovens and hot water tanks, a cold water supply cistern, and apparatus for common cooking purposes ; the floor is laid with metallic lava. This kitchen is for the general accommodation of the occupants of the building, who may supply themselves at the cook's bar, opening on the kitchen, with provisions, which are to be of the best quality, and to be retailed to them at the lowest remunerative prices. Another bar from the cook's department also opens into the coffee-room, for the retail of coffee, &c. ; and, as a general idea of the prices of provisions, we may add, that we have heard that the price of the pint of coffee is to be three halfpence, or exactly the same as that which is given at the commonest coffee shop.

Besides the rooms which we have gone through, there is on the ground floor, to the right of the staircase, a lavatory for day use, and the cook's kitchen, independently of that we have mentioned, and which is also supplied with one of Sherwin's ranges.

From the general kitchen, by means of a stone staircase, we descend to the basement story, which is truly most complete and effective in all its arrangements ; in one portion we find a store department, in which are to be seen the same number of small safes or larders as there are to be occupants in the building ; these larders are raised on brick piers ; they are in ranges, and placed back to back, with an air-passage between, so that the

5

safes which are closed back and front by perforated zinc plates, are thoroughly ventilated. Each stack of larders is lettered, and each separate safe has its number—both letter and number corresponding with a key to be given to each inhabitant, and no two keys will open one larder.

On this same basement floor, we find the engine-room, under charge of an engineer, who is also to superintend other matters relating to his department; there is also the washhouse, with large troughs, supplied with abundance of water; these troughs are as usual divided into compartments, and there is besides, a small division to each compartment for the boiling of linen; this smaller division contains about seven gallons of water, which is heated by means of a small pipe leading the steam from the main pipe to the *bottom* of each tub; we found, by experiment, that seven gallons of water could by this means be brought to a *gallopping boil* in ten minutes. In this washhouse we also found an hydro-extractor or drying-machine, consisting of a cast iron cylinder, containing a wire framing, with a space between the frame and sides of the cylinder; the wire framing being made to revolve with immense velocity, expels the water from the clothes placed within it, without the slightest injury, the clothes being subjected to neither pressure nor wringing; next to the washhouse, there is the ironing-room, supplied with a large ironing-board, and a patent mangle, to be worked by steam. We understand that the accommodation here offered, is to be obtained for two-pence for any time under two hours, and one penny for every hour over. There are also on this floor three bath rooms supplied with hot and cold water by two different cocks, instead of the two-way cock.

Above the ground floor, are three upper stories of sleeping apartments; the sleeping compartments, formed of strong framing of sufficient height for perfect privacy, run along a central corridor; each compartment, measuring eight feet by four feet six inches, has an iron bedstead and bed furniture, and is lighted by half a window, the upper portion of which is opened at the will of the occupier. In each sleeping compartment is a locker for clothes, the key of which is the same as that which opens the larder mentioned above; and in each of these lockers is a false bottom, communicating with an air-flue of half-brick dimensions, running down from below each window-sill, and opening to the exterior. The false bottom of the locker has a flap opening into the sleeping compartment, and which is within reach of the head of the beds, so that the occupant may regulate the supply of fresh air with any degree of nicety he may please or cut it off altogether. For the purpose of the general ventilation of the sleeping-rooms, the framing of the compartments is kept below the level of the ceiling. A spring latch-lock secures the door of each sleeping compartment, and the key of this is given to each tenant, with the key of his locker and safe. On each floor are lavatories and water-closets, for night use. There are large cisterns in the roof, and smaller ones about the building, so as to insure a plentiful supply of water.

The general ventilation of the building is carried on by means of a principal lofty shaft: into this the smoke-flues are led, and by their heat generate an active upward draught. Along the ceilings of the different sleeping rooms, the lecture-room, and other principal apartments, run zinc air-flues, which open into the ventilating-shaft. Through these air-flues hang the gas-pipes, and around each pipe, in the zinc flue is a circular opening for the ingress of vitiated air from the room into the air-flue. By means of slate sliding dampers, at the control of a superintendent, the communication between any air-flue and the ventilating-shaft may be immediately cut off. This plan has been amply tested, and was found eminently successful on the day the building was opened.

To those of our professional readers likely to visit this building (and there are but few who will not find it worth their while), we have but one more detail of arrangement to notice—viz., a small stove, which is truly a *multum in parvo* of its kind; and, from being thoroughly adapted to small "model lodging houses," is well deserving of notice; it is the invention of a gentleman, who had it registered, and who gave the property to the Association.

We must not here forget to return our thanks to Mr. Hudson, the clerk of the works, to whom we were indebted for much attention on our visit to the building, and to whom we think credit is due for an efficient discharge of arduous duties.

One word to the *metropolitan builders*, and we have done. We would wish them to visit this building, and take a *practical* lesson out of an architect's note-book, with reference to comforts wanted in our domestic architecture—comforts which we long to see introduced, instead of so much tumble-down stucco, *mock-Italian* palaces, and *Gothic* villas.

Close adjoining the "Artizan's Home" is another building erecting, and nearly finished, for the use of sixty families.

[For this very interesting description of what we consider a "sign of the times," we are indebted to our contemporary the *Architect and Building Gazette*, which we can freely recommend to all our readers who take an interest in architecture and the building arts.—ED. *Artizan*.]

THE SOCIETIES.

INSTITUTION OF CIVIL ENGINEERS.

This distinguished body having elected Mr. William Cubitt as their President, that gentleman, according to custom, has delivered an inaugural address, wherein he takes a rapid but interesting review of the chief engineering triumphs of the past year and points out the new fields of usefulness opening up to the inventive powers of man in the mechanical sciences. The better arrangement of the business of the institution, so as to secure economy of time and promote familiar intercourse among the members occupies the first part of the address. Mr. Cubitt then announces that a resolution has been come to by the Council to the effect, that all ex-Presidents of the institution have a seat at the council board as honorary councillors, and in order to afford advice and assistance in the discussion of important questions. The address next alludes to the Royal Commission for the promotion of the great industrial exhibition in 1851, and invites the suggestions, counsel, and aid of the members of the institution in fulfilling the objects for which the President's name has been included in that commission.

Mr. Cubitt then proceeds to say—"Although during the past year there has not been so great a demand for the talents, or the energies of engineers, several remarkable works have been finished, or have far advanced towards completion; I will allude briefly to a few of them, and if others of importance escape notice, it must be attributed to the engineers not having brought accounts of them before the institution, or even incidentally mentioned them in the discussions. Among these, the tubular bridges across the river Conway and the Menai Straits, are pre-eminent, for the boldness of the conception, the scientific simplicity of the design, and the difficulty of the execution. In tracing the original idea of the most advantageous disposition of a certain amount of material, in a tubular form; the more definite conception of a hollow beam, to permit the passage and support the weight of an engine and train; the experiments for determining the proper distribution of the material, to prevent compression or disruption; the arrangements for the construction and building up these gigantic masses of material; the means of floating them to their situations, and of raising them to their ultimate destination, at an elevation of 102 feet above the level of the sea (at high water of spring tides); we must feel justly proud of possessing among us the man whose comprehensive mind could originate this magnificent design, and so successfully perform a portion of the work as to leave no doubt of its ultimate accomplishment. The world already duly appreciates this great undertaking, and we should not be behindhand in testifying our estimate of the bold conception of Mr. Robert Stephenson in the original idea, his professional skill in the design and execution, his care and caution in availing himself of the talents and experience of Mr. W. Fairbairn, and Mr. Eaton Hodgkinson, whose scientific investigations, respecting the strength of cast iron, are so well known to the world, and so highly appreciated by our profession, and his intrusting the general construction and elevation to Mr. Frank Forster and Mr. Edwin Clarke. Upon the merits of all these gentlemen we may look with pardonable pride and partiality; their labours speak for themselves. However advantageous may be the results of this construction, in facilitating an important communication, as I shall have occasion to allude to it hereafter, it has already been extremely useful in directing attention to the more general employment of wrought iron for purposes to which it had not previously been deemed applicable;

and it will be found that its introduction to structures of all kinds will become more common, exactly as the method of using it becomes better understood. May I here be permitted to diverge for an instant, in order to direct attention to a subject of considerable importance to the profession. In the year 1847 a commission was appointed (of which I was named a member) for the purpose of inquiring into the conditions to be observed by engineers, in the application of iron in structures exposed to violent concussions and vibration; and for endeavouring to ascertain such principles and forms, and to establish such rules as should enable the engineer and the mechanic, in their respective spheres, to apply the metal with confidence, and should illustrate, by theory and experiment, the action which would take place, under varying circumstances, in the iron railway bridges which had been erected. Numerous witnesses of great theoretical attainment and practical experience, were examined before the commission, and a very interesting series of experiments was carried on, for ascertaining certain points relative to the compression and extension, the tensile and crushing strength, the effect of statical pressure and vibration, concussion, &c. The result of this laborious investigation is (in the words of the report, which will shortly be made public) that 'considering that the attention of engineers has been sufficiently awakened to the necessity of providing a superabundant strength in railway structures, and also considering the great importance of leaving the genius of scientific men unfettered for the development of a subject, as yet so novel and so rapidly progressive as the construction of railways, we are of opinion that any legislative enactments with respect to the forms and proportions of the iron structures employed therein, would be highly inexpedient. It would be foreign to my present purpose to enlarge upon the importance of this decision; but I must recommend the report to your careful perusal and consideration. The harbours of refuge now in progress are works of national utility. Those at Dover and in the Channel Islands, by Mr. Walker, deserve particular attention. The former has already produced extraordinary effects on the littoral currents, and in the movement of the shingle on the coast, and the latter will afford protection to the storm-driven mariner, where he before expected only danger and death. The Breakwater of Portland Island is important, not only as utilising one of the finest bays on our coast, but also as an immense engineering work, intended to be executed almost entirely by convict labour, and on that account it was necessary to render its construction as simple as possible. This has been achieved by Mr. Rendel, whose design is to form along the site of the intended breakwater a timber staging, carried upon screw piles; on this will be laid railways connected by inclined planes with the quarries on the hill, whence the trains of stones will be brought, and their contents be distributed simultaneously, and in regular thickness over given areas, enabling a careful admixture of large and small materials to be effected, and the whole mass to rise gradually to the surface, and being thus self-supporting, to prevent the washing away of the materials, which has been experienced in other works of a similar nature. The harbour at Holyhead, and the new docks at Leith and at Grimsby, also by Mr. Rendel, do equal credit to his comprehensive designs and his executive skill. In conjunction with these maritime works may be mentioned two lighthouses, both possessing remarkable features. The first is an iron structure, erected on the Bishop's-rock, by Mr. Walker. It is situated about thirty miles from the Land's-end, Cornwall, and four miles due west from the St. Agnes Lighthouse, which would probably not have been constructed had our ancestors possessed the modern facilities for the execution of works of this nature. The position is more exposed to the force of the Atlantic than the famed Eddystone Lighthouse, and the surface of the rock is of such an outline as scarcely to admit of a solid building. It was therefore determined to erect such a structure as should offer little or no opposition to the waves, and bear a light at such an elevation as to render it extensively useful. Six hollow cast iron columns, with a strong bar of wrought iron in each, sunk to the depth of five feet into the rock, forming at the base a hexagon 30 feet in diameter, and tapering upwards, support at a height of about 100 feet, the dwellings of the three light-keepers, with stores and provisions for four months, the whole being surmounted by the lantern. The access to the dwelling is by a centre column of cast iron, containing a spiral staircase. The difficulties overcome in the execution of this bold design can scarcely be appreciated without a more detailed account of them, which, however, I trust will be laid before you during this session.

The other is a stone lighthouse called the Skerryvore, erected by Mr. Alan Stevenson, on a small desolate rock situated about 11 miles W.S.W. of the island of Tyree, and fifty miles from the mainland of Scotland. The rock is exposed to the full fury of the North Atlantic, and is surrounded by an almost perpetual surf. The talent and perseverance of the engineer enabled him, however, to complete, without loss of life or limb—great as were the difficulties he had to contend with—a structure far exceeding the dimensions of the famed Eddystone and Bell-rock Lighthouses, their relative heights being—

The Eddystone	68 feet,
The Bell Rock	100 feet,
The Skerryvore	138 feet, 6 inches.

The difficulties of the construction, the merits of the structure, and the system of lighting, are so fully described in Mr. Stevenson's published account of it, that it is not necessary for me to do more than to point to it, as one of the remarkable works of the present day, of which we have justly reason to be proud. In steam navigation, great efforts have been made by some of the principal marine engineers, and the builders of wood and iron vessels. The result has been the production of four steamers, with engines by Messrs. Seaward, Miller, Penn, and Forrester, in vessels built respectively by Messrs. Mare, Miller, Thompson, and Laird, for conveying the mails; and an equal number of engines by Messrs. Maudslay and Field, Forrester and Bury, in vessels by Messrs. Wigram, Mare, Laird, and Vernon, for carrying passengers between Holyhead and Dublin, which have attained the speed of nearly eighteen miles per hour, and accomplish the passage, on an average, in four hours. By these means, when the Britannia tubular bridge is completed, the journey between London and Dublin may be accomplished within eleven hours. This is an extraordinary advance upon the opinions of only a few years since, when it was reported to be possible to perform the same distance in 14 hours. The excellent machinery of Messrs. Maudslay and Field, and of Messrs. Forrester and Co., in the iron steamers built by Mr. C. Mare, and Mr. J. Laird, have also contributed mainly in accomplishing a journey to Paris, as we have recently seen it performed, in eight hours and a half; giving a death-blow to the onerous system of passports, which hitherto interfered so materially with that free and unrestricted communication so essential for the mutual benefit of the two countries. In the accomplishment of this rapid communication with Paris, I may be permitted to feel some pride, as, in my capacity of engineer of the South Eastern, and in my professional connexion with the Boulogne and Amiens railways, the possibility of expediting the intercourse between the two capitals, constantly occupied my mind; and so long ago as in June, 1843, before the present fast steam-boats were placed on the station, I undertook and accomplished the task of conveying the directors and their friends from London to Boulogne, and home again, between six o'clock in the morning, and 10 o'clock in the evening, with a sufficient interval for a public reception at Boulogne. Among the builders of steam-vessels, Mr. Scott Russell must be particularly mentioned, for the successful investigation and application of the wave lines to the forms of vessels, so that the curves of least disturbance can at once be adapted to a vessel, the ultimate or greatest velocity of which has been previously determined; and thus high speeds, and easy motion through the water, can be attained; whilst a given immersion is arrived at with certainty. These points were remarkably shown in the *Manchester*, a vessel for carrying passengers across the Humber, at New Holland, and with its consort steamer, the *Sheffield*, constructed by Messrs. Rennie, becoming, as it were, floating bridges, completing the line of the Manchester, Sheffield, and Lincolnshire Railway, and conveying the contents of the trains, from point to point, at a speed of about 16 miles an hour. In connection with this railway must be mentioned the large pontoon, recently built by Messrs. E. B. Wilson and Co. of Leeds, from the design and under the direction of Mr. John Fowler. This immense iron vessel, which is 400 feet long, 50 feet wide, and 8 feet deep, with a deck area of 20,000 square feet, serves as a floating landing stage for these fast passage steamers, rendering the railway trains independent of the tide and of the muddy shores of the Humber. The deck area of this landing stage is about half that of a somewhat similar structure built a short time previous from my designs, and under my direction at Liverpool, and of which a description and drawings will be prepared for an early meeting of the institution; as an earnest of my intention to practise what I have ventured to impress upon all those, who not only possess the information, but the power of imparting it, for the benefit of their professional brethren. A number of fine steamers have also been constructed for the Government, for private companies, and for Foreign States, in which the beautiful engines of Maudslay and Field, Miller, Seaward, Penn, Napier, Rennie, and others, have fully maintained their European reputation. This incomplete sketch of a few of the engineering works of the past year, leaves untouched that vast subject, the railway system, towards the completion of which, much has been accomplished within the last 12 months, without that public excitement which accompanied all its former progress. There are now nearly 5,500 miles of railway completed in Great Britain, at a cost of about 220,000,000*l.* sterling, which immense sum, derived from private sources, has been expended within the realm, encouraged in an extraordinary degree productive industry of all kinds, and inducing a revolution in all mercantile transactions, and social relations. The steam-engine and the power-loom have been regarded by the soberminded political economist as the real sources of the power and influence of Great Britain, and though the gallantry of her hardy sons, both in the military and the naval services may have been more publicly apparent, and have, in fact, inestimably valuable when called into action, it is the productive classes of this country that constitute its real strength. The example of England, in boldly abandoning the finest roads, and adopting throughout the length and breadth of the land, a network of iron ways, over which, by the aid of steam, passengers and merchandise are conveyed at a velocity, which, at its first proposition, was by the world deemed worse than visionary, first filled our continental neighbours with astonishment, and then compelled their imitation, so that within a few years, by this new power, the relative positions of the continental states are changed, and the ultimate effect must be to introduce wants, and consequently civilisation, to the most remote corners of the world."

The address closes by inviting the particular attention of the association to the sanitary question—to the drainage and sewerage—the paving, lighting, and cleansing of cities and towns—the more copious and less expensive supplies of water and gas, and in conjunction with the architects, the improvements of the dwellings of the labouring classes; the establishment of baths and wash-houses; and the introduction of abbatoirs.

Tuesday, January 15, 1850.

WILLIAM CUBITT, Esq., President, in the Chair.

THE Paper read was "An Account of the Blackfriars Landing Pier," by Mr. F. Lawrence. This pier commences on the Middlesex side of the river, to the east of Blackfriars Bridge, at Chatham Place, and continues parallel to the bridge, and at a distance of forty feet from it, for a length of one hundred and eighty-five feet. The body of the pier (exclusive of the head) is supported on four piers, two of which consist of a single row, and two of a double row of piling, forming three spans of fifty feet each, and having about eight feet headway under them at high-water. The floating barge, or dumby, on which the passengers land, is one hundred feet long and twenty-five feet wide, rising and falling with the tide, in grooves at each end, formed by piles and protected by dolphins. The connection between the dumby and the pier is by a moveable stage eight feet wide and fifty feet long, secured to the pier head, at one end by a hinge joint, and the other end similarly connected to a flight of steps on wheels, which moves on a tramway fixed to the deck of the barge. The principal portion of the timber used in its construction was fir, but the whole, whether of fir or oak, was impregnated by Payne's process, those portions below high-water mark being further protected by a coating of Stockholm tar. The whole of the cast and wrought iron work was galvanised.

The Corporation of London had observed the necessity for an improved landing-place, so early as 1841, but it was not until a fatal accident occurred in 1844, that any decided steps were taken in the matter : then Messrs. Walker and Burges received instructions to prepare a design, which was approved, and the pier was commenced in March, 1845, and completed in October of the same year, under the superintendence of Mr. Hewett, M. Inst. C. E. The total cost was about £4000.

The next paper read was a "Description of a Timber Bridge erected over the River Ouse, on the line of the Lynn and Ely Railway," by Mr. J. S. Valentine, M. Inst. C. E. The total length of this bridge was 450 feet, divided into eleven bays, ten of 30 feet span each, and one over the river of 120 feet span on the square, and one 121 feet 6 inches on the skew. The river-opening consisted of three laminated timber bows, resting upon stone piers, the material for which was procured from the New Leeds Quarries. The dimensions of the bows were, length of chord, 121 feet 6 inches; versed sine, 14 feet 2 inches; and their depth, 3 feet 8 inches; the width of the outer bows was 2 feet 2 inches, that of the centre bow 2 feet 9 inches. They were formed of fifteen layers of three inch deals, abutting upon a cast-iron plate bolted to the tie-beams, which consisted of two whole timbers scarfed and bolted together. Each tie-beam was suspended from the bows by thirteen wrought-iron rods, two inches in diameter, and between these diagonal struts were fitted. Transverse joists, notched on the tie-beams, extended across the whole width of the bridge, and on these the rail bearers were laid, the intervening spaces being filled with three inch deals, laid longitudinally.

The works were commenced in the autumn of 1846, and completed in October, 1847; the total cost of the superstructure being about £3744. When tested, by placing three locomotive engines on each line of rails, the total deflection was only three-eighths of an inch.

Tuesday, January 22, 1850.

WILLIAM CUBITT, Esq., President, in the Chair.

THE paper read was—"On the Periodical Alternations and Progressive Permanent Depression of the Chalk Water Level under London," by the Rev. J. C. Clutterbuck.

The author began by defining the Chalk Water level to be, "the height to which the water rises at any point or continuous series of points in the chalk, or *from* the chalk in perforations, through the London and plastic clays, above the chalk." The term 'Artesioid' was used to describe those wells sunk through the London and plastic clays, in which the water rose from the chalk, or the sands of the plastic clay formation, above the level of those strata, though it might not rise to, or overflow the surface of the ground.

Reference was made to papers read before the Institution in 1842 and 1843, in which it was shown that the Chalk Water level was described by an inclined line drawn from the highest level at which the water accumulated in the chalk, to the lowest proximate vent, or outfall : a general rule, which was found to hold good, not only where the water was found by sinking into a permeable stratum, but where, as in the London Basin, the water rose from a permeable stratum, through perforations in any impermeable stratum above it.

The example treated of in the paper, was described by a line inclining at an average of about thirteen feet in a mile, from the outcrop of the London and plastic clays, to mean tide level in the Thames, below London Bridge.

The height to which water rose in the Paris Basin, from the lower green sand, was adduced in confirmation of that rule.

Before the artesian well at Grenelle was bored, M. Arago calculated that the water would rise above the level of the soil at Paris, as it rose above that level at Elbeuf, near Rouen.

The height at which the water was found in the lower green sand, near Troyes, being one hundred metres above Paris, and one hundred and thirty-one metres above the sea, the author found that a line drawn from that point, to the level of the sea at Havre (where the green sand cropped out), passed over Paris and Elbeuf, at the elevation to which the water actually rose in both places.

A calculation based on the same principle (taking the level of the water in the lower green sand, at Leighton Buzzard, at two hundred and eighty feet above the sea), showed, that if the chalk and gault were bored through in London, the water from the green sand would rise one hundred and fifty feet above Trinity high water mark.

Passing from the natural, to the actual condition of the chalk-water level, under London, there was a general permanent depression of from fifty feet to sixty feet below Trinity high water mark.

Measurements of a well in London, in which the level was seldom disturbed, showed periodical alternations, coincident with the exhaustion and replenishment of the chalk stratum by natural causes, to the amount of four feet six inches, and a permanent depression of one foot six inches per annum, or twelve feet in eight years.

Again, referring to former calculations, it was shown, that the margin of this depression was extending in a greater ratio towards the North, than to the South, or S.E. Since 1843, the level was permanently depressed at Hampstead Road, ten feet ; Camden Town, nineteen feet; Kilburn, twenty feet; and Cricklewood, ten feet. The limit of the depression being, in 1843, between the latter places.

Allusion was then made, to the influx of water at the point where the Thames passed over the outcrop of the sands of the plastic clay formation, and the chalk, as a point to be determined by geological inquiry, and connected with observations as to the action of the tides on the level, and the chemical quality of the water, in that neighbourhood.

The general conclusion drawn from all these facts was, that the rapidity of exhaustion from Artesian wells under London, greatly exceeded the rapidity of supply ; that the amount of defalcation was marked, and could be measured by the extension of a progressive permanent depression, proving that the supply of water from the chalk stratum became each year more precarious, and less to be depended upon, even should there be no addition to the Artesioid wells in and around the metropolis.

In the discussion which ensued, it was shown, that only such a supply of water percolated annually through the chalk stratum, as could be accounted for by the discharge from the rivers of the upper district. The results yielded by Dalton's Rain Gauge, as used by Mr. John Dickinson, were adduced in proof of this position.

The chemical analysis of the water from wells sunk into the chalk, showed the probability of an influx of the tidal water of the Thames, to replenish the vacuum caused by the immense extent of pumping from the London wells.

On the other hand it was contended, that from the great extent of surface whence the chalk derived its supply, there might be such a surplus store of water, as would warrant any amount of pumping, for the domestic supply for the metropolis.

The discussion was announced to be continued at the meeting of Tuesday, January 29th, which would be entirely devoted to it.

CHEMICAL SOCIETY OF LONDON.

ANALYSIS OF THE WELL WATER AT THE ROYAL MINT, WITH SOME REMARKS ON THE WATERS ON THE LONDON WELLS. BY PROFESSOR BRANDE, F.R.S., V.P.C.S., &c.

Previous to the year 1842, the Mint was supplied with water principally from two sources; the dwelling-houses, offices, and a part of the works, by the New River Company, and the steam engines, by wells, partly supplied by so-called land springs, and partly by a tunnel communication with the Tower moat: the principal supplies being derived from the latter, so that when, in consequence of any works carrying on at the tower, the access of the river to the moat was impeded, the operations of the Mint were not unfrequently obliged to be suspended ; besides which, the water derived from that source was always muddy, and often very foul and offensive. In consequence of this bad condition of the water in the tower moat, and the effluvia arising from it in hot weather, it was resolved in the year 1843 to drain and lay it dry. The Mint was accordingly deprived of its supply of water from that source ; and the land springs supplying the wells of the several steam engines, to say nothing of the impurity and hardness of the water thence derived, were found wholly inadequate to the wants of the engines. It therefore became necessary to have recourse to the New River Company for such additional supplies of water as might be wanted for carrying on the business of the Mint, and for this their charges, as far as the steam engines were concerned, were at the rate of £10 per horse-power per annum ; but from various causes, these supplies could not always be depended upon, so that on several occasions a temporary suspension of the business of the Mint was the consequence of a deficient supply of water. Under these circumstances, it became my duty to suggest to the master of the Mint the adoption of such measures as might ensure for the future a regular and adequate supply of water for the use of the whole establishment, and to this end it was necessary, in the first instance to

make myself accurately acquainted with the actual condition of the several wells existing in the Mint, and the quantity and quality of the water which might be derived from them. I was therefore authorized by the Master of the Mint to consult with Mr. Thomas Clark, an experienced well-engineer, in reference to the subject ; and I accordingly desired him to examine into the condition and capabilities of all the wells, shafts, and tunnels, connected with the supplies of water throughout the building. This examination was carefully and effectually accomplished, and it appeared that the several wells were in a very dilapidated, and some of them in a very dangerous state ; that few of them were so situated or conditioned as to admit of being sufficiently or safely deepened, so as to yield an adequate supply of water ; and that, as respected the wells in the several engine-houses, they were mere reservoirs connected with the tunnel-shaft from the tower, and therefore, almost exclusively supplied from the muddy source of the Tower moat.

Having personally convinced myself of the correctness of this report, and having had Mr. Clark's statement corroborated by Mr. George Rennie, I represented the matter in detail to the master of the Mint, and suggested three plans for consideration—namely :

1. To derive the requisite supplies of water from the water companies.
2. To repair the present wells, and to deepen such of them as would admit of that operation.
3. To sink an entirely new well.

And I strongly urged the adoption of the latter alternative, which, after due consideration, was agreed to. I therefore obtained proper plans and estimates from Mr. Clark, which, after having been submitted to the Board of Woods, and by their direction to Major Jebb, were ultimately ordered to be carried into execution.

These plans included the sinking of an entirely new well ; the erection of a capacious water tank, at a sufficient height to supply the ordinary demands of the Mint ; proper pumps for raising the water, and mains for distributing it over all parts of the buildings, together with fire-cocks, and other arrangements, the details of which would be irrelevant to the object of this communication.

It may be right to premise, that the total depth of this new well is about 426 feet; that the depth from the surface down to the chalk is about 224 feet, and the borings into the chalk about 202 feet ; the following being the well-sinker's account of the strata gone through, namely :

	Feet.
Made earth	11
Gravel and sand (with water)	13
Blue clay, with a few sandy veins (no water) ...	98
Coloured sand and pebbles (abundance of water) ...	14
Dark sand, with veins of clay (little water) ..	4
Mottled clay (dry)	6
Loamy sand and dark clay (little water) ...	5
Blue clay with shells	6
White rock (quite dry)	3
Green sand rock, and pebbles (dry)	3
Loamy green sand and black pebbles (little water)	5
Green sand and pebbles (abundance of water) ...	6
Dark sand with shells	40
Flints	10
Chalk	202
	426

The lining of the upper part of the well through the gravel and into the blue clay, is composed of stout cast iron cylinders, 1¼-inch thick, and eight feet clear diameter ; they are made in five feet lengths, with internal flanges three inches wide, packed and jointed with strong bolts and nuts ; these prevent all access of the land springs from above. The shaft is then steined to the depth of 88 feet, (that is nearly through the blue clay,) in 9-inch cemented brickwork ; after which, cast-iron cylinders are resumed of seven feet diameter, and these are continued down to the chalk ; but after passing through the stratum of mottled clay, they include a series of cylinders of six feet diameter, the space between the outer and inner cylinders being filled with gravel-pebbles ; a bore pipe, 20 inches diameter, and 45 feet long, is then driven to about ten feet into the chalk, and through this the boring is continued by an 18-inch augur, to the entire depth of the well. This well, and all the works connected with it, were completed at Christmas, 1846 ; and on the 1st of January, 1847, the whole of the works of the Mint, and the dwelling-houses were supplied with the water, which is raised in a six-inch main to a height of 50 feet above the surface, or 130 feet above the average level of the water in the well, and is delivered at the rate of 240 gallons per minute, by means of three pumps of 9-inch diameter, and 18-inch stroke, into a tank supported upon a building of brickwork. This tank is 100 feet long, 30 feet wide, and five deep; it contains, therefore, 13,000 cubic feet of water, or 93,750 imperial gallons. Two six-inch cast iron mains, furnished with proper slide valves, descend from this tank, one passing on either side of the mint, so as conveniently to supply the whole of the establishment, the daily consumption of water frequently exceeding 4,000 gallons: besides which a daily supply of 6,000 gallons is delivered, by means of a main laid from the mint, across Tower-hill to the Tower, for the use of the inhabitants and the garrison, there being at present no serviceable wells in that fortress, and the water derived from the adjacent river being objectionable in point of cleanliness. The average height which the water attains in the shaft of the Mint well is 80 feet from the surface. After a day's pumping it is lowered, upon an average, 20 feet, but there it remains stationary, the flow of water from below maintaining the level, or in other words, delivering at the rate of about 240 gallons per minute. Before this well was completed, and before the boring into the chalk had been accomplished, the water derived from it contained 44 grains of dry saline matter in the imperial gallon. At present the machinery being complete, and the well in full and daily use, the mean of several experiments in reference to the solid matter contained in the imperial gallon of the water, amounts to 37·5 grains. The substances contained in each gallon of the water are as follows:—

Sulphuric acid	...	...	...	...	...	7·44
Chlorine	...	...	...	...	...	6·31
Carbonic acid (after boiling)	...	...	...	...	5·84
Silica	...	...	...	...	...	0·50
Sodium (combined with chlorine)	...	...	...	4·22
Soda (combined with sulphuric and carbonic acids)	...	10·82
Lime	...	...	...	...	...	1·96
Magnesia ...	...	...	...	...	...	0·71
Organic matter						
Phosphoric acid }	...	...	...	...	traces.
Iron						

The water evaporated to one-fifth of its bulk, and filtered, had lost almost every trace of lime and of magnesia, so that it is probable that the greater part of these substances were held in the state of carbonates, by excess of carbonic acid. The carbonate of lime forms films during boiling, which subside, and appear under the microscope in the form of very minute acicular crystals. The crystalline deposit obtained by slowly evaporating the water, after the precipitated carbonate of lime has been separated by filtration, exhibits, under the microscope, three distinct forms—namely, cubes (of chloride of sodium) prisms, which lie distinct upon the other salts, and are efflorescent (sulphate of soda); and small aggregates of rhomboids, intermixed with small spherical particles, like pin-heads (carbonate of soda). The residue of the evaporation of the water, after having been gradually raised to a dull red heat, acquired a grey tint, and exhaled a slight odour of burning azotized matter; and a piece of moistened turmeric paper, held in the evolved vapour was transitorily reddened.

I have not been able to detect any potassa in this water; and only a slight indication of the presence of a phosphate, in the precipitate deposited by the water during boiling.

Upon the whole, I am inclined to regard the following as a tolerably correct statement of the proximate saline components of this water:—

						Grains in the Imperial gallon.
Chloride of sodium	...	...	...	...	...	10·53
Sulphate of soda ...	...	...	...	...	13·14
Carbonate of soda	...	...	...	...	...	8·63
Carbonate of lime ...	...	...	...	...	3·50
Carbonate of magnesia	...	...	...	...	1·50
Silica	...	...	...	...	...	·50
Organic matter						
Iron }	...	...	...	...	traces.
Phosphoric acid						
						37·80

The specific gravity of the water at 55· is 10,007. Its gaseous contents I have not ascertained.

I have examined the water of several other wells in and about London,

some of which derive their supplies from the sands under the blue clay, and others to a greater or less extent also from borings into the chalk, and I think that in most cases the latter waters are the more pure; that is, that in proportion as the borings are deepened into the chalk, the less are the solid contents of the water. There are in London and its vicinity some very deep wells, which yet do not reach the chalk; and others, of a less depth, which are carried into it; arising out of inequalities in the surface of the chalk, and the varying thickness of the blue clay itself; so that the variations in the relative quantity of solid matter in the waters derived from these wells, is no criterion of their respective depths.

The *shallow wells* of the London district, by which I mean those which do not penetrate the blue clay, but derive their supplies from the gravels and sands above it, yield water of varying quality, but always much less pure than that of the deeper wells, and generally abounding in sulphate of lime, and consequently eminently *hard*, as respects the decomposition of soap, and other common culinary uses. There are many of these wells in which analysis detects indications of contamination by sewers, and by the vicinity of gas pipes, and some of them have been disused and filled up on that account. There are also, as is well known, many which are either in churchyards or upon their boundaries; and it is from these parish pumps that the neighbourhood often exclusively derive their supply of drinking water. I am at present examining the waters of several of these wells. In those which I have already examined, I have been struck with the abundance of *nitrates*, generally nitrate of lime; and this, in some of them, is accompanied by what may be termed a large, proportion of organic matter, so large, indeed, that on proceeding in one case to heat the dry residue of the water to redness, a deflagration ensued; and yet this water is bright and colourless, has no unpleasant taste, and is abundantly resorted to as very superior spring water, by a very populous neighbourhood.

How far such waters may or may not be salubrious is not a question here to be discussed; but in some cases there can, I suppose, be no doubt upon the subject, inasmuch as I have found two of these waters of an evident, though slight, brown or peaty tinge, as furnished from the well, even becoming brown on evaporation, and yielding abundant evidence of containing that species of humic extractive in which the adjacent soil no doubt abounds. I have in no instance been able to detect ammoniacal salts in any of these waters; but I presume that the nitric acid which they contain is the result of the oxidizement of ammonia.

It was my wish to have laid some of the results of these analyses more in detail before the Society. My apology for such imperfect details is, that the important subject of the condition of the waters of London, and its vicinity, may meet with the attention it deserves, and that the comprehensive subject of the metropolitan supply of water may be scientifically, accurately, and dispassionately considered by those who are adequate to the task. As regards the leading question of river supplies on the one hand, and artesian supplies on the other, I cannot, however, help expressing myself decidedly in favour of the former. Deep wells are pre-eminently valuable for local uses, but the peculiarities of the waters which they afford, the depth from which, in many situations, and under most circumstances, those waters must be raised; the possibility, and I think I may say, probability, of the inadequacy of their supply, and the chances of their mutual interference, are some of the circumstances which in my mind, should be well weighed, before the gigantic scheme of the supply of the metropolis from such sources is seriously entertained. On the other hand, pure river water is already upon the surface, in various quarters, in unlimited quantity, and at no great distance, and when filtered, an operation which, as experience has shown, is attainable to any extent, its quality is in all respects superior. That many parts of London are badly and inefficiently supplied with water, and that in some places none is laid on, cannot be denied, but a slight movement in a proper direction would, I think, remedy all real evils under this head. I must further beg leave to express my opinion in favour of the adequacy of the existing water companies to the accomplishment of all that can be reasonably required; the magnitude of their united means, the general excellence of their arrangements, the practical skill with which they have been devised and executed, and the resources which are still open to them, where increase of supply is demanded, are the circumstances upon which I found this opinion.

I shall conclude with a short comparative table, shewing the relative quantity of solid matter contained in such river and spring waters as have been carefully analysed; intending, upon a future occasion, to extend the list to give the details of the analysis, and the names of the analysts: in their present imperfect state, however, the following details will serve to illustrate some of the points touched upon in the preceding notice. The wells which are termed *deep* derive their water from the strata below the blue clay, and some of them penetrate into the chalk; those termed *shallow* are supplied from the strata above the blue clay. This is the case with most of the common London wells, which, however, are often steined to a considerable depth in the clay, for the purpose of forming a reservoir.

					Solid matter in imp. gal.
Thames at Greenwich	...	...	...	...	27.9
„ London	...	...	...	...	28.0
„ Westminster	...	...	...		24.4
„ Brentford	...	...	...		19.2
„ Twickenham	...	...	...	...	22.4
„ Teddington	...	...	...	...	17.4
Average of the Thames between Teddington & Greenwich					23.2
New River	...	...	...	...	19.2
Colne	...	...	...	...	21.3
Lea	...	...	...	...	23.7
Ravensborne, at Deptford	...	...	...		20.0
Combe and Delafield's brewery, Long Acre—deep well					56.8
Apothecaries' Hall, Blackfriars			...	„	45.0
Notting Hill	...	...	...	„	66.6
Royal Mint	...	...	...	„	37.8
Hampstead Waterworks	...	...	„	40.0
Berkley-square	...	...	...	„	60.0
Tilbury Fort	...	...	...	„	75.0
Goding's brewery, Lambeth	...	...	„	50.0
„ „ „	...	...	shallow well		110.0
More's brewery, Old-street	...	...	deep well		38.9
„ „ „	...	...	shallow well		110.0
Trafalgar-square fountains	...	...	deep well		68.9
Well in St. Paul's Churchyard	...	...	...		75.0
„ Bream's-buildings	...	...	...		115.0
„ St. Giles', Holborn	...	...	...		105.0
„ St. Martin's, Charing-cross	...	...		95.0
„ Postern-row, Tower	...	...	...		88.0
Artesian well at Grenelle, Paris	...	...	...		9.86

REPORT OF THE COMMITTEE ON THE REFORM OF THE PATENT LAWS.

WE doubt not that our readers have taken an interest in the portions of the evidence on this subject which have appeared in our pages, and we propose now to sum up the more important points, and to compare the evidence of the various witnesses. The improvements which might be effected in the administration of the present laws, claim the first consideration, both because a step towards reform has already been taken in that direction, and because such observations do not bring us into collision with those spiders—the law-yers, who have thrown their web of technicalities and forms around their prey with their usual unrelaxing grasp.

The first evil is the multiplicity of enrolment offices.

On this subject Mr. Bennet Woodcroft, patentee, thus states his experience of this evil, which, fortunately for all inventors, has been, to some extent, re-medied by closing two out of the three offices—" If, to-morrow, I thought I had made an original invention, and I was desirous of ascertaining the fact, there is another crying evil which I will state. I go first to the Enrolment Office. *There are three Enrolment Offices.* One at the top of Chancery-lane is called the Enrolment Office, another the Petty Bag Office, and the other the Rolls Chapel Office. If I want to see Thomas Savery's patent of 1696, I go and ask ' Have you Thomas Savery's patent of 1696?' They say, ' We will look in the list;' and whether they find it or not, they make you pay a fee, besides unavoidably detaining you some time, and then, per-haps, the answer is ' No, we have not got it.' ' Where can I find it?' ' We cannot direct you to either office.' Then I go to the Rolls Office and say, ' Have you Thomas Savery's patent of 1696?' A search is made, and they say, ' No, we have no such patent.' But there is the fee to pay. Then there is a third search to make, provided the specification had not been enrolled in the last office, and they say, ' No, the patent was granted, but there is no specification.' But there is the fee to pay. It is not the fees alone that I complain of, but the great time lost by the inventor in going

from one office to another; for if you go for a second search that you wish to make, you have all the same ground to go over again."

The patent agents also are unanimous in condemning this ingenious method of wasting the time and money of the public. The next grievance is one peculiarly trying to the non-professional man. We allude to the method of writing the specification in an *engrossing hand* on a *roll* of parchment. When the unhappy inventor, so graphically described by Mr. Woodcroft, has at last, after being bandied from one office to another, caught his specification—that mysterious document which is to enable him to profit by the dearly-bought experience of those who went before him—and the clerk, in his dry official way, has unrolled the seemingly interminable strip of parchment, like a mummy, it is then that his chief trouble begins. By the time that he has deciphered the hieroglyphics on a single skin of parch-ment, at the rate of two lines per minute, and has rolled and unrolled it some dozen times, his patience is pretty well exhausted, and he pulls out his pencil and piece of paper, following Captain Cuttle's maxim—" When found, to make a note on.' The clerk, however, who has been keeping his eye on him, here interposes, and. politely informs him that " Such a pro-ceeding is quite at variance with the rules of the office." We have heard of one daring individual who persisted in defiance of this mandate, but we have no doubt that he knew very well he would never have occasion to go to the office again. Experience, of course, puts the inquirer up to various dodges to evade this monopolizing regulation, but the whole system is, we hope, so near its downfall, that it will not be necessary to give our readers any instruction on this point.

Let us see what professional men have to say on this part of the subject.

Mr. Edmunds.—" I would recommend that specifications should be all written in one shape, that they should be deposited in the Great Seal Patent Office; one search would then suffice and one fee. I would also recommend that specifications should be all written in one shape, that they should be deposited in the Great Seal Patent Office, and be bound in volumes there for the convenience of reference ; thus saving the expense of the engrossment on the roll in the Enrolment Office, and also affording a safe-guard against errors in engrossing."

Mr. Carpmael appears to entertain peculiar views on this subject, for, in answer to question 707, " Could any additional facilities be given in the search for patents?" he answers, " I think not ; it is well conducted at the present time." This gentleman, however, has, it would appear, a very good reason for not wishing to disturb the present state of things, for he tells us (*ante* question 627) that half the patents at present pass through his hands.

Mr. W. Spence.—" There is a defective index (of existing patents). They are a particular document, which only a man accustomed to them knows how to read, so as readily to see where the point of the matter is contained. It would also be better if, instead of keeping the records in the form of a roll of parchment, as they are now and written in ' engrossing hand,' they were transcribed into a book in plain hand-writing ; the drawings, too, being folded to suit the size of the book, which should be folio size. The drawings are now folded so as to come within the ten inches width of the roll, and tacked on to the roll at intervals. This is an inconvenient arrangement when the drawings are large and numerous, especially when the description is long also. In addition to this inconvenience, the hand-writing is often very unintelligible.

Mr. C. Barlow.—Question 1227—" Are the present facilities for searching in the Enrolment Offices sufficient?" " No, they are very objectionable. In the Enrolment Office you are not allowed to copy or to make notes or memoranda. Now, it is necessary and useful for the public that abstracts or reports of such specifications should be made for their benefit, in order, in the first place, that they may know how to improve upon what has already been done; and, secondly, that they may avoid infringing upon other people's rights. Some of these specifications amount to thirty-five or forty skins of parchment, with as many sheets of drawings ; and it is almost im-possible, to any other than a person practically conversant with the peculiar branch of business to which the patent relates, to give even a general out-line of the specified inventions, and, therefore, I think parties ought to be allowed to make memoranda, if not to copy. The reason I apprehend is, that it might interfere with making what are called office copies, if persons could copy for themselves, or make extracts. If you want a faithful verba-tim report of a specification at present, you have to pay for an attested copy. I think it would be extremely desirable that the specifications should be enrolled in book-form by the patentee, not, as at present, upon a skin of parchment, and then afterwards copied upon a roll or skin, which is very tiresome to read, being in old English. They should be enrolled in legible characters in book-form, and kept classified, to be open for reference upon payment of either 6d. or 1s."

We must reserve our remarks on the changes that might be advantageously made in the law itself until our next article.

RECENT AMERICAN PATENTS.

Benjamin M. Otis, Cleveland, Cayuhoga county, Ohio, *for an improvement in self-acting cheese-presses.* March 27.

THE patentee says,—" The nature of my invention consists in the arrangement of two levers, in connexion with certain wheels, in such a manner that a continual and constantly increasing pressure is produced simply by the gravity or weight of the substance to be pressed."

Claim.—" What I claim as my invention is the combination and arrangement of two levers with their corresponding pairs of pulleys, having cords passing around them to their respective barrels."

Benjamin W. Bean, City of New York, *for a machine for sewing cloth of all kinds with a running stitch.* Patented March 4, 1843; re-issued March 10.

THE patentee says,—" My invention consists of a combination of gear wheels and a needle, so applied together, and arranged with respect to each other, that the gear wheels, when they are revolved, and cloth is passed between them, shall make or form what I term the doubles, or the bends, corrugations, or foldings of the edges of the cloth, necessary for the passage of the needle through it, in order to the performance of the sewing of the running stitch."

Claim.—" What I claim as my invention is the combination of a straight or curved needle, and two or more gear wheels, for forming the doubles or corrugations of the cloth, the whole being made to operate essentially as specified. And, in combination therewith, I claim one or more cogged wheels, applied as specified, and for the purpose of advancing the doubles of the cloth along the needle as above explained.

" I also claim the mode of preventing either retrogradation or any improper movement of the needle, viz., by making it with a crook or bend, and placing against said bend one, two, or more wheels, as described."

John Ericsson, City of New York, *for the employment of an auxiliary engine in combination with the condenser pump.* April 3.

THE patentee says,—" The object of my invention is to condense the steam without admixture with the condensing water, and to condense the steam that escapes from the safety valve, and also for the production of fresh water for any other use."

Henry R. Worthington and William H. Baker, City of New York, *for an improved method of measuring the action of the valves in direct action pumping engines.* April 3.

CLAIM.—" What we claim as new is the removing or reducing the resistance against the pump piston, in direct action steam pumps, at the proper time in the stroke, by effecting a connexion between the water on both sides of the piston, in order to allow either the momentum of the moving parts, or the expansion of the steam already within the cylinder, or both conjoined, to act as explained, to throw the steam valve across the ports with certainty, whether at high or low speeds.

" 2nd—We claim the method described of effecting the before-mentioned and claimed object, namely, by making two passages into each end of the cylinder, across one of which the piston is forced, opening, by this means, free communication between the two ends of the cylinder."

William S. Jewett, City of New York, *for an improvement in shaving brushes.* April 10.

CLAIM.—" What I claim as my invention is the introduction of the soap by means of the screw and tube, through the handle into the brush, by which it may be fully impregnated; and also the combination, in one, of the box and brush, thereby saving time and trouble, for it is only necessary to wet the brush, and while the lather is making on the face the beard is softened."

ANALYSIS OF PATENTS.

William Preddy, of Taunton, Somerset, watchmaker, *for improvements in watch-keys and other instruments for winding up watches and other time-keepers.* June 12, 1849.

THIS invention consists in applying a plug to the ordinary watch-key, which serves to fill up the socket, and prevents any dust from accumulating therein, which dust, in ordinary keys, insinuates itself into the interior of the watch when the key is used. A spiral spring at the back of the plug allows it to recede when the key is to be used. Various modifications are described.

Henry Mills Stowe, of Bermuda, master of the brig *James, for improvements in blocks and sheaves.* June 20, 1849.

IN wood blocks, as at present constructed, the sheave pins are supported in the cheeks of the block, and the strain taken through the latter; the patentee proposes to add a fork of metal, embracing the sides of the block, and carrying the sheave pins. The fork-piece has a hook at top, to which the rope is connected. The improvement in the sheaves consists in inserting a metal bush, screwed on the outside, whereby it is fixed in the sheave, which gives a smooth bearing surface on the pin.

Edward Lyon Berthon, clerk, B. A., of Fareham, Southampton, *for an instrument to show the velocity of a ship or other vessel propelled through the water by wind, steam, or other moving power.* June 20, 1849.

THIS invention consists of a mercury guage, which is acted upon by the pressure of the water opposed to the motion of the vessel. A pipe is carried through a stuffing box in the bottom of the vessel, and has its lower end closed, an opening being made in the side to admit the water. This opening may be kept exactly opposite the current by means of a fantail or rudder, or it may be moved by hand, by the observer, until a maximum pressure is indicated. The pipe is connected by flexible tubing with a syphon guage, the two legs of which are connected by a capillary tube (to diminish the sensitiveness, we presume). This guage is placed in the cabin, or other convenient part of the vessel, for observation, and is fitted with mercury, as in the ordinary steam guage. The water contained in the pipes being acted upon by the motion of the vessel through the water, the level of the mercury will vary as the pressure, and its indications, read off on a suitable scale, will give the speed of the vessel, the scale of the divisions being as the squares of the velocities. An index is provided, by means of which it can be ascertained in what position the hole at the lower end of the pipe is, with respect to the keel of the vessel.

Thomas Merchant, of Derby, civil engineer, and Robert Harland, of Derby, carriage builder, *for certain improvements in the construction of railway carriages.* June 25, 1849.

THE first part of this invention consists in connecting together the draw-rods and buffer-rods by two horizontal levers, so that they act in conjunction and keep the buffers together, whether the carriages be passing over curved or straight portions of the line, thereby diminishing the oscillation. The second part, in the arrangement of the break; and the third, in the method of constructing the roofs of railway trucks; one portion of the cover being mounted on a pin, on which it can be turned out of the way.

George Benjamin Thorneycroft, of Wolverhampton, iron master, *for improvements in manufacturing railway tyres, axles, and other iron where great strength and durability are required.* June 26, 1849

THESE improvements consist, first, in forming tyre iron with a centre of charcoal iron, to resist the wear, which is greatest at that part. Secondly, in forming axles of a hollow pile of bars, welded together on the outside, but with the centre bar left unwelded, which is effected by coating it with fire-clay. By this means its fibrous character will be preserved. The patentee also proposes to form hollow axles, either by welding a hollow pile, or by welding two halves, either square or semi-cylindrical, with a semi-cavity in each.

James Nasmyth, of Patricroft, near Manchester, engineer, *for certain improvements in the method of, and apparatus for, communicating and regulating the power for driving or working machines employed in manufacturing, dyeing, printing, and finishing textile fabrics.* June 26, 1849.

THE patentee claims the employment of a number of steam engines to drive a number of machines, in place of using one steam engine for the whole, as is usual. Each machine having its own engine, it can be stopped, or the speed varied at pleasure, without interfering with any of the other machinery, and the patentee imagines that the convenience of this arrangement in certain manufactures where regularity of motion and command of speed are points of importance, will compensate for the increased expense in first cost and fuel. The patentee does not claim any particular form of engine, but the improved method of communicating and regulating the power applied to such machinery, and placing the handle of the steam regulator in such a position that the man at the machine may have perfect control over its motion. We may remark that the same principle was proposed by Mr. Hague, of London, who patented an arrangement in which air was made the vehicle of the power from one large engine to a multitude of smaller ones.

Edward Woods, of Liverpool, *for certain improvements in turn-tables.* June 28, 1849.

THE patentee claims—the construction of the skeleton top, or revolving part of turn-tables, of a ring of malleable iron, as an external band, resting on rollers firmly united to two lines of rails, and combined with an interior frame and central pin.

Hiram Tucker, of Roxbury, Massachusetts, U.S., *for a certain new and improved manufacture of mantel-pieces.* November 2, 1849.

THE patentee proposes to form mantel-pieces of cast iron frames, filled in with stained, or otherwise ornamented, glass, which may be bedded in plaster of Paris.

ROYAL STEAM NAVY.

APPOINTMENTS.

Inspector of Steam Machinery.—W. DINNEN, of the steam-department, Somerset-house, who served under commission in Sir C. Napier's squadron, as inspector of steam-machinery afloat, with a rank corresponding to that of commander, is to proceed to join Commodore Martin's squadron in the same capacity. The utmost advantages were gained from Mr. DINNEN's presence in the former squadron, and we doubt not that in the forthcoming trials of the screw-ships great good will result from his inspection.

Engineers.—GEORGE GLASSON, to the *Gladiator.*

Assistant Engineers.—WILLIAM AUSTIN, to the *Fisgard,* JOSHUA C. ROBINSON, to the *Blenheim.* JOHN WILLIAM SMITH, to *Fisgard.* NOAH D. FRY, to the *Terrible.*—J. MAGNALL, to the *Fisgard.* CHARLES PRESGRAVE, HENRY NEWTON, JOHN SHEIL, and JAMES WHEELER, to the *Gladiator.* THOMAS W. WOODCOCK, WILLIAM L. ROBINSON, and ROBERT C. REYNOLDS, to the *Hermes.*

Second Class Assistant Engineer.—JOHN PATTERSON, to the *Blenheim.*

Third Class Assistant Engineers.—JOHN LAMONT and CHARLES H. PUTT, to the *Blenheim.*

DOCKYARD INTELLIGENCE.—TRIAL OF STEAMERS, &c.

WOOLWICH.—On the 10th instant, the *Enterprise* and *Investigator* departed on their mission in search of Sir John Franklin and his gallant comrades. Nothing has been spared that could add to the efficiency of the vessels, or the comfort of the crews, and we fervently hope that their expedition may be attended with success. Several schemes have been proposed for breaking up the ice, in place of sawing it—the usual method in the arctic regions. The plan of using gunpowder would no doubt be very efficacious in a river, where the current would carry away the pieces of ice; but in cases where they had to be hauled on to the solid ice with ropes, the shape and size to which they would be reduced by the explosion, would render them inconvenient to handle. High pressure steam has also been tried, and a block of ice in layers, 14 inches thick and 3 feet square, was cut through the centre in 55 seconds by a jet at 50lbs. pressure, from 1¼ inch pipe. The ice, however, in the polar regions is a very different article from the comparatively lukewarm stuff we boast of. An experiment promising to be of more use, was tried with a balloon, to which was attached a slow match, and a quantity of slips of paper of various brilliant colours, white of course excepted. The combustion of the thread when the match reached it, would shower down the papers from a considerable altitude, and there is no doubt they would be carried a considerable distance. Messages would of course be written or printed on them, and the chances are—that had the last expedition had some means of this kind, we should not so long have remained in suspense of their whereabouts. A number of these balloons have been supplied to the exploring expedition.

PORTSMOUTH.—*Termagant,* 24, steam frigate, 1556 tons, 620 horse power (screw), by Seaward, was tried again on Thursday, at the measured mile in Stoke's bay, under most favourable circumstances, when the following results were realised:—

Runs			min.	sec.			Knots.
First	...	...	6	40	...	...	9
Second	...	...	6	19	...	...	9.490
Third	...	...	6	13	...	...	9.651
Fourth	...	...	6	27	...	...	9.302
Fifth	...	...	6	0	...	...	10.000
Sixth	...	...	6	45	...	...	8.889

averaging a speed of nearly 9½ knots per hour. Her draught of water was as follows:—forward, 16 feet; aft, 18 feet, with 260 tons of coal on board, in addition to her armament of 10 tons; pitch of the new screw 17 feet 2½ inches; pitch of the former screw, 18 feet; vacuum, 27½; revolutions from 36 to 37; steam, 14lb. Mr. Grant's distilling and cooking galley was in work during the trial, and in 12 hours, with the ordinary amount of fire used for cooking the ordinary meal, distilled 500 gallons of pure water from sea water.

Sidon, 22, steam frigate, 1326 tons, 560 h. p., made her first trial on the 16th since her refit. The weather, contrary to its state for some days, was peculiarly adapted for a favourable trial; there was a top-gallant breeze, the tide mostly slack. The vessel was stowed in all respects as for sea, weights being placed in the various receptacles to the amount of the necessary quantities of provisions and water, for three months' service, for a complement of 300 men. All her sea stores were actually on board, and placed in their proper departments; her sails for sea service, and even her bending sails were stowed in the sail-room. Under these circumstances her draught of water was—forward, 16 feet 4 inches; abaft, 16 feet 3 inches; and her ports out of the water as under—foremost port, 9 feet 8 inches; midship port, 8 feet 1 inch; after port, 7 feet, 11 inches; leaving her tremendous battery 8 feet 1 inch clear of the water. She has made eight runs at the measured mile in Stoke's Bay, but two of them being rejected by the officers as incomplete trials, six runs only were allowed to draw the average from. They were as follow:—

First run	...	...	...	11.009 knots per hour.
Second ditto	...	...	...	10.146 ,,
Third ditto	...	...	...	11.077 ,,
Fourth ditto	...	...	...	9.756 ,,
Fifth ditto	...	...	...	11.390 ,,
Sixth ditto	...	...	...	9.375 ,,

yielding as the result an average speed of 10½ knots per hour Unexpected and gratifying as this result was, she would have achieved even a greater speed had the measured water been unobstructed; the coast was crowded by small coasters, and consequently the *Sidon* had to be steered a circuitous course to avoid collision. The engines worked most satisfactorily, and made from 18 to 19 revolutions per minute; pressure of steam 10lb.; height of engine barometer, 26°: quantity of coal on board on leaving the harbour 190 tons in bunkers. The new boilers afforded an ample supply of steam, and are fitted with steam chests separate from the boilers, so that the steam can be taken either from the one or from the other at pleasure, the great advantage of which is, that in preparing for action the steam is taken from the boilers instead of from the steam chest, and the top of the boiler is three feet below the water line, and consequently, it is presumed, out of the range of shot. On the whole we have reason to believe that the *Sidon* is now by far the most perfect steam frigate in the British navy.

She was again taken out on the 18th, in company with the *Terrible.* The *Sidon's* draught was 17 feet 10 inches on an even keel, being weighted as for sea service, and having 600 tons of coals on board. She gave an average speed of 9.356 knots per hour, with 16½ to 17 revolutions. The *Terrible* was ready for sea, with the exception of powder, shells, &c., about 50 tons. Weight of *Sidon's* guns, 1403 cwt.; broadside, 1196 lbs.; tonnage, 1327 tons.

Weight of *Terrible's* guns, 1672 cwt.; broadside, 13,414 lbs.; tonnage, 1847 tons.

THE "POMONE," *versus* THE "ARROGANT."

These two screw vessels have, it appears, had a trial of speed, in which our vessel, the *Arrogant,* beat her competitor. It is difficult, however, to form any correct opinion of the respective merits, from want of sufficient data. We can only give the arguments on both sides, the particulars of the *Arrogant* being taken from the *Arrogant Journal,* (a name which would excite considerable literary wrath on shore), printed and published on board the vessel, and those of the *Pomone,* from her commander, Captain Favin-Leveque, addressed to the editor of the *Marine,* the French *Nautical Standard.*

The *Arrogant, Encounter* and *Hogue,* have been tried together, and the following is the result, as taken from the *Times,* the *Arrogant* being said to be but an indifferent sailer:—

"The following is about the average speed of the three vessels, working full power, no sail set, and slight head swell:—

"The *Arrogant* averaging 8.6 knots per hour; engines making 63 revolutions per minute, consuming 32 tons of coal in 24 hours, and carrying 8¼ days' coal at full power; horse power, 360.

The *Encounter* 9.2 knots per hour; engines making 75 revolutions per minute, consuming 36 tons of coal in 24 hours, and carrying 4½ days' coal, at full power; horse power same as *Arrogant.*

The *Hogue,* average rate 7.2 knots per hour; engines making 49 revolutions per minute, consuming 28 tons of coal in 24 hours. and will carry 7½ days' coal full speed; horse power 450.

The *Arrogant* and *Encounter's* engines are made by Mr. Penn, of Greenwich, and so remarkably easy do they work that there is not the slightest noise in their engine-rooms; but this is attributable to both vessels being fitted with canvas valves, while those of the *Hogue* (engines by Seaward) are fitted with the brass valves, causing so much noise below that the engineers can, with difficulty, make themselves understood at twelve feet apart. Should the *Hogue* be fitted with canvas, instead of brass valves, it would be of material advantage.

"The greater consumption of coals in the *Arrogant* and *Encounter* in 24 hours' steaming, is probably to be accounted for in the differently constructed boilers of those vessels from the *Hogue's*. The rate per hour, and steaming of such a ship as the *Hogue*, with her immense weight of metal and gigantic hull, caused much astonishment, and brought forth many encomiums from all who witnessed it."

The following is the *Arrogant* bulletin :—

Two trials have taken place between the *Arrogant* and the *Pomone* French screw frigate. The *Arrogant* beat the *Pomone* about 24 hours in a run of 330 miles under steam alone. It appears that generally the *Pomone* is much inferior to the British frigate, both as to her accommodation and to her general equipment. The lower deck of the French ship is taken up with the engines, boilers, and coal bunkers; the crew are therefore obliged to mess on the main-deck between the guns, which is a great encumbrance, and would be extremely prejudicial to the ship in action. Her machinery, boilers, and shaft, are also exposed to great danger from shot. She carries a complement of 390 men, the *Arrogant* a complement of 450. Each carries provisions for 140 days, and the *Arrogant* stores for 12 months, and water for 80 days; while the *Pomone* only carries six months' stores, and water for 40 days. We give their dimensions, &c. :—

	"Arrogant."	"Pomone."
	Ft. in.	Ft. in.
Length on deck...	200 0	170 7
Breadth moulded	44 4	42 7
Depth—upper part of keel to lower water line	18 1	17 3
Load displacement in tons, as built	2632	1891
Constructors' names	J. Fincham	Boucher
Constructors of engines ...	Penn & Co.	Count Rosen
Horse-power of engines ...	360	260

Captain Favin-Leveque gives the following data, which, it will be observed, differ somewhat from the other account as to horse-power and coals. It must also be remarked that the *Arrogant* was built for the screw, while the *Pomone* was a sailing vessel, converted into a steamer.

"*La Pomone* has never before been looked upon as a perfect model, and it is believed the French builders could do much better now.

The power of the *Arrogant* is 360 horses, *La Pomone's* 220 only.

The *Arrogant* has engines of 360 horse power at 700 kilogrammes, (700 cwts.) per horse power, including the water in her boilers, and eight days' provision of coals at 36 tons per diem, are about a load of 540 tons, which being taken on 1,050 tons, that being the full loading capacity of such a frigate; there remains then 510 tons, for artillery, masts, yards, rigging, sails, spare stores, ballast, boats, &c., not including in that list provisions and water. All the objects we have named weigh 550 tons, which, added to the engines and coal, give a load of 1090 tons. With calculation, which is as exact as possible, there remains no room for provisions or water. I must then conclude that the *Arrogant* takes little or no spare stores, that she coals only for five days at the most, and besides takes only 40 or 45 days' provisions. Has the *Arrogant* preserved, as a sailing frigate, the same qualities under sail of fast sailing and evolutions as all sailing frigates? I cannot answer that question; but with the impossibilities of stowage I have signalized, I must class that frigate with common steamers (ships that cannot remain a long time at sea), rather than with "navires mixtes" (auxiliary propellers). By this last name we mean a ship that possesses all the resources of a sailing vessel, in provisions, stores of all kinds, artillery, &c. :—a ship that can either alone, or with a fleet, undertake long voyages, and that possesses moreover a powerful engine that can propel her at the rate of six or seven knots in calm weather, that will always ensure her evolutions, and will permit her to force a passage, even having a line-of-battle ship in tow.

This problem has been solved by *La Pomone*. This frigate possesses all the properties I have mentioned. *La Pomone* takes 140 days' provisions for 390 men; eight days' fuel, and stores of all sorts, for six months; and her artillery and ammunition complete; water for 48 days, and a distilling apparatus. *La Pomone* thus armed and provisioned, steams seven and sometimes seven and a half miles per hour in calm weather, and against strong head breeze she obtains five miles. And without steaming, but with sails only, she has gone "before the wind eleven knots; wind on the quarter eleven knots eight-tenths! close hauled, ten knots;" and in this last situation, *La Pomone* being to the leeward of the 60-gun frigate *Iphigenia* running nine miles, both close hauled under the same sails, out-sailed her and went to windward.

FAVIN-LEVEQUE, Captain, R.N.

PARTICULARS OF THE STEAM-SHIP "REPUBLIC."
(*From the Journal of the Franklin Institute.*)

THIS fine steamer, recently finished at Baltimore, and now running between that port and Charleston, is deserving of particular notice, as being the first vessel built in this country with oscillating engines. Her dimensions are as follows :—

Length on deck, 207 feet; breadth of beam, 30 feet; depth of hold, 18½ feet; average draught of water, 11 feet 9 inches; 2 cylinders, 54 inches diameter, 6 feet stroke; diameter of wheel, 25 feet 6 inches; length of paddles, 8 feet 9 inches; depth of ditto, 2 feet 3 inches; dip of ditto, 3 feet 2 inches; average revolutions, 14 per minute at sea; average pressure of steam, 5 lbs. at sea, cutting off at half stroke; fuel per hour, 1680 pounds of Cumberland coal, with natural draught; 2 boilers, 12 feet wide, 18 feet long, and 8 feet 6 inches high, with 4 furnaces each.

For some years past this form of engine has been coming into favour in England, and it is now used by a large number of river and sea steamers in private service, as well as by many vessels of the British navy. The advantages of the oscillating engine are simplicity, compactness, and a great reduction of weight.

The engines of the *Republic* occupy in the vessel but 10 feet in length, by 20 feet in width, while the ordinary side lever engine would have taken 25 feet in length. This saving of space gives a material increase of room for freight and passengers, and I am credibly informed that the saving in this particular is equal to the expense of coal for the trip. Messrs. Murry and Hazlehurst deserve great credit for their exertions in behalf of this form of engine, as well as for the manner in which they have executed the work, and it is to be hoped that the navy department will be induced to give the oscillating engine that consideration which it deserves.

B.

STEAM NAVIGATION.

SCREW STEAMING.
To the Editor of the Morning Chronicle.

SIR,—The observations which have appeared in your paper recently relative to the proposed lines of steam communication with Australia, and in which the comparative merits of the screw and paddle-wheel have been alluded to, have induced me to request your attention to the following statement of the results of the working of five steamers, belonging to the General Screw Steam Shipping Company, for the year 1849. They have made altogether 170 voyages, outwards and homewards, with cargoes, and have made good a distance from port to port of 110,849 knots at an average speed of 8 to 8½ knots per hour. Only one casualty has occurred to any of the company's vessels during the year; the incident here referred to occurred in the Thames.

I beg also to hand you a report of one voyage of the new screw-steamers *Bosphorus* and *Hellespont*, to and from Constantinople, showing a mean of 7.91 knots. These ships have been laden with 360 tons of merchandize, besides 120 tons of coals.

I am, Sir, your obedient servant,
JAMES LAMING, Managing Director.

General Screw Steam Shipping Company,
2, Royal Exchange-buildings, Jan. 1.

The following statement will show the actual working of the screw, as a propelling power, in the vessels of this company, from the 1st of January to the 31st of December, 1849 :—

City of Rotterdam, 272 tons, 33 horse-power.—To Rotterdam, 20 voyages; Dunkirk, 19; Bayonne, 1; Middleburg, 2.—Total, 42 voyages, 15,850 miles. Average speed, 8 knots.

City of London, 272 tons, 30 horse-power.—To Rotterdam, 8 voyages; Dunkirk, 34; Harlingen, 1; Middleburg, 1.—Total, 44 voyages; 13,327 miles. Average speed, 8 knots.

Lord John Russell, 320 tons, 46 horse-power.—To Harlingen, 49 voyages; Middleburg, 1.—Total, 50 voyages, 25,379 miles. Average speed, 8½ knots.

Sir Robert Peel, 326 tons, 40 horse-power.—Liverpool to Constantinople, 3 voyages; London to Liverpool, 2; to Roche Bernard (Biscay), 1; to Rotterdam, 18.—Total, 24 voyages, 28,206 miles. Average speed, 8½ knots.

Earl of Auckland, 450 tons, 60 horse-power.—To Oporto, 1 voyage; London to Liverpool, 3; Liverpool to Constantinople, 4; to Rotterdam, 1; to Dunkirk, 1.—Total, 10 voyages, 28,487 miles.

Making a total of 110,849 miles.

Performance of the new screw steamers *Bosphorus* and *Hellespont*, on their first voyages from Liverpool to Constantinople, 1849:—

Bosphorus, 536 tons, 80 horse-power.—Sailed from Liverpool, Sept. 15; time on passage, 16 days 15½ hours. Average speed, 8.02 knots. Sailed from Constantinople, Oct. 10; time on passage, 15 days 11½ hours. Average speed, 8.50 knots.

Hellespont, 536 tons, 80 horse-power.—Sailed from Liverpool, Oct. 15; time on passage, 16 days 20 hours 25 min. Average speed, 7.98 knots. Sailed from Smyrna, Nov. 14; time on passage, 18 days 6 hours 30 min. Average speed, 7.20 knots.

Average speed of four passages, 7.91 knots.

Speed at trial of *Bosphorus* the measured mile in Long Reach, 9.68 knots.

Speed at trial of *Hellespont*, the measured mile in Long Reach, 9.65 knots.

Birkenhead.—Mr. John Laird, of Birkenhead, has nearly completed, for the East India Company, a large iron steam-vessel, of a peculiar form, fitted for shallow water, and intended for the navigation of the Ganges. The vessel is upwards of 200 feet long, and 30 feet beam, and will draw, when loaded, about 2 feet of water. Her model resembles that of the *Napier* (a former vessel built by Mr. Laird for the same purpose), with such modifications as experience has suggested. The form is that of the canoe, shovel-shaped at both extremities, and the bottom, amidships,—without keel—forming an inverted gentle segment of an arch; the centre portion, however, or floor, being nearly flat. The rudder is applied at either end, as necessity requires. The vessel is divided longitudinally into three parts, by water tight bulkheads, and traversing these, there are other bulkheads, dividing the whole vessel into 30 water-tight compartments, and adding greatly to her strength. Her depth from the spacious flush-deck varies from 11 feet in the middle, to 8 feet towards the extremities. The floorings, engine-bed, &c., are all of tubular wrought iron, imparting great strength. She is to be propelled by paddle-wheels, to be worked by engines of 180 horse-power. It is expected that she will be capable of towing two or three large cargo or luggage boats. The bottom being of the canoe form, should she go upon a sand bank with the current in her behalf, an anchor may be let gone at the stern end, and the water washing under her will clear away the sand and release her from the danger to which ordinary boats are liable in such navigations, of getting broadside on and being damaged or capsized. Should she take a bank or snag, when running against the tide or current, the anchor may be let go at the bow, and she will drift back into the deep water. Such is the floating capacity of the vessel, and the extent of her decks and accommodations, that she will carry a full regiment of soldiers at a time. All deck or top lumber is avoided. The vessel will, when finished, be taken to pieces, and sent in a ship to India, to be finally put together.—*Liverpool Courier.*

New Peninsular Steam-Fleet.—We understand that, in anticipation of securing the contract for conveying the mails between India and Australia, and of performing the whole of the Mediterranean and Bombay service, the Peninsular and Oriental Company have determined on building seven new and powerful paddle-wheel steam-vessels. Todd and Megregor, of Scotland, are to build two of the number, they having succeeded so well with the *Sultan*, the ship last built. The vessels are to be built of iron.—*United Service Gazette.*

Cork.—Mr. Pike, of Cork, who has already built some fine iron ships, among the rest the *Blarney*, which has been plying between Liverpool and Rotterdam, is at present engaged in building an immense iron vessel for the New York trade. She will be screw propelled, and 1,400 tons burden.

Newcastle.—On the 31st. ult., was launched from the iron ship-building yard of Mr. Thomas Toward, a large iron steam-vessel, intended for a Liverpool firm, and named the *Independence*. She is intended for a tug-boat for the Mersey, for which purpose, from her great strength and judicious mould, she appears to be well adapted. The following are some of her dimensions:—

	ft.	in.
Length on the load water line	124	6
Breadth on ditto	23	0
Depth from keel to gunnel	11	6
Intended load draught of water	6	0

Displacement or weight of vessel at the above draught, including engines, boilers, water, coals, &c., will be about 277 tons. Surface of immersed midship section, 122 feet; surface of load-water section, 2074 feet; centre of gravity of displacement aft of centre of flotation, 1.3; displacement per inch at the load-water line, 4.94 tons. The engines of 120-horse power, by Mr. J. P. Almond, of North Shields, are well calculated to ensure the best success to the boat.

SHIP BUILDING UPON THE CLYDE IN JANUARY, 1850.

[From our own Correspondent.]

Launch of the "Livorno."—On Wednesday, the 2nd ult., a large party of ladies and gentlemen assembled at the building-yard of Messrs. Alexander Denny and Brother (late of Messrs. Denny, Brothers) to witness the launch of a fine iron screw vessel, constructed by that firm for the Liverpool and Leghorn Screw Steam Navigation Company. Amongst the company present we observed George Henderson, Esq., one of the owners, Messrs. M'Kean and M'Larty (of Liverpool), the agents, Mr. George Thompson, of the firm of Messrs. J. and G. Thompson, the engineers, and Mr. W. Clark, the marine artist, from Greenock. On the signal being given, Miss Henderson performed the usual ceremony of naming the vessel, which glided gracefully into the Leven amidst the booming of cannon and the loud cheers of the spectators. The following are the dimensions of the vessel and engines:—

	Ft.	ins.
Length of keel and fore rake	160	0
Breadth of beam	25	6
Depth of hold	15	0
Burden	508$\frac{31}{94}$ tons	
Length of keel	151	0
Length of quarter deck	60	0
Height of do	2	3

Frames 4 × 3 × ½ in. and 1 ft. 3 in. apart. Fifteen strakes of plates from keel to gunwale, tapering from $\frac{11}{16}$ to $\frac{7}{16}$ in. Main deck stringers 2 ft. × ⅝ in. Double rivetted throughout. Launching draught of water, 6 ft. 10 ins. forward, and 6 ft. 8 ins. aft.

A pair of inverted cylinder engines of 100 horse nominal power, attached directly to the propeller-shaft. Two-bladed screw, 10 ft. 6 in. diameter; weigt 22½ cwt. One tubular boiler with six furnaces and 234 tubes.

Description.—Full female figure head; false quarter bridges; three masts; schooner rigged; standing boltsprit; a square stern and clinker built. Port of Liverpool.

The *Livorno* is the first vessel built for the company, and will add to the already well established fame of Messrs. Denny, by whom her lines were designed. She is at present at Finleston Quay, Glasgow, receiving her machinery, and will be commanded by Mr. John Miller, who is well known from his long service in the Canada trade.

Greenock.—Messrs. Robt. Steele and Co. have on the stocks two steamers for the British and North American Royal Mail Company; they are named respectively the *Asia* and the *Africa*—the former will be ready for launching in a month or six weeks. These are the largest vessels ever built of timber in Britain, and combine strength with beauty and symmetry of mould. The following are a few of the principal dimensions:—Length of keel and fore rake, 265 feet; breadth of beam, 39 feet 6 inches; depth of hold, 27 feet; tonnage of hull, 2017$\frac{44}{94}$ tons. The timbers and planking are all of the best British oak. They are to be propelled by two powerful engines on the side lever principle, with strong malleable iron framing, and paddle-wheels, similar to the other celebrated steamers of this enterprising company. Nominal power, 814 horses power; diameter of cylinders, 96 inches × 9 feet length of stroke. The Americans are fitting out two with the same size of cylinders, with 2 feet more stroke. By the end of 1850 we shall know probably the success of both parties.

Messrs. William Simons and Co. have on the stocks a ship classed 13 years at Lloyd's, A 1, to be named the *Jane Ewing*, to form one of the new monthly line of packet ships between Glasgow and Calcutta. The ollowing are a few of the principal dimensions:—Length of keel and fore rake, 120 feet; breadth of beam, 27 feet; depth of hold, 18 feet 6 inches;

and 405$\frac{21}{41}$ tons. She is a very handsome model for carrying and sailing qualities, and is to ply in concert with the ship *Argaum*, 466 tons, class 12 years; ship *Asia*, 524 tons, 10, A 1; ship *Bucephalus*, 557 tons, 10, A 1; ship *City of Glasgow*, 566 tons, 13, A 1; ship *City of Calcutta*, 540 tons, 13, A 1; ship *City of London*, 570 tons, 13, A 1; ship *Deogaum*, 521 tons, 12, A 1; ship *Majestic*, 565 tons, 12, A 1; and the barque *Oriental*, 396 tons, 10, A 1.

Messrs. John Scott and Sons have a large ship for the East India trade, to class 13 years, A 1, at Lloyd's. To have a poop and top-gallant fore-castle; the following are a few of the principal dimensions, &c.

				Ft.	in.
Length of keel and fore rake	...	...		132	0
Breadth of beam	...	...	...	31	0
Depth of hold	...	...	...	21	0
Tonnage	...	...	...	583$\frac{34}{44}$ tons.	

Messrs. Caird and Co., Cartsdyke, have a steamer for the Glasgow and Belfast mail line. The dimensions are—

				Ft.	in.
Length of keel and fore rake	...	...		190	0
Breadth of beam	...	...	...	23	0
Depth of hold	...	...	...	12	6
Tonnage	...	...	...	500$\frac{11}{17}$ tons.	

To have two side lever engines of 180-horses power. Cylinders, 50$\frac{1}{4}$ inches diameter × 4 feet 6 inches stroke. Tubular boilers and feathering paddle-wheels.

Messrs. James M'Millan, Cartsdyke, have a brig in frame, to class 8 years, A 1. To have a break-deck.

				Ft.	in.
Length of keel and fore rake	...	...		95	0
Breadth of beam	...	...	...	23	0
Depth of hold	...	...	...	13	0
Tonnage	...	...	...	230$\frac{61}{94}$ tons.	

GLASGOW.—Messrs. Tod and M'Gregor have upon the stocks a large iron vessel, to be propelled by the screw, and intended to ply between Glasgow and a foreign station. The following are a few of the principal dimensions:—Length of keel and fore rake, 230 feet; breadth of beam, 34 feet; depth of hold, 25 feet, and 1289$\frac{4}{94}$ tons; to carry 1,600 tons dead weight, that is, 1,200 tons of goods, and 400 tons of coals in the bunkers; also 12,500 gallons of fresh water in the tanks, for the use of the crew and passengers. She will have accommodation for 60 cabin, and 100 intermediate passengers, besides steerage passengers. The engines are on the common land engine principle, with masts at top, of 380 horse nominal power. Diameter of cylinders, 66 inches × 5 feet stroke; the screw is three-bladed; diameter, 13 feet; pitch, 18 feet; to be worked by spur wheel and pinion; tubular boilers. She is to have a spar deck; to be rigged as a ship or barque; and promises to be a splendid specimen of naval architecture.

Messrs. Robert Barclay and Curle, Finieston, have at present upon the stocks a large 13 years' timber ship, to be named the *City of Calcutta*, to be launched next month, for the Glasgow and Calcutta new monthly line. Dimensions:—

				Ft.	in.
Length of keel and fore rake	...	...		130	6
Breadth of beam	...	...	...	28	7
Depth of hold	...	...	...	20	6
Tonnage	...	...	...	492$\frac{44}{94}$ tons.	
Length on deck	...	...	...	129.3	
Breadth on ditto	...	...	...	25.8	
Depth of hold	...	...	...	20.2	
Tonnage	...	...	...	541$\frac{72}{94}$ tons.	

Difference in tonnage, 49 tons. This vessel is built of British oak and mahogany, which is coming greatly into use in ship-building in this part of the country. After this vessel is off, there will be laid down the keel of a new ship, for the same trade, to be named the *City of London*, of the following dimensions:—

			Ft.	in.
Length of keel and fore rake	...	...	131	0
Breadth of beam	...	...	29	0
Depth of hold	...	...	20	0
Tonnage	...	...	539$\frac{11}{44}$ tons.	

To be classed 13 years, A 1, at Lloyd's.

There is also upon the stocks and in frame a clipper schooner of timber, for the coasting trade, and of the following dimensions:—

			Ft.	in.
Length of keel and fore rake	...	...	78	0
Breadth of beam	...	...	18	4
Depth of hold	...	...	11	0
Tonnage	...	...	120$\frac{33}{94}$ tons.	

Messrs. Napier and Crichton have upon the stocks three iron vessels, for the Forth and Clyde Canal Company, to be named the *H, I*, and *J*, similar in size to the *A, B, C, D, E, F*, and *G*, launched last year for the coasting trade, and of the following dimensions, viz.:—

			Ft.	in.
Length of keel and fore rake	...	...	65	0
Breadth of beam	...	...	15	10
Depth of hold	...	...	8	0
Tonnage	...	...	44$\frac{44}{94}$	

Messrs. Thomas Wingate and Co., White Inch, have upon the stocks an iron clipper steam vessel, for the Hull and Leith trade, of the following dimensions:—

			Ft	in
Length of keel and fore rake	...	...	175	0
Breadth of beam	...	...	22	7
Depth of hold	...	...	12	5
Length of engine space	...	...	44	8
Tonnage.				Tons
Hull	...	...	443$\frac{41}{94}$	
Contents of engine space	...	...	123$\frac{43}{94}$	
Register	...	...	320$\frac{44}{94}$	

One steeple engine, on Mr. David Napier's 4-piston rod patent principle, of 150-horse power, nominal. Cylinders, 63 inches diameter × 5 feet stroke. Overhung paddle-wheels, 22 feet diameter. 24 floats. 2 tubular boilers; she is a beautiful model, and is intended to be named the *Favourite*.

They are at present lengthening the steamer *Queen of Beauty* 20 feet. To have two perpendicular tubular boilers, and two funnels, to make her similar to the *Plover*, which vessel she will ply in concert with between Glasgow and Rothesay, &c.

			Ft	in
Length of keel and fore rake	...	...	156	11
Breadth of beam	...	...	16	7$\frac{1}{4}$
Depth of hold	...	...	8	3
Tonnage	...	...	229$\frac{14}{44}$ tons.	

Two steeple engines, 70-horse nominal power. Cylinders, 33$\frac{1}{2}$ inches diameter × 3 feet length of stroke; and revolving floats. To condense in double bottom in hull. To be named the *Merlin*.

Messrs. Smith and Rodger have two screw vessels laid down—one for the trade between Liverpool and Constantinople, to ply in concert with the *Pirate* and *Brigand*, of the following dimensions:—

			Ft	in
Length of keel and fore rake	...	...	180	0
Breadth of beam	...	...	25	0
Depth of hold	...	...	15	0
Tonnage	...	...	552$\frac{44}{94}$ tons.	

Screw, diameter, 10 feet 6 inches; 100-horse power. The second vessel is to ply between London and Russia, with a screw 10 feet 6 in. diameter.

			Ft	in
Length of keel and fore rake	...	...	195	0
Breadth of beam	...	...	30	0
Depth of hold	...	...	18	0
Tonnage	...	...	847$\frac{44}{94}$ tons.	

Mr. Robert Napier has an iron steamer upon the stocks, for the Scottish Central Railway Company, for the rivers Forth or Tay.

				Ft	In
Length on deck	...	...	...	140	0
Length of keel	...	...	...	130	0
Breadth of beam	...	...	...	24	2
Breadth over the paddle-cases	...	...	41	8
Depth of hold	...	...	...	9	6
Length of engine room	...	...	42	0

				Tons
Hull	...	...	...	360$\frac{9}{94}$
Contents of engine space	...	...	133$\frac{82}{94}$
Register	...	...	...	229$\frac{82}{94}$

Two oscillating engines and flue boilers. Nominal power, 125 horse-power. Diameter of cylinders, 44 inches × 3 feet 6 inches length of stroke. The frames are 3 feet apart, and the rudders are to be on the box principle. Two funnels.

There is also a clipper screw vessel to ply on the Severn. Length, 100 feet; beam 21 feet; depth, 8 feet; 210$\frac{82}{94}$ tons; screw, 5 feet diameter.

RENFREW.—Messrs. James Henderson and Sons have on the stocks an iron vessel, for the river trade.

				Ft	In
Length aloft	...	...	...	60	0
Breadth of beam	...	...	...	14	9
Depth of hold	...	...	...	4	6
Length of keel and fore rake	...	...	59	0
Tonnage	...	...	...	59$\frac{13}{94}$ tons.

PORT GLASGOW.—Mr. John Wood has on the stocks, and nearly planked, a screw steam-vessel of timber, to replace the loss of the *Kestrel*, on the mail line between Bermuda, Halifax, N.S., St. John's, Newfoundland, &c.

				Ft	in
Length of keel and fore rake	...	...	135	0
Breadth of beam	...	...	...	25	0
Depth of hold	...	...	...	15	0
Tonnage	...	...	...	402$\frac{82}{94}$ tons.

To be propelled by a pair of inverted cylinder engines, of 104-horses power, by Messrs. Caird and Co., Cartsdyke, Greenock. Screw, 10 feet in diameter.

Messrs. John Reid and Co. have on the stocks an iron screw steamer, for Prussia, nearly ready for launching.

				Ft	in
Length of keel and fore rake	...	...	142	0
Breadth of beam	...	...	...	24	0
Depth of hold	...	...	...	15	0
Tonnage	...	...	...	391$\frac{82}{94}$ tons.

Eleven strakes of plates from keel to gunwale, tapering in thickness from $\frac{7}{8}$ to $\frac{5}{8}$ of an inch. Frames, 5 × 3 × $\frac{7}{8}$ inches, and 1 foot 6 inches apart. Keel, stem, and stern-post, 6 × 3 inches. To be propelled by two inverted cylinder engines, of 80-horses power, and one tubular boiler, with 188 tubes and 4 furnaces, by Messrs. James and George Thomson, of the Clyde Bank Foundry.

DUMBARTON.—Messrs. Denny and Rankin have a ship for the Glasgow and Sydney, N. S. W. line. Lewis Potter and Co., of Glasgow.

				Ft	In
Length of keel and fore rake	...	...	149	0
Breadth of beam	...	...	...	31	8
Depth of hold	...	...	...	21	0
Tonnage	...	...	...	670$\frac{41}{94}$ tons.

To have a poop and top-gallant forecastle. To class ten years. Also, a barque which will be ready for launching in four weeks. Class, 10 years. The dimensions are—

				Ft.	in.
Length of keel and fore rake	...	...	104	0
Breadth of beam	...	...	...	25	5$\frac{1}{2}$
Depth of hold	...	...	...	18	0
Tonnage	...	...	...	297$\frac{71}{94}$ tons.

				Ft.
Length on deck	...	...	...	101.8
Breadth on ditto	...	...	...	23.3
Depth of hold	...	...	...	17.8
Tonnage	...	...	...	344$\frac{35}{100}$ tons.

Difference in tonnage, 47 tons.

They have a schooner ready for launching of the following dimensions:—

				Ft	in
Length of keel and fore rake	...	...	64	2$\frac{1}{2}$
Breadth of beam	...	...	...	18	10
Depth of hold	...	...	...	10	0
Tonnage	...	...	...	99$\frac{14}{94}$ tons.

				Ft.
Length on deck	...	...	...	62.8
Breadth on ditto	...	...	...	17.2
Depth of hold	...	...	...	9.9
Tonnage	...	...	...	88$\frac{5}{100}$ tons.

For the trade between Glasgow and Rotterdam, *via* the Forth and Clyde Canal. Intended to be named the *Rankin*.

Messrs. Archibald M'Millan and Son have a schooner for the Irish coasting trade—

				Ft	in
Length of keel and fore rake	...	...	56	0
Breadth of beam	...	...	...	17	0
Depth of hold	...	...	...	9	0
Tonnage	...	...	...	71$\frac{36}{94}$ tons.

To class 8 years.

Also a lighter for the Forth and Clyde Canal and general coasting trade—

				Ft.	in.
Length of keel and fore rake	...	...	62	0
Breadth of beam	...	...	...	14	0
Depth of hold	...	...	...	4	6
Tonnage	...	...	...	55$\frac{27}{94}$ tons.

And a ship for the foreign trade, to class 10 years, A 1—

				Ft	in
Length of keel and fore rake	...	...	115	0
Breadth of beam	...	...	...	27	0
Depth of hold	...	...	...	18	0
Tonnage	...	...	...	386$\frac{82}{94}$ tons.

Also, rebuilding, the barques *Envoy* and *Adam Carr*.

MILLER'S PATENT IMPROVEMENTS IN MORTON'S PATENT SLIP.

THE introduction of the patent slip, as our readers must be aware, afforded a great convenience for repairing vessels in localities where the variations of the tide were but small, and where a dock would have been too costly. The only objectionable part was the wheelwork employed to drag up the vessel; and it is this objection which Mr. Miller's invention is designed to obviate. The hydraulic press offers great facilities for concentrating power, and Mr. Miller has enlisted it in his service. On the upper end of the slip is fixed a hydraulic press, the ram working upwards. Two side rods off the crosshead, connected at bottom by another crosshead, serve to convey the power to the traction rods of the cradle, on which the ship is floated. A small engine and pump, mounted on the cylinder of the press, work up the ram, and the cradle with it. As soon as the ram has made one stroke, the top piece of the traction rod is removed, and the ram and side rods are drawn back by a self-acting apparatus, which opens a waste pipe in the cylinder, and allows the water to escape, while the ram is drawn back by a rope and pulley, thrown in gear with the engine by the same means. The ram is then ready to take fresh hold of the traction rods, and the vessel is drawn up another stroke as before.

Messrs. Morton, the original patentees of the slip, state that this principle can be laid down for less than one-half the cost of the present machinery—for very large slips much less. That ships will be taken up at double the speed, as but a very small proportion of the power is absorbed by friction; and, from the machinery being self-acting, no time is lost by stopping it to take a fresh hold. That the motion in drawing up a ship is so perfectly smooth and uniform, that no part of the carriage or ship is exposed to any undue strain; that it occupies but little space, and is not subject to breakage or derangement; and the same foundation does for both purchase machinery and steam engine.

When the slip is not in motion, the engine may be advantageously used for pumping, sawing, driving grind-stones, blast for smiths' fires, &c.

ANALYSIS OF BOOKS.

*An Essay on the Present and Future Prospects of Farming in Great
Britain.* By W. THOROLD, C. E. London: Ridgway. Pp. 24.

It would only be occupying our readers' time to no purpose to enter into
any disquisition on the causes which have contributed to the present depressed
condition of the agricultural interest. There can be no difference of opinion
as to the propriety of trying to grow corn cheaply, whether it be effected
by diminishing the cost of production, or increasing the quantity and quality
of the produce. Mr. Thorold, as a practical engineer, lays most stress on
the former agency, in which we will imitate him, leaving the question of
artificial manures and green crops to the chemist and the grower.

Mr. Thorold starts with Lord Lyndhurst's axiom, " A difficulty is something to be got over," and argues that, as almost every other interest in
Great Britain has met with and surmounted similar difficulties, there is no
reason why farmers should despair.

The improvement which might be effected in straggling estates and
farms, by combining and exchanging various properties, is first touched
upon by Mr. Thorold in his advice to landowners. This, of course,
would require an act of Parliament, and, although the advantages to
be gained are very great, we fear that the landowners must take some
more active measures than going to Parliament, for "while the grass is
growing, the steed is starving." The author explains how much might
be saved in the way of carting and supervision upon a farm, all in a
piece with the farm-buildings in the centre.

On the plan for farm-buildings, we have the following remarks :—

" It is also essential in carrying out this system, as before stated, that the
farm buildings should be as near the centre of the farm as possible, which,
if it cannot be obtained by exchange, addition, or reduction, the buildings
necessary for occupation should be removed or built new. The old farm
house can remain as a residence, or be converted into cottages, as may be
most convenient in the preliminary stage of proceeding, and as it will
frequently happen that where cottages are wanted, it will be a question
whether the old farm houses that are now on the outside of the farm, and
consequently badly situated for the farmer's occupation, will not be in the
most proper position for cottages ? It is also necessary that good hard roads
should be made, so as to approach one side of every field in all weathers,
and a drift road made from the buildings to the most frequented public
road."

" The object of this design is to convert all the straw, hay, and green crops
into manure, and to retain or prevent the loss of such manure, after
it is obtained, in the most effectual and economical manner ; it is applicable to any sized farm, by merely increasing or diminishing the
feeding and storing departments; but in all cases it should be limited to
farms not exceeding a convenient length or breadth from the homestall, on
account of the expense of road making and carriage. Steam power is intended to be applied to thrashing, dressing, grinding, and bruising corn,
steaming food, cutting hay and straw into chaff, pumping water and liquid
manure, slicing turnips, breaking oil cake, sawing wood, raising manure
from the house by an inclined plane, to load the cart instantly, and prevent the horses waiting for the same ; and probably for the purpose of exhausting foul air from the feeding houses, to excite hunger in cattle, and
thereby diminish the time of fatting. It is here necessary to inform our
readers, that this last plan has been adopted in factories as a principle of
ventilation, and the only objection to it has been, that it makes the work
people always hungry, the very thing of all others, beneficial in grazing or
fatting cattle. Provision should also be made for rendering the feeding
houses perfectly dark for an hour or so after feeding time, in order that the
cattle may take their rest. Cramming may thus be introduced into cattle
feeding, as has long been practised with ortolans, poultry, &c."

" For this purpose a portable steam engine is preferred (with fixed barn
machinery, &c.) on account of its being applicable to more than one set of
buildings, which will render it less expensive, and also more adapted to
meet the possible contingency of steam ploughing, and being sent to the
factory to be repaired, thus avoiding the nuisance of having mechanics on
the premises, or it can further be supplied by a travelling or club engine.
Let us now proceed to a reference to the plate. Figure 1 is the corn barn
open at each end, with a railway running through it, upon which stacks are
to be built upon staddle-frames running upon wheels, instead of standing
as heretofore upon fixed piers or pedestals, and as many staddles are to be
provided as the number of stacks. A stack is to be built on these staddle
frames, upon any part of the railway, and can be run into the barn at
night, and remain there under cover until it is thatched, which it is obvious
can be done either in wet or dry weather. As soon as it is thatched, it is
to be run through the barn, a sufficient distance out of the way, and another
staddle-frame is to be brought empty from the cross line, and a stack built
thereon as before. As soon as it is ascertained that the barn will contain
the remainder of the crop, it can be filled in the usual way, and of course
this last must be thrashed out first; afterwards the stacks on the staddles
can be introduced into the barn, and thrashed by a like process. The
length of railway will be limited by the locality and expense, but it must
be of sufficient length to admit of two or more kinds of corn being stationed
on either side, so that any particular stack can be thrashed when wanted,
by running all those before out of the way ; as it is intended to have the
rails perfectly level, but little power will be required to do this. Hay
stacks may also be stationed on close boarded staddles at one end of the
line, and can afterwards be brought into the barn when they are required
to feed the hay cutter, being thus under cover during the time it would
otherwise be partially exposed to the weather."

" When the stacks are only required to be moved a short distance, it can
be done by a windlass and manual power, or by a capstan driven by the engine, as now practised at the Royal Arsenal in hauling timbers from any
part of the yard to the saw mill. As soon as a stack is thrashed, the
staddle can be run over the centre of the cross line, and by means of a screw,
with a capstan head raised above the line of rails, and being nearly an
equal balance, it can be turned by two men, and lowered into the cross line,
it is then to be covered with a sufficient quantity of wheat straw, to
keep off the weather, and out of the way of the cross line, such
straw being applied in thatching the ensuing year's stacks, and ready
when wanted.—2. The house to contain the portable steam engine, to be
connected through the wall by a universal joint to the driving shaft of the
permanent machinery, and also by a swan-neck joint to the pipe feeding the
steam cookery.—3. The thrashing drum upon the upper floor.—4. Straw
shaker,—5. A Jacob's ladder, whose duty it is to remove the straw from
the shaker into the straw barn.—6. Where it remains until it is wanted
for litter or other purposes ; if required to be cut, it can be brought back
again by reversing the motion of the ladder. It is presumed every grain
of corn will thus be seperated from the straw, and the straw will be in the
most convenient place for its future application ; being connected with the
feeding houses and stables it can be got at with the least labour, and perfectly
dry and clean.—7. The steam cookery ; it will also be desirable to place the
manure and cold water pumps here to keep them from the frost."

We shall return to this subject next month, and examine Mr. Thorold's
propositions more in detail.

To the Editor of the Artizan.

Sir,—I think it is more than probable that I speak the sentiments of
many of your readers when, referring to the Coaling Machinery, so fully
described in your last November and January Nos., I remark what a fortunate circumstance it must be, when such great inventors as Messrs. Summers
and Co. can give that publicity to their talents, which the wide circulation
of the *Artizan* secures, without even the cost of an additional engraving.
No doubt the greatest merit of the latter invention consisted in advertising
it with the smallest possible alteration of the plate already prepared for
Messrs. Blyth's machine, and certainly so well has this been effected that
no laurels will be refused.

It seems to a mechanical mind, to be a pity that any alteration from the
prior invention was found necessary, as the change has conveyed the idea
of a retrograde movement in the inventive process, not befitting the age we
live in. Could you explain to me, sir, whether the buckets, in passing each
other, are apt to kick one another, as, from the limited dimensions of a
collier's main hatch, into which both must descend, such an accident occurred
in a case that came under my own observation ; and what means you would
suggest to remedy the inconvenience ?

Other remarks suggest themselves, which may find their place in a subsequent letter, as I fear I am encroaching on your space.

         I am, sir, your humble servant,
                     COAL WHIPPER.

NOVELTIES.

GREAT EXHIBITION OF THE WORKS OF INDUSTRY OF ALL NATIONS. —We turn to this subject with feelings very different from those with which we regarded it when we penned our remarks last month, and when it appeared to us that the false step on the threshold was very likely to prove fatal to its prospects. The Munday contract, as our readers are aware, has been thrown up, and we trust that the concoctors of that affair will not venture to thrust any more of their schemes on his Royal Highness Prince Albert, whose good sense has saved the undertaking from becoming a mere job. The Manchester folks spoke their mind pretty plainly on the matter, and other towns were preparing to follow their example. As the enterprise is now, however, fairly launched on the current of popular opinion, we will "let bygones be bygones," for we have now not the slightest fear as to the event. Circulars have been sent to the mayors of the various towns, and the local committees formed in the provinces, to request that the names of the proposed representatives of the industrial classes may be sent to the central committee without delay. Lists of the subscriptions will speedily be published, the names of the Queen and Prince Albert having set a good example—her Majesty by giving £1,000, and Prince Albert £500.

BAROMETRICAL MATCH FOR £400 ASIDE. — Mr. L. Vidie, whose aneroid barometer has been frequently attacked on the score of its presumed susceptibility to thermometric influences, has, through the columns of the *Mining Journal*, offered to deposit 400l. in the hands of three competent judges, if one of his opponents, Mr. Negretti, optician, of London, will do the same ; the stakes to be handed over to whichever can produce the most perfect barometer. Mr. Vidie's to be one of his aneroids, and Mr. Negretti's to be the best mercurial barometer he can find. They are to be tested with a variation of temperature of 50° and 100° fahrenheit. Our readers will remember our giving a sketch of the aneroid in our last volume, and giving an instance of the accuracy of one in our possession.

GEOLOGICAL PRIZES.—The council of the Geological Society of Dublin have resolved :—That three prizes be offered by the Society, each of the value of £5 in books, to be awarded for the three most valuable papers in the order of merit, that shall be communicated and read to the society prior to the 31st of December, 1850, on Theoretical or Descriptive Geology, or the application thereto of any of the kindred sciences. Competition to be free to all persons, except to members of the council of the society. The society not binding itself to the publication of any papers presented for such competition, nor to award any prize, unless papers of adequate merit be presented.

LOCOMOTIVE POWER.—German papers state that Mr. Gunther, the head of the locomotive factory at Neustadt, near Vienna, has solved the problem relative to the ascent of trains on inclined planes ; and built an engine which will draw, with ease, up an incline of 40 to 50°, a train of the weight of 2500 tons. (?)

THE FORTHCOMING EXHIBITION IN 1851.—The enthusiasm engendered by the proposal for this exhibition, has extended to America : and already many machinists, manufacturers, and others, are preparing specimens of their skill for the occasion. We understand also that T. Simcox Lea, Esq. of Astley, formerly a large manufacturer at Kidderminster, has issued an address to the working men, calling their attention to the exhibition as a means by which the trade of the town may be promoted. He recommends them to form committees, and liberally offers a prize of 100 guineas to the man, or set of men, in Kidderminster, who shall invent any new and useful article.

THE ORIENTAL INLAND STEAM COMPANY.—A detailed statement has just been issued, containing the objects and prospects of the above company, which proposes the establishment of a line of steamers upon the navigable rivers of India, extending, with their branches, over this great continent—the principal feature being the introducing more extensively of our British manufactures, and receiving the valuable productions of India with greater facility and cheapness. The shallowness of the rivers in the dry season, and the present imperfect mode of transit which is adopted, has hitherto precluded free access to the more important districts of this country. The difficulties which have stood in the way of carrying our commercial intercourse into complete effect is likely to be overcome by the enterprising spirit of the present company. The names of the gentlemen comprising the committees of management afford sufficient guarantee for the effectual carrying out of this important undertaking, whilst their practical experience in similar undertakings is such as to secure confidence in the anticipations of a profitable result.

BERLIN GAS WORKS.—The English Gas Company has published a statement of their losses by fraud, which, they state, amount annually to 2,000,000 cubic feet. What will the shareholders say to this beautiful system of management ?

PEACOCK'S ANTI-SARGASSIAN PAINT.—The Peninsular and Oriental Steam Company's iron steam-ship *Pacha*, after a six months' trial of Capt. Peacock's compound, for preserving the bottoms of iron vessels exposed to the action of sea water, was examined by Captain Engledue, and that part of the vessel subject to constant immersion was found to be perfectly clean and free in every respect from dirt or incrustation of any kind. The result of the survey was a unanimous opinion of the entire success of this composition, one of the peculiar merits of which is its cheapness, as we are informed that the bottom of an iron ship can be coated with it at a less cost than that occasioned by a coat of red lead. The Peninsular Company's iron fleet are now all coated with this composition, and we understand that two tons of it were shipped to India by the steamer *Hindostan* for the use of the Company's iron ships in the Indian seas.

LONDON BRIDGE *versus* SOUTHWARK.—The passage of London-bridge has become a positive nuisance to the pedestrian since the numerous railways have made it their point of entrance into London. The narrowness of the foot-pavement, and its slipperiness, added to the constant and enormous traffic over it, render it anything but a pleasant task to cross it. The completion of the new streets between Southwark-bridge, Queen-street, and Cannon-street, would seem to offer a favourable opportunity for abolishing the paltry toll on Southwark-bridge, and throwing it open to the public. The increased value in the rental of the houses in the vicinity would, we imagine, more than compensate for the few pence taken, a large proportion of which must be applied to pay two toll-keepers. Considering how many passengers must be going in such a direction that Southwark-bridge would be the preferable road, and how small a toll is sufficient to keep them away, it can hardly be doubted that its removal would render the traffic on the two bridges more equal, and be a great public convenience.

RAILWAY EXTORTION.—We often hear of "Railway Extortion"—the term may be applied in more ways than one. The London and N. Western Company required certain lands for the Coventry and Nuneaton line. In one instance, the owner claimed £9578, in another, £6843. A jury, acting on competent and disinterested evidence, awarded the sums of £1350, and £1630, respectively! The law fortunately provides that the extortionate land owner shall, on conviction, pay all the expenses incurred.

JAMAICA.—An Act has been passed exempting the American steamers and their coaling vessels calling there, from tonnage dues, thus placing them on the same footing as the R. W. I. Mail Company's vessels. It is also stated that the copper mines at Mount Vernon, are to be worked by an American company, and that the cultivation of cotton is to be tried. It is gratifying to be able to report the least symptoms of improvement in any of our West Indian Colonies.

PROPOSED BRIDGE ACROSS THE RHINE.—Several plans have been proposed to supersede the bridge of boats across the Rhine, at Cologne, as the traffic, since the opening of the Prussian and Belgian lines of railway, has increased to such an extent, as to render a fixed bridge indispensable. As we mentioned (p. 263,) a tubular bridge has been talked of, but as the question is not yet decided, Mr. Neville, C. E. has proposed to the railway company and the Government to construct a bridge on his system, combining a double line of rails, a cart traffic way, with *trottoirs*, on 12 piers, leaving 13 openings of 100 feet each.

LONDON AND MARGATE STEAM-PACKET COMPANY.—The list of contributories to this defunct undertaking is now being settled before Master Kindersley. From the proceedings it appears that soon after it was started, in 1845, it became utterly unprofitable, and unable to meet its liabilities, which amount to £30,000 on the subscribed capital, with £10,000 assets in hand.

FRENCH WATERPROOF CLOTH OR SILK.—The following is the process adopted by M. Collet :—Take 1 lb. of linseed oil, 1¼ lb. of white lead, 1 oz. of umber, and a clove of garlic ; boil these ingredients for 12 hours over a slow fire, and when this composition acquires a skin upon its surface, it is fit for use. The cloth or silk is then to be immersed, being previously spread over a frame, then hung up to dry, and afterwards rubbed smooth with pumice stone. The material is next to be coated with another composition, prepared in the following manner :—Take 1 lb. of linseed oil, 1 oz. of litharge, 4 drachms of sulphate of zinc, and 4 ozs. of white lead, calcined to a yellow colour ; boil these in an iron pot until they assume the consistence of paste. This preparation is then to be spread over the cloth on one side of it, and then dried in a heated chamber. For covering of silk this last operation should be repeated. Oiled skin cloth, perfectly flexible and waterproof, is thus produced.

LIST OF ENGLISH PATENTS.

FROM DECEMBER 3, 1849, TO JANUARY 17, 1849, INCLUSIVE.

Louis Cesaires Charpillon, of Rue de Luxembourg, in the Republic of France, for improvements in locks for guns and pistols. December 29.

John Read, of Park-terrace, King's-road, Chelsea, gentleman, for improvements in machinery for extracting fluids from animal, vegetable, and mineral substances, and in compressing the same. December 29.

William Palmer, of Sutton-street, Clerkenwell, in the County of Middlesex, manufacturer, for improvements in the manufacture of candles, lamps, and wicks. December 29.

William Barlow, of Blackheath, in the County of Kent, civil engineer, and William Henry Barlow, of Derby, civil engineer, for improvements in the permanent ways of railways. January 3.

Albert Crakell Waterloo, of London-wall, lithographer, for improvements in the means and apparatus for obtaining copies of writings, drawings, and other designs. January 3. —(Communication).

Alexander Brodie Cochrane, jun., and Archibald Slate, of Dudley, in the County of Worcester, engineers, for improvements in the manufacture of iron pipes or tubes. Jan. 3.

Thomas Lighfoot, of Broad Oak, within Accrington, in the County of Lancaster, chemist, for improvements in printing and dyeing fabrics of cotton, and of other fibrous matherial. January 3.

William Buckwell, of the Artificial Granite Works, Battersea, civil engineer, for improvements in compressing or solidifying fuel. January 3.—(To extend to the colonies only).

Joe Sidebottom, of Pandlebury, in the County of Lancaster, manager, for certain improvements in steam engines. January 3.

Henry Dorning, of Kearsley, near Bolton, in the County of Lancaster, brick and tile manufacturer, for certain improvements in machinery or apparatus for manufacturing bricks, tiles, and other similar articles from clay or other plastic materials. January 3.

David Blair White, of the borough of Newcastle-upon-Tyne, Doctor of Medicine, for an improved mode of ballasting and stowing cargo in ships and other vessels. Jan. 8.

Matthew Urlwin Sears, of 36, Burton-crescent, in the parish of St. Pancras, commission agent, for the improved construction of guns and cannons, and manufacture of cartridges for the loading or charging thereof. January 11.—(Communication.)

Samuel Newington, of Knole Frant, in the County of Sussex, doctor of medicine, for improvements in sewing, manuring, and cultivating land; and in certain of the implements used therein. January 11.

Bennett Alfred Burton, of the firm of Bennett, Burton, and Burton, of John's-place, Holland-street, Southwark, engineer, for certain improvements in apparatus connected with sowers, drains, and cesspools; also in suction and delivery pipes, and in connecting such pipes or hose, the apparatus connected with sewers, drains, and cesspools, being applicable to other like purposes. January 11.

John Fayrer, of Surrey-street, Strand, Commander in her Majesty's Royal Navy, for improvements in steering apparatus. January 11.

Alfred Cooper, of Rumsey, in the County of Hants, grocer, for improvements in steam and other power engines, and in the application thereof to motive purposes; also in the method of, and machinery for, arresting or checking the progress of locomotive engines and other carriages. January 11.

James M'Donald, of the City of Chester, coachmaker, for certain improvements in the mode of applying oil or grease to wheels and axles, and to machinery; and in connecting the springs of wheel carriages with the axles or axle boxes. January 11.

John Glasgow, of Manchester, for certain improvements in machinery or apparatus for shearing, shaping, punching, and compressing metals. January 12.

John Milwain, of Manchester, joiner, for certain improvements applicable to the closing of doors, windows, and shutters. January 12.

Andrew Barclay, of Kilmarnock, in the County of Ayr, N.B., engineer, for improvements in the smelting of iron and other ores; and in the manufacture or working of iron and other metals; and in certain rotary engines and fans, machinery, or apparatus, as connected therewith. January 15.

Richard Smith, of Clitheroe, in the County of Lancaster, manufacturer, for certain improvements in looms for weaving. January 16.

Henry Cowing, of Stamford-street, Blackfriars, in the County of Surrey, gentleman, for improvements in obtaining motive power, and in steam and other ploughs, in land carriages, in fire engines, in raising water, for draining and other agricultural purposes, and in apparatus for evaporating saccharine juices and other liquors. January 17.

Joseph Nye, of Mill-pond Wharf, Park-road, Old Kent-road, in the County of Surrey, engine manufacturer, for improvements in hydraulic machinery, parts of which improvements are applicable to steam engines and machinery for driving piles. January 17.

Robert Barber, of Chatham-place, Lock's Fields, in the County of Surrey, for certain improvements in artificial fuel, and in machinery used for manufacturing the same. January 17.

George Henry Taunton, of Liverpool, civil engineer, for certain improvements in obtaining and applying motive power, and in a means to ascertain the strength of chains and ship's cables. January 17.

LIST OF PATENTS THAT HAVE PASSED THE GREAT SEAL OF SCOTLAND.

FROM THE 24TH DAY OF OCTOBER, 1849, TO THE 20TH DAY OF DECEMBER, 1849, INCLUSIVE.

Alexander Parkes, of Harborne, in the county of Stafford, chemist, for improvements in the deposition and manufacture of certain metals, and alloys of metals; and improved mode of treating and working certain metals, and alloys of metals; and in the application of the same to various useful purposes. October 24.

Conrad William Finzel, of the city and county of Bristol, sugar refiner, for improvements in processes and machinery employed in and applicable to the manufacture of sugar. October 24.

William Edward Newton, of Chancery-lane, in the county of Middlesex, civil engineer, for improvements in machinery for planeing, tongueing, and grooving boards or planks. October 24.—(Communication.)

David Owen Edwards, of Sydney-place, Brompton, in the county of Middlesex, surgeon, for improvements in the application of gas for producing and radiating heat. October 24.

John Mercer, of Oakenshaw, in the county of Lancaster, and William Blythe, of Holland Bank, Oswald Hoistle, in the same county, manufacturing chemist, for improvements in certain materials to be used in the processes of dyeing and printing. October 31.

William Henry Ritchie, of Brixton, in the county of Surrey, gentleman, for improvements in fire arms. October 31.

Charles Cowper, of Southampton Buildings, Chancery-lane, for certain improvements in the manufacture of sugar. November 2.—(communication.)

Joseph Lowe, of Salford, in the county of Lancaster, surveyor, for certain improvements in grates or grids, applicable to sewers, drains, and other similar purposes. November 2.

John Holt, of Todmorden, in the county of Lancaster, manager of the Waterside Works, for improvements in machinery or apparatus for preparing cotton and other fibrous substances, parts of which improvements are applicable to machinery used in weighing. November 5,

William Buckwell, of the Artificial Granite Works, Battersea, in the county of Surrey, civil engineer, for improvements in compressing and solidifying fuel. November 5.

Thomas John Knowlys, of Heysham Tower, near Lancaster, Esq. for improvements in the application and combination of mineral and vegetable products: also in obtaining products from mineral and vegetable substances, and in the generation and application of heat. November 5.

Henry Crosley, of the firm of Henry Crosley, Son, and Galsworthy, of Emerson-street, in the county of Surrey, engineer and coppersmith, for certain improved modes or methods of, and apparatus for heating and lighting, for drying substances, and for employing air in a warm and cold state for manufacturing purposes. November 7.

Henry Knight, of Birmingham, in the county of Warwick, for certain improvements in apparatus for printing, embossing, pressing, and perforating. November 12.

Adam Yule, of Dundee, master mariner, and John Chanter, of Lloyds, London, and Arnold-terrace, Bromley, in the county of Middlesex, gentleman, for improvements in the preparation of materials for coating ships, and other vessels. November 14.

John Parkinson, of Bury, in the county of Lancaster, brass founder, for improvements in machinery or apparatus for measuring and registering the flow of liquids. Nov. 14.

Alexander M'Dougall, of Longsight, in the county of Lancaster, chemist, for improvements in recovering useful products from the water used for washing, and in treating wool, woollen and cotton fabrics, and other substances. November 14.

Peter William Barlow, of Blackheath, in the county of Kent, civil engineer, for improvements in parts of the permanent ways for railways. November 14.

George Edmund Donisthorpe, and John Whitehead, of Leeds, manufacturers, for improvements in preparing, combing and heckling fibrous matters. November 16.

Walter Crum, of Thornliebank, in the county of Renfrew, in Scotland, calico printer, for certain improvements in the finishing of woven fabrics. November 16.

Alfred Barlow, of Friday-street, in the city of London, warehouseman, for certain improvements in weaving. November 19.

Charles Edward Amos, of the Grove, Southwark, in the county of Surrey, engineer, and Moses Clark, of St. Mary's Craig, in the county of Kent, engineer, for improvements in the manufacture of paper, and in the apparatus and machinery used therein; part of which apparatus and machinery is applicable for regulating the pressure of liquids, for various useful purposes. November 21.

Joshua Proctor Westhead, of Manchester, manufacturer, for improvements in the manufacture of fur into fabrics. November 21.

John Jordan, of Liverpool, inthe county of Lancaster, engineer, for certain improvements in the construction of ships and other vessels navigating on water. November 26. Four months.

William Garnett Taylor, of Burton Hall, in the county of Westmoreland, gentleman, for improvements in lint, and in linting machines, which improvements in linting machines are, in whole or in part, applicable to other purposes. November 29.

William Edward Newton, of Chancery-lane, in the county of Middlesex, civil engineer, for improvements in stoves, grates, and fireplaces, and in warming or heating buildings. November 30.—(Communication).

George Buchanan, of the city of Edinburgh, civil engineer, for improvements in corks, valves, stoppers, and in the use of flexible substances, for regulating or stopping the passage of fluids, and also in making joints of tubes and pipes, or other vessels. November 30.

Charles Morey, citizen of the United States of America, and now residing at Manchester gentleman, for certain improvements in machinery or apparatus for sewing, embroidering, and uniting or ornamenting by stitches, various descriptions of textile fabrics. Dec. 3. Four months.

Thomas Worsdell, of Birmingham, in the county of Warwick, manufacturer, for certain improvements in the manufacture of envelopes and cases, and in the tools and machinery used therein, part of which may be applied to other purposes. December 7.

John Macintosh, of Berner-street, in the county of Middlesex, for improvements in furnaces, and machinery for obtaining power, and in regulating, measuring, and registering the flow of fluids, and liquids. December 10.

Peter Fairbairn, of Leeds, in the county of York, machinist, and John Hetherington, of Manchester, in the county of Lancaster, machinist, for certain improvements in machinery for preparing and spinning cotton, flax, and other fibrous substances. Dec. 11. (Communication.)

James Smith, of Deanston, in the county of Perth, but now residing in Glasgow, for certain improvements in treating the fleeces of sheep when on the animals. December 26.

Edward Lyon Berthon, of Fareham, in the county of Southampton, clerk, M. A., for certain instruments for ascertaining and indicating the course or way, velocity, time, and draught of ships and the rates of currents; also for discharging water from ships, and for taking altitudes and levels at sea or land. December 20. Four months.

LIST OF PATENTS THAT HAVE PASSED THE GREAT SEAL OF IRELAND,

FROM THE 21ST. DAY OF OCTOBER, TO THE 15TH DAY OF DECEMBER, 1849, INCLUSIVE.

Thomas Beal Browne, of Hampen, in the county of Gloucester, gentleman, for certain improvements in looms, and in the manufacture of woven and worsted fabrics. Oct. 22.

John Goodier, of Mode Wheel, Manchester, in the county of Lancaster, miller, for certain improvements in mills for grinding wheat and other grain. October 22.

William Edward Newton, of Chancery-lane, in the county of Middlesex, civil engineer, for certain improvements in steam boilers. November 6.—(Communication).

Alfred Barlow, of Friday-street, in the city of London, warehouseman, for certain improvements in weaving. November 14.

Henry Knight, of Birmingham, in the county of Warwick, for certain improvements in apparatus for printing, embossing, pressing, and perforating. November 21.

Pierre Armand Lecomte de Fontainemoreau, of South-street, Finsbury, for certain improvements in weaving. November 22.—(Communication.)

Pierre Armand, Lecomte de Fontainemoreau, of South-street, Finsbury, for certain improvements in weaving. November 22.—(Communication).

Sir John Macneill, Knight of Dublin, and Thomas Barry, of Lyons, near Dublin, mechanic, for improvements in locomotive engines, and in the construction of railways November 24.

John Combe, of Leeds, in the county of York, civil engineer, for improvements in machinery, for hackling, carding, winding, dressing, and weaving flax, cotton, silk, and other fibrous substances. November 24.

Conrad William Finzel, of the city and county of Bristol, sugar refiner, for improvements in processes and machinery employed in and applicable to the manufacture of sugar. December 4.

Charles Cowper, of Southampton-buildings, Chancery lane, in the county of Middlesex for certain improvements in the manufacture of sugar. December 4.

William Buckwell, of the Artificial Granite Works, Battersea, in the county of Surrey, civil engineer, for improvements in compressing and solidifying fuel. December 11.

Robert Oxland, and John Oxland, of Plymouth, chemists, for improvements in the manufacture of sugar. December 15.

Robert Urwin of Ashford, in the county of Kent, engineer for certain improvements in steam engines, which may in whole or in part, be applicable to pumps and other machines not worked by steam power. December 15.

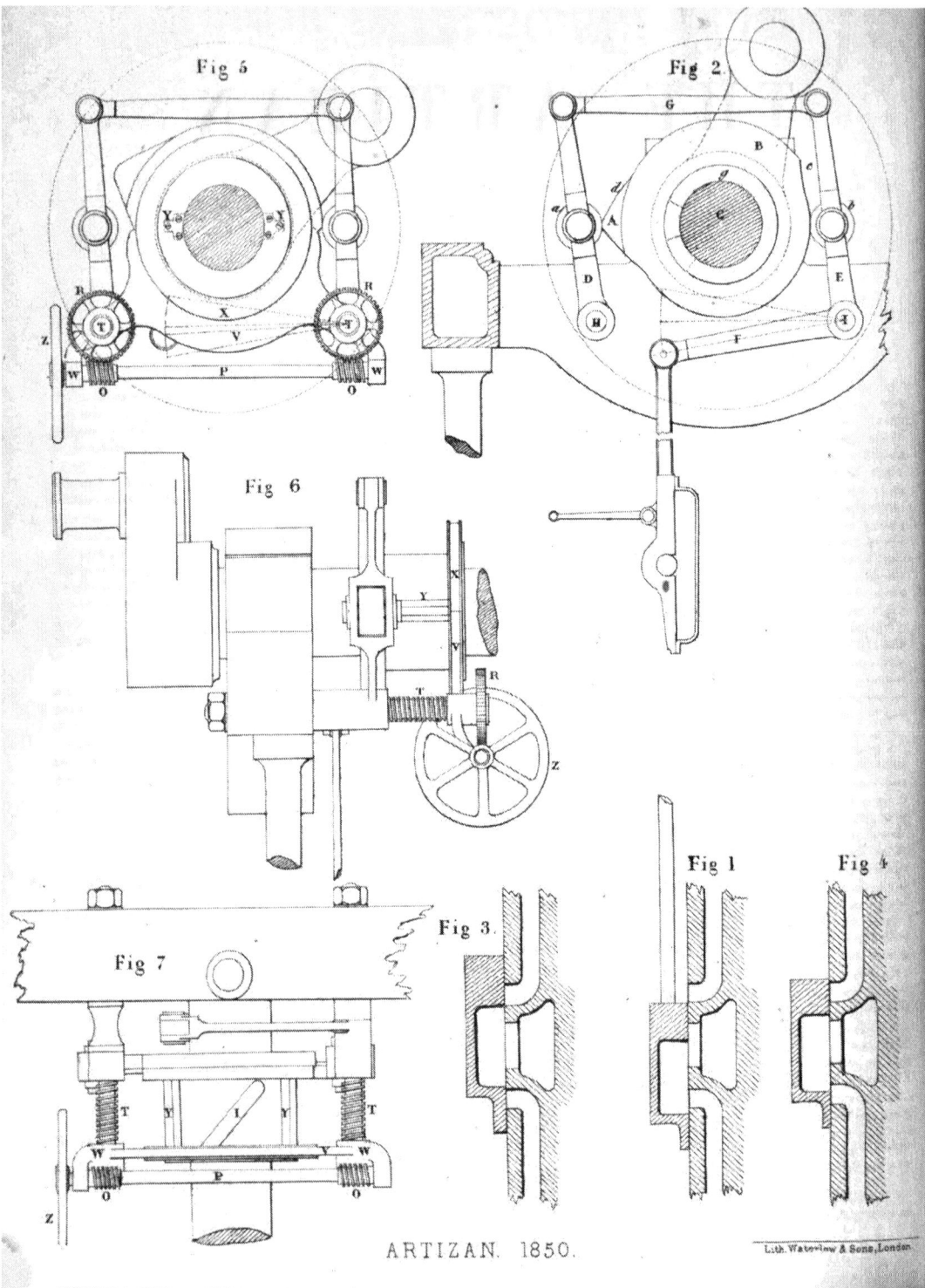

Fig 5

Fig 2

Fig 6

Fig 7

Fig 3

Fig 1

Fig 4

ARTIZAN. 1850.

Lith. Waterlow & Sons, London

THE ARTIZAN.

No. III.—VOL. VIII.—MARCH 1st, 1850.

MECHANICAL ENGINEERING.

ON A NEW FORM OF EXPANSION SLIDE GEAR.

THE benefits to be derived from making use of the expansive principle in steam engines is now so universally acknowledged, and so well understood, that any remarks on this part of the subject appear quite unnecessary. On the best method, however, of carrying out this principle, there is, perhaps, more difference of opinion than on any other detail of engineering. As long as the old-fashioned hand gear and double-beat valves were used, there was no occasion for any separate means of cutting off the steam at any particular part of the stroke, and this system is still used in Cornwall for pumping engines and for crank engines. The superior smoothness of working, however, of the slide, more particularly at high velocities, has caused it to be now generally used in preference to the double-beat valves, although, latterly, Mr. Fairbairn has introduced an improved method of working the double-beat valves, which may obviate some of the objections urged against them.[*]

When the benefits of expansion began to be better appreciated, and steam of a high pressure was introduced, it seemed the most natural way to add a separate expansion valve to the slide, furnished with a separate arrangement of cams for working it. That the expense of this arrangement has prevented its more general use there can be no doubt, whilst at the same time the trouble attending it has often been the cause of its disuse, even where it was applied.

A great variety of plans have been proposed, which it would take too much space to describe, but which I may briefly allude to. Messrs. Seawards' arrangement, in which two sets of valves are used, one for the steam and the other for the exhaust. A number of other plans include a plate or an additional slide on the back or front of the ordinary one, all these, however, requiring a separate arrangement for working them; and, lastly, we have the various modifications of the locomotive slide gear, in which the expansion is varied by altering the stroke of the valve, an arrangement easily managed, but having the defect of not opening the exhaust at the proper time.

In the arrangement which I am about to describe I have endeavoured to avoid all the objections applicable to these several plans, and to render the ordinary slide-valve sufficient for the purpose.

Fig. 1, is a slide valve, of the ordinary description.

Fig. 2, is a side view of the gear for working the slide, independent of the parts necessary to vary the amount of expansion.

A is a cam fixed upon the intermediate shaft C, and acting through the rollers a and b, upon the levers D and E. These levers are connected together by the cross bar G, and consequently both act upon the valve lever F. The studs I and H of the levers E, D, are carried off the entablature in any convenient manner. The crank is shown as having just past the top centre, and the cam has thrown back the lever D, depressing the lever F, and throwing the ports full open for steam and eduction. When the crank has made half a revolution the cam A will act upon the roller b, and raise the valve in a similar manner. The advantage claimed for this particular part

of the gear are, the quick opening of the ports for the admission and eduction of the steam, and at the same time diminishing the travel and size of the valve. Fig. 3 shows the valve that would be required with a common eccentric, viz., 22 inches long, and 3 inches a side cover, and worked with a travel of 12 inches, to give steam for ¾ of the stroke and open full port, with a corresponding shutting up of the exhaust. The valve in figure 1 would be only 18 inches long, with 1 inch a side cover, and 8 inches travel.

The cut-off is effected by giving the valve a partial motion (which can be varied at pleasure), so that, although the steam is cut off, the exhausting port is still partially open for the rest of the stroke, whilst it is kept full open during the time that the steam is admitted on the other side of the piston. This is shown in fig. 4, where the top port is closed whilst the exhaust is still partially open. This motion of the valve is effected in the following manner :—B is a cam fitted on A, so that it can be moved round on it. In figs. 1 and 2, the cam A has just opened the top port full for the admission of steam, and the motion of the levers has brought the roller b in contact with the circular part of the cam B, and the slide will remain stationary in that position until the projection c, on the cam B, raises the valve the depth of the port and shuts off the steam, as shown in figs. 4 and 5, although, as will be seen, it still leaves the exhaust sufficiently open to maintain a perfect vacuum in the cylinder until the termination of the stroke. On the cam A coming round to the roller b, the rest of the stroke of the slide will be completed, and the lower port be instantaneously opened.

It is obvious that, by moving back the cam B, the steam will be cut off later ; and if it be moved so far that the curves c and d coincide, the steam will not be cut off by B at all, but will be admitted for nearly the whole stroke. The engineer will, therefore, have a complete command over the consumption of steam from ¼ of the stroke, (to which the cam is shown adjusted), to the whole stroke.

No alteration is required for going astern. The cam-rod is thrown out of gear, and the engine reversed by hand in the usual manner, the only difference being that the rate of expansion would be reversed, which would be of advantage rather than otherwise, as giving more power when it was most likely to be wanted.

The back part of the projection, B, is so arranged that when the engine is working, cutting off at one-third the stroke (a very good point for general expansion), the astern cut-off will be at two-thirds of the stroke.

The annexed indicator diagram will show the result which may be obtained from the use of this arrangement. The diagram is taken from an engine erected by Messrs. Simpson and Co., of Pimlico, at the Richmond Water Works, which is fitted with expansion-gear from my designs. The cylinder is 20 inches diameter, and 3 feet stroke, and makes 25 strokes per minute. The indicated horse-power is 22.5 h.p. The average pressure 15.75 lbs. per square inch without deducting for friction. Consumption of fuel per 6 hours, 224 lbs., which is at the rate of 1.66 lbs. of coal per horse power per hour. I am aware that exception may be taken to these calculations, and I am, therefore, glad to be able to give the work actually performed by the pump, which fortunately is independent of that *vexatio quæstio*,

---

[*] A drawing of Mr. Fairbairn's expansion-gear, accompanying his paper on the subject, will be found at p. 252 of our last vol.—ED. *Artizan.*

the allowance for friction. From a careful measurement of the water raised, the nett power exerted by the pump is ascertained to be 16 horses, which gives a consumption of fuel of only 2.38 lbs. per horse-power per hour.

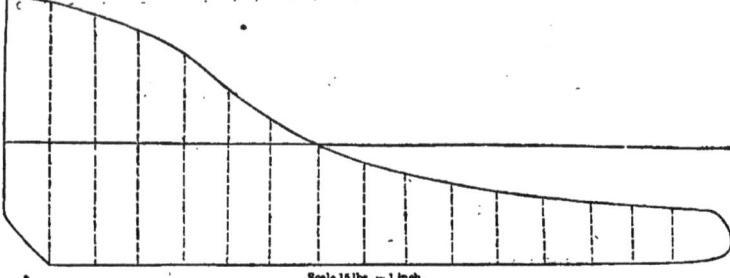

Scale 15 lbs. = 1 inch.

where the steam is cut off. Fig. 6 is an end view, and fig. 7 a reversed plan of the same parts. Two endless screws, O O, are fixed on the shaft, P, and by turning the hand-wheel, Z, the two toothed wheels, R R, are simultaneously turned by the screws, O O. The wheels, R R, are fitted with brass nuts, screwed so as to work steadily on the screws, T T. A clutch plate, V, having two lugs, W W, is fitted to the wheels, R R, so that, by moving the hand-wheel, Z, the plate V is carried longitudinally along. V is fitted nicely to a grooved ring, X , so that X travels with V. The cam, B, is fitted with two strong projecting arms, Y Y, and these run through X, so that B and X stand in the same position to each other. B revolves on the lower part of the cam, A, marked in figure 2 g, and in this lower part are cut two spiral grooves, I I. Strong tongues, forming part of X, are fitted to work in each groove, so that by moving X the relative positions of the cams, A and B, are changed according to the angle of the grooves, and thus steam is admitted in a greater or less degree, according to the direction X is travelling in. X, moving loosely in V, enables this to be done without stopping the engine. I here beg to state that I am indebted to the very talented Messrs. Malcolmson, Brothers, of Waterford, for the idea of the spiral grooves, I I—the application I claim as my own.

It is now some time since I invented this method of working the main valves of a steam-engine, the advantages of which must be obvious to every practical engineer, all secondary expansion valves being liable to objections which are well known. I may here state that I consider the merits of the invention to be simplicity of parts, strength, non-liability to derangement, connection to any common slide, instantaneous admission and emission of the steam, and the effectual accomplishment of expansion to any degree, combined with the best effect from the condenser, accomplished at a very trifling expense. Messrs. Seaward have used my forward cut-off and cross connection in the *Firebrand* and several other vessels where it has given great satisfaction. But it is in long voyage sea-going steam vessels, steam towing vessels, &c., where the advantages of this invention will be felt. In the case of a vessel going against a heavy head sea and wind, and where the speed of the engines is brought down from 18 or 19 strokes to 8 or 9 (a by no means unfrequent occurrence), thus reducing the power of the machinery to one-half, at the very time when a greater power is required both for the safety of the vessel, and making a voyage, here is the remedy at once ; as the resistance to the vessel increases, increase the propelling power to meet it, and with properly constructed engines and boilers, this might be done to the extent of doubling the amount of power given out at each stroke, thus giving a command over the vessel attainable only by these means; while on the other hand, with fair wind or before the sea, reduce the power to the minimum point of expense, an example of which is in diagram No. 1. The use of steam vessels where great distances intervene between the coaling stations has rendered the point of economy in fuel valuable in a degree unknown in short voyages. There are three points for consideration in the matter—viz., for every ton of coal saved there is, first, the value of the fuel itself; secondly, the value

The rate of expansion is varied and the steam regulated, while the engine is in motion, by the following arrangement :—

Fig. 5 shows the position of crank and cam at the point, in this example,

of its stowage room ; and, thirdly, the compound advantage arising from the easier propulsion of the vessel in proportion to the less quantity of water displaced, the less immersion of the paddle-wheel, and the less quantity of steam required to obtain the same speed, and, of course, a correspondingly less quantity of fuel. Take a case where a vessel stows, say 600 tons of coals, for a voyage from Liverpool to New York, and put the whole displacement of the vessel at 1800 or 1900 tons, coals included. The resistance due to the carriage of these coals will amount to one-third of the whole : in fact, to more, in proportion as the paddle-wheel is over immersed—and over immersed it must be at starting—or otherwise the immersion at the end of the voyage must be too little. Now, suppose a means of working the steam so as to get one-fifth more value from it, so that the vessel could start with 500 instead of 600 tons, we should then effect a saving equivalent to the value of 100 tons of coals, and the carriage of 100 tons, which, if not filled up by goods, would give the vessel the advantage arising from the increased speed; or, if the same speed were maintained, the less cost at which it could be so maintained. There is a fourth point worthy consideration ; viz., in our foreign stations, the coals have already had a long sea-voyage carriage, which renders them still more precious : consequently, that carriage is also saved in a corresponding degree—take Aden, Ceylon, &c., for example. Now, I contend that there is no difficulty in constructing marine engines fitted with this gear, or with my equilibrium valve gear (to be described in a future article), so that the expense of working could be reduced to two-thirds its present average amount, and that without any material increase of pressure, or of weight in the machinery—I mean where the common radial paddle-wheel is employed. When we find our neighbours, the Americans, driving larger vessels at as great a speed, and at nearly one-third less expense of fuel, it is certainly time that we, as mercantile men and engineers, were up and doing, or I am afraid the tables will be turned on us, and we shall find our trade pass into their hands, from the simple fact of their being able to do it at a less expense. With new machinery there would be no difficulty in attaining this result of one-third less expense in the working cost, and this result would be at no additional cost for the machinery. A simple attention to the construction of the machinery—that is, boilers, size of cylinders, condensers, &c.,—so as to make use, to the fullest extent, of the powers of this expansion gear, would give out the very greatest practicable result that can be had from the steam ; and in engines already constructed the alteration can be made at a very trifling expense. And so confidant am I of the merits of this invention, that I will undertake by its application to save one-sixth of the fuel in every vessel now crossing the Atlantic, and which is only now fitted with the common eccentric and secondary expansion gear. With respect to its application to towing purposes, it is evident that in towing a small vessel the amount of steam used may be at the lowest point; and when a further development of power, in towing a larger one, is required, the means already described will effect that object.

JOHN DUDGEON,
Inspector of Marine Machinery.

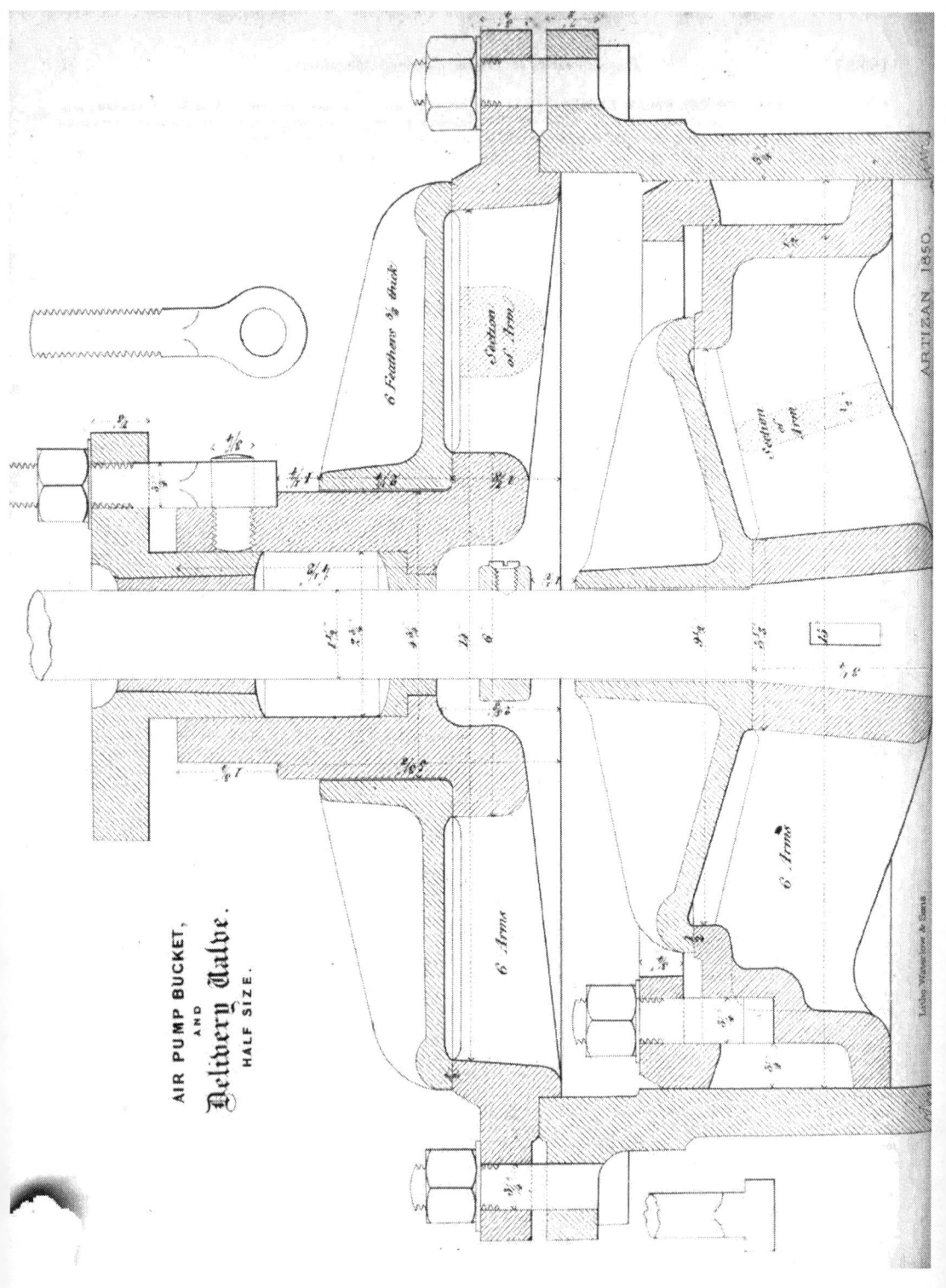

AIR PUMP BUCKET,
AND
Delivery Valve.
HALF SIZE.

6 Feathers ⅜ thick

Section of Arm

Section of Arm

6 Arms

6 Arms

ARTIZAN 1850.

Lithzo Waterstone & Sons

ANALYSIS OF THE STEAM ENGINE.

(Continued from p. 26.)

The half plan of the cylinder, quarter size, in the plate, will serve to explain the packing-chests, which are rectangular in plan. This shape is necessary in the lower one, when the door is put on at the back, to get a flat surface for the joint. Two doors are sometimes used, one on each side at an angle, when, as in the case of marine engines, there may be but little room at the back of the slide-case. Three lugs are shown on the packing-ring to receive the points of the screws: these screws are sometimes made to screw from the inside, the nuts in which they work consisting of a bar of wrought iron bolted across the chest. This plan brings the screws fair down on the packing-ring, and does away with the canting strain on the lugs; but it has the great fault that the engine must be stopped, and the cover removed, before the packing can be screwed down. With the top packing there is no much inconvenience, as the screws pass through the top cover. The top chest is shown square, though it is not actually necessary on this account; but it gives a uniform appearance, and a little more room for handling the packing. Two bosses are cast on the back of the cylinder face 6 ins. from centre, transversely, into which two of the bolts for the top cover are tapped. These bolts ought to be kept as near as possible, without cutting away the surface-joint of the cylinder-cover too much. The bolts in the cylinder-cover are shown about 6 inches pitch; the two opposite ones coming under the cross head, and are tapped (with the thread of a larger diameter to allow the bolt to pass), and serve to screw handles in, by which to lash the cover to the cross head when it has to be lifted. The face of the cylinder is made 23 inches wide over all, to give room for the flanges of the slide-case.

The bottom flange of the cylinder will depend upon the general arrangement of the engine. It is shown with six bosses for $1\frac{1}{2}$ inch bolts—thus, supposing the strength of the bolts to be reduced by screwing to that of $1\frac{1}{4}$ inch iron: area of $1\frac{1}{4}$ inch $= 1.22 \times 6 = 7.32 = 3$ inches diameter, the size of the piston-rod at the strongest part. Taking the bottom flange at $1\frac{1}{4}$ inch thick, the bosses may be $2\frac{1}{2}$ ins. deep in addition.

We have now gone through the various details of the cylinder, with the exception of the slide-gear and the steam-pipe, which we shall consider hereafter. It is a good plan to make a face view of the cylinder, although everything can be fixed without it: it will render the work more easy of comprehension to those who did not make the drawings themselves. Those of our readers who may take the trouble to follow us so far, will find it to their advantage to copy these drawings on larger paper than we can spare, showing the cylinder full length and diameters.

The next point that will engage our attention will be the air-pump and bucket.

The contents of the air-pump are commonly made one-eighth of the capacity of the cylinder, or half the diameter and half the stroke; say 15 inches diameter. If the steam be worked expansively, it will require less injection water, and consequently a smaller air-pump will suffice.

The diameter of the rod, if of iron, may be taken at $\frac{1}{10}$ of the diameter of the pump, or $1\frac{1}{2}$ inch. It is fitted into the rod with a taper end and a key, similar to the piston rod, though, as the strain is chiefly upwards, the key may be lighter in proportion. The bucket is about $\frac{1}{2}$ of the diameter of the pump in depth, say $3\frac{1}{4}$ inches; the outer ring is of the same depth (although this dimension would not be proportionally increased with a larger diameter), and is connected to the centre boss by six arms, $\frac{1}{2}$ inch thick, the same as the ring. Thickness of packing-ring, $\frac{3}{4}$ inch (of brass), held down by $\frac{3}{4}$ bolts with T heads, to receive which, bosses are cast inside the bucket, opposite the arms. Small air-pump buckets are often made without a loose packing-ring, but the practice is not to be commended, and the trifling extra expense is not to be put in competition with the convenience of being able to screw down the packing. The bucket is dished downwards, which makes the delivery of the water more easy when the valve rises. The valve is what is commonly called a "pot-lid valve," a variety which is much cheaper than the butterfly-valves, and which we do not find from experience deserves the bad reputation sometimes awarded it, of striking hard; it is faced in the lathe, and bored to slide freely on the

rod, which guides it, a brass ring being fixed on the rod with two pinch-screws, to prevent the valve rising too high. It is desirable to get the water way as large as possible, but the error must be avoided of making the valve too large, and not allowing sufficient room round it for the water to escape. Taking $\frac{1}{4}$ of the area of the pump as sufficient area for the valves, in this case we ought to have 44 inches area of water way. The diameter of the water way is fixed at $9\frac{1}{2}$ inches, at which the valve clears the lugs on the packing-ring; the area of this is 70 inches, and all this area could be gained (less the space occupied by the arms) if the valve were allowed to rise high enough; but as this would be objectionable, the valve is only allowed to rise $1\frac{1}{2}$ inch, which multiplied by the circumference of $9\frac{1}{2}$ inch ($= 30$ inches) $= 45$ inches for the escape of the water.

The delivery-valve is also of the pot-lid variety, which does away with the necessity of casting a branch on the air-pump. A cover is bolted on the top of the air-pump, consisting of six arms, carrying a stuffing-box for the rod. The outside of the stuffing-box serves as a guide for the valve on the cover, and the water escapes through the spaces between the arms. When a very cheap job is required, the cover and stuffing-box are dispensed with, and the valve slides on the rod, and strikes only on the flange of the pump. This method has the disadvantage, that there are no means of keeping a tight joint between the valve and the rod as they wear; a half-and-half sort of job is sometimes attempted, by putting a stuffing-box on the valve, which stops the leakage, but has a tendency to make the valve stick on the rod from the friction of the packing, and prevents it falling so freely.

Owing to the large diameter of this delivery-valve, it does not need to rise so high. The circumference being 44 inches, one inch rise would be sufficient, but we may say $1\frac{1}{4}$ inch to compensate for the space occupied by the arms.

The gland of the stuffing-box is held down by three eye bolts, for which $\frac{3}{4}$ pins are tapped into the stuffing-box, and which serve as a guard to the valve; the pins are, of course, screwed in, after the valve has been slipped on. Both the bucket-valve and delivery-valve are designed to be made of brass.

It is a point of some importance that the bucket should completely empty the pump at every up stroke, as a smaller pump will then suffice, and the engine will have less load on it. Since the unmechanical practice has been introduced of working the air-pump at the same speed as the piston, even when that has been increased to 400 feet per minute, as in some of the screw vessels, great difficulty has been experienced in devising a suitable valve; a compound of canvas and India-rubber seems now the favourite material, and, as this requires some variation of the parts, we will give in our next article, probably, a sketch of a suitable arrangement.

(To be continued.)

IMPROVEMENTS IN BISCUIT MAKING MACHINERY:

To the Editor of the Artisan:

SIR,

A short time ago a contemporary informed us that Mr. Thomas Harrison of Liverpool, had just patented a machine by which 2,600 biscuits can be produced in one hour. The biscuits have six sides, which prevents any waste in cutting out. The mixing of the flour and water occupies twelve minutes, the kneading five or six minutes, and the baking half an hour. This has been recently very much exceeded by an improved machine-engine, invented by Mr. Bosnell, of Hull, and improved by Mr. Parkinson, Ratcliffe-cross, biscuit baker, by whom they are now manufactured. A sketch of one I send you, which will be readily understood by your readers. I need only state that for the sake of distinctness, I have made the biscuits appear more apart from each other than they are in reality. The dough is put into the trough and is brought down by the flatting rollers, and after being stamped by the docker plate, the biscuits are carried along by the endless web, on to the peal of the man attending the oven. This machine is one of the smallest made, having 2 rows of 14 dockers, making 14 biscuits

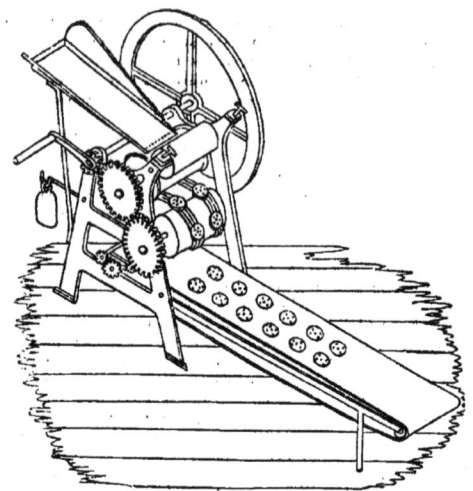

each revolution. The largest machine has 3 rows or 24 dockers, and is worked by one man who can easily turn out 150 biscuits per minute, or 9,000 per hour.

R. ARMSTRONG.

Maritime Invention Office,
Limehouse, Feb. 1850.

To the Editor of the Artisan.

SIR—It is now some twelve months since your columns gave a loud warning on the subject of the Metropolitan Water Supply; since then the cry has flown far and wide. In the space of a few weeks the cholera scourge carried off fourteen thousand souls, and it has been proved beyond the shadow of a doubt that the remedies and preventatives attainable from a sufficient supply of good water, were not only beyond reach, but beyond all hope. For a time, however, though we know not how short, after leaving a large mass of population houseless and helpless, or cast them on the poor rates, the plague has retreated—retreated to one of the fastnesses permitted to exist by Boards of Health, commissioners of sewers, and water monopolists—every parish in London, east, west, north, and south, have lately held meetings on the subject of a fresh supply, and yet in the very teeth of this, we are told by the Board of Health that the works for supplying the public with water should be under the public jurisdiction or management, with works of drainage, paving and surface draining. That, *apart from the merits of any particular scheme of new water works, and pending further investigations as to the practical means of applying the foregoing principle to the metropolis, it is inexpedient to sanction the investment of fresh capital in the same field of supply, as it is probable the new works will have to be re-purchased, and there can be no security that these will be applicable to the arrangements that may be hereafter recommended.* Now, sir, will you allow me, with all respect and with all deference to the members of this Board, and with much of grateful feeling for all their good intentions, will you allow me to ask you, as one of the promoters of the safety of public health, in all matters of engineering, at least, what security the public have that the Board of Health is competent to the task they have undertaken—one entirely dependent upon a mass of practical details, of which they can know nothing practically, since they are not practical men. It is perhaps, the greatest of the misfortunes of science pure, that practical details are overlooked, and necessarily, because purely scientific men never hear of them, and this is certainly one of those important instances in which all such minutiæ require the most careful working and most attentive watching, and this is left to the sole care of a number of scientific gentlemen with the best intentions.

With the slap-dash assertion made by the water monopolists, in the person of such an imposing leader as Sir Wm. Clay, who comes forward with an undaunted daring which would do credit to the boldest leader of a forlorn hope, and who says in his pamphlet (p. 19) that " it is impossible to avoid coming to the conclusion, that water is furnished to London, not only in greater profusion than any other city in the world, but in a degree beyond the utmost wants of its inhabitants, and, when to this is added—that the companies could, if it were required, easily double their present supplies, it must, I think, be considered as demonstrated, that, whatever may be the other improvements required, no outlay of capital could well be more purely in waste, than one devoted to bringing more water to the metropolis." With all this we will have nothing to do, beyond recording such a statement, as a memento of what we may expect, because it has already been most thoroughly demolished. We can, besides, make great allowance for the last struggles of those who are about to lose so much, but I confess to a feeling of extreme surprise, that a Board, established as a guardian of public health, should be the first to throw cold water on the endeavours which the people are making themselves for their own safety.

There is, however, one comfort—that we are not obliged to listen to them; and another solace and subject, I am free to own, of no small pride, is to think that on members of our profession of engineers devolves the duty of removing the affliction under which London is suffering, in the shape of an insufficient supply of impure water. Already numerous schemes are in the field for public approval, and there are more in *embryo*; and, without any design of illegitimately prejudicing any of these, I would call your attention to some of their principal features.

The Henley scheme was alluded to in your columns last year; this company proposes to take the water from the Thames, by an aqueduct near Mednenham Abbey, about 3 miles above Great Marlow. Hambledon Lock, which is about 2 miles above Mednenham, and where there is a lift of 3 feet 6 inches, is to be removed, and another erected below the abbey, so that the river, between the new lock and the one above Henley, will form a nearly level reservoir, 88 feet above Trinity standard.

The works are first to proceed from the abbey, by open cut, 40 feet wide and 10 feet deep, running round the foot of some high grounds between Maidenhead and Great Marlow, approaching Cookham, and running on to the Thames, which an aqueduct crosses above Maidenhead Bridge. Although the distance from Mednenham Abbey to Maidenhead Bridge is only about 6 miles in a straight line, the curve which the open cut takes round the high ground is very nearly 8½ miles in length. From Maidenhead Bridge, this open cut proceeds along the Great Western Railway as far as West Drayton, where it crosses under the Grand Junction Canal, a distance of 10 miles further. From West Drayton the open cut is made 26 feet wide and 7 feet deep, and proceeds on to Bull's Bridge, near Cranford, and to the Brent, for about 5 miles. From here the line proceeds by two brick culverts, each 10 feet in diameter, to a basin at West End, Hampstead.

The aqueduct is to carry 200 millions of gallons per diem as far as West Drayton, and from thence to West Hampstead 100 millions of gallons. The 100 million extra is to be passed from the Thames when there is a surplus, to West Drayton, and then by the Grand Junction Canal to a reservoir at Paddington, 85 feet above Trinity standard, for the sewers. There are to be three collecting and depositing reservoirs; one near Cookham, one near West Drayton, and another near Harrow.

Steam power (3,500 horse) is to raise the water from the West Hampstead Basin, to another reservoir at Hampstead, 165 feet higher, and 250 feet above Trinity standard. From this last reservoir, the water is to be conveyed by large mains to be distributed in the north, and to be carried over Vauxhall Bridge to the south of London; these new mains are to supply the mains and pipes of the present companies.

The engineering estimate is one million for works from Henley to London, including compensation to mill-owners, and one million for cost of extra plant. Total, £2,000,000.

The annual expense as rent charge, for compensation to existing companies, and cost of distribution, is £227,590.

The other scheme, which proposes to take water from the Thames, is the Mapledurham; this company proposes to convey its supply from above Mapledurham lock, which is 17 miles higher up than Mednenham, and 5 miles above the junction of the river Kennet. An open cut, 4½ miles long, is to take the water from here to four reservoirs at Caversham, where it is to undergo the purifying process of Dr. Clarke's patent. Powerful steam engines are to raise the water from these reservoirs, through three 5 feet pipes, over the river into three smaller reservoirs, 35 miles from London, and at levels corresponding with three districts into which the engineers suppose London divided. From these last reservoirs the pipes are continued to the Great Western Railway, near Twyford. From here they are laid by the side of the railway, cross the Thames at Maidenhead, and are continued on to Wormwood Scrubs. Here the high level pipe diverges, and runs on to a reservoir at Primrose Hill, 189 feet above Trinity standard. The other two continue by the side of the Great Western to Paddington, and along Westbourne Terrace and Oxford Street, into a reservoir at St. Giles's. The low level pipe crosses the Thames at Waterloo Bridge, into the south district.

The estimate for this scheme is, for works ... £1,200,000
Annual working expenses 20,000
£1,220,000

Of the effect of either of these schemes on the navigation, I need say nothing, as this has already been done by Mr. James Walker and Mr. Leseh. I will merely point out to your attention, as features in both schemes, the very great distance from which the water is brought to London; the magnitude of steam power required—a wonderful panacea for all engineering difficulties now-a-days; the introduction, in one scheme, of Dr. Clarke's process, which consists in precipitating the carbonate of lime, by the admixture of a certain quantity of water saturated with lime, deprived, by calcining, of carbonic acid. With this process, bye-the-by, Sir W. Clay is very wrath. After expressing his doubts as to its acceptability to water consumers, he observes, at p. 43—"Of course, if it were desirable, it could be done by the present companies, who possess all the necessary means and appliances, in reservoirs, engines, &c., but I repeat I do not believe it would be either practicable or desirable." If not *practicable*, Sir W. Clay, how are the companies to do it? Are they in the habit of achieving impracticabilities? Allow me, however, after this short digression, to return to our subject. You will perceive, by the course which the Henley works are to take, that the crossings are both numerous and of no small significance in an estimate. The long distance of open cut on the Henley scheme is open to the objection which will always lay against schemes of which the line is so much exposed—to receiving impurities along such a lengthy range of country. On the other side, I need scarcely remark on the remarkable feature of 100 miles of pipe of 5 feet diameter, in the Mapledurham scheme, and you may, perhaps, think with me that St Giles's is an odd place for a reservoir. The Mapledurham source of supply is above several villages and towns which drain into the Thames above Mednenham.

The Kingston scheme cannot be called that of a new company. It is here proposed to take the water from Kingston, and to convey it, by 30-inch mains, to the reservoirs of the Lambeth Waterworks at Brixton.

The Wandle project proposes to lift the water from the Wandle to a reservoir to be formed on Wimbledon Common, from whence it is to be conveyed for the supply of the south districts. To preserve the Wandle from sewage contamination, a sewer is to be constructed from Croydon to the Thames—that unfortunate vehicle of all filth.

Of the Watford project, so much has lately been said, besides what they have had to say for themselves—for they are certainly not idle—that I shall be silent on the subject, and pass on to some of the embryo projects.

A correspondent, "F. W.," in the *Times* of the 21st, proposes Bala Lake, in Merioneth, as a source of supply, not only to London, but to Liverpool, Manchester, and other large towns. Bala Lake is, he says, 600 feet above Hampstead Heath, and he proposes to bring the water by a four feet pipe along the North-western Railway, and further observes, that all engineering difficulties are overcome. He admits, however, that there will be certain resting places along the line of transit where the water will lose some of its head, but he does not say anything about rising gradients on the road to London, some of which are very great. North of Tring, for instance, is a gradient rising towards London for several miles, of about 1 in 300. One line of pipe would not deliver the quantities required, and yet at a fair estimate I do not think that a mile of such piping could be had, carted, laid, and jointed under £20,000 per mile, setting all other items and contingencies entirely out of the question.

And there is another consideration, which is, that the North Western Railway does not run to Hampstead Heath, and it would have to be raised some 200 feet before it got there. At the first blush of the thing, 600 feet above Hampstead Heath appears a great height; *but* the distance is immense, and a 4 foot pipe would be found to deliver an inconsiderable quantity, even if the pipes were laid direct to the Heath.

An examination, however, of all these schemes, which are all fair and legitimate, and the productions of high-minded and talented men, is a theme which one can consider with pleasure.

I would now call your attention to an abortive attempt which has just been made to obtain suspension of the standing orders by a scheme connected with the North Kent Railway, an application which I conceive was the more justly rejected that the project possesses less fairness and practicability about it, than any yet brought before the public. The projector of this scheme has imagined that the metropolis is to depend on the operations of the miner for its supply of water, as it does for its supply of fuel; and he would lead us to believe that the North Kent Railway is placed in that felicitous position to be able to convey to London a large proportion of the water which falls upon 6,000 square miles of our chalk district. He considers that some one million and a half of gallons is discharged daily by 250 yards in length on the banks of the river Thames at Erith; in the first place, however, we have not heard at what period or periods of the year the gaugings were taken; and in the second, I no more believe that such land springs are fitted in quality for the supply of London than that the off-scourings of a rabble are adapted to good society. By this assertion of a million and a half of gallons on 250 yards of length, we are led to believe, that this district abounds with water from the chalk, because, as it is said, only one stream, the Cray, crosses the line of railway from the south. On examination, however, I observe and beg to point out numerous streams at Shooters' Hill, and the same at Erith, the Dart and the Darwent with their numerous feeders draining a large tract, two considerable streams running into the estuary at Northfleet, and also draining a considerable district, besides a river running nearly parallel between the railway and the hills for some miles near Chiselhurst and Bromley, and falling into the Ravensbourne. These with the waters of the Ravensbourne, the Cray, and the important river the Medway, all within a distance of 24 miles, are, I think you will allow, sufficient to place this district in a very different position as regards surface drainage to that presented at the first blush by Mr. P. W. Barlow, by the assertion that only one stream, the Cray, crosses the line of railway. But to return to the 250 yards yielding the one and a half million of gallons per diem on this fortunate locality, all over which it is said that similar springs abound, we are led hereby to understand that on a mile we shall have above ten and a half millions of gallons per diem, or 157½ millions of gallons on 15 miles per diem. Now, sir, allow me to observe that the projector of this scheme says that of the 6000 square miles embraced in our great chalk district or basin, one-half or 3000 square miles is a surface of bare chalk, or covered with permeable beds, allowing the water to percolate; upon this surface, *assuming one foot per annum to be absorbed*, the average supply is fourteen hundred and fifty millions of gallons per diem, so that above one-ninth of the rain which is *assumed to be absorbed* by the 3000 square miles, would come to the share of half the North Kent Railway! I think that is what we term proving too much. So I will leave that part of the matter, but I must call your attention to the one foot assumed absorption when we consider that we have only about 24 inches fall of rain. The cost of bringing the water to the Brick-layers' Arms, terminus, is estimated at £150,000, including the cost of heading for intercepting the water flowing from the chalk into the river; I venture to doubt whether this sum would pay for the piping only. I am, Sir, your's faithfully,

London, February 22, 1850, "H."

DIMENSIONS AND DETAILS OF NEW STEAMERS.

THE ARDROSSAN AND BELFAST STEAM-PACKET COMPANY'S IRON VESSELS, "FIRE FLY" AND "GLOW-WORM."

Builder's measurement.		"Fire Fly."	"Glow-worm."
		Ft ins	Ft ins
Length of keel and fore rake...	...	164 0	153 6
Breadth of beam	...	22 3	22 0
Ditto, including the paddle-cases	...	39 0	37 6
Depth of hold amidships ...	...	14 2	12 2
Length of engine space ...	...	49 0	50 2

Tonnage				Tons	Tons
Hull ...	...	...	...	415	360
Contents of engine space	...	...	...	135	128
Register ...	...	...	...	280	231
New measurement				Ft	Ft
Length on deck ...	...	...	...	164.4	153.3
Breadth on ditto amidships	...	...	...	22.0	20.0
Depth of hold ditto	...	...	...	11.8	12.0
Length of poop ...	...	...	...	77.3	9.3
Breadth of ditto ...	...	...	...	21.1	14.6
Depth of ditto ...	...	...	...	2.3	2.3
Length of engine space	...	...	...	49.0	50.2
Tonnage				Tons	Tons
Hull ...	...	...	...	344	288
Poop ...	...	...	...	40	3
Total ...	...	...	...	385	291
Contents of engine space	...	...	...	137	130
Register ...	...	...	...	237	161
Nominal power ...	...	...	...	174 h.p.	102 h.p.
				Ft ins	Ft ins
Diameter of cylinders	...	...	...	0 50	0 40
Length of stroke ...	...	...	...	4 6	3 6
Diameter of air pump	...	...	...	0 44	
Length of stroke ...	...	...	...	2 6	
Diameter of paddle-wheels extreme	...	...	...	22 3	16 6
Ditto, ditto, effective	...	...	...	21 8	16 0
Length of floats ...	...	...	...	6 3	6 0
Breadth of ditto ...	...	...	...	1 8	1 4
Number of arms ...	...	...	...	11	15

Fire Fly—Twenty-two floats. Two tubular boilers, length—13 feet; breadth, 9 feet 2 inches; depth, 12 feet. Six furnaces, three in each boiler—length, 8 feet; breadth 2 feet 6 inches; depth, 3 feet 6 inches. Steam chests—length, mean, 7 feet; breadth, 4 feet; depth, 2 feet. 206 tubes, 103 in each, diameter 4 inches × 7 feet 6 inches. The bunkers are 7 feet long, and all the breadth and depth of the vessel, except the tunnel or passage leading from the engines, breadth, 2 feet 7 inches; depth 6 feet. Also, two tubes through the bunkers, one at each side, 2 feet diameter, to facilitate the draught of the wing furnaces. The frames are 3 × 3 × ½ in. and 1 foot 9 inches apart. Boilers to bunkers, 7 feet 9 inches. Consumption of coals, 19 cwt. per hour; 9¼ lbs. steam pressure; 22 revolutions per minute; average draught of water, 7 feet; average passage, 7½ hours, 80 miles. Two double side rod direct acting engines, by Messrs. Tod and McGregor, Glasgow, 1845, by whom the vessel was built. Boilers by Messrs. Barr and Shearer, Ardrossan. The engines are aft, and the boilers forward. The crew consists of 23 hands—ten in the captain's department, six in the engineer's ditto, and 7 in the steward's.

Description—Bust female figure head, mock quarter galleries, clipper bow, standing bowsprit, three masts, schooner-rigged, square-sterned, and clinker-built vessel. Commander—Mr. Thomas Brown.

Glow-worm—Two sets of 15 arms and floats. Two tubular boilers—length, 10 feet 6 inches; breadth, 7 feet; depth, 9 feet. Four furnaces, two in each boiler—length 6 feet 8 inches; breadth, 2 feet 10 inches; depth, 3 feet 9 inches. Steam chests—length below, 7 feet; ditto at top, 5 feet 6 inches; breadth, 5 feet 4 inches; depth, 3 feet 6 inches. 112 tubes—diameter, 3 inches × 7 feet. Diameter of chimney, 3 feet 6 inches. Bunkers hold 14 tons of coals, consumes 17 cwt. per hour; 28 revolutions per minute. Steam pressure, 7 lbs. Frames, 2¼ × 2¼ × ½ and 3 feet apart. Average draught of water, 6 feet 6 inches. Average passage, 8 hours. This vessel was built upon the wave line principle, for Ashton Smith, Esq., as a pleasure yacht, and is a beautiful model, and an able sea-boat. Has had 83 head of cattle on deck, in a heavy sea, drawing only 6 feet 6 inches of water, and was not in the least crank, and is very buoyant upon the waves. Two side-lever engines, by Mr. Robert Napier, Lance-Field Foundry, Glasgow. Boilers by Messrs. Tod and McGregor, Clyde Foundry. Vessel built by Mr. John Laird, North Birkenhead, and launched on the Queen's birthday, 1838.

Description—Bust female figure head, mock quarter bridges, three masts, schooner-rigged, standing bowsprit, common bow, square-sterned and carvill-built vessel. Port of Glasgow. Commander—Mr. Archibald McLeish.

THE ROYAL MAIL SCREW STEAM VESSEL "KESTREL."

Built by Messrs. Robert Steele and Co.; Engines, &c., by Messrs. Caird and Co., Greenock.

Builders' Measurement			Feet. Inches.
Length of keel and fore rake	...	...	124 0
Breadth of beam, amidships	...	...	25 0
Depth of hold, do.	...	...	14 6
Length of engine space	...	...	32 1
Tonnage.			Tons.
Hull	...	...	365
Contents of engine space	...	...	110
Register ...	...	...	265
New measurement			Feet.
Length on deck ...	...	...	121.1
Breadth on ditto, at midships	...	...	22.9
Depth of hold ditto	...	...	13.8
Length of break deck	...	...	37 0
Breadth of ditto ...	...	...	20.1
Depth of ditto ...	...	...	1.8
Length of engine space	...	...	32.1
Tonnage.			Tons.
Hull ...	...	...	260
Break deck ...	...	...	14
Total ...	...	...	275
Contents of engine space	...	1	
Ditto of engine ditto	...	110 }	112
Register ...	...	...	163

A pair of inverted cylinder engines, of 80-horse nominal power. Diameter of cylinders, 36 inches; × 2 feet length of stroke; diameter of air-pumps 18 inches; diameter of screw (two blades of brass), 9 feet; 79 revolutions per minute, light. One tubular boiler, length at top, 9 ft. 9 in.; ditto, below, 9 feet; breadth, 11 feet, 5 inches; height, 14 feet; three furnaces, length, 6 feet 3 inches; breadth, 3 feet 1 inch; depth, 3 feet 2 in.; 186 tubes, diameter 3¼ inches, × 6 feet, long; chimney, diameter, 3 feet; × 32 feet long. This vessel is the fifteenth fitted with screw machinery, by Messrs. Caird and Co.

Description—Bird figure head, no galleries, round sterned and carvill-built vessel of timber, standing bowsprits, three masts, schooner rigged.

THE IRON SCREW STEAM VESSEL, "SECRET."

Built by Messrs. Denny Brothers, Dumbarton. Engines by Messrs. Caird and Co. Cartsdyke, Greenock.

Builder's measurement.			Ft ins
Length of keel and fore rake	...	...	141 2
Breadth of beam amidships	...	...	23 3¼
Depth of hold at do.	...	...	13 3
Length of engine space	...	...	22 6
Tonnage.			Tons
Hull ...	...	...	373
Contents of engine space ...			75
Register ...	...	...	298
New measurement.			Feet
Length on deck ...	...	...	133.3
Breadth on do. amidships	...	...	22.0
Depth of hold do.	...	...	13.0
Length of break-deck	...	...	43.2
Breadth at do. ...	...	...	18.8
Depth of do. ...	...	...	2.4
Length of engine space	...	...	22.5
Tonnage.			Tons
Hull...	...	...	289
Break-deck ...	...	...	21
Total ...	...	...	310
Shaft space ...	...	3 }	71
Engine space ...	...	68 }	
Register ...	...	...	239

A pair of inverted cylinder engines, of 42 horses nominal power. Diameter of cylinders, 28 inches × 2 feet length of stroke. Diameter of screw, 8 feet. Pitch, 12 to 13 feet (two blades, malleable iron). Engines directly attached to the screw. Crank shaft journals, $6\frac{3}{4} \times 8\frac{1}{2}$ inches. One tubular boiler—length at top, 9 feet 3 inches; ditto at bottom, 8 feet 6 inches; breadth, 10 feet $3\frac{1}{2}$ inches; height, 11 feet. 172 tubes; 3 furnaces. Speed under steam alone, light, $10\frac{1}{2}$ miles. Launched October 13, 1847.

Plying between Liverpool, Constantinople, Smyrna, and Trebizond, with goods and passengers.

Description—A fiddle figure head, no galleries, three masts, schooner-rigged, standing bowsprit, square-sterned and clinch-built vessel.

THE NEW IRON SCREW STEAM VESSEL, "CAMBRTON."

Built and fitted by Messrs. Napier and Crichton, Glasgow.

Builders' measurement.				Ft.	in.
Length aloft	...	...	...	173	9
Length of keel and fore rake	...	...	173	3
Breadth of beam, extreme	...	...	25	8
Depth of hold ...	...	...	...	14	0
Length of engine space ...	...	...	37	6
Length of gearing ditto ...	...	...	12	0
Breadth of ditto	...	...	...	4	0
Depth of ditto ...	...	...	...	5	0
Length of shaft space	...	...	37	6
Breadth of ditto	...	...	...	2	6
Depth of ditto ...	...	...	...	3	3
Tonnage.				Tons.	
Hull ..	...	...	$0\frac{11}{10}$	528$\frac{84}{100}$	
Gearing space ...	...	...	$0\frac{11}{10}$		
Shaft space	...	...	$1\frac{61}{100}$ }	126$\frac{13}{100}$	
Engine ditto	...	...	123$\frac{24}{100}$ }		
Register	...	...	...	402$\frac{44}{100}$	
New Measurement.				Feet	
Length on deck ...	...	...	...	172.1	
Breadth on do. amidships ...	...	...	24.8	
Depth of hold do.	...	...	...	13.5	
Length of break-deck	...	...	41.4	
Breadth of do.	...	...	...	20.9	
Depth of do.	...	...	...	2.2	
Length of gearing space ...	...	...	12.0	
Breadth of do.	...	...	...	4.0	
Depth of do.	...	...	...	5.0	
Length of shaft space	...	...	37.5	
Breadth of do.	...	...	...	2.5	
Depth of do.	...	...	...	3.3	
Length of engine space	...	...	37.5	
Tonnage				Tons	
Hull ...	...	...	...	...	454$\frac{1}{100}$
Break-deck	...	...	...	...	20$\frac{48}{100}$
Total ...	...	...	...	474$\frac{49}{100}$
Contents of gearing space ...	...	2$\frac{70}{100}$		
" shaft space ...	...	3$\frac{71}{100}$ }	141$\frac{41}{100}$	
" engine space ...	...	135$\frac{00}{100}$ }		
Register	...	...	...	333$\frac{70}{100}$	

A pair of beam engines (beam at top), of 102 horse nominal power. Diameter of cylinders, 40 inches × 3 feet 6 inches stroke; diameter of screw, 7 feet ; pitch, 9 feet (three blades). 86 teeth in spur-wheel, and 26 in the pinion. Pitch, 4 inches.

Two tubular boilers—length, 11 feet; breadth, 8 feet 3 inches; height, 10 feet. Steam chests—length at top, 6 feet 6 inches; do. at bottom, 8 feet 6 inches; breadth at top, 3 feet; do. at bottom, 5 feet; height, 4 feet. Six furnaces, three in each—length, 8 feet 6 inches; breadth 2 feet 1 inch; depth, 3 feet 4 inches. 160 malleable iron tubes, 75 in each boiler—diameter of tubes, 4 inches × 7 feet long. Diameter of funnel, 6 feet 6 inches.

Draught of water, with machinery on board, forward, 4 feet 9 inches; aft, 6 feet 6 inches.

Length of keel, cut, 161 feet; fore rake, 12 feet 3 inches; aft rake, 6 inches. Beam, moulded, 25 feet 6 inches. Fifteen strakes of plates from keel to gunwale, tapering in thickness from $\frac{5}{8}$ of an inch to $\frac{3}{8}$ of an inch; bottom and round the bilge, wales, &c., $\frac{1}{2}$ inch. Frames, $3\frac{1}{2} \times 2\frac{1}{2} \times \frac{5}{8}$ in., and 1 foot 6 inches, from centre to centre—stem to stern. Launched 2nd November, 1849.

January 26th, sailed from the tail of the Bank, at Greenock, for Hull, the draught of water forward being 9 feet 6 inches, and 10 feet aft—mean, 9 feet 9 inches; having 300 tons of goods on board, exclusive of coals. Ran the distance from the Clock to Cumbrae in 1 hour and 19 minutes. With the tide, ran the whole distance from the tail of the Bank, Greenock, to the Dock Gates, at Hull, in 84 hours. Steam pressure, 10 lbs. per square inch, the engines making 41 revolutions per minute.

This vessel is the property of Messrs. W. and C. L. Ringrose, merchants, Hull, and is built to ply on the station between Hull and Rotterdam.

Description—Full female figure head, clipper bow, false quarter galleries, standing bowsprit, three masts, schooner-rigged, square-sterned and clinch-built vessel of iron. Port of Hull. Commander—Mr. William Jefson Pattrick.

CORK STEAM NAVIGATION COMPANY'S IRON STEAM-VESSEL, "PREUSSISCHER ADLER" ("PRUSSIAN EAGLE").

Built by Messrs. Thomas Vernon and Co. Engines, boilers, &c., by Messrs. Bury, Curtis, and Kennedy, Clarence Foundry, Liverpool.

Builders' measurement.				Ft.	in.
Length, extreme	...	...	...	218	0
Ditto of keel and fore rake	...	...	180	0
Breadth of beam	...	...	...	29	0
Ditto, including paddle-cases	...	...	51	0
Depth of hold amidships...	...	...	17	10
Length of engine space ...	...	...	45	6
Tonnage.				Tons.	
Hull...	...	...	...	...	732$\frac{51}{100}$
Contents of engine space	...	...	205$\frac{31}{100}$	
Register	...	...	...	527$\frac{22}{100}$	
New measurement.				Ft.	
Length on deck	...	...	...	180.5	
Breadth on deck amidships	...	...	28.2	
Depth of hold ditto	...	...	...	17.6	
Length of engine space ...	...	...	45.5	
Tonnage.				Tons.	
Hull...	...	...	...	...	899
Contents of engine space ...	...	...	245$\frac{48}{100}$	
Register	...	...	...	563$\frac{10}{100}$	

A pair of double side rod direct acting engines, of 336 horses nominal power. Diameter of cylinders, 66 inches × 6 feet 1 inch length of stroke. Diameter of paddle-wheels, extreme, 28 feet 6 inches; ditto, effective, 27 feet 11 inches. Length of floats, 8 feet 10 inches × 2 feet broad. Three sets of 12 arms and 24 floats. Average speed of engines, 17 revolutions per minute, of vessel, $12\frac{1}{2}$ knots, at 12 feet, load draught of water, even keel. Light draught of water, 9 feet 6 inches. The engines are very highly finished. The intermediate shaft, being bent, forms the crank for working one double-acting air pump, and is all bright.

This vessel was built as a war steam vessel for the Prussian Government, and was armed with two heavy pivot guns, one fore and the other aft, and seemed to have answered all the expectations of the proprietors; but having altered their minds, she was subsequently sold to the present owners. They had not had her long in their possession when they got an offer for the re-purchase of the vessel by the Prussian Government, but being well pleased with their bargain they declined. (For boilers see *Artisan Treatise on the Steam Engine*, page 75.) The crew consists of 4 hands in steward's department, 12 in the engineer's, and 16 in the captain's, total 32.

Description — Bird figure head (Eagle), common bow, round-sterned, clinker, and carvil-built vessel of iron; one flush deck, standing bowsprit, two masts, schooner-rigged. Port of Cork. Commander—Mr. William Lane Tooker.

                                                    P. B.

ANALYSIS OF PATENTS.

Richard Archibald Brooman, of London, *for improvements in steam generators.* July 4th, 1849.

This invention consists in a method of applying M. Boutigny's discovery of the speroidalizability of water, and other fluids, to useful purposes—viz. to produce steam of a very high pressure in a generator of very small capacity, as compared with ordinary steam-boilers. By this diminution of size, it is anticipated that the danger of explosion will be obviated, and that the consumption of fuel will be greatly reduced. (At p. 182 of our last volume, this subject will be found discussed.)

The generator consists of a cylindrical boiler, proposed of cast iron, set vertically in a furnace; the bottom convex, and the top flat, with a flange and cover. The inside of the bottom is covered with hemispherical hollows, or grooved channels, the object being to divide the feed water into small portions, and induce the spheroidal state. Two reservoirs are used to supply the feed water, in order that while one is being emptied, the other may be filled. A pipe is carried from the top of the reservoir, and another from the bottom to cocks on the cover of the generator, so that, by opening the cocks, an equal pressure will exist in the reservoir, and the water will enter the generator. The pipe from the top of the reservoir is continued down nearly to the bottom of the generator; so that, should the water in the generator rise above the bottom of this pipe, it will be driven up into the reservoir again by the pressure of the steam. The pipe from the bottom of the reservoir enters the top of the generator, and the water passing through it, is intercepted in its fall by a number of false bottoms, placed at intervals between the top and bottom of the generator, which serve as a heating surface to evaporate a portion of the water. The bottom of the generator the patentee proposes to heat to 500° centigrade, but we confess to be unable clearly to see in what respect his apparatus is superior to various other plans of generators, in which a small surface of highly heated metal is used to produce steam of great pressure, as in Perkins' steam gun, &c.

The patentee claims, first, the employment of steam for manufacturing and other purposes, at a much higher temperature and pressure than has hitherto been the practice, such steam being generated by the combined action of ebullition and spheroidalisation of water. Secondly, the use of perforated trays, spiral wire gauze tubes or gutters, either separate or in combination, in a steam generator, having the bottom hollowed out for the purpose of generating steam by the combined action of ebullition and spheroidalization. Thirdly, the employment of a number of cylinders, meeting at a point where the greater amount of heat is applied in hemispherical ends, and opening at the other ends into a transverse vessel, to which the feed water is supplied, either alone or with the addition of perforated metal trays. Fourthly, the employment of two concentric cylinders, arranged so as to apply the heat both on the interior and exterior surfaces. Fifthly, the use of a waste pipe placed inside the steam generator, and terminating at the bottom just above the hollows and channels in the heating surface, and at the upper part connected with a pipe leading to the feed cisterns, whereby the pressure is equalised in the cisterns and the steam generator, so as to ensure the necessary supply of water to the generator. Sixthly, arranging the several parts in connection with this steam generator, so as to effect the self action of the supply of water. Seventhly—The maintaining the level of the spheroidalized water at a point beneath the highest surface or ridges between the channels in the bottom of the generator, by means of the waste or return pipe; and lastly, placing this improved steam generator within the chimney of the furnace, and also the application of baths of metal, or other suitable material, to the heating of the improved steam generator, as described.

Henry Bessemer, of Baxter House, St. Pancras, Middlesex, *for improvements in the methods, means, and machinery or apparatus employed for raising and forcing water and other fluids.* June 23, 1849.

THIS invention consists of a centrifugal pump, thus constructed—Two discs are cast or bolted together, leaving a water way between them, which is divided by radial ribs into a given number of passages. The disc is mounted vertically or horizontally on a shaft, to which a rapid motion is given by suitable gearing, and the water flows into the discs through an opening in the centre, connected with the suction-pipe. The circular edge of this opening bears against the face of the suction-pipe. The whole machinery is fixed inside a water-tight casing, the shaft of the driving-wheel working through two stuffing boxes, one on each side. An outlet is provided at such a height as to keep the top of the disc covered with water. When the disc is set in motion, the centrifugal force of the water throws it out of the arms into the case, and a vacuum is formed in the suction-pipe, up which the supply of water flows. Another arrangement of the same principle is described, applied to a forcing pump. The disc is placed horizontally, with hanging valves on the suction side; the power, in this case, may be applied by multiplying wheels, from a capstan. The area of the delivering points in the arms ought not, the patentee states, to exceed the area of water way at the centre, but to be rather less. To work one of these horizontal forcing pumps, the patentee also describes an oscillating engine, the trunnions standing vertically, applied direct to the crank-shaft of the pump. (This appears to us an evident infringement of Hastie's patent.) The slide of the engine is described as being worked by the vibration of the cylinder, which is neither a good nor a new plan; the lower trunnion revolves upon a ball, as is done in turntables. In raising water a great height, the patentee prefers to do it by a series of pumps placed at suitable distances, and driven off one shaft. He also proposes to employ a horizontal windmill, a simple emissive engine, a disc engine, or a turbine; or a screw working in the stern of a ship by its motion through the water, and working a pump in the hold, or for other purposes. The peculiar form of screw described may be also employed for propelling, or for raising water, &c., &c.

William Bush, of Great Tower-street, London, civil engineer, *for improvements in lamps and in lighting.* July 4, 1849.

THESE improvements consist in forming reflectors of glass bent into a parabolic, or other suitable shape, and silvered at the back in such a manner that the silvering will not be affected by the heat of the light. The reflector may be mounted in a frame and backed by plaster of Paris to protect it from injury. When a coloured light is required the reflector is to be made of coloured glass. The improved lamp consists of a pressure lamp in which the oil is raised by a piston raised by the weight of a column of mercury. A similar arrangement is proposed to raise a candle. The patentee also proposes to use a number of candles arranged in a circle round a reflector, in place of a single larger light. A floating life preserver is also described, consisting of an air tight case, to receive papers or other valuable property, with ballast at bottom and a silvered reflector at top, which will be visible at a great distance; the case is to be surrounded by a belt of vulcanised Indian rubber to act as a buffer in case of its striking any obstacles.

Thomas Wood Gray, of Limehouse, brass-founder, *for improvements in water-closets, pumps, cocks, lubricators, and deck lights.* June 26, 1849.

THE improved pump consists of a hemispherical chamber, having a shaft at centre on which are mounted two "flappers," or pistons, containing each a valve. A lever is fixed on the shaft by means of which a reciprocating motion is given to the pistons; the piston chamber is fixed on a valve box containing the foot valves and suction pipe. In another arrangement the metal chamber is dispensed with by making it of vulcanised Indian rubber, so that the pump resembles a pair of bellows; in another arrangement the circular bellows form is described. The improvements in water-closets consist in applying these pumps to draw off the soil. The improvements in cocks and valves consist in applying vulcanised Indian rubber tubing to inclose the stem of the plug to prevent leakage, and to act as a spring. An elastic chamber to act in a similar manner to an air vessel is also described, and consists of an enlargement of the delivery pipe of the pump, which is lined with vulcanised Indian rubber tubing of less size than the enlargement, but which stretches to that amount when an extra strain comes on it, and prevents the concussion of the water. The junctions of the hose are proposed to be so constructed that on screwing up the hose, it will lift the valve and allow a free passage for the water, and on removing it the valve will be closed by the pressure from within. The improved lubricator consists of a plunger with a recess in it, working in an oil cup, which at every stroke carries down with it a certain quantity of the soil. The improvements in deck lights consist in mounting the glass in a detached frame, which is screwed into the outer frame, so as to allow of its removal entire.

John Grantham, of Liverpool, engineer, *for improvements in sheathing ships and other vessels.* July 4th, 1849.

The patentee proposes to copper iron vessels, without allowing the two metals to come in contact, in order to prevent galvanic action, and for this purpose ribs are rivetted vertically on the hull, with their edges inclined to form dovetailed grooves, into which wood is driven: over this wood and the ribs, planks or gutta percha are laid, and over this the metal sheathing. When the sides of the vessel are to be coated with cements, and require drying, the patentee uses a portable furnace, consisting of two concentric cylinders; in the inner one is the fire, and air is blown by a fan through the annular space, and being there heated, and afterwards driven against the side of the vessel, produces the desired effect.

Edward Ives Fuller, of Margaret-street, Cavendish-square, coach builder, and George Tabernacle, of Mount-row, Westminster-road, Surrey, coach ironfounder, *for certain improvements in metallic springs for carriages.* July 7th, 1849.

This invention consists in so connecting springs to each other, or to scroll irons, that a free movement is allowed in a horizontal direction, and the inconveniences attending shackles and links are avoided. The end of the spring has a slotted link attached to it, which slides on a block carried by a pin on the other spring or scroll iron. Another method consists in connecting the two springs by a bell-crank, the curve of which coincides with the curve of the spring, when it is at the extremity of its motion.

· REGNANTE · CAROLO · X ·
PRISTINVM · FONTEM · ANGVSTIORI · AREA · JAM · AMPLIFICATA ·
· COMMVNI · VTILITATI · VRBIS · QVE · ORNAMENTO ·
IN · MAIVS · RESTITVERVNT · PRAEFECTVS · ET · AE · DILES ·
ANNO · MDCCCXXVIII ·

T. WRACG.

8

THE FOUNTAIN GAILLON, PARIS.

M. Visconti, Architect.

Our readers sometimes make enquiry of us for designs for various ornamental subjects suitable for cast metal-work. The preceding splendid example of the taste of our neighbours, the French (for which we are indebted to our contemporary, the *Architect*), may be of service to those who are engaged in foundries where ornamental castings are executed. The unanimous cry for water which is now being lustily raised, will, we are quite confident, not be in vain; and great scope will be afforded to taste and ingenuity in carrying out the ornamental and useful application of that necessary of life. Though our climate be not that of the sunny south, we can still enjoy the cooling influence of the sparkling shower and the music of the tinkling drops. Alas! we were just beginning to feel poetical when the remembrance of the Trafalgar-square fountains brought us at one step from the sublime to the ridiculous!

THE SOCIETIES.

INSTITUTION OF MECHANICAL ENGINEERS.

PROCEEDINGS.

The third annual meeting of the members was held at the Queen's Hotel, Railway Station, Birmingham, on Wednesday the 23rd of January, 1850; J. E. McConnell, Esq., V.P., in the chair.

The Chairman said, he was very glad to be able to congratulate the members on the continued prosperity and the increasing success of the Institution, which now comprised more than 200 members; and he proceeded to read the annual Report of the Council upon the proceedings of the last year.

The adjourned discussion on Railway Axles was introduced by reading the following additional paper by Mr. McConnell.

ON THE DETERIORATION OF RAILWAY AXLES, &c.
(With a Plate.)

Having been requested at the last meeting to furnish further proofs of the change from the fibrous to the crystalline character produced in Railway Axles, and feeling convinced that a strict and careful examination of this important subject is a *necessity* in this age of railway practice, the enquiry has been resumed in the hope that the further information and experience gained may tend to a more perfect knowledge of the subject.

Before stating the results of the different experiments which have been made with the view of ascertaining the cause and extent of the change from the fibrous to the crystalline appearance in railway axle iron, it must be observed that in this, as in some other matters of controversy, it is most difficult to produce full and conclusive proof that the iron which is produced of a crystalline character, was once fibrous, as we cannot by any experiment show the change visibly taking place; but surely it is fair and reasonable to admit the *fact* of a change, when we find railway axles when new, from the particular mode of manufacture, present through every part of their substance a tough, strong, fibrous appearance, yet, after several years' use, we find axles of the same description, owing to the various deteriorating causes in action, break short at the back of the wheel, and then present an appearance totally different from the original structure of the iron, as described above.

It has so happened, in strong confirmation of the views stated by the writer at the former meeting, that a very remarkable instance of this change was brought under his notice shortly after that discussion; and he thought the evidence which this case furnishes so important and conclusive, (although produced without any design, and in the ordinary course of business) that the axle has been brought for the inspection of the present meeting.

This axle was fixed in cast-iron wheels, of the pattern in use on several lines of railway, having the H form of spoke, and as this wheel is perfectly rigid, experience has proved that the axles are much more liable to deterioration when working in these kind of wheels, than in those wheels made partly of wood or other construction of wrought-iron, &c., which may have a certain amount of elasticity.

The axle now under consideration broke in ordinary working close at the

back of the wheel as is usually found, and the fractured ends which are now produced to the meeting afford the most distinct proof of the annular space, which was stated on the former occasion to be observable all round the surface of the fracture; and this is not only short grained and crystalline, but there is also in the writer's opinion an evident distinct separation to the extent of the annular space, which it would appear takes place some time before the final fracture, as if each successive blow, heavy or light, lateral or vertical, received or transmitted through the wheels, had each tended to destroy its proportion of cohesion of the previously crystallised substance of the axle at that particular place where the fracture occurs.

On receiving this axle in the workshops, with one wheel still attached, it was allowed by accident to fall a short distance from the waggon to the ground, and so brittle had it become next the wheel, that the other end snapped off simply from the effect of the fall, and shows, as will be observed, a precisely similar appearance to the original fracture.

The writer was anxious to ascertain how far the theory which he held was correct, that the deterioration of the axle was principally local at that point (the back of the wheel), and for this purpose he caused the centre of the axle between the two fractures to be laid on supports, with the view of breaking it. A weight of cast-iron weighing 17 cwt. was then allowed to fall upon it through a space of 14 feet, but, after several attempts, it was found to make no impression upon this centre part of the axle towards effecting a fracture, although it was a frosty day, which would, of course, render the iron more brittle. Finding all efforts to break it by blows fruitless, the axle was then, in order to test its fibrous character, taken to the hydraulic press, and it has been bent to the form of the letter U, until the two ends met, without showing more than the slightest appearance of the skin of its surface breaking, as will be seen, proving still to be of a strong fibrous iron in the centre of the axle. See Fig. 1.

Following up his proposition, the writer wishes to lay considerable stress on the view he previously stated, respecting the effect of the blows or vibrating action given through the wheels to the axle; he attributes the crystallization of the axle at that point close behind the wheel to the sudden stoppage or reaction of the vibratory wave at that place, owing to the check which it meets from the mass of matter, consisting of the wheel, &c., presenting a break of surface, and acting more as an anvil, causing the vibration to re-act like a blow on the neck of the axle (the nearest weakest point), thereby destroying its fibrous character.

Cast-iron wheels, therefore, are objectionable from their rigidity and non-absorption of the lateral and vertical concussion with other strains formerly enumerated, received in course of working, and transmitted to be wholly expended on the axle; and the writer endeavoured to illustrate this by a comparative experiment with two different axles of the same description and age, one being fixed in cast iron, and the other in wooden wheels, those known as the Pimlico make.

First experiment was made on the axle with wooden wheels placed horizontally resting upon the rails; a weight of 17 cwt. was allowed to fall through a distance of 13 feet 3 inches upon the axle, immediately within the wheel, by which the axle was slightly bent at the point where the blow came, and a portion of the tyre resting on the rail was broken clear out. This experiment was repeated four times on the other end of the axle, which was bent but very slightly, and the wheel was rendered completely useless.

Second experiment was made upon the axle with cast-iron wheels placed as in the former case, and the same weight was allowed to fall the same distance at the back of the wheel, when the effect of the first blow was to break the axle at the other end, at the back of the wheel; thus proving that, in the former case, the axle was saved from fracture by the wooden wheel absorbing its full share of the effect of the blow, and the tyre of the wheel breaking proved that in course of working it would receive a portion of the deteriorating forces tending to crystallize, the wheel acting like a cushion to soften the blows before they reached the axle; in the latter case the rail, supporting the cast-iron wheel, was fractured in three places.

A third experiment was tried with another axle with cast-iron wheels placed as before, and received four blows on each end of the axle within the wheels, which caused it to bend, but produced no fracture. This axle had not been much used, and was of a stronger fibrous character.

In order to ascertain the relative appearance of axles which had been in use, and determine the position of the crystalline change, both at the

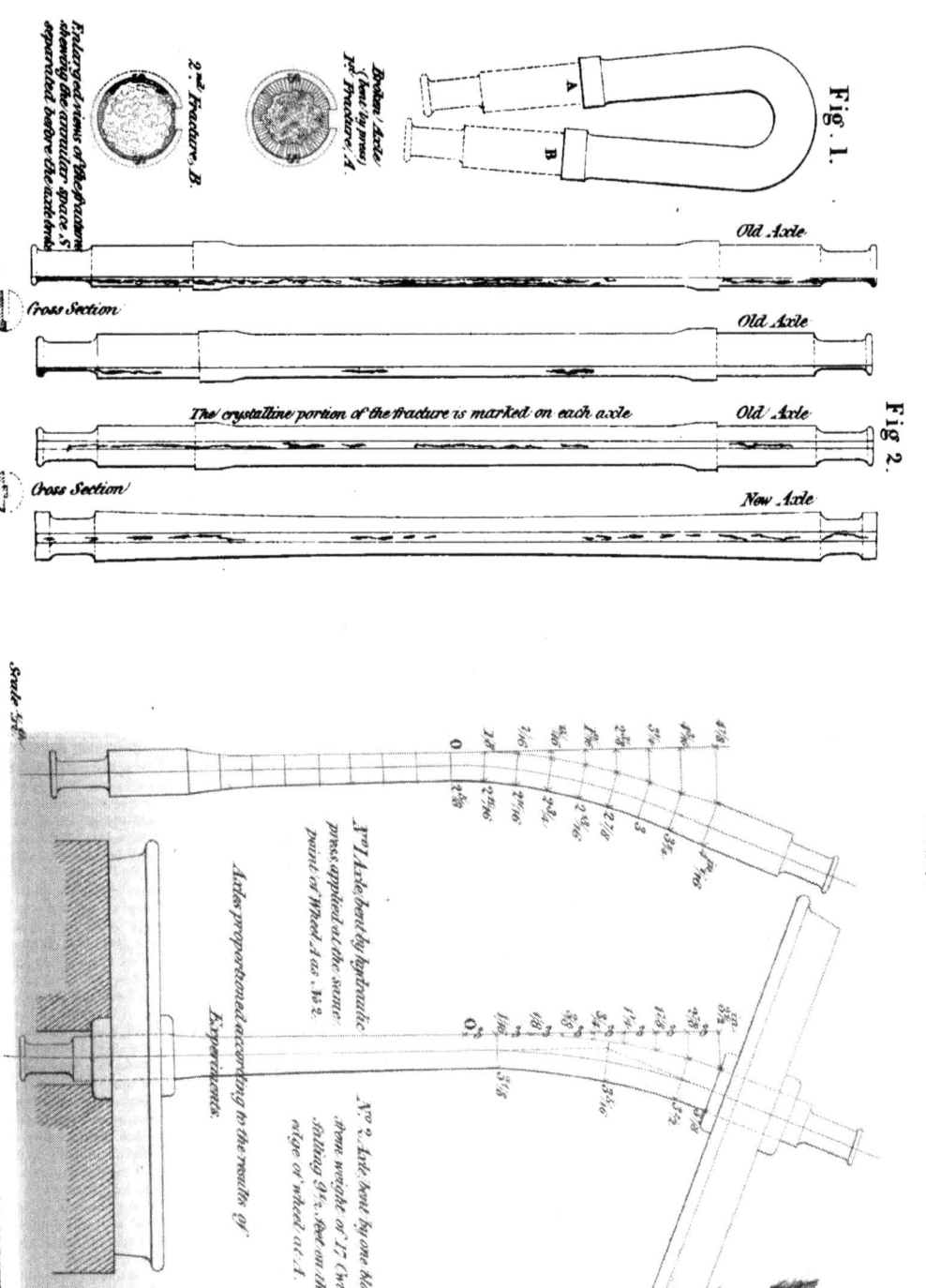

EXPERIMENTS ON RAILWAY AXLES.

Fig. 1.

A

B

Bottom Axle
(bent by press)
1.st Fracture, A.

2.nd Fracture, B.

Enlarged views of the fracture
shewing the annular space S
separated before the axle broke

Cross Section

Old Axle

Old Axle

The crystalline portion of the fracture is marked on each axle   Old Axle

Fig 2.

New Axle

Old Axle

Cross Section

Scale ⅛th

0

1"⅞
1"⅞

2"⅞

2"⅞
2½
2"⅞
3
3¼
3½
3¾

Fig.1 Axle bent by hydraulic
press applied at the same
point as Wheel A as. No 2.

Axles proportioned according to the results of
Experiments.

No 2. Axle bent by one Row
from weight of 17 Cwts.
falling 9½ feet on the
edge of wheel at A.

3¾
3½
3¼
3
2¾
2½
2¼
2
1¾
1½
1¼
1
¾

0*

centre and outer surface of the axle, the writer caused four axles which had been condemned as too small from wear in the bearings to have a groove cut in two cases on each side, to within an inch of the centre, and in the other two, grooved through to within an inch of the outer surface; these were split asunder with wedges, and their appearance will show that a certain change has been going on, and this is more observable in one end of the axle than the other, attributable, he believes, to the break being applied to the end which was on the end where the greatest crystalline change is visible. See Fig. 2.

He has made a number of other experiments in the presence of several of the members of the Institution, with the view of determining the effect produced on the fibre of iron by the cold-hammering process. The following are the principal results :—

No. 1. A piece of ordinary bar iron, $2\frac{1}{2}$ inches wide, and $1\frac{1}{4}$ inch thick, received 20 blows to nick it across, and was broken with 21 blows of a 14lb. hammer, showing a fracture part fibrous and part crystalline.

No. 2. The same bar received 52 blows on one side, and 55 on the other, from the 14-lb. hammer, with 20 to nick it as before, and it broke with 14 blows, showing different layers of fibre and crystal.

No. 3. The same bar received 50 similar blows on each side as No. 2, but each blow on alternate sides successively, and 20 in nicking, and 9 blows broke it.

No. 4. The same bar was not cold-hammered, but received 20 blows in nicking, and required 28 blows to break it, showing a good fracture.

No. 5. Was a $\frac{7}{8}$ inch square bar, received 50 blows on each of two opposite sides, and 25 on each of the other sides, with 4 blows in nicking, and 5 broke it.

No. 6. Without any cold hammering and the same bar, after receiving 4 blows to nick, required 6 to break it.

No. 7. The same as in the case of No. 6, had no cold hammering, with 4 blows to nick it, and required 30 blows to break; in this case it was broken the flat way of the pile of the iron, but in No. 6 it was broken the edge way of the pile.

No. 8. Experiment was made on a shaft $3\frac{5}{8}$ inches diameter, which was cold-hammered at one end, having received 204 blows on all sides from a $3\frac{1}{4}$ ton tilt hammer; 110 blows with a sledge hammer were given to nick this end all round which had been cold-hammered, and it required only 5 blows from the $3\frac{1}{4}$ ton hammer to break it; the other end which had not been cold-hammered, after receiving the same number of blows in nicking, required 78 blows under the $3\frac{1}{4}$ ton hammer to break it, thus proving the enormous amount of deterioration of the strength of the iron caused by the cold-hammering process.

No. 9. A piece of round iron $2\frac{3}{4}$ inches diameter, which had two bearings turned (one at each end) $1\frac{7}{8}$ inch diameter by $2\frac{1}{2}$ inches long, was allowed to run at a considerable velocity for about an hour, with one end oiled and the other dry, the dry end being cooled with water repeatedly when it became hot; the iron was then experimented upon in order to determine by the different force required to break the end which had been injured by want of lubrication, the relative strength of each bearing, but such was the remarkably tough quality of this iron, that although it received 520 blows of a heavy sledge hammer in every possible way to break it in one direction (without being nicked), no fracture could be effected, but the iron seemed to be drawing out at the back of the journal on end, as will be seen by the meeting.

This last case is noticed in particular, as the following experiment of a similar character with an old axle of larger dimensions, shows in strong contrast the altered nature of similar iron from use on a railway, owing to the jar or vibrating action it has suffered.

In the 9th experiment a piece of new iron, intended for part of an axle, although run dry and cooled with water, yet was so fibrous, having received no jar, that it resisted all effort to break it.

No. 10. Another experiment of a similar character was tried on an old axle which had been a long time in use, of the same kind of iron and manufacture as the bar in No. 9 experiment. This axle with the wheels on was run in its own bearings in a lathe at a velocity equal to 10 miles per hour for 5 hours; one journal was kept running dry, and when heated by the friction cooled with water, while the other journal was kept well lubricated with oil. When taken out, the journal which had been heated was broken with 12 blows of a hammer 22 lbs. in weight, while the lubricated journal

required 91 blows with the same hammer to break it, in both cases without being nicked; this appears satisfactorily to prove the injury to the axle which results from the practice of throwing cold water on the journal to cool it when it has become nearly red hot from the want of proper lubrication.

In addition to various other experiments with the view of determining the change which is gradually going on in railway axles, and other iron liable to a jarring, vibrating motion, the writer would refer the meeting to a few of the samples of broken axles sent to him from various quarters, which, if proof were wanting, completely substantiate, in his opinion, the certainty of the crystalline change.

Before reading some of the communications received from other gentlemen containing their experience on the subject, he would first call attention to the two experiments which were tried in relation to the proportion and form of axle, in order to meet the objection raised at the former meeting, "that the slow pressure on the flanches of the wheel to discover where the axles were most exposed to the bending strain, was not a faithful representation of what takes place in practice." The axle was fixed upright so that the wheels were placed in such a position that the violent blow when the wheels of the carriage jarred upon the rail was fairly represented by the blow caused by the descent of a weight of 17 cwt., which was allowed to fall upon the edge of the wheel at A, from a height of $9\frac{1}{2}$ feet. It is most satisfactory to find that the curve into which the axle was bent is quite in accordance with the former results, which were obtained by slow pressure applied at the same points, and establishes the rule of proportion of the axle therein stated. See plate.

The following are some instances of tough fibrous wrought iron being rendered brittle and breaking off quite square with a close-grained fracture from the effect of the concussion of very small blows rapidly repeated for a long period; the blows being very small in force compared to the strength of the iron. These specimens are from the machines for making button shanks, in Mr. Heaton's Mills, Birmingham. The hammer in these machines is about $2\frac{1}{2}$ lbs. weight, and is lifted by a rod $\frac{3}{8}$ inch square, which has a pull upon it of about 12 lbs. from the difference of leverage; the hammer strikes 120 blows per minute, but the cam that drives it acts only during one-fourth of its revolution, so that the velocity of the hammer is equal to four times the number of blows, or nearly 1000 changes of motion per minute. The lifting rods always break with a close-grained short fracture, although made of the toughest and most fibrous iron that can be obtained, and they sometimes last only a few months; the rods break near to the end, which is fixed with a coupling, and the deterioration of the iron appears to be confined within a small portion, the iron remaining quite tough and fibrous within an inch of the fracture, as shown by the specimen, which has been bent double at that part. The hammer is snatched suddenly by the lifting-rod, and is pulled against a strong spring for the purpose of getting a quick recoil and a sharp blow of the hammer much quicker than it would fall by gravity.

Another specimen from the same machines is the lever for pushing off the work from the machine when stamped; the lever is about $\frac{1}{2}$ inch square made of the toughest wrought-iron, it is 9 inches long, and falls back against a stop at one-third of its length from the centre of motion at the bottom, being thrown back sharply by a spring, the total strain upon the lever varying from about 1 lb. to about 12 lbs., according to the accidental circumstances in the working of the machine. These levers all break off quite short and close-grained within an inch of the part that strikes against the stop, but the iron continues quite fibrous and unchanged to within an inch of the point of fracture, as shown in the specimen. They were driven at the same speed as mentioned above, amounting to nearly the velocity of 1000 changes of motion per minute; but they broke so frequently, lasting sometimes only a few weeks, that it was determined at last to reduce the speed of the machines from 120 to about 100 blows per minute, and in consequence of this reduction in speed the levers are much less frequently broken, and last on the average, about four times as long as before.

Communication from Mr. John Kekwick.

"*The Holmes, Rotherham,* 4th *December,* 1849.

"I have been reading in the *Mechanic's Magazine* for last month a report of your able paper on Railway Axles, and I notice Mr. Robert Stephenson said that Mr. McConnell had expressed a strong opinion that a change took place from a *fibrous* structure to a *crystalline* one during the time of its being in use, and it would be satisfactory if an instance could be pointed out where this change had occurred owing to vibration or other treatment, &c.

" I think I can furnish an instance in proof of your opinion on this point.

" In one of our forges we are daily in the habit of using a metal helve or hammer weighing about 4 tons, for the purpose of drawing large sizes of steel, and the shaft of this helve is 17 inches by 9 inches. Finding great inconvenience and danger from the breakage of *cast*-iron helves, we were induced to try a *wrought*-iron one 16 inches by 8 inches. After using this for several months the shaft broke in two about the middle, and the fracture presented the crystalline appearance of 'short' cast-iron : we repaired the shaft, and in the course of a few months it again broke about the same place, and it again presented a similar granulated, cast-iron like crystalline appearance throughout the face of the fracture. I attributed this change solely to the *vibration* and *jar* occasioned in the process of hammering steel, more particularly *cast* steel."

Communication from Mr. BENJAMIN GIBBONS.

" *Shut End House, near Dudley*, 15*th* January, 1850.

" When the heavy cast-iron helves were used for drawing out bars, and the art of *chilling* iron was little understood, the nose or that part of the iron helve struck by the cam to lift it was protected by a wrought-iron plate well fitted, and this was secured by a large pin countersunk into it, and extended through a hole cast through the nose of the helve and screwed as fast as possible on the upper side. The very best and *most fibrous* iron (ascertained to be so by previous breaking) was also selected, and yet when the pin broke by the repeated shocks it had to sustain (about 90 times per minute), it always broke with a large bright grain, *without the least trace of fibre*. This was so regularly the case, that I never knew a pin last for many months.

" Another instance was in a fly-wheel, where wrought-iron arms were used instead of cast-iron, for the purpose of throwing the weight to the outer circumference, and this wheel was applied to a forge hammer engine. It worked well for a time till the arms got loose in the cast-iron rim, and then a violent shock was received every time the cam struck the helve ; after some time the arms began to break one after the other, and though the iron was of the toughest description originally, it was found that any part broken was of a bright crystalline grain.

" The pins of shears for cutting down large cold bars sustain violent shocks ; they perpetually break with the same bright grain, though made of the toughest iron. Also the iron arms of common carts always break with that grain from the same apparent cause.

" I have taken iron of this bright crystalline character which I had previously known to be fibrous, and by drawing it down a little at a proper heat, have never failed to restore the fibrous texture of the iron."

The practical suggestions derivable from the foregoing experiments and enquiries which are confirmed by all the writer's previous experience and information, are—

1st. That the axles of all railway engines, carriages, and vehicles, should be made of the best ascertained quality of iron for the purpose, both tough and strong, and of uniform clean fibrous texture.

2nd. The proportion of an axle in all its parts to be determined from sound experience and calculation ; the load it has to carry, the speed at which it is run, and the description of wheel in which it is placed, and strains to which it is liable in working from curves or inequalities of the road, or other deteriorating causes, being fully considered.

3rd. That previous to any axle being allowed to run on any line, the maker's name should be legibly marked thereon and the date of manufacture, and also when it was first put to work. It is of course manifestly impracticable to record the number of miles run, but as all railway stock in a general way is worked nearly uniform, the above particulars would afford the necessary data to guide the opinion which may be formed, of the age beyond which limit the iron becomes comparatively unsafe.

4th. That it be part of the duty of the proper officer to see that all axles are working in good condition and receiving careful treatment.

5th. The next point the writer would press is, that all in whose power is the opportunity for registering facts in connection with railway axles, should by this or some recognised scientific Institution, be requested to note and carefully collect their information on all the points, in order that a certain average result for the guidance and benefit of all interested may be arrived at.

6th. That attention should be given to ascertain the description and working condition of wheels, which in all points cause the least deteriorating effects on the axle ; and for this he proposes to produce some further experiments, and also results from practice.

7th. That the quality of lubrication and description of bearings used should also be considered, and for this he also proposes to give a paper to the Institution, with the results of experiments and experience.

It is obviously of most material advantage to all who are connected with or have the management of machinery, whether for railway, manufacturing, or mining purposes, to have their attention directed to the phenomena bearing upon the nature, use, stability, and durability of the iron or other material of which that machinery is constructed ; as it must be manifest that we must first obtain a clear knowledge of the best quality, the best form, and the best treatment necessary to select and prepare it for use, and to preserve it from any deteriorating causes as far as possible, in order to obtain the greatest safety, efficiency, and economy in working the machinery for the purpose it is intended to effect.

With the above views kept prominently before them in all their enquiries in this as well as in other branches of practical research in developing improvements of commercial utility, the members of this Institution, from their different positions, with large and varied opportunities, will be enabled to effect great good ; they will assist the progress of useful mechanical inventions, and entitle themselves to the respect and gratitude of all classes, as being the means of producing and encouraging lasting and substantial advantages to the commercial and manufacturing interests of the country.

The Chairman remarked that it was much to be regretted that their President, who took a great interest in the subject, was absent, and perhaps it would be well not to conclude the investigation that evening, in order to afford him an opportunity of being present.

Mr. Cowper enquired with reference to the broken axle exhibited, whether it had been nicked to a square shoulder and broken to test the quality of the iron, or whether it had only been bent by pressure.

The Chairman replied that the axle was broken at one end whilst running on the railway, and was broken off short off at the other end by falling to the ground ; and then in order to see whether the crystallisation was local or otherwise, it was afterwards bent in the centre by three or four blows from a weight of 17 cwt. falling upon it, without the axle being nicked, and it was then doubled up by the hydraulic press, but it did not show any appearance of breaking.

Mr. Wright observed that the fracture was at a very deep square shoulder, and a great deal of the appearance round the fracture might be the result of the shoulder.

The Chairman replied that this, to a certain extent, might be the case, but even without the shoulder there seemed to be an annular crystalline space going on forming.

Mr. Walter Williams expressed his full concurrence in the views stated by Mr. Gibbons in his communication, which were founded on very long experience. He could also speak from the experience of many years, that he had invariably found that iron much used as axles broke in the manner described by the chairman. He was, therefore, quite satisfied that a change takes place in the structure of iron, and was rather surprised that a different opinion was entertained, because he had observed hundreds of instances where after having produced a good tough fibrous iron, yet after hammering it had broken crystalline. But to show how well it was known that iron was affected in its structure, he would mention that in making iron for particular purposes it was desirable to have it of very close fibre, and it was customary to throw the hot iron into a water bosh in the state in which it came from the rolls, and that injured its fibre. The object in thus dealing with the iron was to clean it, and when next put through the rolls its fibrous character was restored ; hence he was of opinion that in the case of axles deteriorated by wear their fibrous character might be restored by drawing down hot, for there was no doubt it was the action of the wheels which made the change.

Mr. Hodge considered the subject as one of great importance, and suggested that the discussion should be deferred until after the members had been furnished with a copy of the paper and the experiments, with such diagrams as were necessary for their illustration. So important was the question which presented itself with reference to changes in the structure of iron that it had occupied the attention of the American Institute for two sessions, and he thought that this Institution should not allow the subject to pass without a long and careful consideration, because it was necessary to have regard to the various circumstances under which the iron was manufactured, and the particular character of the iron itself.

Mr. Henry Smith, in reference to his promise at the last meeting to furnish some results at the present meeting, observed that the experiments on cold-hammering iron, which were described in Mr. McConnell's paper, had been tried at his works, and he fully concurred in all that Mr. McConnell had said with reference to them.

Mr. P. R. Jackson enquired which class of iron the chairman considered best for railway axles—malleable iron or steel. For his own part when he required great strength he employed good steel, and found that answer the best.

The Chairman in reply repeated the first practical deduction contained in his paper, viz., "that the axles of all railway engines, carriages, and vehicles should be made of the best ascertained quality of iron for the purpose, both tough and strong, and of uniform clean fibrous texture." That was his opinion with reference to the quality of iron to be employed, and he thought the Institution would be departing from its province were it to consider any particular district or manufacture. They were now treating of the *deterioration of railway axles*, and the question to be decided by proofs adduced to the members was whether they underwent such a change as from fibrous to crystalline iron; that question being determined, they might then not only consider the quality of iron, but the form of railway axles most advantageous to be adopted.

Mr. Hodge observed, that when steel was employed, it was in order to produce stiffness, and not to resist torsion; he did not think that the mere imparting of carbon to iron would give it the properties required for the present purpose.

Mr. Slate doubted whether the term fibrous, as applied to iron, properly described the state or condition of the material to which it referred. He could understand a fibre of cotton or wool, or other such material, but in the case of fibrous iron, as it was termed, they found a series of small crystals united longitudinally giving the appearance of fibre, and when that changed to larger crystals, the peculiar cohesion seemed to be destroyed, and the whole became a conglomerate mass, without any appearance of fibre.

Mr. Cowper said, it appeared to him that fibre in iron was composed of the separate particles of iron existing in the puddling furnace of different sizes, and that these were afterwards elongated in the process of forging and rolling, so that a number of long particles were obtained lying near to each other though there was not perfect contact owing to the interlying cinder. Crystalline iron was that in which the particles assumed any other form than the elongated form. All iron contained a portion of cinder or silicate of iron, which was more or less squeezed out in the process of forging and rolling.

Mr. Hodge remarked, that to arrive at any true results as to the structure of iron it would be necessary to call in the aid of the microscope, to examine the fibrous and crystalline structure.

Mr. Walter Williams adverted to the well-known fact that the continued working of machinery, such for instance as the crank pins of engines, destroyed the fibrous structure of the iron, and made them crystalline.

Mr. Cowper remarked that it was his opinion that iron could not become crystallized unless it was hammered or so strained by force as to alter its form and produce a permanent set or change of form; he did not think, however, that an iron railway axle became crystallised from the action of the concussions of the wheels, because he did not think that the effect produced was equivalent to cold-hammering; he thought a fair experiment would be to turn a square shoulder in the centre part of the broken axle which had been bent up by pressure, and then to break it with a nick at the shoulder and see if it broke with a fibrous or crystalline fracture, for it was well known that by nicking iron it would break more crystalline.

Mr. Hodge illustrated the subject by reference to the effect produced upon the journal of a picker shaft in a cotton mill, at Lowell in America, where, in order to produce stiffness, a shaft of cast steel was introduced, but it frequently broke off at the journal, particularly when there was a very tight belt on the drum. A collar of cast-iron $1\frac{1}{2}$ inch thick was then shrunk on the journal working in a brass bearing, and it then worked well. He merely adduced this fact to show that the friction caused by high velocity produces a change in the molecular structure of iron.

Mr. Hoby did not think that from the mere appearance of the sectional fracture they could exactly determine the molecular change. They would recollect that Mr. Stephenson adverted to some experiments by Mr. Brunel, where from the mode of producing the fracture the same bar of iron gave out different results; these experiments were perhaps conducted on too small a scale to furnish undeniable results, but he thought it quite possible that the same bar of iron should exhibit different results when twisted slowly in a vice or struck by a smart blow; in the one case the fracture might be crystalline, but fibrous in the other.

A Member said that he had tried an experiment with very tough charcoal iron; he merely attached it to the head of a tilt hammer, which went about 300 strokes per minute, and after a few weeks it broke off brittle without any blow, although the iron was at first as tough as could be made, and this was attributed only to the jarring.

Mr. Hodge observed, that this was quite analogous to the results given in the report of the commissioners on the experiments with reference to the duration of wire bridges in France, that the effect was produced by the constant vibration or jarring between the particles of the iron.

Mr. P. R. Jackson suggested that the opinion of the meeting should be taken whether the change took place or not; but the Chairman observed that such a course would be contrary to the practice of the Institution.

Mr. William Smith said that he produced two specimens of ordinary puddled-bar iron $1\frac{1}{2}$ inch square, on which he had tried the effect of hammering; the first piece was broken off from the bar by 22 blows of a 14 lb hammer, the bar having been nicked, and the fracture was very fibrous; the second piece was 7 inches length cut off from the same bar next to the first piece, and he set it on an anvil and struck it 20 blows on the end, and it was then nicked in the middle and broke off with a single light blow, and showed a square crystalline fracture; another piece was then broken off the same end of the bar as the first piece, to ascertain if the quality of iron in the bar was the same, and it required 21 blows to break it, and was similar in the fracture to the first piece.

Mr. Middleton remarked, that in taking off the tires from the driving wheels of an engine he observed that the bolts were quite crystalline; he was quite satisfied there was a change. And with regard to the hammering which took place on the rails, in his opinion, it was quite sufficient to cause the change observed in railway axles.

Mr. Heaton said, he fully concurred in all that had been said in favour of a change being effected in the structure of iron. He considered the change was generally confined to some particular part, and the rest of the iron was not injured; in his machine for flattening button shanks, which gave a blow of about 12 lbs. (mentioned in Mr. McConnell's paper), the constant action had the effect of breaking the levers, which showed a crystalline fracture, although within half an inch from the part so broken the iron continued unchanged and quite fibrous. The same was observable in the cross pins of corn-spindles, which frequently broke in a few weeks' wear, and he did not know which lasted the longest, steel or iron, but he thought good scrap iron would last as long as a piece of steel, but it would not last half the time if subjected to cold swaging. In the example he produced of broken cross pins the fracture showed a vertical division, because the strain was only at each side, but in the case of a railway axle the fracture showed a circular space in the centre, because the strain was all round the axle on all sides in succession.

The further consideration of the subject was then adjourned to the next meeting, and the Chairman said he hoped the members would come forward with all the information they could collect which bore upon a question of such importance; and for his own part he would take every opportunity of trying further experiments and collecting facts with reference to it.

INSTITUTION OF CIVIL ENGINEERS.

Tuesday, February 5, 1850.

James Simpson, Esq., V. P., in the chair.

The discussion was renewed on the Rev. Mr. Clutterbuck's paper—"On the Alternations and Depressions in the Chalk-water Level under London," and was continued throughout the meeting, so that no original communication could be read.

It was contended, that the area of the chalk district, subject to infiltration, for the supply of the springs and streams uniting in the basin of the Colne, could not possibly exceed the original published estimate of 113½ square miles, and that the proportion of water filtrating through, for that purpose, was much less than had ever hitherto been estimated, inasmuch, as records by Mr. Dickinson's gauge was to a much greater amount, than those afforded by the gauges kept by other experimenters.

It was also contended, that the original position assumed in the paper, had not been weakened by the subsequent discussion; that the observations of the chemists had tended to confirm the statement of the probability of an infiltration of water from the Thames. The practical conclusion to be drawn from the observations, recorded in the author's several papers were:—That the natural drainage and replenishment of the chalk stratum might be traced and accounted for, by observing the alternation of level, in various localities, and at different seasons. That any large quantity of water abstracted from the chalk stratum, at any given point, caused a depression of level around the point ot such abstraction. That in the upper district any such abstraction of water would interfere with, and diminish the supply of, the streams, by which the drainage of the district was regulated; and, lastly, that the depression of level under London, by pumping from Artesian wells, had proved that the rapidity of demand already exceeded that of the supply, and that any attempt to draw a large additional quantity for public use, would be attended with disastrous consequences.

It was suggested that, considering the great works of drainage and water supply which were in contemplation for the metropolis, and looking to the essential importance of having accurate and authentic geological information, in order that those great works might be executed on a sound and certain basis, that the Geological Survey now being carried on by government, in a remote district of North Wales, where no urgent need existed for early geological information, and where no new works of paramount importance were in progress, or in contemplation, should be transferred at once to the metropolitan districts, with a view to throw light on the real structure, mechanical and chemical, of the deep water-bearing strata, on which, opinions so varying and so conflicting had been advanced.

An inquiry was made whether any steps had been taken by the council, in consequence of the statement submitted at the meeting of Tuesday, January 29th, urging the consideration of the manner in which the interests of the public at large, and of the profession, were likely to be affected by the attitude recently assumed by the Railway Commission, in reference to the strength of the wrought-iron bridges used on railways. It was stated that the council had not as yet taken any decided steps in the matter, but that a course had been suggested, which, being followed, would most probably lend to satisfactory results. After this assurance the members expressed their confidence of the interests of the profession being in safe hands, and that every step would be taken for insuring their position and professional reputation.

The motion which had been prepared, was therefore withdrawn; and the chairman requested any communications on the subject, to be made in writing to the Secretary, who would lay them before the council.

At the monthly ballot the following candidates were duly elected:— R. S. Haggar, R. Murray, J. S. Peirce, G. Sibley, H. Smith, and W. Strode, as Associates.

Tuesday, February 12, 1850.

William Cubitt, Esq., President, in the Chair.

The first paper read was, "An Account of the Cast-Iron Lighthouse Tower on Gibb's Hill, in the Bermudas," by Mr. P. Paterson.

The site chosen for this tower was in latitude 32° 14' N. and longitude 64° 50' W., being the southern part of the Bermudas, at which point they are most safely approached. It was at first determined to construct the tower with the materials found in the islands; but, after some progress had been made in quarrying and dressing the stone, it was ascertained to be of too friable a nature for the purpose, so that the Home Government instructed Mr. Alexander Gordon, M. Inst. C. E., to prepare a design for a cast-iron tower, similar to that which had been erected from his designs at Morant Point, Jamaica, and which had proved very successful. The form of this tower was that of a strong conoidal figure, 105 feet 9 inches in height, terminated at the top by an inverted conoidal figure, 4 feet high, in lieu of a capital; its extreme outside diameter was 24 feet at the narrowest part 14 feet, and at the top 20 feet. The external shell was constructed of one hundred and thirty-five concentric cast-iron plates, having inside flanges, and varying in thickness from one inch at the base to about three-quarters of an inch at the top. In the centre of the tower there was a hollow cast-iron column, eighteen inches in diameter in the inside, and of three-quarter inch metal, for supporting Fresnel's Dioptric apparatus, and in which the revolving weight descended; it was also used, in the daytime for the raising and lowering of stores, and likewise contained the waste-water pipe. The lower part of the tower was filled with concrete, leaving a well, faced with brickwork, about eight feet in diameter, and twenty feet in depth, in the centre. Above this were the seven floors, the two lower ones being lined with brickwork, and used as store rooms, and the upper ones, lined with sheet iron, were used as living rooms for the light-keeper. The details were then given of the mode of constructing the floors, the windows, the staircases, and of attaching the lantern and light room to the main structure; it was stated that the light was visible from all points of the compass, excepting when obscured by the high land between Gibb's Hill and Castle Harbour, from the deck of a vessel at a distance of about twenty-seven miles, and possibly even at a still greater distance. The structure occupied less than one year in its actual erection, the different parts having been landed about the end of November, 1844, the first plate being erected on Gibb's Hill on the 19th of December, 1844, and the last plate of the tower on the 9th of October, 18,5. The whole cost of the structure, including the lantern and light apparatus, was stated to have been about £7690, and the annual expense of maintaining it about £450.

The next paper read was "A Description of Sir George Cayley's Hot Air Engine," by Mr. W. W. Poingdestre. After entering briefly into the theoretical considerations of the expansion of heated aeriform bodies, and detailing the attempts made by Lieut. Ericson, for employing hot air, instead of steam, as a prime mover, the author proceeded to state, that in 1837, Sir George Cayley, Bart., Assoc. Inst. C.E., applied the products of combustion from close furnaces, so that they should act at once upon a piston, in a cylinder, similar in every respect to that of a single acting steam engine. The engine consisted of a generator of heat, a working cylinder, and an air pump or blower, the air pump being half the size of the cylinder, and blowing air into, and through, a fire perfectly enclosed within the generator; the doors of the furnace were made perfectly air-tight as soon as the fire was well got up, the first impulse being given to the engine, by throwing a few jets of water upon the fire, which caused the air pump to work immediately, and continued so for hours; the fire being replenished by stopping off the blast from the furnace, and opening the upper bonnet. After the air had passed through the fire, the gaseous products of combustion, generally at a temperature of 600° of Fahrenheit, passed laterally through a chamber, used for separating them from any ashes, or cinders, into the working cylinder before alluded to.

The difficulties attending this description of engine, were the liability of the working parts to be deranged, by the great sensible heat destroying the valves, pistons, and cylinders, and carbonising the lubricating oil. It was stated, that Mr. A. Gordon, M. Inst. C. E., had made a successful experiment, on the application of the heated products of combustion for propelling a boat, without the intervention of any machinery, between the furnace and the water to be acted upon.

INSTITUTION OF CIVIL ENGINEERS OF IRELAND.

The fourth ordinary general meeting of the Institution of Civil Engineers of Ireland, for the present season, was held on the 8th inst., at the Custom-house—Lieut.-Col. Harry D. Jones, R.E., President, in the chair.

A DESCRIPTION OF THE VIADUCT, NEAR QUAKER'S WARD, TAFF VALE RAILWAY, SOUTH WALES.

This viaduct was designed by Mr. Brunel, to carry the main line of the railway over the river Taff, at a point where, from the nature of the locality, such crossing was unavoidable.

The total length of the viaduct was 470 feet, and the greatest height 105 feet, consisting of six semi-circular arches, each 50 feet in span, resting on pillars, whose horizontal section was a regular octagon, 5 feet 9½ inches in the side, giving 14 feet as their diameter. The whole structure was upon a curve of 1320 feet radius, and at the point where it was determined to build, the axis of the river made an angle of 45 deg., with the direction of the tangent to the curve. One of the chief merits of the design was the avoidance of the difficulties and expense of an oblique bridge with spiral courses in addition to those of curving; this was effected by the adoption of that form of pier above mentioned. These pillars were surmounted by a capital of seven feet in height, the base of which, resting on the pier, was, of course identical in plan with it, but in this height of seven feet was corbelled out on four of its faces to the extent of 1 foot 3 inches, changing the regular octagon into another, whose sides were 9 feet, and 3 feet 7½ inches alternately. Two of the 9 feet sides were parallel to the direction of the line of rails, and the other two formed the impost or springing of the arch. The easiest way to have an idea of the form of the soffit of the arches, is by conceiving an ordinary semi-circular arch of 50 span and 14 length, to have the arch quoins bevilled off to an extent of 2 feet 6-in.; and to turn this arch a corresponding centre had to be made, being the ordinary laggings for the cylindrical part, and, what were called by the workmen, saddles for the conical faces. It will be evident to the practical engineer, that the proper bonding of all this work, and especially the arches, must be a matter of great care. A model, cut out of Caen stone, showing four courses of the arch, was produced, which clearly showed the alternate arrangement of the course. The arches being turned, and the spandrils filled up, there was a clear width of 14 feet from outside to outside of the up-stream and down-stream faces of the bridge, giving ultimately 11 feet 6 inches in the clear, between the parapet walls for carrying a single line of rails over, nor indeed, does it seem possible with any advantage to extend the design so as to carry a double way, for thus the pier would be necessarily extended in diameter, or otherwise the chamfering of the soffit increased—both inadmissable, one from interfering with the water-way, and the other from the practical difficulty of bonding the work.

The quarries from whence the stone was obtained were in the immediate vicinity of the works. It was of the blue Pennant grit, called by Sir H. De la Beche, in the Government Geological Survey of this district, "The equivalent of the Pennant grit of the British coal measures;" and very truly characterised by him as being admirably adapted for engineering purposes. Its colour closely resembles that of the common building limestone of this neighbourhood. The lime used was the celebrated Aberthan hydraulic limestone, not only in the foundations, but in all parts of the structure. The foundations on the north side, including one of the river piers, were on rock or indurated gravel, but on the south side the abutment, one land and one river pier, had to be sunk to a far greater depth than originally designed.

From the loftiness and peculiar design of this bridge, it was, during its construction an object of great interest; and most persons who visited it expressed strong opinions unfavourable to its ultimate stability, most of which objections were very futile.

The real difficulty in the construction was found to be the management of the spandril walls on the concave side, so as to gain the true uniform curvature at the string course under the parapets, as on the concave side we had to gather out the courses of the spandrils about four inches, which, from the excellent quality of the stone, we were enabled to do.

It would seem necessary also to explain the reason for crossing the valley, and crossing it at such a height. Such structures seem rather to constitute the difficulty and expense of obtaining good gradients on cross-country lines, which necessarily intersect the rivers at elevations more or less considerable than that of a valley line, which, following the leading of one single stream, ought not, unless for cogent reasons, cross it at all. The consideration of the section of the river, made it clear that no other alternative remained but this lofty and curved viaduct, intersecting the stream at the angle of 45 deg.

The paper was accompanied by a model of the river piers and cutwaters, with the centering and its supports, at a scale of one-twenty-fourth, constructed under the author's direction by Mr. Keenan, and also by a diagram map, at two inches to the mile, showing the general features of the valley of the Taff—and another map, at six chains to the inch, showing the immediate locality of the viaduct, and the natural difficulties of the ground, with the added difficulty of carrying a line of rails through that district, from the great pre-occupation of the surface by the canal and its feeders, and the mineral tram-roads—and also a diagram section of the gradients of the line of railway, with a large isometrical drawing of two of the arches, showing by part section the arrangements of the spandril walls, the mode of closing them over as designed, and as carried out in the construction, with the form of the soffit, the capital, and pillar.

AN ACCOUNT OF THE CONSTRUCTION OF THE MIDLAND GREAT WESTERN RAILWAY OF IRELAND, OVER A TRACT OF BOGS, IN THE COUNTIES OF MEATH AND WESTMEATH, BY GEORGE W. HEMANS, ENGINEER-IN-CHIEF.

The railway from Dublin to Mullingar was projected, from motives of interest and policy, to follow the line, and occupy the banks, of the Royal Canal. The canal banks afforded some facilities for the construction of a railway, but it soon became evident that there were also disadvantages in following them too closely. The earth-works in constructing the canal had been very heavy in character, with some of the deep cuttings through rock, and to relieve them as much as possible, the canal had been laid out to follow every sinuosity of the ground which offered a favourable level. The railway, as far as Mullingar, was also laid out along nearly the whole of these sinuosities, and there being great anxiety to open at least a portion of it at the earliest period, it was at once, on the passing of the Bill, put into a contractor's hands for one-half the distance (as far as Enfield), and rapidly constructed on the canal banks. During the progress of these works, it was found to be desirable to avoid constructing the remainder of the line on a continued system of curves, which, although no longer, by well-informed engineers, considered a source of danger, are decidedly objectionable, as offering a resistance to the trains, causing greater friction, wear and tear, consumption of fuel, and loss of time, besides lengthening the distance. In considering the plans for the second division of the line, between Enfield and Mullingar, the canal bank, which is a continued series of curves, was clearly to be avoided; but another difficulty presented itself on the straight line—the chord to these curves—it would have to traverse a long line of bogs, which, on careful examination with the boring-rod, proved to be from twenty-five to as much as seventy feet deep. Some of them were swell bogs of the softest pulpy nature, having gradually risen to a higher level than the surrounding country, and holding much water in suspension. After an extended examination on the subject, particularly in reference to drainage it was at length apparent that one of the causes of the excess of water, and consequent want of solidity in these bogs, was the position of the canal embankment, traversing the edges of them for a great distance, and completely intercepting all drainage from them along the general fall of the country, towards the river Deal. The following general plan was then at once resolved upon:—First, immediately to open full and sufficient new outlets for the escape of suspended water from the whole area; next, to form a system of drains all along and across the intended line; and finally, as a fixed principle, not to attempt either to excavate or embank the line, but to lay the rails on the natural level of the high bogs, trusting to drainage only to reduce the parts that were too high. With tolerable confidence in this plan, a Deviation Bill was passed through Parliament, and the straight line, traversing about eight miles of deep bog, was immediately commenced. An old wooden shoot, nine inches square, which was the sole outlet for the drainage of a district of about 1,500 square acres of wet bog, was the most ineffective point of the existing drainage, and was, therefore, the first to demand improvement. The banks and bottom of the canal at the place consist of clay artificially superposed on the cut away bog, lying on fine gravel of a very loose, treacherous description, being of a mixed sandy and marly nature. Having resolved on introducing a tunnel culvert, three feet diameter, under the canal at this spot, and that its invert should be six feet lower than the existing shoot, it became a matter of anxious consideration how to do this, in such bad ground, without interfering with the navigation of the canal, or running the risk of bursting a leak in the bottom. The canal level at this stage is twenty miles long, without a lock, and a breach would have been a serious affair.

Mr. Hemans here described very minutely the details of the execution of this very difficult work, which was altogether very successful, which secured the command for drainage of nearly four miles of the line of railway.

While the foregoing work was in progress, a sum of about £1,000 was being expended in the sinking a length of some miles of a river, and under-pinning a culvert, ten feet wide, leading out of the next district of bogs.

This underpinning and building a new invert, at a level four feet below the old one, was also a work requiring great caution. The weight of the embankment and the canal overhead was very great, and here also a breach would have caused extensive damages. As soon as these outlets were ready the drains in the bog were opened.

Mr. Hemans having made some observations on the cost of maintaining railways constructed through bogs, and also on a paper of great interest by the Messrs. Mullens, published in the second volume of the Transactions of the Institute of Civil Engineers of Ireland, concluded by reading a detailed estimate of the cost of these works, which clearly showed the possibility of constructing a double line of railway over deep bogs, when treated as described by him, at a cost not exceeding £6,000 per mile, including all expenses.

SOCIETY OF ARTS.
At the Meeting of the 23d January,
JAMES WALKER, Esq., F. R. S., C. E., V. P., in the Chair.
Mr. A. G. Findlay, M. R. G. S., on Artificial Breakwaters, and the prin-ciples which govern their construction.

Mr. FINDLAY'S paper commenced by stating, that it was not wished to pronounce upon the feasibility or impracticability of any of the numerous plans which have, from time to time, been proposed for the construction of breakwaters, but to submit some facts, drawn from natural effects, shewing the forces to which such structures must be subjected.

The paper, therefore, was naturally divided into two parts. The first, which related to the action of the waves, and its collateral subjects; and the second, to the various forms which have been given to sea-barriers, and the history of the progress of those now in existence.

The principal difficulty in establishing a fixed breakwater was shewn to be the enormous force of the waves. The form and nature of sea-waves generally were alluded to, and Mr. Scott Russell's system described. Of the dynamic force exerted by sea-waves, it was stated that their greatest force was at the crest of the wave before it breaks; and its power in raising itself was measured by a number of facts. At Warberg, in Norway, it rose 400 feet, January 21, 1820: on the coast of Cornwall it rose 300 feet in 1843. Other examples, as the singular "Souffleur"[*] at the Mauritius, &c. were cited, showing that the waves have raised a column of water equivalent to a pressure of three to five tons per square foot; a result in accordance with Mr. T. Stevenson's observations with the Marine Dynamometer.

It was shown by a table that the velocity of waves was dependant on their length; that waves of 300 to 400 feet in length from crest to crest, travelled with a velocity of 90 to 27½ miles an hour, and this whether they were 5 or 54 feet in total height; this velocity alone, should they become primary waves of translation, would give them a great percussive force. That waves travel very great distances was instanced by several facts. That they are raised by distant hurricanes and gales was noticed, by their being felt simultaneously at St. Helena and Ascension, though 600 miles apart; and opinions quoted, that these rollers, or ground-swell, at times originated near Cape Horn, 3,000 miles distant, rendering it more than probable that tropical hurricanes will send storm-waves to our own shores.

That it was not only at their surface that waves exerted great power, but that they reach in their action to the depth of eight fathoms and upwards,

was shown by the operations for the recovery of the treasure from H.M.S. *Thetis*, which was wrecked and sunk at Cape Frio, Brazil, in 1831. The diving-bell was swung four or five feet laterally in calm weather in these operations, much increasing their danger. Besides this, the guns and treasure were found covered by masses of rock of from thirty to fifty tons weight, moved by the action of the water, and weighed or turned over in the second operations by Captain de Roos.

From these facts, it was considered that floating breakwaters generally were not adapted to combat with the waves. Admiral Tayler's plan of timber frame-work sections; Captain Grove's iron cylinders with an at-tached grating; Captain Pringle's frame, moored by its lower edge; Cap-tain A. Sleigh's floating sea-barrier; Mr. Smith's plan, as submitted to the Society, were mentioned; and it was considered that the calculations of their resistance were understated; that Admiral Tayler's section, instead of twenty-five tons' strain, might, if the waves exerted only one-third of their force as known, have to withstand upwards of 1,000 tons; this pro-bably caused the failure of Admiral Tayler's experiment at Brighton, and Captain Groves's at Dover. Major Parlby's principle of the trumpet-mouth sea-weed was compared with the *fucus giganteus* of Dr. Solander, abundant on the Patagonian and Fuegian coasts, and 360 feet in length, which is carried under water in currents, and torn up, and chokes all the bays during storms.

The motion of shingle, an important consideration in establishing break-waters, was shown to be governed by the direction in which the surf strikes the shore, and this is dependant on the direction of the wind. This, from fifteen years observation, by M. Nell de Bréauté, at Dieppe, was shown to be in the ratio of 229 days from western quarters to 132 days from eastern quarters, giving that preponderance to its eastward progress. The mode in which it was arranged on the sloping beach, in the form of a paraboloidal curve, was explained.

Sand, a more powerful agent than shingle in changing the character of a coast, was stated to be deposited by currents, thus rendering the eastern parts of the English Channel much more embarrassed by them than the western portion. The Goodwin Sands were exhibited as examples of the extent of accumulation, and the changeable character of sand deposits. The diagrams exhibited showed the progress of these alterations, and were drawn from, perhaps, the only authentic history we possess of the changeable cha-racter of a quicksand. The different periods, from Graeme Spence's survey in 1795 down to Captain Bullock's in 1850, showed that they had shifted miles in their position and area, evidently refuting the practicability of any principle which would apply to fixing them, and rendering them available more perfectly for breakwater purposes, as was proposed by Capt. Vetch, R.E., to the Royal Commission, 1845.

February 6.—Mr. Findlay commenced the second part of his paper by recapitulating some of the forces and circumstances to which breakwaters are subjected, as cited in the former abstract. The application of these was the subject of the present portion.

The preparations for the great Cherbourg *digue* were noticed; the pro-posals of 1712 and 1777 for a line of sunken ships filled with masonry, as at the siege of La Rochelle in 1573, and the first operations by M. de Cessar, in 1782-4, were described. This latter plan was to sink truncated conical caissons, strongly framed of timber, 150 feet diameter, and 64 feet high, floated by means of a double tier of immense casks around their bases. The first and second was successfully launched; but before the latter could be filled with stones, as intended, a storm carried it away to low-water mark. This led to a great change in the plan; instead of 90 of these cones tan-gent to each other, they were to be placed at considerable distances apart, the intervals to be filled with *pierre perdü*[*]; 18 of them were laid, but they were all destroyed but one before 1789—some of them in two days after their being placed. The method *à pierre perdü* was then resorted to, and continued with, until it was modified by an upright parapet from low-water level by M. Dupare, 1832; the work is still in progress.

---

[*] The "souffleur" consists of a passage worn in the rock, and reaching from below the level of the sea to the top of the cliff, and the waves are driven up this cavity to a considerable height. We have witnessed a some-what similar action of the sea, in what is termed a "blowhole" on the coast of Cornwall. It seems probable that the force of the sea is assisted by the action of compressed air in the cavities of the rocks, like the air vessel of a fire-engine.

[*] *Pierre perdü* is the term applied to work composed of stones thrown promiscuously together, and left to be arranged by the action of the waves.

The series of four different slopes, in which the waves have distributed the stones of the *digue* was described; and the absence of the lowest slope in the Plymouth section was accounted for by the increased force of the waves upon the latter.

The commencement in 1811 by Mr. Rennie, and subsequent proceedings, under its present superintendent, Mr. Stuart, of the Plymouth Breakwater, were then alluded to, and the increased length of foreshore which had been found necessary, from the original design, and the greater effect of the sea at its *west* end described. In 1838, from the great effects of a storm a species of buttress was designed by Mr. James Walker, C. E., for the protection of the base of the lighthouse. This involved a new principle in hydraulic architecture, afterwards alluded to.

This structure resembles in some degree the system of dovetailing and grooves adopted by Smeaton in the Eddystone; but differs in its application. The Delaware breakwater in the United States was then briefly alluded to.

The principal of the presenting a concave face to the waves was then adverted to. In 1734 such a section was proposed, but not acted on, by M. Touros, for S. Jean de Luz. In 1787-95 Don Tournas Munos constructed the sea-walls of Cadiz thus : a straight foreshore of timber planking and a curved masonry termination. This was destroyed by the blocks of stone placed at its foot for protection rolling up the incline against the masonry. M. Emy, who endeavoured to establish the existence of what he denominates the *flot-du-fond*, proposed a cylindrical or other curvilinear face for this purpose in 1818, and in 1820 repaired the works of the fortification of St. Martin, Ile de Ré, in the Bay of Biscay, on his plan, which was so far successful, though not very greatly exposed. Various forms of the concave *revétement* were noticed, and the natural form assumed by the shingle beach was cited as an instance of the effect of beach surf. This form has been adopted in the Dymchurch wall constructed by Mr. Walker. The mode of action of the waves against a cliff was also explained, as producing a similar section.

Mr. Scott Russell's deductions from the wave system, leading also to similar conclusions, were then alluded to, and the sectional form he has proposed described. He preferred a paraboloidal curve for the foreshore; and an over-hanging coping, so as to turn the wave on itself was described.

Mr. Russell, for deep-water structures, preferred the method *à pierre perdú*, forming a straight foreshore. One objection to this system of concave face was, the varying level to which such structures are exposed from tidal influences, and the differences of curve presented at different periods of tide.

From these systems, the vertical, or nearly vertical wall, was then described; and the great national work at Dover, the Refuge Harbour, was stated to be on the principle established by the experience of the buttress at the west end of Plymouth Breakwater. This mode of construction, found effective at that place, counteracts some of the difficulty met with in securing the masonry facing it. In a previous part of the paper it was stated that the stones were blown out of the facing, or towards the sea-wave. This action is attributed to the percussion force entering the joints, and thus the water or air contained within the body of the masonry, being most forcibly driven upwards and outwards, carried single stones out of their beds. The new mode consists of stepping one course of stones into the upper surface of that beneath it, so as to form a ledge to prevent its outward tendency, and also to divert the direct action of the wave on the joint. In addition to this, each stone is so dove-tailed on its horizontal plane, that each course forms virtually one stone; and alternate stones in each course are locked into the course beneath it; so that, throughout the fabric, some portion of each course belongs to the one on either side of it, making the whole into one mass. These stones are faced at the quarries, and fixed in their places by the diving-bell. The situation of Dover Harbour, as being free from the chances of silting up, was considered in reference to the tides, and the improbability that any great amount of shingle would for the future embarrass the work.

Messrs. Staite and Petrie on Improvements in the Electric Light.

Of all artificial lights, that produced by electricity is the most beautiful, pure, and perfect, and only inferior to that of the sun itself. The difficulties involved in its production are manifold; they have, however, been effectually overcome by the inventors' electro-magnetic regulator, which is self-regulating, and not easily deranged.

The carbon used by the inventors is almost chemically pure, of an exceedingly equal structure, and homogeneity, and by a simple process, has been obtained at a very insignificant expense.

The conducting power of carbon is only $\frac{1}{1000}$th part that of copper; but by peculiar arrangements, Messrs. Staite and Petrie have succeeded in supplying their lamps with electrodes for any definite number of hours.

By experiments, the inventors have determined formulæ, which yield, not merely comparative, but direct quantative results as to the relation of the *quantity* of current-electricity to its *intensity* ; and also, in any varying case, give the proper power of the electro-motive elements, their number in series, the diameter of the electrode, the length and section of the wire used for the regulator, its proportions when formed, &c., including the section for conducting wires according to the distance of the light from the battery. The power of the light produced, the limit within which the power of the battery may be suffered to vary, and many minor points—all these being determined by correct laws, and applicable to all possible modifying circumstances. Messrs. Staite and Petrie assert that electricity has been reduced to a system so accurate in detail as to be relied on in practice.

A battery has been constructed by them in which fluid communications between the cells is effected in such a manner as to allow of the battery being charged and discharged in two or three minutes, whilst the strength of the solution used is kept perfectly uniform for very long periods, without the possibility of any local action on the zincs, and requires no sort of amalgamation.

By repeated experiments, Messrs. Staite and Petrie have satisfactorily proved that liquid communication between the cells of a battery, if properly arranged, will not affect either the quantity or intensity of the current, as supposed by many, while, at the same time, it gives the facility of maintaining the power for any given period.

The peculiar economy, which, by great concentration of action and high temperature with very little volume of heat, is obtained by the electric light, may be explained thus: the amount of radiant light increases in a vastly greater ratio than the increase of temperature. A series of curves, illustrated by a diagram, were produced, to show the relative increments of temperature, both in radiant heat and light, from a solid body. As far as experiments have gone, radiant light increases as the sixth power of the excess of temperature above 960° Fahrenheit. If, then, it is very expensive to maintain a given light by keeping a substance at a small increase of temperature beyond incipient luminosity, it will be far less expensive to obtain the same amount of light from a diminished illuminating surface, with a proportionately increased intensity of illumination, because the surface may be diminished in a far greater proportion than the current of electricity required; for the reduced surface must be increased to give the proportionate increase of light. Hence the proportion of luminosity for the given current producing it becomes exceedingly high where the heated surface is so concentrated, as in the case of the tip of the electrode, or rather the spot occupied by the disruptive discharge. The problem of rendering light from electricity continuous and uneconomical has been solved. It has been already introduced by the Barge Steam Towing Company, and is in constant use in the Enterprise tug-boat, and is managed by the engineer on board without difficulty or failure. By the use of this light in houses, &c., all currents of vitiated air and gas are avoided, and a cool, pure, and perfectly steady light is secured.

30th January.

GEORGE MOFFATT, Esq., M.P., V.P., in the Chair.

Mr. Henton, on the Cause and Prevention of Oscillation in Locomotive Engines.

The author, in the outset, calls attention to the necessity and importance

9

of adhering to the natural laws of motion, which cannot be transgressed without loss and inconvenience, and professes to place an old principle in a new light, rather than to lay claim to any new discovery.

When a greater velocity on railroads was attained, the liability of the engine to leave the rails was increased. To obviate this, heavier engines were used, and in many instances the engines and carriages are screwed tightly together, so as to form a rigid bar, and to distribute the weight more equally along the whole train. This, to a certain extent, steadied them, but the oscillation was not entirely got rid of.

The author then mentioned two or three accidents which have occurred from the engines jumping and getting off the rails.

After making experiments, Mr. Heaton ascertained that the oscillation and jumping of the engine arose from the action of the piston and gearing. To correct this defect, Mr. H. has made a model which shows that the disturbing causes arise from the action of the piston in the cylinder. But by applying to it an additional crank moving in the reverse direction to the piston, and driving a weight equal to the resistance of the piston, so that when the piston is at its farthest point in the cylinder from the driving-wheel, the proposed crank is at its nearest, and *vice versâ*, he completely balances the working of the piston, and renders the framework of the machinery, which oscillated to a considerable extent before, entirely steady.

It had been suggested to Mr. Heaton whether, by placing a weight attached to the inside of that portion of the tire of the driving-wheel which, when the piston is at the farthest point in the cylinder, would be directly opposite to it, the same results might not be obtained. Mr. H. tried it, and found that oscillation was prevented, but a new and equally detrimental effect was produced, as at each revolution of the wheel, when the weight was at its highest point from the rail, it had a tendency to fly from the centre of motion, and thus a lifting or jumping action was given.

Abstract of a Paper by Mr. C. F. Whitworth, on an Apparatus for aiding the Drivers of Locomotive Engines in cases of danger, and for preventing Collisions on Railways.

The author proposes that each locomotive shall carry two pendent rods, about six inches long, and moving freely on axes, and acting on triggers. These triggers release two rods, each connected with levers which open their respective valves. One sounds an alarm-whistle; the other admits steam to a piston, in a small cylinder, whose action causes the lever of a throttle-valve to shut off the steam in the dome of the engine.

The piston-rod of this small cylinder, at the same time that it shuts the throttle-valve, applies a lever-break to the wheels of the locomotive, and also registers upon a suitable dial that that has been effected mechanically which the vigilance of the driver, under ordinary circumstances, would have superseded by his obeying the signal some 200 yards before.

The trigger-rods are acted upon by inclined planes of wood, placed parallel with the rails, and a few inches from them laterally. These rods are about four feet long, having hinge-joints at one end, and are capable of an elevation of four or five inches at the other.

This elevation from an horizontal position is, in general, produced by a partial rotation of a transverse spindle placed under the rails, and on which are fixed two cams, which acting by pressure under the inclines, cause them to assume the elevation requisite. The rotation of the spindle is produced by a motion of the lever and wire-rope, which are used for working the semaphore signal; and the cams and lever on the spindle, together with weights for reaction, are so arranged as to cause an elevation or depression of the inclines in perfect accordance with the indication of the signal.

It should be remarked, that when the driver shuts off the steam himself, in accordance with the signal, this action lifts out of gear the trigger-rod, which would otherwise come in contact with the inclines; and that he cannot apply his steam without having replaced the rod, which is liable to expose any neglect of signals.

EVIDENCE ON THE NECESSITY FOR A REFORM OF THE PATENT LAWS.

Continued from page 40.

We now turn to the laws themselves, which, it is not too much to say, are as bad as their administration. In fact, our only difficulty in extracting from the evidence of those best qualified to judge, is the utter want of any defence or palliation of them. They are bad—root and branch. First, as to the expense of a patent. We do not mean to argue on the principle that a man ought to have the same protection for his ideas that a magistrate gives his property. It is quite fair that an inventor should pay for the monopoly which he obtains for fourteen years; for, although the public has the benefit of his invention, at the end of that period it is generally the case that, by the progress of invention, some fresh patent supersedes it, whilst the former patent (from its extensive character) may have kept other inventors out of the field. The grievance is this—that an inventor gets no protection until the patent is sealed. Then, when he has paid his money, he may make experiments and give his invention a fair working trial. He generally finds either that his invention is worthless, or that the improvements which a fair trial suggests are required to be protected by a fresh patent. In either case he has the satisfaction of reflecting that he has paid the same tax as his neighbour who is reaping a fortune from a successful patent. The objection that a man ought only to patent that which is sure to succeed, and that his want of success is a proof of his want of merit, is a sheer absurdity. It is as unjust to make an inventor pay 14 years' tax in advance, as it would be to make him pay his rent in the same manner. The inventor may find it as much to his interest to change his plans as the tenant to change his dwelling. The effect of the laws is to compel a poor inventor to part with, generally, half his invention, merely to defray the cost of protection; whereas, if he could obtain protection for a small sum, he would have the opportunity of publishing his invention, and selling it to the highest bidder.

Mr. Campin says—Some other person may get a knowledge of his invention, and register it, or publicly exhibit it, during the progress of his patent—in either case destroying its validity. "I am in favour of the same policy as that pursued in France, of taking the duties by annual instalments of a moderate amount. The greater part of inventors are in reality men in very humble circumstances.

"A patent should be dated back to the day application was made."

Mr. Carpmael.—"If a patentee could have an opportunity of having it for England, for Ireland, or for Scotland alone, and he also had the power, if he chose, to take it for the three at once, it would be very desirable to reduce the total amount of the three, but not below £100. I think if it extended to the three kingdoms (including the colonies), £150 would not be too much."

Mr. Webster.—"As the law now stands, a person has no protection till the date of the patent, and if any part of his invention should get out during the course of the experiments, he might be deprived entirely of his right." "I was told only yesterday of a case of hearing before the Attorney-General having been postponed, not by reason of want of information, but by reason of his engagements at the chartist trials. The consequence was a postponement of eight days, and the consequence of that was that a party, who had a caveat, obtained information of what the person applying for the patent was about, and, learning something about it, went and registered under the Designs' Act, part of the very invention, and the most essential part of it (which the other intended to patent), well knowing that he could get no protection by patent, because he was either the subsequent inventor, or a person obtaining information improperly. He trusted, therefore, to getting some little advantage by registering it on the moment, and by so doing he destroyed the title of the party to a patent in every part of the United Kingdom." "Nine-tenths of the practical grievances would be got over by allowing the patent right to date from the petition"

"Nothing can be worse than the present system." "I would press upon the attention of the committee the policy of annual payments. I think it is a very good principle indeed. An English patent now costs about £105, a patent for Scotland £80, and a patent for Ireland £150, a most curious difference of charge. I think £350 for the three countries is far too large. What is the reason that you have ten times the number of patents for England that you have for Ireland, and five times the number for England that you have for Scotland? It is because it is not worth people's while, in a commercial point of view, to go to the expense to obtain a patent for the three countries. If you reduced a patent to £150 for the three countries, I believe you would get more money as a matter of fees than you do now." "I am not for cheap patents, still I think £350 is too much; I see no objection to a person paying £150 in the first instance, and a tax annually, if he liked to continue it, or instead of annually, at certain stages. It generally requires half the term of a patent to see if it is worth anything. Then at the end of seven years you might have a second payment if the patent were kept up.

Mr. Webster also mentions another hardship to which the patentee is exposed. When he lodges his specification and drawings, the custom is for the officials to make a copy of them, and return the originals to the patentee. Now, if ever the specification is required to be produced in a court of law, he is bound by *the office copy* (whether it be rightly copied or not), because the original, coming out of his own possession, may have been altered. Mr. Webster suggests, "The practice, as regards wills, is a good one to follow; the original will is kept, and is copied into a book; the public consult the copy."

There is a still worse engine of torment for the unhappy patentee, if he should escape all the preceding. We will quote Mr. Webster's account of it:—" If a party presenting his petition, says that he means to apply for a patent for England only, then he has two months for specifying; if he inserts in his petition his intention to apply for a patent for Scotland and Ireland, he has six months. It sometimes happens that, supposing he applies for all the patents together, that, from accident, the Scotch patent is sealed first; that occurred in a case which was brought under my notice only yesterday; a specification was brought to me, in which it happened that in his Scotch patent he had only four months to specify; he would then have to enrol his specification in Scotland, and thus make a publication of the invention two months previously to the publication in England. If there were a patent running in England for the same invention, but of a prior date to the Scotch patent, a party might steal the invention from the specification published in Scotland, as was alleged to have been done in one case recently before the Lord Chancellor, thus a stranger might put into his English patent, of a prior date, information that he got from the Scotch patent of another person. Then, as the specification relates back to the date of the patent, the stranger so introducing the invention into his patent, is the first inventor in England; and he not only has the whole right in England, but the right under the Scotch patent is gone, by reason of there being a prior patent in England, upon the authority of Brown v. Annandale."

Mr. W. Spence says—" I think the amount of fees now payable on an English patent is not excessive for a monopoly of fourteen years' duration. But, then, I think the patentee is in reason and fairness entitled to more certainty in his property than he at present enjoys, or can enjoy, under the present defective arrangements in the mode of granting patents, and enrolling specifications. I am also favourable to what I will call " small patents,"—that is, a monopoly for a short term for a small fee; something like what the legislature seem to have had in view when they passed the Act for registering designs for articles of utility, but which utterly failed of giving legal protection in the manner desired. " I think the present mode of paying the fees is highly inconvenient, owing mainly to the deferring of the date of the patent to the sealing. This is a source of great uncertainty to the patentee; and in my judgment it exposes him to much risk, without benefiting the public. The early date, with adequate security for restricting the grant of letters patent to *bonâ fide* inventions, would tend greatly to obviate the present difficulty."

Mr. W. Newton:—I think the law ought to be so far altered as to make the patent date from the period of the petition. This early dating of the patent, however, renders some fresh precautions necessary, which Mr. Newton then describes:—

Question 1,105.—If the patent were made to date from the application, would it not be necessary to require that the applicant should prosecute the patent to completion within a limited time?

Answer.—Certainly; most decidedly. And more than that, it would be necessary that he should deposit, *at once*, a preliminary specification, showing the elements of his invention. I should look at the patent in this way; first of all, to get an intelligible title; that title may be " An Improvement in Steam Engines;" but there are a thousand different parts in a steam engine,

and who can tell the part to which the improvement refers? When, therefore, an application is made to the Attorney-general, there should always be deposited at the same time a specification giving a general notion of the invention. As, for instance, that the improvement refers to the valves, or to the packing of the pistons, and that it was intended to effect so and so; just a general idea of the advantages which the inventor contemplated obtaining. Now, that is done at present in cases where there is opposition; but I have often urged that it should be done in all cases. That, in fact, a man may not be able to obtain a " fishing patent," which will serve for the insertion of anything that may fall in his way, before the enrolment of his specification; but that he shall state positively what he has invented, before he gets the Attorney-general's report."

Question 1,106.—Do you think that the present fees upon English patents are excessive?—" Yes, I do, I think it would be desirable if they were reduced." If I remember rightly my former notion was to grant an English patent for 60*l.*, and the other two patents for 20*l.* each, thus making the cost 100*l.*, instead of their exceeding 300*l.* as at present.

" I do not think it would be satisfactory to make the procuring of patents too cheap, for some people entertain the notion that if we were smothered with patents they would lose all their effect, and especially that they would be always in courts of law on questions of infringement. There may be something in that, still I think patents ought to be cheaper than they are. It frequently happens that a man who has an ingenious invention which he cannot find means to secure, is obliged to sacrifice half his interest to some party who finds the money for securing it.

" There is one other observation that I should like to make. The Registration act has been extremely useful as far as it goes—in the protection of forms, but the general impression has been, that that act would protect a combined piece of mechanism as well as a form, and thus we are constantly having registrations for some little piece of machinery; indeed, the practice went so far in the first instance, as to register steam-engines and barrel organs. That, I believe, has been put a stop to now. There are a great many small articles of utility and little novelties connected with the detail of elaborate machines that manufacturers would like to have protection for, and I should think that a seven years' grant of protection for such matters would be amply sufficient and satisfactory, if such protection could be obtained for something like the cost of a patent up to the bill. In France and all the continental countries, they have five, ten, and fifteen years' patents."

Mr. C. Barlow—" I think the fees are too high at present. Assuming that the expense of a patent for England is now about 100*l.*, I think between 50*l.* and 60*l.* would be sufficient. If it could be extended to the three kingdoms, it would be more desirable, but I apprehend there would be a difficulty—say 40*l.* for Scotland, and 35*l.* for Ireland."

Mr. J. C. Robertson—" Assuming the present amount of fees in England upon a patent to be about 100*l.*, I think it is an excessive charge, considering that it takes upwards of 200*l.* more to include Scotland and Ireland. The policy of imposing a fine (as it were) upon inventors, seems in an abstract point of view altogether objectionable, but the question is by no means free from difficulty."

" I think parties would not object to between 25*l.* and 40*l.* I should think the extension to Scotland and Ireland might be put upon a par, for say, half the price of the English patent." " In France, every patentee pays so much per annum; and if that system were adopted here, I think it would produce much more revenue than our own." " In France, if a patent does not turn out well, the parties drop it altogether. The result is, that the government only gets the entire sum upon the successful patents, but successful inventors here would be very willing to pay a per centage on their receipts. It is repeatedly said that the government might get a very large revenue from successful patents."

" The system of deferred payments would, no doubt, tend to a multiplication of patents; but I have recommended, at the same time, that the government should interpose a check to that by causing each application to pass through the sieve of some official examiner, assisted by such men of science or skill as he might see fit to call to his aid." If the expense of patents should be reduced to any considerable extent, I would recommend that each patent should be limited, as in France, to one substantive matter. The practise at present is to crowd as many things into one patent as the words of the title can cover; and to make these words as vague, large, and comprehensive, as possible—a practice arising, no doubt, out of a general feeling that the cost of a patent is too high, and that where so much is exacted—it is but fair to get as much as people can for their money. The consequences of this state of things are, however, very pernicious. The specification of such multitudinous patents become necessarily of great length, so much so as to place office copies of them quite out of ordinary reach, costing very commonly from 10*l*. to 20*l*., and not unfrequently as much as 50*l*. to 60*l*., and increasing enormously the expenses of any legal proceedings, of which they may happen to become the subject. Again, one man pays no more for a dozen inventions than another does for one or two; and, hence, not only a great inequality in the pecuniary operation of the existing system, but a serious loss to the public revenue. Were each patent to embrace one subject matter only, I think it likely, that even though the cost were reduced to about one-third of its present amount (as I have proposed), the aggregate receipts from this source would not be at all diminished."

After this mass of concurrent testimony, is it expecting too much that Government should at once adopt the recommendations of the committee, and not allow the present session to pass without introducing *and carrying* a bill on the subject ? A little outward pressure is all that is required, and we are very much mistaken in our estimation of English Artizans, if they allow the iron to get cool before the final blow is struck.

STOVES AND FIREPLACES.

In a former number we described a portable stove which we had tried and found to answer tolerably well; we mentioned, at the same time, some points in which it might be improved. Whether from reading our remarks, or from an original idea, we cannot say, but these points have been

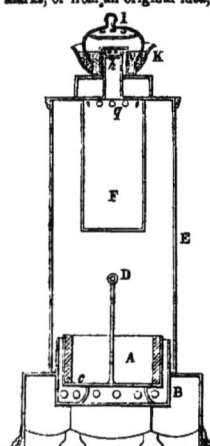

embodied, to a certain extent, in a stove recently registered by M. Harvey, of Dorchester, and entitled the "Neapolitan Stove"—why or wherefore deponent sayeth not. We certainly did not contemplate recommending a stove without a chimney, as we thought we had had enough of those for awhile, albeit in this case the products of combustion are filtered, by passing through a receiver filled with lime and water, and, as lime is known to absorb carbonic acid gas, *of course* the stove is a perfectly safe companion. There is, *of course*, a remote chance that the lime water may get saturated by use and exposure to the atmosphere, and that it may be neglected to be changed; and, after the reports in the daily papers, and our own remarks, our readers will, we hope, duly weigh these chances before they try the experiment. We are not exactly clear, either, how the sulphur is to be got rid of, unless the name, "Neapolitan," is intended to convey that charcoal only is to be used in it. If so, it would be as well to acquaint purchasers with the fact, charcoal being rather expensive as compared with coke.

In the sketch, A is the fire-pan lined with fire brick, with fire bars, *c*, at bottom; in the centre is the rod, D, by which the pan can be lifted out. B is an ash pan. E, the outer case (cylindrical). F, a heat spreader. *g*, holes through which the draught escapes into the pipe, *h*, into an outer pipe, closed at top, but drilled with holes all round, through which the gases escape into the chamber containing lime and water, and finally through the holes at the top into the room, and, we will hope, up the chimney. K is an outer vessel filled with water, which, by its evaporation, will serve to prevent the atmosphere from becoming too dry.

POWER OF THE STEAM JET.

In his evidence before the Committee of the House of Commons on the prevention of accidents in coal mines, J. Mather, Esq. gave some very interesting information on the power of the steam jet; he stated that in a large alkali and muriatic manufactory where it had been applied, it had superseded the use of two chimneys 200 feet and 170 feet high each; he says "six jets, five-sixteenths of an inch big, do the work of a chimney 200 feet high, which cost 2000*l*.; it was the most striking fact I have ever seen." The parties used to be perpetually paying damages for injury to vegetation, and the neighbours were complaining that it was a most offensive manufacture, so much so, that a very extensive work of that kind was about being destroyed altogether, when the adoption of this plan enabled them to discontinue the use of the chimneys, and destroy the source of injury. They produce an enormous current. In the condensation of the gases they pulled the air up 24 feet, through a current of water passing down with great velocity; they drew the muriatic acid gas through this shaft, and got it absorbed altogether, and the furnaces were kept infinitely better than with the 200 ft. chimney. Then there was this additional result, which may be also observed in the mines that this ventilating process in south winds is not affected at all; the furnace is invariably affected in south winds. Frequently you have accidents from the want of pressure in the atmosphere, barometric and hygrometric causes; for we know that accidents frequently come about by south winds, accompanied by the circumstances I name, and they also used to affect similarly the furnaces; but on inquiring amongst the people whether such is the case now, they say invariably, that the jet is so steady that they have no back-puff, as I think they call it, of muriatic acid gas, which was injurious to the health of the men working there; they work as well and as healthily now as in any other manufactory. They have taken a patent (not in justice, I think to the original inventor) to apply the steam-jet to this particular purpose of condensing acid gases in manufactories with the high-pressure steam-jet through a cone, the very suggestion which was thrown out by Mr. Gurney, in 1835. I understand that this operation for the ore-smelting furnaces, if adopted by them, will become of vast importance; that there will then be absolutely supplied by their processes sufficient sulphur, which is now lost, to render it quite unnecessary to have the sulphur of Sicily introduced at all.

The witness further said, he did not think it fair to the public, or individuals, that an invention, the benefit of which was given to the public by the inventor, should be taken advantage of by other parties for their own private gain, and that if any one is to be benefitted, it should be the person whose genius invented, and threw it open to the world. The year previous to the introduction of the jet, the parties mentioned paid 300*l*. for damage to vegetation; the jet had been in use four years, and they had not been called upon for a farthing.

ROYAL STEAM NAVY.

APPOINTMENTS.

Chief Engineers. — JOHN ETHERINGTON, to the *Jackal.* — SAMUEL PEMBERTON, to the *Sphynx.*

Assistant Engineers. — JAMES MOON and REDMOND MAHONY to the *Jackal.* — JAMES WARD to the *Gladiator.* — JAMES SCOTT, LIONEL SWIFT, and JOHN D. LAMONT, to the *Sphynx.*

DOCKYARD INTELLIGENCE.

WOOLWICH.—Jukes' Patent Smoke Consuming Furnace is to be applied to the *Prometheus* steam sloop, of 200 horse power, which has just had new boilers. By a curious coincidence, it has been applied to a French steamer of the same name—the *Promethée.*

SALE OF IRON STEAMERS.—The *Grappler*, of 557 tons, built in 1844 for the Navy, by Messrs. Fairbairn, has just been sold out of the service. Her original cost was 15,000*l*., and she fetched the modest sum of 550*l*. We presume that the extraordinary way in which she was built had some influence on the price, which is hardly that of old iron. The plan is, we believe, a patent of Messrs. Fairbairn, and consists in running the plates vertically with the ribs, instead of horizontally. Whatever success it may have met with on board the *Grappler*, we are not aware that it has been tried in any other vessel.

TRIAL MILE.—Captain Bullock, in the Widgeon steam-vessel, is employed in measuring the ground on the banks of the river below Gravesend for a new measured mile for testing steam vessels, the present measured mile in Long Reach being so often crowded with vessels trading on the Thames.

COAL FOR THE ARCTIC EXPEDITION.—It being desirable that the screw vessels forming part of the Arctic Expedition should carry as much fuel as possible, Mr. Humphreys has proposed a plan for sawing some of the best kinds of coal into the brick form, in order to make them stow closer.

DEVONPORT.—Three of Hall's patent self-feeding and smoke-preventing furnaces, like that at the Post-office, are being fitted up in this yard.

PORTSMOUTH.—Sir B. Walker and Captain Ellice, in conjunction with Captain Chads, form a committee to inquire into and report upon the best method of raising and lowering the propellers of screw steam-ships, so as to dispense with as much as possible of the dead weight near the stern-post. Experiments were tried on board the Blenheim, when with rope tackle, the process was accomplished in six minutes. Mr. Murray, the Superintendent Engineer of the Dockyard, is of opinion he can apply a screw lever, which will do the work in two minutes, and dispense with the manifold appliances now used in performing the same duty.

FRENCH AND ENGLISH SCREW-SHIPS. – The French Government has ordered the line-of-battle ships *l'Ulm*, 100 guns, now building at Rochefort, to be fitted with a screw-propeller, with engines of 300 horse-power. The French have another ship of 120 guns, named *Le Vingt-quatre Fevrier* (the 24th. of February) now fitting with a screw and engines of 900 horse power. The only ship in the English Navy approximating to these powerful screw line-of-battle-ships, is the *Agamemnon*, 80, now building in Woolwich Dockyard, to have engines of 400 horse-power, and which will not be ready for sea for several years.

STEAM NAVIGATION.

INDIAN RIVER STEAM NAVIGATION.—On the 6th instant, a dinner was given at the London Coffee House by the gentlemen who are about to assist Mr. Bourne in carrying out his plans of an improved system of steam navigation on the rivers of India, which offer a vast field for enterprise. We have so recently discussed this subject that we need not repeat our description of the peculiarities of Mr. Bourne's plan which consist of a skilful adaptation of the vessels to the exigencies of the case. On this occasion the chair was occupied by Mr. J. M'Gregor, M.P., and after the usual loyal and patriotic toasts, the important subject of the evening was introduced, and the advantages of the intended project were warmly and eloquently supported by Mr. Byrne, late Deputy-Governor of Bengal, Mr. Duncan, M.P., Sir John Campbell, and Mr. J. O. Walker. The entire absence of any constant and efficient means of communication was held out as the great evil under which India suffered, and by which its almost unlimited resources were crippled in their development; and it was urged that should the present scheme come into operation, the exchange of our manufactured goods against the cotton and other products of the interior of India, would speedily receive a rapid impetus. Towards the close of the proceedings, Mr. Bourne, upon his health being proposed, entered into a detailed statement of the various features of his proposed system, which, there is no doubt, would confer inestimable benefits on our Eastern Empire, and at the same time yield a liberal return for the capital invested in it.

TRIAL OF THE "PROPONTIS."—This fine vessel, the eighth of the General Screw Steam Shipping Company's fleet, the launch of which we previously noticed (p. 285, last vol.) was tried down the river on 12th inst. She was built by Messrs. Mare and Co., and fitted with engines by Messrs. Maudslay, and Co. Her dimensions are, 175 feet between perpendiculars; 25 feet beam, and 17 feet depth of hold; measurement, 560 tons. She has accommodation for 20 first class passengers. A pair of engines of 80 horse nominal power, connected direct to the screw shaft. Cylinders, 36 inches diameter, and 2 feet stroke. Average number of revolutions, 60 per minute. Average speed, 9¼ knots; about the same as the sister vessels *Bosphorus* and *Hellespont*. In going down, she met the *Hellespont* coming up, homeward bound from Constantinople, having effected a very quick passage both ways, viz. :—

				Days.	Hours.
Liverpool to Gibraltar	...	...	...	5	10
Gibralter to Malta	...	...	...	4	18
Malta to Constantinople	...	...	...	4	16
				14	21

RETURN TRIP.

		Days.	Hours.
Constantinople to Smyrna	...	2	2
Smyrna to Malta	...	3	15
Malta to Gibraltar	...	6	10
Gibraltar to London	...	8	23
		21	2

. against head winds and very stormy weather.

We think that these results more than justify the remarks we made on the subject of the vessels intended to be employed for the Brazilian Mail Contract.

NORTHFLEET.—The *Derwent* steam-ship, of 700 tons, built for the intercolonial service of the Royal Mail Steam Packet Company, by Mr. W. Pitcher, was launched from his dockyard on the 31st ult. She was placed immediately in the dry dock, to be coppered, preparatory to her being taken round to Southampton, where her machinery is to be fitted.

MILLWALL.—Messrs. Robinsons and Russell have upon the stocks a beautiful iron yacht, to be named the *Titania*, which is to be launched on 27th instant. Her dimensions are—

					Ft.	in.
Length on deck	...	...	...	...	89	0
Ditto between perpendiculars	...	...	...	...	68	9
Breadth of beam	...	...	...	...	18	0
Draft forward	...	...	...	...	8	0
Ditto aft	...	...	...	...	12	3
Builder's measurement	...	...	...	...	100 tons	
Height of cabins	...	...	...	...	7	6

GREENOCK.—LAUNCH OF THE "ASIA."—This magnificent vessel, built by Messrs. R. Steele and Co., for the British and North American Royal Mail Steam Navigation Company, was launched on the 31st January, between two and three o'clock. The following are her principal dimensions :—

					Feet.
Length on deck	...	...	...	...	265.2
Breadth on ditto amidships	...	...	...	...	37.2
Depth of hold at ditto	...	...	...	...	27.2
Tonnage	...	...	...	...	2226.⁴⁷⁄₉₄ tons.

Launching draught, 10 feet 2 inches forward, and 11 feet 2 inches aft. The *Asia* is the largest vessel ever built in Scotland, and the twenty-second steamer built by the firm.

The intermediate shaft was forged at the Lancefield Forge; rough size, 31 inches, and 21 inches diameter, and 13 feet 6 inches long; weight about 9 tons. The paddle-shafts are 22 inches diameter, and 22 feet 6 inches long; weight, 13 tons. The paddle-wheels will be about 36 feet diameter. Description—A full female figure head, standing boltsprit, no galleries, three masts, schooner or barque-rigged, three flush decks, a round-sterned and carvil-built vessel. She is to be commanded by Mr. C. H. E. Judkins, the commodore of the company's fleet. It is rather curious, whether accidentally or from design we know not, that the names of all the company's vessels end in A—viz., the *Britannia, Acadia, Caledonia, Columbia, Hibernia, Cambria, America, Niagara, Europa, Canada, Asia,* and *Africa*—the last named is not yet ready for launching.

LAUNCH OF THE "JANE EWING."—On Monday the 14th of January this vessel, built for the Glasgow and Calcutta Monthly Line, was launched from the building yard of Messrs. William Simons and Co., Cartsdyke, Greenock. At the appointed time the usual signal being given, Miss Crum, of Glasgow, named her, and she glided smoothly and gracefully into the water, amidst the cheers of the surrounding spectators. The "Jane Ewing" is built of British oak and teak, and is classed A 1 at Lloyds for 13 years. The following are a few of the principle dimensions:—

Builder's measurement					Ft	in
Length of keel and fore rake ...	...	...	...		121	7
Breadth of beam	...	...	...	...	27	10¼
Depth of hold ...	...	...	...	...	18	9
Tonnage	...	...	...	...	433⁸⁶⁄₉₄ tons	
New measurement					Ft	
Length on deck	...	...	...	...	120.8	
Breadth on ditto, at midships	...	...	...	25.4	
Depth of hold at ditto...	...	...	...	18.6	
Tonnage	...	...	...	...	455⁷⁄₁₀₀	

Deck beams, 9 × 9 inches; do., stringers 12 × 6½ inches; between deck, do., 12 × 15 inches; beams, 12 × 12 inches; frames, 8 × 5½ inches; spaced from 4 to 7 inches; ceiling 2½ inches thick, with a round house upon deck; length 26 feet, breadth forward 18 feet; aft 13 feet 8 inches; height 7 feet 6 inches; launching draught of water 6 feet 4 inches forward, and 7 feet 9 inches aft, without masts or spars on board, with the exception of the bowsprit. She is to be commanded by Mr. John Wylie, and is to sail from Glasgow to Calcutta on the 20th of March.

HULL.—On 14th ult., a fine iron screw steamer was launched from the building-yard of Messrs. T. and W. Pim. She has been built for R. M. Sloman, Esq., merchant, of Hamburg, for the Hamburg and New York passenger trade. She is named the *Helena Sloman.* She is 210 feet between perpendiculars, 27 feet beam, and 710 tons burden, and is to have engines of 120 horse-power.

ABERDEEN STEAM NAVIGATION COMPANY.—We understand that Mr. Thomas Anderson, of this city, so long connected with Messrs. Thomson and McConnell, steam-packet managers, has been appointed Manager of the Aberdeen Steam Navigation Company, a situation which he is eminently well qualified for.—*North British Shipping Journal.*

SUNDERLAND TIDE SIGNAL.—A new tide signal has been recently erected at Sunderland, designed by Mr. J. Meik, C.E., which appears an ingenious invention, and one well adapted for such purposes. It consists of a tower carrying a dial, on which is exhibited the height of the tide. The figures are painted on a web of copper wire gauze, mounted on two copper rollers, on which it is wound and unwound by the motion of a float, acted upon by the rise and fall of the tide. In order to increase the scale of the figures, to make them visible at a great distance, the motion of the float is multiplied by a wheel and pinion, as four to one; the wire web will, consequently, pass over four feet while the tide rises or falls one foot. At night the dial is strongly illuminated; and, as the letters are about 21 inches high, they can be seen, and the height of the tide ascertained, at a considerable distance.

THE SCREW PROPELLER.—On Monday, the 11th ult., a question of considerable interest, in respect to steam navigation, was argued before the judicial committee, at the Privy Council-office, Whitehall, Lords Brougham, Campbell, and Langdale, Dr. Lushington, and Mr. Pemberton Leigh, being present. An application was made by Sir Frederick Thesiger, on behalf of the patentees of the screw propeller, for an extension of their patent, which expires in May next. The evidence went to prove that no less than £30,000 had been expended in building the *Archimedes,* and in defraying other weighty charges, to establish the screw-propulsion principle; and it further appeared, that although no less than 32 ships-of-war, and 100 mercantile steam-vessels had been constructed already upon this system, not more than two or three had paid for the patent license. These evasions had been occasioned by the conflicting claims of five different patentees; but, as these have now united in one association, it is expected that all who have adopted the use of the screw propeller will have to pay for their licenses. As the Admiralty are interested either directly or collaterally, in this question, to the amount of about 25,000*l.,* Sir John Jervis, the Attorney-General, assisted by Mr. Crowder, Q. C., opposed the application for an extension of Mr. Frank Petit Smith's patent; but, after examining Capts. Chappell and Crispin, R. N., and Messrs. Brunel and Galloway, engineers, their lordships decided on granting an extension of five years to Mr. Smith's patent upon certain conditions; and there is now, therefore, a fair prospect of that gentleman and his supporters recovering a portion, if not the whole, of the licensing moneys to which they are unquestionably entitled.

VICTORIA DOCKS (OPPOSITE WOOLWICH).—On Monday, 11th ult., the standing orders, were declared to be complied with by the promoters of this measure for the construction of a dock on the north side of the Thames, the incorporated subscribers being Messrs. E. L. Betts, S. Holditch, T. Hayne, R. W. Kennard, R. Till, J. J. Cummins, and T. W. Harby. Proposed capital 400,000*l.,* in 20,000 shares, of 20*l.* each—power to borrow 133,000*l.* Messrs. Peto, M. P.; E. C. Mangles, Kennard, Till, and Cummins, to be the first directors. Land to be taken not to exceed 200 acres. The rates not to exceed those paid in the port of London. It is understood the Admiralty have directed a survey to be made.

ANALYSIS OF BOOKS.

An Essay on the Present and Future Prospects of Farming.—By W. THOROLD, M. Inst. C. E.

(SECOND NOTICE.)

By the concentration of the farm buildings, Mr. Thorold anticipates a saving in manual labour of ten per cent., which amount of labour will not be dispensed with, but will be applied in extracting an additional produce from the soil. Mr. Thorold also assumes that in the majority of farms, useless hedges render unproductive one-tenth of the land, a proportion which we have ourselves seen greatly exceeded, and the evil of which does not stop with the extent of soil wasted, for it is impossible to conduct the various agricultural operations so economically in a number of small fields, as in a few large ones.

The benefit of the application of steam power to farming economy is now fairly established; we do not, however, quite agree with Mr. Thorold in the kind of engine best suited for the purpose. In most agricultural districts coal is dear, and the portability of an engine and boiler is rather at variance with its economy of fuel. The cost of repairs is also much less in a large fixed engine than in a number of small ones. The tubular boiler of the portable engine is also more likely to get out of order, and the whole machinery is more liable to malicious damage. It appears to us, therefore, that it would be a profitable branch of business for a person to erect a steam engine in some central situation, convenient to as many farms as possible, and attach to it the following machinery :—a small flour-mill, thrashing machine, chaff cutting, turnip slicing, and cat bruising machines; a small saw mill, and pumps to pump liquid manure up a stand pipe to a sufficient height to throw the manure over the fields by means of a hose, without poaching the land by using a heavy liquid manure cart, and with a great saving of labour. This would of course necessitate the laying of pipes down from the engine-house to the various fields, but they would not require to be very large, and when the powerful effects of irrigation and liquid manure in increasing the productiveness of the soil are considered, we do not doubt it would pay very well. The proprietor of the mill would do all the work for the neighbouring farmers, and it would be his interest to arrive at the greatest economy of fuel and power, by always keeping the engine fully employed. In many places, too, pure water for domestic purposes, has to be fetched from a distance; and, although the district might not be sufficiently popalous to support a separate water-works, it would pay to lay down pipes if the engine were employed for other purposes.

This system of division of labour is one which we hope to see more introduced into farming, where it will be found as economical as in manufacturing operations. It is not entirely unknown, even now; as we are acquainted with a case, where a clever agricultural mechanic makes a good income by keeping a stock of the most improved drills, &c., and working for all the neighbouring farmers, who find it more profitable to employ him than to lay out their own capital in machines, - capital which they can make a better use of in buying manures, and making bargains for stock. His machines, too, are kept in better order, will do more work, and are idle for a shorter period than theirs would be.

The great advantage of this system is, that it admits of the introduction of the most improved machinery, on estates where individual farmers have neither spirit nor capital enough to venture on such expensive appliances.

Mr. Thorold mentions the fact, that in well, or rather, highly ventilated factories, the workpeople get hungry much sooner than in places imperfectly ventilated, and he proposes to apply the same system to cattle to induce them to eat more; his argument, however, that therefore they would fatten quicker, appears to us a decided *non sequitur*. The current of cool air carries off the animal heat, and renders a larger supply of carbon necessary to keep up that heat. Cattle kept under cover in cold weather, are found to eat less, and fatten quicker, than those exposed: on the same principle that the East Indian gets fat on rice, while the Esquimaux requires train oil, which contains a large proportion of carbon. It would appear, therefore, that the ventilation should only be so much as to preserve health, which will leave more of the food to produce fat.

This reminds us that there is a closer analogy between fattening a beast, and firing a boiler, than many of our readers will be apt to imagine. Your boiler ought to be so designed that it will consume the fuel advantageously, and so some breeds of animals will fatten on much less food than others—Chinese pigs being celebrated for this desirable quality. Some sorts of coals, though higher in price, are found more economical than the cheaper descriptions; just so with the various kinds of food. The careful stoker breaks up the large lumps to burn them to the best advantage, and on the same principle the farmer bruises his oats, and slices the turnips; finally, the boiler is clothed to prevent the escape of heat, and so the farmer finds it more economical to provide shelter for his cattle from the cold, than to allow them to get ravenously hungry by exposure. We regret that we cannot pursue the parallel, for with all the ingenuity of our engineers and boiler-makers, we fear they will never do for the manufacturer what bounteous nature never fails to do for the farmer - return, *in the shape of manure, every penny that he spends in food for his cattle.*

To all interested in farming, and who desire to see both sides of the question, and to decide for themselves, we can recommend Mr. Thorold's pamphlet.

Counsel to Inventors of Improvements in the Useful Arts. By T. TURNER, of the Middle Temple. Pp. 101. London: Elsworth.

This little volume is not of that dry, legal turn, that our readers might expect from the title. The subject is treated in a popular manner, on the principle, we presume, that " every man who is his own lawyer, has a fool for his client." The style is remarkably terse, and the numerous little bits about inventors and inventions, will be particularly interesting to the ingenious. We can only spare room for the following quotations, which, we think, will tempt many of our readers to make a closer acquaintance with the work:—

" Glauber's rule, it is said, was to examine what everyone else threw away."

" The heat in a pound of coal may be sent into the most capricious form of boiler that ever came from a factory, but it will only be the heat of a pound of coal still." " We can only conquer nature by obeying her laws."

These natural hints are infinitely various, and sometimes pop in upon the inventor as unexpectedly as they are unwelcome. The copper sheathing for ships perished by the corrosion of the sea water. Davy, as being peculiarly competent, was called in to prescribe; he duly investigated the

subject, in all points of view that occurred to him, and devised a remedy to his own entire satisfaction. The rusting was stopped, indeed, and the metal remained quite bright. But, Sir Humphrey had been catering for other parties than his employers. The ship's bottom became " an eligible site for building," to all sorts of barnacles, till the ship rapidly became foul, and it was found better to bear the evil of spoiling the copper, than fly to others which they knew not of, and spoil the sailing. Although, however, the canker system could not be entirely dispensed with, the operation was economised by a valuable patent, which only allows corrosion enough of the metal to poison the surface, and make it uninhabitable. Such an indirect benefit, however, even of corrosion and decay, enforces the lesson of turning all to account. " Every lane's end," says Autolycus, " yields a careful man work."

" Hooke says, Whenever his researches were stopped by an (apparently) insurmountable difficulty, he was sure to be on the brink of an important discovery.

RAILWAYS

REVIVAL OF RAILWAY PROPERTY—LIGHT ENGINES.—In the report of the Cork and Bandon Railway Company, submitted at their meeting on the 13th inst., we find the following facts, confirmatory of the belief that much may be accomplished towards the revival of railway property by the introduction of light engines :—

" The passenger trains are conveyed by the ' light ' or small, engines, which continue to afford most satisfactory proof of their efficiency and economy.

The trains frequently consist of the following stock, all fairly laden:—

One large 1st and 2d class carriage, for 58 passengers.
One 3d class carriage, for 40 passengers.
One horse-box, for three horses.
One carriage truck.

Such trains are conveyed between Bandon and Ballinhassig station in 20 minutes, being at the rate of 30 miles per hour, including stoppages.

The daily consumption of coke for each of these engines has been most particularly registered, and the average quality of Newcastle coke consumed per diem is as follows :—

Consumed in lighting engine—time occupied two hours ..Cwts. 2 0 16
Consumed standing in steam —time occupied eight hours....... 2 1 17
Consumed in running 60 miles—time occupied two hours 1 3 26

Total daily consumption...................Cwts. 6 2 3

Which is equivalent to 12 1-5th lbs. per mile per days of 22 hours; but it will be seen that the running time is only 2 hours, during which the consumption is not more than 3¼ lbs. per mile. The average daily consumption of the Company's ordinary-sized engine, with the same work, is 22¼ lbs. per mile per day, or nearly double that of the light engines; and the same difference also arises between the two classes of engines in the consumption of oil, grease, &c., so that an important saving has been effected in the working expenses by the adoption of engines whose powers and dimensions are in proportion to the loads they are required to convey."

CAST IRON RAILWAY SLEEPERS.—Some time since, we alluded to a new system of permanent way—a combined cast-iron chain and sleeper—which had been laid down in experimental lengths upon the South-Eastern line, by the inventor, Mr. Barlow, the engineer-in-chief of the company. Since we directed attention to this application of cast-iron sleepers, other experimental lengths have been laid down upon the most trying curves and embankments of the South-Eastern line, and the new system has, we understand, been found to wear most admirably upon such portions of the railway. Mr. Barlow expresses his conviction that a considerably lighter cast-iron sleeper than the one laid down by him will be strong enough to resist the wear and tear of the engines. Mr. Barlow, in a very valuable report which he has made to the directors of the South-Eastern Company, respecting this new system of permanent way, states. as the result of his experience, that—" The difference in favour of the cast-iron may, therefore, be called, in round numbers, 60*l.* per mile per annum, assuming a durability of 20 years only for the cast-iron, which is a less period than experience justifies in assigning to this material; and no sum is allowed in this estimate for the diminished wear of the rails from the avoidance of the blows and the effect of the expansion. In addition to that of durability, there are other advantages, which there is every reason to expect will be obtained from the iron road. The simplicity in the construction, and the reduction in the number of parts of which the road is composed, combined with the facility of drainage and repair, will, no doubt, have the effect of reducing the cost of maintenance in a larger degree, as well as that of renewal, as the former is necessarily dependent on the latter. The effect of the joint plate is effectually to secure the ends of the rails from motion, and render the joint as even as any other part of the rail, by which all the noise and clatter of the ordinary road is avoided; and from the rails being more frequently supported, and resting on a rigid foundation of iron, instead of an elastic one of wood, which springs under the weight of the engine as its travels, there is no doubt in my mind the tractive force required will be materially reduced."

NOVELTIES.

CHEAP GAS.—There is just now a great stir amongst the scientific folk in New York, by reason of an alleged discovery by a gentleman named Payne, who, it is stated, has practically tested an almost expenseless mode of decomposing water, and reducing it to the gaseous state. By the simple operation of a very small machine, without galvanic batteries, or the consumption of metals or acids, and only the application of less than 1-300th part of 1-horse power, Mr. Payne produces 200 cubic feet of hydrogen gas and 100 feet of oxygen gas per hour. This quantity of these gases, the actual cost of which is less than one cent, furnishes as much heat by combustion as 2000 feet of the ordinary coal gas, and sufficient to supply light equal to 300 common lamps for 10 hours, or to warm an ordinary dwelling-house for 10 hours, including the requisite heat for the kitchens; or to supply the requisite heat for 1-horse power of steam.

THE GREAT EXHIBITION.—Since our last there has been a special meeting of the Society of Arts, for the purpose of ascertaining the position of the society with respect to the Industrial Exhibition of All Nations, proposed to be held in 1851. Mr. Tooke, a vice-president, was in the chair. Mr. C. Barlow proposed two resolutions, one to the effect, that the steps taken by his Royal Highness, with respect to the exhibition, were worthy his high position and general character, and deserved the warmest support of the members, generally, which was carried unanimously; and the other proposed to revoke all the acts of the council with respect to the exhibition, appoint another committee from the body of the members, who should have power to inspect the whole of the minutes of the council, and the correspondence on the subject, and report as to the best means of proceeding in future. The latter resolution excited considerable discussion.—Mr. Scott Russell, the secretary, made a long statement of the steps taken in the great undertaking from first to last. The facts mentioned by him are, however, generally known.—Mr. Whishaw said it was he who had first suggested the exhibition in November, 1844. He had canvassed a considerable portion of the manufacturers of the country, but had not received sufficient support to carry it out; and, he must acknowledge, without the aid of Prince Albert, it could not have assumed the importance it had.—After some conversation, the objectionable resolution of Mr. Barlow was negatived, and an amendment moved by Mr. Murchison, and seconded by Mr. Rotch, requesting the secretary to put his statement, corrected up to the present time, in a form for publication, and to circulate it among the members of the society, was unanimously carried.—It was then resolved to open a subscription at the house of the Society of Arts in aid of the funds for promoting the exhibition.

PUBLIC BATHS AND WASHHOUSES.—The town council of Preston have voted £8,000 for the erection in that borough of public baths and washhouses. They are to contain 100 baths and 100 washing compartments and are to be after the plan of the model establishment in Goulston-square, Whitechapel. With the experience gained in the erection of that building, Mr. Baly, the civil engineer to the Committee for Promoting the Establishment of Baths and Washhouses for the Labouring Classes, has been enabled greatly to reduce the cost for Preston as well as for other places. The plans prepared by him for the baths and washhouses for the parish of St. James, Piccadilly, for which a site has been secured near Messrs. Broadwood's brewery, have been approved by the parochial commissioners. In this parish also, as well as in those of St. Martin's-in-the-Fields, and St. Margaret, and St. John's, Westminster, the plan of the model establishment will be followed.

LIST OF ENGLISH PATENTS,

FROM JANUARY 19 TO FEBRUARY 21, INCLUSIVE.

Macgregor Laid, of Birkenhead, gentleman, for improvements in the construction of metallic ships or vessels, and in materials for coating the bottoms of iron ships or vessels and in steering ships or vessels. January 19.

William Beadon, jun., of Taunton, in the county of Somerset, gentleman, for improvements in conveying away or decomposing smoke and products of combustion from stoves or grates, and in ventilating rooms of residences. January 19.

George Simpson, of Buchanan-street, Glasgow, civil engineer, for a certain improvement or improvements in the machinery, apparatus, or means of raising, lowering, supporting, moving, or transporting heavy bodies. January 19.

William Wood, of Over Darwen, Lancashire, carpet manufacturer, for improvements in the manufacture of carpets and other fabrics. January 23.

Christopher Nickels, of York road, Lambeth, in the county of Surrey, gentleman, for improvements in the manufacture of woollen and other fabrics. January 23.

Walter Westrup, of Wapping, in the county of Middlesex, miller and biscuit baker, for improvements in cleaning and grinding corn or grain, and dressing meal or flour. January 24.

Auguste Reinhard, of Leicester-street, Leicester-square, chemist, for improvements in preparing oils for lubricating purposes, and in apparatus for filtering oil and other liquids. January 24.

Joseph Long and James Long, of Little Tower-street, London, mathematical instrument makers, and Richard Pattenden, of Nelson-square, in the county of Surrey, engineer, for an improvement in instruments and machinery for steering ships, which is also applicable to vices and other instruments and machinery for obtaining power. January 24.

John Dalton, of Hollingworth, in the county of Chester, calico printer, for certain improvements in, and applicable to, machinery or apparatus for bleaching, dying, printing, and finishing textile and other fabrics; and in the engraving of copper rollers, and other metallic bodies. January 26.

Edwin Heycock, of Leeds, in the county of York, merchant, for certain improvements in the finishing and dressing of woollen cloths. January 26.

Thomas Richardson, of the town and county of Newcastle-upon-Tyne, chemist, for improvements in the manufacture of Epsom and other magnesian salts; also alum, and sulphate of ammonia. January 26.

Winceslas le Baron de Traux de Wardin, of Liege, in the kingdom of Belgium, for certain improvements in looms for weaving linen, woollen, and cotton cloths; and in machines for preparing the yarns for such cloths, before entering the loom; and in a machine for finishing grey and bleached linen cloths. January 26.

Thomas Schofield, of Combrook, Hulme, near Manchester, fustian dyer and finisher, and Henry Horabin, of Royton, near Oldham, fustian cutter, for improvements in machinery for cutting fustians and certain other fabrics, to produce a piled surface. January 26.

Thomas Berger, of Hackney, gentleman, for improvements in the manufacture of starch. January 26.

Richard Roberts, of Manchester, engineer, for improvements in the manufacture of certain textile fabrics, in machinery for weaving plain, figured, and terry or looped fabrics, and in machinery or apparatus for cutting velvets and other fabrics. January 29.

Donald Beatson, of Green-street, Stepney, in the county of Middlesex, mariner, for certain improvements in instruments for taking, measuring, and computing angles. January 29.

Ewald Ripe, of Finsbury-square, in the county of Middlesex, merchant, for improvements in the manufacture of steel. January 29.—(Communication.)

Joel Spiller, of Battersea, in the county of Surrey, engineer, for improvements in cleaning and grinding wheat. January 29.

John Mason, of Rochdale, and Mark Smith, of Heywood, both in the county of Lancaster, machine makers, for certain improvements in machinery or apparatus for preparing, spinning, and weaving cotton, and other textile materials; and also improvements in the method of preparing yarns or threads, and in the machinery or apparatus employed for such purposes. January 29.

Francis Edward Colegrave, of Brighton, gentleman, for improvements in saddles, parts of which improvements are also applicable to the standing rigging and other furniture of ships or vessels, and to the connecting links or chains of railway carriages, and other purposes, where tension combined with a certain degree of elasticity are required. January 29.

James Templeton, of Glasgow, in the kingdom of Scotland, manufacturer, for certain improvements in manufacturing figured fabrics, principally designed for the production of carpeting. January 29.

William Edward Newton, of Chancery-lane, civil engineer, for improvements in machinery or apparatus for making hat bodies and other similar articles. January 29.—(Communication.)

Thomas Berry, of Salford, in the county of Lancaster, silk, worsted, and piece dyer and finisher, and Nathan Ramsden, of Salford, in the said county, calendarman and finisher, for certain improvements in the construction of machines for glazing, embossing, and finishing woven fabrics and paper. January 31.

Albert Dummler, of Mark-lane, in the city of London, for improvements in obtaining fibres from textile plants. January 31.—(Communication.)

Etienne Joseph Hanon Valek, of the kingdom of Belgium, miller, for improvements in grinding. January 31.

Edward Highton, of Clarence-villa, Regent's-park, in the county of Middlesex, engineer, for improvements in electric telegraphs, and in making telegraphic communications. February 7.

Charles Atherton, member of the Institution of Civil Engineers, of London, for an improved apparatus or machinery for regulating the admission of steam to the cylinders of steam engines. February 7.

Thomas Auchterlonie, of Glasgow, North Britain, manufacturer and calico printer, for improvements in the production of ornamental fabrics. February 7.

Edward Ormerod, of Manchester, mechanical engineer, and Joseph Shepherd, of Charlton-upon-Medlock, in the same county, mechanical engineer, for improvements in, or applicable to, apparatus for changing the position of carriages on railways. Feb. 2.

Louis Jean Jacques, Viscount de Serioune, of Paris, gentleman, for certain improvements in the manufacture of buttons, and in the apparatus and machinery used therein. February 9.

Bryan Donkin, the younger, of Bermondsey, in the county of Surrey, civil engineer, and Barnard William Farey, of Old Kent Road, in the said county, civil engineer, for improvements in steam engines, and an improved fluid meter. February 9.

Read Holliday, of Huddersfield, for improvements in lamps. February 11.

William Blinkhorn, of Sutton, in the county of Lancaster, glass manufacturer, for certain improvements in machinery, to be used in the manufacture of glass. Feb. 11.

James Webster, of Leicester, engineer, for improvements in the production of gas for the purposes of light. February 12.

John Mackintosh, of Berner-street, Oxford-street, civil engineer, for improvements in obtaining power in the floating of bodies, and in conveying fluids. February 12.

Thomas Whiffen, of Pig's quay, Bridewell Precinct, accountant, for improvements in machinery for registering the delivery of goods. February 21.

THOMAS MEIK ENGINEER

The Transparent Tidal Figures indicating the depth of Water on the Bar

Manufactured only by HENRY WATSON High Bridge Newcastle on Tyne

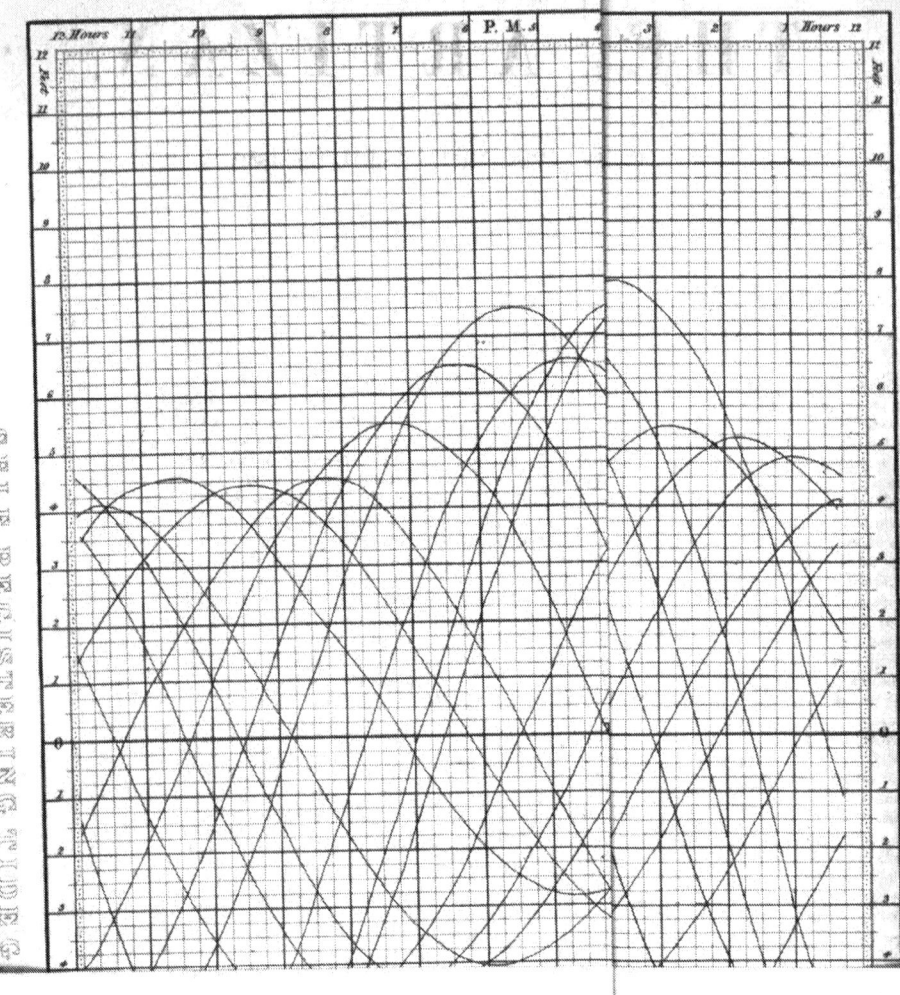

THE ARTIZAN.

No. IV.—Vol. VIII.—APRIL 1st, 1850.

MECHANICAL ENGINEERING.

THE NEW SELF-ACTING TIDE GAUGE AND REGISTER AT SUNDERLAND.

WE alluded last month to the new tide signal erected at Sunderland, and we now present our readers with a view of the pier on which the new Tidal Gauge House is erected, forming one side of the entrance to the South Docks, now in progress. The other engraving shows the diagram traced by the self-registering instrument, with every fluctuation of the tidal wave unerringly delineated for a fortnight together without interruption, and without the assistance of human eyes or hands; a visit once a week to wind up the clock machinery, and once a fortnight to change the diagram paper, is all the superintendence required. When we consider the great difficulty that exists in dark nights and stormy weather, in taking observations of the rise and fall of the tide, so necessary for the purposes of navigation, as well as of science, we have every reason to believe that the observations hitherto used have been, in many instances, a mere approximation to an actual register of the fluctuations. We need not say how necessary it is that all results, in which nature is concerned, should be recorded beyond the shadow of a doubt; this object is fully attained by the instrument we are describing. The principle of the instrument, which delineates the diagram, is not new; instruments assuming to give similar results having been in operation at Sheerness, Bristol, Glasgow, Scarborough, Granton Pier, near Leith, and at one or two other ports and harbours in Great Britain. We believe the credit of the invention is either due to Mr. Wood, of Port Glasgow, or to Mr. Mitchell, of Sheerness. We have before us a fac simile of another of the diagrams drawn by the registering instrument at Sunderland, which shows, in fine and steady lines, the tidal register for fourteen days, no roughness being perceptible, except in very stormy weather, when an indication of the heaviness of the sea is shown in a way which does not shake the accuracy of the record, but leaves a trace of the event after, as in the case of a late storm, painfully interesting. A reference to the diagram, with the subjoined description, will, we trust, explain the working of this instrument. The sheet of paper crossed by lines, like the lines of latitude and longitude, on Mercator's map, is rolled round a barrel like the barrel of an organ; the meridians of longitude are marked with the hours of the day; the parallels of latitude numbered with feet, increasing upwards and downwards from the equator, which is supposed to represent the *mean level of the sea*. The sea is admitted by a small aperture into an upright tube, in which floats a hollow copper ball, suspended round a pulley by a rope of copper wire, and counterbalanced by a weight. As the tide falls, the rope unwinds from the sheeve, and turns a small pinion on the same axle, working a rack to which is fixed a pencil which travels lengthwise along the rollers, from the equator downwards, and marks the tide falling. The barrel is turned round under the pencil at the same time by a clock once in twenty-four hours, and the two motions combined produce the waved line, which curves backwards as the tide begins to rise again. The diagram, therefore, shows that at such an hour, or quarter of an hour, on any particular day the tide had risen or fallen to such a point. The shape of the waved line, if pointed, shows a quick tide; and if rounded, a slack tide; and the comparison of the lines of different days shows clearly the difference of height between neap tides and spring tides.

These self-registering instruments, in addition to the great benefits that would accrue to science and navigation by their general adoption, would afford means of arriving at data that would be of the greatest assistance to engineers in the improvement of our valuable tidal rivers—a subject which, at the present time, is deservedly occupying much attention. Facilities for promoting the general introduction of a *standard datum line* for all engineering purposes in this country, which can only be arrived at by a long series of observations, would then be readily afforded. This datum line, we agree with Captain Denham, should be the *mean level of the sea*. In his valuable work on the Mersey and Dee Navigation, he recommends this datum as a standard for graduating all engineering operations, and a point of departure for engineers when levelling. He also further recommends the desirability of engraving on some rocky spot of every harbour and sheltered portion of coasts, the well-defined *half tide line* DATED. This is distinctly marked in the diagram, and for Sunderland, as far as yet approximated to, is eight feet on the common tide gauge, having low water of spring tides as its zero. When the diagrams for the year are complete, it is proposed at the same port to permanently fix *the half tide line* in a conspicuous part of the harbour, agreeably to Captain Denham's suggestions.

THE SELF-ACTING TIDAL GUAGE.

THIS beautiful apparatus, which has lately been erected and now in operation in Sunderland Harbour, in the same building as the above, is the invention of Mr. Meik, C.E., Engineer to the Commissioners of the River Wear, and Mr. Watson, of Newcastle. We shall best bring its merits before our readers by giving the substance of papers read by those gentlemen before the Royal Society of Arts, Edinburgh, on the evening of January 29th, as extracted from the *Scotsman*—the figures alluded to being distinctly seen in the view.[*]

"The merits of Mr. Meik's paper consisted in directing particular attention to the necessity of all ports and docks having conspicuous gauges for the guidance of vessels inward or outward bound, and of those gauges being of the most simple and intelligible description. Mr. Meik had prepared, and showed in juxtaposition, the present signals used at Leith, and those brought forward by him. For the information of our readers we may mention that the signals used at Leith consist of a series of balls and flags which have to indicate to seamen the depth of water. The new gauge at a single glance, shows the height of the tide in feet by a number in figures corresponding to the depth of water on the bar of a harbour or entrance to a dock. The little attention we often find paid by seamen to the preservation of their own lives, shows the great advantage of having figures that can be at once easily understood, without consulting books, and thereby incurring a loss of time, which in many cases results in the loss of valuable life and property. Mr. Meik proceeded to show that a gauge having the property of being easily understood by all *as soon as seen*, had been erected by himself in conjunction with Mr. Watson for the Commissioners of the

[*] It is in contemplation to erect in the Guage House a barometer with an exterior dial of three or four feet in diameter, visible from a considerable distance, and also a wind gauge and rain gauge, for the purpose of registering meteorological observations.

River Wear at Sunderland Harbour. He then read the following description, which was illustrated by well got up large drawings:—

"A well, carefully boxed in, and of exactly similar depth to the water on the bar, is made below the building which contains the apparatus. Within this well, in an interior pipe or trunk, and rising and falling with the tide, works a float suspended by a copper wire cord, which is carried over a spiral cone fixed in an upper story of the building. By the simple arrangement of a wheel and pinion at the opposite end of the axle to which the cone is fixed, a web of wire gauze works on two rollers fixed at the upper and lower ends of the web. The lower roller is regulated by the movement of this wheel and pinion—the upper one by a balance weight attached to a copper wire cord, which also passes over another spiral cone, having at the extremity of its axle a second wheel and pinion similar to the first. As the float rises and falls with the tide, the wheels and pinions connected with the cones, over which the cords of the float and balance weight respectively pass, move the rollers on which the gauze web travels. On this web are painted in large figures the various depths from high to low water; and as the web works, two points upon it indicate the number of feet and half-feet on the bar at any hour of the tide.

"The web and the figures on it can be made of any size, and to travel 4, 6, 8, 10, or any other proportion, to 1 of the float, by regulating the size of the wheels and pinions. By day the figures on the web are shown white on a black ground: by night they are brilliantly lighted up, the ground still remaining dark. A white transparent varnish is used for the figures, and an opaque black for the ground. The illumination by night is so steady and powerful, that the figures, if made large enough, and the apparatus fixed at a sufficient elevation, will be visible at a considerable distance at sea, and thus afford vessels the means of knowing the exact depth of water, at the mouth of any harbour, before entering it. This simple piece of mechanism is applicable to all places where the want of a correct and conspicuous gauge has been felt—not only in harbours and docks, but at *railway stations for signals*, and such like purposes. The apparatus used occupies so little space, that it can all be contained and worked in a column or pillar without any other building."

ANALYSIS OF THE STEAM ENGINE.

CANVAS VALVES.—The plate represents an air-pump bucket of the same size as the preceding one, but fitted with a valve composed of alternate layers of canvas and indian-rubber, which requires some modification of the details. The diameter of the rod, the depth of the centre boss, the depth of packing, and the packing-ring, are kept the same, but the packing is lowered so as to bring the valve face above the top of the packing-ring. By this means a larger diameter can be given to the valve to compensate for the area occupied by the grating on which the valve face falls. This grating is necessary to support the flexible material of which the valve is composed, and which if the grating holes were too large, would be thrown out of shape by the pressure on the up-stroke. The whole bucket is proposed to be made of brass which admits of the thicknesses being less than in the previous example, which was of cast iron. There are six arms, ⅜ thick, and 3¼ inches deep, and the spaces between the arms are filled with the grating ⅝ inch deep and the ribs, $\frac{3}{16}$ thick. The spaces are not equally divided from the centre, but are made wider as their length becomes less, the object being to support the valve effectually without unduly diminishing the waterway through the bucket. In large buckets, the grating is a separate plate dropped into its place, and secured with small bolts.

The valve is held down by the guard, which has three bosses on it for three bolts, tapped into bosses cast for that purpose on the centre boss for the pump-rod. The guard is made light, being of brass, and not having any violent concussion to sustain, and might be still further lightened, if thought necessary, by making it a grating, similar to the bucket.

The valve is ½ inch thick, and is Mackintosh's patent, compounded of canvass and vulcanised India rubber.*

In large buckets, two or more annular valves may be used, the rings of canvas being held down on their inner edges by an annular guard, with a number of bolts tapped into the bucket, as in the present example.

* Specimens of it can be seen at the *Artisan* office.

It is evident that an arrangement similar to that which we have described, may be applied to the foot and delivery valves; but as the arrangement of these depends in some measure on that of the sole plate, we shall reserve what we have to say about them until we come to that part of the engine.

CONNECTING ROD.—We may next set about a drawing of the connecting rod ends, leaving out of question the length of it at present. The first point to be ascertained is the diameter of the crank pin. This, it is obvious, depends entirely upon the diameter of the cylinder, and is not affected by the length of stroke. The diameter is usually taken at from $\frac{1}{7}$ to ⅛ of the diameter of the cylinder, the larger size being used for large engines. A mean of these will give 4 inches, say—multiply the diameter of the cylinder by 1.3; then 30 × 1.3 = 3.9, or 4 inches nearly. The larger proportionate size in large engines appears to be given for wear, and although the same object may be attained by increasing the width of the bearing, yet it is open to the objection that by doing so the centre of pressure on the pin is removed farther from its support on the crank. As a general rule, however, we should recommend keeping bearings of shafts as small in diameter as is consistent with strength, as the speed of the surfaces is thereby diminished, whilst a proper surface for wear can be readily given by increasing the width of the bearing. The diameter of the connecting rod bearing being fixed at 4 inches, the breadth of the butt will depend upon the thickness of brass allowed at each side. As there is very little wear at the sides, and as thickness there does not strengthen the brass, it is advisable to keep it light—say, ⅜ inch of a side; this will give 4¾ inches for the breadth of the butt. The top and bottom of the brass are kept thick for the wear, and for stiffness—say ¾ inch top and bottom. The flanges do not require to be very wide—say ⅜ at sides, and ½ inch at top, which serves to take off the unsightliness observable when the collar of the crank-pin shows how much the brass is worn away.

It is usual, though perhaps hardly necessary, to cast a small piece between the flange and the top of the brass, and to cut a similar notch in the strap, in order to prevent the top half of the brass turning round in the strap. In any case it is only necessary to put it on one side, as shown. As the thrust upon the crank-pin is not transmitted through the strap, that has only to sustain a tensile force equal to that on the piston rod; but as there is in addition a slight oblique strain tending to force it open, it is usually made of the same strength as the piston rod—say $\frac{1}{10}$ of the diameter, or $\frac{1}{100}$ of the area of the cylinder. Area of 30 inches = 706 inches, which divided by 100 = 7 inches, which must be the area of the two sides of the strap. If the bearing be made 5 inches wide, and the thickness of collars ½ inch, it will leave 4 inches for the thickness of the butt and the strap, or 8 inches for the two sides. Then, 7 inches divided by 8 = ⅞ inch, the thickness of each side. As the strain tending to burst the strap is greater at the junction of the two sides, it is made thicker—say 1⅛ inch. The distance between the end of the butt and the key-way is shown stronger than there is any necessity for, after the fashion of most other engines. We know of no reason for it. Half the diameter of the pin, say 2 ins., would probably be a better rule. The depth of the gib and cutter may be taken at ⅝ the diameter of the pin, say 2½ inches; this depth is usually equally divided between the gib and the key, the former holding the ends of the strap together. The breadth of the ends of the gib may be takenas the same as the average depth—say 1¼ inch, and the depth a little less, say 1⅛. The distance between the cutter hole and the end of the strap, may be the same as the end of the butt, or 2½ inches; although, as we remarked about it, a less depth would have done.

The end of the gib is prolonged to form a guard for the key, which is made to taper about ¼ inch per foot, and of various lengths, there being often no room for a long key—as long again as the distance across the strap, is about the ordinary proportion. The width of the key-way is usually ¼ the thickness of the butt—say 1 inch—the end of the gib is screwed to a diameter rather less—say ⅞ inch—and is made parallel with the under-side of the key, or else the key could not be driven up, as the hole at the end of the lug forged on it is circular. The length of the eight-sided part of the rod, depends for symmetry on the total length of the rod, but we cannot think they look well cut off where the curve commences, as some engineers make them. The neck of the rod is generally made the same in diameter as the piston-rod—say 3 inches.

KEY TO MR. BOURNE'S CATECHISM OF THE STEAM ENGINE.

We propose to devote a series of papers to the arithmetical solution of the various rules Mr. Bourne has given in his Catechism of the Steam Engine, accompanied by such a collection of examples, and by such illustrative drawings, as will constitute a Key to that well-known work. We believe it would be difficult to specify any undertaking which can be esteemed more valuable to the practical engineer, if the execution be only answerable to the design; and with respect to the probable style of the execution, we have only to say that this Key is undertaken with Mr. Bourne's sanction and assistance.

LAWS OF FALLING BODIES.

The laws of falling bodies are applicable to the solution of many problems in mechanics, and it is therefore necessary that the engineer should have a just conception of the nature of those laws. All bodies are drawn to the earth by the force of gravity, and as gravity is a force continually acting, the velocity of falling bodies is continually increased until they strike upon the earth. The force of gravity is not perfectly uniform over the whole surface of the globe, being partly counteracted by the greater centrifugal force of the earth near the equator, and diminished at the poles by the flattened figure of the earth in those situations; but any variation in the force of gravity is inappreciable for practical purposes, and it has been found experimentally that, in the latitude of London, a body will fall $16\frac{1}{12}$ feet in one second. Now, it is clear that, since during this second, the motion must have commenced very slowly, it must have ended much more rapidly than at the rate of $16\frac{1}{12}$ feet in the second, that being the mean of all the varying velocities during the second, and the maximum velocity in all cases of accelerated motion being necessarily greater than the mean. Accordingly, it is found that the velocity of a falling body *at the end* of the first second is $32\frac{1}{6}$ feet, being just double the mean velocity, as might, indeed, be expected, considering that the motion begins from a state of rest. Now, if the velocity attained at the end of the first second be $32\frac{1}{6}$ feet per second, the velocity attained at the end of the second second may be expected to be just twice this, or $64\frac{1}{3}$ feet per second; at the end of the third second, three times $32\frac{1}{6}$, or $96\frac{1}{2}$ feet, and so on. It is found by experiment that this anticipation is correct, and the velocity attained by a falling body at the end of any given number of seconds may easily be determined by multiplying $32\frac{1}{6}$ by the number of seconds, which will give the velocity in seconds required. Since, too, the velocity at the end of the first second is $32\frac{1}{6}$ feet per second, and at the end of the second second $64\frac{1}{3}$ feet per second, the mean velocity *during* the second second will be $48\frac{1}{4}$ feet per second, during the third second $80\frac{5}{12}$ feet per second, and so on. The space through which the body will have fallen at the end of the first second will be $16\frac{1}{12}$ feet; at the end of the second second, $16\frac{1}{12} + 48\frac{1}{4} = 64\frac{1}{3}$; at the end of the third second, $64\frac{1}{3} + 80\frac{5}{12} = 144\frac{3}{4}$, and so on. Taking the space fallen through in the first second as a unit of length, the spaces, velocities, and times of falling bodies are exhibited in the following table :—

Second from the beginning of the descent.	Velocity acquired at the end of that time.	Space fallen through.	Space fallen through in each second of the fall.
1	2	1	1
2	4	4	3
3	6	9	5
4	8	16	7
5	10	25	9
6	12	36	11
7	14	49	13
8	16	64	15

These several relations are expressed by the following rules. To find the velocity in feet per second which a body will acquire in falling during any given number of seconds.

RULE :—*Multiply the number of seconds occupied in the fall, by $32\frac{1}{6}$; the result is the velocity of the body in feet per second.*

Example.—Suppose a stone to be dropped from the top of a tower of such a height that the stone requires four seconds to reach the ground. What velocity will the stone on reaching the ground have acquired ?

Here we have 4 seconds $\times$ $32\frac{1}{6}$ $=$ $128\frac{2}{3}$ feet per second, which is the velocity the stone will have acquired.

To find the total space in feet passed through by a falling body in any

RULE :—*Multiply the square of the time in seconds by $16\frac{1}{12}$; the result is the total space passed through in feet.*

Example.—Suppose a stone to be dropped from the top of a tower, and to reach the ground in four seconds. What is the height of the tower ?

Here we have 4^2 or $16 \times 16\frac{1}{12} = 257\frac{1}{3}$ feet, which is the height of the tower.

To find the velocity in feet per second which a body will acquire in falling through any given number of feet in height.

RULE :—*Multiply the space fallen through in feet by $64\frac{1}{3}$, and extract the square root of the product, which is the velocity required.*

Example.—Suppose an iron ball to be let fall from the top of St. Paul's 404 feet high. With what velocity will the ball strike the ground ?

Here we have $64\frac{1}{3} \times 404 = 25990\frac{2}{3}$, the square root of which is 161.216 which is the velocity in feet per second the ball will have acquired.

To find the number of feet passed through by a falling body in any given second of its descent.

RULE.—*Multiply the number of the second by $32\frac{1}{6}$, and subtract from the product $16\frac{1}{12}$. The remainder will be the number of feet passed through in the second given.*

Example. To find the number of feet passed through by a falling body in the ninth second of its descent.

Here we have $9 \times 32\frac{1}{6} = 289\frac{1}{2} - 16\frac{1}{12} = 273\frac{5}{12}$ which is the number of feet passed through in the ninth second of the descent.

FLY-WHEELS.

The momentum of a body is usually described to be the product of its weight and velocity ; but it will be obvious from the foregoing exposition of the laws of falling bodies that such a standard cannot be accepted as the measure of the power existing in moving bodies, inasmuch as such power is necessarily referable to the height through which the body must have fallen to have acquired its velocity and the height, and the velocity do not vary according to the same law. The height, in feet, from which a body must have fallen to acquire any given velocity will be the square of the velocity in feet per second divided by $64\frac{1}{3}$, or it will be about one-eighth of the velocity squared so that the mechanical energy resident in a body moving with any given velocity may be ascertained by multiplying the weight by the square of one-eighth of the velocity which will represent the amount of weight raised one foot high.

Example 1.—Suppose that a ball, 30 lbs. weight, moves at the rate of 12 feet per second. What is the amount of mechanical force resident in that ball, expressed in lbs., raised one foot high ?

Here 30 $\times$ $(12 \div 8)^2 = 67\frac{1}{2}$ lbs., which is the answer required.

Example 2.—Required, the mechanical effect treasured up in a cast iron fly-wheel, the mean diameter of which is 30 feet, with a sectional area of rim of 60 square inches, and making 20 turns in the minute.

The diameter of the wheel being 30 feet, the circumference will be 94.248 feet, and as the wheel makes 20 revolutions in the minute, the velocity of the rim will be 94.248 $\times$ 20 = 1884.96 feet per minute, or 31.416 feet per second. Again, the cubical content of the rim in cubic feet being 60 $\times$ 94.248 $\div$ 144 = 39.27 cubic feet, and the weight of a cubic foot of cast iron being $453\frac{1}{2}$ lbs., we have 39.27 $\times$ $453\frac{1}{2}$ = 17794.22 lbs. as the weight of the rim. Hence the mechanical effect treasured up in the rim of this wheel is 17794.22 $\times$ $(31.416 \div 8)^2 = 274386.87$ lbs., raised one foot high. This, it will be observed, is about eight actual horse power. The mechanical energy with which the fly-wheel of an engine is generally endowed, is equal to the power exerted in about four half-strokes of the engine, or two complete revolutions; so that the fly-wheel above particularized, is such as would be suitable for an engine which exerts a power of four actual horses, or four times 33,000 lbs., in each revolution.

The following is Boulton and Watt's rule for determining the proper sectional area of the fly-wheel rim :—

RULE.—*Multiply the cube of the mean diameter of the fly-wheel in feet by the square of the number of revolutions per minute, and reserve the product for a divisor: Multiply the square of the diameter of the cylinder in inches by the length of the stroke in feet, and by the constant number 44000, and divide the product by the divisor found as above; the quotient is the proper area of section of the fly-wheel rim in square inches.*

Example.—In Boulton and Watt's 60 horse-power engine, the diameter of the cylinder is 38¼ inches, the length of the stroke 7 feet, and the number of strokes per minute 17½. What will be the proper sectional area of the rim of the fly-wheel for this engine, supposing the mean diameter of the wheel to be 30 feet?

Here $30^3 = 27,000 \times 17.5^2 = 8,268,750$, and $38\frac{1}{4}^2 \times 7 \times 44,000 = 438,053,000$, which, divided by 8,268,750, leaves 53 nearly as the number of square inches proper for the sectional area of the fly-wheel rim.

Supposing that in this engine the actual and the nominal power were the same, as in Mr. Watt's earlier engines was generally the case, the total load lifted in the minute would be $33,000 \times 60 = 1,980,000$ lbs. one foot high, or the load lifted every half stroke would be one-thirty-fifth of this, or 56,000 lbs., or in four half strokes or two whole strokes, 232,000 lbs. Now, the circumference of the ring, being 94.248 feet, and the sectional area of the ring 53 square inches, $94.248 \times 53 \div 144 = 34.688$, which is the number of cubic feet in the ring, and this multiplied by 453½ lbs., the weight of a cubic foot of cast iron, gives 15,718 as the weight of the ring in lbs. The velocity per minute will be $94.248 \times 17.5 = 1649.34$ feet = 27.49 feet per second. Hence the mechanical effect treasured up will be $15,718 \times (27.49 \div 8)^2 = 184,940,698$ lbs. raised one foot high, which, it will be remarked, is more than the power exerted in three half strokes, and less than the power exerted in four half strokes of the engine. In all modern engines it is necessary to reckon the actual and not the nominal power in the application of the foregoing rule, else the fly-wheel will be made too light.

Another rule for determining the dimensions of the fly-wheel is as follows:—

RULE.—*Multiply the mean diameter of the rim by the number of its revolutions per minute, and square the product for a divisor. Divide the number of actual horse-power of the engine by the number of strokes the piston makes per minute; multiply the quotient by the constant number, 2,760,000, and divide the product by the divisor, found as above; the quotient is the requisite quantity of cast iron in cubic feet to form the fly-wheel rim.*

Taking as before the diameter of the rim at 30 feet, the number of horse power as 60, and the number of strokes per minute as 17½, we have $30 \times 17.5 = 525$, the square of which is 2,756.25. The number of horse-power $60 \div 17.5 = 3.428 \times 2,760,000 = 9,461,280 \div 275,625 = 34.326$, which is the proper number of cubic feet of cast iron to form the fly-wheel rim. This agrees very nearly with the amount obtained by Boulton and Watt's rule, which is 34.688 cubic feet.

In many of the modern engines which operate, to some extent, on the expansive principle, and in which great equability of motion is required, the fly-wheel is made so as to have twice the mechanical energy treasured in it that is given by the foregoing rules, and this increased energy may be given either by increasing its weight or by increasing its velocity, or partly by the one mode, and partly by the other. In all engines requiring to impart a very regular motion to the machinery driven, it is advisable to have a short stroke and to cause the engine to make as many strokes in the minute as can conveniently be done.

CENTRIFUGAL FORCE.

The centrifugal force of a fly-wheel or other revolving body increases as the square of the velocity of revolution, or as the height necessary to generate the velocity, so long as no change takes place in the diameter of the circle in which the body revolves; but the centrifugal force increases merely as the diameter of the circle increases, if the number of revolutions remains the same.

To ascertain the centrifugal force of a revolving body:—

RULE.—*Divide the velocity in feet per second by 4.01; the square of the* quotient will be four times the height in feet from which the body must have fallen to have acquired that velocity. *Divide this quadruple height by the diameter of the circle, and the quotient is the centrifugal force in terms of the weight of the body.*

Example.—Suppose that the rim of a fly-wheel 30 feet diameter and weighing 15718 lbs., moves at the rate of 27.49 feet per second, what will be its centrifugal force. Here we have the velocity $27.49 \div 4.01 = 6.86$, which, squared, is 46.9225; and this, divided by 30, is 1.564; so that the centrifugal force is 1.564 times the weight of the body, or 10.97 tons. Another rule is to multiply the square of the number of revolutions per minute (17½) by the diameter of the circle in feet (30) and to divide the product by 5870, which gives the centrifugal force in terms of the weight of the body and $17\frac{1}{2}^2 \times 30 \div 5870 = 1.564$ as before.

THE PENDULUM.

The length of the pendulum vibrating seconds at the level of the sea in London, is 39.1393 inches, and the times in which pendulums of different lengths will vibrate, is as the square roots of their lengths.

To find the length of a pendulum that shall make any required number of vibrations in a given time.

RULE.—*Multiply the square of the number of seconds in the given time by the constant number 39.1393, and divide the product by the square of the number of vibrations, which will give the length of the pendulum in inches.*

Example.—Suppose a pendulum is required to make 35 vibrations in a minute, what must be its length measuring from the centre of suspension to the centre of oscillation.

Here the number of seconds in the prescribed time being 60, we have $60^2 \times 39.1393 = 140901.48$, which, divided by 35^2, or 1225, gives 115.021 inches as the length required.

To find the number of vibrations that a pendulum of any given length will make in any given time.

RULE.—*Multiply the square of the number of seconds in the given time by the constant number 39.1393; divide the product by the given length of the pendulum in inches, and extract the square root of the quotient for the number of vibrations sought.*

Example.—Suppose that the length of a pendulum between the centres of suspension and oscillation is 64 inches, what number of vibrations will it make in the minute.

A minute being 60 seconds, $60^2 \times 39.1393 = 140901.48 \div 64 = 2264.0856$, the square root of which is 47.56, which is the number of vibrations sought.

If a minute be adopted as the unit of time in which the vibrations are to be registered, the foregoing rules may be simplified by bringing this unit into the constant; and as $\sqrt{39.1393} \times 60 = 375.36$, this number serves as a new constant for all cases in which a minute is taken as the unit of time. Hence 375.36 divided by the square root of the pendulum's length, will give the number of vibrations per minute; and 375.36 divided by the number of vibrations per minute, will give the square root of the length of the pendulum, which must be squared in order to obtain the length required.

THE GOVERNOR.

The governor is sometimes termed the conical pendulum, as to the laws of the pendulum its principle of action is referable. If two balls be hung by rods upon a spindle, and the spindle be put into revolution, the balls will diverge until the vertical distance of the plane in which they revolve is equal in length to a pendulum making twice the number of vibrations that the spindle makes of revolutions. To find the time in which a governor should perform one revolution when the vertical height of the governor when in action is given.

RULE.—*Multiply the square root of the vertical height or of the distance in inches between the point of suspension of the arms and the plane of revolution of the balls by the constant fraction 0.31986, and the product will be the proper time of revolution in seconds.*

Example.—In what time should a governor be made to revolve on its axis supposing that the vertical height or the distance of the point of suspension of the arms over the plane of revolution of the balls (when the arms are in the position intended when the engine is at work,) is 39.1393 inches.

The square root of 39.1393 is 6.2561, and 6.2561 × 0.31986 = 2.0011 seconds, which is the time in which one revolution of the governor should be performed. The governor spindle should, therefore, make 30 turns in the minute.

A still simpler rule than this may be deduced from the following considerations; since a conical pendulum makes just half the number of revolutions in the minute that a common pendulum makes of vibrations, and since the number of vibrations per minute due to any given length of a common pendulum is ascertained by dividing 375.36 by the square root of the length; the half of 375.36 or 187.68 divided by the vertical height of a conical pendulum will give the proper number of revolutions per minute. Hence to find the number of revolutions proper for a governor.

RULE.—*Divide 187.68 by the square root of the vertical height or of the distance between the point of suspension and the plane of revolution of the balls when the arms are in their medium position; the quotient is the proper number of revolutions in the minute.*

Example.—Required the proper number of revolutions of a governor of which the vertical height is 39.1393 inches. The square root of 39.1393 being 6.2561 we have 187.68 ÷ 6.2561 = 30 which is the proper number of revolutions per minute.

To find the vertical height of the cone described by the arms of a governor when the spindle makes any given number of revolutions per minute.

RULE.—*Divide the constant number 187.68 by the number of revolutions made per minute: the square of the quotient is the vertical height required.*

Example.—Suppose that a governor makes 30 revolutions per minute what will be the vertical height of the cone described by the extended arms?

Here we have 187.68 ÷ 30 = 6.2561 the square of which is 39.1393 which is the height of the cone in inches.

If the number of revolutions and the length of the arms be fixed, and it is wanted to know what is the diameter of the circle described by the balls.

RULE.—*Divide the constant number 187.68 by the number of revolutions per minute, and the square of the quotient will be the vertical height in inches of the cone described by the arms. Deduct the square of the vertical height in inches, from the square of the length of the arm in inches, and twice the square root of the remainder is the diameter of the circle in which the centre of the balls revolves.*

Example.—Let the number of revolutions per minute be 30, and the length of arm be 45 inches. Required the diameter of the circle in which the balls will revolve.

Here we have 187.68 ÷ 30 = 6.2561, the square of which is 39.1393 inches. Then 39.1393² = 2625 and 45² = 1532 and 2025 − 1532 = 493, the square root of which is 22.2 and twice this is 44.4 which is the diameter of the circle in which the circle of the balls revolve. The arms, therefore, and the plane in which the balls revolve, form an equilateral triangle very nearly.

To find the velocity of revolution proper for any prescribed spread of arms of the governor by the laws of centrifugal force.

RULE.—*Divide the horizontal distance of the arm from the spindle by the vertical height of the cone which will give the centripetal force of the ball, or the force drawing the ball toward the spindle in terms of its own weight. Multiply the centripetal force thus obtained by the constant number 70440, and divide the product by the diameter of the circle made by the centre of the ball in inches; the square root of the quotient is the number of revolutions per minute.*

Example.—Taking as before the horizontal distance of each ball from the spindle at 22.2 inches, and the vertical height of the cone at 39.1393 the centripetal force of the ball being 22.2 ÷ 39.1393 will be .5674 of the weight of the ball. Now .5674 × 70440 = 39967.6, and this divided by 44.4 which is the diameter of the circle in which the balls revolve is 900 the square root of which is 30 revolutions per minute.

THE MECHANICAL POWERS.

The mechanical powers as usually defined and illustrated in mechanical works are a source of profitless perplexity to engineers, and it appears proper to dismiss all the rules which have been elaborated upon this subject, and to refer the question of the increase or diminution of force consequent upon any mechanical combination to the principal of vertical velocities

which will afford an easy solution to all the questions which can arise in practice. It is an established law in mechanics that in proportion as the force or pressure produced in any secondary machine or instrument, such as those known as the mechanical powers, is increased, in the same proportion is the distance through which that pressure acts diminished, and the amount of increase in the pressure is always easily ascertainable by a reference to the diminished velocity caused by the combination. Thus if in turning round a screw the hand travels through a distance of 100 inches, while the screw advances only one inch, the multiplication of the pressure will be 100 to 1, and precisely the same effect will ensue whether this diminution of the velocity and consequent multiplication of the pressure is produced by a windlass, lever, hydraulic press, or any other apparatus. In all mechanical combinations, therefore, it is only necessary to see how much the velocity is diminished in order to ascertain how much the pressure is increased or contrariwise if the velocity be increased the pressure will be proportionately diminished. If the pump plunger of a hydraulic press in descending 8 inches raises the ram ⅛ of an inch, the increase of the power is obviously in the proportion of 64 to 1 supposing the hand to be applied directly to the pump. If, however, a lever intervene divided in the proportion of 8 to 1, the total increase of the pressure will be 8 times 64 or 512 to 1, or by the use of an hydraulic press of the proportions supposed, the pressure of the hand will be 512 times greater than it would otherwise be. The ram, however, will only move through ₅₁₂th of the distance that the hand moves through, and this law applies to all mechanisms for modifying pressure or force. It is generally an easy thing to tell what are the initial and resulting velocities in any machine or mechanical arrangement, and the initial and resulting pressures will always be inversely in the same proportion.

(To be continued.)

HOW'S PATENT SALINOMETER FOR STEAM BOILERS USING SALT WATER.

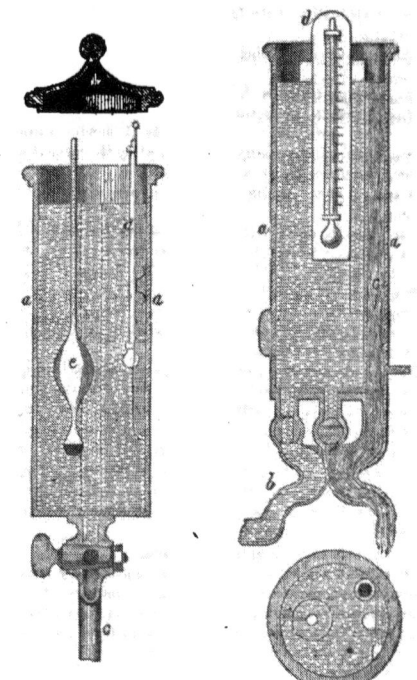

Fig. 1.   Fig. 2.

SEA water in the ocean contains a certain quantity of salt, in the proportion of one pound of salt to 32 or 33 of water, and as all the water evaporated is fresh, all the salt is left in the boiler, which would very soon cause its destruction if not removed; this is done by blowing out at intervals a portion of the partly saturated water from the boiler.

Scale is not formed in a boiler until the water has reached a certain degree of saltness, and if it be kept below that point, the boiler will be kept clean; but if it be allowed to get above it, incrustation takes place, and continues to do so as long as it is above. Hence the necessity of keeping the water in the boiler below a certain degree of saltness, by which a saving of fuel, as well as a saving of the boiler, may be effected.

In most steamers a much greater quantity of hot water is blown off than is necessary, and even then the boilers are not kept clean, because it is not always blown off at the proper time; and when it ought to be blown off, it is not done, there being no means of indicating when, and how much, is necessary. In the first case, fuel is wasted by blowing off too much; and in the second, the boiler becomes covered with an additional stratum of scale, which keeps the water from contact with the metal, and tends to burn out the plates. Besides a loss of fuel resulting from the water not being in contact with the fire surface of the boiler, numerous instances can be re-erred to where the boiler has been permanently injured, and in one case, which came under the notice of the writer, a terrific explosion occurred from this cause alone. This is very easily accounted for, as it is well known that if iron is once over-heated, its strength is very materially diminished.

The gradual increase in the consumption of fuel in most sea-going steamers, is owing to the constant increase of the incrustation in the boiler. Some are removed for no other reason than that they do not generate sufficient steam, in consequence of the fire surface being covered with scale. In other cases the boilers have been burnt out in less than two years' use, from the same cause, while in some instances, boilers running in salt water and kept clear of scale, have been in good order at the end of six or seven years.

This instrument is extremely simple in its construction, and certain in its action; and its utility is evident, as it indicates at all times the exact degree of saltness of the water in the boiler, by which means the quantity of water necessary to be blown out can be regulated with certainty, and reduced to the smallest amount compatible with the safety of the boiler, and economy of fuel.

Figs. 1 and 2 are vertical sections of the instrument taken at right angles to each other. *a* is cylinder connected to the boiler by the pipe *b*, and furnished with a cock, by which the current is regulated. *c* is an overflow pipe, carried down to the bilge, through which the water escapes. *d* is a thermometer, and *e* is the hydrometer, which floats in a copper cage (not shown in the drawing), which protects it from injury. The scale of the hydrometer has marked upon it at the proper height, "Blow," which indicates such a density of the water as requires the operation of blowing off to be performed. *f* is a cock for emptying the cylinder when required.

The following explanation will render its operation easily understood:—

If, as has been stated, 1 lb. of salt enter the boiler with every 32 lbs. of water, then when one-half, or 16 lbs. out of the 32 lbs. are evaporated, the 1 lb. of salt is in the remaining 16 lbs. of water, and is then, in the proportion of 2 lbs. of salt to 32 lbs. of water. Then if one-half of the remaining 16 lbs. of water be evaporated, there will be 8 lbs. left, in which will be the 1 lb. of salt that entered with the 32 lbs. of water; it would then be in the proportion of 4 lbs. of salt to 32 lbs. of water, or what is called 4-32 on the hydrometer. Now if this 8 lbs. of water were blown out, all the salt that entered in the 32 lbs. of water would go out with it, and as long as this proportional part of the water that entered was blown out, the water in the boiler cannot attain a greater degree of saltness than 4-32, from which, it will be seen, that to keep the water in the boiler at 4-32, one-quarter of the water that enters must be blown out; to keep it at 3-32, one-third must be blown out, and to keep it at 2-32, one-half must be blown out, and in proper proportion for any other density when using sea water.

The hydrometer used in this instrument is graduated upon the principle explained above, and is marked, as will be seen on reference to it. O for fresh water; 1-32 for sea water which contains 1 lb. of salt to 32 lbs. of water—2-32 when there is 2 lb. of salt to 32 lbs. of water—3-32 when there is 3 lbs. of salt to 32 lbs. of water—4-32 when there is 4 lbs. of salt to 32 lbs. of water, &c. Each division is divided into four parts, showing halves and quarters of each.

It is also graduated for the temperature of 200 degrees, it being necessary to have some standard of temperature at which the indications were always to be taken, as steam of different pressures has different temperatures; and as a difference in temperature will alter the indications of the hydrometer, it is therefore necessary that the water be relieved from the pressure in the boiler that it may assume a uniform temperature, which it does under the pressure of the atmosphere, and which is accomplished in this instrument, and which renders it applicable to boilers in which the pressure of steam may vary, or in which either high or low pressure steam is used.

The pipe leading to the Salinometer should connect with the boiler at about the height of the tops of the furnaces. A stop-cock is furnished, to be attached to the boiler by two bolts, with a piece of pipe to run into the boiler, nearly closed at one end, and with small holes to prevent anything large from entering. The pipe is connected to the cock by a coupling joint.

When in use, the hydrometer, thermometer, &c., must all be in their places, as represented, and the cock E kept partly open, so as to allow a constant stream of water to pass through, by which means the water in the Salinometer will always be of the same density as that in the boiler; and it will be found that the temperature of the water will be constant at about 200 degrees, if it should vary, by opening the cock E more or less, it can be regulated. If it is within 5 or 10 degrees, it will cause no error of consequence; but if great accuracy is required, allowance can be made for the variation as follows: every 10 degrees in temperature will vary the indication of the hydrometer one-eighth of 1-32; 200 degrees being the standard, therefore if it is 10 degrees above 200, it will show one-eighth of 1-32 less dense than the true density; and for every 10 degrees below 200, it will indicate one-eighth of 1-32 more than the true density: thus, if the temperature is 210 degrees, and the hydrometer indicate a density of 2-32, the true density would be 2 1-8, and if the temperature is 190 degrees, and the hydrometer indicate 2-32, the true density is 1 7-8 of 2-32; but if the stop-cock E is properly regulated, no correction will be necessary, as the proper temperature can easily be produced by opening it more or less.

The loss of fuel by blowing will be nearly as follows, and as it is absolutely necessary to blow, the loss must be submitted to; the actual loss will be less than that given, as in this calculation it is supposed that the boiler is supplied with salt water at 1-32 from the ocean—such is not actually the case, as a small portion of the water supplied to the boiler is part of the condensed steam, and therefore fresh, so that the water fed into the boiler is not quite as salt as that in the ocean; the proportion of fresh thus mixed with the salt water depends upon the temperature of the water used to condense the steam. In the following calculation the latent heat of steam has been taken at 990 degrees; the temperature of the feed water at 100 degrees, and the temperature of the water blown out at 250 degrees, which would correspond to a pressure of steam of nearly 15 lbs. per square inch. The loss varies with the temperature of the water blown out. The loss by blowing at 2-32 and temperature 250 degrees is 11-9 per cent., while the loss by blowing at the same degree of saltness, (2-32,) and the temperature of 293 degrees, which corresponds with about 45 lbs. pressure of steam, 14-9 per cent., being three per cent., more than at about 15 lbs. per square inch.

The loss of fuel by blowing at the different degrees is nearly as follows:

At 1½ of 2-32,	16.9 per cent.		At 3	6.	per cent.
,, 1¾ ,,	14.4	,,	,, 3½	4.9	,,
,, 2 ,,	11.9	,,	,, 4	4.2	,,
,, 2¼	9.4	,,	,, 5	3.2	,,
,, 2½	8.	,,	,, 6	2.5	,,
,, 2¾	7.	,,	,, 7	2.1	,,

To keep the boiler clean, the water should not be allowed to contain, more than 2 lbs. of salt to 32 lbs. of water. To keep it at this density, nearly one half the water pumped into the boiler must be blown out at a loss of nearly twelve per cent. of fuel. It will be observed that the loss is very great if too much water is blown, hence the importance of having some indicator to show when it is necessary, and how much is required to be blown to keep it at a proper and uniform density. Vessels not having Salinometers are compelled to blow at random, sometimes blowing too much, at other times not enough, wasting fuel, and then not keeping the boilers clean, as explained before.

In some vessels, previous to having the Salinometers, the water was kept below 1½ of 2-32, wasting more than five per cent. of fuel.

When on the Southern Coast of Florida, or in the Gulf of Mexico, the density of the water should not get above 1-34 of 2-32.

A. P. How, engineer, U. S. N.

SPRAY'S PATENT LUBRICATOR.

This lubricator is especially designed for the cylinders of engines, and is so constructed that the cup is protected from dust or dirt, and no air is admitted into the cylinder with the oil.

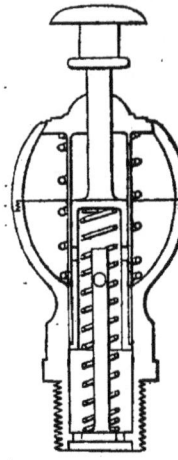

The top of the cup is closed by a conical valve, to which is attached a piece of tubing sliding at its lower end in the stem of the cup. This valve is kept closed against the atmosphere by a spiral spring pressing between it and the bottom of the cup. Inside this tube slides a shorter one, with a rod attached to it, coming up through the valve in the top of the cup. This inner tube is also supported by a spiral spring, and has a flange at the bottom, which is in contact with the outer tube and acts as a stop upwards. Holes are drilled through the outer tube, at the bottom of the cup, and similar holes are drilled through the inner tube; and when these holes are made to coincide by depressing the inner tube by the finger knob, the oil will flow through them, and through holes drilled in the bottom of the stem, into the cylinder. The rod in the stem of the cup serves as a stop to the inner tube. When the cup requires refilling the top valve can be depressed, and the oil poured in. The upper part of the cup is screwed on to allow the parts being put together.

These lubricators have been attached to several engines, and have given great satisfaction. In locomotives a rod may be attached so that the driver can lubricate the cylinders without leaving the footplate, which will, no doubt, be an advantage, more especially in express trains with few stoppages. Specimens of these lubricators may be inspected at our office by any of our readers who may wish to do so.

DUDGEON'S EXPANSION GEAR.
To the Editor of the Artisan.

SIR,—In common, probably, with many of your readers, I was much pleased with the expansion slide gear, delineated and described in your last number, for it appears to me a step in the right direction. But there are one or two points connected with it on which I should be glad to have your opinion and that of your readers. I think it will be allowed that we ought to improve the vacuum to the utmost of our power before attempting anything else, because all the resistance that we can remove is so much clear gain; I therefore, admit that the quickness with which the exhaust is opened, and the duration of its opening, are valuable features in this plan. The point on which I am not so clear is the value of admitting the steam sharply on the piston; and, as it is one on which I think some misapprehension exists in the minds of many persons, I will, with your permission, consider its tenability. I think it was Mr. Parkes who attempted to account for the superior duty of the Cornish pumping engines, by supposing that the steam

had some percussive force, when it was suddenly admitted on the stationary piston. I am not aware whether this opinion is still entertained by any engineers, but I think there are other causes which fully account for the superiority of duty. In any case the pumping engine cannot fairly be compared with an engine working with a crank; not that I suppose there is any loss of power by the crank, but that the expansive principle is better adapted to work where it can have its own way, so to speak, than when it is confined in its effect by a crank. I can, perhaps, better explain my meaning by an illustration. Suppose a direct acting engine with the crank and piston at the bottom point of the stroke; the valve is suddenly opened to its fullest extent, and the steam admitted into the cylinder at its maximum pressure in the boiler. Now, what is the result? Merely that the piston, and through it the moving parts, receive a violent shock, tending to force the crank shaft out of the plummer block, but not producing the slightest useful effect. The fly-wheel ought to be sufficiently heavy to prevent any acceleration of its speed, and the piston travels so slowly at the beginning of the stroke that it is not for some time that it has any material power over the crank. Not so with the pumping engine. There the piston is standing still waiting for the powerful gush of high pressure steam to overcome the inertia of the massive parts and the water in the pumps. When the impetus has been given, the pressure decreases with the expansion of the steam, which is thus used as beneficially as, I think, it is possible to be done. I do not think, therefore, that in crank engines there is any gain by admitting the steam so suddenly, whilst in many mills the shock produced has a very bad effect upon the spinning. So strongly is this felt, that a plan has been for some years adopted, and is now well known, of notching the face of the valve, the lap being increased, and a notch cut out of it on the steam side. Sometimes, instead of a notch, the edge of the valve face is made out of square with the port. In either case the effect is to let the steam in upon the piston, at first through a very small opening, the bottom of the notch, which increases as the slide moves, until the whole width of the port is opened, when the piston is at the quickest part of its stroke. The piston travels so slowly at the beginning of its stroke that a very small opening is sufficient to keep the pressure in the cylinder equal to that admitted by the throttle valve, and I imagine that that is all that is requisite, and that the smaller the opening can be kept, consistent with that equality of pressure, the smoother will the engine work.

By judiciously proportioning the notch and the lap, a considerable amount of expansion can be used, without shutting up the exhaust so much as to be an objection.

The subject is so interesting, that I hope these remarks may induce some of your readers, who are better qualified than myself for the task, may take it up, and give us the results of experiments with different laps and strokes of the valve, with indicator diagrams. Any of your readers who have the opportunity of making a series of experiments on an engine in this way, would, by publishing them, confer a great favour on every one who, like your correspondant, signs himself

Salford.   A COTTON SPINNER.

Sir,

I have read with much surprise in your number for the present month, a description, accompanied with drawings, of a "new form of expansion gear for steam engines," communicated by Mr. John Dudgeon, who styles himself the inventor, and amplifies the subject with a description of the various economical advantages likely to accrue to steam navigation by the employment of the new gearing.

You will share my surprise when I inform you that this plan is my arrangement, and that Mr. John Dudgeon is not entitled to any merit in the matter. To enable you to judge for yourself, I will shortly state the facts; premising that the subject of expansion gear has been a favourite study of mine for some ten years past, and I have kept myself acquainted with the new modifications as they have appeared. I was much impressed with an arrangement which I saw on board a screw steamer in the Thames a few months ago, manufactured by Messrs. Smith and Rodger, on the plan, as I was informed, of Messrs. Macolmson. This plan, although ingenious, is complicated; and it occurred to me that some modifications of it, combined with connected levers, would produce an efficient practical expansion gear.

I embodied my ideas in a working model, arranging and improving as I proceeded, and I have since affixed the apparatus to a small condensing engine. I made no secret of my plan, but freely explained its action to any one who felt an interest in the subject. This arrangement, Mr. Editor, is the one shown by Mr. John Dudgeon, in the article referred to as his own; and the further description added by Mr. John Dudgeon, of the valuable results to be expected, is completely that which I narrated to him when showing him my model and explaining to him very fully, its arrangement and mode of action, the only variations which I can detect, are a few unimportant complications which he has added.

Such a proceeding requires but little comment, and I shall not descend to characterize it, but must leave Mr. John Dudgeon to the judgment of all honest mechanics.

I might add that I am credibly informed that the cross connection of the two roller-levers, as applied in several government steamers, was first suggested by Mr. Dudgeon a few years ago, and as I have used a cross connection between my levers, I wish to render him all the justice that such an unimportant part deserves. This cross connection, however, having been an established method for several years, it cannot be now described as a "new form of expansion slide gear;" the novelty therefore, in the new made can have nothing to do with Mr. John Dudgeon, nor he with it.

Since making my model I have devised several improvements, and if you think the subject of sufficient interest for your readers, shall be most ready to forward you a drawing and description: no doubt had I shown these to Mr. Dudgeon, he would have spared the embarrassment of this offer by appending them to his other improvements.

I am, Sir, your obedient servant,

C. P. STEWART, M.A.

Trinity College, Cambridge.

PLOUGHING BY STEAM POWER.

WHEN we made some remarks in our last number on the economical application of steam power to agricultural operations, we were not aware that our ideas had been so far anticipated, as they appear to have been, by Lord Willoughby on his estate at Grimsthorpe. On his introduction of a steam engine, he was told, we are informed, that it would never be worked for more than a day in a month; but no sooner did the farmers find what a "willing horse" they had got, than they verified the old adage by "galloping him up hill," and have continued to do so ever since, so vigorously, that time has never been found even to clean out the boiler. The latest of its applications has been to steam-ploughing, on which Lord Willoughby has made some important experiments, the results of which he has been kind enough to communicate to us. Time will only permit us now briefly to describe the arrangement employed, but in our next number we shall be able to give a sketch of the machinery, which is very simple and inexpensive. The engine used is one of the portable variety, and is the same which is employed to such advantage on the estate in threshing, grinding, sawing, &c. Three ten-feet lengths of portable railway are laid across the centre of the field, on one of which the engine stands. The power is transmitted from a drum on the crank-shaft to a capstan, provided with bevil and reversing gear. Two ordinary ploughs, one a subsoil one, are drawn by a chain on the capstan, and, in order to save time, ploughs are attached at each end of the chain, so that, while one pair are ploughing, the other pair are being drawn, along with the slack of the chain, to the other end of the field. The chain is therefore little more than half the length of the field, and when the working ploughs have arrived at the capstan, the idle ones are ready to commence their furrow, by reversing the motion of the capstan.

Three ploughs have been tried, and generally the rate has been double that of ordinary work, at twice the depth, and, although the machinery, as might be expected, cannot yet be pronounced perfect, we may safely say that enough has been done to warrant strong hopes of ultimate success.

GREAT CIRCLE SAILING.

IN the *Artisan* for December, 1848, we gave a detailed account of the great circle system of sailing, proposed by Mr. Towson, which, like all new things, has had to struggle very hard against prejudice, but which has lately been brought favourably into public notice, from the publication of the particulars of a voyage performed by the *Constance*, emigrant ship, Captain Godfrey, who, having volunteered for examination at Plymouth, and obtained a first-class certificate, became acquainted during his studies with Mr. Towson's system, and determined to put it into practice on the first opportunity. How well he has succeeded may be judged from the excitement which his second voyage to Adelaide has produced, the run-out having been performed in 77 days, the average being 110 days.

On his first voyage, he resolved to make the composite track, which is thus described in Mr. Towson's work:—"To follow the great circle track rigidly would sometimes lead through latitudes so high as to be impracticable; this generally happens, too, when the greatest amount of distance would be saved; but, though in such cases it would be unwise to attempt the great circle, yet there is a very simple application of these tables, which will give the shortest possible route consistent with a restricted maximum latitude."

The mariner is then directed to choose his maximum latitude, and Capt. Godfrey chose the parallel of 55 deg. This voyage disappointed the expectation of Captain Godfrey, as although far shorter than the average time, it was not the shortest voyage ever made. He discovered that in latitude 55 the winds were light and unsteady; he was therefore obliged to return to the parallel of 50 degrees. Although, however, he failed in the object he had in view, he acquired experience which to himself and the commercial world is of the highest importance. He has ascertained that the composite track on the parallel 50 deg. is the shortest practical route to Australia, for although the route of the parallel of 55 maximum latitude is 100 miles shorter in distance, the advantage of wind gives the unquestionable preference to that of 50 deg. The next voyage he brought this knowledge into practical operation, and has astonished the men of mercantile pursuits by making the shortest voyage ever known.

The composite route to Australia does not differ from other voyages until the mariner has reached about the latitude 24 S. Having cleared the trade winds, he then shapes his route on the arc of a great circle, varying his course by compass, according as the latitude of the ship varies, as shown below; or he sails as near to these courses as the direction of the winds will permit. The courses are as follows:—

Lat.	Course.	Lat.	Course.	Lat.	Course.	Lat.	Course.
25.0	..SE	39.30	..SE b E	46.0	...ESE	49.0	...E b S
30.0	..SE ½ E	41.30	..ESE ½ E	47.0	...ESE ½ E	49.30	...E ½ S
34.0	..SE ½ E	43.0	..ESE ½ S	48.0	...ESE ½ E	49.45	...E ½ S
37.0	..SE ½ E	44.30	..ESE ½ S	48.30	...ESE ½ E	49.57	...E ½ S

This part of the voyage is about 3480 miles, and brings the ship 68 degrees of longitude nearer her destination. She then runs due east on the parallel 50, about 72 deg. 40 min. of longitude, being 4350 miles, and then leaves that parallel by the route of a great circle destination. This last-named part of her voyage is 1866 miles, and about 43 degrees long, making altogether, from the commencement of the composite track, 8154 miles; whereas the same voyage to the Cape, and thence to Adelaide, by Mercator's sailing, is 9080—making a saving of distance to the amount of 935 miles, besides an equal saving of time, from the uniform favourable winds that blow in these latitudes.

EAST INDIAN RAILWAYS.—Amongst the passengers for India by the steamer of the 20th inst., was Mr. George Turnbull, the resident engineer of the East Indian Railway Company, and his staff. A vigorous prosecution of the works is now looked for. From the recent reports of the company it appears that more than 300,000*l.* of the capital is already paid-up, upon which the guaranteed interest of 5 per cent. is accruing, and that arrangements have been made with the India-house, by which, at the expiration of the current year, the paid-up capital will amount to about 500,000*l.*, or one-half of the million required for the first section of the line.

THE SOCIETIES.

INSTITUTION OF MECHANICAL ENGINEERS.

MR. W. A. ADAMS, OF BIRMINGHAM, ON RAILWAY CARRIAGE AND WAGGON SPRINGS.

The object of this paper is to discuss and analyse the various forms and descriptions of springs now in use in Railway Carriages and Waggons, pointing out, to the best of the writer's knowledge and experience, their advantages and defects, and suggesting such improvements in the details as will lead to better effect and economy in the use and manufacture.

Buffing and Bearing Springs are applied to carriages and waggons in order to absorb and neutralise as far as possible the force and momentum of the shocks to which the vehicles are exposed in their ordinary work. A perfect bearing or buffing spring would be that which would absorb the entire power and space of the blow without disturbing the inertia of the vehicle. This in practice is wholly impossible, from the varying loads on bearing springs and varying force on buffing springs. In bearing springs the nearest approach to perfection is in the modern first class carriage, where the disproportion of total weight between loaded and unloaded is less than in any other vehicle.

At the present time, as far as the writer is aware, there is no rule or formula by which Engineers or Manufacturers can ascertain the true form, weight, or quality of material to be used for effectually springing a railway vehicle, and consequently the goods and mineral traffic of the country averaging from 35 to 40 cwt. per spring, is now carried on springs which vary in weight from 35 to 110 lbs. each.

The primary object being in all cases to discriminate between good and bad material, the writer has endeavoured to test the relative quality of spring steel converted from Swedish and from English iron. For this purpose bars of ordinary spring steel were procured from various makers, some being English and the others Swedish; the bars were all 3 inches wide and $\frac{7}{16}$ inch thick. These bars were cut to equal length, marked, and then made into springs and tempered in the ordinary manner; each of the springs consisting of a single plate turned over into an eye at each end, and 18 inches long between the centres of the eyes. These springs were then proved in the presence of Mr. W. P. Marshall, by means of pressure applied at the centre of each spring, the spring being supported by a pin passed through the eye at each end, which rested on rollers to allow the ends to be drawn together freely when the spring deflected.

The results were as follow—

ENGLISH.

No.	Weight.	Deflection.	Permanent set.
1.	15 cwt.	1 inch	no set
	20 „		½ inch
	25 „	Broken	
2.	15 „	1⅛ inch	no set
	20 „	2¼ inch	1 inch
	25 „	Broken	
3.	15 „	1½ inch	⅛ inch
	20 „	3¾ inch	2½ inch
	25 „	much set	
4.	15 „	1⅜ inch	¼ inch
	20 „	2½ inch	1⅝ inch
	25 „	much set	

SWEDISH.

No.	Weight.	Deflection.	Permanent set.
5.	15 cwt.	1⅝ inch	⅜ inch
	20 „	3⅝ inch	2⅝ inch
	25 „	much set	
6.	15 „	2¾ inch	2⅛ inch
	20 „	Broken	
7.	15 „	2⅜ inch	1⅜ inch
	20 „	4½ inch	3⅜ inch
	25 „	much set	
8.	15 „	2⅝ inch	1 inch
	20 „	5½ inch	4¼ inch
	25 „	much set	
9.	15 „	2 inch	¾ inch
	20 „	3¾ inch	2½ inch
	25 „	Broken	
10.	15 „	3¼ inch	2 inch
	20 „	Broken	

From the foregoing experiments it appears that the elasticity, sustaining power, and toughness of the English steel was much greater than that manufactured from the Swedish iron.

The *Laminated Spring* is the most common form for the springs of railway vehicles, consisting of a number of plates, the taper being given by reducing the plates successively in length.

The principle for regulating the taper of the spring is to obtain an equal amount of strain or deflection from each particle of material. If some parts of the spring are deflected less than others, the amount of material might be reduced in those parts without impairing the sustaining power of the spring.

A laminated spring may be tapered either in breadth or thickness, but if parallel in thickness and all the plates the same length, each plate should be uniformly tapered in breadth so that each half of every plate would be a triangle. In practice the plates of laminated springs are made parallel in breadth and thickness, inasmuch as the parallel bar is the most economical form, and the taper is obtained, as before expressed, by the different lengths of plates.

If a spring consisted of only one plate parallel in breadth but tapered in thickness, such taper should be in the form of a parabola, as the strength is in proportion to the square of the thickness. This form is shown in Fig. 2, by the part A A.

Fig. 1, represents one-half of an ordinary waggon bearing spring. Fig. 2 is the same spring pressed flat, but supposing the plates not to slide over one another.

Fig. 1.

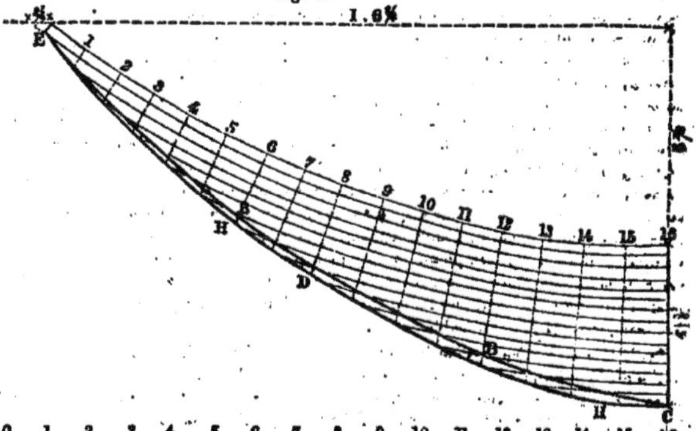

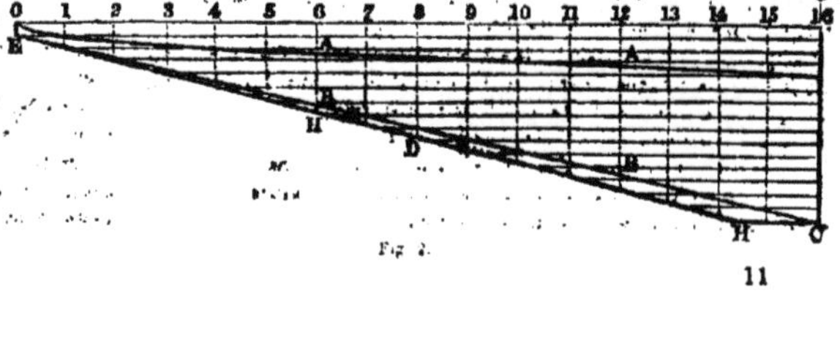

Fig. 2.

If the spring consisted of a number of very thin parallel plates, the correct form would be a uniform taper in thickness from the centre towards the ends, as shown by the portion B B in fig. 2, because the strength of each part of the spring would depend upon the number of plates at that part. In practice the most correct form of spring is between the two forms of the triangle and the parabola, but is nearer the triangle, as the thickness of the plates bears only a small proportion to the average length.

The spring shown in fig. 1 is 3 feet 3 inches long, 3 inches wide, and $4\frac{15}{16}$ inches thick in the centre, and consists of 15 plates $\frac{5}{16}$ inch thick, excepting only the outside plates, which are $\frac{3}{8}$ inch, according to the usual practice to allow for the plate not being supported by plates on both sides.

If this spring were a single plate of the same total strength it would be only $1\frac{1}{4}$ inch thick at the centre, and in the form of the parabola A A in fig. 2, but as it consists of a number of plates the outline must be a line beyond that curve.

The straight line B B in fig. 2 is drawn outside the curve, giving a uniform taper from the centre of the spring to the end of the second plate, leaving the top plate its full thickness to the end. This line B B appears suitable to be adapted for the practical outline of the spring as the deviation from correctness is only very small, and gives a slight diminution in strength at the quarter length D, which is advisable in practice, because the centre C is usually weakened by a $\frac{3}{4}$ inch rivet hole reducing the strength $\frac{1}{4}$ at that point.

The line B B is transferred from fig. 2 to the curved spring in fig. 1 by dividing the length of the top plate into 16 equal parts by the lines from 1 to 16, which are drawn vertical in fig. 2, and radiating to the centre of the curve of the spring in fig. 1. These lines being made of equal length in both cases give the curved line B B in fig. 1. The end of the top plate is lengthened and turned down at E to give a bearing to the spring.

The writer has in practice set out all springs required by him, by drawing through the extreme points C and E a circular arc of the same radius as the top plate of the spring. The line obtained by this method is a singular instance of how near practice has approached theory by this simple method, the extreme difference being only $\frac{1}{8}$ inch.

The line H H is obtained in the same manner as before described, excepting that the spring is not tapered to the centre, but to a set-off of two inches from the centre, viz., from C to H. This is the form universally adopted, but it is clearly incorrect, as the centre is made proportionately weaker than the remainder of the spring, as well as being further weakened by the rivet hole through the centre.

The true and correct form of spring would be, that the centre of the spring should be at H, and the plates connected not by a rivet but with a narrow hoop. In practice the spring is clipped to and bears on the axle box at H, and consequently the mass of steel H to C is entirely wasted.

In two plates of steel of the same length and breadth but of different thickness, the amount of deflection caused by the same weights is in proportion to the cube of the thickness, although the breaking strength is in proportion to the square of the thickness; consequently, if one spring were made with plates double the thickness of those of another spring, the first would require only one-eighth the number of plates, viz., one-eighth the weight of material to support the load with the same amount of deflection; but in that case the extent of the displacement of the particles of the steel in the thick plates would be double of that in the thin plates, and in the practical application of thick plates to springs it is necessary to limit the deflection within the above extent, as the double amount of deflection would break or strain the particles, presuming that in the thin plates the particles were being strained to a reasonable extent.

The *Waggon Bearing Spring* in ordinary use on the Midland, London and North Western, and other railways is shown in fig. 1, and is 3 feet 3 inches long, $6\frac{1}{2}$ inches camber, $4\frac{15}{16}$ inches thick, and 3 inches wide, consisting of 15 plates of which 2 are $\frac{3}{8}$ inch and the rest $\frac{5}{16}$ inch thick, and the spring averages in weight about 93 lbs.

This spring is used to sustain loads not exceeding 6 tons on the four springs exclusive of the waggon body; the waggon body weighs barely 2 tons, making the total load about 8 tons, or 2 tons per spring.

By actual experiments this spring deflects with

1 ton	....	2 tons	....	3 tons
$\frac{7}{8}$ inch	....	2 inches	....	$3\frac{1}{2}$ inches

and will prove flat without setting or breaking.

It is to be noted that in originally proving this spring flat it had set about $\frac{3}{8}$ inch, but that with the same extent of proof it will not again permanently set, having this property in common with other materials.

This spring would well sustain a load of 3 tons in actual work, as the concussions received upon the rails would probably not at any time increase the deflection $\frac{1}{2}$ inch, consequently the load of 2 tons is being sustained on a spring far too rigid, to the detriment of the road and the waggon, and the original first cost is considerably more than it need have been.

Formerly various plans were adopted to lessen the friction at the ends of the springs, by the use of rollers, but these plans are now obsolete, the amount of friction not being found practically detrimental.

The points of the plates of laminated springs were formerly tapered in thickness, but now the usual plan is to form the taper in the breadth by cutting the plates at the ends in a triangular form. This method is found much more certain in its effect, is neater in appearance, and cheaper in manufacture. The cutting is generally performed either with the shearing machine, or between dies in a punching machine, the scraps being used in the melting pot for cast steel.

Fig. 3.

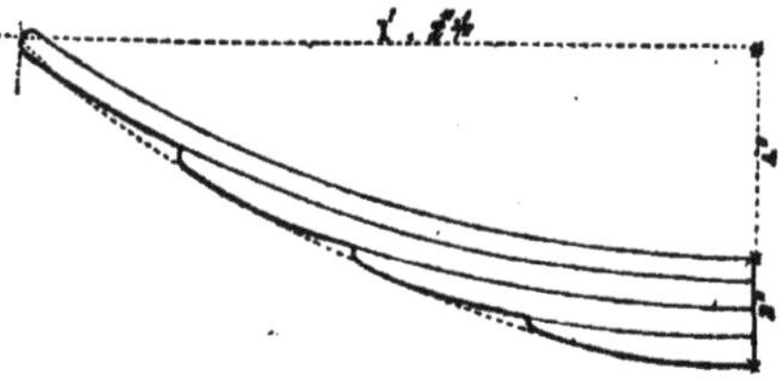

Fig. 3 represents the *Waggon Bearing Spring*, or more correctly speaking *prop*, in extensive use on the North Branch of the London and North Western, the South Staffordshire, Caledonian, and other Railways, which may well be designated by the term *cheap*.

This spring is 2 feet 5 inches long, 4 inches wide, 2 inches thick, camber 4 inches, consisting of 4 plates $\frac{1}{2}$ inch thick, and weighs about 40 lbs. Actual experiment furnishes the following deflections:—

1 ton	....	2 tons	....	3 tons
$\frac{3}{8}$ inch	....	$\frac{3}{4}$ inch	....	$1\frac{1}{8}$ inch

The cause of the immense sustaining power of this spring has been explained before in the observations on thick and thin plates.

The writer has already endeavoured to explain that the ordinary spring (fig. 1) is too rigid, what therefore must be the wear and tear of rails, wheel tyres, vibration to the axles, and general wear and tear to the waggon and load caused by this rigid spring? Compared with fig. 1, this spring affords less relief in the proportion of 6 to 16, and is the furthest removed from the object required to be attained.

The *Waggon Bearing Spring* in extensive use on the Midland Great Western, and other Irish Railways, and on the London and North Western Railway, is the ordinary spring, as in fig. 1, but with eyes rolled at the ends, and hung on scroll-irons.

The advantages of this form of spring are the great space passed through and quickness of adaptation to the inequalities of the road, in consequence of the deflection of the end shackles, caused by the deflection of the spring, and consequent elongation between the centres of eyes of shackles; also the rubbing friction at ends is almost entirely obviated.

The disadvantages are, first, that to carry a given load a much greater quantity of material is required, as from the circumstances of a great portion of the space between the sole-bar and the axle-box being taken up by the scroll irons and shackles, the radius of the curve of the spring is much reduced, and a thicker spring consequently required.

Secondly, the tension on the sole-bars tending to hog the waggon frame, being the reverse of the action of the ordinary spring.

Thirdly, in consequence of the great space passed through by the deflection of this spring, the variations of the load will considerably vary the height of the buffers from the rails.

Fig. 4 represents the new universal *Carriage Bearing Spring*, originally introduced by Mr. Wharton on the London and North Western Railway, as the result of repeated practical trials and improvements; theory would probably have never attained a similar result.

This spring is 5 feet 3 inches long, 2 inches wide, $2\frac{11}{16}$ inches thick, and consists of 9 plates $\frac{5}{16}$ inches thick; the ends of the plates are what is technically termed long spear-pointed.

Fig. 4 represents the spring when loaded, and the peculiar camber before

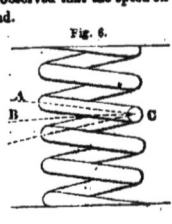

Fig. 4.

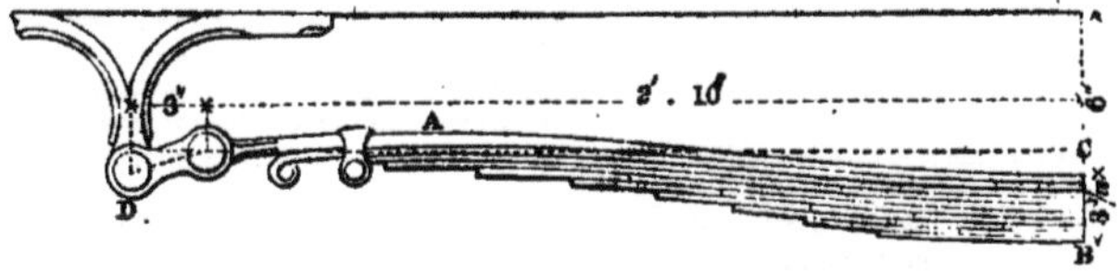

fixing is made by setting the plates entirely at the centre, instead of the plates being set into a curve throughout their whole length, as in other springs. In fixing this spring the tension-brace is adjusted between scroll-irons, with intervening compensating shackles. The tension-brace is 3 inches by $\frac{5}{8}$ inch, and thickened at the ends to $\frac{5}{8}$ inches. The spring is then compressed between the axle-box and the brace.

The action of the spring and brace is that of a lever spring combined with a tension-brace, but the spring is so thoroughly overpowered by the leverage of the brace and the weight of the load, as to have little or no power of reaction or displacing the inertia of the load, beyond that of recovering its original position, thus affording the well-known smoothness and steadiness of action of this construction of carriage spring.

The brace is acted upon principally at the point A, but nevertheless when the blow from the road strikes the point B, and the spring and brace straighten at that point, the curving and straightening of the brace at A is compensated by the straightening and lengthening at C, the amount of tension at D being thus at all times about the same. The tension brace steadies and counteracts the power of the spring, and the spring partly relieves the brace by sustaining it at A.

This combination also affords the means of firmly attaching the axle-box to the spring and brace, and thus holding it independent of the axle-guards, which in this case are wholly *guards*, not *guides*, the guards neither touching the axle-box on the edge or side. Thus the effects of the inequalities of the road laterally and horizontally are only transmitted to the body through the elastic medium of the spring.

Springs of the same construction, but shorter and lighter, are now generally used for horse-boxes, carriage-trucks, and break-vans.

Fig. 5.

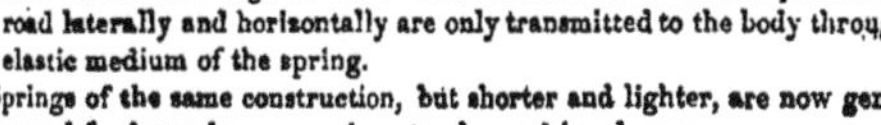

Buchanan's Bearing Spring consists of four flat horizontal plates 4 feet long, 4 inches wide, and tapered in thickness from $\frac{1}{2}$ inch at the centre to $\frac{1}{4}$ inch at the ends, and fastened in the centre and impinging at the ends only.

It does not seem to possess any advantage over the ordinary laminated spring, excepting that the friction between the plates is entirely avoided except at the ends; but at the same time it must be borne in mind, that in ordinary laminated springs the steel is rolled concave, therefore the plates bear at the edges only, which very considerably reduces the friction.

The disadvantages of this spring appear to be—firstly, that the extreme points of support are when the spring is weighted considerably below the centre bearing, necessitating the use of deep scroll-irons in carriages and bearing-blocks in waggons.

Secondly—The manufacture is costly and uncertain, from the fact of the plates being tapered in thickness, and the difficulty of hardening and tempering plates that taper in thickness.

Thirdly—When fixed with scroll-irons, the sustaining power is partly derived from its effect as a tension brace.

Adams's Bow-Spring of the size used for passenger vehicles is 6 feet long from centre to centre of spring eyes, and the versed-sine about 14 inches when weighted; the plates are 8 inches broad in centre, and tapered in width to 5 inches at the eyes, and the thickness is $\frac{9}{16}$ inch.

The advantages of this spring are—

Firstly—It holds the axle-boxes without the intervention of the guards, in the same manner as previously described, with reference to the carriage bearing spring.

Secondly—That the top links permit the wheels, axles, and axle-boxes to traverse laterally in passing curves and other impediments.

Thirdly—That the quick adaptation of this spring to lateral and perpendicular blows preserves the inertia of the body almost wholly from displacement at moderate speeds.

The disadvantages are, that at high speeds, and on a bad road, the reaction of this spring is so great as to cause a rebound, and the gradually increasing momentum from each successive blow occasions very considerable oscillation.

This property has completely negatived its use for 4-wheeled carriages; but it is now used successfully under the 8-wheeled carriages on the North Woolwich branch, and there works to considerable advantage, permitting the wheels to adapt themselves freely to the curves of the road. The oscillation is there almost wholly obviated, from the fact that the blows are received upon eight points, and that the reactive power of a blow on one of the eight points is not sufficient to disturb the inertia of the load.

This spring has been and is now used to a very considerable extent on 6-wheeled carriages in Germany; but it is to be observed that the speed on the Continent is generally slower than in England.

A Spiral Bearing Spring is represented in fig. 6. The dimensions of these springs, as used under the tenders of the Midland Railway, were 9 inches height and 6 inches diameter, and they were made of $\frac{3}{4}$-inch round steel. Within this coil was fixed a second spiral of smaller diameter, coiled the reverse way to prevent the coils interfering.

Fig. 6.

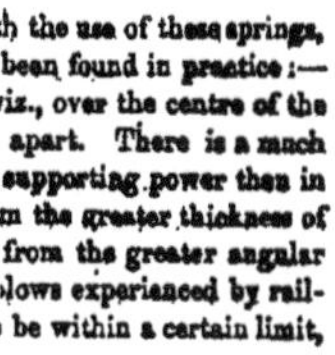

The action of a spiral spring is principally torsion of the steel bar through the angle, A C B, and partly lateral deflection from the increase of diameter, when the spring is compressed.

Practically the writer is not well acquainted with the use of these springs, but presumes that the following objections have been found in practice:—The spring bears upon the sole-bar at one point, viz., over the centre of the axle-box, instead of at two points some 3 feet apart. There is a much greater uncertainty in the degree of elasticity and supporting power than in flat springs composed of many plates, partly from the greater thickness of steel causing uncertainty in the tempering, and from the greater angular strain on the particles of the steel; the sudden blows experienced by railway springs requiring the thickness of the steel to be within a certain limit, say of $\frac{5}{8}$ inch or $\frac{1}{2}$ inch.

Buffer and Draw Springs.—The ordinary Laminated Buffer and Draw Spring is 5 feet $4\frac{1}{2}$ inches long, $5\frac{1}{16}$ inches thick, and 3 inches broad, consisting of 17 plates, the outside plates $\frac{3}{8}$ inches thick, and the remainder $\frac{5}{16}$ inch; the camber when at rest being 13 inches. The same principles of construction apply to this spring as to the laminated bearing spring in fig. 1.

These springs are generally fixed in the centre of the carriage, sliding between four bars of iron, ordinarily termed the "buffer spring cradle." The ends are acted upon by the four buffer rods, and the draw bar is cottered to the centre of the spring. The same methods have been tried to obviate friction at the ends as have been already mentioned with respect to bearing springs, but these plans are now obsolete.

In fixing the springs on carriages they are generally compressed one inch, and in waggons to the extent of about one-third of the stroke. The stroke of the buffer rod is limited to such an extent as will not deflect the spring beyond a straight line.

The sustaining power of this spring is equal to about 2 tons 14 cwt., or equal in all, including both ends of carriage, to about 2¾ tons, developed through a stroke of 2 feet.

As yet this method of buffing has not been surpassed or equalled, as none of the modern substitutes will give this moderate amount of resisting power developed through so great a space as 2 feet; also the weight of the buffer springs being in the centre of the carriage, and the springs acted upon by long buffer rods, cause the action to be very steady.

Fig. 7.

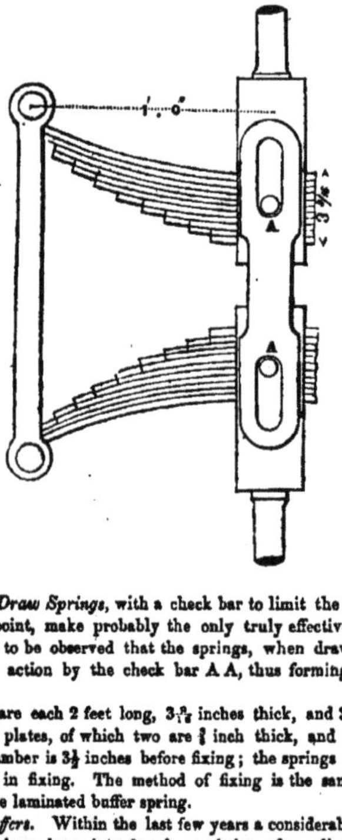

The *Double Draw Springs*, with a check bar to limit the action within the straining point, make probably the only truly effective method yet adopted. It is to be observed that the springs, when drawn home, are limited in their action by the check bar A A, thus forming a continuous rigid draw bar.

The springs are each 2 feet long, 3 1/16 inches thick, and 3 inches wide, consisting of 11 plates, of which two are ⅜ inch thick, and the remainder 5/16 inch; the camber is 3½ inches before fixing; the springs are each compressed ½ inch in fixing. The method of fixing is the same as already described for the laminated buffer spring.

External Buffers. Within the last few years a considerable number of external buffers have been introduced, consisting of a cylinder and piston packed with nearly every available elastic substance, and practically varying only in the material of the packing.

De Bergue's Buffer Spring is packed with rings of vulcanised India-rubber; there are four rings, 5½ inches diameter, and 1¼ inch thickness each.

In the opinion of the writer, this is the least effective of any yet produced, as the stroke is very short, and then only moderately developed under enormous pressure. It is questionable whether, in the event of a collision, the train would not collapse and leave the rails, before the immense sustaining power of these springs was fully developed.

This buffer has an apparent stroke of about 3 inches; but it appears that to drive up the pairs of buffers 1½ inch would require a force of 3 tons.

By reference to the description of the ordinary laminated spring, it will be observed that the stroke is 12 inches with a force of 2¾ tons; being eight times the length of stroke, with a rather less force.

It is also questionable whether the vulcanised India-rubber is of that imperishable nature originally supposed. The writer has had in his possession a considerable quantity of vulcanised elastic band for papers that have become completely rotten.

Todd's Cork Buffer is as nearly as possible the same as De Bergue's, excepting that the packing is cork; there are five plates of cork 7½ inches diameter, and ⅜ inch thick each.

This spring appears to be superior to De Bergue's, inasmuch as the cork is more compressible than the vulcanised India-rubber, but it is questionable whether the cork is not liable to a permanent set.

Fig. 8.

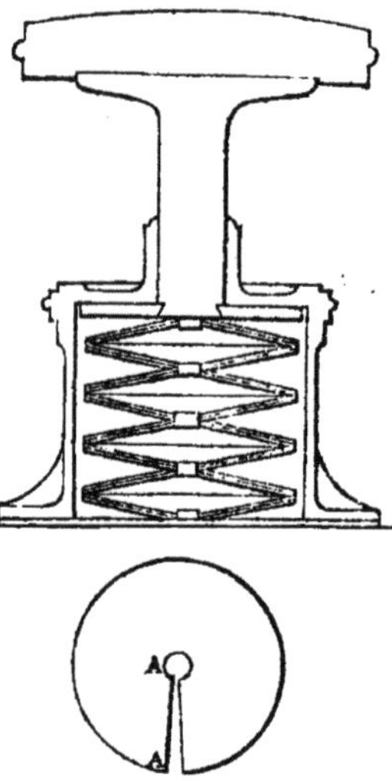

Adams's Disk Buffer has the packing consisting of 16 disk springs, made from flat circular plates of steel, 8 inches diameter, and ⅛ inch thick, with a radiating piece A A, cut out to enable the plates to be pressed to a conical form.

This buffer spring is superior to the foregoing, inasmuch as the total amount of stroke is wholly developed, and the power can be properly adjusted by the thickness of the plates; the total length of stroke is 5½ inches.

Webster's Air Buffer exhibits considerable ingenuity, but is more complicated than the other plans. The air piston is 6 inches diameter, and the leather packing is distended by a vulcanised India-rubber ring; the length of stroke is 4 inches.

In the event of leakage during the stroke, the piston would not return to its original position, and to effect this a small spiral spring is employed, which drives back the piston. A small valve admits air at the time that the piston is recovering its position to compensate for leakage during the stroke.

Spiral Buffer and Draw Springs are used to some extent, but they are liable to the same objections already described with reference to the spiral bearing springs.

Brown's Conical Spiral Spring Buffer appears to be the least objectionable of these. The resisting power is that of a spiral spring made in the form of a cone 7½ inches diameter at the base, and the spring has the advantage of rotating at the point of the cone, there by considerably easing the tendency to fracture or strain the particles of the steel; the steel is 1 inch wide and ⅝ inch thick at the base of the conical spiral, and is tapered for the last three coils to ½ inch diameter at the point of the cone. When driven home the spring forms a complete flat volute.

The sustaining power of the spring is about equal for the space passed through to that of the ordinary laminated buffer spring, but with a shorter stroke, the length of stroke being only 3½ inches instead of 12 inches. From its compactness and comparatively moderate price, it is in the writer's

Fig. 9.

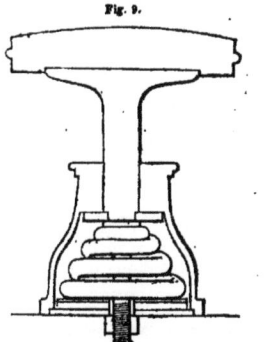

opinion, should the springs be found to stand their work, the most eligible of the external buffers, but yet far from equalling the result obtained by the use of the laminated buffer spring and buffer rods.

The whole of these Cylinder and Piston Buffers are liable to the defect of the piston being guided through only a short length, and consequently they cannot work with the smoothness of the long buffer rod guided in several places. This more particularly applies in the event of an oblique blow upon the buffer.

In conclusion, it is suggested that it would be desirable for a correct table to be formed of the sizes, weight, sustaining power, and deflection of laminated bearing and buffing springs, as a uniform guide in their practical application.

The writer purposes, should it being desired by the meeting, to prepare a laminated waggon bearing spring, with axle-box and adjustments complete, on the principles pointed out at the commencement of this paper, viz., to obtain the present amount of efficient results with the smallest quantity of material.

Mr. Middleton remarked, that the conical spiral-spring buffer had been mentioned in the paper as the most advantageous of the external buffers in respect of the length of stroke, but that a still greater length of stroke was required; and he wished to mention one that he had introduced, consisting of a double-coned spiral spring, which had the advantage of giving a greater length of stroke, and he thought would form a very satisfactory buffer. They had been applied for the purpose of making a long buffer of 7 feet stroke, by using 6 of these spring, 4 in the middle and 1 at each end of the buffer rod.

Mr. Adams observed, that an objection to the double-coned spring would be that it was not free to revolve on its axis like the single-coned spring whilst it was being compressed, because it rested on the large base of the cone at each end, and the friction would be too great to allow of its revolving, but the single-coned spring had so little friction at the small end that it was capable of revolving when compressed. The strain on the steel was increased if a spiral spring was prevented from revolving when compressed, and it was consequently more liable to break.

Mr. Middleton did not understand that it was important for the spiral spring to revolve when compressed.

Mr. Cowper observed that he agreed with the objection made by Mr. Adams; the spiral would necessarily revolve to a certain extent when compressed unless prevented by some obstruction, because the length of each coil of the spiral was a little greater than the circumference of the circle.

Mr. Hodge remarked, that the double-conical spring was not a new invention; and Mr. Middleton replied that he did not claim the invention of the spring, but he considered that its application to the purpose suggested was entirely new.

Mr. Fuller wished to state (for Mr. De Bergue in his absence) with respect to the vulcanised India-rubber in buffer springs, that upwards of 100,000 of the rings had been sent out, and many of them had been in use for two or three years, and as far as he had ascertained, the cases of failure had been very few indeed. In some cases where the material had been used for bearing springs it had failed, in consequence of not having a sufficient amount of bearing surface, but in the application to buffer springs he was not aware of any instance of failure excepting in a few cases where the rings had been over vulcanised.

Mr. Adams replied that he had not any experience of the durability of the vulcanised Indian-rubber applied to buffers, and he had therefore only stated the circumstance he was acquainted with of the bands for papers.

The Chairman thought it would be better to defer the discussion upon the paper until the members had been supplied with a copy in the proceedings of the meeting, and they would then be better enabled to bring such facts and experience as they had to bear upon the subject. He thought that Mr. Adams was entitled to their thanks for the careful research he had exhibited in his paper, which was one of great value and importance; he was one of those who spared no pains to improve every part of the work in which they were engaged. He hoped the Institution would also receive similar communications from many others of the members on practical subjects connected with the various manufactures in which they were engaged.

INSTITUTION OF CIVIL ENGINEERS.

Tuesday, February 26, 1850.

WILLIAM CUBITT, Esq., President in the Chair.

THE paper read was "On the Street Paving of the Metropolis, with an Account of a peculiar system adopted at the London and North-Western Railway Station, Euston Square," by Mr. William Taylor, (of Birmingham).

The paper commenced by directing attention to the importance of a good system of paving, in conjunction with a more perfect plan of sewage for all large towns. The paving of the metropolis had too long been carried on under an antiquated and unscientific system, of using large masses of granite, placed upon an insufficient substratum; the consequences of this were great noise, an imperfect foot-hold for the horses, danger of the constant fracture of the springs and axles from the jolting over an uneven surface, and great expense of repairs. The "Macadamized" streets were manifest improvements on such a system, but the surface was not found capable of resisting the heavy traffic of the main thoroughfares of the City. The defects of the wood pavement so greatly exceeded the merits that it had been nearly abandoned.

Impressed with the disadvantages of the present system of paving, Mr. Taylor tried an experiment about ten years ago, by covering a surface subject to very heavy traffic, and subsequently, about five years since, entirely paving the departure side of the Euston Station of the London and North-Western Railway in a peculiar manner. The system was upon entirely new principles. The method employed was, after removing the subsoil to the depth of sixteen inches, to lay a thickness of four inches of strong gravel, equally and well rammed, then another layer of gravel mixed with a small quantity of chalk, or hoggin, for the purpose of giving elasticity, the ramming being continued as before; a third coat, of the same materials, was then laid and rammed, a regular degree of convexity of surface being preserved. The stones used were of Mount Sorrel Granite, dressed and squared into regular masses of four inches deep, three inches thick, and four inches long: these stones were laid in a bed of fine sand, one inch in thickness, equally spread over the surface of the substratum, and they were carefully placed, so that no stone should rock in its bed. The whole surface was then well driven down with wooden rammers, weighing fifty-five pounds each. The small size of the stones enabled them to be well rammed home, so that the surface of the pavement never sunk, and the hardness and toughness of the material, prevented the stones from being worn down by any traffic, however heavy.

It was stated, that this system was found infinitely preferable to the employment of large stones, and the statement of cost was vastly in its favour; the price of the ordinary kind of granite paving, in London, being eighteen shillings per superficial yard, and the maximum cost of the new or "Euston" pavement, including the substratum, was not twelve shillings per yard, and deducting the value of the old stones, not (in this latter case) claimed by the contractor, the net cost would be only be nine shillings per yard.

The system was stated to have been very extensively employed at Birmingham, and many provincial towns, and it appeared admitted, that the beauty of the pavement when completed, was only equalled by its extreme durability, and by the manifest advantages it offered in its noiselessness, good foot-hold for horses, freedom from jolting, and the small repairs it required.

It was suggested, that the different paving boards should make a trial in streets of small traffic, by lifting the large stones, and cutting them into small cubes, or rectangular pieces, of three inches in depth, for the future pavement; so that a good field would be afforded for the practice of the paviours; which would enable them to be better qualified for the task of extending the system to the more important thoroughfares: by this means, too, a large surplus of stone would be accumulated for paving, and the refuse would be valuable for macadamizing the roads in the outskirts.

Tuesday, March 5, 1850.
WILLIAM CUBITT, Esq., President, in the Chair.

Before the business commenced, it was announced by the Secretary, that an electric telegraphic despatch had been received, communicating the gratifying intelligence, that at seven o'clock in the morning of Tuesday, three locomotive engines and twenty-two loaded coal waggons, weighing in all three hundred tons, had passed through the Britannia tube, over the Menai Straits, with perfect safety, and very satisfactorily to Mr. R. Stephenson, the Engineer.

The discussion was resumed on Mr. Taylor's system of Street Paving, and was extended to such a length as to preclude the reading of any Paper.

It was contended that a rigid and unyielding substratum had been tried by Mr. Telford many years since, and had been used with success in some parts of the City paving, up to the present time. The average duration of the pavement of the streets in the City was stated to be eight years, but that it was constantly subject to injury, from being moved by the water and gas companies. The pavement on London Bridge, by Sir John Rennie, was instanced as a good, but expensive, example of the use of long narrow stones and that by Mr. Walker, on Blackfriars Bridge, was quoted as another instance of the success that might be attained by great care in the preparation of the substratum, which was of concrete, and the stones of the pavement being laid with more than ordinary skill and care. The results in both cases were eminently successful, but it was allowed that such an expensive system, however beautiful, was not applicable to the ordinary streets.

It was admitted, that, although the principal streets of the City and the main thoroughfares of the West and East ends were well attended to, yet it must be allowed, that the paving of the majority of the streets was not in a satisfactory state, and it was attributed, in a great degree, to the want of a definite system being adopted ; there being too many authorities in the shape of parish paving boards, each of which had a separate surveyor, too often equally inefficient and ill paid. The water and gas companies appeared to vie with each other in their endeavours to destroy the paving ; and a portion of the Strand was quoted as having been removed thirty times within two years.

With respect to Mr. Taylor's system of paving, it was contended, that the Mount Sorrel granite was a very superior material, both as regarded its toughness and durability, and that its natural structure enabled it to be worked very advantageously into the small cubes. The main feature of the system was the selection of the material for the substratum, and the careful preparation, so as to afford a sufficiently rigid, but yet imperceptibly elastic bed, whereon the small cube stones should rest. These stones being well driven down by repeated blows of light rammers, attained a degree of solidity which defied the heaviest traffic ; and in the towns where the system was employed, considerable economy had resulted. The surface of the paving approached as nearly as possible to that of a macadamized road, affording even a safer foothold for the horses, and with less noise of passing vehicles. The surface possessed extraordinary durability, and it might be considered as a solid mass of granite. It was announced that within a few weeks there would be specimens of Mr. Taylor's system of paving laid down at the entrances of Hyde Park, where they would be subjected to

regular traffic of a destructive nature, and which would be under constant observation.

A model of an improved Crossing Point was exhibited by Mr. Duncan, of Leeds ; the notch in the rail was shown to be done away with, and the two rails in it were so dovetailed together, as to render any vertical motion between them impossible, thus materially strengthening the crossing.

A piece of brickwork, set in Greaves's blue Lias lime, and which had been kept under water for nine days, was also exhibited. This material was composed of one-third of lime to two-thirds of burnt clay; and it was stated to have been used with great success in the tunnels on the Great Northern Railway, as well as in many hydraulic works, in which it was as durable as cement.

At the monthly ballot for Members, the following gentlemen were duly elected :—Mr. E. O. Tregelles, as Member ; and Messrs. J. A. Agnew, W. Bevan, E. Goddard, J. D. M. Stirling, G. B. Thorneycroft, C. C. Williams, and Lieut. Douglas S. Galton, R. E., as Associates.

Tuesday, March 12, 1850.
WILLIAM CUBITT, Esq., President in the Chair.

It was announced from the Chair, that copies of the ground plan of the intended site in Hyde Park, and of instructions for preparing designs, of the buildings for the Grand Exhibition of 1851, had been presented to the Institution, and that, on application to the Secretary, duplicates of these documents would be forwarded to any of the Members, who intended to devote their attention to the consideration of this question.

The Paper read was, "On Tubular Girder Bridges," by Mr. Wm. Fairbairn, M. Inst. C. E. The author commenced by stating, that the chief points to be taken into consideration were :—First, the application of a given formula, for computing their strength ; Second, the excess of strength that should be given, over the greatest load that could be brought upon the bridge ; and, Third, the effects of impact, with the best mode of testing the strength, and proving the security of the bridge.

In the first place, it had been determined by experiments, that in order to balance the two resisting forces of tension and compression, in a wrought-iron tubular girder, having a cellular top, the sectional area of the bottom should be to the sectional area of the top, as eleven to twelve ; and that until this proportion existed, the usual formula could not be applied ; this formula was, that the breaking weight was equal to the total area, multiplied into the depth, and into a constant (80), and divided by the length of the girder. $\left(w = \dfrac{a\,d\,o}{l} \right)$

Considering the particular case of the Torksey Bridge, the mean sectional areas of the top and the bottom, being respectively 51·08 square inches and 54·93 square inches, the latter was in excess of strength over the former, so that a reduction of the area of the bottom from 54·93 to 46·76 square inches might have been made with propriety, and would have been in conformity with the formula.

By calculation, the ultimate strength of the bridge was found to be 1152 tons, whilst the greatest total load, including the weight of the girders, &c., was only 272 tons ; this gave a strength greater than the heaviest rolling load that could be brought on the bridge, in the proportion of nearly five to one. Although, therefore, the proportion of the girders was not exactly that which the author recommended, he considered that " they were, nevertheless, sufficient to render the bridge perfectly secure." This conclusion was arrived at without taking into consideration, the amount of additional strength derived from the continuity of the girders, across the central pier.

The exact proportions recommended were given in two tables extending respectively to spans of 150 feet, and of 300 feet. The depths of the girders of the first class were taken at one-thirteenth of the span, and those of the second class at one-fifteenth of the span.

The author then investigated the effects of impact at different velocities. It did not appear that experiment established, the fact of increased deflection at high velocities ; for in several experiments on a large scale he had found the deflection as nearly as possible the same at all velocities. He concluded by recommending that the tests to be applied should never exceed the greatest load the bridge was intended to bear.

In the opening of the discussion by Mr. Fowler, Mr. Bidder, and Mr. Eaton Hodgkinson, it was remarked that, satisfactory as it was to have the confirmation of Mr. Fairbairn's authority for the perfect safety of the bridge for all purposes of traffic, it would have been desirable that he should have extended his calculations a little further into the question of the increased strength derived from the continuity of the girder across the central pier, which augmented the total strength fully one-fourth. It was also argued that the excessive proportion of the bottom of the girder, although not an economical disposition of material, was in itself an important addition to the strength of the girder.

The definite proportions assigned in the Paper for girders were disputed, and the attempt to assign empirical rules for the practice of engineers, in structures of this novel character, was earnestly deprecated.

It was important also to remember that the large proportion of the bottom of the beam brought into action a corresponding quantity of the upper part of the side plates in aid of the top. Thus it appeared that if the subject had been pursued further, the proportion of five to one, by which the proportional strength of the beam, over the rolling load, was represented, would have been, from various causes, materially increased.

Tuesday, March 19, 1850.
WILLIAM CUBITT, Esq., President, in the Chair.

The discussion on Mr. W. Fairbairn's paper, "on Tubular Girder Bridges," was renewed, and continued through the evening.

The subject was resumed at the point where it was left on the last discussion of March 12th; and Messrs. Wild, Pole, Rennie, Scott Russell, Eaton Hodgkinson, Walker, Glynn, Bidder, Professor Willis, General Pasley, and Capt. Simmonds, R.E., examined the question at great length, and under all views, illustrating their position by diagrams and models used in the experiments and in the mathematical investigation.

It was stated, that after the remarks made at the last meeting, it was merely requisite to describe the experiments alluded to, and before doing so, to briefly describe their object.

In the Report of the Government Inspector, the limiting strain required for the public safety was defined, and the Torksey Bridge had been condemned for not complying with those conditions. A calculation, therefore, had been made to ascertain the actual strain on the bridge. It appeared, however, that it was really less than the limit prescribed by the Government Inspector. The experiments instituted were for the purpose of testing these contrary results. It was also stated, that in the paper there were many objectionable points, but particularly one that was positively dangerous.

The author had not only omitted the effect of the continuity of the Torksey girders, but stated that it was safer to do so. Now all writers upon the subject, and all who had considered the matter, agreed that in a continuous beam, the effect of continuity was most important, and that in a perfectly continuous beam, the strain over the supports was even greater than elsewhere. It was submitted that this was not the part, the consideration of which it could be "safer to omit."

The form taken by a continuous beam, when uniformly loaded, was convex over the supports, and concave between the points at which the convexity ended; at these points of contrary flexure, the horizontal strains were nil, and the beam might then be severed, without altering its condition. The virtual length of the beam, in the Torksey Bridge was determined by the distance between the exterior support and the point of contrary flexure; and it was to determine this point practically that the experiments were instituted. It was shown that this point was 21¾ feet from the centre support, and that hence the length of the beam was reduced from 130 feet to 108¼ feet.

The compressive strain upon a girder of this length, loaded as prescribed, was 4½ tons per inch, being less than the limit defined. Consequently, it was asserted, that the railway company to whom this bridge belonged, had been deprived of its use, not in consequence of any omission on the part of

their engineer, but in consequence of the inability of the Government authorities to appreciate the strength that had been provided.

In reference to the application of formulæ to the calculation of the strength of the girders, it was considered desirable, in such an important case, not merely to form a general approximate notion of the strength of the bridge, but to ascertain, with all possible exactness, the nature and amount of the strains to which the structure was exposed; and this could only be done, by using a comprehensive process of calculation, which should embrace all the elements affecting the strength of the bridge.

The effect of the continuity of the girders over the two openings, was carefully considered, and the nature of its effect upon the strain was explained, as deduced from the application of the most modern mathematical investigations, and it was demonstrated that the strength of the beam was thereby augmented above one-third.

It was then shown, how the rules for estimating the strength of elastic beams, were rendered applicable to the case of the Torksey bridge, and the results proved, that when the bridge was weighted with the load prescribed by the Government authorities as a test for its strength, the strains of compression and extension were only one half of what competent authorities had stated might be safely applied.

The diagrams exhibited shewed the results of mathematical calculation, as applied to the Torksey Bridge girders, and the remarkable coincidence of these, with experimental results obtained by other investigators in an entirely different manner was insisted on, as a proof of the correctness of the conclusions arrived at.

It was stated, in reply to a remark upon the increased deflection due to velocity, that the result of the experiments tried by the "Cast-Iron Bridge Commission," proved, that "this increase was wholly insignificant in beams of the length and stiffness of those of the Torksey Bridge."

The discussion was summed up by its being stated, that with one exception, all those who had spoken during both evenings, agreed that the formula given in the paper was empirical and not trustworthy; that the effects of percussion and increased velocity were practically only shadowy visions; and as it was admitted, that in the calculations of the Government Inspector, the effect of continuity was neglected, and as it had been proved, that the strain was less on the bridge than that assigned as requisite for the public safety, and that it was, in fact, amply strong, it was evident, that the public had been wrongfully deprived of this bridge, and the Company had been prohibited from gaining the just return for the capital invested, in consequence of an incomplete investigation, and the assumption of untenable formulæ.

THE MANUFACTURE OF BANK OF ENGLAND NOTES.
FROM A LECTURE DELIVERED BY THE REV. JOHN BARLOW M.A., AT THE ROYAL INSTITUTION, FEBRUARY 15.

In attempting to sketch the rise and progress of a bank note, it will not be necessary to go deeply into the paper manufacture generally. Most persons are aware that the many substances resorted to at different periods, such as the tendrils and stalks of various plants, and the bark of certain trees, have been abandoned, and that the staple of the paper manufacture at the present moment is linen rags. The rags, on arriving at the paper manufactures, are first well dusted, then cut into pieces, assorted and bleached. They are then reduced to a pulp, from which the moulder takes a sufficient quantity to form a sheet of paper, holds his mould in a horizontal direction, to allow the water to run off, and leaves a coating of thin fibrous particles, in the form of a sheet, on the bottom of the mould. The sheets thus formed are subjected to pressure, first between woollen cloths, and afterwards alone. Such is a general outline of the stages of this process, which need not be pursued further, the object of these remarks being limited to elucidating the peculiarities of one fabrication.

One of the features of a bank note, which soonest strikes the attention, is its extreme tenuity. Thinness is essential to the ready perception of the real character of the note, and greatly aids the examiner in detecting the marks by which its genuineness or illegitimacy may be determined. But attenuated as is the substance of the paper, it is capable of an unevenness of surface, which forms another most eligible mode of testing the note. The true bank note has a peculiar touch, which may be recognised on passing the paper through the fingers, when the note has a tendency to detain the hand, a property originating in a certain roughness of texture communicated in the manufacture, and inimitable by other means. So valuable is this property as an index to character, that Mr. Jones Lloyd stated the other day, that an experienced clerk could test the notes passing through his hands as rapidly as he could count them.

Another peculiarity of a bank note is the water mark. A certain mark incorporated in the very texture and constitution of the paper is appropriated by the government to these notes, and the exclusive right to its use is guarded by onerous penal sanctions. As none but large capitalists are able to produce a paper liable to be mistaken for the genuine, it is plain that the currency runs little risk of corruption from imitations of this distinction. The water-mark is produced by means of a certain arrangement of wires in the mould, in which the pulp is taken up. The wires, which are of the same form as the mark to be left in the finished product project on the surface of the mould, and hence leave their impression on the paper. To imitate this part of the genuine note, the forger must make his own paper. Why should he not do so? Because the management and manipulation of these moulds is so difficult that it takes the workmen weeks to succeed, and many able artisans, after unsuccessful attempts in this branch of the trade, unwilling to confess their inability, purposely manage to get drunk, and so render their discharge certain, thinking that a less discreditable ground of leaving than admitted want of skill. The nearest approach which the forger can make to the appearance of the wire-work is thus made :—He procures a plate on which the form of the wire-mark is cut in relief, places it and the paper under a press, and so gets a resemblance of the water-lines. It requires, however, but a very limited experience to enable a person to distinguish the wire marked from the impressed paper.

Another important test of the genuine bank note is the bevil edges. Every authentic bank-note has three of its sides rough, and the fourth, which is always a short side, smooth or cut. This is the result of the construction of the mould, and its covering the deckel. When the mould has been plunged into the vat containing the pulp, the deckel, a wooden frame, is placed on it, and giving shape to the borders of the pulp, produces a peculiar thinning off of the edges, which no art has hitherto been able to counterfeit. In all cases of suspicion then, the edges should be observed, and if three of the sides do not differ from the fourth, that fourth being the shortest, suspicion is justified.

No one can have failed to remark the exceeding strength of the notes of the Bank of England. The wear which they are capable of enduring is astonishing. For the sake of accumulating the strain to which a note in circulation is liable, so as to represent in one quality its power of resisting tension, we may secure the edges of a piece of bank paper, of the size and figure of the note, and then load its surface. Such a piece of paper weighs, before sizing, 17½ grains. In this state it will support, without tearing, a weight of 36 lbs. The size, subsequently added, weighs one grain, and its addition enables the note to sustain a strain of 20 lbs. more, or in all 56 lbs. The great tenacity of this kind of paper arises from its eminently fibrous character.

We have now glanced at the more striking features in the paper, its thinness, semi-transparency, its peculiar resistance to the motion of the hand, the watermark, the bevel edges, and its strength. We have now to look further, and to follow the processes by which it is made to assume the character of a promise or undertaking on the part of its issuers. The first of these is the operation of printing.

Printing may be either the pressure of the surface which is to receive certain marks into the indentations of the body that is to be copied, or the pressure of projecting type on the surface to be impressed. The first of these processes is employed by the copper-plate printer; the second is used in letter-press printing, and both are combined in the production of bank notes. The body of the note is printed by the copper-plate process, but the cypher, date, and place, are printed with types. The copper-plate printers' ink used in the Bank of England, is made from charcoal, obtained by burning the tendrils and dried husks of the German grape, commonly called "Frankfort black," which is mixed and ground with linseed oil. The great de-sideratum is a deep black aspect, and in this particular, the notes of the Bank favourably contrast with the brownness of ordinary engraving.

The ink is entirely made, as well as used, on the premises. The other printers' ink is bought from the best samples of the open market.

Until within the last few years, the notes were printed from engraved copper plates; the reasons for which that metal was discarded are interesting. The first grand requirement of the directors is perfect identity of the impression, and were the notes of the hundreth or thousandth, to present a difference even in the heaviness of the engraved strokes, or the length of a hair line—the all-essential power of detecting and demonstrating the real character of a spurious note, would be seriously impaired, if not destroyed. Copper-plates, after the first eight or ten thousand impressions had been taken, would require re-touching, to restore the lines worn away. Now, if two plates were executed by the same hand, there would still be a difference between them appreciable by a practised eye. The bank note must carry through, and carry out, the principle of perfect identity; the paper, the wire mark, bevel edges, even the size and ink are perfectly identical, and should the plates vary never so little, the charm of identity would be broken. Steel is the weapon now uniformly employed. From a steel surface twenty-five times the number of impressions may be taken before the same impairment arises as on copper. But, even if steel were employed in the same way as copper, the difference of wear would only be a question of degree, and the same difficulties would be felt, although twenty-five times seldomer. After twenty-five thousand impressions, recourse must again be had to the human hand, and the chance of discrepancy again be risked. This important result of identity, has been secured within the last fourteen years, in the Bank of England, by means of a process in use in this country for a yet longer time. This process depends on the valuable property of steel, of becoming, by a mere change in its aggregation, at the will of the metallurgist, at one time so soft as to bear the engraver's tool, and afterwards so hard as to scratch glass. A steel roller is engraved while in a soft state, and then, having been heated, suddenly plunged into a bath of cold water, it thus acquires a hardness suitable for any purpose demanding continued wear. The cylinder or roller in which the device has been cut intaglio, thus hardened, is placed in a press, and made so revolve under great pressure, in contact with a cylinder of soft steel, which receives the impression in relief, and which may, in its turn, be hardened. It is obvious that there is no limit to the multiplication of duplicates, by those means, and that identity of impression may be, in this manner, secured to any number of notes.

A plate which has been prepared from one of these rollers, contains an immense number of microscopic curves, into each of which the paper, in the process of printing, must be driven. In order to secure this, the paper must be, to a certain extent, brought back to its former pulpy state. This is accomplished by wetting it, an operation which must be performed under the eye of one of the responsible officers of the Bank. When it is remembered that 30,000 a day is the average number of impressions to be taken, and that every note requires a certain degree of dampness and no more, it will be seen that, without the aid of art, this would be likely to prove a tedious operation. A contrivance to accomplish this object with little delay, is the invention of Mr. Parker; it is founded on the principle illustrated in the following experiment:—Let a packet of dry paper be placed under the receiver of an air-pump, and the jar be exhausted of air; the air which filled the interstices of the paper, and occupied every space between the surfaces, will thus have been withdrawn. Now, let water be admitted to the receiver, and it will immediately ascend, and occupy the space left vacant by the air, and the paper will be thoroughly permeated by the moisture. This process was recommended many years ago, as a means of impregnating meat with the materials intended for its preservation. The press used in the Bank for working the plate, is that invented by Mr. Oldham, called the D press, and the pressure is so strong and well adjusted, that every note leaves its bed with all the sharpness of a proof.

At this stage of the process, the note is deficient in two points requisite for circulation; it wants the cipher, with the place, and further, the signature of the clerk. The cipher, place, date, and number, as formerly stated, are printed with types, and not from a plate or cylinder. In connexion with the numbering of these notes, a most important invention is to be noticed. As every note must bear a number different from the one which precedes it, some means must be employed for shifting the number of the type which is to print it ; 1,001 must be succeeded by 1,002; but how is this to be accomplished ? To suspend the operation for this purpose, is out of the question, where 30,000 impressions a day must be taken off. The instrument by which this feat is performed deserves attention. The handle which works one press actuates a series of wheels, on which the numbers are engraved ; with every elevation of this handle, the wheel is turned round by one figure ; when the nine figures are printed off, a second wheel is thrown into action, and advanced one figure, at which it remains stationary until nine other impressions have been taken, when it again acts. Thus, the second nought in 1,009 is replaced in the next impression by a 1, and the number stands 1,010. The figures thus formed by the motion of the handle, rise and take their place with the more permanent types during the act of impression. It is plain that no printer could depend on himself for numbering 300,000 notes with undeviating accuracy ; but the operation of the machine is certain. Accident might throw the entire operation out of play, but while it proceeds, no mistake can possibly arise.

The signature of the clerk, the last stage of preparation, is a precaution chiefly valuable as a check against forgery, by adding another characteristic by which the note may be identified.

In the last century, from the rudeness of the art, and the want of a system of precautions, great losses were sustained, which led to the offer of a reward of £10,000 for an invention preventive of forgery, and the appointment of a royal commission to inquire what could be done to stay the increasing frauds. For a long time, the gallows was believed to be the great guarantee of a genuine paper currency. Security is now sought in the multiplication of safeguards, simple, yet open to view, and the forgeries on the Bank of England are now fewer than in any other existing monetary institution.

DIMENSIONS AND DETAILS OF NEW STEAMERS.

CITY OF DUBLIN STEAM NAVIGATION-COMPANY'S IRON STEAM VESSEL, "WINDSOR."

Built by Messrs. Thomas Vernon and Co. Engines, Boilers, &c., by Messrs. Bury, Curtis, and Kennedy, Clarence Foundry, Liverpool.

Builder's measurement			Ft	In
Length of keel and fore rake	...	...	206	0
Breadth of beam	...	...	28	0
Ditto including paddle-cases	...	...	47	1
Depth of hold	...	...	16	3
Length of engine space	...	...	50	7
Tonnage.			Tons	
Hull	...	...	763$\frac{20}{94}$	
Contents of engine space	...	...	243$\frac{73}{94}$	
Register	...	...	526$\frac{0}{94}$	
New measurement.			Feet	
Length on deck	...	...	204.7	
Breadth on ditto amidships	...	...	26.9	
Depth of hold ditto	...	...	16.0	
Ditto of poop	...	...	2.4	
Length of engine space	...	...	55.5	
Tonnage.			Tons	
Hull	...	...	797$\frac{75}{100}$	
Contents of engine space	...	...	454$\frac{31}{100}$	
Register	...	...	454$\frac{34}{100}$	

A pair of side-lever engines, of 340 horses nominal power. Diameter of cylinder, 66 inches × 6 feet 3 inches length of stroke. Diameter of paddle-wheels extreme, 26 feet 2 inches ; ditto effective, 27 feet 7 inches. 24 floats, 3 feet × 2 feet 6 inches. Three sets of 12 arms. Load draught of water, 12 feet forward, and 12 feet 6 inches aft. Average speed of engines

26 revolutions per minute, and 20 revolutions per minute, light. Steam pressure, 7 lbs. per square inch. Consumption of fuel, 26 cwt. per hour. Vacuum, 28½ inches. Plying on the station between Liverpool and Belfast (156 miles), usually performed in from 12 to 13½ hours. Three tubular boilers—length, 14 feet ; breadth, 6 feet ; height, 12 feet 7 inches. Nine furnaces, three in each boiler—length, 6 feet 6 inches ; breadth, 2 feet 1 inch ; height, 3 feet 2 inches. 408 wrought iron tubes, 136 in each boiler, 3½ inches diameter × 10 feet. Bunkers hold about 60 tons of coals. Cast iron framing, of the Ionic order. Keel, 190 feet long. Frames (Kennedy and Vernon's patent), 5 × 2½ × ½ inches, and 18 inches apart. The specification of this vessel is similar to that of the *Minerva*, for which see *Artizan*, vol. 7, page 122.) The crew consisted of 37 hands—viz., 5 in the steward's department, 10 in the engineer's ditto, and 14 in the captain's. Vessel designed by Mr. Grantham.

Description—Full male figure head, clipper bow, false quarter badges, square-sterned, clinker, and carvil-built vessel of iron. Two masts, schooner-rigged, standing bowsprit. Port of Dublin. Commander—Mr. Thomas Davies.

DUNDALK AND LIVERPOOL STEAM NAVIGATION COMPANY'S IRON STEAM VESSEL, "PRIDE OF ERIN."

Built and fitted by Mr. Robert Napier, Glasgow.

Builder's measurement.			Ft	In
Length of keel and fore rake	...	...	194	6
Breadth of beam	...	...	27	2
Ditto including paddle-boxes	...	...	47	1
Depth of hold	...	...	15	11
Length of engine space	...	...	63	9
Tonnage.			Tons	
Hull	...	...	719$\frac{43}{94}$	
Contents of engine space	...	...	283$\frac{14}{94}$	
Register	...	...	454$\frac{2}{94}$	
New measurement.			Feet	
Length on deck	...	...	194.6	
Breadth on ditto amidships	...	...	26.2	
Depth of hold ditto	...	...	15.7	
Length of break-deck	...	...	38.6	
Breadth of ditto	...	...	26.3	
Depth of ditto	...	...	2.8	
Length of engine space	...	...	63.8	
Tonnage.			Tons	
Hull	...	...	731$\frac{80}{100}$	
Break-deck	...	...	30$\frac{18}{100}$	
Total	...	...	762$\frac{6}{100}$	
Contents of engine space	...	...	284$\frac{14}{100}$	
Register	...	...	478$\frac{82}{100}$	

A pair of side-lever engines, with malleable iron framing, of 368 horses nominal power. Diameter of cylinders, 70 inches × 5 feet 6 inches length of stroke. Diameter of paddle-wheels extreme, 20 feet 7 inches ; ditto effective, 24 feet 11 inches. Floats, 3 feet × 3 feet 1 inch. Three sets of 20 arms and floats. Two tubular boilers, fired fore and aft—length, 21 feet ; breadth, 10 feet 11 inches ; depth, 11 feet. Steam chests—length 21 feet ; breadth; meah; 4 feet 6 inches ; depth, 3 feet 6 inches. Twelve furnaces, six in each boiler, three at each end—length, 6 feet 6 inches ; breadth, 3 feet 5 inches, with dry bottoms. 180 wrought iron tubes, 90 in each boiler—diameter, 3 inches × 7 feet 6 inches. Space between boilers, 2 feet ; boiler to engines, 6 feet 6 inches ; ditto to ship bulkhead, 6 feet 6 inches. Steam pressure, 7 lbs. per square inch. Consumption of fuel per 24 hours, 50 tons. Average revolutions per minute, 20. Average passage, 12 hours, 159 miles, Dundalk to Liverpool. The frames are 5 × 2 × ½ and 2 feet apart.

Description—Bust female figure head (the Queen), mock quarter badges, square-sterned and clinker-built vessel of iron. Standing bowsprit, three masts, schooner-rigged, clipper-bow. Port of Dundalk. Commander—Mr. John Williams.

DROGHEDA AND LIVERPOOL STEAM NAVIGATION COMPANY'S STEAM VESSEL.—"BRIAN BOIROIMHE."

Built and Fitted by Mr. R. Napier, Glasgow.

Builder's Measurement.	Ft.	in.
Length of keel and fore rake	180	3
Breadth of beam	26	2
Ditto, including paddle-cases	45	5
Depth of hold	16	9
Length of engine space	61	9
Tonnage.	Tons.	
Hull	601$\frac{0}{94}$	
Contents of engine space...	225$\frac{81}{94}$	
Register	375$\frac{81}{94}$	

New Measurement	Ft.
Length on deck	180.0
Breadth on ditto, amidships	25.9$\frac{1}{2}$
Depth of hold ditto	16.5
Length of break-deck	31.7
Breadth of ditto	23.6
Depth of ditto	2.8
Length of engine space	61.8
Tonnage.	Tons.
Hull	626$\frac{26}{100}$
Break Deck	22$\frac{67}{100}$
Total	649$\frac{93}{100}$
Register	363$\frac{37}{100}$
Contents of engine space	286$\frac{56}{100}$

A pair of side lever engines of 306 horse nominal power; diameter of cylinders, 64 inches × 5 feet 6 inches length of stroke; diameter of paddle-wheels, extreme, 26 feet 4 inches; ditto effective, 26 feet 8 inches; floats 8 feet × 2 feet 1 inch; three sets of 26 arms and floats &c. Three tubular boilers; length, 15 feet 6 inches; breadth, 7 feet 11 inches; height, 11 feet 6 inches; steam-chest at mid-boiler, length, 7 feet; breadth, 7 feet 6 inches; depth, 5 feet. Steam-chests of wing-boilers; length, 6 feet 9 inches; breadth at top, 2 feet 2 inches; ditto at bottom, 4 feet 2 inches; depth 2 feet 6 inches. There are 9 furnaces, 3 in each boiler; length, 8 feet 6 inches; breadth, 1 foot 9 inches dry bottoms; having 81 wrought iron tubes, 27 in each boiler, diameter 8 inches × 11 feet long. The coal bunkers are situated between the engines and boilers; the tunnel is 3 feet broad, and 6 feet 7 inches high; and bunker is 7 feet 6 inches, in the length of the vessel, and all the breadth and depth. Steam pressure, 7lbs; average 18 revolutions per minute; average draught of water 10 feet; consumption of fuel 30 cwt of coals per hour; average passage 11 to 12 hours (distance 141 miles) Crew 25 in number, viz—12 on deck, 9 in the engine-room, and 4 in the cabin.

DESCRIPTION.

A full male figure head (King of Munster), clipper-bow, false quarter galleries, square sterned and clench built vessel; standing bowsprit, three masts, schooner-rigged. Port of Drogheda.—Commander, Mr. Peter Owens.

THE WATERFORD STEAM NAVIGATION COMPANY'S IRON VESSEL, "CAMILLA."

Built by Messrs. Joseph Samuda and Co., Bow-creek, Blackwall, London, 1845. Engines, boilers, &c., by Messrs. Fawcett and Preston, Liverpool, 1847. No. 1569.

Builder's measurement.	Ft.	in.
Length of keel and fore rake	175	0
Breadth of beam	24	6
Ditto, including paddle-boxes	41	0
Depth of hold	15	0
Length of engine space	38	8
Tonnage.	Tons.	
Hull...	514$\frac{57}{94}$	
Contents of engine space...	123$\frac{14}{94}$	
Register	391$\frac{43}{94}$	

New measurement.	Ft.
Length on deck	174.5
Breadth on ditto amidships	23.3
Depth of hold ditto	14.8
Ditto of poop	2.8$\frac{1}{2}$
Length of engine space	38.7
Tonnage.	Tons.
Hull...	462$\frac{74}{100}$
Contents of engine space...	144$\frac{43}{100}$
Register	318$\frac{31}{100}$

A pair of oscillating engines of 180-horse nominal power. Diameter of cylinders, 50 inches × 5 feet length of stroke. Two air pumps, lying at an angle, worked off a crank on the intermediate shaft. They have solid buckets, and are force pumps. Diameter of paddle-wheels, extreme, 21 feet 8 inches; ditto effective, 21 feet 1$\frac{1}{2}$ inches. Floats, 6 feet 9 inches × 1 foot 6 inches. Three sets of 16 arms and floats. Two tubular boilers—length, 10 feet; breadth, 10 feet; height, 10 feet. Steam-chests—length, 10 feet; breadth, 5 feet; depth, 5 feet. Six furnaces, three in each boiler—length, 7 feet four inches; breadth, 2 feet; height, 4 feet 7 inches. 528 tubes, 264 in each boiler—diameter, 2$\frac{1}{4}$ inches × 6 feet 3 inches long. Consumption of fuel, 18 cwt. per hour. Average 25 revolutions per minute. Steam pressure, 9 lbs. Bunkers hold 80 tons of coals. Frames of hull, 4 × 2$\frac{1}{2}$ × $\frac{3}{8}$ inches, and 1 foot 6 inches apart. The engines occupy 9 feet in the length of the vessel.

This vessel, formerly *Gipsy Queen*, had a pair of bell-crank engines, of 154-horse nominal power. Diameter of cylinders, 48 inches × 4 feet stroke. They were taken out in 1847, when the present ones were put in.

This vessel formerly, and till lately, plied upon the station between London and St. Petersburg, about 700 miles, and steamed it on an average of 7 days, deducting stoppages at Elsinore, &c. Average draught of water, 10$\frac{1}{2}$ feet. At present plying upon the station between Belfast and Liverpool, &c.

DESCRIPTION.

A bust female figure head, no galleries, round-sterned and clinker-built vessel, common bow, 2 masts, schooner-rigged. Port of Waterford. Commander, Mr. Alfred Brownless.

BELFAST AND LONDON SCREW STEAM NAVIGATION COMPANY'S VESSELS, "ERIN'S QUEEN" AND "LADY SEALE."

"Erin's Queen," built by Messrs. Denny, Brothers, Dumbarton; engines, boilers, by Messrs. Caird and Co., Cartsdyke, Greenock, 1846.

"Lady Seale," built by Messrs. Samuel Follet, and Co., Dartmouth; engines, boilers, &c., by Mr. J. D. Marshall, South Shields. 1846.

Builder's Measurement.	"Erin's Queen." Ft.	in.	"Lady Seale." Ft.	in.
Length of keel and fore rake.. ...	132	0	122	8
Breadth of Beam	21	0	22	0
Depth of Hold	12	9	13	3
Do. of poop		*	2	6
Length of engine space	35	9	34	2
Tonnage.	Tons.		Tons.	
Hull	282$\frac{70}{94}$		304$\frac{4}{94}$	
Contents of engine space	84$\frac{46}{94}$		76$\frac{73}{94}$	
Register ... —	198$\frac{24}{94}$		227$\frac{25}{94}$	
New Measurement	Ft.		Ft.	
Length on deck	132.0		119.5	
Breadth on do. at midships	20.4		20.2	
Depth of hold do.	12.5		13.0	
Length of engine space	35.8		34,2	
Hull	272$\frac{34}{100}$		263[illegible]	
Contents of engine space	61$\frac{16}{100}$		79[illegible]	
Register	211$\frac{18}{100}$		184[illegible]	

Erin's Queen.—A pair of direct acting engines (half lever), attached to the propeller's shaft of 20 horse nominal power; diameter of cylinders,

21 inches × 2 feet length of stroke; diameter of screw, 7 feet × pitch, 9 feet, with two blades. One tubular boiler, length 9 feet; breadth at tubes 8 feet, ditto at furnaces 6 feet 6 inches; height of boiler 11 feet; steam-chest length 7 feet; breadth 7 feet, height 2 feet. Two furnaces length 6 feet 4 inches; breadth 2 feet 6 inches, depth 3 feet 2 inches; 112 tubes, diameter 3 inches × 6 feet, consumes $5\frac{1}{2}$ tons of coals every 24 hours, the engines and screw making 72 revolutions per minute. Steam pressure 8lbs; bunker's hold 36 tons of coals; draught of water (average) forward $9\frac{1}{2}$ feet, aft $11\frac{1}{2}$ feet. Average passage $4\frac{1}{2}$ days, distance about 690 miles. Crew consists of 16 persons, viz—11 on deck, 5 in the engine-room.

DESCRIPTION.

A full female figure head (the Queen), no galleries, square, sterned and clinker built vessel of iron, clipper bow, three masts, schooner rigged, standing bowsprit. Port of Belfast, Commander—Mr. Joseph Humphries.

Lady Seale.—A pair of half lever engines (beam at top) of 40-horse nominal power. Diameter of cylinders, 27 inches × 2 feet 3 inches length of stroke. Diameter of screw, 7 feet × 8 feet 6 inches pitch, with 2 blades. Gearing, for running light; spur-wheel, 64 teeth. Pinion, 22 teeth. Screw making 93 revolutions per minute. Slow gearing spur-wheel, 64 teeth. Pinion, 28 teeth. Pitch, 3 inches; breadth, $14\frac{1}{2}$ inches, screw making 73 revolutions per minute. Both wheels same pitch and breadth. Stroke of crank, 2 feet $8\frac{1}{2}$ inches. Running light engines make 44 revolutions, and with slow gearing 22 revolutions per minute. Steam pressure, 11 lbs. Vacuum, 27 inches. Consuming $6\frac{1}{2}$ cwt. per hour. The screw gearing is shifted by a clutch with a handle and two screws, and can be set at liberty when the vessel is under canvas. The quick gear makes the screw revolve 3 to 1, and the slow gear 2 to 1, of engines. One tubular boiler—length, 9 feet 3 inches; breadth, 9 feet; height, 9 feet 8 inches. Steam-chest—height, 6 feet. Three furnaces—length, 6 feet 9 inches; breadth, 2 feet 7 inches; height, 3 feet 5 inches. 202 tubes, diameter, $2\frac{3}{4}$ inches × 5 feet 6 inches long. In January last, the engineer caused the centre (vertically) row of tubes to be removed, 16 in number, leaving 186 tubes. The tubes could not be properly cleaned before, but they can now do so easily, and a man can get his arm down to saw off the scales, &c., with a hand-saw. Steams $1\frac{1}{2}$ lbs. more than formerly—that is, $9\frac{1}{2}$ lbs. to 11 lbs. now, and the same consumption of fuel, &c. The crew numbers 15, viz., 10 on deck and 5 in the engine room,

DESCRIPTION.

Bust female figure head common bow, square sterned and carvil-built vessel of timber, standing boltsprit, 3 masts, schooner-rigged, false quarter-galleries. Port of London. Commander, Mr. Thomas Silly.

DROGHEDA AND LIVERPOOL STEAM NAVIGATION COMPANY'S IRON STEAM-VESSEL, "LEINSTER LASS."

Built and fitted by Mr. R. Napier, Glasgow.

	Ft.	In.
Builder's measurement.		
Length of keel and fore rake	200	0
Breadth of beam	27	0
Ditto, including paddle-cases	46	3
Depth of hold	16	2
Length of engine space	59	9
Tonnage.	Tons.	
Hull	$718\frac{24}{94}$	
Contents of engine space	$234\frac{0}{94}$	
Register	$484\frac{24}{94}$	
New measurement.	Ft.	
Length on deck	200	3
Breadth on ditto, amidships	26	2
Depth of hold ditto	15	9
Length of break-deck	32	0
Breadth of ditto	27	2
Depth of ditto	2	8
Length of engine space	59	8
Tonnage.	Tons.	
Hull	$670\frac{22}{100}$	
Break deck	$26\frac{31}{100}$	
Total	$696\frac{43}{100}$	
Contents of engine space	$269\frac{65}{100}$	
Register	$426\frac{88}{100}$	

A pair of side lever engines of 372 horse nominal power; diameter of cylinders, $70\frac{1}{2}$ inches × 5 feet 6 inches stroke; diameter of paddle-wheels extreme, 26 feet 6 inches; ditto, effective, 25 feet 10 inches; floats, 7 feet 10 inches × 2 feet 3 inches; three sets of 20 arms and floats, &c. Three tubular boilers, length 18 feet, breadth 8 feet 6 inches; height (including steam chest), 17 feet; breadth of the two steam chests, together, 8 feet; nine furnaces, length 8 feet, breadth 2 feet 1 inch; dry bottoms; 120 tubes, 40 in each boiler, diameter, 6 inches; the bunkers are amidships behind the engines and boilers, and are 6 feet in the length of the vessel, and all the depth and width, having a passage at the middle, 4 feet broad and 6 feet high. The engines have malleable iron framing, light but strong. Steam pressure, 8 lbs. per square inch; average speed, 19 revolutions per minute, consuming 30 cwt, of coal per hour. The bunkers hold 60 tons.

Frames of hull, are $3\frac{3}{4} \times 3 \times \frac{1}{2}$, and 1 foot 6 inches apart. Crew 27 in number, viz., 14 in the captain's department, 4 in the steward's, and 9 in the engine-room.

Description.

A full female figure head, false quarter galleries, square-sterned and clinker-built vessel, clipper bow, standing bowsprit, 3 masts, schooner rigged; Port of Drogheda; Commander, Mr. Edward Toker.

SHIP-BUILDING.

(FROM OUR OWN CORRESPONDENT.)

LONDON.—The *Titania*, of which we gave the dimensions last month, was launched from Messrs. Robinson's and Russell's yard, on 27th ult., at about 3 p.m. The bottle of wine was broken very skilfully by Mrs. Robinson, and the *Titania* obeyed the signal with a promptitude which augurs well for her future success. Through the courtesy of the firm we had the pleasure of inspecting the vessel, which possesses peculiar interest, from the fact of her being built as a yacht for a gentleman, of whom the engineering profession has good reason to be proud—Robert Stephenson, Esq., M.P. Contrary to old-fashioned notions, she was launched with her masts in and rigged. Mr. Stephenson himself was unavoidably absent, but his place was worthily filled by Mr. Bidder. Mr. Russell, in his usual felicitous manner, returned thanks on the health of the firm being drank, and paid a well-deserved compliment to the gentlemen who had contributed their assistance in the various departments, connected with the equipment and decoration of the vessel.

LIVERPOOL, MARCH, 1850.—Messrs. W. B. Jones and Co., Brunswick-dock, have upon the stocks a large timber ship, to class 12 years, to have a poop and top-gallant forecastle, all in frame, and commenced planking.

	Ft.	in.
Length of keel and fore rake	138	7
Breadth of beam	31	10
Depth of hold	21	6
Tonnage, old	$614\frac{44}{94}$ tons.	
Tonnage, new	abt. 800 „	

Owned by Messrs. Henry Moore and Co., of this town, and to be employed in the East India trade.

On January 2, Messrs. W. B. Jones and Co. launched from their building-yard a beautiful 13 years timber-built brig, named the *Fanny Chapman*, for the China coasting trade, and owned in Liverpool. The following are a few of the principal dimensions :—

	Ft.	in.
Length of keel and fore rake	96	$7\frac{3}{4}$
Breadth of beam	23	$4\frac{1}{2}$
Depth of hold	14	$10\frac{1}{2}$
Tonnage, old	$239\frac{33}{94}$ tons.	
	Ft.	
Length on deck	94.8	
Breadth on ditto amidships	21.2	
Depth of hold ditto	14.8	

Tonnage ... ...   230 tons.

Messrs. William Rennie, Johnson, and Co., Brunswick-dock, have upon stocks, and in frame, a 10 years A 1 clipper brig of timber, to be employed in the South American trade, and owned by Messrs. J. Wilson, Machatchan, and Co., and Captain Silk, all of Liverpool. The following are the dimensions, &c. :—

	Ft.	in.
Length of keel and fore rake	106	0
Breadth of beam	21	6
Depth of hold	16	0
Tonnage	233½ tons.	

Messrs. Cato, Miller, and Co., Brunswick-dock, have upon the stocks a large 13 years A 1 ship, for the East India trade, and owned by Messrs. Charles Moore and Co., of this town, all in frame and partly planked and of the following dimensions :—

	Ft.	in.
Length of keel and fore rake	155	0
Breadth of beam	31	0
Depth of hold	21	0
Tonnage	701½ tons.	

Also, a 13 years A 1 Barque, (timber,) on the stocks, partly planked, for the East India or American trade, owned by Messrs. Pryde and Jones, of this town. The following are the principal dimensions :—

	Ft.	in.
Length of keel and fore rake	130	0
Breadth of beam	26	6
Depth of hold	19	0
Tonnage	411½ tons	

Messrs. T. and R. Clarke, jun., Queen's-dock, have in frame a large timber ship, to have a poop and top gallant forecastle, and to class 14 years A 1, at Lloyd's, for the East India trade, and to be all copper fastened.

	Ft.	in.
Length of keel and fore rake	150	0
Breadth of beam	33	9
Depth of hold	22	0
Tonnage	798½ tons	
Ditto by the new measurement, about ...	1000 tons.	

Mr. Joseph Steele, jun., Queen's-dock, has upon the stocks a large timber ship, to class 12 years, A 1, at Lloyd's, to be flush on deck, and of the following dimensions.

	Ft.	in.
Length of keel and fore rake	144	0
Breadth of beam	30	0
Depth of hold	21	6
Tonnage	603½ tons.	

Owned by Messrs. Joseph Steele and Son, Liverpool, for the Calcutta trade.

Messrs. Thomas Roydon and Sons, Queen's-dock, have upon the stocks a 13 years schooner, (timber,) for the Mediterranean trade.

	Ft.	in.
Length of keel and fore rake	104	0
Breadth of beam	22	8
Depth of hold	14	10
Tonnage	249½ tons.	

They also have on the stocks a 13 years A 1, barque, for the Buenos Ayres or La Plata trade.

	Ft.	in.
Length of keel and fore rake	109	0
Breadth of beam	24	3
Depth of hold	15	4
Tonnage	296½ tons.	

Messrs. Peter Chaloner and Sons, Queen's-dock, have on the stocks, a sharp built 12 years' schooner for the fruit-trade (Mediterranean); the dimensions are—

	Ft.	in.
Length of keel and fore rake	76	10½
Breadth of beam	20	2½
Depth of hold	11	2

Tonnage ... ...   146½ tons.

They have also a 13 years' ship for the Calcutta trade.

	Ft.	in.
Length of keel and fore rake	142	6
Breadth of beam	31	8
Depth of hold	21	0
Tonnage	669½ tons	

Mr. William Jackson, Herculaneum-dock, has no new vessels upon the stocks, but is rebuilding a barque and a brig ; and last year he lengthened and raised upon the steamer *Hero*, and made her into a beautiful ship, having a clipper bow, and is a handsome looking vessel, and promises to sail and carry well.

Messrs. Thomas Vernon and Son, Brunswick-dock, have on the stocks a small iron vessel, for California (to ply upon a river there), ready for launching, and of the following dimensions, viz. :—

	Ft.	in.
Length of keel and fore rake	30	0
Breadth of beam	9	0
Depth of hold...	4	0
Tonnage	11½ tons	

This is the only iron vessel upon the stocks here, but they are making several iron houses, stores, and other buildings for California ; likewise making a tubular boiler for the screw steamer *Tintern*, and fitting her out for California.

March 4th:—There was launched a beautiful iron screw steam-vessel from the building-yard of Messrs. John Reid and Co, named the *Marie*, for a Prussian Company, and to trade between Leith and Wolgast, &c.

New Measurement		Ft.
Length on deck	... ...	143.5
Breadth on ditto at midships	... ...	23.7
Depth of hold	... ...	14.4
Length of engine space	... ...	27.2
Breadth of ditto	... ...	24.3
Depth of do.	... ...	15.7
Length of shaft space	... ...	41.1
Breadth of do.	... ...	5.0
Depth of do.	... ...	5.0
Tonnage.		Tons.
Hull ...	... ...	356½
Engine space ...	112 &c.	
Shaft space ...	1½	113½
Register ...	... ...	245½

A pair of direct acting engines (inverted cylinder), by Messrs. James and George Thomson, Clyde Bank Foundry, Finieston, Glasgow, of 80 horse power: Screw, ten feet diameter, with two blades: Tubular boiler.

A full female figure head, false galleries, square sterned and clinker built vessel, standing bowsprit, three masts, schooner rigged, flush deck, clipper bow, port of Woolgast.

February 28th, there was launched from the building-yard of Messrs. Tod and M'Gregor, at Meadowside, a splendid iron screw steam-vessel, named the *City of Glasgow*, for the Glasgow and New York trade. The vessel is advertised to sail in April, and to be commanded by Mr. C. B. Mathews (late of the *Great Western*). The following are the principal dimensions:—

New measurement.		Ft.	in.
Length on deck	... ...	227	0
Breadth on ditto amidships	... ...	33	7
Depth of hold ...	... ...	24	0
Length of shaft-space	... ...	60	5
Breadth of ditto	... ...	5	4
Depth of ditto ...	... ...	6	5
Length of engine space ...	... ...	87	1
Tonnage.		Tons.	
Hull...	... ...	1609½	
Shaft-space	... ...	22½	
Engine-space...	... ...	499½	

Engine and shaft-space	522$\frac{10}{100}$
Register	1087$\frac{33}{100}$

To be propelled by a pair of beam engines (beam at top) of 380-horse nominal power. Diameter of cylinders, 66 inches × 5 feet stroke, having spur-wheel and gearing. The screw is on a new principle of Messrs. Tod and M'Gregor's, and is 13 feet diameter × 18 feet pitch. We have expressed our opinion so often on the subject of screw engines, that it is enough at present to say that toothed gearing and beam engines do not come up to our standard of engineering excellence.

Bust female figure head, false quarter galleries, square-sterned and clinker-built vessel, three decks, all flush, three masts, barque-rigged, standing bowsprit, common bow. Port of Glasgow.

BELFAST.—Messrs. Thompsons and Kirwan have upon the stocks a timber vessel (barque), to class 9 years, A 1, at Lloyd's, to be flush on deck, all in frame, and partly planked, and of the following dimensions:—

	Ft.	in.
Length aloft	104	0
Length of keel and fore rake	103	0
Length of keel for tonnage	88	0
Breadth of beam, extreme	25	0
Ditto, ditto, moulded	23	0
Depth of hold amidships	16	0
Tonnage	284$\frac{14}{94}$ tons.	

Rake of stem, forward, 10 feet; ditto of stern post, aft, 1 foot.

Messrs. Thompsons and Kirwan have just launched a small timber vessel, to be used for carrying linen, &c., on the Lagan Canal, for the use of the Print-Fields Works, and of the following dimensions:—

	Ft.	in.
Length aloft	31	0
Length of keel	29	0
Breadth of beam	10	0
Depth, total	2	8
Tonnage	19$\frac{21}{94}$ tons.	

Messrs. Alexander M'Laine and Sons have upon the stocks, and ready for launching, a large timber schooner.

Messrs. Charles Connell and Sons have on the stocks a clipper schooner of timber, to be flush upon deck, and to class 8 years, A 1 at Lloyd's, all in frame, partly planked, and of the following dimensions:—

	Ft.	in.
Length of keel and fore rake	64	0
Breadth of beam	19	0
Depth of hold	10	0
Tonnage	102$\frac{??}{94}$ tons.	

P. B.

BELFAST, March, 1850.—Steamer *Sea Nymph*, lengthening 15 feet, making her 195 feet long, 28 feet 4 inches broad, and 16 feet deep, and 763$\frac{81}{94}$ tons.

ROYAL STEAM NAVY.

PROMOTIONS.

First-Class Chief Engineer.—JOHN WARD, to the *Blenheim*, at Portsmouth, for service in the steam-squadron in ordinary.

Assistant Engineer.—JAMES MAGNALL, to the *Princess Alice*, Dover steam-packet.

WOOLWICH.—The *Magicienne*, steam-sloop, with engines by Messrs. Penn and Son, was tried at the new measured mile, below Gravesend, on 25th February, under the charge of Lieut. Robertson. She is 214 feet length over all, 28 feet 8 inches beam, and 1,468 tons. Draught 13 feet 7 inches forward, 13 feet 9 inches aft, there being on board coals, anchors, chain cables, boats, and water tanks, &c.—a weight of 456 tons 6 cwt, exclusive of the machinery, which altogether, including engines, boilers, coal bunkers, and paddle-wheels, weighs 272 tons 15 cwt., making a total of 729 tons. The engines are oscillating, with wrought iron entablatures, and are, we believe, one of the six pairs making for government, all of the same design, and from templates, so that, in case of accidents, any of the parts of one of the pairs can be readily replaced. The cylinders are 72 inches diameter, and 7 feet stroke. Paddle-wheels 28 feet diameter, with disengaging gear. The top of the boilers is 3 feet under the load water line and she has two telescopic funnels. The bunkers are constructed over the boilers, at a distance of 4 feet, and hold 400 tons of coals. The average speed, at 21 revolutions, was 11.01 knots per hour. Steam pressure 14 lbs. Indicated horse power, 1,282.

PORTSMOUTH.—The *Basilisk* was tried on the 25th February, after repairs to the engines, and attained a speed of nearly 10¾ knots. She had all her heavy weights on board, and drew 15 feet 10 inches water.

STEAM NAVIGATION.

GENERAL SCREW STEAM SHIPPING COMPANY.—A general meeting of this Company was held on Wednesday last, when a dividend of five per cent. was recommended. The directors stated that an arrangement had been made with the Great Northern Railway Company of France, for the establishment of a line of screw steamers between London and Dunkirk, which has been carried out with great success. The working account from July to December showed that the receipts for that period amounted to £26,298 12s. 4d., and the disbursements to £21,904 6s. 4d., leaving a surplus on the half year of £4,394 6s.

MAIL COMMUNICATION BETWEEN ENGLAND AND IRELAND.—The Board of Admiralty have entered into a contract with the City of Dublin Steam Packet Company, for the the conveyance of the mails between the ports of Kingstown and Holyhead. The arrangements for the future hours of dispatch are not yet notified. In consequence of this unexpected decision of their Lordships, it is manifest that the Chester and Holyhead Company have no other course but to succumb; for, after their spirited but profitless struggle with the Board, it is not to be expected they could much longer play the losing game. They have, however, been the first to establish a 12-hour communication between the two capitals, and their new rivals to be successful cannot well make a retrograde movement. Leaving Dublin at the reasonable hour of half-past 8 in the morning, and reaching London before supper-time on the same night, is too obvious a luxury to be lightly foregone. The City of Dublin Company are to receive £25,000 per annum for the service, and they have given Messrs. Miller and Ravenhill orders to build two new boats.

NEW YORK.—A large steamer, intended for the Hudson river, has just been launched in New York. She is 350 feet long, and is to be fitted with a rotary engine, having a cylinder 16 feet diameter; the wheels are attached direct, and are 40 feet in diameter. This vessel is owned by Messrs. Thompson, and Hicks, of that city, who are determined that no expense shall be wanting to perfect her machinery, which is being constructed at the West Point Foundry, which is a sufficient guarantee that it will be well executed. We hope they will obtain the success they deserve, although, from the repeated failures that have been made, the case appears a bad one.—*Franklin Journal.*

THE STEAM-SHIP "PHILADELPHIA."—This fine steamer having recently sailed on her first trip to Havana, I send you the following particulars relating to her construction and performance. She is 200 feet long on deck 33 feet wide, and 18 feet 3 inches deep, and her hull has been built in the best manner by Messrs. Vaughan & Lynn, from the model furnished by Mr. Thompson, President of the Steam Navigation Company, and she has been much admired for her beauty, as well as for the light draft of water obtained.

Her machinery was began by Messrs. Merrick & Towne, and finished by their successors, Merrick & Son. It consists of two side lever marine engines, with cylinders of 56 inches diameter and 6 feet 9 inches stroke. Water wheels, 27 feet diameter; paddles, 8 feet 6 inches long, and 30 in. deep, and with 200 tons of coals on board they dip under 18 inches; without coal they have but 30 inches dip. Each wheel contains 24 paddles, and the whole 30 inches is placed on one side of the arm, not split, as is usually done. The boilers, two in number, are 26 feet 10 inches long, 12 feet 6 inches wide, and 8 feet 8 inches high, having 4 furnaces each, with grates 7 feet long. Anthracite coal, with natural draft, is used, and found to generate an ample supply of steam. On her trial, the engines made as high as 22 revolutions, and gave an average of 19 with 13 inches of steam, cutting off at half-stroke. The engines are fitted with Sickle's adjustable cut-off, which gave much satisfaction.

On the trip to Charleston, she made the run under steam, to Cape Hatteras, in 27 hours, while from there to Charleston Bar, she was 51 hours, caused by a severe gale of wind ahead, the severity of which may be judged when, during its continuance, a speed of 4 miles per hour was the most that could be obtained, carrying 16 inches of steam and working full stroke. The "Southerner," bound from Charleston to New York, laid by 24 hours behind her time, although the wind would have been with her. The "Philadelphia" is the first side wheel sea steamer built at this port, and her builders may well be proud of their success; she will give them crédit wherever she may go. If our merchants had a portion of that enterprise which distinguishes our sister city, New York, the time would soon come when we would have regular lines to Charleston, Havana, New Orleans, Liverpool, and Havre. Until they attempt to divert the stream, they must be satisfied with such trade as may happen to fall to their share. —*Franklin Journal.*   B.

ANALYSIS OF BOOKS.

Ince's Outlines of English History, p.p., 108.

Ince's Outlines of General Knowledge, p.p., 108.—London 1850, GILBERT.

The significant words "Forty-ninth thousand," on the former, and "Twelfth thousand," on the latter, of those little works speak better than any criticism for their merit. They both contain an immense amount of information, condensed both in style and type. The "History" deserves a place in the artizans' bookshelf. The "General Knowledge" will serve to tempt the young reader to make a better acquaintance with the paths of science.

Rudimentary Dictionary of Terms used in Civil and Naval Architecture, Building, Ecclesiastical and Early Art, Civil and Mechanical Engineering, Fine Art, Mining and Surveying. Part 3. London; J. WEALE.

As far as we are able to judge from a single part of the dictionary, too much has been attempted, and the result is that some of the branches have suffered. The student who looks for the word "Spanner" in vain, will be apt to imagine that "Spiceries and pepper boxes" ought not to have had the preference of the compiler. Nevertheless there is a large amount of information in the work not otherwise readily obtainable, which will cause it to be purchased and read by many.

Hints to all about to Rent, Buy, or Build House Property, by FRANCIS GROSE, Architect, p.p., 104; STARLING.

An amusing as well as a useful little work. The horrors of living in a "cheap house are well depicted, and the radically bad principle of building leases vigorously attacekd. If small capitalists who wish to find a secure investment for their money, ware to employ respectable builders, and "give a fair price," they would possess a species of property, perhaps, less liable to sudden fluctuation or loss than even the public funds, with at the same time, a good interest for their money. The bait of cheapness, and a large percentage often induces them to purchase some batch of houses, "built to sell," which they find, when too late, to be a constant source of annoyance and loss.

The author goes through the various details of a house, and gives hints and advice upon the merits of the various ordinary plans and materials, a knowledge of which cannot but fail to be useful even to those who content themselves with merely renting without purchasing their domiciles.

RAILWAYS.

THE BRITANNIA BRIDGE.—The report of Mr. Stephenson, the engineer-in-chief of the Chester and Holyhead Railway, states that on the 5th instant an uninterrupted communication between Chester and Holyhead was established, by the completion of one line of tubes of the Britannia bridge, and that the last operation of uniting the tubes of the different spans, so as to form one continuous line on beams, by which he calculated upon giving to the structure great additional strength, has been eminently successful, and has fully realised his anticipations. The progressive development of the results of the operation is thus described in the report:—

" When the tubes of the respective spans had been placed in their proper positions, they each, of course, had an amount of deflection due to their then condition, as simple isolated tabular beams, similar to the Conwaybridge, where one span alone exists. In this state of things, the north end of the Anglesea short tube was elevated 15 inches, and a complete junction effected between this tube and the adjacent one; the elevated end was then gradually lowered to its former level, by which operation the upper parts of both tubes being effectually brought into a state of tension; thus, instead of each tube being isolated, they formed one continuous tube, reaching over both spans, one of 230 ft, and the other 460 ft. mutually assisting each other. The extent of this mutual support was accurately and strikingly marked by the central deflection of the larger tube over the larger span, being diminished by 1 inch and 9-10ths. The next step was to unite the two larger tubes together in the Britannia Tower. This was accomplished by first elevating the south end of the Carnarvon large tube 31 inches, in which position the two large tubes were united. When the raised end was lowered to its final level the central deflection of the Anglesea large tube was further diminished by 1 inch and 6-10ths, making a total diminution in the original deflection, when it was an isolated beam of 3½ inches, giving it an additional strength far exceeding the greatest load that it will practically ever be exposed to. The last operation, of lowering the south-end of the Carnarvon large tube, it was to be expected, would produce a corresponding effect upon itself; and, in accordance with our expectations, the deflection was diminished by 2 inches and 4-10ths. It now only remained to complete the junction between the short tube on the Carnarvon side of the Menai Straits and the adjoining large tube. This was done while the south end was elevated 15 inches, being the same amount of elevation as was adopted with the north end of the Anglesea short tube, and the lowering of it was attended with similar results on the adjoining large tube, the deflection being further reduced 1 inch and 3-10ths, making the total reduction of the deflection from that which it possessed when acting as an isolated beam of fully 3 inches and 7-10ths. In addition, however, to this satisfactory result, another was developed during the process of the last lowering, for whilst the deflection of the Carnarvon large tube was gradually lessening, that of the Anglesea large tube was very slightly increased, being precisely what was predicted, and which demonstrated the complete continuity of the now single tube. During the progress of the above operations admeasurements were taken of the elongation of those parts of the top brought into a state of tension, from which the important fact is established, that the strain upon the bottom of the tube is reduced from 5 tons 3 cwt. to 3 tons per square inch, or, in short, that the strength of the bridge is increased in this ratio. Some attempts have been made to produce an impression on the public mind that although the Conway and Britannia bridges evince sufficient strength when first erected, the nature of the structure is such that they cannot continue permanently stable; and, knowing that some opinions of this kind have been hazarded by some in the scientific world, I think it necessary to state that, recently, minute observations have been made in the Conway tubes, which proved beyond question that no change whatever has taken place in their form or deflection, although used daily since May, 1848; and I may add that in the Britannia-bridge there is no strain so great as that to which the chains of Telford's bridge, over the same arm of the sea, have been continually exposed since its erection. This appears to me to be conclusive testimony of the sufficiency of the strength and permanency of these works."

THE EMIGRATION MOVEMENT.

Another amongst the many instances of new applications of the assurance principle is proposed to be carried out, on an extensive scale, by an association called the Colonization Assurance Company. The company, whose bill of incorporation is now before Parliament, will purchase lands in the various colonies and let them on lease in small or large lots to emigrant upon a payment of a yearly rent, coupled with an annual premium, which will entitle them to bequeath the land as freeholds to their heirs. In this way, by a comparatively small yearly outlay, the settler may enter upon his task of cultivation with the same feeling that his efforts are exercised for the permanent benefit of himself and his family, as if he had acquired by the immediate expenditure of capital the actual title to the soil, while it will likewise be in his power, at any period of subsequent prosperity, to become the owner at once, by purchasing his policy at a direct price, calculated according to the usual system of redemption tables. It is also proposed to adopt a plan of terminable premiums, by which, at the end of 10 or 15, or any other period of years, the property may pass over to the assurer or to his representatives in case he should have died before the lapse of the specified term. The success of the entire scheme will depend upon the spirit in which it may be worked out, but it possesses inherent features that might be made to yield great advantages. If the lands are in the first instance judiciously and economically purchased by the company, and the subsequent charge to the tenant is only such as would constitute a fair rate of interest for the outlay and risk incurred, there will be reason to hope good results for all parties; but if, as the prospectus would seem to indicate it is proposed to any extent to take lands at 1*l*. per acre, and to charge the colonists accordingly, it will be out of the question that competition can on such terms be maintained with the United States, where, by the last advices, a measure was actually before Congress to give a free grant of 160 acres to any immigrant who would undertake to cultivate them.

LAKE IN CENTRAL AFRICA. — The Cape papers of the 1st of January refer to the discovery of a great lake in the interior of South Africa during a journey of exploration by two gentlemen named Murry and Oswell. It is situated in longitude 24° east and latitude 19° south, and its limits appear to have been undiscernible. According to the natives, however, it takes twenty-five days to travel round it. The vegetation on its banks is tropical, and palms are abundant, but it contains no crocodiles, alligators, or hippopotami. It is approached by a river, which for some distance is of small size, and which, as it approaches the lake, becomes as large as the Clyde. The lake itself has no islands in it, but it is said that there are many at the mouth of the river, and that these are densely populated by a race entirely different from those near the borders of the lake. Pelicans are numerous, as also fish, some of which resemble perch and carp, and weigh between 40lbs. and 56lbs. There are likewise a great number of elephants, although of a much smaller description than those nearer the colony. The natives, whose language was unlike any known dialect spoken by the other tribes in South Africa, appeared to be of an inferior nature, and to be much afflicted with pulmonary disease.

PATENT NOVELTIES.

M. LOUIS LEMAITRE proposes to make the ferrules for boiler tubes by machinery. The strip of iron is rolled taper, and, having been cut into pieces of the requisite length, they are bent round into the rough shape, and are finally welded by the action of a punch working into a die.

Mr. Arthur Dunn, of Worcester, proposes to stamp cakes of soap with the maker's name much deeper than is ordinarily practised, and to fill up the indentation with a different coloured soap, so that the marks will be legible until nearly the whole of the soap is consumed.

Mr. Robinson, of Huddersfield, proposes an improvement in making orchil and cudbear, by which much time and labour will be saved. The ordinary plan is to mix them into a paste with ammonia, and then to dry them by frequent turning. On the improved system, the paste is squeezed through a cylinder, the bottom of which is perforated with holes, and the paste issues in filaments, which expose a large drying surface to the air. The same process has been long used for the manufacture of vermicelli, with the addition of fanners to cool and dry the material still more rapidly.

AMERICAN PATENTS.

Elijah Slack, of Orchard-street, Renfrew. N. B., gun manufacturer, *for improvements in the preparation of materials to be employed in the manufacture of textile fabrics.* June 2nd, 1849.

The patentee proposes to treat hemp, flax, and other fibrous materials, by soaking them in hot water, and then boiling them in an alkaline solution. The material is then to be bleached with chloride of lime, and then to be boiled in a solution of soapy matter. Finally, it is to be washed clean, and is then ready for manufacture.

James Mulbury, of Parkersburgh, in Chester, county of Pennsylvania, United States, machinist, *for certain improvements in the slide valves of steam engines.* July 4th, 1849.

The patentee proposes to obviate the wear of slide valve faces, by bevilling the corners of the ports and valve faces, alleging that the particles of metal, abraded by the steam, are the cause of the faces wearing in grooves.

NOVELTIES.

THE IRON TRADE IN FRANCE.—A letter dated Liege, March 11, says —Trade is slightly reviving here, though prices are still very low, large contracts of pig-iron being made at 7 fr. 50 c. the 100 kils., about £3 per ton. At Seraing and at Selenin they are putting each one new furnace in blast, and at Ougrée two. Ougrée has contracts with different iron-work in North Germany, Eschweeler, Ruhrort, &c., by which they have to furnish 20,030 tons of pig before the expiration of 1850. There are now in the Liege coal basin 11 out of 20 furnaces in blast, last year there were but eight. Seraing has refused an offer for the construction of a large iron steam-frigate for Egypt, of 1000-horse-power, and which was to cost £100,000., 2,500,000 fr. French money.

NEW VICTORIA DOCKS.—On the 19th instant, pursuant to adjournment, Mr. Rendel, on behalf of the Admiralty, attended at the King's Arm Hotel, Palace-yard, when the promoters of the bill for constructing these docks in the Essex Marshes, opposite Woolwich, with surveys, plans and estimates, appeared for examination. The bill was unopposed, and Mr. Parsons, of the firm of Burchell and Parsons, Parliament-street, and Mr. Bidder, engineer, Great George-street, appeared for the company. The latter was examined at great length, and explained all the plans and drawings; the cost of the docks was estimated at £400,000, and with warehouses, £1,500,000. Mr. Parsons said the docks would be unequalled in extent, and would be a great public benefit, preventing the colliers and foreign steamers from crowding the Pool, and obstructing the navigation as they now did; and it was anticipated that the adoption of free-trade principles would cause a vast increase in the number of foreign vessels. Mr. Elmes, architect, and Capt. C. Rowland, harbour-master, both bore testimony to the requirement of the docks; that they would not interfere with the economy of the tide, but would greatly relieve the river. They considered that, if there were double the number of docks, they would give barely sufficient accommodation. Mr. Rendel said, he would shortly make his report, and render it as brief as possible.

FIRE BRICKS FOR FURNACES.—The *Morning Chronicle* Commissioner in his letter from Merthyr Tydvil, gives an account of a curious branch of industry carried on there—namely, the making of fire bricks for lining the furnaces, and, indeed, for all other purposes where a material is required capable of withstanding intense and long continued heat. There are two substances, found in abundance in the coal and iron districts, which have the property of resisting in a high degree the action of fire; the one is termed "fire clay," a stratum of which is often overlaid by coal—the other is the "farewell rock," a species of stone composed of quartz, blended together by a siliceous cement. Upon this rock repose the whole of the coal and iron-stone "measures." The bricks are used for lining the interior of the blast furnaces down to "the hearth," or receptacle of the fluid iron, which is always constructed of the stone. Experiments on bricks made of this fire clay have satisfactorily shown that its capacity of resisting heat is fully equal to that of the better known, and more generally used, fire-bricks of Stourbridge. The manufacture of fire-bricks at these works is exclusively carried on by women, and a more humiliating and ungenial occupation for the sex is hardly to be found through the entire range of our industrial economy.

Renfrew Patent Slip.—The great want of proper attention which shipowners and others have of late years experienced in getting their vessel repaired, has now, we are glad to say been quite removed. Messrs. James Henderson and Sons' slip at Renfrew offers facilities for every sort of repair, and can accommodate at the same time three of the largest sailing vessels which come up the Clyde, the total length of rails is 600 feet. Breadth of rails 25 feet. Breadth between breast walls 55 feet. The machinery is constructed with all the recent improvements with a condensing engine of 30-horse power, and calculated to take up a vessel of 1000 tons.

LIST OF ENGLISH PATENTS,

FROM JANUARY 19 TO FEBRUARY 28, INCLUSIVE.

John Stephen Woolrich, of Wednesbury, in the County of Stafford, Chemist, John James Russell, of Handsworth, in the same county, and Thomas Henry Russell, of Wednesbury aforesaid, patent tube manufacturers, for improvements in obtaining cadmium and other metals and products from ores or matters containing them. February 21.

Alfred Vincent Newton, of Chancery-lane, in the county of Middlesex, mechanical draughtsman, for improvements in separating and assorting solid materials or substances of different specific gravities. February 21.—(Communication.)

John Slack, of Manchester, in the county of Lancaster, manager, for certain improvements in the manufacture of textile goods or fabrics, and in certain machinery or apparatus connected therewith. January 21.

Alexander Hediard, of Paris, in the Republic of France, gentlemen, for certain improvements in propelling. February 21.

George Holworthy Palmer, of Westbourne-villas, Harrow-road, in the county of Middlesex, civil engineer, and Joshua Horton, of the Aetna steam engine boiler and gasometer manufactory, Smethwick, near Birmingham, in the county of Stafford, for improvements in the arrangement and construction of gas-holders. Feb. 21.

William Cormack, of King-street, Dunstan-road, Haggerstone, in the county of Middlesex, chemist, for improvements in purifying gas; also applicable in obtaining or separating certain products or materials from gas-water, and other similar fluids. Feb. 21.

William Mayo, of the firm of Mayo and Warmington, Silver-street, Wood-street, Cheapside, manufacturers of mineral aerated waters, for improvements in connecting tubes and pipes, and other surfaces of glass and earthenware, and in connecting other matters with glass and earthenware.

John Scoffern, of Essex-street, in the county of Middlesex, M.B., for improvements in the manufacture and refining of sugar, and in the treatment and use of matters obtained in such manufacture, and in the construction of valves used in such and other manufactures. February 21.

Charles Andrew, of Compstall-bridge, in the County of Chester, manufacturer, and Richard Markland, of the same place, manager, for certain improvements in the method of, and in the machinery or apparatus for, preparing warps for weaving. February 21.

James Hall, of Geecross, near Stockport, in the County of Chester, machine-maker, for certain improvements in looms for weaving. February 28.

Brereton Todd, of the Bank, Falmouth, gentleman, for improvements in the manufacture of arsenic, sulphuric acid, and the oxide of antimony, from copper and other ores, in which they are contained, and also the oxide of zinc. February 27.

George Gwynne, Esq., of Sussex-square, in the County of Middlesex, for improvements in the manufacture of sugar. February 27.

Matthew Cochran, of High-street, Paisley, in the County of Renfrew, N.B., manufacturer, for improvements in machinery for the production and ornamenting of fabrics and tissues generally, parts of which are applicable to the regulation of other machinery, and to purposes of a similar nature. February 27.

Julius Jeffreys, of Bucklersbury, in the City of London, gentleman, for improvements in preventing or removing affections of the chest. February 28.

George Tosco Peppe, of Great Marylebone-street, in the County of Middlesex, civil engineer, for improvements in time-keepers. February 28.

George William Lenox, of Billiter-square, in the City of London, chain cable manufacturer, and William Roberts, foreman to Messrs. Brown, Lenox, and Co., of Millwall, for improvements in working windlasses and other barrels. February 28.

LIST OF PATENTS THAT HAVE PASSED THE GREAT SEAL OF SCOTLAND,

FROM THE 21ST. DAY OF DECEMBER, 1849, TO THE 22ND DAY OF FEBRUARY, 1850, INCLUSIVE.

James Usher, of Edinburgh, gentleman, for improvements in machinery for tilling lands. December 24.

John Stoughton Christie, Esq., of Craven-street, Strand, in the County of Middlesex; for an improved construction of wrought iron wheels and machinery for effecting the same. December 24. Four months.—(Communication).

Richard Hobson, M.D., of Leeds, in the County of York, for certain improvements in the manufacture of horse-shoes, and in apparatus for taking the measurement of horse-shoes or horses' hoofs. December 26.

William Ackroyd, of Birkenshaw Mills, near Leeds, in the County of York, manufacturer, for improvements in dressing and cleaning worsted, and worsted mixed with cotton and other fabrics, after they have been woven. December 31.—(Communication.)

John Barsham, of Kingston, in the County of Surrey, manufacturer, for improvements in separating the cocoa fibre from cocoanut husks. December 31. Four months.

John Christophers, of Heavitree, in the County of Devon, formerly merchant and shipowner, for improvements in naval architecture. December 31.

Alexander Brodie Cochrane, jun., and Archibald Slate, both of Dudley, in the County of Worcester, for improvements in the manufacture of iron pipes or tubes. December 31.

Joseph Burch, of Craig Works, near Macclesfield, engineer, for improvements in printing on cotton, woollen, silk, paper, and other fabrics and materials. December 31.

Wenceslas le Baron de Traux de Wardin, of Liege, in the province of Liege, in the kingdom of Belgium, for certain improvements in looms for weaving linen, woollen, and cotton cloths; and in machines for preparing the yarn for such cloths, before entering the loom; and in a machine for finishing grey and bleached linen cloths. January 3.

William Henry Wilding, of the New-road, in the County of Middlesex, gentleman, for certain improvements in engines and machinery for obtaining and applying motive power. January 4.

Charles Cowper, of Southampton-buildings, in the County of Middlesex, for improvements in machinery for raising and lowering weights and persons in mines; and in the arrangement and construction of steam engines employed to put in motion such machinery, part of which improvements are applicable to other useful purposes. January 4.—(Communication.)

Reuben Plant, of Holly Hall Colliery, near Dudley, in the County of Worcester, coal-master, for improvements in making wrought and bar iron. January 7.

Samuel Colt, of Trafalgar-square, in the County of Middlesex, gentleman, for improvements in fire-arms. January 7.

Thomas Lightfoot, of Broadoak, within Accrington, in the County of Lancaster, chemist, for improvements in printing and dying fabrics of cotton and of other fibrous materials. January 7.

Thomas Richardson, of the Town and County of Newcastle upon-Tyne, chemist, for improvements in the manufacture of Epsom and other magnesian salts; also alum and sulphate of ammonia. January 11.

Jerome Andre Drieu, of Manchester, machinist, for certain improvements in the manufacture of wearing apparel, and in the machinery or apparatus connected therewith. January 14.

Thomas Auchterlonie, of Glasgow, North Britain, manufacturer and calico printer, for improvements in the production of ornamental fabrics. January 14.

Andrew Barclay, of Kilmarnock, in the County of Ayr, North Britain, engineer, for improvements in the smelting of iron and other ores, and in the manufacture of working of iron and other metals, and in certain rotary engines and fans, and machinery or apparatus as connected therewith. January 14.

Peter Armand, le Comte de Fontainemoreau, of South-street, Finsbury, for improvements in spinning fibrous substances. January 15.—(Communication.)

Joe Sidebottom, of Pendlebury, in the County of Lancaster, manager, for improvements in steam engines. January 18.

William Edward Newton, of Chancery-lane, in the County of Middlesex, civil engineer for certain improvements in pumps, and in machinery or apparatus for working the same which latter improvements are also applicable for working other machinery. January 18.—(Communication.)

John George Barton, of Regent's-street, in the County of Middlesex, for certain improvements in printing and dyeing materials. January 21.—(Communication.)

Robert Wilson, of Low Moor Iron Works, in the County of York, engineer, for improvements in steam engine boilers, and methods of preventing accident in working the same. January 21. Four months.

J. C. Robertson, of Fleet-street, in the City of London, civil engineer, for improvements in machinery, apparatus, and processes for extracting, depurating, forming, drying, and evaporating substances. January 22.—(Communication.)

William Thomas Henley, of Clerkenwell, in the County of Middlesex, philosophical instrument maker, for certain improvements in telegraphic communication, and in apparatus connected therewith, part of which improvements may be also applicable to the moving of other machines and machinery. January 22.

Christopher Nickels, of York-road, Lambeth, in the County of Surrey, gentleman, for improvements in the manufacture of woollen and other fabrics. January 24.

Edward Riepe, of Finsbury-square, in the County of Middlesex, merchant, for improvements in the manufacture of steel. January 24.

Benjamin Thompson, of Newcastle-upon-Tyne; civil engineer, for improvements in the manufacture of iron. January 31.

Elijah Galloway, of Southampton-buildings, Chancery-lane, in the County of Middlesex civil engineer, for improvements in furnaces. February 1.

Thomas Marsden, of Salford, in the County of Lancaster, machine maker, for improvements in machinery for heckling, combing, or dressing flax, wool, and other fibrous substances. February 1.

Robert Fitzroy, of [illegible], Strand, Commander, Royal Navy, for improvements in steering apparatus. February 1.

Macgregor Laird, of Birkenhead, gentleman, for improvements in the construction of metallic ships or vessels, or in materials for coating the bottom of iron ships or vessels and in steering ships or vessels. February 6.

James Templeton, of Glasgow, in the Kingdom of Scotland, manufacturer, for certain improvements in manufacturing figured fabrics, principally designed for the production of carpeting. February 12.

William Henry Green, of Basinghall-street, in the City of London, gentleman, for improvements in the preparation of peat fuel, and in the mode of applying the products derived therefrom to the preservation of certain substances which are subject to decay. February 12.—(Communication.)

Joseph and James Deng, of Little Tower-street, in the City of London, philosophical instrument makers, and Richard Pattenden, of Nelson-square, in the County of Surrey, engineer, for improvements in instruments and machinery for steering ships, which is also applicable to vices and other instruments and machinery for obtaining power February 12.

William Mayo, of the firm of Mayo and Warmington, Silver-street, Wood-street, Cheapside, in the City of London, manufacturers of mineral aerated waters, for improvements in connecting tubes and pipes, and other surfaces of glass and earthenware, and of connecting other matters with glass and earthenware. February 13.

James M'Donald, of the City of Chester, coach maker, for certain improvements in the method of applying oil or grease to wheels and axles, and to machinery, and in connecting the springs of wheel carriages with the axles or axle boxes. February 13.

Henry Attwood, of Goodman's Fields, in the County of Middlesex, engineer, and John Renton, of Bromley, in the same County, engineer, for certain improvements in the manufacture of starch and other like articles of commerce from farinaceous and leguminous substances. February 14.

William Furness, of Lawton Street, Liverpool, builder, for improvements in machinery for cutting, tenoning, planeing, moulding, dovetailing, boring, mortising, tonguing, grooving, and sawing wood; also for sharpening and grinding tools or surfaces, and also in welding steel to cast iron. February 15.—(Communication.)

Sir John Mac Neil, Knight, of Dublin, and Thomas Barry, of Lyons, near Dublin, mechanic, for improvements in locomotive engines, and in the construction of railways. February 15.

Benjamin Goodfellow, of Hyde, in the County of Chester, engineer, for certain improvements in steam engines. February 21. Four months.

Matthew Cochran, of High Street, Paisley, in the County of Renfrew, North Britain, manufacturer, for improvements in machinery for the production and ornamenting of fabrics and tissues generally, parts of which improvements are applicable to the regulation of other machinery, and to purposes of a similar nature. February 21.

Louis Napoleon Le Gras, of Paris, in the Republic of France, civil engineer, for improvements in the separation and disinfection of fecal matters, in the manufacture of manure, and in the apparatus employed therein. February 21.

Ernest Gaston, of the Erechtheum Club, St. James', in the County of Middlesex, gentleman, for improvements in artificial fuel, and in machinery used for manufacturing the same. February 22. Four months.

THE ARTIZAN.

No. V.—Vol. VIII.—MAY 1st, 1850.

PHILOSOPHY OF ENGINEERING.

NOTES ON THE PHILOSOPHY OF ENGINEERING.

WATER ENGINEERING.

The hydraulic works of the ancients for supplying towns with water, and for performing many other purposes of utility or ostentation, show that they understood water engineering in a general practical way very well; and indeed their proficiency in this department of art would have been quite equal to that of the moderns, but for the investigations into the theory of hydraulics which have been made within the last century, and the important general laws which have been deduced therefrom. There is, perhaps, no department of practical science with which engineers are less conversant than with water engineering in its several important branches; and we propose, therefore, to lay before our readers a brief summary of the results obtained by the various experimentalists who have made this department of knowledge their study, and to add such practical rules and examples as will enable a ready solution to be found for most of the hydraulic questions which can occur in practice. The more important divisions of the subject are the following:—The motion of water in pipes; the motion of water in rivers, drains, and canals; the resistance of bodies moving in water; the operation of hydraulic machines; and the laws of the propagation of waves. Upon each of these subjects we shall have some remarks to offer.

The elementary laws of hydrostatics were laid down by Archimedes, in his work *De Insidentibus Humido*, about 250 years before the Christian era; and *Sextus Julius Frontinus*, inspector of the public fountains at Rome in the reign of Trajan, gives, in his Commentaries on the Aqueducts of Rome, a summary of the hydraulic knowledge of his time. He states, that the discharge of water from an orifice depends not merely on the size of the orifice, but also on the height of the head from which the water comes; but he does not appear to have been acquainted with the law according to which the efflux or velocity of the water varies. After Galileo, however, had discovered the uniform acceleration of falling bodies by gravity, and the laws which regulate the velocity of falling bodies began to be well understood, it occurred to Torricelli, who observed that the jet of water in a fountain ascended nearly as high as the original head, that the velocity of such a jet at any point must be just equal to the velocity which a heavy body would acquire in falling from the height of the jet to the point in question; and consequently that the velocity with which water issues from an orifice in a vessel of water will be as the square root of the height of the water above the orifice. This hypothesis, on being tested by experiment, was found to be correct; and after making a certain allowance for friction and the resistance of the atmosphere, the velocity of water issuing at all pressures was found to be proportional to the square root of the height or pressure, and consequently that the pressure exerted by water against an opposing body must be proportional to the square of the velocity of the water.

No sooner was the law discovered by Torricelli of the velocity of water issuing from an orifice being as the square root of the head completely established by experiment, than it was made the basis of a most erroneous theory of the motion of water in rivers by Guglielmini, inspector of the rivers and canals in the Milanese. According to this author, every particle in the perpendicular section of a river will be impelled with the same velocity as if it issued from an orifice of the same height from the surface, or as if it issued into air instead of issuing into water with nearly the same perpendicular head. By this hypothesis, the water running near the bottom of a river would flow with much greater velocity than the water near the surface; but the very contrary is the fact; and Guglielmini, finding his theory so ill accordant with experiment, instead of abandoning it, propounded another, of an equally inconsiderate character, to supplement the deficiencies of the first. According to this second theory, the reason why the water near the bottom of a river does not appear to have the most rapid flow is, that the irregularities of the bed give to the water transverse motions, so that the apparent velocity is not great, although the actual velocity through these sinuous courses is in reality very considerable. Unfortunately for the credit of this second hypothesis, it was about the time of its promulgation discovered by Mariotte, that a retardation similar to that observed near the bottoms and sides of rivers existed also when water issued through glass pipes, and which, being quite smooth inside, were incapable of imparting that sinuous motion to the rubbing particles which Guglielmini had assumed to be the cause of the retardation. Mariotte consequently attributed the retardation to friction, which is now ascertained to be the just explanation; nevertheless Guglielmini's hypothesis, as is sometimes the fate of pernicious fallacies, has been adopted by several succeeding writers, and has been set forth, with a large ostentation of mathematics, by Varignon, and been adopted by Gravesande, Mushenbroeck, and Belidor.

Mariotte, in his *Traité du Mouvement des Eaux*, published in 1686, gives the results of a great number of experiments made by him at Chantilly and Versailles. He supposes that the particles of water which run along the side of a pipe lose part of their velocity by friction, and that these retarded particles are rubbed upon in their turn by other contiguous particles moving at a greater velocity, which are retarded in their turn: in which way he considers the medium velocity of flowing water may be diminished by the friction of the exterior film. The accuracy of this view was subsequently established by Sir Isaac Newton, who made a number of experiments upon the friction of spheres revolving in water, with the view of controverting the system of celestial vortices propounded by Descartes; and by these experiments it was established, that the velocity of a particle of water moving in a

13

pipe, is an arithmetical mean between the velocities of the particles on each side of it. It was hence deduced by M. Pitot, in 1726, that the total diminution in the discharge of pipes arising from friction will be in the inverse ratio of their diameters. From the inadequate discharge of water through a hole in the bottom of a vessel, as compared with the area of the orifice multiplied by the square root of the height, Sir Isaac Newton was led to entertain doubts of the accuracy of the Torricellian law ; but he subsequently discovered, that the discrepancy arose from the diminished diameter of the jet at a short distance from the orifice, whereby the efficient size of the orifice was diminished ; and it was ascertained, that if the area of this contracted part were taken and multiplied by the square root of the height, the actual discharge would be obtained with great accuracy. This contraction of the efficient discharge was termed by Newton the *contracted vein ;* and in 1718 it was found, by the Marquis Poleni, that the contraction of the vein was diminished, and the discharge of a given orifice with a given head consequently increased, by causing the water to flow through a short pipe, instead of through a hole in a thin metal plate. This result equally took place, whether the water descended perpendicularly, or issued in a horizontal direction.

About this time Newton instituted some experiments to determine the time in which waves oscillate. It appeared to be quite clear, that if water were allowed to fall in the arc of a circle, it would oscillate, setting friction aside, with just the same velocity as any other heavy body pursuing the same path, and the rate of oscillation would be the same as that of a pendulum, with a weight of the configuration of the fluid. Newton proved that the time of oscillation in a U pipe would be the same as that of a pendulum of the length of half the oscillating column ; from whence it is demonstrable, that the undulations of waves are performed in the same time as a pendulum would oscillate if its length were equal to the pitch of the waves, or the distance from apex to apex. The force causing the undulation is the head of water measuring from the level of the hollow to the level of the crest of the wave ; and if we take half of the side of the wave, a pendulum of that length will perform an oscillation while the wave is sinking to its lowest point, and another oscillation while the wave is rising to its highest point, or two oscillations for one undulation.

Newton was followed in his hydraulic speculations by Daniel and John Bernouilli, Maclaurin, d'Alembert, Lagrange, and Euler ; but it does not appear that any substantial addition to our knowledge of the laws of fluids has been made by the investigations of these eminent mathematicians. The discrepancies between theoretical deduction and the actual results, as ascertained by experiment, were in most cases so great as to show that no dependence could be placed upon rules derived from mathematical analysis ; and indeed it daily became more obvious, from the amusing failures of the most eminent mathematicians in the resolution of simple practical problems, that sufficient data did not exist upon which a mathematical theory of hydraulics could be reared. Desaguliers, who had been employed to bring in water to the city of Edinburgh, found, after the execution of the work, that the quantity delivered was only *one-sixth* of the quantity he expected, and only *one-eleventh* of the quantity which Maclaurin expected would be delivered under the arrangements adopted. The frequent recurrence of such cases made it clear that further experiments were needed, and that it was only by a careful generalization of the results of such experiments, that practical rules deserving of any confidence could be obtained. Accordingly in 1764 a series of experiments was instituted by Professor Michelotti, of Turin, in which the discharge through pipes of different sizes and with different heads of water was accurately ascertained. The velocity of water in canals of a given declivity of bed was also investigated, and the whole of the results were published in a work termed *Sperienze Idrauliche*, in 1774.

The results obtained by Michelotti were confirmed by the experi-

ments of the Abbé Bossut, by whose researches the science of hydraulics was first brought into a practical form. By adapting mouth-pieces of different forms to the bottom of a glass reservoir, Bossut found that the particles of water at first descend vertically, but at a certain distance from the orifice they are deflected sideways, and the fluid vein consequently forms a truncated conoid within the vessel, like the contracted vein outside. The greatest base of this conoid is the orifice, and its height is equal to the radius of the orifice. Bossut ascertained also, that when water issues through a thin plate the actual discharge is to the theoretical as 8 to 5, from the contraction of the vein ; but when a tube a diameter or two long is applied, the discharge is increased from 5 to 7½. He found, too, that the contraction of the vein was increased with the height of the reservoir, and that although in cases of water striking a flat board obliquely, the impulse is as the square of the fluid's velocity multiplied by the square of the angle of incidence when the deviation from direct impact is small, yet that from about the angle of 45° downwards the law does not hold, and that the force of the impact becomes smaller than this proportion with greater degrees of obliquity than 45°.

Such was the state of hydraulic knowledge up to 1780, when De Buat, engineer to the king of France, commenced a series of investigations touching the laws of fluid motion, of so complete and practical a character, that all questions relating to the discharge of water by rivers and pipes can now be resolved with nearly the same exactitude and facility as the most ordinary questions of mechanics. De Buat lays it down as a fundamental law, that as the flow of water in a river is caused by gravity, and as gravity is a uniformly accelerating force, the velocity of water in a river would be uniformly accelerated but for the friction of the bed, and the viscidity of the water, which, at a certain velocity, balance the force of gravity. De Buat also, by his experiments, confirmed the observation of Pitot, that the friction of running water in a pipe or channel, is proportional to the amount of rubbing surface; or that the velocities of rivers of a given inclination are nearly as the square roots of their depths. De Buat, in 1786, published the results of his investigations, in a work in two volumes, called *Principes d'Hydraulique*, and this work is made the basis of the articles on Rivers, Water Works and the Resistance of Fluids, contributed to the *Encyclopedia Britannica*, by Professor Robison, and reprinted in his *System of Mechanical Philosophy*. These disquisitions, though disfigured by one or two weighty fallacies, are written with great ability, and constitute perhaps the best summary of hydraulic knowledge that we yet possess. Later writers have simplified some of De Buat's formulæ, but there is no reason to believe that the simplified formulæ give more accurate results, and nowhere are the doctrines of the science of hydraulics set forth with more force and felicity than in the writings of Professor Robison. In 1798, M. Venturi, Professor of Natural Philosophy at Modena, made a number of interesting experiments, illustrative of the lateral communication of motion in fluids, and of the amount of retardation of water in pipes consequent upon a succession of bulgings, instead of a uniform bore. Venturi found that if a stream of running water be directed into a stagnant pool, the whole of the water in the pool lying above the level of the bed of the running stream will be carried out by the current, and lakes and marshes may, consequently, be often drained sucessfully, by sending a stream of water through them.

In 1800, Coulomb investigated the resistance offered by water to oscillating discs. From his enquiries it appeared that the total resistance is made up of two distinct resistances, of which one varies simply as the velocity, and the other as the square of the velocity. He also ascertained that the amount of the resistance is not sensibly increased, either by an increased depth of immersion or by roughening the surface of the disc, and that the fluid particles do not slide so much upon the moving body as upon one another.

One of the most valuable works which have yet appeared illustrative of the laws of fluid motion, is Eytelwein's *Handbook of Mechanics and Hydraulics*, published in Berlin in 1801. Young and Tredgold, in their tracts on hydraulics, derive their facts and formulæ mainly from Eytelwein; and as the rules thus deduced have become interwoven with the practice of engineers in this country, we may here recapitulate the most important of them.

The quantity of water discharged by an orifice, supposing that there was no friction or contraction of the vein, being represented by 1, the quantity actually discharged by an orifice in a thin plate will be ·64 of this theoretical quantity; by the shortest tube that will cause the water to adhere to the sides, the discharge will be ·8125; by short tubes, having their lengths from two to four times their diameters, ·82; and by conical tubes of the form of the contracted vein, ·98. The perpendicular depth of a river, when the total sectional area is spread equally over the total perimeter of the cross section, is what is termed the hydraulic mean depth, and the mean velocity of a river is $\frac{10}{11}$ths of a mean proportional between the hydraulic mean depth and the fall in two English miles. The superficial velocity of a river is nearly a mean proportional between the hydraulic mean depth and the fall in two English miles.

To determine the velocity of discharge of a pipe, when the height of the water in the reservoir above the point of discharge, and the length and diameter of the pipe are given :—

Rule.—*Multiply 2500 times the diameter of the pipe in feet by the height in feet, and divide the product by the length in feet, increased by 50 times the diameter :—The square root of the quotient will be the velocity of discharge in feet per second.*

Example.—Suppose that a reservoir, 50 feet high, is connected with a pipe 48,281 feet long, and ·375 feet in diameter, laid upon a slant of 18 inches in the length of the pipe, and that it is required to know the velocity of efflux, supposing the reservoir to be kept constantly full.

Here 50 feet + 18 inches = 51·5 feet, which is the total amount of the fall, and 2,500 × ·375 × 51·5 = 48,281·25, and 14,637 + 50 × ·375 = 14,655·75, and 48,281·25 ÷ 14.655·75 = 3·3, the square root of which is 1·816, which is the velocity of discharge in feet per second.

To determine the number of cubic feet discharged per second when the velocity in feet per second is known :—

Rule.—*Multiply the area of the pipe in square feet by the velocity in feet per second, and the result will be the number of cubic feet discharged per second.*

To ascertain the velocity of a river or canal of any given declivity of bed, and any given hydraulic mean depth :—

Rule.—*Multiply the hydraulic mean depth in inches by the amount of fall in two miles, also expressed in inches, and extract the square root of the product, $\frac{10}{11}$ths of which is the mean velocity of the river in feet per second.*

Example 1.—In a canal 18 feet wide at the level of the water, 7 feet wide at the bottom, 4 feet deep, and with a fall of 4 inches in the mile, Mr. Watt found that the velocity of the water was 17 inches in a second at the surface, 14 inches in a second at the middle, and 10 inches in a second at the bottom, or on the average about 14 inches in a second. In this case the length of the transverse outline of the bottom will be 20·6 feet, and the sectional area 50 square feet. But 50 + 20·6 = 2·42718 feet, or 29·126 inches, say 29·13 inches, which, multiplied by 8 inches, the fall in two miles = 233·04, the square root of which is 15·26561 inches, and this multiplied by 10 and divided by 11 = 13·8778 inches per second, which is nearly identical with the result Mr. Watt obtained experimentally, as recorded above.

Example 2.—The Red Sea is about 32 feet higher than the Mediterranean. It has been proposed to connect these seas with a canal 21 feet deep, 96 feet wide at bottom, and 180 feet wide at top. The declivity of the bed of the canal would be about 4·731 inches in the mile. It is required to determine the velocity with which the water would flow through it.

Here the sectional area of the canal will be 2898 square feet, and the length of each of the sloping sides will be about 47 feet, which, added to the 96 feet width of bottom, will give 190 feet for the length of the outline of the bottom and sides on the cross section. The mean hydraulic depth therefore will be 2898 + 190 = 15·25 feet, or 183 inches, which, multiplied by 9·462 inches, the fall in two miles = 1731·546, the square root of which is 41·61, $\frac{10}{11}$ of which is 37·83 inches per second, or about 2·15 miles per hour.

It is easy to determine the amount of mechanical power consumed by friction in any river when its volume, depth, and declivity are known. Thus for example :—An inclined plane falling 4 inches in the mile falls in the proportion of 1 in 15840, and the pressure caused by gravity in the direction of the plane will be $\frac{1}{15840}$th of the weight resting upon it. Now as a cubic foot of water weighs $62\frac{1}{2}$ lbs., each cubic foot of water in a river falling 4 inches in the mile will gravitate down the plane with a weight of $62\frac{1}{2}$ ÷ 15840 = ·0039 lbs.; and this pressure per cubic foot, multiplied by the number of cubic feet and by the velocity of the current or the space passed through, will give the amount of mechanical power expended in overcoming the friction. The whole of the mechanical power indeed due to the fall is spent in overcoming the friction, in the case of a river flowing with a uniform velocity, and which is neither accelerated nor retarded.

ANALYSIS OF THE STEAM-ENGINE.

(Continued from p. 74.)

Crank Shaft.—As we have before remarked, the strain upon the crank pin is irrespective of the length of stroke, but the strain upon the crank shaft will increase as the length of the crank, which acts upon it as a lever, increases. The tendency of the strain is to twist off the neck of the shaft, which generally breaks at the collar of the bearing, where it is nicked in. The great diminution of strength which takes place from nicking a piece of iron is well known, and the fact seems to support the opinion that the skin is of more value, in proportion, than the body of the bar. In hammered iron this arises from the improvement which takes place in the exterior particles of the iron, and it would appear advisable, therefore, in cases which admit of it, to forge the shaft as near the finished size as possible, that very little of the skin may be turned off, and to shrink the collars on, instead of turning the bearings out of the body of the shaft.

To avoid the nicking effect, where the bearings are turned out of the shaft, the corners ought to be well rounded out. In locomotive cranked axles this is carried to an extreme, the bearing being rounded for nearly its whole breadth. This has also another effect, in preventing side-play, when the brasses are tightened up.

The strength of shafts to resist torsion is in direct proportion to the cube of their diameters. Thus, if there are two shafts of the respective diameters of 3 and 4 inches, their strengths will be as the cube of 3 is to the cube of 4, or as 27 is to 64.

Rule.—*To find the diameter of the crank shaft, when of wrought iron: Multiply the square of the diameter of the cylinder in inches by the length of the crank in inches; extract the cube root of the product, and divide it by 4, which will give the diameter of the shaft, in the smallest part, in inches.* Thus, the diameter of the cylinder, 30 inches, squared, equals 900, which multiplied by the length of the crank in inches, 30, equals 2700; the cube root of which is 30, and the fourth part of this is $7\frac{1}{2}$ inches—the required diameter.

Crank Shaft Plummer Block.—The diameter of the shaft at the smallest part being fixed, we may proceed to set out the plummer block for the bearing.

The form of the block will depend upon the general arrangement of the engine. The one shown quarter size in our drawing is intended to be bolted, either on the engine sole plate, where there is one, or on a separate plate, bolted down to the masonry.

The diameter being set out, the first point is the thickness of the brasses at the sides. This does not require to be very great, because the weight of the fly-wheel and the strain is mostly downwards, and if the wear should be in one direction sideways, the brasses can be turned end for end when they are worn. Half an inch of aside is shown at the chipping-pieces, which give the brass a bearing at the two ends and in the middle, of an inch each. The top brass, shown in section, shows the form of it between the chipping pieces, the top and bottom being one inch thick. In smaller bearings a chipping piece at each end will be sufficient. The top and bottom brasses are precisely similar, so that one pattern suffices for the two. A flange of about $\frac{1}{2}$ inch at the sides, and $\frac{3}{4}$ inch top and bottom, is struck round, or, as there is no accounting for taste, the flange may be made six sided, parallel with the chipping pieces. The bolts ought to be kept as near the bearing as possible, which will depend upon the metal between the bolt and the brass, for which $\frac{5}{8}$ inch is ample. In marine engines the bolts are sometimes fitted into the brasses, and only just clear the bearing; and it is obvious that the closer they are to the bearing the nearer they will be to their work, and the less strain there will be on the plummer block cap. The tensile strain upon these two bolts is the same as that on the piston rod, leaving out of account the weight of the fly-wheel, to be on the safe side. But as the piston rod is made stronger, as having to stand the thrust, a smaller proportion, say $\frac{1}{17}$ of the diameter of the cylinder for each bolt, will be sufficient. This will give a diameter for each of $1\frac{3}{4}$ inches nearly. Recesses are cast in the under side of the block for the heads of the bolts, and the bolt holes are recessed so that they only bear at top and bottom, in order to diminish the fitting, and that there may be no difficulty in getting the bolts into their places. The plummer block cap fits into the block, and is steadied by it. The proper strength of the cap may be calculated in the following manner. It may be regarded as a girder supported at the two ends by the bolts, and loaded in the middle. The breadth having been settled by the width of the bearing, which is in this case 9 inches, less the thickness of the flanges of the brass, viz., $7\frac{1}{2}$ inches, the depth can be found by a simple rule.

RULE.—*Multiply the distance between the centres of the bolts in inches by the total pressure in lbs. on the piston. This product divided by 7000 times the breadth, gives the square of the depth in inches.*

Thus: Taking the pressure of the steam at 22lbs. per square inch, including the atmosphere, and multiplying it by the area of the cylinder, viz., 706 square inches, gives a total pressure of 15,532lbs. $\times$ $11\frac{1}{2}$ ins. = 178,618. The breadth being $7\frac{1}{2}$ inches, the divisor will be $7\frac{1}{2} \times 7000$ = 52,500. Then, $\frac{178,618}{52,500} = 3{\cdot}4$ nearly—the square root of which is 1·84, and as it is liable to concussions, we may call it in round numbers two inches; from $\frac{3}{4}$ to 1 inch being allowed for screwing down. It was formerly a common practice to cast an oil cup on the top of the cap, but lubricators are now so much used, that this seems unnecessary. The metal round the bolt is made rather more than the diameter of the washer, and a feather is carried from it to the boss for the holding down bolt at the end of the block. The holes for these bolts are generally made a little oblong to allow of the block being shifted on its seat, but this is not always necessary.

The same rule will hold good for the bottom of the block as for the cap, but as it is bolted solidly down, and is not so subject to concussion, we may divide by 10,000 times the breadth, thus, the total pressure 15,532lbs. multiplied by 24 inches, between centres of bolts, equals 372,768, which divided by 75,000 = 5 inches, the square root of which is 2·23 inches, to which may be added another $\frac{1}{2}$ inch for chipping-piece, making $2\frac{3}{4}$ inches, total depth.

(To be continued.)

SPRAY'S PATENT SELF-ACTING FEED APPARATUS.

ONE of the most powerful arguments against the use of high pressure steam has been the difficulty of maintaining a proper supply of water to the boiler; and as most accidents have occurred from want of water in the boiler, it is imagined that a self-acting feed apparatus, which shall be as effective in high-pressure boilers, as the feed head is in low-pressure ones, will materially add to their safety, and tend to remove the prejudices, which still exist in many cases, to their introduction.

With this view Mr. Spray has patented the following arrangement, in which a float increases or diminishes the supply of the feed, as the level of water in the boiler falls or rises.

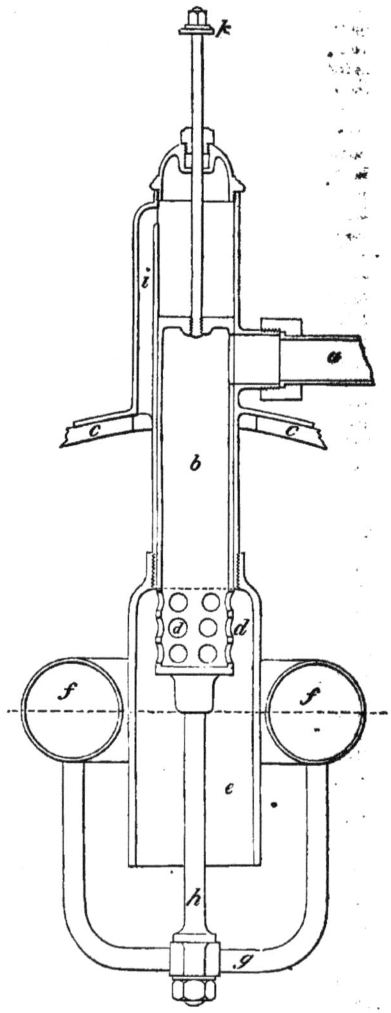

b is a tube, closed at each end, sliding in an outer cylindrical case, bolted on the boiler *c*, *c*. At its lower end is the spindle *h*, which is connected by two arms, *g*, with the circular float *f*, which floats at the water level, and will raise or depress the tube as the water level fluctuates. The water from the feed pump is admitted through the pipe *a*, and when the sliding tube *b* is in the position shown, the whole of the

water will pass through the opening on one side, and through the holes at bottom into the boiler. The pipe *e* carries the feed below the general water level and guides the float in its motion. When the water rises the float will raise *b* and shut off the supply, by closing the holes at top and bottom, until the proper level is arrived at. *i* is a small passage cast on the side of the outer case to allow the steam to press upon the upper side of the tube, and the pressure being the same on the lower side, the one counteracts the other, and renders very little power necessary to move the tube. A small rod is shown attached to the upper end of the tube, working through a stuffing box, and indicating the height of the water in the boiler; a nut and washer, *k*, at the top prevent the float and tube sinking too low when the water in the boiler is blown off.

GALLOWAY'S PATENT BOILERS.

THESE boilers have been extensively introduced in Lancashire by Messrs. W. and J. Galloway, of Manchester, and two of them have lately been put up at the Gutta Percha Company's Works in London. They consist, as shown in the sketches, of a cylindrical shell, containing two furnace tubes, which unite at the end of the bridges into one flue, which is circular for a short length, and then is carried on in an elliptical form to the end of the boiler. To stay this elliptical part, and to give increased heating surface, two rows of vertical water tubes are introduced, connecting the upper and lower water spaces in the boiler. These tubes are tapered from above, which affords more effective heating surface, and facilitates the current of steam and water through them. The flame, after passing the internal flue, is conducted round the sides of the shell as usual.

The junction of the two flues behind the bridges is especially designed to consume the smoke, each furnace being charged alternately; and when the boiler is not too hardly fixed, this very desirable object is

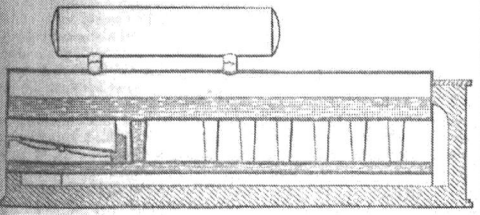

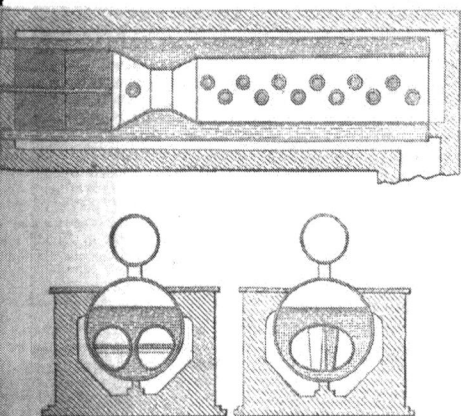

Scale 10 feet to the inch.

effected. The absence of all air valves, or, in fact, apparatus of any kind for the stoker to manage, or rather, to neglect, renders this plan the most practical that we have yet met with.

The boiler shown above is the second boiler erected at the Gutta Percha Works, and differs from the first in the dimensions of the water tubes; those in the first being 12 inches diameter at the top and 10 at the bottom; and those in the second one being 11 inches at the top and 9 at the bottom. There is also one tube more in the second boiler than in the first; otherwise the boilers are alike in their dimensions.

The evaporative power of the first boiler has been satisfactorily tested by R. Armstrong, Esq., C.E., whose experience on the subject of boilers must be sufficiently well known to our readers, and we have been favoured with the following data and results.

"The boiler, which is a cylinder of 7 feet diameter by 30 feet long, was driving a non-condensing engine, nominally of 30 horse power, but during the time of the experiment, it was indicated to average 50 horse power, besides making about 10 horse power of steam, applied to other purposes. The boiler was filled to nearly the top of the glass water gauge, where a mark was placed, and the feed-pump was stopped; at the same time the quantity of fuel on the bars was carefully gauged and the state of the fire noticed, so that they could be left, as nearly as possible, in the same state at the end of the experiment. As the level of the water became lower, the area of the water surface was measured at each inch of its height. The results gave an evaporation of 1 cubic foot per minute, or 60 per hour; the consumption of coal, which was carefully weighed during the experiment, being exactly 336 lbs. per hour, which, compared with the water evaporated as above, is in the proportion of 11·1 to 1. This I believe to be the highest rate ever previously obtained from any kind of boiler, under similar circumstances, and with the same kind of fuel, East Adairs Main, which was by no means of the best quality."

We are not in possession of the details of an especial trial of the second boiler, but its performance is stated to exceed that of the first, the evaporation being 12·5 lbs. water to 1 of coal.

MR. W. B. ADAMS' PLANS FOR THE IMPROVEMENT OF THE LOCOMOTIVE SYSTEM OF RAILWAYS.

THIS title, though not verbally that of the work we are about to notice,[*] expresses that portion of it which we wish more particularly to discuss. Mr. Adams, as must be well known to all our readers, was the constructor of the first locomotive in which the dead weight was attempted to be reduced to a minimum. This machine, the "Express," was constructed for Mr. Samuel of the Eastern Counties' Railway, and we are not aware how far Mr. Adams may be indebted to that gentleman for the idea. Be this, however, as it may, Mr. Adams has the merit of being the champion of the "light" system, in contradistinction to the "heavy."

Mr. Samuel, in his paper, read before the Institution of Mechanical Engineers, and fully reported in our pages, has detailed the first fair trial of the system, so that we need not follow Mr. Adams through the preliminary historical part of the subject, but we will commence with a later date:—

"At this time, Mr. Nixon, the engineer of the Cork and Bandon Railway, who had succeeded to the difficult task of correcting a series of blunders committed by those in authority before him, having heard of the light system advocated by the writer, deemed that he saw in it the true mode of making railways remunerative to the shareholders. A full and clear statement was made to him, and he made an experimental trip to Cambridge with the 'Enfield,' to verify in practice the theory that had been stated. The result was, that he immediately ordered two light engines and trains on the writer's plan.

"Far and near there arose a boding croak among the 'heavies' and their adherents, on the receipt of this intelligence. 'Great are the locomotives of the elect,' was the aphorism of those interested in selling masses of metal, and also of those whose feet were only adapted to

* Road Progress; or Amalgamation of Railways and Highways for Agricultural Improvement, &c., by W. B. Adams, Engineer, 8vo. pp. 76: London, Luxford.

tread on frequented paths. Utter failure was prognosticated, and men of less purpose than Mr. Nixon and his Directors might have been turned away from their object. If Mr. Nixon were right, then the makers of heavy engines were wrong; and, alas! very few are they who, 'filling a mighty space in the world's eye,' are great enough in mind to say, 'Even I am not perfect.' It was asserted that the heavy engines would work light loads with as small a consumption of coke as the light ones, while on emergencies they would take larger loads. Wagers were offered on this point, with the view of demonstrating, by cash power, a mechanical fallacy.

"The light engines on the Cork and Bandon line were of the following construction:—Eight-inch cylinders, 12 inches stroke, on four wheels; driving wheels, 5 feet diameter; leading wheels, 3 feet diameter; distance between wheel centres, 10 feet 6 inches; length of boiler barrel, 9 feet 8 inches; diameter of barrel, 2 feet 4 inches; circular fire-box (90 tubes), 1¼ diameter; length of tubes, 10 feet. The two engines are christened by sonorous Gaelic names, corresponding, in plain Saxon, to 'Running Fire,' and 'Whirlwind.' The weight of these engines is 8¼ tons, empty. They carry the water and fuel on their own frame.

"The heavy engine was of the usual kind, with a tender, the whole being on ten wheels, the cylinders being fourteen inches in diameter.

"The following is the extract from the Engineer's Report, comparing the two classes of engines during five months' performance, from August 1st to December 31st, 1849. He states that the locomotive engines and carrying stock are maintained in good working order, and that a six-wheel ordinary size passenger engine and tender, having 14 inch cylinders, was delivered from the makers, and has been at work from the month of October last, the manufacture as well as the working of which have given him great satisfaction, more particularly from its consumption of fuel being much less than has been known in engines of such dimensions.

"'The passenger trains are conveyed by the 'light,' or small engines, which continue to afford most satisfactory proof of their efficiency and economy in working the passenger traffic on your line.

"'The trains frequently consist of the following stock, all fairly laden:—

"'One large 1st and 2nd class carriage for 58 passengers.
"'One 3rd class carriage for 40 passengers.
"'One horse-box for 3 horses.
"'One carriage truck.

"'Such trains are conveyed between Bandon and Ballinhassig station in 20 minutes, being at the rate of 30 miles per hour, including stoppages. (Gradient 3¼ miles, 1 × 100; total distance 10 miles.)

"'The daily consumption of coke for each of these engines has been most particularly registered by your able station-master at Bandon, Mr. Coglan, from whose returns I find the average quantity of Newcastle coke consumed per diem, as follows:—

	Cwt.	qrs.	lbs.
"'Consumed in lighting engine, time occupied 2 hours	2	0	16
"'Consumed standing in steam, time occupied 8 hours	2	1	17
"'Consumed in running 60 miles, time occupied 2 hours	1	3	26
"'Total daily consumption . . Cwt.	6	2	3

Which is equivalent to 12¼ lbs. per mile per day of 12 hours; but it will be seen that the running time is only 2 hours, during which the consumption is not more than 3¾ lbs. per mile.

"'The average daily consumption of the Company's ordinary-sized engine with the same work, is 22¼ lbs. per mile per day, or nearly double that of the light engines; and the same difference also arises between the two classes of engines in the consumption of oil, grease, &c., so that an important saving has been effected in the working expenses, by the adoption of engines whose powers and dimensions are in proportion to the loads they are required to convey.

"'I have also to notice, that on referring to the working expenses of your railway, as per balance sheet, ending 31st December last, I find the total expenditure for working the line for five months, is £621. 18s. 6d., and which amount, if divided by the mileage, 9780, of that period, will show that the nett cost of working the traffic, inclusive of every expense except maintenance of way, has been 15½d. per mile per train, inclusive of the frequent use of engines for sundry special purposes: and by adding interest and depreciation on rolling stock, the cost per mile, per train, will be about 17d.

"'From the above statement it will be manifest, that the working of your railway has been commenced on the most economical principles.'

"The size of train described above would be sufficient for the transport of 150 passengers instead of 98, supposing the horse-box and carriage-truck changed for passenger carriages. Adding 5¼ cwt. of extra coke for running, and 2 cwt. for lighting an extra engine, with a second driver, stoker, and guard, 24 trains might be run per diem, instead of 6, at an increased expense of about 25s. per diem.

"The present cost for six trains is 85s. per diem, or 17d. per mile for sixty miles, which covers every expense, save maintenance of way. Adding the increase would make up 100s. Dividing this by the increased mileage 240 would give 5½d. per mile per train, or 4s. 7d. for the transit of 150 passengers over ten miles of line, or 3600 passengers per diem at a cost of £5. 10s.

"But to keep working, a spare engine would be requisite, at a cost of 10s. extra per diem for interest, making up 6d. per train per mile, or £6. per diem, total.

"It is obvious, therefore, that with a small addition to the stock, when the twenty miles of the Cork and Bandon line are completed, 1800 passengers may be carried over the whole distance at a cost of £6 per diem, or 650,000 per annum, for less than £2100, including every charge except maintenance of way, which, when well laid and traversed by light engines, will be nearly *nil*.

"Supposing the trains to be half full, at one shilling per head average, the annual amount would be £16,050, from which, deducting expenses £2100, the nett profit would be £14,150, or five per cent., on a capital of £283,000, or seven per cent. on the intended capital of £200,000, without parcels or goods traffic.

"The number of passengers up to Christmas appears to have averaged about 160 per diem. The calculations made above are not on the supposition that such large numbers will be obtained, but merely to show at how small an outlay for stock, provision for transit can be made. But probably, when the line is opened throughout, the numbers will be trebled, or say 500 per diem. At 1s. 6d. per head, this number would leave a clear return of upwards of five per cent. on £200,000, being less than one penny per mile.

"If the Earl of Bandon and the landed proprietors of the south resolve that this thing shall be done—if they be thoroughly imbued with the conviction that the term 'road' is the synonyme of 'civilization,'—that cheap transit is the converse of barbarism, very simple indeed is the process of making the south of Ireland the abode of *wealth*, in the higher sense of the term—the general *weal* of the community. How this may be done will be shown further on.

"While the Cork and Bandon engines were in process of construction, the Directors of the Eastern Counties ordered a second light engine, called the 'Cambridge.'

"No. 6, the '*Cambridge*,' was constructed for the Eastern Counties Railway Company, and was intended to run express between London and Cambridge. The extreme length is 16 feet 9 inches, and it is hung on four wheels, of which the leading wheels are 3 feet diameter, and the drivers 5 feet. Distance between centres of wheels 9 feet 6 inches. Propelled by two outside cylinders, 8 inches diameter and 12 inches stroke, acting directly on to the driving-wheels. The boiler is horizontal, with a barrel 2 feet 6 inches diameter. The driving axle is placed behind the fire-box, which is 2 feet 10¼ inches by 2 feet 6 inches outside diameter. The inner fire-box is 3 feet 1 inch in height, and contains 26 feet of heating surface. The tubes are in number 115, 6 feet 9 inches long and 1½ inch in diameter, with a heating surface of 259 feet. The tank is under the boiler, and holds 240 gallons.

"The 'Cambridge' generally performs the distance between London and Norwich (126 miles) in about four hours, that is, a speed of 30 miles an hour."

"Since that time the 'Cambridge' has been tried at various kinds of work on the Eastern Counties lines. The hardest work has been the traffic on the North Woolwich branch. The distance from London to North Woolwich is 8¾ miles, a considerable portion being reverse curves and steep gradients. At one portion the curve is of three chains radius, one particular part giving a versed sine of 7¼ inches in 30 feet, or two rails length, 1 in 48: the gradient being at that spot a rise of 1 in 89. Over this line the 'Cambridge' has ordinarily worked an eight-wheeled carriage, measuring 40 feet by 9 feet, with accommodation for 116 passengers, and also a luggage break van. On one occasion 180 passengers were brought up, additional carriages being put on for the purpose."

"The 'Fairfield,' and the two Cork and Bandon engines, have a peculiarity of construction. The driving wheels are in front, the former being 4 feet 6 inches in diameter, and the two latter 5 feet. It had been a generally received opinion that it was dangerous to have a large wheel in front, but experience seems to prove the contrary. The Irish engines have been run both ways; but with the driving wheel in front they are invariably steady, while with the small wheel in front they tend to jump. The mechanical reason why this should be, seems very clear: with the driving wheel in front the whole machine is pulled or towed along; with the driving wheel behind, the small front wheel is pushed or propelled. Thus a steam-boat, with the paddle-wheels far forward, is easy to steer, but with them far aft, yaws, and is unruly to the helm.

"The Londonderry and Enniskillen engine will be as follows:—

"No. 8. This engine is being constructed for the Londonderry and Enniskillen Railway Company—the Irish, or 5 feet 3 inch gauge. The extreme length is 19 feet. It is on four wheels, placed at 10 feet 9 inches apart. The leading wheels are 3 feet in diameter, and the trailing wheels 5 feet. Propelled by two outside cylinders, 9 inches in diameter, and 15 inches stroke, acting directly on to the driving wheels. The boiler is horizontal, with a barrel 2 feet 6 inches in diameter. The external fire-box is 3 feet by 2 feet 5 inches, outside measurement. The inner fire-box is 4 feet in height, with 37·5 feet of heating surface. The tubes are 86 in number, 1¾ inches in diameter, and 10 feet 9 inches in length, with a heating surface of 380 feet. The tank is beneath the boiler, and will hold 350 gallons."

The collateral advantages resulting from the use of light engines, are that less power is actually required, as the way will maintain its rigidity and that the expense of maintaining the way will be diminished.

Mr. Adams next proceeds to consider the structure of the rails, and their various means of support; but upon this we do not find much that is new. The following mode is proposed of combining the advantages of various arrangements:—

"Impressed with these advantages, the writer, regarding rails and wheels in the light of 'man and wife,' sought a method of obviating their imperfections. The first question was the joints. His mode of dealing with this evil was as follows:—

"Removing the chair and sleeper altogether from the joint, a pair of iron fishes, 18 inches long, and 4 to 6 inches deep, were applied, one on each side the rail, bearing in the side channels. Four bolts pass through these fishes and rails, tightly screwed up, fitting in the holes of the fishes; but the holes in the rails being left large, to allow for expansion and contraction. The sleepers and chairs being applied to the rails at the extreme end of the fishes, the whole is rendered firm and complete. The fishes would be better 2 feet 6 inches, or 3 feet in length.

"Samples of this having been laid down on the Eastern Counties line for fifteen months, the result was so satisfactory that the Directors ordered a mile to be laid down between Stratford and Lea Bridge, on the northern and eastern division. For this purpose rails were used that had been condemned, the ends having been destroyed in the chairs. It was of course impossible to make a fit of the rails at the outset; but being made fixtures one to the other, they soon became flat, and the drivers now regard this as the best portion of the whole line. The expense of 'maintenance' on this portion is now a mere fraction of the former cost, and the expense of new rails has been saved. The keys do not get out, and thus much risk is avoided.

"But still there remained the difficulty of the small bearing surface of the rails in the chairs, and consequent destruction of the rails. To obviate this, the writer devised a plan of dispensing with the keys and chairs altogether. Two pieces of timber, seven inches square, and thirteen feet long, were grooved out to receive the rail, imbedded to the upper lip. These pieces were bolted together beneath the rail, and held it as in a wooden vice, with a continuous bearing throughout the whole rail surface, where in contact with the wood.

"It was at first supposed by many that the rail would press through the timber, so contrary was the plan to all received notions. But it was easily demonstrable that the bearing surface on the timber was greater than in the common plan; and as metal was not bedded upon metal, the result was general durability, though the sample was laid down on a line of the hardest work known—the Eastern Counties between Bow and Stratford."

"But there is yet another difficulty. Timber, bedded or partly bedded in moist earth or ballast, is very apt to rot. Creosoting and other chemical processes obviate this; but chemical durability is generally gained at the loss of mechanical strength. For this reason stone blocks were formerly considered 'permanent way.' But the impracticability of keeping cast-iron chairs firm on stone blocks, led to attempts to use felt between, as an elastic medium. The best result would have been attained by using longitudinal wood sleepers, between the rails and the stones. Impressed with this, the writer, many years back, in his work on 'wheel carriages,' proposed to bed longitudinal timber in a foundation of brick and cement, forming a groove for the timber in the brickwork. Of late it has been proposed to use

cast iron, altogether dispensing with timber. The numerous experiments will solve the question of practicability; but, in the writer's judgment, the use of timber will be found an essential element of durability, in evading the effects of concussion. The ordinary wood wheel of the highway, shod with a hoop tyre, is probably the strongest existing mechanical construction, when viewed with regard to the work it performs; and in carriages generally, this construction of wood and iron is absolutely necessary to attain durability.

"Mr. Samuel, resident engineer of the Eastern Counties Railway, has lately constructed a cast-iron sleeper, fulfilling some of the above conditions. A cast plate, 16 inches wide and 3 feet 6 inches long, is formed with a trough lengthwise down the centre, wedge-form, 4 inches wide above the top, and 3 inches at the bottom, and about 4½ inches deep. This trough is lined with two pieces of timber, filling up the length, and so grooved by a machine as to embrace the rail between them. Thus the rail only rises 1¼ inches above the surface of the cast iron, and no mischievous leverage takes place, as when chairs are used. The weight of the rail and load compresses the timber into the wedge-form trough, and the rail thus lies in a close-fitting wooden cushion, which cannot be crushed away. Three of these longitudinal sleepers are used to each rail length; and the end of the rail being connected by fishes, as before described, a very good permanent way is attained. The length of the fishes being 18 inches, and the sleepers 10 feet 6 inches, only 3 feet length of a 15 feet rail is left unsupported; whereas by the present plan of chairs and cross-sleepers, only about 14 inches in 15 feet is supported on hard and badly-fitting chairs. Openings are left at spaces in the cast iron, so that moisture may get to the wood, and prevent it from unduly shrinking in hot weather.

The reduction of manual labour in unloading and "man handling" waggons, is strongly insisted upon:

"In the construction of train-carriages and wagons, the principle of four wheels is liable to several disadvantages. The centre of gravity being necessarily high for the convenience of passengers, and the base small, it is impracticable to employ really flexible springs, without involving such an amount of oscillation as to be unbearable to passengers and inconvenient for goods. The striking of the wheel-flanges against the rails while running, causes the body and load to impinge occasionally with three-fourths of the total weight on a single spring. The spring would be broken by the shock; and to prevent this the springs are made so strong, that they are practically not springs at all, save under violence. The amount of damage resulting to permanent way and stock from this imperfect four-wheel mode of construction is very considerable. A short time back an American engineer visited Fairfield Works, and observing a number of four-wheeled wagons in process of construction, remarked—'What! do you make these foolish things still! We turned them off in the States long ago; they wo'nt pay. We use no turn-tables—no man-handling of wagons; that eats up all the goods profits.'"

The system of broad and roomy carriages, to diminish the *length* of the train, and to obtain the greatest room with the least material, is analyzed, and estimates given of the saving that may be effected in first cost. These carriages have been in use for some time on the North Woolwich and North Kent lines, and the only objection that we have heard made to them is, that the lines being laid, and bridges, &c. constructed for narrow carriages, the windows have to be barricaded to prevent the passengers having their heads or arms amputated.

To allow the wheels of these long carriages to traverse the curves conveniently, Mr. Adams makes the wheels loose on the axles; although the axles are still free to revolve on the straight portions of the line, and the slip between the wheel and axle is only supposed to take place on curves. We, however, beg to suggest to Mr. Adams, that a more mechanical plan than this was described by a Mr. Pettit, in the *Artisan* (p. 121, vol. 1846), which consisted of providing each wheel with a separate axle, not reaching across the carriage, and admitting of the centre of gravity being lowered to any desired extent.

To make cheap railways, Mr. Adams proposes to lay rails down on our existing turnpike roads, and to carry the railway to the neighbourhood, instead of bringing the neighbourhood to the railway. For overcoming inclines, Mr. Kollmann's scheme of two sizes of driving-wheels is recommended. The powerful influence which such railways might have on the agricultural interest is enlarged upon, and, indeed, is so important as to deserve a separate treatise. We are informed that a *two-wheeled* engine is in course of designing at the Fairfield Works, to be attached to a four-wheeled platform, like the deck of a steamer, as being the minimum of expense. The plan suggested, of employing two light engines, with their fire-boxes brought together, and attributed to Colonel Colquhoun, is in reality an old scheme of our own, which is fully described in one of our early volumes, and has, we believe, been since made the subject of more than one patent.

We cannot afford any more space this month to this subject : but in our next we will endeavour to show that there are opportunities of further improvements in our existing system, which would have a tendency to "make things pleasant," in a more legitimate way than by "cooking accounts."

"HEAVY" *versus* "LIGHT" LOCOMOTIVES.

As a foil to Mr. Adams' arguments, the following may be found interesting, as showing the difference between the goods and the passenger traffic.

STATEMENT SHOWING THE COMPARATIVE COST OF RUNNING FIRST AND SECOND CLASS LOCOMOTIVES ON THE PHILADELPHIA AND COLUMBIA RAILWAY.

One first-class locomotive will haul, with ease, thirty-five cars at the following cost :—

Cost of locomotive, $8200—10 per cent. wear

and tear,	..	..	..	$820·00
,,	,, ,,	6 ,, interest,		492·00

1312·00

per annum, or at three hundred and ten working days,	$4·23 per day.
Engineer $2 per day, fireman $1·25, ..	3·25 ,,
Sperm oil, four pints, at $1·20 per gallon, ...	60 ,,
Rags, three pounds, at five cents per pound, ..	15 ,,
Wood, two and seven-eighths cords, at $3 per cord,	8·62 ,,

Cost of locomotive per day, hauling thirty-five cars, at 48½ cents per car, ... 16·85

One second class locomotive will haul only twenty cars, and will cost as follows :—

Cost of locomotive $7000—10 per cent. wear

and tear,	..	..	..	$700·00
,,	,, ,,	6 ,, interest,		420·00

1120·00

per annum, or at three hundred and ten working days,	$3·62 per day.
Engineer $2, fireman $1·25 per day, ..	3·25 ,,
Sperm oil, three pints, at $1·20 per gallon, ..	45 ,,
Rags, two pounds, at five cents per pound, ..	10 ,,
Wood, two and one-half cords, at $3 per cord,	7·50 ,,

Cost of locomotive per day, hauling twenty cars, or 74½ cents per car, ... 14·92

120,000 cars per annum, carried in trains of 35 cars each would give	3428²⁷⁄₇ trips.
Same number of cars, hauled in trains of 20 cars each, would give	6000 ,,
Saving, ...	2571⁴⁄₇ ,,

2571⁴⁄₇ trips per annum, at $16·85 each, would be ..	$57,771·43
6000 ,, ,, 15·00 ,, ,, ..	90,000·00
Saving, ...	32,228·57

THE BRIDGE OVER THE RHINE AT COLOGNE.

WE mentioned in our last volume (p. 263) that Mr. Fairbairn had been called in by the Prussian Government, to give his advice on the best method of crossing the Rhine at Cologne, in order to form an uninterrupted railway communication, at present broken by the bridge of boats at Cologne. From its peculiar adaptation to railway traffic, and the fewness of the piers it requires, a tubular bridge is evidently the form best suited to the case ; and accordingly Mr. Fairbairn prepared plans of such a bridge, which received the approval of the King of Prussia and Baron Humboldt, and of all who were competent to form an opinion. A certain Herr Oberbaurathe Lentze, however, whose reputation as an engineer has not yet reached these barbarous regions, had arrived at the conclusion that a suspension bridge was the thing needed, and having enlisted in his favour the Prussian officials, they have between them done their best to "burke" Mr. Fairbairn's plan, and puff off their own. A commission was appointed to inquire into the tubular system, consisting of Herr Lentze himself, and a friend ! The result was as might have been expected ; they visited England, saw the Britannia bridge, and returned with a report against the tubular system.

On the strength of this report, the minister has invited plans in competition for a suspension bridge, which will be a standing monument of folly, if erected. Mr. Fairbairn has addressed a letter to Baron Humboldt, of which we offer an extract :

"And now let me point out the lamentable imperfections which characterize the minister's programme, and the limitations and requirements which will effectually trammel the efforts of men of genius, and deter those of experience and reputation from entering at all upon the competition.

"It is an express condition of the scheme that the railway communication is not to be continuous, and the public will therefore continue to suffer the annoyance and inconvenience of considerable delays ; for it may be safely said that the proposal of disintegrating a train at one terminus and drawing it across to the other by men or horses, bit by bit, and hour by hour, will offer equal, if not greater, obstacles to a rapid journey than the existing system does. How much better would it be that the bridge should embody within itself such elements of strength and durability as would afford at all times and in all seasons a safe transit to those means of locomotion which constitute the wonder and glory of the age! Instead of such a permanent and substantial structure, will the Prussian government sanction the erection of one, the feeble and rickety constitution of which would shudder at the very sight of a locomotive ? Surely not ! Public opinion must step in and forbid it. What is wanted is a bridge to connect the existing railways, not one that will permanently separate them.

"But, again, it is stated that the difference between the levels of the existing railways and that required for the roadway of the intended bridge is too great to be overcome by the locomotive within a short distance of length. This objection is purely imaginary ; for I can state, from personal examination, that the necessary gradient would not be so heavy as several which are worked with great ease in this country. Besides, on the left bank of the Rhine the terminus of the Aix-la-Chapelle line is at the right level ; and that on the side of Deutz may without difficulty be reached by an easy gradient of less than 1 in 100.

"Without meaning the slightest disrespect to the author of the design for the chain bridge, I must repeat my firm and deliberate conviction, that it would prove an incomplete and unsatisfactory structure. A permanent, inflexible, durable, and handsome bridge of enormous strength,[*] adapted, by arrangements which I have now in progress of execution for similar purposes in this country, to give every possible facility to the navigation of the river—calculated to carry across the heaviest railway train at any speed, and which you might cover with the most powerful ordnance from end to end, may be erected at Cologne within the sum which has been demanded for the chain bridge. These statements are not the imaginings of a sanguine mind ; but their accuracy may be corroborated by numerous examples of a similar character which have been erected in this country."

---

[*] The breaking weight of the bridge I proposed, with spans of 310 feet, was equal to 6000 tons, or 120,000 cwts., equally distributed over each span, giving as the ultimate strength of the bridge, with four spans, 24,000 tons, or 480,000 cwts.

EXPANSION SLIDE GEAR.

To the Editor of the Artisan.

SIR,—The best reply I can make to your correspondent, Mr. C. P. Stewart, will be to give you the exact date of my claim to the invention which he so boldly asserts to be his own. In 1842 I was engaged in fitting the expansion gear to the engines of one of H.M.S. frigates, the slides of which were worked by cams in one direction, and by strong springs in the other. It having occurred to me that this arrangement might be improved, I schemed the double system of cam levers (marked D and E in my drawing) with the cross connection between them, and also the forward cut off, by the moveable cam, B. *These are the two cardinal points in the gear*, everything else being a mere matter of detail consequent upon them. As I previously stated, the merit of the hand-gear for moving the cam while the engine is in motion, belongs to Messrs. Malcolmson, for this reason—that the spiral grooves, I I, are the only parts that have any claim to novelty in this part of the invention.

With respect to the other part, if Mr. Stewart could produce a prior claim to mine, I would cheerfully change the name which the gear has borne for the last eight years ; but, sir, I happen to be able to give your readers not only the date of my own claim, but also of that of Mr. Stewart's. About four months ago a friend of mine requested me to favour him, by showing Mr. Stewart and himself the machinery of a new vessel belonging to the Messrs. Malcolmson. I did so, and the engines of this vessel being fitted with expansion gear, in which the spiral grooves were used, I presume that Mr. Stewart will date his knowledge of that part from that period. From the difficulty of making him understand it, I had no doubt that it was the first time, during his ten years' study of the subject, that he had any idea of such an arrangement. Like most tyros, he was rather apt at finding fault, and objected to the gear, &c., as being too complex. My friend explained to him the nature of my gear, showing its simplicity, as being applied to the common slide, &c. I mention this to show how unlikely it is that he had been studying expansion gear of any sort for ten years ; as, had he been doing so, he must have known that the very thing described by him was no secret, being at work on board several vessels, besides the engine at the Richmond water-works, which you have seen at work, and which dates at least twelve months prior to his first knowledge of the matter. About six weeks after this I received an invitation from Mr. Stewart to come and see a model which he had made of my gear.—I accepted the invitation, and found that he had made a rude imitation of it. I can assure your readers that he most carefully avoided anything like an allusion to the gear being his own invention in my presence. I would gladly have given him credit for the idea of applying Messrs. Malcolmson's hand-gear, were it not for the unfortunate circumstance that, before he had even seen it, I had arranged the method described by me in your journal, for the purpose of altering the gear he had seen, in which there is only one screw (T) used : consequently we find that the regulating nut is not sufficiently steady ; and when this is applied to the forward cut off, where the whole strain of moving the slide comes upon it while varying the amount of steam, it would not stand a single day. In his model he had copied even to the single screw—and this is the great talent that is to convert the inventions of practical men into such a shape that they will not even know their own. This plain statement of facts will, I trust, satisfy your readers as to whether I need fear the "judgment of honest mechanics" in this matter. The difference between the matriculated mechanical scholar of Trinity College, Cambridge, and the matriculated mechanic of the workshop will be apparent enough, either as to mechanical design or construction, and I may add, straightforwardness. There is a singular fatuity generally attendant upon a departure from rectitude, as shown in this case ; for how could Mr. Stewart admit that I was the author of the connecting gear, and not see that it is the whole substance of the invention ! Every mechanic must be satisfied at a single glance that the cross connecting gear, the forward cut off, and the spiral grooves, sum up the invention. Mr. Stewart gives the grooves to Messrs. Malcolmson, and the connecting gear to me, and as the forward cut off must follow, it leaves to himself only a puzzling question, as to what part of the matter really is to belong to him :—I think there will be very little more than the consciousness of having (to use the mildest term) made a false start.

I must apologize for taking up so much space in your valuable columns with this reply to Mr. Stewart's letter, and I beg to assure you that this is the only notice that will be taken by me of any communication from him upon this subject. But as it is a wide field that he is now entering upon, I shall hail with pleasure any improvement of his own which he may give the engineering world the benefit of.

JOHN DUDGEON.

To the Editor of the Artisan.

Liverpool, 19th April, 1850.

SIR,—In looking over your number for March, I was much pleased to observe that Mr. Dudgeon had taken advantage of your widely distributed columns, in giving to the public his very ingenious, and, in my opinion, very efficient arrangement of expansion slide gear. The very sensible remarks of your Salford correspondent, in your number for April, shows that it will be the means of drawing the attention of mechanics generally, to a subject of so much importance, particularly to steamers making long voyages.

I was very much astonished on observing, in your last number, a letter signed C. P. Stewart, laying claim to all the merit that may be due for such invention, and stating that he, and he only, was the original designer. Your correspondent commences by stating what he calls the "facts" of the case ; that his favourite study for the last ten years has been expansion gear, but that it was only a few months back that it occurred to him that a modification of Messrs. Malcolmson's gear combined with Mr. Dudgeon's connected levers, coupled with his own arrangements and improvements, would produce what he calls an efficient practical expansion gear.

Your readers will share my surprise at the barefaced attempt of this gentleman, in endeavouring to make it appear that the expansion gear described by Mr. Dudgeon, in your number for March, had been pilfered from him, when I inform you that in 1842, about eight years ago, I was shown by Mr. Dudgeon a drawing of an expansion slide gear, similar to that described in your March number, the only difference being the method of shifting the cams, for cutting the steam off at any part of the stroke, the present method being much simpler, and for which Mr. Dudgeon honestly acknowledges that he was indebted to Mr. Malcolmson.

Your correspondent having offered his services for the benefit of your readers, I hope he will, at an early date, furnish you with a drawing and description of the machine that appears to be used at Trinity College, Cambridge, for the manufactory of "facts," and state if it be his own invention, as it would no doubt tend to the amusement, if not the edification, of most of your readers.

I am, sir,
Your obedient servant,
JOHN BEATTIE.

EXPANSION OF STEAM IN COTTON SPINNING.

SIR,—Your correspondent, "A Cotton Spinner," invites information from your readers touching the best method of carrying out the expansive principle of working steam in engines intended for manufacturing purposes. I therefore, while disclaiming all pretension to superior information relative to such engines, send a few remarks for the consideration of your readers.

Mr. Parkes, as your correspondent observes, did, eight or ten years

14

ago, propound the doctrine, that the superior efficacy of the Cornish engine was due to the percussive action of the steam. But in the second and third numbers of the *Artisan* that doctrine was so completely demolished, that it has never been heard of since that time. It is now acknowledged universally, that the large performance of the Cornish engines in respect to fuel is due to the large expansion of the steam in the cylinder, conjoined with a careful system of clothing, and a large amount of boiler surface ; and it is also very well known, that in rotative engines the same economy of performance is attainable by the same expedients for that purpose. It is no doubt the case, that steam of a high elasticity rushing suddenly against a piston gives a shock to the whole machine ; but I do not believe that this shock is so great in the rotative as in the pumping engine, inasmuch as the momentum of the fly-wheel keeps the piston always moving, whereas the heavy counterweight of a Cornish engine has to be urged suddenly from a state of absolute rest into sudden velocity at every stroke. The method of forming the lap of the valve in the form of a curve or triangle will certainly make the engine work more sweetly, and this expedient was suggested by me fifteen years ago, and was introduced into a steamer on the Clyde, called the *Nimrod*, about that time. But the main objection to a large employment of the expansive action in spinning engines is the irregularity of motion it produces ; and this defect is not to be overcome by the modification of the valve referred to. If your correspondent wishes to employ the expansive action of the steam to a large extent, and at the same time preserve the equability of motion essential to mill engines of every kind, let him attend to the following indications :—1st, let the stroke of the engine be *short* ; 2nd, let the speed of the engine be *as rapid as possible* ; 3rd, let the fly-wheel be *swift and heavy*. These conditions, if fulfilled, will enable the expansive principle to be largely employed ; and the best arrangement for the purpose is probably that of putting sufficient lap upon the valve to cut off the steam at, say, one-third or one-fourth of the stroke, and then to give the further expansion required by *throttling the steam.*

All mill engines work too slow at present. By a suitable arrangement of the air-pump they might be worked at a far higher speed, whereby they would both exert a larger power and impart a more equable motion.

J. B.

Newcastle, April, 1850.

MR. EDITOR,—Sir, in common with many other operative engineers, whose education has been neglected, I would esteem it a great favour from any of your practical or scientific readers, many of whom your journal boasts, if they could furnish me, in simple language, answers to the following questions :

1. In setting out engine work, for instance, valve levers, which generally have a round hole at each end, the centre line is first laid down, and from points on the side of the lever it is required to make lines square with the centre line passing through the eyes of the lever,—a ready method for doing which I would be glad to know.

2. In making bevil wheel patterns, the teeth are cut from pieces dovetailed into the rim of the wheel, but sometimes the pieces are merely fitted to the surface and glued on ; but as it is tedious to fit them one by one on the rim, I want to know the average radius of the curve which the pieces require to have, so that they may be planed to the form without further trouble ; a simple rule for doing so would be of great value to the pattern maker.

3. In the small factory where I am employed there is but one planing machine, so that at times we have to do by hand what might be done easier by the machine ; for instance, I have to cut a long key seat on a shaft, six inches diameter, but as my knowledge of geometry is but small, I am at a loss to know the best method of making the key seat

parallel with the centre line of the shaft : I have to trust to my eye to detect the error ; but this is so unsatisfactory, and in many cases impossible, that I hope some of your readers will put me right on this point.

4. Can the following expression ($\sqrt{\frac{2\ ab}{3\ x}}$) which is termed algebraic, be reduced to simple language ? and if so, why are such expressions made use of ? In many books they are a complete bore, cutting short the study of those who have not been taught the relations letters and figures bear to one another in those peculiar forms. I would esteem it a great favour from any of your scientific readers who would give an explanation.

I am, sir, yours truly,

H. A.

[WE willingly insert our correspondent's letter, and trust that some of our readers will clear away the difficulties in his path. We have no doubt there are many other artizans who will be glad to avail themselves of our columns in a like manner.—ED. ARTIZAN.]

MR. WORM'S NEW PRINTING MACHINE.

THE proprietors of the *North British Advertiser* having resolved upon giving this invention a trial, they have at some length discussed its merits in their columns, and we avail ourselves of an extract from them, which, though rather warmly coloured to our matter-of-fact notions, will afford our readers some notion of the arrangement.

"Monsieur Worms, himself a long time a practical man, and therefore, well acquainted with all the desiderata of machine-printers, appears to have wholly disregarded *the means* by which they have hitherto sought to attain them, to have looked solely and steadily at the *object* in view ; to have dismissed as so many useless incumbrances, the one incomprehensible system of multiplied cylinders, feeders, receiver, tapes, and tape machinery ; and to have *constructed*—not quite perfectly indeed, so far,—but still to have constructed a machine, instead of a pair of machines, capable of printing upwards of nine thousand sheets per hour, on *both sides* of the paper, and that *well*, in good register, with only a *couple* of impression cylinders in place of sixteen, and without an inch of tape. In short, by means of a machine wholly free from intricacy of construction, of small comparative cost, and with only a couple or three superintendents, in place of an equal number of these, and thirty-two feeders and receivers into the bargain, whilst the mode of using it may be briefly described as follows :—

"The types being first set, corrected, and made up into pages in the usual way, the form is then placed upon a hot iron plate, where a *cast* is taken of it by means of a few alternate layers of paper and paste, the latter being thickened with a little Spanish whiting. *Partially* dried by the communication of heat from the hot plate, the said paper cast is now carefully lifted off the form, and placed *inside* of a hot half-cylinder, the *drying* apparatus, *the exact shape* of which it takes, becomes perfectly dry in two or three minutes, and thus stiffens into the form of a half-cylinder. This form or mould, wherein the metal is to be cast, being now complete, is forthwith removed to the casting trough, consisting of another half-cylinder, which it exactly fits ; and a third half-cylinder, of rather smaller diameter, being now brought down and firmly fixed immediately above the mould, the interval is flooded with melted type-metal, and hence *the thickness* of the half cylindrical stereotype plate is equal to the distance between the upper and lower cylindrical iron plates, *between* which it is cast, less always the thickness of the paper mould itself. In short, to obtain a perfectly clear notion of this part of the process, take a pair of compasses, and make therewith half a circle of twelve inches diameter, then from the same point make another half circle, *within the first*, of eleven inches diameter ; now imagine the lower, the larger half circle, to be covered by the paper mould already described, and the space between this mould and the upper, or smaller, half circle to be filled up with melted type metal, and afterwards cooled, and the whole of the stereotyping process is before you.

"The curved stereotype cast, cooled and taken out of the mould, is now put upon one of the machine cylinders, the half of which it covers ; and this process being repeated three times, in addition to the first, the entire pages of the paper are ready for printing, and the inking apparatus, in which there is nothing peculiar, being in order, the driving-belt connected with the steam-engine is transferred in the usual way from the loose pulley to the fast one, when the machine goes to work ; and, without any hands at all, prints the paper in web at the rate—when we saw the machine at work—of 152 sheets in a minute, on both sides ; and as each sheet was 34 inches long, and printed lengthways, this day's *North British Advertiser*, which is only 33 inches in length of column and margin together, may, no doubt, be printed with the same degree of rapidity, by a machine sufficiently wide to take it in breadthways, to receive it, that is to say, in the same way in which it is invariably printed now.

"We have already extended this notice so far beyond our original intention, that a few other remarks that we propose to make, must be given as briefly as possible. It has already been objected to this machine, and that in high quarters, that it can never answer for a newspaper of which two or three editions per diem are printed, containing numerous alterations in their contents. The objection does not apply to ourselves, as we print one edition only for the entire kingdom ; but we doubt its validity in any case, and for this reason, we doubt the absolute necessity of stereotyping at all, but have now merely time and space to throw out the hint that the two *Times* eight-cylinder machines, for example, may one day be reduced to one machine, consisting of but two type and two impression cylinders, with the *et ceteras* already described. Why not? It is quite as easy to print as rapidly upon the new principle, upon both sides of the sheets, as upon one side only ; nor do we see the shadow of a motive for stereotyping at all, provided it be considered better or more convenient to print newspapers with types instead. Patent-right difficulties may, indeed, exist ; but we hardly think that there are any which are purely mechanical.

"But enough for the present ; the difficulties in our own case are sufficiently serious in proposing to adopt the new machine, owing to the circumstance of our habitually using five different sizes of paper, as we chance to have much or little matter to put into them. Still we fancy that we see our way pretty clearly, even through this difficulty, and hence, therefore, we have already secured the first of these machines for any part of Great Britain, provided always the patentees can engage to make us one in such a manner as to do our work as we must have it done ; and whilst, on this head, we feel it but just to state that we consider the inventor of this new machine to have been particularly fortunate in the selection of the gentleman to whom he has intrusted the manufacture of it—for a more substantial or better constructed piece of mechanism than that Mr. de Cotler has produced in the machine we saw in operation, we never desire to see. Indeed, the substantiality, neatness, and excellence of the workmanship, would reflect high honour on any of our best machinists, either in London, Manchester, or Glasgow.

(Signed)   "J. & J. Gray."

SOCIETIES.

INSTITUTION OF CIVIL ENGINEERS.
Tuesday, March 26.

WILLIAM CUBITT, Esq., President, in the Chair.

THE first paper read was a "Description of the Chapple Viaduct, upon the Colchester and Stour Valley Extension of the Eastern Counties Railway," by Mr. P. Bruff, Assoc. Inst. C.E.

This viaduct was thrown across the valley of the Colne, at Chapple ; it consisted of thirty-two semi-circular arches, each of the span of 30 feet, the total length being 1,136 feet, and the extreme height from the foundations to the rail level being 80 feet. The average height of the piers from the foundation to the springing was 45 feet ; they were 27 feet 3 inches wide by 4 feet 10½ inches thick, at the under side of the impost, and tapered downwards to the plinth, with a batter of 1 in 36 ; 23 of the piers only had plinths, which consisted of a set-off of 2½ inches, making the dimensions of the base of those piers 29 feet 6 inches wide, by 7 feet 1 inch thick. The piers were solid below the plinth, but above that level there was a centre opening 6 feet in width, arched at the top and the bottom. The whole of this viaduct was constructed of bricks made in the district, being chiefly set in mortar, but the arches for a distance of 4 feet 6 inches above the springing were set in cement. The viaduct occupied about 20 months in construction, and cost about £55 per lineal yard.

The next paper read was "On the Manufacture of Malleable Iron, with the results of Experiments on the Strength of Railway Axles," by Mr. G. B. Thorneycroft, Assoc. Inst. C.E.

It was stated that malleable iron might be divided into two distinct classes, "red short" and "cold short;" the former being generally produced from the rich ores, and the latter from the poorer or leaner ores. The pig iron made from the rich ores (under the cold blast process only) was not so fluid as that from the lean ores, but when converted into malleable iron it became tough and fibrous, though it was troublesome to work at less than a white heat, which had caused it to be denominated "red short." On the other hand, the pig iron produced from the lean ores possessed greater fluidity, but when malleable it was unfitted to support sudden shocks, or continuous strains, and was hence termed "cold short." It was further stated, that in the manufacture of malleable iron very much depended on the quality of the fuel used in the smelting furnace, and in the subsequent processes ; also that iron became crystalline from two causes ; first, in consequence of being made from naturally cold short pig iron ; and secondly, from a peculiar manipulation during the process of "puddling."

The introduction of hot blast for smelting iron, rendered necessary a careful investigation of the comparative use of hot and cold blast pig iron, in the manufacture of bars, from which it appeared, that if the same quality of materials was used in both cases, equally good bar iron would be produced, though it was more difficult to convert hot blast pig iron into "number one" bars, and the waste was greater. It was certain, that whilst good grey pig iron could be produced, by cold blast, from the best materials, iron of apparently excellent quality could be made, by hot blast, from the most sulphurous ores and fuel ; indeed, to this alone must be attributed the bad reputation of hot blast iron for certain purposes.

As it had been asserted, that the peculiar characteristics of the malleable iron were to be attributed to the ore from which it was produced, and not from the different nature of the processes used in its conversion, which the author had always believed to be the true cause ; he had, at his works near Wolverhampton, made bars of the finest crystalline and of the strongest fibrous texture, from the same Yorkshire pig iron. Another cause which induced great changes in the texture of iron, when cold, was compression, or impact, which would completely alter its texture from a fibrous to a crystalline character, as was well exemplified by the "gag," and the puddling tools used by forgemen, and in several parts of different kinds of machinery the same effect was observed.

The author then proceeded to draw attention to the best shape for railway axles, so as to combine the greatest strength with the least material, illustrating his views by the details of a series of experiments made for determining the question. It would appear that railway axles should be made parallel, from journal to journal, without any shoulder, and with just sufficient strength to prevent any vibration in rotating. The experiments showed that an axle without a shoulder was better able to resist impact than one with a shoulder, in the ratio of 155 to 55, and by leaving the axle parallel, its strength, compared with the same sized axle reduced in the middle, was as 5 to 1½.

Tuesday, April 2.

In the renewed discussion, it appeared to be admitted, that the shoulder on axles was only useful as a gauge, and that it should be curved from, and not square to, the main body ;—that between the journals, the axle should be parallel, for if reduced in the centre, it was sure to bend, and eventually to break. Since the last meeting, Mr. Thorneycroft had made many other experiments, which proved his former opinion, relative to the progressive changes in iron, from compression, which alone caused the destruction of the fibre, and, in fact, that jarring would not do it. Experiments were suggested to ascertain, whether a pressure on the periphery of a wheel, fixed on an axle and kept rotating, would produce the same results, which were admitted to exist in practice.

The next paper read was a "Description of a Lift Bridge, erected over the Grand Surrey Canal, on the Line of the Thames Junction Branch, of the London, Brighton, and South Coast Railway," by Mr. R. J. Hood, M. Inst. C. E.

The act for the construction of this branch, which was a single line, one mile in length, provided that the crossing of the Grand Surrey Canal should be by a swing bridge; but as there were many obstacles in the way of this clause being carried into effect, and as it was not thought to be the most convenient form of construction, it was determined, after due consideration of the advantages and disadvantages of each particular kind of moveable bridge, to erect one on a principle which might be designated a "lift bridge." This consisted, simply, of a rectangular platform, 23½ feet in width, and 35 feet in length, carrying on one side a line of rails, and on the other side a roadway for carts; it was formed of four beams of oak timber, under-trussed with wrought-iron rods, and cast-iron saddles, those for carrying the rails, (which were bridge-shaped,) being stronger than the others, and having a flooring of 3-inch planking; the platform rested, when down, upon piles driven into a bed of hard gravel, met with at a depth of about 20 feet below the water line. The platform, which was about 12½ tons in weight, was suspended at the four corners by galvanized wire-ropes, four inches in circumference, attached to the end of each oak transome by means of strong bow springs, and passing over pullies fixed on four pairs of cast-iron standards, also supported on piles, and fastened at the other end to drums, 3 feet in diameter, each pair of which were keyed on to the same horizontal shaft, situated a few inches under the rail and road level. Upon the same shafts there were also fixed six other drums of a like diameter with the former, carrying, upon coils of wire rope 2½ inches in circumference, balance weights of a total weight of 12½ tons, but not equally distributed, intended to assist in raising the platform, and which descended into cast-iron cylinders or wells. Motion was given to one end of each shaft, by means of simple hand-gearing, consisting of a train of wheels and pinions, by which the power was multiplied twenty-six times.

The level of the rails, above the water line, was 4½ feet, and as the platform was capable of being raised 9½ feet, sufficient room was afforded for the passage of the barges, the greatest number of which ever passing through in the twenty-four hours being fifteen, and since the erection of the bridge not one in a hundred had been detained one minute; though on this point, as well as on many others, the Canal Company had raised factious objections, owing to which, and to the design having to be submitted for approval to the Railway Board, great delay arose in the commencement, and also in the execution of the works, augmenting the actual cost to £1,300, which was beyond what it was presumed a similar work could, under more favourable circumstances, and when the construction was not novel, be executed for.

The bridge was stated to have proved very successful, and in situations where only a given headway was required for a limited span, this kind of construction was recommended.

Tuesday, April 9, 1850.

WILLIAM CUBITT, Esq., President in the Chair.

THE paper read was "On the Construction of Locks and Keys," by Mr. J. Chubb, Assoc. Inst. C.E.

The author commenced by stating, that the most ancient lock, of whose form and construction there was any certain knowledge, was the Egyptian, which had been in use for upwards of four thousand years. The three kinds of modern locks might be thus enumerated.

First,—The letter locks; mostly used for padlocks, and were so far convenient, as a key was not required for opening them. A modification of this lock had been proposed, called the "scutcheon" lock, for securing doors and iron safes, but it was too expensive and complicated to come into general use.

Second,—Locks having fixed wards, in which no real improvement had been made in modern times. These locks were bad in principle, as they could be easily picked; and owing to many thousands of them being yearly made, that could be passed by the same key, little or no security was afforded by them; in fact, it might be safely asserted, that twenty skeleton keys would open all the locks, of a given size, made upon this principle.

Third,—The Egyptian lock; the essential principle of which was, that of moveable pins, or studs dropping into, and securing the bolt, all of which must be raised to the proper height, by corresponding pins in the end of the key, before the bolt could be unfastened. This lock was the foundation upon which most of the ingenious inventions of late years had been based, differing only in the forms of the moveable obstructions to the bolt,—some of which acted vertically, others horizontally, some with a rotatory motion, and many others in an endless variety of ways; but of all these it was thought sufficient to describe only those best known and appreciated, namely, Barron's, Bramah's, and Chubb's.

In Barron's lock, patented in the year 1774, a great improvement was made upon the ancient Egyptian, by the introduction of the over-lift, wards being also used; but, from the fact of there being only two tumblers, it was evident that no great change, or permutation could be made in the combinations.

In Bramah's lock, patented in the year 1784, there was a compound of both direct and rotatory motion given to the key, instead of simply the latter, as in Barron's lock. It consisted of a number of sliders, having notches, of various depths, cut on one edge, so that the motion of the bolt was totally prevented, until each slider was pressed down to its exact depth, which was effected by the key having six cuts in it of different lengths.

In Chubb's lock, first patented in 1818, and since modified and improved by various subsequent patents, there were six separate and distinct tumblers, placed over each other, and capable of being elevated to different heights, but all moving on the centre pin. This lock differed from the others, in having a "detector," by which any attempt to pick, or open the lock with a false key, was immediately notified, on the next application of its own key.

Calculations were then gone into, to show the number of different combinations which might be made in this lock, and it appeared, that with an average sized key, having six steps, each capable of being reduced in height twenty times, the number of changes would be 86,400; that if the seventh step, which threw the bolt, was taken into account, the reduction of it only ten times would increase the number to 864,000. Further, that as the drill pins of the locks and the pipes of the keys might be made of three different sizes, the total number of changes would be 2,592,000. In keys of the smallest size, the total number would be 648,000, whilst in those of the largest size it would be increased to 7,776,000 changes.

In the discussion which ensued, the combinations in the locks of Summerford, and Mc Kinnon, (of New York,) were fully described; an advantage being claimed for the former, in making one tumbler to lift and the other to fall, in order to open it; and, for the latter, that by the addition of a curtain of case-hardened iron, three-quarters of an inch in thickness, radiating from the centre of the pin, and a radiating key, there were no means of reaching the tumblers, for the purpose of taking an impression or otherwise, except by cutting through that curtain. On the other hand, it was positively asserted, that no impression could be taken of, or means invented for picking a lock which had six tumblers, although it could be easily done with locks having fixed wards; further, that Chubb's lock was a decided improvement on all others of the same character, inasmuch as it possessed a "detector," which formed really the peculiar feature of that lock.

April 16th.—The discussion upon Mr. Chubb's paper, "On Locks and Keys," was renewed; and several locks which had not been previously mentioned were exhibited. These bore the names of their inventors—Davis, Parsons, Williams, and Nettlefold.

It was urged, that the curtain which had been mentioned, might be essential for Summerford's lock, but could not be, in any degree, useful in Chubb's lock; in fact, that its only effect would be to induce complication and augment the cost, without increasing the security.

Among numerous instances of ingenious devices for opening locks, that stated to have been tried in America excited much attention. The process was described to be, that the operator, after inserting two pieces of India rubber, to limit the sphere of action, injected from a force-pump, a composition of glue and molasses, in a heated state, which chilled quickly, and, although extremely elastic, had the property of retaining the form and position of the lower side, or bellies of the tumblers, and that after being cut out of the lock, by a thin-bladed instrument, a key could be made from the impression.

In explanation of this, however, it was shown, that in Chub's lock there existed no similarity between the position of the bellies of the tumblers, when at rest, and the figure of the bit of the key; and therefore, that even supposing it to be possible to obtain an accurate impression of the position of the bellies of the tumblers, when at rest, no indication would be afforded of the combination, or any assistance be given for making a false key. In further confirmation of this, a lock by Chubb was shown, in which, when at rest, the bellies of the tumblers were perfectly uniform, and in the same plane, so that an impression of the inside of such a lock must be utterly useless for any purpose.

Although it had been asserted that Chubb's locks had been picked, it was admitted that it had never been proved that those locks had really been made by the inventor; but, on the other hand, it had frequently been shown that spurious imitations of the first expired patent had been sold in large quantities, and had been marked "Chubb's Patent," until the makers were stopped by legal process, when it was ruled, both at law and equity, that although, after the expiration of a patent, any person might manufacture the article, he had no right to pirate a particular trade mark, or to use a distinctive stamp, which was irrespective of any patent right.

The locks used at Pentonville Prison were instanced as uniting goodness and safety with extreme cheapness; but it was admitted that the workmanship was very inferior to that of Chubb's locks.

It was also asserted that Davis's locks, invariably used on the Cabinet Despatch-boxes, which frequently contained important secret papers, were never found to be out of order, or to be susceptible of being picked.

To this it was replied, that Mr. Chubb was prepared to produce a workman, who, without having ever previously seen the locks on the Cabinet Despatch boxes, would open any number, on being allowed half an hour for each; and that the same might be done more easily with the Pentonville Prison locks.

Tuesday, April 23, 1850.

WILLIAM CUBITT, Esq., President, in the Chair.

The paper read was a "Description of the Insistent Pontoon Bridge, at the Dublin Terminus, of the Midland Great Western Railway of Ireland," by Mr. R. Mallet, M. Inst. C.E.

This bridge was stated to be situated on the line of approach from the city to the terminus, and formed a passage over one branch of the Royal Canal, where it crossed the Phibsborough Road, upon the Foster Aqueduct. By the act it was provided, that the navigation of the canal should be as free and unimpeded as possible; and from the circumstance of there being only a height of 16 inches between the intended surface of the road and that of the water of the canal, it necessarily in-

volved the placing of some kind of moveable bridge of rather peculiar construction. After due consideration, the one described in the paper was designed and adopted, as being more suitable to the peculiarities of the situation than any other, owing to the water-channel being only 17 feet 4 inches in width, and that the passage to be made across it required to be at least 50 feet in breadth.

The general idea of this form of movable bridge was that of a pontoon, or flat-bottomed boat, constructed of iron; the breadth being nearly equal to that of the water space to be crossed, and the length about equal to the width of roadway required. The deck beams of this pontoon projected over the sides, and rested, while *in situ*, upon a rabbate, or continuous recess, formed along the top course of each quay wall, but while the pontoon was floating light, the projecting deck beams were two inches clear of this rabbate, and the roadway platform, constituting the deck of the pontoon, was elevated to an equal height above the level of the top of the quay walls, or land on each side; in this state the pontoon could be freely and readily pushed along the canal, for a distance of rather more than its own length, until it was brought opposite to a lye-by, provided by increasing the width of the canal at this point, and being put therein, the navigation was perfectly free.

As a pontoon afloat would form a very unstable roadway for carriages, means were provided for allowing it to settle down in the water, and rest firmly upon the rabbates; and also for again raising it rapidly, so as to float clear of the rabbates, and enable it to be moved away into the lye-by. For this purpose two large valves were placed in the bottom of the pontoon, one near each end, by which water was allowed to enter, and sink the pontoon, until it hung upon the projecting deck beams. For removing this water when it was required to float the pontoon, a large syphon, of a particular construction, was provided, which was capable of being brought instantly into use, and of being as quickly detached, when a sufficiency of water had been withdrawn to enable the pontoon to be moved. These operations were stated to be performed very readily by one man, the navigation being cleared in four minutes, and the roadway restored in less than three minutes.

The details of the construction of the pontoon, of the syphon, and all other parts of the work were then minutely given; also the total cost of the structure, which, exclusive of the masonry, was 1125*l.*, that of the masonry being about 150*l.*; and it was stated to have continued in use, with perfect satisfaction, since its completion in February, 1847.

This form of construction was considered to be applicable in situations where a comparatively narrow water channel had to be crossed by a very wide roadway; but as the particular circumstances of other localities might differ from the one in question, the author suggested various alterations in the details, so as to meet these exigencies.

The next paper read was a "Description of a Wrought-iron Lattice Bridge, constructed over the line of the Rugby and Leamington Railway," by Mr. W. T. Doyne, Assoc. Inst. C.E.

This bridge, which was 150 feet span, carried a public road over the Honingham cutting. It consisted of two girders 156 feet in length, and 10 feet 6 inches in depth, placed at a distance of 20 feet apart, and connected together by means of wrought-iron transverse girders, and by a system of horizontal diagonal bracing. The bottom of the main girders were formed of two angle irons, and wrought-iron plates, eight in number at the centre, but diminishing to three at the ends, and of such dimensions as to make the effective sectional area at the centre, after deducting the loss by rivet holes, equal to 26 square inches; that of the top, which was somewhat differently constructed, so as the better to resist compression, being equal to 40 square inches. The lattices were formed of a series of bars of spoke-iron, intersecting each other at an angle of 60°, being crossed at those points, by longitudinal bars, for the purpose of giving additional rigidity, and of making a closer parapet.

The transverse girders, 7 feet 6 inches apart, were each formed of a plate of wrought iron, with two angle irons at the top and the bottom ; these were covered with corrugated galvanized iron, one-tenth of an inch thick, upon which concrete, and then a layer of gravel and loam metalling, 6 inches thick, was laid. This bridge was erected by Messrs. Smith, Smith, and James, of Leamington, upon a platform which gave to the girders a camber of 7 inches in the centre, which was reduced to 3¼ inches upon removing the platform. The total cost of the bridge was about £3500.

During the progress of the works, the author made some experiments upon the strength of rivets of different sizes, from which it appeared that the average breaking weight, per square inch of sectional area, was 35·10 tons for a chain joint, and 18·89 tons for a lap joint.

The paper announced to be read at the next meeting, Tuesday, April 30th, when the monthly ballot for members will take place, was No. 834, "On the Absorbent Power of Chalk, and its Water Contents, under different conditions," by Professor Ansted.

SOCIETY OF ARTS.
April 17th.
Mr. Antoine Claudet, on Cutting Glass.

The author commenced his paper by a very interesting description of the nature of the diamond, of the form of its natural crystal, and of the mode in which it cuts glass,—quoting a paper on the subject by the late Dr. Wollaston, in the *Philosophical Transactions* for 1816, as well as by a history of the use of glass in windows from the earliest times, when it was used only in ecclesiastical buildings of great splendour, down to its present universal application. He has also, in order the more thoroughly to make apparent the advantage of the use of the diamond, described minutely the very tedious and imperfect methods by which, before its introduction, glass was cut and shaped. The property in question was first found out about the time of Francis I. of France, the well-known anecdote of whom is quoted ; and the different tools used from that time to the present for its manual application are detailed and commented on, many of them being exhibited by the author. The first of these was a mere handle, having the diamond firmly inserted into the lower end. But the handle being round, and the diamond, from the form of its crystal, requiring one unvarying direction to be preserved in order to produce a cut, this was found so imperfect that a step was taken by making the end of the handle flat, to preserve the parallelism against the rule. This, from the shape of the bottom in which the stone was set, was called the "plough diamond." In 1814, Shaw, of London, made a great improvement, and brought the instrument to the shape in which it is still used, by making the metallic setting of the diamond movable on a ferrule at the bottom of the handle, thus putting it out of the power of any deviation of the hand from the proper position to affect the direction of the stone. This, perfect as it may seem, is still difficult to use, and requires long practice for expert performance. The two tests by which the workman knows when his tool is "making a cut" are, the sound and the feel. A modification of the last-named tool, by the brother of its inventor, was formerly used for those who have but little practice ; but it was very little used, and the one shown to the meeting by Mr. Claudet was curious, from being, perhaps, the only one now in existence.

A contrivance for cutting circular plates was shown in action.

The cause of the invention of the machines, the description of which was the principal object of the Paper, was the increased use of glass shades for covering ornaments, the cutting of which, so that they should stand perfectly firm and with an even base, was a most tedious and imperfect operation when done by hand.

The manufacture of these shades, which, under the name of "cylinders de verre," had long been carried on in France, was first undertaken in England, at the instance of Mr. Claudet, by Mr. Lucas Chance of Birmingham, who, in the true spirit of enlightened enterprise, notwithstanding the vexatious pressure of the excise laws, now repealed, embarked largely in the manufacture, getting workmen from France, for making both shades and the sheet glass which had there been for some time made from cylinders. It was now, however, found that some method of cutting the bottom of the shades and cylinders must be adopted surer and less expensive than the manual method, and Mr. Claudet was driven by this necessity to invent his machine.

The principle of the machine expressed in the fewest words, is this: The shade is firmly fixed between an internal support and a transverse bar above it, in a perfectly upright position, above a horizontal, level, and smooth table, its bottom being a few inches above the table. Upon the table travels a small but heavily-weighted base moving on castors, having springing from it two upright pillars, one holding the diamond, and the other forming a support opposite to it. The pillar holding the diamond is fixed, but the other is movable, being by a spring kept close to it. The height of the whole is such that when on the table, the diamond is about an inch above the bottom of the shade. The diamond being introduced inside the shade as it hangs suspended, the pressure of the spring is sufficient to cause it to cut, and it has only to be moved round the shade, the horizontality of the table causing the cut to be perfectly level. This machine was exhibited, and the bottoms of shades cut by it before the meeting. The shape of the shade, whether oval, round, or square, is unimportant in the use of this machine, but Mr. Claudet has contrived another for the cutting of round shades only, in which the shade is laid horizontally,—an elegant system of adjustments being provided, by which shades of any diameter can be cut by the workman with little risk of error.

A vote of thanks to Mr. Claudet for his communication was carried unanimously.

SANITARY IMPROVEMENT OF THE CITY OF COPENHAGEN.

We have much pleasure in giving publicity to the accompanying particulars, for the guidance of Engineers desirous of sending in plans for supplying Copenhagen with Water, Gas, and Sewerage ; and we have no doubt that some of our English engineers, whose railway practice has become so much diminished, will be found amongst the competitors :

With reference to the desirability of effecting an improvement in the present mode of providing the supply of water, as also the public lighting in the city of Copenhagen, likewise the arrangements existing at present for the carrying off of the soil from the town, this business has been submitted to the deliberate consideration of the communal supervision ; and with reference to the same, in both of its divisions, the result has been that the most proper mode of procedure to effect the attainment of their object, was the maturing of plans to be proposed for the adoption of the public, in reference to the requirements and conditions which have been proposed by a Committee convened for the purpose.

The magistracy, with the approbation of the Minister of the Home Department, proceed to announce by these presents, for the information of the public, the Resolution adopted in the business, with the addition of the following appointments to form their basis on the compilation of the anticipated plans.

A.—The Water Works.

1.—The water works must be so constructed, that, if required, they can supply 100,000* barrels of water during the lapse of twenty-four hours.

---

* 1 barrel of water=27 7/10 10,000 Imperial gallons.

2.—In procuring the supply of water mentioned in item No. 1, reference is only taken to the environs, which Copenhagen is entitled to avail itself of, in order to provide itself with water: it is collected and deposited in the reservoirs. Therefore the plan must also include the reservoirs.

3.—In as far as the so-called "Utterslev Marsh" might be taken into consideration in this respect, and whether the entire moor or a portion thereof is proposed to be used, is left to the engineer for the developement in drawing up the plan, to confine himself to report the size and limits of the reservoir, as also the principal points for the re-formation of the same ; whilst the direction of the water works reserves itself to decide more particularly in respect of such eventual re-construction, as to the mode of procedure.

4.—The pressure is required to be such, that the water in the town and suburbs, generally, can reach the height of 90 feet at least above the street, and can be likewise carried to the consumers on the several floors,—also applied instantly in cases of fire,—also to effect the washing of the streets, the gutters, and the sewers which may be found to exist, or which may be constructed in future. To meet the contingency that the inhabitants of the suburb of "Vesterbro" (the West Bridge), who have their distinct supply of water at present, might wish to participate in the general water works of the town, the plan must be so formed as also to include the providing of a supply of water for this suburb.

5.—As the environ specified under the item No. 2, with its reservoirs, supplies the water in a state of contamination or befouled, partly by mechanical action, and partly by particles chemically dissolved, it must be subjected to a purifying process. This must be such, that the water can be used for drinking as well as for household purposes, and in manufactories.

B.—The Sewers.

1.—The plan is required as complete as can be achieved in accordance with the localities existing here ; for carrying off not only the water which collects in the town, but likewise for the removal of all impurities from the houses and privies.

2. On effecting this removal, reference to the utmost degree possible must be had as to the value, in money, of the vast mass of manure found to exist in these collections of filth.

3.—Further care must also be taken that the harbour of this town, where the ebb and flood are devoid of practical influence, be not detrimentally acted upon by the substances which the sewers carry away.

C.—The Public Lighting.

1.—A plan is required for a lighting of the whole town.

2.—In the execution of this plan, in the distribution of the flame, care must be taken that the public lighting of the streets of the town generally, and of its public places, is at least three times as strong as it has been hitherto.

3.—The arrangements must be of that nature, that private persons can be supplied with lighting against an adequate payment for the same, by the public institutions for lighting.

D.—The General Conditions.

1.—It is desirable that the plan should include, under one, all three of the stated operations.

2.—The plans are to be accompanied by the needful drawings and maps essential to examine the plans—as also an estimate of the charges or costs, as well for the first construction as for the annual administration of the repair, fixed according to the prices in Copenhagen.

3.—The plans must be delivered within eight months from this date.

4.—The bidders will be able to obtain the elucidations as to the existing state of things, at present in the possession of the direction (in as far as they are not to be procured of the booksellers), by applying to the offices concerned in this city.

5.—The competition is perfectly free for both natives and foreigners.

6.—The plans received will be adjudicated by a commission, consisting of Colonel Schlegel, of the Royal Engineers, Professor Förchammer, and Mr. Lunde, Member of the Common Council.

7.—A premium of 250 Fredericks d'ors* will be paid for that plan of each of the different branches which is approved by the adjudicating commission ; and if the plan embraces all three branches, and is approved of in its full extent, besides the premiums for each distinct proposal, an additional premium of 250 Fredericks d'ors will be granted. In case only a portion of one of these plans is used, a premium equivalent to such portion will be paid.

8. The plans, in as far as they are adopted, remain the property of the commune of Copenhagen. The acceptation of a plan, or a portion of the same, does not entail any obligation on the commune to make use of the author on carrying the proposed works into effect.

The MAGISTRACY IN COPENHAGEN, the 18th February, 1850.

LOCOMOTIVES FOR THE AUSTRIAN RAILWAYS.

"THE Austrian Government has published in Berlin an offer of a prize of 20,000 full weight Imperial ducats for the best locomotive railway engine, constructed to run on the line about to be carried over the ridge of the Semmering mountains, on the frontiers of Lower Austria and Styria, at a height of 464 Vienna fathoms above the level of the Adriatic sea. From the highest point to the station of Gloggnitz, in Lower Austria, at one end of the railway, the fall is 243·2 fathoms, and the distance, following the course of the railway, 3·8 miles. From the highest point to the station of Mürzzuschlag, in Styria, at the other end of the railway, the fall is 114·2 fathoms, and the distance by the railway 1·6 mile. The greatest rise of the different gradients is 1 in 40 of the length, and the longest of the gradients is 1,671 fathoms. The shortest radius of the different curves is 100 fathoms. But in the steepest rise of 1 in 40 no radius is shorter than 150 fathoms. The longest curve with this radius, and at the greatest rise, extends 296 fathoms. One of the chief qualifications for the required locomotive is, that it should be capable of transporting in ordinarily favourable states of the weather, a gross weight of 2,500 Vienna centner, exclusive of the tender, at a speed of 1½ Austrian miles an hour (4000 Vienna fathoms to the mile), over the greatest ascents at the most unfavourable curves. The locomotive with still greater capability would obtain the preference. It has been determined that the Austrian Administration of State, besides the acquisition of the prize locomotive, should also purchase five other locomotives, at amounts from 6,000 to 10,000 full weight Imperial ducats. The regulations to be observed in the choice of the locomotives have also been fixed."—*Times.*

We have inspected the plans at the Austrian Consulate Office, but there is nothing in them very interesting to English engineers. The railway is on the narrow gauge, but an alteration in the gauge, which will not require any addition to the works, will be entertained, if sufficient reason can be shown for it. The rails are of the double L description, and weigh, as nearly as we can calculate, 64½ lbs. per yard, English measurement. The pressure of the steam must not exceed 127 lbs. per square inch, and the weight on each driving wheel must not exceed 125 centners. The Austrian centner is 100 Austrian lbs., each of which equals 1·234 lbs. English. The weight to be transported, therefore, is 137 English tons, and the weight on each driving wheel 5 tons 11½ cwt. An Austrian ducat is about 9s. 5d. English. The grand prize is therefore about £9400. It is mentioned that the locomotive is to be retained as a *model*, for the instruction, we presume, of Austrian locomotive builders.

ANALYSIS OF BOOKS.

Steam Postal Intercourse and Traffic with the Americas and Austral-Asia. (From the Colonial Magazine.) London ; MORTIMER, 8vo. pp. 16.

THE rapid progress which our Transatlantic cousins have made in ocean steam navigation seems to have caught the Admiralty and our

* 1 Fredericks d'or = about 16s. sterling.

Steam Navigation Companies napping. An American line of steamers between New York and Southampton and Liverpool will be running next month ; and if the Americans are not afraid to organize, at a large expense, an opposition to Cunard's line, what chance will the Royal West India Mail Packet Company have, unless some vigorous and prompt measures are taken to remodel the system? We entered at length (*ante* p. 21) into the proposed alterations in the West India route, which, it was stated, was to enable the company to compete with the American steamers from Chagres *via* New York.

We expressed some incredulity at the time as to the speed proposed to be maintained, on an average, viz., 12 knots, between Southampton and St. Thomas, a distance of 3622 miles, and whether the company are convinced that their calculations will bear the test of experiment or not, we are unable to say; but it would appear so, from the fact of their taking no steps to carry them out. If it be true that they are waiting until a renewal of their contract be guaranteed, it is a pity that so much valuable time has already been lost.

The writer in the pamphlet before us, proposes a scheme which presents a practical solution of the difficulty; viz., that the West India service should be taken from the company, and worked by Cunard's line from New York to Chagres ; and that all the vessels of the West Indian Mail Company should be employed for the Brazilian Mail Contract. On this question we will quote the author :—

"Now, the distance from St. Thomas to England being given at 3622 miles, it will be seen that, to accomplish the passage, as proposed, in twelve days, it would require 12½ knots an hour, and that therefore there is here, at the outset, a palpable and serious miscalculation, the steam-power promised being set down as averaging 12 knots. We will venture, however, to say, that no such average speed will be obtained, that it is preposterous, and that 10½ knots an hour—which would give a 14 days' passage to St. Thomas—is about the outside which may be expected. As regards one day for coaling at this island, (taking a steamer of 1000 horse-power, the consumption of which would not be under 85 tons a-day,) the quantity of coals to be made up at St. Thomas would necessarily occupy from two to three days loading. Thus, we estimate the following final result, at a speed of 10½ knots :—

" Southampton to St. Thomas . . . . 14 days.
  Stoppage at St. Thomas (say) . . . 2 ,,
  St. Thomas to Chagres . . . . . 7 ,,
                                        _____
                    Total . . . . . 23 days.

"We have been considering all this while the navigation of the proposed trunk line ; but as regards the branch steamers, have there also to point out how little reliance can be placed in the practicability of the scheme thus brought before the public. The branch steamer to Vera Cruz is positively made to run from and to St. Thomas, a distance of 3640 miles, while the main and more powerful vessel on the trunk line is accomplishing only 2240 miles, from St. Thomas to Chagres, and back ! How can the practical working of the scheme be in this way ensured ! It is evident that for this Vera Cruz boat alone, and possibly for others likewise, frequent detentions would have to be made at St. Thomas. Taking, therefore, the whole circumstances together, we do not see that the Royal Mail Company can, on their own showing, even with the superior class of boats they propose to build, compete with an organized line of American steamers, now about to run from Chagres to New York, and thence to Liverpool. It is also to be borne in mind that twelve or eighteen months delay in bringing the proposed new boats into activity, would afford ample time permanently to divert the traffic from across the Isthmus of Panama to England, into American hands.

"Yet the necessity for some immediate measure is urgent ; and thus the proposition which the inefficiency of the West Indian Mail service has rendered popular of a line of British boats from Chagres to New York, (in connexion with a collecting service of branch steamers at Jamaica, to meet the Cunard steamers,) is one which it behoves Government seriously to examine.

"On this subject we have been favoured by a communication from an officer of the Royal Navy, of forty-five years' service, the last twenty of which have been passed in the mercantile steam marine ; and if his opinion be sustained, it seems to be decisive of the question of route :—

"' Measuring the two distances from Chagres to England, the one *via*

New York to Liverpool, the other *via* St. Thomas to Southampton, I make, *in the rough*, the former to be 200 miles the longest, taking the distance ' as the crow flies ;' the disadvantages, however, of the latter much more than counterbalance this apparent difference of distance for steam navigation. First, on leaving Chagres to go to St. Thomas, the course is much more against the trade wind than the course to New York, and consequently a greater time is occupied. Secondly, the time taken up to coal at St. Thomas. Thirdly, the course from St. Thomas to Europe, in order to get the soonest out of the trade wind, and to benefit by the gulf stream, is best made by an angle, which renders the actual distance to be steamed over nearly equal to the New York route; perhaps, in most cases, quite equal.

"' Whereas, taking the route by New York, you may benefit more by the trade wind, and by changing ships at New York you save nearly the whole of the time taken up to coal at St. Thomas ; and I make no doubt that, with equal advantages in point of speed, the route by New York must in all cases be the quickest by two or three days. Likewise on the outward route the changing ships at New York is much to be preferred to the re-fitting and re-coaling the same ship at St. Thomas. In the former case you have the ship prepared leisurely, and with time to have everything in first order ; you have a new and fresh set of officers and crew ready to begin a new voyage ; and I take it that these are great advantages over that of having a jaded crew arrived from a voyage, and all their energies called into exercise to lose not a moment's time to get the ship equipped—no rest, and then off to sea with men and officers exhausted—ship in a state of *disorder* and *dirt* from coaling ; no one who has not experienced it can form any idea of the disadvantages attending this, which some may think a trifling matter.'

"On the score of expense, likewise, the New York route would present an advantage.

" The Royal Mail Company are now paid   £240,000
  The semi-monthly route from Chagres
    to New York   130,000
  Proposed three-weekly route . .   185,000

"Thus there would be effected a saving of 55,000*l.* over the three-weekly proposal, and of 110,000*l.* over the present charge.

"The Cunard Company have powerful steamers, they could at once run on the line to Chagres. By leaving the field open to them, the further advantage would be obtained of enabling the Royal Mail Company to enter, without further delay, upon the Brazilian mail-service, for which it has now no steamers disposable.

"In February, 1849, the contract for the performance of this service was assigned to the Royal Mail Company, but up to this time they seem not to have taken a single step to prepare themselves to fulfil their duties. Meanwhile, the merchants connected with the Brazils and the Rio de la Plata trade have been loudly complaining, and with just cause ; conceiving the Government to be showing undue favour to that company in tolerating this remissness. Indeed, the results of it are likely to be most pernicious to our trade, the United States having determined to profit by it, and occupy that field of enterprise with steamers. The mercantile communities of this country, no less than the defaulting contractors, will thus equally suffer, though in different degrees, through their having now to share a traffic with the United States, which they might in a great measure have centred in Great Britain, had due promptitude and energy been displayed in setting this intercourse on foot."

The question of the Australian Mails is also considered, on which we may give the writer's opinions :—

"There are three routes which, geographically speaking, seem to present nearly equally balanced claims : the Eastern route, or that by Suez and Singapore to Sydney, which is named as the point of destination ; the Western route, or that by the Isthmus of the Americas, across the Pacific by New Zealand to Sydney ; lastly, the route by the Cape of Good Hope and Swan River to Sydney.

"Now, turning to these three routes, it is understood that tenders have been made for them as follows :—

"The Eastern route, or that by Suez and Singapore.
  Outward voyage . . . . .   80 days.
  Homeward . . . . . .   71 ,,
                                        _____
                    Total . 151 days.

"The Western route, or that by Panama and New Zealand, allowing twenty-three days from Southampton to Panama.
  Outward voyage . . . . .   65 days.
  Homeward . . . . . .   63 ,,
                                        _____
                    Total . 128 days.

"The Cape of Good Hope route.

Outward voyage . . . . . 72 days.
Homeward . . . . 72 "

Total . 144 days.

"It will thus be seen that by the Western route, a saving in point of time would be effected of no less than thirty-three days over the Eastern route, and of sixteen days over that by the Cape of Good Hope."

The route to Sydney *via* Singapore would be merely a continuation of the Peninsular and Oriental Company's service, and would be cheaply established, but it is indirect. The route by the Cape of Good Hope would require a fresh line, all the advantages of which might be attained at a less cost by a branch of the Brazil service, from Cape Verd Islands. The Panama route offers the quickest communication, and would render us independent of the Isthmus of Suez, which a war might at any time close against us.

We may here mention, that several deputations have endeavoured to impress upon the ministry the necessity of doing something in the matter of the Australian mails; and that it appears that the East India Company, who keep up a communication between Bombay and Suez, are the only parties who object to such an arrangement. The service is performed by them at a great loss, as their charter does not permit of their carrying freight; and it is hoped that this circumstance will have due weight with the authorities.

LIFE-BOATS.

WE have, on several occasions, called attention to the necessity of providing all vessels with efficient means for the preservation of life in the event of shipwreck; and in our number for December 1847, we gave a drawing and description of a life-boat, devised by Messrs. Lamb and White, and constructed by Mr White of Cowes, the eminent shipbuilder, which appeared, from the successful result of a most severe experimental test, to be well adapted for the intended object. Recent events having conspired to recall public attention to the importance of this subject, we have endeavoured to obtain such additional information respecting the performance of this life-boat as would enable the public to judge of its merits. The result of our enquiries has been very satisfactory. It appears that this life-boat has been extensively adopted in sailing vessels and in steamers; and the vessels now fitting out for the Arctic expedition are to be provided with them. The following letter from Captain Engledue, lately returned from India, alludes to the performance of the life-boat in the Madras surf, which it is well known an ordinary boat can scarcely live in, even in the finest weather.

"Peninsular and Oriental Steam Navigation Co.,
"Offices, 57, High-street, Southampton, Jan. 29th, 1850.

"You ask my opinion as to the performance of the life-boat. All I can say, is, that it is the only boat I have ever seen worthy of the name of a life-boat.

"I witnessed the trial of one of your life-boats, in *the surf*, at Madras; and I was delighted with its performance. In fact, from its construction, and the admirable arrangements of the air-tight compartments, it is impossible to capsize it. These boats are suited for all the ordinary work of ships' boats, as well as combining the property of a life-boat. I consider the shape and general construction to be as near perfection as possible.

"The Peninsular and Oriental Company have adopted them in all their vessels; this, at once, will be a sufficient proof as to their known efficiency.

"Should any parties desire any further particulars kindly use my name, and refer them to me.

"Yours faithfully,
"T. W. ENGLEDUE."

The following extract of a letter from the Superintendent of the Peninsular and Oriental Company at Hong Kong, speaks very favourably of the life-boat with which the *Canton*, one of the Company's ships, was provided.

Extract of a Letter received from the Company's Superintendent at Hong Kong, under date 29th Sept.

"During the voyage, when close in with the mainland, the *Canton* was overtaken by a violent *typhoon*, which lasted with great fury for some hours; she was fortunate enough, however, to reach a sheltered place where she lay at anchor, in safety, until it was over. Whilst running for it during the gale, she showed herself a most excellent sea-boat, and gave proof that she was possessed of qualities which would enable her to contend with the most severe weather.

"I must also mention to you that her life-boat rendered important service on one or two occasions during the trip; on one especially, when it kept up a communication with the shore, and carried out hawsers, though the surf was running so high that no other description of boat could possibly have lived in it, and the waves were repeatedly breaking over the boat, and completely burying it beneath them."

At Madras, the Superintendent of the Peninsular Company put a native crew into one of the life-boats, but being unaccustomed to European boats, they imagined it necessary to keep the boat free of water, whereas the boat has actually more stability when filled with water than when empty. Notwithstanding the disadvantage, however, of having an inefficient crew, the letter establishes the fact, that the boat will neither sink nor capsize, which is all that can be wanted in a life-boat.

"On 'Bentinck's' return I shall send back the life-boat. We made several trials with her when the surf was high, but as she is too shallow by two streaks, the first surf filled her, and the crew jumped overboard: but to render a life-boat serviceable here, she ought to be manned with an European crew. The boat has one good quality, she neither upsets nor sinks; but the under surf swamped or filled her, and before water could be baled out; in one attempt, when the crew stuck by her to the last, she was driven a hundred yards along the beach.

(Signed)   "G. BIDEN."

A life-boat has been established at Cardigan, which has given great satisfaction. We subjoin an account of an experimental trial from a local journal, and testimonials from the crew and master of the boat.

"*The Cardigan Life-boat, built at Cowes by Messrs. Thomas and John White.*

"During the late heavy gales and storms which prevailed in Cardigan Bay and on this coast, some experiments were made by a crew selected for the purpose, in order to test the power and safety of the new patent life-boat, recently established by subscription at Cardigan. The crew selected on this occasion consisted of the following persons:—Captain of the boat, Captain George Bowen, Daniel Rees, Griffith Daniel, Thomas Morris, Thomas Evans, Thomas Lloyd, Thomas Lewis, Joseph Davies, John Williams, David Davies, and John Morris.

"At a given signal the gallant little craft, with her hardy crew, scudded merrily into the midst of the foaming and tempestuous waters, the wind at the time blowing a perfect hurricane, and the sea running extremely high, enough to daunt the boldest heart. The boat was soon in deep water, and there every effort was made to waterlog her. She was first placed broadside to the heavy sea, but without the slightest effect being made upon her; she was then turned broadside to the wind, which blew heavy at the time, with the same satisfactory result. The crew then stood up on one side of the boat, but again she fully realised all expectations; her crew then suddenly threw themselves to the opposite side, but again without injury to the boat, or in any way producing a result calculated to lessen confidence. She was also filled to the gunwale with water, but this did not in any great degree affect her buoyancy; and the entire result of the experimental trip sufficiently proved that, should the hour of peril call forth her dauntless crew to assist their fellow-seamen, they can fearlessly trust themselves to the wild wind and waters, with the certainty of a sure rescue to the helpless, and a safe return to themselves. In the new life-boat the arrangements adopted to insure buoyancy, are at the same time conducive to the strength and stability of the boat. The air vessels form a trunk round the inside of the boat, rising as high as the gunwale, but only extending down on each side as far as the bilge, by which means the centre of buoyancy is kept so high that it is impossible to swamp or capsize the boat; the upper part of the air trunk is rounded off inside, to permit the boat to be emptied of water as she rolls, and to facilitate the use of the oars; and the air trunk is divided by partitions into several water-tight compartments, so that no great injury could result from one or more being stove. The gallant crew were hailed with loud cheers by the spectators on their return from the perilous adventure, and the

15

whole crew expressed the most entire confidence in the powers of the boat, and the result of the trial has given general satisfaction.

"It cannot be too generally known that a life-boat of great power is now established at Cardigan, which has hitherto been considered as little better than a yawning sepulchre to the storm-tossed mariners."— *Carmarthen Journal.*

"We, whose names are hereunto attached, forming the crew of the New Life-Boat, lately tried by us, (an account of which has been published in the *Carmarthen Journal*), feel it right to send this our testimonial of the perfect success of the said boat; and that we have every confidence in her, and shall not shrink from facing the most tempestuous weather, when our services are required by our fellow-creatures in distress.

"As witness our hands, this first day of February, one thousand eight hundred and fifty.

	(Signed)	"George Bowen, Master Mariner.
Dated at Cardigan.		Daniel Rees, ditto.
		T. Morris, ditto.
		Griffith Daniel, ditto.
		Thomas Evans, Seaman,
		Jos. Davis, ditto.
		John Williams, ditto.
		John Morris, ditto.
		Thomas Llewis, ditto.
		Thomas Lloyd, ditto.
		David Davies, ditto."

Copy of a Letter received from the Captain of the Life-boat at Cardigan.— Lamb and White's Patent.

"St. Dogmaels, Cardigan, February 15th, 1850.

"DEAR SIR,—I beg to say we were visited on the 6th of this month with a tremendous storm from the N.N.W., and at about 10 in the morning the brig "*Thetis*," of Limerick, 296 tons register, in a sunken state, came on our bar. We immediately manned the life-boat with a picked crew and got very near the vessel, when a tremendous sea broke on the boat and overpowered us. After making several other attempts the boat was manned with a fresh crew, which again failed. Again we got a fresh crew, but before we reached the brig she went to pieces; we, however, succeeded in saving two of the crew, whom we found floating on the water. The remainder of the crew, eleven persons, were drowned.

"The boat answered well, without any fault whatever. It was impossible to pull against the wind. There were thousands of persons looking on and admiring the boat. We are now going to station the boat on the west side of our bay, which will be to windward, but before this can be properly done a kind of breakwater must be made, so as to give us a fair opportunity to start.

"The committee have appointed me Master of the boat, and likewise to get subscriptions to complete our object; I therefore feel satisfied you and your friends will assist us in this important matter, which will give better fair play to the boat.

"Waiting your reply, I remain, yours respectfully,
(Signed) "GEORGE BOWEN
"Master of the Cardigan life-boat."

The crew of the Cardigan life-boat were quite satisfied, from the result of these trials, of the efficiency of the life-boat; but they thought that a longer boat would be desirable, as they could put more power into it when they had a heavy sea and wind to contend with. They therefore sent the boat to the Isle of Wight and, took back, by the same route, a boat three feet longer. We subjoin the log kept by the crew, from which it will be seen that they encountered very bad weather, and that the boat behaved admirably.

Abstract of a Journal in the 24 feet Boat from Cardigan to Cowes.

"1849. Sept. 5th.—1 A. M. Got out over the bar; light winds from S.S.W.; at 3 fine breeze sprang up from S.S.E.; at 8 got through St. David's Sound; at 2 P. M. off St. Ann's; strong breeze from E.S.E.; at 8 off Lundy Island.

"6th.—Strong breeze from E.S.E., with heavy swell; at 6 A.M. abreast Padstow; at 2 P.M. got round the Longships light; winds from the eastward, with heavy swell; tacked boat; at 10 got into Mouse Hole; thick, with variable winds.

"7th.—A.M. Variable light winds; at 6 P.M. got out from Mouse Hole; tacked boat at 9; came to in Mount's Roads at 11; light

breeze sprang up from E.N.E.; got under way, and sailed towards the Lizard.

"8th.—At 2 A.M. abreast the Lizard; strong wind from E.S.E., with heavy swell; tacked boat, with great many vessels in company; at 10 got alongside Falmouth quay.

"9th.—At 2 A.M. light breeze sprang from W.S.W.; got under way; at 8, off the Deadman; fine breeze, with smooth water; at 1 P.M. Eddystone bore S.S.W.; at 5 abreast the Start; strong breeze, with heavy swell.

"10th.—At 1 A.M. abreast the Bill of Portland; strong wind, with sea running very high; at 7 got through the Needles; showery, with strong wind from S.W.; sea running very high; at 10 got to Messrs. White's yard."

Journal of a Voyage from Cowes, Isle of Wight, to Cardigan, in the 27 feet Life-boat. David Owen, Commander. Kept by David Thomas.

"Saturday, Sept. 15th, E.N.E.—Moderate and clear at 9 A.M.; made sail at 12; Needles' lighthouse bore S.W., distance two miles; fine breeze from the eastward and clear; at 4 P. M. St. Alban's Head N.N.W., distance one mile and a half; at 12 Portland light bore N.N.W., distance 10 miles.

"Sunday, 16th, S.E.—Light winds from the southward; drifted into Torbay; at 6 P.M. a light breeze sprung up from N.E.; at 10h. 30m. Start light bore N.N.E., with heavy swell.

"Monday, 17th, N.E. by N.—Strong gale from N.E., attended with showers of rain; at 1h. 20m. A.M., Eddystone light N., distance three miles and a half; at 9h. 30m. abreast the Lizard, E.N.E.; off shore about two miles; sailed along shore into Mount's Bay; at 12h. 30m. P.M. put into Mouse Hole; latter part, strong breeze and clear.

"Tuesday, 18th.—Brisk gale and clear; employed repairing pump, boxes, drying sails, &c.

"19th, E.N.E.—Light winds from E.N.E. and clear; at 8 A.M. made sail; at 10 got through the Longship Sound; tacked boat to the eastward; at 4 P.M. put into St. Ives; at 10 came out of the pier and came to in the bay.

"Sept. 20th, E.N.E.—Fresh breeze from E.N.E.; at 2 A.M. made sail; at 4 P.M. off Trevorse Head; strong gale and heavy swell; at 5 bore for Newquay; at 6 got into the pier; latter part strong gale and heavy rain.

"21st, N.E.—Brisk gale and cloudy; employed drying sails.

"Saturday, Sept. 22nd.—Moderate breeze, thick and cloudy at 9 A.M.; made sail at 11; Trevorse Head bore S E., distance two miles; at noon strong breeze; heavy swell, with drizzling rain; at 8 P.M. Lundy light bore east, distance three miles; blowing strong gale, sea running very high; at 11 boat shipped a heavy sea on the lee bow, and put out the light in the binnacle; at 12 took in the jib foresail and mizen, and hove the boat to under double-reefed mainsail; could not ascertain the drift, on account of having no light in the binnacle.

"Sunday, Sept. 23rd, E.S.E.—Blowing strong, with heavy swell; at 2 A.M. made St. Ann's light on the lee bow; in dread of drifting on the Crow Rocks kept away; St. Ann's light on the weather bow; at 4 out one reef of the mainsail; set foresail and mizen, and hauled on a wind, sea abating a little; at 5 off Skomar island; at 6 got through Broad Sound; tacked into St. Bride's Bay; found all the provisions wet, and could strike no light; bore up for Milford; at 4 P.M. got into Pill and moored boat.

"Sept. 24th, S.E.—Fine weather throughout; employed drying sails and clothes, and getting fresh provisions on board.

"Sept. 25th, S.S.E.—Moderate wind and hazy; at 2 A.M. made sail; at 4 off St. Ann's light; sailed outside the island; at 8 in St. David's Sound; cleared up, with fine breeze, from S.S.E.; at 5 tacked into Fishguard Road; beat up along shore; at 10 off Dina's Head.

"Wednesday, Sept. 26th, S.E.—Moderate breezes and smooth water; tacked up along shore and into Cardigan bay; at 3 A.M. came over the bar; at 3h. 30m. moored at Pioll Cam; at 10 made sail, and beat up the river; blowing strong breeze from the eastward; at 1 P.M. came too abreast Mr. Davies' yard."

SHEPARD'S PATENT SLIDING GATES.

THIS plan, the invention of Mr. Shepard, C.E., is more particularly adapted for large doors and gates, which, if hung on hinges, would require the power of several men to move, but which can by this means be readily opened and closed. It has been applied, amongst other places, to the doors of the coach factory at Euston-square, a sketch of one of which we give. The mode of action is very simple, and will be

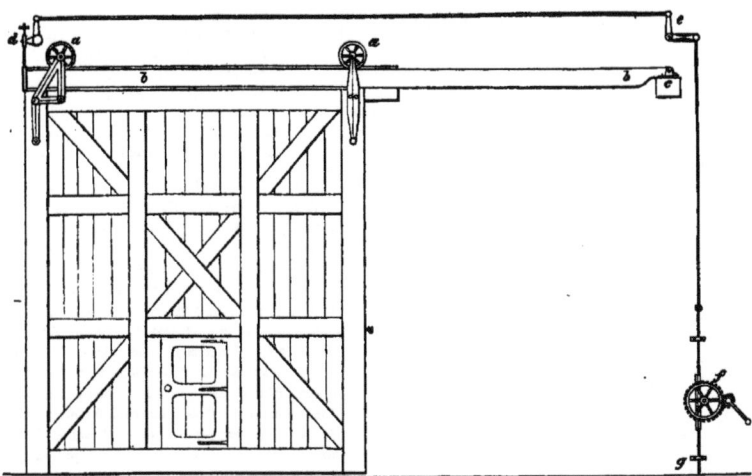

perceived at a glance. The door is hung by two cast-iron frames carrying wheels *a a* running on a bar *b b*, which we may call the railway, overhead. This railway is jointed at the inner end, on a bearer *c*, and at the junction of the two doors is carried by a lever and rod *d*, which is connected to a second similar lever *e*, and finally to the tooth gearing *f*, by working which the extremity of the railway can be raised or depressed, the gravity of the gate causing it to move in either direction, as may be required. The weight of the gate is balanced by a weight connected to the rod *g*, and sunk in a recess provided for it. A similar railway is provided for the other half of the gate; but one regulating apparatus is sufficient; and if the gates are properly balanced, it is evident that the power required to cause them to move is merely that necessary to overcome the friction. Mr. Dockray gives the invention a most satisfactory character, and states—"In reply to your inquiry, I have to inform you, that your apparatus attached to the sliding doors of the coach factory at this station continues to work satisfactorily. These doors are of unusual dimensions—27 feet in length, and 15 feet in height. One man can either open or shut them by means of your invention, with ease."

Mr. Shepard has a numerous list of testimonials, and a very enviable collection of more substantial proofs of approbation, in the shape of gold medals and diamonds from various foreign governments who have patronized his improved gates.

HERTSLET'S PATENT HOLLOW BRICKS.

THE abolition of the Brick Duties seems to have given a spur to the ingenuity of those connected with the trade, and we propose to aid, as far as lies in our power, in the developement of improvement by collecting information on the subject of brick and tile machinery. We have some drawings in hand for the purpose, which we may give in our next Number; but in the mean time we call our readers' attention to an important change now being introduced into the shape of the bricks, and the new principle of making them hollow. While inspecting Mr. Moffat's Patent Sewage Manure Works (of which we have plans in progress), we were struck with the drying-room, which is formed of cast-iron columns and girders, with the intervals filled-in with bricks of the annexed shape.

It will be observed that they are on the cellular principle, which

gives them extraordinary strength, combined with lightness. The stratum of air which they contain renders them bad conductors of heat

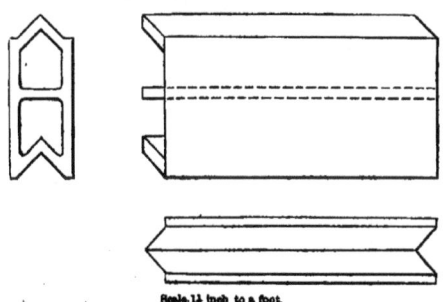

Scale-1½ inch to a foot.

and sound, and peculiarly fits them for partitions, where the weight of common brickwork would preclude its use—for drying ovens, for malt kilns, for closing in boilers, and numerous other purposes, which will readily occur to the reader. We doubt, however, whether any one would be prepared for the enormous strength which the dovetails exhibit in the case of a wall built on Mr. Hertslet's wharf, Adelphi. A small brick building, 7 feet long × 5 feet 7 inches wide, and 6 feet 7 inches high, has, running from one of its longer sides, a wall 2 feet 11 inches high, and about 18 feet long. The whole is of these dovetailed hollow bricks (with the exception of a pier), making the walls 4 inches bare in thickness. A few days since, the horses in a wagon on the wharf took fright, and backed the wagon against this low wall, about 15 feet from its junction with the building. The blow, of course, crushed the unsupported wall, but only where the wheel struck it, and rather than give way at the joints, the wall transmitted the blow through the 15 feet, and lifted the return wall at right angles to it, the further end of which was supported by a pier of common bricks 9 inches × 14. The work was in mortar, and is still standing, inviting the inspection of the curious in such matters.

FRYER AND ROBINSON'S PATENT SAFETY STEERING WHEEL.

This simple and effective invention is designed to give the steersman complete command over the rudder, even in the heaviest weather. It consists merely of the application of a brake to the ordinary steering wheel, and not the least of its advantages is, that it can be readily applied

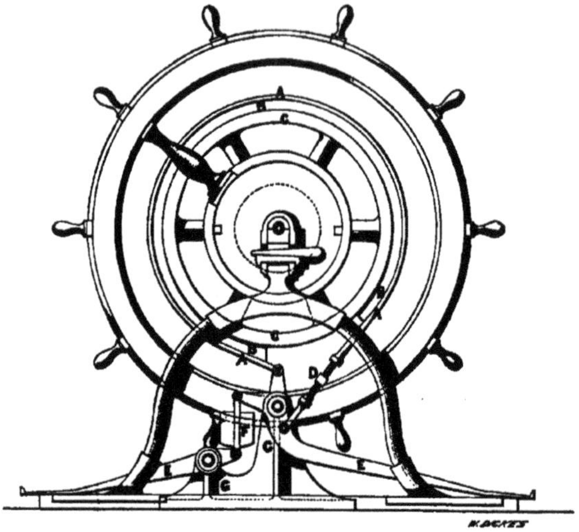

to wheels already made, at a small expense. A A A, is a metal brake band, lined with wood B B B. C is the brake wheel fixed to the steering wheel, D is an adjusting screw, for tightening or loosening the band. E E are two treadle levers, on which one or two steersmen can throw their weight, and which will immediately fix the steering wheel in any required position. F is a balance weight, lifting the brake off the wheel when the man's weight is taken off. G G, the metal framing on which the centres of the levers are supported. It is evident that by varying the pressure of his foot, the steersman can either stop the wheel dead, or allow it gradually to fall away to the force of the sea.

DIMENSIONS AND DETAILS OF NEW STEAMERS.

LIVERPOOL, EGREMONT, AND NEW-BRIGHTON IRON STEAM FERRY-BOAT "FAIRY."

Built by Messrs. Thomas Vernon & Son, Liverpool, 1849. Engines by Messrs. George Forrester & Co., Vauxhall Foundry.

Builder's measurement.	Ft.	In.
Length of keel and fore rake	118	0
Breadth of beam	16	7
Ditto over paddle-cases	31	0
Depth of hold	7	8
Length of engine space	28	4
Tonnage.	**Tons.**	
Hull	$160\frac{29}{94}$	
Contents of engine space	$41\frac{72}{94}$	
Register	$118\frac{51}{94}$	

New measurement.	Ft.	
Length on deck	118	0
Breadth on ditto at midships	16	0
Depth of hold, ditto	7	5
Length of engine space	28	4
Tonnage.	**Tons.**	
Hull	$112\frac{2}{100}$	
Contents of engine space	$36\frac{88}{100}$	
Register	$75\frac{14}{100}$	

A pair of fore and aft oscillating engines, with drag-link (upon the patent principle of Mr. Douglas Hebson) of 62 horse nominal power. Diameter of cylinders, 31 inches × 3 feet 6 inches length of stroke. The air-pumps are two in number, wrought off the crank shaft by a common eccentric wheel on each side of the engines, and work remarkably smooth, and are very compact. Overhung paddle-wheels, diameter extreme, 14 feet 5½ inches; ditto effective, 14 feet 1 inch. Floats, 5 feet 6 inches × 1 foot 4 inches. Two sets of 8 arms, and 16 floats. One tubular boiler, length, 10 feet; breadth, 12 feet; height, 7 feet. Steam chest—length, 10 feet; breadth, 4 feet 6 inches; height, 4 feet 6 inches. Two cylindrical furnaces—diameter 3 feet 6 inches × 6 feet. 160 wrought iron tubes, 3 inches diameter × 7 feet. Average, 36 revolutions per minute. Steam pressure, 11 lbs. Consumes 5 cwt. of coals per hour. Bunkers hold 10 tons. Draught of water 3 feet. Frames, 2½ × 2½ × ¼ inch, and 2 feet apart. Crew, 7 in number, viz.—3 in the engine room and 4 on deck.

DESCRIPTION.

No head or galleries. Both ends built sharp, acting as bow or stern (upon Mr. Laird's patent) with two rudders. No masts nor bowsprit, nor rigging; one deck, and clench built. Port of Liverpool.

DUNDALK AND LIVERPOOL STEAM NAVIGATION COMPANY'S IRON STEAM VESSEL "DUNDALK."

Built and fitted by Mr. Robert Napier, Glasgow, 1843.

Builder's measurement.	Ft.	In.
Length of keel and fore rake	169	6
Breadth of beam	26	1
Ditto over the paddle-cases	46	4½
Depth of hold	15	6
Length of engine space	57	2
Tonnage.	**Tons.**	
Hull	$556\frac{71}{94}$	
Contents of engine space	$206\frac{83}{94}$	
Register	$349\frac{82}{94}$	

New measurement.	Ft.	In.
Length on deck	171	3
Breadth on ditto at midships	25	1
Depth of hold, ditto	15	2
Length of break-deck	36	6
Breadth of ditto	24	5
Depth of ditto	2	8
Length of engine space	57	2
Tonnage.	**Tons.**	
Hull	$574\frac{29}{100}$	
Break-deck	$27\frac{12}{100}$	
Total	$601\frac{41}{100}$	
Contents of engine space	$236\frac{17}{100}$	
Register	$365\frac{24}{100}$	

A pair of side-lever engines of 270 horse nominal power. Diameter of cylinder, 61 inches × 5 feet 6 inches stroke. Diameter of paddle-wheels, extreme, 24 feet 9 inches; ditto effective, 24 feet 1 inch. Floats, 8 feet 8 inches × 2 feet 1 inch. Three sets of 20 arms; average, 21 revolutions per minute. Draught of water, 10 feet 6 inches. Average speed, 13 miles per hour. Common flue boilers; nine furnaces. The former boilers were on board seven years, and a new set were put on board at the beginning of the present year; the company being well satisfied with the first. The speed of the vessel the same as formerly.

DESCRIPTION.

A full female figure head, sham quarter galleries, square sterned, and clinch built vessel. Standing bowsprit, three masts, schooner rigged, clipper bow. Port of Dundalk. Commander—Mr. John Hutcheson.

CITY OF DUBLIN STEAM NAVIGATION COMPANY'S IRON STEAM VESSEL, "ALBERT."

Built by Mr. Thomas Wilson, Liverpool. Engines by Messrs. Maudslay, Sons, and Field, London.

Builder's measurement.	Ft.	In.
Length of keel and fore rake	140	0
Breadth of beam	24	8
Ditto over paddle-cases	41	1
Depth of hold	13	9
Length of engine space	41	4
Tonnage.	**Tons.**	
Hull	400[illegible]	
Engine space	131[illegible]	
Register	268[illegible]	

New measurement.	Ft.	In.
Length on deck	140	5
Breadth on ditto at midships	23	0
Depth of hold	13	6
Ditto of poop	2	7
Length of engine space	41	4
Tonnage	**Tons.**	
Hull	483 3/100	
Contents of engine space	141[illegible]	
Register	342[illegible]	

A pair of side lever engines, of 150 horse nominal power. Diameter of cylinders, 46½ inches × 4 feet 6 inches stroke. Diameter of paddle wheels, extreme, 18 feet 7 inches; ditto, effective, 18 feet 1 inch. Floats, 6 feet 6 inches × 2 feet. Three sets of 14 arms and floats. Two flue boilers—length, 14 feet, breadth of ditto, 8 feet 10 inches, height, 11 feet. Six furnaces, three in each boiler—length, 5 feet, breadth of do., 2 feet 1 inch, height, 3 feet 9 inches. Average, 20 revolutions per minute. Steam pressure, 8 lbs.; consumes 15 cwt. of coals per hour. This vessel was built in 1845 for the present engines, which were formerly on board the steam vessel *Commerce*, built at Liverpool, 1825, but now a sailing vessel.

DESCRIPTION.

No figure head, no galleries, toping-up bowsprit, two masts, schooner-rigged, square-sterned, and carvil-built vessel. Port of Dublin. Commander—Mr. Hamlet W. Geary.

NEW YORK AND ALBANY STEAMER "ISAAC NEWTON."

The largest steamer in the New or Old world.

Dimensions.	Ft.	In.
Length on deck	345	0
Breadth of beam	40	6
Ditto over the paddle-boxes	85	0
	Tons.	
Tonnage (British)	2833[illegible]	
Ditto American	1450	

One over-head beam engine, of 501 horse *nominal* power.* Diameter of cylinder, 82 inches × 12 feet length of stroke. Wrought iron cranks and shafts. Two funnels. Berths for passengers 50; other accommodations for 2200 in the state-rooms, family cabins, &c. Three decks. No figure-head, galleries, or bowsprit. Square sterned and carvil-built vessel. Commander—Mr. W. H. Peck.

ST. LOUIS AND NEW ORLEANS ROYAL MAIL REGULAR STEAM VESSEL, "MARIA."

Built by Messrs. Litherburg and Lockwood. Engines by Mr. Anthony Harkness. Joiner Work by Messrs. Johnson, Morton, and Co. of Cincinnati.

	Ft.	In.
Length on deck	275	0
Ditto of keel	240	0
Breadth of beam	36	0
Ditto including the guards	72	0
Depth of hold	9	6
	Tons.	
Tonnage of hull (American)	1500	
Ditto (British, old)	1746[illegible]	

Two engines, non-condensing. Diameter of cylinders, 30 inches × 9 feet length of stroke; diameter of water-wheels, 30 feet; length of buckets, 16 feet; 8 cylindrical boilers, diameter 3 feet 6 inches; two funnels.

DESCRIPTION.

Main, spar, and hurricane decks, no bowsprit, figure-head, galleries, or masts, square-sterned and carvil-built of timber; the steering-wheel is at the foremost part of the vessel on the spar deck, and the paddles are very far aft. Commander, Mr. Theodore W. Dunnica.

BOSTON AND NEW YORK REGULAR EXPRESS MAIL STEAM VESSEL, "OREGON."

	Ft.
Length on deck	325
Breadth of beam, ...	35
Ditto, over the paddle guards	69
Depth of hold	11
	Tons.
Tonnage	1992[illegible]

One beam engine (beam at top); non-condensing; diameter of cylinder, 72 inches × 14 feet length of stroke; diameter of water wheel, 35 feet; length of bucket, 11 feet. This is a new vessel, and a fast one, plying between Boston and New York, *via* Stonington, Providence, and Newport; leaves New York, from No. 1, North River, every Tuesday, Thursday, and Saturday, and back every Monday, Wednesday, and Saturday.

DESCRIPTION.

Five masts, two funnels, main, spar, and hurricane decks. On the fore part of the spar deck is the pilot's house. No figure-head, galleries, bowsprit, &c. Square-sterned and carvil-built; vessel of timber. Commander—Mr. S. Thayer.

---

* Our Correspondent is quite right in underlining the word "nominal," to put our readers on their guard. The probability is, that 50 lbs. steam is used, and a speed at least double anything on the Thames or Clyde; and that an indicator-card would show 3000 horse power!—Ed. Art.

ROYAL STEAM NAVY.

APPOINTMENTS, &c.

Chief Engineer.—PETER M'DOWALL, to the *Archer*, screw-sloop.
Third Class Chief Engineer.—AUGUSTUS MILLS, to the *Dasher*.
Assistant Engineers.—ROBERT ALLAN, ORESTES N. BROOKER, and HENRY WILKES, to the *Archer.*—JOHN N. RYDER, to the *Intrepid.*

TRIALS OF STEAMERS, &c.—MEGÆRA.—On her late trial, the engines worked well, making 74 strokes, of 2 feet 9 inches each, per minute, with very little noise. The vessel is of iron, 207 feet long, 37 feet 8 inches broad, and 24 feet 3 inches depth of hold; her draught forward, 11 feet 4 inches, and aft, 15 feet 3 inches. Her burthen is nearly 1700, but her actual total displacement during the trial was 2200 tons, and the exact speed at the measured mile in Sea Reach 10·291 knots on the average runs, or 11·895 statute miles per hour. The vacuum in the barometer was 27, and the horse-power exerted 1200 by the indicator.

THE COMPARATIVE COSTS OF STEAM AND SAILING FRIGATES.—The expense of a steam frigate compared to that of a sailing frigate is brought to view by the "Select Committee on Navy Estimates, 1848." It is stated, p. 704 of the Appendix to their Report, that the *sailing* frigate, the Thesis, of 36 guns, 330 men, costs per day in pay and provisions to the officers and men, £42. 4s. 5d., and in wear and tear of hull, masts, yards, &c., £22. 13s.; together £64. 17s. 5d. per day. That a *steam* frigate, the Terrible, of 21 guns, yet of about the same weight of armament as the Thesis, but of lesser number of men, 320, costs per day in pay and provisions, £44. 5s. 2d.; that the Terrible costs in wear and tear of hull, masts, yards, &c., £25; together £69. 5s. 2d. per day. To the £69. 5s. 2d. daily expense of the Terrible is added wear and tear of machinery, and consumption of oil, tallow, &c., £19. 11s. 2d. per diem; altogether £88. 16s. 4d. Thus there is an excess of no less than £23. 18s. 11d. in the daily cost of a steam frigate, over that of the sailing frigate, when the steaming apparatus is not put to use; so that the difference of cost between the two amounts to no less a sum than £8740. 4s. 7d. per annum, independently of coals. When the steam is employed, £4. 5s. 6d. per *hour* is to be added to the extra cost of the Terrible, which, though she were to steam on an average less than 10 hours of the 24, would add another sum of about £15,000 a year to the before-named £8704. 4s. 7d.; making altogether the extra cost of a steam frigate not less than £23,740. 4s. 7d. per annum.

STUDIES FOR MEMBERS PREPARING TO VOTE THE NAVY ESTIMATES.—National Dockyards, and a fleet of unemployed vessels, more or less rapidly decaying at their moorings, are supported and advocated, on the ground that it is necessary to be able to send to sea on an emergency an overwhelming force, and that the army of skilled artificers we keep constantly in pay can be depended upon to fit them out more rapidly and efficiently than private tradesmen. Not a fleet, but two vessels, are wanted to succour Sir J. Franklin: in her Majesty's service they are not to be found, and they are obliged to purchase the vessels out of the despised merchant service, which, according to official blue books, and official bills, ought to be taken charge of by the government. Two steam-tenders are required out of the national steam fleet, which has cost us five millions in the last ten years; none are fit for the service, and the Sir Robert Peel and Free Trade are purchased—much to the joy of their owners. Despatch is necessary; the advantages of the dockyard system, "organized efficiency," &c. &c., will be surely shown. A voyage down the river will dispel that illusion; the united energies of Woolwich and Deptford are unequal to the task, and Wigram and Green have the honour and profit of fitting out the expedition. For the last few years iron steam-vessels have so established their superiority over wooden ones, in the essential qualities of speed, economy, and capacity, that no wooden steamers have been constructed in this country for private individuals or companies exposed to competition. Our government first built a fleet of iron vessels, then condemned them as vessels of war, without a trial, and are now selling them off as useless. All practical inquirers, and the whole steam interest of the country, are aware that a great change is going on in steam navigation, by the substitution of the screw-propeller for the paddle-wheel. Our officials are quietly extending the existing contracts for the Post-office service, by paddle-wheel steamers, and thus doing their utmost to perpetuate the existing monopolies, and to keep back improvement in ocean steam navigation.—*Spectator.*

FOREIGN NAVAL PROGRESS.

THE FRENCH 100 GUN LINE-OF-BATTLE SHIP, PRESIDENT, FORMERLY LE 24 FEVRIER.—The stupendous machinery of this large man-of-war is just finished in the government's work at Indret. It is 960 horse-power, and is looked upon as a master-piece; it is expected to be fitted up in about a month.

SPANISH STEAM NAVY.—The Spanish Government are attempting to negociate a loan of thirty millions of reals, to be applied to the purchase of steamers and other vessels of war for the Spanish navy. We think they had better apply it to pay the interest, if not the principal of their debts.

GREAT NAVAL WORK IN RUSSIA.—In the month of February last, the great naval basin at Sebastopol was completed, and the largest ships-of-war in the Russian navy can now be docked with the greatest ease at that port. Some idea may be formed of the magnitude of the works when it is stated that the basin covers an extent of 10 acres of ground, and has seven dry docks, three on one side, and four on the other. The water in the basin is 30 feet above the level of the Black Sea, and the vessels are taken into it by means of three locks, the iron gates of which were made by Messrs George and Sir John Rennie, and are 64 feet broad, the breadth of the locks, and 28 feet deep. A large reservoir has been constructed at some distance from the basin, and the former is constantly supplied with water by allowing a river to enter it; while the quantity of water in the basin is regulated by sluices from the reservoir. Each of the dry docks has a sluice, which can be opened and the water emptied out in a very limited period, without the trouble of pumping, the plan adopted at the docks adjoining basins in this country when it is found requisite to empty them at high-water. The Emperor of Russia is reported to have about 50 ships of war at present at Sebastopol, and has recently received the best description of machinery for making blocks and other purposes.

STEAM NAVIGATION.

BORRIE'S PATENT TWIN STEAMERS.—We are glad to be able to inform our readers that a boat on this principle is now building, by Messrs. Robinsons and Russell of Millwall, for Mr. Borrie, and as we believe she is intended to run on the Thames, they will have an opportunity of taking a trip to Gravesend in her, before the summer is over.

THE HOLYHEAD STEAM PACKETS.—The City of Dublin Steam Packet Company, who have taken the contract for conveying the mails between Holyhead and Kingstown, are about to purchase two of the Admiralty steam packets, for the purpose of carrying on their contract with the same efficiency, celerity, and regularity that the service has been performed under Admiralty management. They are also about to remove their repairing establishment from Liverpool to Holyhead, as they have obtained possession of the Government at the latter place.

A Cardiff Steam Navigation Company is being formed, to run additional boats between Bristol and Cardiff.

STEAM FOR THE ANDES.—An iron steamboat of small size has recently been built by Mr. George Birkbeck, jun., of New York, which, from its destination, merits some notice. The boat is 55 feet keel, 12 feet beam, and 5 feet hold. She is to be propelled by two high pressure engines of 10-horse power each, connected at right angles. Water wheels 10 feet diameter, and of wrought iron. The whole being fitted together in New York, and each piece marked before being shipped. No piece is to exceed in weight 350 lbs., as, on its arrival at Lima, it has to be transported on the backs of mules to its destination, Lake Titicaca, which is situated near the summit of some of the highest mountains in that country, and several miles above the level of the sea. As yet commerce must be in its infancy in that elevated region, but the lake is 140 miles long, and its coast well timbered, and it is understood that much traffic would be the result of increased facilities. In case the first boat succeeds, a larger one is to be sent out immediately.—*Franklin Journal.*

IRON HOUSES FOR CALIFORNIA.

Messrs. Thomas Vernon and Son, Brunswick Dock, Liverpool, are building iron houses in every variety, the cheapest kind of which are as represented in the sketches. They are portable frame buildings, put together with cast iron dove-tail joints, and the outside is covered with corrugated iron, No. 20 gauge in thickness. This class of buildings is peculiarly adapted for emigrants, by the first cost being low, and the

weight and measure for freight comparatively small. We do not see any reason why they should not be adopted for the peasantry in this country; they are much better than many now in use, and, we believe, would cost less money; besides, a piece of land otherwise almost valueless, might be taken on a short lease at a nominal rental, and the houses

removed at the end of the term, if required. They are quickly put together or taken down again; the joints in the frame-work simply wanting to be fixed in their proper places, and the outside sheeting connected with small bolts and nuts. The buildings are usually sold in pieces and packages suitable for shipment, and for re-construction abroad.

Messrs. Vernon and Son have also on hand, just commenced, a large shed for California, 125 feet long, 25 feet broad, and two stories high, with an office at the one end.

F. B.

RAILWAYS.

UHAMROY'S PATENT HELICAL RAILWAY.—The patentee proposes to lift loads or water in mines, and to apply the same principle to lift railway carriages from one line of rails to another on a higher level. For this purpose, a line of rails is arranged in a helical manner in the shaft of the pit, on which runs a platform on three wheels fixed at different levels. A vertical grooved shaft passes through the centre of this platform from the top to the bottom of the shaft of the mine, and receives rotary motion from any prime mover. The platform is furnished with

a bolt which may be slidden into the groove in the shaft, and a rotary motion thereby imparted to it. Upon the platform rest the wheels of another one, which is fitted with guides that embrace rollers fixed to the sides of the pit, and thereby prevent its revolving. And upon this second platform is placed the load to be lifted. On rotary motion being given to the vertical shaft, the under carriage will also revolve, and travel up the helical railway. By reversing the motion of the shaft the loads will be lowered. Instead of the preceding arrangement, it is proposed to place a number of rollers, arranged in a helical direction, in the shaft of the mine, over which travels a helical projection on the periphery of a cylindrical carriage, which is moved up or down a rotary shaft in the same manner as the second platform first described.

THE ENGINE DRIVERS ON THE NORTH WESTERN had an audience of Mr. M'Connell the other day, to discuss several grievances which they still labour under, the most glaring of which seems to be, the non-payment for overtime, when, as in the case of a train breaking down, they are working more than their usual time, and of course much harder. Mr. M'Connell promised that these and other points should be rectified, and the drivers departed much gratified with the attention paid to their representations.

It is reported that a CONTRACT for thirty LOCOMOTIVES has been taken by a firm at Leeds, for one of the leading lines of railway.

The Eastern Counties Railway Company require a locomotive superintendent, and also a superintendent of the carriage and waggon department.

The Box Tunnel, which is 3192 yards in length, was an object of some interest on the 9th instant, as on that morning, at 25 minutes past 5, the sun shone through it. The only other periods that such an event occurs are on the 3rd and 4th September.

Mr. Rea, of the locomotive department of the Bristol and Birmingham Railway, is to succeed Mr. Sturrock, who has been recently appointed to the Great Northern. Mr. Martly, of the locomotive department of the Great Western, is to be transferred to the same post on the South Wales.

MESSRS. FOX, HENDERSON, & Co. have in hand an iron bridge, 700 feet long, for the Galway Railway, to cross the Shannon at Athlone.

The Engine Drivers of the North British Railway have struck, to the number of 66, refusing to submit to the terms of the directors.

NOVELTIES.

NEW METHOD OF JOINING METALS.—Some interest has been excited by the experiments of a French gentleman, in London, who has, it is stated, discovered a method of joining, by some cement, pieces of metal together so firmly, that when exposed to a tensile strain, they will break through the metal rather than at the joint. Could such an invention be brought to bear practically, it would effect a complete revolution in works of metal.

HOW AXES ARE MADE.—The process has been greatly simplified within the last two years. The iron is rolled out into bars the proper width and thickness of an axe, and 6, 8, and 10 feet long; it is heated and cut off by a large pair of shears propelled by water power; another workman picks up the piece and places it between a die and punch, and the punch comes down and forces the hole for the handle by punching out a piece. An iron mandrill is then inserted into the hole, and it is immediately put under another press, which forms one side of the axe; it then goes into another die, and forms the other side, and is then placed in an upright position, and a chisel comes down and splits the "bit" of the axe ready for the steel; it is then thrown aside. All this is done at one heat, and in less time than it takes to write the *modus operandi*. The blade of the axe is then put in and welded, and passed along to the forger, tempered, and is cast upon the ground to cool. As soon as cool, it is taken up and planed down to an edge by a planing machine, and finished up with the emery wheels—painted, labelled, stamped, and is ready for market.—*American Paper.*

LIST OF ENGLISH PATENTS.

FROM THE 2ND DAY OF MARCH, TO THE 18TH DAY OF APRIL, 1850, INCLUSIVE.

Thomas Richards, William Taylor, and James Wylde, the younger, of Falcon Works, Walworth, Surrey, cotton manufacturers, for improved rollers to be used in the manufacture of silk, cotton, woollen, and other fabrics. March 2.

William Edwards Staite, of Throgmorton-street, London, gentleman, for improvements in pipes for smoking, and in apparatus connected therewith. March 4.

William McNaught, of Rochdale, Lancaster, engineer, for certain improvements in steam-engines, and also improvements in apparatus for ascertaining and registering the power of the same. March 7.

John Fowler, Jun., of Melksham, Wilts, engineer, for improvements in draining land. March 7.

William Benson Stones, of Golden-square, Middlesex, Manchester warehouseman, for improvements in treating peat and other carbonaceous and ligneous matters, so as to obtain products therefrom. March 7.—(Communication.)

William Brown, of Airdrie, Lancashire, electrician, and William Williams the younger, of St. Dennis, Cornwall, gentleman, for improvements in electric and magnetic apparatus for indicating and communicating intelligence. March 7.

Henry James Towling, of Bayswater, Middlesex, commission agent, for improvements in the manufacture of fuel and manure, and deodorizing and disinfecting materials. March 7.

William Church, of Birmingham, engineer, for certain improvements in machinery or apparatus to be employed in manufacturing cards and other articles composed wholly or in part of paper or pasteboard, part or parts of the said machinery being applicable to printing the same, and parts to other purposes where pressure is required. March 7.

Richard Archibald Brooman, of the firm of Messrs. J. C. Robertson & Co., of Fleet-street, patent agents, for improvements in types, stereotype-plates, and other figured surfaces for printing from. March 7.—(Communication.)

Richard Carte, of Southampton-street, Strand, Middlesex, professor of music, for certain improvements in the musical instruments designated flutes, clarionets, hautboys, and bassoons. March 7.

John Tayler, of Manchester, mechanical designer, and Richard Hurst, of Rochdale, in the same county, cotton spinner, for certain improvements in, and applicable to looms for weaving, and in machinery or apparatus for preparing, balling, and winding warps or yarns. March 7.

Gerard John De Witte, of Brook-street, Westminster, Middlesex, gentleman, for improvements in machinery, apparatus, metallic and other substances, for the purposes of letter-press and other printing. March 7.—(Communication.)

John Tebay, of Hackney, Middlesex, civil engineer, for an improved meter for registering the flow of water and other fluids. March 7

Frederick Rosenborg, of Albemarle-street, Middlesex, Esq., and Conrad Montgomery, of the Army and Navy Club, St. James's-square, Middlesex, for improvements in sawing, cutting, boring, and shaping wood. March 7.

Thomas Irving Hill, of Clapham, in the county of Surrey, gentleman, for certain improvements in the treatment of copper and other ores, and obtaining products therefrom. March 9.

Richard Holdsworth, of the firm of Holdsworth & Co., cotton spinner, and William Holgate, engineer, for improvements in apparatus and machinery for warping worsted, cotton, and other fibrous materials. March 11.

William Crane Wilkins, of Long Acre, in the county of Middlesex, engineer, for certain improvements in ventilating, lighting, and heating in lamps and candlesticks; in the manufacture of candles; and in the apparatus to be used for such purposes. March 11.

James Nasmyth, of Lille, in the Republic of France, engineer, for improvements in the method of obtaining and applying heat. March 12.

Robert Milligan, of Harden, near Bingley, in the county of York, manufacturer, for an improved mode of treating certain floated warp or weft, or both, for the purpose of producing ornamented fabrics. March 18.

George Jenkins, of Nassau-street, Soho, in the county of Middlesex, gentleman, for certain improvements in the means of producing motive power. March 18

Thomas Edmondson, of Salford, in the county of Lancaster, printer, for improvements in the manufacture of railway and other tickets; and in machinery or apperatus for marking railway and other tickets. March 19.

William Joseph Horsfall and Thomas James, both of the Mersey Steel and Iron Works, Toxteth Park, Liverpool, in the county of Lancaster, for improvements in the rolling of iron, and other metals. March 19.

Samuel Cunliffe Lister, of Manningham, near Bradford, in the county of York, and George Edmund Donisthorpe, of Leeds, in the same county, manufacturer, for improvements in preparing and combing wool, and other fibrous materials. March 20.

Horatio Carter, of Thirza-place, Old Kent-road, in the county of Surrey, gentleman, for certain improvements in the production of light from ordinary coal gas, by the use of burners consisting of more than one ring or sheet of flame, combined with a suitable chimney, and supplied with atmospheric air, particularly adapted to ventilation. March 23.

Joshua Siddeley, Jun., brass founder, of Liverpool, in the county of Lancaster, for certain improvements in ships' fittings. March 23.

Alfred Wilson, of Myddleton-street, Clerkenwell, in the county of Middlesex, clock case maker, for an improved ventilator. March 23.

John Gedge, of Wellington-street, Strand, in the county of Middlesex, for improvements in lamps and candlesticks. March 23.—(Communication.)

John Stevenson, of Roan Mills, Dungannon, county Tyrone, flax spinner, for certain improvements in machinery for spinning flax and other substances. March 23.

William Sykes, of York-street, in the county of Middlesex, tallow-chandler, for certain improvements in the manufacture of candles and wicks. March 23.

John Varley and Joseph Hacking, of Bury, in the county of Lancaster, engineers, for certain improvements in steam engines, and apparatus connected therewith. March 23.

Henry Robert Ramsbotham, of Bradford, in the county of York, manufacturer, and William Brown, of the same place, mechanic, for improvements in preparing and combing wool. March 23.

William Joseph Curtis, of Port of Spain, in the island of Trinidad, in the West Indies, civil engineer, for improved machinery and apparatus adapted for the manufacture of sugar. March 23.

Nathaniel Mathew, of Wern Tremadoc, in the county of Carnarvon, quarry proprietor, for an apparatus for cutting and dressing slates into various shapes and sizes. March 23.

Alfred Guillaume Roseleur, of Paris, in the Republic of France, but now of South-street, Finsbury, in the county of Middlesex, chemist, for certain improvements in coating or covering metals with tin. March 23.

Alfred Vincent Newton, of Chancery-lane, in the county of Middlesex, for improvements in the preparation of materials for the production of a composition or compositions, applicable to the manufacture of buttons, knife and razor handles, inkstands, door-knobs, and other articles where hardness, strength, and durability are required. March 23.

Edward Welch, of St. John's-wood, London, architect, for improvements in fireplaces and flues, and in apparatus connected therewith. March 23.

Thomas Dickason Rotch, of Drumlamford House, in the county of Ayr, N.B., Esq., for improvements in separating various matters usually found combined in certain saccharine, saline, and ligneous substances. March 26.—(Communication.)

Alfred Vincent Newton, of Chancery-lane, in the county of Middlesex, for improvements in coupling joints for pipes. March 26.—(Communication.)

James Preece, of the city of Hereford, shoemaker, for certain improvements in mills, and machinery applicable to the thrashing and grinding of corn, the manufacture of cider, and other similar purposes. March 26

Joseph Theodore Clenchard, of Paris, in the Republic of France, manufacturing chemist, for certain improvements in the application of arcild to the processes of dyeing and printing in colours; and also an improved apparatus to be employed in the operation of dyeing. March 26.

Evan Leigh, of Mills Platting, near Manchester, cotton spinner, for certain improvements in machinery or apparatus for preparing and spinning cotton, and other fibrous substances March 26.

Thomas Walker, of Wednesbury, in the county of Stafford, iron-master, for improvements in the manufacture of sheets or plates of iron, for certain purposes. March 28.

James Samuel, of Willoughby House, in the county of Middlesex, civil engineer, for certain improvements in the construction of railways and steam engines; and in steam engine machinery. April 5.

Joseph Findlay, of Paisley, in the county of Renfrew, N.B., for an improvement or improvements in machinery or apparatus for turning, cutting, shaping, or reducing wood, or other substances April 5

George Henry Phipps, of Park-road, Stockwell, in the county of Surrey, engineer, for improvements in propelling vessels. April 5.

Jonathan Charles Goodall, of Great College-street, Camden Town, in the county of Middlesex, card maker, for improvements in machinery for cutting paper. April 5.

Charles Seely, of Heighington, in the county of Lincoln, merchant, for improvements in grinding wheat, and other grain. April 5.

John Platt, of Oldham, in the county of Lancaster, engineer, for certain improvements in machinery or apparatus for spinning, doubling, and weaving cotton, flax, and other fibrous substances. April 11.

Richard Prosser, of Birmingham, civil engineer, for certain improvements in machinery and apparatus for manufacturing metal tubes, which improvements in machinery are, in part, applicable for other purposes where pressure is required; also for improvements in the mode of applying metal tubes in steam boilers, or other vessels requiring metal to be applied within them April 11.

Amedee Francis Remond, of Birmingham, for improvements in the manufacture of envelopes. April 15.

Edme Augustin Chameroy, of Paris, for improvements in the manufacture of boilers, and of pipes, of malleable substances, as well as of elastic matter. April 15.

Robert Reid, of Glasgow, manufacturer, for certain improvements in weaving. April 15.

Florid Heindryckx, of Brussels, engineer, for improvements in propelling. April 15.

Cuthbert Dinsdale, of Newcastle-upon-Tyne, dentist, for improvements in the manufacture of artificial palates and gums; and in the mode of setting or fixing natural and artificial teeth. April 15.

John Turner, of Birmingham, engineer, and Joseph Hardwick, of the same place, for a certain improvement, or certain improvements, in the construction and setting of steam boilers. April 15.

George Attwood, of Birmingham, copper roller manufacturer, for a new or improved method of making tubing of copper, or alloys of copper. April 15.

Charles de Bergue, of Authur-street West, London, engineer, for certain improvements in locomotive and other steam engines; also in buffers, for railway purposes. April 15.

John Dove Harris, of the borough of Leicester, manufacturer, for improvements in the manufacture of looped fabrics. April 18.

William Buckwell, of the Artificial Granite Works, Battersea, civil engineer, and George Fisher, of the Taff Vale Railway, Cardiff, civil engineer, for improvements in the construction, and means of applying, carriage and certain other springs. April 18.

William Henry Ashurst, of the Old Jewry, gentleman, for improvements in the manufacture of varnishes. April 18.—(Communication.)

Thomas Ross, of Coleman-street, gentleman, for improvements in machinery for raising a pile upon woven and felted fabrics. April 18.

Abraham Moses Marbe, of Birmingham, chemist, for an improved manufacture of vegetable fluid, to be used in the production of artificial light, and in lamps or burners for consuming the same; which vegetable fluid is also applicable to the manufacture of lacker or varnish. April 18.

William Hargreaves, the younger, of Bradford, in the county of York, ironfounder, for certain improvements in the means of consuming smoke, part of which improvements are also applicable to the generating of steam. April 18.

LIST OF PATENTS THAT HAVE PASSED THE GREAT SEAL OF SCOTLAND.

FROM THE 24TH DAY OF DECEMBER TO THE 31ST, 1849, INCLUSIVE.

James Usher, of Edinburgh, gentleman, for improvements in machinery for tilling land. December 24.

John Stoughton Christie, of Craven-street, Strand, in the county of Middlesex, Esq., for an improved construction of wrought iron wheels, and machinery for effecting the same. December 24.—(Communication.)

Richard Hobson, M.D., of Leeds, in the county of York, for certain improvements in the manufacture of horse-shoes, and an apparatus for taking the measurement of horse-shoes, or horses' hoofs. December 26.

William Ackroyd, of Birkenshaw Mills, near Leeds, in the county of York, manufacturer, for improvements in dressing and cleaning worsted, and worsted mixed with cotton and other fabrics, after they have been woven. December 31.—(Communication.)

John Barsham, of Kingston, in the county of Surrey, manufacturer, for improvements in separating the cocoa fibre from cocoa nut husks. December 31.

DESIGNS FOR ARTICLES OF UTILITY.

REGISTERED FROM 30TH APRIL TO 17TH APRIL

March 30th, 2243, William Robertson, Glasgow, "Mineral discharger."
" " 2244, Thomas Dean and Robert Thorburn, Wishaw, "Drain tile cutting apparatus."
" " 2245, The Ainslie Brick & Tile Machine Company, Piccadilly, "Pipe socket mould, pallet and cutter."
" " 2246, Frederick Parker, Boston, Lincolnshire, "A signal apparatus."
" " 2247, William Harding, New Oxford-street, London, "The Arden clasp."
April 2nd, 2248, Frederick Wilson, Leeds, Yorkshire, "Weighing and driving apparatus, applicable to callendering and other like machines."
" " 2249, Thomas Day and Christopher Martin, Birmingham, "A rotary heel for boots and shoes."
" " 2250, Thomas Waddington, Derby-street, Cheetham-hill-road, Manchester. "Paragon neck-tie."
" " 2251, Samuel Gust, Oxford-street and New Bond-street, "'Tient tout,' or railway portmanteau."
" " 2252, Wellington Williams, Gutter-lane, "Fastening and band for shirt-collars."
" 4th, 2253, W. H. Martin, Burlington Arcade, "The 'Pagetina' parasol riding whip."
" 5th, 2254, Batters, Clements, & Morton, St. John's Wharf, Millbank-street, "Waggon weighing machine."
" " 2255, Robert Gordon & Co., Heaton Foundry, Stockport, "An improved steam boiler."
" 8th, 2256, William Murray, University-street, "A self-cleansing tubular filter."
" " 2257, John Mather, Beaufort-street, Chelsea, "Improved bath valve."
" " 2258, A. Beldham & Co., Portsea, "Self supporting waistband."
" 9th, 2259, Joseph Welch & John Margetson, Cheapside, "The Clarendon cravat."
" 10th, 2260, John Gouger, Wood-street, Cheapside, "The 'Nonpareil' collar."
" 13th, 2261, James Seddon and James Eckersley, Little Bolton, Lancaster, "Cop drier."
" " 2262, John Porter Abbott, Samuel Wright Wade & Robert Walshaw, Bamber-street, Liverpool, "A dead beat pocket or a marine chronometer."
" 15th, 2263, John Hendry & James Murphy, Gifford-street, Kingsland-road, and Honduras-street, Old-street, "A refrigerator."
" " 2264, Louise Smallwood, Rue des Chateaux, Dunkerque, "Improved tile."
" 16th, 2265, Scowen and White, Noble-street, Cheapside, "The 'Uptundum' collar."
" 17th, 2266, Francis Herbert Wenham, Effra Vale Lodge, Brixton, "A parabolic reflector for microscopes."
" " 2267, George Kelly Matthews, Charing-cross, "A pneumo monitor."
" " 2268, George Frederick Hipkins, High-street, Ashted, Birmingham, "Improved nut-cracker."

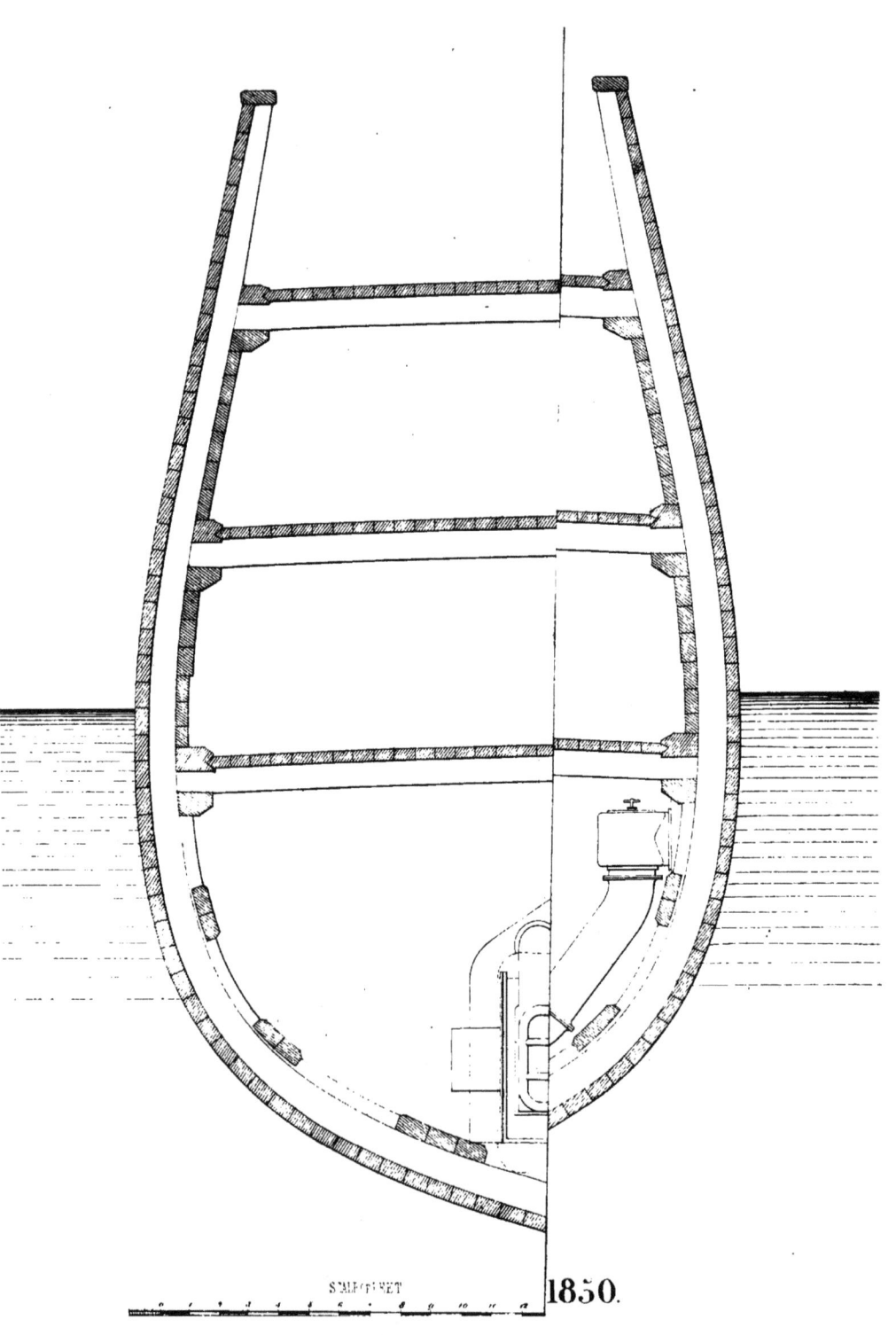

SMERCONET

1850.

④ THE ARTIZAN.

No. VI.—Vol. VIII.—JUNE 1st, 1850.

ENGINES FOR THE SCREW.

PENN'S ENGINES IN THE "ARROGANT" AND "ENCOUNTER."

These engines, constructed by Messrs. Penn & Son, for driving the screw propeller without the intervention of gearing, constitute a new class of screw engines, which appears destined to earn for Messrs. Penn as high a reputation in this undeveloped field as they have already obtained in the department of paddle engines. The drawings which we have given in the present number, and in our last, will enable every one to see that these engines are of the most simple and compact description, and the accounts which have reached us of their performance show that they perfectly realize all the conditions which engines of this kind are required to fulfil. Some of the varieties of engine which have been applied to drive the screw by a direct motion are very complicated and defective, whereas in the fewness and accessibility of their parts, and the efficiency of their operation, these engines leave scarce anything further to be desired. Our readers, however, will require some more conclusive evidence of perfection than can be afforded by our commendatory imputations; and we shall therefore briefly enumerate the main peculiarities of this species of engine, and shall add such facts touching its performance as will enable every reader to form a judgment for himself upon the subject.

The engines of the *Arrogant* and *Encounter* are of that species called the trunk engine. The cylinders, which are 60 inches diameter, lie horizontally, and instead of a common piston-rod being employed to transmit the piston pressure to the exterior of the cylinder, a pipe 24 inches in diameter is employed for this purpose, which protrudes through both ends of the cylinder, so as better to sustain the weight of the piston, and which is of course made tight by means of packing, where it passes through the cylinder top and cylinder bottom This pipe of course partakes of the motion of the piston, being cast in one piece with it, and the bottom end of the connecting-rod is attached to this pipe by means of a pin, the other end embracing the crank-pin in the usual manner. Engines on the trunk principle, it is well known, have occasionally been used before by other engineers. In one of Mr. Watt's early patents a trunk engine is described; and the engines put several years ago into the *Dartford* by Humphreys were on the trunk principle. But in none of the former examples were the peculiar features of this particular species of engine of such obviously eligible application as in the case selected by Messrs. Penn; and there are besides various subordinate features of improvement introduced into the engines of the *Arrogant* and *Encounter*, which remove any objections attaching to the trunk system under former arrangements. The pipe or trunk, instead of being made oval as heretofore, is made cylindrical in these engines, whereby the construction of the engine is facilitated, and the pin to which the connecting-rod is attached becomes at all times accessible. The air-pump is enclosed within the condenser, which lies on the opposite side of the shaft from the cylinder, in order to prevent the ship from being listed over by the weight of the engines. The air-pump, which lies in a horizontal position, is wrought by means of a rod attached to the piston, and passing through a stuffing box in the cylinder cover. The air-pump is double acting, and both the inlet and outlet valves consist of several discs of India-rubber, of moderate diameter, and bound down by a bolt in the centre passing through a cup-shaped washer, so as to enable the disc to rise without encountering any sharp edge. These valves, notwithstanding the rapid speed with which the air-pump bucket moves, are found to work in the smoothest and most satisfactory manner. The cranks to which the connecting rods of the engines are attached are cut out of solid projections forged on the shaft in the same manner as the cranks of locomotives, and the engine imparts its motion to the screw shaft direct, and without the intervention of gearing. The valves are worked by means of a modification of the link motion used in locomotives, whereby the handling of the engines is greatly facilitated. The steam is conducted from the cylinder to the condenser through a large pipe, which slants down towards the condenser so as to prevent any water which may come into that pipe, by condensation of the steam or otherwise, from running back into the cylinder when the vessel lists or rolls. The boilers are in 4 pieces, each piece 12 feet 2 inches long, 10 feet 6 inches wide, and 7 feet high. There are 3 fire-places in each compartment, and each fire-grate is 5 feet by 2 feet 11 inches. There are 264 tubes in each boiler—5 feet 6 inches long, and 2¼ inches diameter; and one chimney —5 feet 6 inches diameter for the 4 compartments. Messrs. Penn find that boilers with the tubes in the same line as the fire-places are not so good as boilers with the tubes at right angles with the fire-places. In both of these cases the tubes are on the same level as the fire-places, so as to keep the boiler below the water-line of the vessel, and out of the reach of shot. The main particulars of the principal dimensions and performance of the screw vessels are exhibited in the following table :—

Principal Dimensions and Performance of the Arrogant and Encounter Screw Steam Ships:—

	"ENCOUNTER."	"ARROGANT."
Length between perpendiculars	190 feet.	200 feet.
Breadth	33′ 2″	45′ 8¾″
Depth	15′ 1″ low. deck 20′ 10″ upp. deck	15′ 1″ lower deck. 20′ 10″ upp. deck.
Tonnage	1053 tons.	1861 tons.
Immersed Sectional Area ...	370 sq. feet.	672 sq. feet.
Draft of Water	14 feet.	20 feet.
Speed of Vessel	10½ knots, 11⅓ miles	8 knots, 9·216 miles.
Diameter of Screw	12 feet.	15 feet 6 inches.
Slip of Screw	⅛th.	⅛th.
Pitch of Screw	16 feet.	15ft. 6in.
Length of Screw	2′ 8″	2′ 7″
Number of blades of Screw ...	2	2
Revolutions per minute ...	80	60
Diameter of Cylinder ...	60″ with 24″ trunk = 55½ dia.	60″ with 24″ trunk = 55½ dia.
Length of Stroke	2′ 3″	3′ 0″
Dimensions of Ports	32′ × 5½″	32″ × 5½″
Stroke of Valve	14″	14″
Lap on Steam Side	3¼″	3¼″
Vacuum by barometer ...	27½″	27½″
Nominal power	360 H. P.	360 H. P.
Actual power	672·7 H.P.	623·3 H. P.
Pressure of Steam in Boiler ...	6lbs.	6 lbs.
Average effective Pressure on Piston	13·31 lbs.	13 lbs.
Steam cut off at — of Stroke	¾ths.	¾ths.

We are sorry that the late period of the month at which the foregoing particulars have reached us, disenables us from going more fully into the merits of these admirable engines, but the drawings we have laid before our readers, and the circumstances of the performance noted above, render any very detailed criticism on our part nearly superfluous. Every one can see that these engines have nearly a minimum of parts and weight, and it is equally obvious that the few parts which do exist are perfectly accessible, without occasioning any material trouble in effecting disconnections. The whole of the machinery is under the water-line, and, what is a most material point in direct action screw engines, the valves of the air-pump are of such a construction as to occasion no shock. Of the quality of the workmanship it would be needless to speak in any engine coming from the hands of Messrs. Penn, and censorious as we are reckoned, we are compelled to say that there is no feature of these engines with which we can find fault—a rare praise from us, and which only in rare instances can be justly bestowed.

NOTES ON THE PHILOSOPHY OF ENGINEERING.

WATER ENGINEERING.

(Continued from p. 99.)

THE quantity of water discharged by an orifice in any given time depends conjointly on the size of the orifice and the velocity of the water. But if a slit or rectangular orifice be made in the side of a cistern of water reaching to the surface of the water from some point beneath it, the water will not issue with a uniform velocity in every point of the slit; and in order to calculate the discharge in the case of such an orifice, it is the mean velocity of the issuing water which must be taken. The actual velocity of the issuing water at any point in the height of the slit will be the same as the velocity which a heavy body would have in falling to that point from the height of the surface of the water, or, in other words, the velocity of the issuing water at any point will be as the square root of the height of the water-level above that point. Now by the laws of falling bodies it appears that a body, when allowed to descend freely by gravity, will pass through $16\frac{1}{12}$ feet during the first second of its descent, and at the end of that time it will have acquired a velocity of $32\frac{1}{6}$ feet; so that the velocity with which water would issue from the lowest part of a rectangular opening in a cistern $16\frac{1}{12}$ feet high is $32\frac{1}{6}$ feet in a second, and the velocities at all the other points will be as the square root of the height or head. If the width of the opening were a foot, and the water flowed with the same velocity from every part of the slit as from the bottom of it, the discharge would manifestly be $16\frac{1}{12} \times 32\frac{1}{6} = 517{\cdot}335$ cubic feet per second; and this volume of water might be represented by a rectangular solid or prism $32\frac{1}{6}$ feet long, $16\frac{1}{12}$ high, and 1 foot thick. But as the upper strata of the water do not flow with the same velocity as the lower strata, it is clear that the figure representing the actual discharge cannot be a rectangular one. If the slit be divided in the direction of its height into any number of equal parts, and the velocity of the water at each of these divisions be represented by a horizontal line or ordinate, then the mean velocity will be obtained with sufficient exactitude for most purposes, by adding together the length of all these lines, and dividing by the number of lines, which will give the mean length of the whole number, or the mean velocity of the water in feet per second, and which will be found to be $344{\cdot}89$ in the case supposed, instead of $517{\cdot}335$, which is the maximum velocity of the issuing water. It is found, however, that a line drawn through the extremity of all the ordinates is a parabola, and by the laws of geometry the area of a parabola is known to be two-thirds of the area of its circumscribing rectangle. Since therefore the area of the parabola represents the actual discharge under the existing differences of velocity, and since its circumscribing rectangle represents what the discharge would be if the velocity of the water in every part of the slit were equal to the velocity

at the bottom part of it, it follows that the mean velocity of the water issuing from a slit reaching to the surface is just two-thirds of the maximum velocity, and two-thirds of $32\frac{1}{6}$ multiplied by $16\frac{1}{12}$ for the height of the slit and 1 foot for its breadth is $344{\cdot}89$ cubic feet, as found above.

From these considerations Eytelwein deduced a rule, for determining the quantity of water discharged over weirs or through sluices reaching to the surface. Here, as in the case of water flowing through pipes, it is necessary to introduce a co-efficient to bring down the theoretical discharge to the diminished discharge consequent upon the friction and viscidity of the water, and Eytelwein found that the discharge of water over weirs is two-thirds of the discharging area multiplied by the maximum velocity of the water, and by a certain coefficient; or since the velocity varies as the square root of the head, the discharge will be two-thirds of the discharging area multiplied by the square root of the head, and by a certain co-efficient for contraction, which he found in the more ordinary cases to be $5{\cdot}1$. Hence to find the quantity of water discharged over a weir, or over the waste board of an overflow sluice,

RULE.—*Multiply the depth of the stream of water running over the waste board in feet, by the width of the stream at the waste board in feet, and by two-thirds of the square root of the depth of the stream running over the waste board in feet, and finally by the constant number* $5{\cdot}1$. *The result is the quantity of water discharged in the second over the weir or waste board in cubic feet.*

Example 1.—A lake has an overflow sluice 3 feet wide, without oblique lateral walls to direct the stream into it. Required the discharge by such a sluice when the water in it runs 2 feet deep. Here $2 \times 3 \times \frac{2}{3} \sqrt{2} \times 5{\cdot}1 = 28{\cdot}845$ cubic feet, which is consequently the quantity of water discharged in the second.

Example 2.—A river falls over a cataract through a rectangular gorge 15 feet wide, and in which the water runs 9 feet deep. Required the quantity of water discharged in a second. Here $9 \times 15 \times \frac{2}{3} \sqrt{9} \times 5{\cdot}1 = 1377$ cubic feet discharged in a second.

Example 3.—A lake has a weir 3 feet in breadth, and the depth of the stream of water running over the weir is 5 feet. How much must the weir be widened to reduce the depth of the water running over the weir to 4 feet? Here the quantity of water to be discharged is fixed, but the velocity which is represented by $\frac{2}{3} \sqrt{5} \times 5{\cdot}1$ must be reduced to a velocity represented by $\frac{2}{3} \sqrt{4} \times 5{\cdot}1$, and the new area must be larger than the original area just in the proportion that the new velocity is less than the original velocity, or $\frac{2}{3} \sqrt{4} \times 5{\cdot}1 : \frac{2}{3} \sqrt{5} \times 5{\cdot}1 :: 3 \times 5 : 7{\cdot}5 \times \sqrt{5}$ feet. The new area therefore being $7{\cdot}5 \times \sqrt{5}$, and the depth of the water being limited to 4 feet, the length of the weir must be $\frac{7{\cdot}5}{4} \sqrt{5}$ or $4{\cdot}19$ feet.

Example 4.—A lake has a weir 12 feet long, over which the water flows with a depth of 4 feet. It is required to know how much the weir must be shortened so that the water may flow over it with a depth of 6 feet. Here the velocity of the water is represented by $\frac{2}{3} \sqrt{4} \times 5{\cdot}1$, and the quantity of the water discharged per second is $\frac{2}{3} \sqrt{4} \times 5{\cdot}1 \times 4 \times 12$. We wish to keep the quantity of water discharged the same as before, but to increase the depth to 6 feet, when the velocity will be represented by $\frac{2}{3} \sqrt{6} \times 5{\cdot}1$. Now the sectional area must be represented by the discharge divided by the velocity, and here the velocity being increased the sectional area will be smaller than before, in the proportion of the increased velocity. Hence $\frac{2}{3} \sqrt{6} \times 5{\cdot}1 : \frac{2}{3} \sqrt{4} \times 5{\cdot}1 :: 4 \times 12 :$ new area, or $\dfrac{\frac{2}{3} \sqrt{4} \times 5{\cdot}1 \times 4 \times 12}{\frac{2}{3} \sqrt{6} \times 5{\cdot}1} = \dfrac{\sqrt{4} \times 4 \times 12}{\sqrt{6}} = \dfrac{96}{2{\cdot}449}$ for the new area, which divided by 6 feet, the new height, gives $6{\cdot}53$ feet for the new length. A weir therefore 12 feet long, with a stream flowing over it 4 feet deep, delivers just the same quantity of water as a weir 6·53 feet long, with a stream flowing over it 6 feet deep.

The investigations of Newton, D'Alembert, and Lagrange, on the subject of waves were pursued by Poisson in 1815, and in 1816 Cauchy gained the prize offered by the French Institute for the best memoir on "The Theory of Waves on the Surface of a heavy Fluid of indefinite Depth." This memoir is published in the third volume of the *Mémoires des Savans.* Experiments on the propagation of waves were made by Weber and by Bidone in 1825, and similar experiments have been made more recently in this country by Mr. Scott Russell, the results of which are given in a series of papers read before the British Association. Bidone has more recently made a number of interesting experiments upon the velocity and percussive force of running water. He found that the greatest contraction of water issuing from an orifice in a plate is at a point as far distant from the discharging aperture as the largest diameter of the discharging orifice, whatever its shape may be; and he further found, that the area of the contracted vein in water issuing from an orifice in a thin plate is from ·60 to ·62 of the area of the orifice, whereby the actual discharge becomes only from ·60 to ·62 of the theoretical discharge. Experiments on the discharge of water through pipes and orifices, and also on the friction of spheres and discs revolving in water and air, were made, in 1830, by Mr. George Rennie, which corroborate the results obtained by Bidone and others. Mr. Rennie found that in the case of small orifices in a thin plate the coefficient for contraction was about ·62, while for additional tubes it was about ·81. Taking the expenditure through a pipe 30 feet long as 1, the expenditure through a thin plate was 3; through a very short tube 4; through a pipe 1 foot long 3·7; and through a pipe 8 feet long 2·6. The resistance of revolving discs and spheres was found to vary as the squares of the velocities, whether their revolution was performed in air or water. The amount of adhesion between a moving body and the air or water in which it moves was first investigated by Du Buat, whose deductions have been confirmed by the observations of Bessel, Sabine, and Baily.

Genley's *Essai sur les Moyens de conduire, d'elever, et de distribuer les Eaux* has a large amount of useful practical information on the subject of proving and laying pipes for conveying water. Matthews' *Hydraulia* also contains a good deal of interesting information, and Hagen's *Handbuch der Wasserbaukunst* is a useful technical work. Rules for the strength of conduit pipes are given by Brix in the *Verhandlungen des Verlins sur Beförderung des Gewerbfleisses in Preussen,* 1834, also by Tredgold and other authors. Wiesbach's experiments on the efflux of water through valves, slides, &c., are given in a work entitled, *Untersuchungen im Gebiete der Mechanik und Hydraulik,* Leipsic, 1842. Bidone's latest experiments on the percussion of water are given in the *Memorie de la Reale Accademia delle Scienze di Torino,* 1838. Poncelet's *Introduction à la Mécanique Industrielle,* 1841, also contains some interesting investigations on the same and similar subjects.

The performance and best proportions of water wheels were first investigated by Smeaton, and the investigation has since been pursued with great ability by Morin, who gives the results of his experiments in a work entitled *Expériences sur les Roues Hydrauliques à Aubes planes et sur les Roues Hydrauliques à Augets,* Metz, 1836. D'Aubuisson, in his *Hydraulique à l'Usage des Ingénieurs,* enters fully into the subject of overshot wheels, and Poncelet, in his *Cours de Mécanique Appliquée,* gives a clear enunciation of the theory. Redtenbacher's *Theorie und Bau der Wasserräder,* Manheim, 1846, is, however, the fullest and most recent work on the subject of water wheels.

A species of horizontal water wheel, called a turbine, operating somewhat on the principle of a smoke-jack, has latterly come into extensive use upon the Continent, and have also been introduced in a few cases into this country. Horizontal water wheels of a rude construction have long been employed in mountainous countries, where water was abundant and an adequate fall readily obtainable; but in these primitive wheels the water operated mainly on the principle of percussion, and a large amount of the useful effect was consequently wasted. In 1827, Poncelet pointed out, in a work entitled, *Mémoire sur les Roues Hydrauliques à Aubes courbes mues par-dessous,* Metz, that the loss of effect in undershot wheels, consequent upon the percussion of the water on the float boards, may be very much reduced by causing the float boards to curve towards the stream, instead of being disposed in the usual radial form, and it was soon perceived that this improvement could be extended to the horizontal impact wheel, which, when the vanes or floats were disposed in a curvilinear form, so as to obviate the impact of the water, became the modern turbine. Numerous varieties of the turbine have now been introduced into practice, with very conflicting pretensions; and several interesting publications on the subject of turbines have appeared in France and Germany. Fourneyron's paper on turbines was published in the *Bulletin de la Société d'Encouragement, &c.,* in 1834. Morin followed with an Experimental Inquiry in 1838. In the same year a paper by Poncelet, on the "Theory of the Mechanical Effects of Fourneyron's Turbine," appeared in the *Comptes Rendus.* Then came Redtenbacher's *Theorie und Bau der Turbinen und Ventilatoren,* Manheim, 1844. The turbines of Koechlin, Jonval, and Fontaine-Baron, are described in the *Comptes Rendus* for 1846. Armengaud's *Publication Industrielle* contains plates of the turbines of Cadiat, Callon, Fourneyron, and Gentilhomme. Nagel's turbine is described in Dingler's Journal, bd. 95; and Passot's turbine in the same journal, bd. 96. Parro's turbine is described in the *Polytechnisches Centrablatt,* bd. 7, 1846; and Bourgeois' screw turbine is described in the same journal, bd. 1, 1847. In *Weisbach's Mechanics,* translated by Professor Gordon, a large amount of useful information is given upon the most interesting questions in hydraulics, and from this source much of the preceding information is derived. A treatise on the turbine, by Professor Ruhlman, was translated by Sir Robert Kane, in 1846, and reviewed in the *Artisan,* in the number for August 1846, page 160. A new variety of turbine is at the same time there suggested and described.

Contemporaneously with the introduction of the turbine on the Continent, a horizontal water mill, operating on the principle of re-action, has been largely introduced in this country by Mr. Whitelaw of Paisley. A similar contrivance, known as Barker's Mill in this country, and Segner's Mill in Germany, has long been in use in Switzerland and other continental countries as a convenient water motor; but Mr. Whitelaw has greatly improved the machine, both as regards compactness and efficiency. The fullest account of the performance of this machine is to be found in a series of communications made to the *Artisan,* by Mr. Whitelaw himself, and which contain the results of a great number of carefully executed experiments, with formulæ deduced from them, to determine the performance in all similar cases. In the Memoirs of the Berlin Academy, 1750—1754, Euler investigates, in a very profound manner, the proper form and theoretical performance of a water mill operating on the principle of re-action; but it does not appear that so large a performance has yet been obtained from this species of mill as he expected, and the form he prescribed has not been adopted in practice.

(To be continued)

[In last month's article on WATER ENGINEERING, a correspondent has pointed out to us that the length of pipe in the example we have given, should be 14,637 feet, instead of 48,281 feet: and 14,637 + 53 × ·375 should be 14,637 + (50 × ·375).]

KEY TO MR. BOURNE'S CATECHISM OF THE STEAM ENGINE.

(Continued from p. 77.)

BURSTING STRAIN UPON REVOLVING BODIES.

MALLEABLE iron will bear a tensile strain of 17,800 lbs. per square inch of section, without permanent derangement of structure, and cast iron 13,500 lbs. per square inch of section; but it is not advisable to throw a greater strain upon the malleable iron employed in machinery than 4000 lbs. per square inch of section, or upon the cast iron employed in machinery than 3000 lbs. per square inch of section.

Let it be required to compute the centrifugal force, or the tendency to bursting of a fly-wheel, 10 feet diameter, with a velocity in the rim of 60 feet per second.

Here by the rule given in a previous number $\left(\dfrac{60}{4\ 01}\right)^2 = 223\cdot8 + 10$ feet $= 22\cdot38$ times the weight of the wheel. Now the weight of a square inch of section of the rim and 1 foot long is $3\cdot15$ lbs., and the circumference being $3\cdot1416$ times the length of the diameter, $3\cdot1416 \times 10 \times 3\cdot15$ lbs. will be the weight of a ring 10 feet diameter and 1 inch square in the section $= 96\cdot96$ lbs. But the centrifugal force at the speed assumed is $22\cdot38$ times the weight of the rim, and $96\cdot96 \times 22\cdot38 = 2214\cdot7248$ lbs.; but as half the wheel endeavours to fly from the other half, or as it is only half the wheel which endeavours to fly off if the other half be fixed on the axis, the separating force will be the half of $2214\cdot7248$, or say 1107 lbs. upon 2 square inches, or $553\cdot5$ lbs. per square inch of section. If the velocity of the rim be increased to $80\cdot2$ feet per second, the separating or bursting force will be 1979 lbs. or $989\cdot5$ lbs. per square inch of section; if the velocity be $100\cdot25$ feet per second, the bursting force will be 3092 lbs. or 1546 lbs. per square inch of section; if the velocity of the rim be $120\cdot3$ feet per second the bursting force will be 4453 lbs. or $2226\cdot5$ lbs. per square inch of section; if the velocity of the rim be $160\cdot4$ feet per second, the bursting force will be 7916 lbs. or 3958 lbs. per square inch of section, and so on. In engines for rolling iron a fly-wheel 16 feet in diameter is sometimes driven with a velocity of 100 revolutions per minute, or with a velocity of rim of 82 feet per second; and the force tending to burst the wheel in such a case is $2079\cdot4$ lbs. or $1039\cdot7$ lbs. per square inch of section.

If a locomotive with wheels 7 feet in diameter travels at the rate of 30 miles an hour, the wheels will make 120 revolutions per minute. The centrifugal force of such wheels will be $120^2 \times 7 + 5870 = 17\cdot17$ times the weight of the wheel. The circumference of a 7 feet wheel is $21\cdot99$ feet, and the weight of 1 foot in length of a bar of malleable iron 1 inch square, being $3\cdot34$ lbs. the weight of a ring of malleable iron 7 feet diameter and 1 inch square in the section will be $73\cdot4466$ lbs. Hence $73\cdot4466 \times 17\cdot17$ or 1261 lbs. is the centrifugal force of such a ring; but as the centrifugal force of half the ring determines the centrifugal strain, and as this strain is borne by the two sides of the ring, the separating force, or force tending to burst the ring per square inch is 315 lbs. At 40 miles an hour the centrifugal strain will be 569 lbs. per square inch of section; at 50 miles an hour 889 lbs.; at 60 miles an hour $1280\cdot5$ lbs.; at 70 miles an hour 1743 lbs.; at 80 miles an hour 2277 lbs.; at 90 miles an hour $2881\cdot5$ lbs.; at 100 miles an hour 3503 lbs.; at 110 miles an hour 4305 lbs. If we take a wheel of 4 feet diameter, the periphery of which runs at the rate of 100 miles an hour, we shall have $700\cdot6$ for the number of revolutions per minute, and $700\cdot6^2 \times 4 + 5870 = 334\cdot473$, which is the number of times that the centrifugal force exceeds the weight of the rim. The circumference of a 4 feet wheel will be $12\cdot566$ feet, and as a bar of malleable iron an inch square and a foot long weighs $3\cdot34$ lbs., the weight of a ring of malleable iron 4 feet diameter and 1 square inch in the cross section, will be $41\cdot87044$ lbs., which multiplied by $334\cdot473$ will give a centrifugal strain of $14,037$ lbs., of which half is to be borne by the two sides of the ring, or 3509 lbs. per square inch

of cross section. This is the same strain very nearly as that which exists in the case of the 7 feet wheel travelling at the rate of 100 miles an hour, and would come out as the same strain precisely if the figures were carried to a sufficient number of decimal places in the respective computations. It hence appears, that the centrifugal strain per square inch of section is the same in all the wheels of a railway train, whatever the diameter of the wheels may be.

It may be useful to extend these investigations to the case of a cast iron disc 10 feet diameter and 1 inch thick, revolving at a speed of 60 feet per second at the rim. Here it is clear that the section of the metal binding the two halves of the disc together is 120 square inches; and 5 multiplied by $0\cdot7071 = 3\cdot5355$ feet is the radius of gyration of the disc, or $7\cdot071$ feet is the diameter of the circle of gyration, or the diameter of a circle into which, if the metal of the disc is supposed to be concentrated, it will have the same mechanical energy as in its natural distribution. The velocity of the circle of gyration will be less than that of the periphery of the disc in the proportion in which 10 exceeds $7\cdot071$, so that if the rim moves at a speed of 60 feet per second the circle of gyration will move at a speed of $42\cdot42$ feet per second Applying therefore the rule for centrifugal force we have $42\cdot42 + 4\cdot01 = 10\cdot58$, the square of which is $111\cdot9364$, and this divided by $7\cdot07$ gives $15\cdot8$ as the number of times the centrifugal force exceeds the weight of the disc. The weight of the disc will be 2950 lbs., which multiplied by $15\cdot8$ gives $46,610$ lbs., one half of which, $23,305$ lbs., is the centrifugal strain tending to separate the disc, or $194\cdot2$ lbs. per square inch of section. It will hence be obvious, that any wheel intended to be put into very rapid revolution should be made in the form of a disc.

We may now inquire what velocity of rotation would burst asunder a revolving body; with which view we may take the case of a millstone 48 inches in diameter, with a central hole 8 inches in diameter. If the density of the stone is 2·5 times greater than that of water, then the weight of a cubic inch of the stone will be $0\cdot0903$ lbs., and the weight of half a circular slice of the stone 1 inch thick will be $79\cdot4$ lbs. The sectional area of such a disc when cut across through the centre will obviously be 40 square inches, and if the tenacity of the stone be 750 lbs. per square inch, the bursting strain will manifestly be 30,000 lbs. To find the velocity of revolution which will give this strain we must first find the circle in which the centre of gyration revolves, which will be $20\cdot8568$ inches in diameter, and the circumference of this circle will be $65\cdot52372288$ inches. By proceeding as in the former cases, it will be found that the bursting velocity is 1130 revolutions per minute.

HEAT AND STEAM.

The latent heat of steam at 212° is about 1000°, by which it is meant that there is as much heat absorbed in raising a given weight of water into steam as would raise the temperature of that water 1000° if its expansion could be prevented. Hence the total heat of steam is 1000° $+212° = 1212°$. The sum of the latent and the sensible heat of vapour is nearly the same at all temperatures; hence the latent heat of vapour at any temperature may be found approximately by subtracting that temperature from 1212°. From these laws it is easy to deduce rules for ascertaining the amount of heat necessary for raising the temperature of a given quantity of water any given number of degrees, or for converting any given quantity of water into steam.

Example.—If a given amount of heat will raise a pound weight of water at 32° to the temperature of 212°, what amount of heat will be required to convert a pound of water at 212° into steam? Here the number of degrees through which the temperature of the water is raised is 212° — 32° = 180°; but the latent heat of steam at 212° is about 1000°, hence the heat required to convert water at 212° into steam at 212° is as 180° to 1000°, or as 1 to $5\frac{1}{2}$ nearly; that is, it will require $5\frac{1}{2}$ times as much heat to raise a pound of water at the boiling point into steam as to raise $5\frac{1}{2}$ lbs. of water from the freezing to the boiling point. In like manner if we raise the temperature of water from 60° to 212°, or through 152°, then to convert it into steam at 212°, the heat required is as 152° to 1000°, or as 1 to 6½ nearly.

To take a practical case; if the water in a boiler be raised from 60° to 100° by 1 cwt. of coal, how much coal must be expended in converting the same water into steam at 212°? If the temperature be raised from 60° to 100° = 40° by 1 cwt. of coal, then to raise it from 60° to 212° = 152° will require a proportionate quantity of coal; hence 40° : 152 : : 1 cwt. : : 3·8 cwt.; but to convert water at 212° into steam at 212° requires 1000°, or about 6½ times as much heat as to raise it from 60° to 212°; hence 152° : 1000° : : 3·8 cwt. : 25 cwt., which is the coal necessary to convert the water at 212° into steam at 212°; and 25 cwt. + 3·8 cwt. = 28·8 cwt. is the total quantity of coal required to raise the water at 60° into steam at 212°.

If in the case we have taken a portion of the water, say one-fourth, had been of the temperature of 100°, which is the ordinary temperature of the feed water of a condensing engine, then the heat necessary to raise the water in the boiler to 212° would be found thus:—there are 3 parts of water at 60°, and 1 part at 100°, hence the total heat is 60° × 3 = 180 + 100° × 1 = in all 280°, which divided by 4, the sum of the number of parts of the water = 70°. The water in the boiler therefore must be raised from 70° instead of from 60°, as in the preceding example. If, as we assumed before, 1 cwt. of coal will raise the water 40° of temperature, then to raise it from 70° to 212° = 142°, will require 40° : 142° : : 1 cwt. : 3·5 cwt. The quantity of heat necessary to convert this water into steam will be the same as before = 25 cwt.; hence the total quantity necessary to convert the given quantity of water at 70° into steam at 212° is 25 + 3·5 = 28·5 cwt.

If the pressure of the steam in the boiler be 15 lbs. above the atmospheric pressure, the boiling point will be at the temperature of 250°, and the latent heat of saturated steam at this temperature is 1212°—250° = 962°. Now to raise the water at 70° to 250° = 180° will require in the proportion of 1 cwt. for every 40°; hence 40° : 180° : : 1 cwt. : 4·5 cwt.; and to convert this water at 250° into steam at the same temperature will require an amount of heat equal to 962°. To raise the temperature of the water 180° took 4·5 cwt.; hence 180° : 962° : : 4·5 cwt. : 24 cwt., and the total quantity of coal expended in converting the water at 70° into steam of 15 lbs. pressure above the atmosphere will be 24 + 4·5 = 28·5 cwt.

From this it appears that the heat necessary to convert a given quantity of water into steam is the same, or nearly so, whatever the pressure of the steam may be; the only difference being that at high pressures the temperature is great and the latent heat small, and at low pressures the temperature is small and the latent heat great.

Since the heat requisite for raising water into steam is known, and the volume of the steam is also known, it becomes easy to compute the quantity of water necessary for condensation in a steam engine. Thus if a given quantity of water, say one cubic foot, be used in the shape of steam of 15 lbs. pressure above the atmosphere, we can easily tell what quantity of water at the temperature of 60° must be used to convert the steam into water at 100°. The latent heat contained in steam of 15 lbs. pressure, or 250° of temperature, is 962°, and 250°+962°=1212° is the sum of the latent and sensible heats. Here we have what is equivalent to a cubic foot of water at a temperature of 1212° to reduce to a temperature of 100°, and an unknown quantity of water to be raised 40°, that is from 60° to 100°; hence 40° : 1112° : : 1 cubic foot : 27·8 cubic feet; that is, 1 cubic foot of water in the shape of steam at a temperature of 250° requires 27·8 cubic feet of water at a temperature of 60° to convert it into water of 100°. From this we see that condensing engines are not of convenient application in situations where water is scarce, as they require nearly thirty times as much water for condensation as for the generation of steam.

ANALYSIS OF THE STEAM-ENGINE.

Continued from p. 100.

The Crank.—Having disposed, in our previous article, of the crank shaft plummer block, we will now proceed to the crank itself, which in land engines, is made of cast-iron for the sake of economy. Cranks more frequently give way than, perhaps, any other part of an engine, the fracture commonly taking place across the large boss, opposite the web. This may be attributed in some cases which have come under our observation, to the practice of heating the crank and shrinking it on the shaft, a plan which ought to be used with care when applied to cast-iron. The shaft being turned larger than the crank eye, the contraction of the crank on cooling is partially arrested, and if this is carried to an excess, it is evident that the molecules of metal are left in a state of tension very unfavourable to their bearing a shock with safety.

The strain upon the crank is a compound one: First there is the direct pressure upon the end of the crank, and if all that pressure could be concentrated upon the centre transversely, it would bear a much greater strain; but as the pressure comes upon the centre of the crank pin, which overhangs considerably, the tendency of that strain is to twist the crank round; consequently the web of the crank ought to be made thicker in proportion to its breadth than theory would indicate, if the strain were a direct one, such as on the beam of an engine.

The diameter of the shaft in the crank is usually made the same size as the bearing, and it is requisite that this should form an element in calculating the strength of the eye of the crank; thus, when Trewhitt's disengaging gear is used, the shaft is enlarged in diameter by a disc, and the crank becomes converted into a band, with a boss for the reception of the crank pin. The strain upon the crank can hardly be worked out in theory, but we shall adopt the far simpler plan of deducing a rule from those proportions which are found to answer in practice.

Rule.—*To find the sectional area of large eye of crank, when of cast-iron. Divide the length of the crank in inches by half the diameter of the bearing; the quotient multiplied by the area of cylinder in inches and divided by 200 gives the sectional area in inches.* Thus: Length of crank = 30 inches, which, divided by half the diameter of bearing 3¾ inches = 8. The quotient 8, multiplied by the area of the cylinder, 706 inches = 5648, which, divided by 200 = 28·24 inches, or 28 in. nearly, for sectional area. It remains to fix the proportion which the breadth of the boss should bear to the thickness, and about the diameter of the shaft, or rather less, is a usual proportion, or, say 7 inches breadth of boss. Then, 28 inches area divided by 7 = 4 inches thickness on each side of the eye of the crank.

The small eye of the crank will depend upon the pin, which we have taken at $\frac{2}{15}$ of the diameter of the cylinder, or 4 inches. The part which enters the crank is made of the same diameter at the face, and is slightly tapered to the end. Various methods are employed for fixing the crank pin, but a nut at the back is probably the most convenient, and is now very generally employed. In this case the pin is not shrunk in, but when that plan is preferred a key may be driven through the pin, either at the back of the crank, or through both crank and pin. Or the pin may be shrunk in, and a round hole drilled through both at once, and a slightly tapered steel pin driven in. In either case, whether a pin or a key through the crank be employed, the boss ought to be rather deeper than we have shown. The pin is reduced to 3 inches diameter, where it is screwed, as the strain to be overcome is only that tending to draw the pin out of the crank.

The breadth of the pin eye may be taken at 1¼ times the diameter of the pin; thus, 4 inches × 1¼ = 5 inches = breadth of small boss of crank. The thickness of eye round the pin may be taken at ½ the depth of the eye, or 2½ inches. Thus the two sides, 27 inches each and the hole 4 inches diameter, will make the boss 9 inches diameter outside.

To be continued.

SELF-ACTING APPARATUS.

London, 13th May, 1850.

Mr. EDITOR,—Sir, In your number for May there is a feed apparatus for high-pressure boilers, patented by Mr. Spray, and as there are one or two objections to it, I beg you will allow me a little of your space to state them, and at the same time to give a modification of the apparatus, which, in my opinion, makes it superior to the original.

In that by Mr. Spray, the tube is closed at both ends, with an orifice at top to the pipe *a*, and a number of holes *d d* at bottom, and being attached by *h* and *g* to the float *f*, is moved upwards and downwards with the rise and fall of the water in the boiler.

In its present position, if the flow of water through *a* is more than that evaporated, then the float rises, closing the openings at both ends of the tube *b*. But suppose the flow of water through *a* is less than that evaporated, which may be caused by the pump leaking air, or superior fuel being used, then the float will fall, carrying the top of the tube *b* below the opening *a*, allowing the water to get on the upper side of *b*, and by-and-bye to be wholly discharged through the opening *i*, rendering useless the tube *e*, which is intended to carry the feed water clear of the steam. This is a serious objection, and one which is sure to render the utility of the whole apparatus questionable. It will also be seen that the part *i* being cast on the side of the upright tube, renders it difficult to be got up bright, if it were wished to be made of brass.

In my sketch the tube *b* is open at both ends, having a nib *d* cast in, so as to secure it to the rod *c*; and on the outside are cast two pieces to which the tube *F* may be brazed. The main part of the apparatus *T* has an inner portion, extending inside the boiler in which *b* slides, and is connected to the outer portion by means of ribs cast in the annular space P. The part inside the boiler having two slots from *S* downwards to allow *d* freely to move up and down, guiding the float *F*. At the top of the tube is a whistle, intended as an alarum when the water reaches a dangerously low level in the boiler, calling the attention of the engineer, who will see that the pump is put in working order, or order the fires to be drawn.

The sketch shows the float in its lowest position, and the whistle in action. A little explanation will show how this is effected. The upper part of the whistle *h* is made fast on the rod *c*, and therefore moves with the tube *b*. The under part of the whistle *r* is in a piece with the main tube *T*, in which *i* is screwed, having fitted in it the piece *n*, which is provided with a small stuffing-box and gland, to make it steam tight on the rod *c*; when the float rises the piece *n* is forced up by the pressure of the steam, which is admitted through the space *p*, displacing the small holes at *o*, and preventing the escape of steam. If we suppose the float may fluctuate 6 inches, then the part of the whistle *h* will therefore be seen to rise 6 inches above *r*, and may be used as an index for the water in the boiler. When it is in its extreme position up, the tube *b* will have covered the orifice *a*, thereby stopping the supply of

feed water. When the float falls and again reaches it present position *h* will come to bear on the gland *e*, and as the water continues to fall the whole weight of the float, &c. will overcome the pressure on *n*, which will be depressed and again bring the whistle into action. An advantage in this arrangement is that the tube *b* may be continued to the bottom of the boiler.

I am, yours truly,

N. D.

WADDELL'S IMPROVED CAPSTAN.

This capstan, the invention of Mr. R. Waddell, engineer of the *Europa* steam-ship, combines the ordinary capstan with a double purchase of considerably greater power, which may be readily disconnected when not required. Fig. 1, (see plate) is a sectional elevation, and Fig. 2 an outside elevation of the improved capstan. A A is the ordinary capstan barrel, provided with purchase holes, B B, to receive the capstan bars, by which it is worked, and moving loose on the fixed central spindle, C C. A double arm piece, D D, shown detached at Fig. 3, is keyed fast on C, and carries a pair of pinions E E, shown also in plan. Fig. 4. F F is a cast-iron cap, forming the top of the capstan, and shutting in the gearing; attached to it is the pinion H, working into, and giving motion to, the two pinions E E. This cap is also provided with purchase holes, I I, for the reception of capstan bars when the slow motion is to be used. The upper part of the capstan is provided with a ring of teeth G G, into which the pinions, E E, work. K is a nut by which the cap is secured in its place.

It will be seen that by applying the capstan bars to the cap F F, the power will be transmitted to the barrel A A, through the pinions H and E, at a speed diminished in proportion to the relative diameter of K, and G G, and therefore with proportionately increased force, whilst by applying the bars to the holes B B, the power will be applied direct to the barrel A A, in the usual manner.

THE ABERDEEN CLIPPER BOW.

ONE of our plates shows a vessel built with the clipper bow invented by Messrs A. Hall & Son, ship builders of Aberdeen, and which is now in very extensive use, as our list of steamers constantly testifies. This form of bow was modelled in 1839, for the first of a series of schooners intended to run in opposition to the steamers between London and Aberdeen. This was found so successful, that between 1839 and 1848 Messrs. Hall built 36 vessels on this principle, all of which have been celebrated for their sailing qualities.

As will be seen, the stem is run out so as to form the cutwater, the effect of which is to run the water lines finer at the bow, to enable her to carry a greater dead weight, and at the same time to diminish the registered tonnage.

The following calculations of the difference between a vessel of this form, the barque *Acasta*, and one of the ordinary proportions, will be found interesting:—

DEPTHS.

Fore	...	$15.9 \times 1 = 15.9$
Midship	...	$16.7 \times 2 = 33.4$
After	...	$15.7 \times 1 = 15.7$
Sum of Depths		65

BREADTHS.

Fore.	Midship.	After.
Upper $15.6 \times 1 = 15.6$	Middle $23.4 \times 3 = 70.2$	Upper $22 \times 1 = 22$
Lower $5.3 \times 1 = 5.3$	Lower $22.1 \times 1 = 22.1$	Lower $8 \times 2 = 16$
20.9	92.3	38

Sum of breadths 20·9 + 92·3 + 38 = 151·2 × 65 = 9828 ×111·4 = 1094839200 + 3500 = ...   312$\frac{1288}{3500}$ tons.

Half poop middle length 24 × average depth 27 = 64·8 × average.

Breadth 20·6 = 1334·88 + 92·4 =   ... $14\frac{51\cdot2}{92\cdot4}$ tons.

Register 327$\frac{3}{4}$ tons.

COMMON DIMENSIONS.

Sum of breadths 175·3 × 66·5 = 11657·45 × 102·8 = 1198385·860 + 3500 = ...   342$\frac{2245}{3500}$ tons,

Half poop same as before   ... $14\frac{51\cdot2}{92\cdot4}$

Register 356$\frac{3}{4}$ tons.

Measurement per former registry act :—Length of keel and fore rake 126·6. Extreme breadth 25·7 = 386$\frac{27}{50}$ tons. Actual burthen when loaded 525 tons.

The above are the actual measurements, as taken by the customs' officer (agreeably to the Register Act, 5 & 6 Wm. 4th), from which it is evident that the registry tonnage is reduced 30 tons; and all the additional length is added, being almost the entire forecastle forward, and a considerable space aft, whilst at the same time the symmetry, sailing qualities, and the dryness on deck are increased.

AUGENDRE'S WHITE GUNPOWDER.

Of the very numerous explosive compounds and mixtures known to chemists, but few admit of any practical application. Some of the most powerful especially are rendered worthless by the danger and difficulty attending their preparation, and by the great uncertainty of their action. Many of these substances have been found to explode, if not spontaneously, yet under conditions not yet fully determined, or from causes which it might be difficult to exclude, such as slight variations of temperature, or of the electrical state of the atmosphere. Gun-cotton, which was at one time the object of very sanguine anticipations, has proved, for most purposes, a failure. Its high price, its tendency to injure firearms, more than compensate for its superior projectile force ; and when we consider that it explodes, according to the experiments of Marx, at 144°, a temperature occasionally produced by the sun's rays, even in temperate climates, we shall conclude that its actual utility is far from considerable. The above-named chemist observed also the very singular fact, that from a gradual rise of temperature it suffers a kind of decomposition, whereby its power is much impaired. Under these circumstances, gunpowder, perhaps the oldest and the feeblest, yet certainly the most manageable of the explosives, seems likely to maintain for some time its practical superiority. Other substances may, however, merit the preference in particular cases, as gun-cotton in mining operations. A new kind of gunpowder, possessing several advantages has been discovered by M. Augendre. It consists of two parts chlorate of potash, one part of lump sugar, and one part prussiate of potash. These ingredients being separately ground to a very fine powder are to be mixed together with a spatula, or, on the large scale, by means of a revolving barrel. The discoverer asserts its superiority over common powder, as more forcible, as less liable to suffer from the action of damp air, and as being more easily and expeditiously prepared. This last property he contends will render it practicable to dispense with large and dangerous magazines in fortresses, ships, &c., as the pulverised materials might be easily and safely stored up in a separate form, and mixed as wanted. On the other hand, he owns that the new powder, from the nature of the vapours generated, would be likely to corrode iron firearms, and that its combustibility is greater

than that of common powder. It may, however, be kept for any length of time at a temperature of 212° with perfect safety.

Friction, however, must be carefully avoided, as it will in many cases cause the mass to explode. The inventor, indeed, maintains that it may be ground dry in an agate mortar with safety. Where the surfaces are perfectly smooth and polished this may hold good, but I have found the very trifling roughness of a Berlin-ware mortar quite sufficient to cause an explosion. A serious accident, indeed, has occurred at Selby, where a druggist's assistant lost one of his eyes, from grinding about two ounces of the mixture in a Wedgwood mortar. The inventor himself suffered severely from an explosion brought on by grinding a quantity, with which a few grains of common powder had got accidentally mingled. Hence he cautions against introducing any particle of sulphur, charcoal, or common gunpowder into the mixture.

When very dry, the new powder may be exploded by a smart blow, but not so readily and invariably as to admit of its application to percussion-caps. The most serious objection to this powder is its price, which will probably not be less than three or four times that of ordinary powder.   8.

THE ARSENIC PANIC.

The pertinacity with which those of our countrymen who are weary of life, or who harbour deadly malice against a neighbour, cling to the use of arsenious acid, is worthy of note. None of your baryta or chrome, your strychnia, or nicotina for plain John Bull; he will be poisoned like his forefathers—with good, solid, old-fashioned arsenic. Hence many well-meaning persons conceive a special horror and indignation against this unfortunate drug, and call loudly upon the legislature to interpose and put a stop to its suicidal and murderous uses. Some propose to interdict the sale of arsenic, except upon certain conditions, which may, they think, prevent it from getting into improper hands. Others actually suggest that no arsenic should be sold, except mingled with some substance that will instantly betray it by colour taste, or smell, if added to any article of food. The problem which these gentlemen have undertaken to solve is by no means easy. If we consider that 4 grains of arsenic will destroy life, and that the amount need not even be administered in one dose, we shall see that the desired adulteration must be very large in amount, if it is to reveal the poison in dark-coloured or highly-seasoned articles of food. And can a substance be found which will answer the desired end, without at the same time frustrating the numerous manufacturing, medicinal, and scientific uses of arsenic? If the adulteration may be easily removed it will lose its value, and if not, the plan would be a gross injustice to the manufacturer and to scientific men, whose rights should not be entirely lost sight of. We have already difficulty enough in obtaining pure reagents without adulteration being made the law of the land. Let rational and practical steps be taken to do away with poisoning, but let no additional hindrance be placed in the way either of chemical research or chemical manufactures.   8.

CORRESPONDENCE.

Sir,—You give us many useful rules and papers in your excellent work, The Artisan, and may I ask for fellow-workmen and myself, the favour of one or two on the construction and method of finding the sizes of the wheels, barrels, &c., in cranes and machines for lifting weights ? I am, Sir, yours, very respectfully,   B. S.
Commercial-road, May 6, 1850.

[We propose, on an early occasion, to give some examples of cranes of good construction; but we may in the meantime explain the principle on which cranes are proportioned, and which will enable the practical man easily to contrive arrangements for raising weights, proper for the particular circumstances he has to meet. The handles of all cranes should have a radius of from 15 to 17 inches, and the spindle on which the handles are fixed should stand about 3 feet 2 inches from the ground. The pressure exerted by each man at the end of the radius of the handle should on the average be from 10 to 15 lbs., though, to overcome an occasional load, it may be as much as double this amount. If, however, the crane be designed to lift any given regular load, say one ton, with two men at the handles, then the impelling or lifting force at the end of the handles will be say 28 lbs., moving in a circle of twice the radius of the handle, or say 32 inches in diameter. If the barrel of the crane be 16 inches in diameter, the surface of the barrel would travel with one-half of the velocity of the men's hands, provided the barrel were upon the spindle to which the handles are affixed, and in such case the weight lifted by a rope wound round the barrel would only be 56 lbs.; but as 2240 lbs. have to be lifted, the wheels intermediate between the handles and the barrel, must multiply in the proportion of 2240 to 56, or 40 to 1, or the diameter of the wheel, supposing one only to be employed, must be forty times greater than that of the pinion by which it is worked. It will be more convenient, therefore, in such a case, to use more than one intermediate wheel, as in the following combination.

On the shaft to which the handle is attached put a pinion of 5 inches diameter, working into a wheel of 30 inches diameter, running upon a second shaft, which shaft also carries a pinion of 6 inches diameter, working into a wheel of 40 inches diameter, fixed upon the shaft which carries the barrel of 16 inches diameter. In order to find the power gained by this crane, multiply together the radii of the handle and the several wheels, and divide this product by the product obtained from multiplying together the radii of the several pinions, and of the barrel. Thus $\frac{16 \times 15 \times 20}{2 \cdot 5 \times 3 \times 8} = 80$, the number of times that the power is increased. If the weight to be lifted is one ton, then $\frac{2240}{80} = 28 =$ lbs., which is the force to be applied at the handle. If two men be employed the force of each will be 14 lbs., which is not too much for moderate lifts ; for occasional short lifts as much as 20 or 30 lbs. may be allowed for each man : so that if two additional men were put to the crane, a weight of $20 \times 4 \times 80 = 6400$ lbs., or 2 tons 16 cwt. could be raised, or even a larger weight than this. With weights of about three-quarters of a ton, the force required to be exerted at the handles is 20 lbs., which would give two men 10 lbs. each, with which resistance they could work habitually with great ease, and for a long time.]

Sir,—In answer to a Querist at Newcastle :—

1. A line running at right angles with the central line connecting the edges of a valve lever may be obtained as follows :—Take a straight edge, with a mark at any point on its edge, and near the middle of its length; measure off from this point, and on each side of it, any convenient length, say a foot. Apply the central point of the straight edge to one end of the line struck along the centre of the lever, and from the *other end* of the central line struck on the lever, describe with a trammels an arc of a circle, of such a radius that the circumference of the circle will pass through the two points previously marked upon the straight edge. The central point on the straight edge must always be kept to the end of the central line struck upon the lever, but the straight edge must be angled upon this point as a centre, until the point of the trammels passes through the other two points, the radius of the trammels being simultaneously adjusted, to make the circle come through these points. When this is done the straight edge

will be at right angles with the central line struck on the lever, and from the straight edge any other measurement may then be made.

2. When the teeth of a bevel wheel pattern are glued on a cone, it is clear that the glued surface of the teeth can no more have an uniform radius than the surface of the cone itself has. No plane therefore will give the proper form to such a surface, but a rasp cut on a part of a conical surface, and which is worked up against a stop, adjusted to the size of the cone on which the teeth were to be placed, would answer the purpose required.

3. To cut a key seat upon a shaft, lay a straight edge flat upon the top of the shaft, and from the edge at each end of the shaft let plumb-lines fall, which will pass through the centres of the shaft. When the plumb-lines are so adjusted, by shifting the straight-edge to one side or the other, that they pass through the shaft centres, draw a line along the shaft close to the edge of the straight-edge, and from this central line lay off on each side half the breadth of the key-seat required.

4. In algebra letters are used to designate quantities, and the advantage of the practice is, that it enables quantities to be multiplied, divided, and otherwise readily dealt with, without incumbering the operation with tedious arithmetical processes. For we know that if any quantity has to be multiplied, and then divided by the same number, the original quantity remains unchanged ; and hence it is obvious that if any number which we may call a, be multiplied by any other number which we may call b, and be then divided again by the same quantity b, we have the original quantity a left ; and this will equally be the case whether this a or b be 1 or 1000. Hence we know that $a \times b \div b = a$, and also $a \times a = a^2$, or the square of a and $a^2 \div a = a$ Thus, by the use of algebra, arithmetical operations may be indicated without being actually performed, whereby the question is cleared of all unnecessary processes before its final arithmetical resolution is performed. The expression $\left(\frac{\sqrt{2\,a\,b}}{3\,x} \right)$ means the square root of the quantity represented by twice a multiplied by b, and divided by $3\,x$. Hence if a be 3, and b be 6, it is clear that $2 \times a \times b$, or $2\,a\,b = 36$, and if $x = 3$, then $3\,x = 9$, and $\frac{2\,a\,b}{3\,x} = \frac{36}{9} = 4$, the square root of which is 2. In all questions, whether algebraical or arithmetical, there are some numbers which are known, and other numbers which are required to be found out. In algebra, for the sake of convenience, the known numbers are always indicated by the first letters of the alphabet, a, b, c, &c., and the unknown numbers, or the numbers required to be found out, by the last letters of the alphabet, x, y, z. This is all only a matter of common sense, and any other kind of notation would answer equally well if as simple in itself, and as generally understood.

J. B.

Kincardine, May, 1850.

Mr. Editor.—Sir, Encouraged by your note appended to the queries of last month, I beg your insertion of the following practical questions, in hopes that some of your readers will give practical answers.

1. In a screw propeller whose pitch is equal to the dia., supposing that it makes a complete thread, I wish to know the relation that a line in the extreme circumference of the thread bears to the circumference of the cylinder from which it is supposed to be cut.

2. Is a collar, or a number of collars, on the screw shaft the best means of taking the thrust ; and for diminishing the friction ?

3. If engines are coupled direct to the screw shaft without the intervention of gearing, what is the best proportion for the dia. and pitch of the screw compared to the length of the crank ?

4. Is the bearing aft of the screw in the rudder-post at all necessary in sea-going vessels ?

I am, yours truly,

O. Y.

INDIAN RAILWAYS.

Letter to the Shareholders of the Great Indian Peninsula Railway Company, from J. CHAPMAN, its Founder and late Manager. London: CHAPMAN, 142, Strand. 1850.

IT is wonderful into what oblique courses Boards of Directors will deviate, however good and honest its individual members may be. Numerous cases have come to light during the recent railway investigations, of respectable and estimable men, who in their private dealings would be incapable of a dishonourable act, lending themselves in their corporate capacity to the most flagrant abuses and frauds; and in this new and singular social law, we must, we suppose, look for an explanation of the injustice Mr. Chapman has sustained at the hands of the Peninsula Railway Directors, who present the strange spectacle of an assembly of respectable men, deliberately perpetrating acts of severity and wrong, and availing themselves of the aid of legal ingenuities, such as all right-thinking men must reprobate and despise. The case is a plain one, and may be told in few words; but, however palpable the impropriety with which Mr. Chapman has been treated may be to all the world beside, the directors of the railway company would now fail to discern the fault, though it were huge as Olympus. Men never reason or reflect after they have once taken a side; and thus directors, of the most honest intentions, if they receive a wrong initial bias from some tricky official, are afterwards carried forward into most indefensible courses by the combativeness of their own dispositions, or the supposed necessity of consistency. Time, however, which cools the heats of controversy, and dispels the mists which assiduous misrepresentation may be expected to create, will one day place these directors in the position we and others occupy—that of impartial spectators; and they will then stand astonished at their own weakness—aye, and their moral delinquency too—in suffering a man like Mr. Chapman to be thrown over on the instigation of unprincipled parasites, whose true character against that time will no doubt be found out. Our business, however, is not with things so difficult of detection as the consciences of railway directors, and we proceed to recapitulate a few of the main facts which are here presented.

Mr. Chapman originated the idea of the Indian Peninsula Railway about 1844, and after having made a most careful digest of all the facts at that time available, a company was formed, and Mr. Chapman was despatched to India to pursue such further enquiries upon the spot as he had found would be advisable. To raise the money necessary to enable this enquiry to be conducted, 1500 paid-up shares were created, of which 1000 were handed to members of the provisional committee, in consideration of a sum of £2400 advanced by them, and 500 were handed to Mr. Chapman, in consideration of his time and services. Under this arrangement Mr. Chapman proceeded to India, and on his return he presented the provisional committee with a masterly report, which was printed, and now constitutes the basis of the company's operations. Public opinion, however, about this time, set in strongly against all railway enterprizes; and there appears to be little doubt that the undertaking would have been abandoned, but for the persevering efforts Mr. Chapman made in its behalf; but his able advocacy of its claims, and the confidence his integrity of character both justified and inspired, carried it over the difficult period, and an arrangement was in the end concluded with the India House, by which the scheme was understood to be established. And now comes the history of Mr. Chapman's requital. To assist in the share or stock-exchange department of the business, a Mr. Nicholson was brought in, with the questionable recommendation of a skill in railway matters, and this diplomatic gentleman, with the aid of some others, appears in the long run to have succeeded in working Mr. Chapman out. Mr. Chapman had stipulated, as a matter of course, for a seat at the Board, and on the occasion of a more profitable situation being offered for his acceptance,

he received an assurance from the chairman that his salary should not be less, as a minimum, when in India, than 1500 rupees a month—which every one acquainted with India must be sensible is a very moderate remuneration for the performance of responsible duties in that country, and which, moreover, was less than half the amount that the manager of the other Indian railway was receiving. But no sooner had the main difficulties incident to the establishment of the undertaking been surmounted, than the seat at the Board was refused; the salary was cut down to the extent of 250 rupees per month below the minimum previously stipulated, and the paid-up shares which Mr. Chapman had received at the outset of the undertaking, were repudiated altogether. It is a significant fact that of the 1500 paid-up shares originally created, Mr. Chapman's 500 shares are the only ones which have been disallowed; though it is difficult to see how, if the 500 are bad, on any technical ground, the 1000 can be good and valid. Lord Wharncliffe, the chairman, by whom the assurance relative to the minimum salary of 1500 rupees per month was given, on being appealed to by Mr. Chapman, to see that understanding faithfully carried out, says, "I have done my best to recal to my recollection the precise incidents of my interview with you, after the discussion respecting your remuneration some time since; but I am sorry to find that I cannot do so with sufficient distinctness to be able confidently to speak as to what passed." Hereupon Mr. Chapman respectfully suggested that Lord Wharncliffe's imperfect recollection should not be suffered to set aside his own distinct remembrance of what occurred; but he submitted that if any difference of opinion existed on the subject, the question might be referred to the East India Company, who, as the guaranteeing parties, had an obvious interest in seeing economy enforced; and he added, that by the decision of the East India Company he was prepared to abide. This offer, however, was rejected; and, as a fitting climax to such a course of injustice, Mr. Chapman was dismissed from the service of the railway company, for temperately urging his just claims, and requesting the fulfilment of promises, which either should never have been made, or never broken. Yet these directors, though plainly convicted of juggling an able and confiding servant out of the just fruits of his talents and industry, are "all honourable men," or are so accounted; and we thus come back to our initial paradox, that there is no iniquity into which a Board of Directors may not be gradually led by crafty officials, however respectable and clear-sighted the constituent members of the Board may be. A Board, indeed, is often only a screen for the designing.

But we think Mr. Chapman blameable also. He has all along been too confiding, and he also delayed too long the distinct assertion of his claims and position, in a business and official manner. While he was only considering how he might best forward the interests of the company, others were considering how they could most effectually throw over a man of such impracticable honesty, and such inconvenient talent. Able men, indeed, have necessarily little of the suspicion proper to small souls; but we think there has been some want of courage in Mr. Chapman's proceedings, as well as an exuberance of faith. We think also that he has committed a grave error in permitting himself to be seduced into that approbation of the fragment of the line now proposed for execution, which is due only to the original line in its integrity. If Mr. Crawford and himself had retired when Mr. Williamson retired, and on the same grounds, he would now have occupied a far higher ground, and attracted a larger sympathy and support, than any question, mainly or apparently personal, can ever command.

There are two railway schemes proposed to be carried into effect in India, which have obtained from the government a guaranteed interest of 5 per cent. upon the capital. One of these projects is that of the East India Railway Company, and the other that of the Great Indian Peninsula Railway Company. The original design of the East India Railway was to connect Calcutta with Delhi, 900 miles distant;

and the design of the Indian Peninsula Railway, was to connect Bombay with the great cotton-fields of Berar, situated 400 miles off, in the heart of the Deccan. Both of these projects, if they had been carried into execution in their integrity, would have been highly useful to India. But the capital necessary for such gigantic schemes was found to be unattainable, and the East Indian Railway has consequently been cut down into a scheme for carrying a line from Calcutta into the jungle, 70 miles off, at an expense of a million; and the Indian Peninsula Railway has dwindled into a scheme for connecting Bombay with the village of Callian, 35 miles distant, at a cost of half-a-million; although those places are already connected by efficient water communication. It was shown by Mr. Bourne several years ago, that although the East India Railway, if carried out in its integrity, would probably pay, the fragment of it at present intended to be constructed, would certainly not; and the same result is equally inevitable in the case of the mutilated scheme now pursued by the Peninsula Railway Company, which there is every reason to believe will never return its expenses. Nobody now, indeed, pretends to believe that either of these projects will be profitable, and their prosecution on the ground that the integral line must eventually be carried out, and that they will then be profitable, is about as reasonable a procedure as building one arch of a bridge, on the hypothesis that the other ten arches must one day be added, and the work will then become one of public utility. The shareholders, we suppose, are indifferent to the question of profits, on the ground that the East India Company has guaranteed them an interest of 5 per cent. upon their investment : but this guarantee is coupled with the condition that the line, if once begun, shall be properly finished, and shall be regularly worked by the railway company, the expenses incident to which may more than swallow up the whole amount guaranteed. It is true the railway companies have the option of selling their lines to the government, if they are found to be unprofitable; but they must be surrendered in a state of perfect repair, and free from all incumbrances. Much of the work of the Indian Peninsula line consists of tunnelling through rock; and if the railway should cost a million to complete it, instead of half-a-million, as now supposed, the prime cost will not be obtained from the government when it comes to be sold, but only the half-million on which the guarantee is given. The country through which the East India Railway is to pass is very subject to floods, which have often carried off the high road, which is carried on an embankment, as is indispensable in that locality. If the railway works be carried off in like manner, the shareholders, and not the government, will have to sustain the loss; for the government has stipulated that it will only purchase the railway if " in perfect repair, and equal to its first state," and cannot be expected therefore to purchase hypothetical works, which have all been swept off. In the alluvial district adjacent to Calcutta stone of any kind is not to be found, and any stone used there is brought from places about as far off as England is from Gibraltar. The cost of stone sleepers for the railway, therefore, would necessarily be very great, and wood is found to be speedily eaten up by the white ants, in spite of any method of impregnating the wood with poisonous substances, which has yet been discovered. If the wooden sleepers of the railway, therefore, be thus destroyed, the expense of renewing them will devolve, not upon the government, but upon the railway shareholders. Add to this the reluctance to relinquish office, which most railway directories have displayed, and the probability of the shareholders being mystified as to their true position, until incumbrances have been accumulated, which will swallow up the capital altogether, and it will be seen how small is the guarantee of a bona-fide dividend of 5 per cent. afforded by the government concession ; and how certain must be the realization of loss and disappointment to all concerned. If the government would agree to take the money from the shareholders as a loan for general purposes of internal improvement, engaging to give for this loan an interest of 5 per cent. clear of all contingencies,

that would be a distinct and safe arrangement for the shareholders to accept. But the present arrangement, with the certainty that there can be no profits over the 5 per cent. guaranteed, involves chances of loss, which to some extent appear to be of inevitable occurrence, and which may eventually swallow up the whole capital invested. It is, no doubt, a very patriotic undertaking to incur these risks, and to suffer these confiscations on behalf of an undertaking of public utility; but we fear that even this object will not be subserved by the execution of these mutilated projects : for we suppose it may be accepted as an axiom that any railway undertaking, which cannot attract to itself sufficient traffic to yield a profit, cannot render material benefit to the district through which it passes. Railways are useful only where they are used, and as the traffic on the proposed fragments at present proposed for execution would be very inconsiderable, their establishment would not only fail to achieve any material public benefit, but by the exhibition of a gigantic failure, they would greatly contribute to deter the investment of English capital in India—a result which, on many grounds, it is so desirable to promote.

SOCIETIES.

INSTITUTION OF MECHANICAL ENGINEERS.
April 24th, 1850.

The usual General Meeting of the members was held in the theatre of the Philosophical Institution, Cannon Street, Birmingham, on Wednesday, the 24th of April, 1850; Robert Stephenson, Esq., M.P., president, of the institution, in the chair.

The minutes of the last general meeting were read by the secretary, and confirmed.

The Chairman then said the adjourned discussion on railway axles, and the fracture of iron, would be opened by reading a few additional observations by Mr. J. E. M'Connell, " On the Deterioration of Railway Axles."

In opening the discussion on Railway Axles, adjourned from the last meeting,* it will be only requisite to refer to the former papers that have been laid before the institution on the form of axles and their deterioration from work.

1st. As regards the proper form for a railway axle, the proportion was shown in which the diameter of the axle should be reduced from the back of each wheel towards the centre, so as to obtain an equal strength throughout the length of the axle, to resist the strains or blows to which it is subjected. This was tested in two different ways, in the one case by a steadily increasing pressure, and in the other by the blow of a weight of 17 cwt. falling 9½ feet; the force in both cases being applied at the same point—namely, at the outer end of one wheel whilst the opposite wheel was fixed. The result given by these tests was, that the axle, when shaped in the proportion ascertained by previous calculation and experiment, was bent into a nearly uniform curve, showing that the object of obtaining an equally proportioned strength was practically accomplished. It may be observed also, that the general experience of practical engineers engaged in the management of railway rolling stock appears to confirm this principle.

2nd. As to the deterioration that takes place in axles, and the change in structure caused by the course of working, several cases were instanced, and specimens were laid before the institution of broken railway axles, showing the crystalline appearance of the fracture. The writer considered that a change was produced from a fibrous to a crystalline structure by the effects of the concussion or jarring that the axles are subjected to whilst running on the railway; and it appears to be generally considered that such change takes place to a greater or less

* Artizan, *ante.* p. 61.

extent according to the circumstances, both in railway axles and in many other cases where iron is exposed to concussion or jarring, though there may be a difference of opinion as to the cause of the change. Another striking instance of the conversion of tough wrought iron into a brittle material, is shown in the chain slings used for carrying the bars during the process of hammering at a forge : the writer lately had an opportunity of observing a chain which had been in use for this purpose, and had become so extremely brittle that it was more like glass in its texture than the tough strong iron which it had been when first made, and he was satisfied that it had only been subjected to this extreme jarring action for a few months, and had not been otherwise employed. And further, it may be mentioned as a circumstance of common occurrence, that the porter-bars that are attached to the blooms whilst under the forge hammer, became so brittle with the constant violent jarring to which they are subjected, that they break in two after a very moderate amount of work : in these instances there appears to have been no cause but the jarring or concussion to produce the change, as the iron was subjected to little strain in proportion to its strength ; and the same may be observed of several of the instances mentioned before, in one of which the wrought iron arms of a fly-wheel were jarred loose in the cast-iron rim, and broke off quite short, from the rapid and continued violent shocks caused by the cam striking the helve, although the iron was of the toughest description originally.

In railway axles there can be no doubt that the same action of jarring or concussion is in force, and may produce corresponding effects upon the strength of the iron ; and that point at the back of the wheel where the effect of the jarring is concentrated, will be most sensibly changed. The action of bending a piece of iron backwards and forwards will, doubtless, result in its fracture at the weakest point, if it be carried on long enough ; and it becomes necessary, therefore, with a given weight of material in an axle, to proportion the strength at every point of its length, so that it may be capable of resisting the breaking force equally throughout, the strength being proportioned so as to cause it to yield as uniformly as possible at every point.

A badly-proportioned axle, which was comparatively unyielding in the centre, would be more affected, both by the bending and jarring forces at that point where the axle is held fast in the boss of the wheel, which is a mass acting as an anvil to break it over. The tendency to break at that point having been, of course, aggravated by the obsolete practice of the axle having a square shoulder of considerable size at the boss of the wheel, instead of the present usual plan of making the least possible difference in the diameter of the axle at that part for the purpose, with a long taper countersunk into the wheel.

It is, obviously, very desirable that every opportunity should be taken by those who are practically engaged in the working of railways, to investigate the facts connected with the failures of axles in process of working, as detached experiments, however carefully and impartially conducted, cannot faithfully represent or afford results corresponding to the effects of the various strains and forces to which axles are subjected whilst working on a railway.

The Chairman observed, that at the first discussion on this subject he took the liberty of drawing the attention of the members to the extreme care that was necessary in coming to any conclusion as to a molecular change in the constitution of wrought iron. He thought that, although there were a number of facts and statements on record, which appeared to render it extremely probable that some change did take place in iron, yet that it only amounted to a change in the particles in their relation to each other, which might in the end produce a brittleness, or impart a crystalline character. These proofs were now multiplied in number, but he thought were not much increased in pointedness, if he excepted the experiment with the chain, which was the most striking and marked instance of which he had yet heard. Hence they must conceive that a change takes place in iron if subject to vibration ; but

an investigation into the precise cause of the change would require more time and care than could at present be devoted to it. He might remark that since their last meeting he had turned his attention to ascertain, if possible, whether any real difference exists in the molecular arrangement of the material or structure of a piece of iron called crystalline, and a piece of iron called fibrous ; and for this purpose he had examined them under a powerful microscope, and it would, probably, surprise the members to know that no real difference could be perceived, and that if he had not previously seen with the naked eye the specimens called fibrous and crystalline, he should not have been able to distinguish the one from the other in the microscope. The best specimen he could select of the kind called fibrous, exhibited to the naked eye a laminal arrangement of dark and light lines, but the light lines composing the apparent fibre were, in point of fact, as crystalline as the other kind of iron, and, therefore, however fibrous it might appear, it was essentially a crystalline mass. Even in a piece of iron, with large facets, which appeared extremely crystalline, when one of the crystals was examined, it gave much the same appearance under the microscope as a fibrous surface gives to the naked eye ; in fact, it would appear to consist of bundles of fibres broken through at certain angles, just as slate was observed in the quarries to break in particular rhomboidal forms. Now, in the instance of slate, there was nothing fibrous or crystalline, but owing to the peculiar arrangement of the particles it exhibited on a large scale something resembling the appearances to be observed in iron — like fibres being broken through in particular planes.

It appeared to him that the fracture taking place in an axle at particular points, might be illustrated by reference to a string being thrown into vibration. There were certain points of the string, called nodes, where no motion took place, because the action on the one side neutralises the action on the other, and the particles at the nodes have double duty to perform, being pulled in opposite directions at the same time : hence what might be called the nodes in the axle had great action upon them, and this might induce a crystalline appearance, although it might not cause much change in the structure of the iron. It appeared to him a matter of extreme difficulty to conceive a change going on in the structure of iron, because it would involve a change from one kind of crystalline structure to another, which was next to an impossibility. He could imagine that a number of particles under the influence of vibration might in time jostle each other into particular forms, and become fibrous ; yet, when they examined most fibrous iron, they would find it already crystalline, which involved the necessity of the molecules leaving one form of crystal and taking another. It would be well for the members to communicate to the institution any well-authenticated facts of crystallization of iron, because nothing could have so important a bearing on the structure of railway axles as the means of tracing fractures to their real cause. Perhaps at their next meeting he might have the pleasure of exhibiting to the members certain microscopic results, but as yet he had not given the subject sufficient consideration to justify him in doing so.

Mr. Adams thought that the appearance called crystalline was caused by nothing more or less than a bundle of fibres, consisting of many small crystals being sheared off square, forming one face.

Mr. H. Smith inquired whether the Chairman thought there was any difference of strength produced. If they took the case of the common gag to the helve, or the prop that was placed under it, they found it became crystalline in the course of time and very brittle, though quite fibrous at first. So also in the case of the chains on inclined planes, they broke very soon. He should like to know whether crystallized iron was not weaker than fibrous.

Mr. M'Connell thought it was so. Whenever iron was subjected to a jar, the fracture was square across, and it seemed as if the whole structure of the iron became brittle like glass. For in the instance he had mentioned of the chain sling, the iron was so brittle that a small tap of a hammer would have broken it ; hence, it must be obvious that whatever might be said as to the relative strength of fibrous and crystalline iron there was a striking difference between tough and brittle. He spoke then guardedly, because, from what he had seen of the appearance of iron under the microscope, he was induced to think that the word fibrous, which they had hitherto applied to the structure of iron, was a misnomer, if applied in the ordinary English acceptation of the term. That, however, an alteration did take place in the quality or condition of iron was manifest, from a great abundance of evidence ; and he thought it would be a decided improvement if they adopted some other word which would express the same quality or condition of iron in its tough state : yet it was clear that a change did take place, making that which was originally tough quite brittle. The effect on a railway axle had been already explained by the instance of a string in vibration. When the axle was at work a node was created at the back of the wheel at each end, and it would be found that although it broke off short at the back of the wheel, yet in the centre it remained quite tough, as if the vibratory wave had passed freely through it. He should be glad to see the matter further investigated, as the subject was one of great importance, and at some future meeting he hoped to be prepared with some further information on the subject.

The Chairman remarked, that the question of comparative strength was one of great importance ; but it must be borne in mind that there was great difference between the two strains of pressure and percussion ; and he doubted whether highly crystalline iron was much weaker than iron which was highly fibrous, if care were only taken of the situation in which it was employed. In the course of the building of the Britannia Tubular Bridge, his attention was called by his assistant, Mr. Clark, to a series of bad plates which had been delivered. Instead of being fibrous boiler plates, they were short-grained and brittle ; and this, in so large a structure, was regarded as a serious objection to them ; accordingly it was decided to remove them from the bottom of the bridge to the top, as in that situation they would be subject to compression instead of tension. He (the Chairman) thought it right to test the tensile strength of those plates, and accordingly they had slips cut from the respective plates, and very much to their surprise the crystalline plates were much the strongest ; for the average strength of the fibrous plates was 18 tons to the square inch, and in a great many instances it ranged as low as 16 tons, whilst the crystalline plates averaged a strength of 21 tons, though they could hardly punch the holes in them, which was a good test as to the quality of the plates. Hence they came to the conclusion, that what is called crystalline iron is capable of a greater steady tensile strain, and that it does not appear less suitable than fibrous iron for an erection of the character in which they were engaged ; and this certainly agreed with the notion of the crystallized facets being bundles of small fibres cut across at one plane. At the same time he thought it would have been objectionable to have put the crystalline plates at the bottom of the tube, because the trains were producing continual vibration, and the two strains—the one under vibration, and the other under steady weight—were very different in their character, and in their effect on iron. The mode of testing the plates at the bridge was by a very direct means, and therefore the results might be relied on with great confidence. They were tested by actual weights suspended direct from the plates themselves, and the strain was not put on by any machine, such as the hydraulic press, or by levers, where the fulcrum was liable to alter a little, causing a material difference in the leverage ; and there was a considerable amount of friction to interfere with the correct result. This would account in some measure for the great discrepancy which prevailed in the results of former experiments with reference to the strength of iron during the last twenty years. Some had thought that the ultimate strength was 24 tons per square inch, but he was satisfied that in no well-conducted experiment would it be found to exceed 21 tons ; and he felt that they could not safely rely upon a greater strength than 16 or 18 tons for practical purposes.

Mr. Slate inquired whether, when the Chairman spoke of 16 or 18 tons being the ultimate limit of elasticity, he meant would it fracture at that point.

The Chairman believed that fracture took place in every instance.

Mr. Slate said he had, with some others, made some experiments on the strength of iron bars, and had minutely tested their elastic power. The result he had arrived at was that after the elastic point was once passed, time became a most important element in the fracture, and the breaking point would depend upon the rapidity with which the weight was put on. In some bars of the best quality of iron, 9 inches by 1 inch, the ultimate strength was 17¼ tons per inch, but the permanent stretching began at about 8 tons per inch, and if that strain had been long enough continued, he considered the bar would have broken with it.

The Chairman observed, that, according to the experiments made by Professor Barlow, the permanent stretching began at 8 or 10 tons per inch, and the bar never came back again to its original length after that limit of strain was passed. It must be borne in mind, that the section of the bar was diminishing, and its density increasing during the stretching.

Mr. Walker observed, that in some experiments he had tried, it was found that 28 tons per inch was the ultimate pressure borne by bar iron, and in some cases it went up as high as 32 tons before breaking, but in these cases the weights had been applied very quickly.

The Chairman concurred in the opinion that time was a very important element in experiments of this nature.

Mr. Slate observed, that the same remark was applicable to cast iron.

Mr. Cowper believed that the point at which the elasticity of iron was overcome and permanent stretching commenced, might be measured at 8 tons per square inch, or by a fine micrometer, at 7½ tons: although by measuring more roughly with beam compasses, it had been stated so high as 10 tons. A bar 3½ inch square and 7 feet 6 inches long, bore 27 tons per square inch before it broke, and it was then extended in length 5 inches ; the elasticity of that bar, after being permanently extended upwards of 3 inches, was as nearly as possible the same as it was at first before permanent extension had commenced, it was stretched one-eighth of an inch by the same increase of strain in both cases, and returned completely.

Mr. Slate doubted the accuracy of this principle.

The Chairman observed, that Mr. Cowper meant, that although the iron was permanently extended, the cohesion among the particles was not so altered as to interfere with the law of its elasticity. The iron itself was not crippled, though the area might be altered ; hence the law of elasticity was not altered, and the constitution of the iron itself was not deteriorated.

Mr. Robinson said, he considered there was an advantage in making experiments with the hydraulic press, because it afforded a good means of detecting the stretching—immediately that extension took place the pump handle began to move faster. It was found in practice, that the moment they got beyond the elastic strain in a bar of iron it became deteriorated ; and they never considered it capable of bearing again with safety unless it came back to the starting point.

The Chairman did not mean to speak with disapprobation respecting the pump, but he thought a little want of accuracy might be created by the use of it, for he thought it quite clear that some better means than the pump handle might be devised, and was in fact in daily use for ascertaining the extension of the iron. Even a little leaking, or an extension of the bar, would detract from the accuracy of the experiment ; and in the complicated pump apparatus there was a great deal of friction, sometimes requiring an additional half-ton per inch to move the ram alone, as had been sometimes observed at the Britannia Bridge. The pump might be out of order, and hence it was a matter of importance to use that mode of testing which was not liable to go wrong, although the use of the dead weight might be the most troublesome.

Mr. Robinson said, he thought no bar was capable of enduring more than 14 or 15 tons per inch, but it was easy to explain the reason why some had stated the results of experiments to range as low as 8 or 9 tons. The accuracy of all such experiments depended on keeping the line of strain in the axis of the bar, and in proportion to negligence in this particular would they fail in obtaining the true results. At the same time he thought it necessary that further experiments should be conducted on as accurate a scale as possible before they attempted to decide a point of such importance.

The Chairman observed, that some experiments had been made by Mr. Parkes, with iron bars, about 3 feet long and 1½ inch square. In order to discover the ultimate strength of wrought-iron he put weights upon the centre of the bars, but the deflection was so great that they bent down between the supports, and the experiment was spoiled. Accordingly he adopted this ingenious mode of ascertaining the point ; he took two bars perfectly similar, heated them in a furnace, and allowed one to cool in a straight position ; the other was bent hot into a curve of 5 inches in 3 feet, and then allowed to cool in that form. When both bars were cold he commenced experimenting with the plain straight bar, and that bent very readily. But before he began to experiment on the bent bar he straightened it cold, and by so doing he brought the particles of the under side of the bar into a state of tension, or in other words into the condition of a tension bar, and the bar broke with very little deflection, because the strain was like that on a trussed girder with a tie rod.

The adjourned discussion on Railway Springs was introduced by reading the following additional paper, by Mr. W. A. Adams, of Birmingham :—

ON RAILWAY CARRIAGE AND WAGGON SPRINGS.

In the paper read at the last meeting, the writer brought before the Institution some Experiments on the relative qualities of Spring-steel manufactured from English and from Swedish iron, and gave a description of the different constructions of Bearing and Buffer Springs, making a comparison between the Laminated Buffer Springs and the various kinds of External Cylinder and Piston Buffers.

An investigation was also given of the principles for regulating the form and thickness of the plates of the ordinary Laminated Springs, and the writer endeavoured to illustrate that the true and correct form for a Laminated Spring is a triangle tapering at a uniform rate from the centre to each end ; and, further, that the Spring should not be weakened in the centre by a bolt or rivet-hole. He intimated his intention of preparing a Laminated Bearing Spring with Axle-box and adjustments complete according to these principles, and thus endeavour to produce the same results as in the ordinary Laminated Spring with the smallest amount of material.

Fig. 11, represents a spring and adjustments of the following

dimensions, which has been made according to the above principles, and is laid before the present meeting :—

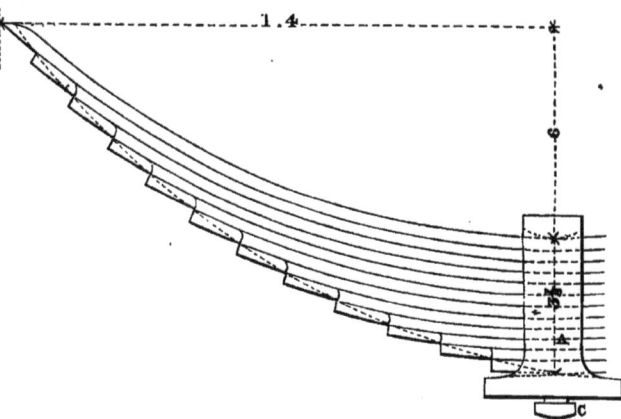

Fig. 11.

Length	2 ft. 8 in.
Camber	6 in.
Width	3 in.
Thickness in centre	3⅞ in.

Consisting of 10 plates ₁₆ inch thick, and 2 plates ⅛ inch thick.

The weight of the spring, exclusive of the hoop, is 59 lbs.

This spring is very nearly a triangle, the base being but ⅛ inch wide. To ensure the correct triangular form, the plates are cut to the correct lengths, as shown in Figure 10, and afterwards cambered.

Fig. 10.

In this spring there is no rivet or bolt-hole, the plates being held together by the clip A. The clip is rounded at the top and bottom, as shown in the section Figure 12, and the spring is therefore confined at the extreme centre only.

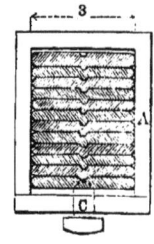

Fig. 12.

To prevent the plates sliding one past the others they are studded one into the other at the centre, as shown at B, Figure 12. To prevent the spring sliding from the hoop, a set screw C, figures 11 and 12, is fixed in the bottom of the clip, the point of the set screw fitting a countersink in the bottom plate. The clip or saddle A is broad at the base, to enable it to rest conveniently on the sides of the Axle-box, in the manner of an ordinary spring hoop, without interfering at all with the grease chamber.

The deflections of the above spring are by actual experiment,

½ ton weight	½ inch deflection.
1 „	1 „
1½ „	1½ „
2 „	2 „
3 „	3 „
4 „	4 „

No permanent set in this experiment.

The smaller improved spring exhibited to the meeting, is of the following dimensions:—

Length	2 ft. 6 in.
Camber	5 in.
Width	3 in.
Thickness in centre	3½ in.

Consisting of ten plates 5/16, and one plate ⅜ inch thick.

The weight of the spring, exclusive of the hoop, is 48lbs.

The deflections by experiment are—

½ ton weight	7/16 inch deflection.
1 „	⅞ „
1½ „	1 7/16 „
2 „	1¾ „
3 „	2⅝ „
4 „	3½ „

No permanent set in this experiment. This spring is somewhat too rigid, and would do better with one plate less, reducing the weight to about 44 lbs.

COMPARATIVE TABLE OF DEFLECTIONS.

Strain on each Spring.	Thick Plate Spring Weighing 40 lbs.	Ordinary Spring Weighing 93 lbs.	New Spring Weighing 59 lbs.	New Spring Weighing 48 lbs.
Tons.	Inches.	Inches.	Inches.	Inches.
½	—	—	½	7/16
1	⅝	⅞	1	⅞
1½	—	—	1½	1 7/16
2	¾	2	2	1¾
3	1⅛	3¼	3	2⅝
4	—	—	4	3½

By reference to this comparative table, showing the experiments with the spring in ordinary use, described in the former paper, it will be noted that the results are nearly the same as those of the Improved Springs now described, but with this difference, that the deflections of the Ordinary Spring are in an increasing ratio, but with the Improved Springs the deflections are in a uniform ratio.

It therefore appears that with a spring weighing about 44 to 50 lbs. the same results can be obtained as with the Ordinary Heavy Waggon Springs, which weigh on the average 93 lbs.

A specimen was exhibited to the meeting of the Ordinary Bearing Spring, with Axle-box and adjustments; and also the Improved Spring, with Axle-box and adjustments. The adjustments of the Ordinary Spring weigh 7 lbs., and of the Improved Spring 5 lbs.

The advantages of the Improved Spring are presumed to be, that, inasmuch as from the correct theoretical form and the absence of the centre rivet or bolt-hole, every particle of the material is doing equal duty, the Spring will be more lasting; and, also, that from the reduction of material the first cost will be considerably lessened.

Mr. Adams briefly explained the drawings, and the specimens of the springs exhibited to the meeting; and added, that having taken 2 tons as the full load on each spring, he had endeavoured to realize the full extent of action with the smallest amount of material.

The Chairman observed, that he thought the proposed spring was a decided improvement in the form of the spring, and avoiding a hole through the centre. In the ordinary spring the centre portion was inactive, and the remainder only was really useful.

Mr. Wright said, the hole in the centre did not appear to him a great objection, and the only advantage in the proposed spring consisted in it being much lighter than those ordinarily in use; but he thought the principle of all that kind of springs was wrong in having so much camber.

The Chairman said, it appeared to him to be intended as a re-production of the advantages of other springs, with less weight and material; and it was certainly incorrect to put a hole in the centre of a girder which was to carry a weight in the centre.

Mr. Wright thought the long flat springs were the best, such as were used in carriages, and that they prevented the axles from breaking, as they did with the other springs used in waggons, and they would not deflect too much, not more than 2 or 2½ inches.

Mr. M'Connell thought the carriage springs were only useful whilst the tension of the load was not enough to bring them flat, but beyond that they would become useless and quite rigid; and with reference to waggon springs, he thought the tension would be too great to make the principle applicable.

Mr. Wright suggested a tension spring, with a loose shackle at each end, on the same principle as some ordinary waggon springs were hung.

Mr. Adams observed, that the form of spring he suggested was very even in its work, and uniform in its deflection throughout. With each additional 5 cwt. of load, it sunk ¼ inch; and with 3 tons upon it the spring was quite as easy, because there was still the same deflection of ¼ inch for each 5 cwt., as with the lighter load.

The Chairman considered it an important advantage that this uniformity of deflection or elasticity extended throughout the entire space.

Mr. Smith thought it a decided improvement to get rid of the hole through the centre, because it enabled them to make use of the whole of the steel in the spring to the very centre.

Mr. Ross did not see any advantage in the nibs in the centre of the spring, instead of a rivet, and thought they would weaken the spring in the centre as much as the rivet-hole. He suggested the introduction of a solid block of ash or oak, for the bearing of the spring in the centre, as he considered there was great benefit resulting from that plan. For three or four years past they had introduced wooden blocks into buffer springs, with decided advantage.

Mr. H. Wright said, in practice, they seldom found a spring break in the centre in the case of carriage springs, owing to the long bearing on a wooden block; but engine springs were liable to break in the centre, where there was only a short bearing, without wood in the centre. But in the carriage springs the material in the centre was certainly inactive, and it was an improvement to save that inactive material.

Mr. Adams remarked, that his object was to improve the present waggon spring, by combining the best action of that kind of spring with the least amount of material; and with regard to the plates being nibbed into each other in the centre, he thought that could not weaken them at all, as there was not any portion of the material removed, as was the case with the rivet-hole; but, on the contrary, from the sectional form of the nib, the strength of the plates was perhaps rather increased than diminished in the centre.

The Chairman observed, that it was desirable to have great elasticity in the spring with a heavy load, and less elasticity with a light load; but springs generally were the reverse of this, and it was an important advantage in the proposed spring, that it was equally elastic with a heavy load as with a light one. In railway waggons it was impossible to keep the loads so uniformly distributed as in carriages.

Mr. Wright thought that the tension spring would yield equally at every point of its elasticity.

Mr. M'Connell observed, that it would diminish in elasticity as the

load increased, because it would become at last absolutely rigid, and could not yield any further.

Mr. Slate considered that the construction of the tension carriage spring was very unmechanical; the strain of the spring was carried through a curve, and though it might do extremely well with a light load, yet when it was applied to waggons varying in their load from 3 to 10 tons, the limits of tension would be exceeded, and between the ends of the scroll irons it would be perfectly rigid. He thought no strength of material that could be put in the tie would be equivalent to support a heavy load in that particular direction, because it must either stretch, or, if not elastic, must certainly break. Besides, he considered there was an immense strain upon the scroll iron, and the form itself was objectionable, however well the curved form might be in appearance.

Mr. Adams explained by the drawing that the straightening of the top plate, as the spring deflected, compensated for the deflection of the shackle, and prevented any undue strain within the limits of load that kind of spring was subjected to in passenger carriages; and the action of the spring was materially assisted by the form in which the plates were set in making the spring, the set being all given at the centre of the plates, thus 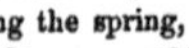 instead of the plates being bent into a uniform curve throughout, thus 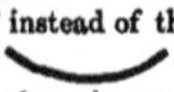

Mr. De Bergue then read the following observations on the India-rubber buffers, in reference to the notice of them in the paper read at the last meeting; the Chairman remarking first, that it was irregular for a paper to be read upon another paper, and could only be permitted as a special exception in the present case, and not as a precedent.

In reference to the observation that the sustaining power of the India-rubber buffers is too great, and that in the event of a collision the train might collapse before this was fully developed; the writer would observe, that the most effective buffers in the event of a collision will be those which will oppose the greatest amount of resistance moving through the greatest space, provided their maximum resisting force should not exceed the pressure that could be sustained by the under frames of the waggons, without injury. Now the maximum sustaining power of a pair of these India-rubber buffers does not exceed 20 tons, and as there are several thousand sets of them in use, many of which have at times been driven quite home without the waggons being collapsed, it follows that their resisting power does not exceed a *useful* limit, and that they must consequently be much more efficient in the event of a collision than any other buffers having the same stroke and only one-third of the resisting power.

But it must be borne in mind that buffers are not solely required for cases of collision, they are more generally serviceable to break the slighter concussions in stopping and starting trains, and in sidings and warehouses; and in order that they should be appropriate to this service, their resisting force must be comparatively very small at the commencement of the stroke; no spring yet produced combines these properties so perfectly as the Vulcanised India-rubber, indeed it is so easily acted upon at the commencement of the stroke that it has been found advisable to compress the four rings in each buffer to the extent of one inch before the stroke commences.

If the immense sustaining power of these buffers were objectionable it could be reduced to any required amount, simply by decreasing the diameter and thickness of the rings, which would also lessen the cost—but, in the opinion of the writer, that would be destroying one of the most valuable properties of these buffers.

A comparison has been made between the relative proportions of effective resistance of a pair of buffers of 12 inches stroke with the ordinary laminated spring, and a pair of the India-rubber waggon buffers; but, in the writer's opinion, the calculations are incorrect. It has been assumed that the India-rubber buffers have only 1½ inch stroke with a final resistance of 3 tons—say 3 tons × 1½ inches = 4½ effective resistance of a pair of India-rubber buffers. Then 12 inches is given as the stroke of the laminated spring with 2¾ tons, which would make 2¾ tons × 12 inches = 33 effective resistance, the proportion being 4½ to 33, or 1 to 7⅓.

But as regards the India-rubber buffers, the length of stroke is exactly 3 inches, and the maximum resistance 20 tons for a pair; and as this large amount of resistance is mainly accumulated towards the end of the stroke (as will be seen from a statement of experiments annexed), it would not be correct to take the half of that as the average resisting power; but it is presumed that it will be keeping within the limits to take only one-quarter of the maximum resistance—say 5 tons, as the average resisting power for a pair of buffers, thus—5 tons × 3 inches = 15 effective resistance.

With regard to the laminated spring—2¾ tons is given as the resisting power of the spring for the pair of buffers with 12 inches of action; but this 2¾ tons is the *maximum* resistance of the spring deflected to a straight line, and being a steel spring, and its resistance not increasing in the same compound ratio as the India-rubber, nearly half its maximum power should be allowed as the average resistance throughout the stroke—say 1⅜ ton × 12 inches = 16½ effective resistance; thus it appears that the proportionate effective resisting force between a pair of the India-rubber 3 inches stroke waggon buffers, and a pair of 12 inches stroke ordinary laminated spring buffers, is as 15 to 16½, instead of being as 1 to 7⅓.

It may be here observed that the India-rubber buffers are not limited to 3 inches stroke; some are made 4½ inches, and some with 6 inches stroke for passenger carriages, and their resisting power is proportionately increased, but this incurs additional expense, which is a matter of no small consideration in the present times, and it is found from lengthened practice that the 3 inches stroke buffers are quite sufficient for all classes of goods waggons, and even for cattle trucks, luggage vans, &c. The size of the India-rubber rings in these 3 inches stroke buffers is 5¼ inch diameter and 1⅜ inch thick.

With respect to the durability of the Vulcanised India-rubber, a reference has been made to elastic bands for papers that have become completely rotten; but it will be sufficient to state the fact, that a great quantity of these bands have been made that were never "vulcanised" at all, and were manufactured under an independent patent for "converting," but they were sold by the same parties, and the public did not know any difference. The India-rubber rings used in the buffers are all vulcanised, and the writer has examined many of them that have been at work for several years, and he has not yet met with a single instance of a bad one.

It has been objected to the External Cylinder Buffers, that the piston or plunger is guided through too short a space, which makes it more liable to break the cylinder in the event of an oblique blow; but it should be observed that this defect is obviated in the India-rubber buffer, where the length of the bearing extends from the mouth of the cylinder to the end of the boss on the base plate, the spindle being fitted so as to form a solid body with the plunger. The India-rubber buffer is superior, in the writer's opinion, to the other external buffers in efficiency and durability, whilst equally compact and economical, as the resistance begins very gradually at the first part of the stroke, and increases to a great power at the latter part, without coming to a dead stop at a moderate pressure, as in the other buffers; the pressure being spread uniformly over the whole surface of the base plate, which is better adapted to preserve the waggon frame from injury, and the elastic material is not liable to break, as steel whether in the form of a spiral or otherwise.

The following table shows the actual compression of one of these India-rubber waggon buffers of 3-inch stroke, with each increase of pressure from ½ ton up to 10 tons, tried with great accuracy in a machine made for the purpose.

Pressure in tons.	Amount of action in inches.
¼	.125
½	.625
¾	1.063
1	1.344
1¼	1.694
1½	1.750
1¾	1.906
2	2.031
2½	2.219
3	2.375
4	2.563
5	2.750
6	2.813
7	2.875
8	2.938
9	2.969
10	3.000

Mr. H. Wright observed, that he had used the India-rubber buffers very extensively in waggons, but not in carriages, and he considered them to act efficiently.

Mr. Henson said, he was not able to speak from his own experience of the India-rubber buffers, as he had only had five sets of them in use; but he thought the material was not durable, as he had seen specimens of the Vulcanised India-rubber which had quite perished in the packing of the air-cylinder buffers.

Mr. Robinson enquired whether there had been any oil in contact with the Vulcanised India-rubber in those specimens, as he understood it would not stand the action of oil; but Mr. Henson said he believed it had been kept free from oil.

Mr. H. Wright said, that on the North Staffordshire Railway all the waggons were made with the India-rubber buffers, and he had not found the material fail in any instances: the only failure of the buffers had been in the cast-iron casings, which had broken at the flange of the cylinder in many instances; but they were easily repaired, and the risk of breaking could be prevented by an alteration in the castings.

Mr. De Bergue explained, that the objection had been obviated by an improved form of the castings, and showed a drawing of the present construction of the buffer.

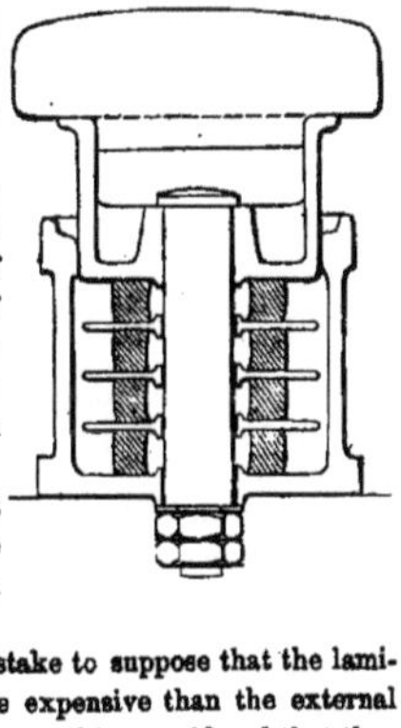

Mr. Adams remarked that his objection to the India-rubber buffer consisted in the circumstance that the length of action was very short for the extent of resistance that was ordinarily called forth in buffer springs; and he should prefer a less resisting power continued through a greater space.

Mr. M'Connell observed, that in that case a laminated buffer spring would be required, which brought them a question of greater cost.

Mr. Adams replied, that it was a mistake to suppose that the laminated buffer springs would be much more expensive than the external buffers, such as the India-rubber buffers; and he considered that they would cost but little more, not so much as 25 per cent. more, including the buffer rods complete, and that the increased cost would be well laid out in laminated springs, being the best in the end.

The Chairman observed, it was an important circumstance if the expense of employing laminated springs was really not greater, as their advantage was obvious from the much greater length of action.

Mr. Wright thought that the increase of cost would be considerably greater, and that it was a question of heavy expense on a large number of waggons. He considered that the repairs would form an expensive item in the laminated springs, as they would be so much knocked about in waggons.

Mr. Ramsbottom remarked, that it was important to have a draw spring, as well as a buffer spring, in all waggons, and the laminated spring might be made to serve both purposes.

Mr. M'Connell observed, that they were much indebted to Mr. Adams for his communication on this important subject, and proposed a vote of thanks to him, which was passed.

INSTITUTION OF CIVIL ENGINEERS.

Tuesday, April 30, 1850.

William Cubitt, Esq., President, in the Chair.

The paper read was "On the Absorbent Power of Chalk, and its Water Contents, under different geological conditions," by Professor D. T. Ansted.

After explaining the nature and extent of the chalk rock of England, both geologically and topographically, and briefly describing its chief physical peculiarities, the author proceeded to detail the results of some experiments made for the purpose of ascertaining the positive and relative absorbent powers of different kinds of chalk, when exposed to moisture under various circumstances.

The specimens experimented on were small cubes, each weighing from three or four ounces, taken from different districts, and geological positions, in the upper, middle, and lower beds of the chalk.

From these experiments it appeared, that the upper chalk, when it was to all appearance perfectly dry, contained about one-third part of a pint of water in each cube foot, which was never parted with under any conditions of dryness of the atmosphere; that in the case of an exposed surface of the rock, the absorption from a moist atmosphere would be unimportant, although when water was presented to it in a liquid form, the upper chalk was found capable of receiving into its mass a quantity of water amounting to more than two gallons for every cube foot of rock, beyond the quantity usually contained in apparently dry chalk, under ordinary exposure.

A specimen of the middle chalk, when thoroughly air-dried by six months' exposure, was found to contain about 23 parts of water in 1000 parts; three-fourths of which water were readily given off by subsequent exposure to a perfectly dry atmosphere, very little more than the original quantity being re-absorbed on exposure to a saturated atmosphere; showing that the absorbent power, in this respect, was even less than in the case of the upper chalk. The quantity of water contained in a cube foot of saturated middle chalk was rather more than two gallons.

A specimen of the lower chalk was found to contain more than 10 parts of water in 1000 parts, about three-fourths of which were rapidly parted with, on exposure to a perfectly dry atmosphere; but the rest, amounting to more than the quantity of water contained in the upper chalk, in its ordinary state, was not parted with by any exposure, short of a vacuum. On subsequent exposure to a saturated atmosphere, more than 15½ parts of water in 1000 parts, were absorbed, and when the specimen was saturated, its water contents exceeded 2¼ gallons per cubic foot.

It was stated, that the upper chalk might generally be regarded as the *conducting*, and the lower chalk as the *containing*, part of the formation, so far as water was concerned; and that chalk must be regarded as a rock, which everywhere admitted the percolation of water, receiving into itself, and conveying to its lower beds, the water that fell on, or was brought to its surface. This readily explained the uniformly dry appearance it presented, and the absence of any streams, arising from mere surface drainage, where extensive exposure of the rock itself occurred. It also appeared that particular bands of rock con-

tained much more water than others, some, indeed, being apparently, though not really, dry, when below the surface of permanent wetness; while others gave off water readily, and to a large extent.

The probable effect of rain-fall upon the surface of the exposed chalk was then considered, and it was estimated, that at least 18 inches descended annually to what was called the surface of permanent wetness, maintaining a general and rude parallelism with the surface of the ground; but when the chalk rock was permanently covered with impermeable soils, as in the London basin, the position of the surface of permanent wetness was liable to extreme variation, and to be most seriously affected, as lateral percolation was then the only source of wetness.

On the other hand, it was thought, that a large portion of chalk rock existed in a state of uniform and permanent wetness, and that wherever the gault extended, under-lying the chalk and keeping up the water, there must be, at and below a certain depth from the surface, a supply of water to the extent of 180 millions of gallons for each square mile one yard in thickness; and that the surface of permanent wetness, dependent chiefly on the present rain-fall, was so far above this lower surface of saturation, as to ensure a supply at least equal to one-half of the rain falling on the immediately surrounding district.

Tuesday, May 7, 1850.

WILLIAM CUBITT, Esq., President, in the Chair.

THE paper read was "On the Application of Water Pressure, as a Motive Power, for working Cranes and other kinds of Machinery," by Mr. W. G. Armstrong, F.R.S., Assoc. Inst. C.E.

The object of the paper was to direct attention to the advantages of a more extended application of Hydraulic Pressure, as a Motive Power, and to point out the means of attaining this desirable end, illustrating the arguments by descriptions and drawings of the engines on this principle, already erected, since the year 1845, when the author first designed a Crane, to be worked by the Pressure of Water from the street water pipes at Newcastle-upon-Tyne.

The principle of these engines, as applied to cranes, was described to be very simple. In order to lift a weight, the water, under a pressure of about 100 feet head, or more, being admitted through a slide valve into a cylinder, exerted a force on a piston, whose rod was connected with the hoisting chain, so arranged by passing over several pullies, as to increase its length of travel to the requisite duty to be performed; the piston receding from the pressure therefore raised the weight to the height required. The lowering of the weight was accomplished by a reverse action, and the crane was turned in either direction by a similar action of a smaller cylinder, whose piston rod was connected with a rack, working into a circle of teeth, fixed to the base of the moveable frame of the crane.

The action of these machines was described to be very smooth and steady, ingenious appliances being adopted for obviating the shock that would otherwise be caused by the sudden closing of the slide valves, and all the different operations being under the perfect control of a few regulating handles. In cases of a great diversity of power being required, separate cylinders were used, so arranged, as that their action could be combined, according to the force required. The speed of working had no other limit than the size of the supply pipe.

Allusion was made to the advantage of employing hydraulic pressure in mercantile docks, for hoisting heavy weights, for whipping light goods out of ships, and for opening and shutting dock gates, swing bridges, and sluices. Its facility of transmission, its safety, and constant readiness for use, rendered it peculiarly suitable for these purposes. It would generally be preferable in such cases to employ steam-power to force the water, rather than to be dependant upon town water-works; and a tank upon a tower, or upon an eminence, would form a convenient magazine of power, enabling the engine to act continuously with an uniform load. Large air vessels had also been successfully employed, instead of an elevated tank.

Hydraulic pressure might, also, in many cases, be advantageously employed for purposes requiring continuous rotation. There were many natural situations where mountain streams might be arrested, or surface-water be impounded on elevated ground, and be conveyed by a pipe into a neighbouring valley, where great mechanical efficiency might be derived from a small supply of water, by the use of water-pressure engines. In mining operations, also, the danger and inconvenience of underground steam engines might be obviated, by substituting water pressure engines, conveying the water down the shaft in pipes, and returning it to the surface by the action of the pumping engine above ground. In such cases the water was merely the vehicle for transmitting power into the mine.

A water pressure engine had been lately very successfully applied by the author, in South Hetton Colliery, for the traction of waggons upon an underground railway. Similar engines had been erected in the lead mines, at Allenheads, for lifting ore, and other purposes. Reservoirs were there formed upon the neighbouring hills, and pipes were carried into the mines to supply the engines, the expended water flowing out by a level. Other engines of the same description were also in course of erection for surface operations at the same place, such as crushing ore, and raising minerals from the shafts.

In their general character, these engines were similar to reciprocating steam engines. The slide valves were balanced by equal pressures in opposite directions, and were constructed to open very spacious water passages. The liability to concussion, on the closing of the education port, was obviated by the application of relief valves, which were lifted by the compressive action of the piston, causing it to act for an instant as a pump, in forcing back the opposing water into the supply pipe. In cases where the engines had been applied to hauling, or winding, four cylinders placed diagonally in pairs, had been used. In other cases, two cylinders had been applied, the uniformity in the motion of the column being maintained by a loaded plunger. The winding engines were reversed by a slot link apparatus, similar to that of a locomotive engine, and which was worked by the pressure of the water, acting under the control of a valve. The regulating and reversing valves were each placed at the mouth of the shaft, at a distance from the engine, the operation of which could thus be directed with great accuracy and safety.

The drawings which accompanied the paper gave representations of an Hydraulic Crane, for shipping coals at Glasgow; Hydraulic Platform Cranes, at the railway station, Newcastle-upon-Tyne; Hydraulic Hoisting Machines, at the warehouses of the Albert Docks, Liverpool; a Water-pressure Engine, for a crushing mill at Allenheads; a similar engine, used at the same place, for winding; and numerous details of all these machines.

At the monthly ballot the following candidates were duly elected:— Messrs. J. G. Appold, C. Clark, W. Crosley, J. Freeman, F. H. Johnson, J. H. Jones, R. W. Kennard, and A. Ogilvie, as Associates.

SOCIETY OF ARTS.

1st May.

Abstract of a Paper on the Causes and Preventives of Mildew in Paper and Parchments; with an Account of Experiments made on the Saturation of growing Wood with Antiseptic Chemical Solutions. By ALFRED GYDE, M.R.C.S.E.

[This Paper was rewarded in 1848 with the Society's Gold Isis Medal.]

OWING to the imperfections formerly existing in the microscope, little was known of the real nature of the class of plants called *fungi* until within the last few years; but since the improvements in that instrument, the subject of the development, growth, and offices of the fungi has received much attention. They compose, with the algæ and lichens, the class of thallogens (Lindley), the algæ existing in water, the other two in air only. A fungus is a cellular flowerless plant, fructifying solely by spores, by which it is propagated, and the methods of attachment of which are singularly various and beautiful. The fungi differ from the lichens and algæ in deriving their nourishment from the substances on which they grow instead of from the media in which they live. They contain a larger quantity of nitrogen in their constitution than vegetables in general do, and the substance called "fungine" has a near resemblance to animal matter. Their spores are inconceivably numerous and minute, and are diffused very widely, developing themselves wherever they find organic matter in a fit state. The principal conditions required for their growth are moisture, heat, and the presence of oxygen and of electricity. No decomposition or development of fungi takes place in dry organic matter; a fact illustrated by the high state of preservation in which timber has been found after the lapse of centuries, as well as by the condition of mummy cases, bandages, &c. kept dry in the hot climate of Egypt. Decay will not take place in a temperature below that of the freezing point of water, nor without oxygen, by excluding which—as contained in the air—meat and vegetables may be kept fresh and sweet for many years.

The process which takes place when moist vegetable substances are exposed to oxygen is one of slow combustion, and has been called by Liebig "Eremacausis," the oxygen uniting with the wood and liberating a volume equal to itself of carbonic acid; another portion combining with the hydrogen of the wood to form water. Decomposition takes place on contact with a body already undergoing the same change, in the same manner that yeast causes fermentation. Animal matter enters into combination with oxygen in precisely the same way with vegetable matter; but as, in addition to carbon and hydrogen, it contains nitrogen, the products of the eremacausis are more numerous—carbonate and nitrate of ammonia, carburetted and sulphuretted hydrogen, and water: and these ammoniacal salts greatly favour the growth of fungi. Now paper consists essentially of woody fibre forming its substance, with animal matter, as size, on its surface.

The first microscopic symptom of decay in paper is irregularity of surface, with slight change of colour, indicating the commencement of the processes just noticed; during which, in addition to carbonic acid, certain organic acids are formed—as cremic and ulmic acid, which, if the paper have been stained by a colouring matter, will form spots of red on the surface. Spots of the same kind are similarly formed on leather coloured during its manufacture. Provided that fungi have not taken root, the colour can be restored by ammonia or any alkali. The same process of decay goes on in parchment as in paper; only with more rapidity, from the presence of nitrogen in its composition. When this decay has begun to take place, fungi are produced—the most common species being penicillium glaucum; they insinuate themselves between the fibre, causing a freer admission of air, and consequently hastening the decay.

The substances most successfully used as preventives of decay are the salts of mercury, copper, and zinc. Bichloride of mercury (corrosive sublimate) is the material employed in the kyanisation of timber, the probable mode of action being its combination with the albumen of the wood, to form an insoluble compound insusceptible of spontaneous decomposition, and therefore incapable of exciting fermentation. The antiseptic power of corrosive sublimate may be easily tested by mixing a little of it with flour paste; the decay of, and appearance of fungi on which are quite prevented by it. Next to corrosive sublimate in antiseptic value stand the salts of copper and zinc. Chloride of zinc has been patented by Sir W. Burnett for the preservation of wood, sail-cloth, &c., and appears to succeed admirably. For use in the preservation of paper, the sulphate of zinc is better than the chloride, which is to a certain extent deliquescent.

A series of experiments were made by the author in the summer of 1840 on the use of metallic and other solutions for the preservation of wood. A deep saw-cut was made all round the circumference of the growing trees near their base, into which the solutions were introduced by forming a basin of clay beneath the cut; thus the solution took the place of the ascending sap, and in periods of time varying from one to three days was found to have impregnated even the topmost leaves of trees fifty feet high. The trees were chiefly beech and larch. After impregnation they were felled, and specimens about five feet long by two inches square cut out, and packed in decaying sawdust in a warm damp cellar, where they were left for seven years. The details of the experiment are given in a table, by which the following general results are made to appear:—The wood saturated with sulphate of copper in the proportion of one pound to one gallon of water, or with acetate of copper, one pound to one pint of vinegar and one gallon of water, were found in perfect preservation, clean, dry, and free from fungus; the remainder, which were saturated with nitrate of soda, prussiate of potash, pyrolignite of iron, sulphate of iron, common salt, and creosote, presented much decay, and a large growth of fungi.

The results obtained from solutions of corrosive sublimate—one-eighteenth of a pound to a gallon of water (Kyan's proportion)—varied in an anomalous manner.

The paper was accompanied by specimens of the wood, showing how complete had been the saturation.

The Patent Safety Steering Wheel of Captain Fayrer, R N., and Lieut. Robinson, R.N., described in the last number of *The Artisan*, was exhibited. Captain Fayrer stated that his experience of the accidents to which the helmsman is liable, during his command of the three large steamers, *President, Liverpool,* and *Forth,* and of the *Lady Flora*, Indiaman, had led to this invention.

A great advantage of this invention is the power which it gives of fixing the rudders of vessels lying in a tide-way or harbour, and thereby preventing the continual wear on the pintles of the rudder, and, in time, the loosening of the stern framing of the vessel.

Letters testifying to the merit of the safety steering wheel, from eminent ship-builders and naval engineers, were read. It is being applied to the large steamers *Asia* and *Africa*, now being built at Greenock for the North American mail service.

May 15th, 1850.

Robert Stephenson, Esq., M.P., Vice-president, in the Chair.

Mr. C. W. Siemens, of Birmingham, on Siemens' Regenerative Condenser.

The paper commences with a historical sketch of the condenser of the steam engine, from the invention of Savery, in which a single vessel served the triple purpose of steam-cylinder, condenser, and water-pump, to James Watt's injection condenser. Hornblower proposed a surface-condenser, which was, however, deficient in extent of cooling surface, and therefore failed, as have many others invented since; the most prominent being that of Mr. Samuel Hall, in which the steam was passed through tubes immersed in a stream of cold water. This condenser has the serious drawbacks of weight, costliness, and difficulty of getting rid of the calcareous deposits from the condensed steam.

Three years ago Mr. Siemens invented his surface condenser for a situation where economy of space and material was essential. It consists of a number of copper plates of $\frac{1}{8}$-inch in thickness, $4\frac{1}{2}$ inches broad, and 2 feet long, which are piled together with two longitudinal flattened wires of the same metal intervening between the adjacent plates, the whole pile being screwed up tight together between the sides of a rectangular cast-iron vessel, constituting the body of the condenser.

The ends of the plates project through the top and bottom of the vessel, and are planed flush with its exterior surfaces. The joints are at top and bottom, secured by means of India-rubber rings, screwed down under small cast-iron frames, and which yield to the difference in expansion of the two metals. The flattened wires are laid parallel, and about three inches apart, and form, with the plates, a large number of narrow passages, through which the cold condensing water flows in an upward direction without entering the vacuous space of the condenser, into which the ends of the plates outside the flattened wires—forming the condensing surfaces—project. The heat of the steam is thus passed through the plates, from their edges towards the centre, to the condensing water,—the limit to its efficiency being the conducting power of the metal. Its dimensions are as follow :—

Heat-absorbing surface by the water	18 sq. feet per H.P.
Condensing surface	9 do. do.
Thickness of metal through which the heat is conducted	1¼ inch.
Weight of copper	60 lbs. per H.P.
Space occupied by plates	·4 cube ft. do. do. = ⅟₇ part of the space occupied by the tubes in Hall's condenser.

Its essential features are its comparative cheapness of construction, the easy access it affords to the water-channels, and reduction in the quantity of condensing-water required.

The Regenerative Condenser.—The origin of this condenser was the suggestion to the author of Mr. Graham of Mayfield Works, "to recover the heat from the condensing-water in the form of a reduced amount of boiling hot water." It consists of an upright rectangular trunk of cast-iron, the lower end of which is cylindrical, and contains a working piston, which performs two strokes for each one of the engine. In the trunk is a set of copper plates, upright and parallel to each other,—the intervening spaces being the same as the thickness of the plates, viz., between ⁴⁄₁₁th and ¹¹⁄₁₁th of an inch.

The upper extremity of the condenser communicates on one side to the exhaust-port of the engine, and on the other through a valve to the hot-well.

The plates are fastened together by five or more thin bolts, with small distance-washers between each plate. There is a lid at the top of the trunk, by removing which the set of plates can be lifted out. Immediately below the plates the injection-pipe enters.

The action of the condenser is as follows. Motion is given to the piston. At the moment that the exhaust-port of the engine opens, the plates are completely immersed in water, a little of which has entered the passage above the plates, and is, together with the air present, carried off by the rush of steam into the hot well, the excess of steam escaping into the atmosphere. The water then, in consequence of the downward motion of the piston, recedes between the plates, exposing them gradually to the steam, which condenses on them. Their upper edges emerging first from the receding water are surrounded by steam of atmospheric pressure, and become rapidly heated to about 210°. The emersion of the plates still continuing, the steam is constantly brought into contact with fresh cool surface, by which the greater portion of it is condensed, until, as the piston descends, the injection enters and completes the vacuum. This is done by the time the working piston of the engine has accomplished ¼th of its stroke. The upper extremities of the plates become heated to near 210°, and the lower to about 160°.

Taking the initial temperature of the condensing water at 60°, the final temperature at 210°, the latent heat of steam at 212°, 960 units, the quantity of water required is 6·6 lbs. to condense 1 lb. of steam of atmospheric pressure. The common injection condenser (supposing the temperature of the condensed steam to be 110°) requires 21·2 lbs. in place of 6·6 lbs.

The advantages of this condenser are :

1. Additional effective power gained on account of the vacuum = 30 per cent., taking the pressure of steam at 40 lbs. above the atmosphere and vacuum in the cylinder 12 lbs.

2. Heat saved in generating steam by the use of boiling feed-water = 10 per cent. over the ordinary method of heating the feed-water to 110°, or 15 per cent. when no use is made of the condensed water for that purpose.

3. The steam which escapes uncondensed may be used to cause draught.

4. The displacing cylinder takes no motive power.

5. The condenser may be started and stopped at any time by turning the injection water on or off. If turned on, it at once forms the vacuum without involving the necessity of blowing through ; and if turned off, it allows the engine to proceed as though it had not a condenser.

6. The air contained in the condenser is at each stroke completely expelled.

7. Greater compactness, and less expense, than the injection condenser.

Its dimensions in terms of parts of the engine are as follow :—Area of plate-chamber = three times that of exhaust-pipe ; length of plates = ⅓ that of stroke of engine ; thickness of plates, ₂₅⁄ of their length ; spaces between plates same as thickness, but never more than ₁₀⁄th of an inch, as with that dimension no sediment can stand against the rush of water. Capacity of displacing cylinder = that of plate-chamber.

It has been attempted to adapt this condenser to the locomotive ; and of the advantages which would be gained if this could be done there can be no doubt. In this case the two condensers were cast in one piece, and placed directly in front of the cylinders. They differed from that just described only in the length of the condenser and stroke of the displacing piston being much shortened ; so that the velocity of the water between the plates may not be too great ; and in having a second set of discharge-valves of peculiar construction for allowing the uncondensed steam to pass freely into the funnel. The ordinary supply of feed-water not being by itself sufficient to maintain the vacuum, this condenser, if applied to locomotives, should only be worked at intervals, on inclines, &c., where its assistance would be needed.

In its application to low-pressure engines, since the steam from the cylinder has not sufficient power to force the air and heated water from the condenser into the atmosphere, a communication is made between the exhaust-valve of the condenser and the lower end of the displacing-cylinder, which, for convenience of arrangement, is here reversed, and which receives the charge of water and air when its piston is at the opposite end of it, and when it is therefore vacuous.

In this case the amount of injection-water is reduced in the proportion of three to one. Ten per cent. is saved by the feed-water being made boiling hot, a great quantity of boiling water being provided which cannot fail to be useful for many purposes.

The first regenerative condenser was applied to a sixteen horse-power high-pressure engine, at Saltby Works, near Birmingham, in September, 1849, where it has been found to answer. One is now being erected at the Paper Works of Messrs. Easton and Amos, at Wandsworth, and will shortly be in action.

A drawing was exhibited, showing the condenser applied to a common high-pressure engine, in connexion with a variable expansion valve, acted on by a governor, which is a modification of Mr. Siemens's chronometric governor, the pendulum being superseded by an expanding fly-wheel.

The principle involved in the regenerative condenser is applicable to many useful purposes, the most remarkable of which are what Mr. Siemens proposes to call his Regenerative Evaporator for brine and other liquids, and the Regenerative Engine, which are now in course of construction at the works of Messrs. Fox and Henderson, near Birmingham, to whose enterprise Mr. Siemens expresses himself as indebted for the carrying out of his several inventions.

The paper was most fully illustrated by drawings and diagrams, and by models of the Surface Condenser, the Regenerative Condenser, a new Water Metre, the Brine Evaporator, and the Chronometric Governor.

After the reading of the paper a discussion took place, chiefly as to the practicability of applying the condenser to locomotives, in which Mr. Scott Russell, Mr. Crampton, and the author took part. It was closed by the Chairman, who said that the circumstances of the locomotive were so peculiar, the requirements of the most perfect simplicity, and freedom from any but the most necessary dead weight so absolute, that he feared this could not be applied to it, even if, which he doubted, the condensation could take place rapidly enough where the cylinder was filled and emptied four times in one second. But the principle was new to him, and certainly highly ingenious, as were the other inventions of Mr. Siemens; and in its application to stationary engines he hoped and believed his ingenuity would meet its due reward.

The thanks of the meeting were given to Mr. Siemens for his highly interesting communication.

AN ACCOUNT OF THE EXPLOSION OF A STEAM BOILER
IN HAGUE STREET, NEW YORK.

From the Journal of the Franklin Institute.

THIS boiler, which exploded on the morning of the 4th of February, was in form what is termed "Montgomery's Patent." It was built in 1847 for Mr. Taylor, but, in consequence of some trouble between him and the builders, (Milligan and Walker,) he then refused to take it, and it was sold by them, to be used in a steamboat at Savannah; but the boiler proving too small, it was sent to Pease and Murphy, in New York, to be sold. While in their possession it was kept in the open air, but was well painted externally, and could have been injured but little. Mr. Taylor recently purchased the boiler from them to use in his machine shop; it was put up in the cellar of his premises, and was first used on Tuesday, the 29th of January, six days previous to the explosion. On using it the first day, with a pressure of 80 lbs. of steam, a loud report was heard, and, on examination, water was found to be running freely out of the boiler from the inverted arch, and the brace A was found to have parted. They were obliged to haul the fire, let out the water, and remove a part of the broken brace that was attached to the tube sheet, cut out the rivets, and then fill the holes with bolts; but no attempt was made to replace the brace. After putting in the bolts and caulking the crown of the inverted arch, the boiler was again filled with water and steam raised; and, although they were aware that the boiler was not strong enough for 80 lbs. pressure, yet, being behind with their work, and having to run during the night, Mr. Ford, the foreman of the establishment, moved out the weight on the safety valve level to 90 lbs.; but before the steam blew off at that point, another loud report was heard, and the boiler found to be leaking badly. Mr. George Birkbeck, Jun., an engineer in business in New York, was then called upon to repair it. Mr. B. reports that, on examining the boiler, he found a fracture across the ends of the legs under the bridge-wall, at the points marked B and C, at which place, and also in the crown of the inverted arch, the boiler had leaked badly,—so bad that, on his arrival, the water had entirely leaked out. Patches were put on over the fractures at B and C in the legs, and the crown of the inverted arch was again recaulked. Mr. Taylor was then informed by Mr. Birkbeck that the boiler was not sufficiently strong to sustain the pressure of steam that they were using, and that in his opinion, the working pressure should not exceed 50 lbs. under any circumstances. Yet, notwithstanding all

these symptoms of weakness, and the opinion of one well acquainted with such matters, the usual pressure of steam (90 to 100) lbs.) appears to have been carried during the remainder of the week.

On Sunday the engineer, for the purpose of stopping the leaks in the boiler, put in it a quantity of horse manure and paper pulp,—articles which are sometimes used for that purpose. On Monday, (the day of the explosion,) the engineer appears to have been in the building as early as usual, but from the testimony of the watchman on the premises, he did not succeed in starting his fire, and called upon him to assist him. In consequence of this delay, steam was not raised sufficiently by seven o'clock, (the hour for commencing work,) and from the testimony of Mr. Brown, the chief smith of the establishment, we learn that his attention was called to the boiler by a peculiar smell emitted from it, as if the gaskets were burning;—that on trying the water-gauge, (one of Worthington's percussion,) he could not find water, and that he then lifted the safety valve lever, when the steam that escaped, to use his own expression, "looked blue," which, being different from what he had often before observed, caused him to speak to the engineer about it, who told him to mind his own business. This was but three or four minutes previous to the explosion. The impression was so strong on his mind that something was wrong, that he was about leaving the building at the time of the explosion, and, by jumping, saved himself from the ruins.

The testimony given at the coroner's inquest, in relation to all the points here stated, is direct and positive. All testify that the boiler was not suitable for the pressure carried upon it; but Mr. Taylor himself says he used it the two days previous to the explosion with 100 lbs. of steam, and that he considered it safe at that pressure.

Having collected all the information I could get from authentic sources upon the subject, and having visited the premises and examined the various parts of the boiler, I am of the opinion that the boiler was entirely too weak for the pressure of steam that it was expected to sustain. It is hardly necessary, in support of this, to give anything more than the testimony that has been referred to; but, on examining the crown of the inverted arch, it will be seen that, for a distance of 3½ feet in length, by the same in width, there was not a single brace,—a piece of gross negligence, and inexcusable in any one professing to manufacture boilers for practical use. All the symptoms of weakness shown in the boiler previous to the explosion were in this part. But, notwithstanding this, I think the immediate cause of the explosion was owing to a short supply of water. I am led to this conclusion from the testimony of Brown, and from the fact that the explosion occurred immediately after starting the engine,—a result which has been demonstrated, from experiment and practice, to be intimately connected with low water. Explosions that take place when there is an abundant supply of water, generally occur while there is no steam being drawn from the boiler, or in cases where the supply of steam exceeds the amount taken away. If we take a boiler with a full supply of water, and secure the safety valve so that it shall raise just previous to the steam reaching that point that will explode the boiler, the raising of the valve will relieve the pressure, and the boiler will be saved; but if we take the same boiler with a short supply of water, and safety valve secured as before, the raising of the valve, by causing the water to rise on the overheated iron, will to a certainty cause an explosion. I therefore assume that, in the absence of positive evidence to the contrary, all explosions that take place at the starting of the engine are caused by the absence of the proper supply of water.

This boiler was 11 feet 3 inches long, 5 feet wide, and 9 feet 7 inches high at the back end; it contained 289 vertical tubes, 4 feet 10 inches long, 2 inches outside diameter. The plate D has as many holes through it as there are tubes, and is secured in its place when the boiler is built. By the use of this plate, the flame is caused to pass between the tubes at their upper end, near the surface of the water, and to return to the

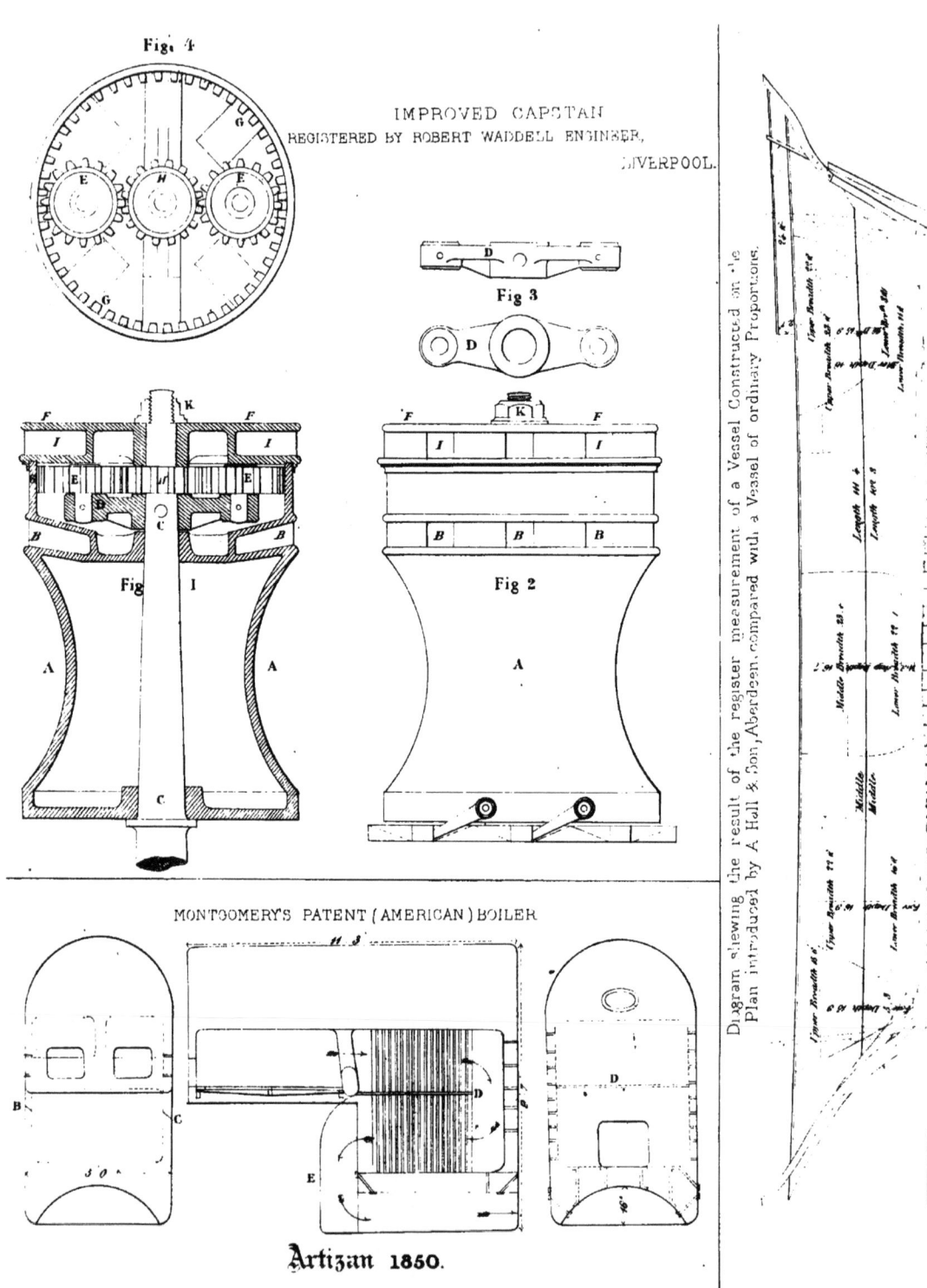

Fig. 4

IMPROVED CAPSTAN
REGISTERED BY ROBERT WADDELL ENGINEER,
LIVERPOOL.

Fig 3

Fig 1

Fig 2

Diagram shewing the result of the register measurement of a Vessel Constructed on the Plan introduced by A. Hall & Son, Aberdeen, compared with a Vessel of ordinary Proportions.

MONTGOMERY'S PATENT (AMERICAN) BOILER

Artizan 1850.

front below near the bottom; it then returns to the back end again under what has been termed the inverted arch. The casing E is of sheet iron. The socket bolts in the legs of the boiler were screwed in, and slightly riveted over. The thickness of the shell and furnace was full ¼ inch. The safety valve was 2¼ inches diameter, and with the weight at the outer notch, indicated 112 lbs.

The building occupied by A. B. Taylor & Co. was of a rectangular form. Front of building about 50 feet, depth about 75 feet; 6 stories high; walls 18 inches thick to the third story, and above that 12 inches. The boiler and engine were in the cellar. The building was situated between other brick buildings, and in contact with them, but its walls were independent. The whole building was destroyed by the explosion, being lifted from its foundation, and falling in one mass of ruins, burying 120 persons who were employed in it. Of that number 70 were killed, and nearly all the rest much injured. An explosion so disastrous in its consequences has never before taken place in this country, and it is incumbent on the authorities of each State that they require all boilers on land to be annually inspected, and prohibit the placing of them inside of large buildings. By this means something will be gained, and the loss of life be materially diminished.

The only portion of the boiler that retains its original shape is the tube-box and tubes,—these are comparatively uninjured, while all the rest is torn to pieces. The inverted arch has not yet been found, but it was separated completely from the rest of the boiler. The shell was divided in two pieces and flattened out; the separation took place midway in the length of the boiler, in line with the water-bridge wall, and one piece, as found, was composed of the sides of the boiler that extended down to the inverted arch, (the socket-bolts which held it to the tube-box were all torn out,) and the portion of the crown above it. The other piece was composed of the crown and sides of the boiler, over and at the sides of the furnace; and also the entire sides and top of the furnace, which were separated lengthwise; the socket-bolts were torn out, and the whole forms one large flat sheet. The entire front end of the boiler, with the front of the furnace and furnace door, was blown off in one piece; the back end is still attached to the tube-box by the socket-bolts, but is very much injured. The safety valve was blown off, taking with it a round piece of the shell of the same diameter as its flanch;—when found it was but little injured, and the weight was secured, (by means of a rope inside of it,) so that it could not have been inside the last notch, or not less than 112 lbs., leaving 1¼ inches of lever outside; if the weight was at the extreme end, then it would retain a pressure of 120 lbs.

The character of vertical tubular boilers is in nowise affected by this explosion. When duly proportioned they will be found economical, and must come into use where economy of fuel and space is an object. B.

CHAPMAN'S PATENT SHROUD AND PURCHASE BLOCKS.

It requires so much moral courage to introduce a new invention, in defiance of precedent and vested interests, that we must not be surprised if we find that the useless "dead-eye" of immemorial antiquity has hitherto maintained its ground against modern innovation. Certainly it is not exactly the thing which a mechanic would choose for the operations it has to perform, but we have been told before now, that "landsmen don't understand these sort of things," and accordingly we believe that the present is the first attempt to improve on a very primitive invention. The dead-eye, we need hardly explain to our readers, is a wooden block without pulleys, through the holes in which the lanyard is rove, by which the shrouds, or supports of the masts, are set up or slacked. A slight idea of its peculiarity may be formed by calculating the power it would take to draw a waggon, deprived of its wheels, up a steep hill. The rope being bent over a (comparatively) sharp edge, and exposed to a severe strain, is, in any case, in a bad

position for durability and strength; but when to this is added, that it has to be dragged over that edge during the operations of setting up or slacking, it is really surprising that no one ever before ventured to give it that simple anti-friction apparatus—a pulley to run upon. The remedies that are usually applied are nearly as bad as the disease. The grease and tar, which are used as unguents to the wood, harden in a cold climate, and by diminishing the flexibility of the rope, which throws the strain upon one part of it, diminish the strength in an equal proportion, and necessitate the use of a much heavier and more expensive rope to commence with, which in its turn aggravates the evil.

The Improved Shroud Blocks, shown in the accompanying sketches, obviate all these difficulties, and give the means of obtaining a great power in a small space, by a simple arrangement, which is applicable to a variety of purposes.

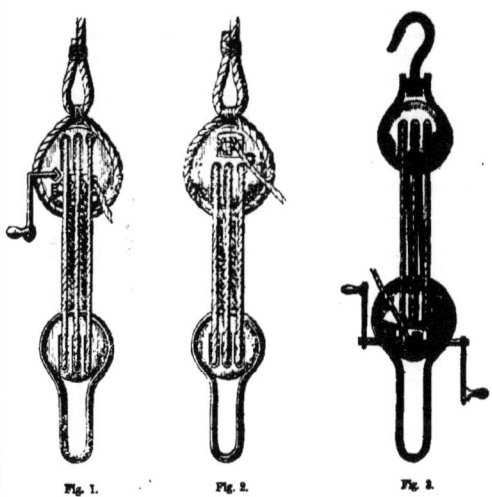

Fig. 1.   Fig. 2.   Fig. 3.

Fig. 1 represents the Improved Shroud Block, the lanyard passing over sheaves and round a double-coned barrel, which has a worm wheel on it, worked by a screw in the shell of the block. The screw is worked by a key, by which a great purchase is obtained, whilst at the same time the worm holds the barrel in any position without trouble. Fig. 2 shows a similar block, but with the coned barrel above the sheaves.

With the common dead-eyes, unless a great number of men are available, only one pair of shrouds can be set up at a time, consequently with considerable danger in bad weather; but with these blocks, from their immense power, one man and a boy are sufficient for each shroud or stay, so that the whole rigging can be set up simultaneously, and in a very short time. From the equal distribution of the strain, it is obvious that smaller lanyards than are now used will be sufficient.

The shells of the blocks are made of cast iron, galvanized, and by the use of this material the risk of blocks splitting in hot climates is obviated. The wheel and worm are made of gun metal for durability; and for yachts the whole block may be made of that metal, thus converting it into an ornamental appendage. The blocks have been severely tested at Woolwich yard, and have met with the unqualified approbation of Admiral Sir J. J. Gordon Bremer, the Master Rigger, and several other gentlemen of great practical experience.

Fig. 3 shows a modification of the blocks adapted to raise the masts of barges. In this case the spindle of the double-coned barrel passes through the block, and a handle being applied on each side, the windlass is entirely dispensed with, a ratchet wheel and paul being employed to hold the barrel.

We have no doubt that these blocks will be found exceedingly useful wherever power in a small space is required; and so many mechanical operations in engineering and building are dependant upon such assistance, that we anticipate they will be very extensively employed.

BOILERS OF THE "CUMBERLAND" AND "PRESIDENT."

THE boilers of the *Cumberland* (see plate) do not present any features of novelty. The space between the crown of the furnaces and the tubes appears to us too small, and we think that the water space at the back of the fire-box ought to have been wider at top than at bottom, to allow the steam to disengage itself freely. The dimensions of the *Cumberland* are given below.

The *President* belongs to the Liverpool Steam Tug Company—cylinders 41 inches diameter × 3 feet 9 inches stroke, 110 horse nominal power. This is not strictly a "tubular boiler," but a flue boiler with elliptical flues. The elliptical form is very weak, and we are at a loss to see what advantage is supposed to be gained by it.

DIMENSIONS AND DETAILS OF NEW STEAMERS.

LIVERPOOL, CARLISLE, AND ANNAN STEAM NAVIGATION COMPANY'S IRON STEAM VESSEL "CUMBERLAND."

Built and Fitted by Messrs. Tod and M'Gregor, Glasgow, No. 46, 1847.

Builder's measurement.				Ft.	In.
Length of keel and fore rake		..	..	197	0
Breadth of beam	..	..	..	25	0
Ditto over the paddle-cases	..	..	44	0
Depth of hold at midships	..	..	13	7
Length of engine space	..	..	..	49	2
Tonnage.				Tons.	
Hull ..	..	..	..	609$\frac{54}{94}$	
Contents of engine space	..	..	167$\frac{71}{94}$	
Register	..	..	..	442$\frac{17}{94}$	
New measurement.				Ft.	Ten.
Length on deck	..		..	197	0
Breadth on ditto at midships	..	..	24	2
Depth of hold, ditto	..	..	..	13	4
Length of break-deck	..	..	50	0
Breadth of ditto	..	..	..	26	3
Depth of ditto	..	..	..	2	0
Length of engine space	..	..	49	2
Tonnage.				Tons.	
Hull ..	..	..	..	489$\frac{94}{100}$	
Break-deck	..	..	..	28$\frac{45}{100}$	
Total ..	..	..	..	518$\frac{39}{100}$	
Contents of engine space	..	..	171$\frac{99}{100}$	
Register	..	..	..	346$\frac{40}{100}$	

A pair of oscillating engines of 298 horse nominal power. Diameter of cylinders, 64 inches × 5 feet length of stroke. Diameter of air-pumps, 38 inches × 2 feet 6 inches. Diameter of paddle-wheels, extreme 25 feet 7 inches; ditto effective, 25 feet. Floats, 7 feet × 2 feet. Three sets of 24 arms and floats for boilers, see plate; fire-bars 8 feet long. 12 streakes of plates from keel to gunwale, tapering in thickness from $\frac{5}{16}$ to $\frac{3}{8}$ of an inch and double riveted. Frames (of Kennedy and Vernon's patent), at midships, 4 × 3 × $\frac{1}{2}$ and 1 foot 6 inches apart, and fore and aft they are 3 × 3 × $\frac{7}{16}$, and 1 foot 9 inches apart. Rivets, $\frac{3}{4}$ to 1 inch. Keel, trough-shape, 8 ins. wide inside, and 2$\frac{1}{4}$ deep; metal, 1$\frac{1}{4}$ thick. Stem, 7 × 2$\frac{1}{2}$ inches. Stern post, 6 × 3$\frac{1}{2}$ inches. Average revolutions per minute, loaded, 20; light, 22. Six floats in water, at a draught of water, 10 feet 6 inches, (mean.) Steam pressure, 8 lbs. Average passage, 13 hours; consuming 16 tons of coals. The *Cumberland* was the first vessel fitted with oscillating engines by Messrs. Tod and M'Gregor, and the second pair, made in Glasgow. The vessel was designed by John Grantham, Esq., C.E., Liverpool. The crew consists of 25 hands, viz., 8 in the engine-room, 5 under the steward, and 12 in the captain's department.

DESCRIPTION.

Bird figure head, (*Eagle*.) Sham quarter bridges. Clipper bow. Square-sterned and clinker built. Standing bowsprit, 2 masts, schooner-rigged. Port of Carlisle. Commander—Mr. David Jones.

GLASGOW.

There was launched from the Iron Ship-building Yard of Mr. Robert Napier, at Govan, on Monday, the 20th, at 8 o'clock in the morning, a beautiful iron steamer for the station between Glasgow and Gareloch; (built to supply the place of the *Superb*, lately sold for the Jersey station;) she was not named at the launch, and will not be named until ready to ply, in consort with the *Duchess of Argyle*.

			Ft.	In.
Length of keel and fore rake	..	..	156	2
Breadth of beam	..	..	16	1
Ditto, over the paddle-cases	..	..	32	0
Depth of hold, midships,	..	..	8	10
Length of engine-space	.	..	33	0
Tonnage.			Tons.	
Hull ..	..	..	213$\frac{41}{94}$	
Contents of engine-space	..	..	48$\frac{5}{94}$	
Register,	..	..	165$\frac{36}{94}$	

To be propelled by a pair of oscillating engines of 70 horse nominal power. Diameter of cylinders 33 ins. 3 feet 6 ins. length of stroke; feathering paddles, 15 feet diameter; one tubular boiler; 5 strokes of plates from keel to gunwale, tapering in thickness from 114 to $\frac{5}{16}$ and $\frac{3}{8}$ of an inch. Frames, 2$\frac{1}{4}$ × 2 × $\frac{1}{2}$ and spaced 3 feet; keel angle iron. Launching draught of water, mean, 4 feet 1 inch. These engines are the second set of oscillating made by Mr. Robert Napier, Vulcan Foundry.

DESCRIPTION.

One deck. No galleries, figurehead, or bowsprit; square-sterned and clinch built vessel; box rudder, common bow. To be commanded by Mr. John Cambell, (late of the *Duchess of Argyll*.)

STEAM NAVIGATION.

THE WEST INDIA MAILS. It is at length announced, that this important undertaking is settled on nearly the same terms as we have already described at p. 21. The company are to have a renewal of their contract for ten years, but the monthly Brazilian mail is to be included under the £240,000 per annum, by which a saving of £30,000 per annum for H.M. vessels between Falmouth and the Brazils will be effected. In deference to the numerous objections that were made to the proposed three-weekly mail, it has been determined to adhere to the fortnightly system. Everything now depends upon getting the new boats out of hand as quickly as possible, and as we hear that the specifications are ready for the contractors, we presume that it will very shortly be announced who are the successful parties. We may here add a report, of which, however, we cannot guarantee the correctness, that a circular having been sent by the directors of the company to our most eminent marine engineers, requesting their opinion on the best form of engines for the service, with but one exception, a verdict was given in favour of side-lever engines, in preference to any others. If side levers they must be, we think it would be worth while to consider whether they might not be of the trussed form, similar to those used in America. Cast iron is objectionable from the enormous weight, and whether malleable iron can be produced of a size and shape suitable for the ordinary form we are not prepared to say.

ACCIDENT TO THE "ACADIA."—We noticed at the time on the occasion of the *Acadia* going ashore at Terschelling, that her preservation was due, in a great measure, to the exertions of the chief engineer;

BOILERS OF THE 'CUMBERLAND'

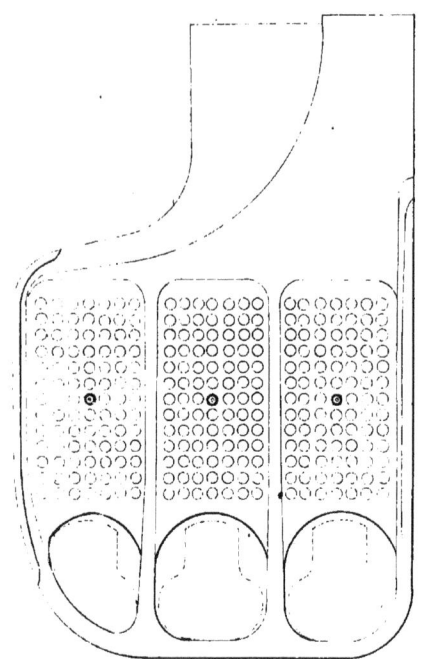
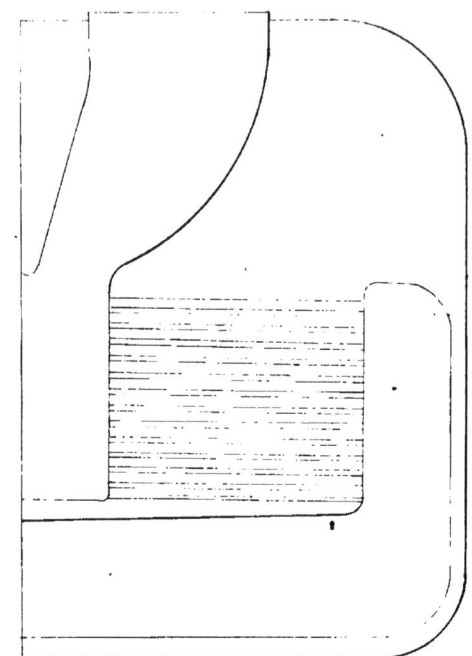

BOILERS OF THE 'PRESIDENT'

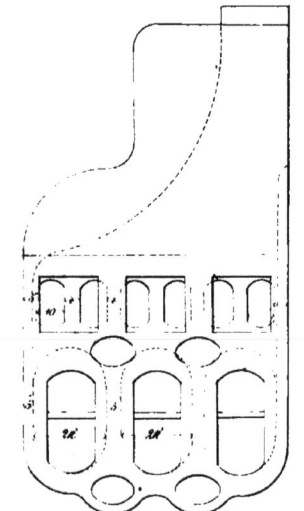
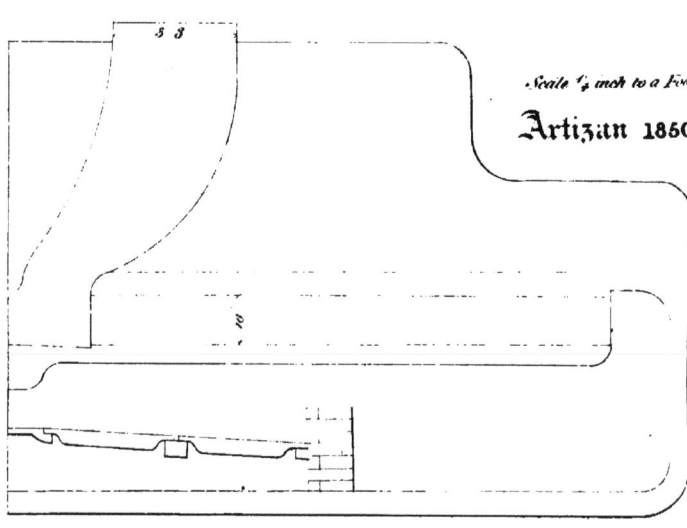

Scale ½ inch to a Foot

Artizan 1850

Mr. Loudon; and we are glad to hear that the underwriters have made him a handsome present to mark their approval of his conduct on that trying occasion.

LIVERPOOL.—The Executive Committee for promoting the Great Exhibition have resolved upon preparing a model of the docks.

NEW DOCKS AT BIRKENHEAD.—Messrs. Thomas Wilson & Co., the eminent shipbuilders of Liverpool, have taken a lease for twenty-five years, of a piece of land fronting the Mersey, of an extent of 3¾ acres, or about 18,000 square yards, for the purpose of shipbuilding. For 14,000 yards of this property the rent is to be £450 per annum, and for the remaining 4000 yards, £20 per annum, the latter portion being reclaimable at three months' notice. The Liverpool corporation, to whom the property belongs, have undertaken to lay out a sum not exceeding £10,000, in building a river wall and graving dock, in order to render the establishment worthy of their flourishing town; and on the money so expended Messrs. Wilson and Co. are to pay 5 per cent. interest for the use of the works. We understand that no expense will be spared to render Messrs. Wilson's building yard one of the most complete in the kingdom.

The Dock Committee have accepted Mr. Thomas Vernon and Son's tender for a new iron light-ship.

ROYAL STEAM NAVY.

APPOINTMENTS, &c.

Chief Engineer.—GEORGE RUSSELL, to the *Prometheus.*

Assistant Engineers.—GEORGE CRICHTON, WILLIAM AUSTIN, and SAMUEL GRIFFITHS, to the *Prometheus.*

Chief Engineer.—WILLIAM DUNKIN, to the *Ajax.*

Assistant Engineers.—W. B. BAIRD, SAMUEL DAVY, THOMAS PATER-SON, and THOMAS DUNCANSON, to the *Ajax.*

FITZ-MAURICE'S ROTARY ENGINE.—The Lords of the Admiralty have inspected Capt. Fitz-Maurice's rotary engine (of which we gave a drawing in our last volume), and have ordered the launch to which it is fitted to be taken to Woolwich, to test the capabilities of it more satisfactorily.

The *Victoria and Albert* has, it is said, been improved in speed a knot an hour by the new boilers, the number of revolutions being increased from 18 to 19½ per minute.

PORTSMOUTH.—TRIAL OF THE DAUNTLESS.—The *Dauntless* was tried on the 13th instant, after having been lengthened 8 feet at the stern. She was brought to her intended draught of water,—16 feet fore, and 16 feet 8 inches aft;—and her speed, at a mean of 8 runs, was 10,266 knots. The engines made 30 revolutions, and the screw 70. Steam pressure 8¼ lbs.; vacuum 25½ inches; screw 14 feet 8 inches diameter, and 18 feet pitch; thermometer in stokehole 88°.

TRIAL OF H.M.S. SIMOOM.—On the 23rd instant this splendid iron vessel had a second trial, and performed the distance between the Clough Lighthouse and Cumbrae (13·66 nautical miles) in 88 minutes with, and 99 minutes against the tide, giving an average speed of more than 8 knots per hour. Her dimensions are as follow :—

	Ft.	In.
Length on deck	234	6
Breadth on ditto amidships	39	4
Depth of hold at ditto	26	1
Length of engine space	56	2
Breadth of ditto	38	8
Depth of ditto	16	3
Length of shaft space	43	7
Breadth of ditto	5	4
Depth of ditto	6	0

Tonnage.				Tons.
Hull	..	..	..	2076¹⁰⁰⁄₁₀₀
Contents of engine space	..	..	384⁴⁵⁄₁₀₀
Contents of shaft ditto	..	..	15⁴⁵⁄₁₀₀
Total	..	..	..	399⁵⁵⁄₁₀₀
Register	..	..	..	1676¹⁰⁄₁₀₀

As we have already pointed out, in noticing her launch, she was built by Mr. R. Napier; but the engines originally designed for her were countermanded, and a pair, or rather two pair, of smaller power substituted. Those now on board are by Messrs. J. Watt & Co. There are four oscillating cylinders, two to each crank—of 42 inches diameter, and 2 feet 6 inches stroke. Four boilers, with three furnaces in each, and a telescope funnel.

NOTES AND NOVELTIES.

EXHIBITION OF 1851.—REGULATIONS REGARDING THE EXHIBITION OF MACHINERY IN MOTION.—Her Majesty's Commissioners for the Exhibition of 1851, being desirous of affording every facility to those persons who may wish to exhibit machines or trains of machinery in motion, have resolved to allow such machinery to be managed and worked, as far as practicable, under the superintendence of the owners, and by their own men. The Commissioners will also find steam, not exceeding 30 lbs. per inch, gratuitously, to the exhibitors, and convey it in clothed pipes to such parts of the building as require steam power. Parties sending machines or articles requiring to be driven by steam should send with the same a small portable steam engine, to which a steam pipe can be laid on. The above will apply to all engines from one horse power to six horse, beyond which power it is presumed no single branch of manufacture or article will require steam power. As regards machines too small to require an independent portable engine, arrangements will be made to place them in groups to be exhibited in communication with some steam engine, also sent for exhibition, in motion. Exhibitors proposing to exhibit portable steam engines, should understand that their engines may be employed for driving other machinery, unless the owners of the steam engines object to such use.

REPEAL OF THE RAILWAY PASSENGER TAX.—Lord Kinnaird, in a letter to G. C. Glyn, Esq., on the subject of the passenger tax, suggests that instead of the companies petitioning for the repeal of this tax, they should persuade Government to take the debentures' debt at 3½ per cent., making it a Government Stock at 3 per cent., the ½ per cent. being in lieu of the passenger duty, and to meet the expenses of working the stock. The companies would save a considerable sum, which would be applicable to increasing dividends, whilst the Government, having a first claim on the property, would be entitled to satisfy themselves with regard to the official position of the affairs of the companies, without any undue interference with the management, and be far preferable to an audit bill.

LIST OF ENGLISH PATENTS.

FROM THE 20TH DAY OF APRIL, TO THE 8TH DAY OF MAY, 1850, INCLUSIVE.

Peter Arkell, of Chapel-street, Stockwell, in the county of Surrey, engineer, for improvements in the manufacture of candle wicks. April 20.

Alfred George Anderson, of Great Suffolk-street, Southwark, in the county of Surrey, soap manufacturer, for improvements in the treatment of a substance produced in soap making, and its application to useful purposes. April 20.

John Timothy Chapman, of Wapping, in the county of Middlesex, engineer, for improvements in apparatus for setting up ships' rigging, and raising weights. April 20.

Richard Archibald Brooman, of the firm of J. C. Robertson & Co., of Fleet-street, London, for improvements in the manufacture of zinc, and in apparatus employed therein. April 20.

Henry Ritchie, of Brixton, in the county of Surrey, for improvements in the manufacture of copper, brass, and other tubes or pipes. April 23.

William Macalpine, of Spring-vale, Hammersmith, general dresser, and Thomas McAlpine, of the same place, manager, for improvements in machinery for washing cotton, linen, and other fabrics. April 23.

Charles Humpey, of Downing College, Cambridge, M.A., for improvements in the manufacture of candles and oils, and in treating fatty and oily matters, and in the application of certain products of fatty and oily matters. April 23.

Antoine Panwels, of Paris, in the Republic of France, merchant, and Vincent Dubochet, also of Paris, in the Republic of France, merchant, for certain improvements in the production of coke, and of gas, for illumination, and also in regulating the circulation of such gas. April 23.

Richard Laming, of the New Chemical Works, Isle of Dogs, in the county of Middlesex, chemist, and Frederick John Evans, of the Horseferry-road, in the city of Westminster, gas-engineer, for improvements in the manufacture of gas for illumination, and other purposes to which coal-gas is applicable; in preparing materials to be employed in such manufacture; and in apparatus for manufacturing and using gas; also improvements in treating certain products resulting from the distillation of coal; parts of which above mentioned improvements are applicable to other similar purposes. April 23.

William Edward Newton, of Chancery-lane, in the county of Middlesex, civil engineer, for improvements in casting type. April 23.

Pierre Armand Lecomte de Fontainemoreau, of South-street, Finsbury, for certain improvements in the manufacture of waters; and in the machinery or apparatus connected therewith. April 23.

Pierre Armand Lecomte de Fontainemoreau, of South-street, Finsbury, for a new and improved mode of conducting, consuming, and disengaging smoke from its deleterious components. April 23.

Ernst Werner Siemens, of Berlin, in the Kingdom of Prussia, electric engineer, for improvements in electric telegraphs. April 23.

Joseph Jean Baranowski, of London, gentleman, for improvements in machinery for counting, numbering, and labelling. April 23.

William Gilbert Elliott, of Blisworth, in the county of Northampton, gentleman, for improvements in the manufacture of bricks, tiles, and pipes, and other articles from plastic materials. April 27.—(Communication.)

Charles May, of Ipswich, engineer, and Robert Leggett, of the same place, foreman of mechanics to Messrs. Ransom and May, of the same place, for improvements in machinery for thrashing and grinding corn, for cutting straw, and other similar substances; also improvements in applying steam power, to give motion to such classes of machinery; and also improvements in machines for depositing seed. April 30.

George Michiels, of London, gentleman, for improvements in treating coal, and in the manufacture of gas; and also in apparatus for burning gas. April 30.—(Communication.)

Evan Protheroe, of Austin Friars, in the city of London, merchant, for improvements in the manufacture of oxide of zinc: and in making paints from oxide of zinc. April 30.—(Communication.)

Robert Dalgliah, of Glasgow, merchant and calico printer, for certain improvements in printing, and in the application of colours to silk, cotton, linen, woollen, and other textile fabrics. May 7.

Gustave Eugene Michel Gerard, of Paris, for improvements in dissolving caoutchouc (India-rubber) and gutta percha. May 7.

George Hurwood, of Ipswich, in the county of Suffolk, engineer, for improvements in grinding corn and other substances. May 7.

Joseph Gibbs, of Devonshire-street, Portland-place, in the county of Middlesex, civil engineer, for improvements in artificial stone, mortar, and cements, and in the modes of manufacturing the same. May 7.

George Robbins, of Forrest-lodge, Southampton, gentleman, for improvements in the construction of railway carriages. May 7.

John Tatham and David Cheetham, of Rochdale, in the county of Lancaster, machine-makers, for certain improvements in machinery or apparatus, and operations connected with the manufacture of cotton, wool, silk, and other fibrous substances and fabrics; and in the application of certain materials to the manufacture of textile fabrics. May 7.

John Youil, of Ardwick, Manchester, brewer, for certain improvements in machinery or apparatus for washing, cleansing, filling, and corking bottles and other vessels. May 8.

LIST OF PATENTS THAT HAVE PASSED THE GREAT SEAL OF SCOTLAND.

FROM THE 25TH DAY OF FEBRUARY TO THE 20TH OF MARCH, 1850, INCLUSIVE.

Auguste Reinhard, of Leicester-street, Leicester-square, in the county of Middlesex, chemist, for improvements in preparing oils for lubricating purposes; and in apparatus for filtering oil and other liquids. February 25.

Onesiphore Pecqueur, of Paris, in the Republic of France, civil engineer, for certain improvements in the manufacture of fishing nets and other net fabrics. February 25.

James Young, of Manchester, in the county of Lancaster, manufacturing chemist, for improvements in the treatment of certain ores, and other matters containing metals, and in obtaining products therefrom. February 26.

Alfred Vincent Newton, of Chancery-lane, in the county of Middlesex, for improvements in manufacturing leather. February 27.—(Communication.)

Eugene Ablon, of Panton-street, Haymarket, in the county of Middlesex, for improvements in increasing the draught in chimneys of locomotive and other engines. March 4.

William Brown, of Airdre, Lanarkshire, electrician, and William Williams, the younger, of St. Dennis, in the county of Cornwall, gentleman, for improvements in electric and magnetic apparatus for indicating and communicating intelligence. March 4.

Alexandre Hediard, of Paris, in the Republic of France, gentleman, for certain improvements in propelling. March 5.

Thomas Richard, William Taylor, and James Wylde, the younger, all of Falcon Works, Walworth, in the county of Surrey, cotton manufacturers, for certain improved rollers, to be used in the manufacture of silk, cotton, woollen, and other fabrics. March 6.

James Hill, of Stalybridge, in the county of Chester, cotton spinner, for improvements applicable to certain machines for preparing, spinning, and doubling cotton, wool, and other fibrous substances. March 6.

John Fowler, Jun., of Melksham, in the county of Wilts, engineer, for improvements in draining land. March 8.

Gerard John de Witte, of Brook-street, Westminster, in the county of Middlesex, gentleman, for improvements in machinery apparatus, metallic, and other substances, for the purposes of letter-press and other printing. March 8.

David Christie, of St. John's-place, Broughton, in the borough of Salford, and county of Lancaster, merchant, for improvements in machinery for preparing, assorting, straightening, tearing, teasing, doubling, twisting, braiding, and weaving cotton, wool, and other fibrous substances. March 13.—(Communication.)

Edward Ormerod, of Manchester, in the county of Lancaster, mechanical engineer, and Joseph Shepherd, of Cholton-upon-Medlock, in the same county, mechanical engineer, for improvements in, or applicable to, apparatus for changing the position of carriages on railways. March 13.

Frank Clark Hills, of Deptford, in the county of Kent, manufacturing chemist, for an improved mode of compressing peat for making fuel or gas, and of manufacturing gas; and of obtaining certain salts. March 15.

Warren De La Rue, of Bunhill-row, in the county of Middlesex, for certain improvements in the manufacture of envelopes. March 20.

William Handley, of Chiswell-street, Finsbury, confectioner, George Duncan, of Battersea, in the county of Surrey, engineer, and Alexander M'Glashan, of Long Acre, in the county of Middlesex, engineer, for improvements in the construction of railway breaks. March 20

LIST OF PATENTS THAT HAVE PASSED THE GREAT SEAL OF IRELAND.

FROM THE 3RD DAY OF JANUARY, TO THE 16TH DAY OF MARCH, 1850, INCLUSIVE.

Osgood Field, of London, merchant, for improvements in anchors. January 3.

Peter Fairbairn, of Leeds, in the county of York, machinist, and John Hetherington, of Manchester, in the county of Lancaster, machinist, for certain improvements in machinery for preparing and spinning cotton, flax, and other fibrous substances. January 12.—(Part communication.)

Richard Hobson, of Leeds, in the county of York, Doctor of Medicine, for certain improvements in the manufacture of horse shoes, and in apparatus for taking the measurement of horse shoes, or horses' hoofs. January 15.

John Jordan, of Liverpool, in the county of Lancaster, engineer, for certain improvements in the construction of ships and other vessels navigating on water. January 17.

Wenceslas, Baron de Traux de Wardin, of Liege, in the province of Liege, in the Kingdom of Belgium, for certain improvements in looms for weaving linen, woollen, and cotton cloths, and in the machinery for preparing the yarns for such cloths before entering the loom, and in a machine for finishing gray and bleached linen cloth. January 17.

Thomas Auchterlonie, of Glasgow, N.B., manufacturer and calico printer, for improvements in the production of ornamental fabrics. January 17.

Alexander Swan, of Kirkaldy, in the county of Fife, manufacturer, for improvements in heating apparatus, and in applying hot and warm air to manufacturing and other purposes, when the same are required. January 28.

Jacques Hulot, of Rue St. Joseph, Paris, in the Republic of France, manufacturer, for improvements in the manufacture of the fronts of shirts. February 1.

Thomas John Knowlys, of Heysham Tower, near Lancaster, Esq., for improvements in the application and combination of mineral products; also in obtaining products from mineral and vegetable substances, and in the generation and application of heat. February 4.

Thomas Henry Russell, patent tube manufacturer, of Wednesbury, and John Stephen Woolrich, of Birmingham, chemist, for improvements in coating iron, and certain other metals and alloys of metals. February 12.

Joseph Stovel, of Suffolk-place, Pall-Mall East, in the county of Middlesex, tailor, for improvements in coats, parts of which improvements are applicable to sleeves of other garments. February 22.

Lucien Vidie, of Paris, in France, but now of South-street, Finsbury, French Advocate, for improvements in conveyances on land and water. February 23.

William Henry Phillips, of York-terrace, Camberwell New-road, in the county of Surrey, engineer, for improvements in extinguishing fire, in the preparation of materials to be used for that purpose; and improvements to assist in saving life and property. February 26.

James Higgins, of Salford, in the county of Lancaster, machine maker, and Thomas Schofield Whitworth, of Salford, in the same county, mechanic, for certain improvements in machinery for preparing, spinning, and doubling cotton, wool, flax, and similar fibrous materials. February 26.

Auguste Reinhard, of Leicester-street, Leicester-square, Middlesex, chemist, for improvements in preparing oils for lubricating purposes; and in apparatus for filtering oil and other liquids. February 26.

Onesiphore Pecqueur, of Paris, in the Republic of France, civil engineer, for certain improvements in the manufacture of fishing nets, and other net fabrics. February 27.

Ernest Gaston, of the Erectheum Club, St. James's, in the county of Middlesex, for certain improvements in artificial fuel, and in machinery used for manufacturing the same. March 1.

Alexandre Hediard, of Paris, in the Republic of France, gentleman, for certain improvements in propelling. March 5.

Alfred Vincent Newton, of Chancery-lane, in the county of Middlesex, for improvements in manufacturing leather. March 6.

Thomas Marsden, of Salford, in the county of Lancaster, machine maker, for improvements in machinery for heckling, combing, or dressing flax, wool, and other fibrous substances. March 8.

Henry Attwood, of Goodman's-fields, in the county of Middlesex, civil engineer, and John Benton, of Bromley, in the same county, for certain improvements in the manufacture of starch, and other like articles of commerce, from farinaceous and leguminous substances. March 12.

James M'Donald, of Chester, coach maker, for certain improvements in the method of applying oil or grease to wheels and axles, and to machinery; and in connecting the springs of wheel carriages with the axles or axle-box. March 15.

James Hill, of Stalybridge, in the county of Chester, for improvements in, and applicable to certain machines for preparing, spinning, and doubling cotton, wool, and other fibrous substances. March 16.

DESIGNS FOR ARTICLES OF UTILITY.

REGISTERED FROM 18TH APRIL TO 6TH MAY.

April 18th, 2269, Richard Edwards, Fairfield-place, Bow, "Knife-cleaning apparatus."

,, 19th, 2270, A. Marshall & Co., Parkside, Hyde-park-corner, "Part of the apparatus used in corsets, denominated the 'Corset à tous Resorts.'"

,, 20th, 2271, J. Robertson, Emmett-street, Poplar, "Apparatus for giving signals by sound."

,, ,, 2272, Mary Ann Nash, Paul's Cray Mill, Kent, "Impressing surface of a dandy roller, for producing water-marks on machine-made paper."

,, ,, 2273, John Weems & Thomas Buchanan, Renfrewshire, "Improved cover for carding and drawing-frame cans."

,, ,, 2274, Alfred Gregory, St. George's-street, St. George's East, "Safety plate for a ship's scuttle."

,, ,, 2275, Henry Potts, Brooke-street, Holborn, "Postage stamp damper and affixer."

,, 22nd, 2276, Reeves, Greaves, & Reeves, Birmingham, "Sword tang."

,, ,, 2277, William Horne, Long-acre, "Improved barouche or barouche phaeton."

,, ,, 2278, Robert Waddell, Liverpool, "Capstan."

,, ,, 2279, Crosse & Blackwell, Soho-square, "Stopper for bottles and jars."

,, ,, 2280, Thomas Kerslake, Exeter, "Improved boiler and furnace."

,, 24th, 2281, William Alexander Adams, Smethwick, "Carriage-spring and centre-clip."

,, ,, 2282, Nicholas Douring, The Phœnix Foundry, Shildon, "Cast-iron railway-carriage wheel."

,, 25th, 2283, John Finlay, Glasgow, "Radiating register-stove."

,, 26th, 2284, James Cuthbert & Co., Great Distaff-lane, "Apparatus for mulling liquids."

,, 27th, 2285, Charles Starkey, Bloxwich, "Lock."

,, 29th, 2286, Hardman, Norton, & Co., Gresham-street, "Attacher for coats and other garments."

,, ,, 2287, Rowland Fothergill, Aberdare Iron Works, Glamorgan, "Sleeper for tram-plates."

,, ,, 2288, Joseph Peace, Sheffield, "Saw-handle."

,, 30th, 2289, Joseph Chatwin, Alcester-street, Birmingham, "Albert gas-burner."

,, ,, 2290, Hall & Wilson, Manchester, "Gas retort."

,, ,, 2291, Edward Thomas Loseby, Gerrard-street, Islington, "Portable crane shower-bath."

,, ,, 2292, Schoolbred & Loveridge, Wolverhampton, "Hip bath."

,, ,, 2293, Barsby & Wells, Dudley, "Day indicator."

,, ,, 2294, Samuel Daniel, Birmingham, "Looking-glass movement."

May 2nd, 2295, Francis Pike Hewitt, Nottingham, "Compound elastic band, or strap for articles of dress."

,, 4th, 2296, Francis Drury, Albany-street, Regent's-park, "Steel bell."

,, 6th, 2297, John O. Eise, Albany-road, Camberwell, "Beer and spirit preserver."

,, ,, 2298, John Holford & Edward Barry Collard, Regent-street, "Frame for carpet and other bags."

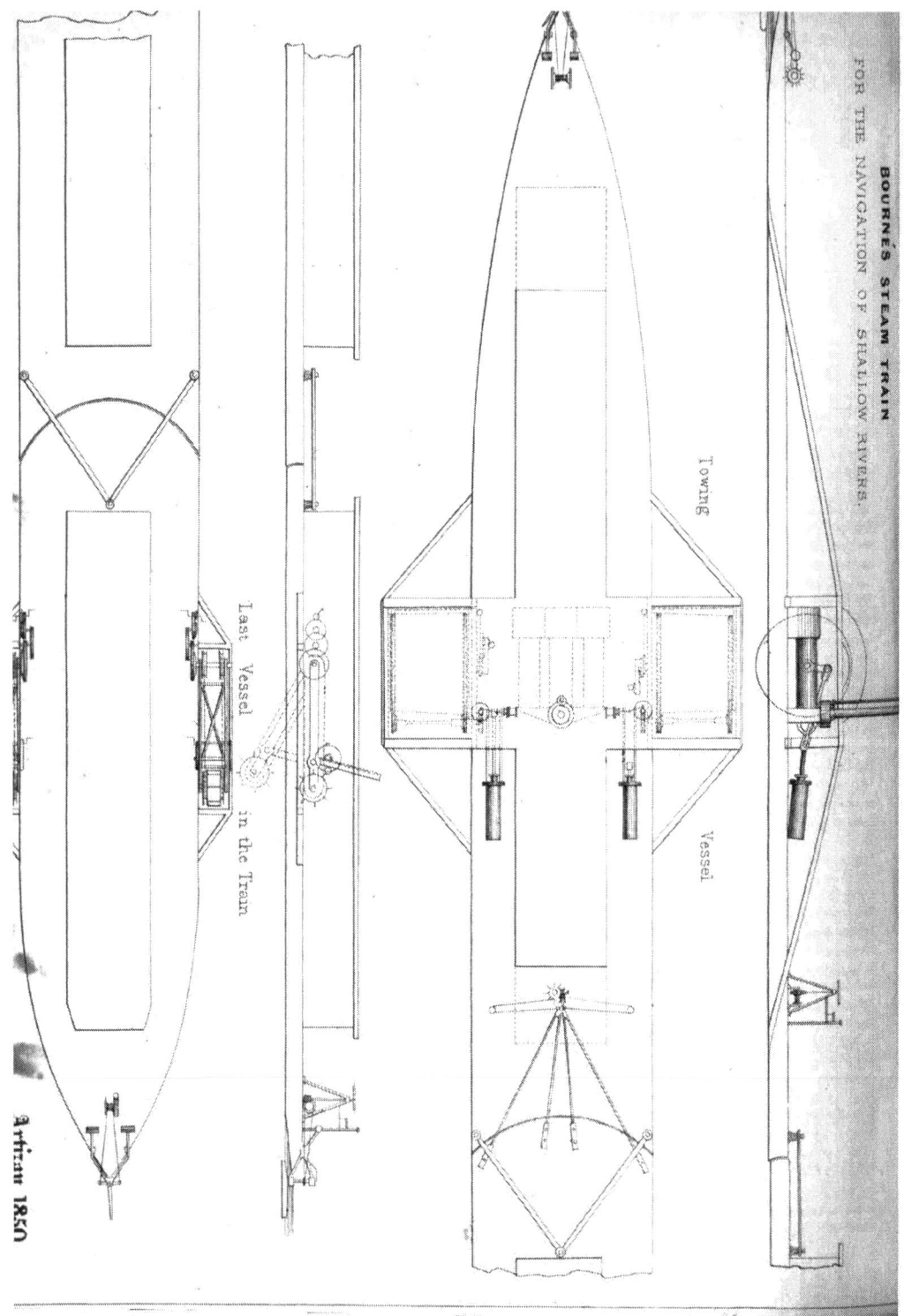

BOURNE'S STEAM TRAIN FOR THE NAVIGATION OF SHALLOW RIVERS.

Towing

Vessel

Last Vessel

in the Train

Artizan 1850

THE ARTIZAN.

No. VII.—Vol. VIII.—JULY 1st, 1850.

INDIAN RIVER NAVIGATION.

INDIAN RIVER NAVIGATION.

A LECTURE ON THE NAVIGATION OF SHALLOW RIVERS, DELIVERED
AT THE UNITED SERVICE INSTITUTION, BY MR. BOURNE.

The navigation of shallow rivers by steam, is a problem which has hitherto obtained but little attention from engineers, partly, no doubt, from the prevailing indisposition of practical men to enter upon new and obscure fields of mechanical research; but mainly from the circumstance that neither in this country nor in America are there any such considerable tracts of river navigation as to render the achievement of material importance. In many countries of the world, however, and especially in India, there are thousands of miles of rivers which, though possessed of a large volume of water, are nevertheless so much obstructed by shallows and sand-banks as to be incapable of efficient navigation by steam vessels of the ordinary kind; and as these rivers ramify in many cases through the heart of the country, so that if susceptible of navigation, they would constitute great steam highways, whereby a cheap and expeditious communication between the coast and the interior could be at all times maintained, the problem of constructing steam vessels by which the navigation of these rivers might be satisfactorily accomplished, is one manifestly which is of great interest and importance. The primary want of India, indeed, is facility of internal communication, and the rivers are the natural highways of the country; but a new species of steam vessel, adapted to the peculiarities of the navigation, must be introduced before the advantages of the rivers can be made fully available. It is hopeless to attempt permanently to deepen the beds or to control the movements of such great rivers as the Ganges or Indus, except at such an outlay as would practically interdict the operation; and any material improvements of the navigation of the rivers of India to be in reality accomplishable, must proceed upon the principle of leaving the rivers as they are, and of introducing upon them a species of vessel which shall not be impaired in its efficiency by the existing impediments. This necessary adaptation would, no doubt, have long ago been effected, if the rivers of India had been situated in England, or if the mechanical engineers of this country had been resident in the East; for the mechanical expedients proper for the accomplishment of the required object would soon have suggested themselves, after a distinct conception had been reached of the nature of the impediments which really existed, and of the conditions it was required to fulfil. It is from the accident of my engagement in India, in connexion with railways in that country, that the function of devising arrangements suitable for the navigation of the rivers has devolved upon me; for I thus became conscious of the importance of rendering the rivers, ramifying, as I perceived they did, over the whole face of the country, available for purposes of internal steam communication, and I had an opportunity of ascertaining, by personal examination upon the spot, what the conditions were which required

to be fulfilled, and the difficulties which must necessarily be surmounted. I saw how insignificant was the area of the country which would be intersected by the railways then proposed for execution, compared with that drained by the great rivers stretching from the Himalayas to the sea, and I perceived that the benefits derivable from opening the rivers to steam would be infinitely larger in amount, and at the same time more prompt and expensive in their realization than those consequent upon the establishment of any possible number of railways. The importance of traversing the rivers by steam in a rapid and efficient manner being thus set beyond dispute, the practicability of the achievement became the next subject of consideration; and I saw no reason to doubt that, under suitable mechanical arrangements, at least ten thousand miles of river in India could be navigated at a speed of from 10 to 15 miles an hour. I could not disguise from myself the fact that the proposed railways, to be of any utility, or to collect to themselves any traffic, must penetrate into the heart of the country, whereby their cost would be made many times larger than was contemplated; and as the persons best acquainted with India concurred in the opinion, that even if the railways were constructed, it would be more advisable to maintain upon them such cheap speeds as 10 or 12 miles an hour, in preference to the high and expensive speeds usual in this country; and as these speeds, it appeared, might be realized on the rivers under suitable arrangements, I did not perceive on what principle the execution of costly, competing, and fragmentary railway works could be defended. The efficient navigation of the rivers by steam would accomplish a large measure of improvement at a very trifling expense; and the cheapest and most extended ameliorations should obviously first be availed of before recourse is had to the costly and microscopic luxuries of railway locomotion. India cannot afford the expense of a duplicate system of transport in some districts, while other districts are destitute of all means of conveyance; and it is the wide diffusion of improvements of a simple and inexpensive character that is required in India, rather than the limitation to a few favoured spots of certain superlative refinements. To introduce railways of the English type into India, is like putting a racer to the plough; and cheaper and less ambitious methods of locomotion, being susceptible of more wide diffusion with any given outlay, will achieve a far larger measure of practical advantage. Where the water-way ends, there should a road-way begin, which in the course of time may ripen into a rail or tram-way, as the traffic grows up into importance; whereas, to begin by laying down fragments of expensive railway in a sterile or undeveloped country, or in competition with commodious water conveyance, is only to ensure the mortification of loss, disappointment, and discredit to all concerned. To enable railways to accomplish the same benefits for India that would follow the efficient navigation of the rivers, the railways must be equally extended; and ten thousand miles of railway, if executed at the cost per mile which appears in the estimates of the East India line, would involve an outlay of 150 millions sterling. The mere yearly depreciation upon such a system, would, if reckoned upon the same data, amount to 15 millions sterling per annum, being nearly as large a sum as the whole revenue of India! This yearly expense is wholly irrespective of tear and wear, of accident from fire and flood, and of all other contingencies whatever, and it supposes, moreover, that no loss would accrue in working any of the lines. On the other hand, the rivers being already made, do not involve the necessity of any outlay; they are not subject to decay or deterioration, and do not occasion any expense for wear and tear. If a steam vessel is not useful or profitable on one river, she may be transferred to another; but a railway once made cannot be removed, or employed for another purpose, whether found to be profitable or the reverse. There is no line of railway in India, of which the execution has yet been sanctioned, which could possibly be worked at a profit, or which is capable of rendering any appreciable benefit, even to the small tract of country it passes through; so that the execution of those lines, even if carried into effect, would practically leave the country as destitute as before of the means of internal communication.

The rivers of India, in common with most of the rivers of tropical climates, are subject to periodical inundations, during which the waters spread beyond the banks, in some cases to a breadth of many miles. At these times there is an abundant depth of water for all the purposes of steam navigation with vessels of the ordinary kind, but as the waters subside numerous sandbanks and shallows in the bed of the river come to light, by which the navigation is seriously obstructed. The larger rivers, however, even under these circumstances, are but rarely fordable in any place, and the general depth of the water is very considerable. But the sandbanks are so numerous, and so frequently changing their position, and there are so many blind channels in which the water gradually shallows, until it becomes inadequate for the purposes of navigation, that it is impossible to navigate even the largest of the Indian rivers during the dry season with vessels drawing more than a few feet of water. In general, the shoals and sandbanks run obliquely across the rivers, in the manner of oblique bars, dividing them in the direction of their length, into long deep pools, which are connected by shallower water. In the bars or shallows there are certain breaks, or deeper places, which constitute the continuation of the channel; but it is very difficult to ascertain where these deeper places lie, and if a vessel in descending the river follows the largest body of water flowing among these banks, as is the natural course, she will generally pass the whole of the deeper channels, and get into a *cul de sac*, from whence she can only extricate herself by retracing her course. A vessel with a very light immersion, however, will generally find sufficient water over the shallows to enable her to pursue a straight course without experiencing these embarrassments, whereas if the draft of water be so great as to render it necessary to keep the deepest part of the channel the course must inevitably be very tortuous, and the vessel will perpetually be getting aground.

The great rivers of India flow, in general, through sandy or alluvial plains, and there are consequently no falls or difficult rapids to be met with in the navigable part of their course. To this rule the Nerbudda and some other smaller streams are exceptions, for those rivers flow in a rocky bed; but as that very peculiarity renders them improvable—seeing that any amelioration effected upon a rocky bed would be permanent and decisive—there is less need to provide special means to enable the navigation of rivers of this class to be effected. The main difficulties which must be encountered in navigating the rivers of India arise from the shallowness of the water, the frequency of the sandbanks, and the shifting nature of the channels, and, indeed, of the river beds themselves, for, generally speaking, the bed of every river shifts its position more or less during every inundation. The sandbanks are of two kinds; the one is hard and solid, and the other partakes of the nature of quicksand, so that it is in effect but a denser kind of water. If a vessel in ascending the Ganges or Indus happens to get aground, a bank will very quickly grow up at the lower side of the vessel, so as to enclose her in a dock; for the sand which the running water carries in suspension is at once deposited so soon as the water comes into the comparatively quiescent place in the lee of the vessel; and this deposition goes on so fast, that in the course of an hour or two a bank will grow up to the surface of the water on which a person may jump out. In time the water deflected by the bottom of the vessel downwards upon the bed of the river will carry away the sand from beneath the bottom and the vessel will get afloat again, but will be unable to move beyond the limits of the dock in which she is enclosed. If, however, she be suffered to drop down with the current, so as to press against the lower side of the dock, the flow of water under the bottom will gradually enlarge the dock on the lower side, and the bank or wave of sand will be carried over and over by the current, until it comes into deep water, when the vessel will get free.

It will be seen from this recapitulation of some of the phenomena incident to the navigation of the rivers of India, that not only must the vessels employed have a very light draft of water, but they must also possess the power of extricating themselves—when they happen to get aground—without delay; inasmuch as if any material delay arises, a new and more difficult state of things will supervene. The only mode of extrication at present attempted is carrying out an anchor upon which a strain is hove by the windlass in the usual manner; but the delay consequent upon this procedure is usually such that the vessel is enclosed in a dock before she can be forced off or over the impediment. The surface presented by an anchor fluke is indeed inadequate to furnish an efficient *point d'appui* for heaving a vessel off a shoal, unless the anchor has been afforded time to sink into the sand, and then its subsequent extrication becomes difficult. Nevertheless vessels of considerable tonnage have been forced over shoals in the Ganges by the agency of their anchors, though there was three feet less water on the shoals than the draft of water of the vessels. Such an operation, however, though fully establishing the practicability of forcing a vessel over shoals by mechanical means, must necessarily be too tedious to be appropriate for vessels in which facility of extrication is indispensable, and in which a high rate of speed is required to be maintained; and however small the draft of water of the vessels may be, yet as there will still be a liability to get aground from an accidental deviation from the channel in navigating these rivers, it is obvious that a prompt and powerful method of extricating the vessel when such an accident occurs becomes altogether indispensable. The vessels must not merely be less liable to get aground than ordinary vessels, but must have more effectual means of getting afloat again when grounding takes place; and no vessels are suitable for the navigation of shifting and shallow rivers which are unable to satisfy those conditions.

When a body moves through a fluid, it carries with it a film, or coating of the fluid; and the thickness of this film in the case of any given fluid depends on the velocity of the moving body. The barnacles, therefore, adhering to the bottom of an ocean steamer repose in comparatively quiescent water; and the seaweeds attached to a fast sailing ship may often be observed to stand nearly straight out from the side, instead of being pressed close in against the side by the current, as might be expected. In the case of the hydraulic belt for raising water, the large adhesion of the water to the surface of the belt is conspicuously exhibited; and in the case of rivers flowing with a current which is neither accelerated nor retarded, the friction of the water upon the bottom of the river just balances the force of gravity down the inclined plane of the bed. It could easily be shown that any agency which removes or sucks away the film of water which a vessel carries with her, must retard the progress of the vessel; as either a new film must be put in motion, whereby power will be expended, or if this ope-

ration be prevented by arrangements adapted to that end, then the friction of the water upon the bottom of the vessel will be augmented. Now when a steam vessel comes into such shallow water that the bottom nearly touches the ground, the film of water moving with the vessel is torn away or retarded by its friction against the bottom of the river, and the speed of the vessel is materially reduced in consequence. At the same time the water is prevented from closing in so readily at the stern of the vessel as would otherwise be the case, in consequence of the increased friction of the water upon the bed, due to the diminished depth. A vacuity, or depression of the water surface is thus caused at the stern of the vessel, which occasions an amount of hydrostatic resistance, such as is due to the difference of level between the stem and stern ; and a current of water sets in from the stem towards the stern, carrying round the paddle wheels like water wheels, whereby the engine runs away at a high speed, without correspondingly impelling the vessel. At the same time the low rate of speed, the diminished immersion of the rudder, and the fact of the water rushing in from all sides to the stem, instead of impinging upon the rudder in the usual manner, seriously interfere with the power of steering, and it has consequently been found that steamers which had achieved a considerable rate of speed in deep water, sometimes realised a progress of only three or four miles a day among the shallows of the Indus. Such cases, it is true, are exceptional ; but all the steamers on the Indus are slow, and even upon the lower part of the Ganges a progress of only fifty miles a day is the speed commonly achieved. A reference to the inexorable laws of science, shows very clearly that the performance must necessarily be very defective in all cases in which the vessels employed to ply upon shallow rivers are of the class proper for the navigation of deeper waters, and it is an indispensable condition, not merely as a means of obviating grounding, but to enable high rates of speed to be attained, that the vessels introduced upon the rivers of India should have the smallest draft of water that is reconcilable with the other conditions which have to be fulfilled. By an examination of the minimum depths of the water during the dry season, it appears that vessels drawing from 12 to 18 inches of water could at all times navigate the larger class of the rivers of India, from the vicinity of the Himalayas to the sea ; and vessels of such a draft would not merely be exempt from the risk of grounding, except by an accidental deviation from the channel, but they would also be exempt from the retardation due to the too near approach of the bottom of the vessel to the bottom of the river, and to the difficulty of filling up the vacuity which the progress of the vessel leaves at the stern.

Such then are some of the principal impediments to the navigation of shallow and shifting rivers, with the conditions indispensable to the success of such an achievement; and it cannot be disguised that the difficulties to be overcome are by no means inconsiderable. At the same time, there is every reason to believe that they will be found completely superable by the resources of engineering science, and the first step towards their effectual supercession is to obtain a distinct conception of their character, and an adequate, perhaps an exaggerated sense of their importance. To conceal or extenuate any of the difficulties attending upon the undertaking would either be to ensure its failure or to cause its success to fall very far short of our just expectations ; and to accomplish a useful result the vessels must not merely be so light and powerful as to achieve a high rate of speed, even in shallow water, but must also be possessed of the capability to carry a remunerative cargo. Numerous plans have suggested themselves to me for the reconciliation of these apparently inconsistent conditions, but the whole of the original conceptions have at length settled into the plan which I will now proceed to describe.

The kind of vessel I propose may be likened to a railway train on water. I intend to carry the cargo and passengers, not in the steamer herself, as is the usual practice, but in a succession of shallow barges towed by the steamer, and so articulated to the steamer and to one another by circular joints as in effect to constitute one long vessel or train, with a single bow to separate the water for the whole train, instead of an independent bow and stern for each of the constituent barges. The same facility in cleaving the water is thus obtained as if the vessel were built on the proportions of a long racing wherry, while facility in turning at bends of the river and exemption from straining, should the vessel ground upon an uneven surface, are at the same time obtained. The steamer or locomotive of the train will be 220 feet long and 36 feet wide, and her immersion will be about 15 or 16 inches of water. The succeeding barges of the train, except the stern barge, will each be about 100 feet long, and will draw about 12 inches of water. The stern barge will be about 160 feet long, and will draw less than 12 inches of water. The average draft of the train will be 12 inches, or a little more, and with this draft each of the barges will carry upwards of 50 tons of cargo. The length of the train will consequently depend upon the quantity of cargo required to be conveyed, and also, it may be, upon the physical peculiarities of the river to be navigated ; but in favourable cases, it is expected that a speed of 12 or 15 miles an hour may be realized with a train of five barges. The steamer carries neither cargo nor passengers, but is laden with her engines only and a small supply of coal. Depôts of coal will be formed at convenient intervals, upon the banks of the river, so that it will not be necessary to encumber the steamer or train with more than a day's supply.

The resistance experienced by any vessel in moving through deep water is made up of two distinct resistances, of which the one is the force requisite to separate the water at the bow and to close it at the stern of the vessel, and the other is the friction caused by the water rubbing upon the vessel's bottom. The bow and stern resistances are manifestly much smaller than usual, under the proposed combination, in consequence of the shallow draft ; but the rubbing surface of the bottom, and consequently the friction, is larger than usual, and there are no data existing by which the total amount of the resistance can be accurately determined. In ordinary steam vessels of any given form, the power necessary for the accomplishment of any prescribed speed, or the speed due to a given amount of power, can easily be told ; but, although we can thus ascertain the total resistance, we are unable to distinguish between the bow and stern resistance and the resistance due to the friction of the water, and are consequently unable to specify what increase in the total resistance any given increase of the rubbing surface will occasion. It is certain, however, that the total resistance of a train of articulated barges will be less than the total resistance of a train of vessels, each provided with a separate bow and stern ; and as the total resistance of such a train of vessels can be readily computed by the ordinary rules, it is obvious that the *limit* of the resistance of the articulated train is readily ascertainable. The ordinary rule for determining the power necessary to be given to a vessel of a specified class, to achieve any prescribed speed, is to multiply the cube of the speed, either in miles or knots, by the broadest sectional area of the vessel in the broadest part in square feet, and to divide by a certain co-efficient, which in vessels of a moderate sharpness is 502, if the speed be taken in knots, but if taken in miles, a different co-efficient must be employed. The result is the number of actual horses power, necessary to accomplish the speed required. In wide and shallow vessels, with a large rubbing surface, this rule will give too low a power, and in the case of a very long vessel, it appears necessary to adopt a rule which will take into account the displacement, rather than the sectional area, as the increase of friction due to increase of length will thus be brought into the calculation. These indications are fulfilled by the following rule :—Multiply the cube of the speed in knots, by the cube-root of the square of the displacement in tons, and divide by the co-efficient 167·3, the result is the number of actual horses power requisite to propel the vessel at the speed required. Now 15 statute miles an hour is 13 knots, or geographical miles, very nearly, and the displacement of a train, consisting of a steamer 220 feet long, 36 feet broad, and drawing 16 inches of water, of two barges, each 100 feet long, 36 feet wide, and drawing 12 inches of water, and of one stern barge 160 feet long and 36 wide, and drawing 12 inches of water, will be in all about 560 tons. Multiplying, therefore, the cube of 13 by the cube-root of 560 squared, and dividing the product by 167·3, we get 894, as the number of actual horses power requisite for the propulsion of such a train at a speed of 15 miles an hour. It is necessary to remark, that an *actual* horse power is a very different unit from a *nominal* horse power, and in some engines every nominal horse power will produce a mechanical effect equal to four actual horses power of 33,000 lbs. raised one foot high in a minute. A nominal horse power is a commercial unit; an actual horse power is a dynamical unit, and is therefore the measure which is properly employed in all dynamical enquiries. But as engines are always bought and sold, and popularly spoken of, in relation to the nominal power, and as 894 actual horses power appears to be a large power for a river steamer to possess, it is necessary to understand, that this power may be exerted by an engine of 225 nominal horses power, and that a train, impelled by from 250 to 300 horses power as commonly defined, will realize the speed required.

It will be useful to test these conclusions by the results of the experiments made by Colonel Beaufoy to ascertain the friction of bodies moving through water, and as nearly the whole resistance of the train is due to friction, we may, without any material inaccuracy, neglect minor sources of retardation. According to Beaufoy, the friction in lbs. per square foot upon a plank moving through the water in the manner of the bottom of a ship is ·014, with a velocity of 1 geographical mile an hour; when the velocity becomes 2 miles an hour the friction is ·0472; 3 miles an hour, ·0948; 4 miles an hour, ·155; 5 miles an hour, ·2264; 6 miles an hour, ·3086; 7 miles an hour, ·4002; 8 miles an hour, ·5008; and by extending the law to 13 geographical, or 15 statute, miles an hour, the friction per square foot would be about 1·2 lbs. The friction appears to increase as the 1·7th power of the velocity, but at high velocities the increase is not so great, and there is every reason to believe that the friction per square foot is less than 1·2 lbs. at a speed of 15 miles an hour. The rubbing surface of the train will be about 18,140 square feet, which multiplied by 1·2 gives 21,768 lbs. as the amount of resistance the vessel experiences when moving at a rate of 15 miles an hour, or 1320 feet per minute; and 21,768 multiplied by 1320 and divided by 33,000, gives us 870·72 as the number of actual horses power which is requisite to overcome the friction of the train at a speed of 15 miles an hour. But this is irrespective of the loss occasioned by the slip of the wheel, which, however, need not be considerable if the floats be of sufficient area, and also of the bow and stern resistance, which, however, from the small immersion of the train, will not be much, so that there appears very little doubt that an engine exerting somewhere between 800 and 900 actual horses power, when worked expansively, will propel the train at a speed of 15 miles an hour. Some of the locomotives on the Great Western Railway exert a greater amount of power than this—as much even as 973 actual horses power—and the weight of those locomotives, as given by Mr. Gooch, is 31 tons 1 cwt. The weight of the engine, therefore, need not occasion any apprehension.

The steamer and the whole of the barges are built of plate iron, and they are all so designed that if any of them was propped up at the ends, and loaded in the middle like a beam, it would bear, without breaking, twice the weight that it will ever be required to carry. This quality of extra strength is indispensable to vessels that will sometimes be getting aground, and the steamer is also strengthened between the paddle boxes, so as to enable the paddle-wheels to sustain a large part of the weight of the vessel without straining, when grounding takes place; the paddle-wheels being made of somewhat extra strength, and the rings being made with a wide bearing surface, like a carriage-wheel, to enable them partially to bear up the vessel without inconvenience. The weight of the hull of the steamer will be about 114 tons, and its displacement, with 16 inches draft of water, is 240 tons, leaving 126 tons of displacement available for carrying the weight of the machinery and the fuel. The weight of each of the cargo flats will be about 50 tons, while its displacement is 100 tons at 12 inches draft, leaving flotation sufficient to enable 50 tons of cargo to be carried. The weight of the last flat of the train will be about 80 tons, and its displacement about 120 tons; but the machinery for drawing back the train when it grounds, will, with the rudder, anchor, and other apparatus, weigh about 20 tons, leaving only 40 tons of displacement available for passengers, &c., in this compartment. The engines will be high-pressure engines, with the common locomotive pressure of 85 lbs. on the inch. High-pressure engines are commonly reckoned objectionable in steam vessels. In this case, however, the passengers are not placed in the same vessel as the engine, but are towed at some distance astern, with cargo barges intervening, so that there is no more danger to passengers under this arrangement than in the case of a locomotive attached to a railway train. There are two engines which are not connected with one another, but each engine turns its own paddle-wheel, so that by slowing one engine and quickening the other the train may be guided in any required direction. There is a rudder at the bow of the steamer, as well as at the stern of the last barge, and an apparatus is provided whereby each barge of the train can be made to assume any position with the rest that is thought desirable, and thus great facility in guiding the train will be obtained.

The cylinders are each 28 inches diameter and 8 feet stroke. The piston will make 30 strokes per minute, which gives a speed of piston of 480 feet in the minute. The steam will be cut off at $\frac{3}{8}$ths of the stroke. The pressure at the end of the stroke will therefore be 37·5 lbs., including the pressure of the atmosphere, for $85 + 15 = 100$ lbs. $\times \frac{3}{8} = 37{\cdot}5$ lbs. The efficiency of steam cut off at $\frac{3}{8}$ths of the stroke is increased 1·86 times, and $37{\cdot}5 \times 1{\cdot}86 = 70$ lbs., from which take 15 lbs. for the pressure of the atmosphere, and 10 lbs. for the resistance due to the blast-pipe in the chimney, and we have 45 lbs per square inch as the average effective pressure upon the pistons. Now a diameter of 28 inches gives an area of 615 square inches, which, multiplied by 45 lbs., the pressure per square inch, and by 480, the velocity of the piston in feet per minute, and divided by 33,000, gives 402 horses as the power exerted by each engine, or 804 as the power exerted by both. This power may at any time be nearly doubled by diminishing the amount of the expansion, so as to fill the cylinder throughout the stroke with steam of 85 lbs. pressure, but the consumption of steam, and consequently of fuel, will be increased in a larger proportion than the increase of power obtained. The quantity of water which will pass through each cylinder per minute, in the form of steam, is three cubic feet, so that the quantity of water evaporated by the boilers per hour will be 360 cubic feet; or say, with waste, 400 cubic feet. There will be two boilers resembling the wide gauge locomotive boilers, each with 2000 feet of heating surface, and weighing about 13 or 14 tons. This will give a total heating surface of 4000 square feet, or 10 square feet to evaporate a cubic foot of water in the hour. The cylinders will lie horizontally on the deck, and the pistons will act on the paddle-wheels in the same manner as the pistons act on the driving wheels in locomotive engines. The paddle wheels, like the driving wheels of locomotives, will be susceptible of some up-and-down motion, to accommodate which the cylinders will give a little more clearance to the piston at the ends than is common in marine engines. The paddle wheels will be 20 feet in diameter, and 15 feet 6 inches broad, and the floats will be 3 feet 6 inches deep, and will be arranged somewhat spirally on the wheel, to facilitate which disposition, and also for other ends, they will be formed of plate-iron. The circumference of the paddle wheels will project below the bottom of the vessel, both with the view of enabling an efficient grip of the water to be obtained, and to afford assistance in getting off or over shoals in the river. In nearly all cases in which shallows of hard sand are encountered, if there is any water at all in advance of the vessel, the paddles, by partly lifting up the vessel, and by partly forcing her forward like a sledge, will carry her over the shallow without stopping at all; and to aid this operation, a multiplying power can be thrown at any moment into gear with the periphery of the paddle wheel, whereby the tractive force applied to the vessel can be increased twelve fold. But for this resource the engines, being unconnected, might sometimes stand still at the end of the stroke when the vessel got aground, at which time there would no longer be any considerable momentum in the wheels or the vessel to carry the crank over the dead point, but by the multiplying gearing the paddle wheels will be compelled to move round, however slowly, and with such a grip of the bottom as these floats will assure, it will be impossible to move the wheels without carrying forward the vessel. And when it is borne in mind that steamers unprovided with any efficient apparatus have been forced over shoals in the Ganges, upon which there is three feet less water than the draft of the vessels, it is plain that there will be comparatively little difficulty in carrying over a vessel with which the deficiency of water can only amount to a few inches, and which has special provision for overcoming such impediments. In the majority of cases, however, in which the shallows consist of quicksand, or where they shelve very gradually, the vessel will not get aground at all, even where the depth of water upon the shoal is considerably less than the draft of the vessel. For the steamer being made with a canoe bow, and a rounding bottom, and the paddle wheels being set in advance of the lowest or deepest part of the bottom, they will in such cases scoop up in their revolution the light sand, so as to make a trench or channel through which the train will pass without touching the bottom of the river, as would otherwise be the case.

Such, then, is a rough outline of the arrangements under which it is proposed to navigate the rivers of India by steam trains, which will carry a large cargo, realize a high speed, and maintain that certainty and regularity of communication, which gives steam locomotion most of its value. It cannot be expected that I can here go into every detail, or meet every objection, but I have probably said enough to show that the undertaking, in all its material features, is susceptible of practical realization. In some of the Indian papers objections have occasionally been raised to the project, but those objections have, in every instance, arisen from a complete misconception of its nature. A late mail from India brought a report on the plan from the Committee of Natural and Physical Sciences at Bombay, and although this report, upon the whole, is drawn up with much intelligence, it falls, nevertheless, into several misapprehensions as to the actual features of the intended arrangement. It appears to be the impression of this committee, that the whole of the coal which is to be used upon the voyage from Calcutta to Delhi, must be put into the steamer when she starts from Calcutta, whereby a dead weight of 470 tons would have to be carried by the train, including the proposed 250 tons of cargo. But no steam vessel at present plying upon the Ganges takes on board sufficient coal at the commencement of the voyage to last to its termination, and I propose that coal should be taken on board, as a general rule, every day, which, with half an hour's delay at each of the stations, can readily be done. The frequency of coaling, however, would in all cases be regulated by the circumstances of the trade in which the vessel was employed, but in most cases a sufficiency of coal could, without inconvenience, be carried in the steamer herself, without sinking her beyond the prescribed draft of water, whereby the whole of the flats, or barges, would be available for the conveyance of passengers and cargo. The train I have just described

would carry only 140 tons, but to enable it to carry 250 tons, it is only necessary that two more barges should be added, and the engines would still be able to impel the extended train at a speed very little short of 15 miles an hour, merely by so adjusting them as to work with less expansion. The Bombay committee seems to be under the impression, moreover, that the barges of the train are set so far asunder, that every barge would have a separate bow and stern resistance of its own ; but it will be obvious, from what I have said, that no such disposition is intended. The barges are so jointed to one another, that there is only a very narrow space between them, and at the joint the plating of the sides and bottom of each barge so overlaps the plating of the barge succeeding it, that the water between the barges is carried as if in a tank, and cannot occasion any resistance to the train. Whatever may be the primary impression in regard to this undertaking, I believe it will be found, on more strict examination, that most of the objections which present themselves on a cursory survey, are either imaginary, or have been foreseen and provided against ; and I have the satisfaction of being able to say, that the most eminent engineers and shipbuilders in this country, as well as the most eminent engineers and naval officers connected with India, completely concur with me in opinion as to the feasibility of this project.[*] The grounds, however, for such a belief, which I have endeavoured in some measure to exhibit, will carry stronger convictions to all minds accustomed to the consideration of such questions than could be afforded by citations of authority, and in addressing this audience, I prefer to rest the question exclusively upon such innate proofs of efficiency as the arrangement may be considered to afford.

Supposing, then, the navigation of the rivers of India by steam in a rapid and efficient manner to be practically accomplishable, it may be worth enquiring what are the main benefits which would result from the innovation. Calcutta is at present more distant in point of time from Delhi than from London for all purposes of commercial intercourse ; and it is obvious that any cheap amelioration, which would reduce the journey from Calcutta to Delhi to 14 days, would be of the utmost importance to Bengal. But it is not merely upon this line of communication that an important advantage would be realized, for the benefit would be extended over the whole of India. The cotton fields of Berar, lying in the heart of the Deccan, 400 miles from a port of shipment, would pour their produce down the Godaveray to Madras, and down the Tapty to Bombay. The Indus would become the highway for the traffic of Affghanistan, Bokhara, and the whole of Central Asia ; which traffic, instead of being monopolised by Russia, in consequence of the facilities of transport, lent by the Caspian and the Volga, would find its natural entrepôt at Bombay. The land contiguous to navigable rivers throughout all India would come into cultivation as soon as a profitable market for its produce could be obtained ; and the revenue derived from the land-tax, and also from the customs, would thus be augmented. The diminution in the cost of transport would lessen the price of salt in the interior, whereby the government would derive the increase of revenue due to increased consumption, and at the same time a great boon would be granted to the people. Local famines would become impossible ; troops and stores would be transportable to any part of the country with economy and expedition, and marauders would be won to the pursuits of commerce. Indeed it may be asserted that the whole country would be quickened in its industry, and awakened in its intelligence by casting a net-work of great steamhighways over the surface of the country, such as the rivers, if opened

* Namely, Messrs. Boulton and Watt ; Miller, Ravenhill, and Co. ; John Penn and Son ; W. Fairbairn, Manchester . Summers, Day, and Baldock, Southampton ; Scott, Sinclair, and Co., Greenock : R. Steele and Co., Greenock : T. and J. White, Cowes ; General Macleod, late Chief Engineer of Bengal ; Colonel Dickenson, late Chief Engineer of Bombay ; Colonel Sim, ate Chief Engineer of Madras ; Admiral Sir C. Malcolm, late Commanding in India : Lieut. Wood, of the Indian Navy ; Capt. Woodley, of the Government Steam Service on the Ganges ; Mr. Childs, Bengal Pilot Service, and many other engineers, shipbuilders, and naval men of experience in the East.

up, would constitute ; and the revenues of the government would, at the same time, be increased, and its expenses be diminished, since the benefit of these highways would be acquired and maintained without any considerable expense.

The Mahanuddy, the Krisna, and the Nerbudda, may all be navigated throughout a considerable part of their length. The Gogra may be ascended to Oude, the Goomty to Lucknow, the Ganges to Gurmucktesir, the Chumbul to Kotah, and the Gunduck to the frontiers of Nepaul. The rivers of the Punjaub are all navigable up to the base of the lower range of the Himalaya. The Indus may be ascended by suitable vessels to a point considerably above Attock. At Attock the Cabool river falls into the Indus, and this river may be ascended by appropriate vessels as high as Jelalabad, thereby obviating the necessity of going through the Khyber Pass on the road from Jelalabad to Peshawur. From Jelalabad there are two routes into Central Asia—the one by way of Cabool and the Pass of Bamian to Balk, and the other by the way of the Panisheer river, and the Pass of Khawak to Koondooz upon the Oxus. The latter route is the best, but all intercourse through it is stopped by the lawless character of the people, and by their conflicts with the adjacent Syash Posh, who are reputed to be the descendants of the Greeks settled at Bactra or Balk, by Alexander the Great.

The Jhelum is navigable to Oin, on the borders of Cashmere ; the Chenaub to Aknur ; the Ravee to Lahore and Umritsir, and the Sutlej to Ropur, at which point a canal, 100 miles long, would join the Sutlej and Jumna, and convert India into an island. This situation was proposed for execution by Lord Ellenborough, but it was apprehended that the soil was too sandy to retain the water. This peculiarity of the soil, however, if it exists, instead of being an objection is in reality an advantage ; for, if the canal be made conical, with its wide end to the Sutlej, from whence the water is taken, the depth of the water, notwithstanding its partial percolation through the sand, would still be maintained, and the water which escaped would go to replenish the wells in the arid region of Hurreana, whereby great benefits to the people of that province would accrue. The friction of the water passing through the sand, and the pressure due to the head of water endeavouring to escape, will always determine the extent of the leakage in any such work ; and the leakage will progressively diminish as the filtering surface silts up, as must happen in all filters, where the water is sometimes turbid from floods.

The Helmund I find to be navigable for a considerable part of its length by vessels of the kind proposed, and it appears probable that this river ran at one time into the Indian ocean, through a channel which still remains, under the name of the Dustee river, and into which the waters, if desirable, could again be turned. The Euphrates also could be navigated by these vessels from Bir, near Aleppo, to its debouch in the Persian Gulf, and a new route to India could thus be obtained. In other parts of the world there are shallow rivers which it would be very desirable to navigate by steam in an efficient manner, but of these I will at present only mention the Niger, the effect of opening up which for commercial purposes, would probably be to repress the slave-trade to a considerable extent. Heretofore the shallowness of the water has made it necessary that any attempt to navigate this river should be made during the wet season, at which time the whole Delta is a pestiferous swamp, and great mortality in the crews of the steamers has consequently been occasioned ; but by steamers on the plan now proposed these African *sunderbunds* could be passed without inconvenience during the healthy season, when the water is low ; and there is every probability, that, with such aids, the river could be ascended to a point considerably higher than Timbuctoo. It would be impossible, however, to attempt any enumeration of the various cases in which steamers of this kind might be usefully employed ; but in all countries in which there are shallow, shifting, and unimproved rivers,

there may they be successfully introduced, provided only there are commodities which require to be conveyed.

INDIAN RAILWAYS AND INDIAN COTTON.

THE mail just arrived from India brings evidence of unanimity of the belief which obtains in that country, as to the utter worthlessness of the railways at present proposed for execution in Bengal and Bombay, and of the consequent impropriety of longer suffering those projects to drag out a wasteful and miserable existence. The *Friend of India* has some very pertinent remarks upon the subject, pointing out the insecurity of the guarantee offered to the shareholders ; but the *Friend of India* is in error when it supposes that the restriction of the Bengal railway to such a small fragment of the work as must render it an unprofitable speculation was the work of the Board of Control ; the fact being, that it is the work of the railway company itself. To make this clear, we shall recapitulate a few facts which we challenge any one to disprove.

The railway company, in the earlier stages of its career, shifted and wavered a good deal in its plans, and in its estimates of expense. But eventually it was considered that the line from Calcutta to Delhi, which it was reckoned advisable to make, would cost at least 15 millions. This, however, was a larger sum than the Board of Control would undertake to give interest upon, as a commencement of such novel undertakings in India ; but the Board of Control gave a guarantee upon three millions, which, it was shown by Mr. Bourne, would enable a line of railway to be carried from Calcutta to Mirzapore, under arrangements he had suggested. This would have been at least a reasonable undertaking ; but the sum guaranteed was reduced from three millions to one million, *on the requisition of the railway company itself ;* and the letter containing that requisition is given in full in a LETTER BY AN EAST INDIA MERCHANT, published a year or two ago, in support of the railways, and attributed to Sir G. Larpent. The reason why this reduced sum and reduced scheme was applied for by the railway company was, that they had no longer the number of shareholders necessary to the execution of the larger project ; for many of the original shareholders having failed to pay their calls, had their shares forfeited, and those forfeited shares were not subsequently taken up by the public. Hence the railway company cut down the project to their means, though it was deprived of worth and vitality by the mutilation. With three millions something might be done—with one million, nothing ; and the reduction of the capital to one million was the work of the railway company itself. Why, then, blame the Board of Control, except, indeed, for yielding too much to railway requisitions ? If they had not yielded, they would have been blamed ; and now, for having yielded, they are blamed by the very parties who would have blamed their recusancy. It signifies little, however, who or what the railway companies may presume to blame, for the real fault lies in their own incompetency and disingenuousness. Here they have marked out for themselves a ruinous scheme ; have deceived their own shareholders as to the real nature of the government assistance, and would now seek to deceive the public by laying upon the Board of Control the fault of the miscarriages which such manifest imbecility must ensure.

The Bombay railway does not stand in a much better position than the East Indian. The project at Bombay is to make a railway from Bombay to Callian, distant 35 miles, although there is at present excellent water communication between the two places. Before the line can be carried from Callian into the interior it has to ascend the Ghauts, a range of mountains rising nearly perpendicularly 2,000 feet ; and here the railway has not merely the steep gradient to encounter, but also nine miles of tunnel, through igneous rock. From the Ghauts the line would have to pass 350 miles into the interior before it reached Oomrowutty, the great cotton depôt, in the heart of Berar, where the cotton is collected for exportation ; and the charge which it is necessary to levy on the conveyance of merchandize, to enable the line to yield a return, is, according to the railway company, 2¾d. per ton, per mile. Mr. Bourne, however, by the aid of his steamers, can bring the cotton down the Godavery from Oomrowutty for ½ per ton, per mile, so that the main object which this so-called cotton railway is intended to accomplish will be achieved by cheaper and more expeditiously effected methods. A railway which has been proposed from Madras to Arcot offers better than either of the others; but Madras, unfortunately, is without a harbour; and perhaps, if the money were spent in common roads or tramways, a better result would be obtained. Madras possesses a peculiar iron stone, called *laterite*, in great abundance, of which tramways could be very cheaply and expeditiously formed. This substance, when in the quarry, is so soft that it may be cut like cheese, but when exposed to the air it assumes a vitrified appearance, and becomes as hard as iron. Numerous structures in the Madras territories are built of this unique material, and, in addition to its great hardness, is found to be totally unaffected by atmospheric influences. Here we have a kind of cast-iron suitable for tramways, ready formed by the hand of nature, by the proper use of which much benefit to the internal communications of the country will be effected. The cotton districts of the Madras presidency are situated on the Bombay side of the peninsula, in the neighbourhood of Coimbatore, and at the extreme south near Tinnevelly, so that a tramway from Madras to Arcot would not convey cotton in any quantities worth mention.

This, nevertheless, is a much better line than either of the others; but it may admit of a question whether Madras does not need a harbour much more than a railway; and certainly the absence of a harbour at the coast terminus of a line of internal communication is a serious disparagement. But upon these topics we need not dwell. It appears to be wholly impossible that Indian railways can rest upon their present basis, and the wrecks of past schemes must be cleared away so as to afford a fair and unencumbered field, before any course can be deliberately and decisively marked out, such as it would be advisable to pursue.

ON WORKING STEAM EXPANSIVELY.

SIR,—The advantage of employing the expansive force of steam in a steam-engine is a necessary consequence of ascertained physical laws; the question of economy attendant on the employment of steam in this manner having been long fully answered both theoretically and practically. Steam-engines are therefore now very generally constructed to carry out this principle to a certain extent, but for the most part only to such a limited degree, that the beneficial effects derivable from it are not fully developed, and they therefore do not receive that extent of appreciation which their merits and importance would otherwise command.

The extent to which expansion may be beneficially carried depends chiefly upon the pressure of the steam; for, to carry out the principle with steam of low pressure, the cylinder has to be increased in size, (in order to obtain a certain amount of power,) in proportion as the degree of expansion is increased, and the amount of friction in a large cylinder, and the resistance offered to an increased area of piston, by the uncondensed vapour in the condenser, constitute so large a deduction from the power as to leave the gain of a very unappreciable amount. In order, therefore, to employ steam in this way, so as to develope its advantages in the best manner, its tension or pressure should be increased in proportion to the degree of expansion intended to be carried out. There existed at one time a bias against the employment of high-pressure steam, and anything more than 2½ or 3 pounds pressure per square inch above the atmosphere was considered dangerous, but this prejudice is rapidly disappearing, as we find in many instances our river-steamers on the Thames using steam at from 20 lbs. to 30 lbs. pressure above the atmosphere; indeed in a judiciously-constructed boiler, adapted for the purpose and properly attended to, there is no more danger in generating steam at a reasonably high pressure, than in generating low-pressure steam in the boilers commonly used for that purpose.

The arrangement which is most generally adopted in rotative engines for carrying out the principle of expansion, is either by the addition of lap or cover to the common slide, worked by an eccentric motion, or by a cut-off valve placed in the passage between the boiler and the working-slide, and worked by a set of variable cams. A very cursory examination of the action of the slide-valve, worked by the common eccentric, is sufficient to show that the principle of expansion can only be carried out to a very limited extent by its use; for, as we increase the cover on the steam side of the valve, so as to cut off the steam behind the piston at an earlier period of the stroke, the exhausting port before the piston is shut proportionally sooner before it (the piston) has reached the end of the stroke; and at the same time the steam behind the piston begins to be exhausted earlier, and the pressure removed from the piston, before it has completed its travel, in proportion to the extent of cover thus given to the valve. On this account, the length of the stroke is as it were virtually diminished; and if the lap or cover given to the slide be of great extent, there will be a considerable loss of the effect of the steam; indeed, I do not consider that in this way the expansion principle can be carried out farther than cutting off at ⅔ths of the stroke with much advantage; that is, expanding the steam to 1½ its volume before expansion. There is a further disadvantage in using the slide-valve worked by an eccentric motion; viz., the wire-drawing of the steam to a certain extent; the gradual opening and shutting of the ports, not allowing the steam to follow up the piston with its full degree of elasticity, on account of the narrowing of the passages; and there is therefore a loss of mechanical effect, for the expansion involved in the steam is not availed of.

The other arrangement in general use in steam-engines working expansively, is a separate cut-off valve, placed between the boiler and the working-valve of the cylinder; but this also has its disadvantages, as it requires a separate, costly, and troublesome apparatus for working it; and, on account of not being placed close to the cylinder, the mechanical effect of the expansion of the steam in the spaces and passages between it and the valve is not fully given out to the piston.

It is therefore obvious, that, in order to take full advantage of the expansive force of the steam, means must be adopted of instantaneously opening and shutting the passages at the proper times, by valves placed as close as possible to the cylinder, and my expansion slide gear, described in your number for last March, will be found to accomplish this in the most satisfactory manner.

In order to show the advantages derivable from carrying out the principle of expansion, I have made the following calculations, which may not be uninteresting to your readers.

We will take as an example a steam-ship having a pair of engines, with cylinders 96 inches diameter and a stroke of 9 feet, making 15 strokes per minute. Suppose that the steam is cut off at ⅔ths of the stroke, by means of lap on the slide-valve, which is worked by a common eccentric; then, if the width of the port be 9 inches, the lap or cover on the steam side will be about 8¼ inches; and if the eduction side of the valve have no cover, the piston will be 7½ inches from the end of the stroke, when the exhausting port before it is shut, and the same distance from the end of the stroke, when the exhausting port behind it begins to open. If we take the initial pressure, that is, the pressure on the piston at the beginning of its stroke at 8 lbs. on the square inch above the atmosphere, (a working pressure now very generally used in sea-going steamers,) the engine would produce an indicator diagram about the same as that below, which is taken from a good engine working in every way under similar circumstances to what is here given.

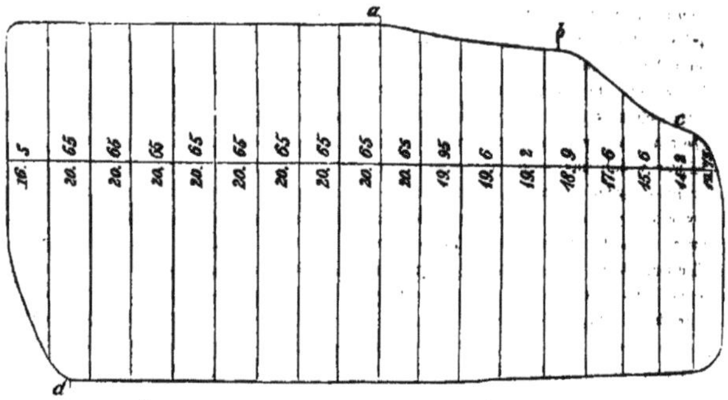

When we examine this diagram we find that when the piston has arrived at the point [a], the slide-valve has shut the port so far that the steam at full pressure cannot follow it up with the required velocity, and therefore it begins to be wire-drawn; which wire-drawing process continues until the piston has arrived at b, (which is one-fourth from the end of the stroke,) when the port is shut, and the expansive action of the steam begins. The steam now expands in the cylinder until the piston reaches the point c, (which in the case we have supposed is 7½ inches from the end of the stroke,) when the exhausting port behind it begins to open, and the pressure is consequently rapidly diminished during the remaining part of the stroke. The vacuum side of the diagram shows that when the piston has arrived at the point d, (7 inche from the end of the stroke in the example,) the exhausting port before it is shut, and the vapour in the cylinder is consequently compressed during the remaining part of the stroke.

From the measurement of this diagram we find the mean pressure on the piston throughout the stroke to be 18·886 lbs. on the square inch; and the mean vacuum 12·216 lbs. to the square inch. Although the initial pressure of the steam is 8 lbs., we will take it at the middle, between the points a and b, where it measures 7·3 lbs. to the square inch. Upon these data the following calculations are founded.

$$\frac{(96^2 \times \cdot7854) \times 18\cdot886 \times (9 \times 2 \times 15)}{33000} = 1118 \text{ H. P.} = \text{indicated horses}$$

power for one engine, or 2236 H. P. for both engines.

$$\frac{(96^2 \times \cdot7854) \times (81 \times 2 \times 15)}{1728} = 10178 \text{ cubic feet of steam per minute}$$

used for each engine, or 20356 cubic feet of steam for both engines. The proportion of steam required for filling the passages and spaces at the ends of the cylinder, &c., will vary with the degree of expansion at which the engines are worked; but at an average, we may take it at 5 per cent., which will make the quantity of steam used by the two engines, per minute, 21374 cubic feet. The volume of steam, at 7·3 lbs. pressure above the atmosphere, is 1174 times that of the water of which it is generated; therefore, $\frac{21374}{1174} = 18\cdot206$ cubic feet of water evaporated per minute; or 1092·36 cubic feet, or 68272·5 lbs. of water converted into steam per hour.

We may take the average evaporative power of coals used in long voyages, with well-constructed boilers, at 10 lbs. of water converted into steam with 1 lb. of coal; therefore, the quantity of coal used per hour in our case will be 6827 lbs., or 3·04 tons; and, if we suppose that in a voyage the steam is on an average used to its full power during 10 days, the quantity of coals consumed in that time will be 729·6 tons.

The following table shows the results that might be obtained from the same engines working to the same power, by using higher degrees of expansion than that which we have assumed in the foregoing calculations. In calculating this table, I have supposed that the steam is cut off by the working valve close to the cylinder; and that the induction and eduction passages are opened and shut instantaneously at the proper time. For the purpose of comparison, I have taken the vacuum the same as in the above calculation; viz., 12·216 lbs. per square inch, although there is no doubt that, from the greater attenuation of the steam, and the clear passage it has to the condenser by the instantaneous opening of the passages, it would be a pound or a pound and a half more than this. Five per cent. is allowed as before on the amount of steam used in the cylinder, for filling the passages and spaces at the ends of the cylinder; but no account is taken of this extra quantity of steam in the calculation of the mean pressure resulting from the expansive action of the steam, so that on this account the results (as far as economy is concerned) are rather below what they would actually be in practice. Although the mechanical effect of the steam of a given quantity of water increases as the temperature at which the steam is generated, yet the advantage thus gained is so very small, within the limits of temperature to which this table is applicable, that it may be set aside without any appreciable error, and I have accordingly left it out in the calculations. It will be seen that No. 1 in the table gives the particulars of the engines as calculated above, and accordingly may be used as a standard with which the other results may be compared.

Number.	Proportion of stroke made before the steam is cut off.	Volume after expansion, that before expansion being unity.	Initial pressure of the steam per square inch above the atmosphere required to allow this degree of expansion, and the engines to work to the same power as No. 1.	Pressure of the steam per square inch at the end of the stroke.	Volume of the steam compared to the volume of the water that has produced it.	lbs. of water required to be evaporated per hour.	Relative proportion of water evaporated, or fuel consumed, No. 1 being taken as unity.	Coals required for a voyage of 10 days' constant steaming.	Economy of fuel indicated in this manner, making No. 1, the standard of comparison.
			lbs.	*lbs.	lb.			tons.	p.cent.
1	¾	1·33	7·300	—	1174	68272	1·000	729·6	—
2	⅔	1·50	8·118	+0·495	1132	62941	0·921	674·3	7·54
3	4/7	1·75	9·277	−1·020	1094	55823	0·817	597·6	18·10
4	½	2·00	10·554	−2·098	1633	51929	0·760	556·3	23·73
5	3/7	2·33	12·354	−3·134	970	47219	0·691	506·0	30·69
6	⅓	3·00	15·864	−4·545	868	41042	0·601	439·7	39·64
7	¼	4·00	21·158	−5·778	749	35671	0·522	382·0	42·61
8	⅕	5·00	26·300	−6·540	664	32191	0·471	344·8	52·61
9	⅙	6·00	31·276	−7·079	598	29736	0·436	318·9	56·34
10	⅐	7·00	36·145	−7·480	545	28014	0·410	300·0	58·84
11	⅛	8·00	40·898	−7·794	503	26559	0·389	284·5	61·04

This table shows clearly the great benefit that would accrue to steam navigation from carrying out the principle of expansion to a much greater extent than what is at present practised; for, if we take the example No. 11, and compare it with No. 1, (which may be considered as a fair specimen of the generality of sea-going steamers as worked at present,) we find that in 10 days' steaming a saving of 445 tons of coals may be effected, the same power being exerted in propelling the vessel in both cases. In a steam-vessel adapted for a long voyage this saving would be of immense advantage, as there is not only the value of this quantity of fuel saved, but the space in the vessel which would be required to stow it would be available for cargo, and thus the carrying properties of the vessel would be greatly enhanced. It must be observed, however, that as the degree of expansion is increased, the strain upon the connections between the piston and the propeller is

---

* In this column the number marked with the sign + is the pressure above the atmosphere, and the other numbers with the sign −, show the number of lbs. per square inch below the atmosphere.

also increased on account of the initial pressure on the piston being greater, and these parts must be made stronger accordingly. Thus the whole initial pressure on the piston in No. 11 is fully 2½ times that in No. 1; the first being 40·898 + 12·216 = 53·114 lbs., and the other, 8 + 12·216 = 20·216 lbs.; so that the connexions would have to be made stronger in the one case than the other in this proportion. But if we take a more moderate degree of expansion, the increase of strain is but little; take for example, No. 6, where the steam is cut off, at ⅓rd of the stroke, we find the pressure is only 15·864 lbs. per square inch above the atmosphere, and the initial pressure on the piston is only about 1⅘ times that of No. 1, although the saving in 10 days' steaming is 290 tons of fuel, or about 40 per cent. of the whole. Hoping that these remarks may be found to be interesting and useful to your readers,

I am, &c. &c.

JOHN DUDGEON.

MR. STEWART IN REPLY TO MR. DUDGEON.

SIR,—If the connection between the two levers is the principal part of the contrivance, or, as Mr. John Dudgeon terms it, the substance of the invention alluded to, under the term of "Dudgeon's Expansion Gear," and all the rest follows as a matter of course, then is Mr. Dudgeon entitled to claim the invention. But, if the contrivance principally consists in the arrangement of the cams, the use of levers with rollers, and the combination of these with Messrs. Malcolmson's spiral grooves to bring the leaf out while the engine is running, and his be only one of the methods that have been adopted to press the rollers against the cam, (that duty having been otherwise performed by counterbalance weights, springs, and vacuum-pumps,) then I deny that Mr. Dudgeon has any right to the claim he makes. Let mechanical men decide. All I say in my letter, and repeat, is, that I claim to have first suggested this arrangement as a whole,—the combination of these contrivances into one practical expansion gear; a claim which I would be the first to relinquish if convinced that it was erroneous: for this arrangement I nowhere claim any merit whatever, never conceiving that I was entitled to any, but simply denying any to Mr. Dudgeon, beyond that attached to the subordinate invention of the cross connexion. The party who writes these letters, if he had read mine, must have seen this; but I am inclined to think that by putting such high-flown expressions into the mouths of these working-men, he has some latent wish to expose them to ridicule. No one of ordinary intelligence could suppose from my letter, that I now, in the year 1850, come forward to claim any part of the expansion gear erected in 1842, which I describe as an "established method for some years;" and, therefore, having nothing to do with the present claim, which is distinctly one of novelty. I simply claim the combination of this with the spiral grooves; a combination which I suggested and carried out, and of which circumstance no one is more perfectly aware than this same injured man, Mr. J. Dudgeon.

Mr. Dudgeon would have your readers believe that in planning some method of strengthening the gear on board Messrs. Malcolmson's vessels, he had made the sketches he sent to you before I saw the engines; all I can say is, that no two plans of gear, as applied to machines bearing the same name, could be more totally different, with the exception of Messrs. Malcolmson's invention of the spiral grooves, which appears in both. But for the false claim set up in Mr. Dudgeon's letter, I should not have come forward in the matter, having no desire for publicity, only studying these objects for my own gratification; and in no case should I have thought of publishing without the express leave of Messrs. Malcolmson. Mr. Dudgeon, in the second letter bearing his signature, states, that his friend explained to me what he misnames "his expansion gear," showing me its simplicity. I beg leave to say, that this is a pure invention on his part, as I was perfectly

acquainted with this gear almost ever since it was first erected in 1842; and having had it daily before my eyes for a period exceeding two years, I was not likely to need any explanation from one who was probably less acquainted with it than myself. No less false is it that Mr. John Dudgeon did me the favour to show me the expansion gear on board Messrs. Malcolmson's vessel, and explain to me this or any other gear; *he was not on board the vessel at all*, and I was permitted to see the engines through the kindness of the engineer in charge. Leaving this matter, I pass on to say that my improvement consists in a method of obtaining motion ahead or astern, not by cams, as at present, shifting their position, but by a cam keyed fast on the shaft, retaining the leaf to alter the degree of expansion; thus doing away with stops, and their concomitant ill effects at high speeds: your readers will be aware that at present the whole arrangement of cams must, like the single eccentric, shift bodily on the shaft from one stop to the other. I am not aware that my plan has been before suggested, and notwithstanding the attempts at wit from Liverpool, and the sneers at that education of which these individuals can know nothing, I renew my offer, if you think the plan interesting, to send you the drawing and description, but I have no wish whatever on my own part to bring it forward in print. I have made the whole thing self-acting, by means of a governor, and have applied it with good effect to an engine with a short quick stroke and heavy fly-wheel, as suggested by your correspondent "J. B."

To conclude the subject: the talented gentleman who invented and brought out the double cams and rollers, has himself assured me that Mr. John Dudgeon had no other connection with the arrangement whatever, except having suggested the junction of the two levers by a rod, and having been employed, with Mr. John Beattie and several others, in a subordinate capacity as fitters in the erection of the gear. The confirmation of Mr. Dudgeon's statement, apparently arising from an indifferent source, is rather weakened by the fact, that being shop-mates together, one might easily show the other the drawing of the gear in question, as the whole of it in the shape of working-drawings would be daily before their eyes, and they would be required to work to them most accurately. On the strength of this one suggestion, of connecting the two levers, instead of showing gratitude to the employer in whose service he learnt what little he knows on the subject of cams, Mr. Dudgeon has the presumption to claim the whole arrangement of cams and rollers, the work of a much better man's brains, and to go about boasting, that *his* cams are fitted to steam-frigates. It may be a thriving trade to go prying about, snapping up other people's ideas, and hastily pushing them into print, but it will always be subject to the inconvenience of exposure.

C. P. STEWART.

NEW BRINE VALVE,

AS USED IN THE BOILERS OF THE ROYAL WEST INDIA MAIL PACKET COMPANY'S STEAM SHIPS.

THIS invention consists of a self-acting valve to discharge the saturated water from boilers using salt water, without incurring the risk of blowing off when the water in the boiler is deficient in quantity, at the same time affording a ready means of regulating the blowing off to any desired amount.

This is effected by connecting the brine valve with the feed valve, so that no water is blown off from, unless a corresponding quantity enters, the boiler.

Fig. 1 is a section of the feed and brine valves, with their connections, bolted in front of the boiler, and fig. 2 a plan of the same. The water delivered by the feed pump entering the feed cock at *e* raises the valve *g*, and with it the lever *h* and the brine valve *i*, which allows a certain quantity to be discharged, in proportion to the quantity entering the

20

boiler; the valves will then close by the pressure within the boiler until the return stroke of the pump. The brine from the boiler enters the valve chest at *o*, and is discharged at *p* into a refrigerator, or overboard.

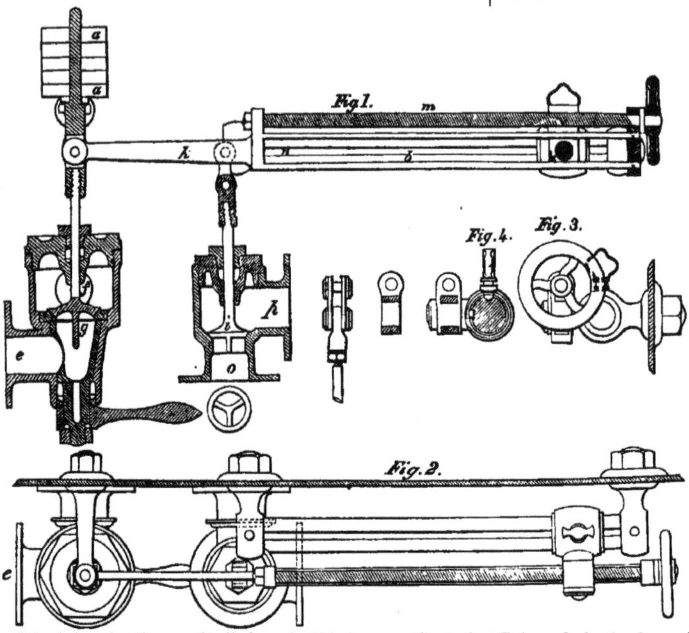

Fig. 1.

Fig. 4.

Fig. 3.

Fig. 2.

It is obvious that the quantity discharged will be in proportion to the respective lifts of the two valves; to regulate this, the lever *h* works on a stud at *k*. This stud is made to move on a shaft *b*, by the screw *m*, to any point on the screw, and the relative lengths of the lever are thus changed, and the lift of the valves made comparatively more or less. The stud is held in position on the shaft *b* by a set screw, which slides in the groove *n*. The valve *g* is loaded with weights, *a a*, equal to the pressure in the boiler, in order to keep the valve *i* closed.

Fig. 3 is an end view, and fig. 4 a cross section at the stud *k*, showing a section of the lever *h* and the shaft *b*.

BARRANS' PATENT RAILWAY AXLES AND BOXES.

THE disadvantages attendant upon the present system of constructing railway axle-boxes, both for the engines and carriages, are well known. The most prominent of these are, the rapid lateral wear of the brasses, which produces oscillation of the engine or carriage, which, in its turn, aggravates the primary evil, and necessitates a frequent renewal of the brasses before they are fairly worn through, or at least, requires that they should be filled in with a softer metal; the carriage, in both of these operations, having to be lifted and thrown out of use for the time. There is, also, a considerable waste of grease with the ordinary axle-boxes, as after being once melted, it is allowed to run away through the bottom of the box; although it may be presumed that it has not become deteriorated in quality, as it has been deprived by evaporation of part of the water it originally contained.

To remove these difficulties, Mr. Barrans proposes, first, to provide an end-bearing piece for each end of the axle, which may be readily adjusted, by which the side oscillation will be reduced to a minimum.

By this means the wear and tear of the whole carriage will be diminished, the comfort of the passengers will be materially increased, and there will be less tendency for the carriages to get off the rails at high speeds. The benefits to be derived will not end here. The rail will also be kept better in gauge, the expense of lifting the carriages will be avoided, and less load will be thrown on the engine, thereby increasing its propelling power.

A reference to the plate will explain how these improvements are proposed to be applied.

Figs. 1 and 2 represent a section and an elevation of the axle-box, in which A is the axle, the end of which is faced with steel; B is an end-bearing piece, let into an hexagonal hole in the end of the socket H, and which being set up by the wedge C to any desired distance from the end of the shaft, will prevent all excess of end-way motion. The wedge is moved by the nut D; E is a set screw which jams the wedge when it is set, and prevents it working loose.

Figs. 3 and 4 show another modification in which the end collar of the shaft is dispensed with. In this case the end-bearing piece B is brought up to the end of the axle A, by means of the screw C, which is secured by the jam nut D and the set screw E, the point of the latter entering a groove cut in the thread.

Figs. 7 and 8 represent another modification, in which the end-bearing piece B is made in the form of a wedge, and is moved by the screw C, and jammed in its place by the set screw E. In all these arrangements the ends of the axles are lubricated by means of the oil-holes O, O, O. The necessary clearance between the bearing pieces B and the ends of the axles, is ascertained by means of a gauge passed through the oil-holes O, O, O.

Figs. 5 and 6 show the method of applying the invention to the existing axle-boxes. In this case, the bearing-piece is formed of a hoop, B, which is brought up against the axle-box by means of the nut D, which bears against the boss of the wheel. This nut is prevented from turning by the guard E, which is attached to the boss of the wheel by the pin F. The hoop is prevented from turning on the axle by means of a key let into both.

The second part of Mr. Barrans' invention consists in applying the boxes H H for the purpose of preventing the waste of grease. These boxes slide into the lower part of the axle-box, and are retained in position by the springs K K. The grease, which would otherwise be wasted, is caught in these boxes, and used over again, until it has lost its lubricating qualities.

The third part consists in a method of preventing the grit and dust set in motion by the wheels, from getting into the axle-boxes. This is effected by a shield, S, fig. 3, attached to the axle-box. A similar shield T, is attached to the axle, and revolves with it, and the flanges of these shields, interlocking with each other, will, it is presumed, offer sufficient impediment to the dust, which would otherwise find its way into the axle-box. The advantage of this is sufficiently obvious.

One of the axle-boxes lies at our office for the inspection of any of our readers.

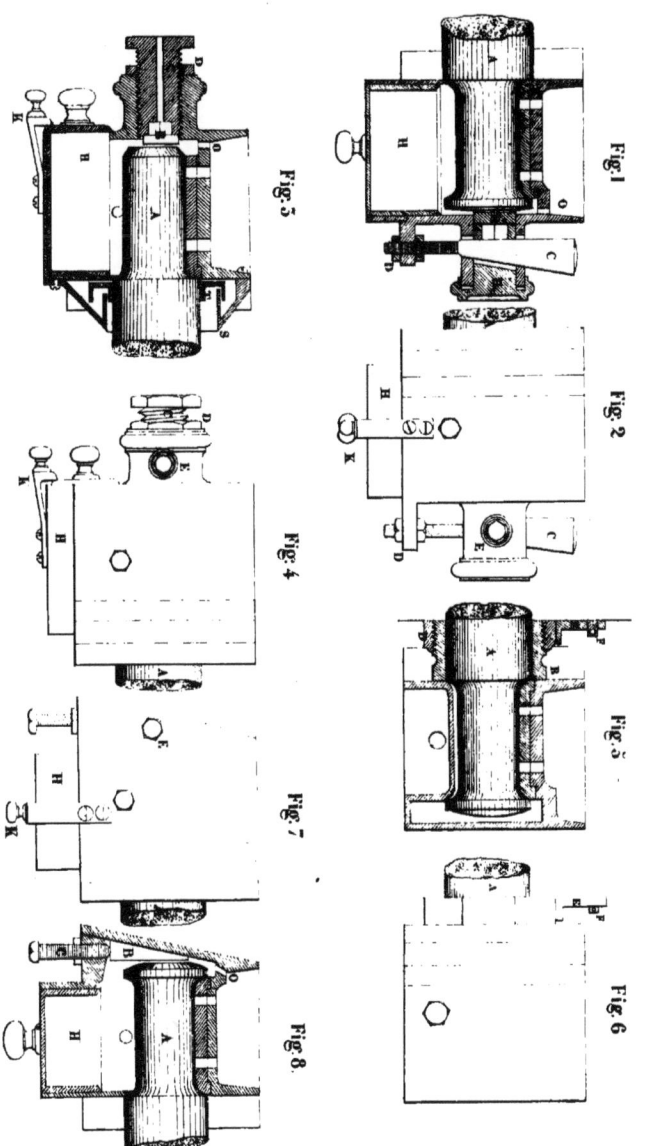

BARRANS'S PATENT RAILWAY AXLES & AXLE BOXES.

Fig.1

Fig.2

Fig.3

Fig.4

Fig.5

Fig.6

Fig.7

Fig.8

Artisan. 1850.

ANALYSIS OF THE STEAM ENGINE.

(Continued from p. 125.)

THE CRANK.—The strain upon the web of the crank depends partly on the length of the crank-pin; but we may take its thickness on an average at half the width of the boss, or 3¼ inches. The width of the web may be taken at ¾ of the diameter of each boss.

Although not strictly in place, we here insert a letter from a Correspondent:

"In the May Number, page 99, you give a rule for calculating the size of the crank-shaft. Is that for a condensing or a non-condensing engine? as the crank-shaft of non-condensing engines would require to be made so much stronger for the same sized cylinder of a condensing engine. Mention how each may be calculated; and how much larger it must be, if made of cast-iron; if of the latter material, which would be best, solid or hollow."

If our Correspondent will turn to our first article on the subject, he will find it expressly stated that the rules were intended to apply solely to condensing engines, using steam not exceeding 10 lbs. pressure per square inch. If a higher pressure be used, the diameter of the cylinder may be diminished, to give an equal power, whilst the sizes of the other parts will remain the same. Thus, with 10 lbs. steam, and 12 lbs. vacuum, = 22 lbs. per square inch, 23·5 square inches of piston is estimated at a horse power; and as 10 inches per horse power is the usual measure for high-pressure engines, it is evident that the pressure must be increased in the proportion of 23·5 to 10. Then, 10 : 23·5 : : 22 : 51·7 lbs. pressure above the atmosphere, being that required for the high-pressure non-condensing engine. Or, to reverse the case: if it is required to find what diameter of cylinder is necessary for a high-pressure engine, multiply the horse power by 10, and find the diameter of a circle with that area in inches. Thus, $30 \times 10 = 300$ inches area, the diameter equal to which is 19½ inches nearly. We shall give specific rules for engines of this class in a future Number.

With reference to cast-iron, it is used on the score of economy for large shafts; but requires to be made somewhat larger than for wrought-iron. Taking a rule of similar construction to that given at p. 99, we have,

To find the diameter of the crank-shaft when of cast-iron.—Multiply the square of the diameter of the cylinder in inches, by the length of the crank in inches; extract the cube-root of the product, and divide it by ·375.

Thus, the diameter of the cylinder, 30 inches, squared = 900, which multiplied by the length of the crank in inches, 30, = 2700; the cube-root of which is 30 and $\frac{30}{\cdot 375} = 8$ inches, the proper diameter of the shaft.

Hollow shafts are only used in cases of large diameters. When it is desired to save weight, as in marine engines, *solid* wrought-iron shafts are employed, although hollow shafts have been used for railway axles; but this is rather an exceptional case.

THE ECCENTRIC AND ROD.—Having fixed the diameter of the crank shaft, and the stroke of the slide, when discussing its proportions, we may design the eccentric; not that any particular proportion of stroke between them is absolutely necessary, because any desired proportion can be obtained by varying the lengths of the levers on the weigh shaft, when there is one, but it is usual to make them of equal stroke, which in this case is 8 inches.

The eye of the eccentric must be of such a diameter as to admit of its being passed over the collar of the shaft, which is here fixed at 8½ inches, allowing half-an-inch of a side collar on the bearing. The shaft being supposed to be swelled at the seat of the fly-wheel, it is evident that the eccentric must be put on the shaft before the crank; and should any accident afterwards occur to it, a new one must be put on in halves, bolted together.

Having set out the diameter of the eye, 8½ inches, fix the thickness of the metal round it, say 1½ inches. The work which the eccentric has to perform varies so much with different engines, that it is difficult to lay down any precise rules for it. With unpacked slides, an approximate estimate of the friction may be made, but when packing is employed, everything must depend upon the workmanship, and the attention paid to the packing. The weight of the eccentric is so insignificant, that it is usually made strong enough for any circumstances. From the centre of the eye, set out half the intended stroke, viz. 4 inches, and from that centre, with a radius of half the stroke, + half diameter of boss, + the thickness of the boss, (4 + 4¼ + 1½) = 9¾, describe the outer diameter of the eccentric, viz., 19½ inches. The thickness of metal of the outer ring is ¾ inch, and the flanges are ¼ inch deep. The boss and the outer ring are connected together by feathers ¾ inch thick, as shown. In large eccentrics, two or more ribs are used, but in one of this size, one seems sufficient; the additional thickness at the junction points out the proper place for the key.

A variety of plans are in use for the rod and its connection with the strap, depending upon the purposes to which it is to be applied. The one we have shown seems well suited for a long rod in a land or marine engine, the tie-rods serving materially to prevent its springing, (a very common defect,) whilst the strain is more equally distributed than if the rod were attached to the lugs only of the eccentric strap. The ordinary design of two bars, filled in with diagonal stay pieces, is both heavy and expensive, none of the work being turned, as is done in the case before us.

As we have not fixed the length of the rod, we cannot state the exact proportion of the length of the tie-rods; but about two-thirds of the total length of the rod will be about the thing. The ends are secured by a bolt passing through them and the centre rod. The dove-tailing of them together is not always practised, but it makes the best job, especially in a large rod. The eccentric gab-pin is shown 2 ins. × 2 ins. which is rather larger than usual, but it is advisable to give it surface to avoid the wear, which always gives trouble. The nose of the rod ought to be made of such a length that it can never fall past the pin when they are at the reverse extremities of their stroke.

The strap is supposed to be made of brass, in deference to ancient example, although we should not object to put cast iron. The two metals wear very well in numerous other instances, and we know no reason why they should not in this. The strap is shown thicker at the centres than at the lugs, to withstand the increased strain. If made of these dimensions of cast-iron, it would be advisable to add a rib on each half, tapering from 1¼ inch at the centre to nothing at the lugs.

The width of the strap is also above the ordinary proportions; 2 inches in width would represent them better; in that case the boss for the centre rod must be made elliptical, and the key way cut obliquely, so as to clear the feather. The width of the boss may be taken at half its internal diameter, or say 4¼ inches.

To be continued.

INDICATOR DIAGRAMS FROM ENGINES OF THE "SABRINA," AND "PREUSSISCHER ADLER."

THE diagram from the *Sabrina's* engine, (S) is of very good form, the expansion-cam working on the third grade. Revolutions per minute, 18¼. The vacuum ought to be much better, however, especially with so much expansion. That of the *Preussischer Adler's* shows a better vacuum, and a very large effective power. The rounding of the diagram, at the end of the steam induction is bad, indicating a wire-drawing of the steam. Engines making 19½ revolutions per minute. (For dimensions of engines and vessel, see p. 55.) When engines are short of steam, and the throttle-valve has to be kept partially shut, to keep up the pressure in the boilers, the steam, of course, is wire-drawn. Say, that the valves are loaded to 10 lbs., and that by throttling, only

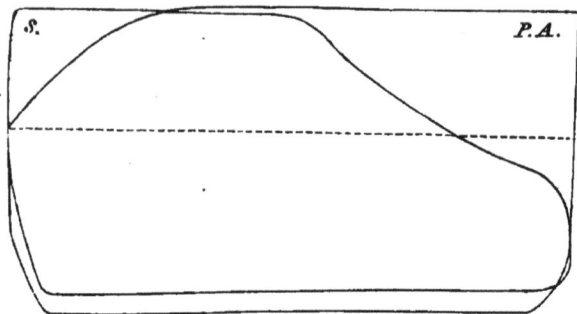

S.   *P.A.*

Scale $\frac{1}{16}$ inch = 1 lb.

7 lbs. is got in the cylinder; then the valve ought to be altered, so as to cut the steam off sooner, to such an extent as will admit of full pressure being got in the cylinder for a portion of the stroke; that is to say, make the boiler produce a smaller quantity of steam, but at a higher pressure. With the same expenditure of fuel this will produce a better effect in the engines.

LOWE'S PATENT STENCH TRAPS.

The absurdity of making our dwelling-houses the receivers of the pestilential gases distilled from sewers and cesspools, seems at length admitted even by the most pig-headed antisanitarian. It is easier, however, to admit the fact, than to provide a remedy. Numerous schemes have been tried, but we have met with none so efficient and so economical as Lowe's Patent Traps, figured in our sketch. It will be

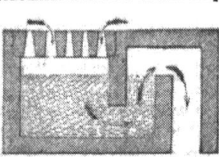

seen that the water they contain acts as a seal to prevent the return of the effluvia from the drain, whilst at the same time it catches the sediment, which would otherwise find its way into the pipe. This is an important point in connexion with the use of the tubular drains. A 3-inch pipe may be a very nice thing to drain a row of houses with, *as long as it is kept free*, but we do not see how this is to be accomplished without a sediment-trap. On a recent visit to Manchester, we found these traps in extensive use, and we observed some, a few days since, being laid down in

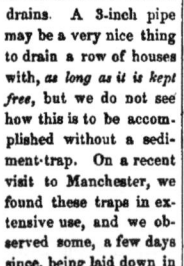

Whitechapel; a pretty severe test. They require, of course, to be periodically emptied; but the value of the manure will probably pay for the trouble.

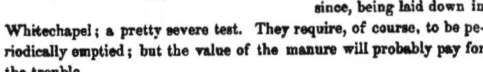

NOTES BY A PRACTICAL CHEMIST.

DISADVANTAGES OF BLACK PAINTS AND DYES.—The choice of colours is usually deemed a matter on which taste or fashion are the only authorities, and many self-styled practical men would smile at the idea of one hue being more advantageous than another, further than might follow from the price of the materials. Yet such is actually the case,

and it happens, moreover, unfortunately, that black, the favourite colour in this country, has, of all others, the lowest claims to utility. Every beginner in physical science must know, that objects with a black surface radiate more freely than those of any other colour; that is, they acquire more rapidly the temperature of surrounding objects, whether this may have been originally higher or lower than their own. This may be shown by a very simple experiment. Take two tin vessels of equal size and shape; blacken one of them in the flame of a candle; then fill both with boiling water, and expose them to the air on a frosty day. The water in the blackened vessel will be found to have reached the temperature of the atmosphere much sooner than that in the other. Or, if we fill the two with cold water, and expose them to the heat of a fire, or to the rays of the sun, the black one will rise the more rapidly in temperature. From these facts it is plain that black garments are hotter in summer, and colder in winter than those of any other colour. But further, every object when heated, expands, and contracts again on cooling. Now, as black substances are liable to more frequent and rapid alterations of temperature, they suffer of course a greater amount of alternate expansion and contraction. Hence their texture is speedily injured, and they fall into decay. And this, be it remembered, is no mere theoretical deduction. It has been found at the dock-yards that the black timbers of ships need renewal much more frequently than the portions painted white, though formed of the same material, and exposed to an equal chance of outward injury. Hence we see the impolicy of using black paint for ships, carriages, doors, outhouses, awnings, and other articles of wood or cloth that are liable to be exposed to the action of the sun. Light brilliant colours, which radiate badly, will be found much more economical, even though the original price be somewhat greater. A praiseworthy attempt to overcome popular prejudice has been made by an eminent firm of shipowners, in London, who have their vessels painted white and wainscot colour, but we believe they stand almost alone in the innovation.

Black substances have besides another more occult, though not less dangerous property; that is, the great facility with which they absorb, and retain infectious and unpleasant gases or vapours. Take a number of bits of cloth of different colours, and fix them over an untrapped sewer, or in any other situation where they may be exposed to offensive effluvia. It will be found that black cloth will absorb the foul odour most strongly, and retain it the most permanently. How absurd then, not to say criminal, is the fashion which compels the medical man and the clergyman, whose avocations so frequently lead them into the midst of infection, to array themselves in this poison-imbibing hue! The scarcity of black colouring-matters might give us a significant warning! Nature loves it not, and does not willingly put it in our hands.

ARTIFICIAL FIRE-CLAY.—The fusibility of common clay arises from the presence of impurities, such as lime, iron, and magnesia. These substances may be easily removed by steeping the clay in hot muriatic acid, then washing with water and drying. Excellent crucibles may be made from common clay prepared in this manner.

OXIDE OF ANTIMONY.—Mix in an iron vessel 15 parts black sulphuret of antimony finely ground, and apply heat, stirring from time to time, as long as sulphurous acid gas is developed. Wash away any superfluous sulphuric acid with water. Decompose the sulphate of antimony thus formed with carbonate of soda, and wash the oxide carefully. This process is considerably more economical than the one in common use.

METALLIC CONSTITUENTS OF HUMAN BLOOD.—According to the analysis of Millon, the amount of lead in the calcined ash of human blood is from 1 to 5 per cent.; that of copper, 0·5 to 2·5; and that of manganese, 10 to 24.

Anhydrous Nitric Acid.—Last year M. Déville succeeded in preparing anhydrous nitric acid by the action of dry chlorine upon nitrate of silver at elevated temperatures. In the "Journal de Pharmacie," for April, he has furnished some additional particulars. The acid is crystalline, forming right rhombic prisms, fusible at 84°—86° F. The liquid acid boils at 118°—122°, with partial decomposition. What gives particular importance to this discovery is the light it is likely to throw upon the hydrogen theory of acids. If Deville's acid, like the dry sulphuric acid, be unable to play the part of an acid until it has met with the elements of water, that hypothesis will receive great confirmation. It is to be hoped that this interesting question may soon be fully investigated.

An Improvement in Lightning Rods.—In fitting up lightning conductors, difficulty is sometimes felt in establishing a good and sufficient connexion with the ground. This is particularly the case in buildings containing large masses of metal, or substances liable to be ignited by the lateral effects of a powerful flash whilst passing down the rods. Many persons, from the damage resulting from a faulty or insufficient system, have been led to condemn conductors as altogether useless. Much of this difficulty might be avoided, by taking advantage of the fact, that an electric charge, traversing a conducting body, gives off a lateral discharge, and is consequently weakened at every roughness or projection upon the surface. Suppose the receiving-rod rise 10 feet above the chimney of a house, and that a horizontal bar run along the ridging, from which connexion with the ground is made in the usual manner. Let then the upper sides of the ridging-rod, and all sides of the receiving-piece be studded with sharp wires about an inch in length. By this means the power of the whole apparatus for gradually and silently discharging a storm-cloud would be greatly increased, whilst, if a flash actually struck the rod, the greater part of the fluid would be instantly scattered in the atmosphere, and the amount requiring to be carried down to the ground rendered comparatively trifling.—S.

ANALYSIS OF BOOKS.

PRACTICAL HYDRAULICS.

Hydraulic Tables, to aid the Calculation of Water and Mill Power, &c. By Nathaniel Beardmore, C.E. London: Waterlow & Sons, 1850.

Every contribution to engineering literature by a practical engineer carries a presumption in its favour, and this work of Mr. Breadmore's does not constitute an exception to this tolerant canon, for it certainly has a practical air about it, which commends it to acceptation in preference to the scientific imbecilities of most of the analogous productions which have appeared in this country. Nevertheless, we cannot say that we by any means concur in all Mr. Beardmore's dicta, and we think his work would have been much more satisfactory if he had more frequently cited his authorities. Every rule must rest either upon theory or upon experiment, and in a collection of tables based confessedly upon experimental researches, the persons by whom the experiments were made, and the circumstances under which they were conducted should be recounted, if it is expected that engineers are to take the computed results as materials for practice. In some cases, no doubt, Mr. Beardmore states his rule, and the reason for it, but in other cases he does not, and the results given differ sometimes from the results given by the most eminent authorities. As an example of this fault we may instance Table 7, and its accompanying explanatory paragraph, which we shall here insert:—

TABLE OF NOMINAL HORSE POWER, FOR ONE FOOT OF FALL, With the different Effective Values as applied to Undershot, Breast and Overshot Wheels and to the Turbine.

Rule.—Add together the numbers, from the column applicable to the case, opposite the several amounts of cubic feet making up the estimated run of the stream, and multiply the sums by the number of feet of fall; the result is the H. power of the mill.

Note.—An ordinary mill will grind about one bushel per horse power per hour—a very good one 1·2 bushels—therefore multiply the tabular numbers by 1 or 1·2 (according to the case), and by the number of hours worked, for the bushels ground per diem.

Discharge of Stream per Minute.	Nominal Horse Power.	Undershot Wheel. Effective H. Power.	Breast Wheel. Effective H. Power.	Overshot Wheel. Effective H. Power.	Turbine. Effective H. Power.
Cubic Feet.					
5	.0095	.0033	.0052	.00615	.0071
10	.019	.0066	.016	.012	.0142
15	.028	.0099	.015	.018	.021
20	.038	.013	.020	.024	.028
25	.048	.016	.026	.031	.035
30	.057	.020	.031	.037	.042
35	.066	.023	.036	.043	.050
40	.076	.026	.041	.049	.057
45	.085	.030	.046	.055	.064
50	.095	.033	.052	.061	.071
55	.104	.036	.057	.068	.078
60	.114	.040	.062	.074	.085
65	.124	.043	.067	.080	.092
70	.133	.046	.072	.086	.099
75	.142	.050	.078	.092	.106
80	.152	.053	.083	.098	.113
85	.161	.056	.088	.104	.121
90	.171	.059	.093	.111	.128
95	.180	.063	.098	.117	.135
100	.190	.066	.104	.123	.142
200	.380	.130	.208	.246	.284
300	.570	.200	.312	.369	.426
400	.760	.260	.416	.492	.568
500	.950	.330	.520	.615	.710
600	1.140	.400	.624	.738	.852
700	1.330	.460	.728	.861	.994
800	1.520	.530	.832	.964	1.136
900	1.710	.590	.936	1.107	1.278
1,000	1.900	.660	1.040	1.230	1.420
2,000	3.800	1.300	2.080	2.460	2.846
3,000	5.700	2.000	3.120	3.690	4.260
4,000	7.600	2.600	4.160	4.920	5.680
5,000	9.500	3.300	5.200	6.150	7.160
6,000	11.400	4.000	6.240	7.380	8.520
7,000	13.300	4.600	7.280	8.610	9.940
8,000	15.200	5.300	[8.320	9.840	11.360
9,000	17.100	5.950	9.360	11.070	12.780
10.000	19.000	6.600	10.400	12.300	14.200

This table gives the nominal value in horse power for 1 foot of fall of streams, discharging from 5 to 10,000 cubic feet per minute; i. e., the weight in pounds of the given number of cubic feet, per minute, divided by the constant 33,000. The effective value of the ordinary applications of water is given according to the best authorities. In estimating the value of a given quantity and fall of water, the mode of application and therefore the commercial effect will vary considerably ; for in low falls, under-shot or breast wheels must be used, which are far more wasteful of water than over-shot wheels (in proportion to the power developed), especially when loaded with tail-water."

Now numerous experiments have been made upon the efficacy of water wheels, of different kinds, by Smeaton, Poncelet, Morin, and others ; but Mr. Beardmore does not condescend to say whose results he adopts, or on what ground his selection has proceeded. Smeaton makes the power obtained from an overshot water-wheel 74 per cent. of the theoretical power ; D'Aubuisson, 76 per cent. ; Weisbach, 78 per cent. ; and in various large wheels, constructed by Rennie and others, the efficiency has been found to be fully 80 per cent. The efficiency of high-breast wheels is nearly as great as that of over-shot wheels, having been found by Morin to be fully 69 per cent. In some exceptional cases, the efficiency of breast wheels has risen as high as 80 per cent. Morin, in his experiments upon turbines, found the efficiency to vary from 69 to 75 per cent., so that turbines and breast wheels appear to be about equal in efficiency, and both are somewhat inferior in efficiency to the overshot wheel. This does not tally with Mr. Beardmore's table, in which it will be remarked that the turbine is set down as the most effective, and yet no authority is adduced for this hypothesis. It will be seen, moreover, that Mr. Beardmore misapprehends the nature of a *nominal* horse power, which is a conventional unit, and not a scientific one, and it is not therefore to be confounded with *theoretical* horse power, which it is Mr. Beardmore's design to indicate. Nominal power is a term only applicable to a machine, and it indicates merely such dimensions of the machine as to be commonly rateable at a certain power; whereas the power due to the gravity and head of a given quantity of water is the theoretical power of the water in an absolute sense, and should be so distinguished.

Table 1 gives the discharge from sluices, reservoirs, and vertical pipes under different heads, and with different forms of the discharging orifice; table 2 gives the discharge over weirs; table 3 gives the velocities of rivers; table 4 gives the velocities of new cuts and arterial drains; table 5 gives the discharge of pipes and culverts; table 6 gives the friction of bends, and table 7 is the table we have extracted. Table 8 is a table of antiquated proportions of steam engines, from Tredgold; table 9 gives the pressure exerted by columns of mercury and of water, and table 10 gives the weight and strength of pipes. Then there are tables showing the quantity of rain that falls in different districts, tables of weights and measure; the weight of materials, areas of circles, powers and roots, logarithms, and other stereotyped things of that character. There is not much originality or talent displayed in the work, and perhaps there is no opportunity for making such qualifications manifest in a work of this character, which is confessedly a compilation. But as an example of systematized information, these tables are creditable and useful, though the utility would have been increased, because more confidence would have been commanded, if the authorities had been more generally given. Mr. Beardmore knows very well himself where he got these results, and *he* may feel warranted in reposing confidence in them; but it is a propensity of practical men to look to the foundations, and no work dealing in facts will be esteemed of practical value (except as containing suggestions) which is destitute of the credentials which a recital of the circumstances of any accepted experiment can alone afford.

Royal Agricultural Society's Prize Model Cottages. London, DEAN & SON.

WE have the detailed plans, specifications and estimates for a pair of cottages for agricultural labourers, for the design of which Mr. Goddard, Architect, received the first prize from the Royal Agricultural Society. The social condition of our agricultural population is far from being the Arcadian one, that we have been too long imagining it. The Rev. S. G. Osborne's well-directed efforts, seconded by the press, have brought to light a state of things which demand instant redress. The problem to be solved is not an easy one. The cottage must be cheap and good. The cottages are built in pairs, but have separate entrances, the only convenience which is common to both, is the pump. The rooms are designed so as to afford no facility for " letting off." The ground-floor of each consists of a living-room, 11 feet × 13 feet, and a scullery, 7 feet × 8 feet 6 inches, a pantry and porch. The floor above contains three bed-rooms, 11 × 10—11 × 7, and 7 × 8 ft. 6 in., respectively. With a liberal estimate for materials and labour, a pair of these cottages, with pigsties, &c., may be erected for £236; or if the bricks are made by the proprietor, or stone be procurable on the estate, 10 per cent. may be taken from these prices.

We can recommend Mr. Goddard's work to all engaged in building, as a useful guide, both in the designs, and in the specification.

HALSTED ON SCREW PROPELLING.

The Screw Fleet of the Navy. By E. P. HALSTED, Capt., R.N. pp. 150. London : SIMPKIN, MARSHALL, & Co., 1850.

THIS work, the first published on a subject at the present moment of peculiar importance, and written by a gentleman who has pursued the subject professionally, and whose official position has given him access to the unpublished experience of others, will be read with great interest. Its appearance is opportune, just at the time when the Brazilian Mail question is about to be decided, and although the author must be regarded rather as an advocate than as a judge, the screw party will gladly hail the accession of so skilful a champion to their cause.

Captain Halsted commences his argument with a definition of the qualities which a steamer of war ought to possess, and by this standard measures the results that have been obtained with the paddle-wheel and the results that may be obtained with the screw. These required qualities may be summed up as follows :—The power of carrying a complete broadside armament;—the means of protecting the machinery to allow of this armament being used in close action;—the means of performing all general service under sail alone, and of performing special service with full, or auxiliary, steam power, to give the maximum of efficiency.

We have not space to follow Captain Halstead through his logical deductions, but must content ourselves with briefly summing up the leading points. First, The paddle-wheel vessel carries an inefficient armament, at the extremities of the ship; hence, inability to meet a fully armed ship, and the necessity of full lines, fore and aft, to carry the guns, involving a loss of power in producing a given speed. Secondly, Her machinery is exposed to shot, which limits her employment to particular service. Thirdly, She is dependent on her supply of coals for all ordinary service, these exhausted, she becomes powerless. Fourthly, She furnishes no efficient school of discipline and instruction for men and officers in practical seamanship.

On the other hand—The screw ship carries an efficient broadside armament; hence, the lines may be made finer, and a higher speed obtained with less power; her machinery is protected from shot; she is a perfect sailing ship, and is therefore independent of coals or accidents to her machinery.

" Distinctive qualifications.—' That whereas the one will sail best without her paddles, and paddle best without her sails ;—the other will screw the fastest with her sails, and sail the fastest with her screw.'

" That there may be no mistake then as to what is here intended by a PERFECT SAILING-SHIP, I now define the term as here applied, practically to mean this ;—' That for the execution of any service demanding no more than the speed of the best classes of our sailing-ships, an Admiral, with both a frigate and a screw-frigate alike at his disposal, should be able indifferently to select whichever it might be desirable to employ, with assurance that, as far as regards speed under sail alone, such service would be performed with equal effect and celerity by either.'

" And further ;—' That as regards services involving her double capacity, the screw-frigate should be in every respect eligible for selection to accompany under sail only an expedition of the fastest sailing-ships to a destination however distant, with assurance of her arriving in company on the scene of action, bringing to the aid of her consorts her unimpaired powers as a steamer.' "

The proper principles on which to rig a screw ship are thus laid down :—

" Those shorter proportions of length to breadth, which obtain in the case of the more ordinary sailing-ship, have compelled her for want of longitudinal room to carry the amount of sail required for her speed, not low, but loftily ; and the increased ' moment of inclination ' thus produced is in her case counteracted by the increased ' measure of stability ' derived from a proportional breadth of beam, supplied at and about the water-line for this very purpose, the ' area of direct resistance ' being kept at a low figure by the fineness of the underform. Now the screw-ship in order to carry her machinery low, is necessarily constructed with a fulness, instead of a fineness, of underform ; but if we also compel her to carry her canvass loftily, we shall then require the increased beam also which is necessary to resist its inclining pressure, and in such case it is clear that we must enlarge the ' area of direct resistance ' to such an extent as to render the attainment of high speed in the screw-ship hopeless. In her case however the conditions of such a necessity do not exist. The room which in the shorter sailing-ship cannot be found, is presented to us in the greater proportionate length of the screw-ship to enable her to carry her canvass,—not loftily,—but low ; and she thus possesses the ability to 'have the ' moment of inclination' of her sails reduced, until her reduced breadth of form is enabled to resist its inclining pressure with the same ' stability ' as that of the sailing-ship."

For purposes of auxiliary power the screw has undoubtedly established a claim to preference of selection; and in the vessels of the navy, in which the maintenance of a high and uniform rate of speed is not the consideration of highest importance, the screw also appears to be the most eligible propeller. But we think Capt. Halsted inconclusive in his proofs when he maintains, that for the mail service of important line, screw vessels are the best adapted. An important mail service requires as its main elements rapidity and regularity of conveyance; and any innovation by which these qualities are rendered of more doubtful attainment cannot be an eligible one, even though it may be attended with some diminution of expense. Now it is contended by the advocates for paddle-wheel steamers, that although in fine weather or with a fair wind the screw is an advantageous propeller, yet that it loses a great part of its efficiency when the vessel has to encounter an adverse wind and sea, so that to achieve a good average velocity under varying circumstances of weather and regularity in the times of arrival, vessels furnished with paddle wheels are much the most efficient ; and whether this doctrine be a just one or not, certainly Capt. Halsted adduces nothing to confute it. He mentions, indeed, that in some of the earlier Halifax steamers there was as much irregularity in the arrivals as is now found to attach to certain screw vessels plying to the Mediterranean. But the causes are manifestly incomparable ; and it is alleged by the advocates for paddle wheels, that the said screw vessels plying to the Mediterranean cannot realize the same regularity of arrival, or obtain the same prices for freight that are realized by paddle-wheel vessels plying to the same ports.

While, therefore, we appreciate as fully as Capt. Halsted the advantages of the screw for naval purposes, and in the cases of vessels plying with auxiliary power, we must maintain that he has not established the position that it is as eligible and efficient a propeller as the paddle, in cases in which a high and regular speed requires to be maintained. Yet we must at the same time confess, that we can see no good reason why it should fail to be as efficient as the paddle under adverse circumstances of wind and weather ; and its deficient performance under such circumstances, if really existing, may perhaps be due to ineligible proportions in the screw itself, or to the position in which it is placed. When a screw and a paddle vessel of equal power are tied stern to stern, the screw vessel gradually overcomes the paddle vessel, and tows it against the whole force of its engines. But the screw vessel under the same circumstances exerts a great deal more power, and there is, we believe, very little doubt, that if the pressure upon the piston of the paddle vessel were so increased as to make the power exerted equal to that exerted in the case of the screw, the paddle would be found to be the more efficient propeller. It would be very useful to have the dynamometric traction of screw and paddle vessels ascertained, both with various pressures of steam upon the piston, and various numbers of horse power exerted in the minute ; and the dynamometer line should in each case be attached before the centre of the ship, so as to render steering necessary to keep the vessel in her right position.

With these remarks we must dismiss Capt. Halsted's present performance, which is very creditable to his talents and industry, and is calculated to illustrate an obscure and interesting subject. We think he has fully succeeded in showing that for naval purposes screw vessels are, on the whole, entitled to a preference over those impelled by paddle wheels, and in the case of vessels moved not by full but by auxiliary power, his proofs we consider to be equally successful. This is much, and we see no reason to despair that in the case of mail vessels a similar superiority of the screw over the paddle may in time

be established. But Capt. Halsted has certainly failed in showing that this superiority, or even an equality of performance under such circumstances, has been established yet, and we probably need more searching experiments and more fastidious investigation, before the information can be collected out of which a result so useful to steam navigation can be expected to arise.

CORRESPONDENCE.

THE SCREW PROPELLER.

To the Editor.—Sir, In answer to the inquiries of a Correspondent at Kincardine in your last number :—

1. A screw propeller is part of a true screw, which is a triangle wound upon a cylinder; and in a screw of which the pitch is equal to the diameter, the edge of the thread in one convolution has the same ratio to the circumference of the screw's disc, that the diagonal of a square has to one side of it.

2. A number of collars on the shaft is the most approved resource for taking the thrust of the screw ; but the bushes into which the bearing fits should be composed of Babbitt's metal, instead of brass. The composition of this metal is given in the second volume of the *Artisan*, page 113.

3. The diameter proper for the screw has no connexion with the length of the crank ; but the screw should be in all cases as large as possible, and the pitch of the screw should be equal to its diameter. The speed proper for the engines will therefore depend upon the intended or expected speed of the vessel, and 10 or 15 per cent. of slip added to the progress or expected progress of the vessel through the water will give the distance to be traversed by the screw in an hour or minute, supposing it to work in a solid. As then the pitch of the screw is known, as well as the distance it must advance in a given time, it is clear that the speed of engine proper to accomplish this advance becomes at once determinable. This will best be illustrated by an example :—

Suppose that a screw vessel has such an amount of engine-power as to warrant the expectation that she will attain a speed of 10 miles an hour. Let the slip be taken at 13 per cent., or 1½ miles an hour, then it is obvious that the screw must travel forward, supposing there was no slip, at the rate of 11½ miles an hour. Let the diameter of the largest screw which can be got in be supposed to be 15 feet, then the pitch will be 15 feet. Now, as 11·5 miles, or 60,720 feet have to be travelled over in the hour, and as 15 feet are travelled over every revolution, there must be 60,720 ÷ 15 = 4048 revolutions of the screw performed in the hour, or 67 revolutions performed in the minute, which, therefore, will be the speed of the engine, if gearing be not interposed.

4. The bearing behind the screw in the stern-post of the ship is found to be very useful in large vessels, and even in the case of small screws it cannot be judiciously dispensed with. There is no doubt that a screw may be overhung with the same facility as a paddle-wheel ; but the bearing in the stern-post causes no inconvenience, and in the case of the screw winding hawsers, or fishing-nets round it, as has sometimes occurred, it is obvious that an end bearing will prevent the shaft from being bent at the neck. Her Majesty's screw-yacht, the Fairy, was at first made without an outside bearing for the screw-shaft ; but the stuffing-box soon became leaky in consequence, and an end bearing was consequently added ; since which time no inconvenience has been experienced. It is manifestly advisable, therefore, to apply an outside bearing to the screw, since, in cases in which this bearing had been omitted at first, it has been subsequently introduced.—J. B.

Mr. Editor,—In your last number there is an account of Mr. Siemen's condenser, in which Mr. Hall's method of condensing is mentioned, which calls to mind another system of condensing I saw on board of the *Neath Abbey*, which plies between Bristol and Neath. It has been running on that station for several years, winter and summer ; and the following particulars I obtained on board the vessel. It is of iron, 97 feet long, 16 broad, and 10 feet deep; propelled by the screw, worked by two 12-inch cylinders, using steam of 45 lbs. pressure. Instead of the steam escaping into the air, it is conducted into two wrought-iron cylinders, one on each side of the vessel, each containing 62 brass tubes, 1¼ inch in diameter, and 64 inches long, open at both ends to the sea ; and as the vessel proceeds, the sea-water passes through these tubes and condenses the steam. This is very different to Mr. Hall's plan, in which the steam goes through the pipes, and the water outside, but the water in this system goes through the pipes, and the steam outside ; by which means the condensing water is much colder, it being a difficult matter to keep the water so cold on Mr. Hall's plan. As fresh water is put into the boilers at starting, and the condensed water returned back to the boiler, less fuel will be required, and the boilers will last longer. There are two boilers, each containing 104 two-inch tubes of 5 feet long to return the flame to the funnel : they consume 5 cwt. of coals in the hour. The engine makes from 129 to 135 revolutions per minute, and she goes from Bristol to the Mumbles, a distance of 90 miles in 5¾ hours. The machinery is very simple, each cylinder lying diagonally ; the piston rods being directly connected to the crank on the shaft. There is no other machinery besides two pumps of 3 inch diameter, one for each engine, to force the condensed water back to the boiler. The maker stated that the *Neath Abbey* would work round the *Lord Beresford*, a large steam-boat plying to and from the port of Bristol.

Will you be so kind as to mention in your next your opinion of the performance and principle of condensing of this boat; and if Mr. Galloway's principle of preventing smoke is preferred to Mr. Chas. Wye William's plan, or is there one better than either ?

"MONA."

Dalkeith, May, 1850.

MR. EDITOR,—Sir, Allow me to suggest answers to one or two of the questions by H. A., of Newcastle.

1. In levers, or other work with a given centre line, square lines may be found from given points, in the following manner. With a pair of compasses, take a distance greater than half the width of the end of the lever, and set one leg in the given point, and with the other cut the centre line in two points, and from these points, with a less radius, find a new point on the opposite side of the centre line ; and a line passing through this point and the given point will be a square line to the centre line.

2. As the radius from any point in the face of a bevel-wheel is different from every other point in it, it follows that a piece of wood planed to one radius will not exactly fit the surface of the wheel ; but in practice, I have found that a line square to the face of the wheel, from a point about ⅓ of the face from the outside edge, and joining the centre line, will answer the purpose. A piece of wood planed to this radius, and afterwards tapered to the shape of the tooth may be made to fit the surface by laying a piece of glass-paper on the wheel, and rubbing the piece of wood slightly in the direction of the tooth.

3. The surest and simplest method I know of laying a key seat on a shaft, is to have two pieces of wood, about the length of the seat, nailed together at right angles, keeping each edge parallel from the inside corner ; the distance from the corner to each edge being about ½ dia. of the shaft. When applied to the shaft, each edge will be parallel with the axis, and any number of lines may be struck parallel to each other, and with the axis. The same piece would answer for shafts considerably larger than the one it is made for, and it may therefore be considered a useful tool. I remain yours,

A. M.

[The foregoing communication ought to have appeared in our last number.—ED. *Artisan*.]

To THE EDITOR.—Sir, I see by the *Builder* that an American has invented a sawing machine, in which the weight of the log sets the saw in motion, and cuts the wood. Will J. B., or some other of your readers, please to calculate for me, how far a log 2 feet square must fall to cut itself up into 2 inch staff ? Yours, &c., J. S.

Liverpool, 24th June, 1850.

MR. EDITOR.—Sir, may I trouble you with the following questions for insertion ? 1. The depth of an engine-beam is 30 inches, web 1¼ thick, top and bottom flanges 7 inches wide, and 2 inches thick; distance between extreme centres 20 feet. I wish to know how to calculate the breaking strain. 2. How must I proportion the web and flanges of a girder for a span of 30 feet ; limited height 2 feet 8 inches, and to carry a weight of 30 tons in the centre, the quantity of metal being a minimum. TYRO.

AMERICAN PATENTS.

Joseph Häygel, Cumberland, Alleghany county, Maryland, *for an improvement in Smut Machines.* June 5.

The patentee says, "The nature of my improvement consists in the combination of two rubbing surfaces of India rubber, and rubbing surface of India rubber with cast iron, to clean the wheat from smut and garlic."

Claim.—"What I claim as new, is the combination with each other of the inclined and horizontal runners, and constructed substantially as set forth, for the purpose of more perfectly separating smut and garlic from wheat."

Edmund Morris, Burlington, Burlington county, New Jersey, *for an improved Door-holder.* June 19.

Claim.—"What I claim as my invention, is the method of constructing turnbuckles, or fastenings for shutters and doors of all kinds, by attaching a plug or knob to the back of the shutter or door, the same fitting or passing into the cavity of a cup-shaped vessel, through an aperture in a disk of India rubber or other elastic substance, the said rubber being so regulated as to grasp the knob, and keep the door or shutter back, substantially as described."

Abner Chapman, Fairfax, Franklin county, Vermont, *for a method of increasing the effective length and cleansing Boiler Flues.* July 17.

The patentee says,—"The nature of my invention consists in furnishing the horizontal flues of a steam boiler with spiral partitions, which partitions can be made to revolve to clear the flue, by which arrangement I am enabled to obtain all the advantages of a spiral flue, which has been heretofore essayed and found useful, till it became choked with ashes, &c., when it was found impossible to clean it ; but, by my construction, the inside or spiral flue can be revolved, and thus be made to clean the flue perfectly, while it retains all the advantages of the stationary spiral flue."

Claim.—"What I claim as my invention, is spiral partitions, forming a spiral flue within the flues of a steam boiler, substantially as described, said thread being affixed to a shaft independent of the flue, so that it can be made to revolve, to scrape the flue, and clear it when it gets foul."

Charles Caples, Savannah, Andrew county, Missouri, *for an improvement in Equalising the Action of Gearing in Horse Powers.* July 31.

The patentee says,—"My invention consists in attaching the wheels to their spindles by flexible bars or springs, instead of the usual rigid methods of keys, plugs, or pins."

Claim.—"What I claim as my invention, is equalizing the strain, and lessening the force of shocks upon a train of cog-wheels, by connecting the wheels with their shafts by springs, substantially as set forth."

MATTER AND ITS PROPERTIES.

MATTER is anything extended, and capable of resisting or transmitting force. A body is a quantity of matter, and every body has length, breadth, and thickness, and resists in a greater or less degree any pressure applied to it. It follows from this definition that a body may not be a substance, and that there may be no such thing in nature as a substance at all. Our ideas of a substance we acquire through the medium of our senses, and any cause which produced the proper sensation, would also produce the corresponding idea, whether the substance existed or not. The recent investigations of Dr. Faraday, and other experimentalists, have rendered it probable that matter is only an aggregation of centres of force. But all the laws relating to matter hold equally true, whether this be its real character, or whether it is an actual substance, as commonly believed.

The inherent properties of matter are volume, inertia, mobility, and divisibility. A fifth property is attraction; but it appears to be rather incidental than essential. Of attraction there are four varieties, namely, gravitation, cohesion, magnetism, and electrical attraction; and there appears little reason to doubt that these are but the different phases of one elementary principle.

Every body must have size or volume, and the limit or termination of a body is a surface or superficies. Thus a dice or cubic inch of ivory has for its superficies six planes, each of one square inch in area. These surfaces meet in edges or lines each one inch long, and the edges meet in corners or points which are destitute of dimension. No finite or imaginable division of a line can ever produce a point, and a line is therefore divisible into an indefinite number of other lines, each of which will have a length inversely proportioned to the number of divisions. In the same way no subdivision of a surface can ever produce a line, and no subdivision of a solid can ever produce a surface. It hence becomes obvious that any quantity of matter, however small, may be made to fill any space, however large, without any pore or interstice occurring, whose diameter shall exceed a given finite line. A cubic inch of ivory or iron might be enlarged into a cube of the diameter of the earth, and yet the matter be equally diffused throughout the space, and be without hole or vacuity larger than the smallest grain of sand; and this enlarged cube might again be compressed into its original volume, without suffering any diminution in the quantity of matter of which it is composed. A cubic inch of water will, by the application of heat, be converted into a cubic foot of steam of the same elasticity as the atmosphere, and by the abstraction of the heat the steam will be again turned into a cubic inch of water. The same effect is no doubt producible by mechanical compression, without any abstraction of heat at all; and as all bodies are compressible by the application of a suitable force, it follows that either the particles of matter are themselves compressible, or that they are not in contact in the natural state of bodies. Now if the particles of matter are themselves compressible, it is clear that the larger the compressing force is, the greater must be the amount of the compression; so that by increasing the compressing force sufficiently, the matter would be forced into a smaller and smaller space, until it disappeared altogether. If, on the contrary, matter be composed of incompressible particles, the further compression of any body will be impossible when the particles of matter composing the body have been brought into contact with one another; and a body in such a state will be incapable of contracting with a diminution of temperature, as it is already in the smallest compass in which it can exist. Thus, if a thousand cubic inches of gold be supposed to contain one cubic inch of matter, the further condensation of gold by pressure will be impossible, after it has been forced into a space equal to one-thousandth of its original bulk; and matter in such a state of density will be incapable of contraction by any amount of cold. As water is about nineteen times lighter than gold, the matter

in a thousand cubic inches of water will only occupy one-nineteenth of a cubic inch when the particles of matter are in contact; and the sum of the vacuous spaces in the gold will be nine hundred and ninety-nine cubic inches, and in the water nine hundred and ninety-nine cubic inches, and eighteen nineteenths of a cubic inch; or, in other words, the sum of the vacant spaces in the water, and in the gold, will be very nearly the same, if gold contain the quantity of matter that we have assumed for the purpose of illustration. Whether matter be a real substance, or an aggregation merely of centres of force, it appears to be at least certain that the ultimate particles or atoms of matter are indivisible—at least, without changing their nature—for, although a space, however small, is obviously divisible into any number of smaller spaces; and although an atom, if occupying space, or if constituting a force, may be supposed to be similarly divisible, yet we have no experience of such a division actually occurring in nature. The laws of atomic combination render it certain that it is only between the atoms of bodies and not between parts of atoms, that action and reaction take place; and although it is conceivable that matter, if consisting of centres of force, may be resolved into some equivalent force manifesting different qualities, and that parts of atoms may consequently assume such a shape; yet, in such a case the parts of atoms are no longer matter, and the supposition does not invalidate the doctrine that the atoms of matter are indivisible. The solid, liquid, and vaporous states of bodies are conditions accidental to their temperature; for every solid may be melted and raised into vapour by an adequate heat, and every vapour or gas may be liquified or solidified by an adequate cold. If a small quantity of gas or vapour be admitted into a large vacuous space, it will expand until the weight of the particles just balances their repulsive force; and at the point where this equibration takes place, the particles will arrange themselves in a level plane, like the surface of a sheet of water. If an electric spark be transmitted through a Torricellian vacuum made over mercury, in a long glass tube, a pale light will be visible in those parts of the vacuum near the mercury, on account of the existence of mercurial vapour there. But if the tube be very long, and be also maintained at a low temperature, there will be a plane in the vacuous space, beyond which the mercurial vapour cannot ascend, and this plane may be ascertained by transmitting sparks through the tube, at points higher and higher up, until such a point is reached that no light is produced within the tube when a spark is transmitted. At this point the weight of the particles of the mercurial vapour will just balance their repulsive force.

Impenetrability is commonly reckoned one of the properties of matter, but from the tenor of the foregoing remarks it will be obvious, that, although in a modified sense impenetrability must continue to be regarded as one of the characteristics of matter, whatever theory relative to the constitution of matter may be adopted, yet in the commonly received sense it may be totally untrue. By impenetrability is meant, not hardness or inseparability, but the impossibility of two bodies being in the same place in the same time; and if matter be an actual substance, the attribute of impenetrability is undoubtedly just. For, although all bodies may contain other bodies in their pores or interstices, in the manner in which water exists in the pores of wood, air in the pores of water, and quicksilver in the pores of gold, yet it is obviously not the matter itself of the wood, water, or gold which is thus penetrated, but merely vacuous spaces in it, which become filled with different matter, or matter in a different state. If matter, however, be not an actual substance, but merely a collection of centres of force, it may be compressed into a smaller and smaller bulk, until the several centres of force become coincident; but the effect of such a compression would be to change it from the principle which we recognize as matter into some other thing. Although, therefore, matter must be impenetrable in a certain sense, inasmuch as if penetration were carried far enough the matter would cease to exist, we are not warranted in asserting that any amount of

21

penetration is impossible, supposing the result to be disregarded. It is by no means certain that bodies resist pressure because their particles occupy space; and in the case of two electrified balls which repel one another, though some distance asunder, we see a resistance exerted, which, if capable of acting on the sense of touch, would no doubt produce the sensation of contact. If the power of repulsion be supposed to be sufficiently great, it will follow that ordinary natural agents will be unable to overcome it, and the phenomena of impenetrability will thus take place, though the matter itself may not be impenetrable or even extended. Since then we know that spheres of repulsion exist, and that the centres of those spheres are, by virtue merely of such repulsion, effectually kept asunder; and since it is superfluous to adduce more causes of natural things than are necessary for the explanation of the observed phenomena, it does not appear necessary that we should suppose an extended atom to exist in the centre of the sphere of repulsion, inasmuch as all the observed phenomena are explicable without such a supposition.

One of the most important properties of matter is that of *inertia*, by which is meant an incapacity of spontaneous change. All matter must be either at rest or in motion, and whatever be its condition in this respect, it can only be changed by the application of some external and counteracting force. There cannot indeed be any such thing as absolute rest in creation, for every particle of matter in the universe is known to be in perpetual motion, but a body may be at rest relatively with the earth, or with other bodies; and it is this relative state that is signified when rest is spoken of in physical dissertation. To put a mass of matter in motion requires the exertion of force, and to stop the motion requires the exertion of an equal and opposite force. A pendulum impelled by gravity, or any other force, through the descending arc of a circle, will, by virtue of its inertia or momentum, rise through the ascending arc to the level from which it originally fell; or rather it will ascend nearly, and would ascend quite to the original level but for friction and the resistance of the air, which occasion some retardation. The air, however, cannot resist a moving body without being put in motion itself, so that although there is less velocity or intensity of motion in the moving body in consequence of the atmospheric resistance, there is a greater quantity of matter moved than would be the case if there were no atmosphere present. If a given force moves a certain quantity of matter with a given velocity it will require twice the force to move twice the quantity of matter with the same velocity; but twice the force will not move the original quantity of matter with twice the velocity, as is sometimes asserted, and of which we shall investigate the reason when we come to speak about falling bodies. A ball rolled along the ground comes in a short time into a state of rest, in consequence of the friction of the rolling surfaces and the resistance of the atmosphere; but if the atmosphere were removed, and the ball and the plane on which it rolls were quite smooth the ball would roll on for ever, and would circulate round the earth continually, supposing the plane to be as extended as to encircle the earth like an equator. By friction heat and electricity are excited, and in this way a part of the force communicated to any moving body may be lost for any useful purpose. It does not, however, follow that any part of the force is absolutely annihilated, any more than the water is annihilated which escapes from a leaky vessel, and all that has been asserted of the indestructible nature of matter, appears to hold true of the indestructible nature of force, which there is every reason to believe can neither be created nor destroyed. Bodies consequently which are brought to a state of rest by friction and atmospheric resistance, are not influenced by any more natural aptitude for rest than for motion; but they merely lose motion in the proportion in which they lose force by its dissipation in friction, and in putting into motion other bodies than those to which the force was primarily applied.

The quantity of matter existing in any body is always reckoned as proportional to the inertia or weight of the body. In bodies of the same kind the quantities of matter are determinable by their respective volumes; but in bodies of different kinds the quantities of matter are only determinable by their volumes and densities conjointly, or by the inertia or weight. Thus, we know that a cubic inch of gold has just one-tenth of the matter in it that ten cubic inches of gold have; but a cubic inch of gold has one-fifth of the matter in it that ten cubic inches of copper have, since ten cubic inches of copper have only the same weight or inertia as five cubic inches of gold. This doctrine, however, of the quantity of matter in bodies being as their weight, though commonly accepted, is by no means demonstrable, and is perhaps untrue; for the weights of atoms of matter may vary from differences in their attractive force, as well as from differences in their size or density; or the total weight of a dense body may be made up of a small number of particles, each with a large attraction, as well as of a large number of particles, each with a small attraction. The physical result, however, is the same whichever supposition is adopted; and it will be more convenient and more conformable to established usage, to regard the quantity of matter in a body as proportional to its weight. Momentum is, properly speaking, the inertia of a moving body, or the measure of indisposition in a moving body to come to a state of rest; and as inertia is measureable by the force requisite to communicate a given velocity to a given quantity of stationary matter, so is momentum measureable by the force requisite to bring to rest a given quantity of matter moving with a given velocity; or, in other words, momentum is measurable by the amount of mechanical power which a given body moving with a given velocity in being brought to rest will impart. Since a force once created can never be destroyed, except by the production of some other equivalent force, it is clear that the whole of the force which a body receives when put into motion, is afterwards surrendered when the body is brought to rest, supposing no loss to have been occasioned by friction or atmospheric resistance, and the momentum of all bodies must consequently be proportional to the force expended in putting them into motion. In most works on Mechanics, however, momentum is defined to be the quantity of motion in bodies, and the respective quantities of motion in bodies is assumed to be in the ratio of their masses and velocities. According to this doctrine a two-pound ball moving at the rate of ten miles an hour, would have the same quantity of motion in it as a one-pound ball moving at the rate of twenty miles an hour. But so far is this doctrine from being self-evident, that it is not even true, and infinite confusion has been created in mechanical enquiries by this erroneous hypothesis. The quantity of motion in a moving body can no more be indicated by the product of its mass and velocity, without reference to the moving force, than the quantity of matter in a cylinder can be indicated by the product of its length and diameter without reference to its density; but as the moving forces of bodies of the same weight vary as the squares of the velocities of motion, the momentum of all bodies will be correctly expressed by the mass or weight multiplied by the square of the velocity. A ball of one-pound weight, therefore, moving at a speed of twenty miles an hour, will have as much momentum in it, or will give as severe a blow as a ball of four-pounds weight moving at the speed of ten miles an hour. A fly-wheel, if its velocity of rotation be doubled, will have four times the momentum to redress the irregularities of motion in the engine; or, if its velocity of rotation be quadrupled, it will have sixteen times the momentum it possessed before. The momentum of a cannon-ball, moving at the rate of 1,700 feet per second, will be 28,900 times greater than if it moved at the rate of 10 feet per second; for the square of 1,700 is to the square 10 as 28,900 is to 1. The momentum of a cannon-ball, therefore, weighing one pound will (if moving at a speed of 1,700 feet in the second) be equal to the momentum of a ball or battering-ram weighing 28,900 lbs., or 12·8 tons, moving with a velocity of 10 feet in the second. Josephus mentions that some of the battering-rams employed by the Romans in Judea were 90 feet long, and weighed 1,500 talents of 114 pounds to the talent, or 76·3392 tons. The weight of a cannon-ball, which will give the same force of impact, when moving at a velocity of 1,800 feet in a second, as such a battering-ram, when moving at a velocity of 10 feet per second, can easily be determined ; for we have only to multiply 76·3392 tons by the square of 10, and to divide by the square of 1,800, which will give ·0023561 tons, or 5·2776 lbs., as the weight of the ball required.

KEY TO MR. BOURNE'S CATECHISM OF THE STEAM ENGINE.

(Continued from p. 125.)

HEAT AND STEAM.

Up to this point we have only taken into consideration steam raised from fresh water, which boils under the atmospheric pressure at a temperature of 212°. In marine boilers, however, sea water is used for the production of steam, and it is found that at the atmospheric pressure sea water boils with a temperature of 213·2°. Sea water contains about 1-33rd of its weight of saline matter, and if by evaporation the proportion of water be diminished, the boiling point will be raised.

If we take steam raised from water containing 4rds of its weight of salt, we find it to be 4·7° hotter than steam of the same pressure produced from fresh water ; hence, if the bulk of the steam in both cases be the same, it follows that the hotter steam consists of a less weight of steam expanded by the addition of 4·7° of heat. A cubic foot of steam from salt water, if reduced in temperature 4·7°, would still retain its gaseous form, as it would then be at the temperature proper for steam raised from fresh water, and its bulk would be reduced according to the law of the contraction of gases, to about ·99 of a cubic foot. If we wish to ascertain the amount of heat expended in raising this steam 4·7° degrees, we must bear in mind that the specific heat of steam is less than that of fresh water in the ratio of ·847 to 1. Hence, to raise a given weight of steam 4.7° requires only as much heat as would raise the same weight of fresh water 3·98° = 4·7° × ·847.

To find the quantity of water required to condense steam of a pressure of 15 lbs. in a marine engine, we must proceed as follows :—
The temperature of the steam at the pressure of 15 lbs. above the atmosphere is 250° for fresh water, and the total heat = 250° + latent heat 962° = 1212°. The feed water has a temperature of, say 100°, hence the total heat given to the steam is 1212° — 100° = 1112° in the case of fresh water. But the boiling point of water containing 4-33rds of its weight of salt, with a pressure of 15 lbs., is 4·7° higher than that of fresh water ; hence the steam must be raised 4·7°. As the specific heat of steam is less than that of water in the ratio of 0·847 to 1, it requires less heat to raise steam of 4·7° than to raise water in that ratio. Hence, 1 : 0·847 : : 4·7° : 3·98° the heat required. The total heat communicated to the steam is, therefore, 1112° + 3·98° = 1115·98° ; or, say 1116°, which, multiplied by 3, the proportionate number of cubic feet evaporated in order to attain the point of saturation represented by 4-33rds of salt, = 3348°.

The cubic foot of brine remaining in the boiler, and which must be blown off to prevent an undue accumulation of salt, has been raised from 100° to 254·7° = 154·7° ; the specific heat of brine, however, is to that of fresh water as ·85 to 1, and hence the heat required to raise the brine 154·7° is less in the same ratio. Hence, 1 : ·85 : : 154·7° : 130·495° the heat required for raising the brine to the temperature of 154·7°. The heat contained in one cubic foot of brine which is blown off may therefore be represented by 130·495°, and the heat contained in three cubic feet of steam evaporated may be represented by 3348° : hence the heat lost by blowing off is $\frac{130·495°}{3348°}$ or about $\frac{1}{25}$th of the heat which is beneficially applied.

Under the atmospheric pressure, or 30 inches of mercury, steam is expanded into about 1700 times the bulk of an equal weight of water : this proportion is so nearly that of a cubic foot (or 1728 cubic inches) to a cubic inch, that the latter proportion is generally employed in practical computations for low pressures, or pressures not greatly exceeding that of the atmosphere. In order to maintain the supply of steam from low pressure boilers it is necessary, therefore, that a cubic inch of water should be supplied for every cubic foot of steam used in the engine. If, for example, the cylinder had a capacity of one cubic foot, and was filled forty times a minute, the feed pump should have a capacity of one cubic inch if filled 40 times a minute ; if the feed pump were to be filled only 20 times a minute it should have a capacity of two cubic inches ;—that is, in engines working with a low pressure, the pump must deliver in a minute as many cubic inches of water as the cylinder consumes cubic feet of steam. In ordinary cases the feed pump is single acting, while the cylinder is double acting, and hence the capacity of the feed pump must be in the case we have taken two cubic inches, or $\frac{2}{1728} = \frac{1}{864}$ of the capacity of the cylinder, supposing that there were no waste or leakage either of steam or water. In practice, however, these conditions cannot be fulfilled, and the feed pump must be able to provide a surplus supply as a compensation for such losses. Hence in practice it is usual to make the feed pump about 2½ times larger than we have mentioned, or $\frac{1}{864} × 2·5 = \frac{1}{345}$ of the capacity of the cylinder.

This rule, however, is, as we have stated, only applicable to engines working with steam but little above the atmospheric pressure ; since steam of twice the pressure contains twice the quantity of water, it requires twice the quantity of water to be delivered by the feed pump to keep up the supply ; where such steam is used, and for such a case, the feed pump must be $\frac{2}{345}$ths of the capacity of the cylinder ; for steam of three times the pressure, the feed pump must be $\frac{3}{345}$ths of the capacity of the cylinder, and so on for all higher pressures.

Our rule then for the atmospheric pressure is thus expressed, $\frac{\text{capacity of cylinder}}{345}$ = capacity of feed pump, but it is clear that this is the same as $\frac{\text{Capacity of cylinder} × 15 \text{ lbs.}}{345 × 15}$ or the same as $\frac{\text{capacity} × 15 \text{ lbs.}}{5175, \text{ or say } 5000}$. In this shape the rule will be available for all pressures, and may be thus stated :—

To find the capacity of the feed pump in cubic inches when the pump is single acting and the engine double acting—

RULE.—*Multiply the capacity of the cylinder in cubic inches by the total pressure in pounds per square inch (including the atmospheric pressure), and divide the product by 5000. The result is the capacity of the feed pump in cubic inches.*

Example 1.—In some of Bury's locomotives the diameter of the cylinder is 12 inches, the length of stroke 18 inches, giving a capacity of 2034 cubic inches ; the diameter of the feed pump plunger is 1½ inches, and the length of stroke 18 inches, giving a capacity for the feed pump of 43·2 cubic inches. Assuming that the pressure upon the safety valve is 35 lbs. per square inch, and applying our rule we obtain $2034 \frac{(35 + 15)}{5000}$ = 40·6 cubic inches, instead of 43·2.

In other examples of locomotives the diameter of cylinder is 13 inches, length of stroke 18 inches, and capacity 2388·6 cubic inches : the diameter of feed pump plunger is 2 inches, length of stroke 18 inches, and capacity 56·52 cubic inches. Assuming the pressure as before to be 35 lbs. above the atmosphere. Then, $\frac{2388·6 × 100}{5000}$ = 47·7 cubic inches, instead of 56·5. Mr. Gooch, in his evidence before the Gauge Commissioners, states that his engines work with as high a pressure of steam as 90 to 100 lbs. on the square inch. If we take 95 lbs. as the pressure, then, $\dfrac{2388 \cdot 6 \times (95 + 15)}{5000} = 52 \cdot 5$ cubic inches capacity of feed pump. 100 lbs. pressure on the inch is now a common pressure in locomotive engines of good construction.

Example 2.—In a marine engine with a cylinder of 20 inches diameter, 24 inches stroke ; and, therefore, with 7536 cubic inches of capacity of cylinder, the feed pump plunger is 2¼ inches diameter, the stroke 6 inches, and the capacity of the feed pump 23·4 cubic inches : in another engine of similar construction of 50 inches diameter of cylinder, 60 inches stroke, and 117,810 therefore of cubic inches of capacity of cylinder, the feed pump plunger is 6 inches diameter, and 15 inches stroke, so that it has a capacity of 420 cubic inches. Taking the pressure on the safety valve at 5 lbs. per square inch, and applying our rule we get, in the first case $\dfrac{7536 \times 20}{5000} = 30$ cubic inches instead of 23·4 :

and in the second case $\dfrac{117{,}780 \times 20}{5000} = 471$ instead 420.

In order to find the quantity of water which the cold water pump must supply for condensation, we must consider the quantity of steam to be condensed. We have already seen that for steam at the atmospheric pressure the feed pump would have to deliver $\frac{1}{864}$th of the capacity of the cylinder, supposing there were no loss from leakage, waste, or priming. We, of course, may neglect all loss for leakage in considering the quantity of water required for condensation, inasmuch as we only require to condense that steam which actually passes through the cylinder. It has been already shown that to condense a cubic foot of water in the shape of steam, requires 27·8 cubic feet of water at 60°, and hence the cold water pump should be $\dfrac{1}{864}$th $\times 27 \cdot 8 = \dfrac{1}{32}$ of the capacity of the cylinder. If the pressure of the steam be doubled the cylinder will contain twice the weight of steam, and hence the rule must take cognizance of the pressure, as in the case of the feed pump. With a pressure of 15 lbs. above the atmosphere, the rule will therefore be, $\dfrac{\text{capacity} \times 15}{30 \times 15} = \dfrac{\text{capacity} \times 15}{450}$. But as the pump does not always draw efficiently, and as the water is sometimes warmer than 60°, a larger proportion of water than what is theoretically requisite must be allowed, and a cold water pump $\frac{1}{16}$th of the capacity of the cylinder if the engine be single acting, and $\frac{1}{11}$th of the capacity of the cylinder if the engine is double acting, answers very well in practice.

To be continued.

SOCIETIES.

INSTITUTION OF MECHANICAL ENGINEERS.
Continued from page 136.

In consequence of the absence of Mr. William Smith, the further consideration of his paper, on the engines of the South Staffordshire Iron District, was adjourned.

The following paper, by Mr. George Heaton, of Birmingham, was then read, " On the Importance of making a Compensation for the Pull of the Air-Pump Bucket in the Condensing Steam Engine."

In the year 1844, the author of the present paper was employed to inspect and ascertain the cause of the irregular motion and inefficient performance of a steam engine and mill used for the purpose of grinding corn. The mill had nine pair of corn stones, five on one and four on the other side of the driving power. The bottom of the corn spindles frequently moved and strained the whole framing which carried them, those most distant from the power having the greatest strain, frequently moving a quarter of an inch, and the end of the horizontal shaft which drove the corn spindles partaking of the same movement and becoming

much heated with its work, and the teeth of the wheels much worn on both sides.

The mill-work was very good and substantial, and had been about four years at work. The steam engine with cylinder of 40 inch diameter, stroke of piston 6 feet, air-pump 26½ inches diameter, and 3 feet stroke, was altogether a strong, well-built engine ; the steam pressure was about 6 lbs. per inch, and the engine was working at 17½ strokes per minute, but if attempted to be run faster a much more irregular motion was produced. The governor was driven with gear at the top of a vertical shaft 14 feet long, and the balls of the governor frequently moved in and out 4 or 5 inches during one stroke of the engine. When running at the speed of 17½ strokes per minute, the governor rod at the throttle valve lever frequently moved ¾ to 1 inch during each stroke of the engine, the greatest opening of the valve being invariably at the end of the pull of the air-pump bucket ; there was a great variation in the distance the rod moved each stroke, moving the farthest every fourth or fifth stroke. The engine appeared to have too much lead, for the reversing blow was struck before the crank arrived at the centre. The time of opening the valves was therefore altered, effecting a saving of steam and requiring the governor rod to be shortened more than 1 inch, (the throttle valve lever being 12 inches long ;) however, the irregular motion continued, and the engine with nine pair of stones appeared to have too much work.

The engine was constructed according to the general practice, to have about an equal weight hanging upon each end of the beam ; the weights of the different parts were stated to be as follows :—

AT THE CRANK END		T. C. Q. lbs.
Connecting rod and block at the top		1 11 3 14
4 brasses		0 0 2 0
Cold water pump bucket and rod		0 2 2 0
Crank and pin		0 14 3 0
Feed pump, plunger and rod		0 2 0 0
		2 11 2 14
Deduct for weight of crank balanced on the main shaft		0 9 0 0
Total weight		2 2 2 14
AT THE CYLINDER END.		T. C. Q. lbs.
Piston rod		0 4 1 19
Piston and ring		0 14 1 0
Pins, gibs, and cotters for ditto		0 1 0 21
Parallel motion		0 11 3 0
Cap and gudgeon to piston rod		0 4 0 0
Plug rod		0 3 2 0
Air-pump bucket		0 4 2 0
Total weight		2 3 2 12

consequently the weights at each end of the beam were balanced within 1 cwt.

The following alteration was then effected in the engine:—

A weight was fixed at the crank end of the engine beam, to assist in the pull of the air-pump bucket, and retard the speed of the engine on the opposite side of the stroke ; this weight was 19 cwt. 3 qrs. 14 lbs., and from its position it was equivalent to about one-half the pull of the bucket, considering the average pull through the whole lift. The engine beam was double, and the balance weight was fixed between the two sides of the beam ; also, the governor was altered, to be driven by a band instead of the former gear and long shaft. The engine was then set to run at 19½ strokes per minute, the speed required by the Company for its work, so as to drive the stones at about 123 revolutions per minute, instead of about 117, the former speed; the corn spindles then ran quite steady, the necks of the horizontal shaft kept cool, the dust remained on the back part of the teeth of the driving wheels, and the governor rod remained steady for a long time together, without anything else being done to either the engine or mill. Since that time the Company have added five pair more corn stones to that end of the shaft the five pair are at, and they run equally steady with the others. The engine appears now to drive thirteen pair of stones with greater ease and freedom than it drove eight pair before the balance weight was added, and the repairs have been considerably diminished in the same space of time. Believing that the pull of the air-pump does not generally receive the consideration it requires in either stationary or marine engines, is the writer's apology for bringing this paper before the meeting.

The Chairman, in moving the thanks of the meeting to Mr. Heaton, said, such subjects were of so much importance that they could not too frequently be brought before the attention of engineers. He trusted that the important statement in this paper had been made with great care, for it was surprising to hear of such great results flowing from such simple means. He should be glad if engineers generally, would communicate all such results as occurred in their experience, because the collection of them would prove of great value.

A vote of thanks having been passed to the writer, Mr. Heaton gave some further explanations of the subject of the paper, and observed, that the engine referred to was working at the Old Union Mill, at Birmingham.

INSTITUTION OF CIVIL ENGINEERS.
Tuesday, May 14, 1850.
WILLIAM CUBITT, Esq., President, in the Chair.

THE paper read was "On the Construction of the Permanent Way of Railways; with an account of the wrought iron Permanent Way, laid down on the Main Line of the North Midland Railway," by Mr. W. H. Barlow, M. Inst. C. E.

The author commenced by entering into the question of the maintenance and renewal of the ordinary railways, analysing very minutely the expenses under the different heads, and showing to what causes the derangement of the line might be attributed. The cost of maintenance was stated to be dependent on two causes, the effect of weather, &c., and the disturbance produced by traffic; and from a summary of the expenditure of the different lines belonging to the Midland Company, it appeared that former amounted to £20 or £30 per mile per annum, and the latter varied from 2d. to 2·7d. per train per mile. After a line was consolidated, by far the greater part of this expenditure was due to the derangement caused by the passage of the trains, which first produced an uneven joint, then loosened the joint key, and then disturbed the sleeper, so that at length the whole of the permanent way generally was degraded.

With regard to renewal, it had been estimated by the officers of the London and North Western Railway, that on their line, the rails would last twenty years, and the sleepers, if 'creosoted,' twenty years, but if unprepared only twelve years; now as the duration of service of the rails was dependant on the amount of the traffic, and that of the sleepers on the weather, it was quite evident, that on lines having less traffic than the London and North Western, the proportionate expense of renewing the sleepers would be much greater, and would increase as the amount of the traffic diminished.

In endeavouring to seek a remedy for this, the author conceived, that, by increasing the dimensions of the bridge rail, sufficient width might be obtained for it to take its own bearing in the ballast, without the use of either traverse sleepers, or longitudinal supports; and,

moreover, that such a construction would possess great strength, be very durable, and be capable of being renewed at a moderate expense. He therefore proposed a bridge rail, 13 inches in width, 5½ inches in depth, and weighing 126 lbs. per lineal yard. There was some difficulty at first in getting it manufactured, but Messrs. Bolckow and Vaughan, of Middlesborough-on-Tees, had overcome all the practical difficulties, and now produced rails of the required size, with hard metal in the upper portion, and ductile metal in the lower, by which both durability and strength were insured. The joint was made by either a cast, or wrought-iron chair, or saddle, which received the ends of the rails, and into which they were keyed with wooden keys. The gauge was preserved by means of a tie-bar, fitted and keyed into sockets on the chairs.

An experimental length of road on this construction had been laid down on the main line of the North Midland Railway, the cost of which was £3,323 per mile; but it was thought, that in future this might be reduced to £2,487 per mile, by reducing the weight of the rails to 100 lbs. per yard, and the chairs in proportion, as it was found by experiment, that these rails were greatly in excess of strength, being as much as three times stronger than that of the ordinary double-headed rail.

A mile of road had also been laid upon the same line, with cast-iron sleepers adapted to the ordinary rail, as introduced by Mr. P. W. Barlow, M. Inst. C. E.; and another mile had been laid with these cast-iron sleepers at the joints only, but having intermediate sleepers of timber.

The motion of the trains over their several experimental lengths was firm and steady, there being no perceptible difference between the two latter descriptions.

In the discussion which ensued, in which Messrs. Hawkshaw, Brunel, Locke, M.P., P. W. and W. H. Barlow, and Glyn, took part, the relative advantages and disadvantages of the different systems of permanent way in present use were discussed, and, also, in some slight degree, compared with that proposed by Mr. W. H. Barlow; but it appeared to be a general opinion, that no one system of laying a permanent road could at present claim a great superiority over any other; and that, in reality, much more depended on the good quality of the materials used in its construction, than in any particular way of laying it. The objects to be obtained were—simplicity of construction, so that there should be as few parts as possible to get out of order, a perfect joint, and economy of maintenance; and though the two first of these desiderata were admitted to be obtained in a permanent way with bridge-shaped rails and longitudinal timber sleepers, it was contended that they were, to some extent, counterbalanced in a road laid in the ordinary manner, with double-headed rails, and cast-iron chairs, as, in some instances, after being turned, the second table was found to be more durable than the first.

Whatever might be the result of the discussion, it was admitted that the subject was one of great importance, and that the introduction of any improvement in so vital a point as the "permanent way" would confer a great boon on railway property.

May 21st.

THE paper read, was "On Printing Machines, especially those used in the printing of the *Times* newspaper;" by Mr. Edward Cowper. This subject was discussed, and a plate of Mr. Applegath's new vertical Machine, described in the Artizan for last December; we need, therefore, only add the additional information which may be gleaned from the abstract of the Paper.

Some interesting statistics, relative to the printing of the *Times*, were mentioned, from which it appeared, that on the 7th of May, 1850, the *Times* and *Supplement* contained 72 columns, or 17,500 lines, made up of upwards of a million pieces of type, of which matter about two-fifths were written, composed, and corrected after 7 o'clock in the evening. The *Supplement* was sent to press at 7 50, P.M., the first form of the paper at 4.15, A.M., and the second form at 4.45, A.M. ; on this occasion 7,000 papers were published before 6.15, A.M., 21,000 papers before 7.30, A.M., and 34,000 before 8.45, A.M., or in about four hours. The greatest number of copies ever printed in one day was 54,000, and the greatest quantity of printing in one day's publication was on the 1st of March, 1848, when the paper used weighed 7 tons, the weight usually required being 4½ tons; the surface to be printed every night, including the *Supplement*, was 30 acres; the weight of the fount of type in constant use was 7 tons, and 110 compositors, and 25 pressmen were constantly employed. The whole of the printing at the *Times* office was actually performed by three of Applegath and Cowper's four-cylinder machines, and two of Applegath's new vertical cylinder machines.

The President afterwards briefly addressed the meeting, congratulating the Members on the continued success and prosperity of the Institution, and adjourned the meeting for business until the second Tuesday in November.

It was moved, seconded, and carried unanimously, that the cordial thanks of the Institution be offered to the President, for the unwearied attention he had paid to the interests of the Institution, and for the urbanity he had at all times displayed in the chair.

SOCIETY OF ARTS.

22nd May.

WILLIAM FOTHERGILL COOKE, Esq., Vice-President, in the Chair.

On the application of Electro-Magnetism as a Motive Power,

by Mr. ROBERT HUNT.

IN this paper the author called attention, in the first place, to the numerous attempts which have been made to apply electro-magnetism as a power for moving machines, and particularly described the apparatus employed by Jacobi, Dal Negro, M'Gauley, Wheatstone, and others, noticing incidentally the machines recently constructed by Mr. Hjorth. Since, notwithstanding the talent which has been devoted to this interesting subject, and the large amount of money which has been spent in the construction of machines, the public are not in possession of any electro-magnetic machine which is capable of exerting any power economically ; and finding that, notwithstanding the aid given to Jacobi by the Russian Government, that able experimentalist has abandoned his experimental trials,—the author has been induced to devote much attention to the examination of the first principles by which the power is regulated, with the hope of being enabled to set the entire question on a satisfactory basis.

The phenomenon of electro-magnetic induction was explained, and illustrations given of the magnetisation of soft iron by means of a voltaic current made to circle around it. The power of electro-magnets was given, and the author stated his belief that this power could be increased without limitation.

A voltaic current produced by the chemical disturbance of the elements of any battery, no matter what its form may be, is capable of producing by induction a magnetic force, *this magnetic force being always in an exact ratio to the amount of matter (zinc, iron, or otherwise) consumed in the battery.*

Several forms of the voltaic battery were explained, particularly those of Daniell, Grove, Bunsen, and Reinsch, the latter being constructed without metals, depending entirely on the action between two dissimilar fluids, slowly combining.

The author had, however, proved, by an extensive series of experiments, that the greatest amount of magnetic power is produced when the chemical action is the most rapid. Hence, in all magnetic ma-

chines, it is more economical to employ a battery under an intense action, than one in which the chemical action is slow. It has been proved by Mr. Joule, and most satisfactorily confirmed by the author, that one-horse power is obtainable in an electro-magnetic engine, the most favourably constructed to prevent loss of power, at the cost of 45 pounds of zinc, in a Grove's battery, in 24 hours ; while 75 pounds are consumed in the same time to produce the same power in a battery of Daniell's construction. The cause of this was referred to the necessity of producing a high degree of excitement, to overcome the resistance which the molecular forces offer to the electrical perturbations, on which the magnetic force depends.

It was contended, that although we have not perhaps arrived at the best form of voltaic battery, yet that we have learnt sufficient of the law of electro-magnetic forces to declare, that, under any conditions, the amount of magnetic power would depend on the change of state-consumption of an element—in the battery, and that the question resolved itself into this :—

What amount of magnetic power can be obtained from an equivalent of any material consumed ?

The following were regarded as the most satisfactory results yet obtained :—

1. The force of voltaic current being equal to 678, the number of grains of zinc destroyed per hour was 151, which raised 9000 pounds one foot high in that time.

2. The force of current being, relatively, 1300, the zinc destroyed in an hour was 291 grains, which raised 10,030 pounds through the space of one foot.

3. The force being 1000, the zinc consumed was 223 grains; the weight lifted one foot 12,672 pounds.

The estimations made by Messrs. Scoresby and Joule, and the results obtained by Œrsted, and more recently by Mr. Hunt, very nearly agree ; and it was stated that one grain of coal consumed in the furnace of a Cornish engine lifted 143 pounds one foot high, whereas, one grain of zinc consumed in the battery lifted only 80 pounds. The cost of one hundred weight of coal is under 9 pence ; the cost of one hundred weight of zinc is above 216 pence. Therefore, under the most perfect conditions, magnetic power must be nearly 25 times more expensive than steam power.

But the author proceeded to show that it was almost proved to be an impossibility ever to reach even this condition, owing, in the first place, to the rate with which the force diminishes through space. As the mean of a great many experiments on a large variety of magnets, of different forms and modes of construction, the following result was given :—

Magnet and armature in contact, lifting force,	220	pounds.
,, distant $\frac{1}{50}$ of an inch	90·6	,,
,, $\frac{1}{25}$	50·7	,,
,, $\frac{1}{5}$	50·1	,,
,, $\frac{1}{10}$	40·6	,,

Thus at one fiftieth of an inch distance four-fifths of the power are lost.

This great reduction of power takes place when the magnets are stationary. The author then proceeded to show that the moment they were set in motion a great reduction of the original power immediately took place ; that, indeed, any disturbance produced near the poles of a magnet diminished, during the continuance of the motion, its attractive force.

The attractive force of a magnet being 150 pounds when free of disturbance, fell to one-half, by occasioning an armature to revolve near its poles.

Therefore, when a system of magnets which had been constructed to produce a given power is set in revolution, every magnet at once suffers an immense loss of power, and consequently their combined action falls in practice very far short of their estimated power. This fact has not been before distinctly stated, although the author is informed that Jacobi observed it.

And not merely does each magnet thus sustain an actual loss of power, but the power thus lost is converted into a new form of force, or rather becomes a current of electricity, acting in opposition to the primary current by which the magnetism is induced.

From an examination of all these results, Mr. Hunt is disposed to regard electro-magnetic power as impracticable, on account of its cost, which must necessarily be, he conceives, under the best conditions, 50 times more expensive than steam power.

The Chairman agreed with Mr. Hunt in his conclusion of the improbability of any result being obtained from electro-magnetism which could enable it to compete with steam as a motive-power. At any rate, the point to which the attention of engineers and experimentalists should be turned at present was, not the contriving of perfect machines for applying electro-magnetic power, but the discovery of the most effectual means of disengaging the power itself from the conditions in which it existed stored up in nature. Mr. Faraday assured us that in a single drop of water is contained as much electricity as is developed in a thunder-storm. The portion of this which we can liberate by any existing battery is very small ; so small, that, as shown by Mr. Hunt's paper, its practical use cannot be profitable. The study of electro-chemistry, he thought, was a more promising field, and one from which might at a future time be developed a power which should supersede even steam.

Mr. Winkworth proposed, and Mr. Highton seconded, a vote of thanks to Mr. Hunt.

The attention of the meeting was called to a model of a three-roomed labourer's cottage, which had been erected by Mr. W. N. Clay, at Harlow, in Essex, at a cost of 10l. only. The walls are formed of clay lumps dried in the sun, having an admixture of straw in their composition ; the roof is of thatch, and the floor of concrete.

Analogous modes of building, used not only for cottages, but for houses of large size, in Cornwall, Hampshire, and the West of England, were mentioned by several members, as well as the "Pisa-work" used in Italy for churches and large buildings.

A chair, ingeniously composed of 492 small pieces of wood dovetailing into each other, and holding together without either glue or pins, was shown to the meeting. It is the work of a farm-labourer, named Selwood, of Charlton, near Pusey, in Wilts, and was entirely executed by him with a knife.

Mr. Varley, jun., explained his improvements in the air-pump. In place of the two barrels and vibrating intermittent motion of the ordinary pump, Mr. Varley has a continuous circular motion in the handle, and one double-acting barrel. The piston-rod is attached to a crank on the motion-shaft, and the cylinder oscillates from its bottom, a packed joint being most ingeniously done away with by having the tube between the barrel and the receiver coiled spirally, which, by its spring, gives play enough for the oscillation of the barrel. Mr. Varley explained his larger pump, in which there are some ingenious contrivances in addition to those already mentioned. Instead of a valve opening inwards into the barrel by the pressure of the air, as in the old pumps, the valve is worked by an eccentric, and is so arranged as to open a communication between the top and bottom of the barrel at each stroke, by which the rarefaction of the air is doubled. He has obtained, with this pump, a vacuum of $\frac{1}{10}$ of an inch of mercury.

5th June.

JOHN LEWIS RICARDO, Esq., M.P., Vice-President, in the Chair.

Proposal for the Formation of a Thames Embankment throughout the Metropolis, having a terraced Highway, and comprising a Railway Arcade and Tunnels for Water, Sewage, and Gas, by Mr. W. H. SMITH, C.E.

The importance of this subject is universally admitted ; but it will be asked, what are the peculiar features of the plans here proposed, and the object of bringing them forward at a period of general depression rather than of enterprise ?

Although various projects have, at different times, been suggested for the conveyance into and through the metropolis of the railways, the sewage, and pure water, and the formation of the Thames embankment, by Mr. Martin, Sir Frederic Trench, Mr. Stephenson, Mr. Walker, Mr. Page, and others, none, like the present, have combined all the great contemplated arterial works in one space—and that space the river-banks, not merely useless in their existing state, but highly pernicious to the health of the largest and most wealthy population in the world.

The reason of their being brought forward at this time is, that, on all sides, steps are being taken which, if carried out, will place serious difficulties in their way, if not prevent their execution altogether. Extensions of railways into the metropolis by tunnels or viaducts have been proposed, and in some instances completed ; a commission exists which purposes to deal solely with the question of sewage; independent pure water companies are now before Parliament; and lastly, powers are granted to individuals to encroach upon the Thames, securing the land as private property.

These efforts, however, tend at the same time to show the general wants of the public, and that such have not as yet been satisfied has been owing to the inefficiency of the plans proposed, their expensive working, and the interruption of traffic which would ensue from their execution separately. The present proposal is for uniting in one work these several objects, avoiding the interruption to commerce, increasing the stability and splendour of the whole, and executing it at a minimum.

The general arrangement is as follows. On the top, about twelve feet above high-water mark, is the terrace, exclusively for the public, without other landing than for passengers. The traffic would be conveyed by the transverse arches beneath, which descend to within a foot of high-water. These arches would be connected with, and the property of, the warehouses or wharfs on the inner side; and thus river traffic would be carried on unimpeded, indeed almost invisibly. Immediately beneath is the railway-tunnel, in the base of which the required culverts for pure water, gas, rain-water, and sewage would be formed at about low-water mark.

Although the remunerative advantages of a railway through London are fully allowed, the enormous outlay required in the first instance has been an insuperable difficulty, as the purchase of property alone, for a viaduct, without any work to the extent here proposed, would amount to more than the entire cost of the improvements contemplated, whilst the steam and noise, together with the walling-out, as it were, of property and free intercourse, are great evils. On the other hand, the objections to tunnels were, the apparently necessary ascent and descent of steep passenger-shafts, and the avoiding of local traffic altogether. Unlike the tunnels of Liverpool, which being in the sandstone create much noise and echo, this hollow embankment, or arcade, would be formed in the sound-deadening London clay ; and the railway passing through would unite all the existing railways, and by branch tunnels convey the passengers to any required part of London. This line of railway would have not alone the combined traffic of the present railways, but a great part of that of London itself, the great objection of the shafts being overcome by a very simple arrangement. Thus passengers might, in the course of a few minutes, proceed from end to end of London, and the two greatest lines of traffic in the world, that of London itself, and that of goods and passengers of the united railways, would be secured and conjoined. It is calculated that this part of the proposition would amply repay the entire works. Some years ago it met with the approbation of one of the first engineers of the day, in connexion with his railway which had its terminus in London. The tunnel would be as well lit up as, and drier than the Thames Tunnel. The Adelphi arches, beneath the Society's house, are an exact illustration of the kind of work, and its position relatively to the houses above. They would, in all probability, from their great extent, be chosen as a depôt, as was proposed by one of the existing companies, thereby removing the street traffic of the metropolis, which is at present in a state of collapse.

Pure water will be obtained from the Thames above the region of manufactories, and conveyed by gravitation, in a culvert within the embankment, through London, where it would be pumped up to supply public fountains and every tenement in London, the present water being employed for cleansing, and flushing periodically, the existing sewers There will likewise be spaces for gas-pipes.

The sewage of the metropolis is intended to be cut off from the Thames, as so strongly recommended in the Report of the Board of Health, and passed longitudinally under the embankment into the marshes; that on the south side being carried by an iron culvert across the Thames, and joining the northern outfall, which would be carried into the estuary of the Thames, near Hollyhaven, below the influence of the tide, to/carry it even as far back as Gravesend. There would be great economy and advantage to the country in employing night trains into which the sewage might be pumped, and conveyed probably for one halfpenny per ton per mile, increasing threefold the productiveness of some of the agricultural districts around London, and thereby, at one and the same time, enhancing the value of property and lowering the price of food. The Thames, being the lowest, is unquestionably the natural outfall of the metropolis, as is agreed on by those who favour its continued impurities; but it does not necessarily follow that because such outfall is preserved, the sewage should not be shut out from the river; and when it can be done, as it may be said, without cost, in connexion with another work, all objection is removed.

The advantage to the community of retaining the present levels and course of the sewers running transversely to the metropolis is self-evident: they have occupied many ages and cost vast sums in their construction, and would be the natural tributaries to these above-named main sewers, the *Cloaca Maxima* of the Thames. These sewers would be cemented; so that there could be no more objection to their proximity to the tunnels than to the drains of every house,—indeed, not so much, they being hermetically sealed. All towns above London should equally be compelled to direct their water from an unnatural to its natural destination, from the river to the land, and thereby restore the Thames to that original purity, which through a succession of ages had been guarded from pollution with jealous scrutiny, so much so as to admit of its being used as a bathing-place for monarchs.

Thus within the embankment there would be contained a railway, with water, sewage, and gas, as at present under all the leading streets, and they would be accessible, like the sewers of Naples, without disrupture of the street above.

Without more capital than is raised by a railway company, would thus be formed a work peculiarly the property of the public, and causing enormous revenues to be derived from that which at the present moment is either diverted into a false channel or wholly lost, or most pernicious in its operation, which may be said of the street traffic, the sewage, and the banks of the Thames.

The estimated cost of two embankments from Vauxhall Bridge, on each side of the river, to the West India Docks on the north, and to Deptford on the south, a distance of ten miles, would be 3,000,000*l*. Admitting for a moment that the reproductive character of the work may have been overrated, it will be no great misfortune to have laid throughout the entire length of London, the ground-work for what would necessarily follow, a line of handsome dwellings, shops and warehouses, with a terraced walk, flanked with trees, adjoining the river, forming truly " the lungs of the metropolis," removing those pernicious

banks and shoals so destructive to health, and taking from our spacious river, with its beautiful changing lines, and its stately and unequalled bridges, that *backdoor* aspect, which is the wonder of foreigners, and a disgrace to our civilization.

On the other hand, it is fully believed that there are no principles involved in these plans of which our existing engineers have not given us successful examples under greater difficulties. The combination of works would surpass in utility and grandeur the cloacæ and aqueducts of ancient Rome, and it would become a monument of the skill and liberality of the present age.

Mr. Boccius explained a plan of which he was the author, in connexion with Mr. Stothert. In this plan the existing sewers are also retained, their contents being pumped up into reservoirs, where their solid contents are, by a process which has just been patented, precipitated and deodorized, the water remaining impregnated only with common salt, and being then used for flushing the sewers; the operations of flushing, pumping-up, and deodorising, continually succeeding each other. The solid manure thus obtained would be of enormous value to the country.

The Chairman, in calling for the thanks of the meeting for the communications and explanations of both these gentlemen, remarked on the imperative necessity that there was that the three great causes of the cholera of last year should be removed,—imperfect sewage, deficient water-supply, and intramural interment. Government had taken the remedies for these into its own hands; a fact which he thought was to be regretted; as in this country all the greatest works had been, and in his opinion, were likely to be, the result of private enterprise.

ROYAL SCOTTISH SOCIETY OF ARTS.

The Royal Scottish Society of Arts met in the Hall, 54, George Street, on Monday, the 22nd April, Patrick Wilson, Esq., Vice-President, in the Chair.

The following communications were made :—

1. "On a New Method of inducing an Upward Current in the Upcast Shaft of Coal-Mines, to promote Ventilation." By Mr. J. Seton Ritchie, Edinburgh.

The author adverted to the vast numbers, as workers, and dependants on them, interested in the adoption of means by which freedom from danger in coal-mines may be attained; then, mentioning the theories by which mine explosions are accounted for, he noticed the numerous methods which have been proposed for maintaining mines in a state of safety, and particularly the method in general use of inducing an upward current of the air of the mine by means of a fire at the lower part of the upcast shaft, that, as the provision of a separate shaft for the removal of the air of the mine is prevented by the great additional expense, even though mechanical appliances may appear highly calculated to maintain a powerful and steady current, difficulty exists in their application, as interfering with the free working of the produce of the mine carried on by the upcast shaft, which is further increased in making provision for continual reliance on them, as spare appliances would require to be provided. The author stated that the method now proposed is free from this obstacle. The current is induced by means of pipes heated by water circulating in them, fixed round the circumference of the shaft, in such manner within the line of it, as shall shield them from injury, leaving sufficient exposure of them to communicate their heat to the air in the shaft; the furnaces for heating the circulating water being at the nearest convenient distance, at a considerably lower level than the orifice of the shaft, as on the depth at which they are placed will depend the perpendicular extent of the upper part of the shaft around which the pipes may be placed. Certainty of action could, with ordinary caution, be relied on, as, even if one of the circulations ceased, from any cause, to act, the others would during that time continue in action. A similar application might also be made at the lower orifice of the shaft, and even extended in some measure to the workings; or the fires now in use at the foot of the shaft might be retained, and the application alone made at the upper part in aid, to promote greater certainty and steadiness in the current. It was submitted that a similar application might be made of steam as of water. It was pointed out that the maintaining of the upward current in the shaft is but one section of the keeping the mine in a state of safety—that, though this will never be effected without a steady and powerful extracting current in the shaft, the latter will be of little avail, unless accompanied by carefully laid out air-courses throughout the mine itself, properly modified as the working advances, attention on the part of those appointed to open and close the doors which it becomes necessary to erect in them to direct the currents, and attention that the building off of exhausted sections of the mine be as frequently as possible accomplished, that they may not become next to permanent reservoirs of noxious gases, ready to lend their aid to a general explosion.

2. "Description of a Design for a Water-Meter." By Mr. F. A. Bucknall, New Swindon, Wilts.

The author stated that the object of this meter is the measurement of the supply of water to private dwellings, breweries, &c. It consists chiefly of a fan-shaped bucket-wheel, revolving within a cylindrical case, and kept water-tight by means of packing, made of India rubber, leather, or other elastic substance, supply and delivery pipes, and wheel and pinion gear, which is connected with an index plate. The revolving action of the meter is maintained by the gravity of the wheel being constantly greater on the one side than on the other, owing to the continuous running off of the water from the opposite side to that at which the water is supplied. The meter is only in action during the time the water is running off.

3. "Description of a New Liquor-Pump, calculated to prevent the Liquor from being contaminated with Verdigris and Oil in the interior of the Pump-Barrel; also applicable to the Pumping of Acids." By Mr. Hay Dall, Brassfounder, Neilson-street, Tradeston, Glasgow.

The author stated the following as the disadvantages of the present system of pumping liquors—1st, That each liquor requires a separate pump. 2nd, That the liquor, in passing through the barrel of the pump, corrodes its interior, especially in the case of fermented liquors, thus producing constant decay in the barrel and valves, and also an accumulation of verdigris in brass pump barrels, which, together with the oil or tallow used to lubricate the piston, is constantly mixing with and contaminating the liquor. The inventor stated that he had his attention frequently directed to the disgusting state of the interior of corroded pump-barrels which had been sent in for repair—that, generally, every crevice and corner of the piston and barrel where it could collect, was clogged with a poisonous and nauseous compound of stale beer and oily verdigris, ready to mix in greater or less quantity with the next liquor that would pass through it. That in the new method one pump can be made to supply any number of liquors, while the liquor never gets into contact with the pump-barrel. The pump is used solely as an air-pump to withdraw the air from the interior of a series of glass or earthenware vessels, properly arranged, and made to communicate with the liquor casks by tubes immersed in the liquor.

When the cocks are properly arranged, and the pump is worked, the liquor rises and fills the vessel, never having passed through the pumped barrel at all, and when the vessel is full, the pumping is stopt, and the liquor is run off into the vessels from which it is to be drunk by a common cock. All the liquors may be pumped up at one time, or any one separately, by properly arranging the cocks; or any one may be pumping while another is being run off. The author stated that he intends this pump also to be used for acids and other corrosive liquids, where the very troublesome leaden pumps are now used. The pipes in this case would be made of lead, porcelain, or glass.

4. "Description of a Model of a Safety-Strap for Glaziers, Slaters, &c." By James R. Dymock, Esq., F.R.S.S.A., Arniston-place.

It was stated that this apparatus has for its object the safety of tradesmen who are employed on roofs or outside of windows, &c. &c. It consists of a balanced iron rod secured inside the window, a strap with shoulder-pieces and connecting cord or rope, each being of sufficient strength not only to sustain the weight of a man, but to endure a sudden jerk without breaking. Its advantages were stated to be simplicity of construction, cheapness, portability, and readiness of adjustment; and that the application of the apparatus might be familiarly illustrated by the ordinary well-known method of securing a watch-dog's chain.

BOILERS OF THE "EXPRESS."

The *Express* is one of the vessels belonging to the Liverpool Steam Tug Company, of the following dimensions: length of deck, 106·5 feet; breadth on deck 19·8 feet; depth of hold, 11 feet; register tonnage, 99 $\frac{42}{94}$ tons. They resemble the boilers of the *President*, (described in our last Number,) in having elliptical flues, but in this instance they are placed with the longer diameter of the ellipse, horizontal instead of vertical. This form of boiler appears to us injudicious. They are long (which renders them inapplicable to anything but a tug,) and at the same time the shell is no stronger than an ordinary tubular boiler of less cubic bulk would be. For tugs, where length can be obtained, the cylindrical or elliptical shell appears the most eligible form.

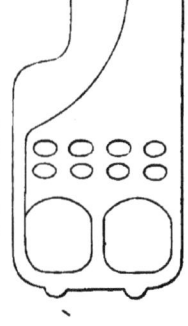 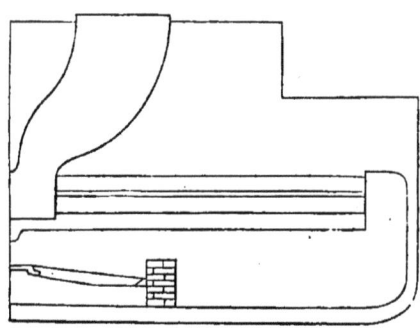

Scale 1/16th of an Inch to a Foot.

DIMENSIONS AND DETAILS OF NEW STEAMERS.

THE BRITISH AND NORTH AMERICAN ROYAL MAIL STEAM NAVIGATION
COMPANY'S NEW STEAM VESSEL, "ASIA."

Built by Messrs. Robert Steele & Co., Greenock. Engines by Mr. Robert Napier, Glasgow.

Builder's measurement.				Ft.	In.
Length of keel and fore rake	..		..	267	0
Breadth of beam	..	..	..	40	6
Ditto, including the paddle cases		..		63	6
Depth of hold, amidships	..		..	27	6
Length of engine space	..		..	92	6
Tonnage.					Tons.
Hull	..	..	..		2128⁷⁄₉₄
Contents of engine space	..		..		811⁵⁄₉
Register	..	..	..		1316³⁷⁄₉₄

New measurement.				Ft.	Tns.
Length on deck	..	..	..	265	2
Breadth on ditto	..		..	37	2
Depth of hold, amidships	..		..	27	2
Length of engine space	..		..	92	5
Tonnage.					Tons.
Hull	..	..	..		2226⁵⁶⁄₁₀₀
Contents of engine space	..		..		1012³⁵⁄₁₀₀
Register	..	..	..		1214²¹⁄₁₀₀

A pair of side lever engines, of 814 horse nominal power ; diameter of cylinders, 96 inches × 9 feet length of stroke ; diameter of paddle wheels, extreme, 37 feet 7½ inches ; ditto effective, 36 feet 10½ inches ; floats, 9 feet 2 inches × (two parts of 19 inches) 3 feet 2 inches ; three sets of 28 arms and floats ; 8 floats in the water, at a draught of 19 feet forward, and 20 feet abaft. The boilers are 4 in number, similar to those of the other vessels, only larger ; they are 20 feet in length, and 16 feet in breadth ; 20 furnaces, 5 in each boiler—length 8 feet, breadth 2 feet 9 inches, depth 5 feet 9 inches ; between boilers, 2 feet ; boilers to bunkers, 7 feet 6 inches ; bunkers hold about 900 tons of coals. 38 men in the engine room, viz. 8 engineers, 18 firemen, and 12 coal trimmers. On the trip from the Clyde to the Mersey this vessel went 15 miles per hour, average. The engines are very handsomely fitted up with malleable iron framing, and the starting wheels are upon the upper platform. On one engine is bolted a dial time-piece, and opposite it is a dial indicator case, with a small rod projecting at the bottom, which acts in concert with an ingenious contrivance on the top of the air-pump cross-head (similar to the buffers used for railway carriages), only small, and at every stroke of the engine the buffer touches the indicator rod gently, thereby giving the number of revolutions made in the whole voyage. The accommodation for passengers may be pronounced perfect, both in elegance and comfort. Nothing is left undone to make the passengers as comfortable as at the best hotels on *terra firma.*

DESCRIPTION.

A full female figure head ; no galleries ; round sterned and carvil built vessel of timber ; 3 decks, flush ; 3 masts ; schooner rigged ; standing bowsprit ; carries 6 boats. Port of Glasgow. Commander—Mr. C. H. E. Judkins.

THE ISLE OF MAN ROYAL MAIL STEAM NAVIGATION COMPANY'S IRON
STEAM VESSEL, "BENN-MAC-CHREE."
(In Saxon—The Woman of my Heart.)

Built and fitted by Mr. Robert Napier, Glasgow.

Builder's measurement.			Ft.	In.
Length of keel and fore rake	..	..	152	0

				Ft.	In.
Breadth of beam	..	..	..	21	0
Ditto over the paddle cases	..		..	38	9
Depth of hold, amidships	..		..	12	9
Length of engine space	..		..	50	0
Tonnage.					Tons.
Hull	..	..	..		330⁴⁴⁄₉₄
Contents of engine space	..		..		113⁴⁹⁄₉₄
Register	..	..	..		211⁵⁹⁄₉₄

New measurement.				Ft.	Tns.
Length on deck	..	..	..	151	9
Breadth on ditto, amidships	..		..	20	3
Depth of hold, ditto	..		..	12	5
Length of engine space	..		..	50	0
Tonnage.					Tons.
Hull	..	..	..		295⁷³⁄₁₀₀
Contents of engine space	..		..		137⁴⁵⁄₁₀₀
Register	..	..	..		158⁴¹⁄₁₀₀

A pair of side lever engines, of 132 horse nominal power ; diameter of cylinders, 44 inches × 4 feet length of stroke ; diameter of paddle wheels, extreme, 17 feet 7 inches ; ditto effective, 17 feet ; floats 6 feet 6 inches × 2 feet ; 3 sets of 16 arms and floats ; tubular boilers—length, 14 feet 9 inches, breadth, 9 feet, depth, 11 feet 3 inches ; length of steam chests, 6 feet 9 inches, breadth, 2 feet 8 inches, depth, 3 feet 9 inches ; round at back. Six furnaces, three in each boiler—length, 5 feet 3 inches, breadth, 2 feet 4 inches, with dry bottoms ; 48 tubes, 24 in each boiler ; diameter, 4 inches ; boiler to bunker, 6 feet 3 inches ; the bunker occupies 4 feet in the length of the vessel, and all the breadth and depth ; holds 25 tons of coals ; tunnel or passage—breadth, 3 feet, depth, 6 feet 8 inches. Frames, 3 × 3 × ⅜ inches, and 2 feet apart ; 8 strakes of plates from keel to gunwale. Revolutions per minute, 28 when loaded, and 31 when light ; steam pressure, 8 lbs. ; consumption of fuel, 1 ton of coals per hour ; draught of water, 7 feet average. Plying between Douglas and Liverpool (75 miles) in 6½ hours. The crew consists of 19 hands, viz. 7 in the engine room, 3 under the steward, and 9 in the captain's department. The engines were made in 1834, the vessel in 1845.

DESCRIPTION.

A full female figure head, false quarter galleries, clipper bow, square sterned and clinch built vessel, standing bowsprit, three masts, schooner rigged. Port of Douglas. Commander—Mr. John Kermode.

These engines were formerly on board of the "Queen of the Isles," built of timber by Mr. John Wood, Port Glasgow, 1834, but converted into a sailing vessel, 1847, by Messrs. Robert Barclay & Curle, Finieston, Glasgow.

				Ft.	Tns.
Length on deck	..	..	..	128	9
Breadth on ditto, amidships	..		..	22	2
Depth of ditto ditto	..		..	16	0
Length of poop	..		..	28	3
Breadth of ditto	..		..	18	1
Depth	..		..	1	8
Tonnage.					Tons.
Hull	..	..	..		337⁷⁴⁄₁₀₀
Poop	..	..	..		9⁷⁷⁄₁₀₀
Total	..	..	..		347⁵¹⁄₁₀₀

Bust, female figure-head. No galleries, square sterned, and carvil built ; three masts, barque rigged, standing bowsprit. Port of Glasgow.

SHIP-BUILDING UPON THE CLYDE IN JUNE, 1850.

(From our own Correspondent.)

GLASGOW.

Messrs. Robert Barclay and Curle, (Finnieston,) have at present upon the stocks, all in frame and planked, an 8 years, A 1, clipper schooner, of timber, for the coasting trade.

	Ft.	In.
Length of keel and fore rake	78	0
Breadth of beam	18	4
Depth of hold at midships	11	0
Tonnage	120⁸⁴⁄₉₄	

This vessel could be launched in four weeks.

They have also upon the stocks, and in frame, a large 13 years' timber ship, for the Clyde and Calcutta Packet Ship service, and to be flush on deck.

	Ft.	In.
Length of keel and fore rake	135	0
Breadth of beam	28	6
Depth of hold at midships	20	0
Tonnage	509⁹⁴⁄₉₄	

At Mr. Robert Napier's yard, Govan, at 8 o'clock on Monday evening, the 3rd June, there was launched from the upper building-yard, an iron paddle steamer, the property of the Scottish Central Railway Company, to ply upon the rivers Forth or Tay, built flush upon deck, square at both ends of the vessel, with a rudder at each end (upon the box principle,) to save the necessity of turning.

	F.	Tnths.
Length on deck	129	0
Breadth on ditto at midships	23	3
Depth of hold, ditto	8	5
Length of engine room	42	0

	Tons.
Hull	234₁⁵⁄₁₀₀
Contents of engine room	90₁⁵⁄₁₀₀
Register	144₁⁵⁄₁₀₀

To be propelled by a pair of oscillating engines, of 125 horses nominal power. Diameter of cylinders, 44 inches × 3 feet 6 inches stroke ; the boilers are of the common flue description ; the frames are 3 feet apart. She is now fitting out at the Lancefield Dock.

Messrs. Tod and M'Gregor have upon the stocks two large steamers for Australian Mail Lines, the property of the Peninsula and Oriental Company. Each vessel to be fitted with a pair of double-side rod direct-acting engines of 470 horses nominal power ; cylinders 77 inches diameter × 6 ft. 6 in. stroke ; diameter of paddle-wheels over the floats 29 feet. One of the vessels is to have Messrs. Summers and Lamb's patent sheet-water transpace-boilers, and the other, ordinary tubular boilers.

GREENOCK.

Messrs. John Scott and Sons have at present upon the stocks, and all in frame, for the East India trade, a large timber ship, to class 13 years, A 1, at Lloyd's ; to have a poop and top-gallant forecastle.

	Ft.	In.
Length of keel and fore rake	132	0
Breadth of beam	31	0
Depth of hold at midships	20	6
Tonnage	583⁹⁴⁄₉₄	

Mr. John Arthur, Cartsdyke, lately launched a beautiful pleasure yacht, flush on deck, and of the following dimensions :—

	Ft.	In.
Length of keel and fore rake	24	6
Breadth of beam	8	2
Depth of hold at midships	4	6
Tonnage	7⅘	

Mr. James M'Millan, Cartsdyke, has upon the stocks, all in frame and partly planked, a brig,—to have a quarter-deck, and to class 8 years, A 1, at Lloyd's.

	Ft.	In.
Length of keel and fore rake	95	4
Breadth of beam	24	0
Depth of hold at midships	16	0
Tonnage	245⁹⁴⁄₉₄	

The Clyde Shipping Company, Greenock, have their steam towing vessel, *Gulliver*, into the New Graving-dock, where they are giving the vessel a thorough overhaul, putting in new paddle beams, and lengthening the keel about 5 feet forward, so as to give less rake to the stem, and sponcering from the keel up to the gunwale, which will be a decided improvement upon the vessel, at all events will be a means of keeping the vessel from falling so heavy into a sea-way. Messrs. M'Onie and Merrilies, engineers, Tradeston, Glasgow, are making a new set of tubular boilers for the *Gulliver*, in lieu of the former, which were on the common flue principle. They are also making a new set of gearing, the engines being on the second motion, and also a new set of feathering paddle wheels, to replace the old common wheel.

Messrs. Robert Steele and Co. have upon the stocks 4 vessels, viz :— A Brig, for the Newfoundland trade, the property of Messrs. James and William Stewart, of Greenock, to class, 9 years, A 1, at Lloyd's, and of the following dimensions :—

Builder's measurement.	Ft.	In.
Length of keel and fore rake	101	0
Breadth of beam	22	9
Depth of hold at midships	14	9
Tonnage	242⁹⁴⁄₉₄	

New measurement.	Ft.	Ten.
Length on deck	99	8
Breadth on ditto at midships	21	0
Depth of hold at ditto	14	8
Tonnage	241⁸⁵⁄₉₄	

This vessel will be launched in about a week hence.

They have also upon the stocks, and in a very forward state, the steam vessel, *Africa*, the property of the British and North American Royal Mail Steam Navigation Company. The following are the dimensions :—

Builder's measurement.	Ft.	In.
Length of keel and fore rake	267	0
Breadth of beam	40	6
Depth of hold	27	6
Tonnage	2,128⁹⁴⁄₉₄	

New measurement.	Ft.	Ten.
Length on deck	265	6
Breadth on ditto at midships	37	2
Depth of hold at ditto	27	2
Tonnage	2,226⁸⁴⁄₉₄	

A pair of side lever engines, of 814 horses nominal power. Diameter of cylinders, 96 inches × 9 feet stroke ; paddle wheels, diameter, extreme, 37 feet 7 inches, and 36 feet 10 inches effective ; 28 floats, 9 feet 2 in. × 3 feet 2 inches, three sets of 28 arms. 8 floats in the water, at 19 feet draft of water. Four flue boilers, 30 furnaces ; bunkers to hold 890 tons of coals ; 38 hands in the engine room. This vessel is built of the best British oak, and planked double out and inside, and between the frames is filled up, from the keel to the gunwale, with rock salt, to preserve the vessel from the dry rot. She is expected to be ready for launching in about three weeks, and is to be commanded by Mr. Alexander Ryrie.

They have also upon the stocks, and in frame, a 9 years' brig, the property of Messrs. William Greene and Co., of Greenock.

		Ft.	In.
Length of keel and fore rake	..	90	0
Breadth of beam	..	20	6
Depth of hold at midships	..	12	6
Tonnage	..	175$\frac{4}{4}$	

Also, a schooner for the coasting trade, owned by Messrs. Ferguson, Henry, and Co., of Greenock, to class 8 years, A 1, at Lloyd's.

		Ft.	In.
Length of keel and fore rake	..	63	6
Breadth of beam	..	18	0
Depth of hold at midships	..	9	0
Tonnage,	..	90$\frac{2}{4}$	

Messrs. Robert Steele and Co. have also converted the steamer *Aurora* into a sailing vessel, and are now fitting the masts and spars, &c. The following are the present dimensions :—

		Ft.	Ten.
Length on deck	..	153	0
Breadth on ditto at midships	..	20	9
Depth of hold at ditto	..	13	8
Length of break-deck	..	10	0
Breadth of ditto	..	21	7
Depth	..	3	5

		Tons.
Hull	..	402$\frac{14}{16}$
Break-deck	..	8$\frac{1}{15}$
Total	..	410$\frac{14}{16}$

This vessel was formerly plying upon the station between Glasgow and Belfast; at the latter place the vessel was built, in 1839. She is now barque-rigged, with 3 masts, and will be shortly ready for sea. Draft of water, 5 feet 3 inches, light.

Messrs. Wm. Simons and Co., Cartsdyke, have upon the stocks, and in frame, a brig for the West India trade, to class 9 years, A 1, at Lloyd's, and of the following dimensions :—

		Ft.	In.
Length of keel and fore rake	..	95	0
Breadth of beam	..	23	0
Depth of hold at midships	..	15	9
Tonnage	..	230$\frac{4}{4}$	

Also, a barque, all in frame, for the Mauritius trade, and owned by Messrs. Dennistoun and Co., Port-Glasgow, to class 8 years, A 1, at Lloyd's, and of the following dimensions :—

		Ft.	In.
Length of keel and fore rake	..	100	0
Breadth of beam	..	24	0
Depth of hold at midships	..	17	3
Tonnage	..	246$\frac{4}{4}$	

Also, a ship for the China trade, and to class 13 years, A 1, at Lloyd's, and of the following dimensions :—

		Ft.	In.
Length of keel and fore rake	..	135	0
Breadth of beam	..	30	0
Depth of hold at midships	..	20	6
Tonnage	..	569$\frac{4}{4}$	

LAUNCH OF THE "TIARA."—On Thursday, the 6th of June, there was launched from the building-yard of Messrs. Wm. Simons and Co.,

Cartsdyke, Greenock, a beautiful pleasure yacht, the property of the builders, and built upon the wave line principle forward; but not in the after part. She is a very peculiarly built vessel, and is expected to sail very fast. The following are the dimensions :—

		Ft.	In.
Length aloft	..	42	0
Length of keel and fore rake	..	33	0
Breadth of beam	..	10	0
Depth of hold at midships	..	7	6
Tonnage	..	14$\frac{4}{4}$	
Rake abaft	..	9 feet.	

New measurement.		Ft.	In.
Length on deck	..	40	6
Breadth on ditto at midships	..	9	0
Depth of hold at ditto	..	5	5
Tonnage	..	10$\frac{21}{100}$	

PORT-GLASGOW.

Mr. James Fagan, Newark, has upon the stocks, all planked, a smack for the coasting trade.

		Ft.	In.
Length of keel and fore rake	..	38	0
Breadth of beam	..	13	0
Depth of hold at midships	..	7	0
Length aloft	..	39	2
Tonnage	..	26$\frac{4}{4}$	

FAIRLIE.

On Saturday, the 25th of June, there was launched from the building yard of Messrs. William Fyfe and Son, a first class yacht, named the *Stella*, the property of W. M. Lang, Esq., of Blackdales. This vessel measures 32 tons, and is a very handsome model, and is expected to sail remarkably fast, if not to excel, at least to equal any yacht of the same tonnage.

DUMBARTON.

Messrs. Denny and Rankin have just laid down a large ship for the Clyde and Calcutta trade, to class 8 years, A 1, at Lloyd's, and owned by Messrs. Peter and Thomson Aikman, of Glasgow.

		Ft.	In.
Length of keel and fore rake	..	151	0
Breadth of beam	..	32	0
Depth of hold	..	22	0
Tonnage	..	707$\frac{4}{4}$	

Also, a smack, all planked and nearly ready for launching, for the coasting trade, to class 6 years, A 1, at Lloyd's, and owned by Messrs. Peter M'Intyre and Co., Dumbarton.

		Ft.	In.
Length of keel and fore rake	..	60	0
Breadth of beam	..	17	0
Depth of hold	..	7	0
Tonnage	..	76$\frac{4}{4}$	

They also launched this year the ship *Admiral*, for Australian trade; the barque *Sylph*, for the Valparaiso trade; and the schooner *Rebecca*, for the Rotterdam trade.

Messrs. Archibald M'Millan and Son have upon the stocks, all in frame, and nearly planked, a ship for the West India and Clyde trade, to class 3 years, A 1, at Lloyd's, owned by Messrs. John Kerr and Co., of Greenock.

		Ft.	In.
Length of keel and fore rake	..	105	0
Breadth of beam	..	25	6
Depth of hold	..	17	0
Tonnage	..	315$\frac{4}{4}$	

Also, a smack, nearly ready for launching, to class 5 years, A 1, at Lloyd's, for the coasting trade, owned by Messrs. John Gibb and Co. Milport, and of the following dimensions :—

Builder's measurement.	Ft.	In.
Length of keel and fore rake	53	7
Breadth of beam	17	6
Depth of hold	7	3
Tonnage	71$\frac{17}{94}$	
New measurement.	**Ft.**	**Ten.**
Length on deck	53	7
Breadth on ditto	16	6
Depth of hold	7	0
Tonnage	45$\frac{88}{100}$	

They have also in frame, and nearly planked, a round-sterned smack, of the class and dimensions for the coasting and fishing trade, owned by Messrs. Archibald Smith and Co., Lochfine.

Messrs. Alexander Denny and Brothers, have upon the stocks a large iron screw steam vessel, plated and nearly ready for launching, the property of the Anglo-Italian Screw Steam Navigation Company, and intended to be named the *Genova*, the following are the dimensions :—

Length of keel and fore rake	166	6
Breadth of beam	25	8
Depth of hold	15	0
Tonnage	501$\frac{78}{94}$	

With a quarter deck 56 feet long and 2 ft. 3 inches deep. The frames are 4 × 3 × $\frac{1}{2}$, and spaced 1 foot 3 inches apart; plates $\frac{11}{16}$ and $\frac{5}{8}$ to $\frac{1}{2}$ inch, and double riveted throughout. To carry 600 tons of measurement goods, and 200 tons of coals in the bunkers. She is expected to sail and steam together from 10$\frac{1}{2}$ to 11 knots per hour. To be propelled by a pair of (inverted cylinder) engines, of 114 horses power, nominal. Cylinders 44 inches diameter, 2 feet 9 inches stroke, with a two-bladed screw, 12 feet 6 inches dia., and 17 feet pitch.

They have also on the stocks and in frame another vessel, similar to the above in the frames and plates, and intended to be named the *Rebecca*, the property of Messrs. Henry Moss & Co., an eminent firm at Liverpool, to ply between Liverpool, Genoa, and Leghorn, and of the following dimensions, &c. :—

	Ft.	In.
Length of keel and fore rake	166	6
Breadth of beam	26	0
Depth of hold	15	0
Tonnage	539$\frac{67}{94}$	

A pair of engines by Messrs. Benjamin Hick and Son, Bolton, of 138 horses nominal power. Cylinders, diameter, 48 inches × 2 feet 10 inches stroke; screw, same as the other. Both vessels to have brass tubular boilers, the former by Messrs. James and George Thomson, Clyde Bank Foundry, Finnieston, Glasgow. The *Rebecca* is to ply in consort with the *Livorno*.

Messrs. William Denny and Brothers, have upon the stocks, a screw steam schooner, for the Belfast and London trade.

	Ft.	In.
Length of keel and fore rake	153	0
Breadth of beam	23	3
Depth of hold	12	0
Tonnage	404$\frac{11}{94}$	

To have engines of 80 horses nominal power.

Also a paddle steamer for the Glasgow and Irish trade, with 184 horses nominal power, of the following dimensions :—

	Ft.	In.
Length of keel and fore rake	180	0
Breadth of beam	23	0
Depth of hold, (moulded)	12	6
Tonnage	471$\frac{33}{94}$	

Also an iron sailing schooner for the Stockton and London trade.

	Ft.	In.
Length of keel and fore rake	95	0
Breadth of beam	32	0
Depth of hold, (moulded)	13	0
Tonnage	210$\frac{72}{94}$	

Launch of the Iron Sailing Ship, "Three Bells," at Dumbarton.

At 9 o'clock, on Thursday morning, the 6th of June, there was launched from the Iron Ship-building Yard of Messrs. William Denny and Brothers, a very handsome iron sailing ship, (with a clipper bow,) named the *Three Bells*. The launch was effected in good style, and that without the slightest accident, although the vessel was full rigged, and sky-sail yards up. She glided gracefully into the water, amidst the cheers of the assembled multitude and the firing of cannon, &c., &c. After the launch, the *Jenny Lind* steam tug took the ship in tow down to the Gairloch, where the compasses were adjusted, after which she proceeded to Glasgow the same afternoon, where the vessel is loading at the berth for Quebec and Montreal, this being a trial voyage, after which she will ply between the Clyde and Australia. The caps on the heads of the lower and top masts are iron instead of wood, as ordinarily, also the bulwarks, coomings, &c.; every thing is iron that can be made of iron; there are 5 water-tight bulkheads.

The following are the dimensions :—

Builder's measurement.	Ft.	In.
Length of keel and fore rake	163	2
Breadth of beam	30	0
Depth of hold	17	0
Tonnage	695$\frac{19}{94}$	
New measurement.	**Ft.**	**Ten.**
Length on deck	171	0
Breadth on ditto, at midships	29	6
Depth of hold, ditto	16	7
Length of poop	40	0
Depth of do.	6	9
Tonnage.	**Tons.**	
Hull	581$\frac{4}{100}$	
Poop	67$\frac{82}{100}$	
Total	648$\frac{4}{100}$	
Difference in tonnage	47	

The pumps are on a new principle by the builders, and were made by Messrs. Smith and Tulloch, Engineers, Cartsdyke, Greenock, and are double acting and communicate with the several compartments, and also with the sea, for the purpose of washing decks or extinguishing fires, &c., &c.; and they are situated between the main-hatch and mast, upon deck, and are a neat job. The frames of the hull are 4 × 3 × $\frac{3}{8}$ and 12 inches apart, or 15 inches between centres at midships. The frames fore and aft are 3$\frac{1}{2}$ × 2$\frac{1}{2}$ × $\frac{1}{2}$, spaced the same; plates, garboard streak $\frac{11}{16}$, above that $\frac{5}{8}$ to $\frac{1}{2}$, and $\frac{7}{16}$ of an inch, the mouth streak $\frac{3}{4}$ of an inch. The enterprising owners of this handsome vessel, are Messrs. John, William, and Finlay Bell, Glasgow.

DESCRIPTION.

A scroll and profile figure head, no galleries, square sterned, and clinch built vessel, three masts, ship rigged, stationary bowsprit, one main poop, and top gallant forecastle. Port of Glasgow.—Commander, Mr. Archibald Campbell.

LONDON.

MILLWALL.—Messrs. Robinson and Russell have on the stocks an iron clipper-schooner, designed to combine fast-sailing weatherly qualities, with great capacity or carrying power, in proportion to her registered tonnage. The following are her dimensions:—

				Ft.	In.
Length between perpendiculars		..	..	71	0
Length on deck	..	..	..	89	6
Breadth of beam	..	..	..	22	0
Depth of hold	..	..	..	13	0
Tonnage, O.M.	..	..	150½½		

WATERFORD.

Mr. Albert White has upon the stocks, and all in frame, and partly planked, a 12 years, A 1, schooner, for the British and Foreign trade : to have a quarter-deck.

				Ft.	In.
Length of keel and fore rake	..		..	82	7
Breadth of beam	..	..		21	10
Depth of hold	..	..		13	0
Tonnage	..	..	..	176½½	
Ditto, new	..	..	..	.. about 166	

May the 9th.—There was launched at the Neptune Iron Works the steamer, *Maid of Erin*, after being lengthened 13 feet. She was originally built by Messrs. Tod & McGregor, Glasgow.—They are about to lengthen the screw steamer, *Dublin*, 30 feet, making the vessel 158 feet in length ; after which it is intended that the *Liverpool* screw steamer shall be lengthened to the same extent.

LAUNCH OF THE U. S. STEAM SHIP, "POWHATTAN."

From the Journal of the Franklin Institute.

This splendid steamer was launched from the Gosport Navy Yard Norfolk, on Thursday, Feb. 14, 1850. The following are her dimensions :—Length of keel, 246 feet ; between perpendiculars, 250 feet ; extreme length from billet to taffrail, 276 feet 6 inches ; on deck, 251 feet 6 inches ; breadth of beam, 45 feet ; over guards, 69 feet 6 inches. She is to have side wheels, be propelled by two inclined engines, with cylinders 70 inches diameter and 10 feet stroke, and will have 4 copper boilers. Her machinery is in course of construction, by A. Mahaffy & Co., whose establishment is adjoining the Navy Yard, and the ship is expected to be ready for trial during the year.   W.

On Monday, the 28th of January, there was launched from the Yard of William H. Brown, in New York, at the same time, three steamers, the *New World*, the *Boston*, and the *Artic*." The *New World* had all her machinery up and steam on, and as soon as she was fairly in the water her engine was put in motion, and she made an excursion about the harbour, and sailed for California about two weeks after. She was 216 feet long, 27 feet beam, and had a single engine, with cylinders 40 inches diameter and 11 feet stroke. She may be called a semi sea steamer, being a compound of the ordinary sea steamer and our river boats. She will, no doubt, make a quick trip around.

The *Boston* was about 750 tons, and the *Artic* was one of the Collins line of Liverpool steamers, and the third launched. She is over 3000 tons burthen, and is to have side wheels and two side lever engines, with cylinders 95 inches diameter, and 10 feet stroke.   X.

UNITED STATES NAVAL DRY DOCKS.

At the present time our Government have in progress four different dry docks, capable of docking the largest vessel afloat. These docks, from their great size and the many improvements that have been introduced, are far superior to any at present in use in Europe, and are such as to merit the attention of the readers of the Journal.

Of the four now building one is at Philadelphia, and is known as the floating *sectional* dry dock. It is patented by Messrs. Dakin, Moody,

Burgess, & Dodge, who are at present constructing this one for the Government, a considerable portion of which is already completed, and the balance in progress. When finished, this dock will consist of 10 sections, each of which has the capacity to raise 800 tons—total power 8000 tons—and will take up a vessel of 350 feet in length. Six sections will raise a ship of the line, and the four remaining sections will raise a frigate. The sections are placed side by side, and connected by timbers at the top of the tanks. The pumps for exhausting the sections are worked by four steam engines,—two of 20 and two of 12-horse power. One of each size is used on each side of the dock, and placed so that the two 20-horse engines exhaust 6 sections, and the two 12-horse engines exhaust 4 sections, a perfect uniformity of level being maintained by suitable connexions.

In connexion with the dock, there is a large stone basin, the sides and bottom being of granite. This basin is 350 feet long and 226 feet wide, and contains a sufficient depth of water, at ordinary high tide, to float the dock and the vessel it may contain.

Immediately adjacent to, and connected with, the basin, are two railways on the main land. These railways are to be of the most substantial character, and fully capable of sustaining any vessel the dock will raise.

The operation of the whole is as follows :—The sections of the dock are hauled out into the river, and the water let into them until they sink deep enough to allow the vessel to be floated in. As soon as this takes place, and the vessel is properly secured, the water is pumped out of the sections, and the vessel raised out of the water. When this has been accomplished, the whole is floated into the stone basin and allowed to ground on the bottom, when the vessel may be hauled on the railway. This is effected by means of a hydraulic cylinder, of 36 inches diameter and 12 feet stroke, worked by an engine of 40-horse power. If necessary, two vessels may be put on the railways, and a ship of the line and frigate left on the dock, so that the capacity of the dock is equal to four vessels of large class. When required, additional ways may be put up in connexion with the basin. The whole will be completed during 1851, but some of the sections will be ready this season.   B.

ROYAL STEAM NAVY.

APPOINTMENTS, &c.

Assistant Engineer.—FREDERICK YOUNG, to the *Plumper*.

HOW TO REPAIR SCREW-PROPELLERS.—Considerable stress has been laid by the opponents of the screw, on the supposed impossibility of repairing it in case of accident without all the resources of an engineering establishment. We find, however, from our Indian news, that Mr. Thomas Oultram, chief-engineer of H. M. S. *Reynard*, has been successful in overcoming the difficulty. One of the arms of the screw broke off at about 11 inches from the boss. The spare screw was shipped in two hours and a quarter, and Mr. Oultram undertook to repair the broken one. Four pieces of boiler-plate were moulded to the required form, riveted together (in double thicknesses, we presume,) and stayed inside, and finally bolted to the stump left on the boss. The steam was got up to full pressure, and the engines reversed whilst at full speed, to test the soundness of the job. The report adds, that the experiment was entirely satisfactory. The screw was repaired in 20 days, and, as may be supposed, with very limited means and tools for doing such a job.

EFFECT OF SHOT ON IRON VESSELS.—The Admiralty, taking Sir C. Napier's advice, have had a butt constructed of iron, representing a section of the main-deck of the *Simoom*, and experiments have been tried of the effect of shot and shell upon it by the gunners of the *Excellent*, under the superintendence of Captain Chads. The firing took place at a distance of 460 yards, with guns of various calibre. On the side the shot entered, a large and tolerably round hole was made in the plate, the edges being jagged and turned inwards. On the opposite side the plate was more jagged, and the rivets started. Some of the shot were *split into fragments*, the effect of which was well shown by a light wooden bulkhead which was shattered to pieces. Shell were also found to be very destructive, the further side suffering the most. These experiments, though apparently conclusive, will, we fear, be of little use, for there will always remain a suspicion that they are got up to serve some party purpose. We are informed, that the West India Mail Company have it under consideration to build their new vessels of iron; but we presume, that as they are intended to be convertible into war-steamers, the Admiralty will withhold their consent. The Peninsular Company have several iron vessels, and are having two more built by Messrs. Tod and M'Gregor, of Glasgow, of 1200 tons, and 500 horses power. Under the title of "End of the Iron Age," the *Nautical Standard* brings to light some experiments undertaken by the Admiralty some 30 years back, to test the durability of wrought-iron gun-carriages then introduced into the navy. The effect of shot upon them was very severe, and as a consequence, they were at once abandoned. There can be no doubt that there are numerous other interesting facts of a scientific nature, collected in the Admiralty archives, which might be published with advantage. As it is, they appear to be lost both to the public and to the officials.

Spanish Steam Navy.—We understand that 12 steam-frigates of 1,400 tons, with engines of 500 horse power, have been ordered to be built for the Spanish government. Two by Mr. Charles Mare, and two by Messrs. Wigram, of Blackwall, are in course of construction. Four are to be built in Spain, and the other four, it is expected, will be built in England. The machinery will all be made in England. Each of these 12 steamers is to mount 14 guns—12 light 68-pounders, and two pivot guns of 10 inches diameter.

Sunderland Docks.—These docks were opened on the 20th instant. Mr. George Hudson, M P., was present, and presided at the dinner in the evening. The *Sunderland Herald* states the length of that portion of the dock which has just been opened, at 2,000 feet, and the average breadth, 440; the width at one point being 360, at another, 440, and at another, 520 feet, and covering in all 18¼ acres. The entrance from the river is between Mr. Meik's Tidal Gauge and the Low Quay, where a spacious tidal harbour has been formed. This communicates with the half-tide basin by two massive lock gates, one 45 and the other 60 feet wide. The lock sill is laid six feet below low-water of spring tides, so there will generally be 20 to 21 feet of water over it. The entrance to the dock itself is 60 feet wide; the depth of water at the quays will be 20 feet, and in the middle 24 feet. The length of quays in the dock is 5,248 feet, which will easily accommodate 40 vessels, while the dock itself will hold 220 more. The length of quays in the half-tide basin, 1,026 feet, accommodating 8 vessels, while 30 more can lie outside these. The dock will thus be capable of containing 260, and the half-tide basin 38 vessels; the depth of water, too, will suffice for ships of the largest tonnage. The estimated cost of the works yet to complete, viz., the sea outlet, the piers, and tidal basin, does not, we understand, exceed £60,000; and it is probable that the whole will be finished in about two years.

LIST OF ENGLISH PATENTS.

From the 22nd day of May to the 20th day of June, 1850, inclusive.

William Edward Newton, of Chancery-lane, civil engineer, for improvements in warming and ventilating buildings. May 22.—(Communication.)

Robert Cotgreave, of Eccleston, in the county of Chester, farmer, for certain improvements in machinery or apparatus to be used in draining land. May 22.

Henry Columbus Hurry, of Manchester, civil engineer, for certain improvements in the method of lubricating machinery. May 22.

William Palmer, of Cottage-grove, Bow-road, in the county of Middlesex, gentleman, for improvements in the manufacture of candles and candle-wicks, and in the machinery applicable to such matters. May 22.

Jules Frederick Maillard Dumeste, of Paris, for certain improvements in reflectors for luminaries. May 22.

Simon Pincoffs, of Manchester, in the county of Lancaster, merchant, for certain improvements in the ageing process in calico printing and dyeing, which improvements are also applicable to other processes in calico printing and dyeing. May 23.

William Radley, chemical engineer, and Frederick Meyer, oil merchant, both of Lambeth, in the county of Surrey, for improvements in treating fatty, oleaginous, resinous, bituminous, and cerous bodies, in the manufacture and application of them, and of their components, and subsidiary products, together with the apparatus to be employed therein, to new and other useful purposes. May 25.

Edwin Pettitt, of Birmingham, civil engineer, for improvements in the manufacture of glass; in the method of forming or shaping, and ornamenting vessels and articles of glass; and in the construction of furnaces and annealing kilns. May 25.

John Hickman, of Walsall, in the county of Stafford, clerk, for improvements in the manufacture of cylindrical and other tubes. May 25.

Alfred Vincent Newton, of Chancery-lane, mechanical draughtsman, for improvements for couplings for carriages, and in the attachment of wheels to axles. May 28.—(Communication.)

James Ashworth, of Rochdale, in the county of Lancaster, woollen manufacturer, and Thomas Mitchell, of the same place, manager, for certain improvements in machinery or apparatus for preparing, spinning, and weaving cotton, wool, and other fibrous materials. May 29.

Jonathan Harlow, of Birmingham, in the county of Warwick, for improvements in the manufacture of bedsteads, and other articles for sitting or reclining on. May 30.

Edwin John Jeffery Dixon, of the Royal Slate Quarries, Brynhafod, near Bangor, North Wales, for improvements in the manufacture of sinks, and other articles of slate or stone. May 30.

Thomas Page, of Middle Scotland-yard, in the county of Middlesex, civil engineer, for improvements in the construction and means of cleansing sewers. June 1.

Ezra Jenks Coates, of Bread-street, Cheapside, in the City of London, merchant, for improvements in the manufacture of bolts, spikes, and nails. June 1.

Moses Poole, of the patent bill office, London, gentleman, for improvements in machinery for punching metals, and in the construction of springs for carriages and other uses. June 1.

Arthur Elliott, machine maker, of Manchester, and Henry Heys, of the same place, bookkeeper, for certain improvements in machinery for manufacturing woven fabrics. June 1.

Guillaume Ferdinand de Douhet, of Clermont Ferrand, in the Republic of France, gentleman, for improvements in the disoxygenation of certain bodies, and the application separately or simultaneously of the products therefrom, to various useful purposes. June 1.

Frank Clarke Hills, and George Hills, of Deptford, in the county of Kent, manufacturing chemists, for certain improvements in manufacturing and refining sugar. June 1.

Samuel Brown, of Lambeth, in the county of Surrey, engineer, for improvements in engines, for measuring and registering the flow of fluids, and substances in a fluid state, which improvements are also applicable to steam and other motive engines. June 1.

John Tucker, of the Royal Dockyard, Woolwich, in the county of Kent, shipwright, for improvements in steam boilers, and in gearing, cleansing, and propelling vessels. June 1.—(Communication.)

George Hayward Ford, of St. Martin's-le-Grand, in the county of Middlesex, gentleman, for improvements in obtaining power. June 3.

Paul d'Angely, of Paris, for certain improvements in the construction of privies and urinals, and in apparatus and machinery for cleansing privies, cesspools, and other places; and in deodorizing the matter extracted therefrom, and rendering it available for agricultural purposes. June 4.

David Napier and James Murdock Napier, of the York-road, Lambeth, in the county of Surrey, engineers, for improvements in apparatus for separating fluid from other matters. June 4.

Theodore Cartali, of Manchester, merchant, for certain improvements in the treatment or preparation of yarns or threads for weaving. June 4.—(Communication.)

William Watson, the younger, of Chapel Allerton, in the county of York, manufacturing chemist, for improvements in the preparation and manufacture of various materials, to be used in the processes of dyeing, printing, and colouring. June 4.

John Sykes and Adam Ogden, both of Dock-street, in Huddersfield, in the county of York, wool-cleaners and machine-makers, for certain improvements in machinery for cleaning wool, cotton, and similar fibrous substances, from burrs, motes, and other extraneous matters. June 4.

Edmund Sharpe, of Lancaster, Master of Arts, for certain improvements in railway carriages. June 5.

William Edward Newton, of Chancery-lane, civil engineer, for improvements applicable to boots, shoes, and other coverings for, or appliances to the feet. June 6.—(Communication.)

George Jackson, of Belfast, Ireland, flax-spinner, for improvements in heckling machinery. June 6.

John McNicoll, of Liverpool, engineer, for improvements in machinery for raising and conveying weights. June 6.

William Robertson, of Gateside Hill, Neilstone, in the county of Renfrew, Scotland, machine-maker, for improvements in certain machinery used for spinning and doubling cotton and other fibrous substances. June 6.

James Alexander Hamilton Bell, of the city of New York, in the United States of America, merchant, for improvements in dressing bran, pollard, and sharps. June 6.—(Communication.)

A grant unto William George Bicknell, of Essex-street, Strand, and James Reginald Torin Graham, of the Grove, Clapham Common, of an extension for the term of six years of letters patent, granted by his late Majesty King William IV. to Miles Berry, of Chancery-lane, for an invention of certain improvements in machinery or apparatus for cleaning, purifying, and drying wheat or other grain or seeds. June 7.

William Newton, of Chancery-lane, civil engineer, for certain improvements in the manufacture of cords, ropes, bands, strong cloths, quilting, sacks, and cushions, and in elastic material for stuffing the latter, in which manufacture caoutchouc forms an essential ingredient; and in the application of parts of these improvements to the manufacture of pads, stoppers, tubes, boxes, baskets, coverings, wrappers, and other like articles of utility. June 8.—(Communication.)

James Colman, of Stoke-mills, Stoke, near Norwich, in the county of Norfolk, mustard and starch manufacturer, for improvements in the manufacture of starch. June 8.

Peter Armand le Comte de Fontainemoreau, of South-street, Finsbury, London, for certain improvements in oscillating engines, put in motion by steam and gas, resulting from combustion. June 8.—(Communication.)

Charles Warwick, of Cheapside, warehouseman, for improvements in apparatus for taking up the work of certain descriptions of knitting machinery. June 8.—(Communication.)

Peter Armand le Comte de Fontainemoreau, of South-street, Finsbury, for certain improvements in the manufacture of sulphate of soda, muriatic and nitric acid. June 8.—(Communication.)

William Edward Newton, of Chancery-lane, civil engineer, for improvements in machinery for carding cotton, wool, or other fibrous materials; and in apparatus for preparing or setting the cards of carding engines. June 11.—(Communication.)

William Jackson, of the town and borough of Kingston-upon-Hull, soap-maker, for improvements in the manufacture of soap, and in the preparation of materials to be used for this purpose. June 11.

William Edward Newton, of Chancery-lane, civil engineer, for improvements in rotary engines. June 11.—(Communication.)

Robert Waddell, of Liverpool, in the county of Lancaster, engineer, for certain improvements in steam engines. June 11.

Alexander Parkes, of Pembrey, Carmarthenshire, experimental chemist, for improvements in smelting and treating certain metals, and in the construction and manufacture of furnaces, and the materials to be used for the same, such furnaces and materials being applicable to the treatment of metals and metallic compounds, and to various other useful purposes of a like nature. June 11.

William Pole, of Great George-street, Westminster, engineer, and David Thomson, of Belgrave-road, Pimlico, engineer, for improvements in steam engines. June 11.

John Henry Vries, of Norfolk-street, Strand, Middlesex, Esq., for improvements in working engines by atmospheric air. June 11.

James Palmer Budd, of the Ystalyfera Iron Works, Swansea, merchant, for improvements in the manufacture of coke. June 11.

John Dearman Dunnicliff, of Hyson-green, in the county of Nottingham, lace manufacturer, and John Woodhouse Bagley, of Radford, in the same county, lace-maker, for certain improvements in lace and other weavings. June 11.

Samuel Ellis, of Salford, engineer, for improvements in machinery or apparatus applicable to all kinds of carriages used on railways. June 11.

Frederick Albert Gatty, of Accrington, in the county of Lancaster, manufacturing chemist, for a certain process, or certain processes, for obtaining carbonate of soda and carbonate of potash. June 11.

William Cox, of the firm of William Cox & Co., of Manchester, cigar merchant, for certain improvements in machinery or apparatus for manufacturing aerated waters, or other such liquids. June 11.

John Sidebottom, of Broadbottom, in the county of Chester, manufacturer, for improvements in looms for weaving. June 11.

William MacLardy, of Manchester, mechanist, for certain improvements in machinery or apparatus for preparing, finishing, and doubling cotton, and other fibrous materials. June 12.

Alfred Vincent Newton, of Chancery-lane, Middlesex, mechanical draughtsman, for improvements in the production of gases, to be used for lighting, heating, and motive power purposes. June 12.—(Communication.)

Gustavus Palmer Harling, of Bartlett's-buildings, in the city of London, artificial florist, for improvements in the manufacture of buttons, and other fastenings. June 12.

Thomas Deakin, of Balsall-heath, in the county of Worcester, Esq., for certain improvements in machinery and apparatus to be used in rolling metals, and in the manufacture of metal tubes. June 12.

John Stopporton, of the Isle of Man, engineer, for certain improvements in propelling vessels. June 12.

William Edward Newton, of Chancery-lane, civil engineer, for certain improvements in the construction of railways. June 12.—(Communication.)

George Allen Everitt, of the firm of Allen Everitt & Son, of the Kingston Metal Works, in the borough of Birmingham, metal and tube manufacturers, and George Glydon, of Birmingham, aforesaid, engineer, and foreman to the said Allen Everitt & Son, for certain improvements in the manufacture of metal tubes for locomotive, marine, and other boilers. June 12.

John Manly, junior, of Birmingham, manufacturer, for certain improvements in the manufacture of nails. June 12.

Charles Lamport, of Workington, in the county of Cumberland, ship-builder, for certain improvements in machinery or apparatus for lifting and moving weights, working chains, and pumping, which improvements are more especially adapted to ship use. June 19.

Charles Greenway, of Green-street, Grosvenor-square, in the county of Middlesex, for improvements in ships' and other pumps, in anchors, and in propelling vessels. June 19.

Benjamin Cheverton, of Camden-street, Camden-town, in the county of Middlesex, artist, for methods of imitating ivory and bone. June 19.

Charles Hanson, of Stepney, in the county of Middlesex, engineer, for certain improvements in steam engines, steam boilers, and safety valves, and in apparatus and machinery for propelling vessels. June 19.

Isaac Hartars, of Wretton-hall, in the county of York, farmer, for improvements in machinery for obtaining motive power. June 19.—(Communication.)

Robert Heath, of Manchester, iron merchant, and Richard Handley Thomas, of Wolstanton, in the county of Stafford, engineer, for certain improvements in the manufacture of iron. June 19.

Ethan Baldwin, of the city of Philadelphia, and State of Pennsylvania, in the United States of America, for a new and useful method of generating and applying steam in propelling vessels, locomotives, and stationary machinery. June 19.

Robert Weare, of Angel-court, Throgmorton-street, clock and watch manufacturer, for certain improvements in the means and apparatus for extinguishing fire, and in galvanic batteries. June 19.

George Roberts, of Tavistock, in the county of Devon, gentleman, for certain improvements in clogs and pattens. June 19.

Gaspard Malo, of Dunkirk, in the Republic of France, shipowner, for certain improvements in propelling vessels. June 20.

William Saunders, of the firm of Randell & Saunders, of Bath, in the county of Somerset, stone merchants, for improvements in sawing and sawing machinery. June 20.

John Hunt, of Stratford, in the county of Essex, engineer, for improvements in forming and moulding plastic substances, and the machinery and apparatus employed therein. June 20.

LIST OF PATENTS THAT HAVE PASSED THE GREAT SEAL OF SCOTLAND.

FROM THE 22ND DAY OF MARCH TO THE 20TH DAY OF MAY, 1850, INCLUSIVE.

James Higgins, of Salford, in the county of Lancaster, machine maker, and Thomas Scholefield Whitworth, of Salford aforesaid, mechanic, for improvements in machinery for preparing, spinning, and doubling cotton, wool, flax, silk, and similar fibrous materials. March 22.

Francois Vouillon, of Princes-street, Hanover square, in the county of Middlesex, manufacturer, for improvements in the manufacture of hats, caps, bonnets, and other articles made of the same or similar materials. March 26.

William Edward Newton, of Chancery-lane, in the county of Middlesex, civil engineer, for improvements in the manufacture of knobs for doors, articles of furniture, or other purposes; and in connecting metallic attachments to articles made of glass, or other analogous materials. March 26.—(Communication.)

Jonathan Charles Goodall, of Great College-street, Camden Town, in the county of Middlesex, card maker, for improvements in machinery for cutting paper. March 27.

Charles Felton Kirkman, of Argyle-street, in the county of Middlesex, gentleman, for improvements in machinery for spinning or twisting cotton, wool, or other fibrous substances. March 28.

Robert Milligan, of Harden, near Bingley, in the county of York, manufacturer, for an improved mode of treating certain floated warp or weft, or both, for the purpose of producing ornamental fabrics. March 28.

Robert White and James Henderson Grant, both of Dalmarnock-road, Glasgow, N.B., engineers, for certain improvements in machinery or apparatus to be used in mines, which improvements, or parts thereof, are also applicable to other purposes of a similar nature. April 11.

William MacLardy, of Manchester, in the county of Lancaster, gentleman, for certain improvements in machinery or apparatus for preparing and spinning cotton and other fibrous substances. April 15.

John Scoffern, of Essex-street, in the county of Middlesex, M.D., for improvements in the manufacture and refining of sugar, and in the treatment and use of matters obtained in such manufacture, and in the construction of valves used in such and other manufacture. April 17.

James Buck Wilson, of St. Helens, in the county of Lancaster, rope maker, for improvements in wire ropes. April 22.

T. S. Prideaux, of Southampton, gentleman, for improvements in puddling and other furnaces, and in steam boilers. April 26.

Charles Cowper, of Southampton-buildings, Chancery-lane, in the county of Middlesex, for certain improvements in the treatment of coal, and in separating coal and other substances from foreign matters; and in the manufacture of artificial fuel and coke; and in the distillation and treatment of tar and other products from coal, together with improvements in the machinery and apparatus employed in the said purposes. April 26.—(Communication.)

Lucien Vidie, late of Paris, in France, but now of South-street, Finsbury-square, advocate, for improvements in conveyances on land and water. April 27.

Robert Dalgleish, of Glasgow, in the county of Lanark, in Scotland, merchant and calico printer, for certain improvements in printing, and in the application of colours to silk, cotton, linen, woollen, and other textile fabrics. April 27.

Ethan Campbell, of the city of New York, in the United States of America, philosophical, practical, and experimental engineer, and a citizen of the said United States, for certain new and useful improvements for generating and applying motive power, and for propelling vessels. April 30.

Robert Reid, of Glasgow, in the county of Lanark, manufacturer, for certain improvements in weaving. May 3.

Maxwell Miller, of Glasgow, in the county of Lanark, coppersmith, for certain improvements in distilling and rectifying. May 3.

Thomas Keely, of the town and county of Nottingham, manufacturer, and William Wilkinson, of the same place, frame-work knitter, for certain improvements in looped or elastic fabrics, and in articles made therefrom; also certain machinery for producing the said improvements, which is applicable, in whole or in part, to the manufacture of looped fabrics generally. May 8.

Peter Armand Le Comte de Fontainemoreau, of South-street, Finsbury-square, in the county of Middlesex, for certain improvements in the production of heat and light, which improvements are applicable to ventilation and the prevention of explosion. May 9.—(Communication.)

Ethan Baldwin, of the city of Philadelphia, and State of Pennsylvania, in the United States of America, for a new and useful method of generating and applying steam, in propelling vessels, locomotives, and stationary machinery. May 9.

Jacob Connop, of Hyde Park, in the county of Middlesex, gentleman, for improvements in melting, moulding, and casting sand, earth, and other argillaceous substances, for paving, building, and various other useful purposes. May 20.

LIST OF PATENTS THAT HAVE PASSED THE GREAT SEAL OF IRELAND.

FROM THE 17TH DAY OF APRIL, TO THE 10TH DAY OF MAY, 1850, INCLUSIVE.

John Fowler, jun., of Melksham, in the county of Wilts, engineer, for improvements in draining land. April 17.

William Garnett Taylor, of Burton Hall, in the county of Westmoreland, gentleman, for improvements in lint, and in linting machines, which improvements in linting machines are, in whole or in part, applicable to other purposes. April 30.

William Brown, of Airdrie, Lanarkshire, electrician, and William Williams, the younger, of St. Dennis, in the county of Cornwall, gentleman, for improvements in electric and magnetic apparatus for indicating and communicating intelligence. May 2.

George Edmond Donisthorpe, and John Whitehead, of Leeds, manufacturers, for improvements in preparing, combing, and hackling fibrous matters. May 10.

DESIGNS FOR ARTICLES OF UTILITY.

REGISTERED FROM 9TH MAY TO 17TH JUNE.

May 9th, 2299, Dent, Allcroft, & Co., Wood-street, Cheapside, "The Osborne cravat."
,, ,, 2300, Thomas Lant, Birmingham, "Fastening for trouser straps."
,, 10th, 2301, John Masters, Welford-place, Leicester, "Calisthenic, or exercising cord."
,, ,, 2302, Pemberton & Son, Birmingham, "Casement fastener."
,, 16th, 2303, W. Baddeley, Alfred-street, Islington, "Portable fire-engine."
,, ,, 2304, Capper & Waters, Regent-street, "The Carlisle jacket."
,, 23rd, 2305, James Nasmyth, Patricroft, Lancashire, "Framing for a portable steam-engine."
,, 24th, 2306, John Sutton, Stamford-street, Blackfriars-road, "Adjustable inkstand."
,, ,, 2307, J. Harrison, John-street, Fitzroy-square, "Boudoir pianoforte action."
,, 25th, 2308, William Brodie, Airdrie, "Tile machine."
,, ,, 2309, Marmaduke Osborn Bergin, Cork, "Automatic fire extinguisher."
,, ,, 2310, Alfred Bird, Birmingham, "Filter."
,, 27th, 2311, John Davenport, Rockingham-street, Sheffield, "Graining comb."
,, 29th, 2312, William Wright Kilworth, Cork, "Improved millstone, furrows, and feeder."
,, ,, 2313, Allan Livingston & Son, Abercorn Works, Portobello, Edinburgh, "Hermetical cradle for joining pipes."
,, 30th, 2314, Francis West, Fleet-street, "Radius rule."
,, ,, 2315, William Pope & Son, Edgeware-road, "Improved stop-valve."
,, ,, 2316, John Roe, West Bromwich, "Lock."
,, 31st, 2317, John Marvin, London Gas Works, Vauxhall, "Portable smelting apparatus."
,, ,, 2318, John Heather, Bedford-court, Covent-garden, "Blackwell's razor guard."
,, ,, 2319, Emanuel Bailey Mather, Oxford-road, Manchester, "Drag with moveable body."
,, ,, 2320, Joseph Fenn, Newgate-street, "Cymameter."
June 3rd, 2321, William Peter Pigott, Oxford-street, "Galvanic belt."
,, ,, 2322, John Hill, Jermyn-street, St. James's, and Regent-street, Westminster, "'The Choretikopas,' a portmanteau of a new construction."
,, 4th, 2323, William John Normanville, Queen's-road, Regent's-park, "Elastic attachment for the side chains of railway carriages, waggons, &c."
,, 4th, 2324, George Godsell, Regent-street, "A Jupon chemise."
,, ,, 2325, George Ingram, Portobello, Scotland, "Improved socket joint for drains."
,, 5th, 2326, John Bessell, Farringdon-street, "The invisible ventilator."
,, ,, 2327, Robert Calvert, M.D., Camden-street, North, Camden New Town, "Self-adjusting brace."
,, 6th, 2328, John Rowan & Sons, The York-street Foundry, Belfast, "Improved factory ventilator.
,, 8th, 2329, George Frederick Hipkins, Ashted-row, Birmingham, "The sportsman's companion," combining nipple-wrench, turnscrew, nipple-pricker, wafer-stamp, and corkscrew.
,, 10th, 2330, Edwin Greenslade Bradford, Teignmouth, Devon, "Fastener for garments."
,, ,, 2331, John Edward Smith, Lawrence-lane, Cheapside, "Shirt."
,, ,, 2332, Thomas Grubb, Dublin, "Improved spindle and bearing, for the dashers of revolving dasher churns."
,, ,, 2333, James William Giles, Aldersgate-street, City, "Dress pin."
,, ,, 2334, George Baddeley, Oxford-street, "Boot."
,, ,, 2335, William Pilbeam, Acton-street, Gray's Inn, "Smoke-preventing chimney-pot."
,, 14th, 2336, Richard Robinson, The Eliza-street Works, Belfast, "Compound bar furnace."
,, ,, 2337, Charles Burton, Trowbridge, "Elastic mauler for a weaver's harness."
,, 17th, 2338, William Bird, Oxford-street, "Boot."
,, ,, 2339, Frederick and Charles Huxham, and James Armitage Brown, Exeter, Devonshire, "Driving motion for hand-mills."
,, ,, 2340, Ann Remington, Shaftesbury-crescent, Pimlico, "Self-acting baster, and vertical heat-reflector for roasting."
,, ,, 2341, Taylor, Henry, & Co., White Lion-street, Spital-square, "Imperial disinfecting filter."
,, ,, 2342, Philip le Capelain, the elder, Long Acre, "Portable oven."

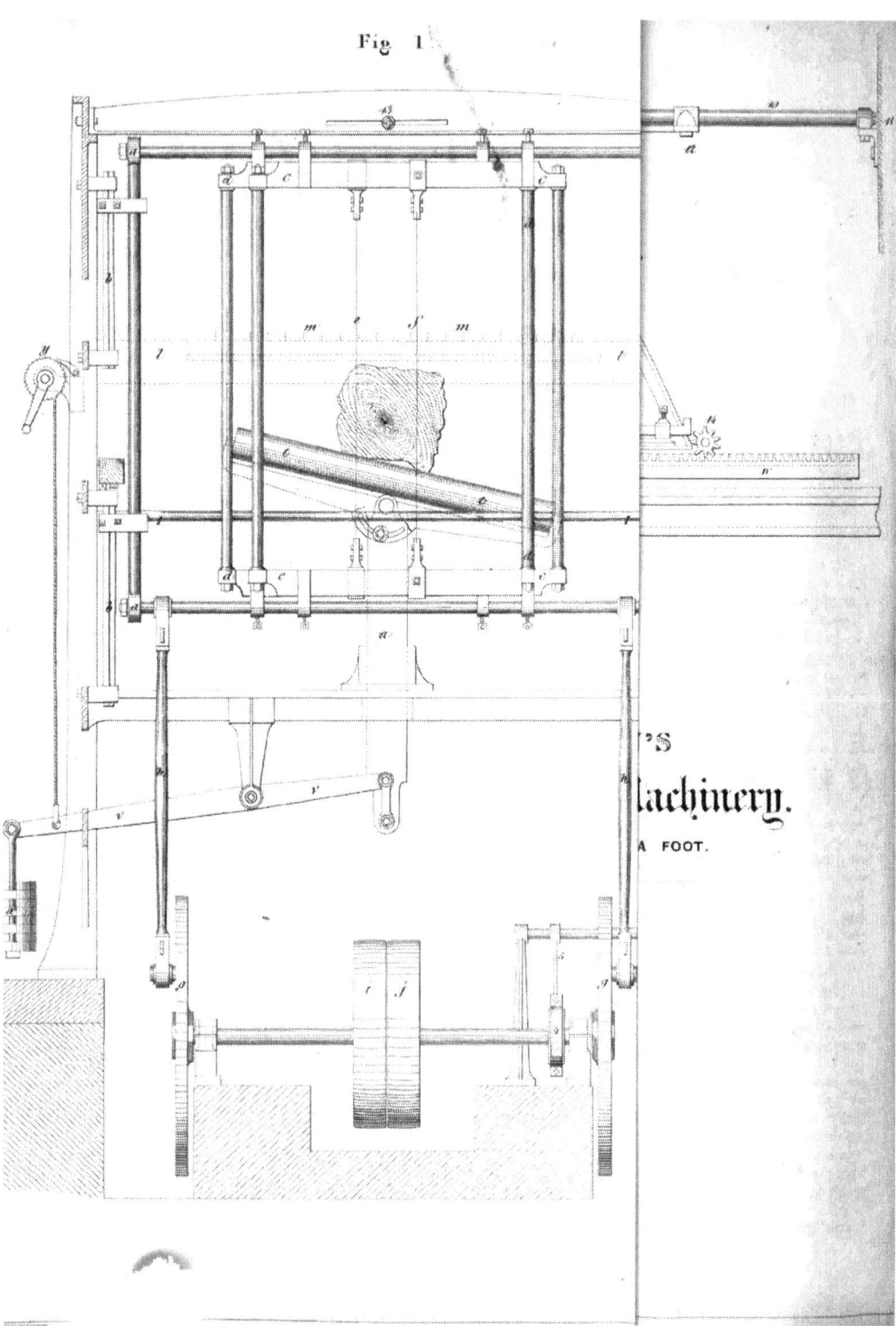

Fig. 1

'S

Machinery.

A FOOT.

THE ARTIZAN.

No. VIII.—Vol. VIII.—AUGUST 1st, 1850.

HAMILTON'S SAWING MACHINERY.

HAMILTON'S PATENT CURVILINEAL AND BEVELLING SAWING MACHINERY.

We believe that it will meet the approbation of those of our readers especially whose avocations bring them in contact with the ship-building interest, to draw attention to the spirit of mechanical improvement in its various operations, which we observe daily growing up around us. It is gratifying also to ourselves to find that our efforts to aid the cause, meet with appreciation from those on whose behalf they are exerted. The introduction of increased economy into the details of construction, seems, however, to be the proper starting point from which to commence the course of improvement, and it is therefore with great pleasure that we lay before our readers, in the present Number, drawings of one of the most important inventions connected with Timber Ship-building that we have yet seen. This invention is a machine for superseding hand-labour in sawing the various curved and bevelled timbers, so largely required in ship-building. The merit of the invention is due to an American gentleman, Mr. Hamilton, who has devoted indefatigable attention to the subject, and whose inventive talent only required London enterprize and skill to develope and bring it to maturity.

The ship-builders of this country are indebted to Money Wigram, Esq., of Blackwall-yard, for having the courage to test this invention and prove its mercantile value. We believe we are correct in saying that Mr. Wigram's establishment is, in consequence of this, at the present time the most complete in the kingdom. In addition to four saw frames, on Mr. Hamilton's patent, there are, in his saw-mill, numerous circular saws, travelling cranes for moving the timber, and railways for its conveyance to every part of the yard. Into all these details we have not space at present to enter; but we may remark that the whole arrangements reflect great credit on Messrs. Fox, Henderson, & Co., the eminent engineers of Birmingham, to whom their execution was entrusted.

In describing the construction of this machinery, it may be necessary to premise that in such delicate operations as the sawing of ship timbers by steam power, the usual powerful machinery of this country must be entirely placed out of view. In the ordinary saw mills which come under our notice, straight cutting is the general rule, and to effect this with the utmost despatch, it is necessary to crowd a frame with saw blades, so that a log may be slit up into planks by once passing through the frame. It is essential to this object that all the saws preserve, without the possibility of deviation, parallel lines, and if from the tortuous grain of the most knotty timber a single blade is induced to either side of its proper course, the whole process must be stopped until the delinquent is returned to the path of duty. As may be supposed, the very constitution of the usual sawing machinery is intended to prevent the possibility of such delay, and amongst the numerous precautions to secure this effect, the saw blades require to be strung very

tightly in the frames, so much so that one ton per inch in breadth of a saw blade is merely considered a safe and judicious strain, to prevent any deviation of the saw from the straight line. The frames, in which perhaps thirty or forty of such saws are strung, require amazing strength. The most ponderous cast and wrought iron is lavished upon their construction. Such a frame of saws when thus strung is tuned like a harp before being trusted upon the timber, and after the minds of mechanical men have become familiarized with such machines, and their no less ponderous driving gear and appurtenances, it is no wonder if they have entirely forgotten the true simplicity of sawing, and require to be conducted to an ordinary and primitive saw-pit to reconsider the very rudiments of the operation.

We cannot explain the mechanism of this invention better than by conducting our readers to the hand saw-pit, and, after first pointing out the perfect ease with which the saw is there guided into any required curve, the total absence of any straining of the saw blade, which is merely stretched in a frame of the lightest timber, the comparative indifference where the points of support may happen to be placed, to show that precisely the same operation is to be performed by the unfailing action of machinery. We shall thus draw the attention of our readers properly to the subject, because the whole operation must not be regarded as an evidence of the invincible power of machinery, such as our ordinary saw mills exhibit, but of the delicacy, and no less certainty and accuracy of operation for which machinery is equally celebrated.

In referring to the accompanying plates, and to those which we purpose shall follow in the subsequent Number, the same figures indicate similar parts of the machinery throughout: a, a, a, a, is a saw frame or "gate," formed of hollow bars of wrought iron, combining great stiffness with the lightest possible construction, and guided upon the square bars, b, b, b, b, in the ordinary manner. The top and bottom rails of this frame are accurately turned, and serve as horizontal guides to the two internal frames, c, c, c, c and d, d, d, d; these two internal frames are fitted to slide with great freedom, horizontally upon the top and bottom bars of the frame a, a, a, a, but with motions perfectly independent of each other, and are made each to receive the buckles of a saw blade, with the power of altering their position to any ordinarily required distance. The saw blades, e and f, are suspended in their buckles upon centres, (see fig 4,) which admit of the saw blades being turned round upon their vertical axes at the will of the attendant. The whole outer frame, with the two inner frames, is put in rapid vertical motion by the usual arrangement of fly-wheels, cranks, and connecting rods, g, g, h, h, and is connected to the motive power by the fast and loose pulleys, i and j. The weight of the frame is balanced as usual by an opposite weight on the arms of the fly-wheels. By this simple arrangement the attendant is able to guide each saw blade, indepen-

23

dently of the other, along any required curved line that may have been marked upon the timber, *k k*. The oblique lateral motion necessary for this being admitted to each saw blade independently, by rotating the blade on its centres between the buckles, and by the traversing the inner frames, *c c* and *d d*, across the bars of the outer frame. This motion is communicated to each saw blade by a forked lever of wood (fig. 5) in the hands of the attendant, which he applies to the back of the saw, and thereby guides it along any required line. The transverse bar, *l, l*, is fixed across the mill frame, the slot in which serves to steady the lever, whilst the pins, *m, m*, serve as fulcra to aid the internal frames in their lateral motion. So far the arrangement for curvilinear cutting is complete. A piece of timber may thus be cut with its sides either straight or curved, either parallel or tapered, as it may have been designed and marked out; but in sawing of ships' timbers every possible curve demands at each point some specific bevel; and in order to meet this requirement a further apparatus is necessary.

The timber, *k k*, is confined in chocks, *n, n*, at either extremity, each of which is mounted on a horizontal axis, allowing the timber to rotate freely; one of these chocks is fitted with a vertical lever, *o*, the upper extremity of which is worked laterally by a horizontal transverse screw, *p*, to which the requisite motion is communicated by the wheel-work, *q, r*, so that by turning the hand wheel *s*, any required bevel can be given to the timber.

These two operations, that of curvilinear sawing and bevelling, by no means exhaust the difficult problem of sawing ships' timbers; in addition, it is necessary to ensure with all the accuracy of which machinery is capable, the regular and systematic changing of bevels from one given angle to another, and this to take effect within certain specific distances marked upon the timber.

We postpone until our next Number our explanations upon this head, which in reality comprehends the most elegant part of the invention, which insures a timber being produced from the saw with that perfect accuracy of form, which can only otherwise be obtained after repeated and expensive adjustments.

We return to some of the details of this ingenious arrangement, and draw the attention of our readers to the means of securing a bearing for the timber in front of the saws. This, however, must be regarded, from the rigidity of the timber, and the little strain exerted by the operation of two saws, rather as an accessory than as a necessary accompaniment of the machine. It may be briefly described as follows: a roller, *t t*, is mounted on a swivelling frame, *u*, and possesses a vertical as well as a bevelling motion. The weight of the roller is balanced through the beam, *v, v*, by the adjustable weights, *x*, and the roller may be either elevated or depressed by the windlass, *y*. It is thus free to follow the surface of the timber, and is made to communicate an upward pressure by the same means; and thus support is given to the timber as may be required.

The method of feeding is, as usual, by means of a rack on each side of the travelling frame, *w w*, worked by the pinions, *z z*, on the shaft, 1 1. The rachet wheel, 2, on the same shaft, is moved by the pall and rod, 3, 3, which is connected to an eccentric, 4, on the crank shaft, through the levers, 5 and 6. A means is provided of varying the feed by shifting the lower centre of the rod, 3, along the lever, 6, which is thus virtually shortened. This is effected by moving the hand lever, 8, into the various notches in the plate, 9, bolted on the side of the stationary frame.

It now only remains for us to explain the method in which the bevelling is marked on the timber, and accurately followed in the machine. This, and the other details, we must reserve until our next Number.

To be continued.

———

COMPASSES OF IRON SHIPS.

THE following able letter was addressed to Mr. Bourne, by whom it has been forwarded to us for publication:—

Southampton, 27th May, 1850.

SIR,—I am favoured with your letter of the 23rd inst., requesting to be informed of my experience in the correction of compasses in iron ships, and on other points to which you have called attention. In reply, I beg to say, I find all *practical* difficulty in navigating iron ships, by reason of their influence on the compasses, overcome.

From the quantity of iron now used in the hull and rigging of timber ships, I frequently find their compasses much complained of, and have had to apply corrections, as in iron ships.

Both in iron and timber ships, the error, though varying in the same direction, alters by efflux of time, and also by change of geographical position.

The compasses of iron ships, though corrected, are also somewhat affected by keeping the same course for several hours with a beam wind, or any influence that causes her to heel over.

There has been great difficulty in ascertaining the exact error in the correction of ships' compasses, either on their voyage or in distant ports: it is natural to attribute all deviations in the course made good to the error of the compasses, though it must constantly arise from bad steering, set, indraught, &c., and if determined by azimuths or amplitudes, no allowance is made for errors in observation, in which two or three observers are generally engaged, and wherein the variation of the compass, which is made the datum, has been erroneously marked on the chart, or even if originally correct, was ascertained at a date so distant as to have altered several degrees since that period, whilst the opportunity of swinging the ship in foreign or distant ports is so rare or inconvenient, as seldom to be attempted.

The modes I have adopted are,

　The Correcting Magnets, as suggested by Professor Airey.
　The Corrected Card, as suggested by Capt. J. S. Sparkes.
　The Table of Errors, as used in H. M. Navy.

The Correcting Magnets have the peculiar advantage of placing a compass on board to all appearance the same as another compass; there is no difference in the card; no directions to give to the commander of the ship or his officers; no alteration in the mode of taking bearings from the compass, and where there is this appearance of simplicity, unless the commander is a scientific man (which is not always the case), the correction by magnets gives most satisfaction, and may be considered preferable; but not much more so than

The Corrected Card.—This, with care, may be constructed more *minutely* correct *at every point* than the compass is with magnets; but it is open to the objection of peculiarity in appearance, and great difference in the distance between the points, *i. e.*, from N. to N. by W., may measure an inch or more, and on the same card from S. to S. by E. only half an inch, gradually reducing or increasing, so that the helmsman is apt to steer with as much allowance S. by E. easterly as he would with the same card N. by W. westerly, and perhaps make a difference of a quarter of a point. A further objection urged is, that you cannot take a bearing from a corrected card, as of course the points of the compass opposite to each other on a common card are not opposite on this, and the several points are only correct when facing the lubbers' point.

This objection has been ingeniously obviated by Captain Sparkes, by placing an equally divided ring on the top, or verge of the compass, from which, when set to the course steered, any bearing may be taken, or (if similarly set) from a common card pasted on a board, used in any part of the ship, with a pair of sights.

These are the popular objections to the corrected card. I do not regard them as serious myself, but they are sufficient to give a preference generally to corrections by magnets.

In using magnets we have to contend with the deterioration of the magnets, and alteration of the local attraction; in the corrected card the alteration of local attraction only.

The *Pottinger*, Peninsular and Oriental steam ship, on a voyage to India, *via* the Cape, found the corrected card more accurate than the correcting magnets, especially after leaving the Cape of Good Hope. Capt. Cooper, who commanded her, thus speaks of his compasses, to which he gave an admirable degree of attention.

" I enjoy great confidence in the binnacle compasses, which are fitted with *Captain Sparkes' Corrected Cards*, and consider them a most valuable invention.

" The accuracy with which the ship has been brought to daily by those compasses, has been so close to the true position of observation, that I consider them perfectly correct,—more particularly in the northern hemisphere."

The corrections by Tables of Errors are, of course, very accurate, but more inconvenient; every course has to be given for the particular error ascertained on that course, in addition to the "variation;" and no bearing can be taken from a compass so used, unless a table of errors be made the standard; without fresh corrections on the voyage there is the probability of the error being allowed the wrong way. This danger is more to be dreaded where a standard compass, fixed on the quarter deck, is made the guide, or standard for the steering, or binnacle compasses aft, to which the corrections are not *directly* applied, the courses to be steered being given by a comparison with this standard compass, the errors of which have been previously, and are from time to time, ascertained. In giving the course to the helmsman, by reference to such a standard, there is a complication, and no doubt errors are occasionally allowed the wrong way.

The mode of ascertaining the accuracy of the compasses is invariably by swinging the ship with her head to the 32 points, and by reciprocal observations with a competent person on shore, finding the difference in the two bearings, that on shore always being the correct one, and the difference gives the error; or else, by taking the bearing of an object six or seven miles distant, such as a church-steeple, the correct bearing of which is well known, and the difference observed on board is the error, and herein no observer on shore is required, as the difference in the angle at so great a distance is imperceptible; in both cases the ship's head must be brought to every point of the compass, and the shore bearing taken with every direction of the ship's head, from every compass in their places on board, *for the error will be different in different parts of the ship, and different in each compass when the direction of the ship's head is changed.*

The mode I adopt of ascertaining the errors is a plan of my own. I place a centre staff with a distinguishing flag near the dockhead, and in the rear describe a semicircle of about 100 feet radius; on that circle every five degrees is marked by a long pole with a flag, and each single degree by a short pole, the magnetic meridian having been carefully laid down beforehand. I have the true bearing wherever the centre staff intersects either of those in the rear, so, as the ship swinging in the dock alters her position, I obtain, *at sight*, from each compass, the true bearing on shore (and without an observer on shore); this is a great convenience, ensures great accuracy, and is peculiarly suitable to places where distant objects cannot be obtained.

Neither of the corrections herein referred to remain true and unaltered by time, but for the most part time effects only a small change, and I find that the commanders gradually increase or decrease the allowance for the change, without requiring to have the ship swung.

Thus, the *Indus*, swung July, 1848, was not required by the Commander to be swung till March, 1850, the change in the error had been 5°, the greatest I have found in the same period. Capt. Soy is remarkably attentive to his compasses, and swung the *Indus* at Alexandria, making a difference in error there and in the same month at Southampton, of 4 degrees.

The *Indus*, however, has always given more trouble in correcting, and required more attention with regard to her compasses than most iron ships, a part of which arises from the inconvenient position in which the deck houses, steering apparatus, and skylight, compel the binnacles to be fixed.

The *Pottinger*, on the contrary, is corrected with the greatest facility, and after being lengthened recently, and her spar deck removed, I was enabled to correct her three compasses, one with magnets, in 2½ hours, and on the conclusion of the only voyage since made, viz., to the Mediterranean, Captain Cooper reported the corrections to be very satisfactory. This ship was previously from two to three years in India, and after her return to England, Captain Cooper writes to say, when removing the compasses for the alteration referred to,—" I was quite pained to move my excellent compasses; they were so perfectly satisfactory as to be the greatest comfort in the ship, during which period they have never been touched since you," (writing to Mr. Stebbing) "corrected them." This ship was the least affected by time, or change in geographical position, that I have yet known.

The *Ripon* was swung in February, 1848, since which the error has altered as much as five degrees in the Channel, but is more correct in the Mediterranean, where Captain Moresby finds the error to differ 4 degrees from the corrections for Southampton.

The *Gauntlet* yacht, swung in the spring of 1847, and furnished with a table of errors, was using the same till the autumn of 1849, with no cause of complaint. When I corrected this yacht I had her heeled over as far as she could be depressed, and the extreme error varied from 2 to 3 degrees. She is a small vessel, and the uplifted, and almost overhanging side, exercised perhaps greater influence than in a larger vessel, from its nearness; the owner, however, has not named this as affecting the accuracy of the Table of Errors, and under weigh she would rarely be so much depressed, and neither so permanently nor stationary; hence the practical result may be less objectionable even in a small craft.

Professor Airey observes, that when the *magnets* are properly placed, the compass will be subject to no error when heeling or pitching. I cannot confirm this at present, but I have no facts to throw a doubt upon it; whilst I have reason to believe other corrections have been disturbed to the extent of ¼ point in a long run, with the wind a-beam, for which I could attribute no other cause.

The *Seaflower* yacht, corrected by magnets, was quite satisfactory to the owner during the yacht season of 1847. I have not a more recent account.

One of the South Western Company's iron vessels has no error of practical inconvenience *on any course*. The rest of the Company's vessels are corrected by magnets, and the corrections have varied by time; no fresh corrections have been made, as these boats run in three or four courses only (to and from Havre and the Channel Islands), and any variation is readily allowed for.

The *Pacha*, having two binnacles with corrected cards, swung and applied July 1847, is reported very accurate. Captain Mehan stated, yesterday, "I found them very correct to and from Gibraltar, except running from Cape St. Vincent to —— when I was out a quarter of a point; but I do not attribute that to the compasses: I often find the same in timber ships.

The *Sultan*, Captain Brooks, to and from Constantinople, was corrected by magnets in July, 1847; the magnets have not been moved since, but soon after this correction, and on her arrival at Southampton, she was swung again, and a table of the uncorrected errors given; the maximum error is 9 to 11 degrees on the N. W., whilst there is only 2 degrees error on the S. E., and some points are correct. The Captain takes great interest in his compasses, he says, " I find a little difference in the errors in summer and winter, but otherwise no difference in the errors since we started. I am quite satisfied with my compasses, and always have been. I find the difference between the errors in England and the Archipelago is 4 degrees."

One of the *Sultan's* compasses is corrected with one magnet, and the other with two, and both have the addition of a box of chain.

The *Ripon* has two magnets, and chain to each compass that is corrected by magnets.

The *Pottinger*, only one magnet and box of chain.

The *Ariel*, with an error of 46°, was corrected with one magnet and no chain; nearly all the points were correct, with this one magnet applied, and the greatest uncorrected error was 4° 40′.

The *Great Britain* had *several magnets* applied, and the uncorrected error on some few points varied from ¼ to ½ point.

The *Madrid* had a compass fixed 20 feet above the deck *aft*, and was still influenced by the local attraction: she carries one now 9 or 10 feet high, which is ¾ point out, and is navigated by a corrected card placed in a binnacle on deck.

The *Ariel* had an error of 16 degrees 12 feet above the deck.

The compasses of the *Euxine* were corrected in Scotland by magnets in June, 1847, and the Captain (Evans) considers them still satisfactory.

The correction *of any one* point of the compass is not always applicable to the correction of the others, although the magnet that corrects the north generally corrects the south, and that which corrects the east generally corrects the west.

If the compass is true for one point it is not necessarily true for other points, and opposite points frequently differ in the amount of error: sometimes the greatest error is north or south, in other vessels east or west; but generally the error is greatest one or two points from a cardinal point, and not at the cardinal point.

The same allowance for variation that is applied to a common compass (by which I understand a compass where the ship has no local attraction), *is applicable* to a corrected compass, but if the corrected compass is in a ship changing her latitude, and thereby causing the corrected compass to vary, then the variation due to that latitude would not be applicable, so that there would be two corrections for the magnetic course:

One variation of the compass.

One deviation of the compass.

For instance, in the Archipelago the *Sultan* has to allow 4 degrees in addition to the variation, and the *Ripon*, in the Mediterranean 4 degrees less, or what is the same thing, one +, the uncorrected error, and the other —.

In the case of large ships, where there are two binnacles, it is difficult to correct both by magnets, unless the binnacles are very far apart, as the large magnets sometimes influence the opposite compass, and are likely to deteriorate each other.

The binnacles should be placed as high above the deck as the view of the compasses by the helmsman will admit, and the errors are generally much lessened by this mode, and the corrections, *ceteris paribus*, more easy, whilst the height above the bulwarks enables bearings to be taken with great facility.

I have constructed an improved compass for iron ships, which I strongly recommend both for standard and binnacle compasses; they are generally adopted for the former purpose in the Royal Mail steam ships, and for both purposes in the Peninsular and Oriental steam ships. They are perfect *azimuth* and steering compasses, and all the observations and corrections are made by the particular compass in the exact place in which it is afterwards to be used, and on long voyages the variation can be determined by azimuths or amplitudes *taken from* either of the *steering compasses*, and the error on the true variation at the ship's position, by the particular compass, is the error directly applicable to that compass, and the same convenience applies to bearings of headlands and other well-determined objects, whilst in the operation of swinging ships to correct the compasses the advantage of taking true bearings from each is very considerable.

This compass has of course no advantage over any other good compass in resisting local attraction, and although I have tried a great number said to have this property, I have never found any one accomplish the object, and much doubt if I ever shall; for when a compass is produced that is insensible to local attraction, I shall expect to find that it is also insensible to the terrestrial attraction, and there are instances of compasses that appeared not to be disturbed by iron placed near them in a drawing-room, that were quite useless in an iron ship. One tried on board the *Indus*, on her experimental voyage, in my presence, failed in this manner.

OBSERVATIONS BY CAPTAIN COOPER ON THE "POTTINGER'S" COMPASSES, OUTWARD VOYAGE, 1847.

Date 1847.	Port Compass with a Corrected Card.	Starboard Compass with a Corrected Card.	Companion Compass corrected with Magnets.	Azimuth Compass.	Latitude.	Longitude.
Mar.	Ship's Head	Ship's Head	Ship's Head	Ship's Head		
15	S.by W.½W	S.by W.¼W.	S.by W.¾W.	S.19W.	13·1N	18·38W.
14	S.½E.	S.½E.	South	South	9·44	18·2
14	S.½E.	S.¾E.	South	South	9·32	18·00
15	South	South	South	South	6·15	17·6
15	South	South	South	South	5·57	17·2
15	South	South	South	S.1·30W.	4·47	16·42
16	South	South	S.½W.	S.5E.	2·24	15·32
17	South	South	S.¼W.	S.3E.	00·10S.	14·52
18	S. by W.	S.by W.	S.by W.¼W.	S.12W.	5·17	14·20
18	S. by W.	S.by W.	S.by W.¾W.	S.12W.	5·21	14·21
19	S.¼W.	S.¼W.	S.¾W.	S.5·20W.	7·13	14·22
27	S.S.E.	S.S.E.	S.by E.½E.	S.12·40E.	10·32	10·48
29	S.E.by S.½S.	S.E.by S.½S.	SE.by E.¾E.	S.19E.	14·31	5·13
April						
3	S.S.E.	S.E.by S.¼S.	SE.by E.¼E.	S.11E.	21·12	0·36E.
May						
11	N.E.½E.	N.E.¼E.	NE.by E.¼E	N.53E.	13·48	65·34
12	N.E.½E.	N.E.¼E.	NE.by E.¾E	N.54E.	11·32	67·51.

"In the differences between the binnacle compasses and azimuth compass, I consider the local error to be with the azimuth compass, and local error to exist in both companion and azimuth compass.

(Signed) "E. COOPER, Commander."

SUMMARY.

1. Corrections by magnets generally have the preference, but are not more *correct* than the corrected card.

2. Corrected cards are a most useful invention, and peculiarly well adapted to iron ships, and essential where the binnacle compasses are near together.

3. Tables of Errors are inconvenient, but correct, but should always be used in reference, *i. e.* directly applied to the steering compass.

4. All iron ships going long voyages should have a table of errors for a compass placed at a particular height, and in a particular position well determined, and the height and position, as well as errors, entered in a book kept below, so that if the binnacles and corrected magnets or cards be washed overboard or shot away, a temporary compass with known errors, may be put up.

5. In over sea voyages it is prudent to have one compass with a corrected card, and the others corrected by magnets.

6. Corrected compasses are affected by time.

7. Corrected compasses are affected by change in geographical position, but the data is as yet insufficient to speak with confidence of the amount, and in some ships the change has been so small as not to receive particular attention.

8. A compass may be very true on one or several points, and three or four points out on others.

9. The errors of one ship are no guide to the errors of another, and

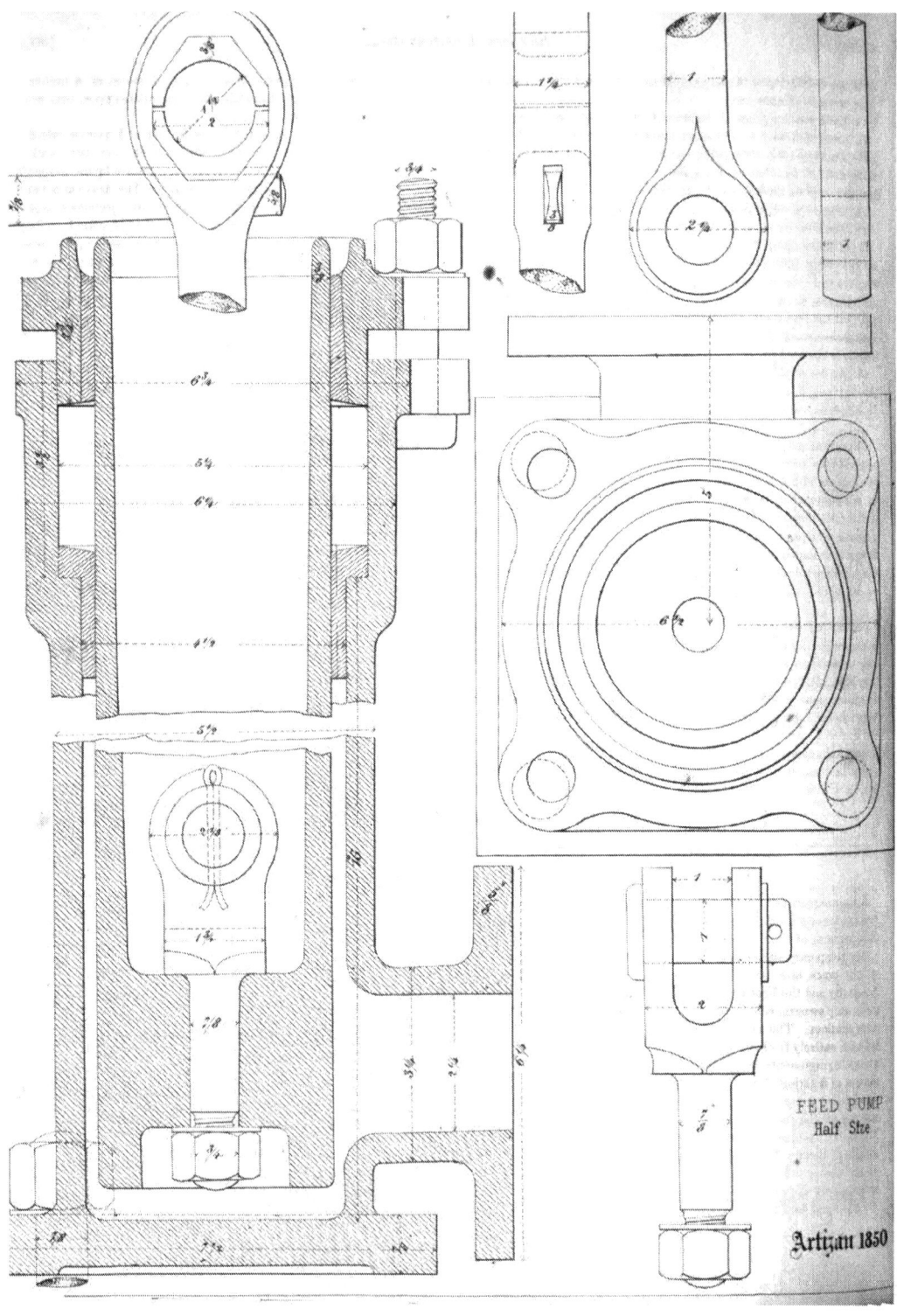

FEED PUMP
Half Size

Artizan 1850

the errors or correctness of one part of the same ship are no indication of the errors of another part.

10. The errors are generally lessened towards midships.

11. Every iron ship is a magnet herself, and some have the north pole aft and some the south pole ; the N. and S. do not always run on the fore and aft line, but in some ships over the port quarter and port bow, and some on the opposite quarters and bows.

12. Whilst there is a general character in the local attraction of iron ships there is rarely any identity, and no general rule appears to apply.

13. In all iron ships, however, there is this invariable rule—that there are two points (not always opposite) at which there is no error, that there are two other points where the error is always at its maximum, and that this deviation gradually goes from right to left and left to right, but not by a regular progression. An error will sometimes not alter more than 3 degrees in a range of 5 points, and then alter 30 degrees in the next 5 points.

14. The deviation is always an accumulating error, or the reverse ; thus it runs 1, 3, 7, 12, 17, 26, 30, 32, 33, (maximum), 31, 28, 24, 20, 17, 13, 9, 6, 3, 0 ; but never 3, 7, 4, 10, 8, 12, 6.

I have thus endeavoured to give you a few notes of my experience in respect to the correction of compasses in iron vessels. I have done so on all points with candour, for I have no prejudice on the subject. I am anxious to elicit truth, and for years have made a particular study of this most interesting branch of science. The practical difficulty of correcting compasses for iron ships is overcome, and they are as safely navigable as timber ships. But I believe we are unable yet to systematize our knowledge of local attraction : we can control its influence, but we can find no uniformity in its results.

*   *   *   *   *

I cannot conclude without impressing on your mind how much the public owe to the Peninsular and Oriental Company, for its great liberality to inventors and experimentalists in reference to ships' compasses ; they have afforded me great facilities, personally, for all my operations, whether connected with their purpose or not ; the managing directors have allowed inventors to take voyages in their ships, and have directed the trial of a variety of projects to overcome local attraction : none of these schemes have succeeded, excepting those to which I have drawn your attention, one being the invention of the Company's superintendent, Capt. J. S. Sparkes.

I have, &c.,
J. R. STEBBING.

ON SURFACE CONDENSATION.

A CORRESPONDENT having requested our opinion on a method of surface condensation differing somewhat from Mr. Hall's, we propose to consider some of the various plans that have been tried for that purpose.

The temporary success of Mr. Hall's system was a curious instance of how much may be effected by skilful working and puffing. The Admiralty and the East India Company adopted it in several cases, but steam ship owners, who looked for some return for their money, were more cautious. The supposed increased durability of the boilers when fed with entirely fresh water, and the saving of fuel, formed, it is true, a tempting argument; but it was discovered, alas ! that there were other sources of deterioration in the boilers of sea-going steamers, which fresh water failed to cure, and that, somehow or other, the saving of fuel did not pay for the constant repairs required by the myriad of joints. In Mr. Hall's condenser, the steam passed through the pipes and the water outside of them. We think that the reverse arrangement, as described by our correspondent, is superior, as it appears to us that in the former arrangement the condensed steam has a greater tendency to choke up the pipes and to diminish their efficiency as cooling surface.

The advantages to be gained from the use of steam of a higher pressure, worked expansively, have been so often insisted upon, that we need not here reiterate them.

High pressure steam leads us to tubular boilers and narrow water spaces, which have long been employed with safety on shore, but which have been limited in their application to marine purposes by the danger arising from calcareous and saline incrustations. The heavy original cost and the necessity of frequent repairs seem fatal objections to any plan on Mr. Hall's principle, even if the room could be spared. We must, therefore, look for a solution of the difficulty in some other direction, unless, indeed, an American invention, of which we have heard, should prove practically efficient. The novelty consists in there being a vacuum on *each side of the tubes*, whereby the leakage is obviated. We do not profess to describe the details—we only announce the fact. Mr. Siemens's surface condenser (see p. 331) ingeniously overcomes the difficulty of making the joints, but must occupy at least as much room as Mr. Hall's apparatus. Mr. Craddock has not succeeded in making many converts to his whirligig system, although the columns of a contemporary bear abundant witness to his indefatigable efforts. His plan will be found fully analysed at p. 104 of our vol. for 1844. It may suffice here to say that it consisted of a cage full of tubes, which was set in rapid motion and was cooled by the air.

Mr. D. Napier's plan is applicable to iron vessels only, and consists in making the bottom of the vessel the condenser, the plates being double. This scheme is a bold one, but is inadmissible in sea-going vessels, where it is most wanted, whilst we have our doubts as to the tightness of all the joints, even in a river boat. All these plans, which may be said to be "dry condensers," relieve the engineer of all trouble with the injection water, but they cannot be said to possess this advantage exclusively, as Mr. Aitken's Patent (see p. 195, vol. 1849) effectually provides against choking the condenser.

The last plan we have to notice is a combination of the injection and surface systems, known as "Symington's," although we believe there are other claimants to the invention. This system requires no alteration in the arrangements of an ordinary injection condenser and air pump ; the water, after leaving the hot wells, passes along two copper pipes placed on each side of the keel, and, after being cooled by the sea water, is again used for injection. There being no vacuum within these cooling pipes, there is no risk of leakage, and if any should take place, it is merely a partial return to the ordinary system. Ordinary sea injection pipes would of course be fitted, which could be used should any accident occur, such as the collapse of the cooling pipes by coming in contact with the ground. From their position, however, such an event could scarcely occur unless the vessel were totally wrecked. The great merit of this plan appears to us to consist in the economy of its application to existing vessels, and the readiness with which the effects of any accident can be remedied. It has been applied to several vessels, but we are not in possession of any *data* to show the results of its working for any length of time. If any of our correspondents can favour us with any information on the subject, they will oblige many of our readers, we doubt not, as well as ourselves.

ANALYSIS OF THE STEAM-ENGINE.

(Continued from p. 155.)

THE FEED PUMP.—At page 163 we have the rule for the proper proportion of the feed pump, when it is single acting, and the engine double acting, expressed thus :—

Multiply the capacity of the cylinder in cubic inches by the total pressure in pounds per square inch (including the atmospheric pressure), and divide the product by 5000. The result is the capacity of the feed pump in cubic inches.

Thus, capacity of cylinder = 706·86 × 60 (area × stroke) = 42411 × 22

(15 + 7 lbs. pressure) = 933042, which, divided by 5000 = 186 inches capacity of feed pump. Assuming a quarter the stroke of the piston, or 15 inches, to be a convenient stroke for the pump, we have $\frac{186}{15} = 12.4$ inches for the area of the plunger, which is 4 inches diameter, nearly.

Having thus fixed the diameter and stroke of the pump, we must consider how it is to be fixed on the sole plate, or on the foundation. It ought to be readily accessible, and yet so placed that if there should be any leakage of water, it may not run about the engine-house floor. If it be made with a square flange at bottom, as we have shown, it can be either bolted directly to the foundation, or on a separate plate as may be most convenient. The trunk principle of a hollow plunger is the most elegant way of working pumps of this description, as it dispenses with the guides required if the rod be attached to the top of the plunger, and makes a cheaper, as well as a better, job.

The diameter of the plunger being set out, a half inch clearance must be allowed on each side for the barrel of the pump, making it 4½ inches diameter. It is not advisable to allow less clearance than this, as in the event of the casting being out of truth, it might be necessary to put in a smaller plunger, or bore it out all the way down. Should, however, it be necessary to place the branch higher up in the pump, that must be considered in determining the proper clearance, as the plunger will descend past the opening, and shut off the escape for the water. The internal diameter of the pump must then be such that as much area be left in the annular space, as is equal to the area of the branch, which will be found by adding together the area of the plunger and the area of the branch. Thus, the area of 4 inches (12·56) + area of 2¼ (3·97) = 16·53, which is about 4 ⅝ diameter. An enlargement must also be cast round the pump on a level with the branch, or the water will be choked at that point, but this is more conveniently done by making the barrel parallel, and of somewhat larger diameter, say 5 inches, and rounding off the corners of the passages.

It seems preferable, where it can be done, to place the branch at the bottom of the pump, for this reason: In some localities the water deposits a great deal of lime, and where that is the case, the pump barrel will get furred up, so that although there might be ample clearance at first, that will gradualy diminish, until the pump break down, if attention be not previously called to it by the difficulty of keeping up the supply of water to the boiler.

The plunger is represented at the bottom of its stroke, ½ an inch being allowed for clearance at the bottom. A wrought-iron jaw-piece is bolted through the bottom of the plunger to receive the pin of the pump rod. This pin ought to be made larger than for strength only, to make it wear longer, as it does not appear worth while, in a pump of this size, to make any provision for tightening up the bearing. The pin and the eye may be case-hardened, if it is thought desirable. One-fourth of the diameter of the plunger is a fair proportion—say 1 inch diameter, and 1 inch wide. The diameter of the shank may be less, as it has only to lift the plunger against the atmosphere, ¾ inch being sufficient; the nut is recessed into the plunger, to diminish its length. Much strength is not needed for the plunger, consequently, it may be cast thin—say, tapering from ½ to ⅜ inch. The metal of the pump is ½ inch thick, and the bottom flange ⅝, including a fitting piece of ⅛ inch all round, to make it steady on its base. It is bolted down with four ⅝ inch bolts.

The proper area for the water ways is a disputed point, but the larger they are the sweeter the pump will work, and the longer the valves will last. About one-third of the area of the pump is usually reckoned a fair proportion, which gives about 2¼ inches diameter. The velocity of the plunger, of course, is an important element in estimating the resistance, but in practice is rarely taken into consideration. On this branch will be bolted a valve box, containing both the suction and discharge passages, and which we shall hereafter describe.

At the bottom of the stuffing-box of the pump is fitted a brass bush 2 inches deep. The length of the pump is made such that the plunger works to within an inch of the top of the bush, which thus affords sufficient guide when it is at the top of its stroke. The stuffing-box allows ⅜ inch of packing round the plunger, and is 3½ deep. The gland is bushed with brass, and is screwed down with four ⅝ bolts. Lugs on the pump 1 inch, and on the gland ⅞ inch deep. The upper eye of the rod, if the gudgeon be outside, may be made close, or if not, with a strap, like the connecting rod. The diameter of this gudgeon is made larger than the lower one, as it has more work on it, and is troublesome to replace. The eye having to slip over the collar of the gudgeon, must be made of corresponding size. The key is nicked into the lower brass, to keep the rod in place.

To be continued.

SICKLES' PATENT (AMERICAN) EXPANSION GEAR.

The extensive use of equilibrium valves for steam engines in America has led to several contrivances for improving their working. With the rapid speed of piston generally adopted in America, the durability of the valves is affected by the momentum, which they acquire in falling, being suddenly arrested. To obviate this difficulty is the object of Sickles' patent, with the accompanying sketch and description of which we have been favoured by an American correspondent. The spindle of the equilibrium valve is connected to the piston rod, *c*, passing up through a stuffing box into the cylinder, *a*, and keyed into the two pistons, *b* and *d*. The bottom of the cylinder, *a*, has a recess bored in it, about ⅛ of an inch larger in diameter than the piston, *b*. The cylinder is filled with water to such a height that the piston, *b*, never rises above the surface, and when the piston falls, with the equilibrium valve, it enters the recess for the last ¼ of an inch of its stroke, displacing the water it contains. The water being able to escape but slowly through the annular space, the momentum of the valve is destroyed without any concussion, the water acting like a buffer, to break the force of the blow. On the cover of this "dash-pot," as it is termed, a small cylinder is placed, in which is fitted the piston, *d*. This piston compresses the air above it, when it rises, which serves, on the down stroke, to prevent the risk of the valve sticking from friction in the stuffing boxes, or any other cause. The whole apparatus is fixed either above or below the cylinder valve, in the most convenient way that the details of the engine will admit. In the engines of sea-going steamers unprovided with such an apparatus, a difficulty has, we understand, been found from the valves not closing promptly when the vessel was rolling.

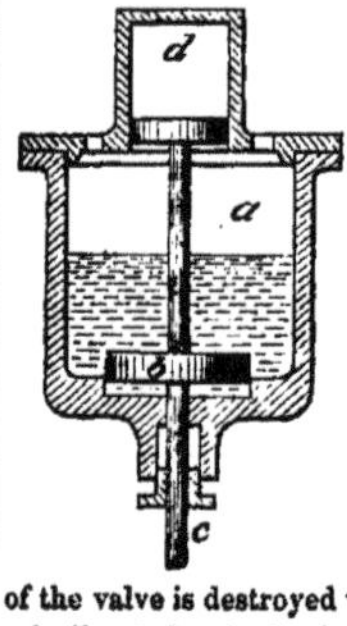

Equilibrium valves for the main valves of marine engines have not met with much favour in this country; but we think that, for large engines especially, the ease with which they may be adjusted, and the little power required to work them, render them deserving of attention. In the American Atlantic boats, one man can handle the engines, while in Cunard's boats, of about the same size, a whole gang of men are required. In cases of collisions, like that of the *Europa* and the *Charles Bartlett*, this point becomes one of serious importance.

AMERICAN ENGINEERING.

The Engineers' and Mechanics' Pocket Book. By C. H. Haswell, Engineer in Chief, U. S. Navy. 5th Edit., New York.

This is the production of a practical engineer, and although he has not entirely thrown overboard the antiquated authorities which figure in all similar works, Mr. Haswell has produced a very useful pocket volume. We say *pocket* volume, advisedly, for its bulk contrasts favourably with some of the so-called pocket companions on this side of the Atlantic. In addition to the ordinary tables, mathematical and arithmetical rules, &c., it contains proportions of gunpowder, dimensions and weight of guns, shot, and shells in the U.S. army and navy, power required to punch plates, calculations for tonnage and displacement of vessels, dimensions of steam engines, water wheels, sugar mills, saw mills, cotton and corn mills, blast engines, &c. We shall best give an idea of the information it contains by a few extracts which may be useful to our readers.

WATER-WHEELS.

" At the mill of Mr. Samuel Newlin, at Fishkill Creek, N. Y., 5 barrels of flour can be ground, and 400 bushels of grain elevated 36 feet per hour, with a stream and overshot wheel of the following dimensions, viz. :

Height of head to centre of opening, 24¼ inches ; opening, 1¼ by 80 inches ; wheel, 22 feet diameter by 8 feet face ; 52 buckets, each 1 foot in depth.

The wheel making 3¼ revolutions, driving 3 run of 4¼ feet stones 130 turns in a minute, with all the attendant machinery.

This is a case of maximum effect, in consequence of the gearing being well set up, and kept in good order.

At the furnace of Mr. Peter Townsend, Monroe Works, N. J., 30 to 34 tons of No. 1 Iron are made per week, with the blast from two 5 feet by 5 feet 1 inch blowing cylinders. The wheel (overshot) being 24 feet diameter, by 6 feet in width, having 70 buckets of 14 inches in depth. The stream is ¾ by 51 inches, having a head 6¼ feet ; the wheel and cylinders each making 4¼ revolutions per minute.

Rocky Glen Factory, Fishkill, N. Y., containing 6144 self-acting mule spindles, 160 looms, weaving printing cloths 27 inches wide of No. 33 yarn (33 hanks to a pound), and producing 24,000 hanks in a day of 11 hours, is driven by a breast wheel and stream of the following dimensions, viz. :

Stream 18 feet by 2 inches, head 20 feet, height of water upon wheel 16 feet, diameter of wheel 26 feet 4 inches, face of wheel 20 feet 9 inches, depth of buckets 15¾ inches, number of buckets 70.

Revolutions, 4⅙ per minute.

" SUGAR MILL.

For expressing 20,000 lbs. of Cane Juice per Day.

NON-CONDENSING ENGINE.—Cylinder, 15 inches in diameter by 4 feet stroke.

Pressure, 50 lbs. per square inch, cut off at ¼ the stroke of the piston. Revolutions, 36 per minute.

Boiler, 1 of 62 inches in diameter by 30 feet in length, with 2, 18 inch return flues. Grates, 36 square feet.

Rolls, two set of 3 each, of 24 inches in diameter by 5 feet in length ; geered 2¼ to 36 of engine, giving a speed of periphery of 15¼ feet per minute.

Fly wheel, 18 feet in diameter ; weight, 5 tons.

This arrangement of a second set of rolls is a late improvement ; its object, that of distributing the cane over an increased surface of rolls, reducing their speed, and affording more time for the juice to run off ; an increase of 20 per cent. is effected by it.

For a Crop of 3000 boxes of Sugar of 500 lbs. each

A non-condensing engine with a cylinder of 11 inches in diameter by 4 feet stroke, making 48 revolutions, with a pressure of steam 60 lbs. per square inch, driving 1 set of rolls, 24 inches by 4 feet, at a speed of periphery of 36 feet per minute.

Boiler, 52 inches by 24 feet, with 2, 16 inch return flues. Grate surface, 25 square feet.

Fly wheel, 16 feet diameter ; weight, 4 tons."

" BLOWING OR BLAST ENGINES.

Dimensions of a Furnace, Engines, &c. At Lonakoning (Md.)

Furnace, diameter at the boshes 14 feet, which fall in, 6.33 inches in every foot rise.

Engine (non-condensing), diameter of cylinder 18 inches, length of stroke 8 feet. Revolutions, 12 per minute, with a pressure of 50 lbs. per square inch.

Boilers, five, each 24 feet in length, and 36 inches in diameter.

Blast cylinders, 5 feet diameter and 8 feet stroke.

At a pressure of from 2 to 2¼ lbs. per square inch, the quantity of blast is 3770 cubic feet per minute, requiring a power of about 50 horses to supply it.

At Mount Savage (Md.)

For blowing four furnaces, 14 feet in diameter, each making 100 tons of pig iron per week.

Engine (condensing), diameter of cylinder 56 inches, length of stroke 10 feet. Revolutions, 15 per minute. Pressure, 60 lbs. per square inch, cut off at ½ of the stroke.

Boilers, 6 of 60 inches in diameter, and 24 feet in length, with 1, 22 inch flue in each, double returned. Grates, 198 square feet.

Blast cylinder, 126 inches in diameter by 10 feet stroke. Revolutions, 15 per minute. Pressure of blast, 4 to 5 lbs. per square inch.

Area of pipes, 2300 square inches, or ⅕ that of the cylinder.

For blowing two furnaces and two fineries, making 240 tons of forge pig per week.

Engine (non-condensing), diameter of cylinder 20 inches, length of stroke 8 feet. Revolutions, 28 per minute. Pressure, 50 to 60 lbs. per square inch (full stroke).

Boilers, 6 of 36 inches in diameter, and 28* feet in length (without flues). Grates, 100 square feet.

Blast cylinders, 2 of 62 inches in diameter by 8 feet stroke. Revolutions, 22 per minute. Pressure of blast, 2¼ lbs. per square inch.

Area of pipes, 3 feet, or ¼ that of the cylinders.

One blast furnace has 2, 3 inch and 1, 3¼ inch tuyeres ; the other has 3 of 3 inches.

One finery has 6 tuyeres of 1¼ inches, and the other 4 of 1¼ inches.

The ore yields from 40 to 45 per cent. of iron. The temperature of the blast is 600°.

" HYDROSTATIC PRESS.

NON-CONDENSING ENGINE. 30 *Bales of Cotton per Hour.*

Cylinder, 10 inches in diameter by 3 feet stroke.

Pressure, 50 lbs. per square inch, full stroke. Revolutions, 45 to 60 per minute.

Presses, two, with 12 inch rams, having 4¼ feet stroke.

Pumps, two of 2 inches diameter by 6 inches stroke."

CORRESPONDENCE.

ON THE POWER OF WATER-WHEELS.

SIR,—Your excellent remarks in the last month's number of the *Artisan*, upon water-wheels, and upon the deduction that must be made from the " actual momentum of the quantity of water employed, multiplied by the height of the fall," in order to obtain the maximum power capable of being realized through the water-wheel, lead me to remark how rare it is to meet with any exposition of the why and wherefore that such deductions require to be made. We are told that an overshot wheel of the best construction can only realize to its proprietor ¾ of the momentum of the water actually expended upon it ; a breast-wheel about ½, and an undershot wheel about ¼ ; but no reasons are adduced why such extraordinary deductions require to be made.

I believe the subject is fitted to draw out the opinions of your scientific readers, and I offer the following remarks with that view, rather than with the idea of clearing up the subject entirely.

It is evident that, when a mass of water reposes in the buckets of a water-wheel in a state of rest, the water presses against the wheel with its full weight ; but that if, on the other hand, the wheel is in such rapid motion, that the water in the buckets descends at the rate of 16 feet in the first second, or the full velocity due to unrestrained gravitation, then the same water cannot press upon the wheel with any part of its weight. And that the wheel would have to be propelled by some other power, to enable it to acquire such a velocity ; or, in other words, all ponderous bodies require their whole weight to enable themselves to descend to the earth at that velocity, and cannot then spare a fraction of that weight to produce any other effect whatever.

<hr/>

* Forty feet would have afforded much economy of fuel.

And, therefore, between the velocity of 0, when the weight is at a maximum, and the velocity of gravitation, when the weight is 0, any number of intermediate velocities may be chosen, each one of which will be accompanied with a proportionate sacrifice of the moving weight.

A good example of this is to be found in the well-known experiment of two bodies of different weights, suspended at the opposite ends of a cord over a pulley. The heaviest weight descends with an uniformly accelerating velocity, but which is less in proportion to the velocity due to unrestrained gravitation, according to the difference between the weights of the two bodies. If the two bodies are represented by A and B, (of which A is the heaviest,) and if g is the velocity generated by gravitation in one second, then $\frac{A-B}{A+B} \times g$ is the velocity with which A will descend. If A = 56 lbs., and B = 28 lbs., g being 32 feet at the surface of our earth, then $\frac{56-28}{56+28} \times 32 = \frac{28}{84} \times 32 = \frac{1}{3} \times 32 = 10\frac{2}{3}$ will be the velocity generated every second by the descent of A, and as the ascent of B is at the same rate, it follows that the greatest weight which 56 lbs. of water, descending at $10\frac{2}{3}$ feet per second, can raise at the same velocity, would be 28 lbs.

In applying this rule to the subject of water-wheels, the difficulty arises of comparing the uniform motion of the wheel with the accelerated motion produced by gravitation. However, a fair computation seems to be, when that velocity is estimated, which would be generated by gravity, at that part of the circumference where the average maximum effect of the water is transferred to the wheel. In an overshot-wheel, receiving the water at the top of the wheel, the height would be taken from the axis of the wheel upwards to a point where the water would be stationary. If, in this case, the wheel were 16 feet diameter, the velocity due to the water, after falling 8 feet, would be $\sqrt{2gs}$ (s being = to the height of the fall = 8 feet) or = 23 feet nearly. If then, we suppose two velocities for such a wheel to describe, say, 4 feet, and 6 feet, per second, and require to know the relative effective power produced by the same volume of water at these velocities, then $\frac{4}{23}$ and $\frac{6}{23}$ would respectively represent the value of the fraction $\frac{A-B}{A+B}$, and the values of A and B would be 13·5 and 9·5, in the first case, and 14·5 and 8·5, in the second, and as $\frac{9·5}{13·5} = ·7$ and $\frac{8·5}{14·5} = ·58$, therefore, these decimals are that per centage of the expenditure of water which would be realized as useful effect at the above respective velocities.

It follows from this that the slower the motion of an overshot wheel, the less sacrifice of the expenditure of water takes place; but when the motion is less than 2 feet per second, the motion of the wheel becomes unsteady. The "regulating" effect of the mass of water diminishing as the square of the velocity decreases.

In undershot wheels, the velocity of the wheel is regulated to $\frac{1}{3}$ of the velocity of the stream at the place of contact. The impulsive effect of the water, multiplied by the velocity of the wheel being then at a maximum. For, if C = the velocity of the stream, and v = that of the wheel, C − v = the velocity of the impact, and the force of impact is proportional to $\frac{2}{C-v}$. The effect on the machinery of this force is also $\frac{2}{C-v} \times v$, and this expression is greatest when $v = \frac{C}{3}$.

To apply the formula to such a wheel, the fraction $\frac{A-B}{A+B}$ is $\frac{1}{3}$, consequently A is = 2, and B = 1; or the greatest effect would be $\frac{1}{3}$ of the expenditure of water.

All kinds of water-wheels must suffer further loss on account of the difficulty of maintaining the water in contact with the wheel to the lowest point, without receiving an impediment to motion on leaving the water, and the undershot-wheel suffers more from this than the overshot, which reduces the effect below the above statement; but these losses may be reduced by careful construction. What I am most anxious to point out is, the causes of loss which are indispensably connected with the force of gravitation, when employed as a moving power. And I propose at a future time to investigate the effects of the same principle, when applied to the power required to propel the paddle-wheels of steamers, to the motion of water in pipes, and many other subjects, the explanation of which is too much monopolised by scientific treatises, and requires to be opened out as the stock in trade of practical mechanics. Trusting that these remarks may not be deemed out of place in your journal, which has done so much to throw open the gates of the temple of science to the artizan,

I am, &c. R. P.

MR. HEATON'S PLAN FOR BALANCING THE STRAIN OF THE AIR PUMP.

Birmingham, 5th July, 1860.

SIR,—I was surprised on reading Mr. George Heaton's paper, on the importance of making a Compensation for the Pull of the Air-Pump Bucket in the Condensing Steam Engine, that the fact of his having applied extra weight to the connecting rod end of the beam, should have been considered a novelty in engineering practice, by the Institution of Mechanical Engineers. I am quite willing to grant Mr. Heaton the merit of having discovered that of which he was before in ignorance, but he and the gentlemen of the above-mentioned institution should be made acquainted of the fact, that engineers of standing have for years been aware of the necessity for doing that which he has done, —and have done it, although in a different way, viz., by casting the connecting-rod very much heavier than is necessary for strength, in order that the engine may be properly balanced. I cannot speak for every engine-maker throughout the kingdom, as there may be many inexperienced men who make such engines as that Mr. Heaton speaks of, but I can vouch for the fact of its having been for years the practice of my employers, who have every right to be considered *engineers*.

I am, Sir,

Your obedient Servant,

J. H.

EXPANSION SLIDE GEAR.

To the Editor of the Artizan.

SIR,—As a reader of your useful journal, I noticed a description of expansion slide gear, by Mr. John Dudgeon, in the number for March last, and also the correspondence that followed, in the numbers for April and May, relative to the originality of the invention of this gear. The rejoinder of Mr. C. P. Stewart, in your last number, is now before me, and, as an artizan, I am not a little surprised at the effrontery displayed, in offering such a communication for publication in the pages of a journal that professes to be one of the principal scientific organs of the artizans of this country; certainly the columns of the *Herald* or the *Morning Post* would have been more congenial to the spirit breathed out in this effusion.

The working men of this country are not insensible to the advantages of education, and only regret that its blessings have not fallen to their lot to so great an extent as they would wish; which condition, however, they endeavour to improve in every legitimate way; hence, our mechanics' institutes, public lectures, circulating libraries, and cheap literature, —marked features of the present age. We accordingly find instances, which, I can assure Mr. Stewart, are by no means rare, of working men toiling from "grey morn to dewy eve," in what he terms a subordinate capacity, for the purpose of procuring as much as barely suffices to keep body and soul together, and yet devoting a portion of the few hours left them for rest and recreation to the improvement of that education, which, although it may have been much more circumscribed than that of their more comfortably circumstanced neighbours, still forms a basis upon which, by perseverance and industry, a substantial superstructure of information may be raised.

Is there anything wonderful then in the possibility that a working man, or an individual who has been a working man, should be able to write a letter in his vernacular language on a subject connected with his every-day avocations? Seemingly it is altogether beyond the conception of Mr. Stewart that he should be able, or has a right to do so, as we may infer from that part of his letter where he says, "I am inclined to think that, by putting such high-flown expressions into the mouths of these working men, he (the party who writes the letters) has some latent wish to expose them to ridicule."

Mr. Stewart seems to belong to that school which considers the working classes mere hewers of wood and drawers of water, amongst whom there is not sufficient mental capacity to imbibe the lights of science, and to whom education is by no means essential, but tends rather to generate a spirit of insubordination, and make them discontented with their lot. But Mr. Stewart, and this class of opinionists, may be assured that there is no deficiency of that talent among artizans, which only requires mental cultivation to make it shine forth with noon-day splendour; and so far from education engendering a spirit of discontent, it rather tends to nourish the seeds of good will in the breasts of the working classes, and to knit the bonds of society more closely together.

It would certainly be disingenuous of artizans to sneer at that education of which Mr. Stewart remarks, "they can know nothing;" but I consider the sneers he refers to are not directed against education, but against the spirit of intolerance, exclusiveness, and conceit, which (it is notorious to the world) is too often imbibed in our great seats of learning. One of Scotia's favourite bards, who, though he "whistled at the plough," occupies a conspicuous niche in the Temple of Fame, gives the following appropriate lines:—

> " A set o' dull conceited hashes,
>   Confuse their brains wi' College classes ;
>   They gang in stirks and come out asses,
>   The truth to speak ;
>   And then they think to climb Parnassus
>   By dint o' Greek.
>
> " What's a' their jargon o' the schools,—
>   Their Latin names for horns and stools !
>   'Gin honest Nature made them fools
>   What soirs their grammars ! .
>   They'd better tak' up spades and sho'ols,
>   Or knappin' hammers !"

The industrious and persevering working man, toiling on his way to the temple of science, has no cause to be disheartened, although he cannot construe Virgil or Homer, or fully understand all the mysteries of the heathen mythology ; neither should he take notice of that favourite dogma of the opinionists here referred to, viz., that "a little learning is a dangerous thing," for, as the talented author of the "Pleasures of Hope" once said, "In comparing small learned acquisitions with none at all, it appears to me to be equally absurd to consider a little learning valueless, or even dangerous, as some will have it, as to talk of a little virtue, a little wealth, or health, or cheerfulness, or a little of any other blessing under Heaven being worthless or dangerous." To abjure any degree of information because we cannot grasp the whole circle of the sciences, or sound the depths of erudition, appears to be just about as

sensible as if we were to shut up our windows because they are too narrow, or because the glass has not the magnifying power of a telescope.

Let not, then, the animadversions of those members of learned institutions, whose erudite acquisitions are too often tainted with a spirit of illiberality, deter the sons of labour from consuming their "midnight oil" in improving their education (however circumscribed it may originally have been), and raising on it a substantial superstructure of scientific and useful knowledge. Let working men reflect that to their class belong the names of Brindley, Smeaton, Watt, Arkwright, Rennie, Telford, Stephenson, Maudslay, Fairbairn, and many others, who form so bright a galaxy of master minds in practical science, and whose stupendous and ingenious works have added so much to the prosperity and glory of this country, and drawn forth the admiration of surrounding nations.

But to return to Mr. Stewart's letter, he says, " The talented gentleman who invented and brought out the double cams and rollers, has himself assured me that Mr. John Dudgeon had no other connexion with the arrangement whatever, except having suggested the junction of the two levers by a rod." Now, did this talented gentleman ever see, before the year 1842, (when this vaunted gear with double cams and rollers is said to have been invented and brought out), a work on the steam engine by Thomas Tredgold, the first edition of which was published in 1827, or fifteen years previous to 1842? If he has, he may perhaps remember that at page 235 of that edition, an arrangement of mechanism (illustrated in plate 9), is described for working the valves of steam engines by double cams acting on rollers; the one cam giving the requisite degree of motion for shifting the valves when the piston is at the ends of the cylinder, and the other acts so as to cut off the steam by the same valves at any part of the stroke, and is capable of being adjusted in order to vary the time of the cut off at pleasure. It is true the rollers in this case are not attached to levers, but are fixed in a frame on the end of the rod, which transmits the motion to the valve shaft, but the principle of both is identical ; and I question much if, taken as a whole, the copy of 1842 would be found to answer the purpose intended so well as the original of 1827.

Mr. Stewart, in his first letter, asserts that the subject of expansion gear has been a favourite study of his for some ten years past, and that he has kept himself acquainted with the new modifications as they have appeared. If this is the case, was Messrs. Malcolmson's application of spiral grooves to shift the cut-off cam on board the screw steamer, he refers to, the first time he had seen this contrivance similarly applied ? for if so his boasted acquaintance with "new modifications of expansion gear as they have appeared," is sadly deficient, as he will find that a similar contrivance was used by both Mr. Fenton and Mr. Longridge (in connexion with their expansion gear for locomotive engines), for shifting the eccentrics round on the shaft, some four or five years ago.

London, July, 1850.   W. H.

PRACTICAL QUERIES.

Norwich, July 4th, 1850.

Mr. Editor,—Sir, Encouraged by the very kind manner in which you have answered the questions of several of your correspondents, I beg the insertion of the following, hoping that some of your talented readers will answer them :—

1st, Which is the readiest way to ascertain the correct position for an eccentric to be placed to work a slide when you have the lap and lead, travel of the slide, and throw of the eccentric given, (say, for instance, a locomotive engine.) Travel of slide, 4½ in. ; throw of eccentric, 4½ in. ; lap on the steam side of slide, 1 in. ; and lead of ditto, ⅛ in.

2nd, In your last number there are some indicator diagrams, which have a line called the atmosphere line on them :—is that line the place at which the indicator point stands previous to the steam being admitted into the cylinder ?

3rd, In the event of the radius rod of a side lever engine breaking when at sea, and not having a duplicate one on board, would it be practicable to work the engine by the remaining one, or by taking it off ?

I am, Sir, yours, obediently,   A WORKING ENGINEER.

ON VENTILATION.

(NOT BY DOCTOR REID.)

VENTILATION seems now the popular subject, if we may judge from the advertisements, which promise us pure air, "fresh from the graveyards and the Thames," in all directions. There is no reason, however, why we should not "set our houses in order," in anticipation of the glorious sanitary reforms that are to be, some of these fine days, and to make provision for enjoying the fresh air, when the presence of that article shall have become a possibility in this overgrown metropolis. The rage lately has been for expedients for letting the air into rooms, and we have perforated glass, perforated zinc, glass Venetian blinds, &c. *ad libitum.* Three gentlemen, Mr. Sheringham, Mr. Bessell, and Mr. Dixon, go a step further, and provide that the cold air entering the room nearly on a level with the ceiling, shall be thrown upwards, and compelled to mix with the heated air, as it descends, thus preventing the danger of a cold draught. It is not enough, however, to let in cold air merely ; the hot air must be also let out. This is attempted to be effected by Arnott's ventilators, which are very well, if the draught of the chimney happens to suit them. But it frequently happens that if they are so adjusted as to let out the air, they also let in the smoke, which to "particular" people, is such a grievous sin that they screw them down, so that they never open at all. The difficulty can hardly be got over, unless by making a special channel for the hot air to escape by, in addition to the chimney. The accompanying sketch shows an arrangement of flues, registered by Mr. W. Walker, of Manchester, by which this object is accomplished.

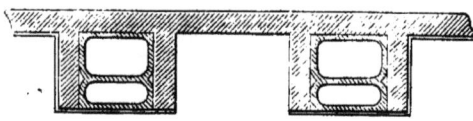

Scale ⅜ of an inch to a foot.

The plan represents a section through the fire-place, with a flue on each side, from the lower stories. These flues are made of burnt-clay, and have a partition in them, forming a larger flue for the smoke, and a smaller one for the foul air. By this means a powerful ventilator would be formed for each apartment, and which could be regulated with the greatest nicety by adjusting a valve on a level with the ceiling. The flues being carried up separately to the top of the building, no smoke can possibly escape into the room. An incidental advantage, but not an unimportant one, gained by the use of these clay flues, is, that there is no loose pargetting or lining, to be raked from the bricks by the sweeping-machines. In old houses, where the chimnies have not been relined, the smoke will frequently find its way into the closets in the room above, and into other chimneys, rather than out of the chimney-top. In 1843, Mr. Denley took out a patent for using circular tubes, and for connecting them to descending flues, in such a way that all the soot might be swept, when required, to the basement, without entering the upper apartments at all. This plan was fully described in the *Artisan* for 1844.

ROYAL SCOTTISH SOCIETY OF ARTS.

The Royal Scottish Society of Arts held an extraordinary meeting in the Hall, 54, George Street, on Monday, 24th June, 1850. Thomas Grainger, Esq., C.E., President, in the Chair.

The following communications were made :

1. Description and four drawings of a large iron roof, recently erected at the Liverpool Terminus of the Lancashire and Yorkshire Railway, by Messrs. Fox, Henderson, & Co., Engineers, London Works, Birmingham. Communicated by Thomas Grainger, Esq.

This roof has been erected under the superintendence of John Hawkshaw, Esq., Civil Engineer to the Lancashire and Yorkshire Railway. The roof covers five lines of rails and three platforms, and a carriageroad 12 yards wide in one span, having no columns nor supports besides the outside walls ; the span varies from 136 feet to 128 feet, and the total length is 638 feet ; the total area thus covered is 83,457 feet. The material used in the construction of this roof is entirely iron. The framing consists of a series of trussed principals placed at intervals of 11 feet from centre to centre ; these principals are attached to the outside walls by cast-iron bed plates or shoes, the whole of which upon one side of the roof are so constructed that the principals may contract or expand freely from variations of temperature. Immediately over the principals are fixed wrought-iron purlines, which support the covering ; this covering is of corrugated sheet-iron galvanised. The roof is both lighted and ventilated along the ridge by four continuous rows of large skylights and two rows of louvres ; half the light is distributed along the ridge, and the remaining half is equally distributed at the eaves ; the total area of light admitted being equal to one-fourth of the entire area of the roof. Considering the immense extent of sheet-iron in the covering of the roof, it was deemed advisable to make expansion joints at various places in the corrugated iron. This principle was also applied to the skylights, and the entire length of roof is thus divided into several portions, which can contract or expand without impairing the efficiency of the work, as being weather proof, or destroying its unity of appearance.

2. Model and additional description of a Self-Acting Water Meter. By Andrew Carrick, Esq., 14, Holmhead Street, Glasgow.

In this meter the water is introduced through a pipe, shut at the end by a projecting flange, but having ports for the passage of the water. At the lower end of these ports, another flange passes round the pipe. An outer case or cover is ground to face the flanges closely, so that, when the cover is up, the supply is shut off. This cover is attached by chain to the end of a beam, whose fulcrum is above the water line, in the meter. From the other end of this beam a perforated bucket is suspended through a boxed-in space, and hangs under the lower end of a syphon which passes up said space, and through its side, down to the bottom of the meter. When the flowing-water reaches the bed of the syphon the bucket is filled, and its superior weight shuts the valve, so that no water is let in till the meter is emptied. The bucket ultimately empties itself through the perforations, and being *now* lighter than the valve cover, the latter descends and the supply is resumed. The cistern is immediately under the meter, and is governed by a float and stopcock, to prevent overflow. The indication of the quantity delivered is taken from the movement of the beam—the *unit* being the *number* of gallons the meter is constructed to contain.

3. Description of a modification of the Paddle Wheel. By Mr. Andrew Mennie, Castle Street, Forfar. A model was exhibited.

The author states that the float boards of this paddle-wheel are attached to axles with two cranks upon each axle, at right angles to each other. That an eccentric apparatus acts upon the cranks, and supports each of the float boards in a position at right angles to the water, during the entire revolution of the paddle-wheel. That the loss of power occasioned by the float boards entering and leaving the water obliquely would be avoided ; and that the objection of liability to derangement cannot be applied to this modification of the paddle-wheel, as one or more of its float boards might be broken without interfering with the remaining ones, any farther than it would with the float boards of the common paddle-wheel; also that a fewer number of float boards would be sufficient to propel a vessel, as they would present a greater resistance to the water than the float boards of the common paddle-wheel.

4. Description of Model of an Improved Coupling for the Springs of Railway and other Carriages. By the same.

The author states that the coupling apparatus for the springs of carriages, is intended to remove the danger and inconvenience arising from the vertical oscillation of the body of the carriage ; that the apparatus regulates the movements of the body of the carriage in a manner similar to the action of the parallel motion of the steam-engine upon the piston-rod, so that the more elastic sort of springs, such as the spiral, could be used with perfect safety.

5. The following Reports of Committees were read and approved of, viz. :
(1.) On Mr. Cleugh's Machine for Boring Coal. Mr. Buchanan, Convener.
(2.) On Mr. Patrick Wilson's Plans of Dwelling-houses for the Working-classes. Mr. Burn Murdoch, Convener.
(3.) On Mr. Smith's method of constructing Wire Fences. Mr. Clerk Maxwell, Convener.
(4.) On Mr. W. R. Douglas' machine for Mortising, Tenoning, Boring, and Ripping Timber. Mr. Slight, Convener.
(5.) On Mr. Stewart Hepburn's method of Disengaging a Railway Train from the Locomotive. Ditto, Convener.
(6.) On Mr. Gregory's Self-acting Disengagement of Locomotive and Tender from the Train on the former leaving the Rails. Ditto, Convener.
(7.) On Shenck and Ghemar's New Method in Lithography. Mr. Cay, Convener.
(8.) On Mr. Fraser's Pressure Indicator. Mr. Paterson, Convener.
(9.) On Mr. Fairbairn's Boiler for Locomotives. Mr. Paterson, Convener.
(10.) On Mr. Dale's Designs for Grate, &c. Mr. Cay, Convener.
(11.) On Mr. Campbell's Railway Points and Crossings. Mr. Buchanan, Convener.
(12.) On Mr. Shedden's Rules for finding the weight of Cast Iron Bodies by measurement. Mr. Slight, Convener.

On a recommendation by the Council, the Society made a donation of £20 towards the local fund for the Great Exhibition of the Works of Industry of all Nations in London in 1851.

The following Prize Committee was appointed to award the prizes for session 1849, viz. :—Thomas Grainger, Esq., President ; Douglas Maclagan, M.D., F.R.S.E., Vice-President ; Geo. Buchanan, Esq., F.R.S.E. ; J. Burn Murdoch, Esq., F.R.S.E. ; William Paterson, Esq. ; John Cay, Esq., F.R.S.E. ; George Lees, LL.D. ; David Rhind, F.R.S.E. ; James Slight, Esq. ; John Clerk Maxwell, Esq., F.R.S.E. ; Professor Kelland, F.R.S.E. ; Thomas Purdie, Esq. ; the Secretary *ex-officio* Convener.

PROLONGATION OF ERICSSON'S PATENT.

Hearing on Petition before the Privy Council, June 24th, 1850.

(Abstracted from the Short-hand Writer's Notes.)

The present case being one of some importance to patentees generally, we have thought it of sufficient interest to demand a special notice, and

having been favoured with the short-hand writer's notes, we now give all the most important portions *verbatim*. The Attorney-General demanded that a condition should be attached to the prolongation, to the effect that the government should have the use of the patent, and with it, of all the other patents for the screw propeller, gratuitously. The argument relied on to extort this concession, appears to us worthy of the narrow-minded policy which has almost invariably characterized the treatment of inventors by the authorities of this country. As our readers well know, the proprietors of the various screw patents have been at law with each other for some years—they receiving the shells while the lawyers swallowed the oysters ;—and when they finally made peace and have a prospect of getting a few of the oysters for themselves, they are coolly told by the Attorney-general—" You are going to make some money now, so you can bear to be fleeced a little." This is really the truth of the matter. If people want to use the Screw propeller in their national capacity, why should they not pay for it the same as they would have to do in their individual capacity ? We confess we can see no difference in the two cases. We had hoped that we lived in more liberal times. Our Exhibition of 1851 will be an unmeaning toy-shop, unless such a radical change is made in our system of Patent Laws as will ensure to the inventor some more equitable treatment, than he seems liable to at present.

Privy Council Chamber, Whitehall, 24th June, 1850.
Before Mr. Baron Parke, the Right Hon. Dr. Stephen Lushington, the Right Hon. T. P. Leigh, and Sir Edward Ryan.

" Sir F. Thesiger.—I have the honour to appear before your lordships in support of this application for the extension of the time of this patent, which was granted on the 13th of July, 1836, to Capt. John Ericsson, and was assigned by him to Count de Rosen, partly for his own benefit, and partly in trust for Capt. Ericsson. My lords, this is an invention for a screw propeller. Your lordships have had the subject of propulsion by screws very frequently before you, and I need not go minutely into that, because you are perfectly familiar with these subjects. Your lordships are aware, probably, that in 1836, when Capt. Ericsson obtained his patent, various experiments at that time had been made from time to time by persons, for the purpose of obtaining what was a great *desideratum*, the power of propelling vessels by means of screws. The only propeller which was in use before 1836 was the old Archimedian screw, which was the entire turn of a screw, and which was a very inconvenient sort of instrument : the length of it prevented its useful action in the water, and, in consequence of its great length, in comparison with its diameter, it was very clumsy, and difficult to apply with convenience to any vessel. There was another sort of propeller, which was with arms, like the vanes of a smoke-jack. That also met with very indifferent success ; and I think, my lords, I am entitled to say, that until Capt. Ericsson's invention, there was no efficient mode of screw propulsion known to the scientific world. Capt. Ericsson perfected his invention and obtained his patent, as I have mentioned, on the 13th of July, 1836 ; and his invention consists of an instrument composed of a series of blades or arms, each being portions or sections of a screw : the whole propelling surface being less than the entire turn of one thread of a screw ; there is an open space left between the arms, which prevents the choking action of the water, and this is applied to a shaft which runs through a stuffing box below the water line of the vessel, and the motive power is applied by cranks fixed on the propeller shaft. The outer end of the propeller shaft is supported by means of a frame fastened to the overhanging stern of the vessel. Round the propeller, as originally invented and introduced by Capt. Ericsson, there is a hoop, and on that hoop additional arms or blades are fixed, the effect of which is to give an increased surface to the propeller. You get the additional power of the propeller without having the arms in the centre of the circumference crowded, and besides that, the interior arms are found to be considerably strengthened by means of this hoop.

Now, my lords, the merit of screw propulsion is mainly attributable to Capt. Ericsson, I think I am entitled to say, in consequence of that opinion having been expressed by a gentleman, who is himself connected with the subject, a person of very considerable science : I mean Mr. Bennet Woodcroft, who has, your lordships know, obtained an extension of a patent for a screw propeller, which was a screw with an increasing pitch, and he, in a work that he has published on this subject states,—' That Capt. Ericsson is a native of Sweden, and held a commission in the Swedish army; but his taste for mechanics was such, as to induce him to leave his native country and establish himself in London, in partnership with the well-known establishment of Messrs. Braithwaite, in which he became a partner, under the firm of Braithwaite & Ericsson. Prior to the construction of his first vessel, he made some experiments with a model boat, which was propelled by means of a screw, in a circular bath in London. The model boat was fitted with a small engine, supplied with steam by a pipe leading from a steam-boiler over the centre of the bath, and descending to within a foot of the water-line, where it was branched off by a swivel-joint, and connected with the engine in the boat. Steam being admitted in this pipe, the engine in the boat was put in motion, and motion was then communicated to the propeller. This model, though less than 2 feet long, performed its voyage about the basin at the rate of upwards of 3 miles an hour.' He then goes on to explain the various modes by which Capt. Ericsson endeavoured to introduce his invention to the public notice, and in page 102 of his work, he says,—' It will thus be seen that Capt. Ericsson accomplished for the screw propeller in America and in England, what Fulton did for the paddle-wheel in the former, and Bell in the latter country, namely, its practical introduction.' Now, my lords, of course I need not say that testimony of that kind is extremely valuable, and I shall produce Mr. Woodcroft before your lordships, to say, in order to explain what he has said in his book, that Capt. Ericsson began his experiments by means of a small model boat. In the month of April, 1837, a vessel called the Francis Ogden was launched, fitted with this screw propeller. She was only 45 feet long, and 8 feet wide, and 3 feet draught; and she was fitted at that time with a double propeller, which I will explain to your lordships. You will observe, by reference to the specification, and the drawings which accompany it, that Capt. Ericsson described his propeller with two wheels; the shaft of the propeller which is nearest to the stern is hollow, and through that shaft another shaft runs, and there is a wheel placed on the external shaft.

The Attorney-General.—Is there not a model.

Sir Frederick Thesiger.—Yes, we have a model; and the wheels have opposite actions, and they move in opposite directions.

The Attorney-General.—Have you not a model? it is impossible to understand it in that way. You never can understand these things by drawings.

Sir Frederick Thesiger.—I was about to explain to your lordships that Capt. Ericsson, in his drawings, shows the double-wheel propeller. The propeller has, in point of fact, been applied both with the double wheel and with the single wheel, and I apprehend there will be no difficulty whatever. We are not here with regard to the validity of the patent; but there will be no difficulty in saying, that if any person, after that invented by Capt. Ericsson, had removed the outer wheel, and had worked with the single wheel only, that would have been an infringement of Capt. Ericsson's propeller, and this is his propeller (exhibiting a model to their lordships.) It is in sections.—These are portions of the screw—segments of the screw (describing on the model.) The hoop, as your lordships see, is calculated to strengthen the interior rim, and at the same time to increase the propelling surface, by means of the arms which are placed on the circumference of the hoop.

The Attorney-General.—That drawing will explain it, (handing a drawing to their lordships.)

Sir Frederick Thesiger.—They turn in different ways. I was about to mention to your lordships, that this propeller has been used with the double wheel, and also with the single wheel, and there is very considerable doubt, I understand, entertained by engineers of the present day, whether for the purpose of towing, for which this was originally principally invented, whether it is not better to use the double wheel than the single wheel. I believe, if you require speed, then the single wheel is preferable to the double. The Francis Ogden was launched, as I have told your lordships, in April, 1837. I have mentioned her dimensions; and, on the first trial, she was fitted with this machinery, and without the slightest alteration, she shot ahead at the rate of 10 miles an hour. The towing powers were then tried; there was a large schooner of 140 tons, which was tugged by means of this miniature steamer, at the rate of 7 miles an hour, and an American ship, called the Toronto, was also towed at the rate of 4½ miles an hour. At the end of the year 1837, Capt. Ericsson was desirous that the Lords of the Admiralty should test the value of his invention, and he took them a little trip, towed in their barge, by his steamer to Limehouse and back, which was a distance of 10 miles; and that short voyage was performed, showing the capabilities of this propeller, to their entire satisfaction; but notwithstanding the merit of the invention was acknowledged, yet there was very great prejudice against it, and great difficulty in forcing it into public notice. In the year

1838, the propeller was attached to some canal-boats that ran from Manchester to London, the diameter of the instrument was only 2 feet 6 inches, and it realized a speed of from 8 to 9 miles an hour. In the month of December, 1837, an iron boat, which was launched at Liverpool in the month of July, 1838, and which was called the Robert F. Stockton, was ordered to be fitted with this propeller, to be worked, I think, by engines of 50 horse power.

The Honourable Thomas Pemberton Leigh.—They were all double wheels, I suppose.

Sir F. Thesiger.—They were all double wheels. The Francis Ogden was tried with a single wheel. Several experiments were made in the presence of Mr. Braithwaite, and other scientific persons, with the single wheel. I believe that was the case with regard to the Robert F. Stockton; she arrived in the Thames in the year 1836, and in the month of January, 1839, there was a trial, in the presence of about 30 gentlemen, official and scientific, English and American, and they were all perfectly satisfied with the powers of this propeller. In that month of January, 1839, an extraordinary experiment was made with regard to the powers of tugging vessels. There were 4 loaded coal-barges, which were collectively 59 feet in the beam, average draught of water being 4 feet 4 inches, besides the sectional area of the steamer, which was 43 feet; and this steamer dragged this enormous load through the water at the rate of 5½ knots an hour. In the early part of 1839, the Enterprise, an Ashby-de-la-Zouch canal-boat, 70 feet long, and 7 feet broad, with engines of 14 horse power, was launched, and her speed was from 9 to 10 miles an hour. At the latter end of 1839, Capt. Ericsson left England for America, where he has been, I believe, almost ever since, if not entirely. There he has fitted no less than 150 vessels with his propeller, and among others, a vessel which was called the Princeton; and the Princeton tried her speed against a celebrated steamer of ours, the Great Western; and we have evidence to show your lordships on that trial of speed the complete success of the Princeton over the Great Western, for I believe she ran round her. Notwithstanding all the merit that was disclosed by means of those different experiments in the scientific world, there was great difficulty indeed in inducing the Admiralty to adopt the invention; but I think it was about the year 1843 or 1844, the French were so much struck with it, that they desired to have one of their frigates, La Pomone, 44 guns, fitted with the propeller, and she was fitted accordingly, and she was the first vessel in Europe.—I believe the Princetown, in America, was the first there—she was the first vessel in Europe—the first man-of-war that had a clear broadside, and which was fitted with this propeller.

The Attorney-General.—Were they all double wheels?

Sir F. Thesiger.—No, that was a single wheel. This seemed to arouse the attention of the Admiralty, and they desired in that year, I think, that a propeller for a 300 horse power engine should be fitted to one of our frigates, called the 'Amphion;' and accordingly, in 1846, or 1847, a propeller was fitted to the Amphion.

The Hon. Thomas Pemberton Leigh.—Was that a single wheel?

Sir F. Thesiger.—That was a single wheel; I believe, generally, your lordship will find that the invention has been applied with the single wheel, and the hoop has, in most cases, been removed, the hoop being no essential part of the invention, but being merely used for the purpose of strengthening the interior arms, and also for increasing the propelling surface by means of blades or arms applied to the circumference.

Mr. Baron Parke.—Is the hoop part of the patent?

Sir F. Thesiger.—Yes, the hoop is part of the patent; the hoop is mentioned in the patent; the double wheel is mentioned, and the hoop beside.

Mr. Baron Parke.—Not the single wheel?

Sir F. Thesiger.—The single wheel is not mentioned. I apprehend, in the first place, we are not here to consider, as your lordships frequently have to consider, whether the patent is a valid patent or not; but you are to enquire into the utility of the invention, and what benefit the party has derived from it, to ascertain whether it is equitably entitled to an extension of the term; and your lordship may remember, that various patents have been taken out with respect to these screws: among others, a person of the name of Lowe took out a patent, which has been the subject of a good deal of litigation in the courts; and I remember perfectly well being myself against Mr. Lowe in the Court of Queen's Bench, that we insisted that Ericsson's patent, which was prior to Lowe's, was completely Lowe's, and that Lowe's was a piracy of Ericsson's. I remember putting the question to one of the engineers who was called for Mr Lowe. I took the hoop off, and I said, ' Is not that precisely Lowe's patent?' He said, ' Yes it is.' ' Well,' I said, ' suppose that Lowe's had preceded Ericsson's, would not Ericsson's have been a piracy of Lowe's!' 'Yes,' he says, 'there is no doubt it would.' 'Well then,' I said, 'Ericsson's preceding Lowe's, why is not Lowe's a piracy of Ericsson's!' Upon which, he began to talk about a table with five legs, and about taking off one of the five legs and leaving the other four legs; he said, the hoop was an incumbrance, and therefore the getting rid of the hoop by Lowe, was, in fact, a practical improvement.

The Attorney-General.—The jury found in that case for the plaintiff.

Sir F. Thesiger.—The jury did so find. The most remarkable thing, as your lordships' experience will tell you, that whenever a question is raised with regard to the infringement of a patent, the jury almost invariably find in favour of the plaintiff; whenever a *scire facias*, the jury almost invariably find for the plaintiff. The Attorney-General knows that perfectly well; and it is not to be wondered at, that the jury found a verdict in favour of Mr Lowe. It is almost according to the course of precedent upon these matters. My lords, I was about to mention that various parties have, from time to time, taken out patents in respect of screw propellers, and among others, there was a company called the Ship Propeller Company, which were using a screw which they had applied to the Great Britain, and which was considered by Count de Rosen, who was here representing the interests of Captain Ericsson when he went to America, an infringement of Mr. Ericsson's patent; and he brought an action against the Ship Propeller Company for this infringement, and the action was pending when proposals for the amalgamation of all the interests of all the parties connected with these patents was made. The Ship Propeller Company stood out for some time, and refused to accede to it; but alternately there was a decision in the Court of Exchequer, in the case of Back v. Sturman, which rather shook their confidence in the validity of their own patent against Captain Ericsson's.

The Attorney-General.—No, against Mr. Lowe. I was counsel in the case.

Sir F. Thesiger.—Yes, but as to this matter with regard to Captain Ericsson's, it shook their confidence, and induced them to come in and agree to an amalgamation with Captain Ericsson and the others; and all the parties met together and proposed they should amalgamate their several interests, inasmuch as it appeared almost impossible that any one of the inventions could be used without a portion of the invention of the others. Mr. Lowe stood out for a considerable time, and various actions were commenced; and it was not until a very recent period indeed that Mr. Lowe consented to come in and join the others. There are five of them altogether, and they have agreed that their interests shall be associated, that they shall be amalgamated together, and that the joint patent of each of them may be used by all indiscriminately.

Now, under these circumstances, your lordships may remember that a Mr. Smith applied some time ago for an extension of his term, he being one of the parties who had consented to this arrangement; and, my lords, my learned friends appeared as they do to-day, for the purpose of getting a clause introduced into the extension of that patent; my learned friend, Mr. Compton, appearing for the Admiralty, and supported by the Attorney-General, who says he appears for the public; and the clause which your lordships were urged to introduce, and if I may be permitted to say so most respectfully, I must regret that your lordships determined should be introduced, for the first time, was a clause compelling the patentee, as a condition of having his term enlarged, to give to the Government or to the Admiralty the absolute right to have this patent invention manufactured for them, without paying anything whatever for the use of the patent. Now, your lordships are aware that it is an ordinary term in all patents, that where they are applicable to public uses, that the public boards to which they would peculiarly belong shall have the use of them, paying according to their discretion; and I believe that discretion has always been fairly and properly exercised. I make no complaint on that account, and I see no reason why the extension of the term should not be coupled with a condition of that kind, extending that sort of clause to the extended term in this case; but it does appear to me, with very great respect to your lordships' decision on that occasion, that it is a very hard thing indeed to say that a party is to give to the government the entire use of his patent without receiving one farthing in return. Just take this case, my lords; suppose an invention which could be beneficially used by the government itself. Your lordships have now made it a principle, and your lordships would be making a precedent against inventors by which they would be very much discouraged, by which the public would be very much injured, if such a term as this is to be imposed for the future; but, of course, if your lordships proceed on this occasion and determine, as in the other case, that it must be so; if for the future no person can expect to have an extension of the term of his patent, how-

ever largely others may have benefited by it, and however he may have bestowed a benefit on the public, without giving to the government, who are the public in fact, the benefit of it——

The Attorney-General.—That was not the intention or ground of it—it was by reason of the amalgamation of all the screw propellers together in combination.

Sir F. Thesiger.—My friend is entirely mistaken. It was never once engaged before your lordships—that was never the foundation upon which it was put. It was the abstract right of the Admiralty to have the benefit of an invention of this kind for the sake of the public, without paying anything for it. The amalgamation at that time could not have been in question, because it was not completed.

Mr. Crowder.—It was mentioned, but it was not completed.

Sir F. Thesiger.—My learned friend, the Attorney-General, and myself have been engaged for a considerable time in promoting to the utmost of our power this amalgamation between the parties, to prevent them tearing themselves to pieces by litigation, and the public being deprived of the benefit of their several inventions; and my friend knows, that when Mr. Smith's patent was under the consideration of your lordships, the final arrangement between them had not taken place. If my friend means to say to-day, that, because you have done it in Smith's case, that inasmuch as Capt. Ericsson is a party to that arrangement, you can make no distinction between them—that, my lords, I apprehend, would enable me to suggest, with great respect to your lordships, the consideration of the propriety of the decision which your lordships have arrived at in the case of Mr. Smith, and whether your lordships think that is a fair and reasonable consideration to be imposed. I know that a party applying for an extension is entirely at your lordships'—I will not say mercy, but at your lordships' discretion. I am quite sure of this, that whatever terms your lordships may impose, those are terms which in your judgment you think just and proper. I am quite certain that no other terms would be imposed on us; but I would humbly suggest a reconsideration of that clause: we have thought it, upon consideration, to be so very hard—it is the first time it has been inserted.

The Hon. T. P. Leigh.—Without saying whether it is a right or wrong clause, we could not possibly alter it; we have no power. As to the use of that patent, the statement that was made on former occasions was, that one patent could not be used without the other, so that if we were to extend the time, and leave it out of this patent, it would be of no service.

The Attorney-General.—That has all been settled.

The Hon. T. P. Leigh.—That is so, and there is no power to alter it. I have no doubt of the propriety of the decision; there it stands, and we have no power to alter it, except by act of Parliament. Therefore I do not see what you would gain by this omission.

The Attorney-General.—There is an agreement between the five patentees, and it is impossible to work one patent without the other. They have taken parts of each. There is an agreement between the five patentees to work their patents in common, and the engineers have agreed to pay a certain amount per horse power, for the use, indifferently, of the screw composed of the whole, as they chose to make them.

Sir F. Thesiger—I have very great doubt, with submission to my learned friend, whether that would bind the engineers to pay so much per horse power in respect to the engines they make for the Admiralty, it being an express term in the patents that the Admiralty is to be supplied without any payment at all.

The Attorney-General.—Whatever the engineers make they are to pay so much per horse power.

The Hon. Dr. S. Lushington.—If all these patents are to be used together one cannot be used without the other, and the effect of your getting a renewal of your patent without that clause in it would be to annul it altogether. Would not that be the effect of it?

Sir F. Thesiger.—Probably it might.

The Attorney-General.—I believe the arrangement entered into by all the patentees is very beneficial for the public and other persons; but of course, unless the same condition is inserted in favour of the Admiralty, I must raise other objections.

The Hon. Dr. S. Lushington.—I do not say whether it is right or wrong; I only ask whether that would not be the effect of it.

Sir F. Thesiger.—Your lordship enlarged Woodcroft's patent without any clause of that kind, and Woodcroft is one of the parties to this arrangement. It only shows the novelty of the introduction of a clause of this kind; it was never dreamt of by the Admiralty, and certainly I would not venture to contrast my opinion and conduct with my learned friend, the Attorney-General's, but when I was in office I should never have thought of insisting on a clause of this kind.

The Attorney-General.—The public have a perfect right to make these screws at the Government yards if they like ;—there is no doubt about that in point of law.

Sir F. Thesiger.—The term of Woodcroft's patent was enlarged without any clause of this kind.

The Attorney-General.—That was long before the contemplation of this amalgamation.

Sir F. Thesiger.—Yes ; so that in point of fact, inasmuch as the others cannot be used without Woodcroft's, at all events, with regard to Woodcroft's, we have, to use a familiar expression, 'the sharp edge of the wedge there.'

The Hon. Dr. S. Lushington.—It was reported on the 11th of March, 1846, for an enlargement for six years.

Sir F. Thesiger.—Of course, my lords, I am in your lordships' hands entirely upon it. I take the liberty of submitting my views upon the subject. Of course, we know perfectly well that, whatever your lordships' decision,—just and right, of course,—are conditions which we are bound to submit to.

The Attorney-General.—Of course it would make a great difference in my course as counsel for the public, whether this clause is inserted or not. I think it very beneficial for the public that it should be inserted. If it is not, I shall have occasion to enquire, perhaps, whether it is useful to make the double wheel ; all of those are matters that will have to be entered into.

Sir F. Thesiger.—I am not at all afraid of that.

The Attorney-General.—Or, in fact, whether there can be any extension in the face of the combination.

Sir F. Thesiger.—With regard to the question, how the accounts stand as between the inventor and the patent, I am afraid it is a very indifferent one indeed, and I shall be able to show your lordships that, notwithstanding the earnest and anxious endeavours that have been made by Count de Rosen, since Mr. Ericsson went abroad, to force this patent on the public notice, that, with the exception of the *Amphion*, which was the last, in 1847, he has not been able to induce persons to take up this screw propeller, and the consequence has been, that in making out the account from the beginning, there is an actual loss on the patent to the amount of upwards of £3000. Considering the merit of this invention, I do trust that your lordships will feel that, at all events, we are entitled to an extension of the term. Of course, I say again, that I am quite willing to submit to any clause which your lordships may think it just and right to introduce into the extension itself. I shall now proceed to prove my case, and leave the matter entirely in your lordships' hands.

(To be concluded in our next number.)

DRAWING FROM OBJECTS,

Being an Abstract of Lessons on Linear Drawing, given at the Home and Colonial Training Schools. Chiefly designed for Teachers. By HANNAH BOLTON. (8vo. pp. 130.) London : Groombridge.

A FEW words in the introduction to this work serve as a sufficient apology for its publication. "Foreigners esteem a practical acquaintance with the art of drawing indispensable to success in business. In every trade, manufacture, or profession, the porte crayon or the pencil is called into requisition." With how little justice this description can be applied to England, we need not say. Our Schools of Design are merely for a class, and are too widely scattered to produce any sensible effect upon the masses, which can only be done by making drawing from objects, as distinguished from drawing from representations on paper, part of the regular routine of ordinary school education. The writer has had some years' experience in instructing pupil teachers, and has here given us an abstract of her lessons in the most simple and elementary form. With the aid of a black board and a piece of chalk, the pupil is taught perspective without being frightened by its name, and the art of sketching from objects as the most natural method. We are as satisfied of the propriety of beginning in this way, as of teaching a child large hand before it begins small; but that is a system which our ordinary "drawing masters" would call rank heresy, and which they banish from their class-room accordingly.

One of the introductory remarks we will notice, as it appears to us to convey, indirectly, an erroneous idea of the relative value of drawing in perspective and without it.

"The ignorance of English operatives, in connexion with diagrams and pictorial illustrations, will be acknowledged by every one, who, through their agency, has attempted to convey an idea of the form of a given object. Show a carpenter a corner view of a stool, (i. e. in perspective.—ED.) and he will say with the utmost gravity, ' But are the legs to be all of different lengths?' "

Now this is hardly fair upon the poor carpenter, because, he being a man of inches and half inches, when he is shown a drawing, expects it to be something that he can readily apply his two-foot rule to, and work from—a want which perspective does not meet. Give him a Side Elevation, End View, and a Plan, and he will have no difficulty in understanding it, because every dimension is truly represented. But ask a person, not a mechanic nor a draughtsman, to make you a sketch, and mark the difference. If it be cylindrical in shape, he will draw two ovals for the ends, and connect them with straight lines, in perspective, by instinct, though wrongly drawn, and with no notion of making more than one view to show all the details. The mechanical system, in our opinion, ought to be taught first, as an exact science, to teach correctness of drawing; perspective will follow. If it should not, it will be more useful to the pupil to be able to make a *correct drawing*, however formal, than a *sketch*, however pleasing and popular.

The authoress deserves great credit for the lucid manner in which she has explained the mysteries of perspective, and her lessons will be especially useful to those who wish to teach themselves, with the view of instructing others.

MACLEAN AND SON'S REGISTERED IMPROVEMENTS IN WINDLASSES AND CAPSTANS.

NUMEROUS attempts have been made to prevent the surging or slipping of the cable to which ordinary windlasses are liable, and which is a fruitful source of accidents, as well as of continual wear and tear. To prevent the cable from riding, it is necessary that it should "fleet," or slip, on the windlass, from the larger to the smaller diameter. This operation, though apparently a very simple one, is not so in practice. The annexed engraving represents one of the most efficacious inventions for the purpose, constructed by Messrs. Maclean and Son, of the Ratcliffe iron works.

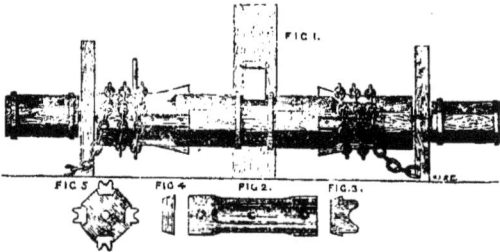

Fig. 1 represents an ordinary windlass, fitted with the improved concave whelps, of which figs. 2, 3, and 4, are views on a larger scale; fig. 5 being a transverse section of the barrel of the windlass. The whelps are made of such a size as to suit the chain cable to be used, and are concave, to receive the link of the chain which falls into it and fleets itself. The right hand or starboard side shows the position of the cable on weighing the anchor, when it would tend to ride up the cone, and the left hand or larboard side, the lowering of the anchor. In the latter case, a bar, called a "Norman," is placed between the first and second coil, to prevent it overrunning itself whilst it slips freely over the plain part of the windlass.

It appears to us that it would be an improvement in windlasses of this description, if the ratchet, instead of being placed in the centre, were double, one being placed at each end, close to its work.

ON THE DETERIORATION TO WHICH MATERIALS SUB-
JECT TO THE INFLUENCE OF SEA WATER ARE LIABLE.

We have at various times remarked on the difficulty to be apprehended from the deteriorating influence of sea-water upon iron vessels,
and long since pointed out, that as far as corrosion was concerned, we
had no cause for fear. There is another point, however, the growth
of grass and barnacles, which is not so easily disposed of. Copper
itself is not proof against the attacks of these insidious enemies, and
when we consider the diminution of speed that takes place, when the
bottom becomes foul, accompanied as it is in steamers with increased
consumption of fuel, it will be seen that the subject is one of the utmost
importance. The expense of coppering prohibits its use in many
situations where it is much needed, as, for example, in the timber work
about harbours, docks, beacons, &c.; and, accordingly, various compositions have been invented, to be applied in the form of paint, to protect
such structures as well as ships' bottoms. One of the most efficient and
economical of these is Captain Peacock's Anti-Sargassian Paint, satisfactory proofs of the merits of which, we had an opportunity of recently
inspecting at Southampton.

The name "Anti-Sargassian" will probably puzzle some of our
readers, we will therefore at once enlighten them, by explaining its
derivation. The Spanish word "Sargazo" means sea-grass; and a large
tract of ocean in the Atlantic, lying between the latitudes of from 20° to
36° N., and longitudes 25° to 40° W., is denominated the "Sargazo," or
"Sargassian Sea," from the presence, in immense quantities, of the
grass, (*fucus natans,*) giving it the appearance of an inundated meadow.
This paint has been applied to all the iron ships of the Peninsular and
Oriental Company. The *Sultan,* which we saw in dock, had not been
scraped or cleaned for eight months, during which time she had made
three voyages between Southampton and Constantinople. A little grass
was visible, about the water line, but not sufficient to impede her progress through the water. Captain Peacock, however, does not propose to
allow its durability to be so severely tried in ordinary cases, but recommends a fresh coating every four months. The value of this, even, may
be estimated by the report of Captain Engledue, the company's superintendent, in which he states—"We have never been able to keep any
of our iron vessels clean for a longer period than a month, or six weeks,
until the application of Captain Peacock's composition."

A curious feature of this composition is, that shortly after immersion
in sea-water, the surface becomes slimy, like the skin of a fish, and this
quality is stated to have a favourable influence on the speed of the
vessel, independently of the freedom from grass and barnacles. We
should hesitate to give such a statement on our own authority, but the
concurrent testimony of the commanders of the ships is hardly to be
explained away. Captain Goodridge, of the mail packet *Courier,* running constantly to and from the Channel Islands, states that half an
hour on the average is saved on the passage, with a proportionate saving
of fuel—the trials not being between a clean bottom and a foul one, but
between the paint and the absence of it. Two pieces of wood that had
been under water at the entrance of the docks for above six months
were taken up for our inspection. One had been painted with Captain
Peacock's composition, and was quite clean and uninjured, with the
exception of two small barnacles having attached themselves to it. The
other, which was unprotected, was honeycombed by some variety of the
teredo, and covered with weeds. The dolphin at the dock entrance was
crumbling to pieces, the tar with which it was coated, and which was
still visible, appearing to have afforded no protection.

We ought not to omit to mention, that the paint may be laid on in a
single tide, whenever a vessel can take the ground, without the necessity
of going into dock, as it dries very quickly. The cost is about the same
as that of red lead.

If these remarks, the result of our own personal inspection and
inquiry, should induce any of our friends on the Clyde or the Mersey to
give Captain Peacock's "Anti-Sargassian" a trial, we shall be glad to
record the results of their experience of its use, in our pages.

STEAM COMMUNICATION WITH THE CAPE OF GOOD
HOPE.

Southampton, July 24.

The Lords Commissioners of the Admiralty have just issued a notifi-
cation, inviting tenders for the conveyance of her Majesty's mails to
and from the Cape of Good Hope.

The contract is to be for seven years, and may be terminated then, or
at any subsequent period, by a notice of 12 months from either party.

The contractors are to engage, to convey her Majesty's mails and
despatches between England and the Cape of Good Hope monthly each
way; at a speed which, on the average of the annual voyages, shall not be
less than eight knots an hour. For this purpose there are to be provided
a sufficient number of efficient steam vessels, propelled on the screw principle, and supplied with engines of not less than 200 horse power, with
competent officers and engineers, and a sufficient crew of able seamen,
—to be in all respects, as to ships, machinery, equipment, and crew,
subject to the approval of the Admiralty. On board of each vessel is to
be provided a secure place of deposit for the mails, and each steamer is
to possess proper boats, and whatever may be necessary for the safe em-
barcation and disembarcation of the mails.

The tenders are to specify the names of the vessels proposed to be
employed, their registered tonnage, horse power, where lying, draught
of water when ready for sea, and speed, together with the date the said
vessels will be ready for survey and complete for sea.

The port of departure is to be chosen by the Admiralty, but parties
tendering are at liberty to restrict their offer to sailing from one particular port, or to mention the compensation they would require, in the
event of the port being changed without their consent.

The vessels are to touch at Madeira, Sierra Leone, and St. Helena,
and at such other places as the Admiralty may from time to time determine.

Proper accommodation is to be provided, free of expense, for the
naval officer in charge of the mails; but parties tendering are permitted
to state whether they would make a deduction in the event of this condition not being required.

The hours of sailing are to be fixed by the Admiralty. The Admiralty
to have the power of surveying the vessels by their officers at all proper
times, and any defect discovered on such survey is to be made good by
the contractors under a penalty of £100. A penalty of £100 will be
incurred if the vessels stop, linger, or deviate from the direct course, or
put back and return, except from stress of weather, or other unavoidable circumstance, or unless authorized by the Admiralty agent in
charge of the mails. A penalty of £30 will be incurred when the contractors fail to provide such steam-vessels, equipped and manned as
stipulated for, or when the vessel does not put to sea according to agreement, and also a sum of £10 for every hour which shall elapse until she
shall actually proceed to sea, but the payment of such penalty is not to
be enforced in the event of such default being proved to the satisfaction
of the Admiralty to have arisen from circumstances over which the
contractors and their servants had no control. A penalty of £4000 will
be incurred by way of stipulated or ascertained damages in case of the
failure of the contractors in the due performance of the contract, and
two sureties to that amount are required. If the contract, or any part
of it, be assigned, underlet, or disposed of without the consent of the
Admiralty, or if it be deliberately broken, the Admiralty are to have
the power of immediately terminating the same.

The tender is to state the time when the parties will be prepared to
commence the contract. The whole postage on letters conveyed in the
vessels employed on this service, whether carried out of her Majesty's

dominions or not, is to be at the disposal of the Postmaster-General. It is understood that the Admiralty do not engage to accept the lowest tender irrespective of all other considerations, and are not bound necessarily to accept any of the tenders that may be sent in.

Such is an outline of the conditions upon which the Lords of the Admiralty are willing to receive proposals for the Cape of Good Hope service. The intention of the Government to establish a regular mail to our South African colonies will doubtless be hailed with great satisfaction, not only by the colonists, but also by the mercantile community interested in the increasing commerce of that part of the world. By superseding the present uncertain means of communication by sailing vessels, all business operations will be greatly facilitated, remittances rendered more regular and speedy, and an inducement will be held out for the middling and better classes of the colonists to revisit their native land, which the prospect of a sailing voyage would in many cases prohibit. Emigration to Southern Africa will likewise be promoted, and altogether it is not too much to say that the establishment of a regular monthly steam communication between England and the Cape of Good Hope will prove a new era in the history and prospects of that and the neighbouring colonies.

It would thus appear that an independent line of steamers is contemplated with which to accomplish this service, quite irrespective of other lines of mail steamers, and that vessels propelled with screws are to be exclusively used. Without attempting to discuss the respective merits of the two principles of propulsion, as applicable to the ocean-going steamers, we would remark, that so far as the requisite speed is concerned, there is no doubt that screw steamers, to go through the water at a rate of eight knots, may be easily procured. Whether, however, an annual average of eight knots an hour can be produced in all weathers, and under all the vicissitudes of so lengthy a voyage, and whether in other respects, screw steamers will be found to combine the desired regularity of arrival and departure with absence from accident, and other qualifications of efficient mail conveyances, are questions that must be solved by experience, as they have hitherto received but a partial test, and therefore the present service (if carried out on the screw principle) will have the effect of deciding whether or not vessels of this particular construction are in the long run sufficiently to be depended upon for lengthened voyages.

There is one point, however, in connexion with the Cape of Good Hope plan, that is well worthy of consideration, and that is, whether it is worth while to incur the expense for an independent line, when a great portion of the route will be regularly traversed by another line of steamers, and whether by a junction with a contemplated line the same, or even greater advantages, cannot be secured to the public at a moiety of the expense.

On examining this subject, we discovered that an arrangement is possible, whereby the Cape of Good Hope mails might be conveyed to and from England, by connecting branch packets at the Cape Verd Islands with the Brazilian mail packets, touching there both out and home.

The packets to Brazil are to call both outward and homeward at Madeira, Teneriffe, and St. Vincent's Cape Verd. The latter port is 2,511 miles, or upwards of three-eighths, of the distance in the direct track from England to the Cape. It follows, therefore, that if a couple of branch packets were to be employed running from St. Vincent's to the Cape of Good Hope, touching at Sierra Leone and St. Helena (as contemplated by the Admiralty), and in correspondence with the Brazilian steamers, they would answer every purpose, and a mail quite equal in regularity, and of greater speed (because of the superior speed and qualities of the Brazil line), would be established to and from the Cape, while the cost to the public service of such branch packets would probably not exceed by a great deal, one-half of what would be necessary to maintain an independent line. The

reduction in expense would be caused by the smaller number of packets necessary, and the lessened distance to be performed by the contractors,—viz., 2,500 miles out, and 2,500 miles home, on each voyage, which, multiplied by 12, would give the annual saving of steaming distance at 60,000 miles.

We cannot doubt that these facts will present themselves to the Lords of the Admiralty, and that their lordships, when adjudicating on this contract, will be guided by a due regard for the public service, and that only such a plan, whether for an independent or a branch line of packets, will be sanctioned as upon public grounds will appear to combine the three indispensable advantages of economy, rapidity, and efficiency.—*Times*

DIMENSIONS AND DETAILS OF NEW STEAMERS.

WHITEHAVEN STEAM NAVIGATION COMPANY'S IRON STEAM VESSEL, "WHITEHAVEN."

Built by Messrs. Thomas Vernon and Co., Liverpool, 1847. Engines by The Butterly Company, Derbyshire.

Builder's measurement.			Ft. In.
Length of keel and fore rake	..	..	180 0
Breadth of beam	..	..	25 5
Ditto over the paddle-boxes	..	..	45 9
Depth of hold ..	..	..	13 10
Length of engine-space ..	..	..	47 9
Tonnage.			Tons.
Hull ..	..	..	574⁷⁄₇
Contents of engine space	..	..	156⁶⁄₉
Register	..	..	407⁷⁄₇
New measurement.			Ft. Tns.
Length on deck	..	..	181 1
Breadth on ditto at midships	..	..	24 1
Depth of hold	..	..	13 6
Ditto of break-deck	..	..	1 8
Length of engine space ..	..	..	47 8
Tonnage.			Tons.
Hull ..	..	..	502⁵⁄₉
Contents of engine-space	..	...	169⁴⁄₉
Register	..	..	333⁸⁄₉

A pair of oscillating engines of 298 horse nominal power; diameter of cylinders, 64 inches × 5 feet stroke. Two inclined air-pumps, diameter, 38 inches × 2 feet 4½ inches stroke. Cycloidal paddle-wheels, diameter, extreme, 25 feet 10½ inches, and 25 feet 2 inches effective; 24 floats, 7 feet 8 inches × 1 foot 9 inches; three sets of 12 arms; floats drawn up 8 inches, making the effective diameter 23 feet 10 inches. Two tubular boilers, length, 12 feet, breadth, 11 feet 5 inches, height, 11 feet 8 inches. Steam chests round at back, length, 12 feet, breadth, 6 feet 6 inches; height, 6 feet; 6 furnaces, 3 in each boiler, length, 7 feet, breadth, 3 feet 1 inch, height, 3 feet 4 inches; 516 (malleable iron) tubes, 3¼ inches × 7 feet 6 inches. Steam-pressure, 10 lbs.; averages 19 revolutions per minute, consuming about 26 cwt. of coals per hour. The engines occupy, fore and aft, 17 feet 9 inches. Centre to centre of cylinders, 11 feet 6 inches. The bunkers hold 28 tons of coals; length of ditto, 6 feet 3 inches. The tunnel or passage is 8 feet in width, and 5 feet 9 inches in height; boilers to bunkers, 7 feet. Plying between Liverpool, Whitehaven, and Belfast. Average draught of water, 10 feet 6 inches. Vessel designed by John Grantham, Esq., C.E., Liverpool.

DESCRIPTION.

A shield figure-head, sham quarter galleries, clipper bow, square sterned and clinch and carvil built vessel, stationary bowsprit, 3 masts, schooner-rigged. Port of Whitehaven. Commander,—Mr. Simeon Vickers Thompson.

THE WHITEHAVEN STEAM NAVIGATION COMPANY'S IRON STEAMER, "QUEEN."

Built by Messrs. Thomas Vernon and Co., Liverpool. Engines by Messrs. Fawcett, Preston, and Co.

Builder's measurement.	Ft.	In.
Length of keel and fore rake	160	0
Breadth of beam	24	4
Ditto over the paddle-boxes	42	1
Depth of hold	13	7
Length of engine space	38	2
Tonnage.	**Tons.**	
Hull	460$\frac{48}{94}$	
Contents of engine-space	120$\frac{81}{94}$	
Register	339$\frac{61}{94}$	

New measurement.	Ft.	Tns.
Length on deck	158	5
Breadth on ditto at midships	23	5
Depth of hold at ditto	13	4
Length of quarter-deck	50	5
Breadth of ditto	24	4
Depth of ditto	2	2
Length of engine space	38	2
Tonnage.	**Tons.**	
Hull	404 [illegible]	
Quarter-deck	29 [illegible]	
Total	433 [illegible]	
Contents of engine space	130 [illegible]	
Register	303 [illegible]	

A pair of Fawett, Preston, and Co.'s patent direct acting crosshead engines of 175 horses nominal power; diameter of cylinders, 50 inches 4 feet 6 inches stroke. Diameter of paddle-wheels, extreme, 20 feet 8 inches, ditto, effective, 20 feet 2 inches; 16 floats, 6 feet 10 inches × 1 foot 9 inches; three sets of 16 arms. Two tubular boilers, which have been in since the vessel was built. Kennedy and Vernon's patent frames, 4 × 2½ × ½ inch, and 1 foot 6 inches apart. Accommodations for 44 cabin passengers. The crew consists of 22 hands, viz., 4 in the cabin, 7 in the engine room, and 11 on deck.

DESCRIPTION.

A full female figure-head (the Queen), false quarter galleries, clipper bow, sham quarter galleries, square-sterned, and clinch and carvil built vessel, 3 masts, schooner-rigged, stationary bowsprit. Port of Whitehaven. Commander,—Mr. James D. Kennedy.

GLASGOW AND LIVERPOOL STEAM SHIPPING COMPANY'S IRON STEAM VESSEL "ORION."

Built and fitted by Messrs. Caird and Co., Cartsdyke, Greenock, 1846.

Builder's measurement.	Ft.	In.
Length of keel and fore rake	210	0
Breadth of beam	28	0
Depth of hold	18	6
Length of engine-space	77	0
Tonnage.	**Tons.**	
Hull	805 [illegible]	
Contents of engine space	321 [illegible]	
Register	484 [illegible]	

New measurement.	Ft.	Tns.
Length on deck	210	6
Breadth on ditto at midships	27	1
Depth of hold do.	18	2
Length of engine space	77	0
Tonnage.	**Tons.**	
Hull	898 [illegible]	
Contents of engine-space	378 [illegible]	
Register	519 [illegible]	

A pair of side lever engines, of 440 horses nominal power. Diameter of cylinders, 74 inches × 6 ft. 9 inches stroke. Paddle-wheels, diameter, extreme, 29 feet 7½ inches, do. effective, 29 feet 0½ inch; three sets of 25 arms and floats, 8 feet 6 inches × 2 feet 6 inches. Malleable iron framing and brass pistons. Tubular boilers with brass tubes. Average speed, 19 revolutions, and 15 miles per hour, in smooth water.

DESCRIPTION.

Full male figure-head, clipper bow, sham galleries, square-sterned, and clinch and carvil built vessel, standing bowsprit, three masts, schooner-rigged. Port of Glasgow. Commander,—Mr. Thomas Henderson.

[This vessel was a fine specimen of iron shipbuilding, and was the largest iron paddle steamer sailing out of Glasgow. We need not here repeat the melancholy particulars of her loss off Portpatrick, on the morning of 18th June, which must be fresh in the memory of all our readers. We trust that the investigation now taking place will have the effect of bringing to justice the persons through whose guilty carelessness so many human beings were unwittingly hurried to destruction.]

THE CITY OF DUBLIN STEAM NAVIGATION COMPANY'S IRON STEAM VESSEL, "TRAFALGAR."

Built and Fitted by Messrs. Tod and M'Gregor, Glasgow, 1847.

Builder's measurement.	Ft.	In.
Length of keel and fore rake	190	0
Breadth of beam	28	1
Ditto including the paddle cases	47	0
Depth of hold	16	11
Length of engine space	56	9
Tonnage.	**Tons.**	
Hull	749 [illegible]	
Contents of engine space	244 [illegible]	
Register	504 [illegible]	

New measurement.	Ft.	Ten.
Length on deck	189	7
Breadth on ditto at midships	27	2
Depth of hold, ditto	16	7
Length of quarter-deck	53	0
Breadth of ditto	26	8
Depth of ditto	3	4
Length of engine space	56	8
Tonnage.	**Tons.**	
Hull	720 [illegible]	
Quarter-deck, ...	52 [illegible]	
Total	772 [illegible]	
Contents of engine space	279 [illegible]	
Register	493 [illegible]	

A pair of oscillating engines of 346 horse nominal power. Cylinders,

68 inches diameter × 5 feet 6½ inches stroke. Air-pumps, 38 inches diameter × 2 feet 6 inches stroke. Paddle-wheels diameter, extreme 26 feet 7 inches; ditto, effective, 27 feet. 26 floats, 7 feet 6 inches × 2 feet. Three sets of 26 arms. Steam pressure, 8 lbs. per square inch; average revolutions 20 per minute; two tubular boilers, 8 furnaces 7 ft. long; consumption of coals 23 cwt. per hour. Average draught of water forward, 10 feet 4 inches, and 10 feet 6 inches aft. Frames, 4¼ × 3¼ × ¾, and 1 feet 6 inches apart. The crew consists of 33 hands, viz., 16 in the captain's department, 6 in the steward's, and 11 in the engine room.

DESCRIPTION.

Bust, male figure head, (Nelson.) No quarter galleries. Standing bowsprit, 2 masts, schooner-rigged, round sterned and clinch built of iron. Port of Dublin. Commander—Mr. Hamlet W. Geary.

THE WATERFORD COMMERCIAL STEAM NAVIGATION COMPANY'S NEW
IRON SCREW STEAM VESSEL, "MARS."

Built by the Owners, at the Neptune Iron Works, Waterford, 1849. Engines, by Messrs. Smith and Rodger, St. James's Foundry, Glasgow.

Builder's measurement.				Ft.	In.
Length of keel and fore rake	..	..	..	165	0
Breadth of beam	..	..	..	30	5
Depth of hold, amidships	..	..	..	15	9
Length of engine space	..	..	..	50	11
Tonnage.				Tons.	
Hull	..	..	..	825	
Contents of engine space	..	..	162	
Register	..	..	..	663	
New measurement.				Ft.	Tns.
Length on deck	..	..	..	184	7
Breadth on ditto amidships	..	..	25	2
Depth of hold ditto	..	..	..	15	6
Length of poop	..	..	..	24	7
Breadth of ditto	..	..	..	22	4
Depth of ditto	..	..	..	6	4
Length of engine space	..	..	50	9
Breadth of ditto	..	..	..	19	9
Depth of ditto	..	..	..	15	9
Tonnage.				Tons.	
Hull	..	..	..	510	
Poop	..	..	..	38	
Total	..	..	..	538	
Contents of engine space	..	..	175	
Register	..	..	..	373	

A pair of steeple engines (upon Mr. David Napier's patent 4-piston rod principle) of 98 horse nominal power. Diameter of cylinders, 40 inches × 3 feet length of stroke; one air-pump. Diameter of spur wheel, 9 feet, and 85 teeth; diameter of pinion, 3 feet 3 inches, and 34 teeth; pitch, 4 inches; breadth of ditto, 1 foot 6 inches; diameter of screw (two blades), 10 feet 2 inches; pitch, 11 feet 6 inches; breadth of blades, 4 feet 6 inches. Shaw's gridiron slide valves, worked by bevil wheels off the intermediate shaft, by means of two horizontal and two vertical shafts; upon the vertical shafts there are two cams for working the expansion and slide valves, which work horizontally across the cylinders; the spindles of both valves work through the back of the casing, with a stuffing-box at each side; on the horizontal shafts there is a disengaging clutch for throwing the engines out of gear; there is only one starting wheel for both shafts; by moving it forwards and throwing the clutches in gear the engines go a head, and hauling it back they go astern. Steam pressure, 12 lbs.; revolutions per minute,

46. The bunkers hold 40 tons of coals. Plying upon the station between Waterford and Liverpool, 229 miles; average passage, 20 hours; draught of water, 13 feet forward and 14 feet aft; two tubular boilers, length 9 feet 4 inches; breadth, 8 feet 4 inches; depth, 11 feet; 4 cylindrical furnaces, 2 in each boiler—length, 6 feet × 3 feet 6 inches diameter; 150 tubes in all; diameter 3½ inches × 7 feet; malleable iron. The smoke box is built on the front of the boilers, with the funnel upon the top—a very good principle for lightness, but it makes the engine room very hot.

DESCRIPTION.

A bust male figure head, sham quarter galleries, clipper bow, square sterned and clinch built vessel, standing bowsprit, three masts, schooner rigged. Port of Waterford. Commander—Mr. William Clarke.

THE WATERFORD AND NEW ROSS STEAM NAVIGATION COMPANY'S NEW
IRON STEAMER, "NORAH CRIENA."

Built and fitted at the Neptune Iron Works, Waterford, 1849.

Builder's measurement.				Ft.	In.
Length of keel and fore rake	..	..	135	0
Breadth of beam	..	..	..	18	6
Ditto over the paddle cases	..	..	33	9¼
Depth of hold, amidships	..	..	8	0
Length of engine space	..	..	31	11
Tonnage.				Tons.	
Hull	..	..	..	236	
Contents of engine space	..	..	69	
Register	..	..	..	167	
New measurement.				Ft.	Tns.
Length on deck	..	..	..	133	0
Breadth on ditto, amidships	..	..	18	0
Depth of hold, ditto	..	..	..	7	7
Length of quarter-deck	..	..	34	5
Breadth of ditto	..	..	..	16	5
Depth of ditto	..	..	..	1	4
Length of engine space	..	..	31	9
Tonnage.				Tons.	
Hull	..	..	..	132	
Quarter deck	..	..	..	8	
Total	..	..	..	140	
Engine space	..	..	..	47	
Register	..	..	..	93	

One steeple engine (on Mr. David Napier's patent 4-piston rod principle) of 77 horse nominal power; diameter of cylinder, 48 inches × 4 feet stroke; diameter of paddles, extreme, 16 feet 4 inches; ditto, effective, 15 feet 9 inches; floats, 5 feet 9 inches × 1 foot 3 inches; 2 sets of 8 arms, and 16 floats; steam pressure, 8 lbs.; consumes 9 cwt. of coals per hour; 27 revolutions per minute; 2 tubular boilers; 4 furnaces. 2 in each; frames, 2½ × 2½ × ¾ inches, and 2 feet apart. Crew, 10 in number, viz. 6 on deck, 2 in the cabin, and 2 in the engine room. The distance from New Ross to Waterford, 18 miles, on an average in 2 hours, including stoppages. The draft of water, 6 feet.

Same valves as the *Mars, Apollo, Diana,* &c., &c.

DESCRIPTION.

No figure-head, or galleries, or bowsprit. Square sterned, and clinch built vessel, 2 masts, schooner rigged. Port of Waterford. Master—Mr. Richard Jones.

SHIP-BUILDING ON THE CLYDE AND THAMES.
(*From our own Correspondent.*)
GLASGOW.

Mr. R. Napier has upon the stocks a new iron steamer for the Glasgow and Londonderry trade, to be named the *Rose*, of 527¾ tons : will soon be ready for launching. She is to be propelled by side-lever engines, by the same firm, of 212 horses nominal power. Diameter of cylinders, 54 inches × 5 feet length of stroke, and 20 feet paddle wheel ; to ply in consort with the *Shamrock* and *Thistle*, the property of the same owners ; to be commanded by Mr. James Turnbull, late of the *Shamrock*.

They have just commenced another vessel of 518¾ tons, same power as the above ; the property of the General Steam Navigation Company.

They have also upon the stocks, and ready for launching, an iron lighter, of 56¾ tons, for the Forth and Clyde Canal, and coasting upon the Clyde.

Messrs. Smith and Rodger, (Govan,) Glasgow, have at present upon the stocks, and nearly ready for launching, a large iron screw steam vessel, the property of the Cork Steam Ship Company, to be named the *Albatross*, of the following dimensions :—

		Ft.	In.
Length of keel and fore rake		195	0
Breadth of beam		30	0
Depth of hold		18	0
Tonnage		847¾	

To be propelled by a pair of steeple engines, of 124 horses nominal power. Diameter of cylinders 45 inches × 3 feet length of stroke ; worked by spur wheel and pinion, having Malcolmson's steam and expansion valves ; two-bladed screw, diameter, 10 feet 6 inches, pitch, 13 feet ; (expanding) ; two tubular boilers, with 294 tubes, and 4 cylindrical furnaces ; frames, 4 × 3 × ⁷⁄₁₆, and spaced 18 inches from centre to centre ; 12 strakes of plates from keel to gunwale, tapering from ⁷⁄₁₆ to ¼, and ⁷⁄₁₆ inch ; keel and stern, 6 × 2 inches ; stern post, 6 × 3 inches ; propeller frame, 9 × 3½ inches, designed by Mr. E. Pascoe, of London. A common bow, and the hull with a poop deck. To be commanded by Mr. Dennis O'Sullivan, late of the *Gannet*. Mr. William Lyle, of the *Blarney* is transferred to the *Gannet*, also the property of the Cork Steam Ship Company.

They have also just laid down the keel of an iron screw vessel, for the London and Hamburgh trade, and of the following dimensions :—

		Ft.	In.
Length of keel and fore rake		180	0
Breadth of beam		26	0
Depth of hold		17	0
Tonnage		591¾	

Nominal power, 98 H. P. ; screw, diameter, 9 feet 6 inches × pitch, 13 feet ; spur wheel and pinion, similar in size to the *Mars*, *Diana*, and *Apollo*.

They have also just laid the keel of another iron screw steam vessel for the trade between Grangemouth and Hamburgh, and of the following dimensions :—

		Ft.	In.
Length of keel and fore rake		165	0
Breadth of beam		25	0
Depth of hold		14	6
Tonnage		502¾	

Nominal power, 56 H. P. ; diameter of cylinders, 32 inches × 2 feet 6 inches length of stroke ; same size of screw as the former one ; both having spur gearing and engines similar to the *Albatross*. Both vessels to have clipper bows, &c.

The Liverpool, Malta, and Constantinople Screw Steam Navigation Company's iron steam vessel, *Astrologer*, was launched from the building-yard of Messrs. Smith and Rodger, Govan, Glasgow, on Saturday, the 25th of May, at the appointed time, one o'clock, upon the signal being given. The vessel was named by Mr. Richard Gilchrist, of the firm of Messrs. Lewis Potter & Co., the owners. The weather being extremely stormy and wet, there were not many people assembled. The launch was effected in good style. The following are the dimensions :—

			Ft.	In.
Length of keel and fore rake			180	0
Breadth of beam			25	0
Depth of hold			15	0
Length of engine space			39	0
Ditto of gearing space			11	8
Breadth of ditto			5	6
Depth of ditto			4	0
Length of disconnecting gearing ditto			10	4
Breadth of ditto			6	9
Depth of ditto			8	3
Length of shaft gearing ditto			23	11
Breadth of ditto			1	2
Depth of ditto			4	1

	Tons.
Hull	552¾
Contents of engine space	132¾
ditto gearing ditto	1¾
ditto disconnecting ditto	1¾	135¾
ditto shaft ditto	0¾
Register	417¾

New measurement.

			Ft.	Ten.
Length on deck			186	0
Breath on ditto (at midships)			24	0
Depth of hold ditto			14	2
Length of quarter-deck			35	0
Breadth of ditto			19	7
Depth of ditto			2	3
Length of engine space			39	0
Ditto of gearing ditto			11	7
Breadth ditto ditto			5	5
Depth ditto ditto			4	0
Length of disconnecting ditto			10	4
Breadth ditto ditto			6	8
Depth ditto ditto			8	3
Length of Shaft			23	9
Breadth of ditto			1	2
Depth of ditto			4	1

Tonnage.	Tons.
Hull	459¾
Quarter-deck	17¾
Gross	476¾
Contents of engine room	143¾
ditto gearing ditto	3¾
ditto disconnecting ditto	6¾	154¾
ditto shaft ditto	1¾
Register	322¾

With a pair of steeple engines, (upon Mr. D. Napier's patent four-piston rod principle,) of 124 horses nominal power. Diameter of cylinders, 45 inches × 3 feet length of stroke ; two-bladed screw, diameter, 10 feet 8 inches, pitch 13 feet 6 inches, worked by spur wheel and pinion ; two tubular boilers, with four cylindrical furnaces ; frames of vessel, 4 × 3 × ⁷⁄₁₆, and 18 inches from centre to centre ; 11 strakes of plates from keel to gunwale, tapering in thickness from ⁷⁄₁₆ to ¼ ; and ⁷⁄₁₆ of an inch ; keel and stem, 6 × 2 inches ; stern post 6 × 3 inches ; propeller frame, 9 × 2½ inches. This is a very handsome clipper-built screw steam vessel, and was designed by Mr. John Ferguson. The launching draught of water forward was 5 feet and 7 feet 3 inches abaft. This vessel was built to ply upon the station between Liverpool, Malta, and Constantinople, &c., &c., in consort and in connection with the screw steamers *Pirate* and *Brigand*, also built by Messrs. Smith and Rodger, Glasgow.

DESCRIPTION.

Full male figure-head, no galleries, square sterned, and clinch built of iron, standing bowsprit, three masts, schooner rigged, Port of Glasgow.—Commander, Mr. John Millburn, late of the *Brigand*.

Messrs. Thomas Wingate & Co., White Inch, Glasgow, are at present fitting out a new steamer, lately launched by them for the Leith and Hull Steam Navigation Company, and to ply upon that station in concert with the *Brilliant*. It is named the *Courier*. The dimensions are, builder's measurement :—

	Ft.	In.
Length of keel and fore rake	170	0
Breadth of beam	22	7
Depth of hold	12	6
Length of engine space	44	8
Tonnage.	Tons.	
Hull	428 $\frac{62}{94}$	
Contents of engine space	122 $\frac{33}{94}$	
Register	306 $\frac{29}{94}$	
New measurement.	Ft.	Ten.
Length on deck	175	8
Breadth of ditto, at midships	21	8
Depth of hold, at ditto	12	1
Length of quarter-deck	41	7
Breadth of ditto	23	3
Depth	3	1
Length of engine space	44	7
Tonnage.	Tons.	
Hull	340 $\frac{48}{100}$	
Quarter-deck	39 $\frac{95}{100}$	
Gross	379 $\frac{7}{100}$	
Contents of engine space	127 $\frac{60}{100}$	
Register	245 $\frac{47}{100}$	

One steeple-engine, (on Mr. D. Napier's patent 4-piston rod principle,) of 150 horse nominal power; diameter of cylinder, 63 inches × 5 feet length of stroke; overhung paddle-wheels, diameter extreme, 21 feet 8 inches, ditto effective, 21 feet 1 inch; 20 floats, 6 feet 6 inches, × 2 feet (in two parts of 12 inches;) 2 sets of 10 arms and 20 floats. Two tubular boilers; 8 furnaces, 4 in each. Length of boilers, 13 feet 8 inches; breadth of ditto, 10 feet 10 inches; depth of ditto, 10 feet 4 inches. Length of furnaces, 3 feet 8 inches; breadth of ditto, 1 foot 9 inches. Area of fire-grate, 133 feet. Frames, 3½ × 2¼ × ½, and 1 foot 6 inches apart. Launching draught of water 4 feet even keel. With machinery, water, and coals, 6 feet 6 inches, even keel. This is the handsomest paddle-steamer launched at Glasgow for some time back.

DESCRIPTION.

Clipper bow, shield or profile figure-head, round-sterned and clinker-built vessel, of iron. No galleries; standing-bowsprit; 2 masts; schooner-rigged; port of Leith.

On Thursday, the 6th of June, at 9 A. M., there was launched from their yard a new iron-steamer for the river, the property of Alexander M'Kellar, Jun., Esq., and called the *Eclipse*, of the following dimensions, builder's measurement.

	Ft.	In.
Length of keel and fore rake	156	6
Breadth of beam	16	0
Depth of hold (moulded)	7	0
Length of engine-space	41	11
Tonnage.	Tons.	
Hull	198 $\frac{37}{94}$	
Contents of engine space	57 $\frac{18}{94}$	
Register	141 $\frac{19}{94}$	
New measurement.	Ft.	Ten.
Length on deck	156.	7
Breadth on ditto, at midships	15	3
Depth of hold, ditto	6	6
Length of engine space	41	9
Tonnage.	Tons.	
Hull	117 $\frac{84}{100}$	
Contents of engine space	45 $\frac{73}{100}$	
Register	72 $\frac{71}{100}$	

One steeple-engine of 62 horse power nominal (on Mr. David Napier's patent 4-piston-rod principle.) Diameter of cylinder, 44 inches × 3 feet 6 inches length of stroke. Overhung paddle-wheels, diameter extreme, 16 feet 5½ inches, and 15 feet 11½ inches effective; 16 floats, 5 feet 9 inches × 1 foot 3 inches; 2 sets of 16 arms, &c. This engine is the best arranged of any on this principle that I have seen. One upright tubular boiler, 2 furnaces, and 4 fire-places (two forward and two aft). The after and fore fire-places are in one furnace. Launching draught of water, 2 feet 2 inches; sailing trim, 3 feet 4 inches, even keel. On Friday, the 14th, was the trial trip, which was very satisfactory to all parties.

DESCRIPTION.

This is a plain-built steamer, having no masts, bowsprit, figure-head or galleries; square-sterned and clinch-built vessel; 1 deck. Port of Glasgow.

Messrs. Thomas Wingate and Co. have upon the stocks, and nearly ready for launching, a very long and low steamer for river navigation, the property of Mr. David Napier, of the following dimensions :—

	Ft.	In.
Length of keel and fore-rake	146	6
Breadth of beam	12	0
Depth of hold (moulded)	6	6
Length of engine-room	32	9
Tonnage.	Tons.	
Hull	106 $\frac{64}{94}$	
Engine-room	25 $\frac{4}{94}$	
Register	81 $\frac{61}{94}$	
New measurement.	ft.	in.
Length on deck	146	4
Breadth on ditto, at midships	11	3
Depth of hold	6	1
Length of engine space	32	8
Tonnage	Tons.	
Hull	74 [illegible]	
Contents of engine space	24 $\frac{46}{100}$	
Register	49 [illegible]	

A pair of fore and aft diagonal engines, with oscillating piston-rods, (on Mr. David Napier's patent principle,) of 32 horse power nominal power. Diameter of cylinder 25 inches × 2 feet 1 inch length of stroke. One vertical tubular boiler, having 458 composition tubes; 2 furnaces. Condenses at bilges, with Mr. D. Napier's patent two small half-beam engines with beam at top for working the air-pumps and the feed and bilge-pumps. The large engines are solely to propel the vessel. Five strakes of plates from keel to gunwale.

This steamer is similar to the *Eclipse*.

GREENOCK.

Messrs. Caird and Co., Cartsdyke, launched from their building-yard, at one o'clock, P.M., on Monday afternoon, the 27th of May, a beautiful new iron paddle-wheel steam vessel, named the *Laurel* (named by Miss Paterson, daughter of Alexander Paterson, Esq., of Drumry,) and is the property of Messrs. G. and J. Burns, of Glasgow, and is to ply in consort with the *Lyra, Thetis,* &c., on the mail line between Glasgow, Greenock, and Belfast. She is a splendid specimen of marine architecture, and is expected to sail fast. The following are the dimensions, &c.

			Ft.	In.
Length of keel and fore rake	..	..	190	0
Breadth of beam	..	..	23	0
Depth of hold ..	..	..	12	9
Length of engine space ..	..	..	55	8
Tonnage.			Tons.	
Hull ..	..	..	500⁵⁹⁄₉₄	
Contents of engine space	..	..	157⁷⁴⁄₉₄	
Register	..	..	342⁵⁵⁄₉₄	
New measurement.			Ft.	Ten.
Length on deck	..	..	187	4
Breadth on ditto at midships	..	..	22	0
Depth of hold at ditto	..	..	12	5
Length of quarter-deck ..	..	..	45	4
Breadth of ditto	..	..	19	4
Depth of ditto ..	..	..	2	6
Length of engine space ..	..	..	55	7
Tonnage.			Tons.	
Hull	..	..	404⁷⁶⁄₁₀₀	
Quarter-deck ..	..	..	24⁷⁷⁄₁₀₀	
Total ..	..	..	428⁵³⁄₁₀₀	
Contents of engine space	..	..	165⁷⁷⁄₁₀₀	
Register	..	..	263⁷⁶⁄₁₀₀	

With a pair of side lever engines, formerly on board the *Camilla,* (mentioned in a late number.) Made by Messrs. Grendon, Mackay, and Co., Drogheda; nominal power, 180 horses power; diameter of cylinders, 50¼ inches × 4 feet 6 inches length of stroke; feathering paddle wheels, and one tubular boiler. Launching draught of water, 3 feet 6 inches; even keel.

DESCRIPTION.

Clipper bow; bust female figure-head; mock quarter galleries; square sterned and clinch built vessel; standing bowsprit; two masts; schooner rigged. Port of Glasgow.

Messrs. Scott, Sinclair, and Co. have at present in hand, and nearly finished, a pair of horizontal engines, for H. M. screw steam frigate, *Brisk,* at present building at Woolwich, of 172 horses nominal power; diameter of cylinders, 52 inches × 3 feet 6 inches stroke, with tubular boilers.

Messrs. Campbell and M'Nabb, of the Ingleston Foundry, Greenock, are at present constructing a steeple engine, for a new steamer building by Messrs. Barr and Shearer, Ardrossan, to supply the place of the late steamer, *Isle of Arran,* which was burned.

ARDROSSAN.

At one o'clock in the afternoon of Friday, the 14th, there was launched from the building yard of Messrs. Barr and Shearer, a beautiful brig, named the *Pioneer,* for the New Zealand trade, of 148 tons burden. Classed 8 years, A 1, at Lloyd's.

CORK.

On Tuesday evening, June 11th, there was launched from the building yard, Brickfields, by the Cork Steam Ship Company, a large iron screw steam vessel, named the *Pelican,* to be commanded by Captain Hall, and the property of the builders.

FAIRLIE.

June.—There was launched from the building yard of Messrs. William Fyfe and Son, a beautiful pleasure yacht, named the *Coralie,* of the following dimensions:—

			Ft.	Ten.
Length on deck	..	..	46	5
Breadth on ditto at midships	..	..	11	4
Depth of hold ditto	..	..	6	9
Tonnage	..	..	18¹⁸⁄₁₀₀	
Ditto, old	..	..	29	

Commander—Mr. Charles R. Dunnage.   F. B.

GREENWICH.

Messrs. W. Joyce and Co. have upon the stocks, and nearly ready for launching, an iron steamer, to be named the *City of Paris.*

		Ft.	In.
Length between perpendiculars	..	165	0
Breadth between paddle-boxes	..	23	0
Depth a-midships, clear	..	13	0
Deep water line	..	6	9
Burden, tons O.M.	..	425⁵⁵⁄₉₄	

She is the property of the Commercial Steam Navigation Company, and is intended to run between London and Boulogne. Messrs. W. Joyce and Co. are also constructing for her a pair of double piston rod direct acting engines, of 120 horses power; cylinders 44 inches diameter, and 4 feet stroke. To be fitted with tubular boilers.

AMERICAN PATENTS.

G. S. Langdon, Rising Sun, Maryland, assignee of Patrick S. Devlan, Reading, Berks county, Pennsylvania, *for an improvement in Metallic Boot Heels.* July 24.

The patentee says,—" My invention and improvement consists in making a hollow metallic heel for boots and shoes in two parts, one placed within the other, with a spring between them, to support the weight of the body, and prevent the unpleasant shocks produced by the concussion of the ordinary boot heel upon a hard surface when the wearer is walking fast.

Claim.—" What I claim as my invention, is making a metallic tread for the heels of shoes and boots, separate from, but secured within, the casing of the heel, in such a manner that it shall be free to change its position, to accommodate itself to the inequalities of the surface of the ground, whereby it wears more evenly, and is less fatiguing to the foot than a rigid heel, in the manner set forth."

STEAM NAVIGATION.

WAR STEAMERS FOR THE SPANISH GOVERNMENT.—It appears that a considerable increase is making in the Spanish navy. Messrs Maudslay, Sons, and Field have contracted to make four pairs of engines, of 500-horse power each pair, for the Spanish government, at an estimated cost of £200,000 for the whole. Messrs. John Penn and Son have also contracted to make two pairs of engines, of 350-horse power each pair, and Messrs. Miller, Ravenhill, and Co., two pair of engines, of 350-horse power each pair, for the same government. Messrs. Wigram are building a war steamer, and Mr. Green, at Blackwall, another of a similar class, to be fitted with their engines in this country. The other steamers for the 500-horse power engines are on the stocks in Spain, and will soon be ready for their reception.

THE NEW WEST INDIA STEAM FLEET.—SOUTHAMPTON, July 17.— The directors of the Royal Mail Steam-packet Company have accepted tenders for the immediate construction of five magnificent Atlantic steam-ships, for performing the through voyages from Southampton to the Isthmus of Panama. One of these vessels is to be built in South-ampton by Mr. Wigram, of London, but her machinery is to be put on board in the Clyde. The following is a list of the ships, their names, tonnage, and power, with the names of the builders, viz. :—The Oronoco, 2,250 tons, 750 horse power, to be built by Pitcher, at Northfleet, the engines by Messrs. Maudslay, Sons, and Field, of London. The Magdalena, 2,250 tons, 750 horse-power, to be built by Pitcher, of Northfleet, the engines by Messrs. Napier. The Demerara, 2,250 tons, 750 horse-power, to be built by Messrs. Patterson, of Bristol, the engines by Messrs. Caird and Co., of Greenock. The Amazon, 2,250 tons, 750 horse-power, to be built by Messrs. Green, of Blackwall, the engines by Messrs. Seaward and Co., of London. The Parana, 2,250 tons, 750 horse power, to be built at Southampton by Messrs. Wigram, the engines by Messrs. Caird and Co., of Greenock. Thus the builders most celebrated in naval architecture, and firms the most remarkable for the construction of marine steam-engines are to be employed in producing these ships, which it may confidently be expected will embrace every improvement of merit that has yet been introduced, and which will doubtless, by their speed and general efficiency for transatlantic voyaging, be unsurpassed by any of the magnificent steam-ships now engaged in regularly crossing the ocean. The whole of the vessels are to be built of wood, and will be ready for sea in a year, or perhaps less. They will be propelled on the paddle-wheel principle, and are to be pressed forward with the greatest possible despatch. In an article in *The Times* of the 11th inst., detailing the distance to be steamed annually by the West India and Brazilian steamers, a small error has been committed. The number of miles to be steamed in order to perform the combined service is 547,296 miles, while 29,640 miles will have to be traversed by sailing vessels, the total mileage being 567,936 miles, instead of 577,936 miles, as mentioned on that occasion, and which was so rendered by a clerical error. The number of ships employed in performing the West India and Brazil services, including a proper provision for reserve, will be 20, including the five new ships above named and the following, namely :—Steamers, Avon, Clyde, Conway, Dee, Derwent, Eagle, Great Western, Medway, Severn, Tay, Teviot, Thames, Trent, Esk (screw), and Larne (sailing-vessel.)

NEW LINE OF STEAMERS TO AMERICA—We observe it stated by one of the Liverpool papers, that the proprietors of Cunard's line of steamers are about to commence building a line of large screw steamers, for the purpose of conveying goods and passengers at low rates. We are glad to see that the *City of Glasgow* is performing very satisfactorily. She is, we believe, the property of the builders, Messrs. Tod and McGregor, of Glasgow. Will nobody have pity upon the *Great Britain* ! she deserves a better fate than rusting at Liverpool.

IRON STEAM-BOAT BUILDING IN TURKEY.—On Saturday, the 23rd of January, we walked from Mrori-keui to the iron-works of Barout-Khaneh, and to an iron steam-boat which was building on the bank of the creek, not 30 yards beyond the walls of the great powder-works. The sparks from the tall chimney of old H——'s steam-engine were flying about on one side of the powder-mills, and here were the chimneys of one furnace and two forges! It was difficult to conceive how it happened that the whole of Barout-Khaneh was not blown up. There had been terrible explosions in former times, before the powder-mills had such inflammable neighbours. The iron boat looked like a reel in a bottle. They were building in a place which had no exit to the sea, except by a narrow mouth choked up by a sandbank. "This boat," said Mr. Phillips, the builder, "will cost the sultan five or six times the sum for which he might have bought a good iron boat in England. When she is finished, if that day ever comes, they will have to spend a great sum of money to clear out this choked creek, so as to get her afloat in the Sea of Marmora; and then I must send her out without her engines. She ought to have been built at the arsenal on the Golden Horn. There are 50 good places for the purpose, without any impediments, where she might have been launched from the stocks into the clear deep water, without any expense."—*Turkey and its Destiny.*

NOTES BY A PRACTICAL CHEMIST.

PREPARATION OF HYPOSULPHITE OF SODA.—A neutral sulphite is first obtained by dividing a solution of the common carbonate into two portions, saturating the one with sulphurous acid gas, (best obtained by heating powdered charcoal in sulphuric acid,) and then neutralizing with the remainder of the carbonate. The neutralized liquid is now placed in a flask and boiled for some time to drive off the sulphurous acid retained in solution by the water. When acid fumes no longer escape, sulphur is added, and the boiling continued. The clear liquid is finally poured off from any residue of sulphur, and set to crystallize. To purify the salt thus formed, gentle heat is applied, so as to melt it in its own water of crystallization, and continued until a portion of the water evaporates. On cooling, the hyposulphite alone crystallizes, whilst the impurities, especially sulphate of soda, remain dissolved in the mother liquid. If perfectly pure, the hyposulphite does not precipitate dilute solutions of barytic salts.

TESTS FOR IODINE.—Free iodine, even in very minute traces, may be easily detected by means of the well-known blue colour which it forms with starch. When found in combination with other bodies it must first be set at liberty, and for this purpose we have a variety of methods. The usual process is to add to the substance in question chlorine water, or to treat it with gaseous chlorine, which by its stronger affinity for the metals, hydrogen, etc., displaces the iodine. This method requires various precautions, and is often wanting in delicacy, as chlorine has a considerable affinity for iodine; and if added in excess, which is often difficult to avoid, it enters into combination with the latter body, and thus enables it to escape detection. Diluted nitric acid is also employed for the same purpose; but it cannot effect the decomposition if chloride of mercury be present. Mr. Watt proposes to fuse a little chloride of zinc in a test-tube, adding a small quantity of manganese, and then drop in the substance to be examined. The iodine, if present, is then made manifest on applying starch. The author states that by this method the presence of iodine was shown by the colour of its vapour on testing one drop of a solution of iodine of potassium, containing one grain to the ounce of water. M. Reynoso has invented a most delicate process, where the iodides are decomposed by the peroxide of hydrogen. The method is to place in a test-tube a small fragment of the peroxide of barium, (or calcium,) add then a little distilled water, pure hydrochloric acid and starch paste; wait then a moment until some bubbles rise to the surface and add the suspected substance. If the amount of iodine is small, a pink tinge appears in the liquid, if in greater quantity the colour is, of course, blue. By this process $\frac{1}{10000}$th of iodide of potassium may be detected; and its delicacy is not impaired by the presence of chlorides, sulphurets, sulphites, or hyposulphites.

By substituting ether for starch the same method can be used to detect bromides. The above-mentioned processes do not apply to the oxygen compounds of iodine. M. Thorel's method embraces these also. He puts into a phial 50—60 grammes (77—92 gr.) of the suspected liquid, or if a solid body, diffuses it in a small quantity of water. Six drops of pure nitric acid, and the same quantity of hydrochloric acid are then added. A small piece of paper coated with thin mucilage of starch is then placed at the mouth of the phial, and heat is applied; if iodine be present, either as iodide or iodate, a blue tinge appears on the paper. If this is not seen when the liquid has been brought to boil, the same quantity of the acids must again be added and the phial shaken. If still no blue spots are formed, the author adds to the suspected liquor 10—20 centigrammes (1½—3 gr.) tartrate of potash, dissolved in a very small quantity of water. Heat is then applied for an instant before adding the acids, which are now used in the proportion of 8—10 drops of nitric to 4 of hydrochloric.

Lastly, Dr. Cantor has succeeded in discovering iodine in many mineral waters by the following process. The watery solution of the substance to be examined is concentrated by heat in a porcelain dish ; absolutely pure carbonate of potash is then added in slight excess and boiled for some time. Cool, filter, and evaporate cautiously to dryness. The residue is powdered, and treated with alcohol of 40°, which dissolves any bromides and iodides that may be present. The alcoholic solution is then evaporated to dryness, and if organic matter be present, exposed to a low red heat. Dilute acetic acid is now added in slight excess, to neutralize the small amount of carbonate of potash taken up by the alcohol. It is now again evaporated to dryness, carefully avoiding a heat sufficient to decompose the acetate. The residue is now dissolved in a very small quantity of water, adding two or three drops of a weak solution of starch. A little of a test-acid (consisting of 10 parts sulphuric acid at 66° with 1 part nitric acid at 25°) is placed in a narrow-bottomed glass, and the saline solution is poured carefully down upon it, so as not to mix. If iodides and bromides are both present, there will appear two zones in the saline solution, one of a bright yellow, and the other of a blue.

New Red Colouring Matter.—A colouring matter has recently been obtained from the roots of rhubarb, which promises to be of considerable practical importance, and may even, to a considerable extent, supersede cochineal. One part of the cleaned root is treated at a gentle heat, with 4 parts of nitric acid. After red fumes have entirely ceased to escape, there remains a mass of a yellow or orange colour, which the discoverer, M. Garot, names *erythrose*, and which combines with the alkalies forming crimson and purple compounds. An excess of nitric acid must be carefully avoided, otherwise much oxalic acid will be produced. The ammoniacal compound dissolved in water, or by preference in alcohol, imparts to silk and wool beautiful and permanent colours, resembling those obtained from cochineal, but which it considerably exceeds in tinctorial power. The common garden rhubarb yields 8—10 per cent of erythrose, and the Asiatic 15—20 ; but as the former imparts the more brilliant red, and can be obtained at a very trifling price, it will deserve the preference.

Chalk as a Protection for Copper.—Some time ago it was stated that copper rubbed over with common chalk was thereby almost entirely protected from the corrosive action of sea water. To determine this, 2 pieces of clean sheet copper, the one coated with chalk were placed in solutions of sea-salt of equal strength. The former slip weighed 11½ gr., and the latter 8. After remaining for three weeks in the solutions they were taken out, washed and weighed. The former was found to have lost ⅜ gr., and the latter ½, which, allowing for the weight of the chalk, brings them to an equality, and shows that no protection can be obtained in this manner.—S.

NOTES AND NOVELTIES.

Building for the Great Exhibition.—The Commissioners for the management of the Industrial Exhibition of 1851 met on the 26th, for the purpose of deciding finally on the details of the building plan ; and came to the resolution that Mr. Paxton's original plan should be adopted, with the addition of transepts and a barrel-roof for these transepts alone. The roof of the longitudinal portion is to be flat, as proposed in the first instance. The transepts will be useful as breaking the monotony of the long straight line of glass :—the keel-shaped roof for the transepts, though more costly than a flat roof, is justifiable by the reason that the additional elevation gained will permit the inclosure of a line of trees which stand about the middle of the space. The building is to be prepared with galleries. The following statistics will convey a notion of the extent of its capacities. " There will be on the ground-floor alone seven miles of tables. There will be 1,200,000 square feet of glass,—24 miles of one description of gutter, and 218 miles of ' sash bar ;' and in the construction 4,500 tons of iron will be expended. The wooden floor will be arranged with ' divisions,' so as to

allow the dust to fall through. The contract has, we believe, been signed with Messrs. Fox and Henderson, of the Smethwick Works, Birmingham, for the sum of £77,500."—*Athenæum.*

Bird's Improved Filter.—This appears to us a very ingenious way of taking advantage of the syphon, to form a simple and convenient filter. Filtering *upwards*, our readers is, is the most approved mode, and this principle may be, by this arrangement, applied to every cistern and water-butt in existence. A small cylindrical vessel is filled with the filtering medium, which is composed of silica, in layers, the first being coarse, and the rest gradually increasing in fineness. Apertures are made in the bottom, and to the top is fitted a gutta-percha tube, say five or six feet long, provided with a stopcock at the end. The filtering vessel, when in use, is hung in a water-butt, or even a bucket of water on a shelf, and the tube hanging over, forms the longer leg of a syphon, which may be set to work in the usual way, by exhausting the tube. The rapidity of the filtration may be increased by increasing the length of the tube and the height of the column of water, where convenient to do so. Hydrostatic pressure may be employed to clean out the filter when it requires it, by merely reversing the apparatus ; that is, putting the discharge-pipe into the water-butt, and allowing the water to run back through the apertures at bottom, bringing the sediment with it. As regards convenience of application this invention strikes us as the *ne plus ultra.*

Babbitt's Patent Metal.—In answer to a correspondent we now repeat the recipe for the composition of Babbitt's Patent Bearing Metal, which has come into very general use :—

First melt 4 oz. copper, and while melted add 12 oz. best quality Banca tin ; then add 8 oz. regulus antimony, then 12 oz. more tin. After the copper is melted, and 4 or 5 lbs. tin have been added, the heat should be reduced to a dull red colour, in order to prevent oxidation ; then add the remainder of the metals as above named. In melting the above, there should be a small quantity of powdered charcoal upon the surface of the metal. I make the above-named composition (which I call " hardening") in the first place ; then, as I want to use lining metal, add 2 lbs. of Banca tin to every one pound of hardening ; this will produce the metal I now use for lining boxes. I find by experience that this is the best composition I have ever used ; so that the proportions for the lining metal should be 4 lbs. copper, 8 oz. regulus antimony, and 96 lbs tin.

Approach of Patent Reform.—The propositions for reform of the patent laws, which have been so often advocated in the *Artisan*, and pressed upon the notice of the government and legislature, by our correspondent, Mr. F. W. Campin, the patent agent, seem likely to become law in a very short time, two bills being now before parliament. One for amending the practice of passing patents under the Great Seal, and the other, amending the Designs Acts, and enabling inventors to *provisionally register* designs and inventions for *one year,* (which may in some cases be extended to eighteen months,) within which period they may take a patent for the invention, or completely register the design, under the existing Designs Act. And this, notwithstanding the public exhibition at any institution, not being a place of sale, (*the Great Exhibition of* 1851, for instance,) provided the same be not brought into operation commercially. The effect of the first-mentioned Act depends very much on the regulations made under it by the Lord Chancellor. We hope they will prevent the clashing of patented inventions and designs.

LIST OF ENGLISH PATENTS.

From the 24th day of June to the 17th day of July, 1850, inclusive.

Robert Andrew Macfie, of Liverpool, sugar refiner, for improvements in manufacturing, refining, and preparing sugar : also, improvements in manufacturing and treating animal charcoal. June 24.

Henry Stephens, of Stamford-street, Blackfriar's-road, writing fluid manufacturer, and Edwin Wylder, of Paddington, mechanist, for certain improvements in ever-pointed pencils, pens, and penholders. June 24.

William Laird, of Liverpool, merchant, for improvements in life-boats, and in apparatus for filtering and purifying water. June 24.—(Communication.)

Joshua Vickermann Binns, of Lockwood, near Huddersfield, in the county of York, mechanic, for improvements in piecing wool, cardings, and in a machine called a piecing machine. June 24.

Edward Mitchell, of Great Sutton-street, Clerkenwell, gentleman, for improvements in fastenings for articles used for writing and drawing, and other purposes; and improvements in articles to be used for writing and drawing. June 24.

John Percy, of Birmingham, M.D., and Henry Wiggin, of the same place, manufacturer, for a new metallic alloy or new metallic alloys June 24

Thomas Fulljames, of Old Kent-road, gentleman, for certain improvements in machinery or apparatus for raising, lowering, and moving weights or other heavy bodies. June 26.

James Forster, of Liverpool, merchant, for improvements in filtering water and other liquids. June 27.

Joseph Foot, of Spital-square, in the county of Middlesex, for improvements in boilers. June 27.

James Thomson, of Glasgow, civil engineer, for improvements in hydraulic machinery, and in steam engines. July 3.

Richard Winter of New Cross, in the county of Kent, gentleman, for improvements in metallic vessels for measuring and holding liquids. July 3.

James Ward Hoby, of Blackheath, engineer, for certain improvements in the construction of parts of the permanent ways of railways, and in shaping iron. July 3.

Paul Rapsey Hodge, civil and mechanical engineer, of Adam-street, Adelphi, for improvements in certain descriptions of steam-engines; and in the apparatus and management for cultivating and manuring the soil, and in treating the produce thereof. July 3.

Wakefield Pim, of the town or borough of Kingston-upon-Hull, engine and boiler maker, for certain improvements in the construction of the boilers and funnels of steam-engines. July 3.

William Lancaster, of New Bond-street, in the county of Middlesex, gunmaker, for improvements in the manufacture of fire-arms and cannon, and of percussion tubes. July 3.

John Coope Haddan, of Bloomsbury-square, in the county of Middlesex, civil engineer, for improvements in the construction of carriages, and of wheels, and in brickwork. July 3.

Francis Edward Colegrave, of Brighton, Esq., for improvements in the valves of steam and other engines, in causing the driving wheels of locomotive engines to bite the rails, and also in supplying water to steam boilers. July 3.

Charles Phillips, of the city of Bristol, engineer, for improvements in apparatus or machinery for cutting turnips, and other similar substances, as food for cattle. July 3.

Richard Hornsby, of Spittlegate Grantham, in the county of Lincoln, agricultural implement manufacturer, for improvements in machinery for sowing corn and seeds, and in depositing manure; in thrashing machines, in machines for depositing or winnowing corn; and in steam-engines and boilers for agricultural purposes. July 3.

Charles Starr, of New York, for improvements in bookbinding. July 3.

James Kingsford, of Essex-street, Strand, Esquire, for improvements in refrigerating and freezing. July 3.

Weston Tuxford, of Boston, in the county of Lincoln, for improvements in machinery for crushing or pressing land, and for shaking straw; also improvements in applying steam power to agricultural machinery. July 4.

Henry Pratt, of New Bond-street, in the parish of Saint George, Hanover-square, in the county of Middlesex, camp equipage manufacturer, for improvements in the construction of portmanteaus and travelling trunks. July 9.

Alfred Vincent Newton, of Chancery-lane, in the county of Middlesex, mechanical draughtsman, for improvements in the preparation and manufacture of caoutchouc or india-rubber. July 9.

Robert Rumney Crawford, of Warden Paper Mill, in the county of Northumberland, paper maker, for an improvement in drying paper. July 10.

Jacob Connop, of Hyde-park, in the county of Middlesex, gentleman, for improvements in melting, moulding, and casting sand, earth, and argillaceous substances, for paving, building, and various other useful purposes. July 10.

James Hill, of Stalybridge, in the county of Chester, cotton-spinner, for improvements in, or applicable to, certain machines for preparing cotton, wool, and other fibrous substances, for spinning and doubling. July 15.

Tempest Booth, of Ardwick, in the county of Lancaster, gun manufacturer, for certain improvements in the method of, and apparatus for, obtaining and applying motive power. July 15.

Edward N. Smith, of West Brookfield, of the State of Massachusetts, in the United States of North America, for a machine to fold paper. July 17.

Edward John Dent, of the Strand in the county of Middlesex, chronometer maker, for improvements in compasses for navigation, surveying, and similar purposes. July 17.

William Herbert Gossage, of Stoke Prior, in the county of Worcester, chemist, for improvements in obtaining certain metals from some compounds containing such metals, and in obtaining other products, by the use of certain compounds containing metals. July 17.

Jean Jules, Varillat, of Rouen, in the republic of France, manufacturing chemist, for improvements in the extraction and preparation of colouring, tanning, and saccharine matters from various vegetable substances, and in the apparatus to be employed therein. July 17.

John Melville, of Upper Harley street, in the county of Middlesex, Esq., for certain improvements in the construction of railways and locomotive engines and carriages. July 17.

Henrietta Brown, of Long-lane, Bermondsey, widow and executrix of the late Samuel Brown, for improvements in the manufacture of metallic casks and vessels. July 17.—(Communication.)

John Silvester, of West Bromwich, in the county of Stafford, whitesmith, for improvements in straightening, flattening, setting, and shaping hardened steel. July 17.

Ezekiel Edmonds, the younger, of Bradford, in the county of Wiltshire, cloth manufacturer, for improvements in the manufacture of certain descriptions of woollen fabrics. July 17.

LIST OF PATENTS THAT HAVE PASSED THE GREAT SEAL OF SCOTLAND.

FROM THE 24TH DAY OF MAY TO THE 21ST DAY OF JUNE, 1850, INCLUSIVE.

George Jackson, of Belfast, Ireland, flax-dresser, for improvements in heckling machinery. May 24.

Frederick Rosenborg, of Albemarle-street, in the county of Middlesex, Esquire, and Conrad Montgomery, of the Army and Navy Club, St. James's-square, in the same county, Esquire, for improvements in sawing, cutting, boring, and shaping wood. May 24.

George Hayward Ford, of St. Martin's-le-Grand, in the county of Middlesex, for improvements in obtaining power. May 27.

Joseph Barrans, of St. Paul's, Deptford, in the county of Kent, engineer, for improvements in axles and axle-boxes of locomotive engines, and other railway carriages. May 27.

Samuel Fisher, of Birmingham, in the county of Warwick, engineer, for improvements in railway carriage wheels, axles, buffer, and draw-springs and hinges for railway carriage and other doors. May 28.

Thomas Chandler, of Stockton, Wilts, for improvements in machinery for applying liquid manure. May 28.

Thomas Dickson Rotch, of Drumlanford House, in the county of Ayr, North Britain, Esq., for improvements in separating various matters, usually found combined in certain saccharine, saline, and ligneous substances. May 28.—(Communication.)

Henry Columbus Hurry, of Manchester, in the county of Lancaster, civil engineer, for certain improvements in the method of lubricating machinery. May 29.

John Dalton, of Hollingworth, in the county of Chester, calico-printer, for certain improvements in, and applicable to, machinery or apparatus for bleaching, dyeing, printing, and finishing textile and other fabrics; and in the engraving of copper rollers, and other metallic bodies. June 5.

Frederick Albert Gatty, of Accrington, in the county of Lancaster, manufacturing chemist, for a certain process, or certain processes, for obtaining carbonate of soda and carbonate of potash. June 5.

Jules Le Bastier, of Paris, in the republic of France, but now of South-street, Finsbury, in the county of Middlesex, gentleman, for certain improvements in machinery or apparatus for printing. June 6.

William Robertson, of Gateside Mill, Neilston, in the county of Renfrew, Scotland, machine maker, for improvements in certain machinery used for spinning and doubling cotton and other fibrous substances. June 7.

Francis Tongue Rufford, of Prescott-house, in the county of Worcester, fire-brick manufacturer, and Isaac Mason, of Cradley, in the same county, potter, and John Finch, of Pickard street, City-road, in the county of Middlesex, manufacturer, for improvements in the manufacture of baths and wash tubs, or wash vessels. June 19.

Baron Louis Lo Presti, of Paris, in the republic of France, for improvements in hydraulic presses, which are in whole, or in part, applicable to pumps, and other like machines. June 10.

Arthur Elliott, machine maker, of Manchester, in the county of Lancaster, and Henry Heys, of the same place, book-keeper, for certain improvements in machinery for manufacturing woven fabrics. June 14.

Simon Pincoffs, of Manchester, in the county of Lancaster, merchant, for certain improvements in the ageing process, in printing and dyeing calicoes, and other woven fabrics, which improvements are also applicable to other processes in printing and dyeing calicoes, and other woven fabrics. May 30.

James Palmer Budd, of the Ystalyfera Iron Works, Swansea, merchant, for improvements in the manufacture of coke. May 31.

William Macalpine, of Spring-Vale, Hammersmith, in the county of Middlesex, general draper, and Thomas Macalpine, of the same place, manager, for improvements in machinery for washing cotton, linen, and other fabrics. May 31.

Charles Andrew, of Compstall Bridge, in the county of Chester, and Richard Markland, of the same place, manager, for certain improvements in the method of, or apparatus for preparing warps for weaving. May 31.

Charles Cowper, of Southampton-buildings, Chancery-lane, in the county of Middlesex, for improvements in instruments for measuring, indicating, and regulating the pressure of air, steam, and other fluids, and in instruments for measuring, indicating, and regulating the temperature of the same, and in instruments for obtaining motive power from the same. June 14.—(Communication.)

William Watson the younger, of Chapel Allerton, in the parish of Leeds, in the county of York, manufacturing chemist, for improvements in the preparation and manufacture of various materials to be used in the processes of dyeing, printing, and colouring. June 18.

William Edward Newton, of Chancery-lane, in the county of Middlesex, civil engineer, for improvements in rotary engines. June 21.—(Communication.)

James Ward Hoby, of Blackheath, in the county of Kent, engineer, for certain improvements in the construction of parts of the permanent way of railways, and in shaping iron. June 21.

LIST OF PATENTS THAT HAVE PASSED THE GREAT SEAL OF IRELAND

John Stevenson, of Roan Mills, Dungannon, county of Tyrone, flax-spinner, for certain improvements in machinery for spinning flax and other substances. May 25.

DESIGNS FOR ARTICLES OF UTILITY.

REGISTERED FROM 21ST JUNE TO 16TH JULY.

June 21st, 2344, Joseph Lester, Cambridge-street, Hackney, "Filtering funnel."
„ „ 2345, H. B. Hewett, Holborn, "Chaud Froid."
„ 22nd, 2346, Samuel F. Hattersley, Westbrook Works, Bradford, "A shaping plate for forming the cop or spool in spinning yarns."
„ 24th, 2347, John Goulding, J. G., and A. Goulding, Eldon-street, Finsbury, "Omnium office table."
„ 25th, 2348, A. A. Neuberger, South-street, Finsbury, "Improved night lamp boiler."
„ „ 2349, Thomas Dowler, Birmingham, "Match box."
„ 26th, 2350, Thomas Ryan Pinches, Oxenden-street, Haymarket, "Purse envelope."
„ „ 2351, Leonard Hicks, Leeds, "Cape coat."
„ „ 2352, John Sellers, Sheffield, "Razor."
„ „ 2353, Stephen Sharp, Stamford, "Lump-sugar cutting machine."
„ „ 2354, Webb and Greenway, Birmingham, "Cupboard fastener."
„ 27th, 2355, J. and G. Johnston, Paisley, "Cutting apparatus for bonnet tops."
„ 28th, 2356, Hopwood and Armstrong, St. George-street, Wellclose-square, "A door, and apparatus for closing ships' scuttles."
„ 29th, 2357, A. Ettrick, Highbarnes, Sunderland, "Travelling bag or portmanteau."
July 1st, 2358, C. Cowper, Southampton-building, "An addition to a braiding machine."
„ „ 2359, Henry A. Jowett, Sawley, near Derby, "Parts of a signal lamp."
„ 2nd, 2360, James Woods, Stowmarket, Suffolk, "Improved bruising and grinding mill."
„ 3rd, 2361, George Simpson, Spurrier Gate, York, "The York coat and paletot."
„ 4th, 2362, William Walker, Manchester, "Improved ventilating chimney tube."
„ „ 2363, John Ashford, Birmingham, "Umbrella-rail and water-box, for church and chapel pew, carriage, and other doors."
„ 5th, 2364, Joseph Foxall and Co., Thavies Inn, London, "The Triumfante pen."
„ „ 2365, Charles Wilford, Brompton, Yorkshire, "Rotary steam-engine."
„ 6th, 2366, William Collins, jun., Glasgow, "Security envelope."
„ „ 2367, Thomas Pardon, Hull, "Portable bureau."
„ 9th, 2368, Thomas Yates, Coleshill-street, Birmingham, "Improved preserve-pot, for mustard, pickles, and other articles."
„ „ 2369, Anna Maria Breton, Lower Berkeley-street, London, "Embroidering frame."
„ 10th, 2370, James Carter, Lamb's-buildings, Bunhill-row, London, and Johnson Wood, Leadenhall-street, City, "The nautical state-cabin basin."
July 12th, 2371, William Garnett, Tarporley, Cheshire, "Spring for a saddle."
„ „ 2372, William Crosskill, Beverley Works, near Hull, Yorkshire, "Improved feeding apparatus for thrashing machines."
„ „ 2373, Deane, Dray, and Deane, King William-street, London-bridge, "Improved steam boiler."
„ 13th, 2374, William Reynard Lane, Strand, Middlesex, "The economic percolator."
„ „ 2375, William Thomas Loy, King-street, Westminster, "The Tudor razor guard."
„ „ 2376, Richard Robinson, Belfast, "High combustion furnace."
„ 15th, 2377, R. Gray and Sons, Uddingstone, Glasgow, "Draw spring lever."
„ 16th, 2378, Richard Howson, and Henry Howson, Manchester, "Improved differential screwing apparatus for presses."
„ „ 2379, Thomas Key, Charing-cross, London, "Improved regimental cased serpenticlede."

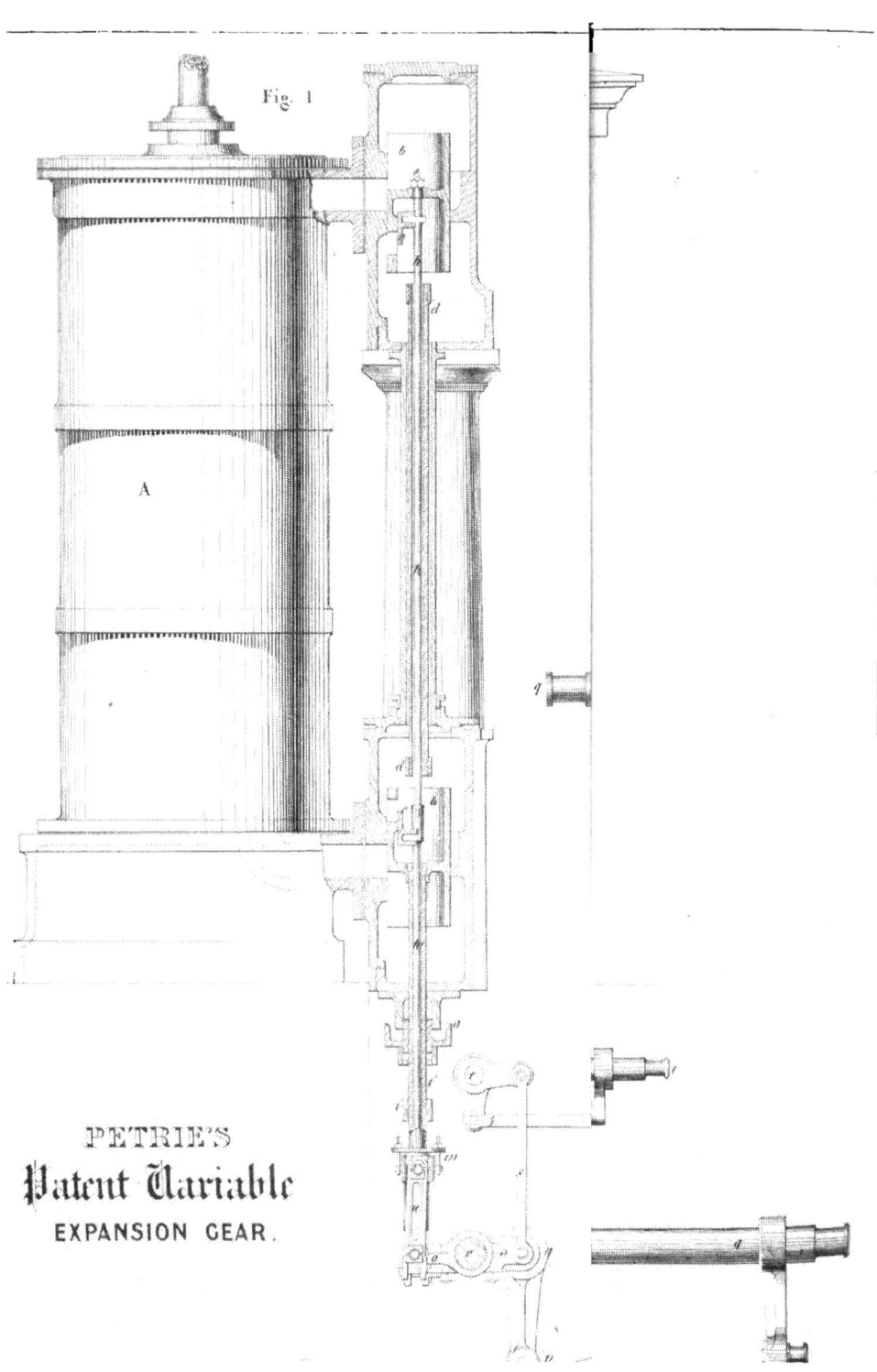

Fig. 1

A

PETRIE'S
Patent Variable
EXPANSION GEAR.

THE ARTIZAN.

No. IX.—Vol. VIII.—SEPTEMBER 1st, 1850.

PETRIE'S EXPANSION GEAR.

PETRIE'S PATENT EXPANSION GEAR.

In our last volume, at page 60, we gave an indicator diagram from an engine at Messrs. Hargreave's calico works at Accrington, fitted with Messrs. Petrie's Patent Self-Acting Variable Expansion Gear, of which we promised details in a future number. We are now able to redeem our engagement, having lately had the advantage of inspecting a number of engines fitted with this gear, and of taking the indicator diagrams figured below. The subject of working steam expansively has been so lately discussed at length in our pages, that we need not occupy our space with a repetition of the advantages to be gained by its more extensive adoption. The peculiarities of Messrs. Petrie's arrangement for accomplishing this desirable object are,—1st, that the steam is cut off close to the cylinder face; 2ndly, that there is no pressure upon the expansion slide, and consequently that very little power is required to work it, which materially conduces to the durability of the parts; 3rdly, that advantage is taken of every diminution of the load to work more expansively; and 4thly, that the apparatus being self-acting, nothing is left to depend on the vigilance of the attendant.

The plate represents the parts of an ordinary beam condensing engine, to which the invention is applied. It will be seen that the cut-off slides work on the inside of the ordinary D slides, opening and closing steam passages in them, and that the cam by which the cut-off slides are worked is so connected to the governor, that when the speed of the engine is accelerated by work being thrown off, the steam is cut off sooner, and that when the speed of the engine diminishes, the steam is admitted for a longer portion of the stroke.

Fig. 1 is an elevation of the cylinder and working gear, with the slides shown in section; fig. 2 is a transverse section of the same through the valves; fig. 3 is a side elevation of the gear on the crank shaft; fig. 4 a plan of the same; fig. 5 a plan of part of the weigh shaft. In the different views the same letters refer to the same objects.

A is the cylinder of the engine; b b the ordinary D slides; c c the cut-off slides, working on the inner faces of the D valves, which are planed to receive them. The D valves are coupled together by a hollow rod, d d, and the cross-heads and rods, e e, e e; the lower slide rod, f f, passing through the inverted stuffing-box, g, and being also hollow, to admit of the rod h h, for working the cut-off slides, passing through it. The main slide rod, f f, is connected by the cross-head, i, and the links, k k, to the levers, l l, on the weigh shaft q (see fig. 5). The cut-off slide rod, h h, is attached at the lower end to the sliding stuffing-box or boot, m, connected by the links, n n, to the lever, o o. From fig. 5 it will be seen that the end of this lever and the ends of the levers l l very nearly coincide, so that if o o had no independent motion, the D slides and the cut-off slides would have the same motion communicated to them by the eccentric and rod, p p, through the weigh shaft; that is to say, the cut-off slides would remain stationary inside the D valves.

But to give the cut-off slides the requisite motion, the lever o o is centred upon a gudgeon r, fixed to the weigh shaft q q, and the other end of o o being attached by the link s to the cut-off weigh shaft, t t, an independent motion can be communicated to the cut-off slides, which is applied to shut the passages in the D valves, and so cut off the steam at any desired point of the stroke.

It now remains to be shown how the requisite motion is obtained for the cut-off weigh shaft t t. On the crank shaft u u is keyed the toothed wheel v, driving a similar wheel w, which is keyed on the boss of the bevel wheel 1, and driving through the bevel pinions 2, 2, the bevel wheel 3, on the boss of which is keyed the cam x. The revolution of the cam x gives motion to the frame y (provided with friction rollers) sliding on a suitable sole plate z. To the frame is attached the rod 4, 4, thus completing the required connexion between the motion of the crank shaft and the cut-off weigh shaft and cut-off slides.

To make this arrangement variable and self-acting, the governor is applied to alter the position of the cam x in the following manner: The governor is driven, as usual, by bevel gear, and the spindle is made hollow, to communicate the motion of the balls to the inner rod 5; through this rod passes a key 6, which acts as a driver to the bevel wheels 7 and 8, both of which are loose on the spindle. On the face of each wheel are two pins of such a length that, as the driver rises and falls by the varying speed of the governor, as soon as it is out of gear with one bevel wheel it engages the other. Both of these wheels take into the wheel 9, so that when the governor rises, the wheel 8 is thrown in gear, and drives 9 in one direction, and when the governor falls, 7 is thrown in gear, and drives 9 in the opposite direction. The motion of wheel 9 is conveyed through the change wheels 10, 10, to the bevel wheels 11 and 12, and transmitted by the vertical shaft 13 to the worm 14, which takes into the worm wheel 15. This worm wheel carries the two bevel pinions 2, 2, and through them, the wheel 3 and cam x have their position changed with respect to the crank of the engine, thus setting the cam to cut off earlier or later as the work may require it. Teeth are required on only a portion of the periphery of the worm wheel, so as to allow of its making one fourth of a revolution, which will shift the cam half a revolution earlier or later, or from beginning to end of a stroke. The bevel wheel 9 is attached to its spindle by friction, in order to prevent the governor driving the worm beyond the teeth on the periphery of the worm wheel.

In order to indicate at what portion of the stroke the steam is cut off, the vertical shaft, 3, is screwed for a part of its length, and by its revolution raises or depresses a nut carrying a pointer, 16. A scale representing the stroke of the engine on the column which carries the shaft indicates the point at which the steam is cut off.

The change wheels, 10, 10, are necessary, as in engines where the load fluctuates very suddenly, the cam requires altering with greater quickness than in engines where such is not the case.

26

We have had the opportunity of examining a number of engines working on this principle, but from their similarity we need only notice two or three, of which we took the annexed diagrams, which represent the state of working of the engines just as we found them, without any attempt to improve their working order, or to render the cases exceptional. We mention this, because the vacuum in No. 1 is only 12 lbs., which is below any other of Messrs. Petrie's engines that we have tested, and is to be attributed to slackness of the packings.

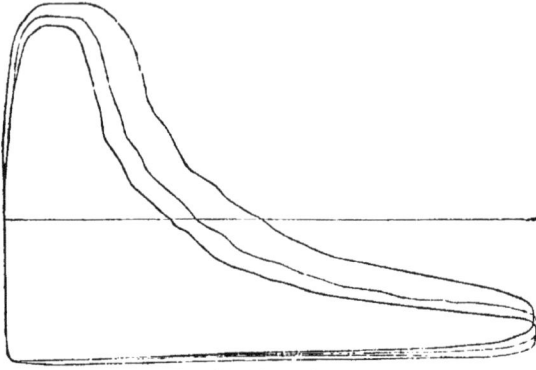

Fig. 1.—Scale 12 lbs. to an inch.

The above diagrams are from an engine at the mill of Messrs. Radcliffe, Brothers, Oldham Road: cylinder, 34½ inches in diameter and 6 feet 6 inches stroke, making 25½ revolutions per minute; pressure in boiler, 20½ lbs.; highest pressure in cylinder, 18½ lbs.* This diagram was taken especially with a view to test the self-varying power of the gear, as the load was diminished. The line showing the highest power is the ordinary full work of the engine. It will be observed that the valves are nicely adjusted to let the steam gradually on to the piston, and the good effect of this is found in the entire absence of any tremor or lifting in the main centre columns. Two scutchers were thrown off, and in the course of a few strokes, the engine came back to her

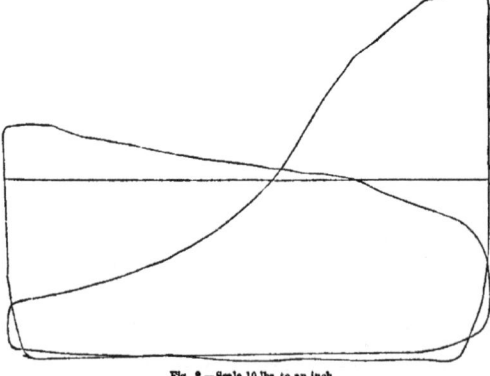

Fig. 2.—Scale 10 lbs. to an inch

* The experiments made by Messrs. Radcliffe show that the consumption of coal of their best engine, not having this expansion apparatus applied, is 41·7 per cent. more than their expansive engines. By exact experiment they have also ascertained, that when not using steam for any other purpose than the engine, the weight of coal required by their new 20 horse heavily-loaded expansive engine is only 2·8 lbs. per horse power per working hour.

regular speed, and gave the intermediate diagram. The variation of speed was very slight, entirely dispensing with the attendance of the engine-man to shut off the steam, as is commonly done, on a signal being given by a bell in the engine room. Six throstle frames were then thrown off, giving the diagram of least power, with the same satisfactory result. In fact, a more perfect automatic regulator can hardly be imagined, and until the day arrives when we can endow an engine with a quantum of foreknowledge, we may say that no better results will be obtained.

Diagrams No. 2 are taken from one of a pair of 60 horse engines in a mill of Messrs. Bright and Brothers, at Rochdale: cylinders 40 inches diameter and 8 feet stroke, making 20½ revolutions per minute.

These two diagrams exhibit the result of an experiment undertaken to determine the saving of fuel, by working the engines with and without the cut-off valves. The average pressure 13.1 lbs., and the work performed is the same in both cases, and the respective quantities of fuel consumed are 7 tons 6 cwt., and 10 tons, showing a saving of 27 per cent. by the use of the gearing. This saving, it will be observed, is effected in a case where the D slides cut off earlier than usual; but for this, the saving would have been still greater.

The diagrams No. 3 are from the top and bottom of one of the same pair of engines, which, as will be seen, were only lightly loaded when we tested them.

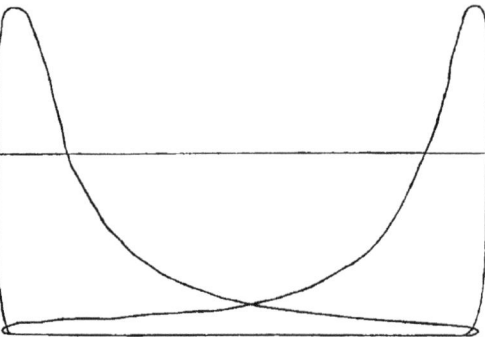

Fig. 3.—Scale 10 lbs. to an inch.

The engines are supplied with steam by two boilers, each 8 feet diameter, and 35 feet long, with two fire-place flues through; a kind of boiler now in very general use in the manufacturing districts. Steam is also taken from the same boilers to heat the mill, supply three dressing frames, and heat a large cistern of water in which the weft used in carpet weaving is soaked. The saving above mentioned is on the whole quantity.

These engines are a beautiful specimen of their class. Their high speed of piston, 328 feet per minute, (a principle we have long advocated), their regularity and smoothness of working, and their economy of fuel, present a judicious combination not frequently met with. The engine house is 57 feet long and 21 feet wide, the two engines being coupled together, and their power transmitted through a large spur fly-wheel, 24 feet diameter. They are, we believe, the longest stroked pair of engines in Lancashire, and reflect great credit upon Messrs. Petrie and Co., the makers. A similar pair have been made by the same firm, for a company in Russia, and are now working in St. Petersburg.

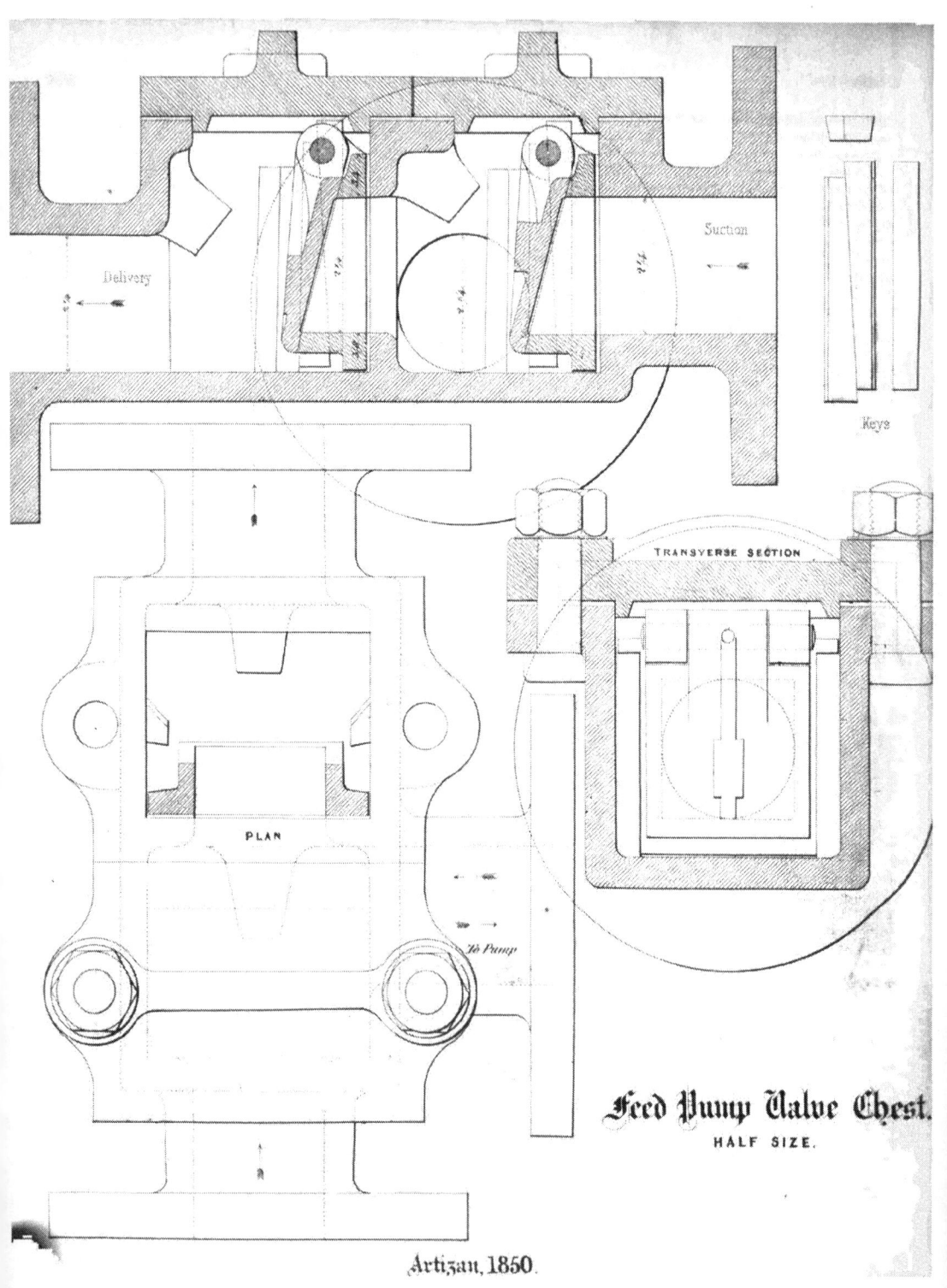

Delivery

Suction

Keys

TRANSVERSE SECTION

PLAN

To Pump

Feed Pump Valve Chest.

HALF SIZE.

Artizan, 1850.

ANALYSIS OF THE STEAM-ENGINE.

(Continued from p. 182.)

Feed Pump Valve Chest.—The feed pump we have described having only one branch, is designed for a valve box containing both the suction and delivery valves, which appears preferable to using two valve boxes, on account of its being more compact, and saving a joint and other fitting; but in a case where it is desirable to keep the suction and delivery valve boxes separate, two branches must be cast on the pump, and each valve placed in a suitable box, with a passage and flange at each end. The description of valves to be used is an important point, as the efficiency of the pump depends upon their proper action. The three varieties most commonly used are the ball valve, the spindle valve, and the hanging valve. The first of these is used in locomotives, and is found to answer better than any other kind with a high velocity of pump-plunger. The trouble of getting up the spherical valve and seat has prevented its more extended use. The spindle valve is the cheapest form, most of the work being turned, and admits of a very simple arrangement, of which we shall probably give an example in some future number. It has the objection, however, that it is more liable to be gagged by chips, spun yarn, and other articles, which find their way into the suction pipe, than the hanging valve of which we have given an example. The hanging valve, on the other hand, has the disadvantage that it offers a greater obstruction to the passage of the water than either of the others, but it still commands the preference, more particularly for large valves.

As the passages in the valves are shown 2¼ inches *square*, the area will be larger than the pipe, which is only 2½ inches *diameter*; this, however, will compensate for the want of escape at the sides and top of the valve.

Presuming that we commence with the left hand, or the delivery valve, its depth being drawn, the surface necessary to make the valve-seat tight must be fixed, say ¼ of an inch; this will give the bottom of the chest, the general thickness of which may be taken at ½ inch. The thickness of metal of the valve-seat face is $\frac{5}{16}$ inch, and the valve is set at a slight angle, to ensure its closing and to make the lift of the valve less. The seats are fixed by double keys, which are more convenient for getting out than single ones. Bevelled strips are cast on the sides of the box to receive the keys, which do not require to be driven in, as some people imagine, to jam the seats, for the pressure has always a tendency to keep them in their place, and they are often sprung and made to leak by being over tightly keyed, although they may have been fitted true in the vice. The valve seats, and joint pins are made of gun metal, and a small pin is driven through the valve to fix the joint pin, which thus works in the lugs on the seat. Care must be taken to allow sufficient area for the water to pass when the valve rises, by making the box of proper length. The branch to the pump is kept as far as possible from the suction valve, to allow the water to pass freely clear of the seat. Guards are cast on the box, to prevent the valves rising too high, which is an evil, both from their being later in closing and striking harder on the seats; the valve is strengthened where it strikes the guard. Each valve has a separate cover, as it may not always be necessary to break both joints, and each is bolted down by two ¾ bolts. Lugs are cast on the box and covers to receive the bolts, and also ribs on the latter, to prevent the pressure springing the covers and causing them to leak. When both faces are got up true, it is sometimes difficult to stop a leak, as the cover will spring, however hard the nuts are screwed down; this may be remedied by filing either face a little convex in the direction of the bolts, so that the cover may be sprung a little in the opposite direction by the bolts.

To be continued.

INSTITUTION OF MECHANICAL ENGINEERS.

"On a Blowing Engine working at high velocities." By Mr. Archibald Slate, of Dudley.

In introducing to the Meeting the proposal for Working Blowing Engines at High Velocities, the writer of the present paper wishes shortly to direct attention to the various changes through which this description of engine has passed, the better to elucidate the difficulties to be overcome, and the advantages to be derived from the further change now proposed.

The first records he has been able to collect show the blowing cylinders to be single-acting, or having the power of propelling the blast when the piston was moving in one direction only; three or more of these blowing cylinders appear to have been attached to one crank-shaft, worked by a water wheel, and thus a tolerable steady pressure of air has been obtained. When the gradual improvements of the steam engine and the demand for increased means of manufacture caused it almost entirely to supersede all other power, the blowing apparatus appears to have been accommodated as much as possible to the steam engine, so as to afford the character of engine for the time being, the fullest development of its power.

In pursuance of this object the single-acting atmospheric engine of Newcomen was attached to a blowing cylinder, which propelled the air from the upper side of the piston only, and in addition to the water regulator, which appears to have been known at an earlier date, there was attached a cylinder, now known as the regulating tub, which was equal to or larger in diameter than the blowing cylinder. In this was fitted a piston with a rod moving in a guide fixed on the open top of the regulating tub, the bottom of the latter being close, and having an open connection to the main from the blowing cylinder. The piston in the tub was loaded to the pressure of blast required, and in the intervals between the discharges of the blowing cylinder, the descent of the piston in the tub kept up the discharge of air into the water regulator, which intervened between it and the furnace; thus in effect, as far as possible, making the engine double-acting. To prevent the piston being blown out of the regulating tub, a large safety-valve was attached to the top of the rod by a strap, long enough to allow the desired play of the piston, and short enough to lift the safety-valve, or snorter, as it is usually termed, if the piston at any time exceeded its limits; and the number of strokes of the engine was also regulated by the tub piston, as to it the cataracts were attached.

When the double-acting engines of Watt were introduced, the regulating tub was still retained, though not nearly so essential a part of the machine as in the former instance.

The next change that took place was the general abandonment of the water regulator (though some of these are still at work, or have been within a few years); the reason for this change was the discovery that the air in summer, already surcharged with moisture, took up an additional quantity from passing over the surface of the water in the regulator, and that this was prejudicial to the working of the furnaces.

When the large area of the water regulator was shut off, it was then found that the tub was by no means such a perfect regulator as it was supposed to be, as the momentum of the engine passed too sudden into the heavy piston of the tub, and throwing it up much beyond the height due to the pressure of the air, caused an irregularity that was even more aggravated by its descent; to counteract this, a spring beam was placed on the top of the tub so as gradually to check the momentum of the piston, and this had some effect, but not at all a satisfactory one.

The next alteration which appears to have suggested itself, was the application of large air chambers, from twelve times to thirty times the area of the blowing cylinder, in which the elasticity of the compressed air acted as the regulator of the discharge, the tub with its piston being in some cases retained to work the cataracts, and as a telltale against the engine men, in case of their allowing the steam to slacken and the piston to descend. In other cases the tub was dispensed with altogether.

We now enter upon the last change which took place some fifteen years ago, namely, the coupling of two double-acting engines, and double-acting blowing cylinders upon the same crank shaft at right angles, so as to keep up a regular discharge. This effect was in some measure obtained, but an air chamber or what is equivalent to it, very large mains, were still required to obtain what was considered a satisfactory result.

At this point the realized improvements of the blowing engine stop short, leaving it still a large, cumbrous, and expensive machine, and not capable of moving through its valves the HIGHLY ELASTIC MEDIUM, AIR, at a greater rate than the absolutely NON-ELASTIC FLUID, WATER, is moved through an ordinary pump. Under these circumstances, it must be obvious that after all the engineering talent that has been spent on this description of engine, there is still (if the expression may be applied) a wide range of discovery open.

The immediate cause of the writer's attention being attracted to the improvement of the blowing engine, was the difficulty experienced in regulating one of the old construction of blowing engine in the latter part of 1848, and having at the same time occasion to employ some small 9 inch cylinders driven by the air of the large blowing engine. These small cylinders, when driving the shafting only, sometimes at-

tained a velocity of upwards of 200 revolutions per minute, suggesting the idea of the possibility of reversing their motion and taking in the air in place of blowing it out through them; there was, however, a difficulty in the slide valve, which did not open and shut fast enough. After some consideration it was agreed that another cylinder should be prepared, and the centre port made much larger, and the slide over-travelled nearly half its stroke in excess, which had the desired effect; a cylinder of 9 inches diameter, and 1 foot stroke, having been driven 320 revolutions or 640 feet per minute, discharging the air at a pressure of 3½ lbs. per square inch, through a tuyere of 1½ inch diameter, or ₆th of the area of the blowing piston. This performance, as is well known, is more than double that of any ordinary engine, the total area of the tuyeres with a 90 inch blowing cylinder, being at a pressure of 3½ lbs., about 52 circular inches, or ₇₂th of the area blowing piston.

We are all acquainted with the tremour which is felt even in the best form of the large sized engines; but in the experiments at a high velocity with the small sized cylinders, not the slightest jar was felt or noise heard, it is therefore proposed to increase the speed of the piston in actual practice, from 640 to 750 feet per minute, the length of stroke being 2 feet in place of 1 foot; this is somewhat under the speed of a locomotive piston at 40 miles per hour, which is about 800 feet per minute, so that it is conceived no difficulty can present itself to this. The proposed speed of 750 feet per minute, is three times the usual speed of the present blowing engines, 250 feet per minute.

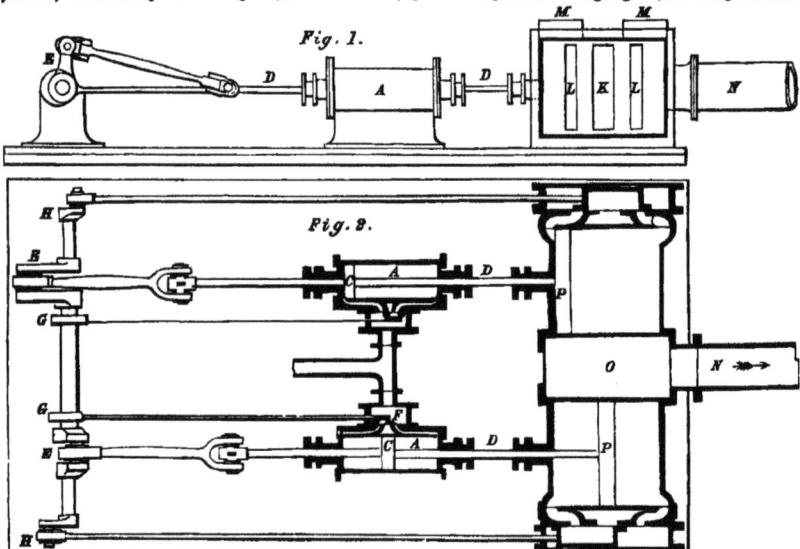

Fig. 1.

Fig. 2.

The construction of the proposed engine is shown in the accompanying drawings; fig. 1, is an elevation, and fig. 2, a plan of the engine, showing the pair of steam cylinders and blowing cylinders; AA are the steam cylinders, 10 inches diameter and 2 feet stroke; BB the blowing cylinders 30 inches diameter and 2 feet stroke, with their pistons C and P, fixed on the same piston rods D, which are connected to two cranks E, fixed at right angles to each other on the same shaft. The slide valves F of the steam cylinders are worked by the eccentrics G on the cranked shaft, and the cranks H at the outer ends of the same shaft, work the slide valves of the blowing cylinders. The centre port K passes downwards to an external opening for the admission of the air, and the discharge ports LL deliver into the passages M on the

top of the cylinder, which communicate with the air main N by the chest O formed between the cylinders. The piston of the blowing cylinder is intended to be made without any packing, being a light hollow cast-iron piston turned to an easy fit; and the slide valve of the blowing cylinder to have a packing plate at the back, working against the cover of the valve box, with a ring of india-rubber inserted between this plate and the back of the valve, to give a little elasticity.

It appears that 30 inches diameter is somewhere about the most convenient size for a stroke of 2 feet, and as it is considered an advantage to have the stroke as short as possible, to increase the regularity of the blast, the comparative cost of the different engines which follows has been taken upon this basis, two 10-inch steam cylinders and two 30-inch blowing cylinders, costing together (exclusive of the boilers) about £400, being reckoned equal to blow one of our largest furnaces, making 160 tons of iron per week, and having a surplus equal to blowing a cupola or refinery, as is generally allowed, as such an engine would give at 640 feet per minute the same speed of piston as in the experiments, very nearly 30 circular inches of tuyere, at a pressure of 3½ lbs. to the square inch; the circular inch is used in speaking of the area of the tuyere, as the blast that any furnace is taking is usually reckoned by simply squaring the diameter of the tuyere, but the pressure is taken on the square inch.

The experiments on which these calculations were founded, having been made upwards of 12 months ago, were repeated last week, and the results were found to be as nearly as they could be measured the same, the blowing cylinder had in the interval been driving the lathes in the pattern shop, and the slide was found perfect. An indicator was applied with a view to test the amount of friction of the air in entering the cylinder at the high velocity, and a simple method was adopted of ascertaining this. A tuyere was made as large as the inlet port, and the engine was driven to nearly or quite 700 feet per minute, when the gauge showed a pressure of ¼ of a lb. per square inch, and as the friction would be the same through the same sized openings at other pressures, it follows that the loss by friction on a pressure of blast of 3½ lbs. per inch would be $\frac{1}{15}$th or 6⅔ per cent. loss; as the port in this case was $\frac{1}{11}$th of the area, and the port proposed is ⅛th, it is assumed that the loss would not exceed 5 per cent. from this cause, or indeed from any other cause, as the friction from propelling the air through a given sized tuyere, at a given pressure, must be the same in both cases.

Following up the comparison of first cost, we find that (exclusive of boilers, which are assumed the same in both cases, but taking into account the cost of the engine house), there would be a saving by the proposed plan of between 65 and 70 per cent.; the cost of a pair of the best engines in Staffordshire blowing three furnaces being £3,650, while on the proposed plan they would cost £1,100 if high pressure only, or, if high pressure and condensing £1,350, including in each case the engine house but not the boilers.

Many will prefer high pressure only, on account of its simplicity, but as it appears evident that a given quantity of steam can be condensed in the same time, in the same condenser, whether admitted in a few large jets or in a great number of small jets, there is no reason whatever why a condensing apparatus may not be attached to the short stroke engine at high velocities; the only condition being that it must be equivalent to the power of the engine, without relation to the size of the cylinder. The air-pump in this case must be double acting with slide valves, or it may be rotary and placed round the crank shaft, and there appears to be no advantage in a fly wheel for such an arrangement of blowing engines.

The speed of the engine should be regulated by a hydrostatic governor, communicating with the blast main, and attached to the throttle valve, exactly similar to those used in gas works for regulating the engine driving the exhausters; this would regulate the engine with greater delicacy, and maintain a more uniform blast than can be done with the present engines; and the rapid succession of the strokes of the two small blowing cylinders acting alternately, would render the present large reservoir quite unnecessary.

Supposing the advantages claimed for this description of engine to be realized, which the writer has no reason to doubt, it may be applied to assist the present blowing engines where they are overpowered, which is in many instances the case, as there is no ready means of increasing their power as the works develope themselves, and greater calls are made on the engine; but in the case of the proposed engines, if at any time an increase were desired another blowing cylinder might be added to the shaft, at a comparatively small cost.

Referring again to what first drew the attention of the writer to this subject, the employment of small cylinders worked by the pressure of air, where it was inconvenient or impracticable to employ shafting; it has been found that a 12-inch air cylinder with 3 lb. pressure attached to a large foundry crane, under which 15·30 inch pipes are cast vertically every ten hours, does the work of double the number of men that could by any possibility work at the crane.

This suggests the possibility of a very considerable advantage to railway companies, by the use of the proposed engines, as the blowing cylinders for compressing the air might be attached to the end of the piston rod of any of the small-sized engines now laid up at several stations, and the air conveyed to the various cranes, to which cylinders might be attached for about £25 per crane, without disturbing the present arrangement for the use of manual power in cases of emergency. The saving of manual labour by such an arrangement will be best estimated by the managers of goods departments, some of whom are amongst the members, and with reference to the mechanical application of the power, the writer hopes to have the pleasure of presenting the Institution with another paper at some future meeting.

The Chairman inquired if Mr. Slate could furnish them with any comparison of the advantages of the proposed blowing cylinder, and the fan-blast, which had been so well developed by Mr. Buckle at a former meeting.

Mr. Slate said he had used fans made according to Mr. Buckle's principle, and could speak to their excellence and superiority; they were the least expense in construction, being made with light wood arms, and he had obtained from 4½ to 5 oz. per square inch pressure with them. He had tried both the cylinder-blast and the fan-blast for melting iron, and indeed had them both now in use; but he was of opinion the cylinder-blast was decidedly the best for the purpose, as the fan-blast caused the lining of the cupola to burn away quicker, and also consumed a larger proportion of fuel. He had found they could not blow so continuously with the fan-blast, and required to stop more frequently for repairs of the lining than with the cylinder-blast. The pressure of the fan-blast was not sufficient to carry it through the burden, so that the passage of the air was more at the sides of the cupola, which caused the lining to be cut away, and hence he considered the cylinder-blast was the best for melting iron; and though it might not be so cheap at first cost, there was no doubt of its ultimate economy.

Mr. Davies inquired whether the iron manufactured was equally good with the cylinder-blast as with the fan-blast; and whether the hard blast did not harden the iron.

Mr. Slate had at one time entertained a similar idea, but he had tried both extensively, and in the thousands of tons which he had melted, he had been unable to detect any difference between the quality of iron made under the influence of the fan, and that made by the cylinder-blast.

Mr. Robinson inquired what pressure and what sized tuyeres Mr. Slate had used with each kind of blast.

Mr. Slate replied, that the pressure with the cylinder-blast was about 3½ lbs. per inch at the cupola, and they had six 1 inch or 1¼ inch tuyeres. In the case of the fan they had two tuyeres about 6 inches diameter. They used best Durham hard coke, because light coke was useless with the cylinder-blast, which would blow it away.

Mr. Davies said, he made an exhauster that had been used extensively for blowing copper-melting furnaces, but he believed the fan was preferred, though it gave less pressure of blast.

Mr. Robinson thought the fan-blast was best for a cupola, and he could not see the reason why the cylinder-blast should not injure the sides of the cupola more than the fan-blast, because it had greater pressure, and must have more power to force its way through to the opposite side.

Mr. Slate said, the result of his observations had been that the cylinder-blast caused the least injury to the lining, and he considered that it forced its way better amongst the coke and material, on account of its pressure being so much greater than the fan-blast. He found the lining of their cupolas that had the fan-blast seldom lasted more than a few days without stopping for repairs, but those with the cylinder-blast would work for some weeks with only casual repairs.

Mr. Cowper was of a different opinion, and thought there would not be any greater destruction of the lining with the fan-blast, unless there were some other cause; the circumstance of blowing with 6 tuyeres in the one case, and only 2 in the other, might cause a difference. At the London works the cupola was blown with a fan-blast, and had two 10 inch tuyeres at 5 oz. pressure, but they did not find the sides cut away; on the contrary, with some trifling repairs each morning before starting work, the lining of the cupola lasted for many weeks. In his opinion the fan-blast was preferable to the cylinder-blast for a cupola.

Mr. W. Smith remarked, that he did not know any instance of the fan being applied to blast furnaces in that district, and it was for those more particularly that Mr. Slate's engine was proposed; the question raised by the paper was, whether in the case of blast furnaces it was better to employ a small cylinder at a high velocity, or a large cylinder at a slow speed. This small blowing engine was proposed to supersede the ponderous machines which were employed for the purpose at the blast furnaces; he considered it was an important suggestion, and he saw no reason why it should not accomplish the object intended.

Mr. Slate observed, that the practicability of working the blowing cylinder at the quick speed, had been proved by his trials with a cylinder driven by indirect power; and although he had not yet been able to try a complete blowing engine driven direct by a steam piston as proposed, there was no difficulty to be overcome in driving the piston at the speed required, and the cost of the steam used would not be increased.

Mr. Cowper was of opinion that the proposed quick motion would give a more regular blast, which was a matter of great importance as affecting the make of iron; but it was a question whether the great speed at which it was proposed to be worked, would not injuriously affect the durability of the working parts of the engine.

The Chairman did not think there was reason to fear any serious objection from that cause, when it was borne in mind that the piston of a locomotive engine frequently worked at the velocity of 800 feet per minute, and the proposed engine would be stationary instead of locomotive.

A vote of thanks was passed to Mr. Slate, who promised to communicate the results of further experiments on the subject.

IMPROVED RAILWAY POINTS AND CROSSINGS.

Abstract of a Paper read before the Royal Scottish Society of Arts, March, 1859. By W. Campbell, C.E., Resident Engineer, Edinburgh, and Bathgate Railway.

In the crossing point, fig. 1, the dotted lines indicate the web of the rail, and show where the rail has been bent and the flanges on the top side cut away, to give a bearing at the bolt-holes, shown by dotted lines at the point. Fig. 2 is a transverse section of the improved model, where the rail is cut into the bottom flange only. Fig. 3, the ordinary make, cut into both top and bottom flanges; and fig. 4, the patent make, cut into the under side of top flange only.

In this paper Mr. Campbell proceeded to describe a sketch of rail-

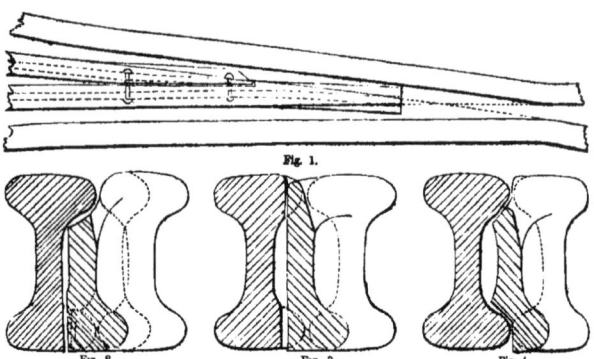

Fig. 1.

Fig. 2.　　　　　　　Fig. 3.　　　　　　　Fig. 4.

ways, sidings, &c., showing the positions of the points and crossings and the crossing rails as executed on the Edinburgh and Bathgate railway. The improved switch is on its bottom side the same as the common make, while on its top side it resembles the patent switch, but is simpler to make, is equally efficient, and will stand more fatigue. He had made careful examination of the points on the principal lines, and observed their great tear and wear; therefore, in the model the bearing surface is neither notched nor under-cut, the inside of the top of the switch being bent with a twist so as to pass under the top flange of the stock rail. The top of the switch not being mitered into the under side of the bearing surface of the stock rail, it is not liable to be locked by the barbing over of the stock from the pressure of the wheels, as happens to the general make of the patent switch and others which resemble it in cutting under the top flange of the stock. A cut of rail, rusted and varnished on the end, showed the laminated structure of the top of the rail, which is the part that gives way under traffic by scaling off from the constant impact of the wheels. This is kept in view in the make of the improved switch. The cutting away part of the under-flange of the stock, while it does not materially weaken it, allows a broader and steadier base for the switch, and stones will not so readily rest between and prevent the shutting of the switch. The drawings showed how the common make of switch possessed the advantage of a straight face and continuous bearing surface in great perfection, although, from consisting of two parts, it is much less durable at the point than the model. The author was not aware of anything having been done to meet the tear and wear of the crossing point, notwithstanding the weight of the engines in use: any contrivance for the main road must be very secure, but at stations where there is much traffic while the transit is slow, the wheels might be assisted over the interval at the crossing point by a piece of iron keyed between the rails, having its surface one inch below the top of the rail, and tapering down at each end, on which the flange of the wheel would run till the face again touched the rail, and so be prevented from falling, as it does, off the steel point with a blow on the knee of the wing rail, which is the point that gives way. This is similar to what is done at the crossing of the bars on a turntable. The chair is laid level on the sleeper, but the seat of the rail is inclined 1 in 15 in the chair, so as to give the rail an equal cant its whole length, to meet the cone of the wheel. The inside jaw of the joint chair should fit close up under the flange of the rail, but the intermediate chairs should not rise quite so high, and be slightly rounded on the inner face to allow the rail to adjust itself to the joints, which are first keyed and spiked firm.

CORRESPONDENCE.

IMPROVEMENTS IN ANCHORS.
(To the Editor of the Artizan.)

SIR,—As the safety of much property and many valuable lives depend upon the efficiency of the Anchor, it is natural to suppose that any improvement in the construction of an instrument of such vital importance will meet with the most serious consideration and cordial support of every person connected with the shipping interest.

Under this impression, I am desirous of explaining, as briefly as possible, the principle of construction of my improved small-palmed Anchor, in order to show, that notwithstanding it may have, at first glance, the appearance of being formed to cut through the ground, it does in reality possess a much greater power of resistance than the ordinary large-palmed anchors of the same weight.

The limits of this paper will not permit me to enter into a lengthened discussion on the merits of the different sectional forms hitherto used in the construction of anchors, in order to obtain the greatest amount of strength, with a given weight of iron : I will therefore at present confine my remarks principally to their holding qualities.

In the first place, then, it appears that the inefficiency of the large palm is owing to its loosening the ground in front of it, and to its liability to get " shod," and consequent tendency to rise out of the ground; and when this takes place, no dependance can be had on its again taking hold, and therefore another anchor must be let go, when it would otherwise have been desirable to ride by one.

The small palm, however, does not disturb the ground, which, on the contrary, passes freely over it; and this is to be attributed to its making a more favourable angle with the resisting medium, which gives the anchors thus constructed a natural tendency to penetrate deeper, and without the least liability to get " shod."

This being the case, a ship will never run away with an anchor with small palms, of the form represented by the accompanying drawing, which, if dragged by riding too short, will again hold on, with a sufficient scope of cable; for it has no tendency whatsoever to rise out of the ground.

This penetrating property is likewise possessed, but in a minor degree, by my former small-palmed anchor, which has stood the test of several years' trial, and met with general approbation. But the holding quality of the plan now under consideration is, in a great measure, based upon a principle hitherto entirely overlooked in the construction of anchors. Nevertheless its peculiarly advantageous effect can be made quite obvious to the most cursory observer, although at first glance it may appear somewhat paradoxical.

In the first place, then, it will be seen by the sections, Figs. 14 and 15, that the arms of the anchor, Fig. 1, are formed on the principle of a wedge, the inside or front being made thinner than the outside or back part. The object of this form is to avoid disturbing the ground in front of the arms, and to augment the lateral pressure of the ground against the sides of the arms. For the same reason, and in order to retain as long as possible the rubbing action of the ground against the sides of the arms, the chamfer on the outside or back part is made smaller than that on the inside or front part; and I have ascertained, by actual experiment, that the ground, by reason of its elasticity, immediately closes in and reunites behind the anchors thus constructed; whereas the large-palmed anchors of the usual construction, when dragged, leave a wide rut or trench behind them. And, moreover, the arms of anchors of the ordinary construction are usually made of an oval form, or of an oval flattened a little at the sides, and sometimes nearly round.

Now, it is obvious that when any body of a round or oval section passes through the ground, the friction and lateral pressure of the ground ceases, for the most part, to produce any retarding effect, beyond the centre of that body; and it should also be borne in mind that these sectional forms are far from being the best in regard to strength. All curvilinear figures indeed are highly objectionable when opposed to a transverse strain, for in that case nearly the whole force of extension on the one side, and compression on the other, is confined to a few fibres or particles lying on the surfaces, at the greatest distance from the neutral axis; whereas the forms adopted in the construction of the improved anchor present surfaces of greater extent, parallel to the axis of rotation, and therefore bearing an equal strain, and, consequently, much less likely to give way under any severe trial. The square and rectangular forms are, moreover, better calculated for insuring sound workmanship. To return, however, to the holding qualities, let us again refer to the drawing, but more especially to the section Fig. 13, by which it will be seen that the form of the improved palm is widely different from all the forms of palms hitherto used, for instead of presenting a flat surface at right angles to the resisting medium, the front of the palm is " bevelled," and thus presents two surfaces obliquely to the line of traction, with one intermediate surface (comparatively small) at right angles thereto; and as any two sides of a triangle are longer than the third, these surfaces present a greater area of resistance than could be obtained by a flat palm of the same length and breadth.

And, moreover, their centre of resistance is considerably deeper in the ground, which is another decided advantage. In fact, if the lower arms of two anchors of equal weights be buried in the ground up to the middle of their shanks, it will be seen that the broadest part of the palm of the improved anchor is below the point, or termination of the arm of the anchor of the usual construction; and the tendency of the former is to penetrate deeper, whilst that of the latter is to rise out of the ground.

It should also be observed, that when the improved anchor is buried up to the middle of the upper arm (and it frequently sinks entirely under the surface,) the back of the palm is in contact with the ground, and its rubbing action greatly augments the holding power of the anchor. This may be easily demonstrated by showing

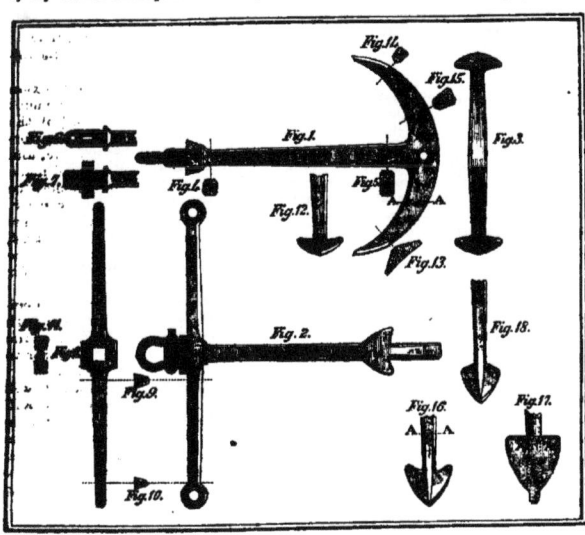

that the friction upon the back of the palm is greater than that upon the front, inasmuch as the ground on which it rests has not only to support the weight of the superincumbent ground, which denotes the friction upon the face or front of the palm, but likewise the weight of both arms, together with that of the crown, and a considerable portion of the shank.

It is now proper to advert to a principle which has been as yet only slightly glanced at, for it is, in fact, by its powerful operation that the plan now under review obtains such a manifest superiority over every other anchor hitherto used.

If, for example, a wedge having parallel sides be placed flatwise, at the depth of two or three feet beneath the surface of the ground, its resistance to any impelling force in the direction of its point, whether by traction, or by propulsion, would be in proportion to the superincumbent weight, which would have to be raised up as the wedge advanced. But if the wedge be placed edgewise, at the same depth as before, it will be found that its resistance would be greatly increased by the indefinite extent of the ground laterally, and therefore the wedge could not be moved forward, without compressing the ground on either side of it, to such an extent as to allow the thick end to pass.

This then is precisely the action of the edges of the improved palms, when the arm of the anchor is buried to a certain depth in the ground, as represented by Figs. 3 & 12.

The action of the oblique surfaces of the palm, being in the direction of the perpendiculars thereto, is partly lateral, and partly vertical, and will be clearly understood by a reference to Figs. 3, 12, and 13 ; but the palm is always buried to such a depth that its vertical action upon the ground does not produce any perceptible elevation of it at the surface.

It is only necessary here to add, that the holding power of the anchor is greatly augmented by the peculiar shape of the arm, which acts in the same manner as the edges of the palm ; for it is obvious that the friction and lateral pressure of the ground against its sides, is much increased by its wedge form ; and the friction, and consequent resistance, may be still further increased by making the sides of the arms a little hollow or concave. There is, in fact, in constant action upon the surfaces of the improved arms and palms a sort of concentrated resistance which does not obtain in any other anchor.

The improved stock is now to be explained ; and its principle of construction, and peculiar advantages, will be perhaps best understood by contrasting it with the stocks now in use.

For large anchors then, the practice at present is, to use a wooden stock, which is doubtless stronger than that of iron, and therefore less liable to be broken. It is likewise better calculated for " canting " the anchor quickly ; but then it should be borne in mind that it is liable to be " wormed," and is more subject to deterioration by " wear and tear " than the iron stock. And moreover, its power of holding is very questionable; for it is obvious from its lightness when submersed, and the extended base on which its rests, that it cannot sink much beneath the surface of the ground, and therefore it prevents the arm from penetrating beyond a certain depth, and this depth is limited by the resistance of the ground against the lower part of the shank, which is in a manner suspended by the wooden stock.

For small anchors, however, the stock is generally made of iron, of a round or oval form, to reeve or pass through a hole in the shank for that purpose.

. This arrangement is very convenient for stocking or unstocking the anchor, but it is highly objectionable in regard to holding, and more especially when there are large knobs or balls on the ends of the stock ; which, however, are almost indispensable for facilitating the " canting " of the anchor. But after the anchor is " canted," these balls tend to keep the stock off the ground, over which it passes with but little resistance, and this tendency is further increased by the protuberance on the shank, caused by the formation of the stock-hole.

In fact, the entire action of the iron stock in common use very much resembles that of a sledge, which has its front end turned upwards, in order that it may oppose the least resistance to the ground, and slide along as smoothly as possible.

Now, it must always be borne in mind that the intention of an anchor is to obtain the greatest possible amount of resistance compatible with a sufficient degree of strength; and, with this object in view, the sectional form of the improved iron stock is made widely different from any of the forms hitherto used. This will be obvious by reference to Figs. 9 and 10, by which it will be seen that the sections are somewhat of a triangular shape, and consequently the stock is of a prismatic sort of form, having its front thicker than its back part ; which form gives it a tendency to sink into the ground when the anchor is dragged ; for it will be observed that the stock generally rests on its front edge, and its lower side does not come wholly into contact with the ground, until the crown of the anchor is buried to a considerable depth beneath the surface.

It will therefore be quite evident that if the improved stock, by reason of its weight and penetrating tendency, sinks to the depth of one, two, or three feet beneath the surface of the ground, the arm will also penetrate so much deeper. And moreover, this penetrating tendency is increased by the projecting part in the middle of the stock, Fig. 8, which forms a rut or trench for the shank to fall into, and thereby still further augments the holding power of the anchor, as well as that of the stock. The discs at the ends of the stock are to prevent its sinking into the ground in " canting " the anchor, and the holes therein are for the purpose of saving iron, and in order to lessen the obstruction to the sinking of the stock after the anchor is " canted."

By Fig. 18, it will be seen that the palms of the stream and kedge anchors are formed in such a manner as to prevent their hooking the boat's gunwale; and it may be proper to mention that, for the convenience of stocking and unstocking, the stocks are rove through the shanks of the anchor as usual ; but with a hole at one end, and a bend and " button " at the other.

Trusting that the importance of the subject will sufficiently justify my occupying so much of your valuable space, and that it may elicit some further discussion to add to our common stock of information.

         I am, &c., WILLIAM RODGER, R.N.

To the Editor of the Artizan.

                       London, August, 1850.

SIR,—In reply to the engineer at Norwich, I beg to offer the following solutions to his queries.

No. 1. In a locomotive where the eccentric rod is in direct connexion with the valve, the eccentric is placed before the crank, the amount being ruled by the lap and lead, which in this case is equal to ¼ of the whole travel of valve. Therefore, when the crank is on the (say forward) centre, the valve has only ¼ of its backward stroke to make, and were it not for the angle of the eccentric rod, the eccentric would make an angle of 135° with the crank. But the correct position may be found, by describing, on a board, a circle equal to the path of eccentric, from the centre of which, in a straight line in direction of crank, set off a distance equal to eccentric rod, minus the amount of lap and lead, and with the eccentric rod as radius, from this point cut the circle, the intersections on either side of the straight line will be the centres for backward and forward eccentrics, as the case may be.

No. 2. The atmospheric line on indicator diagrams shows the position at which the pencil stands previous to being put in connexion with the cylinder, or when there is an equal pressure on each side of the indicator piston, and is made by allowing the barrel of the indicator to make one or two strokes before opening the cock to the cylinder.

No. 3, If one of the radius rods of a side-lever engine breaks, it will be better to leave the other at work ; but by the loss of one there will be an undue strain on the piston rod, and it would be advisable to make a temporary one, by filing the ends of a bar of iron hollow, to suit the pins in motion lever, and side rod ; and another bar having its ends doubled over the two pins, to be lashed to it, which might do till reaching port. It would not be safe to start the engine having no radius rods.   I remain, yours truly, N. D.

PROLONGATION OF ERICSSON'S PATENT.

Hearing on Petition before the Privy Council, June 24th, 1850.

(Abstracted from the Short-hand Writer's Notes.)

Continued from page 190.

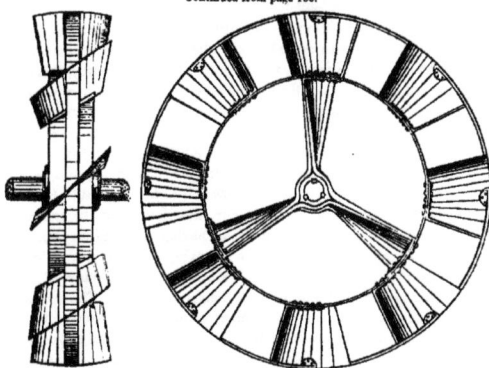

Mr. Horwood sworn.—Witness proceeds to prove the publication and service of the necessary notices of the petition for the prolongation.

The Attorney-General raised an objection to the petition, as being advertised in the name of the Assignee, and not of the person to whom the patent was granted, which was overruled.

The letters patent and an office copy of the specification were then put in, and also a copy of the assignment of a portion of the patent to Count Adolph de Rosen.

Mr. Bennet Woodcroft sworn.—Is Professor of Machinery at King's College, and is a patentee of a screw propeller, which patent has been extended. The parties having patents for the screw propeller have united ; they are Messrs. Smith, Lowe, Ericsson, Blaxland, and myself. I do not know the terms of the arrangement; but after fighting each other for many years we have got tired of it and want to be amicable.

By the Attorney-General.—You were to be a partner in the profits ?
A.—Profits ! we have had none.

Took out a patent for screw propulsion in 1832, and is well acquainted with Mr. Ericsson's patent, and the history of screw propulsion. Published a work called the *Origin and Progress of Steam Navigation.* Believes that through the patent of Captain Ericsson the screw propeller was practically introduced to the world. In Captain Ericsson's invention there are two axes passing out of the stern post of the vessel under water, a hollow and solid axis ; and to each of those axes is a portion of a wheel having uniform blades placed in contrary directions upon them. The wheel nearest to the ship revolves in one direction, and the one farthest from the ship in a contrary direction. in order to overtake the current formed by the first portion of the wheel. I never saw the propeller as applied. I have seen the vessel in which the screws were fixed, but they were under water, and the Thames' water is not very clear. They were entirely submerged. There were no other screws practically in use at that time.

The ring in Captain Ericsson's screw is not an essential part of the invention ; if you put a ring on, it enables one or two or more intermediate blades to be added on the surface of that ring, but if you take away the ring, then it leaves the arms in the form you have got, the three there project from the axis. The wheel or ring certainly would have the effect of strengthening the arms to a certain extent, and then additional blades would give a greater propelling power. One wheel would act without the other, and I think the speed of the vessel would be as great ; you would put the whole power into one wheel instead of two. Judging from what I have seen, I think the two wheels would act very well for towing, but I have had no particular experience in that respect.

Cross-examined by the Attorney-General.
Q.—Did not Capt. Ericsson first introduce a fixed shaft, or a shaft running horizontally below the water-line ?
A.—Yes ; Capt. Ericsson did.
Q.—He was the first that introduced the shaft running below the line of the water through the stuffing-box outside the stern ?
A.—Yes.

Q.—Then if you take off one of the wheels, and the arm and use it with a fixed shaft below the water-line, that is Lowe's, is it not ?
A.—That is what is called Lowe's.
Q.—But to make it Lowe's you must take Smith's segment of a screw ?
A.—No ; there were segments of screws before Smith's and Lowe's.
Q.—What they call the Ship Propeller Company's. Smith had got the cut screw, had he not ?
A.—No ; not in his original patent.
Q.—Had he not a turn of a screw ?
A.—No ; Smith had an entire screw of two turns.
Q.—You had a screw likewise ?
A.—Yes ; I had a screw likewise.
Q.—With an inclined pitch ?
A.—With an increasing pitch.
The Honourable Thomas P. Leigh.—What do you call the increasing pitch ?
A.—Here is a model. The increasing pitch is a screw that varies in its angle with the axis. If the succeeding parts do not overtake the current it would gain no resistance. That was the theory on which the screw was made.
The Attorney-General.—Yours was a screw or thread upon a cone.
A.—It is a portion of a screw wound round a cylinder, instead of an entire worm wound round a cylinder.
Q.—This is Smith's, one turn of a screw.
A.—That is one turn of an Archimedian screw.
Q.—Yours is a screw with an increasing pitch ?
A.—Yes ; no part of it is of a uniform pitch.
Q.—What is Blaxland's ?
A.—A portion of Smith's, cutting out a little bit of the blade.
The proprietors of the screw patents have agreed to divide the amount payable by the Admiralty for the bygone use of the screw. Does not know that that amount is £20,000. The solicitor, who is acting for the company, says he does not think it will be nearly so much as is generally supposed.
Sir F. Thesiger.—It is stated that Mr. Carpmael is appointed to be the arbitrator between the parties, and according to the merits of each he is to award the respective sums that the engineers have from time to time contracted to receive from the Admiralty.
The Attorney-General.—Are the parties to take each of them one-fifth ?
A.—No; I think not. I think we are to be put into the scale of merit, but I do not know the actual amount we are to receive.
— Galloway, Esq., sworn.—Is a civil engineer, and has devoted considerable attention and time to the screw propeller. Has closely examined Capt. Ericsson's patent. In 1838 saw the single wheel applied to the *Robert F. Stockton.* The propeller consists of segments of screws in contradistinction from one entire screw. I think it was the first time I had seen the segment of a screw so applied. The whole apparatus is submerged, and is worked by direct action, in all previous arrangements the power being communicated by wheel gear or straps. This plan is particularly adapted to war steamers, as being less exposed to shot, and occupying less space. The others were all exposed to shot. That is a very important matter, and no doubt goes to the merit of these parties.
Sir F. Thesiger.—It may now be necessary to produce some evidence with regard to the accounts.
Mr. Baron Parke.—There is no doubt about the merits of the patent, but we cannot take that about the accounts for granted.
The Attorney-General.—No doubt, if we are going into the accounts, unless your lordships shall intimate some opinion upon this condition, I shall put some questions, which are very awkward as to the accounts, and we may go into the accounts elsewhere. I understand that there are £20,000 coming to you.
Sir F. Thesiger.—Not to us.
The Attorney-General.—But a large portion. You say you have had £3000 loss ; then you will have to set against it one-fifth of the £20,000.
Sir F. Thesiger.—Supposing we were to have one-fifth of the £20,000 that would be £10,000, and the difference would be only £1000.
Mr. Baron Parke.—We cannot tell what the amount is. Supposing the account should be in your favour then you may get more.
The Attorney-General.—I do not want to interrupt or go into that if I can help it, or to interpose any obstacle, because I think that it is a *bonâ fide* arrangement, and should be carried out.
Mr. Baron Parke.—I believe we have none of us any doubt that that condition must be imposed; it would be impossible to do otherwise,

because, as they are all amalgamated together, they all five must be worked together, and if we did not introduce that condition in this case, it would be neutralized; they are all working together, and we must pursue the same course that was pursued before, and impose the same condition on the extension generally on these patents, just as we have done before.

The Attorney-General.—Yes, my lord, the same as before. With reference to the extension, Smith's was extended for five years, and every extension which is given day by day to one of these five patents, extends the other four. I only mention that so that your lordships may see at once how that is.

Sir F. Thesiger.—I am quite sure your lordships will not act upon any consideration of that account. The only question is, what is the merit of this particular invention before your lordships, and what the expense has been, and what the object has been.

Mr. Baron Parke.—The question is about the expense incurred ; the time is extended with a view to the expense which the patentee has incurred, so that the patentee may be remunerated for his beneficial invention.

Frederick Braithwaite, Esq., sworn.—Was a member of the firm of Braithwaite, Milner and Co., and was connected with Captain Ericsson ever since he came to England, sixteen or seventeen years ago. We were the only manufacturers in England of his screw propeller. (Produces an abstract from the books of the firm, showing the expenses incurred on account of the patent, and showing an actual loss of £3172. 16s. 2d. The Attorney-General, after taking objections to some of the items, expressed himself satisfied.)

JUDGMENT.

Mr. Baron Parke.—Their lordships are satisfied in this case to report that the patent ought to be extended for the same period as Smith's patent, that is, for five years ; and we think there ought to be the same clause annexed as there was to Mr. Smith's patent, that the Crown may have the use of the patent without paying any of the parties for it.

The Attorney-General.—I understand your lordships to grant this extension upon the same terms and the same conditions as Mr. Smith's !

Mr. Baron Parke.—Yes.

The Attorney-General.—And further, the Crown using it may employ engineers to make it.

Mr. Baron Parke.— Yes.

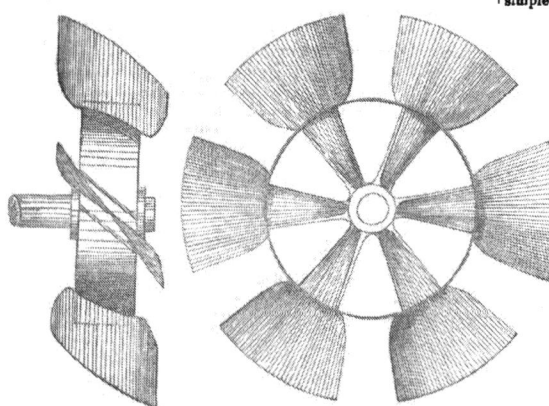

Ericsson's Propeller, as applied to the American Steam-Frigate *Princeton.* Diameter, 14 feet ; pitch, 35 feet.

NOTES BY A PRACTICAL CHEMIST.

NEWLY DISCOVERED METAL.—According to a paper read before the Stockholm Academy of Sciences, a new metal has been discovered by M. Ulgren, and has received the name *Aridium.* This substance is found principally in the chrome-iron ores of Reoras. Its oxides show some analogy to those of iron, but may be distinguished from them by

several reactions. Thus, with prussiate of potash, a solution of the peroxide gives, indeed, like iron, a dark blue precipitate, but on adding excess of the prussiate, it passes into a dirty green. Metallic aridium has not yet been obtained.

THE GASES OF WATER AS A SOURCE OF LIGHT AND HEAT.—Much speculation has been caused by the alleged discovery, in America, of a method of decomposing water so rapidly and abundantly, that the disengaged gases are practically available as fuel. "A new principle of electricity," obtained, it would seem, by "turning a crank," is the decomposing agent ; but the discoverer, Mr. Paine, of Worcester, has not yet made known his process. It must be owned that such statements are not quite free from suspicion. "A new principle of electricity" is a very vague term. How is it to be obtained ! But if all be correct, if the anticipation of our illustrious Davy be realized, Mr. Paine may congratulate himself on having achieved an epoch in the career of practical science. The discovery of Watt, vast as have been its results, must assume, in comparison, a secondary rank. The collier will no longer ply his dreary and dangerous trade. The possession of coal will cease to form an element of national greatness, nor will its proximity now decide the value of metallic ores. The smoke-consumption question will be finally settled, and Manchester and Birmingham may breathe the pure air, and bask in the free sunshine. Our steamers will no longer be burdened with coal, but will suck up their fuel from the bosom of the ocean. The mixture of hydrogen and oxygen may be made to yield any temperature required up to the melting point of platinum, and though their flame is not in itself highly luminous, yet when urged upon a fragment of lime, it affords the purest and most brilliant light. In short, Mr. Paine's invention leaves us nothing to wish, but that it may be found correct.

M. GILLARD, of Paris, has invented another method of decomposing water for lighting purposes, which may be seen in operation at the works of Mr. Kurtz, Cornbrook, Manchester. The gas is obtained by passing steam over charcoal at a white heat, the carbonic acid produced being removed by means of lime. The mechanism employed is very simple. A common D retort, set in the usual manner, is traversed from front to back by a steam-pipe, ¾ inch in diameter supported at about 4 inches above the bottom. The lower part of this pipe (except for about a foot nearest the mouth of the retort) is set with numerous fine apertures, in three rows, the middle row opening downwards, and the two others in a lateral direction. A white heat is first raised, then the bottom of the retort charged with fragments of charcoal and the steam turned on. The supply of gas is then abundant, the hydrogen being exceedingly pure. As this gas, however, as in the case of Mr. Paine's process, has but a feeble illuminating power, some further contrivance is needed. A kind of cage or basket of fine platinum wire is placed over each burner, and the flame is thus rendered intensely luminous. The light is very bright and pure, whilst the air of apartments into which it is introduced is not liable to be contaminated with carbonic acid and sulphurous acid, frequently great sources of annoyance where common coal gas is burned. The manufacture also is perfectly free from nuisance. According to the statement of the inventor, it is well suited for warming rooms, culinary purposes, &c. Whilst such practical applications are thus made of the decomposition of water, we may perhaps hear with surprise this decomposition utterly denied. A Mr. Stevenson, some years ago, published a pamphlet, entitled, "Errors in Chemistry, Electricity, and Magnetism." Lest any doubt should prevail as to his competence to treat on such topics, he took care to add that he had never "made a single experiment, personally or by proxy," in any of the above sciences. In this pamphlet water is termed a simple, elementary substance, on the *authority of Aristotle* (!) and of the *Scrip-*

tures (!!). On being reviewed in a somewhat caustic manner in the *Athenæum*, he waxed wroth, and threatened the editor with *legal proceedings!* Latterly he has been maintaining his theory in the columns of the *Lancet*. His method of arguing is to bring forward the heat, or electricity employed in the decomposition of the water, and to treat them as material substances, entering into chemical combination. But if we view heat and electricity as mere actions, or vibratory properties of matter, all falls to the ground. If Mr. Stevenson be correct, analysis and synthesis are henceforth no proofs at all of the composition of a body, and chemistry, as a science, has ceased to exist.

CONSPECTUS OF EXPLOSIVE BODIES.—Explosion is nothing more than the rapid expansion or sudden generation of gaseous matter, and may accompany either combination or decomposition. From the development of vapour from boiling liquids it differs only in degree. Its mechanical force is due to the violent motion of the evolved gases, or to the impulse which they communicate to the atmosphere. Explosives may be divided into three classes : 1st, Chemical compounds, which explode on decomposition; 2nd, Elementary bodies, which explode on combination ; and 3rdly, Mixtures where various bodies are decomposed and formed. To the first class belong hypochlorous and chlorous acids, chloride and iodide of nitrogen, sulphurets of phosphorus, cyanide of phosphorus, ammoniurets of silver and gold, fulminates of mercury, silver, platinum, and copper, the salts of picric and chrysammic acids, nitrate of mannite, and gun-cotton. To the second class belong oxygen and hydrogen, chlorine and hydrogen, bromine with phosphorus. Many other elementary bodies also ignite on coming into combination, but not being able to assume a gaseous state with sufficient facility, they do not, properly speaking, furnish instances of explosion. The third class comprises chlorates mixed with charcoal, sulphur, phosphorus, arsenic, sugar, sulphurets of arsenic and antimony, prussiate of potass, and organic substances in general; permanganates with similar substances; nitrate of potash with carbon, sulphur, phosphorus, with sulphur and carbonate of potash (fulminating powder) ; other dry nitrates with the same bodies : iodate of potash with charcoal, sulphur, or phosphorus ; phosphuretted hydrogen with oxygen, or with common air ; vapour of ether with oxygen, nitrous oxyde with hydrogen, carbonic oxide with oxygen, bromide of sulphur with hot water, ammoniacal gas with oxygen, carburetted and sulphuretted hydrogen with oxygen.

In almost all explosives the constituent elementary bodies are united by a very feeble degree of affinity, which may be overcome by a slight rise of temperature, by the electric spark, and even by mechanical action. The latter need not surprise us, as friction and percussion invariably alter the calorific and electric state of the bodies to which they are applied. Some substances are even caused to explode by the gentlest contact with bodies whose chemical action is insignificant. Thus, the chloride of nitrogen, probably the most formidable of all fulminating compounds, explodes at once on touching any kind of oil or grease. So-called spontaneous explosions depend probably upon the influence of light, of some variation in barometrical pressure (which evidently modifies the affinity of oxygen for phosphorus), or upon the electric state of the atmosphere.

TO KEEP THE PROTOSULPHATE OF IRON FROM OXIDATION.—M. Ruspini dries the crystals rapidly upon bibulous paper, and then places them in a drying apparatus at 81° F., until it effloresces. It may now be preserved in well-stoppered bottles for any length of time, without absorbing oxygen.

PROTOCHLORIDE OF CARBON AND OIL OF OLEFIANT GAS AS SUBSTITUTES FOR CHLOROFORM.—According to the experiments of M. Reynoso these substances may be employed with safety for anæsthetic purposes, and the state of insensibility which they produce lasts much longer than that from ether or chloroform.   S.

TWENTIETH MEETING OF THE BRITISH ASSOCIATION FOR THE ADVANCEMENT OF SCIENCE.

THE modern Athens has this year been honoured with the presence of the British Association, which commenced its proceedings on the 31st ultimo. Our readers will have already been made acquainted with the transactions by our weekly contemporaries, who have more available space for such subjects. We must content ourselves with briefly noticing such papers as bear upon the practical subjects to which the *Artizan* is devoted.

Dr. Robinson, on abdicating the presidency, and introducing Sir D. Brewster, congratulated the Association, alike on its prosperity and its good fortune in securing the services of so eminent a philosopher to conduct its future government. Sir D. Brewster, in assuming his office, delivered an eloquent address, from which we extract a few portions :—

"Within the bounds of our own system, and in the vicinity of our own Earth, between the orbits of Mars and Jupiter, there is a wide space which, according to the law of planetary distance, ought to contain a planet. Kepler predicted that a planet would be found there—and strange to say, the astronomers of our own times discovered, at the beginning of the present century, four small planets, Ceres, Pallas, Juno, and Vesta, occupying the very place in our system where the anticipated planet ought to have been found. Ceres, the first of these, was discovered by Piazzi, at Palermo, in 1801 ; Pallas, the second of them, by Dr. Olbers, of Bremen, in 1802 ; Juno, the third, by Mr. Harding, in 1804 ; and Vesta, the fourth, by Dr. Olbers, in 1807. After the discovery of the third, Dr. Olbers suggested the idea that they were the fragments of a planet that had been burst in pieces ; and, considering that they must all have diverged from one point in the original orbit, and ought to return to the opposite point, he examined these parts of the heavens, and thus discovered the planet Vesta. But though this principle was in the possession of astronomers, nearly forty years elapsed before any other planetary fragment was discovered. At last, in 1845, Mr. Encke, of Driessen, in Prussia, discovered the fragment called Astræa, and in 1847 another, called Hebe. In the same year, our countryman, Mr. Hind, discovered other two, Iris and Flora. In 1848, Mr. Graham, an Irish astronomer, discovered a ninth fragment, called Metis. In 1849, Mr. Gasparis, of Naples, discovered another, which he calls Hygeia ; and within the last two months, the same astronomer has discovered the eleventh fragment, to which he has given the name of Parthenope. If these eleven small planets are really the remains of a larger one, the size of the original planet must have been considerable. What its size would seem to be a problem beyond the grasp of reason. But human genius has been permitted to triumph over greater difficulties. The planet Neptune was discovered before a ray of its light had entered the human eye ; and by a law of the solar system just discovered, we can determine the original magnitude of the broken planet long after it has been shivered into fragments ; and we might have determined it even after a single fragment had proved its existence. This law we owe to Mr. Daniel Kirkwood, of Pottsville, a humble American, who, like the illustrious Kepler, struggled to find something new among the arithmetical relations of the planetary elements. Between every two adjacent planets there is a point where their attractions are equal. If we call the distance of this point from the Sun the radius of a planet's sphere of attraction. then Mr. Kirkwood's law is, that in every planet the square of the length of its year, reckoned in days, varies as the cube of the radius of its sphere of attraction. This law has been verified by more than one American astronomer, and there can be no doubt, as one of them expresses it, that it is at least a physical fact in the mechanism of our system. This law requires the existence of a planet between Mars and Jupiter, and it follows from the law, that the broken planet must have been a little larger than Mars, or about 5000 miles in diameter, and that the length of its day must have been about 57½ hours. The American astronomers regard this law as amounting to a demonstration of the nebular hypothesis of Laplace; but we venture to say that this opinion will not be adopted by the astronomers of England. Among the more recent discoveries within the bounds of our own system, I cannot omit to mention those of our distinguished countryman, Mr. Lassell, of Liverpool. By means of a fine 20-feet reflector, constructed by himself, he detected the satellite of Neptune, and more recently an eighth satellite circulating round Saturn—a discovery which was made on the very same day, by Mr. Bond, Director of the Observatory of Cambridge, in the United States. Mr. Lassell has still more recently, and under a singularly favourable state of the atmosphere, observed the very minute, but extremely black, shadow of the ring of Saturn upon the body of the planet. He observed the line of shadow to be notched, as it were, and almost broken up into a line of dots—thus indicating mountains upon the plane of the ring—mountains, doubtless, raised by the same internal forces, and answering the same ends, as those of our own globe.

" It is to the influence of Lord Rosse's example that we are indebted for the fine reflecting telescope of Mr. Lassell, of which I have already spoken; and it is to it, also, that we owe another telescope, which, though yet unknown to science, I am bound in this place especially to notice. I allude to the reflector recently constructed by Mr. James Nasmyth, a native of this city, already distinguished by his mechanical inventions, and one of a family well known to us all, and occupying a high place among the artists of Scotland. This instrument has its great speculum 20 feet in focal length, and 20 inches in diameter; but it differs from all other telescopes in the remarkable facility with which it can be used. Its tube moves vertically upon hollow trunnions, through which the astronomer, seated in a little observatory, with only a horizontal motion, can view at his ease every part of the heavens. Hitherto, the astronomer has been obliged to seat himself at the upper end of his Newtonian telescope; and if no other observer will acknowledge the awkwardness and insecurity of his position, I can myself vouch for its danger, having fallen from the very top of Mr. Ramage's 20-feet telescope when it was directed to a point not very far from the zenith.

" It has been long known, both from theory and in practice, that the imperfect transparency of the earth's atmosphere, and the unequal refraction which arises from differences of temperature, combine to set a limit to the use of high magnifying powers in our telescopes. Hitherto, however, the application of such high powers was checked by the imperfections of the instruments themselves; and it is only since the construction of Lord Rosse's telescope that astronomers have found that, in our damp and variable climate, it is only during a few days of the year that telescopes of such magnitude can use successfully the high magnifying powers which they are capable of bearing. Even in a cloudless sky, when the stars are sparkling in the firmament, the astronomer is baffled by influences which are invisible, and while new planets and new satellites are being discovered by instruments comparatively small, the gigantic Polyphemus lies slumbering in his cave, blinded by thermal currents more irresistible than the firebrand of Ulysses. As the astronomer, however, cannot command a tempest to clear his atmosphere, nor a thunder storm to purify it, his only alternative is to remove his telescope to some southern climate, where no clouds disturb the serenity of the firmament, and no changes of temperature distract the emanations of the stars. A fact has been recently mentioned, which entitles us to anticipate great results from such a measure. The Marquis of Ormonde is said to have seen from Mount Etna, with his naked eye, the satellites of Jupiter. If this be true, what discoveries may we not expect, even in Europe, from a large reflector working above the grosser strata of our atmosphere! This noble experiment of sending a large reflector to a southern climate has been but once

made in the history of science. Sir John Herschel transported his telescopes and his family to the South of Africa, and during a voluntary exile of four years' duration he enriched astronomy with many splendid discoveries. Such a sacrifice, however, is not likely to be made again; and we must, therefore, look to the aid of Government for the realization of a project which every civilized people will applaud, and which, by adding to the conquests of science, will add to the glory of our country."

" On Cotton Manufactures." By Mr. G. R. Porter.

The importance to this country of a certain and ample supply of the raw material of our cotton manufactures can hardly be overrated. As an assurance against the fluctuations of the supply of cotton, the author proposes to extend the cultivation of another material, viz. flax, to which the existing machinery, with some slight modifications, would be applicable. Flax can be cultivated in any part of England, would afford a profitable crop to the farmer, and employ the surplus labour, while the millowner would, to a certain extent, be rendered independent of the supply of cotton.

" On the Sugar Produce of the South of Spain, chiefly in connexion with the employment of the Acetate of Lead and Sulphurous Acid as purifying agents." By Dr. Scoffern.

On the southern coast of Spain, in a region limited by Almeira on the east, and Malaga on the west, bounded on the north by mountain ranges, and on the south by the Mediterranean, is a tract of land which, so far as its climate and productions are concerned, may be aptly denominated tropical. In it the date, palm, indigo, cotton, and sugar-cane flourish with vigour, yielding products equal both in quantity and quality to those of the tropics themselves. The sugar-cane, first introduced by the Arab conquerors, is not only consumed in large quantities as a dessert, but also gives rise to a considerable manufacture of raw and refined sugar, a circumstance which, beyond Spain itself, seems to be very little known. There is perhaps no example on record of any operation involving a commercial result attended with such an enormous destruction of material, as the operation of extracting sugar from the cane. One portion of this loss is due to mechanical, another to chemical causes. The sugar-cane has been stated by most writers who have found opportunities of practically examining the subject, to contain no more than 10 per cent. of solid non-saccharine matter, leaving 90 per cent. of juice to be extracted. Of this 90 per cent., most writers concur in testifying that in practice scarcely 50 per cent. are actually obtained; at least in the British West India possessions. Cane juice itself has usually been stated to contain from 17 to 23 per cent. of crystalline sugar, of which scarcely 7 per cent. in practice is actually extracted. Considerable doubts having been expressed as to these statements of the amount of juice in the cane, and sugar in the juice, I have lately gone through a series of experiments having for their object the settlement of the doubt, and with the result of amply confirming the testimony of other experimenters. Having operated on canes from various parts of this district, by slicing them,—exhausting first by hot water and then by hot alcohol, and finally drying, I obtained as my mean result about 10 per cent. of woody or insoluble matter—whilst the sugar extracted and crystallized ranged from 17 to 23 per cent., as had previously been stated. It would consequently appear that 40 per cent. of juice is actually lost in the practice of our West India workings; and now arises, as a most important consideration, the question as to what extent this loss is inevitable, and to what extent it might have been obviated by altered machinery or improved manipulation. Instead of 50 per cent. of juice extracted, 70 per cent. is much nearer the average amount yielded by the sugar-mills of this coast, although occasionally the result is as high as 75 per cent., and this, in some cases, with mills of very inferior construction. The cane, however, is passed between the rollers of the mill four times, until the refuse or megass, as the pressed cane is called, has been reduced to a state of disaggregation resembling ground tan, whereas the West India cane refuse is represented to be in the form of long strings, a sufficient proof that the pressure applied has been very inadequate. After the cane has finally left the mill it is immediately, in the Spanish sugar regions, subjected to the operation of pressing, sometimes by the agency of a screw, but in many cases by hydrostatic force. By the latter method, I have seen 13 per cent. of juice extracted from megass which had already yielded up 73 per cent. of juice to the mill, thus elevating the total quantity extracted to 86 per cent. out of the original 90, and consequently as a manufacturing operation leaving very little more to be desired. The hydrostatic press I consider to be an apparatus which is indispensable to the economy of every sugar estate :—not only does it largely contribute to the amount of juice extracted,—but what is most remarkable is, the juice resulting from hydrostatic pressure of megass is invariably, so far as my observations have gone, richer in sugar than juice yielded by the mill,—a fact which seems to be only explicable on the supposition that the hydrostatic press, in virtue of its great power, is enabled to extrude those particles of sugar which microscopic examination demonstrates to exist in the cane in the solid and crystalline form. The subsequent stages of the sugar manufacture, as carried on in Spain, do not materially differ from those in operation in Cuba, and many other tropical countries. The juice is defecated or purified by lime, skimmed, evaporated to the requisite degree, and poured into earthenware moulds, the contents of which are finally exposed to the operation of claying. In one manufactory, however, witnessed by me, at Almunecar, lime is no longer used, on account of its well-known injurious effects on sugar: —no other agent having been substituted in its stead, but sole reliance being placed on the coagulation by heat of albuminous matters present in the juice, and their final removal by skimming. Under this system of manufacture the sugar produced is light coloured, but badly grained, and the unseparated albuminous matters are present in such quantity, that every 100 parts of the concentrated saccharine juice, as it comes from the teache, or last evaporating pan, only yield 40 parts of crystallized sugar on cooling, the other 60 per cent. remaining in the condition of molasses, perfectly uncrystallizable until some adequate means for defecation be had recourse to. The chief object of my residence in this sugar district was to superintend the erection of machinery for manufacturing sugar, by means of my own process. The site of our operations is Montril, about forty-five miles south of Granada,—in a manufactory furnished with apparatus of the rudest character. Up to this period (July 9) our own vacuum apparatus has not been sufficiently advanced to enable us to pursue our operations by its aid; nevertheless, owing to the superior defecating power of the sub-acetate of lead, we have, even with the old and rude machinery, obtained a result of more than 16, instead of 7 per cent. of sugar. Our striking teaches, or final evaporating pans, we were under the necessity of removing, in order to afford the requisite space for our own machinery; hence we were reduced to the necessity of concluding our process of concentration in a brass pan of conical form, and holding about 600 imperial gallons, thus materially increasing the difficulty of the evaporative process. Hitherto only one-sixth per cent. on the juice of sub-acetate has been used,— but I imagine the quantity may be advantageously increased. As filtration is indispensable for the conducting of this process, considerable fear was entertained lest fermentation might supervene. This fear, however, practice has demonstrated to be groundless, inasmuch as we possess, in sulphurous acid, an agent most antagonistic to fermentation. Another speculative fear was, lest danger might arise from the lead employed: this fear, too, practice demonstrates to be entirely without foundation, for not only is the sulphite of lead most easily removed,—but even were it to remain no injury could supervene, inasmuch as this agent is as harmless as chalk.[*]

In continuation :—Observations on the Sulphite of Lead were made by Dr. Gregory,—who stated that he had made experiments on the sulphite of lead formed in this process. He admitted that an infinitely small proportion might still remain in the sugar, but that he considered it quite innocuous. He had indeed fed rabbits and dogs with food which had been united with this sulphite of lead, and the result was that they thrived amazingly, showing no symptom of any of the known effects of lead. Dr. Gregory also remarked that, in testing sugar for lead with the hydro-sulphuret of ammonia, iron was often mistaken for the former metal.

Dr. Christison contended that we had no evidence that the sulphite of lead was innocuous. It was true that in cases of poisoning by carbonate of lead, sulphuric acid was administered to convert it into the comparatively insoluble sulphate; but this was a case widely different from the slow accumulation of lead upon the system. Dr. Christison adduced some examples of exceedingly small doses of lead being taken in water for more than twelve months before its evil effects became apparent. He, therefore, thought it yet remained to be proved that the sulphite of lead was without action on the system, since we know nothing of the influence of the solvents it would meet with in the system, or of the influences of vital action. Rabbits, he was prepared to say, should be entirely rejected in these inquiries, since he had found that they were not affected by many poisons. Dogs and cats were the only animals which could, from their internal structure be regarded as the representatives of the human system in these investigations.

"On the Incrustations in Boilers." By Dr. J. Davy.

Contains nothing with which our readers will be unacquainted.

Mr. J. Scott Russell, "On the Wave System."

Mr. Scott Russell read a report from Rio Janeiro, which narrated the progress that had been made in the Brazils, within the last six years, in the application of the principles of the Wave System to the practical construction of ships, both of steam vessels and of sailing vessels. Mr. Butler Dodgson is a naval architect, employed in the Parts de Aria Iron Works and Dockyard, an establishment largely engaged for Government in the construction of ships and steam vessels. He had early read the reports of the British Association which contained an account of the wave system, and had been enabled to construct a number of vessels upon that system, and the present communication showed that he had done so with perfect success. The vessels built on this principle possess, not only greater speed than others, but also every other good quality as sea-going vessels. Mr. Butler Dodgson encountered the usual opposition from the interests of rivals, and the prejudices of men in office; but having tested and established the value of the principle, he is now employed to build large steamers for the Government on that principle.—Dr. Robinson expressed his regret that knowledge of which foreign Governments were thus enabled to avail themselves was not turned to practical account by Government at home. The British Association had made application to the Government of this country, to render the researches of Mr. Scott Russell, which had been carried on under the auspices of the Association, available to the public service; but hitherto without success.—A discussion arose regarding the recent applications of the wave principle to the con-

---

[*] It was lately stated in the House of Commons, that sugar prepared on Dr. Scoffern's patent process had been analysed by several eminent chemists, and that no traces of lead were found to exist in it, but that lead was found in the treacle. Dr. Scoffern had, however, very fairly offered that he and his family would eat any reasonable quantity of the said treacle, to prove its innocence. So little is the self-denial of the man of science appreciated, that we are informed the Hon. House received the announcement with "loud laughter".—ED.

struction of sailing-yacht schooners in England. The *Titania** had proved herself to be the fastest yacht of her size, and to possess in a high degree the qualities of a sea-going vessel, and she was built on the wave principle.

Section G.—Mechanical Science.

Mr. Nasmyth gave an account of his new arrangement of the reflecting telescope, by which great additional comfort was afforded to the observer. This consisted in having the centering or trunnions at the centre of gravity; through one of which, in a tubular form, the rays from the reflector within were thrown into the eye thus placed, as in the Newtonian telescope at the side. The advantage from this arrangement is, that the eye does not require to move upon a movement of the telescope. Mr. Nasmyth then described his plan of casting specula, by which unsoundness was avoided.

Prof. Smith explained a new form of equatorial at present constructing for the Edinburgh Observatory, and a folding dome for extra meridian instruments. After this he explained a mode of cooling the air in tropical climates. This was in the first instance to condense air by mechanical means. Then to allow the air thus condensed, and consequently heated, to fall to the common temperature. The condensed air thus let loose, and allowed to fall into a room, would, by its expansion, lower all the air with which it comes in contact. He had tested the principle on a large scale, and found it to answer his expectations. Mr. Taylor knew of men working in one of the Cornish mines at a temperature of 110°. It would now be possible to send them down a treat of cold air, which he had no doubt they would relish as much as a lady does an ice on a hot day.—Mr. Rankine said, in reference to the power required, that he had made the calculation, and the result was, that one horse working for one hour lowers 9,000 cubic feet of air 20°; and, of course, in this proportion for all other cases. This was exclusive of friction.

Mr. Lassell, of Liverpool, gave an account of his new method of supporting a large speculum free from sensible flexure in all positions. This he proposed to do when in a horizontal position, by supporting it at eighteen different points on which the weight might bear equally; and by casting the speculum with ribs, he proposed to adapt levers, that when the telescope is elevated, they might bear the weight among them, and thus prevent it from disturbing the true form of this speculum.—The President of the Section said that the evil arising from flexure was much felt in Lord Rosse's telescope, and of course lay much in the way of its efficiency.

"On a Register Hygrometer for regulating the Atmospheric Moisture of Houses." By Mr. Appold.

This instrument, with a variation of one quarter of a degree in the hygrometric state of the atmosphere, opens a valve capable of supplying ten quarts of water per hour, conveying it on to the surface of warm pipes covered with blotting paper, by which the water is evaporated until the atmosphere is sufficiently saturated, and the valve thereby closed. A lead pencil attached registers the distance the hygrometer travels, and thus a sheet of paper moved by a clock would show the hygrometric state of the atmosphere at any period of time.

"On a Gas Stove." By Mr. W. S. Ward.

The novelty of this consists in constructing the stove in a vertical position, so as to expose considerable surfaces for the absorption of

* For dimensions of the *Titania* see *ante*, p. 69.

heat from gas burners, and for the radiation of the heat. The author found that his apparatus was sufficient to raise the temperature of a moderate-sized room from 5 to 10 deg. Fah., with a consumption of about 3 feet of gas per hour, costing about 2d. for ten hours; and that it was particularly useful in warming a bed-room, where only a slight elevation of temperature was required, and free from the production of dirt or smell.

Mr. Whitworth's communication "On a New Duplex Turning-lathe." was then read by Mr. Scott Russell.

The improvement suggested not only doubled the quantity of work, but did it in a much better style. It was to have two cutters on opposite sides of the cylinder to be turned, thus at once increasing the performance, and rendering that better by removing the tremor which would necessarily arise.

"On the Value of the Gaseous Escape from the Blast Furnaces at the Ystalfera Iron Works," in continuation of a paper read at the meeting of the Association in 1848. By Mr. Palmer Budd.

Mr. Budd stated that, since the meeting of the Association at Swansea, he had continued, and with increased success, to apply the waste gases that escaped from the top of blast furnaces, to the manufacture of iron; and it was the result of his further experience applied to the whole of his furnaces (nine in number) since that period, that he now wished to submit to the Section. Mr. Budd then referred to his mode of applying the gaseous escape, and said it was well known that there were two descriptions of furnaces used for metallurgic purposes. The one was the blast furnace, into which air was injected, by mechanical means, at a great density, so as to penetrate upwards of 40 feet of dense materials; and the other was the reverberatory furnace, where the fire was produced by means of the draught of a chimney stack. What he had accomplished was by combining these two, so that the gaseous products of the furnace, instead of escaping through the tunnel head, were drawn sideways by a high stack, and passing through the stoves and boilers, leave behind the necessary temperature of the blast and of the steam. In a blast furnace the ores are smelted before the *tuyères* by the conversion of the solid carbon into carbonic acid, which, passing up through the middle region of the furnace into a bath of carbon, was reconverted into carbonic oxide, capable of combining with a further dose of oxygen. It would be thus seen that the whole of the carbon of the fuel should be present at the top of the furnace in a gaseous form. When the British Association met at Swansea, he had not used the gaseous escape at any great distance from the furnace, his stoves and boilers being very closely contiguous. Further experience, however, had proved that by the aid of a stack at the end of the chain of sufficient dimensions, the gaseous escape from the furnace might be made to travel in the most tortuous directions, descending to the stoves built for heating by the usual fire-places, and traversing the boilers; the only condition absolutely necessary being that there should be an unbroken communication with the high stack at the end, into which the gaseous escape might at last pass, and by which it was drawn forward, instead of passing off wastefully at the tunnel-head. When, however, the draft was carried downward, and to long distances, he had found it necessary to drop into the top of the furnace a hopper or funnel, made of sheet-iron, which acted as a shield at the mouths of the horizontal flues, and prevented them from either being affected by high winds, or from being choked up by materials thrown into the furnace. The reason, no doubt, why this funnel was not applied before was the great apparent temperature at the funnel-head. In practice, however, it was found that until the gaseous escape mingled with the atmosphere, its heating power was not such as to injure sheet-iron, or even to make it red-hot. In fact, so long as there was an escape upwards, the iron funnel would not be injured. The damage arose during and after stoppages of the furnace, when the blast was obstructed in its passage upwards by the settlement of the materials in the furnace, so that the atmosphere rushed down to meet the ascending gases, and, of course, caused a very high local temperature. His practice was to exclude the atmospheric air as much as possible. The affinity of the gases for oxygen was so great that the air leakage raised the temperature quite sufficient for safety, whilst the full combustion of the gaseous escape would melt down the bricks in the flues, and destroy the texture of the iron tube. It was not possible for him to say what combinations took place at high temperatures, where carbonic oxide, carbonic acid, hydrogen, and nitrogen, were mixed in such proportions. At any rate, he found a smothered combustion to be the most suitable and economical for the purposes in view. He was happy to say that, at length, the application of the gaseous escape had been tried in Scotland ; and that at Dundyvan and elsewhere it was now in successful operation. The peculiar quality of the furnace coal of Scotland being what was called in South Wales "free burning," which, when put into the furnace raw, coked sufficiently in its descent, gave out an enormous escape, so much so that, upon a rough estimate, he calculated that the waste from one furnace in Scotland was sufficient to heat the blast, and to raise the steam for three. With anthracite coal, the minimum effect was obtained, as it was a dense fuel of nearly 95 per cent. of solid carbon ; but in Scotland there would be an enormous surplus at the tunnel-head. He observed that the saving at the Dundyvan Iron Works was stated to be about 1¼ tons for each ton of iron produced. Supposing, therefore, 600,000 tons of iron to be the produce of Scotland, and supposing the value of the coal used to be 3s. a ton, the saving that would thus be effected on the make of Scotland would amount to £112,500 a-year; to which might be added £20,000 a-year of saving in wages and repairs, which would make a total saving of £132,500, or about 4s. 5d. a ton on the produce of Scotland, which on the present price of 44s. per ton, was about 10 per cent. on the value. If the gaseous escape could be extended to the use of the forge, a further saving of three tons of coal would be effected,—thus making, at least, a saving of 20s. a ton on all the iron manufactured into bars, sheets, and rails.

Mr. G. Beattie gave a description of his new Door Spring, and exhibited one of the springs in working order—the motive power being the pressure of the atmosphere. Mr. Beattie's application of this natural law is simple in the contrivance. When the door is opening, it withdraws a tight piston from the closed end of a cylinder, which leaves a vacuum behind the piston, and the pressure of the atmosphere upon the piston forces it back to its place, and closes the door. This cylinder has an exhausted chamber in connexion with it for giving the door a maintaining power when shut. There is also working with the first cylinder and piston a dwarf cylinder and piston for regulating the speed the door is wished to be closed at, which has perfect control over the travel of the door, either in allowing it to shut at once or to take any given time. The advantages this door closer possesses are that the resistance is uniform when opening the door ; and when shutting it there can be no increase of speed beyond that to which it is set, and consequently no slamming or noise.

Mr. Stevenson made a statement of the result of certain observations made by him on the Force of the Waves with reference to the Construction of Marine Works.

The object of Mr. Stevenson's experiments is to ascertain by means of a self-registering instrument the force of the waves per square foot of surface. The instrument consists in a disc on which the sea impinges, and the impact is registered by means of a spiral spring. The result of the experiments hitherto made, may be stated to be a force of about 1½ tons per square foot for the German Ocean, and of 3 tons for the Atlantic Ocean. The experiments from which these results were obtained being made at the Bell Rock and Skerryvore lighthouses.

"On the Limits to the Velocity of Revolving Lighthouse Apparatus, caused by the time required for the production of Luminous Impressions on the Eye." By Mr. Swan.

Mr. Swan having referred to the well-known fact that the impressions of light remain for a definitive portion of time, about one-tenth of a second, said that no experiments so far as he knew had been made as to the time required for making the impression. His experiments had been undertaken with this view. The brightness of the impression he found to be in proportion to the time of making it. When the time was one-fifticth of a second, for example, the brightness of the impression was about one-tenth of the brightness of the full light. From this Mr. Swan inferred that the light could not exceed a certain rate of revolution, otherwise a sufficiently vivid impression could not be made upon the eye.

The President then communicated the substance of a note which he had received from M. Jules Guyot, claiming the priority of the invention of the tubular bridge, and contending, it would appear, that English engineers had taken the idea from him.

Sir C. Pasley said that Mr. Stephenson laid claim to the invention of iron girders, whether great or small, and upon this he rested his claim to the invention of the tubular bridge. He had seen his first idea, which was rejected by the Admiralty from its not affording space enough for the navigation of the Strait. His next idea was two oval tubes, resting upon a pillar on the Britannia Rock. He believed that up to this time no idea had been formed of a tubular bridge. The next step was the rectangular form, which was shown to be the best, by the experiments of Fairbairn. He thought that the particular form was due to Fairbairn, while he believed the original idea of the tubular bridge to be due to Stephenson.

Sir D. Brewster observed, that if Stephenson admits, which he seems to have done, that the invention of the girder was the invention of the tubular bridge, then it certainly did follow that, just as a telescope of a foot long was as much a telescope as that of Lord Rosse's, the invention was due to Stephenson. He did think, however, that Stephenson had claimed too much, and the risk was, he would get credit for less than was his due.

Dr. Robinson remarked that if the letters arising out of the controversy touching this affair between Stephenson and Fairbairn were to be relied on, he was of opinion that Stephenson had extended his claim too far. It did appear to him (Dr. Robinson) that up to a late period Mr. Stephenson had no idea at all of any other than the tensile force, and that the resistance to a compressive force had not yet entered his mind.

The Astronomer Royal expressed his great regret that a controversy of this kind had been admitted into the British Association. He protested against all discussions of this kind, as being foreign to its objects, and calculated in no small degree to disturb the harmony of its deliberations.

Sir D. Brewster having been boldly told when in France that the idea of the tubular bridge had been stolen by the English, he felt bound to defend his countrymen from such an allegation. He did not see why the discussion could not be conducted in kindness, and with the simple idea of determining the truth.

BUILDING FOR THE EXHIBITION OF 1851.

At a public meeting in Bakewell, last week, Mr. Paxton gave some interesting explanations of the construction of his design of a building for the Show of Industry and Art in Hyde Park.

Mr. Paxton stated that it was not till after the rise of the squabble in the newspapers about the site that he had turned any attention to the matter. When his attention was fixed on the subject, he resolved, without knowing anything of any other plan, or even obtaining a prospectus, to attempt something which he thought suitable for the occasion. The building would be 2,100 feet long by 400 broad. The centre aisle would be 120 feet broad, or ten feet wider than the Conservatory at Chatsworth. So vast a structure as this must necessarily be made as simple as possible in its details, else it would be impossible to carry it out: therefore the glass and its iron supports comprise the whole structure. The columns are precisely the same throughout the building, and will fit every part; the same may be said of each of the bars; and every piece of glass will be of the same size, namely, four feet long. No numbering or marking will be required, and the whole will be put together like a perfect piece of machinery. The water is brought down valleys on the roof, and thence down the columns; the water in no instance has further than twelve feet to run before it is delivered into the valleys or gutters; and the whole is so constructed as to carry the rain water outside, and the condensed water inside. The building is divided into broad and narrow compartments, and by tying these together there is little for the cross-ties of the centre to carry. It is entirely divided into twenty-four places—in short, everything runs to twenty-four, so that the work is made to square and fit, without any small detail being left to carry out. The number of columns fifteen feet long is 6,024; there are 3,000 gallery-bearers; 1,245 wrought-iron girders; forty-five miles of sash-bars; and 1,073,760 feet of glass to cover the whole. The site will stand upon upwards of twenty acres of ground; but by a special arrangement the available space which may be afforded by galleries can be extended to about thirty acres, if necessary. With regard to the ventilation and the rays of light, he would say that the former was a very peculiar part of the plan. The whole building, four feet round the bottom, will be filled with louver boards, so placed as to admit air but exclude rain. On the inside of that there will be a canvass to move up and down, and in very hot weather this may be watered and the interior kept cool. The top part of the centre building is put up almost entirely for the purposes of ventilation; and he thought it would be found that if he had erred at all in respect of the means of ventilation, there would be found too much rather than too little. By covering the greater part of the building with canvass, a gentle light will be thrown over the whole building; and the whole of the glass at the top of the northern side of the building will give a direct light to the interior. If more light be wanted, the means of affording it are provided.

The building will be covered in by the 1st of January next: he was as firmly persuaded that the contract would be accomplished to the day, as he was certain that he then addressed that meeting.

The gallery of the building will be twenty-four feet wide, and will extend a distance of six miles. Now if, after the purposes of the exhibition are answered, it were thought desirable to let the building remain—and he sincerely hoped it would not be pulled down nor shipped to America—if they chose to let it remain, see to what a purpose it might be applied. There might be made an excellent carriage-drive round the interior, as well as a road for equestrians, with the centre tastefully laid out and planted; and then there would be nearly six miles of room in the galleries for a promenade for the public.

The Duke of Devonshire assured the meeting that they might depend upon it there is no doubt of the success of this admirable plan; "for Mr. Paxton has never attempted anything which he has not succeeded in fully carrying out."

Mr. Paxton rose again, and observed, that simple as the details of the work might appear, people must not imagine that it was the invention of a dream—an Arabian night's entertainment.

It was the growth of a number of years of deep thought and practice; and unless the conservatory at Chatsworth had been first made this would not have been erected. The experience he gathered in the erection of that building had not been lost upon the one about to be erected; which was a better design, in some respects, and constructed upon a more economical principle. Such a design, however, could not have been erected twenty-four years ago, on account of the cost of the glass, which would have been more than the whole cost of the proposed building. The erection of the conservatory was the principal cause of introducing this particular form of glass into this country. He was anxious, in order to avoid the collection of dirt, not to have a lap in the glass; and he went to the establishment of Chance, of Birmingham, where he met with a French and a Belgian manufacturer, whom he prevailed on to make the glass for the conservatory four feet long. They did so; and the introduction of it led the Birmingham manufacturers to prepare the same, and they now make the best of any country,—a striking illustration, among many that might be given, of the benefits to be derived from the exhibition itself.

Mr. Barker, who seems to be a local owner of mines and a manufacturer, made an interesting speech in illustration of the benefits we have derived by admitting foreign competition: the fact is, we have more to gain than to lose by seeing the productions of foreigners.

The art of inlaying in marble was a striking illustration of the truth of this. It was practised to some extent in that neighbourhood, and the execution of the work was far superior to the Florentine mosaic of that description. But the fertility and beauty of design among the Italians secured them a ready sale for their works in this country, to the exclusion of the productions of Derbyshire. He exhibited a beautiful table of black marble, inlaid with flowers of various colours, the work of Mr. Woodruff, of Bakewell; and he showed, by some smaller specimens, the mode in which the inlaying is executed, and the extreme minuteness and accuracy with which the parts to be inlaid are fitted to the groundwork. Mr. Woodruff has asked for a design of some work which he desires to execute in a style worthy of the Show next year; and he has no fear of being excelled by foreigners in execution. Mr. Barker pointed to some products of lead, and declared himself willing to explain their manufacture to foreigners. He had always found that those smelters and manufacturers of lead who kept their doors closed to their competitors in the trade were invariably surpassed by those who freely exchanged information at the same time that they carried on an honourable and vigorous spirit of emulation.

Lately, at the laboratory of the Ecoles des Mines in Paris, the chemical professors gave him the analyses of various metallic products, which he had never before seen analyzed; and with the utmost liberality they offered to submit to analysis all mineral substances which he would at any time send to them, and to furnish him with the results without any charge. Such an offer made him blush with shame to think that England, the richest country in the world in metals and minerals, was without any school of instruction in mining and metallurgy; while France, so comparatively poor in her metallic products, possessed the finest school in the world. He felt that, standing there with all his English associations and prejudices weighing upon him, he was not in so fit a condition to give an impartial judgment on the merits of this great exhibition as if he were on the Continent of Europe or in America among his Anglo-Saxon brethren. But if he might judge from what he had recently heard from enlightened foreigners of various nations, he should say, that this gathering of all nations was viewed by them as the grandest design which had ever been conceived by any nation in the world, and calculated to produce most important results, both in a social and commercial point of view, to the inhabitants of every country who may participate in it.

DIMENSIONS AND DETAILS OF NEW STEAMERS.

THE UNION (AMERICAN) STEAM NAVIGATION COMPANY'S IRON VESSEL, "FOYLE."

Length on deck, 196 feet; beam, 25 feet; depth of hold, 16 feet; length of quarter deck, 44 feet; breadth, 26 feet; and depth, 2 feet.

Tonnage, 761 tons. Contents of engine room, 259 tons.

Draft of water, 8 feet 6 inches.

Cylinders, $68\frac{3}{8}$ inches in diameter, with 6 feet 6 inches stroke of piston.

Air Pumps, 42 inches in diameter.

Cylinder Trunnions, 25.5 inches in diameter, and 8 inches in length.

Water Wheels, 26.5 feet in diameter by 8.5 feet in width. Buckets, 27.5 inches in depth. Arms, three sets of 24 in each wheel.

Boilers, two tubular boilers, with 3 furnaces at each end; length, 16 feet 1.5 inches; breadth, 9 feet 7 inches; height, 13 feet 10 inches. Grates, 12.5 square feet in each. Furnaces, 5 × 2.5 feet, and 3.25 feet deep, including ash pit. Tubes, 165 at each end, 3.25 inches internal diameter, and 4.625 inches from centres.

Revolutions, 21 5 per minute. Nominal power of engines, 372 horses.

Hull, of wrought iron. 13 strokes of plates from keel to gunwale diminishing upwards from $\frac{3}{4}$ to $\frac{1}{2}$ inch in thickness. Frames 18 inches apart a-midships, and 22 inches fore and aft, $\frac{7}{16} \times 2\frac{7}{8} \times 4$ inches of L iron.

PROGRESS OF SHIP BUILDING AND STEAM NAVIGATION.

(*From our own Correspondents.*)

LONDON.

Trial of *Her Majesty.*—On the 7th instant, we had the pleasure of being present at the trial of a very elegant little vessel, named *Her Majesty*, built and fitted by Messrs. Robinsons & Russell, for the Portsmouth and Ryde Royal Mail Steam Packet Company. The engines are oscillating, fitted with feathering paddle-wheels, and tubular boiler. The ports and slides are double, and placed at an angle; the air-pump is oblique and worked with a trunk, dispensing with cross-head and guides. The entablature is of wrought iron, and lightness has been studied in every detail. The cabins are very neatly finished, and the boat throughout does the builders very great credit. The masts are made to lower, the feet being stepped in cast-iron shoes, turning on a joint fixed to the deck. The *London Pride*, one of the fastest of the above-bridge boats, accompanied her to Gravesend, to bring back the company, but proved no match for her speed. The following are her dimensions:—

	Ft.	In.
Length between perpendiculars	123	0
Breadth of beam	14	0
Depth of hold	7	0
Tonnage, O. M.	119$\frac{32}{94}$	

Immersed sectional area, 46 square feet; draft of water, 4 feet; speed of vessel, 12⅜ knots = 14⅜ miles; diameter of paddle, effective, 9 feet, extreme, 11 feet; length of floats, 5 feet; breadth of do. 2 feet, number of do. 9 feet; revolutions per minute, (average,) 58. Diameter of cylinder, 27 inches; length of stroke, 2 feet 6 inches; dimensions of ports, 10″ × 1″¾ inches; stroke of valve, 3¼ inches; lap on steam side, 1¼ inches; nominal power, 40 horses; pressure of steam in boiler, 15 lbs.; steam cut off at ⅜ of stroke.

Messrs. Robinson & Russell have at present on the stocks, two iron steamers of the following dimensions:—

	Ft.	In.
Length between perpendiculars ..	166	0
Breadth of beam	26	0
Depth of hold	10	6
Breadth including paddle-boxes ..	43	0
Burden in tons O. M. ..	519$\frac{32}{94}$	

A pair of oscillating engines of 160 nominal horse power, with malleable iron framing, forming part and combined with hull of vessel.

	Ft.	In.
Diameter of cylinders	0	48
Length of stroke	4	6
Diameter of paddle-wheels, extreme ..	17	0
ditto effective ..	16	0
Sets floats	18	0

Four tubular boilers to each vessel; stipulated speed, 15 miles per hour.

BRISTOL.

Messrs. C. Hill & Co. have on the stocks, a 12 years, A. 1, brig.

	Ft.	In.
Length between perpendiculars ..	88	6
Breadth	23	6
Depth of hold	16	4
Register measurement ..	240 tons	

They have also lately built the 12 years, A. 1, barque *Moultan*.

	Ft.	In.
Length between perpendiculars ..	96	7
Breadth	23	6
Depth	18	2
Register measurement	372 tons.	

Messrs. Paterson are converting the timbers for the new West India Mail boat, which will make some work for the shipwrights at this port.

NEWCASTLE.

Messrs. Joseph and John Mair, St. Peter's Quay, have upon the stocks, nearly ready for launching, a 12 years' barque, for the foreign trade, half-poop.

	Ft.	In.
Length of keel and fore rake	113	0
Breadth of beam	28	2
Depth of hold	18	6
Rake of stem	9	0
Tonnage	406$\frac{41}{94}$	

Messrs. Ambrose and Richard Hopper, North Shore, have re-built the French brigantine, *Esther*, of Caen, where the vessel was built in 1838. She was abandoned at sea, and afterwards brought in and sold. Now named the *Nancy*, of Newcastle, and sheathed with zinc. Classed 7 years, A 1, at Lloyd's.

	Ft.	Tns.
Length on deck	67	6
Breath on ditto	18	7
Depth of hold	8	9
Tonnage	87$\frac{1}{10}$	

Messrs. Mills and Fulton, North Shore, have upon the stocks a brig to class 7 years, A 1, at Lloyd's, for the foreign trade, and nearly ready for launching. Flush on deck.

	Ft.	In.
Length of keel and fore rake ..	101	0
Breadth of beam	27	0
Depth of hold	17	0
Rake of stem	7	0
Tonnage	281$\frac{41}{94}$	

They launched, in 1849, a brig for the coal trade, named the *Wrights*, of South Shields, to class 7 years.

	Ft.	In.
Length of keel and fore rake ..	90	0
Breadth of beam	25	0
Depth of hold	16	6
Tonnage	240$\frac{41}{94}$	
New measurement.	Ft.	Tns.
Length on deck ..	92	5
Breadth on ditto at midships ..	22	5
Depth of hold	16	4
Tonnage	255$\frac{52}{94}$	

Carries 18 keels of coals.

BLACKWALL (DURHAM).

Mr. Jonathan Robson has upon the stocks an iron paddle steamer, all plated, to ply upon the river Volga, in Russia, and is only to draw 2 feet 8 inches, with all on board.

	Ft.	In.
Length of keel and fore rake ..	89	0
Breadth of beam	16	6
Depth of hold	7	9
Tonnage, ...	114$\frac{41}{94}$	

One half lever engine of 30 horse nominal power. Diameter of cylinder, 30 inches × 3 feet 6 inches length of stroke; one iron tubular boiler, length 8 feet 9 inches, breadth 8 feet, depth 7 feet 6 inches, with

28

3 furnaces and 58 tubes 4 inches in diameter. There are 7 strakes of plates from keel to gunwale; frames $3\frac{1}{2} \times 2 \times \frac{3}{8}$, and from 24 to 28 inches apart. This steamer is built flush upon deck, with a round stern and clinch built, and seems well adapted for her destined service.

TYNE MAIN (DURHAM.)

Messrs. Gady and Lamb have upon the stocks, all planked, a barque for the India trade, with a half-poop, and to class 9 years, A 1, at Lloyd's, of the following dimensions :—

	Ft.	In.
Length of keel and fore rake	116	6
Breadth of beam	28	6
Depth of hold	18	9
Rake of stem, forward	8	6
Tonnage	$436\frac{71}{94}$	

In 1849 there was launched from this yard the brigantine, *Doughty*, of the following dimensions :—

	Ft.	Tns.
Length on deck	77	2
Breadth on ditto, at midships	20	3
Depth of hold, ditto	11	8
Tonnage	$143\frac{1648}{3500}$	

FRIAR'S GOOSE (DURHAM.)

Messrs. Irwin and Fair have upon the stocks a brig, built flush, for the foreign and coasting trade, nearly planked, to class 7 years, A 1, at Lloyd's, of the following dimensions :—

	Ft.	In.
Length of keel and fore rake	80	6
Breadth of beam	23	0
Depth of hold	12	8
Rake of stem, forward	4	6
Tonnage	$189\frac{14}{94}$	

In 1849, there was launched from this yard the brigantine, *Mary Ogle*, for the coasting trade, of the following dimensions :—

	Ft.	Tns.
Length on deck	72	5
Breadth on ditto, at midships	19	3
Depth of hold, at ditto	11	4
Tonnage	$125\frac{231}{3500}$	

BILL QUAY (DURHAM.)

Mr. Eccles has no vessels building.

Mr. Wm. Boutland has none upon the stocks. There was launched from this yard this year, the sloop *Sunbeam*, for the coasting trade, of the following dimensions :—

	Ft.	Tns.
Length on deck	45	9
Breadth on ditto at midships	15	0
Depth of hold do.	5	6
Tonnage	$28\frac{351}{3500}$	

There was also launched this year, from this yard, the schooner *Emily*, for the coasting trade, of the following dimensions :—

	Ft.	Tns.
Length on deck	53	7
Breadth on ditto at midships	16	1
Depth of hold, ditto	7	7
Tonnage	$53\frac{1146}{3500}$	

PEEL MAIN (DURHAM.)

Mr. William Rennieson has no vessels building, but several being repaired.

HEBURN-QUAY (DURHAM.)

Mr. Thomas Redhead has upon the stocks the brigantine *Theodorick*, which has been lengthened 11 feet 6 inches. This vessel was built at Yarmouth, in the year 1836, and the following were the previous dimensions :—

	Ft.	Tns.
Length on deck	73	0
Breadth on ditto at midships	18	7
Depth of hold at ditto	13	5
Tonnage	$138\frac{1231}{3500}$	

WEST JARROW (DURHAM.)

Mr. Trotter has no vessel building.

EAST JARROW (DURHAM.)

Mr. D. Bider, given up business.

SOUTH SHIELDS (DURHAM.)

Mr. James Young, West Docks, has upon the stocks, all in frame, and nearly planked, a barque for general foreign trade, to be flush upon deck, and to class 8 years, A 1, at Lloyd's, of the following dimensions:

	Ft.	In.
Length of keel and fore rake	98	0
Breadth of beam	27	0
Depth of hold	17	0
Rake of stem, forward	8	0
Tonnage	$319\frac{87}{94}$	

Messrs. Edwards and Shield, High Dock, have just launched (July) a clipper-barque, for the foreign trade, and classed 7 years, A 1, at Lloyd's, of the following dimensions :—

	Ft.	In.
Length of keel and fore rake	93	0
Breadth of beam	24	0
Depth of hold	14	0
Rake of stem, forward	13	0
Tonnage	$241\frac{63}{94}$	

In 1849, they launched the brig *Queenstown*.

Mr. Thomas Forsyth has upon the stocks, and all in frame and nearly planked, a barque for the foreign trade, flush upon deck, to class 9 years, A 1, at Lloyd's, of the following dimensions :—

	Ft.	In.
Length of keel and fore rake	107	0
Breadth of beam	26	8
Depth of hold	17	6
Rake of stem, forward	10	0
Tonnage	$347\frac{11}{94}$	

Messrs. Thomas Metcalfe and Son have upon the stocks, partly planked, a flush built barque, for the foreign trade, to class 9 years, A 1, at Lloyd's, of the following dimensions :—

	Ft.	In.
Length of keel and fore rake	106	0
Breadth of beam	26	0
Depth of hold	16	6
Rake of stem, forward	10	0
Tonnage	$325\frac{1}{94}$	

Messrs. M'Leod and Henderson, Middle-Dock Company, have upon the stocks, and nearly ready for launching, a brig for the foreign and coasting trade, flush on deck, and to class 8 years, A 1, at Lloyd's, and owned by Mr. Thomas Gibson, of North Shields, of the following dimensions :—

	Ft.	In.
Length of keel and fore rake	84	0
Breadth of beam	21	9
Depth of hold	12	6
Rake of stem, forward	6	0
Tonnage	180½	

On the 13th of February, there was launched from this yard, a 13 years, A 1, barque of 500 tons, named the *Mary Florence*, intended for the India trade. Built with poop and top-gallant forecastle.

Also, in July, the brig *Maude*, for the foreign trade, classed 8 years, A 1. In 1849, also, the 13 years, A 1, ship *Havering*, for the India trade.

Messrs. Thomas Young and Son, West Docks, have upon the stocks, all in frame, a ship, to have a poop and top-gallant forecastle, for the East India trade, to class 13 years. A 1, at Lloyd's ; she is the property of the builders. The following are the dimensions :—

	Ft.	In.
Length of keel and fore rake	124	6
Breadth of beam	29	8
Depth of hold	19	10
Rake of stem, forward	8	6
Tonnage	507½	

There was launched from this yard, this year, the barque *Oliver Cromwell*, of 464 tons old, and 504 tons new measurement, classed 13 years, A 1, at Lloyd's, for the East India trade, the property of the builders.

In 1848, there was launched from this yard, the brig *Cambyses*, for the Black Sea trade, of 258 tons old, and 278 tons new ; classed 7 years, A 1, at Lloyd's.

Mr. Thomas Wallis has upon the stocks, nearly planked, a barque, flush upon deck, for the foreign trade, and to class 9 years, A 1, at Lloyd's.

	Ft.	In.
Length of keel and fore rake	102	0
Breadth of beam	26	0
Depth of hold	17	0
Rake of stem, forward	8	0
Tonnage	310½	

The following are the vessels launched since the commencement of the firm, viz., brig *Ocean Child*, 1842, snow, *John and Eleanor*, 1844, ship, *Jenny Lind*, 1846 ; brig *Mellisa*, 1847 ; schooner *Equity*, 1847 ; brig *Terpsichore*, 1848, and schooner *Warbler*, 1849, being 7 vessels in all.

Mr. Luke B. Bushell has upon the stocks, partly in frame, a brig, to class 8 years, A 1, at Lloyd's, and flush upon deck, for the foreign trade, of the following dimensions :—

	Ft.	In.
Length of keel and fore rake	87	0
Breadth of beam	25	6
Depth of hold	15	6
Rake of stem, forward	7	0
Tonnage	252½	

In 1849, launched a brig, sold to a Sunderland firm.

Mr. Andrew Woodhouse has upon the stocks a clinch built steamer, about half built, for the Tyne, of the following dimensions :—

	Ft.	In.
Length of keel and fore rake	71	0
Breadth of beam	14	0
Depth of hold	7	0
Rake of stem, forward	7	0
Tonnage	65½	

One half-lever engine, by Messrs. Hepple and Landells, North Shields.

Messrs. T. W. Wawn and Co. have upon the stocks, all in frame and partly planked, a brig for the foreign trade, to class 8 years, A 1, at Lloyd's, flush upon deck, of the following dimensions :—

	Ft.	In.
Length of keel and fore rake	94	0
Breadth of beam	26	2
Depth of hold	16	0
Rake of stem	7	6
Tonnage	285½	

From this yard, in 1849, there was launched a brig, the *Alfred*, for the coasting trade, of the following dimensions :—

	Ft.	In.
Length of keel and fore rake	82	6
Breadth of beam	24	6
Depth of hold	12	6
Rake of stem, forward	7	6
Tonnage	217½	

NORTH SHORE (NORTHUMBERLAND.)

Messrs. Ambrose and Richard Hopper have just rebuilt the French schooner *Esther*, of Caen, in France, where the vessel was originally built in 1838, but was abandoned at sea, brought in and sold, and is now the brigantine *Nancy*, of Newcastle, and is classed 7 years, A 1, at Lloyd's. She is sheathed with zinc, which is allowed to stand for 7 years if properly coated. The following are the dimensions :—

New measurement.	Ft.	Ins.
Length on deck	67	6
Breadth on ditto at midships	18	7
Depth of hold ditto	8	9
Tonnage	87½	

Messrs. Hills and Fulton have upon the stocks, and planked, a brig, for the foreign trade, flush on deck, to class 7 years, A 1, at Lloyd's, of the following dimensions :—

	Ft.	In.
Length of keel and fore rake	101	0
Breadth of beam	27	0
Depth of hold	17	0
Rake of stem, forward	7	0
Tonnage	331½	

In 1849, there was launched the brig *Wrights*, of South Shields, classed 7 years, A 1, at Lloyd's, of the following dimensions :—

New measurement.	Ft.	Ins.
Length on deck	92	5
Breadth on ditto	22	5
Depth of hold	16	4
Tonnage	255½	

Carries 18 keels of coals.

ST. LAWRENCE (NORTHUMBERLAND.)

Mr. John Elliot has upon the stocks a river steamer, clinch built, all in frame, and nearly planked, of the following dimensions :—

	Ft.	In.
Length of keel and fore rake	67	0
Breadth of beam	12	8
Depth of hold	7	0
Rake of stem, forward	9	0
Tonnage	51½	

One half-lever engine, by Mr. Robert Sharp, Newcastle, of 12 horse nominal power ; diameter of cylinder, 20 inches × 3 feet 3 inches length of stroke ; diameter of paddles, 9 feet ; one flue boiler, with 2 furnaces.

Mr. William Cunningham has upon the stocks, and nearly planked, a barque for the India trade, flush upon deck, to class 8 years, A 1, at Lloyd's, of the following dimensions :—

				Ft.	In.
Length of keel and fore rake	..	..		111	6
Breadth of beam	..	..		27	7
Depth of hold	..	..		18	3
Rake of stem, forward	..	..		9	6
Tonnage	..	..	..	391⁴⁄₉₄	

This vessel is owned by Mr. Thomas Bell, South Shields.

Messrs. Joseph and John Hair and Co. have upon the stocks, all in frame and partly planked, a barque for the India trade, built with a quarter-deck, to class 12 years, A 1, at Lloyd's.

			Ft	In.
Length of keel and fore rake	..	..	113	0
Breadth of beam	..	..	28	2
Depth of hold ..	..	..	18	6
Rake of stem, forward	..	..	9	0
Tonnage ..	..	..	466⁵⁄₄	

Messrs. Thomas and William Smith have upon the stocks a very large poop ship, all in frame and partly planked, about 1000 tons builder's measurement, and classed 14 years, A 1, at Lloyd's, to be employed in the London and East India trade, (belonging to the Messrs. Smiths of Newcastle.) In 1849, this firm launched a very beautiful ship, named the *Blenheim*, and we believe this is the largest timber vessel ever launched into the Tyne: the following are its dimensions, (with spar deck.)

				Ft.	Tns.
Length on deck	..	..		175	6
Breadth on ditto at midships	..	..	37	0
Depth of hold ditto	..	..		29	7
Tonnage ..	..	..		1666¹³⁴⁄₃₅₄	

ST. ANTHONY'S, (NORTHUMBERLAND.)

Mr. Cuthbert Potts has upon the stocks a schooner for the coasting and foreign trade, flush on deck, to class 8 years, A 1, at Lloyd's ; all in frame, (bow to the river,) and of the following dimensions :—

				Ft.	In.
Length of keel and fore rake	..	..		74	0
Breadth of beam	..	..		22	0
Depth of hold	..	..		12	6
Rake of stem, forward	..	..		8	6
Tonnage ..	..	..		154¹⁄₉	

Mr. Joseph William Wilkinson, has upon the stocks, all in frame and partly planked, a schooner for the coasting and foreign trade, flush on deck, to class 7 years, A 1, at Lloyd's, and of the following dimensions :—

				Ft.	In.
Length of keel and fore rake	..	..		86	3
Breadth of beam	..	..		25	0
Depth of hold	..	..		13	0
Rake of stem, forward	..	..		6	3
Tonnage ..	..	..		239⁸⁄₄	

They have also upon the stocks a clinch built river steamer, ready for launching, of the following dimensions :—

				Ft.	In.
Length of keel and fore rake	..	..		75	6
Breadth of beam	..	..		14	0
Depth of hold	..	..		7	0
Rake of stem, forward	..	..		9	0
Tonnage ..	..	..		71¹⁄₄	

LOW WALKER (NORTHUMBERLAND.)

Mr. Thomas Seymour has upon the stocks a brig for the coasting or foreign trade ; flush upon deck, to class 7 years, A 1, at Lloyd's, and of the following dimensions :—

				Ft.	In.
Length of keel and fore rake	..	..		80	0
Breadth of beam	..	..		24	0
Depth of hold	..	..		13	0
Rake of stem, forward	..	..		7	0
Tonnage ..	..	..		201¹⁄₁	

In 1849 there was launched from this yard the brig *Edward and Ann*, employed in the Baltic trade ; also the brig, *Eleanor Grace*, for the same trade ; the following are the dimensions :—

				Ft.	Tns.
Length on deck	..	..		86	8
Breadth on ditto, amidships	..	..	22	3
Depth of hold, ditto	..	..		14	6
Tonnage ..	..	..		224⁴⁄₄	

And the brig *Volusia*, for the Mediterranean trade :—

				Ft.	Tns.
Length on deck	..	..		80	0
Breadth on ditto, amidships	..	..	20	5
Depth of hold	..	..		12	8
Tonnage ..	..	..		158⁹⁹⁄₁₀₀	

Also for the same trade the barque *May Queen* :—

				Ft.	Tns.
Length on deck	..	..		106	6
Breadth on ditto, amidships	..	..	24	4
Depth of hold, ditto	..	..		18	2
Tonnage ..	..	..		361⁵⁶⁄₁₀₀	

WILLINGTON (NORTHUMBERLAND).

Messrs. Charles Smith & Son have upon the stocks, and ready for launching a brig, built with a break-deck :—

New measurement.

			Ft.	Tns.
Length on deck	..	..	90	3
Breadth on ditto, amidships	..	..	21	7
Depth of hold	..	..	15	6
Length of break-deck ..	..	..	15	2
Breadth of ditto	..	..	16	9
Depth of ditto	..	..	1	0
Tonnage.				Tons.
Hull	..	..	..	232¹⁹⁴⁄₅
Break-deck	..	..	..	2¹¹⁶⁄₅
Total	..	..	..	235⁴⁰⁄₅

Messrs. Coutts & Parkinson are laying the keel of an iron sailing ship, for the London and East India trade, same as the *Courier.*

At half-past 5 o'clock, on Thursday afternoon, the 11th of July, there was launched from the iron ship-building yard of Messrs. Coutts and Parkinson, a very handsome iron sailing ship, named the *Courier.* On the usual signal being given, Miss Milne named the vessel, and in a few seconds this beautiful specimen of iron naval architecture floated upon the Tyne, amidst the cheers of the assembled spectators. After the launch about sixty ladies and gentlemen, friends of the owners and builders, sat down to a cold collation, laid in a large workshop on the premises. The chair was filled by John Smith, Esq., the owner, who in the course of the evening discussed at some length the capabilities of wood and iron ships, giving a decided preference to the latter. The *Courier,* he said, would carry at least 300 tons more cargo than a wooden vessel of the same dimensions, which in a long voyage would yield a considerable increase of freight, &c., &c. Both cabins are placed upon deck, so that the holds are entirely appropriated to the stowage of goods. The fittings will be very elegant, the carved work being executed by Messrs. Helyer & Son, of London, and the accommodations will be of the very best description. The following are the dimensions, &c. :—

			Ft.	In.
Length between perpendiculars	..	..	134	0
Length at 15 feet load line	..	..	130	0
Length of keel	..	..	125	0
Breadth of beam	..	..	30	0
Depth of hold	..	..	19	3
Tonnage ..	..	..	555$\frac{87}{94}$	

New measurement.

			Ft.	Tns.
Length on deck	..	..	130	0
Breadth on ditto, amidships	..	..	29	0
Depth of hold, ditto	..	..	18	9
Length of poop	..	..	33	2
Breadth of ditto	..	..	23	4
Depth of ditto	..	..	6	7

Tonnage.

				Tons.
Hull	..	..	..	601$\frac{111}{123}$
Poop	..	..	..	56$\frac{148}{163}$
Total	..	..	..	658$\frac{46}{63}$

The keel, stem, and stern post are all welded into one piece of bar iron 9 × 2 inches, the plates taper from $\frac{3}{8}$ to $\frac{5}{16}$ of an inch, and the frames are 4 × 3 × $\frac{1}{2}$, and 1 foot 4 inches apart. She is divided into water-tight compartments.

Description.—A shield figure-head, mock quarter galleries, square sterned, and clinch built vessel of iron; standing bowsprit, 3 masts, ship rigged. Port of Sunderland.

They also launched this year the iron brigantine *Sally Gale* of the following dimensions :—

			Ft.	Tns.
Length on deck	..	..	85	5
Breadth on ditto at midships	..	..	20	0
Depth of hold	..	..	13	1
Tonnage ..	..	..	193$\frac{118}{153}$	

EAST HOWDEN (NORTHUMBERLAND.)

Mr. Thomas has upon the stocks a brig, classed 9 years, A 1, at Lloyd's, flush on deck, named the *Partisan*, of the following dimensions :—

			Ft.	Tns.
Length on deck	..	..	94	3
Breadth on ditto at midships	..	..	23	6
Depth of hold, ditto	..	..	17	3
Tonnage ..	..	..	293$\frac{117}{163}$	

Also another brig ready for launching, of the following dimensions :

			Ft.	Tns.
Length on deck	..	..	95	0
Breadth on ditto at midships	..	..	23	6
Depth of hold ditto	..	..	17	0
Tonnage ..	..	..	295$\frac{118}{163}$	

Both vessels for the foreign trade, and both plain vessels, except that the *Partisan* has a male bust figure-head.

Launch of the *Queen of Sheba.*—On Saturday, the 10th of August, there was launched from the building-yard of Mr. Thomas Brown, a beautiful clipper timber ship, named the *Queen of Sheba*, of the following dimensions :—

			Ft.	Tns.
Length on deck	..	..	121	0
Breadth on ditto at midships	..	..	22	8
Depth of hold ditto	..	..	15	6
Length of poop	..	..	29	1
Breadth of ditto	..	..	20	1

			Ft.	Tns.
Depth of poop ..	..	..	6	5

Tonnage.

				Tons.
Hull ..	..	..	..	315$\frac{114}{163}$
Poop	..	..	..	43$\frac{57}{63}$
Total	..	..	..	358$\frac{171}{163}$

This vessel is the property of the Commander, Mr. Caddell, and is to load at Newcastle for California, and is a very clean model, and will carry about 22 keels of coals, besides other goods.

Description.—A full female figure-head, no galleries, round sterned and carvil built vessel, 3 masts, ship-rigged, standing bowsprit. Port of Aberdeen.

HOWDEN (NORTHUMBERLAND.)

Mr. Morrison has lately launched a floating dock, named *Limekiln Shore*, of the following dimensions :—

			Ft.	Tns.
Length on deck	..	..	118	0
Breadth on ditto at midships	..	..	34	3
Depth of hold at ditto	..	..	6	5
Tonnage ..	..	..	251$\frac{117}{163}$	

Mr. William Oliver has upon the stocks, all in frame, a barque for the East India trade, to have a poop and top-gallant forecastle, to class 12 years, A 1, at Lloyd's.

			Ft.	In.
Length of keel and fore rake	..	..	150	0
Breadth of beam	..	..	30	0
Depth of hold ..	..	..	21	6
Rake of stem, forward	..	..	10	0
Tonnage ..	..	..	631$\frac{31}{94}$	

Mr. Jas. Lovie, Coble Dean, has upon the stocks a (timber) schooner, for the coasting trade, to be a clinch and carvil built vessel.

			Ft.	In.
Length of keel and fore rake	..	..	53	0
Breadth of beam	..	..	16	0
Depth of hold	..	..	8	0
Rake of stem	..	..	3	0
Tonnage ..	..	..	59$\frac{3}{94}$	

Built bow to the river.

Messrs. Thoburn and Grant, Coble Deane, have upon the stocks, and nearly planked, a river tug boat for the Tyne; clinch built (of timber,) and laid with bow to the river.

			Ft.	In.
Length of keel and fore rake	..	..	71	0
Breadth of beam	..	..	15	6
Depth of hold	..	..	8	6
Rake of stem	..	..	8	0
Ditto of stern post	..	..	1	0
Tonnage ..	..	..	81$\frac{3}{94}$	

One half-lever engine, by Messrs. Hepple and Landell, North Shields.

Mr. James Dowey, Coble Deane, has upon the stocks all planked a river tug boat (of timber) for Wales ; clinch built, laid with bow to the river.

			Ft.	In.
Length of keel and fore rake	..	..	74	6
Breadth of beam	..	..	16	0
Depth of hold ..	..	..	7	6
Rake forward	..	..	9	0
Tonnage ..	..	..	87$\frac{31}{94}$	

One half-lever engine, by Mr. J. D. Marshall, South Shields.

BOILER EXPLOSION AT BRISTOL.

A FEARFUL explosion occurred at Bristol on the 29th ult. on board a small steamer named the *Red Rover*, by which fifteen persons lost their lives, the engineer of the boat included. We have been favoured by a correspondent with some particulars of the vessel and boiler, which we will now give, with some remarks on what appears to us the extraordinary manner in which the inquests were conducted. The *Red Rover* was built and fitted in Ireland, and was 47 feet 3 inches long over all; 5 feet deep in hold, and 7 feet 3 inches beam. The engines were high-pressure, direct acting ones. The boiler is represented in the accompanying sketch.

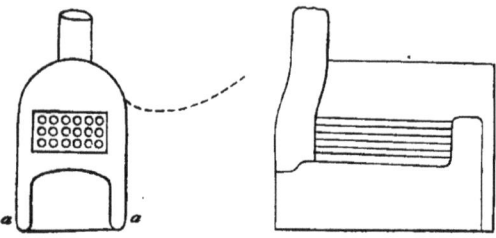

Scale—¼ inch to a foot.

The boiler was repaired on its arrival at Bristol, a few stays being put in, and it was tested with water to 20 or 30 lbs. pressure. The plates were ⅜ thick, and it would appear that there were no stays put in originally, and that there were only three in when the explosion took place. A man was put on board as engineer who had never driven an engine before; and a youth who was employed as cheque taker, stated in his evidence, that passengers sometimes put their feet on the safety-valve lever,—when they were particularly anxious to get to their journey's end, we presume.

Under this system an explosion does not seem a very improbable contingency. Accordingly, an explosion did take place, the sides of the boiler rending at *a, a*, and flattening out on each side, as represented by the dotted line, the heads of the stays being drawn completely through the plates. One piece, weighing 1¼ cwt., was thrown 100 yards. An inquest was held, and the following evidence elicited :—

John Nicholas.—Has been a smith and boiler-maker thirty years. Three weeks before the explosion, Mr. Anderson, the owner of the *Red Rover*, employed him to inspect the boiler. "The state of the boiler was very bad. All the stays of the boiler were just gone through, pushed in by the pressure of the steam. In the end of the boiler there was a crack all along by the stay, 18 inches long." Witness said, "He could do nothing to make it a safe job." Mr. Anderson then said, "We will have a new boiler." Witness's son is a boiler-maker, and put a patch over the crack, without consulting witness. His son came home and said, "Well, father, we have got a fire in the *Rover* again." Witness said, "You must know that boiler is not safe; it is not safe for a cat."

By a Juror.—My son did not express any uneasiness when I saw him on Sunday. Nuts would sink into new iron with thin plates, but not in thick plates. There was a leak in the boiler, which had on one occasion put out the fire. Parties were obliged to keep constantly pumping into the boiler—a boiler requiring that would be no good. Could not say that in the present case the iron of the boiler was so weak in consequence of the wear as to occasion the accident.

The Coroner.—I cannot allow any opinion to be taken theoretically, because that opinion may be well or ill founded. His opinion appears to be that the explosion was caused by a defective boiler, but his son, a boiler maker, 26 years of age, and a competent engineer,(!) thought it was perfectly safe, and had no scruple in going in her.

Albert Brain, a carpenter, deposed that he was on board the *Red Rover* at the time of the explosion. He was sitting on the rail at the after part of the vessel. Shortly before the boat started, he heard Mr. Anderson and the engineer conversing together, and Mr. Anderson said to him, "Had you better not give her a few strokes of the pump, as when there is such a pressure of steam on, it is always well to have

plenty of water." The engineer replied, that they would start immediately, when she would fetch up. Shortly after the vessel started the engines were reversed, and the vessel put back to the lock, when the explosion took place. Within a minute of the explosion, Puddy (the captain !) tried the safety valve, and the steam blew off. Directly afterwards the engineer came up and extended the weight, and the steam no longer blew off. No other person touched the safety valve.

A juror suggested that they ought to have before them the man who made the boiler, and the previous engineer, as he considered there had not been sufficient evidence given either as to the precise state of the boiler, or the cause of the explosion.

The Coroner "was at a loss to see what object could be gained by it. They must all be aware that the eyes of the public were directed upon them, and that great anxiety was manifested as to the result of this enquiry. If it was likely that any fresh light could be thrown on the matter, he should be the first to propose an adjournment; but they had now been sitting three days, and the public of Bristol was perfectly aware where they were sitting; they were, therefore, extremely unlikely to obtain any more evidence."

The suggestion was accordingly overruled; but, we may ask, did it never occur to the worthy coroner that the "public of Bristol" were not the most likely or proper people to come forward and give such evidence as would enable the jury to give a true verdict? If a man dies, exhibiting strong symptoms of being poisoned, do we trust to the public coming forward, to procure evidence to point out the guilty party, or do we not rather employ the highest chemical talent that can be obtained? We regret that our space will not admit of our giving the summing up *in extenso*, but the tone appears to us to evince a decided usurpation of the province of the jury, thus :—"It certainly did not appear to him (the Coroner) that anything had been proved by which crime could be attached to any individual.—No doubt had been thrown on any part of the vessel but the boiler, on that boiler doubt had been thrown by several witnesses; but the jury would not fail to bear in mind that those doubts were rebutted by witnesses equal in number and experience to the others who were of a different opinion (?) The majority of the witnesses were in favour of the opinion that if the vessel was worked with care and plenty of water, the boiler would continue good for some time to come."

The room was then ordered to be cleared, and after the jury had deliberated for nearly an hour, they returned as their verdict, "That the deceased had met with their death in consequence of the bursting of the boiler of the *Red Rover*, which was at the time in an unfit state for use."

We cannot discover that any of the following points were settled, although we would suggest them to the coroner in the next case that may occur in Bristol, as his view of the law, as expressed in his summing-up, seems likely to make more work of a similar kind.

What was the pressure of the steam at the time of the explosion?

Was the boiler of such a form as any competent engineer would make to work at high pressure?

Does the fact of a man having been brought up a boiler-maker, and of his never having previously driven an engine, render him a competent engineer, to whom the lives of a boatful of passengers may be safely entrusted!

To the Editor.

Chelsea, August, 1850.

Sir,—Will any of your correspondents inform me how large a balloon must be to carry a weight of 1 ton, to an altitude of 10,000 feet, supposing hydrogen gas to be used for inflation.

No. 2. Is it possible, considering the present state of science, to navigate the air by means of aerial machines.

A. E.

To the Editor.

London, August, 1850.

Sir,—Seeing the queries for July are still open for solution, I beg to offer the following answers.—

In that by J. S. If the log be of oak, and 8 feet long, and each foot weighing 925 lbs., the total weight being $925 \times 32 = 29600$ lbs. Now Navier shows that this is very little more than the friction, which has to be overcome in sawing one square foot; therefore the log would have to fall through one foot, in order to cut one square foot, and as there are to be 11 cuts, 8 feet long, the total number of square feet of sawing will be 176, which also equals the distance fallen through by the log.

In query, No. 1, by Tyro, of Liverpool, the breaking strain of the engine beam may be found in the following manner:—

From the square of the depth, multiplied by the width of flange $= 30^2 \times 7$, deduct the square of the depth, less the thickness of flange increased by $\frac{1}{4}$ multiplied by the width, less the thickness of web which would equal $(30-\overline{2+\frac{1}{4}})^2 \times 5\cdot5$ and dividing the remainder by the length in feet, will give the breaking weight in tons. The question would stand thus: $\dfrac{30^2 \times 7 - (30 - \overline{2 + \frac{1}{4}})^2 \times 5\cdot5}{20} = \dfrac{6,300 - 4,2009\cdot7}{20} = 104\frac{1}{2}$ tons.

No. 2. The proportions for the girder of 30 feet span would be as follows:—

If the weight to be carried is 30 tons, we may safely take the breaking strain to be 100 tons, a piece of it one foot long, would break with 3000 tons. Now the limit in depth is 27 inches, and let the bottom flange be also 27 inches, and such a girder would not be safe to cast at less than one inch thick in web; hence to get the thickness of bottom flange, $27 - \sqrt{\dfrac{27^3 - 3000}{26}} = 1\cdot67$, and $1\cdot67 - \dfrac{1\cdot67}{7} = 1\cdot43$ inches, say $1\frac{1}{2}$ = thickness of bottom flange. The top flange being the same thickness, the width would be to the bottom one, as 1 to 6, or $4\frac{1}{2}$ inches. The proportions would then stand as follows:—

Depth, 27 inches, width of bottom flange, 27 inches, width of top ditto, $4\frac{1}{2}$, thickness of both flanges, $1\frac{1}{2}$, thickness of web, 1 inch, to carry a permanent weight of 30 tons in the centre.

I am, yours truly,
N. D.

ANALYSIS OF NEW BOOKS.

Tables of the Strength and Deflection of Timber. By W. LEA, Surveyor. London: Simpkin, Marshall, & Co. Birmingham: Osborne.

THESE tables purport to give the dimensions and strengths of different varieties of timber, under all the varying circumstances in which they can be placed in the usual course of construction. Red pine is selected as the standard of comparison, and the formulæ are stated to be the results of the experiments of Professor Barlow, whose name is a sufficient guarantee for their correctness. It is obvious that the value of such tables as these must depend upon their accuracy and their copiousness. Assuming the presence of the first of these qualifications, we are glad to see that Mr. Lea has not forgotten the second, for we have frequently found, when endeavouring to save ourselves the time and possible inaccuracy of a tedious calculation, that the tables to which we have had recourse, do not go quite high enough, or quite low enough, and so, for our purpose, might as well have never been made. Tables of figures are hardly "quotable," we must therefore beg of our readers to search for themselves.

Marshall's Index Ready Reckoner for the Calculation of Wages, &c. London: Longman & Co.

THE remarks we have made above on the necessity of *copiousness* in works of this kind, apply equally well here. The author has made a great step in advance by carrying out the calculations by quarters of a day, from ¼ to 30 days, thereby saving the necessity of making two calculations when fractions are involved. Another novelty consists in placing the daily rates of wages in the margin, so that the book can be instantly opened at the right place. From some little experience of our own in paying workmen, we can testify to the saving of time arising

from the use of a good set of wages' tables, and we would recommend the author, should his work reach a second edition, to extend the rate from five shillings a-day to seven shillings, which would make the tables more generally useful.

PATENT REFORM.

THE two bills which we noticed last month—the one relating to patent law, entitled, "A Bill to Simplify the Form of Appointment to certain Offices, and the Manner of passing Grants under the Great Seal;" and the other, the "New Designs Act"—have experienced a most melancholy fate, the first has been *burked*, and the second maimed and mutilated in a most parliamentary manner, so that instead of having any good effect upon the patent system, by aiding inventors to protect their inventions in a preliminary manner, as it would have done, it is now much more likely to lead them astray.

We trust, however, that inventors will not give up the good fight, and that our correspondent, Mr. CAMPIN, will renew his labours at the proper season.

The Act as it now stands enacts:—

1. That designs may be provisionally registered for *one year*, and during that period may be published and exhibited under certain circumstances, and then completely registered for three years, but it *does not enact that they may be patented.*

2. The sale of any article of such design during provisional registration is to render the said registration void, but the design itself may be sold.

3. The Board of Trade may grant an extension for six months in certain cases of provisional registration.

4. Sculpture, models, &c., to be allowed registration, and the benefits of the Acts.

5. Designs for ornamenting of ivory, bone, papier mâché, and other solid substances not already comprised in the 1st, 2nd, or 3rd classes of the Designs Act of 1842, are henceforth to be considered as included in class 4 of that Act.

6. The Board of Trade may extend registration of ornamental designs, power being also given to them to revoke such extension, if deemed necessary.

7. The registrar of designs, in certain cases where it may appear reasonable, may dispense with drawings, and may accept a specification in lieu of them.

8. The documents of the office are not to be produced in courts of law without a judge's order, and sealed copies ordered by a judge are to be received in evidence.

LIST OF ENGLISH PATENTS.

FROM THE 22ND DAY OF JULY TO THE 16TH DAY OF AUGUST, 1850, INCLUSIVE.

Henry Bessemer, of Baxter House Old St. Pancras-road, civil engineer, for certain improvements in figuring and ornamenting surfaces; and in the blocks, plates, rollers, implements, and machinery employed therein. July 22.

James Bradford, of Torquay, in the county of Devon, jeweller, for improvements in locks and other fastenings. July 22.

Thomas Mills, of Bow, in the county of Middlesex, engineer, for improvements in steam engines and in pumps. July 22.

Joseph Paxton, of Chatsworth, in the county of Derby, gentleman, for certain improvements in roofs. July 22.

Leonard Bower, of Birmingham, in the county of Warwick, manufacturer, and Thomas Fortune, of Harborne, in the county of Stafford, mechanic, for certain improved machinery for manufacturing screws, bolts, rivets, and nails. July 23.

William Beetson, of Brick-lane, St. Luke's, in the county of Middlesex, brass founder, for improvements in water-closets, pumps, and cocks. July 23.

William Edward Newton, of Chancery-lane, civil engineer, for improvements in obtaining, preparing, and applying zinc, and other volatile metals, and the oxides thereof; and in the application of zinc, or ores containing the same, to the preparation or manufacture of certain metals, or alloys of metals. July 23.—(Communication.)

George Hazeldine, of Lant-street, Southwark, in the county of Surrey, carriage builder, for improvements in the construction of waggons, carts, and vans. July 23.

Henry Constantine Jennings, of Great Tower-street, in the city of London, practical chemist, for improvements in rendering canvas, and other fabrics, and leather, waterproof. July 23.

William Edward Newton, of Chancery-lane, in the county of Middlesex, civil engineer, for improvements in machinery for cutting files. July 23.

George Dunbar, of Paris, Esquire, for improvements in suspending carriages. July 23.

Langston Scott, of Moorgate-street, in the city of London, wine merchant, for improvements in a mode or modes of preparing certain matters or substances to be used as pigments. July 24.

Charles William Bell, of Manchester, for improvements in apparatus connected with water-closets, drains, and cesspools; and in gas and air-traps. July 25.

Rodolphe Helbrouner, of Regent-street, in the county of Middlesex, for improvements in preventing the external air, dust, and noise from entering apartments. July 31.

Thomas Dickson Rotch, of Drumlanford House, in the county of Ayr, N. B., Esq., for an improved mode of manufacturing soap. July 31.

Matthew Trattles, of Rochester, in the county of Kent, tool maker, for certain improvements in saw sets, mallets, and other tools; and in apparatus and machinery for manufacturing the same. July 31.

John Sheafe Gaskin, Jun., of the Island of Barbadoes, in the West Indies, gentleman, for improvements in the manufacture of rum. (To extend to the Colonies only.) July 31.

Richard Archibald Brooman, of Fleet-street, in the city of London, for an improvement or improvements in abdominal supporters. July 31.—(Communication.)

James White, of Holborn, in the county of Middlesex, mill maker, for improvements in machinery for bruising, crushing, and for expressing juice from certain vegetable substances. July 31.

Henry Bessemer, of Baxter House, St. Pancras-road, in the county of Middlesex, engineer, for certain improvements in apparatus acting by centrifugal force in the manufacture of sugar, and other improvements in the treatment of saccharine matter by such apparatus. July 31.

Juan Nepomisceno Adorno, of Golden-square, in the county of Middlesex, gentleman, for improvements in manufacturing cigars, and other similar articles. July 31.

Henry Rishton, of Kendal, in the county of Westmoreland, plumber, for certain improvements in water-closets and urinals. July 31.

Joseph Poole Pirsson, of the city of New York, United States of America, civil engineer, for certain improvements in steam machinery, and apparatus connected therewith. July 31

John Hynam, of Princes-square, Finsbury, in the county of Middlesex, chemical light manufacturer, for improvements in machinery for placing splints of wood, and wax and composition tapers, in frames for dipping. July 31.

John James Greenough, of George-street, Hanover-square, in the county of Middlesex, gentleman, for improvements in obtaining and applying motive power. July 31.

Peter Fairbairn, of Leeds, in the county of York, machinist, and John Hetherington, of Manchester, machinist, for certain improvements in machinery or apparatus for preparing, spinning, and weaving cotton, flax, and other fibrous substances; also in constructing and applying models or patterns for moulding, preparatory to casting parts of machinery employed in preparing, spinning, and manufacturing fibrous substances; and also in certain tools to be used in making such machinery. July 31.

Matthew Gray, of Morris-place, in the city of Glasgow, practical engineer, for an improved method of supplying steam boilers with water. July 31.

Edward Gabriel Leroy, of Paris, in the republic of France, gentleman, for certain improvements in locomotive engines, and in the means and apparatus to be employed for generating and condensing the steam to be used therein. July 31.

Joseph Shaw, of Paddock, near Huddersfield, in the county of York, cloth finisher, for improvements in constructing and working certain parts of railways. August 3.

John Gwynne, of Lansdowne-Lodge, Notting-hill, merchant, for improvements in obtaining motive power, and in applying the same to giving motion to machinery August 5.—(Communication.)

Francis Kane, of Berner's Mews, in the county of Middlesex, chair maker, for improvements in reclining chairs, in castors for chairs, and other articles of furniture; and improvements in presses. August 5.

William Crosskill, of Beverley, in the county of York, civil engineer, for improvements in mills for grinding, splitting, pulverizing, and crushing grain, bones, bark, ore, and other hard substances, and for grinding paint, and other soft substances; and for shelling or removing the skin from rice, and other grain; and in machinery for giving rotary motion to mills, thrashing machines, and any other machine requiring rotary motion to be communicated by any horse or other animal. August 6.—(Communication.)

Joseph Steele, of Chancery-lane, for improvements in coating and impregnating metals and metallic articles. August 9.

Henry Meyer, of the Strand, gentleman, for certain improvements in power looms for weaving. August 10.

Selim Richard St. Clair Massiah, of Alderman's-walk, in the city of London, for improvements in the manufacture of artificial marble and stone; and in treating marble and stone. August 10.

Alfred Holl, of Greenwich, engineer, for improvements in steam engines. August 12.

Arnaud Nicholas Freche, of the city of Paris, merchant, for improvements in obtaining power. August 12.

Charles Cadby, of Liquorpond-street, in the county of Middlesex, piano-forte maker, for improvements in stringed musical instruments. August 12.

George Thompson, of Park-road, Regent's-park, gentleman, for certain improvements in machinery and apparatus for cutting, digging, or turning up earth, applicable to agricultural purposes. August 12.

Samuel John Pittar, of Church-place, Clapham, in the county of Surrey, civil engineer, for certain improvements in umbrellas and parasols. August 13.

Peter Claussen, of Great Charlotte-street, Blackfriars, in the county of Surrey, manufacturer, for certain improvements in bleaching, and in the preparation of materials for spinning and felting, and in yarns and felts. August 16.—(Communication.)

William Keates, of Liverpool, merchant, for improvements in machinery for manufacturing rollers and cylinders used for calico-printing, and other purposes. August 16.

Alexander Melville, of Baker-street, Portman-square, in the county of Middlesex, gentleman, and Edward Callow, of Park-road, Stockwell, in the county of Surrey, gentleman, for certain improvements in muskets, cannon, and other fire-arms; and in explosive compositions and instruments. N.B.—This patent, being opposed at the Great Seal, was not dated until after the publication of the last list, but bears date the 6th instant, the day it would have been sealed but for the opposition.

Charles Heard Wild, of St Martin's-lane, Middlesex, civil engineer, for improvements in certain structures for retaining water. August 17.

Henry Holland, of Birmingham, umbrella furniture manufacturer, for improvements in the manufacture of umbrellas and parasols. August 22.

Edmee Augustin Chameroy, of Paris, for improvements in paving streets and other surfaces. August 22.

Frederick Hale Thompson, of Berner's-street, Middlesex, gentleman, and Thomas Robert Mellish, of Portland-street, same county, glass cutter, for improvements in cutting, staining, silvering, and fixing articles of glass. August 22.

William Dick, of Edinburgh, professor of veterinary medicine, Veterinary-college, Edinburgh, for improvements in the manufacture of steel and gas. August 22.

Benjamin Rotch, of Lowlands, Middlesex, esq., for a factitious saltpetre, and a mode by which factitious saltpetre may be obtained for commercial purposes. August 22.

William Edward Newton, of Chancery-lane, Middlesex, civil engineer, for improvements in refining gold. August 22.—(Communication.)

William Edward Newton, of Chancery-lane, Middlesex, civil engineer, for improvements in the construction of ships' magazines. August 22.—(Communication.)

William Edward Newton, of Chancery-lane, Middlesex, civil engineer, for improvements in machinery or apparatus for producing ice, and for general refrigeratory purposes. August 22.—(Communication.)

William Edward Newton, of Chancery-lane, Middlesex, civil engineer, for improvements in the construction of ships or vessels, and in steam boilers or generators. August 22.—(Communication.)

Daniel Illingworth, of Bradford, in the county of York, worsted-spinner, for certain improvements in machinery for preparing all descriptions of wool and hair grown upon animals, for the carding, combing, and other manufacturing processes. August 22.

Duncan Bruce, of Paspebiac, in the district of Gaspé, in Canada, but at present at Liverpool, in the county of Lancaster, esq., for certain improvements in the construction of rotary engines. August 22.

Richard Prosser, of Birmingham, civil engineer, for improvements in supplying steam-boilers with water, and in clearing out the tubes of steam-boilers. August 22.

LIST OF PATENTS THAT HAVE PASSED THE GREAT SEAL OF SCOTLAND.

From the 24th day of June to the 22nd day of July, 1850, inclusive.

William Wood, of Over Darwen, Lancashire, carpet manufacturer, for improvements in the manufacture of carpets and other fabrics. June 24.

Moses Poole, gentleman, for improvements in machinery for punching metals; and in the construction of springs for carriages, and other uses. June 28.

Peter Armand le Comte de Fontainemoreau, of South-street, Finsbury, in the county of Middlesex, for certain improvements in the manufacture of sulphate of soda, muriatic and nitric acids. July 3.—(Communication.)

Thomas Dickson Rotch, of Drumlanford House, in the county of Ayr, Esq., for an improved mode of manufacturing soap. July 3.

William Cormack, of King-street, Danston-road, Haggerstone, in the county of Middlesex, chemist, for certain improvements in purifying gas, also applicable in obtaining or separating certain products or materials from gas, water, and other similar fluids. July 10.

Robert Andrew Macfie, of Liverpool, in the county of Lancaster, sugar refiner, for improvements in manufacturing, refining, and preparing sugar, also improvements in manufacturing and treating animal charcoal. July 10.

Richard Roberts, of Manchester, in the county of Lancaster, engineer, for improvements in the manufacture of certain textile fabrics; in machinery for weaving plain, figured, and terry or looped fabrics; and in machinery or apparatus for cutting velvets and other fabrics. July 12.

John Stevenson, of Roan Mills, Dungannon, county Tyrone, flax spinner, for certain improvements in machinery for spinning flax and other substances. July 17.

James Thompson, of Glasgow, in the county of Lanark, civil engineer, for improvements in hydraulic machinery, and in steam engines. July 17.

Tempest Booth, of Ardwick, in the county of Lancaster, gum manufacturer, for certain improvements in the method of, and apparatus for, obtaining and applying motive power. July 19.

Peter William Barlow, of Blackheath, in the county of Kent, civil engineer, and William Henry Barlow, of Derby, civil engineer, for improvements in the permanent ways of railways. July 22.

LIST OF PATENTS THAT HAVE PASSED THE GREAT SEAL OF IRELAND.

From the 24th day of June, to the 17th day of July, 1850, inclusive.

Thomas Dickson Rotch, of Drumlanford House, in the county of Ayr, Esq., for improvements in separating various matters usually found in certain saccharine, saline, and liquous substances. June 24.—(Communication.)

James Hard Hoby, of Blackheath, in the county of Kent, Esq., for certain improvements of parts of the permanent way of railways, and in shaping iron. July 15.

Francis Tongue Rufford, of Prescott House, in the county of Worcester, fire-brick manufacturer, Isaac Marson, of Cradley, in the same county, potter, and John Finch, of Pickford-street, City-road, in the county of Middlesex, manufacturer, for improvements in the manufacture of baths and washtubs or wash-vessels. July 17.

George Jackson, of Belfast, Ireland, flax spinner, for improvements in heckling machinery. July 17.

DESIGNS FOR ARTICLES OF UTILITY.

Registered from 17th July to 13th August.

July 17th, 2380, Arthur Samuel Hobson, Kew, Surrey, "Contracting and elongating parasol."
" 19th, 2381, Charles Ledger, Clarence-street, Sheffield, "Table cutlery."
" " 2382, James Dannott, Bishopwearmouth, Durham, "Domestic mangle."
" " 2383, Isaac & Campbell, St. James's-street, Pall-mall, "Barrack, college, and cabin portable furniture."
" 22nd, 2384, John Schofield & William Barker, Cornbrook, Hulme, near Manchester "Improved face-plate and cutters, for rasping and chipping dye-woods."
" " 2385, William Randel, Birmingham, "Hook and eye."
" 23rd, 2386, Francois Jules Livin Tigé, Arthur-street West, London, "Bath."
" 25th, 2387, Ann Remington, Shaftsbury-crescent, Pimlico, "Improved roasting apparatus."
" 26th, 2388, John Wright, New George-street, Sheffield, "Tempering and straightening plates."
" " 2389, Andrew Campbell, Tottenham Court-road, "Argyll bouquet-holder, and watch-protector."
" 27th, 2390, Samuel Perkes, Birkenhead, "Metallic folding bedstead."
" " 2391, George Boulton, Great Dover-street, Southwark, "Improved chrosha (or crochet) and tambour hook."
" 29th, 2392, Henry Broadhead, Beech Grove Terrace, Leeds, "Improved flat whitening brush."
" 30th, 2393, Joseph Mackenzie, Bideford, Devon, "The Cheirosthenicon."
" 31st, 2394, James Thornton & Son, Birmingham, "Signal lamp."
Aug. 2nd, 2395, John Sanders, Birmingham, "Set of dies for making-pressed hinges."
" " 2396, William Palmer, Sutton-street, Clerkenwell, "Candle-lamp."
" 3rd, 2397, John Goode, Jun., Birmingham, "Swivel."
" " 2398, William Palmer, Western-road, Brighton, Sussex, "Sculptors, statuaries, and modellers' revolving table."
" 6th, 2399, John Martin, Killyleagh-mills, county of Down, Ireland, "An arrangement of steam and water pipes, to be applied in spinning flax, tow, and other fibrous substances."
" 7th, 2400, Robert Davis, Globe-yard, South Molton-street, London, "A pipe-mouse."
" 8th, 2401, George Hart & Sons, Union-street, Southwark, "Spring folding collegian cap."
" " 2402, Joseph Welch & John Margetson, Cheapside, "Folding trencher cap."
" 9th, 2403, H. C. Windle & W. D. Blyth, Walsal, "Latch."
" 10th, 2404, Susan Hooper & Co., Cottage-lane Works, Birmingham, "Register stove top, with extra moveable door."
" 12th, 2405, Thomas & Charles Clark, Wolverhampton, "Spring hinge."
" 13th, 2406, Capt. Wm. Henry Armstrong, Claremont Lodge, Cobham, Surrey, "Rose tree and flower girdle."
" 15th, 2407, Y. D. Stewart & Co., St. Rollox, Glasgow, "Core carriage, for making and drying cores for metal pipes."
" " 2408, T. M. Sharp, Donegal-street, Belfast, "Sack elevator."
" 16th, 2409, Joseph Salt, Uxbridge, "Pipe socket die."
" 19th, 2410, Michael Neville, Great Charlotte-street, Liverpool, "Improved joint for elbow and other pipes."
" " 2411, Thomas Busby, St. Marylebone Baths and Washhouses, New Road, "Improved valve apparatus for baths."
" " 2412, Henry Fletcher, Manchester, "Drawing roller for cotton machinery."
" " 2413, Thomas Brooks, Spital-square, Norton Folgate, "The Sutherland silk"
" 20th, 2414, Lewis Lee, Woodbury, Exeter, "Combined cultivating plough."

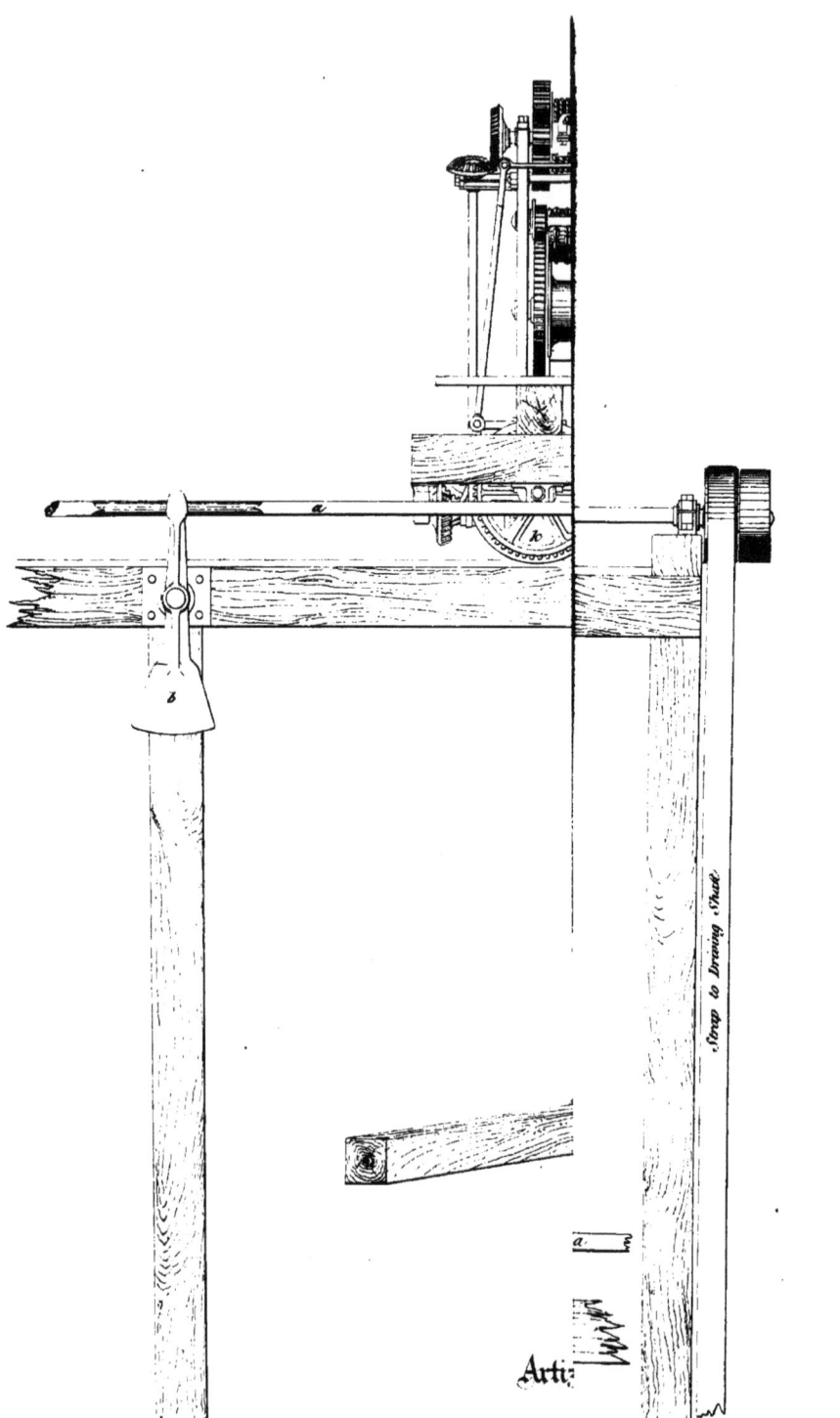

Strap to Driving Shaft.

THE ARTIZAN.

No. X.—VOL. VIII.—OCTOBER 1st, 1850.

PATENT STEAM TRAVELLING CRANE.

McNICOLL & VERNON'S PATENT STEAM TRAVELLING CRANE.

The travelling crane, although an introduction of recent date, has proved such a convenient auxiliary in the multifarious operations involving the lifting and removal of heavy weights, that its use has spread very rapidly, and it is now to be found in almost every situation where it is applicable. In the erection of all large buildings, docks, &c.; in engine shops, like those of Woolwich Dock Yard and Swindon, and in those of several private firms, the Travelling Crane effects an important saving, although worked by manual labour. How much greater then will be the economy, both of time and money, obtained by the use of steam power, in place of the numerous men at present employed? The problem of its application to this purpose has been satisfactorily solved by Messrs. McNicoll & Vernon, of Liverpool, at the saw mills of the former of whom two Steam Travelling Cranes may be seen in constant operation.

We saw one of these machines performing its ordinary daily work, and its most striking feature is the remarkable ease with which it can be made to perform all its movements. It is worked by a youth of 16 or 17 years of age, who stands on the platform, and by moving two or three handles is able to lift weights varying from 1 to 5 tons, to put them on or take them off carts or timber carriages, pile them one upon the other, or convey them from one side of the yard to the other, a distance of 127 feet. This distance might of course be increased to twice or three times the length, if the amount of work required it, and the premises were of sufficient extent.

The amount of work that these machines will perform, and the consequent saving in wages which they effect, are truly surprising. One of them has displaced two of the ordinary hand travelling cranes. The latter employed 4 men each, 3 men on the platform to hoist, &c., and 1 man below to fasten on the logs, in all 8 men, at 16s. per week each, or £332. 16s. per annum. The patent steam crane is worked by a youth at 10s. per week, and a man fastening the logs to the hooks or chains, at 16s. per week, or £67. 12s. per annum. Thus the one machine not only effects a saving of £265. 4s. per annum, but does the work of the two cranes which it displaced, doing it, at the same time, in a much more efficient manner.

The following experiment, which was performed on the 26th of July last, will enable persons to form an accurate idea of its capabilities. 13 logs of timber, containing 1050 cubic feet, were piled in a cess at one side of the yard. A plot of ground on the opposite side of the yard, 100 feet distant from the place where the timber was lying, was cleared, in order that the timber be removed from the former and piled on the latter place. At one o'clock precisely the crane started, travelled 100 feet where the timber was lying, hoisted a log, returned to the place from whence it started, and deposited it on the ground in exactly

2 minutes. It immediately proceeded on a second journey, and at precisely 4 min. 10 sec. after one o'clock it deposited the second log. The remaining logs were, one by one, conveyed over the distance, and in 27 min. 30 sec. the logs had been removed and piled in a cess at the opposite end of the yard. The average weight of the logs was 30 cwt., the total weight 19½ tons, allowing 54 cubic feet to the ton. The machine had travelled 2600 feet, or within 40 feet of half a mile, for half the distance carrying a load of 30 cwt., in addition to its own weight, besides having made 26 stoppages. During the whole of the operation only two persons were engaged,—the youth who directed the machine, and the man who fastened on the logs.

This experiment has been repeated several times, and the time occupied has never exceeded 27 min. 30 sec. On one occasion it was performed in 26 minutes. To those persons conversant with the difficulty and expense that, under ordinary circumstances, attend the removal and piling of so bulky an article as timber, the result of this experiment will appear startling, as the wages of the two persons employed could not exceed sixpence for half an hour's work.

We are glad to be able to furnish our readers with plans and a description of this ingenious invention, which, however, requires to be seen to be properly appreciated.

This machine, like the ordinary hand travelling crane, moves upon a tram road laid upon longitudinal beams, raised from 15 to 20 feet above the level of the ground, the beams being supported at intervals by uprights. A square shaft, a, (2½ inch diameter) runs the entire length of the tram road, and is attached to the longitudinal beams by moveable supports, b b b. This shaft is connected at one extremity to the engine. Upon it, and revolving with it, is placed a drum, c, which works by means of a leather belt, the pulley, d, attached to the moving platform. The pulley, d, is fixed on the shaft, e, upon which are placed the bevil wheels, which impart the threefold motion to the crane. The bevil wheels, $f f$, which revolve freely on the shaft, are made so as to turn the bevil wheel, g, by means of the clutch box, h, which is attached to the shaft; so that by withdrawing the clutch box from one of the bevil wheels and putting it in gear with the other, the motion of the bevil wheel, g, is reversed, and when the clutch box is out of gear the bevil wheel, g, is stationary. The bevil wheel, g, is fastened upon the small shaft, i, to the other end of which is attached the pinion, j, which works the spur wheel fixed to the roller wheel, k, and imparts the longitudinal motion to the whole platform. As the platform would otherwise move away from the drum, c, which communicates the motion, it is made to slide freely upon the shaft, and being attached to the moving platform, by means of the rod, l, it always preserves its relative position with regard to the pulley, d. The difficulty of making the drum pass over the numerous brackets, that a long shaft must necessarily have to support it, is overcome by making the brackets swing on a centre, so that when the drum, c, protected by the guard, n, comes in contact with one of the brackets, b b, it yields, as shown in fig. 1, and allows the drum to pass over it. Immediately it has so passed, the weight of the lower extremity of the bracket causes it to resume its position, and the machine passes on to the next bracket, where the operation is repeated. In order to prevent the shock that would be felt in putting in motion so heavy a body as a travelling crane of 50 feet span, carrying, in addition to its own weight, a load of 3 or 4 tons, a friction roller, o, is made to press upon the leather belt that passes round the drum, c, and the pulley, d, so that before putting the machine in gear, the friction roller is raised ; the machine is then put in gear, and the friction roller gradually lowered. The momentary slipping of the belt round the pulley, d, when the weight of the friction roller is only partially resting upon it, causes the machine to move forward with an easy motion, and directly it is under way the friction roller is allowed to bear with the whole of its weight, and the crane then moves forward with its load, at its usual speed of 100 feet in 45 seconds.

The hoisting motion is obtained by communicating the power through the bevil wheels, q q, and the shaft, r, to the barrel, s, round which the chain revolves. In order to render the hoisting motion independent of the transverse motion, the hoisting chain passes from the barrel round which it is coiled to the truck, t, and after passing over the pulley, u, under the snatch block, v, and over the pulley, w, it is finally attached to the point, x, at the extreme end of the platform. To hoist a weight, therefore, it is merely necessary that the handle, y, which communicates with the clutch box, z, should be moved a few inches.

The transverse motion is imparted to the load by means of the barrel, 'a, which is worked from the shaft, e, by the bevil wheels, 'b 'b, and clutch box, 'c, in the same manner as the longitudinal and the hoisting motions. Two chains are attached to the barrel, in such a way that one winds when the other unwinds. One of these chains is attached to the small truck, t, at 'd, and the other is carried round the pulley, 'e, and fastened to the truck at 'f, so that by alternately putting the clutch box, 'c, in gear with one or other of the bevil wheels, 'b 'b, by means of the handle, 'g, the truck, and with it the load, is moved backwards or forwards along the platform, at right angles with the motion of the platform itself.

Each of the above—the longitudinal, the transverse, and the hoisting —motions can be used independently of either of the others ; or any two of the motions may be used in combination ; or the whole three may be used simultaneously. For instance, at the same time that a weight attached to the hook, 'h, is being raised from the ground by the barrel, s, the truck, t, and consequently the load suspended on the chain, may be moved in the direction 'i or 'j, at the same time that the whole platform may be moving in a longitudinal direction.

We would recommend such of our readers as have the opportunity, to pay Mr. M'Nicoll's saw mill and timber yard a visit, and witness the working of this crane with their own eyes, which will give them a better idea of its usefulness than we can hope to do by a written description.

The numerous applications of which it is susceptible, such as to the goods traffic at railway stations, the unloading of vessels, and the general work in foundries, quarries, builders' yards, &c., lead us to imagine that before very long, travelling cranes worked by manual labour will become the exception, rather than as at present the rule. We ought not to omit to mention (for it is a very important point), that steam power can be readily applied on this plan to nearly all the existing cranes, and that therefore the cost of making the addition will be the only expense where they are already in use.

HAMILTON'S PATENT CURVILINEAL SAWING AND BEVILLING MACHINERY.

(Continued from p. 178.)

HAVING described, in our former illustration of Mr. Hamilton's in-

vention, the methods of communicating motion to the saws and to the timber, we will now proceed to analyse the plan for laying off the bevils, and regulating the motion of the timber with that accuracy which enables the attendant to turn out his work *finished*, and obviates the necessity of any dubbing or dressing the timber by hand.

The method by which a saw cut, when once entered upon a piece of timber, is changed, so as to form a different angle with the surface, has been already explained, by rotating the timber upon the centre of the dogs in which it is securely held at each end. Fig. 3, which is an end view, shows the arrangement by which the dog at the back end of the timber is rotated to any required angle. The bar, o o, is formed of two pieces, which slide upon each other, and are retained in a straight line by two coupling boxes. The lower extremity of one bar forms the dog carrying the timber, whilst the upper extremity of the other bar is connected by a joint to the nut of the screw, p p, which travels across the dovetailed grooves by the action of the wheels, q, r, which are put in motion by the hand wheel, s. The upper end of the compound bar, o o, is thus moved in a horizontal direction across the machine ; and whilst one position of this bar accords with the first entrance of the saw cut, the gradual change of the bar from one angle to another whilst the sawing of the timber proceeds, must give to the sawn surface any degree of twist required. In the shaping of ship timbers each piece is first " sided ;" that is, two opposite faces are sawn straight and parallel to each other. The twisted form required to be given to the two remaining faces, and which is technically called " moulding " the timber, can thus be measured at any part by applying a bevilling square to either of the parallel surfaces, and thus any degree of twist becomes in fact a change of bevil. The practical method of transferring the required bevils of any one timber to the arm, o o, so that a twisted surface may be produced having certain given bevils, will be best illustrated by an example. A A represents a piece of timber already sided, and upon one of the flat surfaces of which the curvilineal form of a ship's timber has been traced out. The bevils required to be given to the curvilineal edge have also been indicated, according to the usual custom of shipwrights, by the angular figures, b, c, d, e, f ; it being understood that after the said timber shall have been cut out a bevil set to the angle 1 c 2 shall apply itself correctly in the direction c c (at right angles with the curve), from the upper surface to the sawn edge of the timber. The intended centres upon which the timber is to be rotated during the operation of sawing being determined as x x, it is evident that all bevils must be resolved into one direction, and that at right angles with the line, x x. A temporary board, H, is attached to the nut of the bevilling arm, o o, upon which the resolved bevils are marked, at such distances as that each bevil shall converge to the centre of the dog, u. This is easily accomplished by a common bevil square applied to the edge of the board, and, guided by a temporary straight-edge, radiating round the axis of the dog. The bevils, b b, c c, d d, e e, f f, are thus transferred to the board, and are there indicated by the same letters. The log being now fixed in the dogs, so that the saw may enter at the end, b, and the first bevil, b b, struck on the end of the log, the arm, o o, is to be moved until b b becomes perpendicular, to admit of the entrance of the saw. The board, or template, is now to be fixed to the nut of the arm, o o, by the thumb screw, so that the upper end of the bevil, b, coincides with the centre of the machine. As the sawing proceeds the arm o, o, is moved to the left hand, carrying the template along with it, until by the time that the part c on the log has reached the edge of the saw, the line c on the template has also reached the centre point of the machine, previously occupied by b. The motion of the arm is continued until the points o, e, and f, have each in succession passed underneath the centre at the several times that those parts of the log have reached the cutting edge of the saw. In order to secure a perfect uniformity of change from one bevil to another, the distances of b, c, d, e, and f, from each other are measured along the

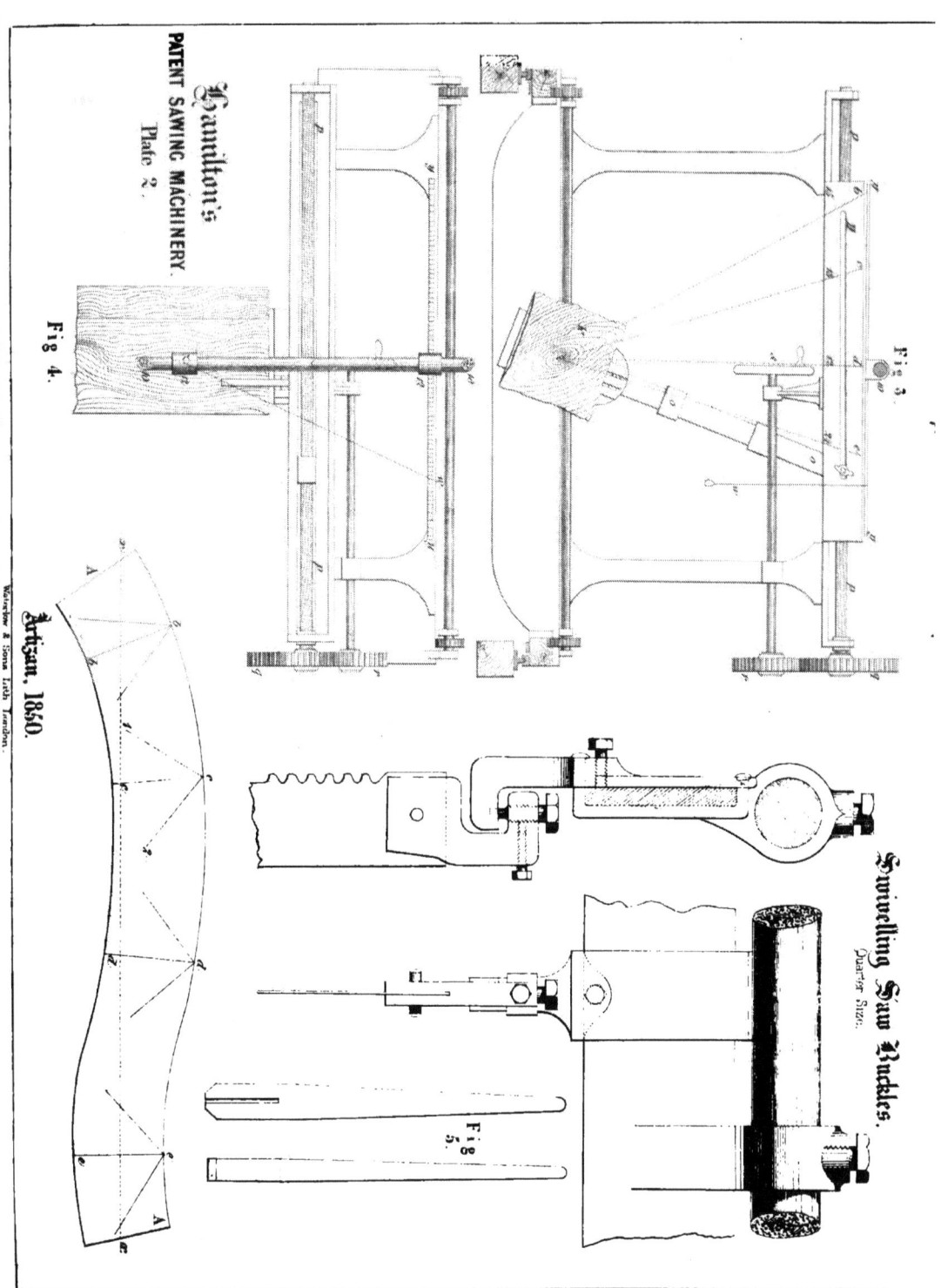

Hamilton's
PATENT SAWING MACHINERY.
Plate 2.

Fig. 4.

Fig. 3

Artizan, 1850.

Waterlow & Sons Lith. London.

Swivelling Saw Buckles.
Quarter Size.

Fig. 5.

axis of the log, and are recorded on the template between the different bevils as the figures 15, 18, 12, and 24, which are supposed to indicate the number of inches that are contained between the several points marked on the log. The bar 10, 10, in fig. 2 (see plate), is accurately fitted to receive the sliding bar 12, 12, and is fixed to the centre of the machine at one end, and to a bracket, 11, on the wall of the building at the other, so as correctly to indicate the centre of the machine, and be perpendicular over the axis of the log. Fig. 4 is a plan of the same. The sliding bar, 12, 12, is graduated with inches from the centre *s* towards the cross bar *y y*. This cross bar being attached to the slider is finely notched all along its length, so as to retain the cord *s w*, wherever it may be placed ; as soon as the saw had entered the log on the line *b, b*, fig. 3, the slider was pushed forwards until the centre *s* numbered 15 inches in advance of the edge of the template. The cord *s w* was then thrown over the cross bar *y y*, so that radiating from the centre *s* it passed exactly over the mark *o* on the template; as the sawing advanced towards *o* on the log the lateral motion of the template was so regulated that the mark *o* was kept constantly under the line of the cord, and thus arrived under the centre *s* precisely at the same instant that it also arrived into the position formerly occupied by *b*. The slider was again pushed forward 18 inches, and the cord stretched so as to lie over the mark *d* on the template, and the sawing continued till in succession all the log had been thus passed over.

It will be obvious, from the foregoing explanation, that whatever curve the saw may have been describing on the surface of the timber, the operation of bevilling is precisely the same.

In order to prevent any difficulty to the attendant in following the curved lines marked upon the timber, he is provided with a flexible hose and nozzle, connected to a blowing machine, by which the saw-dust, which would otherwise accumulate on the lines, is readily blown away.

We have thus described at length the various details connected with the construction and operation of this ingenious and useful machinery; but we still have some doubt whether any degree of explanation, short of an actual examination of the machinery itself, can give our readers complete satisfaction. We look forward, therefore, with great pleasure to an opportunity which will shortly be afforded the scientific world of examining and witnessing the operation of one of the machines at the works of Messrs. J. & A. Blyth, engineers, London, who are about to construct a set for the patentees.

AGRICULTURAL ENGINEERING.

Since we last noticed Lord Willoughby's steam plough (*ante*, p. 80), considerable progress has been made towards solving the problem of the economy of steam ploughing, by the construction of a very light and powerful locomotive, built at Swindon works, by Mr. Gooch, for the express purpose, and named the "California." The engine is on four wheels, and the tender on two only, being supported by the engine. The cylinders are placed at the smoke-box end, above the barrel of the boiler, and no fly-wheel is used, the chain barrels being on a second motion, worked by bevil gear. We can add but little to our former description of the method of ploughing, but we may give the following particulars from the description accompanying the plates, published for his Lordship by Mr. Ridgway:—

"The machinery employed consists of the "California," a locomotive engine, weighing 3½ tons, and of twenty-six horses power. (It was designed by Mr. Gooch, to whose friendship on this, as on many other occasions, I am so greatly indebted.) It has a double capstan attached, removable when the engine is required for other purposes.

"The engine moves across the centre of the field on a light portable railway. The ploughs advance and recede on either side of the railway, at right angles to it.

"The plough employed consists of four ordinary, and the like

number of subsoil ploughs, fixed in a frame: it is directed by a person standing upon a small platform.

"Two such ploughs, one on either side the railway, alternately advance and recede ; the advancing plough working, the other idle until it regains its proper position for ploughing the next four furrows. On the completion of the four furrows both ways, the engine and side frames advance each 3 feet.

"The ploughs are attached to an endless chain 150 yards in length. They can be detached at pleasure, or shifted from one side the chain to the other. They travel at the rate of 5 miles an hour. Provision is made in case they strike against any impediment. There is also a provision on the carriage for tightening the chain at the fences, by which the length may be varied 40 feet, to suit irregularly-shaped fields. If any further alteration is necessary, the chain is made in 80 feet lengths, one of which can be added or taken out as required.

"The full power of the engine is not exerted with the ploughs above described ; and the number of blades can therefore be increased, if experience proves it to be advisable.

"In the present state of things it is difficult to form a correct estimate of the value of the invention in a commercial point of view. I will only say, that a machine of the power, and with the arrangements described, would perform the work usually done by 16 ploughs, driven by as many men, and drawn by 32 horses. Requiring itself the attendance of 8 men, and a horse to draw the water for the engine, it would thus save the labour of 31 horses and 8 men. Against this must be set an expense of five shillings a day for coals, as well as 10 per cent. upon the value of the machinery, say three shillings a day upon an original cost of 450*l*. to 500*l*. This latter item, however, would be fully compensated by the saving in the interest of capital now laid out on horses.

"The machinery is only calculated for the cultivation of flat land. It might possibly be used with advantage in the West Indies.

"Willoughby de Eresby."

Mr. Caird, who, by the by, does not seem much the worse for the "harrowing" he experienced at the hands of *Blackwood*, continues his reports on the agricultural districts, and much interesting information may be gleaned from them. The farmers are often taunted with their supposed slowness in adopting any improvements in their operations ; but a more hopeful picture is drawn by the Commissioner, who may be considered, too, rather hard to please. Near Mansfield we are told "the land is drawn into ridges 27 inches apart, on the top of which the turnip seed is sown with a drill, which at the same time deposits beneath it a layer of ashes, soaked in liquid manure, at the rate of 20 quarters an acre. *The seed, falling on this moist bed, springs at once*, and the chief difficulty in clay land, that of getting the small seed of the turnip to strike, is thus completely obviated."

"Mr. Paget, near Nottingham, farms 300 acres, and sends 1100*l*. worth of milk and butter to Nottingham annually."

In Staffordshire, we are told that the experience which has been acquired in mining has led to a more scientific and successful system of drainage than in most other districts ; a hint which ought not to be lost on some of our civil engineers, who might turn their attention to this subject with great advantage.

On Sir Robert Peel's estate, at Tamworth, some trouble has been experienced by the choking up of the drains by an ochrey deposit. One main drain pipe, 12 inches' diameter, was nearly closed by it, and had to be cleaned out by drawing a long iron wire, with a bunch of straw tied to it, right up the pipe, for which purpose it was necessary to sink openings every hundred yards or so into the drain. After the ochre is loosened by the rubbing of the straw, the drain is flushed, and the deposit washed away. On a neighbouring estate the wheat is drilled on what we suppose may be called the "ventilating system." "Instead of drilling in the usual way, at 9 inches between the rows, two rows are put in at 4 inches apart, and then with an interval of 14 inches, thus getting the same number of rows in the same space, but with alternate intervals so wide as to admit of very effectual horse hoeing, the smaller interval being cleaned with the hand hoe."

The manufacture of concentrated milk seems likely to offer a fresh field for profit. The milk is evaporated by a steam heat of about 110°, in a shallow copper vessel, with a certain proportion of sugar, and is kept constantly stirred for four hours, when it is reduced to about one-fourth its original bulk. It is then put in tin cases, the covers soldered on, and then exposed to a boiling heat. It will keep for a long time, and must be valuable on board ship. The emigration movement ought to supply a good market for this "manufactured article."

Another speculative individual manufactures an "English Guano," by converting bones into superphosphate of lime. The bones are boiled in a perforated cylinder, and yield about 5 per cent. of grease, which is sold to soapboilers for 25*l.* a ton. The bones are then crushed, moistened with water, and treated with sulphuric acid, which dissolves them. They are finally crushed to powder, and either sold alone or mixed with equal weights of guano. It is an invariable fact, and one that ought to be borne in mind by those who are connected with the drainage of towns, that whenever a farmer is found to be doing particularly well, a liquid manure tank forms part of his economy. We cannot do better than conclude our gleanings with an account of a strictly engineering piece of work.

The part of Lord Hatherton's estate at Teddesley, near Penkridge, which is farmed by his lordship, embraces about 1700 acres, a large proportion of which was originally part of Cannock Chase. It extends from the river Penk over the wooded heights which bound the view eastward from the Penkridge station, on the London and North-Western Railway. Thirty years ago the whole of this tract was in a most neglected state, great part of it was a worthless waste, without roads, undrained, and open and exposed to the wintry blasts which sweep over the elevated grounds of the Midland counties. It is now a rich and fertile domain, carrying luxuriant crops of wheat and barley, the upper parts ornamented with sheltering woods, the pastures folded over with flocks of Southdown sheep, the extensive farm-buildings filled with cattle, while the lower slopes are covered with verdure produced by irrigation. The skill which has been shown in turning to advantage every provision of nature in each step of pro-gressive improvement is what is chiefly instructive here. The water which soaked through the bogs and elevated swamps, rendering them barren, is drained and collected into a reservoir. From this it is con-veyed to the farm buildings, which it supplies with water for the stock; it turns the machinery which manufactures the products of the farm, and then glides off to enrich by irrigation a tract of meadows, 111 acres in extent, the produce of which has been doubled by the process, at an annual cost of 4s. 6d. an acre for attendance in laying on the water.

The ease with which a constant supply of water for driving ma-chinery may be obtained is well illustrated here. A bog, 30 acres in extent, left unplanted in the middle of a plantation, having been con-sidered irreclaimable, was thoroughly drained. Besides the surface water, some strong land springs were tapped, and the whole conveyed by main drains to a reservoir, a few acres in extent, whence the water flows underground about half a mile to the farm buildings. The drainage of this swamp, and that of 140 or 150 acres more adjoin-ing it, gives an ample supply for working machinery of twelve horses power every day throughout the year; and before the lands were drained, this water was not only lost as a motive power, but did im-mense injury by stagnating beneath the surface, and extending its chilling effects to every portion of ground through which it slowly oozed from its source. At the farm buildings to which the stream is conveyed a mill-wheel, 38 feet in diameter, is sunk into the solid sand-stone rock to such a depth that the water discharges itself into it "overshot." The tail water is taken from the bottom of the wheel by a tunnel driven through the solid rock for nearly 500 yards, whence it is conducted into channels for irrigation. When the mill is stopped, the water between the reservoir and the wheel, which would otherwise run to waste, is conveyed by pipes to the different yards and buildings, for the use of the stock, from which any surplus finds its way to the

meadows. The purposes to which the water power is applied are these:—It turns two pairs of stones (one, as we saw it, grinding wheat, the other pease), it grinds malt, works a circular saw, a lathe, a chaff-cutter, and a thrashing-machine. The whole of these can be worked at the same time, though in practice that is seldom necessary. It has been in operation for several years, working every day, and all day, summer and winter. Independent altogether of the improvement of the land by drainage, and the subsequent use of the water in irrigation, its direct value as a motive power is estimated to exceed 500*l.* a year, and that was obtained by a total expenditure of about 1,700*l.* In a multitude of cases a similar power to this could be as easily got, which at present is suffered to stagnate in the ground, or if collected in drains, then heedlessly allowed to run to waste; for there were no unusual facilities on this estate for obtaining a supply of water. All that is re-quired is procured from the drainage of about 200 acres of land. It is carried in earthen pipes along a gentle declivity, and with very little leakage, about 600 yards from the reservoir to the mill, and is then dis-charged through a tunnel; the whole distance from the reservoir to the outfall being 1,200 yards, and the total fall being about 50 feet. On this point we take the opinion of Mr. Williams, civil engineer (page 26 of his pamphlet, published by Ridgway), "*On the Application of Drainage Water to Mill Power* :

"There is surely nothing here described which would lead a casual observer to imagine that water power equal to 12 horses was to be found in such a situation. The estimate usually formed of the requisites for the use of water as a motive power, is a large stream or brook of water, having a considerable fall in its course, and the term 'mill-stream,' which is given to such currents, invariably conveys the im-pression of a large body of water, flowing very rapidly down a channel having considerable inclination; the only other idea which seems to be associated with the driving of waterwheels is the nearly vertical descent of a comparatively small body of water down the face of some sharp declivity, and in cases of this kind large overshot wheels are occasion-ally to be met with; but I am not aware of any other instance where the water derived from the under-drainage of the land, and that alone, has been converted to purposes so valuable, and where so much in-genuity has been displayed in the adaptation of means which, to a superficial observer, would appear totally inadequate to the production of such important results. The merit of the plan consists in its originality; there is nothing in the practical adoption of the principle which suggests difficulty, and every one who examines it on the spot naturally asks himself—why has not this been adopted elsewhere."

ATHERTON'S PATENT EXPANSION GEAR.
To the Editor.

SIR,—I beg to submit, for the consideration of Steam-Engine Pro-prietors, the following particulars, in illustration of the defects of the *Cam-motion* Expansive Gear usually adopted in steamers; and also to describe my recently-invented *Eccentric* Expansion Gear, whereby the defects of the Cam-motion Expansion Gear are obviated, and whereby the economy derivable from the principle of expansion may be practi-cally realised.

The advantages of working steam expansively being admitted, the mode of effecting that object is a matter which deeply affects the interests of Steam-Engine Proprietors; particularly the interests of Steam-Shipping Companies; and more especially the Owners of Screw Vessels, of which the engines are worked at unusual speed.

In marine engines, the expansion of steam is effected either by the steam slide, or by the cam-motion expansion slide. When the steam slide only is used, the steam is not usually *cut off* at less than two-thirds of the stroke; and to obtain the remaining small degree of expansive action, through about one-third of the stroke only, the danger of break-ing down the engine is incurred, by the liability to water being confined in the cylinder, or else the steam does not act with its full force on the piston, by reason of the steam-ports not being fully opened; and in all cases, the very limited extent to which steam is worked expansively by means of the steam-slide alone, is far short of the limit to which the principle of expansion may be advantageously carried out; consequently, an additional slide is employed, which is driven by the apparatus known as the *cam-motion*, by the operation of which the expansion slide receives a *sudden motion* or impulse, whereby the steam-way is opened, and again another sudden impulse in the opposite direction, whereby the steam-way is closed; so that, in *each* revolution of the engine, the steam-way having to be opened twice and closed twice, *four* such impulses, or sudden motions, *in alternately opposite directions*, require to be communicated by the *cam-motion* to the expansion slide. It follows, therefore, that in marine engines, making, for example, 20 revolutions per minute, the expansion slide, and all the apparatus connected therewith, weighing probably several hundred weight, have to be started into motion, and as suddenly arrested 80 times per minute; and in the case of direct-action engines making *seventy-five revolutions per minute*, as is frequently required of engines, even of large size, driving the screw-propeller, the number of such distinct movements to be communicated by the cam-motion to the expansion slide, *amounts to 300 per minute;* and, further, supposing the steam to be taken on at the turn of the stroke, and to be cut off at one-eighth of the stroke, the expansion slide will require to be started into motion, arrested, and again started upon its back motion, all in the period of about *one-tenth of a second*, a requirement obviously unattainable.

Such being the attempted action of the Cam-motion Expansion Gear, it fails of attaining the required precision: the joints soon become loose, and the noise of its operation insufferable; consequently, its constant application is soon dispensed with, and the *economy* which ought to be derived from the principle of working expansively fails of being realized.

To obviate the defects above referred to, it is now proposed to drive the expansion slide by means of an Eccentric Motion, as by the drawings annexed. It will be observed that the expansion slide being driven by an eccentric wheel, *is not subject to any sudden impulse*, but is kept in continuous motion, like the steam slide; it will consequently operate as *noiselessly* as the steam slide; be as little liable to derangement; and work with the same *invariable precision*, whatever be the number of revolutions at which the engine may be driven.

Referring to Fig. 1—the engine is supposed to be taking on the steam at the extremity of the stroke; C is the axis of the crank-shaft on which the expansive eccentric wheel is supposed to be placed; C g is the medium direction of the eccentric rod, on which the distance C a is taken, *equal* to the steam aperture E through the slide. Also, C b is taken equal to C a, and from the points (a), (C), (b), the lines (a x), (C y), (b x), are drawn perpendicular to (C g). It will be found that if the slide be driven by an eccentric wheel, having its centre at (a), and the connexion with the slide be completed, as shown by the drawing, C a will be the radius of the circle described by the centre of the eccentric wheel, the throw will be twice C a, and the aperture E of the slide will *not* pass beyond the corresponding port E', consequently steam will be admitted throughout the whole revolution; if, however, on the line (a x), we take any point (p), and bring the centre of the eccentric wheel up to that point, then C p will be the radius of the circle that will be described by the centre of the eccentric wheel, which circle will pass beyond the limits of the lines (a x) and (b x), and it is evident that whilst the centre (p) of the eccentric wheel is in the act of passing between the lines (a x) and (b x), the aperture, E, of the slide will be passing the port E', and steam will be *admitted;* but when the centre of the eccentric wheel is beyond the limits of (a x) and (b x), the faces F of the slide will be opposite the port E', and the steam will be *cut off.*

It will be observed that the angles p C s, s' C p', represent the portions of the revolution during which the steam will pass the expansion-slide, and the angles s C s' and p' C p represent the portions of the revo-

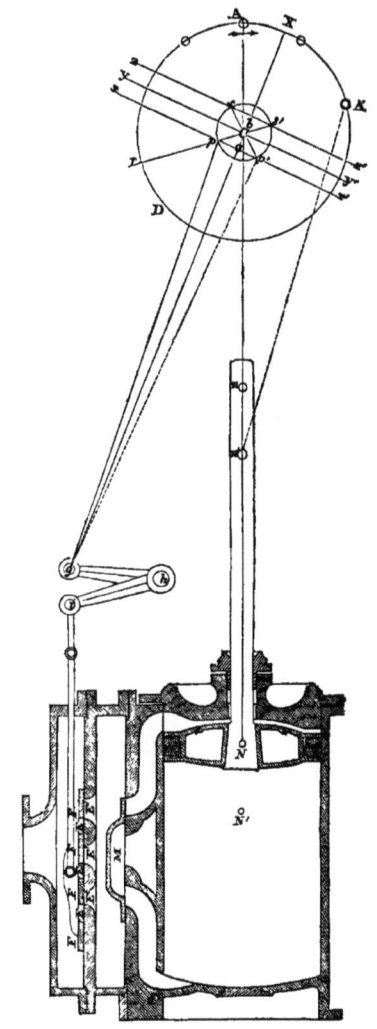

lution during which the faces F of the slide will be *opposite* the ports E', and consequently for these periods the steam will be cut off; and it is apparent that the farther the point (p) is distant from the point (a), the smaller will be the angles p C s and s' C p', in comparison with the angle s C s' and p' C p; that is, the smaller will be the period during which the steam is admitted, in comparison with the period during which the steam is cut off.

If, therefore, we so construct an eccentric wheel, that it be properly seated upon the shaft, and be so arranged that *its centre may be made to traverse at pleasure on the line* (a x), we shall, by thus altering the position of the eccentric wheel, produce the effect of varying the degree of expansion at pleasure, as may be required.

Figs. 2 and 3 show one of the numerous methods of construction whereby an eccentric wheel may have the required property above referred to; viz., its centre being made to traverse at pleasure on the line (*a p*) the line (*a p*) not passing through (C), the axis of the shaft, but passing at a given distance (C *a*) therefrom.

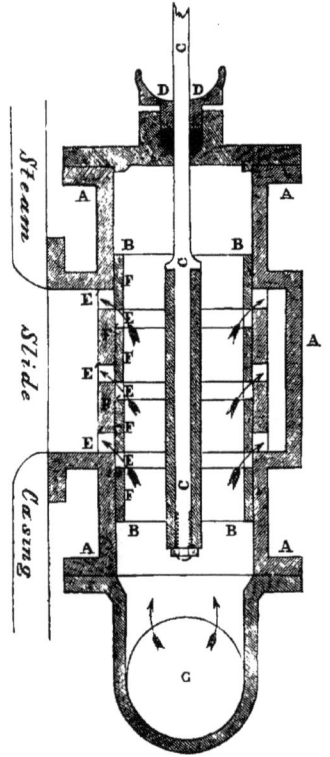

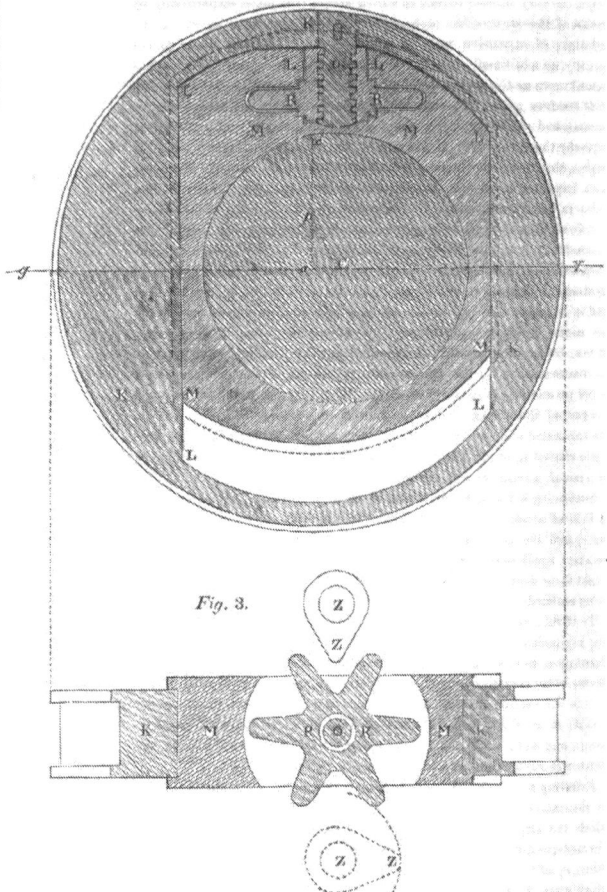

Fig. 3.

K is a skeleton eccentric wheel.

L, the void space of the skeleton eccentric wheel.

M, a block fitted upon the shaft, and either fixed or connected with a clutch, the opposite sides being parallel to each other and to the line (*a p*), upon which block the skeleton eccentric wheel is made to slide or traverse the required distance (*a p*) or any part thereof.

O, a screw fixed to the rim of the eccentric wheel, and called the leading screw.

R, a nut fitted within the block M, working upon the screw O, and made to turn like a swivel by means of the arms projecting from it forming a ratchet wheel, whereby the nut R may be turned by hand when the engine is not in motion, or by one or other of the moveable finger-pieces, Z Z, when the engine is in action. Or, instead of the nut R being furnished with the ratchet-wheel arms, it may be furnished with a screw-wheel, and be operated upon by a tangent screw.

It is apparent that by this construction the centre of the eccentric may be made to traverse at pleasure upon the line (*a p*), even whilst the engine is in motion.

The expansion-slide may be either flat, as in Fig. 1, with one, two, or more apertures, E, or it may be cylindrical, as in Fig. 4; but, in constructing it, care must be taken that the width of the respective faces, F, between the apertures of the slide, may give a sufficient range for the *extreme travel* of the slide when working the steam expansively in the *greatest* required degree.

CHARLES ATHERTON, Chief Engineer.
H. M. Dockyard, Devonport.

ON ADJUSTING THE COMPASSES OF IRON SHIPS.
To the Editor.

SIR,—I have the honor of acknowledging the receipt of your note, requesting any information in my power regarding the loss of the *Orion*, and the general phenomena of the variation of the compass in iron vessels.

The evidence given at the trial of the officers of that unfortunate ship was to this effect :—After I had completed the adjustment of her compasses the maximum error was 2¼° with the one by which she was steered, and the aberration of the second on the bridge amounted only to 2°. Yet, notwithstanding all the accuracy that may be accomplished in the adjustment of the compass, I would not have the temerity to declare its infallibility, or that a deflection of the needle might not take place that would jeopardize many a noble ship ; for my experience has shown me that there are circumstances of an accidental character to which compasses are liable, calculated to produce considerable error, without being attributable to inaccuracy of adjustment.

Mr. Stebbing, in his remarks, has stated a broad and simple truth, —"that all practical difficulties are surmounted in the adjustment of the compasses of iron craft, and that they may be navigated with as much safety as those built of wood." But having had nine years' experience in this department, it may not be uninteresting to state the results of my experience on one or two important points, and endeavour to remove a prejudice that may arise from the belief that the errors produced from heeling over have not been entirely conquered.

This additional and distinct adjustment I have adopted for a long period with complete success ; but the disturbance from this cause does not characterize the whole, for in some vessels, where the original error is small and a number of magnets are employed in the correction, the heeling over produces scarcely any effect ; yet in others an enormous deviation is produced from this cause. This is exemplified in a vessel called the *Lion*, of Hull, a large Hamburgh steamer. Previous to commencing the adjustment I had her listed over, and found a deviation of 40° ; this formidable error I surmounted, and then proceeded by the acknowledged system of Professor Airy (to whom we are all indebted for his invaluable investigation in this most important branch of science,) and I have the pleasure of stating, that at the completion of her adjustment, she was as correct as any wood-built ship afloat, either when heeling over or when upright, and has given perfect satisfaction to her commander.

The following observations, although simple in their nature, may be of use to those ignorant of the subject. After the adjustment of iron vessels I would recommend attention to the weight of the card, and the length, quality, and intensity of the needles ; for in time, when there may be a necessity for a change in the compass, arising from friction, or other causes, an alteration in any of the above points would be likely to produce a difference from the original correction. I would likewise impress strongly on nautical men the necessity for examining, or causing to be examined, very frequently the agate, or jewel, on which the centre moves ; for in steam vessels the vibration is a great evil, and that which is created by blowing off their boilers, will do more mischief in five minutes than could be produced in a sailing vessel in as many months ; in fact, with some this vibration will cause the agate and centre to be affected so seriously that the card would stand anywhere, and consequently if trusted to, would be worse than having none at all. The state of the agates may be easily ascertained by feeling the surface with a pin or fine point ; if any roughness is discovered the agate is no longer fit for use.

The effects of vibration were shown very remarkably in a screw steamer, called the *Dublin*, in a very short period, and was the cause of our constructing a compass to remedy this evil, which proved perfectly successful; for when supplied to this vessel she was enabled to steer with accuracy for two or three months without requiring repair.

Our idea was :—If the bowl containing the card could be floated in any liquid, without coming in contact with the metal, the effects of vibration would very materially be cut off, and the result was, after having been well tested, they were ordered for the North American Mail Steamers, and numerous others, and have given great satisfaction.

I may here pay a well-deserved compliment to Charles Mc. Iver, Esq.,

for his extreme vigilance in not only personally examining the aberration of the compasses in that fleet, but in giving instructions to swing each vessel at every available opportunity, in order to ascertain and register, the deviations upon each point, which may enable me to discover whether a change occurs from sudden magnetic disturbance, effluxion of time, or other causes.

I have every reason to believe that in some vessels the change is rapid, and shows the necessity for the process of swinging to be more generally adopted.

In carrying out my former observations with regard to adjustment on Professor Airy's principle, there is one point of a very satisfactory nature ; when magnets are made properly, and placed in situations not exposed to the production of oxide, their permanent quality is of a very high order, and the reduction of power in the great majority of cases is so exceedingly slow in its operation, that no serious inconvenience may be apprehended from that cause.

I would likewise impress upon parties interested, the absolute necessity for a careful determination of the truthfulness of the stations on which their shore compasses may be placed, and in order to inform those unacquainted with the process, the following simple instructions will suffice.

Let a compass of the exact description necessary for the vessel, (fitted with revolving sights) be placed in the binnacle, and your assistants (each with a compass) be placed at localities which you consider free from local disturbance ; to determine which let a repetition of cross bearings be taken from each of the compasses, before placing the vessel in the required position for adjustment. All must perfectly agree on shore with the amount of error as shown by the binnacle compass ; you will thereby be able to place the ship's head in any position you may require, without the necessity of taking the line of the masts, for upon the quays of many docks there are obstacles to its accomplishment in that way.

When I wish to bring the ship's head due north, I direct my sights, (after the signal is given) to one of my assistants, who directs his sights to me. Should his observation be 30° W., and mine 20°, I refer to my second shore compass, and if I find the results agree, of course there is a deflection of the needle to the westward of 10° ; and if that is the amount from due north, the vessel's head is due north, ready for the first adjustment.

In adopting this process, it enabled me to discover at Goole a local disturbance of a very serious character, produced by iron land ties, running into the made land, which, with a party dependant on one compass, and taking the line of the masts, would have caused him no little perplexity.

I beg now to conclude my few remarks, by stating that the unremitting attention to this subject displayed by Capt. Johnson, R.N., and many others of late years, has had the effect of drawing attention to the necessity of great accuracy and vigilance, in the process of rectifying the aberration, and of constructing, in the most perfect manner, an instrument, on which the lives and fortunes of so many of our fellow-countrymen depend.

I remain, Sir,

Your obedient Servant,

JOHN GRAY,

Liverpool, September, 1850.   Of the firm of Gray and Keen.

ON EQUILIBRIUM VALVES.
To the Editor.

SIR,—It is with anything but pleasant feelings I observe the bragging of the Americans about their crack boat, the *Atlantic*, beating our boats in their voyages to and from America ; but from the Liverpool Mercury of the 9th of August last, it is some consolation to observe that the *Asia* has made the quickest trip ever yet performed.

If there is anything that gives the superiority to their boats, it is their having much larger space for eduction, and their valves being balanced; in proof of which, I have read in an American paper that after her first voyage, the eduction pipes and passages of the *Atlantic* were much enlarged, which much increased her speed; and in your description of Sickle's expansion gear, page 182, you state that " in the American Atlantic boats, one man can handle the engines, while in Cunard's boats, of about the same size, a whole gang of men are required ;" so these last boats' valves destroy a great deal of the power. As a further proof, I will relate what I have done to my own nine-inch engine, which drives my threshing mill. I am not an engineer, but sufficiently acquainted with engines to know when they are going wrong, and to give directions for their alteration. When I first had mine, I found the steam and eduction pipes were what is generally considered a good proportion, that is, one-fifth the diameter, or $\frac{1}{25}$ the area of the cylinder, the ports being 4 by $\frac{1}{2}$ with $\frac{1}{8}$ inch lap on valve; it then required the steam 50 before it would do any work, and then not longer than $\frac{1}{4}$ of an hour, when it stopped, and would not start again under 50 lbs. pressure. I had a new nozzle with ports 6 × 1$\frac{1}{4}$, and the passages increased to $\frac{1}{4}$th the area of cylinder, and the lap increased, so that when the engine was at top centre, the top port was just opening, and the lower port was $\frac{3}{4}$ open to eduction; it then worked well with steam about 33. But here a difficulty arose; the extra pressure on the enlarged valve required stronger apparatus to work the valve, and not being strong enough, it bent and would not work the valve; so stronger work was applied. I found that it took 378 lbs. to move the valve when the pressure of steam was 25 lbs. and having a four inch cylinder by me, I placed it at the back of the slide case at *a*, after the inclosed plan, fig. 1, and it took only 190 lbs. to move the valve, and the engine then worked very well with only 25 lbs. pressure; it would have taken a larger cylinder at back of slide case.

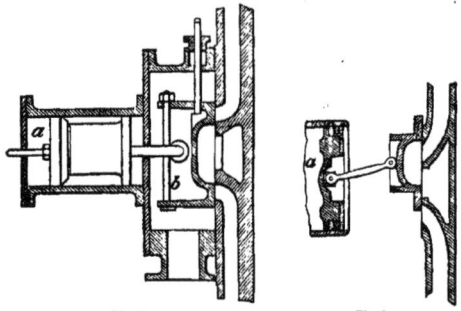

Fig. 1.   Fig. 2.

I had seen a plan of a cylinder something like it, the valve and the piston being connected by a rod with two hinge joints, but as the connecting rod would move in the arc of a circle, part of the stroke would push the piston and part would draw it; considering that when the piston was being drawn in, it increased the pressure instead of diminishing it, I adopted the roller, it having a regular pull against the back of the valve; say if I am correct? Did not alter the steam pipe, so did not open the ports to the steam but about $\frac{1}{2}$, which had about as much area as the 2 inch steam pipe, so the travel of the slide was short. I consider it is the steam left in the cylinder of a non-condensing engine after the valve is shut, by being compressed when passing the centre, which causes the back pressure; this is obviated by the increased lap; but as no steam remains in a condensing engine, such an increased lap is not required. When I put the extra lap to my valve, the engine passed the centres very free, and it cut off the steam at three quarters of the stroke.

Another contrivance our first rate engineers should adopt, that is to admit beyond the grate, sufficient atmospheric air in jets for its oxygen to ignite, first, the carburetted and bi-carburetted hydrogen gas, and then the carbonic oxide; this would save a great many tons of coal

during the voyage, the vessel would not be so deep in the water, and of course take less power to move her, as there would be less water to displace.   Yours, &c.,   ISLE OF MAN.

[Our correspondent deserves credit for his ideas, but he has fallen into a slight error on the subject of the proportions, which we will explain. In *low pressure* engines, $\frac{1}{15}$ the area of the cylinder is often taken for the area of the ports; but in *high pressure* engines, the cylinder being so much smaller for the same power, the same rule does not obtain. As from 22 to 25 inches on a low pressure cylinder are commonly reckoned equal to a nominal horse power, it follows that the former rule is nearly equivalent to one inch of port per horse power. This way of stating the question would give too large a port for the high pressure cylinder; 4 × $\frac{1}{2}$ is too small, and 6 × 1$\frac{1}{4}$ is needlessly large, with a short slide, wasting a great deal of steam. About $\frac{1}{30}$ the area of the cylinder will be found a good proportion for high pressure engines, and will admit of considerable speed of piston without any back pressure, particularly if there is a little lap on the slide. This would give a port of about 4$\frac{1}{2}$ × 1 inch. We have given a sketch, fig. 2, of the method of balancing the valves employed in the Great Western locomotive, " Iron Duke," which we understand has not been found to answer satisfactorily. His plan has the disadvantage that it can only be said to be in equilibrium when the centre of the roller is over the centre of the slide, at half stroke. It would require two rollers and a stiff rigid bar, to prevent the unequal pull that the one roller has on the slide, when it is at either extremity of its stroke. A description of a new form of equilibrium slide, patented by M. Mazeline of Havre, will be found in our last vol., at page 169, with a calculation by Mr. Holm of the power required to work the slides of a locomotive. Mr. C. Wye Williams, or some other of the numerous band of smoke burners, would, we are afraid, come down on our correspondent, if he were to attempt to put his plan in practice, of admitting jets of air behind the fire-bars. It is strictly scientific, but unfortunately you cannot get stokers to measure off the precise number of cubic feet of air to the shovel of coals, and as any excess of cold air passing into the flues, can only cool them down, " our first rate engineers," (including our humble selves, if we may be allowed to pass in such good company,) have come to the conclusion that ample heating surface, a moderate rate of combustion, and thin fire-bars, are more likely to *pay* in the long run, than most of the various ingenious combinations, into which boiler furnaces have been tortured.—ED. ART.]

To the Editor,

Belfast, September, 1850.

MR. EDITOR,—Sir, Will any of your correspondents solve the following problem ? Suppose a hollow cast-iron shaft of such a diameter and such a height so that the weight shall be sufficient to crush the metal in the base, and when filled with water to the top the weight of water shall equal the weight of the shaft, and suppose the thickness of metal at the top to be 2 inches,—required, the height and weight; the thickness at the base to be such as just sufficient to restrain the pressure of the water; and with what force and velocity would a slice cut from the top, 1 foot deep, reach the ground, and with what velocity would the water issue from a jet at the base, and how long would it take to empty itself through an orifice 12 inches diameter.

———   I am, &c., B. A.

To the Editor.

London, September, 1850.

MR. EDITOR,—Sir, The diameter of the balloon in A. E.'s query of Chelsea, may be found in the following manner:—first, to find the pressure or density of the atmosphere at an altitude of 10,000 feet we have log. 30 — $\frac{10000}{63946}$ =log. of pressure = 20·93. The weight of one cubic foot of this atmosphere is as 30 : 20·93 : : 553 : 386 grains, and deducting $\frac{1}{14}$ for weight of hydrogen, we have 386 — 27·5 = 358·5 grains = the available buoyancy of each cubic foot, then to find the diameter of balloon we have $\sqrt[3]{\dfrac{2240 \times 7000}{358\cdot5 \times \cdot5236}}$ = 20·3 feet.

I am, yours truly, N. D.

CORRESPONDENCE.

WHITELAW'S STEAM-ENGINE EXPANSION GEAR.

To the Editor.

Johnstone, Renfrewshire, 17th Sept., 1850.

SIR,—If your readers interested in the matter take the trouble to examine the number of the *Repertory of Patent Inventions*, new series, published in January, 1835 ; some parts of the London *Mechanics' Magazine*, issued betwixt that date and 1840 ; Appendix B to *Tredgold on the Steam Engine ;* and the numbers for May, August, and September of the present year, of the *Glasgow Practical Mechanics' Journal*, they will see that the plan of expansion gear published in this month's number of the *Artizan* is mine, and that Messrs. John Petrie and Co. have not even the slightest claim to it.

I write to let parties who may require steam engines know, that they need not pay, in the shape of patent right, £1 per horse power for the use of the invention referred to, as it is and has, for a great length of time, been public property.

It may be as well to mention that what appears with my name to it in the present month's number of the Glasgow periodical above referred to, contains an inaccuracy or two, owing, I suppose, to the editor not forming a correct idea of what I wrote before he modified my letter to suit his pages.

The steam engines Messrs. John Petrie and Co. have made are not so simple and complete as they would have been if they had had the courage to adopt the whole of my improvements; but as hitherto they have, from time to time, laid aside an expedient of their own to replace it with something taken out of my plan, it is reasonable to suppose that by and by they will make a good steam engine. Their complicated governor will not help them out of their difficulties. I think I can let them know where they will find a description of something very like it, that was published prior to the first date above given.

I am, Sir, yours very respectfully,

JAMES WHITELAW.

ON CALCULATING EARTH-WORKS.

To the Editor.

SIR,—In calculating quantities of earth-work, the tables published by Sir John Macneill have been extensively used by both engineers and contractors, and I may add, deservedly so, for, with the exception of one formula, I am of opinion that they are correct. I allude to his rule for calculating the area of the transverse section of a cutting on "sidelong ground ;" which is, "to the rectangle of the depths, multiplied by the ratio of the slopes, add half the sum of the depths multiplied by the bottom width of the cutting, and the sum will be the area."

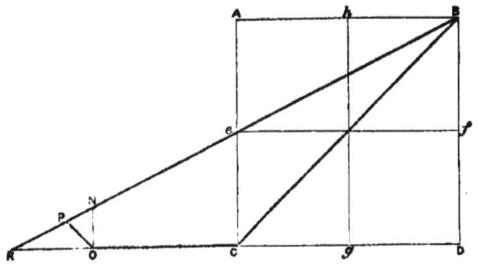

Now if we make N O in the above figure

$$
\begin{aligned}
\text{N O} &= 4 = d' \\
e\,\text{C} &\quad\cdots\quad = 12 = d \\
\text{O C} &\quad\cdots\quad = 16 = b \\
\text{Ratio of slope 1 to 1} &\quad\cdots\quad = r
\end{aligned}
$$

The rule becomes $r\,d'\,d + \dfrac{d'+d}{2} \times b$, or in figures the result is

$$1 \times 4 \times 12 + \frac{4+12}{2} \times 16 = 176 \text{ feet area of section.}$$ But this falls far short of the actual quantity. To illustrate which as simply as possible, construct the square A B C D, making its side 24 feet, bisect it by the lines $e f$, $g h$, and draw the diagonal C B, which will represent the slope of the cutting at an angle of 45° or " 1 to 1 :" next draw the line B e N, the surface of the ground, at an angle of 26° 34′ or " 1 in 2," and complete the section by drawing the other slope, the bottom, &c.

As the angle P O N is known to be 45°, and the angle O R N 26° 34′, it is obvious that the angle P N O is 63° 26′, and the angle O P N 71° 34′, consequently as the side O N and the three angles are known, you have ample data to ascertain that in this instance the area of the

		Ft.
Triangle N O P	=	5·63
Quadrilateral N e O C $= \dfrac{4+12}{2} \times 16$	=	128·00
Triangle C e b $= \frac{1}{2}(12 \times 24)$ ..	=	144·00
		277·63

the correct area of the section P O C B, which exceeds that obtained by Sir John Macneill's formula by 101·63 feet.

As this is a matter of great importance to parties engaged on public works, I shall feel obliged by your giving it a place in your valuable publication.

I am, Sir,

Your obedient Servant,

Brigg, Lincolnshire,   W. C. ATKINSON.

September 2nd, 1850.

INSTITUTION OF MECHANICAL ENGINEERS.

THE usual General Meeting of the members was held at the house of the Institution, Newhall Street, Birmingham, on Wednesday, the 24th July, 1850 ; J. R. M'Connell, Esq., Vice-President, in the Chair.

In opening the proceedings, the Chairman regretted that, on this occasion of the first meeting of the members of the Institution in their new house, they had not the presence of Mr. Robert Stephenson, their respected President, who was prevented from attending the meeting in consequence of being engaged at the floating of the last tube of the Britannia bridge.

The minutes of the last General Meeting were read by the Secretary, and confirmed.

The Chairman then said, he had the pleasure to announce to the members, that their President had given to the funds of the Institution the very handsome donation of £100, to mark his sense of the importance of the Institution ; and never were their prospects and finances in so flourishing a state as at the present time. They were now in possession of rooms for the meeting of the members at any time they came, where they would always find their Secretary to receive them, and afford information and assistance with reference to the proceedings and objects of the Institution. He hoped that they would soon be able to add to the usefulness of the Institution by a good mechanical and scientific library for reference, but this would of course depend upon the contributions towards so desirable an object ; they had already the nucleus of a library, and received the various engineering periodicals. He trusted that great practical benefit would result from the intercourse amongst the members which the Institution was calculated to afford. In conclusion, the Chairman proposed a vote of thanks to the President for his handsome donation, which was passed.

The Secretary then read the following paper, by Mr. William Smith, of Dudley :—" ON THE CONDENSATION OF STEAM IN THE ENGINES OF THE SOUTH STAFFORDSHIRE IRON DISTRICT, AND THE IMPROVEMENTS TO BE EFFECTED IN THEM."

THE object of the present paper with the accompanying series of Indicator Diagrams, which have been taken from the several engines by the author of the paper, is to show the present working condition of forty-eight of the largest class of mill, forge, and blast engines in South Staffordshire, with some remarks as to the practicability of improving them.

The general character of the Indicator Diagrams of the majority of these engines, shows a considerable pressure of steam, continued nearly uniform throughout the whole stroke of the piston, and averaging about 12 lbs. per square inch above the atmosphere in the forge and mill engines, and about 7 lbs. per square inch in the blast engines; with a very defective vacuum, commencing about the atmospheric line, and reaching only from 7 lbs. to 11 lbs. per square inch below the atmosphere at the end of the stroke, the average vacuum being about 6¼ lbs. per square inch below the atmosphere throughout the stroke. Some of the Indicator Diagrams from blast engines show a considerable expansive action, but not a good vacuum.

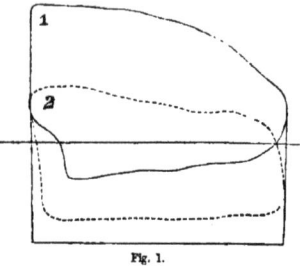

Fig. 1, shows the Indicator Diagram from a mill engine of 42 inch cylinder and seven feet stroke, making 17 strokes per minute, which was working very imperfectly in the condensation of the steam, and has been improved to a remarkable extent, by an alteration made for the purpose of improving the vacuum, which has effected a very considerable saving in the consumption of fuel. This engine was working with 19¾ lbs. pressure of steam at the beginning of the stroke, continued to 17⅓ lbs. pressure at the middle, and reduced to 6 lbs. per inch at the end of the stroke, by wire-drawing the steam without any cut off expansion valve; the average pressure being 16·37 lbs. per square inch throughout the stroke; the average vacuum was only 2·72 lbs. per square inch below the atmosphere, beginning a little above the atmospheric line, and reaching only 5 lbs. below the atmosphere at the end of the stroke. This performance being so bad it was considered necessary to examine the engine, and the cause was found to be from the valves, thoroughfares, and condenser being much too small for the proper proportion, the steam and eduction valves being only 7 inches diameter, and the thoroughfares of the same size; these were therefore removed and replaced by others, the steam valves being 10 inches diameter, and the eduction valves and thoroughfares 12 inches diameter, or three times the area of the original ones. The condenser was also nearly doubled in capacity by attaching a large vessel on the top of it, which made it rather larger than the regular proportion; the air pump was only 24 inches diameter, with half the stroke of the steam piston, or about ⅓th less contents than the regular proportion for the size of the cylinder, this was not altered, but there was an abundant supply of cold water for injection.

The result of the above alteration is shown in Fig. 2, the steam pressure being 8 lbs. at the beginning, and reduced to about the atmosphere at the end of the stroke, the average being 5·40 lbs. instead of 16·37 lbs. per square inch pressure throughout the stroke; the vacuum commenced at 10½ lbs. and ended at 11 lbs., the average being 10·15 lbs. instead of 2·72 lbs. per square inch below the atmosphere throughout the stroke. The improvement in the vacuum amounts therefore to a constant average pressure of 7·43 lbs. per square inch throughout the stroke; the total power of the engine, as shown by the first Diagram, was 19·09 lbs. per inch on the piston throughout the stroke, being 190 horse-power, consequently this improvement of the vacuum amounted to 39 per cent. of the total power of the engine or 74 horse-power.

The engine before the alteration had the steam valves, the eduction valves, and the thoroughfares only 7 inches diameter. By the alteration, the steam valves were increased to 10 inches diameter, and the eduction valves E and thoroughfares T to 12 inches diameter; the new valves being so much larger than the old ones, a different arrangement was required to make room for them, the spindle of the lower steam valve being carried up the side pipe, and the upper eduction valve placed over the other side pipe, so that three of the valve spindles are worked at the upper steam chest, and one only at the lower.

The addition made to the condenser, was a circular vessel constructed of boiler plate, 3 feet 6 inches diameter, and 15 inches high, fixed on the top of the condenser. A further improvement was also made in the condenser, by cleaning out the deposit of lime, and adding an internal injection pipe and rose; there was no internal injection pipe previously, but simply a hole in the side of the condenser, where the injection-cock was fixed on, and consequently the injection water was much less efficient in condensing the steam, being poured into the condenser in a single stream, instead of being scattered in a number of small jets from the rose end of the pipe.

The majority of engines in this district are similar in this respect, and the reason that has been given, is, that the rose is apt to get the holes choked up by deposit from the water, which is very much impregnated with lime. This is a matter requiring particular attention in this district, and cases have come under the writer's observation, where condensers were filled up by the deposit in the course of two or three years' time, to such an extent, that the capacity was reduced fully one half, as well as the passage through the foot valve; it is a very hard calcareous deposit, which adheres firmly to the cast iron, and requires considerable labour to cut it out, involving a serious stoppage of the engines, and they were consequently worked as long as possible before taking off the condenser cover to cut out the deposit, which increased to 7 inches thickness, and as much as half a ton weight in one engine.

Besides the very important saving effected by the greater power obtained from the steam, in consequence of the improvement of 39 per cent. in the vacuum, as described above, the engine has been found to do the work more regularly and satisfactorily since the alteration, than before; it was liable to be pulled up by any extra strain of the rolls, &c., whenever the piston was getting in want of repacking, as the leakage of steam injuring the vacuum on account of the very deficient condensing power; but that has not occurred since the alteration was made.

The engine drives a merchant mill of 3 pair of rolls, a guide mill of 3 pair, 2 pair of forge rolls, a forge hammer, 2 shears, and a pump for draining the foundations. It was not stopped longer than three days to make the whole of the alterations described above.

Another similar engine of the same size as the preceding, (No. 17) was also examined, in consequence of the imperfection in its condensing, and the valves and thoroughfares were found to be 10 inches diameter, but the valves had not sufficient lift; the eduction pipe to the condenser was 9 inches diameter, and the condenser was 2 feet 4 inches diameter, and 4 feet 6 inches high; the eduction pipe was then removed and replaced with one 12 inches diameter, also a large vessel was fixed on the top of the condenser, which increased its capacity about one third. The lift of the valves was then increased from 1¼ inch to 2⅜ inches, and the result of the alteration was an improvement in the vacuum of from 1·50 lbs. to 7·97 lbs. per square inch below the atmosphere, or 6·47 lbs. per square inch increase of average pressure throughout the stroke.

The saving of fuel from these alterations has not been well ascertained, as the engines in both cases are worked from a series of boilers which also supply steam to other engines upon which the load is very unequal, but the saving is admitted to be very considerable, and in the case of No. 17, the proprietors have been enabled to use an inferior description of slack, and also to throw off one boiler, with a fire grate about 7 feet square, and 45 square yards of heated surface, without any diminution in the power employed.

The aggregate power of the 45 mill, forge, and blast engines from which the indicator diagrams are taken, is nominally 3240 horse power, according to Boulton and Watt's proportions of the cylinders, but by the calculation of the indicator diagrams, the total is 7919 horse-power; the average vacuum obtained in the present working of all the engines, is about 6 lbs. per inch below the atmosphere throughout the stroke, omitting from the average four, which are exceptions to the general run of these engines; and the average vacuum obtained in the 6 expansive engines, of which indicator diagrams are also given, is 10½ lbs. per inch below the atmosphere throughout the stroke. The loss of power from the imperfect vacuum in the former engines may therefore be taken at the difference between these pressures, or 4½ lbs. per square inch pressure throughout the stroke, which amounts to 1930 indicated horse power upon these engines, or in other words, an additional power of 1930 horse power, or 26 per cent. increased power might be obtained from the same expenditure of steam, and consequently of fuel, if the vacuum were improved so as to be as good as the average of the 6 expansive engines, or 10½ lbs. per inch throughout the stroke. This vacuum has been obtained in the two engines, Nos. 12 and 17, which have been altered as before described, although in these engines the alteration was carried out only to a limited extent, and at a comparatively trifling expense; but if it were carried out efficiently by attaching expansive gear in addition to the alterations that have been made, a much better effect would be obtained by using the same volume of steam expansively.

In many cases the expansive action is accomplished by the addition of a separate expansion valve in the steam pipe, which is worked by a cam, so as to cut off the steam at any portion of the stroke that may be desired, this valve opening and shutting twice for each double stroke of the engine; the steam and eduction valves are worked by a common eccentric motion, the top and bottom valves opening and shutting together. But this is an imperfect mode of obtaining expansion, because the steam filling the side pipe and the two steam chests expands after the cut off valve is shut, and this steam forms a considerable proportion to the contents of the cylinder.

The only efficient mode of applying expansive action, is by lifting each valve by a separate cam, so adjusted as to shut each steam valve at whatever point of the stroke may be desired, whilst the eduction valve is held open till the termination of the stroke; by which means the full effect of the expansive action is obtained. The difference in effect between these two modes of cutting off the steam, is shown by the Diagrams Nos. 3 and 4, which are taken from a pair of blast engines working coupled together, and with no difference between them except that in No. 4 the steam is cut off by a separate expansion valve in the steam pipe, and in No. 3 the valves are lifted by separate cams.

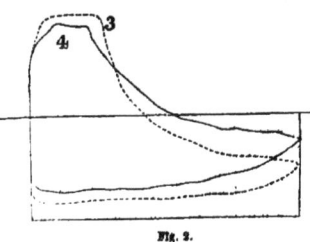

Fig. 2.

But independent of the loss sustained by not working expansively, the loss of power in the engines described being 1930 horse power as shown before, the annual loss in money by extra consumption of fuel in these engines, calculating 20 lbs. of slack per hour, for one horse power, at a cost of 3s. per ton, will amount to £18,610, or £2. 7s. 7d. per horse power per annum.

The total power of the steam engines employed in the manufacture of iron in this district, may be computed to be fully ten times the nominal power above named; and the total annual loss to the proprietor from the causes described in the present paper, may be therefore taken in round numbers at £180,000 per annum, as the more ex-

pansive engines described above may be considered a fair average of the engines in the district.

It has been generally considered hitherto, that the improvement of expansive action of steam was not applicable advantageously to the engines of this district, because of the small cost of the fuel employed; but this will be seen to be an erroneous conclusion from the actual results of the alterations described above, where the improvement was only effected in the vacuum, and the expansive principle was not carried out, which would have effected a still greater saving. The total quantity of fuel consumed at present is so large, that although the price per ton is insignificant, the total amount of saving effected by the per centage on the whole is very important.

In addition to the saving in cost of fuel consumed, a very important saving would also be effected in the tear and wear of the boilers, which is fully in proportion to the extra fuel burnt under them, and the repairing of which is invariably attended with serious inconvenience and expense.

The description of boilers in general use in the district, and the further saving to be effected by improvements in their construction and mode of setting, is also an important practical subject for consideration, and it is intended to form the subject of another paper, to be laid before the Institution at a future meeting.

The Chairman said he believed the writer was quite within bounds, when he estimated the saving in fuel which might be effected in that district alone at £180,000 per annum; nor was the subject of importance in that light merely, because it was found to prevail as a general rule, that the amount of destruction in machinery and boilers was nearly in proportion to the quantity of fuel consumed. He had remarked at a former meeting on the practical importance of obtaining comparative accounts as complete as possible of the consumption of fuel, and economy of working of the steam engines in the different districts of the country, and he thought that all information of that kind was of great practical value.

Mr. Bowman inquired whether, in most of the engines mentioned, the proportions of Boulton and Watt were observed in the condenser?

Mr. W. Smith replied, that, speaking generally, he believed that was the case, but the bad working of the engines was accounted for by the extraordinary pressure of the steam used. The error was, that engines intended and proportioned for 3 lbs. steam were worked up to 12 or 16 lbs. per inch throughout the stroke, and consequently, they were very imperfect in their condensing; as there was so much larger quantity of steam to be condensed at each stroke, when the cylinder full of high pressure steam expanded down to the same pressure as the low pressure steam.

Mr. Bowman observed, that this would seem to imply that the size of the condenser should be regulated by the pressure of the steam in the cylinder.

Mr. Cowper said, the pressure of the steam was certainly a necessary element to be taken into consideration, as well as the size of the cylinder, in determining the size of the condenser. There was not only a greater quantity of steam to condense when a higher pressure was employed, but also a greater quantity of air to pump out at each stroke of the air pump. He mentioned a case which came within his own observation in that district, where 18 lbs. steam was employed; there was no barometer guage, but the parties were satisfied that they had a good vacuum; however, the fact was, that the injection water was forced into the condenser by means of a cistern at the top of the engine house, 22 feet in height.

Mr. Slate remarked, that he fully concurred in the results obtained by Mr. Smith, but feared they were so startling that there would be a disinclination to give them credence in the district. It was highly important then that the truth of the deductions should be practically admitted.

Mr. T. Thorneycroft, as an iron master of the district referred to, felt extremely obliged to the author of the paper for pointing out the means whereby any saving could be effected, more especially at a time when, owing to the state of the trade, economy in the manufacture was so essential.

Mr. W. Smith said, it had often occurred to him, that a steam engine was like no other machine. A time-piece, if out of order, was sent back to the maker to be repaired, and in the case of machines of other descriptions, if they did not do their work well they were immediately stopped, because they wasted and injured the material upon which they were employed. But when the old steam engine, after 20 or 30 years of hard labour, showed some symptoms of disorder, it could not be stopped, so with an extra application of the coal shovel, and some hammering at the cotters, &c., it was set to work again, and with its powerful steam arm it wound round all the complicated machinery. This, however, was done at an enormous expense to the proprietor of the engine, and it would be much better if he were to renovate its constitution. He trusted that the exertions of the members of the Institution would have some influence in showing to persons of the description referred to, the necessity of carrying out these things on more efficient principles than they had hitherto been conducted.

Mr. Bowman thought it a matter of great importance that the injection water should spread itself out amongst the whole quantity of steam immediately on its passage into the condenser, and the alteration made by Mr. Smith in the mode of injection was very advantageous.

Mr. Cowper observed, that they ought all to add their testimony to the value of the indicator figures produced by Mr. Smith, because they showed the character of the engines much better than any judgment which could be formed with reference to them, inasmuch as it was the character of each engine written by itself, and could not be erroneous. He had not the slightest doubt, that a loss of £180,000 at least, as stated by Mr. Smith, was sustained in that district, because the mode of condensing ordinarily adopted was exceedingly defective. It had occurred to him many years ago, that a valve might be put at the side of the condenser, and connected with an injection pump, so that a gush of cold water might be injected at every stroke, at the very moment of the entrance of the steam into the condenser, and shut off again immediately, by which means the greatest possible use might be made of the injection water, and the condensation of the steam effected with a smaller quantity of injection water.

He then explained the drawing of an improved injection valve which he had constructed, and found to work very successfully: the object was to maintain the full pressure of the water at the point of entrance into the condenser, and to obtain a more efficient distribution of the jet of water without danger of its getting choked. In Fig. *a* is the condenser, *b* the eduction pipe, *c* the air pump, *d* the cold water cistern in which they are immersed; *e* is the injection valve, a conical valve rising a little above the bottom of the condenser, with a perforated cap below in the cold water cistern: this valve is lifted by the screwed rod *f*, and the admission of the injection water can be regulated with the greatest accuracy by the screw. The water enters the condenser in a fine sheet all round the valve, which strikes the sides of the condenser and fills the whole space with a fine spray; he had ascertained this by trying the valve in a box similar to the condenser, but partially open, with a column of water of the same pressure as the injection, and he found the distribution of the water was so perfect as to fill the box with a complete spray or fog. There was also a different construction in the air pump, which he considered advantageous; the bottom dropped into a well *g g*, in the bottom of the condenser, and the water rose up the space *g g*, when the air-pump bucket dipped into it, forming a water-valve instead of the ordinary foot-valve, and giving pressure enough to ensure the bucket-valve opening if there was any obstruction.

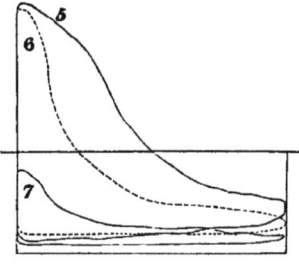

Fig. 5, shows the indicator figure, taken from the engine when in full work, at 24 revolutions per minute, driving shafting and two fans, and amounting to 72¾ indicated horse power. Fig. 6, is the indicator figure of the same engine when part of the work was thrown off, amounting to 38¼ horse power; and Fig. 7, is the indicator figure for the engine and four lines of shafting alone, without any work, amounting to 14 horse power, at the same speed of 24 revolutions per minute. The engine is high-pressure, expansive and condensing, and is one of a pair working coupled together: there was originally in their place, a pair of high-pressure engines, non-expansive and non-condensing, and the comparative economy of power effected by the present engines is so great, that although the same boilers only are used, there is 2¼ to 2½ times the power obtained.

The indicator figures exhibited by Mr. Cowper to the meeting, were drawn to the scale of 20 inches length of stroke, and ½ inch for each lb. of pressure; and he begged to suggest that scale as a convenient one to be adhered to, for indicator figures intended to be exhibited to the Institution.

Mr. Slate thought the plan of injection proposed by Mr. Cowper was a very eligible one. With reference to the alternate injection of the water, he had experienced the difficulty in marine engines, of too much water being admitted by the injection cock, whenever the engines were working slowly, causing the injection water to choke up the condenser and even get up into the cylinder, and he had adopted a slide valve in the injection pipe, admitting only water enough at each stroke of the engine for the condensation of the steam; the jet of water was thrown against a perforated distributing plate.

The Chairman remarked that there would be a tendency in the rose of the injection pipe, as adopted by Mr. Smith, to become choked up.

Mr. Cowper observed that, in the plan he had described, that difficulty was quite obviated, as in the case of the circular valve becoming choked,

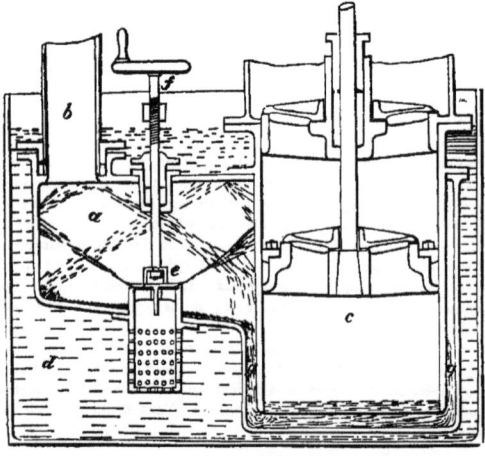

they had only to lift it up an inch or two by the screw handle, and then screw it down again, and the rush of water would effectually wash out any obstruction.

The Chairman considered that a great advantage, as it would prevent any stoppage of the engine. He thought the members of the Institution were much indebted to Mr. Smith for his researches, but their obligations were small compared with those of the iron manufacturers of the district, with whom he had been more immediately brought in contact, as the saving proved to have been effected by the improvement of the engines, formed so serious a proportion to the whole expense of working them. It was important that this subject should occupy the attention of the iron masters, because their material must bear a proportion in its price to the management bestowed in its manufacture. He hoped Mr. Smith would not lose sight of the subject, but keep it prominently before, not only the iron manufacturers of South Staffordshire, but the owners of steam engines throughout the country; and he thought this Institution was an excellent vehicle for the purpose, because it was only by such an Institution that information could be collected in a practical form, and the results be duly investigated and considered. In conclusion, he proposed a vote of thanks to Mr. Smith, which was passed.

BRITISH ASSOCIATION.—EDINBURGH.
(Continued from p. 215.)
"On Atlantic Waves." By Dr. Scoresby.

Dr. Scoresby had had, for many years, opportunities of observing the magnitude and velocity of waves, and more recently, in returning by the steamer *Hibernia* from Boston, in the spring of 1848. For such observations steam-ships present peculiar advantages. In scudding before the wind, the paddle-boxes on either side prevent the rolling of the vessel to any great extent, and the ship, when in the trough of the sea, is almost perfectly steady for several seconds together. There are also different platforms from which observations may be made from the deck, the saloon or cuddy deck, and the paddle-boxes. In the case of the *Hibernia*, on the occasion referred to, he had ascertained that the height of the eye on the saloon deck, above the line of flotation, was about twenty-three feet three inches, and on the paddle-boxes thirty feet three inches. On the 5th of March, 1848, lat. 51.28, lon. 30, it blew a hard gale at sunset, with the barometer at 29.50. Next morning, at ten o'clock, it stood at 28.30, when the scene was terribly magnificent. Looking from the saloon-deck, almost every wave was above the eye, and consequently more than twenty-four feet above the trough, or twelve above the mean level of the sea. He then ventured on to the paddle-box, and when the ship was completely within the trough of the sea, which even its great length could not span, at least half the waves rose above the paddle-boxes, and many, as determined from the angle of elevation (above 2¼ deg. at a distance of 300 feet), about 3 feet higher; adding 30 feet for the level of the eye, the height of the average highest waves must have been 43 feet above the level at which the ship floated. The appearance the ocean then presented was one of the grandest he had ever beheld. During the swell, which continued after the storm, the waves were still of great height, but reduced, on the average, to about 24 feet. Whilst the mean elevation of the highest waves, from the hollow of the trough, was 43 feet, occasional wave-crests were raised still higher. The general average of the time occupied by the waves in overtaking the ship was 16½ seconds. The length of the vessel was 220 feet, and the waves were six seconds in passing from stern to stem, thus giving (after variations for ship's progress and obliquity of course) the probable distance of the waves, from crest to crest, of 559 feet. In determining the mean velocity of the wave, reference must of course always be had to the velocity of the ship at the time. During the time which elapsed between successive waves overtaking the ship, the vessel, as was ascertained by her rate of sailing at the time, had advanced so much as to make the actual distance accomplished by the waves in 16½ seconds, 790.5 feet, so that

their velocity was about 32.67 English miles per hour, or assuming the largest possible error, certainly 30 miles per hour.

Mr. Scott Russell observed that Dr. Scoresby's observations have thrown much light on this subject, and he bore testimony to the accuracy of Dr. Scoresby's mode of measuring the height, which is perhaps the most difficult point, and also the velocity of the waves. From smaller waves, only 16 inches broad, Mr. S. Russell has predicted, in tables published some time ago in the Transactions of the Association, that waves 559 feet long will be found to have a velocity of from 30 to 31 miles per hour. And it must be gratifying to the lovers of science to learn that, until Dr. Scoresby came into the room this morning, he had never heard or seen anything of these tables. In such observations as those which had just been read, the three main points to be noted were—1st, The greatest height of the wave; 2nd, The distance from the top of one wave to the top of another; and 3rd, The period of oscillation of the wave.

"The Patent Laws." By Professor Hancock.

In this paper Professor Hancock clearly and forcibly exposes the injurious operation of our present system of Patent Laws. The subject, however, has been so often handled in this journal that we can only give the following table, which may be found useful for reference, and the author's recommendations:—

Countries.	Species of Patent of Invention.	Average Cost.		
		£.	s.	d.
United Kingdom .	Copyright of ornamental designs (under 2 Vic. c. 17, and 5 and 6 Vic. c. 100) for from 9 months to 3 years.	From 0 to 4	6 11	0 6
United Kingdom .	Copyright of design in configuration of articles of utility (under 6 and 7 Vic. c. 65) for 3 years.	From 11 to 15	11 4	6 6
Bavaria	Patent for 5 years.	12	0	0
United States of America	Patent for 14 years for an American.	13	0	0
Bavaria	Patent for 10 years.	15	0	0
Prussia	.. 5, 6, or 8 years.	15	0	0
Sweden	.. 5 years.	15	0	0
Bavaria	.. 15 years.	20	0	0
Belgium	.. 5 years.	23	0	0
Austria	.. 5 years.	25	0	0
France........	.. 5 years.	31	0	0
Belgium	.. 10 years.	37	0	0
Holland	.. 10 years.	37	0	0
Austria	.. 10 years.	45	0	0
Spain	.. 5 years.	50	0	0
France...	.. 10 years.	52	0	0
Belgium	.. 15 years.	70	0	0
Holland	.. 15 years.	70	0	0
France........	.. 15 years.	73	0	0
Austria	.. 15 years.	75	0	0
Scotland	.. 14 years.	75		
United States of America	Patent for 14 years for any foreigner except a British subject.	77	10	0
Russia	Patent for 1 to 6 years.	From 20 to 80	0 0	0 0
England	.. 14 years.	110	0	0
United States of America	Patent for 14 years for a British subject.	120	0	0
Ireland	Patent for 14 years.	135	0	0
United Kingdom, including British Colonies, and including specifications.	Patent for 14 years.	376	0	0

From what has been already said, it is obvious that the cost of obtaining British patents can be readily reduced.

1st. By having only one patent or certificate of registration for the United Kingdom.

2nd. By adopting for all inventions the simple forms of granting certificates of registration now used with respect to ornamental designs and designs of configuration; and so rendering unnecessary the prolix and complicated forms now required in obtaining patents.

3rd. By substituting with respect to all inventions, the moderate fees and stamps of registration of designs, for the official fees and stamps on patents.

Were these changes adopted—and they are changes at once conformable to the policy of recent legislation on the subject, and to the teachings of common sense—the cost of obtaining a patent or privilege of property in inventions, for the entire British dominions, would be at once reduced from 376*l.* to 15*l.*; and Great Britain, instead of being inferior to every other country in this important branch of human legislation, would occupy her natural position in showing the greatest care for the most noble and valuable species of human property.

" On the Self-Imposed Taxation of the Working Classes of the United Kingdom." By Mr. G. R. Porter.

The object of the author is to exhibit the amount expended on three articles of luxury, the use of which he presumes might advantageously be dispensed with, viz. spirits, beer, and tobacco; the respective values of which are £24,091,458, £25,383,165, and £7,588,607, making a total of £57,063,230.

NOTES BY A PRACTICAL CHEMIST.

IMPROVED METHOD OF ESTIMATING TIN.—Hitherto in chemical analysis tin has always been estimated in the form of stannic acid (peroxide of tin). The difficulty of the manipulations, or rather the minute care that they require, the time necessarily spent in its preparation, washing, and drying, as well as the inevitable inaccuracy of the process, form often a hindrance to the analysis of this metal. The new method depends on the employment of a normal test liquor, and possesses a simplicity and correctness not otherwise attainable. The process depends on the facility with which protochloride of tin withdraws chlorine from bodies capable of furnishing it. If we pour the orange-coloured solution of perchloride of iron into protochloride of tin (which is colourless), the former salt will give up one atom of chlorine, converting it into the colourless perchloride, and will itself be reduced to the (colourless) protochloride of iron.

$$Fe^2 Cl^3 + Sn Cl = 2 (Fe Cl) + Sn Cl^2$$

The decoloration of the iron takes place therefore as long as the tin requires more chlorine; but as soon as the protochloride is perchlorinized, the smallest additional drop of the iron liquor will give a strong orange tint, and thus show that the operation is at an end. If the strength of the iron solution be known, we know at once the quantity of tin sought for. This system of analysis (with normal test liquors) is so much in use that I may omit all particulars, except those relating expressly to tin.

For this purpose 1 or 2 grammes (15 to 30 gr.) of the substance to be examined are placed in a pint flask with a mixture of 1 part nitric with 6 parts muriatic acid, and boiled until the liquid turns yellow, and emits a strong odour of chlorine. The tin is now in solution as protochloride. Zinc is now added, until the liquid becomes clear, colourless, and transparent. Then, with a graduated dropping tube, a solution of perchloride of iron of a known strength is added, until a faint tinge appears, and the amount of tin is found by a simple computation.

The addition of some water to the liquor to be tested is useful,

especially in examining alloys which contain copper. Arsenic is the only metal which interferes with this process. Tin containing this substance must be strongly heated for some time in a crucible, when the arsenic is volatilised, and the residue may be treated as above.

To prepare perchloride of iron I employed peroxide of iron, or, better still, colcothar, which I boiled for about 10 minutes in muriatic acid, and filtered immediately. This liquid does not change, and may be kept for any length of time. To make the solution of perchloride of iron of a known strength, we should weigh out exactly 1 gramme of tin, find what number of degrees on the dropping tube is required for the perchloride, and compare it with the results of analysis.

NEW MODE OF PREVENTING THE INCRUSTATION OF STEAM BOILERS.—This is effected by placing sugar in the boiler. A manufacturer of Lyons has employed, instead of sugar, dextrine, as obtained from potatoe starch. About 6 pounds of this syrup were placed in the boiler of an 8 horse power engine, working for a month at the rate of 14 hours a day. At the end of this time, the boiler when examined was found clean.

CHEAP AND DURABLE BLUE COLOUR.—Calcine for 2 hours at a forge heat, a mixture of 60 parts of quartz sand, 45 of soda, and 9 or 10 oxide of copper. This colour, which was used by the ancients, resists the action of the most powerful agents, and is not affected by air, light, or moisture.

CLARK'S SOAP TEST FOR DETERMINING THE HARDNESS OF WATER.—According to a paper by Mr. Dugald Campbell, read before the British Association, this test cannot be absolutely depended upon in the presence of magnesia, which substance appears to mask in some degree the amount of lime present. Thus a standard of lime of 18° takes 32° test measures; one of lime of 16° + 1° magnesia, takes 31·6, and 1 of lime 16° + 16° magnesia, only 27 9.

ON THE NUTRITIVE VALUE OF FOOD AS DEPENDING UPON ITS PERCENTAGE OF NITROGEN.—Dr. Voelcker has shown that the method of determining the value of articles of food, by estimating the nitrogen which they contain is fallacious, on account of the presence of ammoniacal salts. Thus of the 6·61 per cent of nitrogen contained in dry mushrooms, (Agaricus prunellus) 1·82, or nearly ⅓ was present as ammonia, and was consequently valueless. In this manner the nutritive power of fungi, and of several other vegetables, have, according to the author, been considerably overrated.

METHOD OF HARDENING PLASTER-CASTS, AND GIVING THEM THE APPEARANCE OF MARBLE.—Take 2 parts stearine, 2 parts Venice soap, 1 part pearlash, and 24 to 30 parts caustic potassa in solution. The stearine and soap are cut in slices, mixed with the cold solution of potassa, and then boiled for half-an-hour, constantly stirring. Whenever the mass rises, a little more of the cold solution is added. The pearlash, first moistened with water, is then added, and the whole boiled for a few minutes. The paste is then stirred until cold, and then mixed with so much cold potassa liquor that it becomes perfectly liquid. Before this composition is used, it should be kept well covered for several days. It may be preserved for years. Before applying it, the plaster objects should be well dusted, then covered with the liquid by means of a thick brush as long as it is absorbed, and left to dry. The surface is then dusted with leather. If the coating has not become glossy, the operation must be repeated.

ON THE PRESERVATION OF COPPER.

To the Editor of the Artizan.

SIR,—In the *Artizan* for August, page 199, a paragraph, signed S., states that chalk does not protect copper from the corrosive action of sea-water; and gives an account of an experiment with two pieces of clean sheet-copper placed in solutions of sea-salt of equal strength for the same period, and after three weeks were each found to have lost precisely the same weight, and proves " that no protection can be obtained in this manner."

It appears to the writer that an important feature has been overlooked by S., who summarily disposes of the vulgar error about chalk, as a protective for copper sheathing.

The instances in which the preservation of the copper has been most remarkable, are those in which the sheets have been marked and numbered with lime, as is the practice in India. Where unburnt chalk has been used for numbering the sheets, the traces of the chalk are soon obliterated, and of course the corrosion of the copper is prevented to but a very trifling extent.

The lime appears to be decidedly protective to the surface of the copper in all cases where it has been laid on with a brush in a liquid state; whether it would be equally protective if used in a dry state is very doubtful.

The writer remembers to have seen instances where a complete coating of lime was applied; the result was, that certain portions of the surface were completely protected, and remained perfectly smooth and prominent, whilst other parts were deeply corroded: although this prevented the waste of metal, it rendered the surface rough and prejudicial to the speed of the vessel.

The great secret is to procure a clean metallic surface, which can only be secured by constant abrasion.   A.

To the Editor.

Sir,—I should be very happy to learn, through the medium of the *Artizan,* a ready way of ascertaining the presence of nitrates of soda and potash in colouring liquors.

Yours, &c.,
A Calico Printer, Glasgow.

RECENT AMERICAN PATENTS.

John J. De Haven, Reading, Berks county, Pennsylvania, *for a removeable Fire Box for Locomotives.* April 24.

Claim.—" What I claim as my invention, is attaching an independent fire box to the steam boiler, in such a manner as to render it easily removeable, without displacing the boiler dome, machinery, or frame work, for the purpose of being repaired or replaced by another, whether the means of attachment be those herein described, or others capable of effecting the same object, and which have been used for analogous purposes.

" I do not claim making the dome to project from the end of the boiler, over the fire box, but when it does so project, I claim making it with a fixed and tight bottom sufficiently strong to resist the pressure of the steam, in order that it may be unnecessary to rivet it to the fire box, as has heretofore been the practice, and that one or more pipes, arranged so as to be easily detached, and of sufficient capacity to allow the free passage of the steam generated in the casing of the fire box, may be all the connexion that is necessary between the latter and the dome."

Paul K. Hubbs, Holmesburg, Philadelphia county, Pennsylvania, *for a Filtering Apparatus for Steamboat Boilers.* April 24.

The patentee says,—" The nature of my invention consists in providing for steam boilers on board of steam vessels, a filtering apparatus, so placed as to receive the double action of pressure from the river below and a suction of a pump above the filter plate."

Claim.—" What I claim as my invention, is placing a boiler filter near or upon the bottom of a vessel, with a pump elevating the water from its upper surface, when the reservoir beneath the filter is connected with the outside water by means of two inclined apertures, with stops or valves for closing them, constructed as described, whereby the greatest amount of pressure may be exerted upon the filtering diaphragm, and it may be washed by a current produced by the motion of the boat, as described."

Edwin Allyn, assignee of Joseph E. Andrews, Boston, Massachusetts, *for an improved variable Power Capstan.* April 24.

Claim.—" What I claim as my invention, is a capstan constructed as herein specified, so as to be susceptible of producing a quick and direct action to overcome a slight resistance, and a slow and more powerful action to overcome a great resistance, by merely turning the drum head round in the opposite directions while the barrel of the capstan always moves in the same direction; and the same being accomplished without any shipping or unshipping of gears, and by a system of rachets, pawls, and gear wheels, pinions, &c., all arranged so as to turn with the capstan for the direct and quick action, but, for the slow and more powerful action, to turn the capstan barrel in the same direction by reversing the motion of the drum head: said parts being combined and operating as set forth."

William D. Berry, Boston, Massachusetts, *for an improvement in Iron Pavements for Streets.* July 12.

The patentee says,—" The nature of my improvement consists in covering the surface of the street with boxes made of iron of any convenient form and size, divided into sections, (which sections are to be so small as not to admit the hoofs of a horse,) by compartments of iron, which are so arranged as to strengthen the whole, and together with the rim of the boxes, are groved in such a manner as will most effectually prevent the feet of horses, or wheels of carriages, from slipping. The boxes are keyed or linked together, and the interstices or sections are to be filled with any composition which may be procurable in the section of country where the pavement may be used, and which may be found suitable to the purpose. Among the compositions which may be used, I name asphaltum, and a composition made of stone and shells, broken small and mixed with hydraulic, or other cement."

Claim.—" What I claim as my invention, is the manner of using iron in the pavement of streets, by means of boxes connected by flanches or keys and commissures, and divided into small sections, which leave openings or interstices, to be filled inside and between the rims with any composition which may be best adapted to the purpose. Using for that purpose boxes of any form, divided into sections in any manner which will produce the intended effect."

William Duff, City of Baltimore, Maryland, *for an improvement in the Safety Valve for Steam Engines.* July 28.

The patentee says,—" My improvement consists in causing a portion of the water from the boiler to constitute a portion of the weight that is to bear upon the safety valve of a steam engine."

Claim.—" What I claim as new, is the employment of a portion of the water contained in a steam boiler, to constitute the weight, or a part of the weight, by which a safety valve is to be held down, and which water will cease to constitute such weight when it has descended to a given level; the said weight of water being rendered effective by means of apparatus, constructed and arranged substantially in the manner set forth."

John Street, City of Philadelphia, Pennsylvania, *for an improvement in Artificial Writing Slates.* November 21.

The patentee says,—" The nature of my invention consists in applying a silicious composition to wood, for the purpose of forming a wooden writing slate."

Claim.—" What I claim as my invention, is a wooden writing slate of a variety of colours, formed by the application of the composition set forth, to smooth surfaces of wood of any desired size and thickness."

Waring Latting, City of New York, *for an improvement in Umbrellas.* November 21.

Claim.—" What I claim as new and as of my invention, is, 1st, the construction and arrangement of the hollow handle of the umbrella, so that the covers, stretchers, &c., can be attached to or detached from it, substantially as set forth, and when disconnected can be put into said hollow handle, by which means the apparatus becomes a walking stick. 2nd. The combination of the cylinder, with its shoulder, latch and button, and screw to receive the runner cylinder and thimble with the grooves and small washer to mount the ribs and form an umbrella that can rotate on its centre when in use."

Gail Borden, Jun., Galveston, Texas, *for a Preparation of Portable Soup Bread.* February 5.

The patentee says,—" The nature of my invention consists in extracting the nutritious parts of flesh or animal meat of every description, and combining this concentrated extract with flour or vegetable meal, and baking the two substances in an oven, thereby forming a portable desiccated soup bread, containing a large amount of the most important alimentary substance, in a very small bulk and convenient form, well adapted to seafaring purposes, travellers, hospitals, and also for family use, which will save the trouble and expense of much cooking."

Claim.—" I claim the new and useful manufacture of desiccated soup bread, formed of the concentrated extract of alimentary animal substances, combined with vegetable flour or meal, made into cakes and baked into bread, in the manner substantially as herein described, for the purpose set forth."

Edwin B. Bowditch, New Haven, Connecticut, *for an Improvement in Sofa Bedsteads.* February 26.

The patentee says,—" My invention consists in arranging the ordinary seat of a sofa in such a manner as to revolve upon pivots at the ends, in a frame which is hinged to the front of the sofa in such a manner as to be thrown open, and, by revolving the ordinary seat in this frame, bring the stuffed side up, and on a level with another seat or bed placed under the ordinary seat, thereby forming a bed."

Claim.—" 1st, What I claim as my invention, is the ordinary seat of a sofa or other suitable article of furniture, so arranged as to revolve on a centre at each end, in a frame so constructed as to turn over and bring the top or stuffed side of the seat (by revolving the same) on a level with another seat or bed placed under the ordinary seat.

" 2nd, I also claim the use of the stuffed ends forming the support for the top seat when turned over and used as a bed.

Jos. Dixon, Jersey City, New Jersey, *for an Improvement in Firing Kilns for Pottery Ware, Black Lead Crucibles, &c.* March 5.

The patentee says,—" My invention consists in substituting rosin for the kinds of fuel heretofore used for these purposes, the distillation of which readily, and at a low temperature, evolves a great quantity of highly inflammable gas, which, in an inflammable or inflamed state, extends through all the parts of the kiln, giving an equal, or nearly equal, heat throughout, that will bake equally, while at the same time it contains more carbon than the supporter of combustion can take up in passing through the flues of the kiln formed by the ware, and thus prevents the injurious action of the heated oxygen on the surface of the ware, particularly when baking black lead crucibles."

Claim.—" What I claim as my invention, is the use of rosin, or the distillation thereof, as a combustible for baking pottery and all other kinds of earthenware, substantially as described, as a means of preventing such articles from being ' over fired' or ' slack-burned,' and whereby, also, the injurious action of atmospheric air on the surface of black lead crucibles, pottery ware, bricks, &c., is avoided, as described."

James Cunningham, Reading, Berkshire county, Pennsylvania, *for an Improvement in Ventilating Railroad Cars.* March 12.

The patentee says,—" My invention consists in attaching to one of the cars of a train a centrifugal fan, which is driven from one of the axletrees of the car, the blast thus generated being conveyed through the car by pipes, whence it is discharged by adjustable adjutages of peculiar form in the direction required, to prevent the dust from entering the car."

Claim.—" What I claim as my invention, is the employment of jets of air, produced substantially in the manner herein set forth, for preventing the entrance of dust into railroad cars or carriages of any description."

E. Henry Parsons & Sanford E. Parsons, Wilkesbarre, Luzerne county, Pennsylvania, *for an improvement in Hanging Saws in Saw Mills.* April 30.

The patentees say,—" Our invention consists in hanging the saw in advance of its front or cutting edge, in such manner that the pressure of the log advanced against it will tend to keep it in line with the direction in which the carriage is advancing, thus dispensing with the heavy saw gate usually required to strain the saw."

Claim.—" What we claim as our invention, is the method of hanging a mill saw from guides in advance of its front edge, which will sustain the whole pressure caused by the advancement of the wood on the carriage against the saw teeth, the plate of the saw swinging on the advanced guides as pivots, so that when cutting it is kept running in a plane passing through the guides in the direction in which the carriage moves, as a vane is kept by the wind in the direction in which it blows."

PROCEEDINGS OF THE FRANKLIN INSTITUTE, U.S.
May, 1850.

Mr. Seth E. Winslow exhibited and explained to the members present a model of his patented substitute for the pulleys and weights of windows. It consists of a spring attached to the side of a window sash, upon which a roller runs. When the window is hoisted the roller does not bear against the window frame, and hence the window may be easily raised ; but when the sash tends to descend, the roller runs along the spring and is pressed against it, so as to hold the sash firmly in its place. A simple modification locks the window sashes when both in place, so as to prevent the window from being hoisted from the outside.

Mr. B. H. Bartol made some interesting remarks in relation to Pirson's Fresh Water Condenser, now in use on board the steamer *Osprey.* The peculiar feature of this condenser, which distinguishes it from all others previously known to the public, is the placing of the condensing tubes horizontally within the ordinary shower condenser, which is made of enlarged dimensions for the purpose. By this arrangement, the water required for condensation is admitted through the ordinary injection cock, and rises to the top of the external condenser, where it is discharged on a scattering-plate, from whence it passes directly on to the tubes of the internal condenser, which are below it and arranged in three ranges or sets, one above the other ; the steam from the cylinder is admitted into the upper range, and passes through the three before being discharged at the bottom. The fresh water produced by the condensation of the steam is pumped out by a small pump and immediately returned to the boilers, while the water used to produce condensation is taken out by the air-pump of the engine. The internal condenser is not attached to the external one, but merely laid in it. The three ranges are separately made, and the outlet from the upper slips loosely into the one below it, so that when the whole internal condenser is together, it may be moved from ¼ in. to ½ in. in any direction. This freedom prevents any liability to fracture from unequal expansion, and the tubes being in vacuum relieves them from all pressure. As the condensing water reaches the bottom of the tubes it is immediately pumped out, so that there is not at any time any water around the tubes other than the thin sheet passing over their surfaces. On the *Osprey,* the vacuum within the tubes of the internal condenser is 26 inches, and the same in the external one ; the internal vacuum is the result of condensation, while the external vacuum is produced by the air-pump. The *Osprey* has made three passages, or 2,750 miles in all, and has no trouble in keeping a full supply of fresh water in her boilers.

AMERICAN STEAM VESSELS.

THE AMERICAN STEAM NAVY.

In the October number of the Journal, I alluded to the steam vessels belonging to our navy, and which at that time, including all classes, numbered seven. Since then, the Edith has been lost in the Pacific, so that we are now reduced to six, and five of that number are very indifferent vessels, leaving the Mississippi alone to sustain the credit of the country, and, so far as one vessel can, she will nobly do it.

There are now building four steamers, the Powhattan, Susquehanna, Saranac, and San Jacinto. The first at Norfolk, the second at Philadelphia, the third at Portsmouth, N. H., and the last at New York. The first two are 250 feet long, and 45 feet beam, and the last two are 196 feet long, and 37 feet beam. The first two have side wheels, and two inclined engines, each with cylinders 70 inches diameter, and 10 feet stroke; the third has side wheels and 2 inclined engines, with 60-inch cylinders, 9 feet stroke, and the fourth has a propeller and two inclined engines, working across the ship, with cylinders 60 inches in diameter, 4 feet 2 inches stroke.

When it is taken into consideration that, in war steamers, every foot of room possesses a double value from the large number of men that have to be accommodated, we may well inquire why it is that all of these vessels have engines that take up so much space in the ship, to the discomfort of every one on board. The space between bulkheads, on the Susquehanna, is 89 feet of the widest part of the vessel. Without disturbing the arrangements of the boilers, engines of equal efficiency, and less weight and cost, could have been put in, and the whole space occupied reduced to 60 feet. In fact, no other form of marine engine at present known could be spread over as much space as the inclined engine adopted in these vessels. To be sure, by adopting some other form, we could not have used several so called valuable American Patents, but what was lost by the inventors would have been doubly gained to the country.

The Board of Engineers, who determined the form of engines for these vessels, were of one opinion, that nothing but inclined engines should be used. Their reasons have never been made public, and while all the engineers of this country and Europe are in the dark as to the advantages of this form of engine, the Navy Department very unfairly keeps all the information to itself.

The use of the inclined engine has heretofore compelled the decking over of the lower part of the engine, to obtain room for stores, &c., and in some cases, the firemen, who are roasted while on duty, have been almost boiled when in their rooms. The Missouri was burnt by having a store room over the engine.

The forms of engine most used in the English Navy at present, are vertical direct action and the oscillating, and they have been well proved as worthy of confidence. But the fact of their being well tested there appears to have been an objection to their use here. We must have American engines; our flags are entirely different, why should not our engines be so! And we have the satisfaction of knowing that our engines are independent and original.

In examining a list of the builders of machinery for the English Navy, the names of Maudslay, Napier, Seaward, Fawcett, Boulton & Watt, Rennie, Fairbairn, Penn, and other celebrated builders, appear, all of whom design the engines they build, the plans being first approved by the Government, and a superintending engineer being stationed at the works. By this means, the talents of all the builders in the country are made available, and the competition between them stimulates all to active exertion, and the cost of Government engines does not exceed that for private service; while here, the system that prevails is opposed to improvement, and while it enhances the cost of the engines at least one-third, is productive of no good to any one, not even to the contractors, who would much prefer a different system.

It is hoped that the present Secretary of the Navy, who is not committed to the errors of the past, will take a proper view of the matter, and if so, any steamers that may be built during his term will be done in one half the time, and at two-thirds or three-fourths the present cost, while their machinery will take less room, and give more comfort to all on board.—Journal of the Franklin Institute.

[In order to understand the force of this writer's remarks, our readers ought to be acquainted with the manner in which the contracts for marine engines are managed by the United States' Admiralty. The parties tendering give in prices for the materials and labour according to a schedule, much in the same way as in our railway contracts, and engineers are appointed on behalf of the Admiralty to attend constantly at the factory, to take the men's time and inspect the materials and workmanship. Detail drawings are supplied by the Admiralty, to which the contractors are compelled rigidly to adhere. The fruits of this system may be readily imagined. It is to the interest of the contractors to make the engines as expensive as possible, whilst they have no spur to produce any improvement.—ED. ARTIZAN.]

PARTICULARS OF THE STEAMSHIP "OHIO."

This fine mail steamer, recently finished for the line between New York and New Orleans, via Charleston and Havana, has just left on her third trip, and the following particulars concerning her may be of interest to the readers of the Journal:

Length of keel, 240 feet; length on spar deck, 265 feet; depth of hold from spar deck, 33 feet; do. do. from main deck, 25 feet; breadth of beam, 46 feet; by government measurement, 2300 tons. She is fitted with two side lever marine engines, having cylinders of 90 inches diameter. Length of stroke, 8 feet; diameter of water wheels, 36 feet; width of wheel, 10 feet,

The general arrangement of the engines does not vary materially from those of the Canada and Europa, but some of the details are different. They have the long D slide valve, the Ohio has (double) balance valves, and while the steam valves are worked by one eccentric, so adjusted as to cut off the steam at any part of the stroke, the exhaust valves are worked by a separate eccentric, which may be set to give any desired lead. The valves being nearly balanced, may be worked with ease by hand.

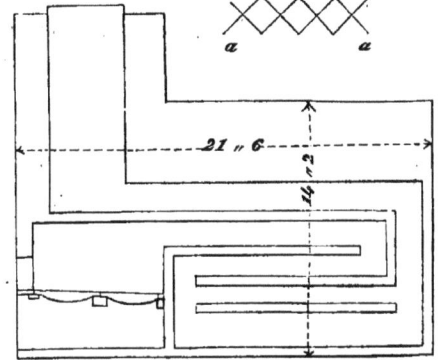

The engines are a creditable piece of work, both as to design and finish, and appear to have proper strength for the duty they will have to perform. The boilers are four in number, two forward and two abaft the engines, each one being 15 feet wide, 21 feet 6 inches long, and 14 feet 2 inches high, having 4 furnaces, with grates 8 feet long. Using anthracite coal, with fan blast, 15 lbs. of steam can easily be maintained. The flues of these boilers are arranged somewhat different from any heretofore built, and are the only ones of the kind. After passing to the bottom, as is usual to drop flue boilers, they rise and pass to the front again, where each pair of boilers unite in one chimney. By placing the boilers before and abaft the engines, the firemen are at all times in sight of the engineer, the weight is more evenly distributed, and any liability to strain the ship from that cause avoided. The *Ohio* has a diagonal framing of 3-inch round iron extending her whole length, between the centre kelson and main deck beam, as at *a, a*, which insures greater strength, and is not usually done. She can accommodate 500 passengers of various classes, and recently left New York with that number. She connects at Havana with the *Falcon*, for Chagres, and a good portion of her passengers leave at that port.

The owners of the *Ohio* have another vessel, the *Georgia*, of equal power but different model, nearly done, and as these vessels will be the same in all other respects, a very good comparison can be made between them. On the completion of the *Georgia*, I will announce the result.

The engines of the *Ohio* were built by T. F. Secor & Co., New York; the hull by Bishop & Simonson; the whole being under the supervision of Joseph N. Scott, Esq., Chief Engineer of the line.—*Journal of the Franklin Institute.*

PROPORTIONS FOR AMERICAN STEAMERS.

RIVER ENGINES, WITH SIDE WHEELS.

'NIAGARA.' CONDENSING. *For 123 square Feet of Immersed Section.*

Length of vessel, 265 feet; beam, 28 feet 6 inches; depth of hold, 9 feet 3 inches; draught (loaded), 4 feet 9 inches.

Cylinder, 216 cubic feet in capacity. Condenser, 88 cubic feet. Air pump. 33.5 cubic feet.

Force Pumps, 5½ inches diameter by 4½ feet stroke.

Pressure, 40 to 45 lbs. per square inch, cut off at ½ stroke of the piston. Revolutions, 24 per minute.

Water Wheels, 30 feet in diameter by 11 feet face. Arms, 24 in each flange. Buckets, two, of 15 inches deep. Dip (at load line), 30 inches.

Shafts wrought iron), Journal, 14 inches.

Boilers, two, of 27 feet in length by 10 feet front Shell, 8 feet 6 inches in diameter. Fire and flue surface, 3000 squarefeet. Grates, 108 square feet. Steam room, 1200 cubic feet.

Fuel, 3200 lbs. of anthracite coal per hour (maximum).

Blowers, two, of 9 feet in diameter. Fans, ten of 24 inches by 3 feet face.

Blowing engines, two, of 10 inches diameter of cylinder by 12 inches stroke. Revolutions, 150 per minute.

Weights.

Engines	... ...	186,000 lbs.
Boilers ...	... ...	65,000 „
Wood, in engines and wheels	...	29,000 „
Water in boilers ...	... ...	76,000 „
Total	... ...	356,000 lbs.

'SOUTH AMERICA.' CONDENSING. *For 132 square Feet of Immersed Section.*

Length of vessel, 250 feet; beam, 27 feet; depth of hold, 9 feet; draught (loaded), 5 feet.

Cylinder, 175 cubic feet in capacity. Air pump, 38.5 cubic feet.

Condenser, 72 cubic feet. Force pumps, 5 inches diameter by 4 feet stroke.

Pressure, 35 to 40 lbs. per square inch, cut off at ½ the stroke of the piston.

Revolutions, 23·5 to 24 per minute.

Water wheels, 29 feet in diameter by 11 feet face. Arms, 24 in number. Buckets, two divisions, and 30 inches deep. Dip (at load-line), 30 inches.

Shafts (wrought iron), diameter of journal, 13 inches.

Boilers, two, 27 feet in length by 9.5 in width. Fire and flue surface, 3000 square feet. Shell, 8 feet in diameter. Grates, 100 square feet. Steam room, 1000 cubic feet.

Consumption of fuel, 3000 lbs. of anthracite coal per hour (maximum).

Blowers, four, 4 feet diameter by 26 inches face. 4 arms. Fans, 13 inches deep. Revolutions, 75 per minute.

Blowing engines, Cylinder, 8 inches in diameter by 12 inches stroke.

Weight of boilers, 62,000 lbs.

The above engines and boilers were designed and constructed at the Phœnix Foundry, New-York.

CONDENSING. *For 160 square Feet of Immersed Section.*

Length of vessel, 335 feet; beam, 35 feet; depth of hold, 11 feet 6 inches.

Cylinder, 313 cubic feet in capacity. Air pump, 54 cubic feet.

Pressure, 38 lbs. per square inch. Revolutions, 22 per minute.

Water wheels, 34 feet in diameter by 10 feet 8 inches face. Buckets, 30 inches deep.

Boilers, Shell, 9½ feet in diameter. Surface, 3660 square feet. Steam room, 1570 cubic feet. Grates, 145 square feet.

Blowing Engines, two cylinders, of 14 inches diameter by 14 inches stroke. Two blowers, 10 feet in diameter by 2 feet in width. Ten fans in each, of 26 inches in depth. Revolutions, 100 per minute.

Fuel, 3000 lbs. of anthracite coal per hour.

NON-CONDENSING. *For 300 square Feet of Immersed Section.*

Vessel, 260 feet in length, 38 feet beam, and 8 feet draught when loaded

Cylinders, two, each 30 inches in diameter by 10 feet stroke of piston (98.3 cubic feet). Force pumps, 6¾ inches in diameter by 25 inches stroke.

Water wheels, 33 feet in diameter by 15 feet in width, 19 arms in each; buckets, 36 inches deep. Shafts cast iron. Diameter of journals, 16 and 14 inches.

Connecting rod, 35feet in length. Piston rod, diameter, 6 inches.

Steam valves, 50 square inches each. Exhaust valves, 63 square inches.

Boilers, 5 of 42 inches in diameter by 34 feet in length, with 2 return flues in each, 16 inches in diameter, having 2278 square feet of heating surface. Grates, 84 square feet.

Boiler plates, (shells), quarter of an inch in thickness. Flues, full quarter of an inch.

Pressure, 75 to 100 lbs. per square inch, cut off at ¾ the stroke of the piston.

Revolutions, 16 to 21 per minute. Dip of wheel, 5 feet when loaded.

Consumption of fuel, 2.3 cords of yellow pine per hour.

Weights, Engines, 160 tons; boilers, 9000 lbs.

Pressure of Steam, 100 lbs. per square inch, cut off at ½ stroke. Revolutions, 22 per minute.

Cylinders, 42½ cubic feet. Boilers, 1393 square feet of fire and flue surface.

Water wheels, 22½ feet in diameter by 10 feet 4 inches face, with 13 inches depth of bucket.

Smoke pipe, 42 inches in diameter × 45 feet high. Area of flues, 1600 square inches. Fuel, 36 cords Western wood in 12 hours.

Furnace, 17 feet in width by 42 in length, and 17 inches in height. Grates, 68 square feet.

NOTE.—32.75 square feet of fire and flue surface is the proportion for each cubic foot in the cylinders at the above given revolutions.

AMERICAN MEASUREMENT LAWS.

By a law of Congress, the tonnage of vessels is found as follows:—

For a Double-decked.—Take the length from the fore part of the stem to the after side of the sternpost above the upper deck; the breadth at the broadest part above the main wales; half of this breadth must be taken as the depth of the vessel; then deduct from the length ⅗ of the breadth, multiply the remainder by the breadth, and the product by the depth; divide this last product by 95, and the quotient is the tonnage.

Example.—What is the tonnage of a ship of the line, measuring, as above, 210 feet on deck, and 59 feet in breadth.

59 ÷ 2 = 29.5, depth.

210 — ⅗ of 59 = 174.6 × 59 × 29.5 ÷ 95 = 3198.8 tons.

For a Single-decked.—Take the length and breadth as above directed for a double-decked, and deduct from the length ⅜ of the breadth ; take the depth from the under side of the deck-plank to the ceiling of the hold ; then proceed as before.

Example.—The length of a vessel is (as above) 223 feet, the breadth 39¼ feet, and the depth of hold 23½ feet ; what is the tonnage ?

$$223 - \tfrac{3}{8} \text{ of } 39.5 = 199.3 \times 39.5 \times 23.5 + 95 = 1947.3 \text{ tons.}$$

A ton will stow 3½ bales cotton.

NOTE.—The burden of similar ships are to each other as the cubes of their like dimensions.

CARPENTERS' MEASUREMENT.—*For a Single-decked.*—Multiply the length of keel, the breadth of beam, and the depth of the hold together, and divide by 95.

For a Double-decked.—Multiply as above, taking half the breadth of beam for the depth of the hold, and divide by 95.

DIMENSIONS AND DETAILS OF NEW STEAMERS.

THE NEW IRON STEAM SHIP "PRINCE"

			Ft.	In.
Length between perpendiculars	..	..	160	0
Breadth amidships	..	..	24	0
Depth amidships	..	..	13	0
Load draught	..	..	7	6
Burthen, builder's measurement		..	446.¾	

A pair of oscillating engines, of 200 horse nominal power, by Messrs. J. Penn & Son, of Greenwich. Cylinders, 55½ inches diameter × 4 feet stroke. Feathering paddle wheels, 20 feet diameter. Floats, 7 feet × 3 feet. Two tubular boilers, 9 feet 1 inch long, and 18 feet 9 inches wide ; containing 792 tubes 2½ inches inside diameter × 6 feet 6 inches long. Six furnaces, 2 feet 6½ inches wide, 8 feet 6 inches long. Bunkers hold 70 tons of coals. Consumption of fuel, 16 cwt. per hour. Number of revolutions, when light, 30 per minute. Average speed, 15½ miles per hour.

The hull of this vessel was built by Mr. Fairbairn, at Millwall, from the lines of Mr. Pasco, and having since become the property of Capt. W. S. Andrews, of Lowestoft, she has had various improvements made on her equipment, as originally designed. The completion of the vessel, and the decoration of the cabins, have been executed by Mr. W. Taylor, of Deptford, under the superintendence of Mr. W. Wilton, engineer.

We were much pleased with an inspection of this vessel, which is one that the Thames may well be proud of. The engines are in Messrs. Penn's usual style of excellence, and are fitted with expansion gear and brine pumps. The tubes of the boiler struck us as being rather small in diameter, at least unless a smokeless coal is to be used. The auxiliary engine can be connected to the deck pumps to form a fire engine, and there are two 6-inch metal bilge pumps to the after hold. The saloon is very lofty, being about 7 feet 6 inches under the deck beams, and is fitted up with a careful regard to comfort, as well as elegance. There are two tiers of sofas, and the lower ones are constructed so as to draw out to increase their width for sleeping berths. The panels are ornamented with landscape paintings, of great beauty. In fact, she is more in the style of a yacht than anything else. The vessel is schooner rigged, and is built with three water-tight bulk heads, fitted with valves to connect the compartments whenever necessary.

THE BRITISH AND NORTH AMERICAN ROYAL MAIL STEAM NAVIGATION COMPANY'S STEAM VESSEL, "CALEDONIA."

Built by Mr. Charles Wood, Dumbarton, 1840. Engines, boilers, &c., by Mr. Robert Napier, Glasgow.

			Ft.	In.
Length on deck	..	..	..	202	5

			Ft.	In.
Breadth on ditto, at midships	..	..	31	0
Depth of hold, ditto	..	..	22	5
Length of engine-space ..	..	..	69	4

Tonnage.			Tons.
Hull ..	..	..	1138½⁴ᵒ⁄₁₀₀
Contents of engine-space	..	..	583₁⁰⁄₁₀₀

Register	..	..	..	615

A pair of side lever engines with Gothic cast iron framings, of 416 horses nominal power ; diameter of cylinders, 72 inches × 6 feet 10 inches length of stroke ; diameter of paddle-wheels, extreme, 28 feet 5 inches, ditto, effective, 27 feet 4½ inches ; floats, 6 feet 9 inches × 2 feet 10 inches ; three sets of 21 arms and floats ; air pumps, 42½ inches diameter ; main centre, 14 inches diameter. Four flue boilers, length, 14 feet, breadth, 11 feet, height, 11 feet 6 inches ; 12 furnaces, 3 in each boiler ; length, 6 feet 10 inches ; breadth, 2 feet 9 inches. Average draft of water, 17 feet ; engines make 19 revolutions per minute.

Description.—A full female figure-head, sham quarter galleries, square sterned and carvil built of timber, one deck, standing bowsprit, 3 masts, schooner-rigged. Port of Glasgow ; Commander,—Mr. James Leitch.

The *Caledonia* has since been sold to the Spanish Government.

CORK STEAM SHIP COMPANY'S IRON STEAM VESSEL, "NIMROD."

Built by Messrs. Thomas Vernon and Co., Liverpool, 1846. Engines by Messrs. Bury, Curtis, and Kennedy, Clarence Foundry.

Builder's measurement.			Ft.	In.
Length of keel and fore rake	..	..	180	0
Breadth of beam	..	..	25	11
Ditto including paddle-boxes	..	..	45	10
Depth of hold	..	..	16	4
Length of engine space	..	..	39	4

Tonnage.			Tons.
Hull ..	..	..	532¼¼
Contents of engine space	..	..	127¼¼

Register	..	..	404½½

New measurement.			Ft.	Tns.
Length on deck	..	..	177	6
Breadth on ditto at midships	..	..	25	3
Depth of hold ..	..	..	16	0
Ditto of break-deck ..	..	..	2	7
Length of engine space	..	..	39	4

Tonnage.			Tons.
Hull ..	..	..	618₆⁴⁄₉₄
Break deck ..	..	..	47₇²⁄₉₄

Gross	..	..	..	665₈⁷⁄₉₄
Contents of engine space	..	..	172₄⁵⁄₉₄

Register	..	..	..	493₄¹⁄₉₄

A pair of direct acting engines (double side rod principle) of 320 horse nominal power ; diameter of cylinders, 66 inches × 5 feet 3 inches length of stroke ; diameter extreme, of paddle-wheels, 23 feet 3 inches ; ditto, effective, 22 feet 8 inches ; twenty floats, 8 feet 3 inches × 2 feet 4 inches ; three sets of 20 arms ; average 22 revolutions per minute ; engines occupy 9 feet × 20 feet 6 inches ; bunkers hold 60 tons of coals ; tubular boilers. Plying upon the station between Cork and Liverpool, (283 miles.) Draft (average) of water, 10 feet 6 inches forward, and 11 feet 6 inches aft ; average passage, 24 hours ; speed of vessel about 11½ miles per hour. The crew are 28 in number, viz., 12 in the engine room, 12 in the captain's, and 4 in the steward's department.

DESCRIPTION.

A bust, male figure-head, sham quarter badges, standing bowsprit, 3 masts, schooner-rigged, common bow, square-sterned, clinch and carvil built vessel, one main and a break deck, (from the stern to fore part of engine room). Port of Cork. Commander,—Mr. John Pile.

THE LEITH AND NEWCASTLE STEAM NAVIGATION COMPANY'S IRON VESSEL, "BRITANNIA."

Vessel and Engines, by Messrs. Smith and Rodger, Glasgow, 1845.

Builder's measurement.	Ft.	In.
Length of keel and fore rake	165	0
Breadth of beam	22	6
Ditto, including the paddle-boxes ..	37	0
Depth of hold	10	9
Length of engine space	49	0
Tonnage.	Tons.	
Hull	$411\frac{81}{94}$	
Contents of engine space	$111\frac{80}{94}$	
Register	$300\frac{1}{94}$	
New measurement.	Ft.	Tns.
Length on deck	165	6
Breadth on ditto, amidships	21	2
Depth of hold	10	7
Length of quarter-deck	51	0
Breadth of ditto	20	6
Depth of ditto	2	4
Length of engine space	49	0
Tonnage.	Tons.	
Hull	$300\frac{13}{100}$	
Quarter-deck	$27\frac{34}{100}$	
Total	$327\frac{47}{100}$	
Contents of engine space	$120\frac{29}{100}$	
Register	$207\frac{18}{100}$	

A pair of steeple engines, (upon Mr. David Napier's patent 4-piston rod principle,) of 146 horse nominal power; diameter of cylinders, 45 inches × 5 feet length of stroke; diameter of paddle-wheels, extreme, 21 feet 3 inches; ditto effective, 20 feet 9 inches; floats, 5 feet 6 inches × 2 feet; three sets of 10 arms and 20 floats; two tubular boilers, with six furnaces, by Messrs. Hawthorne and Co., Leith, 1849; steam pressure, 7 lbs.; 22 revolutions per minute; draught of water, mean, 8½ feet; average passage, 9½ to 10 hours. The cabin has fifty berths for passengers; and the crew consists of 17 persons, viz. 7 on deck, 4 in the cabins, and 6 in the engine room.

DESCRIPTION.—A shield, or profile figure-head; no galleries; round sterned and clinch built vessel; clipper bow, standing bowsprit, 2 masts, schooner rigged. Port of Leith. Commander,—Mr. Duncan Buchanan.

THE ABERDEEN AND NEWCASTLE STEAM NAVIGATION COMPANY'S IRON VESSEL, "VICTORIA."

Built and Fitted by Messrs. Tod and McGregor, Glasgow, 1848.

Builder's measurement.	Ft.	In.
Length of keel and fore rake	148	0
Breadth of beam	20	4
Ditto including the paddle-boxes ..	38	5
Depth of hold	10	5
Length of engine space	57	4
Tonnage.	Tons.	
Hull	$289\frac{92}{94}$	
Contents of engine space	$116\frac{69}{94}$	
Register	$173\frac{23}{94}$	
New measurement.	Ft.	Tns.
Length on deck	148	5
Breadth on ditto amidships	19	9
Depth of hold ditto	10	2
Length of break-deck	42	8
Breadth of ditto	19	9
Depth of ditto	2	0
Length of engine space	57	4
Tonnage.	Tons.	
Hull	$260\frac{88}{100}$	
Break-deck	$18\frac{43}{100}$	
Gross	$279\frac{31}{100}$	
Contents of engine space	$126\frac{9}{100}$	
Register	$153\frac{22}{100}$	

A pair of side lever engines of 100 horses nominal power; diameter of cylinders, 39½ inches × 3 feet 6 inches length of stroke; diameter of paddle-wheels extreme, 15 feet 0½ inch, ditto, effective, 14 feet 6½ inches; floats, 7 feet × 1 foot 6 inches; two sets of 15 arms and floats. One flue boiler, length, 16 feet, breadth, 16 feet 6 inches, height, 8 feet; six furnaces, length of bars, 6 feet, breadth, 1 foot 10 inches, height 3 feet 9 inches; steam-chest, breadth, 6 feet 3 inches. There is a bunker between the engines and boiler, length, fore and aft, 8 feet 9 inches; passage breadth, 2 feet 6 inches, depth, 5 feet 9 inches; holds 35 tons of coals; two side bunkers, one on each side of the boiler, both holding 25 tons of coals, making a total of 60 tons in the bunkers; boiler to bunkers, 6 feet. Frames, $2\frac{3}{4}$ × $2\frac{1}{4}$ × ½ inches, and 1 foot 9 inches apart. The crew are 17 in number; viz, 9 in the captain's department, 3 in the steward's, and 5 in the engine room. Steam pressure, 9 lbs.; consumes 10 cwt. of coals per hour; engines making 25 revolutions per minute; average draught of water, 7 feet fore and aft. The engines were constructed in 1835. There is accommodation for 30 cabin passengers.

DESCRIPTION.

A bust female figure-head, sham quarter galleries, square-sterned, and clinch built vessel, clipper bow; standing bowsprit, 2 masts, schooner rigged. Port of Aberdeen. Commander,—Mr. J. T. Willett.

THE AUSTRIAN IRON STEAM VESSEL, "PRINCIPE STIRBEY."

Built by Mr. Jonathan Robson, Iron Shipbuilder, Blackwall, 1850, (Durham). Engine, Boilers, &c. by ditto, Engine Maker, Gateshead-upon-Tyne.

Builder's measurement.	Ft.	In.
Length of keel and fore rake	106	7
Breadth of beam	18	4
Ditto over the paddle-boxes	36	8
Depth of hold	9	3
Length of engine space	42	11
Tonnage.	Tons.	
Hull	$172\frac{13}{94}$	
Contents of engine space	$77\frac{6}{94}$	
Register	$95\frac{7}{94}$	
New measurement.	Ft.	Tns.
Length on deck	106	6
Breadth on ditto amidships	17	7
Depth of hold ditto	9	0
Length of engine space	42	9

Tonnage.	Tons.
Hull	124
Contents of engine space	73$\frac{1}{10}$
Register	50$\frac{9}{10}$

One half-lever engine of 57 horses nominal power; diameter of cylinder, 41 inches × 4 feet 3 inches length of stroke; diameter of paddle-wheels, extreme, 14 feet 9 inches; ditto, effective, 14 feet 4 inches; floats, 7 feet 2 inches; and varying in breadth from 17 to 21 inches; mean, 19 inches; three sets of 14 arms and floats. Launching draught of water, forward, 1 foot 11 inches; aft, 2 feet inches. (Engine. No. 43.)

THE AUSTRIAN IRON STEAM VESSEL, "PRINCIPE CARAGIORGIEVICH."

Also built and fitted by the above.

Builder's measurement.	Ft.	In.
Length of keel and fore rake	107	3
Breadth of beam	18	3
Ditto over the paddle-boxes	35	7
Depth of hold	9	2
Length of engine space	40	3
Tonnage.	Tons.	
Hull	171$\frac{50}{94}$	
Contents of engine space	71$\frac{74}{94}$	
Register	99$\frac{70}{94}$	
New measurement.	Ft.	Tns.
Length on deck	107	2
Breadth on ditto amidships	17	6
Depth of hold ditto	8	9
Length of engine space	40	3
Tonnage.	Tons.	
Hull	126	
Contents of engine space	68$\frac{3}{10}$	
Register	57$\frac{7}{10}$	

One half-lever engine (No. 44), of 57 horses nominal power; diameter of cylinder, 41 inches × 4 feet 3 inches length of stroke; diameter of paddle-wheels, extreme, 14 feet 8 inches; ditto, effective, 14 feet 3 inches; floats, 7 feet × 19 inches; three sets of 14 arms and floats; launching draught of water, forward, 2 feet 3 inches; aft, 2 feet. Launched on the 13th of July last. Both vessels have 2 round flue boilers—length 20 feet, breadth 7 feet 10 inches, height 8 feet 3 inches; steam chests—length 3 feet 6 inches, breadth 3 feet 2 inches, height 2 feet; four furnaces, two in each boiler,—length 6 feet; bars 5 feet 9 inches, breadth 3 feet, height 3 feet 1 inch. There are 8 strakes of plates; the frames are 3½ × 2¼ × ½ inches, and 2 feet 1 inch apart. On the 14th of August was the trial trip of both vessels, when a speed of 10¼ knots per hour was obtained: the engines of both vessels made 37 revolutions per minute; the draft of both vessels, with all on board, was 4 feet 2 inches. Each vessel has 4 water-tight bulk-heads. The engines are the strongest and best finished, made upon this principle, that I have yet seen. These vessels are to ply upon the Black Sea, with goods and passengers, and are owned by Signor Gogseivich.

Description.—A griffin figure-head, no galleries, round sterned and clinch built vessels, one deck flush, standing bowsprit, 2 masts, schooner rigged.

PROGRESS OF SHIPBUILDING AND STEAM NAVIGATION.

NORTH SHIELDS.

Messrs. Thomas Young & Son, launched in July, 1850, a barque named the *Anglo Saxon*, classed 8 years, A 1., at Lloyd's, 334 tons old, for the Ceylon trade; owned by the builders; also in February, 1849, a brig named the *Maize*, classed 8 years, A 1, at Lloyd's, 157 tons for the Danube trade.

Mr. Thomas Anderson, Low Lights, North Shields, has upon the stocks, a clinch (timber) steamer, for towing at Blyth; laid bow to the river.

	Ft.	n.
Length of keel and fore rake ..	71	0
Breadth of beam	14	3
Depth of hold	8	3
Rake forward	6	0
Tonnage	67$\frac{13}{94}$	

One half-lever engine, by Mr. J. P. Almond, North Shields. Nominal power, 25 horses power; diameter of cylinder, 28 inches × 3 feet 6 inches length of stroke; diameter of paddle wheels, 10 feet 6 inches.

SHIPBUILDING ON THE WEAR,

(SUNDERLAND AND SUBURBS,)

In September, 1850.

MONKWEARMOUTH.

Messrs. G. W. and W. G. Hall, Bridge Dock, have on the stocks, ready for launching, a ship for the East India trade, with a poop and top-gallant forecastle, to class 13 years, A 1, at Lloyd's; owned by the builders.

	Ft.	In.
Length of keel and fore rake	125	0
Breadth of beam	29	9
Depth of hold	19	9
Rake of stem	11	0
Tonnage	512$\frac{39}{94}$	

They have also in frame a schooner for the coasting trade, to be flush upon deck, and to class 10 years, A 1, at Lloyd's, owned by a party in Banff.

	Ft.	In.
Length of keel and fore rake	78	0
Breadth of beam	21	9
Depth of hold	11	4
Rake of stem	6	0
Tonnage	194$\frac{57}{94}$	

They have also in frame a keel for the river, owned by the builders, of the following dimensions:—

	Ft.	In.
Length of keel and fore rake	48	8
Breadth of beam	23	4
Depth of hold	5	8
Rake of stem	3	8
Tonnage	92$\frac{19}{94}$	

BISHOPWEARMOUTH.

Mr. Sam. Peter Austin has upon the stocks, all in frame and partly planked, a brig, to be named the *Briton*, for foreign trade, to be flush upon deck, and to class 12 years, A 1, at Lloyd's.

	Ft.	In
Length of keel and fore rake	106	0
Breadth of beam	26	9
Depth of hold	18	1
Rake of stem	9	0
Tonnage	360$\frac{13}{94}$	

Also, a keel for the river, the property of the builders, of the following dimensions:—

	Ft.	In.
Length of keel and fore rake	38	0
Breadth of beam	22	0
Depth of hold	3	0
Rake of stem	3	0
Tonnage	64$\frac{8}{94}$	

Messrs. Ralph and William Hutchinson have upon the stocks, and in frame, a barque for the East India trade, owned by the builders, to have a poop and top-gallant forecastle, to class 12 years, A 1, at Lloyd's.

	Ft.	In
Length of keel and fore rake	118	0
Breadth of beam	28	0
Depth of hold	19	0
Rake of stem	10	0
Tonnage	422$\frac{8}{94}$	

Mr. John Thomas Alcock has upon the stocks a brig, to class 9 years, A 1, at Lloyd's, for the foreign trade, all in frame and partly planked.

	Ft.	In.
Length of keel and fore rake	88	0
Breadth of beam	25	6
Depth of hold	14	6
Rake of stem	9	0
Tonnage	264$\frac{8}{94}$	

Messrs. R. N. Potts & Brothers have upon the stocks, and in frame, partly planked, a barque to class 8 years, A 1, at Lloyd's, and to be flush on deck, to be employed in the India trade.

				Ft.	In.
Length of keel and fore rake				105	0
Breadth of beam	..		..	27	3
Depth of hold ..		..	..	18	0
Rake of stem ..		..	..	8	0
Tonnage	..		..	*354⅓	

Built bow to the river.

———

Mr. John Hutchinson has upon the stocks, and in frame, a brig, to class 8 years, A 1, at Lloyd's, to be flush upon deck, for the foreign trade.

			Ft.	In.
Length of keel and fore rake			98	0
Breadth of beam	..	..	26	6
Depth of hold ..		..	17	6
Rake of stem ..	..	..	9	0
Tonnage	..	..	308⅔	

They have also just laid another vessel similar to the above.

MONKWEARMOUTH.

Mr. Ralph Hutchinson has upon the stocks, and ready for launching, a brig for the foreign trade, to class 9 years, A 1, at Lloyd's, and flush on deck.

				Ft.	In.
Length of keel and fore rake		..		93	0
Breadth of beam	..		..	24	6
Depth of hold ..		..	..	15	0
Rake of stem	..		..	7	0
Tonnage	..		..	252¼	

Also, a brig, all in frame, partly planked, also for the foreign trade, to class 9 years, A 1, at Lloyd's, and flush on deck.

			Ft.	In.
Length of keel and fore rake			87	0
Breadth of beam	..	..	23	6
Depth of hold ..		..	13	0
Rake of stem ..	..	..	7	0
Tonnage	..	..	215¾	

Also, just laid down, the keel of a barque, for the India trade, to class 13 years, A 1, at Lloyd's, to have a poop and forecastle deck.

	Ft.	In.
Length of keel and fore rake	131	0

			Ft.	In.
Breadth of beam	..	..	30	0
Depth of hold ..	..	..	20	0
Rake of stem ..	..	..	10	0
Tonnage	..	..	540⅔	

LIVERPOOL.

Messrs. Cato, Miller, & Co. have lately launched the following vessels, both classed 13 years, A 1, at Lloyd's.

Peruana, for the East India and China trade.

			Ft.	In.
Length for tonnage	..	..	131	1
Breadth for ditto	..	..	26	4
Depth of hold	..	..	19	1
Tonnage	..	..	425¾	

Koh-i-noor, for the East India and China trade.

			Ft.	In.
Length for tonnage	..	..	157	1
Breadth for ditto	..	..	31	0
Depth of hold	..	..	21	6
Tonnage	..	..	707⅜	

Peruana launched on July 10th, 1850; and *Koh-i-noor* on September 7th, 1850. The latter is the largest merchant-ship yet built in Liverpool, and is fitted with Robertson's (American) steering apparatus.

STEAM COMMUNICATION WITH THE CAPE OF GOOD HOPE.

It is now officially announced, that the tender of the General Screw Steam Navigation Company to perform the Cape of Good Hope mail contract has been accepted by the Admiralty; and it is also rumoured, that the contractors will accept of certain of the screw vessels of the navy as part payment for their contract; thus at the same time expediting the commencement of the mail service, and relieving the Admiralty from the dilemma in which the recent experiments on the effects of shot upon iron vessels have involved them. The amount to be paid is 30,000*l.* per annum.

It gives us great satisfaction to know that so important a colony as the Cape is at last to be united to the mother country by the powerful aid of steam navigation, which must have a most beneficial effect on our mutual trade. There can be little doubt that private enterprise will, ere long, continue the line to India, even if the government and East India Company should agree to send the Australian mails by the Isthmus of Suez,—a route which is always liable to interruption in the event of a war, when it might be most needed. In a recent article in the *Times* (Sept. 9) it is shown, that as far as Australia is concerned, the route by Panama has an advantage over the Suez and Singapore route of 1798 miles, and over the Cape route of 2,390. The high rate of charges on the Suez, or Peninsular & Oriental Company's line is also alleged as sufficient reason why it would be inadmissible as a route to Australia. The writer appears very fearful that a line of screw steamers may be organized from the Cape to Australia, and so spoil his pet project; but as we think there can be no doubt that the line to the Cape will pay, independently of any extension, it cannot be considered as interfering with the Panama line. His anxiety also to prove that a branch from the Cape Verdes, in connection with the West India Company's Brazil mail line, would be more for the interests of the public than the arrangement adopted, seems to savour too much of the partizan to have much weight. The Cape people do not want, and cannot afford to pay for, a speed of 12 knots an hour, which the West India boats are to make on the average. A transhipment at the Cape Verdes might be all very well for letter-boxes, but does not strike us as the best arrangement for heavy goods and passengers, which by screw boats

will be conveyed at a rate that will set in motion a stream of emigration and commerce, advantageous alike to both countries. "But," says the critic, "the establishment of this communication will be the first practical test of the merits of steam ships propelled by screws, as applicable to lengthy transatlantic voyages. There are not wanting persons of experience in nautical affairs, who are thoroughly persuaded that screw vessels of small power in proportion to tonnage will never make their passages in the time prescribed by the government." This reminds us of the history of oscillating engines; first, they wouldn't do at all; then they would only do for very small engines; then they would only do for *moderate-sized engines*, and so on, until the question only became,—what power a "moderate-sized" engine really was. And so the opponents of auxiliary screws will, we presume, always be able to find "persons of experience" who, after the regular voyages of the screw boats to the Mediterranean, and the *City of Glasgow* to New York, will declare they only want to see a "lengthy voyage" performed, to effect their conversion.

THE GREAT EXHIBITION.

Some observations having been made reflecting upon the conduct of the Commissioners, in awarding the contract for the erection of the building in Hyde-park to Messrs. Fox, Henderson, and Co., without having submitted it to public competition, the *Morning Chronicle* remarks that such observations could only be made by parties ignorant of the circumstances under which the contract was obtained. The Commissioners, as is well known, decided upon one of the plans sent in to them by the various competitors, and tenders were required for the erection of the building so selected. Instructions were issued by the Commissioners to all parties desirous of tendering, with general specifications of the several works required to be done in the erection of the building. Among the instructions so issued was the following:—"Tenders for methods of construction other than those shown upon the drawings and described in the specifications will be entertained, but on condition only of their being accompanied by working drawings and specifications, and fully priced bills of quantities." Among the parties who sent in tenders were Messrs. Fox, Henderson, and Co., their tenders being at the same time accompanied by Mr. Paxton's beautiful plan, with specifications and bills of quantities and prices, in pursuance of the regulation above referred to. The Commissioners abandoned the plan they had originally chosen, and selected that of Mr. Paxton. In coming to that decision, however, they had the fullest opportunity of comparing the prices of the work required to be done—not only with those contained in the tender of Messrs. Fox, Henderson, and Co., for the building first selected, but also with those contained in the whole of the other tenders; and the result of a most careful comparison of the prices so given, was to prove that the tender of the present contractors was considerably below that of any other person. It is difficult, therefore, to conceive how, in the face of such facts, it is possible to cast any blame upon the Commissioners for their conduct in this respect. The terms upon which the contract was taken were also highly favourable to the progress of the great undertaking, as the contractors undertake to receive only 35,000*l*. during the progress of the works, the remaining 40,000*l*. to be paid when the receipts of the Exhibition produced that sum.

The first lot of iron bases and columns have arrived on the ground; as specimens of casting they are clear and beautiful, and have a light and elegant appearance. Of these columns not less than 3,230 will be required for the building, and, as they are hollow, they are intended to serve as water pipes, to convey the water from the roof of the building; and as it is contemplated to construct the roof of a series of ridges and valleys of 8 feet span, running transversely with the valley at the head of each column, they can be applied with perfect ease to that purpose. Not less than 34 miles of iron gutter pipes will be required to convey the water to the heads of the different columns. Of the 50,000 deals ordered for the flooring of the building, a large proportion has arrived, as well as a considerable quantity of balk timber. The hoarding, which is a circuit of nearly a mile, is formed of 6000 1¼ inch 12 feet deals, and is so constructed as not to injure the wood by the use of nails. The hoarding is formed by fixing two battens in the ground upright, at about 1¼ inch apart, and at equal distances; the deals are then laid edge upon edge, the ends being "clipped" by the battens, the tops of which are fastened by iron hooping. A large quantity of the castings have already arrived, and more are on their way to the metropolis. Several tons weight of glass have also arrived in London during the week.

Arrangements have been made for protecting from piracy the design of any article exposed to view at the Exhibition, and a circular, recently issued by the Commissioners, states that there are reasonable expectations that the Board of Trade will grant the right of provisional registration, free of charge, to all exhibitors, of articles which would fall within the provisions of the Act for the Registration of Designs.

Some very beautiful specimens of Honiton lace are in course of preparation for the Exhibition, and the local committees have stated that some fine specimens of Devonshire marble are intended to be exhibited. It ought not to be forgotten that the 31st of October is the last day on which applications for space can be received from intending exhibitors. The space already demanded by the metropolitan districts is 27,774 square feet of floor or table, and 24,243 square feet of wall space. Ten thousand square feet have been granted to Manchester, and we believe 80,000 to America. The total area of the ground floor and galleries of the building will be 855,360 square feet. Messrs. Fox, Henderson, and Co. are confident that they will be able to complete the works within the specified time.

NOTES ON ENGINEERING.

INVENTION OF BEVIL GEAR.—I believe the merit of the invention of bevil gear is due to Messrs. Conacher & Nisbett, formerly millwrights, of Edinburgh. This would be probably about the year 1770.

It was called "conical gear" in Scotland. Previous to its introduction, the common trundle and face wheel, the "rong" and "cog," were the only substitute; and, as may be imagined, but a very poor one for heavy work.

ORIGIN OF THE TERM "NAVIGATOR."—I remember noticing an odd mistake on this subject in some journal or another a short time since. A correspondent, who inquired the origin of the word "navigator," as applied to the men employed in constructing railways and similar works, was informed, in reply, that they were so called because they were men who went to sea when out of employment on shore. The writer, however, was "at sea" rather than the navigators. In the first place, if these men ever did go to sea, they would be *sailors*, not *navigators*, the term, in that sense, meaning a person understanding the art of navigating a ship. The term really arose during the construction of the system of inland navigation, when the men who worked on the canals obtained the name of "navigators," now familiarly shortened into "navvies."

A SUBSCRIBER.

EFFECT OF SHOT ON IRON VESSELS.

Two sections of new iron, each 10 feet square, were built similar to the *Simoon* at the wales, as to plates, ribs, and security, with the exception of the occasional filling-in pieces of oak between the ribs on the main deck and the inside planking, and which would not have added to the safety of a vessel or crew. The plates were ⅝ths of an inch thick. These sections were placed 35 feet apart, and at a distance of 450 yards, secured to piles, driven firmly into the ground. A screen of 1-inch fir boards was placed 10 feet behind the front section, to test the severity of the splinters, and another of extended canvas, to ascertain their number. The guns and charges made use of were such as all the steam vessels carry. The accompanying drawing, for which I am indebted to Captain Savage, of the Royal Marine Artillery, will show more clearly than can be expressed the nature of the holes made by the shot on passing through the sections, to which a detail of the practice is annexed.

The result of these experiments is the reverse of those made on the *Ruby*, in 1846, a small, light-built iron vessel, when the great damage was found to be sustained on the shot passing out on the opposite side to that fired at, making clear round holes only on the first side. On the present occasion, the resistance being so much greater, the principal injury has been on the front side; and the fractures made are of that description that two or three shot, and sometimes even a single one, striking under the water-line, must endanger the ship. There is also another most serious evil attending this great resistance, which was not anticipated, and which has caused great surprise. The shot or shell on striking are shivered into innumerable pieces, passing on as a cloud of langrage with great velocity, sufficient to pass through the 1-inch fir-boards, the larger pieces going to a considerable distance (400 or 500 yards), and some through the rear section, making large irregular holes; this would be most destructive, and I firmly believe men could not stand behind it.

It will be observed that all description of shot, from the 10-inch down to grape, have been used, and all with similar destructive effect.

The last shot fired, an 8-inch with a 5 lbs. charge, established the point that the wood-work will not prevent the evils before stated; it struck a rib that fastened it to the pile of 14 inches; it cut away everything, and made the effect worse.

These experiments, I consider, prove that whether iron vessels are of a slight or substantial construction, iron is not a material calculated for ships of war.

(Signed)   H. D. CHADS, Captain.

Excellent, June 21, 1850.

LIST OF ENGLISH PATENTS.

From the 29th day of August to the 19th day of September, 1850, inclusive.

Alfred Vincent Newton, of Chancery-lane, in the county of Middlesex, mechanical draughtsman, for improvements in cutting types, and other irregular figures. August 29.—(Communication.)

George Augustus Huddart, of Brynkir, in the county of Caernarvon, Esq., for certain improvements in the manufacture of cigars, and certain improved apparatus for smoking cigars. August 29.

Sir John Scott Lillie, Companion of the Most Honourable Order of the Bath, of Paris, France, for certain improvements in the application of motive power. September 5.

John Saul of Manchester, cotton spinner, for certain improvements in machinery or apparatus for spinning and twisting cotton and other fibrous substances. September 5.

George Smith, of Manchester, engineer, for certain improvements in steam engines; and also improvements in feeding or supplying the boilers of the same, part or parts of which improvements are also applicable to other similar purposes. September 5.

William Watt, of the city of Glasgow, N.B., manufacturing chemist, for certain improvements applicable to inland navigation; which improvements, or parts thereof, are also applicable generally to raising, lowering, or transporting heavy bodies. September 5.

Andrew Barclay, of Kilmarnock, in the county of Ayr, N. B., engineer, for improvements in the smelting of iron and other ores, and in the manufacture or working of iron and other metals, and in certain rotary engines and fans, machinery, or apparatus, as connected therewith. September 5.

Wm. Erskine Cochrane, of Cambridge-terrace, Regent's-park, and Henry Francis, of Princes-street, Rotherhithe, for improvements in propelling, steering, and ballasting vessels, in the pistons of steam engines, in fire-bars of furnaces, and in sleepers of railways. September 5.

Frederick Woodbridge, of Old Gravel-lane, in the county of Middlesex, engineer, for improvements in machinery for manufacturing rivets, bolts, and screw blanks. September 5.

John Beattie, of Liverpool, engineer, for certain improvements in steering vessels. September 5.

James Mather, the younger, of Crow Oaks, Pilkington, in the county of Lancaster, bleacher, and Thomas Edmeston, of the same place, calenderman, for certain improvements in machinery or apparatus for scouring, finishing, and stretching woollen, cotton, and other woven fabrics. September 5.

Christopher Cross, of Farnworth, near Boston, in the county of Lancaster, cotton spinner and manufacturer, for certain improvements in the manufacture of textile fabrics; also in the manufacture of wearing apparel and other articles from textile materials; and in the machinery or apparatus for effecting the same. September 5.

James Rennie, of Gowan Bank, Falkirk, in the county of Stirling, in the kingdom of Scotland, gentleman, for a certain improvement or improvements in the construction of gas retorts and furnaces, and in apparatus or machinery applicable to the same. September 5.

Pierre Erard, of Paris, for improvements in the construction of piano-fortes. September 12.

Robert Longdon, the younger, of Derby, in the county of Derby, glove manufacturer, and Thomas Parker Tabberer, of Derby aforesaid, manufacturer of elastic fabrics, for improvements in the manufacture of looped fabrics. September 12.

Astley Paston Price, of Margate, in the county of Kent, chemist, and James Heywood Whitehead, of the Royal George Mills, Saddleworth, near Manchester, for improvements in filters. September 12.

Thomas Lucas Paterson, of the city of Glasgow, N. B., manufacturer and calico printer, for certain improvements in the preparation or manufacture of textile materials, and in the finishing of woven fabrics, and in the machinery or apparatus used therein. September 12.

Richard Archibald Brooman, of the firm of J. C. Robertson & Co., of Fleet-street, in the city of London, for improvements in purifying water, and preparing it for engineering, manufacturing, and domestic uses. September 19.—(Communication.)

Henri Jeremy Christen, of Paris, engraver, for improvements in cylinder printing. September 19.

Jasper Wheeler Rogers, of Dublin, civil engineer, for certain improvements in the preparation of peat, and in the manufacture of the same into fuel and charcoal. September 19.

William Eccles, of Walton-le-dale, in the county of Lancaster, cotton spinner, for certain improvements in looms for weaving. September 19.

Samuel Brisbane, of Manchester, pattern maker, for certain improvements in looms for weaving. September 19.

James Nasmyth, of Patricroft, in the county of Lancaster, engineer, and John Barton, of Manchester, in the same county, copper roller manufacturer, for certain improvements in machinery or apparatus for printing calicoes, and other surfaces; and also improvements in the manufacture of copper or other metallic rollers, to be employed therein; and in the machinery or apparatus connected with such manufacture. September 19.

LIST OF PATENTS THAT HAVE PASSED THE GREAT SEAL OF SCOTLAND.

From the 26th day of July to the 22nd day of August, 1850, inclusive.

Richard A. Brooman, of Fleet-street, in the city of London, for improvements in types, stereotype plates, and other figured surfaces for printing from. July 26.

Donald Beatson, of Stepney, in the county of Middlesex, mariner, for certain improvements in instruments for taking, measuring, and completing angles. July 29.

Joel Spiller, of Battersea, in the county of Surrey, engineer, for improvements in cleaning and grinding wheat and other grain. July 29.

William Edward Newton, of Chancery-lane, in the county of Middlesex, civil engineer, for improvements in machinery or apparatus for making hat bodies, and other similar articles. July 30.

John Gwynne, of Lansdowne Lodge, Notting-hill, merchant, for improvements in obtaining motive power, and in applying the same to giving motion to machinery. July 31.

Walter Neilson, of Hyde Park-street, in the city of Glasgow, N. B., engineer, for improvements in the application of steam for raising, lowering, moving, or transporting heavy bodies. August 2.

George Gwynne, of Sussex-terrace, in the county of Middlesex, Esq., for improvements in the manufacture of sugar. August 7.

William Cox, of Manchester, in the county of Lancaster, cigar merchant, for improvements in machinery or apparatus for manufacturing aërated waters, or other such liquids. August 7.—(Communication.)

William Edward Newton, of Chancery-lane, in the county of Middlesex, civil engineer, for improvements in obtaining, preparing, and applying zinc, and other volatile metals, and the oxides thereof; and in the application of zinc, and ores containing the same, to the preparation or manufacture of certain metals, or alloys of metals. August 8.—(Communication.)

Mathew Grey, of Morris-place, in the city of Glasgow, in the county of Lanark, practical engineer, for an improved method of supplying steam boilers with water. August 9.

William Watt, of the city of Glasgow, N. B., manufacturing chemist, for certain improvements applicable to inland navigation, which improvements, or parts thereof, are also applicable generally to raising, lowering, or transporting heavy bodies. August 13.

George Augustus Huddart, of Brynkir, in the county of Caernarvon, Esq., for certain improvements in the manufacture of cigars. August 14.

James Rennie, of Gowan Bank, Falkirk, in the county of Stirling, N. B., gentleman, for a certain improvement, or improvements in the construction of gas retorts and furnaces, and in apparatus or machinery applicable to the same. August 14.

William Charles Bell, of Manchester, in the county of Lancaster, for improvements in apparatus connected with water closets, drains, and cesspools, and gas and air traps. August 14.

Henry Meyer, of the Strand, in the county of Middlesex, gentleman, for certain improvements in power looms for weaving. August 14.

Read Holliday, of Huddersfield, for improvements in lamps. August 14.

William Mac Naught, of Rochdale, in the county of Lancaster, engineer, for certain improvements in steam engines, and also improvements in apparatus for ascertaining and registering the power of the same. August 16.

Alfred Holl, of Greenwich, in the county of Kent, for improvements in steam engines. August 16.

William Edward Newton, of Chancery-lane, in the county of Middlesex, civil engineer, for improvements in the construction of ships or vessels, and in steam engines, boilers, or generators. August 20.—(Communication.)

Edward Highton, of Clarence Villa, Regent's-park, in the county of Middlesex, engineer, for improvements in electric telegraphs, and in making telegraphic communications. August 21.

Charles William Lancaster, of New Bond-street, in the county of Middlesex, gun-maker, for improvements in the construction of fire-arms, cannon, and projectiles, and in the manufacture of percussion tubes. August 21.

William Dick, of the city of Edinburgh, professor of veterinary medicine, in the Edinburgh Veterinary College, for improvements in the manufacture of steel and gas. August 22.

LIST OF PATENTS THAT HAVE PASSED THE GREAT SEAL OF IRELAND.

From the 31st day of July, to the 16th day of August, 1850, inclusive.

Eugene Ablon, of Panton-street, Haymarket, in the county of Middlesex, for improvements in increasing the draft in chimneys of locomotive and other engines. July 31.

Joseph Barrans, of St. Paul's, Deptford, in the county of Kent, Esq., for improvements in axles and axle boxes of locomotive engines, and other railway carriages. August 1.

Thomas Dickson Rotch, of Drumlanford-house, in the county of Ayr, Esq., for an improved mode of manufacturing soap. August 1.

Louis Napoleon Le Gras, of Paris, in the Republic of France, civil engineer, for improvements in the separation and disinfection of fecal matters in the manufacture of manure, and in the apparatus employed therein. August 3.

Thomas Keely, of the town and county of the town of Nottingham, manufacturer, and William Wilkinson, of the same place, framework knitter, for certain improvements in looped or elastic fabrics, and in articles made therefrom; also certain machinery for producing the said improvements, which is applicable in whole, or in part, to the manufacture of looped fabrics generally. August 3.

John Gwynne, of Lansdowne Lodge, Notting-hill, merchant, for improvements in obtaining motive power, and in applying the same to giving motion to machinery. August 6.

George Augustus Huddart, of Brynkir, in the county of Caernarvon, Esq., for certain improvements in the manufacture of cigars, and certain apparatus for smoking certain cigars. August 16.

DESIGNS FOR ARTICLES OF UTILITY.

Registered from 22nd August to 18th September.

Aug. 22nd, 2415, Schofield, Brown, Davies, & Halse, Gresham-street, "The University cravat."

" 23rd, 2416, J. Swain & Co., Oxford-street, "The registered Syrian paletot."

" " 2417, J. Swain & Co., Oxford-street, "The registered Syrian jacket."

" 24th, 2418, Samuel Rooke, Jun., Whittall-street, Birmingham, "Oxonian ink pot."

" " 2419, Bernhard Samuelson, Banbury, Oxfordshire, "Beater to be used in making butter."

" 27th, 2420, William George Armstrong, Elswick Engine Works, Newcastle, "Hydraulic equalizer."

" 31st, 2421, William Elliot Carrett, Leeds, "Steam pump."

" " 2422, William Bird, Oxford-street, "Boot."

" " 2423, Michael McMinnus, Blackburn, "Parexograph, or self-acting copying guide."

" " 2424, David Hodge & Thomas Roberts, Hatton-garden, "Candle lamp, for burning magnum candles."

Sept. 3rd, 2425, John Tanner, Broad-street, Bristol, "Cloth trowsers."

" " 2426, William Newman & William Newman, Jun., Stafford-street, Wolverhampton, and Henrietta-street, Birmingham, "Imperial door-spring."

" " 2427, Alfred Moring, Artillery-place West, Bunhill-row, "Nepaulese braces."

" 4th, 2428, Levy D. Smith, Little Knight Ryder-street, St. Paul's, "A colouring embossing apparatus."

" 6th, 2429, Hugh Booth, Swinton, Lancashire, "Fork, for the weft stop motion, used in looms or machinery for manufacturing woven fabrics."

" 7th, 2430, William Craig & Isaac Whitesmith, Glasgow, "Brake for slubbing and roving frames."

" 9th, 2431, Lewis Cooke Hertslet, Fitzroy Park, Highgate, "Double socket joint for connecting tubes or pipes without flanges."

" " 2432, Lamen Zox, Long Acre, "Cape or cloak with hood, for travelling or walking."

" " 2433, James Isaac Sands & Henry Edward Outtram, Holborn Hill, "A pair of self-supporting trousers."

" 10th, 2434, George Wolstenholm, Washington Works, Sheffield, "Doubly carbonized I X L razor."

" 12th, 2435, Thomas Honnor, Leadenhall-street, City, "The 'Utilis' over coat."

" " 2436, Henry Phillips, Graham-street, Birmingham, "Improved shield for brooch pins."

" 13th, 2437, E. O. Tindall & L. Tindall, Scarborough, Yorkshire, "Cooking range."

" 16th, 2438, H. J. Nicoll & D. Nicoll, Regent-street, "Wrapper cloak."

" " 2439, Charles Roper Mead, Charlotte cottages, Arthur-street, Old Kent-road, "Gas Meter."

" 17th, 2440, Edward Bing, Effingham-place, Ramsgate, "Window and door weather joint."

" " 2441, Thomas Royle, Wolverhampton, "Trouser strap."

" 18th, 2442, Welch & Margetson, Cheapside, "Cantab braces."

" " 2443, Joseph Guise, Clerkenwell-green, "Catoptric deflector and bracket for a gas burner."

" " 2444, Richard Bright, Burton-street, Westminster, "Portable safety carriage lamp."

THE ARTIZAN.

No. XI.—Vol. VIII.—NOVEMBER 1st, 1850.

IMPROVEMENT OF RAILWAY DIVIDENDS.

SUGGESTIONS FOR THE IMPROVEMENT OF RAILWAY DIVIDENDS.

If an apology were wanted for approaching this delicate subject, we might refer our readers to the railway share list, and bid them compare "paid" with "present prices." We are beginning to hear of railways "being closed," or "worked by horses," "rolling stock being taken in execution," and the like. We are opening, too, competing lines now and then, like the Great Northern, which must necessarily abstract traffic from the North Western and North Eastern railways, and tend to diminish dividends already cut down pretty close. These facts seem to indicate that ere long the shareholders of numerous lines will have to choose between no dividends at all, or some change in their system of working. Increasing fares and diminishing accommodation seem to be given up for a bad job, not because they are unfair to the public, but simply because liberal measures are found to pay better.

Shareholders are so little accustomed to act in unison, that the majority of railway meetings are allowed to pass over with only a few indistinct mutterings of discontent, which, if they ever assume any tangible shape, are referred as "the excellent suggestions of my worthy friend" to "our engineer, or secretary," who puts an extinguisher over them with true official tact. Indeed the inducement to any man to attempt to improve by fair means the dividend of a railway company, is infinitesimally small. Should any large shareholder by chance possess the engineering and business knowledge necessary to enable him to meet the officials on their own ground, the only effect of his labours, for a considerable period, will be to deteriorate the market value of property in which he holds a large stake, and should he eventually carry through his measures of reform, he will find in the tardy improvement which they will occasion, but a very poor remuneration for the loss of time and money which he will incur in combating, single-handed, the ignorance and prejudice, if not corruption, that will inevitably be arrayed against him. The more natural course for a capitalist is to withdraw as quietly as possible, and seek some other investment, over the management of which his influence may be more beneficially exercised.

It may not be uninteresting to our readers to consider some of the causes which have led to the depreciation of a property so vast, and so widely diffused. We will not attempt to explain the enormous sums which have been lavished in buying off the opposition of landowners, in fighting rival companies in parliament, and in contracts made for the advantage of firms intimately connected with the directors, but will rather confine ourselves to some of those points on which errors of judgment have occurred, which have contributed to diminish the profits of the trunk lines.

The construction of branch lines, with guaranteed dividends on the capital expended, has been one of the most fatal errors which have been committed, not because a railway passing through a thinly populated and poor district must necessarily be a bad investment *per se*, but because they have, in most cases, been constructed without any regard to the exigences of the case. Deeply rooted notions as to the impracticability of working a railway safely with a single line of rails, and of the necessity of erecting expensive stations, bridges of masonry, and similar engineering luxuries, have led to an outlay of money which a due estimate of the traffic would have shown to be unjustifiable. It does not seem to have occurred to directors that a railway may be made *too well*—in fact, to last 100 years, and never pay a dividend. Thus many branches are worked at a positive loss to the parent line, from their extravagant cost and inconsiderable traffic. To make a line pay which runs through a poor district requires a judicious outlay of capital to make its advantages available to the population, and to develope the traffic. In America the increased value which a railway gives to the property through which it passes, justifies the construction of a line merely to connect two termini, perhaps 100 miles apart, whilst the landowner who receives the benefit, has to pay towards the railway instead of being allowed, as in this country, to bring forward extortionate demands for damages caused by severance, compulsory sale, &c. Circumstances with us are different, but still advantage may be taken to a great extent of the improvement effected. Taking the case of a purely agricultural district, through which a cheap single line of railway has been carried, it seems to be assumed that it must necessarily absorb all the existing traffic in the conveyance of lime and other manures, live and dead stock, and crops, without considering that the *conveyance to the nearest station* is half the battle. We all know that the peculiar advantage of a railway is found in moving large masses of goods at very low rates when once on the railway, compared with the expense of haulage on common roads, and therefore its superior economy is only felt to a small extent by the farmer, unless his establishment happens to be situated on the line of rail. An occasional visit to the station near some rural village will satisfy the inquirer on this point. He will see a team bringing a load from a farm a few miles off, over an indifferent road, and may watch the slow process of unloading into the shed (rarely at once into the railway truck), and the take-it-easy sort-of-way in which matters are managed, and he will then understand why the traffic does not flow of its own accord into the desired channel, in spite of the canvassing which some few companies have at length condescended to make use of. As, then, we cannot bring the farm to the railway, we must bring the railway to the farm, by laying down branch lines on the existing turnpike roads, and running through the main streets of the towns and villages, and into the main farm establishments. These branches would be constructed very cheaply, being of sufficient strength only to take an ordinary loaded truck. They would be worked by horse power, and thus obviate any danger that might arise from fire or from collisions in the thoroughfares. When we consider that a horse will draw a load of from 15 to 20 tons on a railway, or about 15 times as much as on an ordinary road, we see at once that where speed is not required, the locomotive may be dispensed with, and the cost of making the permanent way of corresponding strength avoided. These inexpensive branches would, like the fine filaments which nature supplies to draw sustenance for trees of the largest growth, collect the traffic of a district to one central point on the main line, where it would be managed with greater economy than by a number of smaller establishments. An immense amount of loading and unloading would be saved, to the advantage both of the consumer and producer. Where tenants from short leases, and landowners for want of capital, were unable to avail themselves of these plans, it would appear a strictly legitimate use of a company's capital to construct all the works themselves, and charge an interest on the capital so expended ; retaining possession meanwhile as security, but giving the landowner the power of purchasing the works whenever he had the means of doing so. Some of these branch lines would probably, when the traffic and population had increased, become converted into locomotive lines, for which they would form the pioneers and creators of traffic. The jealousy of the existing companies would, perhaps, hardly permit it, or a systematic plan might be adopted by a company which would obtain a general Act of parliament, like an enclosure Act, which would enable them to execute the works without involving the necessity of separate Acts of parliament, the expense of which falls heavily upon schemes on a moderate scale. It would be very far from our object if these remarks were merely understood to refer to rural districts, for we are assured that there exists ample room for the beneficial introduction of such branch lines into most of our large towns. The Blackwall Railway has never answered the purpose for which it was originally intended, because to bring a few casks of sugar three or four miles, it is not worth while, practically, to put them into a railway truck, and then again into a cart at the Minories, to get them to their destination. At Southampton the principle is partially carried out, with evident good effects. A branch line runs through the dock warehouses and along the river, so that each of the numerous manufacturing establishments on its banks have the railway at the gate of their premises. Bristol is very deficient in railway accommodation of this kind, although from the large area of ground over which the docks and river frontage extend it seems peculiarly to want it to foster the rising trade of the port. Here, as in a vast number of other cases, there is ample room for the introduction of a complete system of branch railways, which would form a great public convenience as well as a source of revenue to the company.

The improvement in railway property in this direction has been well argued by Mr. W. B. Adams, in his "Road Progress," (noticed *ante*, p. 101,) and it is much to be regretted that his views, the soundness of which are every day becoming more apparent, have not met with a more extended support. A strong and involuntary compliment has, however, been paid to him and to Mr. Samuel, by the constructors of the "light engines," of the performances of which we now hear so much. To judge from the tone assumed by many on this subject, it might be supposed that such a thing as a light engine had only just been discovered. If our readers, however, will turn to our journal for 1843, p. 44, they will find a plate and description of a four-wheeled engine by Messrs. Bury, Curtis, and Kennedy, the type of, we are afraid to say how many, hundreds constructed by that firm, and which were "improved upon" by other engine makers, until it became a race which should build the biggest engine, much as children try which shall blow the biggest bubble, the analogy being unfortunately carried out too far to suit the pockets of the shareholders.

Our engineers have not yet thought fit to give the American system of carriages a trial, although they appear not unworthy of it.

For our own part, we are induced to think that it would be a

great convenience to be able to stand upright in a carriage when tired of sitting—that we would rather take a cup of coffee, or a chop on the way, than be compelled to leave a half-tasted meal at Swindle'em station, (where we have paid at a rate that justifies the present occupant giving 20,000*l.* for the good will), or else have to stop at Birmingham an hour, when we don't want to stop at all—that a little artificial warmth during winter would not be unacceptable in this climate—and that, finally, after enduring all this, and much more, it would be a more sensible plan to take our tickets toward the latter end of the journey, than to keep us waiting some ten minutes outside the station, while that enlivening ceremony is being performed. The complaint of a traveller, that the draught is unpleasant in a long undivided carriage, would apparently be met by giving each double seat a blind, which might be drawn at pleasure, but we do not think there is much weight in this objection, or the Americans, who provide iced water in summer, and a place of convenience for the comfort of their passengers, would not tolerate such an arrangement.

We have purposely abstained from going into any minute details, in our remarks, because we are persuaded that there are enough defects visible on the surface of our present system. If we can but induce shareholders to insist upon a change of principles in the management of railway property, the details may be safely left to that ingenuity and competition, which has produced a speed of fifty miles per hour, and a trip to Brighton and back for three shillings and sixpence!

CARRETT'S PATENT STEAM-PUMP.

This simple, cheap, and efficient apparatus is arranged and constructed for the supplying with water, either high or low pressure, marine, locomotive, or stationary, boilers, or forcing water to great heights, for various hydraulic purposes of domestic and general economy. It can be set at work at any moment, independant of the engine or other machinery belonging to the boiler, being in itself an engine, a lifting, and a force pump combined.

The greatest difficulty to be overcome in the application of any apparatus to this purpose, is to insure an equal and constant delivery, and at the same time be able to work the pump at a good and effective speed, without injury to the water-pipes, joints, clacks, and machinery.

By the ordinary apparatus this becomes next to an impossibility, in consequence of the *vis inertia* of the water, which cannot be made to start instanter throughout the whole length of the pipes at the precise moment that the plunger changes the direction of its motion ;—the result is, the pump-barrel gets only partially filled at each stroke, and the ram comes down through the remaining empty space upon it with an accelerating force, causing a severe shock to the whole apparatus, and producing in consequence a whole series of unavoidable evils, which operate to the speedy destruction of the whole machinery.

In the Registered Steam-Pump these evils are entirely obviated, by the interposition of suitable air-vessels, working together and in conjunction with the pump ; the effect of which is to produce a constant stream of water throughout the whole length of the pipes, which will continue without intermission so long as the pump is suffered to perpetuate its motion.

The *modus operandi* is as follows :—At every ascent of the plunger the bottom valve draws its amount of water from the bottom of the first air-vessel, which is shortly replenished by the constant stream through the suction pipe connecting this reservoir with the well. When the plunger descends, the water beneath it is driven through the top clack into the second air-chamber, where, after it has accumulated sufficiently to overcome the pressure, it will finally make its exit in one constant stream into the boiler or vessel provided for its reception.

In this novel apparatus, the pump and air-vessels are all enclosed in an ornamental base, above which is placed an inverted steam cylinder,

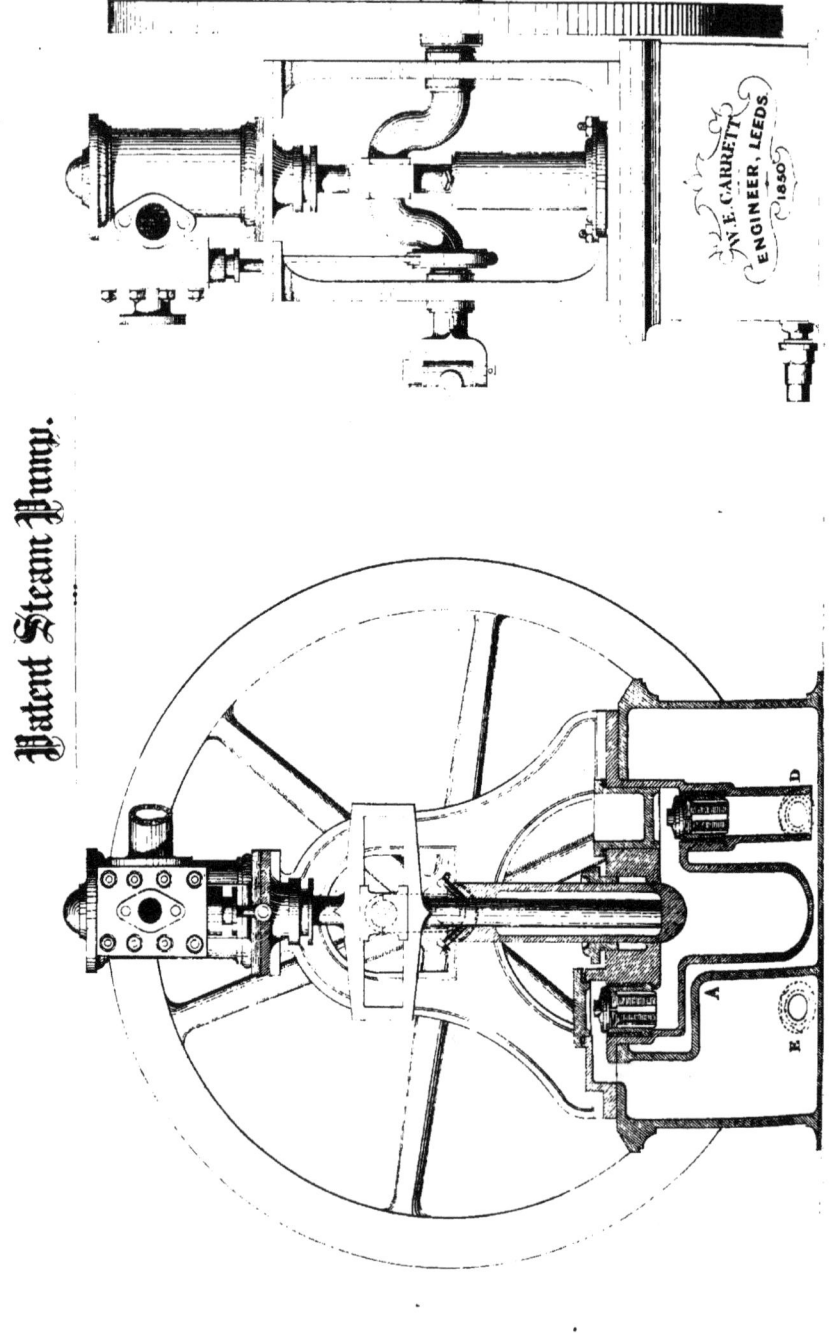

Patent Steam Pump.

W. E. GARRETT,
ENGINEER, LEEDS.
1850

working in direct action with the ram. The whole machine is quite portable and compact, requiring no other fixing than the attachment of the steam and water pipes : while the size of the entire apparatus is very little more than that of the diameter of its own fly-wheel.

W. E. CARRETT, Engineer, Leeds.

The construction of this pumping engine will be readily understood from the plate, which shows a side elevation in section, and an end view. The cistern which contains the pump is divided into two compartments by the plate A, forming the air-vessels for the suction and delivery pipes, and constitutes the sole plate of the engine. Two side frames are bolted upon it, on the top of which is fixed the steam cylinder. The piston rod and pump rod are in one piece, and have between them a slotted piece to receive the crank pin, which works in a brass block sliding in the slot. The pump rod is connected to the pump plunger by two set screws, which have merely to withstand the strain on the up stroke, as the point of the rod bears on the bottom of the plunger. By slacking these screws the plunger, which then forms a guide for the rod, is disconnected from the engine, which may then be applied to drive other work by means of the universal joint on the end of the crank shaft, or by a strap off the fly-wheel.

The valves are constructed of the simplest form, and have four wings instead of three, as ordinarily made, to give more surface for wear; and the water-way is increased just where it is required, by cutting away a portion of each wing. The outsides of the valve seats are not turned, nor are the sockets for their reception bored, but after being dropped in place, the vacancy between them is filled up with iron cement. With the same object of diminishing the fitting, the covers (which form the guards to prevent the valves rising too high) are not faced, but the joints are made by the interposition of a ring of vulcanized India-rubber which answers very well for water, but which our own experience does not lead us to recommend for steam; and it will be noticed that the seat and cover are made of such a shape that the vulcanized ring is wedged in, and any internal pressure only tightens the joint.

We do not altogether hold with Mr. Carrett in adopting the slotted crosshead principle instead of a connecting rod ; but taking into consideration the fact that in general it is only used to limit the stroke of the engine, and that it diminishes the height and expense of the machine, it may be tolerated. If the power is to be transmitted through the crank shaft it would be advisable to give the sliding-block ample surface, and a lubricator travelling with it. The air-vessel is a very important adjunct to all pumps working against a high pressure, but we are not convinced that the air-vessel on the delivery side, E, is arranged in the best form. It is well known that under high pressure the air in the vessel is absorbed by the water, and after working some time the vessel will be found full of water instead of air, and consequently of no use. Now, to obviate this it seems advisable to let the water delivered from the pump pass by a pipe to the *bottom* of the *air-vessel*, which is preferable when tall and of small diameter, so as to expose but a small surface of air to the water. To do this in the case before us a pipe could be carried down from the delivery port of the pump in the same way as is done on the suction side, and the water would not thus have to pass through, and in contact with, the air to reach the delivery branch.

Considerable credit is due to Mr. Carrett for his attempt to produce a small engine at a minimum of cost, which may, for aught we know, eventually become as common an appendage to our household as the turnspits formerly used to be. Many houses have already the boiler to warm the rooms and baths, and for cooking operations ; and the engine will no doubt soon follow as a matter of course.

AGRICULTURAL ENGINEERING.

THE economy of the application of steam power to agricultural operations is now fairly admitted, but very few accurate experiments have been made to show the precise figures of the results. We therefore have great pleasure in bringing before our readers a valuable practical paper, by Mr. Peter Laws, read at a late meeting of the Newcastle Farmers' Club.

The subject is divided into two main branches—the production and conveyance of the crop, or raw material ; and the manufacturing at the homestead of that raw material, so as to fit it for the market, or for human food.

Under the first head Mr. Laws describes the application of steam power to drainage, by means of pumps and scoop wheels—to irrigation —to ploughing and cultivating the soil, and to the conveyance of agricultural produce.

With respect to drainage and irrigation, all our readers will be aware that much has been done in the fen districts, though more remains to do. It is not, however, so well known that a considerable portion of the steam-power employed in draining the fens might be dispensed with if the proprietors would be content with making merely *drains* instead of *canals*. That the latter are eminently useful for inland transit it cannot be denied ; but the convenience may be purchased at too dear a rate, as the canals, to be available, must always be kept full ; and consequently in many districts the water has to be lifted by steam power solely on account of their consequent high level.

Mr. Laws, we see, inclines to our opinion (*ante* p. 70) that for irrigation, and the application of liquid manure, steam power may be employed to force it through pipes more economically than by liquid manure carts, which, from their weight, are apt to poach the fields. He holds out very little hopes to ploughers by steam, and common road locomotists ; and if we differ with him it is only in degree, whilst at the same time we admire the preference which he gives to those objects within his present reach.

For the rest we must allow Mr. Laws to speak for himself, only premising that all questions of profit and loss in the employment of machinery turn very much on the *time* that it can be kept at work. If an engine pays when only used for 5½ hours per day, what would it do if kept going for the 10 hours ? The high pressure non-condensing engine is justly preferred for small powers, as the waste steam may be used to advantage after it leaves the engine, so as to obtain the power almost for nothing. We will, however, now leave the field to Mr. Laws.

ON THE APPLICATION OF STEAM TO AGRICULTURE, BY MR. PETER LAWS.

Turning to the fourth subject under consideration, namely—the conveyance of agricultural produce, we may divide it into the conveyance of the raw material to the homestead to be manufactured for the market, and to the conveyance of the manufactured produce to the market.

Beginning with the conveyance of the unmanufactured, or raw material. All that has been said previously upon steam ploughing is equally applicable to the present subject, which is neither more nor less than that, in the present state of our engineering knowledge, it is quite impossible to construct any engine to be used upon the unprotected soil, or common farm roads, to enter into competition with animal power. As a further proof, I will instance the mode of thrashing pursued in the south of England, which, as you all know, is by means of portable thrashing machines, which are now frequently driven by portable steam engines. Now these engines, instead of being able to remove the thrashing machine from place to place, are themselves to be removed by horse labour. So much for the extended use of steam power upon common roads. I need hardly tell you there is little chance of the railway system being adopted, even upon the large farms, for the above-mentioned purpose.

With regard to the conveyance of the manufactured produce from the farm to the market, very different results may be, and are accomplished. No one, coolly considering the subject, will attempt to deny that the quick and cheap conveyance of such bulky and perishable commodities, as the most of agricultural productions are, must be a very great desideratum indeed. And although the farmer in the immediate vicinity of large towns may have some reason to complain of his inability of obtaining such high prices as he formerly got, previous to the introduction of railways and steamboats, yet to the distant and inland cultivator, and to the city consumer, the change has been a most beneficial one ; for to the former it has been the means of obtaining higher prices and greater demand for the articles he raises and deals in, and to the latter it furnishes a cheaper and better supply. Thus, though steam communication may have crippled or destroyed particular trades, yet we must confess that it has greatly benefited the public at large, and we must bear in mind the adage that,

"All partial evil's universal good."

But before dismissing the present subject, I think it my duty to mention the benefit that would probably have accrued to the farmer had our railway speculators, instead of ruining themselves by constructing railways, at enormous expense, to towns where there is little traffic, made a few light cheap branch lines, running through our agricultural districts, conveying coal, lime, and manure to the farmer, and transporting our heavy and perishable productions of corn, green crops, milk, &c., to the towns. With light engines and carriages, no doubt can exist of such railways being remunerative. With these remarks I will conclude the out-door application of steam to agriculture, and proceed with its in-door application, or the manufacturing of the raw material to fit it for the market.

In commencing this subject, I need scarcely mention that thrashing is the principal farming purpose to which steam power is applied in this neighbourhood, and it fortunately happens that its application to barn-work is very simple, and easily accomplished. The steam engine for such purposes differs but little or none from the usual construction, although certainly what is called the over-head crank engine is the one most generally employed, as it costs less, is simpler in its parts and fittings, and is easier managed than the beam engine, all of which advantages are of consequence to the farmer. The non-condensing is generally preferred to the condensing engine, on account of requiring less water, and for the reasons I have already given in favour of the crank engine. The non-condensing certainly consumes a little more fuel than the condensing engine ; yet, upon the whole, it is the most suitable for farm purposes, and if well-made and managed, a four horse power engine will not consume more than a hundred weight of common coals in the hour ; and, during the above time, it will thrash from 25 to 30 bolls of wheat, according to the yield, and oats and barley in proportion. I am of opinion that where steam power has been applied in this district, in the majority of cases, the steam engine and machinery have been erected upon too extensive a scale, for, in its present form and proportions, it is only upon the largest farms that it can be beneficially employed. Here, I think, our millwrights are wrong, because a well-made horse machine is quite competent to thrash the crop, even upon a moderately large farm ; and to erect an engine of six or seven horse power upon any farms not employing more than three draughts is preposterous in the extreme. In such a case, even setting aside the expense, the boiler requires as much fuel to raise the steam as to thrash the crop, besides demanding more hands to attend the machinery than can generally be spared upon such a farm ; indeed the advantage of steam power is very questionable upon any farm not working more than three pairs of horses, unless part fattening stock are kept upon it ; in such a case a steam-engine is a most valuable acquisition, as it not only thrashes the crop, but affords the means of crushing and grinding inferior grain, pulse, &c., and, if required, cutting hay and straw for fodder. The spare steam may also, when needed, be used for cooking

or preparing the food for horses and cattle. I am quite aware many of you will consider the latter operations as not of much consequence, but I must also recollect that there are many agriculturists who do attach much value to them, and my object is merely to point out the most suitable means of performing such operations, leaving the adoption of them to such as have the means and will to carry them out.

But to proceed. I will pass over a large farm, because, if situated in this coal district, no doubt exists of the superiority of steam in preference to horse power for thrashing, and take the case of one working three pair of horses, and feeding off in the house a dozen cattle or so, besides dairy stock and pigs. We will also take it for granted that a considerable quantity of inferior and refuse grain, pease, &c., is used for the fattening of cattle and pigs, besides cut hay and straw for the remainder of the stock. Upon such a farm the engine need not be more than three horse power ; indeed, if well managed it may be less, and yet perfectly sufficient for the purposes to which we wish to apply it. The thrashing machine ought to be simple, and as lightly constructed as is consistent with durability. One rake is sufficient, and is less liable to entangle the straw than when two are used. It ought also to be furnished with elevators for carrying away the thrashed corn into a chamber, apart from the barn, and immediately above the dressing machine, which ought also to be driven by the engine, along with or separate from the thrashing mill, at the pleasure of the manager. The thrashing mill is generally driven by gearing, and the subordinate machines by means of straps running on fast and loose pulleys, so as to be set in motion or stopped while the engine is at work. The engine will have a six-inch cylinder and eighteen-inch stroke, making about seventy strokes per minute. The boiler will be about two feet nine inches diameter, and twelve feet long ; or if used for steaming food for cattle, it may be preferable to use two boilers, each about nine or ten feet long, and two feet in diameter. They ought to be constructed so as to be used independently of each other ; and although they will cost a little more than a single large one, will in the end effect a considerable saving in fuel, by obviating the necessity of using the large boiler when wanted for steaming, or when little work is to be done. The engine ought to have what is technically called lap and lead of the slide, so as to use the steam expansively, and effect a still further economy in fuel, and the full working pressure ought never to exceed 45lb. per square inch. Such a machine will thrash from 16 to 24 bushels in the hour, according to the yield, and will thoroughly separate the corn from the straw, and carry the thrashed corn into the clean chamber, there to lie until the thrashing is finished. The dressing may then commence, which is better than carrying them on simultaneously, as a better sample can be thus obtained, owing to the greater regularity of the feed and blast. The cost of such a machine and engine, including dressing machine and elevators, ought not to exceed £120 at the outside, the interest upon which, together with the wear and tear, may be taken as amounting to about £7. 10s.

The hands required will be as follows :—A man to attend the engine and machinery, another to feed the machine, two girls to hand up the sheaves, and two women to take away the straw—in all six hands.

The expense will be as under—beginning at six in the morning, allowing half an hour at eight o'clock for breakfast, and a quarter at ten, finishing at noon—in all five hours and a quarter. The expense will be as under, setting aside interest upon the prime cost :—

	s.	d.
1 Man attending engine and machine, at 2s. per day	1	0
1 Man feeding machine	1	0
2 Girls handing the sheaves, &c., at 6d.	0	6
2 Women taking away the straw, at 10d.	0	10
Fuel for the engine, a cwt. per hour, including raising the steam, 7 cwt , and carriage at 3s. 6d. per ton	1	3
Oil, tallow, &c., for engine and machinery	0	3
	4	10

The quantity thrashed in the above time would be about ninety bushels, costing in round numbers rather more than ½*d.* per bushel. The dressing of the corn fit for market, requiring a man and a boy to attend the machinery, take away the sacks, &c., time required, about two hours or two hours and a half, according to circumstances, would stand as under. The engine might be grinding or crushing grain at the same time and with the same hands.

	s.	*d.*
Wages of man attending the machinery	0	6
Wages of boy assisting ditto	0	1½
Fuel required for the engine, oil, &c., about	0	3½
	0	11

Or less than half a farthing per bushel. Stated cost of thrashing and dressing ninety bushels of wheat, 5*s.* 9*d.*; or under a penny per bushel.

Now let us see what the above would cost by horse power. To thrash the above quantity would require four good horses and driver, besides an extra hand to clear away the thrashed corn. The cost of the machinery would be about 60*l.*; the interest upon which, together with the wear and tear, would amount to about 4*l.* 10*s.* in the year.

The cost of thrashing a hundred bushels of wheat would be as under:

	s.	*d.*
Man to feed in the thrashing mill, at 2*s.* per day ..	1	0
Boy to drive, at 8*d.* per day	0	4
2 Girls to hand up the sheaves, at 6*d.* per day	0	6
2 Women to take away the straw, at 10*d.* per day ..	0	10
4 Horses, at 2*s.* 3*d.* each	5	0
Oil, &c.	0	1½
Per hundred bushels	7	9½

To dress this corn as it is generally done, putting it once slowly through the machine as in the former case, will require as follows:—

	s.	*d.*
Man to measure up the corn	0	6
2 Women to turn the machine	0	2½
1 Woman to hold the sacks	0	2½
1 Girl to feed in	0	1½
Total cost of thrashing and dressing a hundred bushels	8	10

Showing a balance in favour of steam power of 3*s.* 1*d.*, or in other words, effecting a saving of 35 per cent.

But, as I have already said, it is not from the thrashing that the full benefit of steam power is to be derived; inasmuch as when applied to crushing and grinding grain for home use, it is found immeasurably superior to horse power, affording, as it does, the means of using up the whole of his inferior corn. In fact, since such corn can now scarcely meet with a buyer in the market, the farmer is almost necessitated to use it at home, and afterwards sell it in the form of beef or pork. It may not be amiss to mention that common millstones answer best for the above purpose, when all things are taken into consideration.

The same saving in favour of steam *versus* horse power applies equally to the chaff-cutter. Whether cutting hay or straw is of real service would be presumptuous in me to say—as even amongst the gentlemen here assembled, scarcely two opinions will be found alike; all that I can do is simply to point out the best and cheapest method of performing such an operation, and I again say the steam engine will effect it much cheaper than either horse power or human labour.

Amongst the miscellaneous purposes to which steam can be applied, I have already mentioned the conveyance of liquid manure and the preparing of food for cattle. In addition to those there are many subordinate machines to which it may form the motive power, such as pumps for supplying the homestead with water, churns, and such like; and, however trivial these appear to people who have not seen, or do not need them, still they are useful in their proper station, and I am accordingly bound to give them a place in the present paper.

I must not omit to state that the spare steam from the engine can be most economically used for heating purposes, and for drying corn. In fact, there are many modes of employing this truly useful servant, far more indeed than the generality of people ever dream of. And now for one word regarding the danger attending its use. That there is a danger no one need pretend to deny, but that that danger is very remote I fearlessly venture to assert, and that with common care no fear of accident from either fire or explosion need be apprehended, even by the most timid or nervous mind.

THE PRESENT SYSTEM OF STEAM-BOAT INSPECTION.

EXPLOSION OF THE BOILER OF THE "QUEEN" STEAMER.

On Wednesday, July 10th, a fatal explosion occurred at Devonport, on board the steamer, *Queen*, the boiler of which burst just as she was coming from her night moorings to the Quay, for the purpose of taking on board a large party who, in a few moments more, would have been all on board.

Upon an examination of the boiler, immediately afterwards, it was found to have been driven forward about 2 feet from its former position, and the back plates had been entirely removed; and so great had been the amount of force exerted on it that it was completely torn off, the line of separation being through the centre of the angle iron which connected the sides, bottom, and top of boiler to the back, which had now been blown overboard. The area of the open end was found on measurement to be about 40 square feet, or about 8 feet by 5 feet. The tubes, which were of iron, and about 2¼ inches diameter, were covered with a slight incrustation, or scale, and on examining the top ones, no indication of their being left dry for want of water was to be found, as there was no sign of recent oxidation, and the scale was adhering to the top of them as firmly as on any of the surrounding parts of the boiler. On the back of the fire-box, between which and the back there had been a water space of between 4 and 5 inches, were two angle iron stays of about 3 inches wide, and 12 inches long, fastened to the plates with ¾ inch rivets, with three holes ¾ inch diameter to connect with similar pieces riveted to the back of the boiler, by means of cotter pins, each overlapping the other; one of the stays was split through these pin holes from top to bottom, and on the fractured surface there was an amount of incrustation about equal to that on the surrounding parts, indicating that the stay had been in that state for some considerable time, and of course was of *no use* as a stay; the other stay, situated in a similar position on the back of the fire-box, was of the same general dimensions, but entire, with two of the three connecting pins in their places; clearly showing that its fellow stay connected to the missing back must be split also, which, upon subsequent examination, was found to be the case, and which also, from the amount of scale on the fractured surface, proved that it had been long useless. The distance horizontally between the two stays was about 28 inches; there were no stays to bottom of boiler, to connect it with any other portion. There were six diagonal stays of about 1¼ inches round iron, connecting the bottom of the steam-chest with the sides of the boiler, which merely prevented the angle at the top of the sides being distorted by the upward and lateral pressures, the bottom and back being unsupported at the time. We should suppose that the first part to give way under these circumstances would be the junction of the bottom and back, in the centre of their length, as the two forces acting downward and backward would resolve themselves into one great force on that particular spot; and so it evidently had been, for the middle of the back edge of the boiler bottom was bent down about 3 or 4 inches, leaving two legs of flat iron which had been fastened to the bottom of the fire-box for support, about that much clear of the bottom of the boiler, and the bottom edge of the back part, when found at low water, was bent backward in the middle in a similar manner, and presented every indication of having been the first point to give way.

Upon a subsequent examination of the safety valve, it was found that there was insufficient space for the escape of steam from it, *by the box above the valve being nearly filled with the lead weight on the spindle,* the area of which space was only about ⅓ the area of the valve itself. There was nothing which indicated a *sticking* of the valve at the time of the explosion. In addition to the weight on the spindle in the valve-box, there was a lever resting on the top of the spindle outside, with a shifting weight on it; this lever was accessible to the engineer, and by it he could vary his pressure to the extent of some 4 or 5 pounds per square inch on the valve. Upon weighing the weights, valve, lever, &c., it was found that the whole weight on the valve was about 253 lbs ; area of valve 15 inches; which would give as a maximum pressure as follows :—

Whole weight .. = 253 lbs.

$$\frac{253 \text{ lbs.}}{15 \text{ ins.}} = 16\tfrac{13}{15} \text{ lbs. per square inch.}$$

Area of safety valve = 15 ins.

But at the time of the explosion the weight on the lever was not at its maximum, but giving a pressure of 15.15 lbs. per square inch, and it appears in the evidence before the coroner, that the person in charge of the engines at the time was on deck about three minutes before the explosion, and the steam was *not quite up.* This would lead us to suppose that the back of the boiler was in a very weakened state, produced by the continual warping or bulging out and in, as the steam might be up or down, until it had destroyed, to a very serious extent, the cohesive power of the angle iron, and that power had become less than was necessary to withstand the force of the accumulated pressure of the steam. The back of the boiler being at the time unsupported by stays, which, on account of their mal-construction, had long before been rendered useless, was, from its shape, the weakest part, and gave way accordingly.

There appears to have been a very lamentable amount of ignorance, or negligence, perhaps both, displayed in this affair. Ignorance on the part of the designer or constructor of the boiler, clearly shown in the character and extent of the stays ; and negligence on the part of the inspector, who had inspected and given a certificate, only 30 days prior to the occurence, although, as shown on the inquest, he knew there was *no mercury in the steam guage ;* or on the part of the proprietors, or persons in charge of the engines and boiler. One or more of three parties are highly culpable. But since the passing of the Act 9th and 10th Vict., *legal* responsibility is removed from the shoulders of steam-boat proprietors, as long as they get their boats and engines *legally* inspected at the appointed times, and it is hardly to be expected that persons who are not thoroughly acquainted with the internal structure and general principles of steam engines and boilers, will think there is anything materially wrong so soon after the inspection, especially in this case, where the boiler was only thirteen months old.

We must be allowed to think that the extent of the inspection is too limited. The inspector should not only examine the general structure of the engines and boiler, but he should also be empowered to try in his balance the capabilities of the person in charge, and search him as to his knowledge of the machine he professes to be master of. We hesitate not to say, that in many instances we have found persons in charge of marine and other engines who are not fit for the positions they fill. But when we say that those persons should undergo the examination of the inspector, we mean of course that the inspector shall be a person who understands his business thoroughly,—a man acquainted with the practical working of steam machinery; and when he makes an official inspection of engines or their boilers he shall personally examine such portions as are likely, by failure, to jeopardize

human life; or if not personally, his proxy shall be accountable for the truth or genuineness of his report.

There is an important fact connected with this affair ; for, says the "Mining Journal," "*The maker of the boiler was the Government inspector, and in giving his evidence, (at the inquest, we presume,) he manifests a degree of subserviency to the opinion of the owners, which is too likely to exist when the interest of the employer is submitted to the tribunal of the judgment of the employed.*" And from the evidence of Mr. Simpson, "it appears that it was not usual for the inspectors to make an internal examination of the boilers." If this be the truth, what guarantee have the public against a repetition of such calamitous results, and to what an extent may we not suffer from this fact ! Before the passing of the 9th and 10th Vict. steam-boat proprietors were in the habit of employing some one capable of making an examination of the state of their machinery, and of reporting thereon ; especially if it were supposed that things were not right, or as they should be ; but now, as before stated, the responsibility is taken from their shoulders, and a *legal* inspection, followed by a certificate, is reckoned a sufficient security against immediate danger. But the case of the *Queen* proves that however good the provision may be, taken on its merits, the working in detail is not in a healthy state. For here was a boiler which was inspected, and certified to be in a safe condition and good working order, whilst it is proved that such was not the case, and it is known that that part of the boiler which gave way was not examined. Indeed, were those very stays in as perfect a state as good materials could make them, the boiler was not a safe one ; for, in the first place, there were not a sufficient number of stays, there being none in the boiler bottom to stay *it* to any other portion, neither were there any to the top of the furnaces, or across the boiler, and the only two stays on the back, although of a flat form and very extensive area, were made of angle iron, and so fixed as to present but little resistance in the direction of the force exerted on them with the steam up. The only mystery is that the accident did not happen sooner ; only the very best of materials could have prevented it.

We hear that the boiler is now in the hands of her original maker for thorough repair, and will now have *plenty* of stays of the proper shape, upon the principle, that if two are not enough, four may be.

These facts, added to some other similar accidents that have occurred lately, seem to indicate that the system of the inspection of steam-machinery is not so efficient as it ought to be, and that some change in its enactments is needed. A most important point, and one that has been most strangely overlooked by the legislature, is the obtaining the services of engineers, whose business engagements are not likely to interfere with their duties as inspectors. Under the present system a foreman or manager may be called upon to inspect a boiler made by his employers ; or, what is scarcely less objectionable, by some competing firm. No honest man would wish to be placed in such a position, whilst, at the same time, it unfortunately happens that there are but few competent practical engineers, to whom the objection does not apply. This may arise from the low scale of fees payable to the inspector, which render some other source of income necessary, in all but one or two of the largest ports. The only way in which this difficulty could be overcome, would be to diminish the number of inspectors, and unite several ports under one supervision. This would have the effect of raising the remuneration and position of the inspector, and of rendering him independent of patronage. Our experience does not lead us to anticipate that any step will be taken in the matter, until the public have been startled by some very glaring case, when we may probably have to report on the grand discovery that will then be made of the inefficiency of the present system.

We should add that at the time of the explosion one of the stokers was killed, another man had his leg broken, and a third, who was the engineer and part-owner, was so severely scalded that he died, after lingering about three weeks.

AERIAL NAVIGATION.

To the Editor.

Sir,—Your correspondent, A. E., in the land of balloons, has started a question which I think worthy the attention of the scientific world, as the nature of the subject appears to have prevented its proper investigation, otherwise we should not meet with the constant repetitions of the same blunders in the plans of succeeding inventors. The theme is a tempting one, and I had hoped that some other correspondents would have favoured you with their ideas on the various plans that have been propounded to enable man to assert his dominion over the air as he has already done over the earth and water; but as such is not yet the case, I beg the favour of your inserting the accompanying notes on the principles which come into play, when we attempt to deal with the subtle element air.

We have, during the present century, had many balloon ascents, and a few startling announcements of flying by means of wings, or some such mechanism; and within these eight or ten years we have been told that a machine had been constructed for flying, the same being propelled by a *bona fide* steam engine. How far that has succeeded we are most of us aware,—it has not yet made a trip; but for all that our patent lists have swelled with specifications of " Aerial Machines," and improvements in transmitting goods and passengers through the air. We in London have been gulled more than once in this way;—for instance, on a certain day about April, 1843, we were told that the famous Henson Machine would start from Primrose Hill, and half of London was on tiptoe of expectation to catch a glimpse of the wondrous thing.

Then a great many of our notables were led a dance to the west end, where, by paying their shilling, they were to have a peep at the veritable machine itself. This was very well in its way. But the people of 1843 are expected to be more enlightened in the year 1850; but so far from this being the case we have been favoured last month with a drawing in the *Illustrated News,* of a monstrous machine, invented by a French gentleman, who, it is said, had the satisfaction of haranguing and convincing a large audience in Paris of the efficiency of his machine. Lastly, I read in the daily papers that a Spaniard has at last solved the problem, and intends, at no very distant day, to make a trip to France, and across the Channel to England (no proviso is mentioned of winds or weather permitting), and thence to London, to claim from the British government the reward offered for such a machine.*

I will now go into the detail of the several machines, and endeavour to show how far each has succeeded, and in what point they have failed.

The main feature in the Henson machine was a large platform, or sail, stretched on a light frame of wood or other material, inclined to the horizon at a small angle. The steam engine and boiler were suspended from below, and the paddles were placed, one on each side of the platform, the whole being properly braced and stayed together. The platform was also intended to receive the passengers and goods, which might also be covered over in case of need. The weight of the apparatus I have supposed to be 10 tons, which is certainly under the mark. Here, then, we have a weight of 22,400 lbs. to be supported in the air, by means of machinery carried in the machine. Let us suppose that this includes passengers, cargo, &c., and that the platform, or sail, is 150 feet long, and 50 feet wide, which gives a surface of 7500 square feet, and that the whole of this surface is in a horizontal position. To keep this weight in equilibrium there must be a pressure acting on the under side equal to the whole weight; that is, on each square foot there

must be a pressure of $\frac{22400}{7500} = 3$ lbs., and this pressure must be generated by the machine itself; that is, power must be given out by the engine sufficient to impel a column of air at such a velocity, as shall make the pressure per square foot = 3 lbs. By the laws of fluids we find the formula for the resistance per square foot to be as follows :—

Putting v = the velocity per second, then, $\frac{v^2}{64\frac{1}{2}} \times .076 \times 1 = 3$, .076 being the weight of a cubic foot of air. This formula reduced becomes $v = 50$, therefore the velocity of the column of air, to give a resistance of 3 lbs. per square foot, must be 50 feet per second. The horses power necessary to do this will be $\frac{50 \times 3 \times 7500 \times 60}{33000} = \frac{67500}{33} = 2042$ H.P.

It must be remembered that this power is necessary solely to keep the machine from falling to the earth, and has nothing to do with the propelling power, which we will now proceed to find. In fixing on the speed at which the aerial machine may be expected to travel, we must consider the present speed of railway travelling, and if it is to be superseded by aerial travelling, the slowest speed of the aerial machine must be at least equal to the quickest of our locomotives. For the present case we will suppose 60 miles per hour. To determine the power necessary to do this, I have supposed the whole opposing surface of passengers and machine, &c., to be 100 square feet; this is certainly under the real amount; 60 miles per hour is 88 feet per second, and to find the resistance per square foot, we have as before $\frac{88^2}{64\frac{1}{2}} \times .076 \times 1 = $ resistance in lbs. per square foot = 9.15. The propelling power is therefore $\frac{88 \times 9.15 \times 100 \times 60}{33000} = \frac{4831.2}{33} = 146$ H. P., adding to this the former power of 2042, we have a total power of 2188 horses. But the whole power is intended to be used in a horizontal direction, and by inclining the sail at a small angle to the horizon, the resistance to the atmosphere was intended to overcome the gravity. To determine the amount of inclination, we have 2042 horses power to dispose of, and which determines the angle of inclination. Putting $x =$ to the sine of the angle, then, $\frac{88 \times 9.15 \times 7500 \times x^2 \times 60}{33000} = 2042 = \frac{67386}{362340 x^2}$ or $x^2 = .18507$, and $x = .43125$, angle of inclination = 25½ degrees; the power required, however, will be more, owing to the angle at which the air strikes the sail, and the slip. We see, then, that we require at least a power of 2188 horses to propel a machine weighing 10 tons through the air, at the rate of 60 miles per hour, and every mechanic cannot fail to perceive that this is a practical impossibility. Even in our advanced stage of engineering we have not yet been able to develope upwards of 2000 horses power out of 10 tons of material; and indeed in our lightest marine engines we think it very smart if we can get one horse power out of ⅛ of a ton of material,† and at the same rate we should require 729 tons for the 2188 horses power. It might be supposed that the machine would be of a description best adapted to the case, so as to act in an efficient manner on the air. Instead of this a pair of paddle wheels are placed, one on each side, intended to propel the machine. We might as well submerge the common paddle-wheels on the sides of our steamers, and expect the vessel to be propelled as usual ! It is evident there is no power in the wheel to propel in this position, for whatever resistance there is on the lower float there would be the same on the upper, and the whole power would be expended in giving a

---

* Can you tell me if such a reward is really offered by the British Government ? If so, or if it were generally known, I think we should have many more like inventions.

† Locomotives would afford a case more nearly parallel. The Great Western heaviest locomotives are said to be capable of exerting 800 horses indicated power, and weigh, including tender, 50 tons. Supposing that the weight could be reduced to 30 tons for the engine alone, including coke and water, we have $\frac{600 \text{ cwt.}}{800} = \frac{3}{4}$ cwt. per horse power.—Ed. Art.

rotatory motion to the water. This is analogous to the paddle-wheel working in air. The efficiency of the paddle-wheel as a propeller depends on its working in two fluids whose specific gravities are widely different; for instance, the specific gravities of air and water are, respectively, 1.216 and 1000, the denser fluid being used as the resisting medium, and the greater the difference of their specific gravities, the greater will be the efficiency of the propeller.

But the calculations I have made have only had reference to the power required to support and propel the machine at the earth's surface, and in order to clear *terra firma*, and all earthly objects, the flight must be taken at a considerable distance from the earth,—say, in general, 1000 feet. But it is known that the density of the air decreases rapidly as we leave the earth's surface, and of course a greater column of air, travelling at a greater velocity, will be required to give a resistance of 3 lbs. per square foot, which was shown to be required to keep the weight in equilibrium. Thus, at 1000 feet from the surface, the pressure would be, by the acknowledged formula:—Log. 30 − $\frac{1000}{63946}$ = log. of pressure, and pressure = 28.95 lbs., the density or weight of a cubic foot would be as 30 : 28.95 :: .076 : .073. The velocity of the column of resisting air would be $\frac{v^2}{64\frac{1}{4}}$ × .073 = 3, which, reduced, becomes v = 51, and the horses power would be found as before, $\frac{51 \times 3 \times 7500 \times 60}{33000}$ = 2101 horses power. The power required to overcome the horizontal resistance at the same velocity, however, will be less: the pressure per square foot will be $\frac{88^2}{64\frac{1}{4}}$ × .073 = 8 78 lbs., and the power will be $\frac{88 \times 8.78 \times 100 \times 60}{33000}$ = 140. The sum of the powers being 2241, the odds increasing against the success of the machine.

And it may also be added, as it is intended nothing shall oppose its transit through the air in a direct line, as the bird flies, that to do this in our own isles would require a height of 5000 feet, some of our mountains being nearly that height : and proceeding as before, we find the power necessary to be 2372 horses. It would be folly, from what we have seen, to think of crossing the Alps,—Mont Blanc being 15.780 feet, and I think it will be allowed by most of your readers that such a machine is totally unfit for navigating the air.

Many schemes have been proposed for navigating the air, but the one just spoken of created the greatest sensation, I believe. I dare say many of your readers have heard of artificial wings being applied by some inconceivable means to men's arms, which were to be moved rapidly by the man-bird, whereby he would be carried through the air at any rate or height he pleased. It will not be necessary to go much into detail on this point. Let us suppose the weight of the man, wings and all, to be 10 stone = 140 lbs., and allowing 47 feet for the area of his wings, this gives a pressure of 3 lbs. of resistance on every square foot. The velocity equal to this is 50 feet per second : the power necessary for this resistance is $\frac{50 \times 3 \times 47 \times 60}{4000}$ = 106 men, 4000 being the units of work a man is supposed to be capable of performing in one minute as a maximum, so that we see it would take 106 men doing their best to support one man in the air. Besides, I cannot conceive by what mechanical arrangement an artificial wing could be made so beautifully adapted to its purpose as the wing of a bird, which is perfection itself. And if attached to the arm, the man would be incapable of exerting much power, because the mechanism of the arm is not adapted to support much weight in an extended position, and it is only in rowing or lifting heavy weights, that he can exert a force of 4000 units of work per minute, and at once we may pronounce the impossibility of man, by means of wings, navigating the air.

We come now to the method of using balloons to explore the upper regions, and the present century has had its full share of them. Science has been assisted very much by the experiments made by some of the astronomers of the present day by means of balloons, but so far they have only been guided by the currents of air in which they chance to be. There have been, it is true, many schemes proposed to overcome the effects of the currents ; and to illustrate the same, I recollect, about ten years ago, seeing a miniature balloon sent up in the large room of the Polytechnic, to the astonishment of an admiring audience ; it was provided with some clock work in a miniature car, attached to a small propeller ; and as the clock-work set the propeller in motion at a great velocity, for a short period, it succeeded in propelling the balloon from one side of the room to the other, which, coupled with the remarks of the learned lecturer, half persuaded the audience that it might be practicable on a large scale.

But it may be easily imagined that the air in the room was perfectly still, and although motion was given to the balloon, yet the speed of, say 2 feet in 3 or 4 seconds, was so small, and required so little power, that the experiment was almost worth nothing.

Let us take an example of a balloon 20 feet diameter, travelling at a height of 1000 feet from the earth, and at the slow rate of 6½ miles an hour, the power required would be .3 horse power,—this is supposing that there is not a breath of wind ; but suppose the wind blowing in the opposite direction to that of the balloon, a pleasant breeze of 6½ miles an hour, then it is evident that the whole power in the balloon would be absorbed in overcoming the tendency of the wind to blow it away, or the power would be just sufficient to keep it stationary over one place. And if it be required to proceed at the rate of 6½ miles an hour in opposition to the wind, it would require eight times the power,— .3 × 8 = 2.4 horses power. But this is slow work. People now-a-days would never patronize such travelling, except for the novelty of the thing. Even at 16 miles an hour, which is still slow, the power required would be 4.5 horses power, and at that rate against a head-wind at the same rate, 4.5 × 8 = 36 horses power would be required. But let us see what it would be at 60 miles an hour—this is 3.75 times quicker than 16 and the cube of 3.75 = 52.7, and 52.7 × 4.5 = 237 horses power. It seems quite clear that no balloon could stand this: it would be torn in shreds, and balloons in general could only travel in calm weather.

This does not say much for the success of aerial travelling ; for even on the ocean, in the greatest storms, we have our mails wafted from shore to shore, in spite of wind or weather. And on the land our iron horse rides on his iron way, and heeds not the roar of the tempest.

Next month I will return to the subject, and notice the invention of M. Petin.

N. D.

CALCULATION OF THE POWER OF CENTRIFUGAL FORCE.

To the Editor.

Sir,—In your June number, in the Key to Mr. Bourne's Catechism a rule is given for calculating the bursting strain of revolving bodies, and takes the case of a fly-wheel 10 feet diameter, velocity of rim being 60 feet per second, the centrifugal force, or bursting strain, of which is said to be 2214 lbs. Now, if this be really the bursting strain, the pressure on each square inch of section is 1107 lbs., and not 553¼, for the case is analogous to a steam boiler 10 feet diameter, and 1 inch thick, with a pressure of 18.45 lbs. per square inch above the atmosphere.

In it there is 120 × 18.45 = 2214 lbs. on every inch in length tending to burst ; giving, as in the wheel, 2 square inches to support that

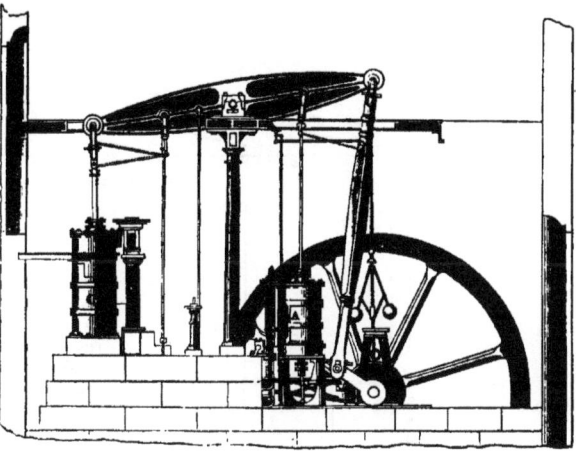

pressure, or 1107 per inch. But I think, although that is the general rule for calculating the centrifugal force of a fly-wheel, that it gives a result just double what it ought to be.

Let us suppose that the wheel is cut in two, and the metal of one half formed into a ball on the end of a rod 5 feet long, and revolving in a circle 10 feet diameter, with a velocity of 60 feet per second. The centrifugal force would be $\left(\dfrac{60}{4.01}\right)^2$ × 48.48 = 1107 lbs.

Now this would be an unbalanced force, continually tending to break or bend the shaft about which it revolves. But again, let us suppose that the rod be extended 5 feet in the opposite direction, and the other half of the wheel be made into a ball, and placed at the same distance from the centre as the other, then will its centrifugal force be equal, and acting in the opposite direction. There will then be no tendency to break or bend the shaft, as the two forces being equal, balance each other ; and although the rod has a force of 1107 lbs. at each end, pulling in opposite directions, the whole strain on the rod is only 1107 lbs., or one of those forces.

This reasoning in its simplest form would be, in the case of a rope over a pulley, with an equal weight at each end, the strain on the rope being equal to only one of these weights.

From this I infer that the bursting, or centrifugal force of the fly-wheel in question, is 1107 lbs., instead of 2214.

I am, yours truly,

N. D.

[The conclusion to which our correspondent comes is precisely that given in our June number, but as he has called our attention to the subject, we shall endeavour to clear up some of its obscurities. Strictly speaking, a wheel, or any other symmetrical body in which the axis of rotation coincides with the geometric axis, has no centrifugal force ; for the mass of the body being equally disposed around the axis, the centrifugal force of each particle is balanced by an equal and opposite force. We may, therefore, consider the body as divided into two equal masses, having each a centrifugal force, equal and opposite to that of the other, and therefore exerting no force upon the axis of the body. Either of these masses, however, will fly off from the centre so soon as its centrifugal force exceeds the cohesive force which retains it in its place; and hence, at the moment of bursting, the cohesive force is equal to the centrifugal force of half the body. The bursting strain is not in any way affected by the circumstance, that two equal forces are acting in opposite directions, for the case is similar to that of two men of equal strength pulling at either end of a spring balance, where it is clear that the extension of the spring is precisely the same as if it were attached to any immoveable object, and pulled by one man only.—ED. ART.]

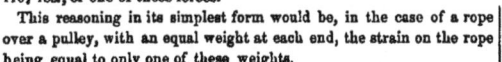

McNAUGHT'S PATENT DOUBLE CYLINDER ENGINE.

WE have before noticed this invention, which is making rapid progress in the manufacturing districts. It is of so simple a character, that the drawing leaves but little to do in the way of description. To the ordinary low pressure condensing engine is applied a high pressure cylinder, A, on the *crank side* of the beam, the steam passing from it into the low pressure cylinder, C, where it expands, and whence it finally escapes into the condenser. By this means, therefore, an ordinary low pressure engine may be converted into a high pressure expansive engine, with an important saving of fuel as well as an increase of power. The reason for placing the high pressure cylinder on the opposite end of the beam to the low pressure cylinder is readily seen. The strain on the main centre and pillars and wall being double that on the end of the beam, any additional load placed on the same end as the low pressure cylinder would aggravate the evil which always exists in overloaded engines, but which is entirely removed by the additional strain being placed at the opposite end, whereby the engine is brought into equilibrium, and the strain removed from the main centre, which has the effect of causing the engine to work much more smoothly, and with a corresponding diminution of wear and tear.

It is such a common practice for manufactures to increase their works and add machinery, without considering that their engines are probably already fully loaded, that we are not surprised that they have availed themselves so readily of the relief offered by this simple and inexpensive arrangement. From the numerous testimonials which Mr. M'Naught has received, we gather that the saving of fuel accomplished is from 30 to 40 per cent., and the increase of power in about the same proportion, but of course varying with the previous state of the engine.

ON WINDMILL SAILS.

To the Editor of the Artisan.

Brigg, Lincolnshire, Oct. 8, 1850.

SIR,—As the sails of Windmills are yet in extensive use, it is to me a matter of surprise that no well-defined rule has been established for constructing them upon correct principles. Mr. Smeaton, many years ago, gave the following angles of " weather " as the most effective, viz. :

1st, or top bar of the sail,	18 degrees from the plane of motion.		
2nd bar,	„	19	„
3rd bar,	„	18	„
4th bar,	„	16	„
5th bar,	„	12½	„
6th, or point bar,	„	7	„

But the improved self-regulating sails, patented by Cubitt, which move at a less velocity and require more weather, have caused this method to be long since abandoned ; and Maclaurin's angle of 96° 34', or 6 inches to the foot weather for the top bar, has been almost universally adopted : yet as no rule for the construction of the remaining portion of the sail has hitherto been determined, the result is anything but satisfactory.

33

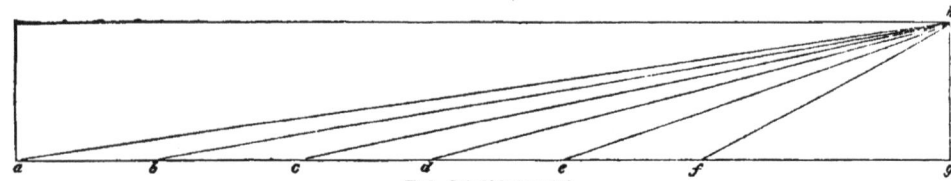

Fig. 1.—Scale, 16 feet to an inch.

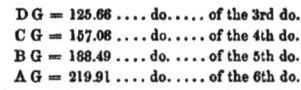

Fig. 2.　　　　　　Fig. 3.

Scale, ¼ inch to a foot.

It appears to me obvious that the surface of the sail must be a portion of a regular spiral, that the momentum of the wind may be the same at all the different distances from the centre of motion. Hence the following construction :—In fig. 2 the top bar of the sail is 10 feet from the centre of the axis, and the other 5 bars are placed at intervals of 5 feet each. The distance passed over by each bar in one revolution of the sails will be as follows :—

1st, or top bar = 20 × 3.1416 = 62.83 feet.

2nd bar .... = 30 ×　　,,　　= 94.24 ,,

3rd bar .... = 40 ×　　,,　　= 125.66 ,,

4th bar ...... = 50 ×　　,,　　= 157.08 ,,

5th bar ...... = 60 ×　　,,　　= 188.49 ,,

6th bar ...... = 70 ×　　,,　　= 219.91 ,,

And the first bar, being placed at an angle of 6 inches to the foot, if it were working in a solid, would advance half the length of its path, or 31.41 feet,—and, to make every other bar advance the same distance, and thereby form a spiral surface, is the object of the diagram No. 1.

In that diagram make

F G =　62.83 feet, the path of the top bar.

E G =　94.24 .... do. .... of the 2nd do.

D G = 125.66 .... do. .... of the 3rd do.

C G = 157.08 .... do. .... of the 4th do.

B G = 188.49 .... do. .... of the 5th do.

A G = 219.91 .... do. .... of the 6th do.

From the point G, and at a right angle to A G, set off G H equal to half the path of the top bar (31.41 feet), and draw lines from A B C D E and F to H. The angle these form with the base of the diagram, will, when transferred to the corresponding bars of the sail, give its surface the spiral form required. The base of the diagram corresponds with the sail's plane of motion.

It is an easy matter to calculate the ratio of weather of each bar, as the base and perpendicular of each triangle are given, but the construction of the diagram being so simple, it will in most cases be preferred. It is scarcely necessary to add that F H in fig. 1 applies to *f h* in fig. 2, and *f' h'* in fig. 3, &c.

The error which most millwrights fall into is in carrying the extreme weather too near the point of the sail, by which the cloth is made to "*flap*," as it is technically termed ; or, in other words, the resistance it meets with in passing through the air becomes greater than the pressure of the wind on the driving surface, and great loss of power is the result. Mr. Smeaton's rule is not free from this defect, as the weather of his sail only varies 2° from the 1st to the 4th bar.

To obviate the "flapping of the cloth," I have known some millwrights weather the point bar in the wrong direction and thereby neutralize the power of a considerable portion of the sail. But these errors will be avoided by giving the sail *a spiral surface.*

I am, Sir, your obedient servant,

W. C. ATKINSON.

P.S.—The first self-regulating windmill sails were invented and patented by a relation of mine, the late Mr. Robert Sutton, of Barton-on-Humber, a description of which was written and published by W. S. Heselden, Esq., in the year 1807. The principle of these sails was afterwards modified and improved by Cubitt.

SAFETY BOAT PLUGS.

To the Editor of the Artizan.

Devonport, 9th Oct., 1850.

SIR,—The late steam vessel disasters, in which a frightful loss of life has occurred by the plugs for the boats having been lost, has naturally drawn attention to the means of avoiding similar casualties, and a very ingenious contrivance, which I have just had an opportunity of examining, devised some time ago, by Lieutenant Stevens, of the *St. George* guardship, of this port, has been fitted in so many cases, and with so much success, that I believe you will consider it ought to be made more generally known, and that its merit cannot fail to ensure its extended application. The plug, or little apparatus, consists of two brass plates, *a a* and *c c*, three inches in diameter, and of about one-eighth of an inch in thickness, with an intervening disc, *d d*, of leather ; one of which brass plates, *c c*, is secured by four brass screw nails on the inside of the bottom of the boat ; and the other plate, *a a*, by being screwed like a nut on a stud, *b*, projecting upwards from the centre of the under plate, *c c*, can be forced down by a simple twist of the finger and thumb

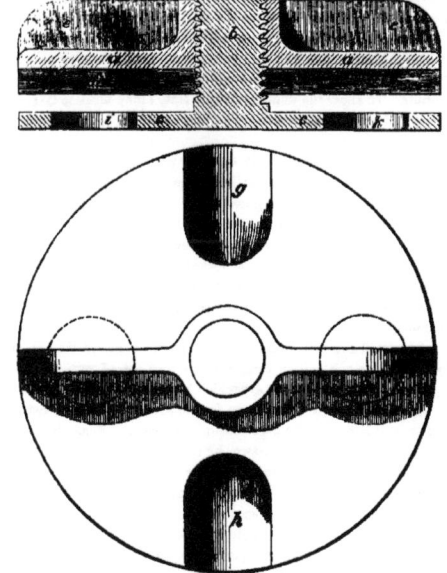

acting on the feathers, *e e*, upon the disc of leather, *d d*, and it again upon the stationary plate, *c c*, so close as completely to seal and prevent the passage of water betwixt the plates. Each of the brass plates has two holes, three-fourths of an inch in diameter, and by placing the two plates so that the holes, *g h*, of the upper one are over those, *i k*, of the under one, a free passage for the water exists, but by twisting the upper plate round, so as to be close upon the under one, the holes are no longer over each other, and the bottom of the boat is rendered completely tight.

This simple contrivance, which can be fitted at a cost of half a crown, has already been applied with complete success to the boats of the following ships :—

Phaeton, 50.	St. George, guard-ship.
Inconstant, 36.	Albion, 92.
Hydra, Steam vessel.	Portland, 50.
Agincourt, guard-ship.	Thetis, 36. &c. &c.

I am, Sir, your most obedient servant,

AN ENGINEER.

PETRIE'S EXPANSION GEAR.

To the Editor.

Rochdale, 24th October, 1850.

SIR,—We are much surprised that the publication of our steam-engine expansion apparatus, in your September number, should have brought forth such a communication from Mr. James Whitelaw, as appears in this month's *Artisan*. Its tone and object we will not now characterize, but express our earnest hope that all persons interested will act upon the advice Mr. Whitelaw gives them, and examine the articles he refers to, *not omitting* those parts of the *London Mechanics' Magazine*, the dates of which he has not given, but which, so far as we have been able to find them, we now supply, viz :—August 11th, 1838; March 9th, and November 16th, 1839 ; and August 8th, 1840.

We are satisfied that such an examination will lead to a conclusion exactly the reverse of that which Mr. Whitelaw asserts ; the same examination will show how unsuccessfully he laboured, from the year 1834 to the year 1840, to effect the objects which are so perfectly attained by our patent expansion apparatus, that every person to whose steam engine we have applied it, is ready to testify to the truth of the statement made by you, in the *Artisan* of September, viz. :— " In fact, a more perfect automatic regulator can hardly be imagined, and until the day arrives when we can endow an engine with a quantum of foreknowledge, we may say that no better results will be obtained."

We do not wish to reflect upon Mr. Whitelaw for the non-attainment of his object, and might easily show the utter inefficiency of his governor and apparatus for regulating the speed of the steam engine, but the fact of its never having succeeded, and of his laying aside all publication on the subject for the last ten years, may be deemed sufficient.

As to the validity of our patent, we assure Mr. Whitelaw that the more persons he can induce, by his writing or otherwise, to use our patent expansion apparatus, the more he will promote our interest, whether such persons make application to us *previously* to their adoption of it, or not.

Soliciting insertion of the above in your next month's number,

We are, yours respectfully,

JOHN PETRIE & Co.

PRACTICAL QUERIES AND ANSWERS.

To the Editor.

SIR,—In glancing over my reply to the fourth query of H. A., at page 128, I perceive I have made a mistake, which I wish to correct, as it may mislead your correspondent. The expression there given $\left(\dfrac{\sqrt{2\,a\,b}}{3\,x} \right)$ means that the square root of the numerator of the fraction is to be divided by the denominator, whereas the expression $\left(\sqrt{\dfrac{2\,a\,b}{3\,x}} \right)$ means that the square root of the whole fraction is to be taken. In the first case we have, $\dfrac{\sqrt{36}}{9} = \dfrac{6}{9}$; in the second case we have $\sqrt{\dfrac{36}{9}} = \sqrt{4}$ $= 2$; a simpler example, perhaps, is the following, $\dfrac{\sqrt{16}}{4} = 1$, but $\sqrt{\dfrac{16}{4}}$ $= 2$.

J. B.

To the Editor.

SIR,—In answer to J. S., page 160 :—

A log of yellow pine 30 feet long by 2 feet square, contains 120 cubic feet, which multiplied by 40 lbs., the weight of one cubic foot, gives a weight of 4800 lbs., and this falling 3 feet, which is as much as the length of an ordinary saw blade will allow, gives a power of $\dfrac{4,800 \times 3}{33,000}$ $= .436$, or less than half a horse power, which is manifestly inadequate.

Allow me to suggest that it would be highly useful if your correspondents would furnish you with detailed statements of the power actually expended in driving saw mills and other kinds of machinery, as I am not aware of any such information being accessible to the public.

J. C.

To the Editor.

SIR,—In attempting to solve the question proposed by one of your correspondents, respecting the distance which a log of wood would require to fall to develope sufficient power to cause itself to be cut up by a saw mill, I see that I have made a very gross blunder, p. 233, having taken a cubic foot of oak to weigh 925 *pounds* instead of *ounces.* This will make the distance to be fallen through 16 times as great as I have given, which shows still more strongly the absurdity of the proposed scheme. Apologising for the error,

I am, &c.,

N. D.

To the Editor. Lincoln.

Sir,—Perceiving that you have begun to devote some space to chemical questions, you would, perhaps, be able to afford me some hints as to how I must proceed in analysing soils.

I am, sir, yours, &c.,

A. F.

NOTES BY A PRACTICAL CHEMIST.

Answers to Correspondents.—"A Calico Printer."—The usual tests for nitric acid, or soluble nitrates (such as those of potash and soda) are as follows :—The liquid in question is placed in a test-tube, with about ⅓ its bulk of strong sulphuric acid, and a crystal of green vitriol added. A deep brown colour appears in the liquid. The same test may also be applied by cautiously evaporating the liquid in question to dryness, placing a portion of the residue in a test-tube, adding sulphuric acid, and then a solution of green vitriol. A deep brown ring of colour appears at the junction of the two liquids. If, however, the liquor be so dark as to render such tests inconclusive, it may be evaporated to dryness, placed along with some copper filings in a test-tube, and drenched with sulphuric acid, slightly diluted. The presence of nitric acid is shown by ruddy fumes. Or the liquid may be placed in a retort, with about a ⅓ its bulk of sulpuric acid (free from nitric acid), heat applied, and the evolved fumes conducted into a solution of carbonate of potash, which may then be tested according to the first-mentioned methods.

Paine's Hydro-electric Light.—We are still in uncertainty about the real nature and merits of this alleged discovery. Very circumstantial reports have been circulated that the whole is merely hydrogen gas, generated in the ordinary manner by the action of dilute sulphuric acid upon zinc, and then passed through oil of turpentine, which substance, it is further maintained, suffers no diminution in the process! Should this account be correct, the invention is alike devoid of scientific interest and of practical utility, as the gas thus obtained must be far more expensive than coal gas. On the other hand, a recent letter in the *Manchester Examiner* emphatically denies the above statement, which is ascribed to the hostility of the American gas companies. Time will show. In the mean time editors of non-scientific journals cannot be too cautious in their comments upon this and similar topics.

Mr. Staite's electric light is at present undergoing a careful examination by a committee of scientific men at Manchester, whose report may be soon expected. Mr. White's hydro-carbon gas is now in use at Southport, where it gives universal satisfaction both as to price and quality. There is, in short, every reason to hope that the reign of coal gas, with its manifold nuisances and its exorbitant price, will soon be at an end.

Test for Strychnia.—Put a drop of sulphuric acid on a slip of glass, add a little of the substance to be examined, and stir them together so as to promote solution. Then place on the mixture a little bichromate of potash in fine powder, and draw a glass rod through the liquid. The presence of strychnia is shown by a beautiful violet tinge, which, in a short time, fades into a kind of orange, but may be renewed by the addition of a little more of the bichromate.

Test for the Compounds of Protine.—The highly acid liquid procured by dissolving mercury in an equal weight of nitric acid with 4½ equivalents of water (40 parts of water to 101 of mercury), is a very delicate reagent for the substances allied to albumen. The liquor gives a very deep rose colour to these substances, and thus we may easily detect ₁₀₀₀₀ of albumen dissolved in water, and even still smaller amounts. To show the delicacy of this test, I may mention that cotton, starch, and gum-arabic assume, when touched therewith, a distinct rose colour.

The nitro-mercurial liquor is made by pouring on the pure metal an equal weight of nitric acid with 4½ equivalents of water. A lively action ensues without the application of heat ; when the effervescence becomes slow, heat is applied till the mercury is entirely taken up. Two measures of water are added to each measure of the mercurial liquid. In a few hours the clear liquor is decanted off from the deposit of crystals and preserved for use. The re-action of this liquid upon albuminous substances is complete at a temperature of 140° to 150° Fahr.—E. Millon.

Delicate Test for Gold.—Digest about 5 gr. of the ore, finely powdered, in strong nitric acid, for the purpose of removing all the sulphurets. That portion of ore which is insoluble in nitric acid is then well heated on a piece of platinum foil, so as to drive off any remaining sulphur, and is next to be digested in aqua regia. From the solution thus obtained, take a drop or two, by means of a glass rod, and place it upon a piece of white porcelain, so as to form a streak. Warm the porcelain over the flame of a spirit lamp, and when the liquid portion has evaporated, throw on the spot where it was placed a jet of flame by means of a blow-pipe : if any gold be present, it will be indicated by a beautiful and characteristic purple colour, which, to a certain extent will disappear when the flame is withdrawn. The same colour may be made to appear and disappear at will, by heating and cooling the spot in question.

To Coat Glass and Porcelain Vessels with Copper.—The outer surface of the vessel is smeared over with Canada balsam, then strewed over with fine powder of graphite, and the latter connected with the copper pole of a galvano-plastic apparatus. Dr. Mohr recommends the vessels to be first coated very thinly with copal varnish, then to be strewed over with bronzing powder, and this coating afterwards made perfectly smooth. The vessels are then filled with water, and placed in a solution of sulphate of copper.

Chinese Silver.—This alloy is a German silver, coated with silver by the electrotype process, but it is distinguished from the ordinary electro-plated German silver by its density, and by the thickness of its silver coating. Articles made of Chinese silver are two-thirds less in price than those of ordinary plate, and wear equally well. Its composition appears to be :

Silver	..	..	..	..	2.05
Copper	..	..	..	..	63.24
Zinc	..	..	..	..	19.52
Nickel	..	..	..	..	13.
Cobalt and iron	..	..	..	..	0.12

Solder for German Silver.—Five parts of German silver, four of zinc. This alloy is run out into thin plates, and afterwards powdered.

Bronze Powders.—1. *Red.* Mix 100 parts sulphate of copper, 60 parts carbonate of soda ; heat till they unite into a mass ; cool, powder, and add 15 parts of copper filings ; mix well and keep them at a white heat for about twenty minutes ; then let them cool, powder, wash and dry. 2. *Gold Coloured.* Verdigris, 8 oz. ; tutty powder, 4 oz. ; borax and nitre, each 2 oz. ; biobloride of mercury, ½ oz. ; work them with oil into a paste, and fuse them together. 3. *Silver White.* Melt together 1 oz. each of bismuth and tin ; then add 1 oz. of pure mercury ; cool and pulverize.

S.

INSTITUTION OF MECHANICAL ENGINEERS.

"ON THE FORM OF SHAFTS AND AXLES." By Mr. Thomas Thorneycroft, of Wolverhampton.

IN order to arrive at proper proportions for any of those principle media of power, which are so fully employed in almost every branch of manufacturing science peculiar to this kingdom, two or three leading points obtain, as axioms on which to reason, in order to arrive at satisfactory results.

Taking, for instance, iron as the material in question, it is required to apply it in an entire new sphere of mechanical movement; the first leading point for examination is the law which limits the tensile and compressive powers of that material, and should the various forces which are about to be put into operation, be by any means calculable quantities, the tensile and compressive powers of the material being determined, there is before us an easy mode of arriving at satisfactory results.

It has, however, been found of equal importance thoroughly to investigate the cause of every failure in this material, and mark those parts where the greatest amount of weakness appeared, so that in re-construction, the simple laws of strength, as determined by experiments, are applied in connexion with the results of practice, in producing principles of form, and mechanical arrangement, better and safer than either of them alone would have done: yet, notwithstanding that by these means safer results have been obtained and brought into use, from the rapid advance of mechanical contrivance, the moving parts of machinery are being daily subjected to untried and incalculable forces; hence the necessity of uniting to former experiments and practice, experiments and contrivances as closely analogous to the peculiar circumstances which are found to operate so powerfully in deteriorating and destroying that most valuable material now under consideration.

It would be deeply interesting to trace the many changes which have taken place in the formation of the various structures, both of cast and wrought iron, which have been brought into use during the last fifty years; some of these remain to the present, monuments of the skill of their projectors, and at the same time proofs of the soundness of the principles on which they have been constructed: on others, causes have been in constant operation, gradually reducing the strength of the original mass until they have become unfitted for the purposes of their erection.

In not a few instances these causes of weakness have been detected, and proper remedies applied, by better arrangement of materials; and, in some instances, by the adoption of entire new principles of construction.

If our attention is directed to the bridge class of structures, we perceive that, previous to the introduction of railways, the more general form was the simple arch, which, whether constructed of cast or wrought iron, there is left indisputable proof that the arch, as a principle, cannot be excelled, either for stability or durability, and that, simply because there are in it fewer elements of self-destruction than in any other form or principle which has been applied for the like purpose. Hence it is not too much to presume, that just in proportion as we leave the principle of the arch, and approach that form which necessity, in many cases, has rendered imperative, we introduce elements which, if not carefully watched, must sooner or later prove fatal to the stability of the mass.

To determine what these elements of self-destruction are, and to what extent they are in operation, has lately occupied the highest mathematical and practical talent of this kingdom; and they have recorded as the result of their experiments and investigation, that to resist the effects of reiterated flexure, iron should scarcely be allowed to suffer a deflection equal to one third of its ultimate deflection, for should the deflection reach one half of its ultimate deflection, fracture will sooner or later take place. It is, therefore, reasonable to conclude that the greater the amount of rigidity it is practicable to introduce into structures of this nature, the fewer will be the self-destroying elements in operation, and, consequently, the greater their durability.

These deductions will receive very considerable support from the history of the various descriptions of shafting employed in the different manufactories of this country; previous to the introduction of the slide lathe, the shafting employed in the spinning manufactories was a constant source of vexation and expense, the want of that perfect parallelism which is now obtained, exposed the shaft to vibration and bending at every revolution, the consequence was constant fractures. The same results have been observed and recorded in reference to the shafting in use in the iron works of this district; and if we pass to the main shafts of water wheels, or the intermediate shafts of marine engines, we see that what at one period of their history was considered good in principle, (viz.—parallel shafts), have had to give place to others, more generally of increased diameter at the centre, or if parallel greatly in excess of former practice. Perhaps no better case could be selected than that of the intermediate shaft of a marine engine to illustrate the subject now before the institution, for there might be traced an almost perfect agreement in all the forces which act upon that shaft, and on the axles of either engines or carriages on a railway.

The author of this paper being a manufacturer of railway axles, has had his attention drawn to the subject of the form of axles for some considerable time; and from his knowledge of the properties of iron, and his observations of the fractures of shafts and axles, has concluded that various forms of shafts and axles possess elements of self-destruction—that the fractures which take place are generally confined to given parts, and that those parts where fracture takes place, exhibit errors of mechanical construction, or errors of mechanical arrangement, when in motion.

A very extensive course of experiments has been gone through by the author, approximating as closely as possible to the forces on axles when in use; and these have satisfied his mind, that just in proportion as there are departures from certain fixed principles of construction in either shafts or axles, in the same proportion will be their liability to fracture.

Before passing to an examination of the experiments, it may assist to a more correct elucidation of the subject if the railway axle is viewed as having certain relations to a girder in principle. Girders generally have their two ends resting on two points of support, and the load is either located at fixed distances from the props, or dispersed over the whole surface; just so with the axle; it has its points of support and its loaded parts; but it is not clearly evident which are the loaded parts and which the props. It has been stated that the wheels may be considered the props, and the journals the loaded parts; but it is thought that with equal propriety the journals may be considered the props, and the wheels the loaded parts: if this latter opinion is at all admissible, we then have the load brought much nearer the centre of the axle than in the case where the journals are considered the loaded parts; and, besides, it brings more immediately before us the influence which the inclined bearing surface of the wheels will necessarily have in increasing the power of any lateral or vertical blow, which the axle will receive through the wheels. It is found that the inclined surface of the wheel tire ranges from 1 in 12 to 1 in 20, and, as a matter of course, the direct tendency of the wheels under a load is to descend that incline, so that every vertical blow which the wheels may receive is compounded of two forces, viz.:—the one to crush the wheels in the direction of their vertical plane, and the other to move the lower parts of the wheels together; it will be seen that these two forces have a direct tendency to bend the axle somewhere between the wheels; should that yielding or bending extend no farther than one half the elastic limit, if long continued, fracture will ultimately take place; but should the elastic limit be exceeded, the axle takes a permanent bend, the wheels are then diverted from their vertical plane, and, as a matter of course, leave the rails. To demonstrate this is the object of the first experiment. An axle reduced in the middle to $1\frac{3}{4}$ inch dia. was placed upon two props 4 feet 9 inches apart, and loaded in the middle, the utmost of its deflection without a per-

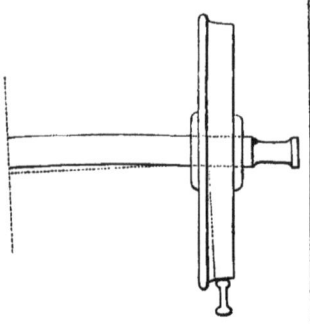

manent set, was .232 inches, the load carried 7 tons. An axle reduced to 4 inches in the middle, and then placed upon the props 4 feet 9 inches apart, its utmost deflection without a permanent set was .281 inches, the load carrried 9 tons. Another axle, but parallel, $4\frac{1}{8}$ inches diameter, was placed upon the props 4 feet 9 inches apart, its utmost deflection, without a permanent set, was .343 inches, the load carried 14 tons. Hence, by reducing an axle of $4\frac{1}{8}$ ins. diameter in the middle to $3\frac{1}{4}$ inches, its limit of elasticity is reduced from .343 inches to .232 inches, and the load, to produce that elasticity, from 14 to 7 tons. Fig. 1 shows the position of the wheels to the rails when the bending of the axle has exceeded its elastic limit.

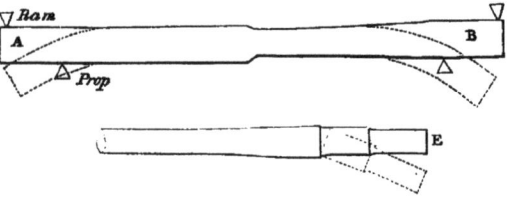

The object of the second experiment was to ascertain what influence the reduction of an axle in the middle would have on its strength to resist sudden impact, compared to an unreduced one; this axle was made as represented by fig. 3, which shows the end A parallel to the centre $4\frac{1}{4}$ inches diameter, and the end B is drawn down from the back of the wheel towards the centre, where it is 4 inches diameter. The end A was then subjected to impact—the relative position of prop and ram was the back of the wheel and the neck of the journal, this end received 46 blows of the ram, and bent to an angle of 18°. The end B was then subjected to impact—the prop and ram in the same relative position, when it bent back to an angle of 22° with only 16 blows of the ram, (as shown by the dotted lines in fig. 2.) The object of the third experiment was to ascertain what influence a shoulder behind the wheel would have on the strength of the axle at that part, compared to one without a shoulder. Fig. 3 and 4 were one axle cut in two, the end E

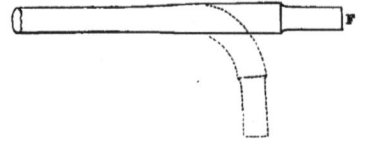

was turned from the neck of the journal, leaving a shoulder $\frac{1}{8}$th inch

deep as a stop to the wheel; the end F was turned from the neck of the journal to the same diameter, but no shoulder left. The end E was subjected to hydraulic pressure, the load being in a direct line with the shoulder, when it broke in two with a load of 60 tons. The end F subjected in the same way to hydraulic pressure, when it bent into the form shown by the dotted lines, with 84 tons. The object of the fourth experiment was to ascertain what influence the position of the wheel, in relation to the neck of the journal, would have on the strength of the journal under impact. Fig. 5 was a piece of an axle

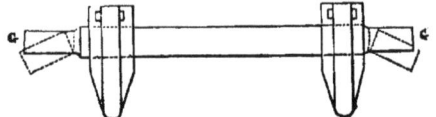

with a journal taken down at each end; the end G was keyed into a cast iron frame, the face of the frame in a line with the neck of the journal, the journal was then subjected to the impact of a ram falling 10 feet, when it broke off at the 7th blow. The end H was keyed into the cast iron frame in the same way, but with the neck of the journal projecting $1\frac{1}{4}$ inches from the face of the frame, the journal was then subjected to the impact of the same ram falling 10 feet, when it broke at the 24th blow.

From these experiments, and from the acknowledged deteriorating influence of vibration or bending on iron, especially when continued any great length of time, it is the author's opinion that neither shafts nor railway axles ought to be reduced in the middle, but rather, if there is to be a departure from the parallel form, they should be made thickest in the middle, and thus effectually prevent any vibration or bending whatever; for it is the introduction of this principle into almost every description of beam and girder, also into the connecting rods of every description of steam engine, and into a large quantity of the shafting now in use, that has rendered the whole of these articles so superior in point of durability, to what they were when other principles of form were in use.

Mr. Thorneycroft gave a further illustration of the paper by reference to several specimens of axles which were exhibited to the meeting. Having obtained an axle which had a shoulder at both ends, he turned the shoulder off one end but left it on the other, and he found that in the instance where the shoulder was turned off, it required a pressure of 120 tons to break it, and $1\frac{1}{4}$ inch deflection; while the other end, where the shoulder was not turned off, broke with a pressure of 106 tons and $\frac{7}{8}$ of an inch deflection.

The Chairman observed that, as there was not time for the discussion of the paper at that meeting, it had better be adjourned to the next meeting, more especially in the absence of their president, who took so great an interest in the subject.

Mr. Thorneycroft said, that between that time and the next meeting, he would be happy if any members of the Institution would visit his works, and test the truth of the positions advanced in his paper, and suggest any other experiments to investigate the subject.

ROYAL CORNWALL POLYTECHNIC SOCIETY.

The usual annual meeting of this Society took place on the 18th ult., and, judging from the reports, was not a whit inferior in interest to any of its predecessors. We give abstracts of a few of the papers, reserving others for which illustrations are in progress.

BALANCE BOXES OF STEAM PUMPING ENGINES.

Mr. Francis Michell, jun., of Redruth, communicated the following:—The shifting of the weight in balance boxes of steam pumping engines has always been attended with much labour and waste of time, the engine always remaining idle whenever balance has been thrown out of the boxes, the operation being too dangerous to admit of its working. Several instances have occurred in which the engine-man has preferred to run a risk to obviate the difficulty he would have in again setting the engine to work, and frightful accidents have ensued in consequence. There is also much steam wasted when there is too much balance in the boxes, by the piston never reaching the top of the cylinder, and any-thing is more agreeable to an engine-man than going out of the warm engine-house by night (perhaps in a flood of rain) to lift great stones, or broken masses of cast-iron out of the box. To obviate these incon-veniences the idea has occurred to me of using a trimming balance plunger, instead of a box, the pole case being fixed at or above the adit level. At the bottom of the lift of pumps is fixed a cock valve, which can be opened by fastening one end of a copper or iron wire to it and carrying the other end up the shaft and into the engine-house, so as to enable the engine-man to manage it at pleasure, letting out as much of the column of water as is necessary. The cock would shut itself, if loaded with a weight, as soon as the wire was let go. When more balance was wanted a supply could always be obtained from the waste water of the engine, which should be regulated by a valve, also com-municating with the engine-house. I do not anticipate any difficulty from the leaking of the stuffing box of the plunger, as, by a little prac-tice, the engine-man would be able to regulate the cock at the surface, which, for greater nicety, should be opened by a screw, so as to make up exactly for any leakage that might occur. Balance plungers have been in use for several years, but I have not yet heard of any attempt having been made to use them for trimming steam engines.

NAVAL ARCHITECTURE.

THE judges reported that having examined the different specimens of copper, iron, and wood, they are decidedly of opinion that there is a striking and manifest difference in those parts to which Mr. Peacock's anti-sargassian paint has been applied, and much in favour of his composition.

PRODUCTION OF PLASTER AND OTHER CASTS.

Mr. J. H. Medlen, of Redruth, communicated the following :—At a recent exhibition of ancient and mediæval art in London, particular attention was attracted to certain specimens of earthenware, statnettes, busts, &c., (manufactured in 1465) on account of the peculiar sharpness of the figures forming the ornamental portions of them. This sharpness was so striking as to present rather the appearance of spirited carving than of moulded patterns. This ware was named the "Della Robbia," after the inventor. The art of producing it appears however to have been lost during the sixteenth century, no specimens of later date having been procured. From seeing a notice of the above, I have been led to experiment on the effect of producing a vacuum in the moulds used for casting such articles, as small portions of air confined in the insterstices of such moulds often prevent the impression from being perfect. It is well known to persons engaged in plaster casting, that several casts in succession are often missed, in consequence of the moulds containing air, thus preventing the plaster from filling the mould. This difficulty would be entirely obviated. The same remark will apply to medallions made of sulphur, wax, &c. Pressure alone will not accomplish the same end, owing to the compression of the air below the substance employed; but with a vacuum in the mould the advantages of both are combined, the weight of the atmosphere on the surface of the fluid forcing it into the most minute interstices.

THE PATENT LAWS.

A MEETING, convened by the parties composing "The Inventor's Patent Law Reform League," was held on the 22nd inst., at Anderton's Hotel, Fleet-street, for the purpose of explaining the objects of the association, and adopting an address to the Queen, praying for an adequate protection of inventions. It was announced that Mr. Hume, M.P., had been invited to take the chair ; but the honourable gentleman not presenting himself, Mr. J. Ellis, the chairman of the "League," was called on to preside.

Mr. J. D. Mahon, the secretary, read a report from the provisional committee, stating that they had consulted many persons interested in the progress of manufacture and art, who were generally of opinion that no adequate protection was afforded by the Provisional Registra-tion Designs Act of last session, owing to the way in which it had been mutilated in committee. This had led to the formation of the League in August last, who sought, by eliciting a strong public demonstration, to secure such an alteration of the patent laws as might afford adequate security to inventors

The Chairman said that individual members of the League had taken steps as early as May last in support of the object now sought. Their cause had been advocated by the press generally, in particular by the *Morning Chronicle*, and one or two other of the daily papers. It would no doubt strike foreign visitors with the utmost surprise, when they came to London next May, to find that our inventors, and especially poor men of genius, who had produced many valuable machines now in operation, had been absolutely neglected, and had had to battle with all the difficulties arising from inadequate means. Mr. Townley, a poor inventor in the metropolis, finding that the late act protected designs only, and not inventions, wrote to Prince Albert on the subject, and received the following answer :—"I am directed to acknowledge the receipt of your letter of the 22d inst., addressed to his Royal Highness Prince Albert, on the subject of the means to be adopted for the security from piracy of unpatented machines which may be exhibited ; and I am to call your attention to No. 8 of the 'general conditions,' which is herewith inclosed. The subject, however, is one of much difficulty, and is now under the consideration of the Commissioners." It had been proposed, as a half-measure, that some step should be taken, giving security to inventors for one year, or until a patent could be taken out ; but he was convinced that nothing short of a thorough reform of the existing patent laws would meet the necessities of the case. While the capitalist had ample security for his money, and for the interest which it would bear, was it not monstrous that a poor man could not call his invention his own unless he could expend £400 on a patent !

Mr. Price, who was described as "an inventor and patentee," and who stated that he was the "founder of the London Inventors' and Mechanics' Society," moved the first resolution, which was in the fol-lowing terms :—"That the great event of the exhibition of the industry and inventive talent of all nations has prominently exposed the many defects of our patent laws, and the non-fulfilment of the promised pro-tection of original inventions thereat, render it expedient and proper for those who are thereby withheld from exhibiting, to consider and enforce by all legal and available means the institution of reasonable patent laws, and thus remove this slur from the exhibition, and secure a permanent industrial benefit to society at large." In proof of the want of information on this subject amongst public men, he stated that he waited upon Sir De Lacy Evans, M.P., to solicit his support, and found that he was not aware of the enormous cost of patents for Eng-land, and for Great Britain—(hear).

Mr. James Weston, inventor and patentee, seconded the resolution, and pointed out the hardship of the existing laws.

Mr. A. Campbell said the law in this country ought at once to be assimilated to that of France ; where, as was stated by the *Morning Chronicle* a few days ago, complete protection might be secured by a poor inventor for an outlay of about 8l.—(hear, hear). The terms were equally favourable in Prussia, Austria, and other countries of Europe. In a letter which he had received from Mr. Wyatt, one of the secretaries to the exhibition, that gentleman stated that the subject of security to inventions would be considered by the Royal Commis-sioners at their next meeting ; but it was not probable they would meet before November. He was convinced that the redress of the existing grievance must come from the people themselves—(hear, hear).

The resolution was then put, and unanimously agreed to.

Mr. Ward, inventor, moved a resolution declaratory of the defects of the existing patent laws, and of the delays and expense which were engendered by the legal tribunals. He chiefly dwelt on the latter point, observing that if a patent cost only 5s., the expense of maintain-ing it through the present legal processes would of itself be ruinous. Patentees were constantly exposed to infringements, and the first step in defence cost the poor patentee 200l.—(hear). He (Mr. Ward) had experienced these difficulties; he had had to proceed in Chancery, and had been occupied five months in examining witnesses in that court, owing to the system pursued of daily hours and half-hours. He had had to go through all this though the party proceeded against made no defence.—(shame!) The case occupied five, yes, and nine months; and he had to pay 1,400l. as costs, though he gained his cause triumphantly, and though there was not a shadow of pretence for the opposition—the case being at last decided in an hour—(hear, hear). He believed his opponent, who was an enormously rich man, would never have given in but that his health had suffered from the vexation caused by the suit—(laughter). At present, a patent simply gave a right to go to law ; and hence a poor patentee was frequently ruined.

Mr. Campin, of the Patent-office, Strand, seconded the resolution. He said the material difficulty in the way of obtaining a patent, even where the inventor was prepared with the money, was the great risk of its being lost by the inventor not deriving any beneficial interest therefrom before the date of the Great Seal, which is always some time after the first application, and sometimes not till the specification. It was clear from what had been recently done by the Legislature, that they were quite disposed to reduce the exorbitant cost of patents; but he anticipated very little benefit from this alone, as, if a patent were even obtainable for nothing, other parties would be the more easily induced to take out similar patents, running the risk of infringement—(hear, hear). So imperfect were the present means resorted to by the courts for deciding on controverted patents, that he imagined the juries must frequently have recourse to the process of "tossing up"—(laughter).

Mr. Lee said he had a valuable invention, which he was determined to keep in abeyance till an alteration of the patent laws took place.

A further resolution suggested that it would be highly beneficial to British and Foreign inventors, and to society at large, if international arrangements could be made to assure to inventors protection in all countries for all inventions approved by the authorities of the Great Exhibition.

It was resolved that a petition, founded on the foregoing resolutions, should be addressed to the Queen, and a committee was appointed to wait on Sir George Grey to make arrangements for its presentation.

The proceedings were closed with a vote of thanks to the chairman.

A POOR MAN'S TALE OF A PATENT.
From Household Words.

I am not used to writing for print. What working-man that never labours less (some Mondays, and Christmas Time and Easter Time, excepted) than twelve or fourteen hour a day, is? But I have been asked to put down, plain, what I have got to say ; and so I take pen-and-ink, and do it to the best of my power, hoping defects will find excuse.

I was born nigh London, but have worked in a shop at Birmingham (what you would call Manufactories, we call Shops), almost ever since I was out of my time. I served my apprenticeship at Deptford, nigh where I was born, and I am a smith by trade. My name is John. I have been called " Old John " ever since I was nineteen year of age, on account of not having much hair. I am fifty-six year of age at the present time, and I don't find myself with more hair, nor yet with less, to signify, than at nineteen year of age, aforesaid.

I have been married five and thirty year, come next April. I was married on All Fool's Day. Let them laugh that win. I won a good wife that day, and it was as sensible a day to me, as ever I had.

We have had a matter of ten children, six whereof are living. My eldest son is engineer in the Italian steam-packet " Mezzo Giorno," plying between Marseilles and Naple, and calling at Genoa, Leghorn, and Civita Vecchia." He was a good workman. He invented a many useful little things that brought him in—nothing. I have two sons doing well at Sydney, New South Wales—single, when last heard from. One of my sons (James) went wild and for a soldier, where he was shot in India, living six weeks in hospital with a musket-ball lodged in his shoulder-blade, which he wrote with his own hand. He was the best looking. One of my two daughters (Mary) is comfortable in her circumstances, but water on the chest. The other (Charlotte), her husband run away from her in the basest manner, and she and her three children live with us. The youngest, six year old, has a turn for mechanics.

I am not a Chartist, and I never was. I don't mean to say but what I see a good many public points to complain of, still I don't think that's the way to set them right. If I did think so, I should be a Chartist. But I don't think so, and I am not a Chartist. I read the paper, and hear discussion, at what we call " a parlour " in Birmingham, and I know many good men and workmen who are Chartists. Note. Not Physical force.

It won't be took as boastful in me, if I make the remark (for I can't

put down what I have got to say, without putting that down before going any further), that I have always been of an ingenious turn. I once got twenty pound by a screw, and it's in use now. I have been twenty year, off and on, completing an Invention and perfecting it. I perfected it, last Christmas Eve at ten o'clock at night. Me and my wife stood and let some tears fall over the model, when it was done and I brought her in to take a look at it.

A friend of mine, by the name of William Butcher, is a Chartist. Moderate. He is a good speaker. He is very animated. I have often heard him deliver that what is, at every turn, in the way of us working-men, is, that too many places have been made, in the course of time, to provide for people that never ought to have been provided for; and to that we have to obey forms and pay fees to support those places when we shouldn't ought. "True," (delivers William Butcher), "all the public has to do this, but it falls heaviest on the working man, because he has least to spare ; and likewise because impediments shouldn't be put in his way, when he wants redress of wrong, or furtherance of right." Note. I have wrote down those words from William Butcher's own mouth. W. B. delivering them fresh for the aforesaid purpose.

Now, to my model again. There it was, perfected of, on Christmas Eve, gone nigh a year, at ten o'clock at night. All the money I could spare I had laid out upon the Model ; and when times was bad, or my daughter Charlotte's children sickly, or both, it had stood still, months at a spell. I had pulled it to pieces, and made it over again with improvements, I don't know how often. There it stood, at last, a perfected Model as aforesaid.

William Butcher and me had a long talk, Christmas Day, respecting of the Model. William is very sensible. But sometimes cranky. William said, "What will you do with it, John?" I said, "Patent it." William said, "How Patent it, John?" I said, "By taking out a Patent." William then delivered that the law of Patent was a cruel wrong. William said, "John, if you make your invention public, before you got a Patent, any one may rob you of the fruits of your hard work. You are put in a cleft stick, John. Either you must drive a bargain very much against yourself, by getting a party to come forward beforehand with the great expenses of the Patent ; or, you must be put about, from post to pillar, among so many parties, trying to make a better bargain for yourself, and showing your invention, that your invention will be took from you over your head." I said, "William Butcher, are you cranky? You are sometimes cranky." William said, "No John, I tell you the truth ;" which he then delivered more at length. I said to W. B. I would Patent the invention myself.

My wife's brother, George Bury of West Bromwich (his wife unfortunately took to drinking, made away with everything, and seventeen times committed to Birmingham Jail before happy release in every point of view), left my wife, his sister, when he died, a legacy of one hundred and twenty-eight pound ten, Bank of England Stocks. Me and my wife had never broke into that money yet. Note. We might come to be old, and past our work. We now agreed to Patent the invention. We said we would make a hole in it—I mean in the aforesaid money—and Patent the Invention. William Butcher wrote me a letter to Thomas Joy, in London. T. J. is a carpenter, six feet four in height, and plays quoits well. He lives in Chelsea, London, by the church. I got leave from the shop, to be took on again when I come back. I am a good workman. Not a Teetotaller ; but never drunk. When the Christmas holidays were over, I went up to London by the Parliamentary Train, and hired a lodging for a week with Thomas Joy. He is married. He has one son gone to sea.

Thomas Joy delivered (from a book he had) that the first step to be took, in Patenting the invention, was to prepare a petition unto Queen Victoria. William Butcher had delivered similar, and drawn it up. Note. William is a ready writer. A declaration before a Master in Chancery was to be added to it. That, we likewise drew up. After a deal of trouble I found out a Master, in Southampton Buildings, Chancery Lane, nigh Temple Bar, where I made the declaration, and paid eighteenpence. I was told to take the declaration and petition to the Home Office, in Whitehall, where I left it to be signed by the Home Secretary (after I had found the office out) and where I paid two pound, two, and sixpence. In six days he signed it, and I was told to take it to the Attorney-General's chambers, and leave it there for a report. I did so, and paid four pound, four. Note. Nobody, all through, ever thankful for their money, but all uncivil.

My lodging at Thomas Joy's was now hired for another week, whereof five days were gone. The Attorney-General made what they called a Report-of-course (my invention being, as William Butcher had delivered before starting, unopposed), and I was sent back with it to the Home Office. They made a Copy of it, which was called a Warrant. For this warrant I paid seven pound, thirteen, and six. It was sent to the Queen, to sign. The Queen sent it back, signed. The Home Secretary signed it again. The gentleman throwed it at me when I called, and said, "Now take it to the Patent Office in Lincoln's Inn." I was then in my third week at Thomas Joy's, living very sparing, on account of fees. I found myself losing heart.

At the Patent Office in Lincoln's Inn, they made "a draft of the Queen's bill," of my invention, and a "docket of the bill." I paid five pound, ten, and six, for this. They "engrossed two copies of the bill; one for the Signet Office, and one for the Privy-Seal Office." I paid one pound, seven, and six, for this. Stamp duty over and above, three pound. The Engrossing Clerk of the same office engrossed the Queen's bill for signature. I paid him one pound, one. Stamp-duty, again, one pound, ten. I was next to take the Queen's bill to the Attorney-General again, and get it signed again. I took it, and paid five pound more. I fetched it away, and took it to the Home Secretary again. He sent it to the Queen again. She signed it again. I paid seven pound, thirteen, and six, more, for this. I had been over a month at Thomas Joy's. I was quite wore out, patience and pocket.

Thomas Joy delivered all this, as it went on, to William Butcher. William Butcher delivered it to three Birmingham Parlours, from which it got to all the other Parlours, and was took, as I have been told since, right through all the shops in the North of England. Note. William Butcher delivered, at his Parlour, in a speech, that it was a Patent way of making Chartists.

But I hadn't nigh done yet. The Queen's bill was to be took to the Signet Office in Somerset House, Strand—where the stamp shop is. The Clerk of the Signet made "a Signet bill for the Lord Keeper of the Privy Seal." I paid him four pound, seven. The Clerk of the Lord Keeper of the Privy Seal made "a Privy Seal bill for the Lord Chancellor." I paid him four pound, two. The Privy-Seal bill was handed over to the Clerk of the Patents, who engrossed the aforesaid. I paid him five pound, seventeen, and eight; at the same time, I paid Stamp-duty for the Patent, in one lump, thirty pound. I next paid for "boxes for the Patent," nine and sixpence. Note. Thomas Joy would have made the same at a profit, for eighteenpence. I next paid "fees to the Deputy, the Lord Chancellor's Purse-bearer," two pound, two. I next paid "fees to the Clerk of the Hanaper," seven pound, thirteen. I next paid, to the Lord Chancellor again, one pound, eleven, and six. Last of all, I paid "fees to the Deputy Sealer, and Deputy Chaff-Wax," ten shillings and sixpence. I had lodged at Thomas Joy's over six weeks, and the unopposed Patent for my invention, for England only, had cost me ninety-six pound, seven, and eightpence. If I had taken it out for the United Kingdom, it would have cost me more than three hundred pound.

Now, teaching had not come up but very limited when I was young. So much the worse for me you'll say. I say the same. William Butcher is twenty year younger than me. He knows a hundred year more. If William Butcher had wanted to Patent an invention, he might have been sharper than myself when hustled backwards and forwards among all those offices, though I doubt if so patient. Note. William being sometimes cranky, and consider Porters, Messengers, and Clerks.

Thereby I say nothing of my being tired of my life, while I was Patenting my invention. But I put this : Is it reasonable to make a man feel as if, in inventing an ingenious improvement meant to do good, he had done something wrong ? How else can a man feel, when he is met by such difficulties at every turn ? All inventors taking out a Patent MUST feel so. And look at the expense. How hard on me, and how hard on the country if there's any merit in me (and my invention is took up now, I am thankful to say, and doing well), to put me to all that expense before I can move a finger ! Make the addition yourself, and it 'll come to ninety-six pound, seven, and eightpence. No more, and no less.

What can I say against William Butcher, about places ? Look at the Home Secretary, the Attorney-General, the Patent Office, the Engrossing Clerk, the Lord Chancellor, the Privy Seal, the Clerk of the Patents, the Lord Chancellor's Purse-bearer, the Clerk of the Hanaper, the Deputy Clerk of the Hanaper, the Deputy Sealer, and the Deputy Chaff-wax. No man in England could get a Patent for an India-rubber band, or an iron hoop, without feeing all of them. Some of them over and over again. I went through thirty-five stages. I began with the Queen upon the Throne. I ended with the Deputy Chaff-wax. Note. I should like to see the Deputy Chaff-wax. Is it a man or what is it ?

What I had to tell, I have told. I have wrote it down. I hope it's plain. Not so much in the handwriting (though nothing to boast of there), as in the sense of it. I will now conclude with Thomas Joy. Thomas said to me, when we parted, "John, if the laws of this country were as honest as they ought to be, you would have come to London—registered an exact description and drawing of your invention—paid half-a-crown or so for doing of it—and therein and thereby have got your Patent."

My opinion is the same as Thomas Joy. Further. In William Butcher's delivering "that the whole gang of Hanapers and Chaff-waxes must be done away with, and that England has been chaffed and waxed sufficient," I agree.

GURNEY'S STEAM JET.

"This steam-ventilator is in constant use at the Orrell colliery near Wigan. A cylindrical boiler of twenty-four horses' power, twenty feet long, by six feet diameter, is set in brickwork in the usual manner, above the ground near the mouth of the up-cast shaft, which is 900 feet deep. A pipe proceeds from this boiler down the shaft to a depth of 600 feet, where it turns off into a drift or passage sloping downwards, and leading into some of the galleries of the mine. At a distance of fourteen feet along this drift the pipe is divided into four smaller branches, each of which stands up across the drift, and is perforated with three apertures fitted with conical mouth-pieces. These mouth-pieces or jets (twelve in number) point upwards in a direction parallel with the floor of the drift, and are so spaced in their respective pipes as to be distributed equally over its entire sectional area. The boiler supplies steam at a pressure of 50 lbs. per square inch, which is considerably reduced before it reaches the jets by condensation within the pipe, which ought to be lapped. The steam issuing from these jets expands conically, the bases of the inverted cones of steam occupying space in the shaft, and acting on the air as pistons; the jets by their upward force also communicating motion to the air laterally, much in the same manner that a running stream of water communicates motion in the same direction to standing water in its immediate vicinity ; or as the air in a chimney is drawn out and carried on in the same direction as the prevailing wind. Probably upward motion is also imparted to the air on the principle of continually-expanding concentric rings of steam curling over each other as they issue from the jets, and drawing air into the inverted cones of steam, whence it is driven onward, as before described. These several causes combine with the high temperature of the steam in producing an upward motion within the main shaft ; just as the steam discharged from the blast-pipe into the chimney of a locomotive causes a strong current of air to follow through the fire-bars. The above arrangement of steam-jets and general mode of ventilation has been also adopted at the Seaton-Delaval Colliery, near Newcastle-on-Tyne.

"From data kindly supplied by Mr. G. Gilroy, viewer of the Orrell colliery, the absolute effect produced by this arrangement, as indicated by the anemometer, amounts to 46,143 cubic feet of air passed through the mine per minute, being equal to 1922.6 feet per horse per minute. This result, taken in connection with the power required to produce it, is considerably below that which has been obtained by the writer with a double-action air-pump, which passed upwards of 13,000 cubic feet per minute with a power of four horses, being equal to 3,250 cubic feet per horse per minute. The difference may probably be owing to the more indirect action of the steam-jets upon the air, which can hardly be expected to operate with the same efficiency as when the expansive energy of steam is confined within a cylinder, and concentrated upon a piston fitting closely into it, as in the steam engine ; but before any just comparison can be made, more precise experiment must be instituted. The avoidance of all machinery on the steam-jet principle is an argument in its favour in many cases."—*From "Hints on Ventilation," by W. Walker.*

ANALYSIS OF BOOKS.

Chapel and School Architecture, as appropriate to the Buildings of Non-conformists, particularly to those of the Wesleyan Methodists ; with practical Directions for the Erection of Chapels and School-houses. By the Rev. F. J. JOBSON. October. pp. 191. London : Hamilton, Adams, & Co.

THIS book may be hailed as one of the signs of the age. Methodism and Gothic Architecture will seem to most of our readers, we doubt not, subjects the most incongruous. But Methodism is progressing with the world around it ; and her sons, with a more refined education, and less contracted views than the generation that has passed away, have ceased to confound the use with the abuse of the effect of external objects on the human mind. We need not here discuss the extent to which the mind is influenced by the objects by which it is surrounded, nor how far art continues to be the handmaid to religion ; it is sufficient to our present purpose to know that a re-action is taking place in the right direction in chapel architecture, the present volume forming the first permanent record of the progress that has taken place. Mr. Jobson had the good fortune in his early days to have studied ecclesiastical architecture as a profession, and it may well be imagined that his experience and technical knowledge made him a valuable accession to the chapel-building committee, who have to report on the eligibility of the plans, for carrying out which pecuniary assistance is expected by the local Wesleyan committees.

His investigations, we need hardly say, showed that "they were as excessive in cost as they were unsatisfactory in appearance." How far these defects have been remedied the present volume bears evidence.

After examining the various orders of architecture, and the reasons which point out the Gothic as the most suitable for ecclesiastical edifices, examples are given of the early, the decorated, and the perpendicular English, on which are the following remarks :—

" The architectural works of these three periods are, in number, and many of them in magnitude, sources of amazement to beholders now living ; and especially when we consider that the Reformers and Puritans demolished nearly as many buildings and ornaments as they spared. The highest names in English ecclesiastical history are found classed as the scientific guides and superintending architects of the periods in which they lived. Bishops did not refuse to take the compass and the square, and to make designs for the House of God. Some of them, like Hugh of Lincoln, used the chisel and mallet. and carried up steep ladders the 'goodly stones' they had prepared. Masons were, in those days, accounted most honourable in their employment. God's house was, uniformly, what it ought always to be—the best house in every city, town or village. Who, on entering such cities as Durham, York, or Lincoln, can behold their superb Cathedrals rising in solemn grandeur, and towering above all other buildings, and not admire them ! Who can view the magnificent pile of Lincoln Cathedral, as it strides more than five hundred feet along, on its ' sovereign hill,' (to use the words of Wordsworth, in his fine apostrophe to it,) so that when seen from the main street below, (from which it may be viewed to the extent of more than mile,) it seems as if the House of God was enthroned in regnant grandeur,—and not say that it stands as a lasting memorial, if not of the pre-eminent spirituality, yet of the laborious service and sacrificing zeal of them who built it ?

The prevailing style of chapel building is well described.

" I would not, unless rendered necessary by unsupported contradiction, give pictorial illustrations of the inappropriateness of forms that have been employed for Methodist chapels, considering the object of their erection,—by contrasting drawings made from such buildings with Gothic designs ; although such contrasts would fully sustain the statements made in this chapter, and would strengthen what I have yet to advance on the ground of economy. To say nothing of the barn-like Chapels in country-places, that might have been erected with better forms and proportions at no additional cost, (and in most instances with less,—for disproportions in buildings are usually very expensive,) I could refer to large Chapels in commercial and manufacturing towns which are more like warehouses or factories than Houses of God ; and where, if in any case, a tall chimney were added on one side, the building would immediately appear ready for use as a cotton-mill or wool-factory. And others might be named that look much more like concert-rooms or theatres, than erections for Christian worship ;—others,with made-up shop-like fronts, having sham windows, readily seen to be such,—by their situation,—being placed higher than the roof ; and the whole, perhaps, propped up behind by an iron bar ; while the sides are as plain and barn-like as could well be conceived, and disfigured by a clumsy heap of chimneys. But I forbear to give exact copies of such, and offer as an accompanying illustration of my statements, a general, and what any observant and candid person will admit is not an exaggerated representation of what has often been built,—in contrast, also, with the design of a chapel such as might have been erected instead.

The notion as to the difference in cost is thus upset :—

" As to *Expense*, it is a mistake, fostered by prejudice, to suppose that Gothic Architecture is necessarily more costly than Grecian or Roman. In the forms most frequently employed in the erection of ecclesiastical buildings, it is the cheapest. The District Church Building Committee, and the Free Church of Scotland, have proved this for themselves. And the Methodists have *proved* it. The Model Plan Committee, appointed by the last Bristol Conference, applied to six of the most able architects, residing in different parts of the kingdom, for de-

signs, specifications, and estimates, in their quantities and prices, of a chapel to accommodate seven hundred and fifty persons, in Gothic, Grecian, or Roman styles : each architect to supply two designs—one in Gothic and the other in Grecian or Roman—with their estimates. The result was, that in *every* case, the estimated cost of the erection of the Gothic design was *less* than the estimated cost of the others ; and, in some instances, considerably less. And this is what might be expected ; for one great recommendation of Gothic Architecture is, that it employs no unnecessary forms *merely* in the way of ornament, as other styles do. It requires no expenditure of 500*l.* on five or six heavy and lofty columns to support nothing, as does Pagan Architecture. I know of one Grecian front of a Methodist Chapel which must, with its quadrangular tiers of columns and entablature. and with its flight of numerous steps, (necessary for its elevation, but most dangerous in frosty weather.—and, at all times, difficult for the aged,) have cost as much as all the chapel besides. And I could name another Grecian Chapel in Methodism that had no less than 500*l.* expended on its fluted-columned recess for the Communion-Table, almost wholly hidden behind the Pulpit and the Reading-Desk ; and which Chapel left the Trustees with a debt, that by its many thousands, has oppressed them most grievously. But I forbear, for while I write *freely*, I must not even seem to condemn good and generous men, who, in their great zeal for God, committed, unintentionally, some improprieties.

Gothic architecture requires no such extravagant outlay for ornament. All its ornaments are parts *necessary* for the strength and convenience of the building. Its buttresses support and strengthen the walls, and make them as strong as if twice as thick. Its mullioned windows prevent the blinding glare of a mass of light, such as shines in at a large Grecian opening. Its pillars, if within, support the middle roof, and hold fast the gallery. Its pinnacles, by their pointed forms, throw off the wet from the buttresses, and prevent injury ; and its parapets, cornices, and basement mouldings, are all, if properly employed, conductors of water from the building. It requires no artificial accompaniments,—such as do-nothing front gables with blank windows and with iron-bar supports behind. It is—incontrovertibly—the most *consistent* and the most *economical* style of Chapel Building that can be employed."

Some practical hints on school buildings, and builders' contracts, we must reserve for another notice.

PROGRESS OF SHIP-BUILDING AND STEAM NAVIGATION.

DIMENSIONS AND DETAILS OF NEW STEAMERS.

THE IMPERIAL RUSSIAN STEAM YACHT, "PETERHOFF."

Built by Messrs. Mare, of Blackwall, and fitted by Messrs. George and Sir John Rennie.

	Ft.	In.
Length between perpendiculars...	187	0
Breadth (extreme)	21	6
Depth	9	0
Draught of water	4	0
Tonnage	412 Tons.	

As she is intended principally for river navigation, the vessel is flat-bottomed ; she is frigate rigged, with wire rope rigging. She has four watertight bulkheads, and the bulwarks and wood fittings generally are of mahogany.

The frames of the ship are disposed in the ordinary way ; the keel is wrought iron, and the engine-bearers, which are constructed of boiler plate in the box form. run fore and aft the entire length of the engine. room, to stiffen that portion of the bottom carrying the machinery.

The engines are on the oscillating plan, and have one inclined air pump between the cylinders, which is worked by a crank on the intermediate shaft.

The valves of the air-pump are all of vulcanized India rubber.

The slides are worked by Stephenson's Expansive Link Motion, whereby the engines may be reversed with the greatest ease by one man, without shutting off the steam ; and the amount of expansion altered to any extent when the engines are in motion.

The paddle wheels are of the most approved feathering construction

The feed and bilge pumps are horizontal, and are worked by wrought iron levers, secured to the cylinder trunnion flange; the valves of these pumps are also of vulcanized India rubber.

The upper frame, or headstock of the engines, is made of wrought iron plates, 7-8ths thick, with gun metal bearings, lined with soft metal.

The following are the principal dimensions of the engines:—

				Ft.	In.
Diameter of cylinder	..	..	..	0	47¼
Stroke	..	..	..	3	6
Diameter of air pump	..	..	..	0	33
Stroke	..	..	..	0	21½
Diameter of paddle wheel, effective		..	15	11
Area of paddle float	..	..	..	19	0
Diameter of main shaft	..	..	..	0	9

The boilers are tubular, two in number, occupying the entire width of the ship. There are six furnaces, 3 feet 1 inch high, and 2 feet 7 inches broad, the tubes returning over them. The tubes are brass, 7 feet long, 2¼ inches diameter outside, and 496 in number.

The average of six runs, at the measured mile, sea-reach, gave a mean speed of 16⅔ miles; the engines making 36½ revolutions, steam in boilers blowing off at 15lbs, with a vacuum in the condenser of 27 inches of mercury. The indicated power taken during the runs was 602 horses power.

DESCRIPTION OF THE UNITED STATES STEAMER "SUSQUEHANNA."

This fine naval steamer, one of the four now building for the Government, was launched on the 13th of April from the Philadelphia Navy Yard. As she is one of the largest war steamers belonging to the Navy (the other of the same size being the *Powhattan*), her dimensions will be of interest to the readers of the Journal.

				Ft.	In.
Length of deck	..	..	..	256	6
Breadth of beam	..	..	..	45	
Depth of hold	..	..	..	26	6
Draft of water when loaded	..	..	19	

Tonnage, 2436 tons.

She is to be propelled by two inclined engines, the frames being of wrought iron.

			Ft.	In.
Diameter of cylinders	..	..	5	10
Length of stroke	..	..	10	
Diameter of air-pump	..	..	4	
Length of stroke	..	..	3	4
Diameter of condenser	..	..	6	3
Height of condenser	..	..	3	3
Diameter of water wheels	..	..	31	
Width of water wheels	..	..	9	6

Number of arms in each centre, 26, having 26 split paddles, forming 52 of 17 inches by 9 feet 6 inches.

Number of flanches in each wheel, 3.

Whole number of arms in each wheel, 78.

Size of arms, 5¼ × 1¼.

Diameter of shafts in main journal, 18 inches.

Diameter connecting rods, in necks 7 inches, in centre 9½.

Diameter piston rod, 7 inches.

Steam passages in cylinders, 42 × 8½.

Area of foot valve, 752 inches.

Four copper boilers, 15 feet 9 inches long, 14 feet 1 inch wide, 12 feet 9 inches high.

Number of furnaces in each boiler, 3.

Length of grate, 6 feet 6 inches.

Diameter of chimney, 8 feet 4 inches.

Height of chimney 45 feet 9 inches.

The engines were designed by Charles W. Copeland, Esq., and constructed by Murry & Hazlehurst, of Baltimore. The whole will be completed by the 1st of August.   B.

THE AMERICAN STEAMSHIP "ATLANTIC."

This gigantic steamer, the first finished of Collins' New Liverpool Line, made a trial trip on the 20th of April, and performed to the satisfaction of all on board. A good deal of interest was felt as to the success of her boilers, but they are reported to have given an abundant supply of steam with a moderate amount of fuel. The boilers are four in number, back to back, having one common chimney. Each boiler is 22 feet 2 inches long, 13 feet 8 inches wide, and the same in height in front. There are two rows of furnaces, one above the other, or eight furnaces to each boiler; the lower furnaces have grates 7 feet 4 inches long, and the upper ones are 5 feet 4 inches long. Back of the bridgewalls are 37 rows in depth of 2-inch tubes, placed vertically, through which the water circulates. The external surface of these tubes, in connexion with the water legs or division between the furnaces, constitutes the principal amount of fire surface. The tubes are 5 feet and 4 feet 6 inches in length, about equally divided, or one-half of each. The engines are two in number, with side levers; cylinders 95 inches diameter, 9 feet stroke; water wheels 36 feet diameter, 12 feet 6 inches wide, and with 1000 tons of coal on board, carrying 10 lbs. steam at sea, and cutting off at half stroke, made 12 revolutions.

The engines are the best specimen of marine engines yet produced in this country, and the frames are particularly worthy of note, as being braced in a very secure manner. They were designed and built by Stillman, Allen, & Co., Novelty Works, New York; and the boilers were designed by Mr. John Faron, jun., recently deceased, who was chief engineer of the line.

The hull is a splendid specimen of naval architecture, and has never been surpassed for strength or beauty. There is a diagonal frame-work of iron extending from the bilge to the upper deck, and running the whole length of the vessel. It is composed of bars 45 feet long, 6 × 1 inches, placed at a distance of 4 feet apart, and let into the timbers their thickness. This iron frame-work is firmly secured to the wooden frame, so as mutually to support each other. The extreme length on deck is 290 feet, breadth of beam 45 feet, depth of hold 32 feet, and by custom-house measurement she is 2,900 tons. The finish of her cabins can hardly be described: it is of the richest character, and composed principally of rose-wood, satin-wood, oak, &c., inlaid.

She has accommodations for 200 first class passengers; and, besides her fuel, can carry 1000 tons of goods. Great expectations are entertained in relation to her speed, but I am glad to see that her owners and builders have not countenanced any high-wrought statements. A few trips will soon test everything; and I have no fear but she will be a credit to her builders, whether in speed she surpasses the new Cunard steamers, *Asia* and *Africa*, or not.

The cost of the *Atlantic* is £550,000, one-half of which sum was expended on her machinery. She is commanded by Captain James West, formerly of this city, and the 1st, 2d, 3d, and 4th officers are past midshipmen of the U. S. Navy. The chief engineer is Mr. J. W. Rodgers, one well known in his profession, and he has six assistants.

The *Pacific* will succeed the *Atlantic* in about two months; her machinery is building at the Allaire Works. The *Baltic* and *Artic* will not be ready before fall.—*Franklin Journal.*   B.

SHIPBUILDING ON THE WEAR (SUNDERLAND), SEPT. 1850.

(Continued from p. 246.)

WASHINGTON STAITH.

Mr. William Reid has upon the stocks, and nearly in frame, a brig, for the coasting and foreign trade, to be flush upon deck, and to class 8 years, A 1.

	Ft.	In.
Length of keel and fore rake ..	95	0
Breadth of beam	25	6
Depth of hold	15	0
Rake of stem	9	0
Tonnage	280$\frac{7}{94}$	

Will carry about 20 keels of coals = 428 tons.

NORTH HYLTON.

Mr. John Haswell has upon the stocks, nearly planked, a barque for the foreign trade, to be flush upon deck, to be classed 8 years, A 1.

	Ft.	In.
Length of keel and fore rake	115	0
Breadth of beam	27	9
Depth of hold	18	9
Rake of stem	9	0
Tonnage	410$\frac{18}{94}$	

There was launched from this yard, in July, a barque (not named), for the coasting or foreign trade, flush upon deck, to be classed 8 years, A 1.

	Ft.	In.
Length of keel and fore rake	105	0
Breadth of beam	27	0
Depth of hold	18	4
Rake of stem	9	0
Tonnage	347$\frac{73}{94}$	
New measurement.	Ft.	Tns.
Length on deck	104	6
Breadth on ditto at midships	24	4
Depth of hold ditto ..	18	4
Tonnage	379$\frac{3424}{3500}$	

Will carry 27 keels of coals = 577.8 tons.

Messrs. Lister and Bertram have upon the stocks, and all planked, a barque for the Mediterranean trade, to be flush upon deck, and will class 8 years, A 1.

	Ft.	In.
Length of keel and fore rake	111	6
Breadth of beam	27	6
Depth of hold	17	6
Rake of stem	8	6
Tonnage	381$\frac{31}{94}$	

Will carry 26 keels of coals = 556.4 tons.

Messrs. Hodgeson and Gardiner launched from their yard, on the 5th September, a barque named the *Leander*, of Newcastle, owned by Messrs. Grey, for the East India trade, flush upon deck, classed 8 years, A 1.

	Ft.	In.
Length of keel and fore rake	116	6
Breadth of beam	28	0
Depth of hold	19	6
Rake of stem	8	6
Tonnage	480$\frac{4}{94}$	

Mr. William Taylor has upon the stocks, all planked, a brig, for the coasting and foreign trade, flush on deck, to class 8 years, A 1.

	Ft.	In.
Length of keel and fore rake	90	0
Breadth of beam	23	7
Depth of hold	14	0
Rake of stem	7	0
Tonnage	226$\frac{6}{94}$	

Will carry 16 keels of coals = 342.4 tons.

There is also upon the stocks, a barque for the India trade, to have a half-poop, to class 12 years, A 1, will carry 27 keels of coals = 577.8 tons.

	Ft.	In.
Length of keel and fore rake ..	111	0
Breadth of beam	24	0
Depth of hold	18	6
Rake of stem	9	0
Tonnage	301$\frac{33}{94}$	

Mr. H. Carr has upon the stocks a barque for the foreign trade, to class 8 years, A 1, to be flush on deck, and will carry 30 keels of coals = 642.0 tons.

	Ft.	In.
Length of keel and fore rake	119	0
Breadth of beam	27	6
Depth of hold	18	4
Rake of stem	9	0
Tonnage	418$\frac{88}{94}$	

There was launched from this yard, on the 27th of August, a brig named the *Petrel*, of Sunderland, for the coasting and foreign trade, flush on deck, classed eight years, A 1; will carry 14.6 keels of coals = 312.44 tons; bust female figurehead.

	Ft.	Tns.
Length on deck	88	7
Breadth on ditto at midships ..	21	8
Depth of hold ditto ..	13	8
Tonnage	202$\frac{2724}{3500}$	

Messrs. Todd and Brown launched from their yard, on the 24th of August, a barque (not named) for the foreign trade, flush upon deck, classed eight years, A 1, at Lloyd's, will carry 30 keels of coals = 642.0 tons; bust female figure-head.

	Ft.	Tns.
Length on deck	113	9
Breadth on ditto at midships ..	24	4
Depth of hold ditto ..	18	6
Tonnage	420$\frac{2529}{3500}$	

Also from this yard, on the 5th of September, there was launched a brig (not named) for the coasting and foreign trade, flush on deck, classed 8 years, A 1, at Lloyd's, will carry 16.8 keels of coals = 359.52 tons; bust female figure-head.

	Ft.	Tns.
Length on deck	85	5
Breadth on ditto at midships ..	21	9
Depth of hold	14	9
Tonnage	232$\frac{1078}{3500}$	

Mr. Edward Brown has upon the stocks a brig, all planked, for the foreign trade, flush upon deck, to class eight years, A 1, at Lloyd's; will carry 16 keels of coals = 342.4 tons.

	Ft.	In.
Length of keel and fore rake	88	0
Breadth of beam	24	0
Depth of hold	14	0
Rake of stem	7	0
Tonnage	225$\frac{33}{94}$	

HYLTON DEAN.

Mr. Thomas Lightfoot has upon the stocks a brig, in frame, for the coasting and foreign trade, to be flush upon deck, and to class eight years, A 1.

	Ft.	In.
Length of keel and fore rake ..	85	0
Breadth of beam	24	0
Depth of hold	12	6
Rake of stem	7	0
Tonnage	216$\frac{57}{94}$	

There is also upon the stocks a barque, all in frame, for the India trade, to have a half-poop and top-gallant forecastle, to class 9 years, A 1, at Lloyd's; will carry 31 keels of coals = 727.6 tons.

	Ft.	In.
Length of keel and fore rake	128	0
Breadth of beam	28	6
Depth of hold	19	3
Rake of stem	8	0
Tonnage	574$\frac{27}{94}$	

LOW-SOUTHWICK.

Mr. James Hardy has upon the stocks, all in frame, a barque for the foreign trade, to class 8 years, A 1, will carry 30 keels of coals = 642.0 tons.

	Ft.	In.
Length of keel and fore rake	110	0
Breadth of beam	27	0
Depth of hold	18	0
Rake of stem	9	0
Tonnage	366$\frac{37}{94}$	

Mr. Andrew Leithead has upon the stocks, and in frame, a brig for the foreign trade, to be flush upon deck, and will class 8 years, A 1, at Lloyd's, about 230 *tons*.

Mr. Wilson Chilton has upon the stocks, and planked, a brig for the coasting trade, to be flush upon deck, and will class 8 years, A 1, will carry 19½ keels of coals = 417.30 tons.

	Ft.	In.
Length of keel and fore rake	95	0
Breadth of beam	25	0
Depth of hold	15	9
Rake of stem	8	6
Tonnage	234$\frac{11}{94}$	

From this yard, in April, there was launched a barque for the foreign trade (not named), classed 9 years, A 1, will carry 27.19 keels of coals = 581.866 tons; a full female figure-head; sham galleries.

	Ft.	Tns.
Length on deck	106	3
Breadth of ditto at midships ..	25	0
Depth of hold	18	7
Length of half-poop	31	5
Breadth of ditto	21	2
Depth of ditto	3	2
Tonnage.	Tons.	
Hull	387$\frac{1834}{3500}$	
Half-poop	23$\frac{443}{3500}$	
Total	410$\frac{2277}{3500}$	

Messrs. Briggs and Clarke have upon the stocks, and in frame, a brig for the coasting trade, to have a break-deck, and to class 10 years, A 1; will carry 19 keels of coals = 406.6 tons.

	Ft.	In.
Length of keel and fore rake ..	93	0
Breadth of beam	25	0
Depth of hold	16	0
Rake of stem	8	0
Tonnage	261$\frac{28}{94}$	

Messrs. Doxford and Crown have upon the stocks, and in frame, a ship for the East India trade, to have a full poop and top-gallant forecastle, will class 10 years, A 1.

	Ft.	In.
Length of keel and fore rake ..	125	0
Breadth of beam	27	6
Depth of hold	19	3
Rake of stem	10	0
Tonnage	444$\frac{7}{94}$	

Also upon the stocks, and in frame, a brig for the coasting trade, to be flush upon deck, to class 8 years, A 1; will carry 18 keels of coals = 385.2 tons.

	Ft.	In.
Length of keel and fore rake ..	90	0
Breadth of beam	25	0
Depth of hold	15	6
Rake of stem	8	0
Tonnage	251¾¼	

Mr. George Worthy has upon the stocks, all planked, a barque for the foreign trade, flush upon deck, to class 10 years, A 1, at Lloyd's.

	Ft.	In.
Length of keel and fore rake ..	109	0
Breadth of beam ..	27	6
Depth of hold	18	6
Rake of stem	9	0
Tonnage	377¾¼	

Mr. John Crown has upon the stocks, and in frame, a ship, for the East India trade, to have a poop and top-gallant forecastle, to be classed 10 years, A 1.

	Ft.	In.
Length of keel and fore rake ..	147	0
Breadth of beam ..	30	0
Depth of hold	21	0
Rake of stem	10	0
Tonnage	617¾¼	

Messrs. Austin and Mills have upon the stocks, all planked, a brig for the coasting trade, to be flush upon deck, and to class 8 years, A 1.

	Ft.	In.
Length of keel and fore rake ..	94	0
Breadth of beam ..	24	4
Depth of hold	14	4
Rake of stem	8	6
Tonnage	251¾¼	

There was launched from this yard this year, the barque, *Aberaman*, of London, classed 10 years, A 1, at Lloyd's, with a half-poop and top-gallant forecastle. will carry 30 keels of coals = 642.0 tons ; a full female figure-head, mock galleries ; to be employed in the London, Singapore, and China trade.

	Ft.	Tns.
Length on deck	113	4
Breadth on ditto at midships ..	25	4
Depth of hold ditto ..	18	7
Tonnage	454¾¼	

Also from this yard, on the 9th of September, there was launched, the ship *Quito*, for the East India trade, classed 13 years, A 1, will carry 32.11 keels of coals = 687.154 tons ; a bust male figure-head (Indian) ; sham galleries.

	Ft.	Tns.
Length on deck	114	2
Breadth on ditto, at midships ..	25	5
Depth of hold ditto ..	19	0
Length of poop	29	9
Breadth of ditto	21	1
Depth of ditto	6	4
Tonnage.		Tons.
Hull	459¾¼	
Poop	43¾¼	
Total ..	**503¾¼**	

Mr. Matthew Stothard, has upon the stocks, all planked, a barque for the foreign trade, to be flush upon deck, and will class 8 years, A 1.

	Ft.	In.
Length of keel and fore rake ..	104	0
Breadth of beam ..	27	0
Depth of hold ..	18	0
Rake of stem	9	0
Tonnage	353¾¼	

Mr. William Petrie, has upon the stocks, ready for launching, a brig for the coasting trade, flush upon deck, classed 8 years, A 1, at

---

Lloyd's ; will carry 17 6 keels of coals = 376.64 tons.

	Ft.	Tns.
Length on deck	85	3
Breadth on ditto, at midships ..	22	7
Depth of hold, ditto ..	15	8
Tonnage	244¾¼	

Also upon the stocks, and in timber, a barque for the foreign trade, to be flush upon deck ; will class 8 years, A 1.

	Ft.	Tns.
Length of keel and fore rake ...	104	6
Breadth of beam ..	27	0
Depth of hold ..	17	0
Rake of stem	11	0
Tonnage	353¾¼	

Messrs. John and Robert Candlish, have upon the stocks, all planked, a ship, for the East India trade, with a poop and top-gallant forecastle, to class 14 years, A 1.

	Ft.	In.
Length of keel and fore rake ..	138	1½
Breadth of beam ..	32	10
Depth of hold ..	22	0
Rake of stem ..	10	0
Tonnage	684¾¼	

Mr. William Worthy has upon the stocks, nearly in frame, a brig, for the coasting trade, to be flush upon deck, to class 8 years, A 1 ; will carry 12½ keels of coals = 267.50 tons.

	Ft.	In.
Length of keel and fore rake ..	76	6
Breadth of beam ..	22	0
Depth of hold ..	12	6
Rake of stem	6	0
Tonnage	162¾¼	

RAVEN'S-WHEEL.

Mr. Thomas Stonehouse has upon the stocks, all planked, a barque, for the foreign trade, flush upon deck, to class 8 years, A 1 ; will carry 29 keels of coals = 620.6 tons.

	Ft.	In.
Length of keel and fore rake ..	107	0
Breadth of beam ..	27	0
Depth of hold ..	18	0
Rake of stem	9	0
Tonnage	355¾¼	

WREATHS' QUAY.

Messrs. Wallace and Peverley have upon the stocks, and in frame, a schooner for the coasting trade, to be flush on deck, with a round stern, to class 5 years, A 1, at Lloyd's.

	Ft.	In.
Length of keel and fore rake ..	60	6
Breadth of beam ..	18	3
Depth of hold	8	6
Rake of stem	6	0
Tonnage	92¾¼	

Messrs. Thomas and Benjamin Tiffin have upon the stocks, and in frame, a barque, for the foreign trade, to be flush upon deck, to class 8 years, A 1.

	Ft.	In.
Length of keel and fore rake ..	104	0
Breadth of beam	27	0
Depth of hold	18	2
Rake of stem	7	6
Tonnage	353¾¼	

Mr. John Barker has upon the stocks, ready for launching, a barque for the East India trade, (owned by J. Sharer, Esq., of Sunderland,) flush on deck, to class 12 years, A 1, at Lloyd's.

	Ft.	In.
Length of keel and fore rake ..	123	0
Breadth of beam	29	6
Depth of hold	19	6
Rake of stem	9	0
Tonnage	494¾¼	

MONKWEARMOUTH BRIDGE DOCK, (SUNDERLAND BRIDGE).

Messrs. G. W. Hall have upon the stocks, and ready to launch, a ship for the East India trade, to class 13 years, A 1, at Lloyd's, with a poop and top-gallant forecastle, owned by the builders ; will carry 37.9 keels of coals = 811.06 tons ; with a full male figure-head, and mock galleries.

	Ft.	Tns.
Length on deck	120	8
Breadth on ditto, at midships..	26	7
Depth of hold, ditto ..	19	9
Length of poop	37	0
Breadth of ditto ..	21	2
Depth of ditto	6	6
Tonnage.		Tons.
Hull	527¾¼	
Poop	56¾¼	
Total ..	**583¾¼**	

THREE CRANES WHARF.

Mr. Ralph Hutchinson lately launched the barque *Cleopatra*, of Glasgow, for the East India trade, classed 12 years, A 1 ; will carry 34.2 keels of coals = 731.88 tons ; full female figure-head, and false galleries.

	Ft.	Tns.
Length on deck	119	8
Breadth on ditto, amidships ..	26	0
Depth of hold ditto ..	18	7
Length of poop	30	6
Breadth of ditto ..	21	9
Depth of ditto ..	6	5
Length of wings of poop ..	2	6
Breadth of ditto ..	6	1
Depth of ditto ..	6	2
Tonnage.		Tons.
Hull	478¾¼	
Poop	46¾¼	
Wings (each)	1¾¼	
Total ..	**526¾¼**	

STRAND SLIP-WAY.

Mr. William Byers and Brothers have upon the stocks, nearly planked, a brig for the foreign trade, to be flush upon deck ; will class 8 years, A 1.

	Ft.	In.
Length of keel and fore rake..	88	0
Breadth of beam	25	6
Depth of hold	15	6
Rake of stem	8	0
Tonnage	255¾¼	

Also, upon the stocks, and ready for launching, a barque for the foreign trade, classed 8 years, A 1 ; will carry 29.12 keels of coals = 623.168 tons.

	Ft.	Tns.
Length on deck	109	0
Breadth on ditto at midships ..	24	7
Depth of hold, ditto ..	18	8
Length of half-poop	25	5
Breadth of ditto ..	21	0
Depth of ditto ..	3	5
Tonnage.		Tons.
Hull	418¾¼	
Half-poop ..	20¾¼	
Total	**438¾¼**	

NORTH SAND.

Mr. George Barker has upon the stocks, and in frame, a brig for the foreign trade, to be flush upon deck, and will class 6 years, A 1.

	Ft.	In.
Length of keel and fore rake ..	88	0
Breadth of beam	22	0
Depth of hold	12	0
Rake of stem	6	0
Tonnage	197 $\frac{31}{94}$	

Also, upon the stocks, and in frame, a barque for the foreign trade, to have a poop and top-gallant forecastle; will class 1° years, A 1.

	Ft.	In.
Length of keel and fore rake..	120	0
Breadth of beam	29	0
Depth of hold	19	0
Rake of stem	9	0
Tonnage	462 $\frac{15}{94}$	

Mr. William Pile, jun. has upon the stocks, all planked, a brig for the Baltic trade, flush upon deck; classed 8 years, A 1, at Lloyd's.

	Ft.	In.
Length of keel and fore rake ..	98	0
Breadth of beam	26	0
Depth of hold	17	0
Rake of stem	8	0
Tonnage	299 $\frac{4}{94}$	

Also, upon the stocks, and in frame, a ship for the Sunderland and Calcutta trade, to have a poop and top-gallant forecastle, to class 10 years, A 1.

	Ft.	In.
Length of keel and fore rake ..	156	0
Breadth of beam	31	6
Depth of hold	21	6
Rake of stem	9	0
Tonnage	732 $\frac{21}{94}$	

Also, upon the stocks, and planked, a brig for the coal trade, flush upon deck; classed 7 years, A 1.

	Ft.	In.
Length of keel and fore rake ..	89	0
Breadth of beam	23	0
Depth of hold	12	6
Rake of stem	7	0
Tonnage	213 $\frac{11}{94}$	

Messrs. Robert Thompson and Sons have upon the stocks, ready for launching, a ship for the East India trade, classed 13 years, A 1.

	Ft.	In.
Length of keel and fore rake ..	144	0
Breadth of beam	31	0
Depth of hold	21	0
Rake of stem	11	0
Tonnage	645 $\frac{12}{94}$	

They have also just laid down the keel of a brig for the coasting trade, to be flush upon deck, will class 8 years, A 1.

	Ft.	In.
Length of keel and fore rank ..	86	0
Breadth of beam	24	0
Depth of hold	13	6
Rake of stem	6	0
Tonnage	219 $\frac{62}{94}$	

They have also commenced a ship for the East India trade, to have a poop and top-gallant forecastle, to class 13 years, A 1.

	Ft.	In.
Length of keel and fore rake..	141	6
Breadth of beam	30	6
Depth of hold	20	9
Rake of stem	10	0
Tonnage	591 $\frac{76}{94}$	

Mr. William Harkas has upon the stocks, and ready for launching, a ship for the East India trade, classed 11 years, A 1; will carry 37·3 keels of coals = 698 22 tons.

	Ft.	Tns.
Length on deck	124	7
Breadth on ditto, amidships ..	25	6
Depth of hold, ditto	19	5
Length of poop..	32	0
Breadth of ditto	20	6
Depth of ditto	6	1

Tonnage.	Tons.
Hull	521 [illegible]
Poop	43 [illegible]
Total	565 [illegible]

Messrs. Booth and Blakelocks have upon the stocks, and in frame, a brig for the foreign trade, to be flush upon deck; will class 8 years, A 1.

	Ft.	In.
Length of keel and fore rake..	90	0
Breadth of beam	25	0
Depth of hold	15	6
Rake of stem	7	3
Tonnage	251 $\frac{31}{94}$	

Also, upon the stocks, and in frame, a barque for the foreign trade, to be flush upon deck, to class 8 years, A 1.

	Ft.	In.
Length of keel and fore rake ..	114	0
Breadth of beam	27	6
Depth of hold	18	6
Rake of stem	9	0
Tonnage	398 $\frac{31}{94}$	

NORTH DOCK.

Messrs. Ratcliff and Spence have launched this year the snow, *Saxon Maid* (of Sunderland), for the coasting trade: carries 18.11 keels of coals = 387.554 tons.

	Ft.	Tns.
Length on deck	91	6
Breadth on ditto atmidships ..	23	2
Depth of hold, ditto	15	9
Tonnage	255 [illegible]	

Also the snow *Isis* (of Dundee), for the coasting trade: carries 13.1 keels of coals = 280.34 tons.

	Ft.	Tns.
Length on deck	84	2
Breadth on ditto at midships ..	21	2
Depth of hold, ditto	13	8
Tonnage	192 [illegible]	

F. B.

HOW MUD-HOLE DOORS OUGHT *NOT* TO BE PUT ON.

A SHOCKING accident occurred on 10th inst., on board the "Erin's Queen," a screw steamer, trading between London and Belfast, by which the chief engineer, John Fergusson, was scalded to death. It appeared from the evidence that the mud-hole doors over the furnaces were *put on outside*, and the attention of the chief engineer being drawn to one of them leaking when steam was up, and the boat about to proceed down the river, he attempted to tighten up the nut, and in doing so the bolt broke, and the door was blown off, and the unfortunate man was blown with it to the other side of the stoke-hole, and of course instantly scalded to death. Mr. Edmund Green, the engineer of another vessel, and Mr. W. K. Whytehead, C.E., were examined to show the error which had been made by the constructor of the boiler in putting the doors on the outside instead of the inside of the boiler. At the suggestion of the latter, the coroner read, for the guidance of the jury, the following passage from Bourne's *Treatise on the Steam Engine*:—

"It is much the safest way to put on both mud-hole and man-hole doors from the inside, with cross bars on the outside to keep them closed. The plan sometimes followed of putting on mud-hole doors from the outside, and securing them by one or two bolts, is a practice we have already reprehended as full of danger, as if the thread strips, or the bolt breaks, the door will fly off, and the boiling water rush out, scalding every one in the vicinity. Mud-hole doors of this kind, even if they leak, cannot be screwed up to tighten them when the steam is up, as there is a perpetual risk in tightening the doors of stripping the thread, or breaking the bolt." (p. 230.)

The jury returned a verdict of "accidental death," coupled with a strong recommendation that in future the practice of making these doors outside should be avoided.

EAST INDIA RAILWAY.

According to the advices by the recent Overland Mail, the plan for the construction of the first division of the East Indian (Bengal) Railway, has been settled by the Government of India, in accordance with the suggestions of the railway company in London. It is understood that for the first 40 miles, from Calcutta to Pundooah, the line will be double, and that it will be carried thence as a single line a further distance of 90 miles to the Runegunge Collieries, near Burdwan. These mines supply Calcutta with coal, and they will therefore constitute a large source of traffic, while at the same time they are situated on the direct route which would naturally be chosen for a trunk road to Mirzapoor and Delhi. The Government at Calcutta have already sanctioned contracts for the construction of the first 40 miles, and one provision of these contracts is, that the parties are to maintain the line in complete order for a period of three years. An act also has been read for the first time in Council, to enable the company to take the requisite land, and it likewise appears that from the calculations thus far made the entire length of 130 miles will be completed within a cost of £1,000,000.

VICTORIA DOCKS.

THE Victoria Docks will occupy a vast tract of land, extending across the marshes in front of the town of Woolwich. One entrance will be in the Gallions, the other in that reach of the river known by the expressive, but not very euphonious, title of Bugsby's Hole. The mainwater channel, therefore, will extend entirely across the marshes, (forming what is now called North Woolwich into an island,) and being nearly three miles in length. The only point at which it will intersect the North Woolwich Railway will be at a point near Blackwall, where the upper lock will be crossed by the railway, on an incline varying from 1 in 100 to 1 in 200. The breadth of the dock will average about a quarter of a mile ; but the limit of deviation extends to double this distance. To afford some idea of the enormous magnitude of this undertaking, it will be sufficient to adduce the comparison used by the projectors of the company: The entire water area occupied by the various docks on the northern and southern banks of the Thames amounts to 211 acres ; the water area of the Victoria Docks will extend to 270, being considerably more than the area of all the other docks put together. The number of ships which entered the existing docks in 1848 was 4,915, with an aggregate of 1,172,707 tons. The Victoria Docks alone will afford accommodation for nearly six thousand vessels, with an aggregate of nearly one million four hundred thousand tons.

The plans of the Victoria Docks are exceedingly comprehensive, and the details of the arrangements is as perfect as can be conceived. It is the first example of the application of a scientific and well-methodised plan to a great commercial enterprise. The extended plans show three large docks for the accommodation of shipping, as well as a half-tide dock, with one canal running through the entire line, and connecting the four docks together. It is at first proposed to excavate only one dock and the grand canal, leaving the remaining docks to be excavated as necessity shall arise. The first peculiarity to which our attention is directed, is the formation of a double entrance lock : the one of smaller dimensions, adapted for barges and other small craft; the other much larger, and fitted for vessels of the greatest size. This arrangement, which exists in no other docks, has advantages too manifest to be descanted upon. It admits of the exit and entrance of small craft at all times, with the smallest possible loss of water, and the smallest exertion of force. Another grand provision is, the construction throughout all the docks of landing stages, projecting into the water, and enabling a much larger number of vessels to be accommodated than could be provided for with ordinary quays. On the landing stages lines of rail, with turn-tables, are laid down, so that merchandise can be landed at once from the vessel on to the truck that is to convey it to the metropolis. These lines communicate directly with a line of rails traversing the docks, which in their turn run at once into the main line of the North Woolwich Railway. The cranes and other machinery will be worked by steam power ; and attached to each of the principal docks will be graving docks for the repair of vessels. It is almost impossible to conceive of plans more unique, more comprehensive, or more perfect than those which Mr. Bidder has put forth for these docks.

Up to the present moment the progress made in the construction of the docks has been confined to the operation of boring, to ascertain the amount of water made by the land springs, in order to provide the engines necessary for keeping the ground clear during the progress of the excavations. The engine has already been purchased, and early in the spring the work of construction will be commenced with great vigour, and prosecuted to completion.—*Architect.*

NOTES OF THE MONTH.—SELF-PRIMING MUSKET.

A MOST interesting experiment was tried at Portsmouth on the 25th ult., by order of the Major-general commanding, which, if adopted in the service, will greatly facilitate the loading and firing of the forces, either afloat or ashore. This was a self-priming musket, the patented invention of Manton and Harrington. In the stock along the barrel of the piece runs a groove or well containing 70 percussion caps, which by the agency of a fitting appliance in connexion with the ramrod, fall into their place over the nipple of the gun simultaneously with the withdrawal of the ramrod from the stock for the purpose of ramming home the charge. In cold weather or a cold climate such an improvement would be inestimable in its value to our troops, as the difficulty in fingering so diminutive an article as a cap with benumbed fingers can only be imagined by those who have been so unfortunate as to be so circumstanced. Colonel Maxwell, of the 82d regiment, has tested the invention, and its performances yielded the most satisfactory result. Seventy rounds were fired with the regulation cartridge, and not one cap failed. The self-priming machinery is entirely independent of the lock, and might be fitted to any musket at the expense of a few shillings. The

Major-general commanding is highly pleased with the invention, which will enable the soldier to fire 70 rounds without stopping to prime—no mean advantage in close firing.

CAPE OF GOOD HOPE MAILS.—It is understood to be definitely settled that Southampton, in preference to Plymouth, is to be the port chosen for embarking and landing the Cape mails, owing to the Post-office and Admiralty stations being already in operation there. If the Cornish men had acted up to their favourite motto, "one and all," they might have had a railway ere this to Falmouth, which would then stand unrivalled, from its position saving a tedious and dangerous passage up channel, and the security and convenience of its harbour.

EAST INDIAN STEAM NAVIGATION.—We are informed that the Peninsular and Oriental Company are about to run some of their vessels between Hong Kong, Canton, Shanghai, and other northern ports in China, and that they also propose to put boats on the station between Singapore and Sydney, in continuation of their present line to the former port. This, we presume, is done with the intention of keeping everybody else out.

A COMPANY is also being formed for the purpose of running a line of screw steamers from Aden to Ceylon and Australia, and connecting Aden with the Mauritius and the Cape of Good Hope.

THE Pacific Steam Navigation Company have also ordered two new boats of Mr. Robert Napier, to carry out an arrangement with the West India Mail Company. All these facts seem to show that steam navigation has received a fresh impetus, and that our marine engineers and shipbuilders have a prosperous time before them.

A NOTION FOR 1851.—For a genuine novelty commend us, by all that is ingenious, to our transatlantic cousins. We saw an American rat-trap once, in which the first rat that was caught, in trying to make his escape, reset the trap for the benefit of his fellow rats, and we thought the idea a good one. But it must yield the palm to another recently patented, which is thus described by the inventor, who, we imagine, will produce something that will be a caution to us Britishers in 1851.—"My invention consists in a trap constructed in such a manner that the rat who looks at the bait shall see his own image reflected by a mirror in such a position as will lead him to believe that a second rat is endeavouring to get before him in seizing the bait ; and when the first rat has been caught his image will also be reflected by a mirror, so that the next rat who shall look at the bait shall see two rats apparently striving to seize it, thus decoying him upon the turning floor, which yields to his weight and precipitates him into the body of the trap."

LIST OF ENGLISH PATENTS.

FROM THE 26TH DAY OF SEPTEMBER TO THE 24TH DAY OF OCTOBER, 1850, INCLUSIVE

Henry Houldsworth, of Coltness House, in the County of Lanark, North Britain, iron master, for improvements in the manufacture of iron and other metals. September 26.

Alfred Vincent Newton, of Chancery-lane, mechanical draughtsman, for improvements in dyeing yarn, and in manufacturing certain woven fabrics. September 26.—(Communication.)

James Hamilton, of London, engineer, for improvements in machinery for sawing, boring, and shaping wood. September 28.

Charles Harratt, of Royal Exchange Buildings, in the City of London, merchant, for improvements in rolling iron. September 28.

Joseph Burch, of Craig Works, in the county of Chester, printer, for improvements in printing terry and pile carpets, wool and silk, and other fabrics. September 28.

Joseph Crossley, of Halifax, carpet manufacturer, George Collier, of the same place, mechanic, and James Hudson, of Littleborough, printer, for improvements in printing yarns for, and in weaving carpets, and other fabrics. September 28.

Cyprien Theodore Tifferean, of Paris, in the Republic of France, gentleman, for certain improvements in hydraulic clocks. October 3.

Jean Pierre Paul Amberger, of Paris, in the Republic of France, civil engineer, for certain improvements in the application of magnetic power for moving and stopping carriages, for giving adherence to wheels upon rails, and also for transmitting motion. October 3.

William Tudor Mabley, of Manchester, for certain improvements in the manufacture of soap. October 3.—(Communication.)

William Bogrett, of Saint Martin's-lane, in the county of Middlesex, gentleman, and William Smith, of Margaret-street, in the said county, engineer, for improvements in producing and applying heat, and in engines to be worked by steam, or other elastic fluid, which engines are also applicable as pumps. October 3.

Julian Bernard, of Buchanan-street, in the city of Glasgow, N.B., artist, for improvements in pneumatic springs, buffers, pumps, and stuffing-boxes. October 4.

Charles Bury, of Salford, in the county of Lancaster, manager, for certain improvements in machinery or apparatus for preparing and spinning, doubling or twisting, silk, waste, cotton, wool, flax, or other fibrous substances. October 10.

Charles Bury, of Salford, in the county of Lancaster, manager, for certain improvements in machinery or apparatus for cleaning, spinning, doubling, and throwing raw silk. October 10.

Robert Beart, of Godmanchester, for improvements in the manufacture of bricks and tiles. October 10.

John Scott Russell, of Great George-street, Westminster, engineer, for improvements in the construction of ships and vessels propelled by paddle-wheels, with a view to better arming the same. October 10.

William Wood, of Over Darwin, Lancashire, carpet manufacturer, for improvements in the manufacture of carpets, and other fabrics. October 10.

William Henry Ritchie, of Kennington, in the county of Surrey, gentleman, for certain improvements in machinery for preparing and carding fibrous substances. October 10.—(Communication.)

William Edward Newton, of Chancery-lane, civil engineer, for improvements in manufacturing yarns. October 10.—(Communication.)

James Hamilton Browne, of the Reform Club, Pall Mall, Esq., for improvements in the separation and disinfection of fecal matters, and in the apparatus employed therein. October 10.—(Communication.)

William Francis Fernihough, of London, engineer, for improvements in locomotive and other steam engines; and improvements in obtaining motive power. October 10.

Whiting Hayden, of Windham, in the State of Connecticut, of the United States of America, for an improved regulator, or apparatus, for regulating the draft of the sliver, on the machine termed the "drawing frame." October 10.

Ardolf Frederick Gurit, of Manchester, gentleman, for an improved method of extracting silver from argentiferous minerals. October 10.

George Michiels, of London, gentleman, for improvements in treating and preparing potatoes for seed. October 17.—(Communication.)

John Fowler, jun., of Melksham, in the county of Wilts, engineer, for improvements in steam-engines, in raising and forcing fluids, in irrigating and draining land, and in machinery for cutting wood for drain pipes and other uses. October 17.

Daniel Trowers Shears, of Bankside, in the county of Surrey, copper merchant, for improvements in the manufacture and refining of sugar. October 17.—(Communication.)

John Robert Johnson, of Crawford-street, chemist, for improvements in fixing colours on fabrics made of cotton or other fibre. October 17.—(Communication.)

James Henry Baddeley, of Shelton, in the county of Stafford, engineer and designer, for improvements in the manufacture of ornamental articles of earthenware. October 17.

Thomas Richards Harding, of Lille, in the Republic of France, manufacturer, for improvements in machinery for heckling and carding flax, in machinery for combing and drawing wood and other fibrous materials, and in machinery for making parts of such machines, and for a new arrangement of the steam engine for driving flax and woollen mills, which arrangement is also applicable to other purposes where motive power is required. October 17.

Henry Bernoulli Barlow, of Manchester, consulting engineer, for improvements in spinning cotton, and other fibrous materials. October 17.

James Henry Williams, of Birmingham, manufacturer, for certain improvements in the manufacture of buttons. October 17.

James Young, of Manchester, manufacturing chemist, for improvements in the treatment of certain bituminous mineral substances, and in obtaining products therefrom. October 17.

Jean Louis Pascal, of Moorgate-street, London, civil engineer, for an improved apparatus for the cure or prevention of smoky chimneys, and also for the ventilation of ships, rooms, and buildings in general. October 24.

Thomas Beale Browne, of Hampen, near Andoversford, Gloucester, gentleman, for improvements in weaving and preparing fibrous materials, and staining or printing fabrics. October 24.—(Communication.)

Alexander Dixon, of Abercorn Foundry, Paisley, for improvements in moulding iron and other metals. October 24.

John Mercer, of Oakenshaw, within Clayton-le-Moors, Lancashire, gentleman, for improvements in the preparation of cotton and other fabrics and fibrous materials. October 24.

John Oliver York, of Boulogne-sur-Mer, France, for improvements in the mode or manner of generating steam in locomotive, marine, and other boilers. October 24.

John Grant, of Hyde-park-street, Middlesex, for improvements in heating and regulating temperature. October 24.

Aaron Rose, of Halesowen, Worcester, manufacturer, for a certain new or improved method or certain new or improved methods of manufacturing twisted gun and pistol barrels. October 24.

Samuel Jacobs, of Highgate Kendall, Westmoreland, cabinet-maker, for certain improvements in printing on woollen, cotton, paper, and other substances, parts of which improvements are applicable also to the purposes of colouring, shading, tinting, or varnishing such substances. October 24.

Bryan Millington, of Brant Broughton, Lincoln, and of the firm of Millington and Sons, of Newark-upon-Trent, Nottingham, millers, for improvements in corn-cleaning and flour-dressing machines. October 24.

Edward Clarence Shepard, of Parliament-street, Westminster, gentleman, for certain improvements in electro-magnetic apparatus, suitable for the production of motive power, of heat, and of light. October 24.—(Communication.)

LIST OF PATENTS THAT HAVE PASSED THE GREAT SEAL OF SCOTLAND.

FROM THE 22ND DAY OF AUGUST TO THE 20TH DAY OF SEPTEMBER, 1850, INCLUSIVE.

Thomas Lucas Paterson, of the city of Glasgow, North Britain, manufacturer and calico printer, for certain improvements in the preparation or manufacture of textile materials, and in the finishing of woven fabrics, and in the machinery or apparatus used therein. August 22.

Henry Houldsworth, of Coltness House, in the county of Lanark, North Britain, iron master, for improvements in the manufacture of iron and other metals. August 28.

James Hall, of Geecross, in the county of Chester, machine maker, for certain improvements in looms for weaving. August 28.

Robert Westmorland Hutchinson, of Camberwell, in the county of Surrey, gentleman, for certain improvements in saw sets, mallets, and other tools, and in apparatus or machinery for manufacturing the same. August 28.

Charles Lamport, of Workington, in the county of Cumberland, shipbuilder, for certain improvements in machinery or apparatus for spinning or twisting cotton and other fibrous substances. September 2.

Astley Paston Price, of Margate, in the county of Kent, and James Haywood Whitehead, of the Royal George Mills, Saddleworth, near Manchester, for improvements in filters. September 2.

Frederick Woodbridge, of Old Gravel-lane, in the county of Middlesex, engineer, for improvements in machinery for manufacturing rivets, bolts, and screw blanks. September 3.

Wakefield Pim, of the town or borough of Kingston-upon-Hull, in the county of the same town or borough, engine and boiler maker, and builder of iron steam ships, for certain improvements in the construction of boilers and funnels of steam engines. September 4.

William Joseph Horsfall, and Thomas James, both of the Mersey Steel and Iron Works, Toxteth Park, Liverpool, in the county of Lancaster, for improvements in the rolling of iron and other metals. September 6.

George Attwood, of Birmingham, in the county of Warwick, copper roller manufacturer, for a new or improved method of making tubing of copper and alloys of copper. September 6.

Thomas Priestley, of Shuttleworth, in the county of Lancaster, manager, and Richard Hurst, of Rochdale, in the same county, cotton spinner, for certain improvements in machinery or apparatus, to be used for preparing, spinning, and doubling cotton, wool, flax, silk, and similar fibrous materials; and also in machinery or apparatus for preparing, balling, and winding warps and yarns. September 7.

George Thompson, of Park-road, Regent's-park, in the county of Middlesex, gentleman, for certain improvements in machinery and apparatus for cutting, digging, and turning up earth, applicable to agricultural purposes. September 16.

Christopher Cross, of Farnworth, near Bolton, in the county of Lancaster, cotton spinner and manufacturer, for certain improvements in the manufacture of textile fabrics; also in the manufacture of wearing apparel, and other articles from textile materials, and in the machinery or apparatus for effecting the same. September 16.

Joseph Long, and James Long, of Little Tower-street, in the city of London, mathematical instrument makers, and Richard Pattenden, of Nelson-square, in the county of Surrey, engineer, for an improvement in instruments and machinery for steering ships, which is applicable to vices, and other instruments and machinery for obtaining power. September 17.

John James Greenough, of George-street, Hanover-square, in the county of Middlesex, gentleman, for improvements in obtaining and applying motive power. September 17.—(Communication.)

John Sidebottom, of Broadbottom, in the county of Chester, manufacturer, for improvements in looms for weaving. September 18.

James Scott, of Falkirk, in the county of Stirling, North Britain, shipwright, for certain improvements in docks, slips, and apparatus connected therewith. September 20.

George Robbins, of Forrest Lodge, near Hythe, in the county of Southampton, gentleman, for improvements in the construction of railway carriages. September 20.

LIST OF PATENTS THAT HAVE PASSED THE GREAT SEAL OF IRELAND.

FROM THE 24TH DAY OF AUGUST, TO THE 18TH DAY OF SEPTEMBER, 1850, INCLUSIVE.

George Gwynne, of Sussex-square, in the county of Middlesex, engineer, for improvements in the manufacture of sugar. August 24.

Robert Reid, of Glasgow, in the county of Lanark, manufacturer, for certain improvements in weaving. August 27.

Richard Archibald Brooman, of the firm of Messrs. Robertson and Co., of Fleet-street, in the city of London, for improvements in types, stereotype plates, and other figured surfaces for printing from. September 6.

James Rennie, of Gowan Bank, Falkirk, in the county of Stirling, North Britain, gentleman, for a certain improvement or improvements in the construction of gas retorts and furnaces, and in apparatus or machinery applicable to the same. September 10.

Peter Fairbairn, of Leeds, York, machinist, and John Hetherington, of Manchester, for certain improvements in machinery or apparatus for preparing, spinning, and weaving cotton, flax, and other fibrous substances; also, in constructing and applying models or patterns for moulding, preparatory to casting parts of machinery employed in preparing, spinning, and manufacturing fibrous substances; and also in certain tools to be used in making such machinery. September 13.

George Thompson, of Park-road, Regent's-park, Middlesex, gentleman, for certain improvements in machinery and apparatus for cutting, digging, or turning up earth, applicable to agricultural purposes. September 14.

George Attwood, of Birmingham, for a new or improved method of making tubing of copper, or alloys of copper. September 18.

DESIGNS FOR ARTICLES OF UTILITY.

REGISTERED FROM 19TH SEPTEMBER TO

Sept. 19th, 2445, A. W. Smith and Co., Paisley, "Centrifugal agitating churn."
,, 20th, 2446, Alfred Koepe & William Watkins, Stourbridge, "Parts of a vice."
,, 21st, 2447, Frederick A. Frimely, Cannon-street, City, "Improved registered oval brush."
,, 21st, 2448, H. J. & D. Nicoll, Regent-street, "Inner lining or wadding for garments and other articles."
,, 21st, 2449, Samuel Harrison, Stanhope-street, Clare Market, "Ventilator."
,, 24th, 2450, John G. Taylor, Great St Thomas Apostle, "Safety mount for fastenings."
,, 25th, 2451, W. James Epps, Bower Nurseries, Maidstone, "Improved sulphurator."
,, 26th, 2452, George Boulton, Great Dover-road, Borough, "Improved globular shield pin."
,, 26th, 2453, William Cutler, St. James'-street, "The Duplexa coat."
,, 26th, 2454, Joseph Morris & Sons, Astwood, near Redditch, "Needle case."
,, 28th, 2455, Hurst & Reynolds, New-street, Birmingham, "Improved fastenings for stays and other articles of dress."
Oct. 1st, 2456, Thomas Thompson, Leith, "Safety plug for boats and vessels."
,, 1st, 2457, George Aldred, Primrose-street, Bishopsgate-steet Without, "Plate mortice nut, for a looking glass."
,, 1st, 2458, Walter Raymond, Albion-square East, Dalston, "A life raft."
,, 1st, 2459, Frederick Clowes, Ann-street, Birmingham, "Self-adjusting vertebral brace."
,, 1st, 2460, Samuel A. Hayes, Strand, "Apparatus for fractures of the lower extremities."
,, 3rd, 2461, Thomas Key, Charing-cross, "New improved regimental case'd clarinet."
,, 4th, 2462, Clayton, Shuttleworth, and Co., Stamp End Works, Lincoln, "Combined threshing, shaking, and riddling machine."
,, 4th, 2463, Henry Kilby & William Harris, Cheltenham, "Portable hot-house."
,, 4th, 2464, J. G. Taylor, Great St. Thomas Apostle, "Self-securing spring for pins, broaches, and ornaments."
,, 4th, 2465, Allen and Moore, Birmingham, "Match-box lid."
,, 4th, 2466, Mortiboy & Herbert, Newman-street, Oxford-street, "Clasp fastener for bracelets, chains," &c.
,, 5th, 2567, J. Cartwright, Newton Wood, Chester, "Improved steam boiler."
,, 5th, 2468, Geo. Harrow, Old Bond-street, "Improved railway travelling trunk—the Panelasticon."
,, 7th, 2469, Geo. Boulton, Great Dover road, Borough, "Improved safety pin."
,, 7th, 2470, Roger Brown, Division-street, Sheffield, "Magnetic lightning conductor."
,, 8th, 2471, Elkington and Co., Birmingham, "Fountain."
,, 8th, 2472, W. Culverwell, Charlotte street, Blackfriar's-road, "Portable domestic vapour bath."
,, 8th, 2473, Fox, Henderson, and Co., Birmingham, and Spring-gardens, London, "Luffer for a ventilator."
,, 8th, 2474, Miall, Marshall, and Co., Ingram-court, Fenchurch-street, "Duplex flanged pipe joint."
,, 8th, 2475, W. Chapman, Johnson-street, Clonmel, Ireland, "Grain crusher, and regulating feed for facilitating the grinding of meal and flour."
,, 9th, 2476, W. Lowe, Birmingham, "Bolt."
,, 10th, 2477, Louis Dutralh, Wellington-street, Strand, "Plantoform, or instrument for measuring the feet of horses for facilitating shoeing."
,, 10th, 2478, Morris Gardiner, Ashill, near Watton, Norfolk, "Lever spring drop."
,, 11th, 2479, John Gray & Robert John Keen, Liverpool, "Anti-vibration elastic compass disc."
,, 12th, 2480, John Smith, Albert Works, Uxbridge, "Revolving sifter."
,, 14th, 2481, Thomas Smith Freeman, Fenchurch-street, "Safety pocket for waistcoat."
,, 15th, 2482, Charles Beinhauer, Hamburg, "Charles Beinhauer's economical registered stove."
,, 16th, 2483, George Rolfe & William Stacey, Bradford, "Perforated ventilating valve cover."
,, 16th, 2484, John Nurse, Crawford-street, Bryanstone-square, "The cabriolet or curricle Brougham, with self-acting step-piece."
,, 16th, 2485, John Raphael Isaac, Castle-street, Liverpool, "Cork or stopper."
,, 17th, 2486, Gustavus Edward Beckers, C.E., Railway station, Paddington, "Self-acting siding stop."
,, 18th, 2487, Cook & Williams, Prince's street, Hanover-square, "Respirator stock or tie."
,, 18th, 2488, Cook & Williams, Prince's-street, Hanover-square, "Face and chest protector."
,, 18th, 2489, Susan Walker, The Grove, Hersham, Surrey, "A patinette."
,, 21st, 2490, William Towns, B.A., St. John's College, Cambridge, "Spirit meter."
,, 22nd, 2491, John Scholl, Berwick-street, Oxford-street, "Smoke consumer for gas-burners."
,, 23rd, 2492, George Mosley, John's-place, Grange-road, "Safety-pin."

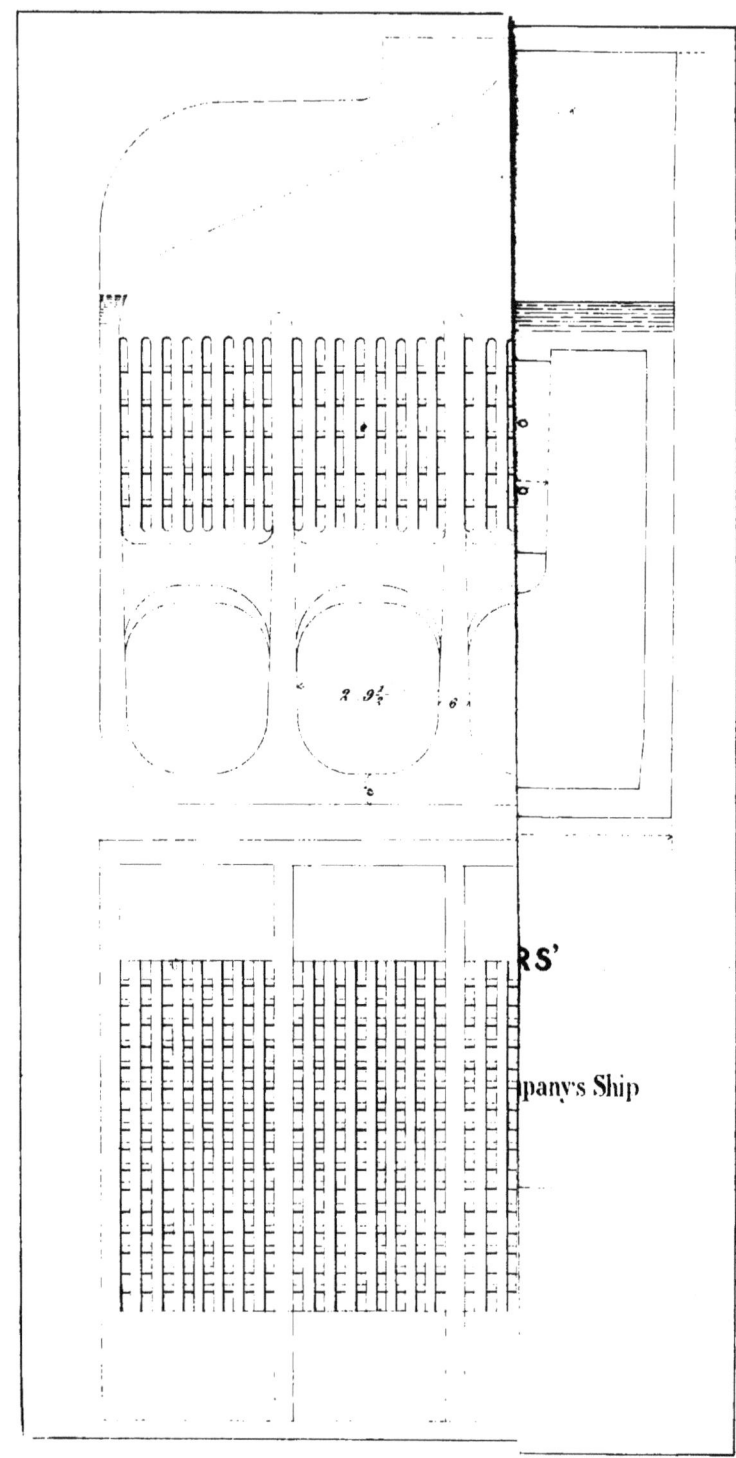

RS'

pany's Ship

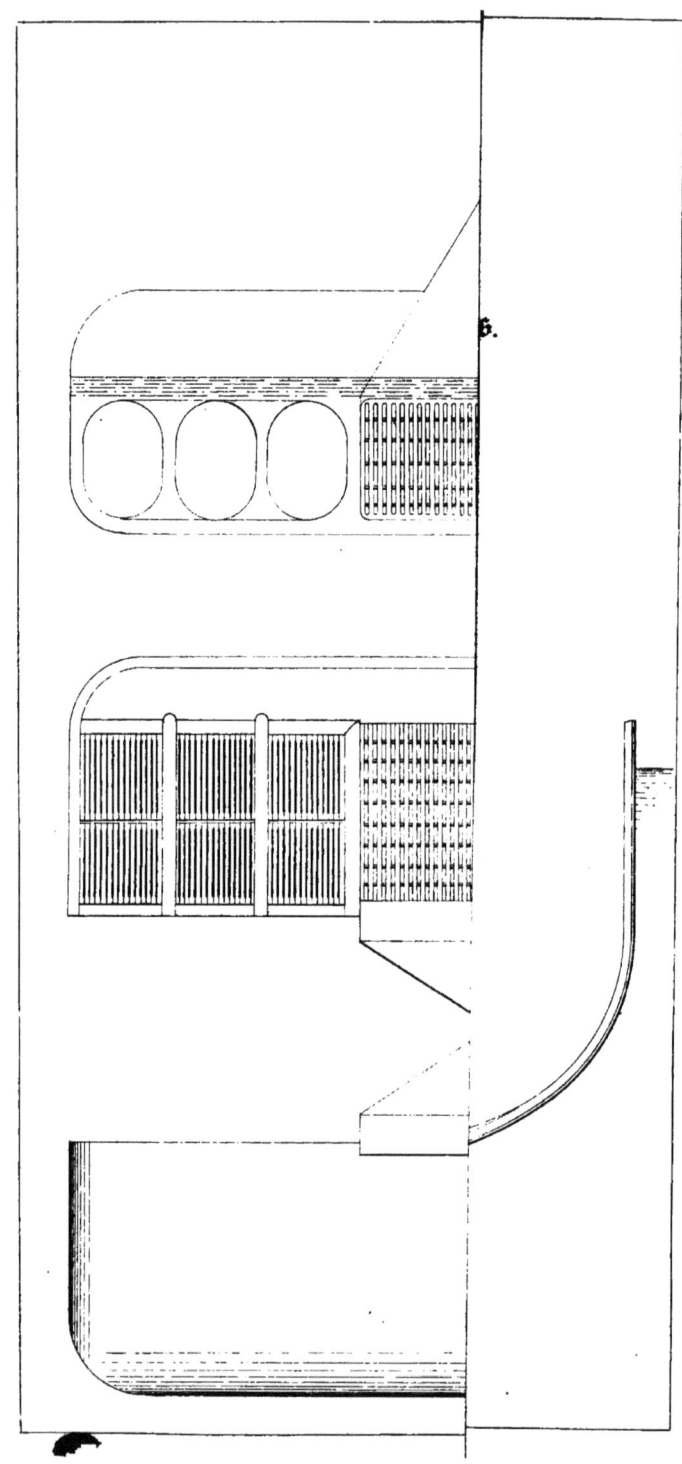

THE ARTIZAN.

No. XII.—Vol. VIII.—DECEMBER 1st, 1850.

LAMB AND SUMMERS' PATENT BOILERS.

THE introduction of the marine tubular boiler, although not marking so important an era in steam navigation as its locomotive prototype in our railway system, yet was the most important step in advance which had then been made in that branch of engineering; and although at first strongly resisted, eventually supplanted, for river boats, its predecessor, the common flue boiler. When, however, it was attempted to be applied to sea-going steamers the difficulty of removing a deposit of scale upon the tubes (which had always been the strongest argument against them), was found a serious drawback to their economical employment. Not only was the durability of the boiler affected, and frequent repairs rendered necessary, but its steam-generating powers were diminished, so that on long voyages, where economy of fuel was most important, it was most difficult to be attained. The difficulty admitted both of a chemical and a mechanical solution. The failure of Dr. Ritterbrand's scheme, as our readers will remember, we did not hesitate to predict, and the result has verified our anticipations. Mr. Lamb's scale-preventer deserved, and met with, a better fate, but did not entirely get rid of the difficulty; and that gentleman has now, in conjunction with Mr. Summers (of the firm of Summers, Day, and Baldock, of Southampton), produced a novel arrangement of flues, which may be briefly described by saying that they combine the accessibility of the common flue-boiler with the diminution of cubic contents of the tubular one. The plates which accompany this paper will render any lengthened description unnecessary. One of these plates represents the boilers of the Peninsular and Oriental Steam Navigation Company's vessel Pacha, which was originally made with tubes, which were replaced, when worn out, with the patent flues. The other plate represents their application to the boilers of steamers of war, in which the flues are placed on a level with the furnaces to keep them below the water line, out of the reach of shot.

In the boilers of the Pacha, the smoke spaces in the flues are 1¾ inches, and the water spaces 2½ inches, but these dimensions will vary with circumstances; the plates are ¼ inch thick. It will be remarked that the stays necessary for the flat flues are in the *fire spaces, not in the water spaces*, so that no nucleus is offered round which the scale can collect, as in the reverse system; and no impediment to interfere with the complete and rapid cleansing of the water spaces from scale by means of the scrapers usually employed. The shells of the boilers are stayed in the ordinary way. The same amount of surface can be got in the same capacity as with tubes, and the boiler will hold about the same quantity of water. The only difference is that if the tubes are $\frac{3}{16}$ thick they will, of course, be rather lighter than ¼ inch plates; but the difference, as compared with the gross weight, is so small as to be unimportant.

In the event of an accident to any of the flues they may be taken out separately, or collectively, to be repaired or replaced with new ones; but, from the facility with which they can be kept clean, they ought, as in the old-fashioned flue boilers, to wear out the shell : indeed, the length of time a *thin* plate will last if kept clean and never overheated, would astonish some of the advocates for thick plates in boilers.

Patent flues were fitted to two of the furnaces of the Pacha's boilers in October 1849, and in December following the whole were fitted with them, in consequence of the successful results obtained from the first partial alteration. As the flues were inserted in the same space formerly occupied by the tubes, and no alteration was made in the pressure of steam, the engines, or the vessel, the saving in fuel effected may be fairly attributed to the alteration in the flues. Previous to the alteration the average consumption of the Pacha's boilers on a voyage from Southampton to Gibraltar and back, 2,400 miles, was 276 tons : after the patent flues had been applied, 235 tons, giving a saving of 40 tons in round numbers. The speed of the vessel was also increased in a slight degree—.3 knots per hour—owing to the increased steam generative power. The boilers of the Tagus have also been fitted with these flues, with a saving of 25 tons of coals per voyage, and a considerable increase of speed; but as the engines were repaired at the same time, and the radial floats replaced by feathering ones, the success cannot be so accurately meted out, as in the case of the Pacha, where no other alteration of any kind was made. The Ruby (Isle of Wight steamer) is also fitted with patent flues, which have effected a saving of fuel, making, with two others, five boilers at work on this plan, and all are giving good results.

We think our readers will agree with us in accepting these data as promising well for the success of this invention, which turns upon one of those points which can never be conclusively settled upon paper merely, but which deserves the serious attention of all who are interested in steam navigation.

35

ON THE STRENGTH OF IRON.

Summary of the principal Facts ascertained by the Commissioners appointed to inquire into the Application of Iron to Railway Structures.

AN inquiry into the strength of cast and wrought iron naturally divides itself into two great heads : First, the power of resisting unvarying statical pressures, such as those to which the girders supporting a water tank, or any other stationary weight, are subject ; and second, the power of resisting shifting pressures, vibrations, and concussions, such as those found to obtain in various kinds of machinery, and in the girders of a railway bridge, over which heavy trains, moving at a high rate of speed, are continually passing. The latter case, however, finally resolves itself into a modification of the former, inasmuch as any determinate amount of shock and vibration is equivalent in its effect to a determinate increase of the statical pressure ; and accordingly, while it is a common practice among engineers to make girders intended to sustain an unvarying load only so strong as to carry three times the load without breaking. girders intended to withstand irregular pressures, such as those which obtain in a railway bridge, are usually made strong enough to carry from six to ten times the maximum load, without breaking. The circumstance therefore of the load being a moving one, is tantamount to an increase of its statical amount, and it was one of the functions of the Commission appointed to inquire into the application of iron to railway structures, to ascertain what increase of the statical pressure would occasion the same strain as a given velocity of the load under certain specified conditions. It is clear that this relation once determined, the statical pressure is all that has thenceforth to be considered, and the question of the strength proper for all kinds of constructions is consequently narrowed to the determination of the strength necessary to withstand a certain statical strain, which is greater in an ascertained proportion than that due to the quiescent load.

It has heretofore been a prevailing impression that the breaking tendency of a moving load is, in reality, less than that of a stationary load, and in corroboration of this view, the fact is recited, that ice may be skated over with impunity, which, if stood upon, will be broken through. But disturbing influences are here in operation which vitiate the conclusion arrived at, for a sheet of ice is generally supported by water, which, by its inertia resists any sudden change of position, and the more rapidly ice is bent by a moving weight, the more powerfully will it be supported or pressed up by the water. It does not follow, therefore, that even although a moving weight may pass over ice, which would break through it, if the weight were stationary, that the breaking pressure is diminished by motion ; for the result may follow from the ice being more effectually supported by the water in the case of rapid deflections, instead of being imputable to any diminished pressure of the moving weight, as commonly assumed.

If a load be placed upon a beam, propped up in the middle, and the prop be suddenly withdrawn, so as to allow deflection to take place, it is clear that the strain must be greater than if the load had been gradually applied. For the momentum of the weight, and also of the beam itself, falling through the space through which it has been deflected, has necessarily to be counteracted by the elasticity of the beam, and the beam will therefore be bent momentarily to a greater extent than what is due to the load, and after a few vibrations up and down, it will settle at the amount of deflection due to the load. This action is very conspicuously exhibited in the steam engine indicator, which consists of a small cylinder fitted with a piston, which is pressed down by a spring and pressed up by steam admitted through a pipe in the bottom. If steam of any considerable pressure be suddenly admitted into this instrument, the piston is shot up like a projectile, and its momentum compresses the spring to a much greater tension than what is due to the pressure of the steam. This undue tension next sends the piston back to a point of tension considerably beneath that which is due to the

pressure of the steam, and, after a few rebounds, like that of an elastic ball let fall upon a pavement, the point of tension answerable to the actual pressure of the steam is finally attained. It is obvious that the spring must be strong enough, not merely to sustain the tension due to the pressure of the steam, but also that accession of tension due to the momentum of the piston ; and, in like manner, a beam or girder exposed to the sudden imposition of a heavy weight must not merely be strong enough to bear that weight, but also to withstand the strain due to the momentum called into existence in every case where rapid deflection takes place.

If a railway train, moving at a high rate of speed, comes to a declivity in the line, the pressure of the wheels upon the rails will be diminished ; and, in like manner, if the train comes to an acclivity the pressure of the wheels upon the rails will be increased. The cause of this variation in the pressure, or apparent weight, is not of difficult apprehension, for the velocity with which a body falls by gravity, being a certain determinate quantity, which is incapable of spontaneous increase, it follows that if the fall of the plane in any given horizontal distance is greater than the space through which gravity would carry the body perpendicularly in the time the horizontal distance is being passed through, then, in such case the body will leave the plane altogether, and advance in the manner of a projectile. It is equally clear that the defect of pressure upon the rails when a train descends an inclined plane must be compensated for by an excess of pressure over that of the simple weight at the next acclivity, for the pressure upon the rails at any acclivity must not merely balance the weight, but it must also suffice to overcome the inertia of the train, and raise it gradually against the force of gravity up to the level from which it originally descended. Now, as any beam which is deflected by a load passing over it forms both a falling and rising plane, it follows that upon the first half of the beam the pressure will be less than what is due to the load ; and on the second half of the beam, the pressure will be greater than what is due to the load, so that the maximum stress, and consequently the maximum deflection, will not be in the middle of the beam, but at a point nearer one end, and consequently the shape of the beam should be such as to give the greatest strength, not at the middle, but at a point between the middle and one of the ends. The same benefit as regards strength might be attained without this modification, by so curving up the beam in the centre that it would become a straight line when passed over by its heaviest load ; and this method of adjustment would equally apply in whatever direction the train travelled. In practice the deflection is usually so small, that such adjustments are disregarded—the deflection proper for a girder bridge of 30 feet span, not being more than one-fourth of an inch, or one 1440th part of the length of the bridge ; but in some experiments tried by the Commissioners, in which a carriage weighing 1120 lbs., was passed over cast iron bars 9 feet long, 4 inches broad, and 4½ inches deep, the deflection when the carriage was at rest was $\frac{6}{10}$ths of an inch ; when the carriage moved at the rate of 10 miles an hour, the deflection was $\frac{8}{10}$ths of an inch, and when the carriage moved at the rate of 30 miles an hour, the deflection was 1¼ in., being more than double the statical deflection ; and as the strain, or breaking weight is nearly proportional to the deflection, it follows that if a stationary load of 4150 lbs. is required to break two bars when applied at their centres, a moving load of 1778 lbs. will break them when the velocity is 30 miles per hour. And however small the natural stationary deflection may be, the actual momentary deflection will be considerable where the pressure of the load is suddenly applied. This is exemplified in the deflection occasioned by the pressure of the steam in some of the cylinder covers of the Cornish engines, where the steam is suddenly admitted upon the piston ; for although the deflection due to the pressure is small, yet as the pressure has been very suddenly applied and the deflection very suddenly accomplished, the velocity and, consequently, the momentum of the particles of matter composing the cylinder cover must be considerable; and as this velocity when arrested must go to increase the deflection, the actual deflection momentarily caused is greater than what would have been expected. In most machines and structures exposed to sudden strains an analogous action exists, and since the maximum strain, however momentary in its duration, is to be taken as the strain which has to be withstood, it is necessary, in considering the dimensions of any structure proper to withstand a given pressure, to pay regard not merely to the amount of deflection due to the load, but also to the shortness of the time in which the deflection is produced.

In seeking for a mathematical expression of the law of the deflection of iron girders sustaining moving loads, the Commissioners called in the aid of Mr. Stokes, of Cambridge, and they give the following account of the results of that gentleman's investigations:—"Mr. Stokes has shown that when the inertia of the bridge is supposed small the trajectories of the load and the corresponding deflection of the bridge depend upon a certain quantity, which he terms β; this quantity varies directly as the square of the length of the bar, and inversely as the product of the central statical deflection (namely, that which would be produced by the load set at rest on the centre of the bridge), and of the square of the velocity with which the load passes over the bridge. When β is small the increase of deflection due to the velocity of the load becomes very great; so much so, that if β be equal to 1.3 the statical deflections are doubled, and are tripled when β becomes 0.8, becoming still greater as lesser values of β are taken. On the contrary, greater values of β correspond to small deflections; and it has been shown by our researches, that in the cases of real bridges β is rarely less than 14, and is commonly very much greater, and that, consequently, the greatest increase of deflection from velocity would be, upon this theory, never greater than $\frac{1}{70}$th, varying from that to $\frac{1}{100}$th or less. As β varies directly as the square of the length of the bridge, it is plain that the nine feet bars of the Portsmouth experiments will correspond to much less values of β than the 20 and 30 feet length of actual bridges; while the values of β in the former cases are still further diminished by the greater deflections necessarily employed in experiments, as explained above. It is thus shown, that the enormous increase of deflection produced by the velocity in the Portsmouth experiments cannot occur with real bridges, since it appears that the phenomena in question are developed to a great extent, when the magnitude of the structure is diminished. But these calculations are made upon the supposition, that the inertia of the bridge is very small; and experiments made with the apparatus above mentioned have shown, that while β is less than about unity, the inertia of the bridge tends to diminish the deflection; while, on the other hand, when β is greater than unity (including, of course, all practical cases), the inertia of the bridge tends to increase the deflections obtained upon the above supposition. Lastly, the total increase of the statical deflection, when the inertia of the bridge is taken into account, will be found much greater for short bridges than for long bridges. Supposing, for example, the mass of the travelling load and of the bridge to be nearly equal, the increase of the statical deflection at the highest velocities for bridges of 20 feet in length, and of the ordinary stiffness, may be more than one-half, whereas for bridges of 50 feet in length the increase will not be greater than one-seventh, and will rapidly diminish as greater lengths are taken. But as it has been shown that the increase *cæteris paribus* is diminished by increasing the stiffness of the bridge, we always have it in our power to reduce its amount within safe limits. Hence, in estimating the strength of a railway bridge, this increase of the statical deflection must be taken into account, by calculating it from the greatest load which is likely to pass over the bridge, and from the highest possible velocity. It must be remembered, also, that this deflection is liable to be increased by jerks produced by the passage of the train over the rails."

It needs no mathematical process to discover that, setting aside the question of the inertia, the extra strain upon a beam deflected by a moving weight will, with any given length and deflection, be proportional to the square of the velocity of the moving load; and in the same manner, the length of beam remaining the same, the strain will, with any given velocity of the load, be proportional to the square of the deflection. For the momentum of any moving body being proportional to the square of its velocity, it follows, that, in the case of a railway train deflected either sideways or upwards by a curve or incline, the strain will be proportional to the square of the amount of motion in a new direction, given in any specified time; or with any given velocity of the train the strain will be proportionate to the square of the amount of the deflection of the rails from a perpendicular or horizontal plane in any given distance along the line. It is equally obvious that the inertia, and subsequently the momentum, of the beam itself, introduces a new element into the question, with which the previous question of the deflection caused by the momentum of the train must by no means be confounded, and in the case of the cover of a steam cylinder, momentarily bulged out to a greater extent than what is due to the pressure, it is mainly to the momentum of the particles of matter composing the cover that the excess of bulging is to be attributed. It is also clear that the mass of matter in a beam first resists deflection by its inertia, and then promotes deflection by its momentum; but whether in practical cases increased mass, without reference to strength or weight, will, upon the whole, increase or diminish deflection, will very much depend upon the magnitude of the mass relatively with the magnitude of the deflecting pressure, and the rapidity with which that pressure is applied and removed. Thus if a small pressure be very suddenly applied to the middle of a ponderous beam, and as suddenly withdrawn, the inertia of the beam will, as in the case of the collision of bodies, tend to resist the force, and thus obviate deflection to a considerable extent; but if the pressure be so long continued as to produce the amount of deflection due to the strength, the effect of the inertia in that case will be to increase the deflection, since the mass must, under these circumstances, move through a space equal to the deflection, whereby a momentum will have been acquired that will afterwards expend itself in increasing the deflection. Hence in all very short beams passed over by a rapidly moving load, the inertia or mass of the beam tends to diminish the deflection, whereas in all beams of the ordinary lengths employed upon railways, the inertia of the beams tends to increase the deflection. By far the severest strains, however, to which railway structures are habitually exposed, from the motion of the load, arise from the jerks and concussions caused by the imperfect junction of the rails at the ends, or other similar irregularities of surface, and a large amount of inertia in a beam will enable it to withstand such shocks much better than it could otherwise do. For the effect of a large inertia will be to compel the train to deviate from the horizontal plane to an extent answerable to the difference of weight of the bridge and train, whereby but little deflection of the bridge will be occasioned, and the less the bridge is deflected the smaller will be the strain upon it. It appears to be highly conducive, therefore, to the security of railway bridges, 1st, to so tie the several parts together, laterally, as to constitute them into one mass, that will move together or not at all; and, 2nd, to load the bridge well with ballasting attached to the beams when the natural weight of the bridge is small; to the end that there may be adequate inertia to resist any sudden shock or concussion, such as is caused by the imperfect adjustment of the ends of the rails.

(To be continued.)

ON THE VENTILATION OF COAL MINES.

BY W. BRUNTON, C. E.

THE numerous instances of loss of life from the explosion of carburetted hydrogen in coal mines render an apology for any attempt to lessen or remove the evil unnecessary, while it is hoped that the elucidation of the subject, causing it to be better understood, will lead to the adoption of better means of rarefaction than the furnace, and in time obviate the necessity for the use of the safety lamp by the ordinary working collier, which has been one of the most prolific causes of the appalling events alluded to. The late accident at Oldham is another proof of the truth of this statement. That scores of men for hours together should be breathing a highly explosive atmosphere, ready to ignite and destroy them in a moment upon the indiscretion of any one of the party with relation to his safety lamp, the principles of which he does not understand, or upon an accident befalling any one of these frail and fragile implements, is a condition of danger without a parallel.

In the following pages I propose to describe the ordinary means used for the ventilation of collieries; to point out what appears to be the inherent defects of the principle of heat as a ventilator to a coal mine; and to describe the apparatus which I have invented and erected for Thomas Powell, Esq., of the Gaer, near Newport, Monmouthshire, which possesses much greater power of rarefaction than the best furnaces, and is in many respects better adapted to the varying circumstances of coal mines.

The ease and facility with which atmospheric air moves, upon its receiving an increase of temperature, is the principle upon which the ordinary method of ventilation is conducted.

In sinking a shaft, the heat communicated to the air in descending, and its contact with the bodies of the men, is usually sufficient to create an ascending and descending current for the supply of fresh air; and this is greatly promoted by a partition dividing the shaft into two compartments, the downcast on one side, the upcast on the other. But little progress can be made in working a colliery till a more effectual means of ventilation is applied. For this purpose a furnace, or large open grate, is constructed near to the bottom of the upcast-shaft, upon which a constant fire is maintained, over which the air passes from the workings of the colliery, and is thereby rarefied in its progress before it enters the upcast-shaft, when its buoyancy creates a draught through the ramifications of the mine back to the downcast-shaft, by which the fresh atmospheric air enters and passes through the workings or avenues of the colliery at a velocity proportionate to the rarefaction or draught attained in the upcast-shaft, acting as a chimney.

I will now advert to some circumstances constituting the inherent defects of the system of rarefaction by heat, which depends on the difference of temperature between the air in the downcast and that in the upcast-shaft. This is greatly affected by atmospheric changes, such as the difference of temperature, as well as that indicated by the rise or fall of the barometer; for during the night the atmosphere may be at freezing, and during the day at 72°; and, supposing the heat of the upcast-shaft to be 182°, this change would cause during the day a reduction of the rarefying power equal to 33 per cent. or $\frac{1}{3}$; and this may often be simultaneous with a rapid fall of the barometer, whereby the exudation of fire-damp is very much promoted, inducing a state of things in the direction of danger, without a visible cause, apparent to the miner, and over which there is in this mode of ventilation very little or no control; for the same atmospheric change that tends to danger from the efflux of gas diminishes the power of the furnace to expel it. Secondly, the power of the furnace to rarefy mainly depends on the depth of the shaft; so that in shallow mines the rarefaction is much more languid than in those of great depth. The amount of rarefaction effected by three large furnaces, in a shaft of about 400 yards deep, is 12½ lbs. on the square foot, or 2¼ inches of water. Thirdly, it is a special part of the late improvements made in the ventilation of collieries subject to fire-damp that a portion of the air conducted through the fiery workings is not permitted to approach the furnace, but is carried by a distinct air-course into the upcast-shaft sufficiently high or distant from the furnace

to avoid explosion. This necessity supplies a strong proof of the inadaptation of fire as a ventilator in a fiery colliery.

I may here observe, that the depth of the shaft and the heat of the upcast, which I have assumed in illustration of rarefaction by the furnace, are taken from some of the best conducted collieries in the counties of Northumberland and Durham. In none of the pits in South Wales where the furnace is used have I found the rarefaction to exceed $\frac{7}{10}$ of an inch of water. There the ventilation is so languid and dependent upon the agitation created and kept up by the transit of waggons and horses through the colliery during the day, while the men are at work, that in the absence of this bustle the whole atmosphere becomes stagnant, and too dangerous to be re-entered by the workmen in the morning, until the stalls have been explored by the aid of a Davy lamp and pronounced safe. This deficiency of power in the furnace when applied to shallow collieries demonstrates the want of a more powerful, mechanical, and controlable means of rarefaction, possessing universality of adaptation.

Fourthly, the air, impregnated in its passage with all the exhalations of the colliery, and then heated by the furnace, is found to be exceedingly corrosive and injurious to iron, more especially where there is moisture. This circumstance alone occasions great expense and much anxiety to the proprietors of collieries, where iron tubbing in the shaft is continually exposed to this deteriorating influence. Fifthly, in the event of an explosion, the position of the furnace, the difficulty of getting to it (as the means of descending are often destroyed), and the dread of a second explosion while the fire in the furnace is unextinguished, all operate as a preventive to reaching the sufferers from choke-damp. If the fire-damp kills its scores, the choke-damp often kills its hundreds. Witness the accident at Aberdare, in August, 1849, where of fifty-two found dead in the colliery only seven appeared to be burnt. In the recent explosion at Oldham the means of ventilation were destroyed, and the density of the choke-damp rendered it for a while impossible to enter the colliery; so that while in all probability many were being suffocated whom the fire had spared, there existed no means of rescuing them or supplying them with fresh air. Surely these events call loudly for the adoption of some means of ventilation more competent to prevent explosions, and able when they occur speedily to clear the atmosphere of the colliery from the choke-damp, and thus save the lives of those who have not suffered from the fiery blast.

I will now describe the mechanical means I have substituted, and the particular advantages it possesses over the furnace as a ventilator.

I construct over the upcast-shaft, or over a chamber immediately connected therewith, a hollow drum of sheet iron, with radial compartments, through which the air is discharged with that degree of force due to the velocity with which the drum revolves upon its axis. The diagrams represent a drum, 22 feet exterior diameter, with compartments of 6 feet long, measured radially; 16 feet being, therefore, their mean diameter, the centrifugal force at 120 revolutions per minute will be 39·25, which, multiplied by the weight of 6 cubic feet of air, $=\frac{444}{1000}$ of a pound, will give a pressure of 17·5 pounds on the square foot, as the amount of rarefaction produced in the interior of the drum, and consequently in the upcast-shaft with which it is connected; this is much beyond what can be obtained by the furnace, yet greatly within the limits of the capability of this machine.

Figures 1 and 2 represent an elevation and plan of the machine, connected by a short tunnel with the upcast-shaft *g*, which in this case is also the pump-shaft, and is therefore closed at the top by a strong cover, with a hole through which the pump rod works. The drum is driven by a small engine, *f*, placed horizontally on the masonry supports, and connected directly to the vertical shaft of the drum; *a, a*, are ribs of wood fastened to the centre plate of the drum; *c*, wrought iron suspension rods; and *d*, a curb of sheet iron; *e e*, are timber joists supporting the bearing of the central spindle of the machine.

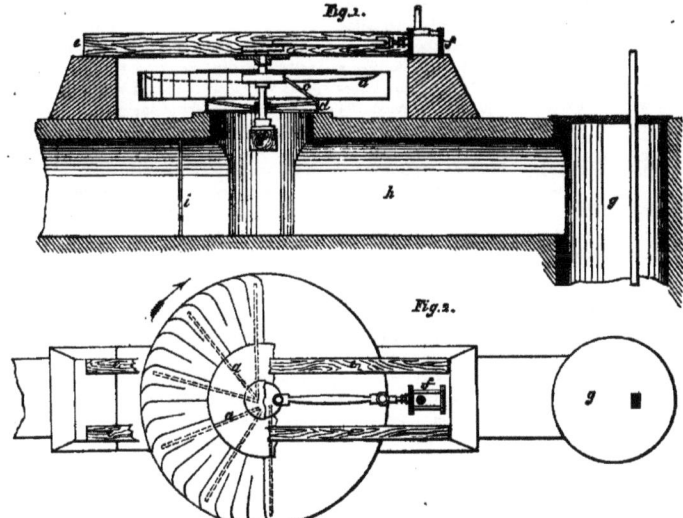

Fig. 1.

Fig. 2.

will discharge the noxious gas by a current of fresh air more copious than can be produced by any other means in use, before the men re-enter the mine. All that is needful to effect this is, that upon the retirement of the workmen and their lights, the air be prevented entering the workings from the downcast shaft; the exhaustion alluded to will immediately commence, for the quantity of air ascending the upcast-shaft being decreased, the drum acted on by the same amount of power, will be accelerated, and the rarefaction consequently increased, whereby the whole extent of the workings will be subjected in a few minutes to the full measure of rarefaction obtained in the upcast-shaft. Upon the fresh air being permitted to enter, the colliery will be found in a state of **extraordinary purity** of atmosphere, and freedom from the risk of explosion; for it is the concurrent testimony of all intelligent underground men, that the fire-damp exudes copiously during the fall of the barometer, and also that during its rise the reverse takes place; the fissures that during the fall were discharging gas, now absorb or draw in atmospheric air; but the effects attendant upon a fall of the barometer must necessarily be more or less dangerous in proportion to the time it had been rising or nearly stationary, when a large portion of the gas evolved during that period will have accumulated in the goaf basins or vaults. The nature of this is so well described in the Report of Messrs. Lyell and Faraday upon the explosion at the Haswell colliery in 1844, that I have requested and obtained permission to make the following extracts :—

It has been often proved that the blast of an explosion will avoid a sudden bend if it can escape by a straight passage; therefore the chief force of an explosion would find an outlet by lifting the cover over the upcast-shaft, and the remainder by driving open the door *i* at the end of the air culvert *h*. The machine would thus be uninjured, and might be immediately applied to clear the colliery of chokedamp, and thereby preserve the lives not destroyed by the fiery explosion.

The machine is an entirely new modification of the fan. Its construction is of the most simple integral character; it has no valves or separate moving parts; has no attrition, and all the friction is resolved into a foot pivot moving in oil; when at rest it offers no impediment to air ascending from the shaft, is very inexpensive, and liable to no derangement; in short, it is a simple mechanical implement, whereby any degree of rarefaction necessary to ventilation is rendered certain and regular, being subject to the law of central forces, which is as fixed and determinate as that by which a stone falls to the earth.

In contrasting it with the furnace, it may be observed, that it is subject to no sensible difference upon the changes of the barometrical column, but, on the other hand, is capable by increase of velocity at such seasons of obviating or counteracting the danger connected therewith, and is equally applicable to all depths.

There will be no necessity for the separate conveyance of air by a stone drift into a higher part of the upcast-shaft to avoid the furnace, as now practised.

All the injurious effect upon the iron in the upcast-shaft will be entirely prevented, and no part of the workings need be stinted of air as to quantity.

But beyond the ordinary requirements of ventilation, as now practised, there is an advantageous application of this machine, which can in no respect be effected or imitated by the furnace. It possesses such power of rarefaction that the atmosphere of a colliery may be subjected in half an hour to an artificial exhaustion of 3, 4, or 5 tenths of an inch of mercury, producing in the colliery, during the absence of the workmen and their lights, the very same exudation of the gases that would have taken place during the natural change of the atmosphere indicated by a like fall of the barometrical column; and the machine

"The goaf may be considered as a heap of rocky fragments rising up into the vault or cavity from which it has fallen, perhaps nearly compact in the parts which are the oldest, lowest, and nearest the middle, but open in structure towards and near its surface, whether at the centre of the goaf or at the edges; and the vault or concavity of the goaf may be considered as an inverted basin, having its edge coincident with the roof of the mine all round the goaf.

"Let us now consider this goaf as a receptacle for gas, or fire-damp, a compound of hydrogen and carbon, known as light hydrocarbonate, and by other names. The weight of pure fire-damp is little more than half that of air; it gradually and spontaneously mixes with air, and the weight of any mixture is proportionate to the quantities of air and fire-damp. Any gas that may be evolved in the goaf, or that may gradually creep into it along the roof of the workings, against which it will naturally flow, will ascend into the goaf vault, and will find its place higher in proportion to its freedom from air; and this will go on continually, the goaf vault forming the natural basin into which all gas will drain (upwards) from parts inclining to the goaf, just as the concavity on the side of a gentle hill will receive water draining downwards from its sides, and from the parts above inclining towards it.

"Thus goafs are evidently in mines subject more or less to firedamp, reservoirs of the gas, and explosive mixtures; giving out their gas into the workings of the mines by a gradual underflow in smaller or larger quantities under ordinary circumstances, or suddenly, and in great proportion, on extraordinary occasions; and they may either supply that explosive mixture which first takes fire, or they may add their magazine of fire-damp and explosive mixtures to increase the conflagration when the fire reaches them from an explosion in some other parts of the mine.

"There is one point connected with what may be called the action of the goaf, and the occasional, sudden, and temporary discharge of gas from it. One of the witnesses on the inquest, Mr. G. Hunter, pointed out the effect he had observed in the mine on a change in the barometer,—that as the barometer fell fire-damp would tend to appear, and that it did this the more suddenly and abundantly if the barometer, having continued high for some time, fell suddenly ; and Mr. Buddle has already strongly stated his opinion that accidents from fire-damp always occur with a low barometer.

" A fall of an inch in barometer, of a sudden, is rare, but a fall of the one-tenth of an inch is not, and that in such a goaf as the one supposed, viz. 13 acres, would place 7,550 cubic feet below the edge of the cavity ; this all tends to issue forth at one place, and that generally a place where the ventilation is weakest. Hence it does appear to us that the goaf, in connection with barometer changes, may in certain mines be productive of sudden evolutions of fire-damp and explosive mixtures, and that the indication of the barometer, and the consequent condition of the mine, ought to be very carefully attended to."

The artificial exhaustion of the atmosphere of a colliery is not now a doubtful question. It has been most perfectly realized, as the following report will show.

"COLLIERY VENTILATION.—On Wednesday, the 29th of August, J. K. Blackwell, Esq., the government inspector of coal mines, visited Gelly Gaer, the colliery of Thomas Powell, Esq., the Gaer, near Newport, and examined the mechanism, and witnessed the performance of the ventilator erected there by Mr. Brunton, for the proprietor, who, together with Mr. Rogers, of Abercarn, Mr. James, of Woodfield, Mr. Thomas Williams, &c., accompanied the inspector through the colliery. The rarefaction maintained by the machine being fully two inches of water, or 10 lbs. on the square foot, was found more than sufficient for the ventilation of this, one of Mr. Powell's minor collieries, but selected by himself purposely, to ascertain the capability of this novel apparatus, before his application of it to his other extensive works. After traversing the extent of the workings, in an abundant supply of air, the party retired into the bottom of the downcast pit, when the most interesting part of the performance was exhibited, by shutting the inlet air-door, which was instantly followed by a loud rushing of air through all the crevices of the doors and stoppings ; and during the application of the water-gauge (not more than a minute) the whole extent of the colliery, six or eight acres, was thus artificially subjected to the same circumstances as if by a natural atmospheric change, the barometer had fallen $\frac{4}{10}$ths of an inch, leaving no doubt as to the practicability of exhausting a colliery to 3, 4, or $\frac{1}{10}$ths, if needful, thereby drawing off the fire-damp, or other gases, during the absence of the workmen ; and as a further demonstration of the capability of discharging the gas thus drawn out, and of restoring fresh air, the velocity of the machine was increased, till the rarefaction was $4\frac{3}{4}$ inches of water, or 24 lbs. on the square foot. This machine being satisfactorily tested, is to be removed to the old Duffryn colliery ; another put up upon the new Duffryn colliery ; and in a few weeks one will be in operation at Giffyllion colliery, belonging to J. Calvert, Esq."—*Monmouthshire Merlin.*

From the data of Messrs. Lyall and Faraday the exhaustion effected at Gelly Gaer, viz., $\frac{1}{10}$ths of mercury, would have drawn from the goaf of the Haswell colliery 15,000 feet of fire-damp, besides what would have issued from the blowers and fissures in the whole coal, and upon the restoration the colliery would have been supplied with an atmosphere of fresh air, rendering the goaf so much less dangerous from any sudden internal fall, and the fissures in the whole coal would have been brought into that state of safety in which they are found upon the rising of the barometer, viz., drawing in air.

A change like this, artificially effected in the course of 6 or 8 hours upon an extensive colliery subject to fire-damp may appear to many startling and dangerous, but let them remember that such changes actually take place when they are neither expected nor provided against, but, on the contrary, the men with their lights are in the mine, ready to fire the exuded fire-damp, which often results in a fatal explosion. But the change that takes place by the natural rise of the barometer after explosion will in no case be attended by the same beneficial effects, as the sudden and powerful restoration of the air after an artificial exhaustion.

From these observations it is obvious that if the fire-damp be drawn off at short intervals, as at every twenty-four hours, the accumulation and consequent danger will be very little compared with what it frequently is through the continuance of weeks of fine weather ; and the daily discharge of these minor accumulations will maintain the colliery, whilst the men are at work, in that state of safety (but better ascertained), experienced whilst the barometer is rising.

Possessing thus the power of anticipating the sudden exudation of gas by drawing it off when it can do no harm, and of rendering the colliery much more safe and healthful for the workmen, may we not reasonably hope that the subject will receive the attention it deserves, and that a system of alternate exhaustion and restoration will be judiciously brought into practice as experience will dictate, until the Davy lamp is no longer necessary for the common collier, the danger of explosion almost or altogether obviated, and the health of the miner greatly promoted !

The very recent explosions powerfully appeal to our humanity, to legislative influences, and to the general interests of the coal owner and miner, for the necessity of some important step being taken towards the better ventilating, management, and general safety of our coal mines.

AERIAL NAVIGATION.

(Concluded from p. 254.)

IN continuing the subject of aerial navigation, I come now to notice the boldest scheme of the day, viz. M. Petin's " System of Aerial Navigation," by which he hopes to attain the long-desired power of rendering the balloon subservient to our will.

I have already alluded to the fact of a large Parisian audience being inspired by him with the idea of the success of his invention ; and in proceeding to notice the several features of the machine, we may be able to judge for ourselves how far he has succeeded.

He commences by saying, that hitherto those who have sought to direct balloons in the air have not fully investigated natural laws. This is indeed a truth ; but at the same time he endeavours to prove that he alone has penetrated the veil, and discovered that all animate and inanimate bodies never move but by the combination of the action of the heavy body with the resistance of the surrounding medium. This is his starting point, which is only true for birds and fishes, animals and machines on the surface of the earth using the earth as their fulcrum, in which case the surrounding medium, or air, only causes resistance. He says, in order that there may be motion, " intelligence must direct the action of the heavy body ;" and it might be added,—intelligence, or at least nature, would place effectual means at the disposal of those actions to generate motion. This, however, M. Petin has neglected, and in this he has erred.

The system of aerial navigation may be described as follows : four immense balloons, 90 feet diameter, are arranged behind each other, connected by a frame-work of timber 490 feet long by 212 feet broad, stayed and braced, having a sort of gallery all round for containing the passengers, and open in the centre. To this frame the balloons are connected,—one at each end, and two intervening, below each of which are strong cross-stays ; and on each side of each balloon is placed an upright standard, carrying another platform or plane at a level a little below the centre of the balloons. This is the plane by which he proposes to produce his movements. The lower frame is supported by suitable cordage from the balloons, and the upper plane, looking from above, would appear an irregular figure, having the upper surface of the two middle balloons like two hemispheres placed in the centre, and the corresponding halves of the outside balloons will appear overhanging each end. Each end of this plane is composed of wooden splats, like Venetian blinds, so as to open and shut at pleasure. In the centre are placed four parachutes, two to open in ascending, and two in descending. In the middle of the lower frame below the balloons are placed a number of spiral surfaces and wheels, which are proposed to be used in elevating and depressing the machine, and propelling it in a horizontal direction.

There is a prow placed in front against the balloon of a conical form and insignificant dimensions, intended to diminish resistance in passing through the air.

The whole affair has a most imposing appearance, and looks as if intended to give battle to the elements. The mode of action the inventor proposes shall be as follows : when the machine leaves the earth it will have a great ascensional force, and by opening the splats in the upper plane at one end the resistance to ascend at that end will be removed, and as a consequence that end will rise above the level of the other end. This being accomplished, the machine will no longer ascend in a vertical line, but will shoot up in an inclined direction with great velocity ; and by closing the splats again the pressure is restored, and the machine becomes horizontal, when it is expected that the momentum acquired will carry it in a horizontal direction, and thus pass over great distances ; these momentums being repeated as often as desired, either in front or in rear, by which means it is expected to move in any direction whatever. The wheels and spiral surfaces are to be used when the machine attains such a height as to have no longer any ascending power, then, instead of allowing the gas to escape, the aeronaut is to apply himself dexterously to the wheels or screws, and bring the machine to a lower level, and again allow it to ascend with great velocity, as before, in the inclined and horizontal directions, and so on, *ad libitum.* Here is a monstrous conclusion for any one to arrive at who has investigated nature and its laws ! whose machine is intended as a type of nature's actions ! Such a conclusion may be swallowed by an audience of amateurs, but certainly no mechanic could for a moment believe that this was truth.

In the first place, then, in order to show how far this may succeed, let us look more minutely at the details of the machine. There are four immense balloons 90 feet in diameter, the capacity of each will be $90^1 \times .5236 = 381704$ cubic feet, and will displace a weight of air = 28628 lbs. ; and supposing common coal gas to be used for inflation, the specific gravity of which is .6, that of air being 1.2, there will be a weight of gas equal to half that of the air, or 14314 lbs., leaving 14314 lbs. as the available buoyancy of each balloon at the earth's surface ; and $14314 \times 4 = 57256$ lbs. being the total buoyancy. From this has to be deducted the weight of the balloons, wheels, and framework of the machine. Each balloon, allowing 1 lb. for every square yard of surface, will weigh $1\frac{1}{4}$ tons ; the whole frame, wheels, and tackle I have estimated at 10 tons ; and $1\frac{1}{4} \times 4 + 10 = 15$ tons $= 33600$ lbs., and deducting this we have $57256 - 33600 = 23656$ lbs. for goods and passengers. 150 passengers, averaging 10 stone each, or 140 lbs. = 21000 lbs., leaving only 2656 lbs. for ascending power. This unbalanced weight would allow the machine to ascend to a height corresponding to this difference in the weight of the displaced air, and to find the height we must first find the difference of pressure, which is as $57256 : 57256 - 2656 : : 30 : 28.6 =$ the column of mercury corresponding to the pressure. Then by applying the rule given at page 232* the height may be found. Putting $x =$ height — then log. 30 — log. $28.6 \times 63946 = x$ log. 30 $= 1.477121$

$$\text{log. } 28.6 = 1.456366$$
$$\overline{\cdot020755} \times 63946 = 1327 = x.$$

The machine in ascending to this trifling height could not gain any

* I find that the diameter of the balloon there given does not correspond with the formula, and ought to be 44 instead of 20.3.

great velocity ; but, on the contrary, its motion would be comparatively slow, for the great amount of surface exposed would offer an effectual resistance, and the supposed action of the inclined plane would be *nil.*

If we suppose only 50 passengers in the machine it would attain a height of 9537 feet. This height might lead one to suppose that the velocity acquired would cause the inclined action the inventor speaks of; but it will be seen, that in opening the splats at one end, in order to remove pressure, the plane, such as it is, would be broken, and all that remains are only two irregular pieces, one on each side of the two balloons at the opposite end of the machine ; and to make matters worse, the two parachutes opening downwards have the same effect on the machine that an exceeding bad road, full of gaps and ruts, would have on a carriage being moved over it. We have supposed the splats to be opened at one end, but although there is no resistance offered by them, there is a sufficient quantity of cordage and framework, &c., immediately below them, which would cause almost as much resistance ; and if, as very probable, two or three passengers be at that end more than at the other, the equilibrium will be undisturbed. But I think the better plan to throw the machine on its "beam ends" would be to ask the passengers in a polite manner to walk to the other end of the carriage, and then, for the *vice versa* movements, they would surely not object to walk to the other end, and so on, rushing from one end to the other, as the crowd does on the deck of a newly-launched vessel, to rock her out of her cradle. It would be necessary, however, to have cleats nailed on the floor of the carriage, to assist the obliging passengers in clambering up the inclined plane, something like the landing stages for our river steamers.

Even if it were possible for this machine to ascend in an inclined direction, in order to progress in a horizontal direction it ought to have only one position in ascending, and not as proposed alternately, in one direction and another, something like a person ascending a staircase, who at last finds himself in a vertical position over that from which he set out.

The inventor of this vast machine was fully aware of the lawless winds of heaven, which direct at their own wild will, and accordingly has prepared for the contest, by placing some large wheels and helical surfaces in the midst of his machine, to be used for screwing into a head wind, or directing the machine to any point of the compass. These wheels and surfaces are utterly insignificant to effect these objects, and the remarks in my last paper will show what an enormous power would be necessary to accomplish this ; and although the inventor proposes other than manual power, if that is insufficient, it can easily be shown that the available buoyancy is far from being sufficient for such a purpose. 200 passengers would more than outbalance it. There is, therefore, little chance of any propelling power being carried, even against a moderate current ; also their position in the carriage is such that the mass of cordage, &c., surrounding them would go far to prevent any useful effect. This *monstrous* fragile barque would be driven by the lawless winds like a crystal barque in the currents of the ocean, and would share no better fate. It would accomplish no more than what has been already done, that is, it would carry its occupants a considerable distance in a little time by drifting with the current ; and no man acquainted with nature's simple laws would endeavour to thwart her in the upper regions, which are peculiarly nature's own. There is no known power capable of competing with the warring elements, electricity excepted ; but a thousand years may yet elapse ere this power be developed.

Navigation of the air is very different from navigating the waters of the ocean, but aeronauts are have classed them under one head. In ocean navigation we see a buoyant vessel floating on the surface, and propelled by a paddle-wheel, or screw, which acts in an efficient manner in the water. On the other hand, in aerial navigation the vessel, or balloon, does not float on the surface, but is wholly immersed in the fluid, and the propellers applied so insignificant as to be incapable of propelling the balloon, even against a moderate current. It would be an analogous case to attempt to propel a vessel wholly immersed in water against the currents of the ocean. But we know that it is the great aim of the engineers of the present day to avoid deep immersion, and, use every means to curtail the weight of the vessel, engines, and boilers, to give as small a draft of water as possible. It is surprising that men should have devoted so much study to accomplish such aerial schemes, which are next to impossibilities.

There is yet another point in this "System of Aerial Navigation " which I have not mentioned, and which will go far to prevent even a trial of the machine (I venture to say it will not even be constructed)— that is, the gas for inflation. Each balloon being 70 feet in diameter will have a capacity of 381704 cubic feet, the total for 4 = 1526816. This number of cubic feet of coal gas, supposing it manufactured at the cheapest possible rate, cannot be less than 1*s.* 6*d.* per 1000 feet ; but the selling price in London is 4*s.* In Paris it must be considerably more, seeing that coal is dearer. And 1526816 cubic feet will cost in London £305 4*s.*, and however short the trip may be this sum, or nearly so, must be expended. It might, however, be economised by allowing only so much gas to escape as to allow it to touch the earth if the journey is to be continued ; and at every station an enormous gas work must be erected for the supply of gas. The gas for one inflation, generated at one charge of 6 hours' duration, would require sixteen hundred retorts, which is nearly double the product of the largest existing gas-work in London.

I fear I have occupied too much of your valuable space with this subject ; but if it meet the eye of any one still endeavouring to solve the problem (by the newspaper reports it would seem we are to have some locomotive balloons for the Exhibition next year) it may prevent needless waste of time and money in such foolish projects.

The last attempt at navigating the upper regions in this country was by Mr. Bell, during the past summer, from Vauxhall gardens. The shape of the balloon was an elongated cylinder, with hemispherical ends, floating horizontally ; and in the car were placed some small propellers, in the shape of screws and vanes, to be worked by the aeronaut. I was eye-witness to his ascent, which, like all former experiments, failed to accomplish the purpose.

This is no more than was accomplished nearly seventy years ago ; for in 1784 two brothers, of the name of Roberts, constructed a balloon 46 feet by 27, with 5 wings or oars attached to the car, 13 feet long. These oars enabled them, in a perfect calm, to describe a segment of an ellipse, whose shortest diameter was 6000 feet. This was the most that could be accomplished. In October, 1843, we find M. Leinberger, of Nuremberg, had been exhibiting a model of a steam flying machine, with so much success that he had commenced to construct one on a large scale. It is needless to say that it has not yet appeared. His model, I suppose, was on a similar principle to that exhibited in the Polytechnic, in 1840.

From these facts and conclusions it may be said that the upper regions cannot be turned to account as the high-way of life. In fact, the Creator seems to have intended that it never should be so ; for the oxygen, or life-sustaining principle of the atmosphere, is intimately diffused in the same ratio at all densities. In leaving the surface of the earth the density rapidly decreases, and at an elevation of 10,000 feet the density has decreased ½, or nearly so ; at 3½ miles it is reduced to ¼ ; so that a person breathing this atmosphere would inhale at every breath one half less oxygen. Few persons could exist long under such circumstances, and there are many who find the ordinary atmosphere hardly sufficient for their wants. There is yet another serious con. sideration ; it is found that for every 1000 feet of ascent the temperature decreases 3° Farenheit, and, consequently, at the height of 10,000

feet there would be a difference of 30°. If that of the earth's surface be 60° then at this height it would be 2° below the freezing-point ; and thus aerial travellers would be taken from the midst of summer to the depth of winter in the space of 15 or 20 minutes.

This would have a most injurious effect on the human system. We are already heirs to ills enough, and our ingenuity should be taxed to lessen those ills, instead of being misdirected in search of the unattainable.   N. D.

INDICATOR DIAGRAMS FROM A DOUBLE CYLINDER ENGINE.

At the request of a correspondent, we give an example of indicator diagrams taken from a double cylinder engine of the following dimensions : high pressure cylinder, 12 inches diameter and 3 feet stroke ; low pressure cylinder, 21 inches diameter and 3 feet stroke ; speed, 54 revolutions per minute. The average pressure throughout the stroke of the high pressure cylinder is 30 lbs., and in the low pressure cylinder 10.86 lbs ; the contents of the cylinders being as their areas, or as 113 to 346, that is as 1 to 3, nearly. The gross horse power indicated then, will be as follows : $113 \times 30 = 3390$, and $346 \times 10.86 = 3757$. Then $3390 + 3757 = 7147$ lbs., the sum of the pressure on both pistons. Then $\frac{7147 \times 54 \times 6}{33000} = 70.1$ horses power, without any deduction for friction. This engine would probably be nominally 20 horses power, but it will be observed that it is pretty nearly loaded up to a maximum, and that the speed of piston, 324 feet $(54 \times 3 \times 2)$ per minute, is one half more than Boulton & Watt's standard, although not higher than many of our best engines are now working.

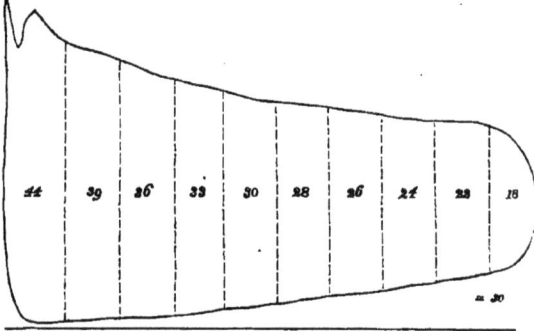

H. P Cylinder—scale 10ths.

L. P. Cylinder—Scale 20ths.

METHOD OF SHIFTING EXPANSION CAMS.

In the use of cams, in various forms of expansion gear, they have to be shifted round upon their centre to cut off the steam, sooner or later; and this motion cannot always be obtained without complex gear. One of the simplest and most elegant arrangements with which we are acquainted is that of M. Trésel, a French engineer, which we are glad to be able to present to our readers. It will be readily understood, from the sketch below, which represents a side and end view of two cams, *a* and *b*: *a*, being for the ordinary slide, is immoveable on the shaft; *b*, which works the expansion slide, is loose on the shaft. On the end of the shaft is a handle attached to a bevil wheel, by turning which the screw turns in the nut *c*, which it raises or depresses as the handle is turned to the right or left. The nut *c* is attached to the link *d*, which connects it with the cam *b*; and the frame which carries the screw and nut *c* being fixed on the shaft, the motion of the nut turns the cam *b* round on the shaft, as required.

We have made arrangements to give our readers some further specimens of French engineering, which cannot fail to be interesting to English mechanics.

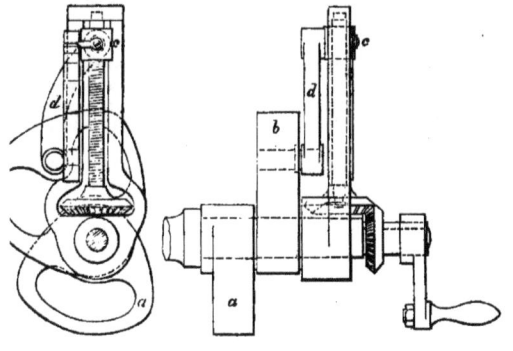

CARRETT'S PATENT STEAM-PUMP.

To the Editor.

Sir,—Your remarks upon the particulars of detail of my Patent Steam Pump, need, I think, some further notice, since the scale of illustration could not easily represent them in a self-explanatory form.

The slotted cross-head application for converting an alternate into a rotatory motion, introduced for its compactness and simplicity, being in accordance with the rest of the machine.

The slide-frame and block, when properly case-hardened, are by this means rendered capable of lasting some half-dozen years, as I have seen from similar ones in actual practice.

The expense of renewing such block at the end of that period not being very great, I advocate that this arrangement is best suited to the case in which I have applied it.

In construction, the slotted frame is closed up on both sides, where it is not necessary for the crank pin to traverse; the interior is filled with oil, along which the slide-block is continually traversing. Further, the power of the steam cylinder is transmitted direct to the ram; the purpose of the fly-wheel being simply to work the valve, and carry the piston over its dead points.

In the application of this pumping machine to larger purposes of from 3 to 6 horse power, a connecting-rod is then contrived to be made use of, along with other necessary alterations which a larger apparatus would require.

If an air-vessel is connected with a pump in a proper manner it will never lose its elastic medium, and should such an escape by leakage, or other accident occur, there will soon, by the pump's action, more air collect to supply its place, the surplus passing off *per se* at the discharge pipe.

The entrance of the atmosphere into a pump is with difficulty prevented, neither is it at all easy to be got rid of when required.

The steam pump in question is so constructed that this elastic medium cannot become permanently lodged in any part, and thus baffle the effective stroke; since the discharge valve has its outlet from the very top of the barrel, and all air bubbles must in consequence find their way through along with the water.

The application of India rubber is intended for water joints solely, and not for steam, as you seem to have understood. This self-accommodating medium answers admirably well for joints that have to be opened repeatedly, requiring no cement of any kind to make it tight every time it is disturbed. It should be confined between two inclined surfaces in all cases, so that the tendency to escape is always counteracted by the pressure of water within; thus it will tighten itself rather than suffer any leakage.

I am, Sir,

Leeds, 14th August.   Yours respectfully,
                                                          W. O. Carrett.

[We willingly give Mr. Carrett the opportunity which he desires of setting himself right with our readers on the subject of his steam pump; but we do not clearly see his argument. We must still be allowed to express our opinion, that air vessels, *however arranged*, are apt to fill with water, when the air vessel stands below the level of the discharge pipe, as in this case. The remark on the use of vulcanized India rubber could hardly be understood to mean that Mr. Carrett had recommended it for steam joints, but as he had not warned the reader against it we thought it right to do so, having a case now before us, where a serious loss of money and time has been incurred, through its use in a system of steam drying pipes. Neither could we be supposed to know that Mr. Carrett had other arrangements (with connecting rods) which he would recommend, as our only information on the subject was obtained from himself, and the plate was submitted to him for correction before it was printed.—Ed. Art.]

INSTITUTION OF MECHANICAL ENGINEERS.

The General Meeting of the members was held at the house of the Institution, 54, Newhall-street, Birmingham, on Wednesday, the 23rd October, 1850; J. E. M'Connell, Esq., Vice-President, in the Chair.

The minutes of the last General Meeting were read by the Secretary, and confirmed.

The Chairman announced that, according to the rules of the Institution, the President, Vice-Presidents, and the following five of the council in rotation, would go out of office at the end of the present year; and that at the present meeting the council and officers for the succeeding year were to be nominated for the election of the next annual meeting.

President.—Robert Stephenson, Esq., M.P.

Vice-Presidents.—Charles Beyer, Esq., Manchester; J. E. M'Connell, Esq., Wolverton John Penn, Esq., London.

Council.—E. A. Cowper, Esq., Birmingham; Edward Humphrys, Esq., Woolwich; Edward Jones, Esq., Bridgewater; W. A. Matthews, Esq., Sheffield; and Archibald Slate, Esq., Dudley.

Treasurer.—Charles Geach, Esq., Birmingham.

Secretary.—Wm. P. Marshall, Birmingham.

These were proposed for re-election, with the addition of any other members who might be proposed by the meeting.

Mr. James A. Shipton, of Manchester, was proposed by Mr. Bowman for one of the council, and no other names having been added by the meeting, the list was adopted.

The Secretary then read the following supplementary paper, by Mr. Thomas Thorneycroft, of Wolverhampton:—

ON THE FORM OF RAILWAY AXLES.

Since the reading of the paper on the form of Railway Axles, the author has had his attention specially directed to some of those points which it was the object of the paper to introduce and support.

In that paper, as well as in others on the same subject, a parallel had been drawn between the railway axle and the girder, as being somewhat alike in principle; admitting the correctness of this opinion, the question would arise, why is the principle upon which every girder is made departed from in the case of the axle? If it is pleaded that the close proximity of the prop and load, and these acting at the extreme ends of the axle, has justified this departure from the girder principle; then it might be expected that girders loaded under very similar circumstances would in like manner be reduced in th middle; but not so; as a case in point, reference might be made to the girders which suspended those parts of the Britannia tubes which pass through the towers, where the prop and load are at the extreme ends of the girder, and within a few inches of each other; yet these girders are parallel, although for a distance equal to the width of the tube there is no load whatever.

The principal reason which has been assigned for reducing axles in the middle, is the supposition that when parallel, the effect of the forces from lateral and vertical percussion tends to break the axle behind the wheel; that being the point where the greatest amount of fractures have taken place: the author is, however, of opinion, that the simple and only cause of the fracture of axles at that particular point is the shoulder, which it has been the practice to leave on the axle as a stop to the wheel; some of the experiments now before the Institution prove, at least, that where a shoulder exists the strength of the axle is reduced more than one-half, which affords presumptive proof that there are other causes in constant operation (beside the arrestment of the wave of vibration), inducing fracture at that particular point.

It has now become the opinion of some engineers that in every case of collision or other derangements of a train when in motion, that axles reduced smaller in the middle are unable to keep their form, and that such axles exposed to violent lateral blows are easily sent beyond the limit of their elasticity, the consequence is the wheels leave the rails and contribute directly to greater damage than would ensue were the train to keep the line.

A short time ago some disarrangement of a train took place on the Shrewsbury and Birmingham railway, in which case three or four carriages were nearly broken to pieces; the axles of these carriages were all reduced in the middle, and nearly all of them were more or less bent, while some of the carriages in the same train with parallel axles suffered little or no damage, and there was not one parallel axle bent in the slightest degree. Such a result might have been anticipated when it is remembered, that the resistance which the middle of an axle offers to a bending force is as the cube of its diameter. Hence, if we take the diameter of the centre of a reduced axle at 2½ inches, the cube of which is 18·06, and then take the diameter of a parallel axle of the same weight, which would be 3¼ inches, the cube of which is 34·32, we find that with the same quantity of material the parallel axle has the advantage of the reduced one, to resist all the forces to which axles are subject by 90 per cent. So early as 1842 the Mechanical Section of the British Association had the subject of the fracture of railway axles fully discussed, after a number of excellent remarks by Mr. Nasmyth on the different causes which tended to destroy the fibre of iron, and render it brittle; he observed, that simply nicking iron to the extent of only $\frac{1}{100}$th of the area took away $\frac{1}{10}$th of its strength. Mr. Fairbairn at the same time expressed his opinion that the two chief causes of the breakage of railway axles were bending and percussion, these changed the fibrous to the crystalline structure. In a paper read by Mr. J. O. York before the Institution of Civil Engineers, in 1843, reference was made to the fleeting bars used as levers for turning the large screws for forcing forwards the shield in the Thames Tunnel, that they never lasted longer than three or four weeks, although very strong and made from the best materials; and that when fracture took place they exhibited a bright crystallized appearance, clearly showing that oft repeated bending without any concussion had destroyed the fibre of the iron, and rendered it quite brittle.

A mass of evidence might be adduced to prove that the internal structure of iron undergoes no change, unless there be a change of form; and that simple jarring or vibration will not destroy the fibre of iron, whereas bending, if long continued, will change the most fibrous iron into crystalline, therefore the author would fully subscribe to the opinion of one of the railway commissioners, who has stated, "that it

was of importance to avoid deflection on railway axles, as deflection was almost as fatal as fracture in causing accidents."

Mr. Thorneycroft gave an explanation of the experiments which he had laid before the preceding meeting, and the specimen axles exhibited on the table. Supposing that an axle bent in the centre, it must have a tendency to throw the wheels off the line; and as every time it turned round it would bend backwards and forwards, if it were bent more than the point of elasticity, it would have a tendency to snap off at the point where it was firmly fixed. If the axle were bent beyond its elastic limit, it would take a set and would not completely go back again; and, consequently, as the bending would alter the shape, as there was a constant action going on it would have a tendency to produce permanent injury of the iron, and in time it would break off short, because whenever there was an alteration from the fibrous into the crystalline state, it would snap off at the point where it was rigidly fixed, namely—at the inside part of the wheels. The object was to get at the best form of axle possible, and to shew that there might be improvements in the generality of axles at present used. Axles had generally been reduced in the middle, but the experiments appeared to show that in point of security great advantages would be gained by making the axle parallel all the way along, instead of reduced in the middle, since the latter were found very frequently to snap close to the wheels.

Mr. Bowman expressed his opinion that it was unphilosophical and unmechanical either to reduce axles in the middle, or to make a shoulder behind the wheel. He considered the reduction of an axle in the middle must have a tendency to reduce its strength; and that by taking away the shoulder from behind the wheel, the principal cause of fracture at that point would be removed.

Mr. Slate fully agreed with the view expressed as to the removal of the shoulder behind the wheel, but if the illustration given in the paper derived from the girder suggested anything, he thought it was like strengthening a girder in the middle when it proved weak at the ends· When a strain was put on the flange of the wheel, the point of fracture would be behind the wheel; but if there were any analogy between the cases of the axle and the girder, it would tend to show that the axle would break in the middle. The proposition brought forward was, that if the axle were made so stiff that there was no vibration, it would not be so liable to break behind the wheel; but he did not conceive that any addition of strength in the centre would produce strength behind the wheel. Indeed, where the elastic action was the greatest the fracture would take place, and by making the axle stronger in the middle the elastic action would be greatest at the wheel, and the liability to fracture at that point would be increased, because the flexibility would be confined to the part at the wheel instead of being diffused over the whole axle.

Mr. T. Thorneycroft remarked, that the girders alluded to were parallel all the way along, and they supported the whole weight of the tube from the two extreme ends. Such, also, was the case with the axle which supported the weight, not in the middle, but at both ends.

Mr. Peacock remarked, that the material must be taken into account, because the girder alluded to was of cast-iron, and if it had been reduced in the centre the strength might have been injured before it left the foundry by unequal contraction; but in the case of the axle, being of wrought-iron, there was a great difference.

Mr. T. Thorneycroft said, the girder had to sustain a great weight, and so had a railway axle; and in process of time the structure of the iron would be injured by bending backwards and forwards. He fancied that the object in view was the same which he entertained in giving the railway axle strength in the centre, because by bending they destroyed the original form of the iron, and thereby changed its structure, and that the object was to prevent the girder bending in the centre.

Mr. Slate remarked, that if the girder were reduced in the centre it would be liable to be broken there by vibration. If there was any analogy the axle also would break in the centre ; but that was not the fact.

Mr. Bowman said, that axles broke in the centre ; two or three cases had come to his knowledge, though he had not much experience on railways.

The Chairman observed, that as it was an important point, he should like to elicit from such members as had experience, what number of axles they had seen broken in the centre.

Mr. H. Wright said he had never seen one, that he was aware of.

Mr. Ramsbottom had frequently seen axles broken near the end, but had not met with a single case of an axle breaking in the centre.

Mr. Peacock concurred with the preceding speaker.

Mr. Allan said, he had seen a leading engine axle broken within a few inches of the centre, but for that one he had seen probably 500 axles broken at the wheel.

Mr. Owen had seen some thousands of broken axles, but he was not aware, through many years experience, of one axle breaking directly in the middle.

Mr. Henson had never seen one break in the middle, and thought that many thousands broke at the wheel compared to one at the middle.

The Chairman said, the result of his experience fully agreed with the preceding observations, that it was very rare for axles to break in the centre.

Mr. T. Thorneycroft inquired whether any member had seen any of the parallel axles broken close by the nave of the wheel.

Mr. Henson said, he had seen a large proportion of them so broken ; some of these had very slight shoulders, the others larger ones.

Fig. 1.

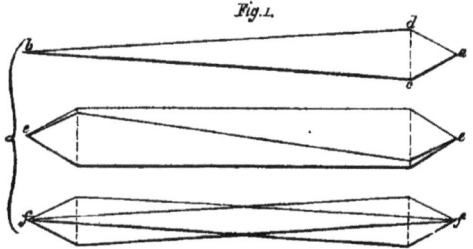

Mr. Cowper said, it seemed to him that Mr. Thorneycroft's conclusions were arrived at by experiment, unaided by theory. In the accompanying sketch, fig. 1, if they took *a b* as the axis of a railway axle, *a* and *b* as the centres of the journals, and *c* as the centre of one wheel, they would have the case of a girder weighted at *a* and *b*, and supported at *c;* the proportionate *strength* ought, therefore, to be as a triangle *a c d*, and a triangle *b c d.* Now if they put two of these triangles together, as at *e e*, they would at once arrive at the result that the strength of the axle should be uniform between the wheels, and consequently parallel, and from the wheels to the journals, the strength should be as a triangle ; and if they had merely to do with a strain due to the weight on the journals of the axle, these proportionate strengths would be strictly correct. But they had another enemy to deal with—they had to provide against the lateral strains from the flanges of the wheels suddenly striking the switches and crossings in passing through them ; and this was so much greater than the mere weight on the axle, that it must be considered chiefly in determining the form of an axle ; if, therefore, the figure *a c b d* were reversed on itself, the outline thus given would represent the proportionate *strength* of an axle, as at *f f*, which was fully in accordance with the usual tapered form of axles. *The actual diameters* could, of course, be easily arrived at, by taking the cube root of the width ; as it was well known the *strength* of solid cylinders are as the cubes of their diameters.

Mr. Shipton observed, that experience showed that an axle should be a rigid body ; hence he understood the idea of the writer of the paper to be—that elasticity in the centre tended to ultimate fracture.

Mr. Bowman said, the parallel axle was adopted to do away with the deflection. In the cases of parallel axles referred to as being broken there were shoulders behind the wheel, but what they wanted to find was an instance of a parallel axle without a shoulder being broken.

Fig. 2.

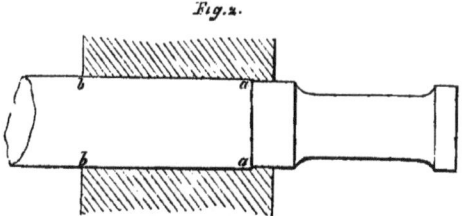

Mr. Slate observed, that he had suggested the introduction of a small shoulder inside the boss of the wheel, near the outer side, (see *a*, fig 2,) which he thought would have all the advantage of the shoulder at the inner side of the boss, without weakening the axle at all. The wheel was to be bored out a tight fit, and forced on to the axle by a press, but the first 1¼ inch from the inner side was to be slightly coned as shown at *b*, so as to remove the grip on the axle from the extreme edge of the boss, and prevent the tendency for the axle to break at that point.

The Chairman said, they had found, a considerable time ago, that in the use of the square shoulder there was a great liability to cause fracture ; hence they adopted the present form, which is countersunk into the wheel, from the inner edge of the boss, with as small a taper as possible : the difference of the axle in its rough state and when turned true, being sufficient for the purpose, bevilled off into the wheel, as the wheel boss was bored accurately, and forced on tight by an hydraulic press. The shoulder was thus entirely avoided.

Mr. Middleton observed, that he had proposed some time ago that a cone of about one third the length should be carried into the boss of the wheel, or rather a large hollow ; and in turning up the axle he would leave no shoulder at all.

Mr. Williams said, there was no doubt a parallel axle would be the stiffest, but the question was, whether it was the most efficient. If a bar of iron was repeatedly bent backwards and forwards in the middle, it would certainly become crystalline and would break in the centre ; but axles did not break in the centre, hence the illustration did not hold good.

Mr. Cowper remarked, that a parallel axle or bar of iron, fixed near one end in a vice, and worked about at the other end, would break at the vice, no doubt, like the axles breaking at the point where they are fixed in the boss of the wheel ; but he could conceive the possibility of it being reduced from that point to the other end in such a taper that they could not tell where it would break, and it would be equally strong throughout.

Mr. H. Smith said, whether the shoulder were square or not, he was of opinion that axles were more liable to break at that part than any other. He might observe, that the axle-trees of gentlemen's carriages were made parallel, and he had known many of them broken in the centre as well as at the shoulder.

Mr. Peacock observed, there was no doubt a collar behind the wheel was bad. The question was only whether the parallel axle or the taper axle was best. He considered that if Mr. Thorneycroft's experiments had been tried, by giving the blow on the wheel instead of the journal, he would have arrived at very different results, and at results also which bore much more upon the practical determination of the question. In the experiment mentioned, where the short end of an axle broke off with seven blows, as contrasted with the other end which took twenty-four blows to break it, he thought that the fracture was not caused by weight alone, but by vibration, otherwise the short end must have borne a greater weight than the long projection. As the results of the experiments did not coincide with his own experience, he would suggest to Mr. Thorneycroft, that he should try other experiments, by applying the blows to the flange of the wheel instead of the journal ; and that he should apply this test both to the parallel and taper axles, dispensing with the collar in both cases.

The Chairman referred to the experiments on the form of axles that he had laid before the Institution on a previous occasion (pp. 58, 130), in which he had applied the force to the edge of the wheel, and the results confirmed the taper form of axle.

Mr. G. B. Thorneycroft remarked, that it was simply with the view of determining the most philosophical and mechanical form of axle that he had paid attention to this subject. He considered that a shoulder, whether inside the wheel or outside, was decidedly objectionable. When force was applied, either by pressure or by a blow to a parallel bar of iron, it bent and the fibres drew out ; but the moment they turned a shoulder in any part of the bar, they cut through the outer fibres of the iron, and they could not draw out the inner from under the outer fibres, and the bar snapped short like a stick. He did not maintain that the parallel axle never broke, but he considered that it would take half as much more force to bend a parallel axle as would be sufficient to bend a tapered one. Neither did he say that axles, parallel or taper, broke in the centre ; he did not think they did, but that if an axle was prevented bending in the centre, strength and security were thereby gained.

The Chairman observed, that in order to institute a fair comparison of the relative strength of the taper and the parallel axle, it was necessary to take care that the same weight of iron was employed between the wheels in both cases ; if the parallel axle weighed more than the taper axle, it was not a fair comparison of strength. The diagrams exhibited did not show as much strength of metal in the taper as in the parallel forms.

Mr. G. Thorneycroft replied, that he considered a parallel axle of the same weight with a taper axle would be much the stronger.

Mr. Ramsbottom remarked, that the conclusions as to the correct form of axles arrived at by the writer of the paper were entirely different to his own conclusions and experience. He always considered that, whether in the case of axles or machinery of any kind, there must be an error in the proportions, if any one could say beforehand at what point a fracture was likely to occur. There could not be any question that a shoulder behind the wheel was objectionable, since any sudden variation in the strength must lead to a disturbance of the forces, and eventually to fracture. He could only conceive one instance in railway practice where axles should be parallel, and that was in the case where the forces were applied in a line directly parallel to the

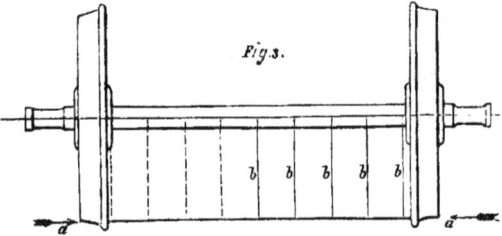

Fig. 3.

axle ; as at *a a*, fig. 3. If a pair of wheels were running, for instance between rails converging to a point, the axle should be parallel, since

the effect of the leverage was the same at all points *b b* between the wheels. But there was another and more important force resulting from a lateral blow upon one wheel only, coupled with the load of the vehicle on the axle, the direction of which would be tolerably well

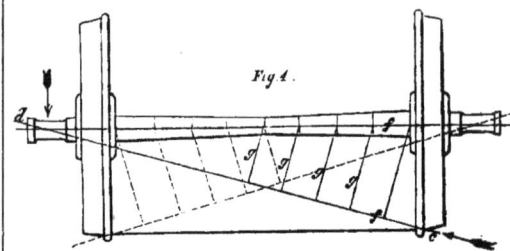

Fig. 4.

indicated by a line *c d* fig. 4, drawn from the circumference of the wheel on one side to the centre of the journal on the other side ; and if the line *f f* was drawn perpendicular to this, from the axle close to the wheel, it would represent the greatest effective leverage, tending to break or strain the axle at that point ; and the strain upon any other point of the axle might be found by drawing lines *g g* parallel to this, in fact the cube roots of these lines would give the diameter of the axle at the points where they fall.

He had remarked that some of the early axles were parallel throughout, but an alteration had been introduced, and they now found the least weight of metal in the centre. Notwithstanding this he believed the principle was not carried out sufficiently far, since he had never seen a single case of a fracture in the centre of an axle, whilst he had seen a great many broken close to the wheel or near it. This, in his opinion, was sufficient proof that they were not carrying out the principle of taper axles so far as mechanical science and experience suggested.

Mr. T. Thorneycroft suggested, that the further consideration of the question should be adjourned, and offered before the next meeting, to try further experiments and lay the results before the members. He would take a long axle, cut it into two parts, each the same weight, and reduce one in the middle, and keep the other parallel all the way along, taking care that the same weight or metal should exist between the props in each case. He invited members to attend and inspect the experiments whilst they were going forward.

Mr. G. B. Thorneycroft remarked, it was at the point where the strain took place that the axle broke, and experience showed that by bending iron frequently backwards and forwards it may be rendered crystalline.

The Chairman observed, that a considerable degree of light had been thrown upon the subject by the discussion. In the conducting of any experiments on axles, it was necessary that they should be subjected to natural blows or forces, as similar as possible to those that they are subjected to in practice, because the point which they wanted to ascertain was the positive result in actual working. It had been well observed that the wheel was the anvil or hammer from which the axle received its blow ; but, in addition to this, there was a jarring force, as well as a bending force, all tending to break it. The experiments that he had previously made had been conducted on that principle, and the force had been applied to the wheels, which was requisite in order to obtain true results. As the subject was one of vital importance to railway interests, and materially affected the question of safety in travelling, he thought too much attention could not be bestowed upon it ; and the discussion had better be adjourned to a future meeting.

A paper was then read by Mr. W. Buckle, of Soho, "On the Inventions and Life of William Murdoch," which we must postpone for a future number.

INSTITUTION OF CIVIL ENGINEERS.
NOVEMBER 12, 1850.

William Cubitt, Esq., President, in the Chair.

The proceedings of the evening commenced with the announcement of the dates of the ordinary meetings of the Session; the appointment of December 17th, for the Annual General Meeting for the election of the President, Council, and Officers; and of the 27th May, 1851, for the President's Conversazione.

The paper read was, "A Comparative View of the Recorded Explosions in Coal Mines," by Mr. William West, of Leeds, Assoc. Inst. C.E The reports of Faraday, Lyell, De la Beche, Playfair, and others, were carefully analyzed and tabulated, from which it appeared, that tendencies towards a dangerous condition existed in mines reputed to be comparatively safe, and that these tendencies were so numerous, and varied so suddenly in their nature and extent, as to necessitate attention to every kind of precaution.

The proposed appointment, by the Government, of Inspectors of Mines, was noticed, not with the intention of showing that their supervision would diminish the responsibility of the mining engineers and overmen, but of demonstrating that by establishing more constant communication between the various districts, they might induce the general adoption of those measures of precaution which were found in certain mines to be so efficacious in averting accidents, or in affording means of safety when they did occur.

The different depths of mines, varying from seventy-five yards at Darley, to three hundred yards at Haswell, did not appear to have any influence on the accidents. The tendency to the emission of carburetted hydrogen gas from certain seams, would have appeared a more rational reason, though the records did not appear to bear out that theory, as mines receiving a tolerable character, had been the scene of repeated explosions; for instance, the Jarrow mine, where, although reported "to be not very fiery," there had been six explosions in the course of 28 years, and 140 persons had been killed.

The compatability of general good ventilation with the occasional occurrence of the most fatal explosions, was particularly dwelt on. The witnesses on the inquests after the Haswell and the Jarrow accidents agreed that the "ventilation was perfect," "the pit full of air," and "the air quite good, and plenty of it." The fault, then, did not lie in the quantity of air, but rather in the difficulty of directing it so generally throughout all parts of the mine, as to sweep away the gas as it was produced. The "splits" for the air were noticed, and the condition of the goaf, the pockets of gas formed in the roof, and the sudden irruptions from the occasional falls in the goaf and old stalls, were dwelt on at great length, and, combined with the injudicious use of unprotected lights, and the liability of accident to the lamps, were shown to have been the probable cause of all the explosions. The miners' lamps were passed over somewhat too cursorily, as at the present moment, when so much has been done for their improvement, that part of the subject might have been descanted on with advantage.

The precautions for saving life on the occurrence of accidents, such as abolishing bratticed shafts, and sinking a pair at each mine, at such distances apart as should insure one remaining intact, in case of an explosion injuring the other; the "soaling off" of a portion of the fresh air for the exhausting furnace, and conducting the return air into the upcast shaft at some height above the fire; together with several minor details for insuring the constant working of the exhausting apparatus,

to draw off the fatal "after-damp, or choke-damp," were strongly insisted on.

The rashness and carelessness of the miners was instanced with regret; but it was shown that by education and good example, their better qualities must be brought out, and that then, the best safeguard against accident would be the instinctive love of life, and a knowledge of impending danger from the infringement of any of the precautionary regulations established in the mines. The improvement of the workmen was, therefore, strongly insisted on, as more real benefit would probably result from such measures, than from the appointment of a host of government inspectors.

Nov. 19, 1850.

The subject of the paper read was "The Ventilation of Collieries, theoretically and practically considered," by Mr. William Price Struvé (of Swansea), M. Inst. C. E.

The author commenced by showing that the general principles which ought to govern the ventilation of collieries were:

1st. That a current of air through the channels of collieries, at a velocity of five feet per second, was sufficient for most purposes.

2nd. That a current exceeding that velocity would only be attained at the expense of leakage and other evils.

3rd. That in order to obtain the requisite supply of fresh air, the channels of a colliery or mine ought to be enlarged, according to the exigency.

In the process of laying out a mine, a subdivision occurred by which the workings were apportioned into numerous compartments, which facilitated the system of splitting the current of air, or diverting it into numerous channels, giving to each compartment a separate and therefore, more effective ventilating force; at the same time the area of the channel was enlarged, and the aggregate length of the air tube shortened, so that it was quite practicable to pass through the workings of a mine, three hundred cubic feet of air per minute for each man employed.

The velocity of the air current in a mine was so easily affected, that it was important to consider by what accidents, and under what circumstances, any changes took place.

It could not be supposed that the excavated space of old workings was completely filled by the 'falls' of the roof and 'creeps' of the floor; extensive rupture of the stratification occurred, and through this broken ground great leakage must take place. This would seriously affect a long continuous air course, therefore the way to meet this difficulty was to split, shorten, and enlarge the air channel. The details of two experiments at the Eaglesbush and Ynis's David collieries, where the air was pumped out by Mr. Struvé's mine ventilator, showed that a large proportion of the air was drawn from the old workings, and the 'goaf,' or broken ground surrounding the colliery, and did not come down the intake shaft, and traverse the actual workings, as it ought to have done.

In both these cases the enlarging and splitting of the air channels, so as to reduce the velocity of the air to about three feet or four feet per second, would have produced most beneficial results.

These principles were shown to have been lost sight of in the majority even of the great collieries, and the power of rarefaction by a furnace, was trusted to for dragging the long column of air over and through innumerable impediments. In some cases this was left to be produced by the increased temperature of the mine, from the candles, and the respiration of the men, aided by the cooling effect of water trickling down the intake shaft. These scarcely sufficed to produce an average difference between the two shafts of thirteen degrees in winter, whilst in the summer, and in certain states of the atmosphere there was no difference at all, and, consequently, little or no ventilation. Where rarefaction by heat was used, the temperature in the upcast shaft varied from ninety degrees to one hundred and sixty degrees ; this, however advantageous for ventilation, was injurious to the shaft itself, and absolutely dangerous to the men who had to traverse it.

A comparison of the dimensions of the air passages and the velocities of the currents in numerous collieries, led to an estimate of the motive power required to produce the results attained in the best ventilated mines, in case of the employment of a steam engine and air pumps. This power would have varied between 23 horse power and 26 horse power.

The efficiency of furnace ventilation was always increased by the depth of the shafts, especially if they were entirely devoted for the purposes of ventilation, irrespective of the working of the pit.

The experiments of Mr. Nicholas Wood, Mr. G. Elliot, Mr. H. Vivian, and other mining engineers, were then quoted, to demonstrate the insufficiency of the "steam jet," as a means of promoting ventilation, showing that it was a most wasteful application of power, when compared with the steam force employed to work Struvé's mine ventilator at the Eaglesbush colliery. This apparatus consisted of two hollow pistons, resembling large gasometers, plunging into cisterns of water, and having inlet and outlet valves. The pistons received alternate motion from a small steam engine of 5 horse power; and being filled and emptied at each revolution of the crank, produced a regularity of current and a degree of copious ventilation hitherto unknown in the mines to which they had been applied. The small cost of their establishment—only about one hundred pounds for an extensive mine—joined with the little liability to getting out of order, was much in their favour.

The paper terminated with copious extracts from the able mining reports of Mr. John Phillips and Mr. Kenyon Blackwell, confirming all the positions assumed by the author.

[The apparatus described above seems to resemble very closely the gas exhauster constructed by Messrs. Blyth, of London, for the Commercial Gas Company, described in the *Artizan* for November, 1848.—ED. ART.]

ROYAL CORNWALL POLYTECHNIC SOCIETY.
(Continued from p. 203.)

CAST-IRON MAGNETS.

Mr. R. W. Fox read and commented on an essay by Mr. Hearder, of Plymouth, on the application of cast-iron as a substitute for steel in the construction of very powerful permanent magnets. The magneto-electric machine—that is to say, the machine which develops electricity by the inductive action of permanent magnets upon masses of soft iron, is, of course, limited in its power by the degree of magnetic intensity existing in the inducing magnet ; and as the difficulty as well as the expense of constructing permanent steel magnets, increase in a very much higher ratio than the relative amount of power obtained, it becomes extremely desirable to obtain this power at a cheaper rate. Mr. Hearder, in the course of his experience in the working of cast-iron, had observed a vast number of apparently trifling circumstances which influenced very materially the mechanical properties and molecular arrangement of the iron employed. And, as certain peculiarities in the character of steel are found to modify considerably its susceptibility to magnetic action, and as certain conditions which were found unfavourable to magnetic developement in straight bars, were indispensably necessary for it when curved or horse-shoe bars were used, it was presumed that although cast-iron might not be adapted for *straight* magnets, yet the very conditions on which its unsuitability depended, might be just those which would adapt it for the construction of *horse-shoe* magnets. Acting on this idea, Mr. Hearder had a pattern made from which 24 horse-shoe bars were cast, from good pig-iron in green sand. A hole was drilled near each pole, and one in the bend of every magnet, through which three screwed wires were passed, which, by

means of tightening nuts bound the whole into one *fasciculus*, 4½ inches thick. No attempt was made to make the poles flat, beyond simply holding the magnet upon the face of an ordinary grindstone, to take off the edging produced by the flasks. A soft iron keeper was made, 4½ inches by 3 inches, and one inch thick. The bars were then severally magnetized, by bringing them in contact with the poles of a powerful electro-magnet ; their magnetism, when compared with steel of equal size, and their power of retaining it also was apparently feeble ; the strongest would not lift more than 4 to 5 lbs., whilst the weakest were as low as 2 lbs. As they were magnetized and severally placed in the bundle, the keeper was kept in contact with the poles ; and, after they were all screwed up, the magnet, weighing 72 lbs., was readily lifted by the keeper, and required an addition of more than 30 lbs. to break. The faces of the poles were in a very unfavourable state to allow of the adhesion of the keeper, as they had never been flattened ; but, nevertheless, the power here developed was, contrary to general experience, greater than the sum of its elements. After repeated separations of the keeper from the magnet, the attractive force was still upwards of 80 lbs., and at the end of 12 months the power was still as much as 50 lbs. Its power of magnetizing bars was very considerable, as well as its inductive power through soft iron. The hardness of the metal rendering it impossible, without great expense and labour, to grind the faces of the poles true, and economy being the main object in their construction, Mr. Hearder was desirous of trying the effect of soft-iron false poles. The readiest way of trying this experiment which suggested itself, was the use of short soft-iron straps, which might be applied to the sides and inserted between parts of the magnet, so as to serve at the same time to bind on the false poles, and transmit to them any attractive power obtained from the parts of the magnet with which the straps were in contact. Upon magnetising the bars and mounting them with the soft-iron poles, it now required upwards of 250 lbs. to separate the keeper the first time, and subsequently 150 ; and after having been magnetized 4 years, during nearly 6 months of which the keeper was off, it still retained a power of 80 lbs. This arrangement of soft-iron poles is, strange to say, not accompanied by the same results when applied to *steel* magnets ; for, although very great care was taken in mounting in this way an extremely powerful steel magnet, which would lift 250 lbs., yet its power sustained a loss when the poles were attached, showing a remarkable difference between the properties of cast-iron and steel in this respect.—Mr. Hearder proceeds to say that he believes he has fully accomplished the object he had in view, viz., to introduce a material for the construction of permanent magnets of great power, which combine cheapness with efficiency, and at the same time simplicity of construction. He had purposely delayed bringing the invention formally before the public until now, in order that he might have the experience of the fairest test of magnetic permanency, viz., time, before he would take upon himself to recommend its adoption. He believes that it offers advantages which are not to be despised. The peculiar adaptation of the soft-iron poles, which can be made of any shape, to suit the requirements of circumstances, fits them admirably for all purposes where rotating armatures are required, since the soft-iron poles may be made to suit the sweep of the rotation body. In the magnetizing of bars, &c., the soft-iron poles appear to facilitate considerably the communication of magnetic power. The expense of a steel magnet to lift 150 lbs. would be about 10*l*. ; whereas a cast-iron one of equal power may be made for 30*s*. or 40*s*. Since the cast-iron magnet of 72 lbs. lifts 150 by a rough experiment, and a steel magnet of the same weight is not expected to lift much more than 170, it follows that cast-iron is not far inferior in its magnetic properties to steel, whilst it is vastly superior in convenience of manufacture, leaving the great point of economy out of the question.—Mr. Hearder proceeded to detail a few remarkable facts connected with the magnetic conditions and arrangements which had taken place in these bars by their mutual influence upon each other. When first these bars were magnetized, their individual powers were noted, and when after 12 months they were dismounted, they were again separately tested, and a most extraordinary series of results was obtained. One magnet alone would lift its own weight; another lifted 2 lbs.; and none of the rest lifted as much as 1 lb. The sum of their individual powers amounted to only 13 lbs., whilst in the mass they lifted more than 50 lbs. But the most remarkable peculiarity was the fact that the two outer magnets, numbers 1 and 24, had their poles reversed, with the trifling power of a few ounces; numbers 2 and 23 being the next two, were perfectly neutral; numbers 3 and 22 maintained their original polarity, with a trifling force of 2 or 3 ounces; and each successive pair similarly taken off, manifested, with some few exceptions, greater power as they approached the centre. One or two of the middle ones were, however, weak. Upon comparing their present power with that formerly denoted by the marks upon them, very little relation could be observed between their original and present intensities, but there appeared to be a much more intimate relation between their observed conditions and their respective situations in the magnet. With this impression, when they were re-magnetized, and fitted with the soft-iron poles, their arrangement was altered; those which had before been in the centre were placed outside and were marked afresh to denote their powers when they last came out of the magnet; and after a lapse of 4 years, when the magnet was again dismounted, precisely the same results were obtained as before. The whole amount of their individual lifting powers when added together was barely 11 lbs.; whilst in the bundle their lifting power was 80.

In addition to the cast-iron magnet, which formed the subject of this paper, Mr. Hearder sent for exhibition a permanent steel magnet, which, he believed, was the most powerful in relation to its weight, that had ever been constructed. It consisted of 100 thin horse-shoe plates of steel. The entire weight is about 39 lbs. When first magnetized, with the keeper attached, the force required to separate it was upwards of 450 lbs.; and subsequently it remained stationary at 240 lbs., which weight it has repeatedly sustained. Although it has been magnetized 3 years, it still lifts more than 150, under all the unfavourable circumstances of unequal surface, when the keeper is applied. In this magnet, the author believes he has just doubled the power hitherto obtained, and he believes, for the first time, the price of permanent magnets may now be rated at per cwt. of lifting power.

NOTES BY A PRACTICAL CHEMIST.

INFLUENCE OF LIGHT ON THE CHEMICAL ACTION OF OXYGEN.—At the recent meeting of the Swiss Association for the Advancement of Science Professor Schönbein read a paper on the Influence of Light upon the Affinities of Oxygen. He finds that oxygen, either pure or as found in the air, combines with sulphuret of lead under the influence of the solar rays, converting it into the white sulphate. In the dark, all other circumstances remaining the same, there was no perceptible action. In a strong summer sunshine the change took place in 15 minutes. Hence paper coated with the sulphuret of lead may be used for photographic purposes. It is not, however, sensitive enough for the camera. The sulphurets of arsenic and antimony are less easily affected. He shows likewise that the affinity of oxygen for some other substances is much increased by solar action, independent of heat. Thus he has, by the same means, transformed common oxide of lead into a compound of the protoxide and peroxide. To this existing power he refers various instances of slow oxidation in the open air, especially common bleaching. He further supposes that the electricity of the clouds has a voltaic origin, arising from the electromotive action of oxygen, under the influence of light, upon the water contained in the atmosphere.

ON A METHOD OF FIXING COLOURS UPON TISSUES.—When an egg is boiled in a colour bath the colour immediately fixes itself to the shell. Egg-shells contain, like bones, an organic tissue and mineral salts. If it is attempted to dye these mineral salts, the phosphate or carbonate of lime, separately, it fails, and therefore neither of these salts can be the mordant. If, on the other hand, we attempt to colour the organic tissue of egg-shells, or of bones, this immediately becomes dyed; hence it follows that the organic matter of the bones and egg-shells is the mordant. Now in the same manner as mineral mordants have hitherto been employed to fix colouring matters upon cotton, organic mordants may be used, and Broquette has already employed caseine for this purpose. The coating of vegetable fibres with animal matter was first carried out by Hausmann, as observed by Barreswil, but is said never to have reached any importance. The caseine must of course be first dissolved, in order that the tissues may be penetrated by the solution, but it must then be rendered insoluble in the tissues. Now it has been shown by Braconnet that caseine forms a soluble compound with ammonia, which is again decomposed by boiling. Broquette therefore impregnates the goods with a solution of caseine in ammonia, then heats them to expel the ammonia, upon which the caseine remains in an insoluble state in the tissues. Cotton goods thus treated are saturated with animal matter, and may be now dyed in the same colour baths as those used for wollen tissues. Frequently the dyes are alcaline; they then dissolve the caseine instead of being fixed by it. But since Bachelier used a mixture of lime and caseine as a cement, it has been known that such a mixture hardens and becomes fixed. Broquette therefore employs the caseine sometimes with lime alone, sometimes with ammonia and lime together, and saturates the goods with this caseate of lime, which, in a warm atmosphere, soon sets, and then resists the alcalies and rinsing with alcaline liquids. By this treatment the cotton acquires a peculiar stiffness; so that although its capacity for dyes has become nearly equal to that of wool, it is far behind the latter in lustre. But this evil also can be remedied by mixing the mordant with oil. Oil, caseine, and lime form a mordant which fixes the colours with remarkable lustre. When the goods to be dyed consist of wool and cotton a different plan has to be followed; the mordant, in this case, is not adapted for the two materials; the wool is deprived of its natural lustre, and the cotton is not sufficiently penetrated. For such goods Broquette employs the mordant before the weaving; it is applied to cotton in the spinning, when it can afterwards be woven and bleached like wool, without the mordant receiving any injury. When threads thus prepared are woven, the tissues can be dyed just like woollen stuffs without further treatment. By means of the solution of caseate of lime, mineral colours which are insoluble in water can be adapted to the dying of stuffs; they are mixed with the solution in the state of very fine powder. These liquid colours, which can be prepared with ultramarine, ochre, etc., can again be removed with water, unless they have been dried; but as soon as they coagulate, they adhere firmly to the tissues inclosing the colouring principle. A farther application of this mordant of caseine, oil, and lime is in the printing of stuffs; in this case we are not limited merely to mineral colours, which by its aid may be fixed upon the goods, but the numerous vegetable colours may likewise be very well applied, by first converting them into lakes by means of alumina or protoxide of tin, and then using these lakes in the same manner as the powdered mineral colours. After being printed the goods are wrapped in moist linen, and left for about half an hour in the moist vapour in a warm atmosphere. During this time the impressed colour does not dry superficially, but is absorbed into the interior of the fibres, and is then completely fixed in a subsequent drying.

This new method of mordanting has already had considerable influence upon several pigments, such as archil, which has only been used for dying exceptionally. By Broquette's process some very beautiful colours are obtained from it, modifications of the peculiar colour of the archil by lime. It will be evident that in this process of dying it is requisite to pass the goods through a lime bath, which will not do for many dyes, as the colours have their tints altered by such treatment. In such cases magnesia is to be substituted for lime. When goods are printed with the mineral colours or lakes according to the above process very full colours are obtained, which in the case of many patterns is not desirable. To bring out the shades and half colours in the full coloured impressions the printed goods are placed with the coloured surface upon an absorbing ground, and the forms pressed on the back. The printed portion pressed upon the absorbing surface is deprived of some of its colour, and numerous patterns can be produced in this manner.

New Compound of Resin and Lard.—Professor Olmsted read a paper before the American Association for the Advancement of Science, on a new and important compound of resin and lard. It is best made by adding one part of resin, in fine powder, to three parts of lard, and stirring the mass well, without the application of heat. The compound is more easily fusible than lard, running freely at 72°. The addition of resin prevents, in the lard, its tendency to spontaneous decomposition or rancidity. Hence it is valuable for lubricating articles of brass and copper, such as the barrels of air-pumps, stop-cocks, &c. It may be used, either with or without the addition of black lead, to protect stoves, grates, and iron piping from rust. The new compound forms also an excellent waterproof paste for leather, which does not rub off, and admits of the subsequent application of blacking.

The addition of a small quantity of resin to lamp-oils, greatly increases their illuminating power, and renders them less liable to coagulate.

Tenacity of Metals.—M. Baudrimont has obtained the following results:—1. That the tenacity of metals varies with their temperature. 2. That with some exceptions it generally decreases as the temperature rises. 3. That in the case of silver, the tenacity decreases more rapidly than the temperature. 4. That the tenacity of gold, platinum, palladium, and copper diminishes less rapidly than the temperature. 5. That the case of iron is very peculiar: at 212° its tenacity is not so great as at 32°; at 392° its tenacity is greater than at 32°.

Distribution of Iodine.—The *Comptes Rendus* for August 26th contains a paper by M. Chatin, on the presence of iodine in waters, rocks, and organic substances. The following are some of his conclusions: Iodine appears in coal, in anthracite (in a smaller proportion), turf, and graphite. Fresh-water animals contain more iodine than the plants grown in the same water. Iodine is found in variable proportions in all fresh water, probably as iodide of iron. Its amount increases with the ferruginous nature of the soil drained. River water contains more iodine than that of springs. Commercial potassa contains iodine, but nitrate of potassa, cream of tartar, tartar emetic, and double tartrate of soda and potassa contain none. Rock salt is almost entirely pure. Wines, cider, and perry contain more iodine than fresh water; milk more than wine; and asses' milk more than that of cows. An insufficient supply of iodine in food and drink leads to scrofula.

New Test for Nitrates.—Professor Schaeffer adds to the suspected solution one or two drops of ferrocyanide of potassium (not enough to tinge the liquid); a little acetic acid is then added, and in a short time the liquid assumes a strong yellow colour.

                                      S.

BUILDING FOR THE GREAT EXHIBITION.

So much has already been said in the public papers upon the all-engrossing subject, the Building for the Industrial Exhibition, that we must presume our readers are acquainted with the general features and facts in connection with it; our present object will, therefore, be to supply a few of the details of construction gained from a visit to the Works, and from the Drawings exhibited at a Meeting of the Society of Arts in the Adelphi, at which Mr. Paxton read to the Members a paper descriptive of his design, with its history as gradually developed in his own mind, after the many years' experience he has had in the erection of buildings of a similar nature, though on a very minute scale as compared with this giant superstructure: this fact, that the design of the construction is the result of years of study and experience,—and not, as is imagined by those who hear Mr. Paxton's name mentioned for the first time, some sudden flight of theoretical genius,—must tend greatly to satisfy the public mind upon the question of its stability; a question, which the extremely light appearance of its construction, when compared with its vast extent, is liable to suggest to all of us. Neither is the public eye accustomed to large glass structures; and we have, therefore, no recognized standard of strength with which to compare the Exhibition building. Doubtless, the novelty of the construction raises the anxiety of those unable to estimate for themselves by calculation its strength; and as we think there must be few who do not feel great interest, the national credit being staked upon the satisfactory completion, ultimate stability, and suitable adaptation of the present structure, all information should be afforded to satisfy the public mind, and dispel their fears.

The first remarkable character that is observed in examining the building is the uniformity existing through all the parts of the construction, so that the whole is made to consist of a repetition of the same detail over and over again. If we examine a plan, we shall observe a centre aisle, 72 feet in width, extending the whole length of the building; on either side occur aisles 24 feet wide, then next 48 feet, next again 24 feet, then 48 feet, and outside of all 24 feet: total width being 408 feet. The pillars supporting the roofs over the several aisles are all exactly similar; they are surmounted by girders, over the 24 and 48 feet spans, 3 feet in depth; the additional strength for the wider span being obtained by the girders being of wrought iron, while the other is of cast metal. We subjoin a sketch of the cast girder, showing the method of attachment to the pillar. The 72-feet girder is of wrought iron, 9 feet 6 inches in depth, divided by Queen-posts, and double diagonal trussing, or lattice-work; this has a camber of 9½ inches.

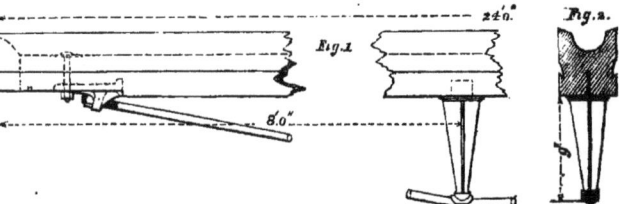

Figs. 1 and 2 are the elevation and section of the Paxton trussed girder, forming also a gutter for carrying off the water: it consists of a wooden beam cut by machinery to the form shown in the section; it is trussed beneath by a ⅞ rod, attached to cast-iron shoes, fastened on the ends of the beam, as shown in Fig. 1. There are two cast-iron stretchers, and by means of a nut on the end of the straining rod the beam is bent to a camber of about 2 inches, so that when the girder is

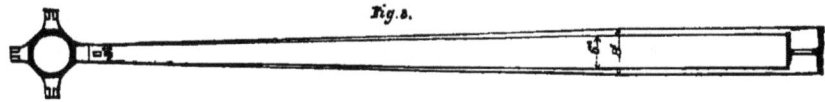

Fig. 3.

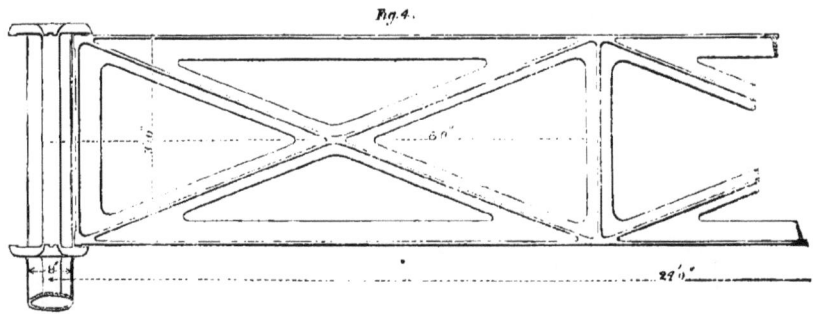

Fig. 4.

laid horizontally the gutter has a fall each way from the centre. In the section of the beam is shown, on either side a small gutter, the purpose of which is to catch the moisture that condenses on the under side of the glass, and carry it off with the other water, just as is done in the hatchways over marine engines. The ends of these girders rest upon troughs laid along the top of the transverse girders: these troughs convey the water to the columns, down which it falls, and is carried off by pipes laid below the flooring. This arrangement prevents any liability of the roof being flooded, as the extreme distance that any portion of water has to be conveyed by the troughs is 24 feet; and to each superficial area of 24 feet square the column forms a pipe to carry off the water.

The Paxton girders are placed 8 feet apart, so that each cast-iron girder supports two of them, and the wrought-iron girder four.

In the accompanying sketch of the cast-iron girders, Fig. 3 is a plan and Fig. 4 an elevation: the top of the column is given for the purpose of showing the mode of attaching the girders. To all the columns, except those at the very outside, 4 ends of girders have to be attached, for which 4 upper and 4 under lugs are cast on the top of the column. These lugs have projections on their interior surfaces, between which and corresponding projections on the upper and under surfaces of the beam, there is space sufficient for a key, and by it the girder is made a fixture to the column in direction of its length. In order to fix it transversely there is a projection and recess on the under side on the girder and lug, and a key is driven in on the upper side, longitudinal recesses being made to receive it in the lug and girder. In fixing the girder it is lifted to the height of the lugs, then slid into its position sideways, and the keys driven into their places.

The wrought-iron girders are on the trussed principle, and, for the sake of uniformity, of the same depth as the cast-iron ones. The upper web consists of two pieces of light angle iron, about 5 × 3 inches; the lower web of two pieces of flat iron ¼ thick and 5 inches deep. The vertical stretching pieces occur every 8 feet, and are of double T iron; and diagonal straining pieces, 5 inches by ¼, are fixed in the 8 feet spaces, and rivetted between the two angle irons of the upper web and the flat bars of the lower web.

The ridge and furrow form of the covering is the great novel feature in the building, and Mr. Paxton has devoted much attention and trouble to bring it to its present complete style. The span (or width between the Paxton girders) is 8 feet, and the pitch such as to make the inclination of the glass 2½ to 1. The panes of glass are 49 × 10; so that

between the top of the ridge and bottom of the furrow is one piece of glass, and thereby all unsightly joints are dispensed with. The glass weighs 16 oz. per foot, and it was not without great trouble that the sheet glass was made of such dimensions as to cut to 49 inches in length; and great credit is due to the spirited manufacturers, Messrs. Chance, of Birmingham, for effecting such an improvement as to produce this large size. A join between the ridge and furrow would have involved the necessity of giving a much steeper inclination to the glass to prevent the wind blowing any wet between the joints. It would also have been an insuperable objection that the condensed moisture on the inside would be liable to drop from these joints on objects exhibited.

For the foundation on which the whole building rests, a hole is sunk in the ground under each column, three feet deep, and about the same across each way: this is filled with concrete to within six inches of the surface; the end of the column has a foot cast on it 18 inches long by 12 broad: this rests on the surface of the concrete, and it is considered unnecessary to have anything to prevent the column being shifted on its base horizontally, the weight upon it being sufficient to prevent such an accident.

(To be continued.)

ANALYSIS OF BOOKS.

Chapel and School Architecture. London: Hamilton, Adams, & Co.
(Second Notice.)

THE author, in confirmation of his remarks on the suitability and economy of the Gothic style of architecture, notices several examples in the metropolis as well as in the provinces, which have been built in accordance with the general principles adopted by the model committee. Amongst these we may mention, in London, Poplar chapel, which we some time since minutely inspected, rather puzzled at the time, we must confess, to account for the taste displayed in its design. Portwood chapel, near Stockport, is also a good example, being one built after the model design, for which a premium of fifty guineas was awarded to James Wilson, Esq., architect, of Bath, by the committee. Of the Islington chapel, we will quote the particulars, which may be useful as a guide to our professional readers.

"The chapel is erected on the angle of ground at the Islington end of the Liverpool-road, and has, underneath, on the basement floor, a morning-chapel, which accommodates upwards of five hundred persons, and seven vestries. The whole of the ground floor of the chapel itself is fitted up with pews and free-seats, side-aisles, and communion,

37

which, together with the side and end galleries, will accommodate fifteen hundred persons. The chapel measures 90 feet long by 54 feet wide, the height from the floor to the apex of the roof is 50 feet, and the height from the outside ground-line to the top of the turret on the front gable is 76 feet. The design is in the decorated style of Gothic architecture, or coeval with the buildings of the fourteenth century. The centre of the west front is occupied by a deeply-recessed and richly-moulded doorway, beneath a large and handsome window; filled, in its upper compartments, with flowing tracery: square massive buttresses divide the centre from the wings of this elevation, which contain a centre window, and are flanked by double angle buttresses. In the sides of the chapel are five handsomely enriched windows (each varying in design,) occupying spaces of equal width between buttresses. A clerestory has the same number of windows, the walls of which, with those of the side aisles, are surmounted with an enriched parapet, pierced with trefoils and quatrefoils. The clerestory is supported by arches, springing from octangular columns, with foliated capitals, over which are inserted moulded and carved corbels, from whence spring the carved ribs of the roof, with carved spandrils, supporting the principal rafters. The timbers of the roof are moulded on the under side, and stained in imitation of oak. At the south-east angle of the building, an octangular turret is attached, the lower portion of which serves as a staircase to the side gallery, and the other part is occupied by flues, which carry off the vitiated air from all parts of the building;—the warm air being supplied from the circulation of hot water in pipes, laid in the basement, and conveyed, by a warm air culvert, to the open space under the pew floors. Openings are made in the upright face of the steps to the pews, and covered with gauze wire, which allows the warm air to disseminate itself uniformly throughout the building. An entrance for cold air communicates with the apparatus in the basement, so that, in summer, it may be admitted through the same channels as the warm. Openings are left in the inner soffit of the roof, to give the vitiated air access to the space between it and the slate surface, which space is in immediate connection with the ventilating tower. This tower contains a fire-place, which will be put in use when the peculiar state of the atmosphere needs its assistance, to cause the required current of air for perfect ventilation. The walls of the chapel are built of Kentish rag-stone, and the ashlar and carvings are executed in Bath stone. Its entire cost was about £6000; and it was erected, from the design, and under the superintendence, of Mr. James Wilson."

Into Mr. Jobson's arguments on the moral training to be supplied in public schools, we need not here enter. It will suffice if we express our hearty concurrence in his remarks on the necessity of due provision being also made for the *physical* training of the rising generation. There is a vast field for improvement in this respect. A flower garden and swings are very well, but a carpenter's shop would not be out of place. The object is not to make all boys carpenters, but to save those whose talent is mechanical from being tied behind the counter or desk all their lives. Franklin, in his autobiography, speaks strongly of the advantages he obtained from a knowledge of mechanical operations which his father encouraged him in observing, in order to discover the natural bent of his inclination. But to return; plans are given for schools of various designs, from the small village school to the complete educational establishment, where, as in the normal training schools at Westminster, provision is made for the education and residence of juniors and seniors of both sexes; suggestions are offered to be observed in choosing a site, and the benefits to be ultimately obtained by care in the selection, and in obtaining, if possible, additional space, to provide against future enlargement, are explained. Forms are given for the deeds necessary to secure the safe and permanent settlement of property so acquired. The false economy in attempting to dispense with the services of a duly qualified architect, is exposed, as it deserves, and the author's statements need no corroboration.

" An architect, who understands his profession, knows how to dispose of the materials in building so as to save more than the cost of his commission." "If the principle of competition among architects be adopted, and the gentleman supplying the most approved design is to be employed, then it is much better to select three or four professional men, who are known to be fully competent for the undertaking as

competitors, than to invite, by public advertisement, all the architects to send in designs who may choose to do so. In the latter case, besides the confusion and bewilderment of the trustees, through the large number of designs presented to them for comparison, and from which they will find it extremely difficult to select, with unanimity, the one most suited to their requirements; they will not, by open and indiscriminate competition, be likely to obtain the best designs; for architects of the greatest ability and experience, having full employment, will not enter into such competition with a number of speculative and unemployed persons."

The competition system is attended with such manifest evils that we can only express our surprise that architects, as a body, have not set their faces against it; but so long as there are to be found professional men who are content to take the hundredth part of a chance of getting a £20 or £30 premium, so long will trustees and building committees play their fantastic tricks.

"The instructions to architects should all be in writing, and should be given by only *one* of the trustees, appointed to do so, so that the architects may have equal advantage; and that none of them may be misled by verbal communications from an individual trustee."

. " The builders allowed to estimate for the work should *all* be such as have the confidence of the trustees, so that the lowest offer may be safely accepted. On this account, it is better to make a selection of builders, from whom estimates shall be obtained, than to throw open the work to all builders who may choose to tender estimates for it. By this precaution the dissatisfaction may be avoided, which usually arises, when, for want of confidence, the lowest offer is not accepted by the trustees."

A form of contract for the builder is given, and general instructions on the particulars which ought to be supplied to the architects.

From our extracts our readers will judge with us that Mr. Jobson's work is of a practical and useful character, and none the less acceptable for the earnestness of its tone.

PROSPECTS OF ATLANTIC STEAM NAVIGATION.

The rapid passages of the new American Atlantic steamers have attracted some attention to their boilers, which are constructed with vertical water tubes behind the furnaces. In a late number of the *Journal of the Franklin Institute*, is a paper showing the progress made with the principle since 1825, when Joseph Eve patented an arrangement of vertical tubes connected with receivers at top and bottom. In 1828, Paul Steenstrup patented a boiler, in section somewhat like a waggon back, with a fire-flue, flat at top and bottom, and supported by vertical tubes. Four tubes were in the furnace, so as to heat them more highly than the rest, and so determine an upward current through them. This boiler, with more tube surface, would make a boiler equal to the present ones in use, with the exception that its shape is weak. Dr. Nott, of New York, designed, in 1830, a boiler consisting of a number of vertical tubes, with a semi-cylindrical chamber at each end. This was obviously bad, on account of no provision being made to obtain a due circulation of water through the tubes, which is indispensable to prevent their being burnt out. In 1835, Thomas Holloway, of Philadelphia, constructed a boiler which has answered well, and is now in use. Over two ordinary rectangular furnaces are placed two rectangular flues, which return the flame to the front of the boiler, where the two combine in one smoke-box, and the draft is finally carried through horizontal fire tubes to the back smoke-box, over which is the chimney. In the furnaces are horizontal water tubes, connecting the side water spaces, with one vertical junction tube in each, to the top of the furnace. The upper flues are also supplied with vertical water tubes, which also, we presume, act as props or stays. The great objection to this arrangement (which combines both the water and fire tube systems), seems to be the difficulty that would be felt in getting at the water tubes to clean or repair them, as they all terminate in narrow water spaces. This would be fatal to a sea-going boiler, but on the Delaware it is said to have answered.

Returning to English progress, we find that in 1841, a patent was granted to John Hall for a boiler composed of vertical water tubes, but having the peculiarity of being made in three distinct pieces, so as to be easily taken apart, with the idea apparently of facilitating repairs. In 1843, the Earl of Dundonald patented an arrangement, which consists of a furnace with vertical tubes set behind it. The novelty consists in carrying the flame from the furnace up to the *top of the tubes:* after diffusing itself among them it escapes at the bottom, the object being to heat the tops the most, and so create a current through them. A steam blast pipe is provided to blow out the ashes from among the tubes, and a small flue direct from the upper part of the tube space to the chimney, by opening which the draft would be increased and steam be got up more quickly. In 1845, J. Montgomery, of Tennessee, patented a form of boiler, an engraving of one of which will be found in the June number, p. 141, together with an account of its explosion, arising from a want of stays and over pressure. These boilers have, it would appear, been adopted in various cases in the United States with good results, and when the steamers *Atlantic* and *Pacific* were begun by Mr. E. K. Collins, he caused a number of experiments to be made with these boilers working in salt water, the duration extending over the time necessary for a trip to Europe. Finding, as is stated, that the tubes kept free from scale, he determined to adopt the principle, and the form of Montgomery's boiler being objectionable from the necessity of returning the flue below the boiler, his engineer, Mr. J. Faron, junr., designed a set of boilers without the diaphragm in the tube space, being, in fact, Dundonald's boiler. The only difference, indeed, is that there are two tiers of furnaces, a plan not to be commended, if sufficient grate surface can in any other way be obtained. It will thus be seen that the form which has been arrived at is simply the old-fashioned flue boiler, with the flues filled with vertical water tubes connecting the top and bottom of the boiler. We know that this form of boiler was tried some years back at Hull, in steamers running between that port and Hamburgh. We believe that they were addicted to priming, and we will endeavour, before our next publication, to get some particulars of their employment and qualities.

If it be asked why this arrangement, which is said to answer so well in America, was not more generally adopted in this country, we may suggest that the introduction of the locomotive boiler turned the attention of all our engineers to its adaptation to marine purposes, and that the water-tube system had never had a fair trial on the Thames, where it was introduced by Mr. Spiller. His arrangement consisted of a water casing and fire-box, the space above the furnace being filled with nearly horizontal water tubes, a slight inclination being given to create a current through them.

The fault which we conceive attaches to the vertical tube boiler, both American and English, is that the tubes are too small in diameter in proportion to their length, and that they are parallel. An attempt, which appears to have been very successful, has been made by Messrs. Galloway, of Manchester, whose boilers are figured and described at p. 101 of the May number, and which fulfil these conditions. We may here mention that the credit of the large saving in fuel, and diminution of the smoke nuisance, stated in the daily papers to have been effected by an eminent firm in Manchester, is entirely due to the employment of these boilers, the report of which, from Messrs. Whitbread's brewery, entirely bears out the statement furnished to us by Mr. Armstrong, in our notice of those at the Gutta Percha Works, City Road.

Amongst those who have turned their attention to the vertical tube boiler, we must not omit to mention Mr. David Napier, whose arrangement will be found described at p. 67 of the *Artizan* Treatise on the Steam Engine. We may here reiterate our objection that the tubes are too small in diameter, and that their lower ends are inaccessible. Still these points seem not to prevent their partial adoption, as we notice from our Glasgow correspondent's report, that Messrs. Smith and Rodger have constructed several, and still persevere in their use.

Taking the *Franklin Journal*, then, alone as an authority, we should be justified in saying that the merit of the invention and introduction of water tube boilers must be claimed for England, whilst to America is due the credit of being the first to venture on a trial of them for a transatlantic voyage,—on a scale, the magnitude of which would have made a failure proportionately serious.

To judge from the statements of some of our contemporaries, the time has arrived when America is to bear off the palm of ocean steam navigation from this country; and the ground for this opinion seems to be that the West India Mail Company have decided upon having side lever engines and common flue boilers (?) for their large vessels of 800 horses power. Without entering at present into the question of what would have been, under the circumstances, the best form of engines for these boats (which we will take an early opportunity of discussing), we will only remind our readers that the present competition between the rival steamers resembles, in some measure, the trial of strength between the broad and narrow guage engine builders. When the narrow guage party boasted that they could show an engine on their guage, superior in heating surface to any on the broad, they were met with the fact, that although by straining every point they had breasted their rivals, the latter had still room for an extension which would put them as far in advance as they were at starting. And so with respect to the Atlantic steamers; if our builders were commissioned to turn out a fleet, unlimited as to first cost, and regardless of a dividend, we should fear no competition as to speed in a field which English engineers and ship-builders have made peculiarly their own. As it is, we have no objection to back the *Asia* and *Africa* against the *Atlantic* and *Pacific*, on the average of their service for the next two or three years.

PROGRESS OF SHIP-BUILDING AND STEAM NAVIGATION.

THE GLASGOW CASTLE ROYAL MAIL STEAM NAVIGATION COMPANY'S IRON STEAM VESSEL, "MERLIN."

Built and fitted by Messrs. Thomas Wingate & Co., White Inch, Glasgow. 1850.

Builder's measurement.	Ft.	In
Length of keel and fore rake ..	149	11
Breadth of beam	16	$7\frac{1}{2}$
ditto, over the paddle boxes	31	4
Depth of hold	8	3
Length of engine space	49	0
Tonnage.	Tons.	
Hull	$207\frac{45}{94}$	
Contents of engine space ..	$73\frac{4}{91}$	
Register	$134\frac{43}{94}$	

New Measurement.	Ft.	Tns.
Length on deck	150	8
Breadth on ditto, amidships ..	16	1
Depth of hold, ditto ..	8	0
Length of quarter-deck ..	14	5
Breadth of ditto	13	0
Depth of ditto	2	8
Length of engine space	49	0
Tonnage.	Tons.	
Hull	$153\frac{41}{100}$	
Quarter-deck	$5\frac{71}{100}$	
Total	$159\frac{12}{100}$	
Contents of engine space ..	$68\frac{40}{100}$	
Register	$90\frac{85}{100}$	

A pair of steeple engines, of 70 horse nominal power; diameter of cylinders, 34 inches × 3 feet length of stroke; feathering paddle wheels, (overhung,) diameter, 13 feet 1 inch; ten floats, 5 feet 2 inches × 2 feet 6 inches; condensers in iron bilges of hull, consisting of 319 composition tubes in each, diameter, $\frac{5}{8}$ of an inch × 10 fee —total 638 tubes; two auxiliary engines, one for feeding the boilers, the other for working the air-pump. Two vertical tubular boilers, the one before and the other abaft the engines, diameter 8 feet × 13 feet 10 inches high, containing 884 tubes (composition), 442 in each boiler, diameters (varying) from $1\frac{1}{8}$ to 2 inches × 6 feet long; four furnaces, two in each boiler; two funnels. The frames of hull are $2\frac{1}{2} \times 2\frac{1}{2} \times \frac{3}{8}$ inches, and

2 feet 9 inches apart; the bunkers hold 24 tons of coal, 7 tons 4 cwt. being the quantity taken on board for the station the vessel is plying upon, viz. Glasgow, Greenock, and Ardrishaig; distance from the latter, 50 miles; time, 3 hours and 10 minutes, average—the draft of water forward being 3 feet 9 inches and 4 feet aft; total distance 71 miles, or, going and returning, 142 miles; steam pressure, 20 lbs.; average revolutions per minute, 44; consumption of fuel, 12 cwt. of coals per hour. The crew are 20 in number, viz.—7 in the captain's department, 9 in the steward's, and 4 in the engine room.

DESCRIPTION.

A plain steamer, having no bowsprit, figure-head, or galleries; two masts, latteen rigged; common bow; square sterned and clinch-built vessel. Port of Glasgow. Commander,—Mr. Peter Turner.

THE CORK STEAM SHIP COMPANY'S NEW IRON SCREW VESSEL, "ALBATROSS."

Built and fitted by Messrs. Smith & Rodger, Glasgow.

Builder's measurement.	Ft.	In.
Length of keel and fore rake..	196	2
Breadth of beam (2 feet sponcing each side)	30	0
Depth of hold	16	0
Length of engine space ..	49	6
Tonnage.	Tons.	
Hull	$853\frac{8}{94}$	
Contents of engine space ..	$236\frac{19}{94}$	
Register	$616\frac{36}{94}$	
New measurement.	Ft.	Tns.
Length on deck	195	2
Breadth on ditto, amidships..	26	7
Depth of hold, ditto	15	8
Length of poop	24	7
Breadth of ditto	22	8
Depth of ditto	6	3
Length of engine space ..	49	5
Tonnage.	Tons.	
Hull	$607\frac{85}{100}$	
Poop	$38\frac{03}{100}$	
Total	$645\frac{88}{100}$	
Contents of engine space ..	$142\frac{70}{100}$	
Register	$503\frac{18}{100}$	

A pair of steeple engines (upon Mr. David Napier's four-piston-rod principle), of 124 horse nominal power, diamoter of cylinders, 45 inches × 3 feet length of stroke; one air-pump, diameter, 34 inches × 1 foot 6 inches stroke; diameter of screw-propeller, 10 feet 6 inches; pitch, 11 feet 6 inches (2 blades), worked by wheel and pinion. The engines are fitted with india-rubber valves, and Malcolmson's gridiron steam-slide valves. A pair of tubular boilers before the engines, length, 10 feet, breadth, 10 feet, height, 12 feet 6 inches, each having a cylindrical steam-chest, 4 feet diameter × 5 feet high; four cylindrical furnaces, two to each boiler, diameter, 4 feet × 6 feet long, area of fire-grate, 96 square feet; 154 malleable iron tubes, in each boiler, diameter, 3¼ inches × 7 feet 6 inches, with a dry smoke-box on the front of the boiler; steam pressure, 17 lbs.; consumption of fuel, 18 cwt. of coals per hour; average revolutions of engines 42 per minute, and 126 revolutions of the propeller. speed of vessel, 11½ to 12 knots per hour. Frames, 4 × 3 × ½ of an inch thick, spaced 1 foot 6 inches apart; 12 strakes of plates from keel to gunwale, tapering in thickness from ⅝ to ⅜ inch. Launched on the 8th of August; the draft of water forward being 4 feet 10 inches and 7 feet 2 inches aft—mean 6 feet; commenced to ply in September, between Dublin and Liverpool, 138 miles. This is a very fast vessel in proportion to power and tonnage; the hull was designed by Edward Pasco, Esq., of London.

DESCRIPTION.

A bird figure-head (albatross), sham quarter-badges, standing bowsprit, common bow, three masts (tall, with short top masts), schooner rigged, square sterned, and clinker built. Port of Cork. Commander,—Mr. Thomas Lyle.

THE DUMBARTON STEAM NAVIGATION COMPANY'S NEW IRON VESSEL, "QUEEN."

Built by Messrs. William Denny and Brothers, Wood-yards, Dumbarton. Engines, boilers, &c., by Messrs. Smith and Rodger, St. James's Foundry, Glasgow.

DIMENSIONS.

Builder's measurement.	Ft.	In.
Length of keel and fore rake ..	140	0
Breadth of beam	17	2
Ditto, including the paddle boxes	34	1¼
Depth of hold	7	8
Length of engine space ..	32	7
Tonnage.	Tons.	
Hull	$206\frac{19}{94}$	
Contents of engine space ..	$52\frac{5}{94}$	
Register	$154\frac{14}{94}$	
New measurement.	Ft.	Tns.
Length on deck	138	1
Breadth on ditto, amidships ..	16	7
Depth of hold, ditto ..	7	0
Length of engine space ..	32	6
Tonnage.	Tons.	
Hull	$131\frac{34}{100}$	
Contents of engine space ..	$41\frac{2}{100}$	
Register..	$90\frac{32}{100}$	

One steeple engine (upon Mr. David Napier's patent four-piston-rod principle) of 62 horse nominal power; diameter of cylinder, 44 inches × 3 feet 6 inches length of stroke; diameter of paddle wheels, extreme, 16 feet 2 inches and 15 feet 8 inches effective; 18 floats 6 feet 3 inches × 1 foot 2 inches, two sets of 9 arms; average revolutions per minute, 38; steam pressure, 25 lbs.; consumption of coals, 8 cwt. per hour; one vertical tubular boiler, diameter, 9 feet 8 inches × 13 feet 6 inches; steam chest, diameter, 3 feet 6 inches × 2 feet (2 feet above top of boiler); 344 tubes, diameters varying from 2¼ to 4 inches × 7 feet 6 inches; diameter of chimney, 3 feet; two furnaces. Six strakes of plates from keel to gunwale; frames 2¼ × 2¼ × ¼ inches, and 2 feet 6 inches apart. The Queen plies upon the station between Glasgow, Port Glasgow, Greenock, Gourock, Killcregan, Ardintenny, and Arochar (Loch-goil). Launched March 25, 1850.

DESCRIPTION.

A plain-built vessel, having neither bowsprit, figure-head, nor galleries, but having figures upon the top of rail on each side of bow; one mast, sloop-rigged, common bow, square-sterned and clinch built (Port of Dumbarton). Port of Glasgow. Commander,—Mr. John Wilson.

SHIP-BUILDING ON THE WEAR,

Concluded from p. 270.

(FROM OUR OWN REPORTERS.)

COXGREEN.

Messrs. Sykes, Talbot, and Sykes, have upon the stocks and in frame, a barque, to have a half-poop, and flush forward, to class 12 years, A 1.

	Ft.	In.
Length of keel and fore rake ..	110	0
Breadth of beam	26	0
Depth of hold	17	0
Rake of stem	9	0
Tonnage	$339\frac{41}{94}$	

They have also a barque, all in frame, to have a half-poop and top-gallant forecastle, and to class 13 years, A 1.

	Ft.	In.
Length of keel and fore rake ..	117	0
Breadth of beam	28	0
Depth of hold	18	0
Rake of stem	9	0
Tonnage	$417\frac{70}{94}$	

Also a ship, nearly in frame, with a full poop and top-gallant forecastle, to class 12 years, A 1.

	Ft.	In.
Length of keel and fore rake..	126	6
Breadth of beam	30	0
Depth of hold	19	0
Rake of stem	10	0
Tonnage	$567\frac{31}{94}$	

All these vessels are for the East India trade.

There was launched from this yard this year the snow, *Dorothy Alice*, of Sunderland, flush on deck, to class 8 years, A 1.

	Ft.	Tns.
Length on deck	87	2
Breadth on ditto, at midships	22	5
Depth of hold	15	3
Tonnage	$228\frac{1788}{3500}$	

Carries 16.4 keels of coals = 350.96 tons, employed in the coasting trade.

Also, the snow, *Nethania*, of Colchester, for the coasting trade; flush upon deck, classed 8 years, A 1. Carries 11.7 keels of coals = 250.38 tons.

	Ft.	Tns.
Length on deck	79	0
Breadth on ditto, at midships ..	21	0
Depth of hold, ditto ..	12	3
Tonnage	$161\frac{1444}{3500}$	

Also, the snow, *Elizabeth Nicholson*, of Shields, flush on deck, for the coasting trade, classed 8 years, A 1. Carries 18.6 keels of coals = 398.04 tons.

	Ft.	Tns.
Length of deck	90	3
Breadth of ditto at midships ..	22	5
Depth of hold ditto	16	0
Tonnage	$255\frac{1611}{3500}$	

WHITE-HEUCH.

Mr. Wm. Spoor has upon the stocks, nearly ready for launching, a barque for the foreign trade, flush upon deck, to class 9 years, A 1.

	Ft.	In.
Length of keel and fore rake	107	0
Breadth of beam	26	6
Depth of hold	17	0
Rake of stem	7	0
Tonnage	$313\frac{76}{94}$	

There was launched from this yard this year the barque, *Herald*, of Goole, flush on deck, classed 9 years, A 1, for the foreign trade. Carries 21.13 keels of coal = 452.182 tons.

	Ft.	Tns.
Length on deck	97	2
Breadth on ditto at midships ..	22	6
Depth of hold ditto ..	16	4
Tonnage	$307\frac{1739}{3500}$	

Also, the snow, *Tiberias*, of Sunderland, for the coasting trade, flush upon deck. Carries 20.4 keels = 436.56 tons.

	Ft.	Tns.
Length of deck	90	0
Breadth of ditto at midships ..	23	3
Depth of hold, ditto	15	9
Tonnage	284 [illegible]	

SOUTH HYLTON.

Mr. William Carr has upon the stocks, and ready to launch, a brig, flush upon deck, classed 8 years, for the southern trade.

	Ft.	In.
Length of keel and fore rake ..	95	6
Breadth of beam	25	0
Depth of hold	16	0
Rake of stem	7	6
Tonnage	270$\frac{7}{94}$	

There was launched from this yard this year, the snow, *Stephen Huntly*, of Sunderland, for the coasting trade, flush on deck, classed 8 years, A 1. Carries 19.10 keels = 387.554 tons.

	Ft.	Tns.
Length on deck	90	3
Breadth on ditto at midships..	22	8
Depth of hold, ditto ..	16	2
Tonnage	276$\frac{39}{3500}$	

Also the keel, *Fanny*, of Sunderland, classed 8 years. Carries 1.9 keels of coals = 40.66 tons.

	Ft.	In.
Length on deck	45	0
Breadth on ditto at midships ..	20	0
Depth of hold, ditto	3	2
Tonnage	23$\frac{122}{3500}$	

Mr. J. Rogerson has upon the stocks, nearly planked, a brig for the Mediterranean trade, flush upon deck, class 8 years, A 1.

	Ft.	In.
Length of keel and fore rake ..	88	0
Breadth of beam	24	8
Depth of hold	14	6
Rake of stem	8	0
Tonnage	241$\frac{74}{94}$	

Also, upon the stocks, nearly in frame, a schooner for the coasting trade, to class 8 years, A 1.

	Ft.	In.
Length of keel and fore rake ..	69	0
Breadth of beam	20	0
Depth of hold	10	6
Rake of stem	7	0
Tonnage	121$\frac{44}{94}$	

There was launched this year, the snow, *Endeavour*, of Sunderland, for the coasting trade, flush on deck. Carries 15.7 keels of coals = 335.98 tons.

	Ft.	Tns.
Length on deck	86	5
Breadth on ditto at midships ..	21	6
Depth of hold, ditto	14	6
Tonnage	217$\frac{1516}{3500}$	

Also, the snow, *John and Jane*, of Sunderland, for the coasting trade, flush on deck, classed 8 years, A 1. Carries 14.11 keels of coals = 301.954 tons.

	Ft.	Tns.
Length on deck	83	0
Breadth on ditto, amidships ..	21	4
Depth of hold, ditto	14	7
Tonnage	207$\frac{1521}{3500}$	

Also, the snow, *Nina*, of Sunderland, flush on deck, for the coasting trade. Carries 19.12 keels of coals = 409 18 tons.

	Ft.	Tns.
Length on deck	90	9
Breadth on ditto at midships ..	23	2
Depth of hold, ditto	16	7
Tonnage	278$\frac{73}{3500}$	

Mr. George Bainbridge has upon the stocks, and in frame, a schooner for the coasting trade, flush on deck, to class 8 years, A 1.

	Ft.	In.
Length of keel and fore rake ..	75	0
Breadth of beam	19	0
Depth of hold	10	0
Rake of stem	5	0
Tonnage	123$\frac{44}{94}$	

There was launched from this yard, in 1850, the snow, *Temperance Star*, of Sunderland, for the coasting trade, flush on deck, classed 8 years, A 1. Carries 10.1 keels of coals = 216.14 tons.

	Ft.	Tns.
Length on deck	74	0
Breadth on ditto, amidships ..	20	0
Depth of hold ditto ..	11	5
Tonnage	121$\frac{47}{94}$	

Also, the snow, *William*, of London, flush on deck, classed 8 years, A 1. Carries 21.6 keels of coals = 562.24 tons.

	Ft.	Tns.
Length on deck	92	8
Breadth on ditto at midships ..	24	1
Depth of hold, ditto	16	2
Tonnage	300$\frac{122}{3500}$	

Mr. Lawson Gales has upon the stocks, ready for launching, a barque for the Mediterranean trade, classed 9 years, A 1, with a half-poop; no galleries; bust, male head.

	Ft.	In.
Length of keel and fore rake..	99	6
Breadth of beam	25	9
Depth of hold	17	2
Rake of stem	8	6
Tonnage	302$\frac{3}{4}$	

Also, upon the stocks, and in frame, a barque for the foreign trade, to have a poop and top-gallant forecastle; will class 9 years, A 1.

	Ft.	In.
Length of keel and fore rank ..	131	0
Breadth of beam	30	0
Depth of hold	21	0
Rake of stem	11	0
Tonnage	541$\frac{44}{94}$	

Launched from this yard, 1850, the barque, *Candahar*, of London, for the East India trade, with a poop and top-gallant forecastle; classed 10 years, A 1.

	Ft.	Tns.
Length on deck	131	8
Breadth on ditto at midships ..	28	9
Depth of hold, ditto	22	2
Tonnage	780$\frac{133}{3500}$	

Also, the barque, *Viking*, of Sunderland, for the foreign trade, with a half-poop; classed 10 years, A 1.

	Ft.	Tns.
Length on deck	93	7
Breadth on ditto at midships ..	23	1
Depth of hold, ditto	17	0
Tonnage	319$\frac{353}{3500}$	

Messrs. Forrest and Jackson launched from their yard, September the 5th, the brig, *Sultan*, of Sunderland, for the foreign trade, flush upon deck, full man figure-head, no galleries. Carries 16.13 keels of coals = 345.162 tons.

	Ft.	Tns.
Length on deck	93	8
Breadth on ditto at midships	22	4
Depth of hold ditto ..	14	6
Tonnage	247$\frac{153}{3500}$	

FORD DOCK-YARD.

Mr. Wm. Naizby has upon the stocks, ready for launching, a brig for the foreign trade, classed 9 years, A 1, flush upon deck ; carries 21.10 keels of coals = 451.540 tons.

	Ft.	Tns.
Length on deck	93	6
Breadth on ditto at midships ..	23	8
Depth of hold, ditto	16	9
Tonnage	304$\frac{163}{3500}$	

Also, upon the stocks, and in frame, a ship for the foreign trade, classed 9 years, A 1.

	Ft.	In.
Length of keel and fore rake ..	114	6
Breadth of beam	27	0
Depth of hold	18	6
Rake of stem	8	6
Tonnage	383$\frac{3}{4}$	

Launched this year, the barque, *Constantine*, of Sunderland, for the foreign trade, flush upon deck, classed 8 years, A 1, carries 36.9 keels of coals = 789.66 tons.

	Ft.	Tns.
Length on deck	117	9
Breadth on ditto at midships	25	3
Depth of hold, ditto ..	20	1
Tonnage	513$\frac{136}{3500}$	

Also, the barque, *Felton Park*, of Sunderland, for the foreign trade, flush on deck, carries 27 keels of coals = 587 8 tons, classed 9 years, A 1.

	Ft.	Tns.
Length on deck	100	5
Breadth of ditto at midships ..	24	3
Depth of hold	18	3
Tonnage	378$\frac{153}{3500}$	

CLAX-HEUGH.

Mr. John Hodgeson Robson has no vessels upon the stocks at present, but launched this year two vessels, viz., the snow, *Ellen*, of Sunderland, for the coasting trade, with break-deck ; classed 7 years, A 1.

	Ft.	Tns.
Length on deck	82	2
Breadth on ditto at midships ..	22	7
Depth of hold ditto	14	7
Tonnage	216$\frac{153}{3500}$	

Also, the snow, *Royal Thistle*, of Sunderland, for the coasting trade, flush upon deck, class 8 years, A 1.

	Ft.	Tns.
Length on deck	91	8
Breadth on ditto at midships ..	24	3
Depth of hold ditto ..	16	1
Tonnage	290$\frac{153}{3500}$	

Carries 20.10 keels of coals = 430.140 tons.

MOWBRAY'S QUAY.

Mr. George Short has upon the stocks, nearly ready for launching, a brig for the Mediterranean trade, flush upon deck; class 8 years, A 1.

	Ft.	In.
Length of keel and fore rake	98	0
Breadth of beam	26	6
Depth of hold	17	0
Rake of stem	8	0
Tonnage	310$\frac{44}{94}$	

PALLION.

Mr. John Watson has upon the stocks and in frame, a barque for the foreign trade, to have a half-poop and top-gallant forecastle, to class 9 years, A 1.

	Ft.	In.
Length of keel and fore rake ..	115	0
Breadth of beam	27	0
Depth of hold	18	3
Rake of stem	9	0
Tonnage	386$\frac{34}{94}$	

Launched this year, from this yard, the ship, *John Ritson*, of Sunderland, for the East India trade ; carries 34.5 keels of coals = 738.30 tons ; classed 13 years, A 1.

	Ft.	Tns.
Length on deck	119	4
Breadth on ditto at midships ..	26	4
Depth of hold ditto ..	18	7
Length of poop	35	5
Breadth of ditto	22	1
Depth of ditto	3	1

Tonnage.	Tons.
Hull	481$\frac{2849}{3500}$
Pork	26$\frac{1125}{3500}$
Total	508$\frac{163}{3500}$

Mr. Richard Wilkinson has upon the stocks, all planked, a barque for the foreign trade, flush upon deck, to class 8 years, A 1.

	Ft.	In.
Length of keel and fore rake	93	0
Breadth of beam	25	2
Depth of hold	15	3
Rake of stem	9	0
Tonnage	269$\frac{29}{94}$	

There was launched from this yard this year, 3 vessels, viz., the snow, *Addison*, of Stockton, for the coasting trade, flush on deck, carries 17.4 keels of coals = 372.36 tons; classed 8 years, A 1.

	Ft.	Tns.
Length on deck	88	5
Breadth on ditto at midships ..	22	6
Depth of hold, ditto ..	15	4
Tonnage	242$\frac{186}{3500}$	

Also the barque *Meander* (of Sunderland), for the foreign trade, flush upon deck; carries 29.6 keels of coals = 633.44 tons; classed 12 years, A 1.

	Ft.	Tns.
Length on deck	104	9
Breadth on deck, amidships ..	24	8
Depth of hold, ditto	18	7
Tonnage	412$\frac{2967}{3500}$	

And the barque *Star in the East* (of Sunderland), flush upon deck, employed in the foreign trade; carries 22.6 keels of coals = 483.64 tons; class 8 years, A 1.

	Ft.	Tns.
Length on deck	94	4
Breadth on ditto, amidships ..	23	7
Depth of hold, ditto	16	6
Tonnage	314$\frac{1503}{3500}$	

Mr. John Watson (Old Yard), has upon the stocks a brig, all in frame, for the foreign trade, to be flush on deck; classed 8 years, A 1.

	Ft.	In.
Length of keel and fore rake ..	94	0
Breadth of beam	26	0
Depth of hold	17	0
Rake of stem	6	0
Tonnage	281$\frac{85}{94}$	

Messrs. Simpson and Short launched this year the snow *Isabella and Dorothy* (of Shields), for the coasting trade, flush on deck; carries 21.12 keels of coals = 451.968 tons; classed 8 years, A 1.

	Ft.	Tns.
Length on deck	92	7
Breadth on ditto, amidships ..	24	1
Depth of hold, ditto	17	1
Tonnage	306$\frac{227}{3500}$	

Also the keel *Isabella* (of Sunderland), flush on deck, owned by Mr. Greenwell; carries 2.4 keels of coals = 51.36 tons.

	Ft.	Tns.
Length on deck	52	8
Breadth on ditto, amidships ..	21	4
Depth of hold, ditto	3	0
Tonnage	32$\frac{712}{3500}$	

Mr. Joseph Simpson has upon the stocks, and ready for launching, a barque, for the foreign trade, flush on deck, a full female figure-head; carries 28.3 keels of coals = 606.12 tons; classed 8 years, A 1.

	Ft.	Tns.
Length on deck	103	9
Breadth on ditto, amidships ..	24	8
Depth of hold	18	0
Tonnage	395$\frac{2045}{3500}$	

Mr. John Smith has upon the stocks, and in frame, a ship, for the East India trade, to have a poop and topgallant forecastle, to class 13 years, A 1.

	Ft.	In.
Length of keel and fore rake ..	145	0
Breadth of beam	32	0
Depth of hold	21	4
Rake of stem	11	0
Tonnage	685$\frac{70}{94}$	

There was launched this year from this yard the ship *Janet Willis* (of London), with a poop and top-gallant forecastle, employed in the East India trade; classed 13 years, A 1.

	Ft.	Tns.
Length on deck	126	8
Breadth on ditto, amidships ..	28	6
Depth of hold, ditto	20	0
Tonnage (total)	666$\frac{1764}{3500}$	

Mr. Arrow Leithead has upon the stocks, and in frame, a brig, for the foreign trade, to be flush upon deck; to class 8 years, A 1.

	Ft.	In.
Length of keel and fore rake ..	90	0
Breadth of beam	24	0
Depth of hold	15	2
Rake of stem	9	0
Tonnage	231$\frac{87}{94}$	

Launched this year, the ship *Cambodia* (of Sunderland), for the East India trade; carries 59.11 keels of coals = 1264.954 tons.

	Ft.	Tns.
Length on deck	143	2
Breadth on ditto, amidships ..	31	7
Depth of hold, ditto	22	0
Length of poop	40	0
Breadth of ditto	25	7
Depth of ditto	6	5
Length of wings	2	8
Breadth of ditto	6	1
Depth of ditto	6	3

Tonnage	Tons.
Hull	837$\frac{2657}{3500}$
Poop	47$\frac{431}{3500}$
Wings (each)	1$\frac{[illegible]}{3500}$
Total	914$\frac{738}{3500}$

Mr. William Wilkinson has upon the stocks, all planked, a schooner, for the coasting trade, flush upon deck; to class 8 years, A 1.

	Ft.	In.
Length of keel and fore rake ..	69	0
Breadth of beam	17	5
Depth of hold	10	0
Rake of stem	7	0
Tonnage	96$\frac{31}{94}$	

Also, upon the stocks, and in frame, a brig, for the foreign trade, with a clipper bow, flush upon deck; to class 8 years, A 1.

	Ft.	In.
Length of keel and fore rake ..	88	0
Breadth of beam	20	6
Depth of hold	12	6
Rake of stem	17	0
Tonnage	160$\frac{41}{94}$	

DEPTFORD.

Mr. William Williamson has upon the stocks, and ready to launch, a ship, for the London and East India trade, owned by Mr. Lindsay, of London; will carry 52.13 keels of coals = 1115.582 tons; classed 9 years, A 1.

	Ft.	Tns.
Length on deck	149	3
Breadth on ditto, amidships ..	28	3
Depth of hold, ditto	21	4
Length of poop	40	8
Breadth of ditto .. .	26	0
Depth of ditto	6	4

Tonnage.	Tons.
Hull	741$\frac{[illegible]}{3500}$
Poop	74$\frac{2123}{3500}$
Total	815$\frac{2817}{3500}$

There was launched this year, from this yard the barque *Nepaul* (of Sunderland); carries 30.12 keels of coals = 644.568 tons.

	Ft.	Tns.
Length on deck	112	1
Breadth on ditto, amidships ..	25	7
Depth of hold, ditto	19	0
Length of quarter-deck ..	31	0
Breadth of ditto	21	4
Depth of ditto	3	3

Tonnage.	Tons.
Hull	432$\frac{846}{3500}$
Quarter-deck	23$\frac{1124}{3500}$
Total	455$\frac{1970}{3500}$

Mr. John Robinson has upon the stocks, and ready to launch, a snow, for the foreign trade, flush upon deck; to class 8 years, A 1.

Builder's measurement.	Ft.	In.
Length of keel and fore rake ..	90	0
Breadth of beam	25	0
Depth of hold	15	3
Rake of stem	9	0
Tonnage	251$\frac{31}{94}$	
New measurement	Ft.	Tns.
Length on deck	87	9
Breadth on ditto, amidships ..	22	9
Depth of hold, ditto	15	2
Tonnage	240$\frac{775}{3500}$	

Will carry 17.2 keels of coals = 368.08 tons.

There was launched from this yard this year, the ship *Alipore* (of London), for the London and East India trade, owned by Mr. Lindsay, of London; to class 9 years, A 1.

Builder's measurement,	Ft.	In
Length of keel and fore rake ..	150	0
Breadth of beam	31	0
Depth of hold	15	5
Rake of stem	12	0
Tonnage	676$\frac{1}{94}$	
New measurement.	Ft.	Tns.
Length on deck	147	0
Breadth on ditto, amidships ..	28	3
Depth of hold, ditto	21	2
Tonnage	811$\frac{190}{3500}$	

Figure-head—" Hercules strangling a lion."

Also the barque *Branscombe* (of Bridgewater), for the foreign trade, with a poop; classed 10 years, A 1.

	Ft.	Tns.
Length on deck	111	1
Breadth on ditto, amidships ..	25	6
Depth of hold, ditto	18	9
Tonnage	481$\frac{719}{3500}$	

Mr. James Laing has upon the stocks three vessels, viz.:—a ship, all planked, with a poop and top-gallant forecastle; to class 13 years, A 1.

	Ft.	In.
Length of keel and fore rake ..	143	6
Breadth of beam	33	0
Depth of hold	22	0
Rake of stem	10	6
Tonnage	721$\frac{4}{94}$	

F. B.

OUGHT WE TO BE CONTENT WITH OUR PRESENT MEANS OF EXTINGUISHING FIRES?

In our last volume, p. 145, we drew attention to the manifest inefficiency of all the means at present in use in this country for extinguishing fires. The general apathy which prevails on this subject may be traced to the system of fire insurance, which, like ship insurance, does not attempt to prevent loss, but taxes the whole country to pay for the carelessness or fraud of a comparatively few individuals. The tax of fire insurance seems light, individually, but the aggregate sum paid in the United Kingdom is enormous, and might be very greatly reduced, were fire engines of sufficient power employed. It is rather out of character in this mechanical age, to hear of such fires as those at Gravesend and in Mark-lane, *actually burning themselves out.* As to *putting out* a fire, or saving the building in which it originates, it is rarely done,—" the efforts of the firemen being directed to saving the adjoining buildings," as the stereotyped phrase is. Some years back Messrs. Braithwaite & Milner constructed a steam fire-engine, of immense power, but the only patronage it received was that the hoses were cut by the men belonging to the other engines, out of jealousy of its superior powers. It was ultimately sent to Berlin, where it was of essential service on the occurrence of a large fire; and some others were constructed for various parts of the continent.

We have been led to make these remarks from having recently witnessed the performance of a fire-engine worked by steam power, in the West India Docks. The dock company employ a steam tug to move the vessels using the docks, and their assistant engineer, Mr. P. Clark, has designed a simple method of making the power of the engines of the boat available in case of fire. A large Downton's pump is fixed on deck, and connected by gearing to the engines, so that they can be readily disconnected from the paddle wheels, and their power applied to the pump. The power of the engines is 30 horses, which, nominally, would be equal to 240 men, or 10 of the ordinary fire-engines, but, in reality, to a much greater number. Without using the whole power of the engines, a stream of water equal to 600 GALLONS, OR 3 TONS, per minute, is projected 20 feet higher than the highest warehouse in the docks, forming a "fire annihilator" of the best description. As the fires in the boilers are never allowed to go *out entirely,* this machine is always in readiness, and in the event of a ship taking fire could tow her out of danger, and extinguish the fire at the same time. In such a case as the burning of the Irongate wharf warehouse, one or two of the ordinary tugs on the river, fitted in this manner, would have prevented a very serious loss of property. The time necessary to row the present floating engines on the river to the scene of operation, or to procure the service of a tug to tow them, and then to arrange the services of the vast number of hands required to work them, will always prevent their proving of any real services. We congratulate the Dock Company on the possession of such a valuable aid in case of fire, and hope that the example will not be lost upon government and other public bodies.

McNICOLL & VERNON'S STEAM CRANES.

WE are glad to hear that the Hull Dock Company have decided upon working the quays of the new Victoria Dock by means of McNicoll & Vernon's Patent Steam Travelling Crane; a detailed description of which, it will be remembered, was given in our October number. This will afford an extremely favourable opportunity of exhibiting the peculiar merits and advantages of this invention. We understand that the scheme is designed ultimately to include no fewer than 16 travelling cranes, each crane to be of 53 feet span, and to travel over a space of 300 feet, thus covering a total area of upwards of 280,000 square feet. The whole of these machines will be worked by one stationary engine. It is intended to draw the timber out of the bow port of the vessel, to deposit it on the quay for measurement and examination by the Cus-

toms, to remove it to a distance, and ultimately to pile it in cesses, by the agency of these machines, without the assistance of horses or manual labour, with the exception, of course, of the man and boy required to attend on each crane. Orders have already been given for the execution of a portion of the scheme, and when the whole is carried out it is confidently expected that the expense of landing and storing timber will be reduced from about 2*s.* per load of 50 feet to about 4*d.*, or one-sixth of the price now paid for similar operations in Liverpool and Hull. We learn also that four of these machines are in the course of erection at Manchester; and we have no doubt that before long they will be generally adopted at the goods' depôts of railway stations, timber yards, foundries, and in all those places where hoisting, moving, and transporting of heavy weights are carried on.

A working model of the crane is in course of preparation for the great Exhibition of 1851, in which we have no doubt it will attract the attention to which the ingenuity and importance of the invention entitle it.

ZINC PAINT *VERSUS* WHITE LEAD.

WE of the nineteenth century are apt to boast of our progress in the arts and sciences, but it is only within the last few months that we have succeeded in producing, as a marketable article, a substitute for the abominable pigment—white lead. Our posterity will, doubtless, be astonished to find for how long we were content to line our houses with a material whose deadly properties paralyzed the hand that used it, and they will not form a very favourable opinion of the charity which allowed it to poison our workmen, or the sense which could not detect its baneful influence on ourselves. It is proved beyond a doubt that the evil effects of white lead extend beyond the time during which its offensive smell remains apparent, and that consequently it ought never to be used for the interior of dwelling houses. The readiness with which it is affected by foul air is also a strong objection to its use under many circumstances, rendering frequent renewal necessary, even if it had no other fault. Under these circumstances then, we hail as an important boon, the present which chemical science has made us in zinc paint, as a substitute for white lead. Its freedom from any noxious quality would alone make it eminently valuable; and in addition it possesses the advantages peculiar to itself,—of freedom from change under exposure to sulphuretted hydrogen and ammonia, and of a brightness of colour which has no rival. Its power of reflecting artificial light is also very remarkable, and is a not less valuable property. We should hesitate to speak so confidently had we not witnessed its application and tested its good qualities. To our nautical friends it will be valuable as a paint for ships' holds, and the wood and metal work about marine engines, where, as is well known, white lead is of little use. Messrs. Hubbuck, the patentees, have sent some specimens to our office, where they may be inspected by any persons who may desire to do so.

PATENT TRIPLE FILES.—On the principle that "many a little makes a meikle," we have here an ingenious attempt to diminish the time spent by the workman in laying down and taking up his files. Half the round edge of an ordinary half round file is cut flat, so that it combines a flat, a half round, and a three square file, all in one. The practical man cannot fail to be delighted with them. The manufacturers, Messrs. Earl, Smith, & Co., of Sheffield, have sent some samples of them to our office, where they lie for inspection.

LIST OF ENGLISH PATENTS,
FROM THE 2ND TO THE 21st DAY OF NOVEMBER, 1850, INCLUSIVE.
Matthew Hodgkinson, of Red-street, near Newcastle-under-Lyne, in the county of Stafford, mine agent, for improvements in furnaces, or apparatus for smelting ores and minerals, and for the making of pig iron. November 2.
Victor Emile Warmont, of Neuilly Seine, in the Republic of France, for improvements in dyeing wood and other fibrous materials and fabrics. November 2.
Joseph Christian Davidson, of Yalding, in the county of Kent, brick maker, for improvements in lime and other kilns and furnaces. November 2
John Matthews, of Kidderminster, foreman, for improvements in sizing paper. November 2.
Jonas Bateman, of Upper-street, Islington, cooper, for improvements in life boats. November 2.

Archibald Slate, of Woodside Iron Works, Dudley, for improvements in canal navigation. November 2.

Pierre Antoine Auguste de la Barre de Nanteuil, of Leicester-street, in the county of Middlesex, for improvements in propelling carriages. November 2.—(Communication.)

William and Colin Mather, of Salford, engineers, and Ferdinand Kaselowstry, of Berlin, in the kingdom of Prussia, engineer, for improvements in machinery for washing, steaming, drying, and finishing cotton, linen, and woollen fabrics. November 2.

John Borland, of Norfolk-street, Strand, engineer, for certain improvements in weaving machinery. November 2.

John Slate, of Wandsworth, in the county of Surrey, accountant, for improvements in stoves and furnaces, and in chimney pots and regulators. November 2.

John Tatham and David Cheetham, of Rochdale, in the county of Lancaster, machine makers, for certain improvements in the manufacture of cotton and other fibrous materials, and fabrics composed of such materials. November 2.

Richard Clyburn, engineer to the firm of D. Maclean and Son, of Saint George-street East, in the county of Middlesex, for improvements in wheel carriages. November 2.—(Partly a communication.)

James Black, of Edinburgh, machine maker, for a machine for folding. November 7. (Partly a communication.)

Richard Archibald Brooman, of Fleet-street, for improvements in railways. November 7. —(Communication.)

William Fairbairn, of Manchester, in the county of Lancaster, civil engineer, for improvements in cranes and other lifting or hoisting machines. November 7.

William Crane Wilkins, of Long-acre, in the county of Middlesex, engineer, for an invention for lighting, and in apparatus for lighthouses, signal, floating, and harbour lights. November 7.

Samuel Edwards, James Ansell, and Patrick Heyns, of Shadwell, in the county of Middlesex, engineers, for certain improvements in obtaining and applying motive power, and in pumps. November 7.

John Alexander Lerow, of Boston, in the United States of America, gentleman, for certain improvements in sewing machines. November 7.

Benjamin Guy Babington, of George-street, Hanover-square, in the county of Middlesex. doctor of medicine, for improvements in preventing incrustations of steam and other boilers, November 7.

George Frederick Morrell, of Fleet-street, London, gentleman, for improvements in obtaining and applying motive power, and also in pumps. November 7.

John Clare, jun., of Exchange-buildings, Liverpool, gentleman, for improvements in the manufacture of metallic casks. November 7.

John Robinson, of Stepney, in the county of Middlesex, engineer, for improvements in lifting and moving fluid and other bodies, and in apparatus for steering ships and other vessels. November 7.

David Christie, of St. John's-place, Broughton, in the borough of Salford, and county of Lancaster, merchant, for improvements in machinery or apparatus for preparing, carding, spinning, doubling, twisting, weaving, and knitting, cotton, wool, and other fibrous substances; also for sewing and packing. November 7.—(Communication.)

Robert Lucas, of Furnival's-inn, in the city of London, mechanical draughtsman, for improvements in telegraphic and printing apparatus. November 7.

Thomas Main, of the Strand, printer, for improvements in printing machinery. November 8.

James Rock, jun., of Hastings, in the county of Sussex, coach-builder, for certain improvements in carriages, which are also applicable, in whole or in part, to other machines. November 9.

William Palmer, of Sutton-street, Clerkenwell, manufacturer, for improvements in the manufacture of candles and night-lights. November 9.

James Scott, of Falkirk, N. B., shipwright, for certain improvements in docks, slips, and apparatus connected therewith. November 9.

Sir Francis Charles Knowles, of Lovell, in the county of Bucks, baronet, for improvements in the manufacture of charcoal. November 9.

Lucien Vidie, of Rue du Grand Chantier, Paris, in the Republic of France, French advocate, for improvements in measuring the pressure of air, steam, gas, and liquids. November 9.

Joseph Nye, of Mill Pond Wharf, Old Kent-road, engineer, for improvements in hydraulic machinery, parts of which improvements are applicable to steam engines and machinery for driving piles. November 12.

George Robins Booth, of London, engineer, for improvements in the manufacture of gas. November 12.

Peter Spence, of Pendleton, Manchester, manufacturing chemist, for improvements in the manufacture of alum, and certain alkaline salts: and in the manufacture of cement, part of which improvements are applicable in obtaining volatile liquids. November 12.

Edwin Clark, of Palace New Road, in the county of Middlesex, civil engineer, and Henry Mapple, of Child's-hill, Hampstead, electric engineer, for improvements in electric telegraphs, and in apparatus connected therewith. November 12.

Henry Medhurst, engineer, in the employ of Messrs. Shears and Sons, of Bankside, Southwark, for improvements in gas meters. November 12.

Etienne Masson, of Place St. Michel, at Paris, gardener, for improvements in the preparation of certain vegetable alimentary substances for the provisioning of ships and armies, and other purposes, where the said substances are required to be preserved. November 12.

John Ball, of Ashford, in the county of Kent, engineer, for improvements in applying heat to bakers' ovens, and their appendages. November 12.

Henry Wimshurst, of Limehouse, in the county of Middlesex, ship builder, for improvements in steam engines, in propelling, and in the construction of ships and vessels. November 12.

Charles Marsden, of Kingsland-road, in the county of Middlesex, engineer, for improvements in scissors and in thimbles. November 12

William Duckworth, of Liverpool, coffee merchant, for certain improvements in the manufacture of chicory, with certain improvements in the machinery or apparatus for the manufacture thereof. November 14.

Thomas Shore, of Exwich, in the county of Devon, miller, for an improved method of dressing flour. November 14.

Robert Howarth, of Chapman-street, Oldham-road, Manchester, for improvements in machinery for raising a nap on cotton, woollen, silk, and other fabrics. November 14.

Abraham Haley, of Frome, in the county of Somerset, machinist, for certain improvements in looms for weaving. November 14.

Edward David Ashe, of Brompton, in the county of Middlesex, lieutenant in her Majesty's navy, for a new or improved nautical instrument or instruments, applicable, especially amongst other purposes, to those of great circle sailing. November 14.

John Swindells, of the firm of Swindells and Williams, of Manchester, and Ince, near Wigan, manufacturing chemist, for certain improvements in obtaining products from ores and other matters containing metals, and in the preparation and application of several such products for the purpose of bleaching, printing, dyeing, and colour making. November 14.

Joseph Conrad Baron Liebhaber, of Paris, in the Republic of France, for improvements in blasting rocks; also in working marble and stone; and in preparing products therefrom. November 14.

Charles Allemand, of Paris, in the Republic of France, gentleman, for an improved apparatus for producing light November 14.

Thomas Coats, of Ferguslie, in the town of Paisley, and county of Renfrew, Scotland, thread manufacturer, for certain improvements in turning, cutting, and shaping wood and other materials. November 16.

Joseph Martin, of Liverpool, in the county of Lancaster, rice miller, for improvements in machinery and apparatus for cleansing and otherwise treating rice and certain other grains, seeds, and farinaceous substances. November 16.

Thomas Allen, of St. Andrew's-square, Edinburgh, printer and publisher of the "Caledonian Mercury," for certain improvement in electric telegraphs, and in the application of electric currents for deflecting magnets, or producing electro magnets. November 16.

William Laird, of Liverpool, in the county of Lancaster, merchant, and Edward Alfred Cowper, of Handsworth, in the county of Warwick, engineer, for improvements in machinery for loading and discharging certain descriptions of cargo in ships and other vessels, and in the construction of such vessels. November 16.

John Hosking, of Islington, in the county of Middlesex, engineer, for certain improvements in valves, applicable to pumps; and also in apparatus to regulate the pressure and flow of water or air in and through pipes. November 19.

Thomas Dunn, of Windsor Bridge Iron Works, Pendleton, near Manchester, in the county of Lancaster, engineer, for improvements in machinery and apparatus for moving engines and carriages from one line of rails to another, and for turning them; also for compressing certain substances, and for raising and lowering heavy bodies. November 19.

Paul de Foistoy, of Paris, in the state of France, General in the service of His Majesty the Emperor of Russia, for improvements in dredging machines. November 19.—(Communication.)

Clement Augustus Kurtz, of Manchester, in the county of Lancaster, practical chemist, for improvements in dyeing. November 19.—(Communication.)

Alfred Vincent Newton, of Chancery-lane, in the county of Middlesex, mechanical draughtsman, for an improved composition, applicable to the coating of wood, metals, plaster, and other substances, which are required to be preserved from decay, which composition may be also employed as a pigment or paint November 19.—(Communication.)

Robert Brown, of Liverpool, in the county of Lancaster, plumber and brass-founder, for improvements in the application of pumps for raising and forcing water. November 19.

Henry William Ripley, of Bradford, in the county of York, dyer, for improvements in dyeing and finishing piece goods. November 19.

John James Greenough, of the Strand, in the county of Middlesex, gentleman, for improvements in the construction of chairs, couches, and seats; parts of which improvements are also applicable to various purposes where springs for supporting heavy bodies, and resisting sudden and continuous pressure are required. November 21.—(Communication.)

DESIGNS FOR ARTICLES OF UTILITY.

Registered from 24th October to 20th November.

Oct. 24th, 2493, F. B. Geithner, Birmingham, "Expanding dining table."
„ „ 2494, W. Poupard, Wych-street, Strand, "Curvilinear beam for weighing machines."
„ 25th, 2495, E. O. Tindall & L. Tindall, Scarborough, York, "Tindall's smoke elevator."
„ „ 2496, Key, Mitchell, & Fries, Newgate-street, "Convertible bedstead."
„ „ 2497, Edward Greaves, Sheffield, "Variable pendulum, or portable metronome."
„ 26th, 2498, Bryan, Donkin, & Co., Grange-road, Bermondsey, "Rotary rag boiler for paper makers."
„ „ 2499, W. F. Robinson, Charles-street, St. James's, "Self-acting safety plug or stopper for boats and other vessels."
„ „ 2500, Robert Watts, Peter-street, Manchester, "Improved metallic packing for pistons."
„ 28th, 2501, Joseph Harvey, Westminster bridge-road, and Heron-court, Richmond, "The Richmond car."
„ 29th, 2502, Charles Maschevitz, jun., Birmingham, "Box or case for postage stamps."
„ „ 2503, David Duthoit & Job Roof, Finsbury-pavement, "The bush tent."
„ „ 2504, Thomas Parker, Kensington, "Knife and fork cleaner."
„ 30th, 2505, Charles Rowley, Birmingham, London, and Manchester, "The prince's vest button."
„ „ 2506, J. Smith & H. M. Ditchett, St. Augustine's-parade, Bristol, "Improved blind roller."
„ 31st, 2507, Swain & Adeney, Piccadilly, "Swain & Adeney's universal whip socket."
„ „ 2508, C. A. Ferguson & T Ferguson, Mast-house, Millwall, Poplar, "Improved gun-carriage, to facilitate the training and working of heavy guns"
„ „ 2509, Chapman & Son, Frith-street, Soho, "A moveable button."
„ „ 2510, Laurie & Marner, Oxford-street, "Invisible carriage step."
„ „ 2511, Earl, Smith, & Co., Hallamshire Works, Sheffield, "The triple file."
Nov. 1st, 2512, William Leschallas Budge-row, City, "Pentagon envelope."
„ „ 2513, Isaac Naylor, Burton, near Barnsley, "Alarm gun."
„ „ 2514, John Furnihough & Sons, Victoria Works, Dunkinfield, Chester, "Steam boiler."
„ 2nd, 2515, W. C. Hugman, Great Ormond-street, Queen's-square, "Portable folding truss."
„ 4th, 2516, G. P. Tye, Birmingham, "Hyacinth glass and support."
„ „ 2517, D. Duthoit & J. Roof, Finsbury-pavement, "The aerial tent."
„ 5th, 2518, Thomas Lambert & Son, Short-street, New-cut, Lambeth, "Fountain lamp."
„ „ 2519, R. & J. Garrard, Leman-street, Gravel-lane, Southwark, "Hat."
„ „ 2520, W. E. Jenkins, George-street, Euston-square, "Embossing machine for stamping with ink."
„ 6th, 2521, E. A. Gaillard, Bedford-street, Strand, "New travelling case."
„ „ 2522, Browning & Rigby, Adelphi Iron Works, Salford, Manchester, "Compound cylinder steam engine."
„ 7th, 2523, John Verrinder, Lincoln, "Box table and sofa bedstead."
„ „ 2524, Jenkins & Ashford, Birmingham, "Mattrass."
„ „ 2525, James Tonkin, Oxford-street, "Improved spring lath."
„ „ 2526, William Wilson, King-street, Manchester, "Hot water cistern, for baths, &c."
„ 8th, 2527, J. H. Sharpe, Belfast, "Improved paddle-wheel."
„ „ 2528, George Horton, Thomas-street, Manchester, "A joiner's brace."
„ 9th, 2529, George Broughall, Willenhall, Staffordshire, "Improved steam stamp."
„ 11th, 2530, C. & J. Clark, Street, near Glastonbury, Somersetshire, "Parts of shoes."
„ 12th, 2531, Fowler & Fry, Bristol. "Improved cart."
„ 13th, 2532, Martin Billing, Newhall-street, Birmingham, "A lithographic perforating and registering machine."
„ 14th, 2533, Frederick Grosjean, Regent-street, "A railway rug or wrapper."
„ „ 2534, T. F. Griffiths, Birmingham, "A saucepan lid."
„ „ 2535, Lord, Brothers, Canal-street Works, Todmorden, York, "Improved hook for the weight hooks of lap and other machines."
„ 15th, 2536, T. F. Griffiths, Birmingham, "Candlestick."
„ „ 2537, Lorant Poirier, Bucklersbury, "Lithographic press."
„ „ 2538, Jeakins & Wolmershausen, Curzon-street, Mayfair, "A lady's riding habit."
„ 18th, 2539, Waddington & Son, Coleman-street, "Etui bisutile, or parasol and knitting case."
„ 19th, 2540, Thomas Rutter, Harborne, "Nail."
„ „ 2541, Arthur Jermingham, Portsmouth, "Letter-clip."
„ „ 2542, Martindale & Bowman, Globe-road, Mile-end, "Poché-au-chapeau."
„ 20th, 2543, Joseph Last, Haymarket, "The continental wardrobe portmanteau."
„ „ 2544, J. W. Smith, Birmingham, "Button."

Lightning Source UK Ltd.
Milton Keynes UK
UKHW020226160221
378861UK00003B/24